A History of Cuban
Baseball, 1864–2006

A History of Cuban Baseball, 1864–2006

PETER C. BJARKMAN

McFarland & Company, Inc., Publishers

Jefferson, North Carolina, and London

For Mark Rucker, who shared the adventure,
and for Ronnie Wilbur, who shares the dream.

Peter C. Bjarkman is the author of numerous books,
including McFarland's *Baseball with a Latin Beat:
A History of the Latin American Game* (1994)

All uncredited photographs are from the author's collection

LIBRARY OF CONGRESS CATALOGUING-IN-PUBLICATION DATA

Bjarkman, Peter C.
A history of Cuban baseball, 1864–2006 / Peter C. Bjarkman.
p.   cm.
Includes bibliographical references and index.

ISBN-13: 978-0-7864-2829-8
ISBN-10: 0-7864-2829-5
(illustrated case binding : 50# alkaline paper) ∞

1. Baseball — Cuba — History.
I. Title.
GV863.25.A1B53   2007   796.35709729'1— dc22   2006027779

British Library cataloguing data are available

On the cover: (top) Alejandro Oms; Fidel Castro with fellow revolutionaries;
(bottom) Cuba's 2003 World Cup championship team

Manufactured in the United States of America

*McFarland & Company, Inc., Publishers
Box 611, Jefferson, North Carolina 28640
www.mcfarlandpub.com*

Table of Contents

Preface

In the most elaborate previous history of Cuban baseball, Roberto González Echevarría advances his thesis that the island's national pastime reached its zenith at the tail end of the 1946–47 professional winter league season. Readers of *The Pride of Havana* are led to believe that after the pennant-deciding clashes between Almendares and Habana in February 1947 Cuban baseball suffered a long and steady decline toward oblivion. First came a decade of rapid disintegration for the once popular professional league affiliated with Major League Baseball; next followed the half-century (Echevarría was writing in 1999) of virtual isolation which transpired while a post-revolution amateur league system blocked top Cuban stars like Agustín Marquetti, Antonio Muñoz, Braudilio Vinent and Omar Linares from their destined true Valhalla in the American big leagues; during the same wasteland half-century (from González Echevarría's perspective and that of not an insignificant number of other professional-baseball-oriented authors) Cuba's often over-rated national teams won endless international titles only because they competed against inferior talent culled from the sport's amateur backwaters.

Professor González Echevarría is an enthusiastic fan of Cuba's early professional heyday and an informed student of baseball's earliest roots and evolution on the now communist-controlled island that today houses perhaps the most vibrant baseball universe found outside the American major leagues. But like so many enthusiastic fans of the diamond sport, the author of *The Pride of Havana* also falls into the trap of assuming that his sport's Golden Age settled in the fondly remembered and nostalgia-colored seasons of his own youth — the age when all things (baseball included) were seen with a much rosier hue. Nothing in the world is more conservative than a middle-aged male baseball rooter. And there is no more distorted form of history than one tinged with heavy layers of youth-inspired nostalgia.

Cuban baseball does not — despite the contentions of many of its recent chroniclers — live entirely or even primarily in a realm of backward-looking nostalgia; nor does the island's national pastime depend on deep-rooted memories to recover its greatest seasons, most glorious triumphs, or most celebrated individual ball-playing heroes. The reality — demonstrated on the diamonds of Hiram Bithorn Stadium in San Juan and Petco Park in San Diego — is that the apex moments of Cuban baseball history have only of late been unfolding with the still-fresh events of March 2006. The focal point of Cuba's baseball nostalgia will now for the long foreseeable future assuredly lie in the early months of the sixth year of the twenty-first century. The Golden Age is not at all a distant fading memory to be sought out in some remote lost era, but rather a firsthand experience to be savored in the living present. Never has Cuban baseball been any better than it is at the present moment; never has the talent been deeper, the game more celebrated, or the triumphs more pronounced.

Professor González Echevarría's portrait of Cuban baseball, though one informed by many valuable details and much painstaking research into the game's earlier epochs, thus in the end leaves us with a major distortion of the island's true sporting saga. The game's zenith on the island is not centered in the middle of the past century but lies instead in the opening decade of the new one. But the triumphs of the Cuban national team in the recent WBC were also not an overnight aberration. They are best viewed as the final chapter of a steady four-plus-decade evolution of modern-era Cuban baseball that represents the island sport's true Age of Valhalla. Nearly twelve million devoted native fans have thrilled to more than forty seasons of a competitive island-wide league that has produced the game's greatest legacy and provided the bulk of its greatest stars. Sluggers Marquetti, Muñoz, Wilfredo Sánchez and Luis Casanova can match any heroes of the early twentieth century blackball era; Cuba has never produced a better all-around player than Omar Linares or a purer natural hitter than Osmani Urrutia; the recent heroics of Liván and El Duque Hernández and of José Contreras seem to seal the issue that Cuban pitchers in the big leagues have never been better than they are in the present era (and this despite the fact that the best Cuban pitchers like Pedro Lazo, Lázaro Valle and Norge Vera have never left their homeland).

The true tragedy for American fans is not the one universally assumed — that cold war politics has prevented Cuban stars from flooding into the major leagues. The true loss is that the prized league in Cuba — as much on a par with the majors as either the Japanese Central League or Japanese Pacific League — has remained as hidden from North American eyes as once the Negro circuits of the early twentieth century were also similarly obscured from view. The last half-century of baseball in Cuba has not in any sense been the lamentable decline reported ad nauseam by Cuban ex-patriots in Miami or by ill-informed champions of major league baseball; it has instead been an era of steadily building momentum that has now resulted in the Cuban national pastime finally reaching its destined appointment with long-overdue recognition during the eye-opening events of March 2006.

Much of Havana (then a city of little more than a million inhabitants) may well have paused for the 1947 Almendares versus Habana showdown pennant series as described by González Echevarría. In contrast, an entire island nation of more than 12 million — citizens from all walks and not merely baseball fans — was totally paralyzed by the dozen days of the recent World Baseball Classic. This is neither an exaggeration nor an aberration. When the Cuban team played in San Juan and San Diego all commerce on the island literally ground to a halt. Perhaps as much as ninety percent of the country — a nation well accustomed to pausing for public spectacles — was glued before television sets and radios to follow every pitch with mixtures of joy and agony. This was no longer the fair-weather fans of local professional clubs like the post-war Blues or Lions, but followers of a team carrying an entire nation's self-esteem. This was professional baseball's closest-ever approximation of the twentieth-century phenomenon of world cup soccer.

Not only the baseball-oriented male population (as back in 1947) was now engrossed by the spectacle, but also a more universal audience that included women and children and even the occasional male who was not normally a follower of sporting events. It was patriotism and ethnic pride that was now on the line. A land where baseball has a lengthy history as a proving ground for nationhood and a symbol for patriotism now discovered its fondest dream on the distant baseball diamonds of the north. It was the dream that their own all-stars could indeed compete head-to-toe with the world's top professionals. There was now full justification in the offering that a league long enjoyed at home was far more than only a precious domestic entertainment. Cubans now relished the fact that their beloved home-grown brand of "pelota" was indeed equal to any version found in the outside world.

Two myths, both fostered by most of the earlier treatments of island baseball, were laid aside by the recent MLB-sponsored World Baseball Classic. One was the notion that Cuba's Olympic triumphs in Barcelona, Atlanta and Athens were in the end false measures of the transparent powerhouse teams that represented Cuba's national pastime. A second was the idea that the denizens of the past-era Havana professional circuit of the 1940s or 1950s represented a higher level of play on the island. The reality of course is that the native Cuban pros of the immediate post-war era were in the main minor leaguers, sprinkled with a few marginal big league all-stars (Miñoso, Pascual, Pedro Ramos) who made preciously little impact on diamonds up north. One simply can not imagine a representative squad of top Cubans — say one with Camilo Pascual on the hill, Julio Bécquer at first, Willie Miranda at short and Miñoso batting cleanup — beating true big league

all-stars whose lineup might include Mantle, Mays, Aaron, Clemente, Snider and Berra. Yet the WBC found today's Cuba all-stars triumphing over the likes of Pujols, Bernie Williams, David Ortiz, Omar Vizquel and a pair of Cy Young starters named Colón and Santana. The WBC sufficiently showcased that the Cuban Leaguers are indeed big leaguers capable of holding their own with the best squads assembled from the majors. The recent tournament also suggests that books like *The Pride of Havana* which have downplayed the modern-era Cuban League have in the process largely distorted the historical record. This current volume has been written with the primary goal of finally setting that record straight.

*   *   *

Major League Baseball's first World Baseball Classic did not turn out to be quite what either the moguls of American professional baseball or any of the rest of the world had quite expected. MLB's WBC was advertised from the start as the first legitimate global championship tournament in which top stars from the world's self-anointed best professional league would battle for patriotic pride while wearing the uniforms of their native countries. After nearly three weeks of exciting action that had gripped television audiences throughout Latin America and Asia, as well as much of North America, we arrived at a most surprising if altogether intriguing grand finale in San Diego's showcase Petco Park. Japan (without any of its recognizable big league exports except Mariners nonpareil Ichiro Suzuki and Rangers closer Akinori Otsuka) and Cuba (the only team in the tournament with no pro leaguers in its stable) together proved to the world that their brand of team-oriented baseball is the style best adapted to winning in short-duration and tension-packed international tournaments.

Before the first pitch of the Cuba-Japan showdown was hurled on March 20, big league superstars filling the showcase lineups of teams representing pre-tournament favorites Venezuela, Dominican Republic, Puerto Rico and the USA had already all rejoined their pro clubs at spring training sites scattered throughout Florida and Arizona. When all-stars representing baseball's two other top leagues — the Cuban League and the Japanese Professional League — assumed the field for the final nine innings of the WBC there was no Derek Jeter, Albert Pujols, Pudge Rodríguez, Johann Santana, Bartolo Colón or Carlos Beltrán anywhere on the scene. With the single exception of Japan's Ichiro Suzuki, the only true star remaining here at San Diego's Petco Park was the white five-pointer that adorns the Cuban flag. It was not the scenario originally envisioned by Commissioner Bud Selig, Players' Union head Gene Orza or other architects of MLB's effort at remaking Olympic baseball in its own image. But few could deny that it was a grand enough spectacle for all its unaccountable turns and twists.

For MLB executives the final weekend of this showcase tournament, in fact, had to be the worst possible nightmare. Japan's Central and Pacific leagues, while a valued source for a few select star imports like Ichiro, Hideki Matsui, and Hideo Nomo, have never been judged on a par with the U.S. majors.

And the Cubans have always been discounted by North American baseball forces as highly overrated for all their past international successes. Cuba has dominated the international baseball scene since its 1959 socialist revolution and new form of amateur sport reshaped the island. Cuban teams have captured three of four Olympic crowns, 25 of 28 World Cups, and nine of 12 Intercontinental Cup titles. The only time they have not won a World Cup title since 1976 was in 1982, a year when they did not compete. But such a record of unchallenged supremacy has long been dispatched as ill-won and even illegitimate.

In truth, the very motivation for the WBC in the first place had in large part been to put the Cubans back in their rightful place by stacking international baseball with the cream of the professional talent pool. The consensus reaction stateside has always been that Cuba's reputation was overblown, that their miraculous string of successes was earned in cheap fashion against amateur or collegiate level opponents. The prevailing wisdom was that the Cuban Leaguers could never compete head-to-head against top big leaguers. Just how wrong that perception had always been was soon underscored with a string of convincing victories over Venezuela (featuring Cy Young starter Johann Santana), Puerto Rico (playing on home turf before a packed arena of 20,000 fanatics), and universal favorite Team Dominicana (also boasting its Cy Young starter Bartolo Colón). Never again should the strength and resilience of Cuban baseball be so callously doubted.

Of course MLB was not entirely a loser — despite such an unpredictable turn of events on the field of play. The stated WBC goal of spreading a message that baseball is truly an international sport was by all measures a resounding success. Merchandize was peddled in record numbers. Stadiums were jam packed in Orlando and San Juan and also cozily populated in the larger venues of Phoenix and Anaheim. All-important television ratings far exceeded expectations, despite the underwhelming underperformance of a star-studded Team USA. The atmosphere was truly electric for second round matches in San Juan's Hiram Bithorn Stadium — where four Latin American powers faced off in a first true "Caribbean Series" matching the Cuban juggernaut against top big leaguers from Venezuela, the Dominican and host Puerto Rico. And most importantly, a huge North American television audience had its eyes rudely opened to the undeniable fact that top flight baseball is no longer restricted to the United States and the Dominican Republic. Mexico and Canada both upended the USA Dream Team. Korea, without a single household name big leaguer, ran the table undefeated until a semifinal loss to rival Japan. And the two international powerhouses left standing on the final night claimed only a single recognizable major leaguer between them. What could possibly have been a better scenario for growing baseball as a mature international sport?

The biggest shock in an event full of more than mild surprises was without doubt the wild successes of the Cuban national team. Cuban baseball has long awaited the hour when it would find a main stage to demonstrate that its quality was on a true par with that of any league in the world — especially the celebrity-stunted, high-salaried forces of the U.S. major leagues. That hour finally arrived and the new-generation Cuban Leaguers were more than up to the challenge. There will now, of course, be skeptics quick to assert that the WBC was an unfair test simply because big leaguers were in the early stages of spring training, with pitchers not yet fine-tuned and batters struggling with timing and lacking mid-season conditioning. But Dominican manager Manny Acta was quick to dismiss this perception. "Everyone knew we were going to play this tournament as far back as the last All-Star break. Everyone therefore had the same opportunity to prepare themselves." It must be remembered that if the Cubans were coming into this tournament in the middle of their own National Series, they were also at a severe disadvantage because of pitch-count limits established to load the dice in favor of the less-conditioned big leaguers.

Cuba's victories in the WBC have not been quite as surprising to those of us who have closely watched the Cuban National Series on island soil over the years, or followed the triumphs of the Cuban team for two decades in distant outposts such as Barcelona, Sydney, Atlanta, Athens, Rotterdam and Taipei. The Cubans have long-since mastered the art of playing in short tournaments with a single-elimination championship round format. The Cuban brain trust, including manager Higinio Vélez, commissioner Carlitos Rodríguez and technical director Benito Camacho, did a remarkable job in selecting the best possible roster from numerous top National Series stars, and then in preparing their ball club physically and psychologically for the stiffest challenge in their nation's century-plus sports history. The results were the biggest string of victories in the proud history of Cuban baseball — either before or after the 1959 revolution. Despite a one-sided meltdown loss to Japan in the finale, Cuba had already savored on U.S. soil the true apex of its gold-studded 140-year-long baseball saga.

The North American press — partly from shameful lack of information and partly from its ongoing fascination and even obsession with the storyline of possible defections by star Cuban players — once again wrote endlessly before the first pitch of the WBC that either Cuba would not send its top stars to compete in San Juan and San Diego, or that showcase players would likely abandon their homeland in droves. Such stories were, as always, the result of wishful thinking and unfortunate disinformation. They failed to take into account the seriousness with which Cuba's baseball brain trust would prepare for this showcase tournament. They relied on speculations that Cuba's baseball forces were now weakened by retirements and defections. They discounted pitchers like Pedro Lazo and Yadel Martí and sluggers like Yulieski Gourriel, who *Baseball America* would soon enough be touting as the top overall WBC prospect.

What most of American and international media failed to recognize on the eve of the WBC was that new stars had already emerged at Athens (2004 Olympics) and last fall in Rotterdam's World Cup. Pedro Luis Lazo is every bit as devastating on the mound as José Contreras. Yadel Martí and

Vicyohandri Odelín may already be, despite their young ages, superior to any of the handful of Cuban hurlers who have abandoned the island. Ariel Pestano is a big-league quality catcher and switch-hitting Frederich Cepeda a sure-fire big league outfielder. In Osmani Urrutia and Michel Enríquez the current squad boasts two of the top five hitters (career batting average) in Cuban League history. And at 22, Yulieski Gourriel is already drawing comparisons with the legendary Omar Linares, comparisons that have now been rubber-stamped by two weeks of WBC action. American media has continued to ignore the fact that despite the departures of El Duque and Contreras, the large majority of the island's top stars have remained safely planted at home, awaiting the opportunity to test themselves against big leaguers while wearing the jersey of their homeland and not the uniforms of commercial big league ball clubs.

This was indeed the strongest Cuban lineup in recent memory and arguably the best ever. If there was a flaw it might have been pitching depth, yet that chink in otherwise solid armor proved to be minimal at best since Cuba won in the end on the strength of clutch pitching. The offensive lineup Cuba brought to San Juan was filled with productive batsmen named Garlobo, Cepeda, Gourriel and Urrutia (now the Cuban League's all-time leader in batting average), all equal to any sluggers of the past. And in the end the Cubans won big games over their three Caribbean rivals on the strength of their underestimated but always clutch hurling. Contreras might be gone. But Lazo was still there and proved himself the one truly dominant closer on the WBC scene. With young arms like Martí, Odelín and Yunieski Maya, the Cuban talent well is now anything but dry.

The first WBC was not only a resounding success by every measure, but it was also — in a way MLB officials had not anticipated — a turning point for international baseball. In the end there would be no anticipated marquee match-up of big league superstars representing baseball's two strongest bastions — the USA and the Dominican Republic. There was, instead, a far more intriguing clash between the two best leagues outside the majors — the Cuban League and the Japanese League. MLB had unwittingly managed to shine the spotlight directly on its two main competitors.

When the dust (and in San Diego the raindrops) finally cleared, the debut WBC had proven at least three things. One was that Cuban baseball is absolutely for real. The Cubans have not won so relentlessly because they only face collegians or pros of lower classification. Cuban talent has now proven quite capable of rising to the level of whatever challenge it faces. A second eye-opener in this tournament had to be the quality of pitching now found around the world. Dominican manager Acta stressed that perception after his team's semifinal loss to Cuba. A final lesson of this tournament has been that Team USA can not expect to win on the world stage simply by throwing together a team of super celebrities at the eleventh hour. The American big leaguers need to learn about playing with the same intensified patriotic passion long found in the camps of the Dominicans, Japanese, Koreans and Cubans.

The first WBC will leave an indelible impression on the baseball world until the next round is played sometime in 2009. As others have observed in the aftermath, a legitimate question has now been raised about MLB's centerpiece position in the baseball universe: perhaps the big leagues no longer possess the highest quality baseball in the world, only the most expensive. Cuban skipper Higinio Vélez — who managed his pitchers throughout the tournament with the consummate skills of a big league bench boss — uttered the most memorable line of the final weekend in San Diego when he pointed out that his Cubans were a team of "hombres not nombres" ("men not names"). Vélez was quick to clarify that he was claiming that his team had great and dedicated ballplayers even if they were still "unknowns" on the world professional stage.

One of those "unknowns" was slugging outfielder Frederich Cepeda — the only ballplayer to hit safely in all eight WBC games — who best captured the theme of Cuba's stunning successes when he reminded the American press that "you can not judge baseball teams by the prices the athletes are paid, but only by the heart with which they play." Cepeda concluded that "our team has always fought with unity and control, as a team of unity." That unity has now sent shockwaves throughout the baseball universe.

Where has the Cuban baseball come from that shocked fans in American and Asian venues during March 2006? What indeed has been going on in Cuba during the nearly half-century of so-called "amateur" league play that followed Cuba's 1959 political upheaval? And what are the links between this post-revolutionary diamond heritage and the three-quarters of a century of professional action that had preceded and that fills most of the volumes previously devoted to the island's rich baseball saga? The answers are all here in this first extensive study of Cuba's baseball heritage that gives equal weight to ballpark history both before and after the fateful social and political transformations of January 1959, and both before and after the arrival in power of Cuba's most notable baseball fan, Fidel Castro.

* * *

Cuba's baseball history — like the 20th-century social and political history of the island as a whole — thus falls into two equally remarkable chapters, seemingly quite separate and defined by a wide chasm standing squarely between the two, a deep gulf resulting from the island nation's irrevocable break with its neighboring American overlords which came near the end of the century's sixth decade. But these two chapters are not nearly as divorced, one from the other, as a first superficial survey might seemingly dictate. The amateur baseball tradition which has been fostered under the Cuban socialist/communist government since 1962 finds its roots deeply embedded in a native Cuban amateur ball-playing tradition which reaches back to the thirties and even decades before that. At the same time, the aura of myth and mystery endemic to Cuban professional baseball of the blackball era and of the winter league heyday has never quite left the scene, even once the bats became aluminum, the championship prizes were re-

Manager Higinio Vélez is at the center of the home plate greeting party as Yulieski Gourriel completes a home run trot against Panama that launched Cuba's run to the World Baseball Classic finals.

duced to world cup trophies and Olympic gold medals, and the ballpark action became a showcase piece of the larger program of politicized and socialized government-run sports.

If Fidel Castro has often used baseball in recent decades as a propaganda tool to advance the cause of national identity and promote his perceived advantages of a socialist society, it must be remembered that the sport's 19th-century roots were also bound up with a nationalistic cause of rebellion against the then-hated Spaniards. If the island has taken pride of late in thrashing U.S. professionals at Olympic tournaments, the same was the case during barnstorming trips into Cuba by brash major leaguers nearly a century ago, when the burdens of American occupation and U.S. imperialism seemed every bit as threatening to Cubans as they later would under Batista and in the shadows of the Bay of Pigs. And if the Cuban national team has won many glorious victories in international amateur competitions over the last three decades, it was also regularly doing so almost before Fidel Castro was even born.

The chapters and appendices that follow tell of the rich history of Cuban baseball since its origins in the mid–19th-century. This is a subject that has not gone untreated in the recent literature. Celebrated Yale University literature professor Roberto González Echevarría (*The Pride of Havana*, 1999) contributes substantially to knowledge of the Cuban pastime with a massive work that purports to be a thoroughgoing history of the subject and at least partially serves precisely that function. University of Texas historian Milton Jamail (*Full Count*, 2000) has also treated the contemporary Cuban League scene but with emphasis more on the structure and post-revolution organization of Cuban baseball and the seeming full-blown crisis the island sport faces at the outset of the 21st century. *Sports Illustrated* staff writer S.L. Price (*Pitching Around Fidel*, 2000) has also emphasized baseball on the island in his more expansive look at the overall plight of crack athletes in Cuba during declining economic conditions of the past decade. My own earlier contribution was an elaborate coffee table picture book (*Smoke*, 1999), a collaboration with baseball photo archivist Mark Rucker designed to preserve a rare pictorial record of the Cuban pastime. But there are obvious shortcomings in each of these books that now justify a more searching look at the Cuban national game.

One special problem remains a maze of inconsistency

that surrounds reporting of Cuban baseball history down through the decades. The sparse collection of noteworthy books published through the years in Cuba itself also share this not unimportant deficiency. A landmark early-century island-published tome by Raúl Díez Muro (*Historia del base ball profesional de Cuba,* 1949) reveals to the careful reader or researcher an almost endless catalogue of errors in its reported scores, seasonal standings and player statistics. The few works treating post-1960 Cuban League action hardly fare much better. The somewhat more contemporary *Viva y en Juego* (Casas, Alfonso and Pestana, 1986) is far more accurate but reveals a post-revolution socialist enthusiasm strewn with excessive rhetorical cliché. My own text in *Smoke* regrettably failed to substantially correct many of these existing flaws. There are, for example, entries found in *Smoke*'s "Cuban Baseball Chronology" that sustain myths or repeat earlier sloppy reporting, which only my own most recent research has begun to unravel and supplant with more accurate accounts. González Echevarría's *The Pride of Havana* (published the same year as *Smoke*) still offers the most detailed and comprehensive history of island professional and amateur baseball while at the same time failing to escape its own nightmare of factual errors and infelicities. Most notable perhaps are difficulties González Echevarría experiences in sorting out ballplayer names (also officials and writers) and maintaining consistency in their correct spellings (Bart Giammatti/Giamatti, Moises Quintana/Quintero, Laird Bergard/Bergad, Murray Franklyn/Franklin, Santiago Ulrich/Ullrich, Ron/Don Blasingame, Lourdes Gorriel/Gourriel, Buck O'Neill/O'Neil, Willy/Willie Miranda, Bobby Thompson/Thomson, Sendaharu/Sadaharu Oh, Robert Fynch/Finch, Adrian Zavala/Zabala, Wilbur/Wilmur Fields, Johny/Johnny Lipon, Gerald/Donald Honig, etc.). Some of these nagging inaccuracies admittedly fall into the category of mere unsightly typographical errors. If this is a minor distraction in the end, more troubling is the profusion of incorrect dates, chronologies, event names and locations when it comes to reporting Cuba's many glorious triumphs and few rare stumbles during 20th-century world amateur competitions. (I return to this issue in Chapter 7.)

In the spirit of complete fairness, my own work in *Smoke,* as noted, reveals its own share of errors, oversights, and inaccuracies — a certain portion of which were again a result of less than perfect editing. I have applied myself in this more thoroughgoing work to setting the record straight on some of these earlier missteps, as well as adding substantially to that record as amended by nearly five years of subsequent arduous research into Cuba's often murky baseball past. All of us tackling the existing records of the island sport have suffered substantially from the dense jungle of errors carried by primary texts such as those by Diéz Muro and by Delgado and Nieto (*Béisbol Cubano: Récords y Estadísticas,* 1955) that have long been taken too uncritically as bibles on the subject. My hope here is to finally expunge some of the worst inconsistencies. That is to say, hopefully to clear up some of the mess once and for all to the degree that this is today even possible. One aid in this effort has been the unpublished yet invaluable research carried

on in Havana in recent decades by eighty-year-old Severo Nieto Fernández himself, and also by an equally dedicated and authoritative Alberto Pestana (still today employed as a Cuban League statistician and historical archivist). Both men have been generous in discussing and sharing their many emendations and corrections of earlier works — both their own and those of others. Nieto, especially, has sorted out much of the record on early-century professional Cuban League play. And Pestana is the best living source for notebooks crammed full of data on Cuba's international play both before and after the baseball-reshaping 1959 revolution. (Some of Pestana's invaluable data on World Cup and Olympic events has been also reprised in Chapter 10 of my recent *Diamonds around the Globe: The Encyclopedia of International Baseball,* 2005.)

Professor González Echevarría has provided the most thoroughgoing history to date, for all his book's minor editorial shortcomings. *The Pride of Havana* nonetheless suffers as a scholarly work from an affliction not uncommon to even the best of baseball historians. The author's frequent tendency is to color events with personal nostalgia. Cuba's Golden Age is thus quite predictably found to be the one he grew up with and the one when he himself was first thrilled by island play as an impressionable youngster. Couple this with a tenaciously held political opposition toward the Castro government and thus nearly all changes it soon brought to the island and González Echevarría's view is one that inevitably over-plays baseball glories from the thirties and forties while at the same time sweeping conveniently under the carpet as nearly worthless all baseball achievements of the past near half-century.

There is also substantial weakness in González Echevarría's efforts at establishing a 1947 pennant-deciding series between Almendares and Habana ball clubs as the true apogee for all of Cuban baseball. There were indeed glorious achievements to be found everywhere throughout the early and mid–20th-century seasons on Cuban diamonds, both in Havana's winter professional circuit and the amateur games and leagues that spread across the island. But it is equally true that Cuba never owned what could be considered a truly national baseball enterprise before the transforming events of the late-fifties socialist revolution. And the league baseball being played during the vaunted (by González Echevarría) 1940s and fifties era was as much as anything a reflection of a decadent sport already falling into rapid decline.

The late fifties saw public interest waning (particularly outside Havana) in Cuban League professional games, especially with the wildly popular Almendares and Habana teams now falling on hard times and the fan-poor Cienfuegos and Marianao clubs thus capturing five of a final half-dozen pennants. The AAA Cuban Sugar Kings drew small and even negligible crowds at the new Havana Gran Stadium throughout their brief history that commenced in 1954 and died suddenly with revolutionary furor surrounding the anti-Batista guerrilla movement. After the 1959 revolution, however, baseball once again seized an entire island as it had not done for years and even decades. Stadiums overflowed throughout the island during the 1960s and '70s and new parks were soon being built in most provincial capitals (Camagüey, Pinar del Río, Matanzas, Sancti Spíritus, Holguín, Santiago de Cuba, etc.). The baseball re-organization under Cuban government control that emerged in the sixties was for the first time one that existed solely for benefit of the collective Cuban people and thus was no longer controlled and exploited as a convenient talent farm by U.S. professional organized baseball (which had established its hold over Cuban League affairs in the wake of an aborted 1946 attempt by Mexican millionaire Jorge Pasquel to establish his own rival major league operation by ruthlessly raiding American and Cuban talent). Cuba, after 1962, for the first time truly boasted its own genuine national sport — one that was not merely an outpost of the American white or black professional game — just as on other social, economic and political fronts the regenerated country at long last had finally achieved its own non-American and non-Spanish national identity.

University of North Carolina cultural historian Louis Pérez, Jr. eloquently captures much of the connection between Cuba's nineteenth-century national origins and the foundations of the island's national game of baseball. Professor Pérez demonstrates exhaustively in his marvelous recent book *On Becoming Cuban* (1998) how Cubans of the fifties had ultimately become fed up as a society with their loss of national identity and with related wholesale submergence of everything that was natively Cuban to the pervasive intrusion of all that was covetously and embarrassingly North American. Baseball was certainly no exception in this danger-fraught cultural equation. It is no more surprising, then, that the Cubans would reject American control on the baseball diamond (in the guise of MLB-controlled organized baseball) than that they should — in a fit of patriotism and national pride — finally throw off the economic bonds that had long exploited their sugar industry, utility companies and other natural resources for exclusive benefit of absentee foreign investors or profit-driven North American imperialists.

In sum, Roberto González Echevarría has written a valuable book recapturing baseball's lost Caribbean origins born in Cuba during the final decades of the 19th century and matured with Havana's winter league scene during the first half of the 20th century. But his portrait remains rather incomplete in detail and somewhat wrongly focused through ideology. What I am suggesting here is that if *The Pride of Havana* is intended as a comprehensive history of baseball played in Cuba — and not merely as the nostalgic portrait of Cuba's long-gone winter league scene from a half-century distant — then fully half of its 400-plus pages might well be expected to treat Cuba's contemporary (post-Fidel) baseball scene. Dismissal of the current amateur Cuban League on the excuse that it is not of big-league caliber is in the end a major disservice to the rather substantial impact of Cuba's full baseball history. The subject should never be reduced to Cuban baseball as seen solely in the glare of major league events and achievements. Cuban baseball of the past forty years — played altogether free from organized pro baseball's iron grip — is in and of itself a most engaging untold story. It is not important

what arguments may rage about levels of play in Cuba as measured by pro standards of fundamental skill or consistent performance. The quality of baseball as fan spectacle must never to be judged solely by the raw talent of participating athletes alone. (It is also equally defensible that the value of pre-integration Negro league baseball as an American cultural institution never rested on any convincing argument that a majority of Negro league stars could have performed successfully in the majors, or may now merit bronze plaques at Cooperstown.) There are other relevant factors at play, like unwavering fan enthusiasm, arresting and colorful on-field spectacle, spontaneous growth of underpinning legends and myths, and — most important of all — the sport's reflection of a sustaining and recognizable national character.

Other major histories of Cuban baseball — those written in Spanish and not English — are also marred by often debilitating incompleteness. The standard reference work of Delgado and Nieto (*Béisbol Cubano: Récords y Estadísticas,* 1955), published only in Cuba, is a half-century out of date and thus misses altogether all important baseball of post-revolutionary Cuba. The same is true of the classic tome provided by Díez Muro (*Historia de base ball profesional de Cuba,* 1949), which provides most data and guidelines for the subsequent handbook by Delgado and Nieto. Both books are also either maddeningly inaccurate or regrettably incomplete when it comes to providing year-by-year standings and individual player statistics. More recent but still unpublished data compiled by Severo Nieto over the past four decades (and subsequently shared with this author in Havana) allows for a good deal of correction and updating of these two helpful but altogether unreliable classics.

A self-published Spanish-language illustrated history by California-based Cuban expatriate Angel Torres (*La Leyenda del Béisbol Cubano,* 1996) makes the identical assumptions found in *The Pride of Havana* about post-revolutionary baseball, and thus also leaves some of the more important chapters of the sport's island saga completely blank. Yet the Miami-published (Torres) and Havana-published (Delgado and Nieto) volumes actually both surpass González Echevarría when it comes strictly to details of the pre-1961 Cuban professional winter league seasons. Both Spanish "encyclopedias" provide much in the way of background statistics ignored by González Echevarría's exclusively narrative account of pre-Castro-era baseball. Year-by-year recaps provided by Torres include not only pennant-race reviews but also helpful summaries of individual league leaders and team standings. Delgado and Nieto also offer semi-complete Cuban League records for several dozen of the island's top professional winter league performers (Negro leaguers like Monte Irvin, Joe Black and Terry McDuffie and white American major leaguers like Ed Roebuck, Ken Boyer and Don Blasingame are included). These were the best encyclopedic works previously available, at least as far as what they cover; but by reading them one gets the distinct impression that the entire island of Cuba mysteriously sank into Caribbean waters immediately after the final pitch of the 1961 Havana professional season.

Milton Jamail (*Full Count*, 2000) is one American writer who does not shy away from baseball in the Castro era, but rather takes the contemporary Cuban League as his own main story line. Jamail is thoroughgoing in his detailing of precisely how the current Cuban baseball system works and he is especially helpful in describing such background matters as the organization and function of Cuban sports academics and training schools. His pointed analysis of current/recent problems on the Cuban scene and his recommendations for solutions will not, however, sit easy with many Cuban baseball observers. Jamail's beat as a *Baseball America* reporter has long been major league scouting and recruiting in Latin America, and he thus not surprisingly approaches Cuba from precisely this perspective. He sees defecting players largely as liberated slaves finally able to achieve the financial rewards they merit by playing in baseball's most glorious realm of the U.S. major leagues; he also assumes Cuban fans will one day extract great pleasure from watching local stars performing via television in the far distant venues of New York or Houston; he ignores any notion that these same Havana fanatics will be just as likely dismayed by resulting empty stadiums in Havana or Santiago once the bulk of local talent has fled northward. My own opinion is that Jamail has misread much of what today's Cuban baseball is all about, and thus what it has to offer both the Cuban and visiting North American spectator. He is right on target with many of his assessments, such as his notion that Fidel repeatedly views baseball as a legitimate arena for scoring large-scale propaganda victories on a convenient international stage. But Jamail seems never to see the proverbial forest for the trees when it comes to an overall assessment and appreciation of what are Cuban baseball's most glorious elements. From his perspective the 45-year isolation of Cuban baseball has been largely a tragic loss to U.S. big league fans and general managers, rather than a huge boon to Cuban fans who — as an unintended by-product — still own baseball's single remaining alternative universe.

My own focus in this book is fixed precisely on those special elements that make Cuba's game one of the true treasures of international baseball play. My approach has been historical, and I detail Cuba's baseball past as a means to understanding and more fully appreciating its inherited baseball present. My position is not strictly political in tone, though I doggedly maintain a largely pro-revolution posture on Cuba when it comes to matters of baseball aesthetics and the continued purity of the non-commercialized Cuban pastime. One does not have to support the entire scope of Fidel Castro's political enterprise in order to value a Cuban baseball system still free from the big business trappings that have nearly wrecked our current corporate major league sport.

My slant on Cuban baseball admittedly also reflects strong bias toward the beauties of international amateur sport, plus equally outspoken misgivings about what I take to be the sad state of today's major league baseball industry — rampant commercialism and a greed-driven business focus that together have sadly warped a former national pastime into a made-for-television entertainment event today so unpalatable to most past-era fans. I do not argue either for or against the Castro socialist experiment per se. I do largely agree with Milton Jamail and others that the long-standing U.S. economic sanctions aimed against Cuba have over the years benefited only Havana and Washington politicos, while at the same time ignoring disenfranchised citizens in both nations. I fully realize, as well, that Cuban baseball in the final analysis will have to change drastically in the not too distant future, if only because the tired and largely failed Cuban revolution must soon give way little by little to more open economic and culture exchanges with the colossus to the north. Cuba's post-revolution national pastime will soon regrettably lose its innocence, just as big league baseball long ago also did, once exclusive focus in the sport inevitably becomes financial gains for franchise owners, ballplayers, and media moguls rather than innocent pleasures of fans longing only for the unrestrained joy of experiencing the most perfect game among man's inventions. But I am certainly not rooting for any acceleration in that inevitable process.

My approach here in retelling Cuban baseball history is to divide my volume into four distinct sections. The first celebrates four truly legendary idols of Cuban baseball; Martín Dihigo, Adolfo Luque, Orestes Miñoso and Conrado (Connie) Marrero each receive their own biographical and analytical chapters. Martín Dihigo (a versatile black giant who once paced the exotic Mexican League in both batting and pitching in the same season) was unarguably Cuba's greatest-ever sporting icon. Luque (winner of a still-franchise-record 27 games in 1923 for the National League Cincinnati Reds) made the first substantial Cuban splash in the American big leagues. Miñoso (Chicago's original "Go-Go" White Sox speedster) first brought the novel flash and pizzazz of Latino-style baseball to our North American consciousness during the post-integration nineteen-fifties. And the pixie-like, cigar-puffing Marrero (best remembered by American fans as an enigmatic 40-year-old Washington Senators rookie) was the island's biggest amateur-era star, even though his career came well before the post-revolution apex of Cuba's celebrated amateur game.

Part II is devoted to Cuba's various showcase leagues — amateur and professional, pre-revolution and post–Fidel. Chapter 5 summarizes the full history of Cuba's professional winter league that was first launched on the island a mere two years after the founding of America's granddaddy National League and only survived (sometimes just barely) as a jewel of winter Caribbean baseball until the mid-century arrival of the fateful Castro-led revolution. Chapter 6 recounts the careers and contributions of lesser-known stars (Cuban and American) from a glorious blackball barnstorming era that was Cuba's special legacy during a blighted epoch existing before racial integration in U.S. organized baseball. Had segregation of the races never existed on North American diamonds, it is more than likely that forgotten players named Dihigo, Méndez, Torriente and Oms (among numerous black Cuban legends of that era) might well have been the Clementes, Marichals, Miñosos and Alous of the explosive big league decades separating the two great wars.

The heady tale of Cuban amateur baseball and the miraculous domination of Cuban teams on the world tournament scene also merits its own thorough-going coverage (Chapters 7 and 8), complete with extensive details on each and every top international competition played during the 20th century and beyond (including World Cup, Intercontinental Cup, Pan American and Central American Games, and Olympics). Here an exciting story unfolds of numerous major world tournaments, beginning with the world amateur championships inaugurated in the early 1940s and lately called the Baseball World Cup, and culminating with bitterly-fought USA-Cuba Olympic showdowns in Atlanta and Sydney at century's end. Special focus is placed here on a landmark 1999 Pan American Games confrontation at Winnipeg between skilled Cuban amateurs and the Canada, Dominican and American squads stocked for the first time with rosters of high-level minor league professionals. The Winnipeg Olympic-style experiment (one this author witnessed first-hand) provided perhaps the most thrilling international baseball competitions found anywhere on record.

Part III of the book is devoted to the lasting and far-reaching legacies of Cuban baseball history. Chapter 9 both explores and explodes the wildly popular myth portraying Fidel Castro as reported big league pitching prospect of the forties and reviews the consequences of that enduring quasi-legend. Also reviewed in a separate chapter (Chapter 10) is the entire saga of Cuba's substantial contributions to big league baseball before the fluid Cuban talent pipeline was rudely closed down after 1960 in the shadow of worsening USA-Cuba diplomatic relations. Additional chapters treat unknown superstars (Chapter 11) from recent decades of Cuban League play, plus the full story of the past decade's tentative efforts at baseball détente (Chapter 12), including the over-hyped if under-analyzed saga of Cuba's big league defectors during the 1990s, and the generally misunderstood Baltimore Orioles vs. Team Cuba exhibition series in spring 1999 with its intriguing implications for possible future working accords between the world's two foremost baseball-playing nations.

The fourth and final part offers the most comprehensive collections of Cuban baseball statistics (for both pre-revolution and post-revolution eras) found in any English language publication. Year-by-year team champions and individual league leaders are provided in Appendix D for both pre–1959 and post–1962 Cuban leagues, including the season and career individual pitching and batting leaders and all major category record holders. There is a detailed 140-year Cuban baseball chronology (Appendix A) collecting the important landmark events involving both Cuban big leaguers and island-based play. For Negro baseball enthusiasts there is also a Blackball Register (Appendix B), which documents, year-by-year, all legitimate Cuban teams and individual Cuban ballplayers on both barnstorming teams and established Negro league clubs. And there are also complete rosters and career statistics for all Cubans who played in the major leagues (Appendix C), as well as for all players (Appendix D) who appeared on Castro-era Cuban national teams between 1962 and 2005.

*   *   *

Nearly a decade of extensive Cuba travel has provided this author with something closely akin to a life-altering experience. My ingrained perspective on my own native land—which so centrally prizes its avowed commitments to personal freedom and political democracy—could not help but be somewhat filtered by experiencing firsthand a foreign land which I had long been taught to believe existed under a grueling reign of political oppression and offered few opportunities for unfettered self-expression. It does not take much time in Cuba to discover that alternative forms of political administration do not always mean obliteration of all cherished political liberties. My own first-hand experience in Cuba—if not altering my deep appreciation for the many blessing of our own native land—has also increased my awareness of callous American excesses. While residents of New York, Chicago or Miami may boast greater liberties at the polling places and greater freedom of choice in the market place, they enjoy little of the average Cuban's freedom from fear of walking local neighborhood streets, freedom from rank abuses of a capitalist marketplace, or freedom from the insidious forces of institutionalized racism and sexism. Havana is not only the most charming but also easily the safest capital city whose streets I have been privileged to visit. And if the structures of local government and the pressures of cultural expectation are indeed quite different, Cuba today is anything but a brutal police state or a virtual political prison. The Cuban people are among the most hospitable, charming, life-loving and resilient of any I have ever known. And when it comes to our present subject of baseball, the Cuban version of the game — more because of than in spite of its freedoms from U.S. major league style professional spectacles — has restored for this writer a love for the American/Cuban game that had earlier been almost entirely destroyed in the late 1980s and early nineties by the self-serving shenanigans of big league players and owners alike.

Many have shared quite intimately my personal Cuban adventure over the past nine-plus years. First on the scene was Mark Rucker, my partner in the project that produced *Smoke*, my first book about the Cuban national pastime and the publishing project of which I remain most proud to this day. It was Mark who conceived and fostered the original idea to visit the island and to write about Cuban baseball, and without Mark's hefty push in the early stages of the *Smoke* enterprise I would have never known either Cuba or the life-shifting experiences that it has gifted to us both. *Baseball America* writer Milton Jamail and Texas Rangers radio broadcaster Eric Nadel — two transplanted Texans who comment on the game with eloquence and insight — have crossed my path on more than one Cuban junket and have provided endless valuable input on the subject of *pelota cubana*. Bob Weinstein has beaten more byways and pathways in Cuba with me than anyone else and has inevitably enriched my days there as much as anyone. I would be remiss not also to mention that my first reading in 1999 of Roberto González Echevarría's *The Pride of Havana* was an inspiration as well as an extensive education, even if the esteemed professor and I occupy distinctly opposite corners in any debate about either Cuban politics or Cuban baseball.

But I am most heavily indebted to my two constant Cuban companions and *compañeros,* Ismael Sené and Martín Hacthoun (no pseudonyms here, thank you!), spiritual brothers without whom Cuba over the years simply would never have been anywhere near the same *béisbol paradiso. Gracias por todo, mis hermanos.*

Introduction

All men dream, but not equally. Those who dream by night in the dusty recesses of their mind, wake in the day to find that it was vanity. But the dreamers of the day are dangerous men for they may act their dreams with open eyes. This I did.
— T.E. Lawrence

An almost surreal scene of flood-lit infield ballet enveloped a most perfect of all possible baseball backdrops. The arresting setting on this special night was a classic concrete and steel ballpark of immediate post-war vintage. Stretched out before me was a true picture-post-card scene — a cavernous stadium filled with ghostly shadows of countless ballgames past, fading green paint peeling from sprawling wooden grandstand seats, a single-decked arena tucked under a cantilevered ceiling that reached from foul pole to foul pole, distant green-hued cement outfield bleachers topped by a massive quartet of towering electric light stanchions. In the background fifty thousand-plus raucous fans kept up their constant din of enthusiasm to support on-field action as the home club edged toward a narrow and thus especially thrilling victory. Remarkably absent from this scene were any of the more commonplace distractions that define more familiar late-twentieth-century big league theme-park stadiums — with their erector-set retractable roofs, their skyscraper-proportion video scoreboards, the endless corridors of food courts and gift shops, and the ever-present surrounding blare of screaming electronic commercial chatter. In my own mind's eye this was truly baseball resurrected from a time long past and but dimly remembered — from an epoch long before our North American professional league parks were somehow converted *en masse* into garish shopping malls while at the same time being transformed into oversized and plastic-carpeted television sound stages.

The time frame is late October of 2003 and the exotic locale is Havana, Cuba. The game on tap this particular night was a nail-biting struggle between national teams representing heavily favored reigning champion Cuba and upstart, upset-minded yet outmanned Brazil. It was opening night of medal round games in international baseball's World Cup XXXV, an event unknown to American fans but now being staged for the fifth time since the mid-fifties on the tradition-riddled diamond of Havana's Estadio Latinoamericano (and for a tenth time overall here in amateur baseball's world capital). The ballpark itself was a key player in the charming scene, an unparalleled fifty-five-year-old crumbling edifice that had somehow ruggedly survived

the full half-century of virtual isolation imposed by Cold War politics on a still-proud Cuban national pastime. On this recent warm October night the vaunted Cuban national team — equal in talent to almost any big league twenty-five-man roster — would be surprisingly extended to the very brink of disaster by an overachieving Brazilian club, itself boasting little in the way of recognized baseball tradition, yet on this night nonetheless riding the potent arm of a talented Japanese-trained industrial league hurler who fittingly picked this precise moment to uncork the surprise game of his life.

The nostalgic setting and thrilling play experienced this special night in Havana's Latin American Stadium perfectly captures Cuba's rare baseball enterprise at its showcase best. But this was also a marquee moment for a more-muted parallel world of "amateur" international championship baseball — a universe long collectively ignored by U.S. baseball fans, major media outlets, and the head-stuck-in-the-sand corporate power-brokers today guiding the fortunes of North America's professional organized baseball. This moment alone seemed proof positive that there is indeed a thriving alternative baseball universe, one as far off the beaten path of mainsteam baseball action as were — in another earlier era — outlawed Negro leagues and unwanted dark-skinned ballplayers who also performed in unheralded games staged in the dim shadows everywhere across back-roads America.

Such showcase games found in today's baseball-crazy Cuba do not come without a steep price for curious North American visitors; they even extract a heavy toll on native island rooters immune to luxurious trappings of big league games matching millionaire athletes and housed in gaudy pleasure-dome settings. First and foremost is the issue of creature comforts: the wooden seats in Havana are unbearably hard and uneven, the ballpark restrooms are distastefully unsanitary and even quite primitive, concession and souvenir stands are rare, and the only ballpark fare usually available is steaming hot and stale black Cuban coffee dispensed in small squirts from lunchbox-style fifties-era thermos bottles and then gulped from tiny finger-scorching paper cups. Stadium outfield and grandstand lighting is reminiscent of backwater rookie-league ball fields of the 1940s and scoreboards rarely carry anything beyond the batting orders and line scores. Cuban League uniforms of late also look more appropriate to local industrial league softball attire: caps are one-size-fits-all adjustable items and a single design for home and away nylon shirts (differing in color and team name only) is universally adopted by the entire league.

Yet even if the physical setting and outward trappings are more suggestive of semi-pro venues than of top-level pro ball, it is nonetheless a small price to pay for recovering the spectacle of baseball as it was once played in our own youth. Cuban baseball is — in every sense, positive and negative — a very far cry from the bat-and-ball spectacles today altered almost beyond recognition by made-for-TV versions of North America's floundering national pastime.

Just reaching a Cuban ballpark has become exceedingly difficult of late for any American *aficionado* pursuing such extraordinary entertainment pleasure. The largest hurtle remains a long-standing U.S. government travel ban, one sanctioned by Helms-Burton legislation designed to force political change on the island by stemming the flow of American dollars into Fidel Castro's faltering economy. This restriction on the rights of our citizens to visit the communist nation takes the form of long-standing requirements for a U.S. Treasury Department travel license issued by OFAC (Office of Foreign Assets Control) and only available for certain approved academic research or humanitarian and cultural exchanges. American tourism to Cuba remains strictly taboo under Helms-Burton sanctions, despite forty years of evidence that such restrictions have done nothing to shake the foundations of Castro's socialist government or to bring about any of the fuzzy American political objectives.

Big Brother's watchful eye on Americans attempting to sneak through OFAC's protective net has only intensified in the aftermath of our 9–11 inspired war on terrorism. The Bush Administration's increased nation-building efforts aimed at Iraq and other perceived evil empires (countries, like Cuba, outspokenly opposing what many in Third World outposts increasingly see as American "imperialism") have now meant further elevated hassles for those intrepid Americans who would exercise their freedoms by venturing into such forbidden foreign territory. Even legal (OFAC licensed) travelers to Cuba have in recent months had to battle with increased surveillance inspired by President Bush's intensified attentions to these celebrated (if not entirely popular) Homeland Security measures.

My own travel to Cuba since 1996 has been entirely legal under OFAC provisions that provide for trips by fulltime academics engaged in legitimate Cuba studies and capable of demonstrating likely probability of publication. Having made more than thirty trips to the island since February 1997, to collect data and photographs and conduct interviews related to my earlier book *Smoke* (co-authored with Mark Rucker), as well as to this present volume, I have rarely encountered more than routine questions from U.S. immigration officers about my appropriate OFAC license status on either departure for or arrival from Cuba. With my regular venue for travel being the sanctioned charter flights that depart several times weekly from Miami International Airport, I had always found legal (OFAC approved) travelers to be courteously treated and rarely hassled by Miami-based immigration and customs authorities. But that picture would change quite radically on one recent trip in late October 2003.

On route to Havana for a final round of fact checking related to this current volume — and also on assignment to cover World Cup XXXV for *Baseball America* — I received a bitter taste of the new OFAC enforcement efforts that had kicked into effect only that very week, on the heels of President Bush's latest national radio address once more promising to get tough on Americans who persisted on venturing behind enemy lines in Fidel's forbidden island. Despite the continued validity of my general license permission — still very much on the OFAC books — and despite a normal procedure of filing required travel affidavits with the charter airline on which I was flying, my progress was blocked at the boarding gate by uniformed Homeland Security officers for the first time checking passports and OFAC travel licenses of all Americans attempting to board the Havana-bound flight.

Excessive details about the tense momentary scene that followed are neither welcome nor appropriate in a book devoted to baseball; and yet the raw facts do bear on the subject of Washington's iron-fisted control over everything Cuban, including baseball. In brief, I had to convince attending agents that specific licenses (ones issued on OFAC letterhead with specific dates for a sanctioned trip) were indeed not required for general license category academic researchers. The day was only saved when in desperation I unpacked from my carry-on luggage one of my earlier-issued "specific license" OFAC permissions dated from December 1999 (I always carry one with me) and also agreed to a possible interview with OFAC officials upon my return stateside. The upshot of the matter was that Homeland Security guards newly assigned to monitor Cuba flights in October 2003 had never been briefed about general license provisions and were apparently instructed to clear specific license travelers only, regardless of what existing laws might still sanction. Upon my return to Miami I was told by a U.S. Customs inspector examining my bags for permitted Cuban rum and cigars (licensed travelers are allowed one bottle and one box) that he indeed knew of my right to travel on general license provisions but that he had now been instructed by OFAC administrators to tell general license travelers that they were being "unofficially discouraged" from choosing this still-legal travel route, and that they ought to seek a specific license for each trip if they "didn't want to be hassled" either when leaving or re-entering homeland borders. The point of such personal history — however extraneous to baseball matters at hand — is merely to underscore a fact that even for legal Cuba travelers, efforts to reach the distant venues of Cuba's isolated alternative baseball universe today constitute anything but a routine or comfortable adventure.

But on the night of October 22, 2003, all such annoyances were temporarily obliterated by the purity of the Cuban baseball scene at hand. The night was truly electric as a boisterous if not quite overflowing partisan throng welcomed each base hit and every slick fielding play made by their beloved Cuban national team. Partisans and more neutral observers alike anticipated a laughably one-sided affair — likely even a "knockout" that would end prematurely with the rule suspending play once either team amasses a ten-run lead after seven "official" innings (6½ frames if the home club is leading). The hosts anticipated breezing to another patented easy victory in their opening medal round match against a Brazil team boasting few names recognizable even to regulars on the international baseball scene and carrying no trappings of historical tradition in the sport that is Cuba's very national lifeblood.

But such are the potential marvels of any baseball game that a single masterful pitching performance might well equalize almost any mismatch; on this rare night that unexpected virtuoso performance came via a Brazilian hurler

Cuban super fan and local baseball expert Ismael Sené (center), with the author (left) and fellow author-photographer Mark Rucker at Regla ballpark near Havana in December 1999 (courtesy Transcendental Graphics).

named Kleber Tomita whose ancestral roots were Japanese and whose baseball training was also the product of recent summer service in a top-level Japanese industrial league. Tomita handcuffed a befuddled Cuban lineup for eight innings and soon disaster stared the home forces squarely in the face after a solo homer put the Brazilians on top in the opening half of the final frame.

Yet the legacy of more than a half-century of Cuban domination in international baseball venues is so palpable at times that miracle finishes have all but become an anticipated culmination of almost any such nail-biting tournament challenge. The teeming Havana crowd of better than 50,000 would be forced to hold their collective breath only briefly before this year's young slugging stars — infielders Yulieski Gourriel and Kendry Morales — would offer up the joy-unleashing lightning strokes to rudely burst Tomita's impossible dream and scuttle Brazil's near-miracle. Yulieski's towering opposite-field-triple topped by Kendry's follow-up ringing homer deep into the right-field grandstand capped the night's exciting near-upset with stunning suddenness. For this enthralled observer it seemed nothing short of one of those once-in-a-lifetime climactic finishes — a moment resplendent with images of Bobby Thomson, Bill Mazeroski and Joe Carter all rolled into one, a rare instant which coalesced the innumerable thrills and unsurpassed beauties which for me have become the very warp and woof as well as the yin and yang that is today's incomparable Cuban baseball.

* * *

Each and every outsider who has chased after nostalgia in Cuba's quaint ballparks has his favorite indelible images of a remarkable island baseball culture that is today fast-fading and even threatened with imminent if not immediate demise. For Milton Jamail in his recent book *Full Count* it is a scene that the author witnessed outside Havana's aging Estadio Latinoamericano only hours before a league game between the formidable Pinar del Río club and the local favorite Havana Industriales nine. Arriving two hours before game time Jamail stumbled upon a pickup game in the streets fronting one of the park's main entrances. It was a contest featuring rag-tag players mostly pushing middle age, competing with carved sticks and broom handles for bats, tightly wound twine for a makeshift ball, and flattened cardboard boxes serving for bases. Surrounding the informal pickup match was a crowd of rapt spectators that included the entire roster of the just-arrived Industriales team already attired in their uniform pants, tee shirts, and baseball cleats. While the hometown league players joined a growing crowd to cheer on rivals in this commonplace street pickup game, fans mixed with local diamond heroes and everyone remained fixated on the heated stick-ball action. No one pestered the mingling Industriales stars for handshakes or for autographs, or even seemed to acknowledge their presence. In Jamail's own words it was an inspired moment "harkening back to images of the game long past in the United States."

Such rare moments, shared by just about any visitor to the engaging and often disarming Cuban baseball scene, never fail to expose the warts as well as the considerable wonders of a national pastime that is nearly as old as its North American predecessor and every bit as much — perhaps even more — a vital element of the national consciousness that sustains it. If Jamail's personal version of such mind-binding moments of "surprise filled with inspiration" surrounding Cuban ballpark culture came with that one pickup game outside Havana's Latin American Stadium, my own similar moments seem almost too frequent to catalogue. They may also seem less remarkable in any subsequent retelling. Yet they are nonetheless burned indelibly into my own growing inventory of Cuban baseball images.

Perhaps my own most cherished recollection came after a league game in Pinar del Río and unfolded when Mark Rucker and I joined a pair of Cuban hosts for a two-hour auto ride (in their rust-eaten Russian-model Lada) along the desolate rural highway linking Pinar with Havana. Our companions — officials of Cuba's national sports ministry who had driven us to the western province on one of our earliest visits to Cuban ballparks in February 1997 — were almost as unfamiliar with the maze of village streets surrounding Estadio Capitán San Luis as we were. The result was an increasingly futile backstreet search to locate an avenue that might take us directly to the lost highway entrance.

Disoriented amidst tangles of similar-looking dark side streets, we eventually stumbled on the lighted entrance to what appeared to be a combination bar and grocery shop offering assorted staples and soft drinks. Requesting help at the shadowy doorway after explaining our sad plight, we were promptly joined by a smiling and strapping bare-chested black-skinned athlete attired only in dirt-stained baseball pants and stocking feet, sporting a gym bag slung over one shoulder and a handsome female companion clinging to the other. A shocking realization hit us immediately that the familiar face was that of Pinar ace pitcher Pedro Luis Lazo, still in partial uniform and obviously wending his own way home on foot only moments after the final ninth-inning out. The amused pitcher merely chuckled at the confusion of these "foreigners" from Havana and immediately jumped on his hardscrabble Chinese bicycle rescued from inside the shop entrance way. As though this were a normal nightly occurrence, Lazo waved to us to follow and then proceeded to peddle through several blocks of dusty streets the size of alleyways until he had safely deposited us alongside the highway entrance ramp. Having a good laugh with Mark over the surreal incident as we raced through the night-time darkness on route back to Havana, I could only keep asking myself (as I have many times since) what the chances would ever have been of running into Whitey Ford or Allie Reynolds or Roger Clemens trudging on foot a dozen blocks from Yankee Stadium and then enlisting the assistance of a bicycle-peddling big leaguer in guiding us back in the direction of the Major Deegan Expressway.

A far sadder if equally amazing moment — also set in the distant island outpost of Pinar del Río — exposes the distinct downside of such all-pervasive Cuban baseball innocence. Traveling with a group of American photographers in February 2002, Mark Rucker and I again encountered the highly unexpected during a brief rest stop on the outskirts of the island's westernmost city. Waiting for the remainder of the contingent to attend to nature's callings before the long ride back to Havana, I innocently wandered into a small alcove adjacent to the Pinar del Río Hotel bar, located behind the main entrance-way lobby. What first caught my eye was shocking enough in its own right. Hanging against the wall, on ordinary wire coat hangers, were a trio of sharp red Cuban national team jerseys, displayed to reveal the numbers and names of local heroes Pedro Luis Lazo, Omar Ajete, and pitching coach Julio Romero — all current members of the Pinar del Río Cuban League team. The snazzy shirts were easily identifiable as game-worn jerseys from the Atlanta Olympic Games and thus constituted a primitive local excuse for something approximating a miniature hometown

The author (right) and a fellow American traveler (front) in dugout of Capitán San Luis Stadium with three members of Pinar del Río Cuban League team in February 2001.

Capitán San Luis Stadium in Pinar del Río, the prototype 1960s-era Cuban League ballpark.

baseball hall of fame. Nothing appeared to be in place (in the form of locks, cameras or even an attentive watchman) to provide even minimal security protection for such valuable pieces of memorabilia. The Olympic baseball shirts were easy pickings for any American visitor with a clue about their likely eBay market value. My first impulse was unobtrusively to search out Mark and quietly call to his attention something which I didn't want the rest of our party knowing about. But as I turned to depart the small room I was nearly floored by an even more disquieting sight. Next to the entranceway was something that had escaped my notice during my haste to view the display of treasured jerseys. Against the wall stood a modest unlocked glass display case (marred by an ugly crack across the top) boldly displaying original Atlanta gold medals earned in July 1996 by the same three ballplayers. There they rested, completely unguarded and yet apparently nonetheless relatively safe from any local tampering in this Third World town where petty theft or memorabilia profiteering are still completely foreign notions.

All such quaint and other-worldly moments do not necessarily transpire on the streets or in byways found outside the local ballpark. Game day action in the Cuban League stadium can also be surrounded by truly magical scenes — visions inconceivably far removed from the electronic din and commercial trappings encountered in today's big league venues. Cuban League games provide a North American visitor with a level of action and a collection of unknown yet polished stars hardly if at all distinguishable from those of any major league setting. But there are always unsettling surprises: often the spectacle has its own most disarming moments.

The most memorable big-time baseball game I have ever

witnessed was staged in January 2000 in the most unlikely environs of Havana's famed psychiatric hospital campus, the same locale where future "defector" and big-league post-season MVP Orlando "El Duque" Hernández labored in exile from the Cuban League during several months immediately preceding his much-celebrated 1997 dash to fame and riches with the professional American League New York Yankees. The contest, between Havana's hometown Metropolitanos and visiting Ciego de Avila, crystallized perfectly a chaotic world comprising much of Cuban League baseball.

Even before the day's first pitch was tossed or first bat swung, my constant Havana ballpark companion Isidro Saenz (an obvious if transparent pseudonym) would on this occasion provide an enriching historical backdrop for the afternoon's festive outing, as he had often done for so many others. This time it would take the form of some cogent insights drawn from Isidro's endless inventory of political humor, much of which — like this particular offering — features Cuba's indestructible *líder máximo* and supreme cultural father figure — Fidel Castro himself. But first some background scene-setting is in order.

Isidro and I had on the previous night witnessed a marvelous pitching duel staged by the same two tail-ender ball clubs at Latin American Stadium — a 2–1 13-inning nail-biter that seemed to reflect an entire 2000 National Series season that was being hobbled by an uncomfortable transition to wooden bats in the aftermath of a full quarter-century of using aluminum war clubs. Heavy slugging for which the Cuban League had long been noted would not be at all in evidence this particular winter. Home-run bashing had fallen off to such a degree that the individual league leader boasted only four

An outside view of Cristóbal Lara Stadium in Nueva Gerona, capital city of Isla de la Juventud. Cristóbal Lara, with its only grandstands and both dugouts along the first base line, provides Cuba's most unique baseball setting.

total dingers nearly halfway through the campaign. Batting averages around the circuit were anemic, and even run-of-the-mill pitchers were posting ERAs more appropriate for big-leaguers with names like Grove, Gibson, Clemens, Ford and Mathewson. When we arrived at tiny Manuel Fajardo Stadium on the Havana hospital campus for the rematch, we therefore had little reason not to expect yet another low-scoring squeaker of the type that had filled most of the past several months.

Before settling back in the languid sunshine to enjoy some classic game action, the unusual ballpark setting would briefly take center stage. It has become routine practice in recent seasons to stage Wednesday afternoon league contests in the smaller parks dotting each and every province, thus providing citizens outside the regional capitals with a chance to experience games close to home — one of the practices designed to lend truth to the notion that Cuban baseball (and Cuban sports in general) is truly "the peoples' right and privilege." Of these once-a-week venues, Manuel Fajardo Stadium ranks at the top of the list for both charm and quaintness. Seating only about 3,000 fans in the covered grandstand that runs from slightly outside third base to a few dozen feet beyond first base, the park features green tile-covered outfield walls about a dozen feet in height and backed from foul pole

to foul pole by an array of 30-foot-high green Lebanon cedars offering the most bucolic of possible settings.

External trappings in Fajardo Stadium are primitive to an extreme: all seats are merely numbered squares painted on thirty rows of smooth concrete bleachers; the infield is clay-filled and the outfield grass features an array of worn brown patches; a single scoreboard teetering above the right-field fence is little more than a schoolyard-style wood structure without any electronics, on which the line scores are strung out with painted tablets hung manually from wooden pegs. Behind the outfield wall, largely hidden amongst the ancient cedars, stand three silent rusty sentinels that once functioned as electric-light towers but long ago were stripped of all wiring and lamps. It all seemed lifted from some Hollywood film capturing American baseball between the world wars, a perfect setting for local high school action somewhere in Nebraska's corn belt, vintage late thirties or early forties.

Fajardo Stadium nonetheless bears a name with considerable historical significance, plus a tradition of some luster in post-revolution Cuban baseball. Officially christened *Campo Deportivo Manuel "Piti" Fajardo* (Fajardo Sports Field), it memorializes a revolutionary hero who once served bravely as the platoon medic in the 1957–1958 Sierra Maestra campaign

Pre-game setting and pastoral view at Nueva Gerona's Cristóbal Lara Stadium in January 2000.

alongside Fidel and Che. Constructed adjacent to the hospital grounds (a stone's throw from Havana's José Marti Airport) the structure served as setting for numerous amateur games for several decades; at one point the hospital even boasted a crack team at the provincial league level. After a period of relative neglect during the "Special Period" of economic hardship in the early nineties, the field was again resurrected as a part-time Cuban League venue in time for the 1998–99 National Series season.

The hospital grounds ballpark is also, quite coincidentally, home to one of Cuba's most delightful baseball legends clothed in political humor. And this is the very tale that Isidro Saenz began to relate only moments after our arrival in the grandstand on this particular January afternoon. As the humorous tale unfolds, Fidel and brother Raúl, Cuba's chief military commander, paid an inspection visit to the then-new hospital grounds in the mid or late sixties, shortly after the launching of Cuba's nearly two-decade entanglement with war-torn Angola. Passing by the stadium Fidel casually noticed a ballgame in progress and detoured to the grandstand to relax briefly while enjoying his own favorite pastime. The game in progress was a recreational outing for institutionalized inmates and both the field and surrounding stands were packed with residents who seemingly had minimal knowledge of Cuba's

national sport. As the strange game continued, Fidel and Raúl were astonished by such scenes as the pitcher winding up and tossing his deliveries over the backstop or into the dugout, some batters swinging and then running directly to third or second base, outfielders preoccupied not with chasing down fly balls but rather with scaling up the distant fences, and umpires tossing a dozen and more balls into play simultaneously.

As the story recounts, the sudden presence of Fidel and Raúl did not go unnoticed by one apparently very alert inmate seated in the nearby grandstand; the young man wasted little time in hastily approaching *el presidente* and attempting to gain an intimate personal audience. "Please *Comandante,*" the fellow pleaded, "You have to help me. I am not crazy like these others but instead am a victim of jealous family members who had me committed here to serve their own perverse ends. I am as sane as any man in the street and you must redress this wrong and have me released before I truly do go mad!" Temporarily distracted by the visitor's babble, Fidel politely suggested that the poor fellow join his compatriots out on the field and stop running on so and thus interrupting the amusing spectacle.

But the desperate inmate only persisted. "*Comandante,* I am truly NOT crazy!" he barked. "Look how those fools carry on at baseball. Sane people like you and me know how this beautiful game of ours is supposed to be played." At which point he launched into a detailed discussion of the finer points of *pelota* and in the process quickly had Fidel's full attention. The commander and chief was soon enough convinced that any man who knew the game so well could indeed not be nuts like the others and must indeed be a victim of some mix-up that had brought him to these grounds. Turning to Raúl, a magnanimous Fidel suggested an appropriate resolution for the poor man's plight. "Raúl," he instructed, "you can plainly see this fellow is a baseball connoisseur and not at all a crazy man. Make sure you get his name and begin procedures for his immediate release when we return to the office tomorrow morning. We need good citizens and truly bright men like this to help our cause in Angola." But before Fidel could utter another word the inmate had already begun fleeing toward the wall separating the grandstand from the field of play. "Excuse me," *Comandante,* he shouted over his shoulder while in full flight. "I hear my teammates shouting my name and I can't delay a moment more because they must need me now as a pinch hitter!"

The gag was not only precious but indeed most appropriate, as I was to discover as action began to unfold in Cuba's only ballpark housed on the grounds of a mental hospital. Although ballpark entry is free of any admission charge at Fajardo Stadium (Cubans are now charged one peso or four American cents for a grandstand ticket at Latin American Stadium, or three pesos for the prime reserved seats), the opening pitch was tossed with only perhaps five hundred fans scattered throughout the galleries. By the third inning, however, the stands began to fill to overflowing as several hundred in-

mates were released onto the grounds for afternoon recreation and many soon began making their way into the ballpark. It was a rare crowd of rooters to say the very least.

Most distinctive about the late arrivals was their uniforms consisting of faded blue jeans plus dingy blue or gray-toned long-sleeved canvas work shirts. Each carried (or rather wore) a tin drinking cup tied with a short, thick twine string to a side belt loop. Most were middle-aged or beyond, and the entire crowd seemed at first to be composed exclusively of men, though a few women with the identical close-cropped hairstyles would later be noticed as the game wore on. The first wave of two dozen or so denizens clustered together in rows immediately behind home plate; but as the population of inmates gradually swelled to six or seven hundred a few innings later, some had located only a few feet from us, closer to the first base dugout. While many sat statue-like through passing innings on the spot originally selected, others began to wander around aimlessly as the game droned on. As my attention occasionally returned to some of these locals — especially during between-inning lulls in play — I began to notice that some carried tattered backpacks containing a few personal items which appeared to consist of combs, paper-wrapped sandwiches and even a few school-style notebooks. It was during one of these interludes that I became aware that one crew-cut inmate puffing on a huge foot-long cigar and sporting brightly rouged cheeks after the fashion of a circus clown was indeed a sixty-something female and not the old man I at first mistook her for. By her side was a much younger black male with a bright costume feather lodged carefully behind his left ear.

Such local color was not restricted to the grandstands alone. One old-timer among the "crazies" (likely he was seventy-something), sported a floppy oversized white straw hat while wandering amongst the crowd near home plate; soon he ambled onto the field itself behind home during the bottom of the fourth, then strolled casually around in front of the third-base dugout — all to no one's apparent concern — before, just as unfettered, again exiting near home through the same grandstand barrier. A few innings later the arresting character danced lasciviously around home plate as between-innings rock music blared from the PA system. (The music itself was a rare occurrence for Cuban ballparks.) The self-appointed clown/mascot also stationed himself back on the field outside the third base foul line during late innings and began doing animated service as a retriever of foul balls drilled out in his direction. Whether he was only a tolerated inmate, a regular ballpark employee, or perhaps both, would remain an unsolved mystery. But his antics were soon to be overshadowed by

Mark Rucker (left) and the author at Palmar del Junco ballpark in Matanzas, site of Cuba's legendary first reported ballgame in December 1874.

other amusing grandstand high jinks, including a brief violent tug-of-war between two "crazies" over a backpack that one possessed and the other coveted, as well as a disheveled fifty-plus female inmate systematically working small clusters of grandstand "outsiders" and loudly inquiring after possible offers of a tasty cigar.

Such idyllic trappings and quaint historical overtones would only momentarily distract us from the circus of unfolding on-field baseball action. Offensive fireworks began quite early with Ciego de Avila's muscular catcher Roger Machado first awakening a drowsy crowd by poling a towering blast far into the trees behind the left field fence in the top half of the second frame. Teammate Franklin López responded immediately with a nearly identical poke that provoked the rattled Metros pitcher to plunk the following batter on purpose and thus earn an immediate ejection from play. This was unusual action indeed in a season when novel wooden bats had seemingly pulled the plug entirely on offensive fireworks. But it was only a foreshadowing, for in the third López smacked yet another dinger, this time with the bases jammed. Before the onslaught finally spun to a halt with a knockout-rule-shortened seven-inning 18–5 victory for the visitors, a new league mark for single-game homers had been set with eight (one even poetically socked by a Metros outfielder named Cervantes). The true impact of the day's extraordinary display of hitting could only later be fully appreciated when set against the fact that this was a season in which the eventual league home run champ would boast a mere ten. Two long smashes by López were his only pair of round-trippers for the entire campaign. Six homers by Ciego de Avila that day represented a full thirty percent of the club's entire season's total. Craziness on this rare Cuban League afternoon was hardly confined to exotic behaviors in the grandstand alone.

The rivals on this day were admittedly two of the league's least talented rosters, a fact that might have either excused or explained at least something of the abnormal style of play. The local Metros (short for Metropolitanos) have long suffered a reputation as Havana's "other club" and seemingly always play their games with little appreciable fan following. The Metros are almost an "unofficial" farm club for the more popular Industriales team also housed in the capital city. It has become common practice of late among league officials to reassign promising young players who debut with Metros onto the Industriales roster and thus improve prospects for Havana's crowd-pleasers. National team outfielders Yasser Gómez and Carlos Tabares are two recent illustrations of such player transfers (which remain quite rare in a league which normally has no trading of ballplayers). Ciego de Avila for its part fares little better when it comes to either fan following or serious runs at National Series league pennants. Since first appearing as a league team in 1978, the club representing one of Cuba's smallest provinces (population-wise) has boasted only five winning seasons and but one post-season playoff appearance.

The rarified atmosphere coloring this usual game in January 2000 was certainly only enhanced by circumstances of a first season in decades featuring wooden bats. It was thus dou-bly ironic that on this occasion Cuban batters would awaken in two normally light-hitting lineups with a fireworks display rarely topped even during a heyday of aluminum slugging. And on-field chaos was plausibly amplified almost exponentially by the off-beat locale and related background chaos constantly breaking out in the grandstand itself. In the end such exceptions once more seemed merely to prove a rule concerning the tenacious reign of the unlikely and the unusual that infuses each and every corner of the Cuban national pastime.

Nothing better captured this extraordinary mix of big-time baseball fare with bush-league histrionics than the day's backdrop comedy in record keeping. With balls already flying out of the park and runners circling the bases in profusion before many had even reached their seats, it soon became apparent that few in attendance had any idea what the game score actually was — though a repetition of blue jerseys racing toward the plate convinced most that visiting Ciego must be comfortably in the lead. The actual score stood at 9–1 after three frames and then 17–2 by the time we reached the halfway mark during the home portion of the fifth. But we had no grasp of these tallies at the time. The crude outfield scoreboard was manned by a dedicated denizen whose attire alone signaled permanent attachment to the institution (a silver drinking cup occasionally flashing reflections from his hip). If he was perhaps better prepared to handle the responsibilities of his post on other occasions, on this high-scoring day he was simply overwhelmed by the higher mathematics. The scoreboard top line (that for the visiting club) first read "2 2 5 2" after four innings, but when gusts of wind temporarily removed the numerical signs from the pegs that had once held them they were quickly replaced with "4 0 6 8" to indicate the Ciego de Avila tally. Hefty wind blasts were soon scattering scoreboard totals landward as freely as they were lifting fly balls skyward. As the score on the field changed rapidly, that on the scoreboard was also subject to even greater and more drastic alterations. The game finally finished, it was truly doubtful that any among even the sanest spectators filing out of the ballpark had the faintest idea of what the final score might actually have been.

One final delightful footnote remains to punctuate the rare afternoon's fare. It was also during the ongoing scoreboard fiasco that for the very first time in nearly five years of wandering Cuban ballparks I suddenly became conscious of an especially curious feature of Cuban League baseball; and it was one that most other American visitors most likely stumble upon during their very first outing at a ballgame in Havana. Yet it was a trivial treasure that had somehow to date completely escaped my own consciousness. Cuba's outfield fences are distinctive for their hand-lettered and oversized propaganda slogans praising triumphs of the revolution or spiritual virtues of socialist sport; it was that afternoon in Fajardo Stadium that I first became aware that even a Cuban scoreboard itself gets into the act of celebrating baseball's proud ties to Fidel Castro's forty-year communist revolution. The right edge of the scoreboard line score — the part were summary totals are placed and which carries the headings R-H-E in English-speaking North America — naturally reads **C-H-E** in every baseball stadium throughout Cuba. (While "Hits" and "Errors" are indicated by their customary English initials, runs scored here becomes "C" for the Spanish *carreras*.) Thus one merely has to glance at a scoreboard in any Cuban ballpark to discover this most permanent reminder of Cuba's most world-renowned individual revolutionary icon. Che indeed lives!

I was also left with more than Che Guevara's eerie symbolic presence to fill my thoughts at the end of perhaps my most unusual afternoon spent in a Cuban ballpark. The day's events had seemingly unfolded in a fashion reminiscent of what could only have been an altogether surreal baseball dream. Could such a game have transpired in Fenway Park or Forbes Field or even in the quaintest Florida or Arizona spring training venue? It was hardly likely and less than imaginable. Despite all surface appearances, this was not a sandlot or rookie league game plucked from some backwater bush league setting. It was a crucial mid-season league contest in a pro-level circuit featuring many athletes and even a few entire teams that were seasoned big-league equivalents. It constituted a typical mini-chapter from the ongoing chronicle of one of the world's leading baseball stages. This was only business as usual in one of international baseball's primer center-stage venues.

One had no option but to leave such a scene entirely stunned and thoroughly drained by what had been witnessed. As the collection of no more than a couple hundred visiting fans filed from Manuel Fajardo Stadium, some institutionalized residents remained transfixed at their posts, staring motionless as they had done for the preceding two hours. Some gazed blankly at the field now vacant of both players and action while others faced in an opposite direction as though transfixed by some unseen side show transpiring in the upper regions of the equally sparse grandstand. Their engrossing private movies were apparently still screening behind their vacuous stares. None in this modest throng seemed even vaguely conscious of a more transient crowd that was now melting away from around them.

Tomorrow ballplayers for both Ciego de Avila and Metropolitanos would board cramped, uncomfortable buses for long dusty rides to some other point on the island, where a new home stand or road trip would be launched. The Cuban baseball cycle remains resistant to any encroachments from passing time, and today as yesterday remains entirely unbroken.

* * *

Is there anywhere a land where baseball passions run deeper or where baseball tradition stands more ingrained in the national psyche than it does right here in the United States of America? The answer — perhaps somewhat surprisingly to those raised on the indelible myths of Abner Doubleday, Babe Ruth and Jackie Robinson — is a resounding "YES!" on both counts. And that privileged land would most certainly have to be Fidel Castro's always mysterious island nation of communist Cuba.

Cubans, after all, were playing their own version of the North American national pastime on an organized professional level as early as 1878, a mere two years after the founding of our own granddaddy National League. The first reported "organized" game occurred on the outskirts of Havana (in the sun-bathed seaport city of Matanzas) during December 1874, but baseball was widely known to exist on Cuban soil as early as 1864. It was the Cubans, furthermore, who transmitted the sport to other outposts of the Caribbean in the late 19th century and who also provided a first few waves of Latin American big league talent during early decades of the 20th century. And of course it has been Cuban teams that have relentlessly dominated a near-half-century of international-level competitions — IBAF world junior and senior championships (the latter today known as the Baseball World Cup), the Intercontinental Cup, the Pan American Games, and finally the Olympic Games — staged since Fidel Castro seized power and thus also since the island's overnight conversion from professional action to strictly amateur play in the second winter season of the 1960s.

Yet despite the strength of Cuban baseball tradition, the persistent depth of Cuban talent imported by Negro league (Martín Dihigo, Cristóbal Torriente, José Méndez, Alejandro Oms) and major league (Dolf Luque, Minnie Miñoso, Bert Campaneris, Mike Cuéllar, Tony Oliva, Tony Pérez) teams across most of the past century, and the undeniable presence of Cuba's national teams on the world amateur scene, arguably the most prominent feature of Cuba's baseball enterprise has nonetheless always remained the relentless mystery that surrounds ball-playing on the oversized island nation. Myth and mystery have indeed long remained the very bywords — perhaps even the very defining elements — of almost every aspect of Cuba's cherished diamond sport.

Negro league and big league barnstormers visiting the island — from John McGraw's first forays with his vacationing New York Giants near the turn of the century through the barnstorming heyday of the 1930s and forties — contribute some of winter baseball's most enduring legends. Cuban baseball pride was first inflamed by the "Black Diamond" José de la Caridad Méndez dominating befuddled big leaguers in 1908 (also 1909–1911) and by firebrand Cristóbal Torriente reputedly outperforming the behemoth Babe Ruth in 1920, even if precise details of these embellished legendary encounters between touring white big leaguers and native island blackball legends would subsequently always frustrate Negro league researchers attempting to amass revealing portraits or verify surviving accounts.

Cuban big league pioneers like Steve Bellán (the first Latin major leaguer when he appeared with the Troy, New York, team of the National Association in 1871), Rafael Almeida and Armando Marsans (the first Latinos to play in the majors during the 20th century when they debuted with Cincinnati in July 1911), pitcher Dolf Luque (a rarely acknowledged pioneering Caribbean star who figured prominently in both the 1919 and 1933 World Series), and the trailblazing Minnie Miñoso (the flamboyant "Cuban Comet" who crossed racial barriers as Chicago's first black big leaguer) are all remembered more as exotic stereotypes (hot-blood Latinos exhibiting comical broken English and flaming tempers) than as living, breathing genuine ballplayers. Most often these early Cuban stars have been relegated to history's dustbin as quaint exceptions to Latino baseball's trickle of early-twentieth-century "good field, no hit" hackers and rank journeymen.

Luque especially has suffered in the pages of history due to a distorted 1923 on-field incident (one which resulted in his kayoing Casey Stengel in the New York Giants dugout) which has long overshadowed his many pitching milestones: Luque was the first Latin American ballplayer to appear in a World Series, first to win 20 games in a National League season, and first to pace a big league circuit in both ERA and victories. Yet few existing accounts (an exception being my own earlier *Baseball with a Latin Beat* published a decade ago} have accorded Adolfo Luque his due as the first genuine Hispanic big league star, a legendary figure of Cuban League history (as both manager and pitcher), and one of the top pitchers in Cincinnati Reds annals (as owner of the best single season pitching mark in that ball club's rich National League history).

If Luque has rarely received his due, North American fans know almost nothing about four-nation Hall-of-Famer Martín Dihigo, considered by many Negro league researchers to be the best and most versatile blackball performer of all-time. Negro baseball's most renowned historian Robert Peterson (writing in his *Only the Ball Was White* in 1970) once found it necessary to recall that forgotten Negro baseball voices like owner Cum Posey and all-star Buck Leonard had often stressed Dihigo's combined ball-playing talents as never approached by any one man, black or white. Cooperstown enshrinement in 1977 by the major league veterans committee has so far done little to rescue Dihigo's reputation among American enthusiasts who rarely see beyond the horizons of the white man's organized baseball realms. And if Dihigo himself has been unaccountably lost to popular baseball history, other Cuban greats like Méndez, Torriente, Claro Duany, Silvio García and Alejandro Oms remain even today the most shadowy of all the golden-era blackball stars.

The mysteries obscuring Cuban baseball are remarkably even greater when it comes to the second half of the just-closed twentieth century. The chaotic story of the final winters of professional baseball on the island which unfolded in the immediate wake of Fidel Castro's sudden rise to power has never been accurately recounted and is surprisingly for the very first time rehearsed in some detail within this present volume. A wildly popular yet totally groundless myth still persists that Fidel himself was once a promising pitching prospect who had almost been signed by either the New York Giants, Washington Senators or New York Yankees (depending on the particular source of the circulating legend), though this tale is pure hokum, as is revealed with painstaking care in chapters that follow. Yet despite the groundlessness

of the Castro pitching legend, it has doggedly remained for many the best-known Cuban baseball "fact" in current circulation.

It has even been repeated *ad nauseam* that if only 1940s-era Washington Senators super scout Joe Cambria had been more cognizant that some prospects develop slowly and had thus risked inking a hot-prospect named Castro, then perhaps the whole future direction of hemisphere 20th-century politics might have been quite radically altered. The actual facts of Fidel's less-than-mediocre amateur pitching talent have never been properly sorted out by gullible commentators largely because this runaway legend — like so much touching Cuba's mysterious baseball heritage — is far more tantalizing than any bare-bones truths.

North American fans (even rabid followers of Latin American baseball) remain almost entirely in the dark when it comes to details about the numerous individual headliners, organizational structure, and rapid evolution of a hidden Cuban League that has remained the island's sports showcase (aluminum bats, quaint ballparks, neon-lit foul polls, and all) since its inauguration in 1962. Just as American fans of the

Cuba's revolutionary icon Che Guevara stands on muddy dugout steps in 1963, prepared to take part in an exhibition pick-up baseball game.

twenties, thirties and forties missed out on now-resurrected past-era stars like Josh Gibson, Oscar Charleston, Satchel Paige and an array of other crack black leaguers forced into the shadows by baseball's institutionalized racism, so too have more recent generations of rooters missed witnessing Muñoz, Marquetti, Vinent, Linares, Pacheco, Urrutia and dozens more buried in Cuba by the specter of America's Cold War politics. Some of these missing Cubans from the past thirty or forty years may well have qualified as Cooperstown legends; many more were likely legitimate big-league all-stars.

And the most recent small flood of Cuban defectors — Rey Ordóñez (Mets), Ariel Prieto (A's), Osvaldo Fernández (Giants), René Arocha (Cardinals), Rolando Arrojo (Devil Rays, Red Sox), Liván Hernández (Marlins, Expos), Orlando "El Duque" Hernández and José Contreras (Yankees, White Sox) and Danys Báez (Indians, Devil Rays) — have fostered the growing notion that current Cuban baseball is indeed a hidden potential pipeline of unlimited and untested big league talent which is now again about to explode upon the big league scene. Such speculation is fueled in the main by serious miscalculation of what in reality today's Cuban League actually is, and by sparse accurate scouting data available on even the top Cuban stars.

Impressive 1992 Barcelona and 1996 Atlanta gold medal performances by such muscle-bound Cuban sluggers as Omar Linares and Orestes Kindelán, such acrobatic middle infielders as Germán Mesa and Eduardo Paret, such talented flychasers as Yasser Gómez, Luis Ulacia and Osmani Urrutia, and such dominating hurlers as Omar Ajete, Maels Rodríguez and Pedro Luis Laso, have only further enhanced a popular notion of Cuban baseball as a veritable gold mine of seemingly uncollectible professional talent.

In truth the Cuban League appeared to fall on hard times during recent winters near the end of the 20th century, due perhaps to a large confluence of related factors. These factors seemingly included long isolation from modern coaching innovations; some questionable policies by Cuban League officials involving suspensions of top players charged with tainted loyalty (those perceived as threats to defect); shipping of prospects to amateur and semi-professional leagues in Italy, Colombia, Nicaragua and Japan; and the subsequent disappointment of die-hard Cuban fans (especially those in Havana) in response to this dissolution of the league's overall level of talent.

The past nine winters (1998–2006) have nonetheless witnessed a rather considerable rebounding of fan interest and thus of renewed excitement surrounding Cuban League seasons. Central to the revival have been spirited overall league play, a number of record-busting performances (José Ibar's 20 pitching wins in 1998, Maels Rodríguez's 263 strikeouts in 2001, and Osmani Urrutia's remarkable string of .400-plus batting topping the list), a lengthened Cuban League schedule (to 90 games), a renewed mid-season All-Star Game and revised format for the summertime second season (now called the Super League), further heights achieved by the national team in international play (especially the triumph over the big-league Baltimore Orioles and also a more recent "trifecta" of World Cup victories in Taipei, Havana and Rotterdam), and welcomed news concerning reversals in Cuban League policies regarding exporting of some stars and the suspensions of others. The ultimate peak, of course, would arrive with the amazing title-game run achieved during an inaugural MLB World Baseball Classic last March. Cuban baseball thus remains, as always, an unrivaled hotbed of regularly regenerating talent and an almost idyllic scene for American fans soured by stateside professional baseball's current rash of steroid scandals, cheapened slugging records, and ongoing debilitating over-commercialization.

But where did these glories of Cuba's national pastime come from, how did they emerge and evolve, and what accounts for their unrivalled uniqueness? It is a complex tale indeed, and one needing a far more balanced treatment than anywhere earlier attempted. So let the remarkable saga — of Cuban diamond legends both heralded and obscure, of a panoply of professional and amateur leagues that have filled nearly a century and a half, and of the indelible legacy that has only expanded under the manipulations of Fidel Castro's fifty-year communist experiment — now finally begin to unfold.

PART I

The Cuban Legends

1

Martín Dihigo — Baseball's Least-Known Hall of Famer

Cuban baseball — for all the glamour it now seemingly holds for American diamond *aficionados* — is hardly a matter of household names in Chicago, Los Angeles, New York, or even Miami. The biggest stars on the current Cuban national team — a big-league-quality outfit which has more than held its own in recent seasons with both the American League Orioles and AAA-level USA, Canadian, Australian and Japanese Olympic nines — are virtually unknown to all but the most dedicated Cuba watchers. Twenty-one-year-old Maels Rodríguez (before his career-ending arm injury in 2002) hurled a scorching fastball clocked in Cuban League play in excess of one hundred miles per hour, and equally proficient flamethrowers Faustino Corrales, Norge Vera and José Ibar have of late set big-league scouts to salivating with their repeated mastery of U.S. pro hitters in Winnipeg (1999 Pan Am Games), Sydney (2000 Olympics), and Taipei (2001 world championships). Yet none of these headlining island stars would receive even a knowing nod from perhaps one in fifty thousand self-proclaimed USA ballpark experts.

The first Cuban-born big-leaguer to be enshrined in Cooperstown? Big Red Machine icon Tony Pérez finally cracked that barrier with the final Hall of Fame balloting of the 20th century. Minnie Miñoso, Camilo Pascual, Bert Campaneris and Tony Olivia may be familiar enough names from earlier Cuban big-league infiltrations, but the Cuban presence in the United States has seemingly always been more a matter of colorful role players than one of legitimate front-line stars. Yankees and Chisox ace "El Duque" Hernández with his much-embellished tale of heroic escape from Cuban baseball servitude is, admittedly, a recent headline grabber — as was half-brother World Series MVP Liván Hernández a few short Octobers back with the Florida Marlins. But in Cuba itself Orlando Hernández would never have been classed among the island's true diamond immortals. And Liván was hardly a blip on the radar scope of Cuban baseball (posting a lifetime 27–16 mark over three seasons) before defecting from the junior national team early in the last decade. Far heftier stars on the

Cuban scene like sluggers Omar Linares and Orestes Kindelán and hurlers Lázaro Valle and Norge Vera (owner of a league-best 0.97 ERA in 2000 and ace of the 2003 World Cup) are all but invisible anywhere but on their native island.

This is an old story for Cuban baseball. Light-skinned Dolf Luque (a two-decade major leaguer of the 1910s, '20s and '30s, who still owns the best-ever season for a Cincinnati Reds hurler) and swarthy-toned Martín Dihigo (legendary denizen of the invisible Negro leagues) remain the indelible Cuban baseball icons of the first half-century. Yet such can be claimed only within the boundaries of Fidel Castro's off-the-beaten-track communist-controlled island. Both Luque and Dihigo are entirely overlooked by stateside diamond historians — even those of a most industrious bent who ply their trade under the banner of the august Society for American Baseball Research and thus pride themselves in leaving almost no stone unturned when it comes to mining baseball's rich past.

Despite nearly 200 wins and one dominating National League season boasting twenty-seven victories and a microscopic 1.93 ERA (both NL bests in 1923), Luque was never a genuine star in the big leagues, even if he was the most visible and renowned among exotic Caribbean ballplayers who labored on the major league scene between the two world wars. Dihigo — more tragically — remained virtually unknown to North American ballpark denizens, along with the bulk of his fellow Negro league stars, at least until his strange-sounding name was belatedly added decades later to the list of immortals housed in Cooperstown. On the annual winter tour back home in Cuba — as well as in Venezuela, Mexico, and the neighboring Dominican Republic — the lanky and trim six-foot-one-inch Dihigo was a true giant among itinerant diamond barnstormers. His absence from big-league parks nonetheless meant certain anonymity among white American fans and white American sports writers up north, where the biggest crowds and biggest headlines were always drawn.*

The fates of Dihigo and Luque were anything but

*The given family names of Cuba's two most famous past-era stars are frequently mispronounced and often misspelled — prime indications of the injustices that have befallen island ball-playing legends. Luque (LOU-kay) is properly stressed on the first syllable; his first name was Adolfo and the short form — Dolf — should be spelled with an "f" and not a "ph." Dihigo (DEE-go) is also stressed on the first syllable, but the given name carries a written stress mark — Martín — and is (cont.)

unique, to be sure. Lurking back on the island there were still other Cuban stalwarts who rivaled even Luque and Dihigo in athletic stature, even if none ever quite surpassed "The Pride of Havana" (Luque's popular moniker) or "El Inmortal" (Dihigo's) for the sheer dimension of their outsized homespun legends. Among the most notable of the island stars from the century's earliest decades was a brief and brilliant comet known everywhere on the winter ball scene as the Cuban "Black Diamond" — José Méndez — who turned big league heads and warmed Cuban pride with his dominations of McGraw's Giants and Cobb's Tigers during island barnstorming visits in 1908 and 1909. The rubber-armed, ebony-faced Méndez stood only five feet nine inches and tipped the scales at a mere 155 pounds, but he flung a dancing fastball that appeared to even the most seasoned pro hitters to weigh more than the pitcher himself.

Méndez amazed the baseball world almost overnight in the winter of 1908 when he was first discovered by baseball's white establishment, much to the dismay of one set of big-league batsmen who performed off-season duties that year for the Cincinnati Reds. When the visiting National League club arrived in Havana that winter for their celebrated whirlwind

Dapper retired Martín Dihigo poses in Cerro Stadium in late 1940s with son Martín Junior, who later played on the same minor league club in Kansas as Pete Rose and Tany Pérez.

tour, they could hardly have anticipated the rude greeting they would receive from an unheralded set of island blackball strikeout artists. First came Méndez's 1908 exhibition contests versus the bedazzled Cincinnati ball club. In November of that year the diminutive Cuban first shut down the big-leaguers with a brilliant 1–0, one-hit masterpiece. (It was spoiled only by Miller Huggins's scratch single in the ninth.) To prove that the first one-sided encounter was no fluke, Méndez hurled another seven shutout innings of relief only two weeks after the first surprise blanking. He then punctuated the issue with a second complete-game shutout, 4–0, just four days later.

"El Diamante Negro" had suddenly thrown twenty-five straight scoreless frames against the bewildered Cincinnati team. Trading his Cuban League uniform representing Havana-based Club Almendares for the jerseys of various barnstorming outfits, he reportedly then continued his miraculous string of outings with twenty more consecutive runless frames, though now admittedly working against somewhat lesser competition: a nine-inning shutout against a touring semipro team from Key West; a no-hitter in a return engagement against the same ball club back in Key West (perhaps the first integrated game ever played in Florida); and finally two additional shutout innings for Almendares in Cuban League play.

The magic which Méndez began against the shell-shocked Cincinnati ball club in 1908 continued against four additional big-league visitors over the course of the next three winters. Things started a bit roughly for the celebrated Cuban ace the following winter when the touring Detroit Tigers (even sans front-line stars Ty Cobb and Sam Crawford) administered a 9–3 drubbing. Returning to form against Tigers ace Ed Willett (21–10 that summer in the American League), Méndez fell again, 4–0, despite yielding just six hits and one earned run while enduring four costly fielding errors committed behind him. But Méndez did manage a victory against the Tigers in 1909, a 2–1 five-hitter in his third and final outing. The 1909 series against Detroit also saw a second black Cuban ace, Eustaquio Pedroso, dazzle the once-more humiliated visiting big-leaguers with his own eleven-inning no-hitter.

Manager McGraw desperately wanted Méndez for his own roster despite the Cuban's taboo swarthy skin tone, and even compared "El Diamante Negro" to the immortal Christy Mathewson — the current ace of his own National League staff back in New York. It was Dolf Luque, however, who somewhat later offered perhaps the highest praise for the talents of the remarkable José Méndez. Returning to Havana for a public celebration honoring his own twenty-seven-win 1923 National League campaign, the successful big-leaguer spied Méndez lurking in the grandstand and approached the aging and injured thirty-six-year-old Negro leaguer with a most memorable greeting. "This parade should have been for you,"

thus pronounced Mar-TEEN. Dihigo's Cooperstown enshrinement in 1977 was not enough to prevent renowned baseball historians Lawrence Ritter and Donald Honig from referring to him several times as "Martin Dihago" in their 1979 book The Image of Their Greatness. Such casual treatment has been even more egregious with 2006 Cooperstown electee Cristóbal Torriente, whose first and last names have regularly been subject to a myriad of variations (Christobel, Cristobel and Torrienti being the most common abuses).

remarked a humble and politic Luque. "Certainly you're a far better pitcher than I am."

There was also another blackball star from Cuba — this one named Torriente — who once outslugged Babe Ruth during a memorable island visit by the Bambino most notable for the Babe's epic carousing. Much of Cristobal Torriente's own legend is indeed founded not on his stellar decade of blackball play (with Rube Foster's Chicago American Giants), but upon his brief encounter with John McGraw's touring team of big-leaguers (mostly New York Giants) in Havana during the late fall following the 1920 major league season. And no lesser figure played a key role in this memorable face-off than Babe Ruth himself, fresh from his stunning fifty-four-homer debut with the Yankees the previous summer and enticed to perform in Havana by a then-incredible offer of $1,000 per game in hard cash from Cuban promoter Abel Linares. With regular Giants first baseman George "Highpockets" Kelly taking the mound for the big leaguers against the same Cuban Almendares club that had once featured Méndez, Torriente seized advantage by smashing booming back-to-back opposite field homers. When Ruth (who himself failed at the plate three times) assumed the hill to silence the Cuban slugger, he was greeted rudely enough by Torriente's third prodigious blow — a ringing double to left which nearly removed the legs of Giants third sacker Frankie Frisch.

The final count saw Torriente going four for five with three round trippers and six runs batted home; Ruth stood zero for two, having walked twice and reached once on an error. (That the legitimacy of this game might be challenged — due to rumors of goldbricking by the Americans — is discussed further in Chapter 6 of this volume.) Frisch would later lionize "The Cuban Strongboy" when he remembered the particular blast that nearly amputated his limbs: "In those days Torriente was a hell of a player! Christ, I'd like to whitewash him and bring him straight up (to the majors)!"

Thus, for three full decades — 1910 through 1940 — Cuba was a genuine *béisbol paradiso,* a true island paradise of wintertime barnstorming heroics. The big-leaguers visited frequently and seemingly always returned home with awestruck assessments like the one Torriente had inspired from Frankie Frisch, or the one Méndez elicited from John McGraw. So did the best among U.S. blackball stars, who were tested regulars on the November–January Cuban League scene. Oscar Charleston fashioned a .361 batting mark over nine Cuban seasons and was once part of a Santa Clara Leopards outfield in 1923–24 (with Cubans Pablo Mesa and Alejandro Oms) often considered the best flychasing trio pro baseball ever produced; James "Cool Papa" Bell ("Jimmy" Bell in Cuba) spent four seasons flashing on the base paths with the Cuban League Cienfuegos entry. Lesser black stars like Preston Hill, Rube Foster and Oliver Marcelle were as lionized on the island as they were in the shadowy blackball circuit back home. And the legends they left behind still vibrate in the island's baseball soul: Jimmy Bell's three homers (one struck against Dihigo) in a single 1929 game, Ray "Jabao" Brown's first twentieth-century Cuban no-hitter, and native Cuban Alejan-

Artist's rendering of legendary Cuban League and blackball star Martín Dihigo in the uniform of the Cuban X-Giants (courtesy Bob Carroll).

dro Oms's prodigious slugging (featuring powerful blasts sprayed to all fields), daring base-paths feats, and circus outfield catches spread over two full decades.

But as far as most white North American fans of the major league game were concerned, these tropical barnstormers might just as well — in the phrase of historian Douglass Wallop — have been "playing doubleheaders on the dark side of the moon." They were altogether invisible in the lands up north where baseball was strictly a summertime affair — and strictly a white man's affair when it came to mainstream reporting. It would be more than half a century before the efforts of dedicated revisionist historians (like Robert Peterson, Donn Rogosin, and John Holway, to mention only the most noted scholars) would bring their legends back to life for the bulk of a major-league-oriented (and largely white) North American baseball fandom.

For all the unappreciated glories of Luque, Torriente, Méndez and the island's other forgotten white and black stars, one name nonetheless still towers above all the rest — when it comes to ball-playing denizens most badly treated by the fickle winds of ill-fortune or shifting social mores of their own eras. When a special committee of Hall-of-Fame electors was established in 1971 for the overdue task of selecting past-eras greats from among excluded blackballers, one of the committee's earliest choices (1977) was inevitably the versatile Cuban pitcher-infielder-outfielder who stands head and shoulders above all his Latin countrymen. Among fourteen greats tabbed to date (through 2005) by this special Negro leagues enshrinement committee — Satchel Paige was the first in 1971 and Josh Gibson and Buck Leonard followed close behind — Dihigo was only the ninth chosen and so far remains the only player of Latin American origin to merit such nomination. The perhaps-surprising selection of Martín Dihigo for Cooperstown enshrinement, coming at a time when only Roberto Clemente among Latin-born ballplayers was a member of the unique fraternity of the game's greatest stars, was a decision that, in retrospect, was beyond criticism — even under the most exacting of standards. Yet without careful study of long-buried blackball and winterball records (sparse as they are), perhaps few at the time could have truly appreciated the fitting justice underlying the belated honor.

Martín Dihigo was certainly no latter-day case of admission into the Hall of Immortals driven by a guilt-ridden sympathy vote. Many rare distinctions marked Dihigo's résumé alone and thus justified immediate Cooperstown enshrine-ment. Dihigo would, for one thing, eventually claim distinction as the only ballplayer elected to halls of fame in three separate nations — Cuba and Mexico would also eventually enshrine him. Here was also a ballplayer soon to be chosen (in an early 1980s poll) by surviving Negro leaguers as the all-time best black second baseman, while remarkably also receiving numerous votes as best-ever performer at both third base and the outfield. And if these unparalleled achievements in North American Negro league venues and on island barnstorming tours were not hefty credentials enough, Dihigo had also once been an incomparable Mexican League legend, hurling that country's first-ever pro league no-hitter (1937) while surprisingly also pacing the Mexican League circuit in batting percentage during the following summer season. Perhaps for icing — if icing be needed — so entrenched is Dihigo's stature on his native island that his living memory has even overcome forty years of post-revolutionary efforts to belittle if not stamp out altogether all earlier achievements of professional baseball from collective island memory. Thus despite the many glories amassed by amateur baseball tradition in Cuba after the 1959 revolution, it is pre–Castro professional hero Martín Dihigo who still towers untouched as the baseball-crazy island nation's greatest diamond treasure.

When this author reminisced with Cuban legend Conrado Marrero in Havana in January 1999 (Chapter 4) the venerable grand old man of island baseball was lucid about tabbing his nation's biggest star. Marrero's own pitching career stretches back to the 1930s when Dihigo was still active on the mound and still a star performer throughout the Caribbean region. And Marrero himself followed a later-in-life big-league career in the early 1950s with the Washington Senators (he was nudging 40 as a rookie) by keeping his hand in top-level baseball even after the 1959 revolution. For years he has been a part-time Cuban League pitching coach and has thus seen firsthand all the Cuban greats down to the present national team stars. But for Marrero it was indisputably Dihigo who was the greatest among the lot.

Most Cubans who religiously followed their national sport in the first half of the past century — before Fidel Castro rose to power and in the process changed the direction of Cuban baseball as drastically as everything else in daily Cuban life — would concur to the last man (Cuba has few rabid women fans) that Dihigo was the unparalleled best at any diamond position (save catcher) that their native island ever produced. In Cuba in the years before communism and the rise of amateur sport, Martín Dihigo was everywhere acknowledged as Babe Ruth, Joe DiMaggio and Walter Johnson all wrapped up in one muscular dark-skinned package. Unfortunately it was that dark skin which also made him Cuba's greatest loss for several generations of North American baseball watchers.

Artist's rendering of Dihigo in the uniform of the Cuban League Santa Clara Leopardes (courtesy Bob Carroll).

*   *   *

There is special fascination with the truly versatile ballplayer. Baseball is not a game made for specialists; true diamond heroes hit with power or at least relentless precision, are possessed of glue-filled gloves and rifle-like throwing arms, and run the base paths with pure abandon. It is for this reason alone, more than all others, that baseball traditionalists abhor the concept of a designated hitter or rue the age of the single-inning relief specialist. Ballplayers who perform efficiently at multiple positions most often capture fans' hearts and stoke a manager's eternal gratitude.

Nowhere have truly versatile ballplayers been more plentiful and noteworthy than among the Latino big leaguers of past and present generations. For starters, only two men have ever played all nine positions in a single "official" big league game, and both were predictably Latins. First Bert Campaneris turned the trick (September 9, 1965) in one of Charlie Finley's notorious publicity stunts with the Kansas City Athletics; later César Tóvar of the Minnesota Twins would imitate Campaneris (September 22, 1968) with his own inning-by-inning whirlwind around the diamond. Admittedly these were both cheap publicity events designed to entertain fans of also-ran ball clubs. Yet Tóvar was truly as versatile as they come and played regularly at four different positions (outfield, third, second and short) while also leading the junior circuit in 1967 in game appearances. (Tóvar was also a clutch batsman who broke up more no-hitters — five — than any single batter in baseball history.) Campaneris, for his part, was equally as comfortable at any of the three infield slots (exclusive of first base) and occasionally saw outfield duty in a rare pinch. The nine-position single-game feats of these two Latin utility men may well have been more showmanship than anything else, and yet no other big leaguers in history have ever been up to the task of pulling off such a spectacular feat.

There is of course another ballplayer of Latin birthright who stands in a class by himself when it comes to such defensive versatility. Imagine a ballplayer who played all positions (or all but one) not as a once-in-a-lifetime stunt but as an everyday occurrence. And imagine such a ballplayer being praised by skilled rivals and teammates alike for his unparalleled mastery at each position he manned. Imagine such a ballplayer and you have Martín Dihigo — baseball's greatest all-around Negro leaguer and in the eyes of many old-timers the best ballplayer ever seen on the planet. It is little wonder that Cubans long called him "The Immortal" and that far and wide — in the Dominican Republic, Mexico, Puerto Rico, Venezuela, and on the Negro league diamonds of Chicago, New York, Pittsburgh and Kansas City — he was known simply as "The Maestro" in fitting tribute to his on-field grace, star quality, and unrivalled technical knowledge and mastery of the game.

Martín Dihigo during mid-career in the 1930s. Location and exact date of the photo remain unknown, but scene was probably Havana in the mid–1930s.

It is reported (though nowhere documented) that Dihigo often showed off his all-around skill by taking his own turn at all nine positions in numerous Negro league contests. In a career that stretched to a quarter century in Cuba and included at least a dozen Mexican winter seasons and fourteen Negro league campaigns (1923–1936), the black Cuban giant was always most dominant as a pitcher. His mound credentials would eventually include no-hitters in three countries (Mexico, Venezuela and Puerto Rico), a documented 119–57 Mexican League record (18–2, 0.90 ERA in 1938), a recorded 93–48 won-lost mark over his last dozen Cuban seasons

Martín Dihigo's Country-by-Country Career Pitching Breakdown

Country (Years)	W–L Record	Teams
Cuba (1922–1947)	107– 56 (.656)	Habana, Almendares, Marianao, Santa Clara, Cienfuegos
Mexico (1937–1947)	119– 57 (.676)	Aguila, Veracruz, Mexico City, Torreón, Nuevo Laredo, San Luis
Venezuela (1933–1935)	26– 4 (.867)	Concordia, La Guaira
Dominican Republic (1937)	6– 4 (.600)	Aguilas Cibaeñas
Negro Leagues (1923–1945)	30– 21 (.588)	Cuban Stars, Homestead Grays, Hilldale, Baltimore, New York Cubans
Totals	**288–142 (.670)**	

(1935–1946), a 218–106 (.673) winter league and Negro league ledger in games officially documented, and perhaps dozens more victories lost to history through shoddy record-keeping that marred the barnstorming circuits.

As a hitter he was equally devastating on the opposition: a .317 lifetime BA in Mexico, where he paced the circuit at .387 in 1938 (the same season he posted his unthinkable 0.90 ERA upon the mound); nine seasons of documented .300 hitting in his native Cuba; more than 130 career homers with more than eleven seasons for which his home run numbers are entirely missing. If the home runs were sometimes few and far between during Caribbean seasons it was likely due to the cavernous Cuban, Dominican and Venezuelan playing grounds. As tribute to Dihigo's raw power at career peak author John Holway cites Schoolboy Johnny Taylor's eyewitness of a roof-clearing blast in Havana (the roof was on a house beyond the outfield enclosure) and Buck Leonard's report of a 500-foot-plus shot onto a hospital roof adjacent to Pittsburgh's Greenlee Field.

While the numbers of hits and pitching victories were

Dihigo (left) conducting a pre-game interview with Fermín Guerra in Havana's Cerro Stadium during his post–playing-days career as baseball radio commentator.

never very well recorded the anecdotal evidence for Dihigo's greatness is often almost overwhelming. Stories abound of the Cuban's flaming fastball, his deadly throwing arm, his fence-rattling lumber, and his rare grace at virtually every field position except the catcher's slot. (He did occasionally move behind the plate to catch, even though the backstop position was never a strong point or an assignment for which he showed much enthusiasm.) But as first an infielder, later an outfielder, and finally a pitcher he was a true nonpareil on whatever part of the diamond he chose to take his stance.

By all accounts, he was also a most crafty diamond opponent. Stories are common of Dihigo's clever and sometimes highly entertaining — even humorous (if treacherous) — on-field ploys. He once shagged an outfield hit and then jogged the ball into the infield to communicate with his shortstop; on the return trip to his garden post (still clutching the baseball) he politely asked a runner stationed on second if he could adjust the dust-covered base — and promptly achieved an unexpected putout by tagging the all-too-cooperative opponent who had foolishly stepped off the sack. A more celebrated (if not apocryphal) incident — reported by one longtime Cuban fan to researcher John Holway — has the Cuban ace strolling from third to the plate screaming "you balked, you balked" at a stunned rival pitcher, who remained frozen on the mound until Dihigo was halfway to the dugout with an unorthodox home plate steal tucked in his pocket.

Such documented testimonies to Dihigo's versatility are legion and make impressive reading indeed. Blackball great Buck Leonard leads the parade of those who once spoke reverently of Martín Dihigo as the game's undisputed "greatest all-around talent." Leonard (himself frequently labeled the Black Lou Gehrig) was unequivocal in his enthusiastic assessment (reported in an interview with Holway): "He was the greatest all-around player I know. I'd say he was the best ballplayer of all time, black or white. He could do it all. He is my ideal ball player, makes no difference what race either. If he's not the greatest I don't know who is. You take your Ruths, Cobbs, and DiMaggios. Give me Dihigo and I bet I'd beat you almost every time."

And most of Leonard's blackball sidekicks apparently agreed almost to a man. When surviving Negro leaguers were polled in the early 1980s regarding an all-time Negro lineup it was Dihigo, not surprisingly, who wound up as the second baseman of choice. His selection was all the more remarkable, however, when one considers that numerous ballots were cast for "The Maestro" at two other positions as well — outfield and third base.

Dihigo, of course, did not start out as a player of quite such remarkable skill, but raw talent was observed from the outset. He commenced learning the game as an eager teenager when taken under the wing of black barnstorming greats (especially Oscar Charleston and John Henry Lloyd) visiting Cuba at the close of the World War I era. As a seventeen-year-old rookie of little polish with the powerhouse Habana Reds (also known as the Lions) the tall skinny kid from Matanzas (a two-hour cart ride from Havana) would bat an anemic

.179 and hold his roster spot only by gaudy displays of defensive potential.

A first trip northward with Alex Pompez's Cuban Stars in 1923 (the exact same season when Luque emerged as a big league star in Cincinnati) dramatically demonstrated two things about the lanky youngster to all who saw him play at second and short. One was that you simply couldn't hit a ball by him in the infield; the second was that it was no difficulty at all to throw almost any curveball right past the overanxious youngster when he was in the batter's box. His speed and range around second base drew highest praise from most sportswriters on the blackball circuit, and despite weak hitting, he was quickly hailed as the best Cuban import since mound ace José Méndez.

At first his impact as a Negro leaguer was minimal due to befuddlement in the face of the teasing curveball. But the slow start didn't last long for a player of such natural talent, dedication, and willingness to work out his proven defects. In a few years Dihigo had emerged as one of the true greats of Negro league play. Diligently practicing his timing against the curveball delivery of batting practice hurlers, Dihigo was soon pushing his batting average skyward: in two years he would hit .370 (with twelve homers, for the 1927 Eastern Colored League Cuban Stars) and in two more (playing for the American Negro League Philadelphia Hilldale club in 1929) his mark would climb to .386, along with a league-best eighteen homers to pace the top U.S. summertime Negro league circuit.

Yet Dihigo did not restrict his baseball challenges to North American Negro league play, nor did he merely hit and field the baseball for a living. Soon he was also tearing up Mexican League ballparks. And he was doing so as a dominating moundsman as well as an airtight infield defender and part-time outfielder with a throwing arm that veteran Negro leaguer Ted Page would later call even better than Clemente's. Dihigo once stunned blackball great Judy Johnson with an unparalleled throwing exhibition at the Havana ballpark (supposedly La Tropical) in the early 1930s. In a show of pre-game skill Dihigo had been matched against a professional jai alai player who first displayed his own athleticism by slinging a ball with his basketlike cesto that hit the centerfield fence on a single bounce; standing on home plate the rubber-armed baseballer then uncorked a heave that sailed off the same wall on the fly.

It was in Mexico that Dihigo would first prove his special prowess as a pitching wonder, hurling the league's first recorded no-hitter (in 1937) and establishing its all-time standards for single-season ERA and lifetime winning percentage. The conversion to pitching did not mean a slacking off in other aspects of his balanced game. The late 1920s and early 1930s saw Dihigo's winter league batting averages in his native

A rare image of Dihigo (right) during his brief playing career with the Caracas team in the Venezuelan winter league (c. 1934).

Cuba soar from .300 to .344 to .415 to .450. In one remarkable individual performance the black Cuban giant would nip out teammate Willie Wells for a Cuban League batting title by registering a five-for-five outing on the season's final day, a shade better than Wells' own four-for-four in the same ballgame.

Despite a fastball that was often compared with that of Satchel Paige, it was as a devastating hitter that Dihigo was perhaps always the greatest late-game threat. Blackball historian John Holway has reasonably ranked Dihigo among the greatest of all blackball sluggers, season after long season. And some of Dihigo's hitting feats indeed border on the legendary. Holway reports one ex-blackball ace as witnessing a Dihigo line drive which nearly decapitated a paralyzed shortstop, then scorched against the outfield fence before the amazed infield defender could raise his helpless hands in self-defense. The skinny kid who arrived in the early 1920s with the Cuban Stars — looking most like a beanpole version of scarecrow-shaped Marty Marion (of St. Louis Browns fame) — soon filled out and developed wrists of steel since seen only on the likes of Ernie Banks and Hank Aaron. He regularly led the Cuban circuit in round trippers in ballparks where outfield fences (if they existed at all) were a long pony ride from home plate. While ballpark size and the short league schedule might well diminish the impact of Dihigo's raw hitting numbers, Holway's somewhat incomplete reconstructed blackball record for the Cuban great today makes impressive reading by almost any standard of measure.

What is often most overlooked is Dihigo's rare accomplishment on the pitching rubber, where he reversed Babe Ruth's versatility as slugger-turned-hurler. The Dihigo pitching legend was most pronounced, of course, in Mexico, where he won in double figures on a half-dozen occasions and twice

Another rare image of Dihigo (center, with "A" on shirt) after his pitching victory for Aguila, during the top single season in 1938. Dihigo was the Mexican League's best pitcher (0.90 ERA, 18–2) and its champion batter (.387 BA) that same summer (courtesy Transcendental Graphics).

piled up twenty or more victories. The true showcase season was his second (in 1938, when he posted his 18–2 ledger with a miniscule 0.90 ERA across 167 innings). In a Mexican circuit recently strengthened by the importation of such frontline blackball stars as Josh Gibson, Ray Dandridge, Willie Wells and the ageless Satchel Paige, Dihigo not only pitched and batted (with his league-best .387 BA) but also managed his Aguila club in a pitched battle against Paige's Mexico City–based Agrario outfit. The season was highlighted by a pennant-showdown game between the two teams on September 5, when Dihigo and Paige dueled on the hill for eight tense innings of a 1–1 tie. Dihigo himself settled the matter with a resounding homer which he crushed off fellow Cuban ace Ramón Bragaña, who had relieved a wilted Paige in the ninth frame.

Sparingly used on the hill during most of his North American Negro league seasons, the versatile Cuban nonethe-less again managed to make his mark from time to time as a recognized mound ace. At no time was this more true than during the 1935 campaign — one of his best and at the same time most disappointing — and a year marked by two memorable if ultimately disastrous pitching outings. In that summer's East-West All-Star Game, Dihigo recovered from a sixth-inning wall collision (while chasing down a Josh Gibson 400-foot blast) to relieve Luis Tiant, Sr., in the tenth frame, unfortunately yielding the tying runs during that fateful inning and then also giving up perhaps the most famous gopherball in blackball annals to Mule Suttles in the eleventh. A more fateful outing would also follow for the New York Cubans ace hurler and playing manager at season's end. It came in the series-turning playoff game with the Pittsburgh Crawfords, when Dihigo stubbornly inserted himself in relief of ace hurler Johnny Taylor, promptly yielding a long game-

Major League Baseball's Top Career Pitchers (Ranked by W-L Pct.)
(with comparison to Martín Dihigo's Career Winning Percentage)
Including only Modern-Era Twentieth-Century Seasons (1900–2000)

Pitcher	Years (Seasons)	Won-Lost (Pct)	Professional Leagues
Pedro Martinez	1992–2000 (9)	125– 56 (.691)	National League, American League
Whitey Ford	1950–67 (16)	236–106 (.690)	American League
Robert "Lefty" Grove	1925–41 (17)	300–141 (.680)	American League
Martín Dihigo	**1922–47 (24)**	**288–142 (.670)**	**Negro Leagues, Cuba, Mexico, Venezuela**
Vic Raschi	1946–55 (10)	132– 66 (.667)	American League, National League
Christy Mathewson	1900–16 (17)	373–188 (.665)	National League
Sam Leever	1898–1910 (13)	194–100 (.660)	National League
Sal Maglie	1945, 1950–58 (10)	119– 62 (.657)	National League, American League
Sandy Koufax	1955–66 (11)	165– 87 (.655)	National League
Johnny Allen	1932–44 (13)	142– 75 (.654)	American League, National League
Randy Johnson	1988–2000 (13)	179– 95 (.653)	National League, American League
Ron Guidry	1975–88 (14)	170– 91 (.651)	American League

tying homer to Oscar Charleston and then a game-winning double to Judy Johnson in a fateful season-crushing ninth inning.

Such disasters aside, Dihigo's overall mound achievements would in the end rank him with the game's greatest — black or white, major league or Caribbean winter circuit. His verifiable career won-lost mark — spread over a quarter-century, four countries and four leagues — was sufficient to stand him alongside the big-league's top statistical achievers. Only Lefty Grove and Whitey Ford, among Cooperstown immortals, can today boast a more successful won-lost ledger, and Grove and Ford certainly did not also post all-star credentials at three or four other diamond positions. Nor did they match Dihigo's twenty-plus seasons.

When playing days finally faded for the ageless Cuban, Dihigo had other baseball challenges to conquer and other immense contributions to make. As a player-manager he piloted teams to league titles in Cuba (1936, 1937), Venezuela (1953), and Mexico (1942), and also managed a 1953 Venezuelan entry in Caribbean Series play. A cheery personality and considerable facility with English made Dihigo equally popular with Negro leaguers, native Hispanics and North American big-leaguers seeking winter league experience. It has been claimed that it was Dihigo's immense popularity (as well as the pure fun of playing for the easy-going bench boss) which attracted the large number of blackball stars who made their winter diamond homes in Cuba during the thirties and forties. Each time a new Negro league great inherited his rightful spot as "greatest ever" at a new slot on the diamond — say Satchel Paige on the mound, Oscar Charleston in the outfield, Judy Johnson at third, or Buck Leonard at first — it was common practice to note repeatedly that the new immortal had no parallel at his chosen position except, of course, the past-era immortal Dihigo.

* * *

Dihigo's lengthy span of playing days came to an end in the late 1940s in the shadows of World War II. He would continue to manage for several more years but never did achieve

his goal of managing the Habana Lions team, which was still under the long-time tutelage of Miguel Angel González, a light-skinned Cuban former big-league catcher, third base coach and fill-in manager, mostly with the St. Louis Cardinals. (It was González who coined the phrase "Good field, no hit" in a scouting report on Moe Berg and also González who waved Enos Slaughter home from third in the famous dash around the basepaths in Boston which clinched a 1946 World Series victory.)

Cuba's most versatile diamond star also tried his hand briefly at umpiring in both Cuba and Mexico. He even became an announcer/commentator for radio broadcasts of Cuban League games but only had minimal success in the latter occupation. By the early 1950s Dihigo seemed to have turned a tad bitter and was uncharacteristically outspoken with a microphone in his hands. He often criticized the achievements of younger stars in the most acrid tones. Perhaps the strain of being so long ignored by the white baseball world (especially after 1947, when blacks finally entered the big league game) was finally catching up with him. Dihigo's playing days had closed in the very year that Jackie Robinson ended baseball's apartheid on diamonds up north, and the irony could not have been entirely lost on baseball segregation's most egregious victim.

When the Cuban revolution came in the late fifties, Dihigo faded out of sight behind the dense sugar cane curtain which surrounded the island following Fidel Castro's sudden rise to power. Once more Cuba's greatest baseball icon was invisible everywhere outside the island of his birth. All indications are that Dihigo was a strong supporter of the socialist revolutionary cause. He reportedly helped fund Fidel and his rebel forces during his later years of umpiring and managing in Mexico, while the rebels were themselves only a rag-tag band of outmanned insurgents camped out in the Sierra Maestra foothills of Oriente Province. Dihigo had left his native country in protest when strongman Fulgencio Batista grabbed power in March 1952 and he returned home permanently only after Fidel's revolution had finally succeeded.

Dihigo's final years were reportedly spent working in

quiet support of Fidel's now-entrenched revolutionary movement. He served as an instructor with newly established programs institutionalizing amateur baseball on the island. Occasionally he appeared at "official" ceremonies such as school openings or stadium dedications. One widely published photo displays him tossing a ceremonial first pitch at the César Sandino Stadium in Santa Clara, nattily attired in straw hat and traditional *guayabera*. His elder son and namesake carried enough proper family genes to be signed to a minor league contract with the Cincinnati organization (1959) and enjoyed a brief U.S. minor league stint (playing alongside Pete Rose in Geneva, New York, and Tony Pérez in Topeka, Kansas) just before tensions between Castro and Washington escalated and the doors to the island finally slammed shut in 1961. Martín Dihigo, Jr. then returned home and took up residence in Cienfuegos, as well as his own active support of revolutionary causes. A second and younger son named Gilberto followed a different career path as a sportswriter and eventually abandoned his homeland (in the early 1990s) to write and live in Mexico City. (Gilberto Dihigo was an important informant on Cuban baseball history for author Milton Jamail during the writing of *Full Count: Inside Cuban Baseball*.)

The life of Cuba's top diamond star also ended — not surprisingly — in the same relative obscurity that had marked so much of his nonpareil diamond career. Boarding with his eldest son near Cienfuegos, Dihigo suffered increasing health problems soon after he passed his sixty-fifth birthday. The onetime robust athlete was actually hospitalized on several occasions early in 1971 (he was only 66 at the time) reportedly suffering from a cerebral thrombosis. He finally died quietly in the early evening hours of May 19, 1971. What followed was a period of country-wide mourning truly befitting a national idol. There were public ceremonies featuring the nation's number one fan, Fidel Castro, and newspaper tributes that recounted every past diamond triumph of the figure universally acknowledged among his countrymen as "El Inmortal." The celebrated baseballer was even treated in death as a fallen hero of the revolution, though his island-wide reputation had all been earned in another era and far away from the arenas of national politics.

Of course, all this was never enough to bring Dihigo into the baseball limelight of the North American big leagues or the North American sporting press. He was born with the wrong skin color and raised in the wrong decade for such a dream ever to flourish. If there was an ironic appropriateness to fellow Cuban Minnie Miñoso's popular moniker (Miñoso was tagged "The Comet" and his fame once burned brightly yet all too briefly), there is also an equal irony in the black-ball nickname ("The Maestro") that Dihigo once proudly bore.

Dihigo's winterball contributions would eventually receive tardy recognition with his afterthought enshrinement in Cooperstown as a one-time Negro league great. Long before Cooperstown recognition, the Cuban legend already had been "officially" sanctioned as a Hall of Famer in his homeland and in Mexico and Venezuela for good measure. He today thus remains baseball's only four-nation hall-of-fame hero. Yet "The Maestro" would never have a chance to work his artistry on the grandest stage of all — an American League or National League ballpark. He had played a rich diamond music that was doomed to fall upon the deaf ears of a white-oriented sports press up north. His concert halls simply always lay too far off the beaten baseball paths.

Ultimately, the real tragedy of Dihigo's exclusion from the fan-soaked white major leagues is today impossible to dismiss — legendary status and belated hall of fame enshrinements aside. Beyond all else there was the incalculable loss for two full generations of white fans of the thrill of seeing him play. There was the lamentable absence of a smoke-tossing Dihigo on the major league mound in legendary combat with Lefty Grove or Bob Feller or Dizzy Dean; or perhaps an agile Dihigo roaming the same outfield with the young DiMaggio or plugging the same infield with Marty Marion, Luke Appling or Billy Herman. Dihigo himself never would know the sweet taste of glory that might have been his in a true big-league venue. And for a game so soaked in historical records and fed by statistical

Martín Dihigo, Jr., with the author (wearing cap) at the small memorial Martín Dihigo Museum near Cienfuegos in February 2001.

documentation, the unarguable numbers by which each hero is measured are in this case simply not there in the open for our latter-day perusal and admiration.

Mid-century Cuban star Minnie Miñoso's childhood baseball idol, not surprisingly, was none other than the immortal Martín Dihigo. Both hailed from Matanzas Province and both would travel a similarly rocky path through racial harassment to eventual hard-earned baseball stardom. Miñoso has often recorded his debt to the idol of all those who knew the heyday of Cuban baseball:

"Dihigo once let me carry his shoes and glove and that's how I got into the ball park down there when I was a kid. He was a big man, all muscle with not an ounce of fat on him. He helped me by teaching me how to play properly. When I played a few years in the Negro leagues, with the New York Cubans, Dihigo was past his prime and just a manager then, so I never really competed against him as a player. But it is difficult to explain what a great hero he was in Cuba. Everywhere he went he was recognized and mobbed for autographs. I'd have to say he was most responsible for me getting to the major leagues. He was a big man, but he was big in all ways, as a player, as a manager, as a teacher, as a man."

As Miñoso's so eloquently states, it is indeed perhaps virtually impossible — especially in today's transient world crammed with instant celebrities but void of lasting heroes — to apprehend just how large a national treasure Dihigo actually once was in the baseball-crazed nation of Cuba. Here was a disadvantaged youth from Miñoso's own sugar cane plantation background of grinding poverty who had somehow ignored all insult and exclusion to achieve ultimate hero status. The reasons for Miñoso's choice of ball-playing hero are therefore quite obvious. The irony — perhaps quite unapparent to Miñoso in his youth, or even at his career's end — was just how alike their truly parallel careers actually were.

Miñoso himself might have resided in Cooperstown if his full career (winter leagues and Mexico, in addition to the majors) were ever taken into justifiable account. And while Martín Dihigo does own a Cooperstown plaque, he remains nonetheless a top candidate for a tarnished distinction of baseball's most overlooked and under-appreciated genuine Hall of Famer.

Cienfuegos pitcher Dihigo (far left) listens in during a 1939–40 season home plate dispute involving veteran Almendares manager Adolfo Luque (number 32) (courtesy Transcendental Graphics).

References and Suggested Readings

Bjarkman, Peter C. *Baseball with a Latin Beat: A History of the Latin American Game.* Jefferson, NC, and London: McFarland, 1994.

Brock, Lisa, and Bijan Bayne. "Not Just Black: African-Americans, Cubans and Baseball," in: *Between Race and Empire: African-Americans and Cubans Before the Cuban Revolution.* Edited by Lisa Brock and Digna Castañeda Fuentes. Philadelphia: Temple University Press, 1998, 186–204.

Burgos, Adrian, Jr. "Jugando en el norte: Caribbean Players in the Negro Leagues, 1910–1950," in: *Centro: Journal of the Center for Puerto Rican Studies 8,* nos. 1–2 (1996), 128–149.

González Echevarría, Roberto. *The Pride of Havana: A History of Cuban Baseball.* New York: Oxford University Press, 1999.

Holway, John. *Blackball Stars: Negro League Pioneers.* New York: Carroll & Graf, 1992 (Westport: Meckler, 1988), 236–47.

Jamail, Milton. *Full Count: The Inside Story of Cuban Baseball.* Carbondale: Southern Illinois University Press, 2000.

Riley, James A. *The Biographical Encyclopedia of the Negro Baseball Leagues.* New York: Carroll & Graf, 1994.

Rucker, Mark, and Peter C. Bjarkman. *Smoke: The Romance and Lore of Cuban Baseball.* New York: Total Sports Illustrated, 1999.

Santana Alonso, Alfredo. *Martín Dihigo: El Inmortal del Béisbol.* Havana: Editorial Científico-Técnica, 1997.

Torres, Angel. *La Leyenda del Béisbol Cubano, 1878–1997.* Montebello, California (self-published), 1996.

Martín Dihigo's Mexican League (Summer) Pitching Record

Year	Mexico League Club	Games	W–L	Pct.	CG	IP	SO	BB	ERA
1937	Aguila	5	4–0	1.000	4	38.2	51	8	0.93
1938	Aguila	22	18–2	.900	16	167.0	184	32	0.90
1939	Aguila	23	15–8	.652	20	202.0	202	42	2.87
1940	Veracruz	17	8–6	.571	8	109.1	65	43	3.54
1941	Mexico City-Torreón	23	9–10	.434	9	157.0	93	43	4.01
1942	Torreón	35	22–7	.759	26	245.1	211	77	2.53
1943	Torreón	36	16–8	.667	18	194.1	134	64	3.10
1944	Nuevo Laredo	31	12–10	.554	18	212.1	90	88	3.13
1945	— — — —		Did Not Play						
1946	Torreón	20	11–4	.733	11	140.0	63	49	2.83
1947	San Luis-Veracruz	10	4–2	.667	3	55.2	16	13	4.37
Totals	**9 Seasons**	**212**	**119–57**	**.676**	**133**	**1521.2**	**1109**	**559**	**2.84**

*Dihigo also pitched in 3 Mexican League All-Star Games (1942, 1943, 1944), logging 8 total innings, allowing 2 earned runs, striking out 6 batters, walking one.

Martín Dihigo's Composite Lost Blackball Statistics

Year	Club	G	AB	H	2B	3B	HR	BA	W–L	ERA
1922–23	Habana (CL)	13	31	5	0	0	0	.161	Did not pitch	
1923	Cuban Stars (NL)	12	48	11	NA	NA	NA	.230	1–1	NA
1923–24	Almendares (CL)	1	2	0	0	0	0	.000	0–0	NA
1924	Cuban Stars (NL)	32	132	31	1	0	0	.263	1–1	NA
1924–25	Habana (CL)	27	50	15	3	3	1	.300	2–3	NA
1925	Cuban Stars (NL)	28	96	28	3	1	2	.292	4–7	NA
1925–26	Habana (CL)	9	32	11	3	2	1	.344	0–0	NA
1926	Cuban Stars (NL)	40	169	55	8	3	11#	.421	Did not pitch	
1926–27	Habana (CL)	28	95	40	5	3	3	.421	3–0	NA
1927	Cuban Stars (NL)	61	246	77	3	1	12#	.370	1–0	NA
1927–28	Habana (CL)	33	130	54#	12	3	2	.415	4–2	NA
1928	Homestead (NL)	5	20	4	1	0	0	.200	0–1	NA
1928–29	Habana (CL)	42	152	46	14	4	2	.303	2–1	NA
1929	Hilldale (NL)	23	79	24	2	0	18	.386	4–2	NA
1929–30	Almendares (CL)	51	180	51	6	6	0	.282	1–2	NA
1930	Cuban Stars (NL)	14	60	26	1	2	6	.433	Did not pitch	
1930–31	Almendares (C)	14	54	18	1	2	0	.333	2–0	NA
1931	Hilldale (NL)	65	245	65	2	3	5	.265	6–1	NA
1931–32	Almendares (C)	3	10	3	2	0	0	.300	Did not pitch	
1933	Venezuela	NA	NA	NA	NA	NA	NA	NA	6–0	0.15
1934–35	Venezuela	NA	NA	NA	NA	NA	NA	NA	20–4	NA
1935	NY Cubans (NL)	46	161	52	11	4	9#	.372	7–3	NA
1935–36	Santa Clara (CL)	48	176	63	7	9#	2	.358#	11–2#	NA
1936	NY Cubans (NL)	28	92	36	9	1	11	.391#	5–3	NA
1936–37	Marianao (CL)	69#	229	74	6	2	5#	.323	14–10	NA
1937	Aguila (ML)	7	28	10	1	2	1	.357	4–0	0.93
1937	Dominican Republic	25	97	34	6	2	4	.351	6–4	NA
1937–38	Marianao (CL)	52	165	50	5	4	0	.303	11–5	NA
1938	Aguila (ML)	42	142	55	8	2	6	.387#	18–2	0.90#
1938–39	Habana (CL)	51	145	37	7	1	1	.255	14–2	NA
1939	Aguila (ML)	51	187	63	11	3	5	.336	15–8	2.87
1939–40	Cienfuegos (CL)	25	79	23	2	2	1	.291	6–4	NA
1940	MC-Veracruz (ML)	78	302	110	17	6	9	.364	8–6	3.54
1940–41	Habana (CL)	35	110	20	4	2	0	.182	8–3	NA
1941	Torreón (ML)	92	329	102	25	4	12	.310	9–10	4.01
1941–42	Habana (CL)	40	123	28	6	0	1	.228	8–3	NA
1942	Torreón (ML)	85	279	89	12	4	8	.319	22–7	2.53#
1942–43	Habana (CL)	39	135	36	6	1	1	.267	4–8	NA
1943	Torreón (ML)	75	238	66	14	3	7	.277	16–8	3.10
1943–44	Habana (CL)	29	87	22	2	1	0	.253	8–1	2.23
1944	Nuevo Laredo (ML)	60	189	47	10	2	4	.249	12–10	3.13
1944–45	Habana (CL)	17	29	6	1	0	0	.207	3–3	3.84

Year	Club	G	AB	H	2B	3B	HR	BA	W–L	ERA
1945	NY Cubans (NL)	17	54	11	0	0	3	.204	1–2	NA
1945–46	Cienfuegos (CL)	34	71	16	3	0	0	.225	5–4	NA
1946	Torreón (ML)	66	177	56	9	2	3	.316	11–4	2.82
1946–47	Cienfuegos (CL)	15	10	1	0	0	0	.100	1–3	10.80
1947	SL-Veracruz (ML)	20	46	9	3	1	0	.196	4–2	4.32
Totals	**24 Years**	1647	5511	1680	252	91	156	.305	288–142	NA

NA = Not Available; # = League Leader; NL = Negro Leagues; CL = Cuban League (Winter); ML = Mexican League (Summer); Totals column at bottom reflects partial totals based on numbers known and is thus an approximation.

Martín Dihigo's Cuban League (Winter) Batting Record

Year	Cuban Club	Games	AB	R	H	2B	3B	HR	RBI	B.A.
1922–23	Habana	13	31	3	5	0	0	0	NA	.161
1923–24	Almendares	1	2	0	0	0	0	0	0	.000
1924–25	Habana	27	50	12	15	3	3	1	NA	.300
1925–26	Habana	9	32	11	11	3	2	1	NA	.344
1926–27	Cuba-Habana	22	75	20	31	4	1	3	NA	.413
— —	Marianao	6	20	8	9	1	2	0	NA	.450
1927–28	Habana	33	130	32	54#	12	3	2	NA	.415
1928–29	Habana	42	152	29	46	14	4	2	NA	.303
1929–30	Almendares	51	180	23	51	6	6	0	NA	.282
1930–31	Almendares	14	54	8	18	1	2	0	NA	.333
1931–32	Almendares	3	10	2	3	2	0	0	NA	.300
1935–36	Santa Clara	48	176	42#	63	7	9#	2	38#	.358#
1936–37	Marianao	69#	229	38	74	6	2	5#	34	.323
1937–38	Marianao	52	165	21	50	5	4	0	28	.303
1938–39	Habana	51	145	24	37	7	1	1	12	.255
1939–40	Cienfuegos	25	79	10	23	2	2	1	17	.291
1940–41	Habana	35	110	16	20	4	2	0	5	.182
1941–42	Habana	40	123	19	28	6	0	1	9	.228
1942–43	Habana	39	135	14	36	6	1	1	17	.267
1943–44	Habana	29	87	11	22	2	1	0	17	.253
1944–45	Habana	17	29	3	6	1	0	0	3	.207
1945–46	Cienfuegos	34	71	9	16	3	0	0	8	.225
1946–47	Cienfuegos	15	10	0	1	0	0	0	2	.100
Totals	**23 Seasons**	675	2095	355	619	95	45	20	190	.295

NA = Not Available; # = League Leader; Note = These statistics are drawn from records available in Cuba and differ from incorrect/incomplete numbers provided in John Holway's book (1988) *Blackball Stars* (Meckler).

Martín Dihigo's Cuban League (Winter) Pitching Record

Year	Cuban League Club	Games	W–L	Pct.	CG	IP	SO	BB	ERA
1922–23	Habana	Did not pitch (played as infielder only)							
1923–24	Almendares	1	0–0	.000	0	NA	NA	NA	NA
1924–25	Habana	20	2–3	.400	1	NA	NA	NA	NA
1925–26	Habana	1	0–0	.000	0	NA	3	0	0.00
1926–27	Habana	2	2–0	1.000	1	NA	NA	NA	NA
1926–27	Marianao (CT*)	1	1–0	1.000	0	NA	NA	NA	NA
1927–28	Habana	6	4–2	.667	5	NA	NA	NA	NA
1928–29	Habana	5	2–1	.667	2	NA	NA	NA	NA
1929–30	Almendares	3	1–2	.333	2	NA	NA	NA	NA
1930–31	Almendarista	2	2–0	1.000	2	NA	NA	NA	NA
1931–32	Almendares	Did not pitch (played as infielder only)							
1935–36	Santa Clara	18	11–2	.846#	13	NA	NA	NA	NA
1936–37	Marianao	30	14–10	.583	22	NA	NA	NA	NA
1937–38	Marianao	20	11–5	.688	12	NA	NA	NA	NA
1938–39	Habana	21	14–2	.875	14#	NA	NA	NA	NA
1939–40	Cienfuegos	13	6–4	.600	9	NA	NA	NA	NA
1940–41	Habana	13	8–3	.727	10	NA	NA	NA	NA
1941–42	Habana	17	8–3	.727	11#	NA	NA	NA	NA
1942–43	Habana	14	4–8	.333	7	NA	NA	NA	NA
1943–44	Habana	15	8–1	.889#	4	72.2	30	29	2.23

Year	Cuban League Club	Games	W-L	Pct.	CG	IP	SO	BB	ERA
1944–45	Habana	13	3–3	.500	2	61.0	30	18	3.84
1945–46	Cienfuegos	17	5–4	.556	4	NA	46	31	NA
1946–47	Cienfuegos	8	1–3	.250	0	16.2	16	13	10.80
Totals	**20 Seasons**	**240**	**107–56**	**.656**	**121**	--	--	--	--

NA=Not Available; #=League Leader; CT = 1926–27 second championship season known as the Campeonato Triangular; Note=These statistics are drawn from records long available in Cuba and thus differ somewhat from incorrect and incomplete numbers in John Holway's *Blackball Stars* (1988).

2

Adolfo Luque — The Original "Pride of Havana"

Luque's heart failed him in the clutch? It never did before.

— Frank Graham, 1957 Eulogy

Baseball was already a fixture on the Cuban scene by the early 1870s and it had arrived burdened with its own home-grown Cuban apostles and its own full-blown and homespun creation myths. If American sailors truly had any hand in introducing a fledgling North American pastime to Cuban longshoremen and dockhands at Matanzas harbor sometime in 1866 (as persistent legend relates), the baseball already being played on the island in years immediately following the United States Civil War was definitely not an exclusive Yankee import.

For starters, it is well documented that a pair of Havana-bred brothers named Guilló (often spelled Guillot) had returned home from Mobile, Alabama's Springhill College as early has 1864 with bats and balls stuffed in their luggage; and Nemesio and Ernesto Guilló were soon organizing impromptu pickup matches among former schoolmates in the central Havana barrio of Vedado. Within a mere handful of summers (1871) the first native Cuban baseballer — one "Steve" Bellán, who had earlier joined the college nine at Fordham University — had also gained a toehold within American professional ranks as an infielder with the Troy (NY) Haymakers ball club of the then "major league" National Association. Although it would be another four full decades (in 1911, to be precise) before any more Cubans would follow Bellán into the true "big leagues" of the north, Havana was nonetheless already featuring its own professional circuit before the end of the 1870s, a mere two years after the founding of North America's venerable and still-standing National League.

Yet despite this primitive-era debut of island baseball and the surprisingly early trickle of Cuban players northward, there was but a single Cuban who ever garnered even moderate attention in the U.S. leagues during pro baseball's initial three-quarters of a century. Racial barriers had almost everything to do with this, of course. The grandest of the early Cuban hurling and slugging phenoms were simply too black in skin pigment ever to penetrate America's exclusively white-toned national sport during the eras of Adrian "Cap" Anson and Kenesaw Mountain Landis.

Thus but one lonely pioneer — Adolfo Luque (LOO-kay), a fireplug right-hander who debuted with Boston's National Leaguers in 1914 and was already a veteran mound-corps mainstay with the Cincinnati club when the infamous 1919 Black Sox World Series rolled around — was left to carry the Cuban big league banner throughout the half-century preceding World War II. More embarrassing for Cuban baseball perhaps than the mere lonesomeness of Luque's big-league career was the persistent flavor of Luque's negative image in Chicago, Boston, New York, St. Louis and all points north. For the light-skinned if dark-tempered Cuban idol maintained a lasting reputation with big-league fans and ballpark scribes alike that was unfortunately never quite what most Cuban fans would have wished for back home.

Adolfo Luque today, of course, holds a rare place in Cuban baseball lore — the only Caribbean islander to earn even a modicum of big league fame during the first half-century of modern major league history. Between Nap Lajoie and Jackie Robinson the few dozen Cubans who worked their way north were either brief curiosities in organized baseball (journeyman "coffee-tasters" like receiver Miguel Angel "Mike" González with the National League Boston and St. Louis outfits, and erratic outfielder Armando Marsans with Cincinnati) or else passing shadows that barely tasted the proverbial cup of big league coffee (altogether forgettable names like Rafael Almeida, Angel Aragón, José Acosta and Oscar Tuero). Numerous others — included some of the most famous and talented back home in Havana — toured with black barnstorming outfits that rarely if ever passed before the eyes of a white baseball press.

Luque — by contrast — was something altogether special. His big league credentials would by career's end nearly approximate the numbers posted by many of his contemporaries destined for Cooperstown enshrinement once the game decided to formalize its history with a sacred hall of immortals. Twice (with the Reds in 1919 and the Giants in 1933) he experienced the pinnacle of World Series victory. As a near-two-hundred-game winner he blazed trails that no other Latin ballplayer would approximate for decades. And back in Cuba he generated a feverish following for the big league game and in the process carved out as well a lasting loyalty for "our beloved Reds" ("*nuestros queridos rojos*") among baseball-crazed Habaneros. Yet, for all that, his career was destined to be cursed by the fate that eventually became a personal calling card for nearly all early Latin ballplayers blessed with appropriate talent and skin tone to make their way to the baseball big-time. Among North American fans and writers Dolf Luque would always remain a familiar stereotype — a cartoon figure rather than a genuine baseball hero. At least this was the case at all stops north of Key West or Miami.

* * *

Perhaps the most spurious of apocryphal tales within the ample catalogue of legends that often substitute for serious baseball history is the one surrounding the fiery-tempered Cuban hurler Adolfo Luque, who pitched a dozen seasons for the "Roaring Twenties"–era Cincinnati Reds. Legend has it that Luque, after taking a severe riding from the New York Giants bench, stopped in mid-windup, placed the ball and glove gingerly alongside the mound, then charged straight into the New York dugout to thrash flaky Giants outfielder Casey Stengel to within half an inch of his life.

Veteran Dolf Luque with the National League's New York Giants ball club in 1933. Luque clinched a World Series victory that year in his final big league hurrah (courtesy Transcendental Graphics).

This tale always manages to portray Luque within the strict parameters of a familiar Latin American stereotype — the quick-to-anger, hot-blooded, and somewhat addle-brained Latino who knows little of North American idiom or customs of fair play and can respond to the heat of combat only with flashing temper and flailing fists. The image has, of course, been reinforced over the long summers of baseball's history by the unfortunate (if largely uncharacteristic) real-life baseball events surrounding the most notorious among Latin hurlers. Juan Marichal once brained Dodger catcher Johnny Roseboro with his Louisville Slugger when the Los Angeles receiver returned the ball to his pitcher (with the Giants ace at bat) by firing too close to Marichal's head. The Giants' Rubén Gómez was equally infamous for memorable head-hunting incidents featuring Brooklyn's Carl Furillo and Cincinnati's Frank Robinson. Gómez once plunked heavy-hitting Joe Adcock on the wrist, released a second bean ball as the enraged Braves first sacker charged toward the mound, then retreated to the safety of the dugout only to return moments later wielding a lethal unsheathed switchblade knife.

The oft-told story involving Luque's kamikaze mission against the Giants bench seems, in its most popular version, either a distortion or an abstraction of real-time events. Neither the year (it had to be between 1921 and 1923, during Stengel's brief tenure with McGraw's club) nor circumstances are usually mentioned when the legend is related, and specific events are never detailed with any care. The true indiscretion here, of course, is that this story always seems to receive far more press than those devoted to the facts and figures surrounding Luque's otherwise proud and productive twenty-year big-league career. This was, after all, a premier pitcher of the early lively-ball era, a winner of nearly 200 major league contests, the first great Latin American big league ballplayer ever, and the first among his countrymen to pitch in a World Series, win 20 games in a single summer or 100 in a career, or lead a major league circuit in victories, winning percentage, and ERA. Dolf Luque was, indeed, far more than simply the hot-spirited Latino who once, in a fit of temper, silenced the loquacious Charles Dillon Stengel.

For the record, the much ballyhooed incident involving Luque and Stengel does have its basis in raw fact. And like the Marichal-Roseboro affair four decades later, it appears to have contained events and details infrequently if ever properly reported. The setting was actually Cincinnati's Redland Field (later Crosley Field) on the day of a rare packed house in mid-summer of 1922. The overflow crowd — allowed to stand along the sidelines, thus forcing players of both teams to take up bench seats outside the normal dugout area — added to the tensions of the afternoon. While the

Giants bench, as was their normal practice, spent the early innings of the afternoon disparaging Cincinnati hurler Luque's Latin heritage, these taunts where more audible than usual on this particular day, largely because of the close proximity of the visiting team bench, only yards from the third base line. Future Hall-of-Famer Ross Youngs was reportedly at the plate when the Cuban pitcher decided he had heard about enough from offending Giants outfielder Bill Cunningham, a particularly vociferous heckler seated boldly on McGraw's bench. Luque did, in fairness of fact, at this point leave both ball and glove at the center of the playing field while he suddenly charged after Cunningham, unleashing a fierce blow that missed the startled loudmouth and landed squarely on Stengel's jaw instead. The unreported details are that Luque was at least in part a justified aggressor, while Stengel remained a totally accidental and unwitting victim.

The infamous attack, it turns out, was something of a humorous misadventure and more the stuff of comic relief than the product of sinister provocation. While the inevitable free-for-all that ensued quickly led to Dolf Luque's banishment from the field of play, the now-enraged Cuban soon returned to the battle scene, again screaming for Cunningham and brandishing an ash bat like an ancient lethal war club. It subsequently took four policemen and assorted teammates to escort Luque from the ballpark yet a second time. Thus the colorful Cincinnati pitcher had managed to foreshadow both Marichal and Gómez—later club-wielding Latin moundsmen—all within this single moment of intemperate high-spirited action. Unfortunately what originally passed for comic interlude had dire consequences in this particular instance. Luque had suddenly and predictably played a most unfortunate role in fueling the very stereotype that has since dogged his own career and that of so many of his countrymen. Yet like Marichal, he was in reality a fierce competitor who almost always manifested his will to win with a blazing fastball and some of the cleverest pitching of his age. He was, as well, a usually quiet and iron-willed man whose huge contributions to the game are unfortunately remembered today only by a diminished handful of his aging Cuban countrymen. So buried by circumstance are Luque's considerable and pioneering pitching achievements that reputable baseball historian Lonnie Wheeler fully reports the infamous Luque-Stengel brawl in his marvelous pictorial history of Cincinnati baseball—*The Cincinnati Game*, with John Baskin (Orange Frazer Press, 1988)—then devotes an entire chapter of the same landmark book to "The Latin Connection" in Reds history without so much as a single mention of Dolf Luque or his unmatchable 1923 National League campaign in Cincinnati.

It is a fact now easily forgotten in view of the near tidal wave invasion of Latin players during the 1980s and 1990s—especially the seeming explosion of talent flooding the majors from the hardscrabble island nation of the Dominican Republic—that before Fidel Castro shut down the supply lines in the early '60s, Cuba had dispatched a steady stream of talented players to the big leagues. The first and perhaps least notable

Dolf Luque during his peak and record-setting season with the National League Cincinnati Reds in 1923. His 27 wins that summer are still a Cincinnati club record (courtesy Transcendental Graphics).

was Esteban Bellán, an altogether average infielder with the Troy Haymakers and New York Highlanders of the National Association in the early 1870s; the earliest National Leaguers were Armando Marsans and Rafael Almeida, who both toiled over a few brief seasons with the Cincinnati club beginning in 1911. After the color barrier was dismantled in 1947, the 1950s ushered in quality players from Cuba as widely known for their baseball abilities as for their unique pioneering status—Sandy Amoros of the Dodgers, Camilo Pascual, Pete Ramos, Connie Marrero and Julio Bécquer with the Senators, Minnie Miñoso, Mike Fornieles and Sandy Consuegra of the White Sox, Chico Fernández of the Phillies and Tigers, Román Mejías with the Pirates, Willie Miranda of the Orioles, and stellar lefty Mike Cuéllar, who launched his illustrious pitching career with Cincinnati in 1959.

The best of the early Cubans, beyond the least shadow of a doubt, was Luque, a man who was clearly both fortunate beneficiary and ill-starred victim of racial and ethnic prejudices that ruled major league baseball of his era. While dark-skinned Cuban legend Martín Dihigo was barred from the majors, the light-skinned Luque was quietly welcomed by management, if not always warmly accepted by the full complement of southern mountain boys who staffed most big league rosters. Ironically, Havana-born Luque had been raised only a decade and a half earlier and less than fifty miles distant from Dihigo, who himself hailed from the coastal village of Matanzas. Yet while Luque labored at times brilliantly in the big leagues during the second, third, and fourth decades of the century, his achievements were always diminished in part because he pitched the bulk of his career in the hinterlands that were Cincinnati, in part because his nearly 200 big-league victories were spread thinly over twenty years rather than clustered in a handful of 20-game seasons (he had only one such watershed year). And in the current Revisionist Age of baseball history writing—when Negro Leaguers have at long last received not only their belated rightful due, but a huge nostalgic sympathy vote as well—Martín Dihigo is now widely revered as blackball icon and even enshrined within Cooperstown's portals for his wintertime Cuban League and summertime Mexican League play, while Luque himself lies nearly obscured in the dust and chaff of baseball history.

The memorable pitching career of Dolf Luque might best be capsulated in three distinct stages. Most prominent were the glory years with the Cincinnati Reds spread throughout the full span of the Roaring Twenties, baseball's first flamboyant and explosive decade after the pitching-rich but offense-poor Dead-Ball Era. But first came the formative years of apprentice moundsmanship divided between two distinct baseball-oriented countries. Launching professional play in Cuba in 1912 as both a pitcher and hard-hitting infielder, Luque displayed considerable talent at third base as well as on the mound. A mere six months later the talented youngster was promptly recruited by Dr. Hernández Henríquez, a Cuban entrepreneur residing in New Jersey and operating the Long Branch franchise of the New Jersey–New York State League. A sterling 22–5 record that first New Jersey summer, along with a strange twist of baseball fate, soon provided the hot-shot Cuban pitcher with a quick ticket to big-league fame. This was the epoch when professional baseball was still banned in New York City on the Sabbath, and thus visiting major league clubs often supplemented sparse travel money by scheduling exhibition contests with the conveniently located Long Branch team on the available Sunday afternoon open dates. It was this circumstance that allowed Luque to impress Boston Braves manager George Stallings sufficiently to earn a big-league contract late in the 1914 season, the very year in which Boston surprisingly charged from the rear of the pack in late summer to earn lasting reputation as the "Miracle Braves"— winners of an unexpected National League flag. In his debut with Boston, Dolf Luque became the first Latin American pitcher to appear in either the American or National League, preceding Emilio Palmero with the Giants by a single season and Oscar Tuero with the Cardinals by a full four campaigns.

Brief appearances with Boston in 1914 and 1915 provided little immediate success for the Cuban import, who soon found himself toiling with Jersey City and Toronto of the International League and Louisville of the American Association in search of much-needed minor-league seasoning. A fast start (11 wins in 13 appearances) in the 1918 campaign, however, brought on Stage Two for Luque: a permanent home in Cincinnati that would span the next dozen seasons. The Cuban fastballer was an immediate success in the Queen City, winning 16 games in the combined 1918–1919 seasons, throwing the first shutout by a Latin pitcher, and playing a major role out of the bullpen as the Reds copped their first-ever National League flag during the last year of the century's second decade. Luque himself made history that fall of 1919 as the first Latin-bred thrower to appear in World Series play. He tossed five scoreless innings in two Series relief appearances while the underdog Reds outlasted Charlie Comiskey's Chicagoans in the infamous Black Sox Series.

But it was Luque's 1923 campaign that provided his career hallmark and that was, by any measure, one of the finest single campaigns ever enjoyed by a National League hurler during any epoch. Few moundsmen have ever so thoroughly dominated an entire league for

Luque (left) and Mike González, two of the Cuban League's greatest managers, participate in a dedication ceremony at Cerro Stadium memorializing their lengthy careers.

a full campaign: Luque won 27 while losing but 8, leading the circuit in victories, winning percentage (.771), ERA (1.93) and shutouts (6). The six shutouts could well have been ten: he had four scoreless efforts erased in the ninth inning. His 1.93 ERA would not be matched by another Latin hurler until Luis Tiant registered an almost unapproachable standard of 1.60 in the aberrant 1968 season (the one known as The Year of the Pitcher, when the entire league checked in with a 2.98 mark and five American Leaguers posted sub–2.00 figures). That same summer Luque also became the first pitcher among his countrymen to sock a major league homer, while himself allowing only two opposition round-trippers in 322 innings, the second stingiest home run allowance ever for a pitcher in the senior circuit and close on the heels of the 1921 standard of one homer in 301 innings pitched, recorded by Cincinnati Reds teammate and Hall-of-Famer Eppa Rixey.

One can best appreciate Luque's 1923 performance merely by reviewing the day-in and day-out consistency of his remarkable summer-long craftsmanship. The game-by-game record is worth reviewing here and has been reproduced below for leisurely perusal. The tally shows the Reds' top ace winning both of his decisions in April, standing 3–1 in May, 5–1 in June, 7–1 in July (including wins in both ends of the twin bill on the 17th), 4–2 for the dog days of August, and 6–3 down the stretch run of September. So consistent was the Cuban's overall performance that he registered 28 complete games (second in the league to Brooklyn's Burleigh Grimes), paced the senior circuit with six shutouts, trailed only Grimes again in innings pitched (322 to 327), gave up the league's fewest hits per game (7.8), yielded the lowest opponents' batting average (.235), and outstripped the league's second stingiest hurler by almost a full run per game (teammate Eppa Rixey with a 2.80 ERA).

In the terms of John Thorn and Pete Palmer's Total Pitcher Index (which rates a pitcher's effective performance against that of the entire league), Luque's 1923 campaign ranks fourth best in the two decades separating the century's two great wars (1920–1940). Only Bucky Walters in 1939, Lefty Grove in 1931, and Carl Hubbell in 1933 outstripped Luque by the yardstick of the Thorn-Palmer statistical measure. And yet despite Luque's top-drawer performance (coupled with added 20-victory campaigns by teammates Eppa Rixey and Pete Donohue), Cincinnati nonetheless saw the pennant slip away to John McGraw's powerhouse Giants. It was the front-running New Yorkers who bested Luque in three of his seven losses (the other defeats coming at the hands of Chicago twice and Brooklyn, Philadelphia and Pittsburgh, which each took the measure of the Cuban righty on but a single occasion). Havana's pride and joy was especially devastating on opposing ball clubs in their own home parks, winning a dozen decisions against a mere pair of road-trip setbacks registered in Chicago in late June and Pittsburgh in early September.

Dolf Luque's 27 Victories in 1923 for the Cincinnati Reds

Date	Location	Linescore (Runs-Hits-Errors)	Record (W-L)
April 20	Cincinnati	Cincinnati Reds 10-8-2, St. Louis Cardinals 2-8-3	1 Won–0 Lost
April 24	Cincinnati	Cincinnati Reds 5-8-1, Pittsburgh Pirates 4-9-3	2 Won–0 Lost
May 2	Cincinnati	Chicago Cubs 2-6-6, Cincinnati Reds 1-1-1	2 Won–1 Lost
May 18	New York	Cincinnati Reds 7-10-1, New York Giants 0-6-2	3 Won–1 Lost
May 27	Cincinnati	Cincinnati Reds 2-5-2, St. Louis Cardinals 1-7-1	4 Won–1 Lost
May 31	Chicago	Cincinnati Reds 7-9-0, Chicago Cubs 2-6-1	5 Won–1 Lost
June 2	Cincinnati	Cincinnati Reds 7-10-1, Boston Braves 1-6-1	6 Won–1 Lost
June 10	Cincinnati	Cincinnati Reds 2-8-2, Philadelphia Phillies 1-5-3	7 Won–1 Lost
June 15	Cincinnati	Cincinnati Reds 3-6-1, New York Giants 0-5-0	8 Won–1 Lost
June 19	Cincinnati	Cincinnati Reds 1-7-1, Brooklyn Robins 0-5-2	9 Won–1 Lost
June 24	Chicago	Chicago Cubs 2-8-1, Cincinnati Reds 0-3-0	9 Won–2 Lost
June 29	Cincinnati	Cincinnati Reds 2-8-2, Pittsburgh Pirates 0-7-1	10 Won–2 Lost
July 4	Chicago	Cincinnati Reds 6-12-1, Chicago Cubs 1-7-1	11 Won–2 Lost
July 8	New York	Cincinnati Reds 5-12-1, New York Giants 3-7-0	12 Won–2 Lost
July 12	Philadelphia	Cincinnati Reds 2-6-0, Philadelphia Phillies 0-3-1	13 Won–2 Lost
July 17 (DH)	Boston	Cincinnati 4-9-1, Boston Braves3-8-1 (1st Game)	14 Won–2 Lost
July 17 (DH)	(Boston)	Cincinnati 9-10-3, Boston Braves 5-10-0 (2nd Game)	15 Won–2 Lost
July 21	Brooklyn	Cincinnati Reds 10-19-0, Brooklyn Robins 6-12-3	16 Won–2 Lost
July 25	Cincinnati	Brooklyn Robins 6-10-2, Cincinnati Reds 3-7-2	16 Won–3 Lost
July 29	Cincinnati	Cincinnati Reds 2-8-0, Boston Braves 1-8-1	17 Won–3 Lost
August 4	Cincinnati	New York Giants 14-20-0, Cincinnati Reds 4-11-1	17 Won–4 Lost
August 7	Cincinnati	New York Giants 6-12-1, Cincinnati Reds 2-8-1	17 Won–5 Lost
August 15	New York	Cincinnati Reds 6-11-1, New York Giants 3-9-0	18 Won–5 Lost
August 20	Philadelphia	Cincinnati Reds 6-13-1, Philadelphia Phillies 3-9-1	19 Won–5 Lost
August 24	Brooklyn	Cincinnati Reds 4-10-0, Brooklyn Robins 0-4-3	20 Won–5 Lost
August 28	Boston	Cincinnati Reds 4-8-1, Boston Braves 1-3-3	21 Won–5 Lost
September 1	Cincinnati	Cincinnati Reds 4-9-0, Chicago Cubs 3-9-2	22 Won–5 Lost
September 5	Pittsburgh	Pittsburgh Pirates 6-13-1, Cincinnati Reds 2-12-2	22 Won–6 Lost
September 9	Cincinnati	Cincinnati Reds 8-12-0, Pittsburgh Pirates 3-12-3	23 Won–6 Lost

(continued on page 44)

Date	Location	Linescore (Runs-Hits-Errors)	Record (W-L)
September 14	Cincinnati	Cincinnati Reds 9-12-2, Boston Braves 1-4-4	24 Won–6 Lost
September 17	Cincinnati	Cincinnati Reds 7-8-1, Boston Braves 4-14-0	25 Won–6 Lost
September 20	Cincinnati	Philadelphia Phillies 2-6-0, Cincinnati Reds 0-6-4	25 Won–7 Lost
September 23	Cincinnati	New York Giants 3-12-0, Cincinnati Reds 2-8-1	25 Won–8 Lost
September 25	Cincinnati	Cincinnati Reds 5-8-2, Brooklyn Robins 1-5-2	26 Won–8 Lost
September 29	Cincinnati	Cincinnati Reds 11-17-1, St. Louis Cardinals 1-4-2	27 Won–8 Lost

Luque's remarkable campaign may well stand as one of the handful of best seasons ever produced by a National League moundsman. No Cincinnati pitcher has done better in the nearly eight-decade span that has followed (Bucky Walters won an equal number in 1939). But it is again a telling fact that Luque's 1923 performance rarely if ever is brought to the fore when discussion turns to all-time best pitching performances. Evidence for both the achievement and dismissal of Luque's 1923 season is found in an astute research article by one SABR writer who advances the 1968 summer of Bob Gib-

son as perhaps the true single-season high-water mark for pitchers. In his 1993 essay Peter Gordon compares 40 top campaigns that he selects as "overall bests" and reprises each in some numerical detail. The conclusion is that Gibson in 1968 — despite a rather mediocre 22–9 won-lost mark — edges out such competitors as Walter Johnson in 1913 and Three-Finger Brown in 1906 once performance against overall league averages in taken as an appropriate defining measure.

Gordon's method is to rank his forty stellar pitching performances by what he takes to be the most insightful measures: these are the comparisons of the pitcher in question with the winning ratio of his own team and with the ERA total for the entire league that year. What percentage of his team's victories did the star hurler garner in his stellar season, by what amount did his winning percentage surpass the percentage of his own club, and what is the ratio of his own ERA to the overall league ERA for that season? It is the final standard that Gordon employs for his ultimate rankings since "won-lost records do not reliably reflect a pitcher's true worth" (Gordon 67).

What is relevant for the current discussion is neither the validity of Gordon's methodology nor the accuracy of his own ratings of all-time best single seasons. Rather it is the remarkable fact that Luque's 1923 season (fourth best of the mid-century era when measured by Thorn and Palmer's Total Pitching Index) does not even appear any-

Marianao manager Luque (center) in Cerro Stadium in 1950 with Cleveland Indians GM Frank "Trader" Lane and star outfielder Orestes "Minnie" Miñoso.

25 Greatest Single-Season Pitching Performances, 1892–1987
Based on Peter Gordon's Published Listing

Player (Year)	W–L	Pct.	ERA	TW–L	TPct.	LERA	TW%	TWD	LERA%
Rollie Fingers (1981)	6–3	.667	1.04	62–47	.569	3.66	9.7	.098	.284 (1)
Bob Gibson (1968)	22–9	.709	1.12	97–65	.598	2.99	22.7	.111	.375 (2)
Walter Johnson (1913)	36–7	.837	1.13	90–64	.584	2.93	40.0	.253	.386 (3)
Three-Finger Brown (1906)	26–6	.813	1.04	116–36	.763	2.99	29.5	.109	.425 (5)
Christy Mathewson (1905)	31–8	.795	1.27	105–48	.686	3.59	22.2	.190	.426 (6)
Dwight Gooden (1985)	24–4	.857	1.53	108–54	.581	3.66	41.8	.187	.443 (7)
Cy Young (1901)	33–10	.767	1.62	79–57	.592	2.75	34.4	.164	.444 (8)
Pete Alexander (1915)	31–10	.756	1.22	90–62	.613	3.77	25.0	.280	.462 (9)
Ron Guidry (1978)	25–3	.893	1.74	100–63	.704	4.38	29.0	.181	.470 (10)
Lefty Grove (1931)	31–4	.885	2.06	107–45	.586	3.61	28.4	.164	.479 (11)
Sandy Koufax (1966)	27–9	.750	1.73	95–67	.642	3.99	8.0	.108	.481 (12)
Willie Hernandez (1984)	9–3	.750	1.92	104–58	.704	4.00	29.6	.180	.483 (13)
Dolf Luque (1923)	**27–8**	**.771**	**1.93**	**91–62**	**.591**	**4.29**	**25.0**	**.170**	**.490**
Warren Spahn (1953)	23–7	.767	2.10	92–62	.597	4.29	25.0	.170	.4969
Spud Chandler (1943)	20–4	.833	1.64	98–56	.636	3.30	20.4	.197	.4970
Carl Hubbell (1933)	23–12	.657	1.66	91–61	.599	3.34	25.3	.058	.504
Lefty Gomez (1937)	21–11	.656	2.33	102–52	.662	4.62	20.6	-.006	.507
Tom Seaver (1971)	20–10	.667	1.76	83–79	.512	3.47	24.1	.155	.514
Jack Coombs (1910)	31–9	.775	1.30	102–48	.680	2.53	30.4	.095	.524
Vida Blue (1971)	24–8	.750	1.82	101–60	.627	3.47	23.8	.123	.525
Dazzy Vance (1930)	17–15	.531	2.61	86–68	.558	4.97	19.8	-.027	.538
Mort Cooper (1942)	22–7	.758	1.78	106–48	.688	3.31	20–8	.070	.539
Hal Newhouser (1945)	25–9	.735	1.81	88–65	.575	3.36	28.4	.160	.558
Dazzy Vance (1924)	28–6	.824	2.16	92–62	.597	3.87	30.4	.227	.558
Steve Carlton (1972)	27–10	.730	1.97	59–97	.378	3.46	45.8	.352	.569

Dolf Luque does NOT appear in Gordon's original published list

Note: Pitchers ranked by ratio of personal ERA to league ERA (far right-hand column); Gordon's original list included top 40 seasons, while this present listing has been pared to the top 25 for convenience of presentation.

Key: TW–L = won-lost record of pitcher's team; TPct. = team's victory percentage; LERA = league ERA for that season; TW% = ratio of pitcher's victories to his team's victories; TWD (Team Wins Differential) = percentage points by which pitcher's won-lost percentage surpasses or falls short of team's winning percentage; LERA% = ratio of pitcher's ERA to that of entire league.

where on Gordon's listing of forty remarkable pitching seasons. When one adds in Luque "career season" and then applies Gordon's own statistical measures it turns out that the excluded Cuban stands proudly in thirteenth slot on Gordon's honor roll. Why is it that Luque somehow did not make it onto Gordon's imperfect radar screen? Is it that he is not yet among the immortals in Cooperstown, that he is not a household name among our amateur baseball historians, or that he is simply to be dismissed as a clownish character whose one great year had to be an mere aberration? Gordon is of course not the first to give Cuba's greatest big-league pitching export such unwarranted short shrift.

It is all-too-characteristic of Luque's entire quixotic career that baseball scholars ignore his numerous top performances in this off-handed way. What in the end is the overriding reason? There seemingly are several explanations at least. An inability to speak polished English always fed the image of the comical foreigner. Americans didn't yet take a shining to foreign stars during Luque's era and he has continued to pay the price for his contemporary negative assessment. There were few of these dusky imports on the big league scene and none seemed to be appreciated beyond their convenient roles as images of comic relief. And of course the rest of Luque's career admittedly didn't measure up to initial successes in 1919 and

1923, and this fact didn't help any either. Yet it is hard to think of another near-200-game winner with such little positive press.

* * *

The 1923 season was a high-water mark never again to be equaled by the imported hurler today known back home as "The Pride of Havana." Next in the evolution of Luque's career came the dozen waning seasons as a role player, even if he was still a significant contributor with the Reds, Dodgers and Giants. After losing 23 ballgames with the second-place Reds in 1922 and then pacing the league in victories with the runner-up Cincinnati club of 1923, Dolf Luque would never again enjoy a 20-victory season, though he did come close on both ends of the ledger with a 16–18 mark (plus a league-leading 2.63 ERA) during the 1925 campaign. He did win consistently in double figures, however, over a ten-year span extending through his first of two brief seasons with Brooklyn at the outset of the next decade. It is one of the final ironies of Luque's career that while he was not technically the first Latin ballplayer with the Cincinnati Reds (following Marsans and Almeida in that role), he did actually hold this distinction with the Brooklyn Dodgers team which he joined in 1930. And while it was with the Reds that he had made his historic first World Series appearance, it was with the Giants a decade and a half later that he made a truly significant World Series contribution at the very twilight of his career, gaining the crucial fifth and final game victory in the 1933 Series with a brilliant four-inning relief stint against the then-powerful Washington Senators in the nation's capital.

The third and final dimension of Luque's lengthy career is the one almost totally unknown to North American fans, his brilliant three decades of seasons as both player and manager in the winter league play of his Caribbean homeland. As a pitcher in Cuba, Luque was quite legendary, compiling a 93–62 (.600 Pct.) career mark spread over twenty-two short seasons of wintertime play, ranking as the Cuban League's leading pitcher (9–2) on a single occasion in 1928–29. In 1917 he was also the league's leading hitter (.355), and he capped it all by managing league championship teams on eight different occasions (1919–20, 1924–25, 1934–35, 1939–40, 1941–42, 1942–43, 1945–46, 1946–47).

Luque's reputation in the wintertime Cuban League was unarguably in the end most durable as a manager. This claim stands despite the fact that his pitching achievements were considerable, with his 93 victories and a a .600-plus career won-lost percentage, and also despite the additional fact that Luque was for most of his career a playing manager and not simply a bench-riding skipper. But as a field manager Luque has few rivals anywhere in Cuban League annals, as any mere statistical summary will attest. As a pitcher, by contrast, he was remarkable but hardly unique. His record does not match that of Martín Dihigo who recorded 106 victories in 19 winters. Yet no one else pitched 22 winter seasons in Cuba, nor were there any other 93-game winners outside of Dihigo. (Cup-of-coffee big leaguer Adrián Zabala also compiled 90 victories over the course of 16 Cuban seasons.) But José Méndez, Adolfo Luján and Bebé Royer did record higher lifetime winner percentages (as did of course Dihigo) and all logged more seasons as individual league leaders. Luque's victory totals on the mound in Cuba are as much a testament to his longevity as to his year-in and year-out dominance.

But as a manager there is only the venerable Miguel Angel González to rival Luque for years of service and overall winning success. Luque was notably the only manager to serve with each of the "big four" teams in Cuba, serving the bulk of his career at the helm of Almendares (where he first managed in 1920), but also spending three seasons on the bench with Habana (1924, 1955, 1956) and one each with Cienfuegos and Marianao. His one bench assignment with *Los Elefantes* (1946) gained for Cienfuegos the club's very first pennant in team annals.

Luque posted seven outright titles during his 19 years at the helm of Almendares (where he won 401 over-

Dolf Luque (right) with the Cuban League's Habana Leones mid-career in the 1929–30 winter league season.

all games), his career winning mark stood at 565 and 471 (.545), and he experienced only seven losing ledgers (five with *Los Alacranes*). Luque's total 24 winters as Cuban League manager is outstripped only by Miguel Angel González with 38 (all served with Club Habana), and his 565 wins is also outdistanced only by the unapproachable 917 rung up by Miguel Angel. But while Luque was a regular winner with Almendares (finishing first or second in 14 of 19 years with the Blues), González like venerable Connie Mack amassed his victory totals largely through relentless accumulation. Miguel Angel suffered a handful of the most embarrassing Cuban League seasons on record during his marathon career (including an unimaginable 8 and 58 ledger in 1938) and yet still posted a career winning percentage of .538 (a fraction behind Luque). González's record 13 league pennants outstrips Luque's total by a half-dozen but were earned over a career 37 percent longer. And Luque's managerial record is also augmented by back-to-back Mexican league pennants earned with Nuevo Laredo in the early fifties.

Perhaps Dolf Luque's most significant contribution to the national pastime was his proven talent for developing big-league potential in the players he coached and managed over several decades of winter-league play. One of Luque's brightest and most accomplished students was future New York and Brooklyn star hurler Sal (the Barber) Maglie, who learned his tough style of "shaving" hitters close to the chin from his famed Cuban mentor. Luque (who had developed his own "shaving" techniques with Senior Circuit hitters two decades earlier) was Maglie's pitching coach with the Giants during the latter's rookie 1945 season, as well as his manager with Cienfuegos in the Cuban League that same winter, and at Puebla in the Mexican League in the winter seasons of 1946 and 1947. Maglie has often credited Luque above all others for preparing him for the major leagues. So did Latin America's first big league batting champion, Roberto "Beto" Avila, who also played for Luque in Puebla during the Mexican League campaigns of 1946 and 1947. It was this very talent for player development, in the end, which perhaps spoke most eloquently about the falseness of Luque's widespread popular image as an emotional, quick-tempered and untutored ballplayer during his own big-league playing days.

When it comes to selecting a descriptive term to summarize Luque's career, "explosive" has often been the popular choice. For many commentators, this is the proper phrase to describe his reputed temperamental behavior, his exaggerated on-field outbursts, his infrequent yet widely reported pugilistic endeavors (Luque never shied away from knocking down his share of plate-hugging hitters, of course, but then neither did most successful moundsmen of his era). For still others, it characterizes a career that seemed to burst across the horizon with a single exceptional year, then fade into the obscurity of a forgotten journeyman big-leaguer. But both notions are wide-of-the-mark distortions, and most especially the one that sees Luque as a momentary flash upon the baseball scene. "Durable" would be the far more accurate epithet. For Dolf Luque was a tireless warrior whose pitching career seemed to

stretch on almost without end. His glorious 1923 season was achieved at the already considerable age of thirty-three; he again led the senior circuit in ERA (2.63) two summers later at age thirty-five; he recorded 14 victories and a .636 winning percentage in 1930 while laboring for the Dodgers at the advanced age of forty; his two shutouts that season advanced his career total to 26, a mark which was unsurpassed among Latin pitchers until the arrival of Marichal, Pascual, Tiant and Cuéllar in the decade of the '60s. Referred to widely as the rejuvenated "Papá Montero" by 1933, he recorded eight crucial wins that summer and the clinching World Series victory at age forty-three. His big league career did not end until he was forty-five and had registered twenty full seasons, only one short of the National League longevity standard for hurlers held jointly by Warren Spahn and Eppa Rixey.

Luque's unique claim on durability and longevity is even further strengthened when one takes into consideration his remarkable winter league career played out over an incredible thirty-four winters in Cuba. Debuting with Club Fe of Havana in 1912 at age twenty-two, the indefatigable right-hander registered his final winter-season triumph at age forty-six in 1936, then returned a full decade later to pitch several innings of stellar relief work in the 1945–1946 season at the unimaginable age of fifty-five. Luque's combined totals for major league and winter league baseball — stretching over almost thirty-five years — comprise 284 wins, a figure still unrivaled among all his Latin countrymen. And for those critics who would hasten to establish that longevity alone is not sufficient merit for baseball immortality, it should also be established that Luque's twenty-year ERA of 3.24 outstrips such notable enshrined or wannabe Hall-of-Famers as Bob Feller, Early Wynn, Robin Roberts, Nolan Ryan and Lew Burdette, to name but a few of baseball's most unforgettable moundsmen.

Perhaps the greatest irony surrounding Dolf Luque's big-league career in the end is the misconception that he was a cold, laconic and hot-tempered man, either on the field or off. Upon the occasion of the Cuban hurler's premature and largely unnoticed death at age sixty-six (of a heart attack in Havana in July of 1957), legendary sportswriter Frank Graham provided the final and perhaps most eloquent tribute to this "Pride of Havana" who had reigned so stoically as the first certified Hispanic baseball star:

> It's hard to believe. Adolfo Luque was much too strong, too tough, too determined to die at this age of sixty-six ... he died of a heart attack. Did he? It sounds absurd. Luque's heart failed him in the clutch? It never did before. How many close ball games did he pitch? How many did he win ... or lose? When he won, it was sometimes on his heart. When he lost, it was never because his heart missed a beat. Some enemy hitter got lucky or some idiot playing behind Luque fumbled a ground ball or dropped a sinking liner or was out of position so that he did not make the catch that should have been so easy for him.

No claim should ever be made that Luque was a ballplaying saint or inspiring role model. As player, manager and ball club owner (the latter two roles in the winter leagues of his homeland), the redoubtable Luque was not at all free from displays of fiery temper and volcanic outbursts that fleshed out his colorful reputation. One incident recorded by Negro league historian Donn Rogosin (in *Invisible Men*, 157–158) is likely as typical as it may be apocryphal. As manager of his hometown Havana Almendares club in the mid–'40s Luque reportedly established instant dominance over Negro leaguer Terris McDuffie when the imported star refused to take the mound for a pitching assignment with but two days rest. Summoning his reticent hurler into his pigeonhole dressing room office the menacing skipper calmly pulled an oversized pistol from his desk draw and patiently repeated his lineup assignment. The terrified McDuffie is reported to have seized the offered ball without further protest, then tossed a brilliant two-hitter against the far less threatening opposition.

Luque's career now lies largely buried, yet not so buried that a careful reader of the *Baseball Encyclopedia* does not find the full measure of his greatness. New focus on Latin players in recent years has also brought Luque's name (if not full mem-

ory of his career) back into our collective baseball consciousness. Any proper list of all-time Latin American hurlers reveals him as surpassed in accomplishment only by that "Dominican Dandy" named Marichal, and by his own modern-day alter-ego and fellow countryman, Luis Tiant, Jr. Even today Luque still far outdistances all other Latin hurlers, including such memorable figures as Mike Cuéllar, Camilo Pascual, Juan Pizarro, Fernando Valenzuela and Dennis Martínez (the latter did surpass Luque's career victory total in 1993). And in the now-forgotten category of hitting by pitchers, Dolf Luque stands in a class by himself, having once led the Cuban winter circuit in batting, posting a career .252 average in winter league play, and batting over .227 during twenty major league seasons, an achievement unrivalled by all other usually weak-sticking Hispanic hurlers. He will perhaps never receive his full due in the hindsight of a big league history so filled with flashy Hispanic players of the past two decades. Yet for the educated fan who has poured religiously over the game's rich archives, Dolf Luque is a presence unmatched by all other Hispanic heroes of sport's golden decades between the two great wars.

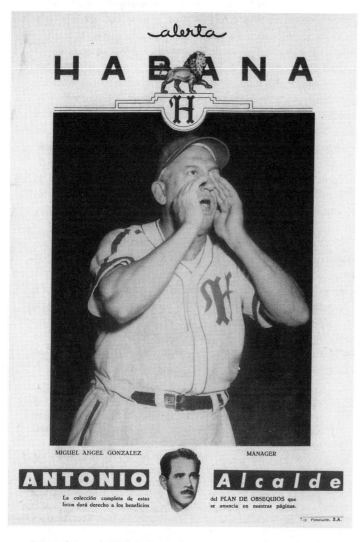

Miguel Angel (Mike) González, Luque's longtime managerial rival in Cuban League winter seasons and fellow Cuban pioneer in the big leagues.

An older and more jovial Dolf Luque as coach for the Cuban League Habana ball club in the early 1950s.

Luque was far more than the man who courted baseball legend by once belting the loud-mouthed Casey Stengel. It would surely be an exaggeration to argue for Luque's enshrinement in Cooperstown solely on the basis of his substantial yet hardly unparalleled big-league numbers, though some have grabbed immortality with far less impressive credentials. It would be equally a failure of historical perspective to dismiss him as a journeyman pitcher of average talent and few remarkable achievements. Few other hurlers have enjoyed such dominance over a short span of a few seasons. Fewer still have proved as durable or maintained their dominance over big-league hitters at so hoary an age. Almost none have contributed to the national pastime so richly after the door slammed shut upon an active big-league playing career. Almost no other major league pitcher did so much with so little fanfare.

The case for depositing Cuba's most renowned hurler of the post Dead Ball Era in the hallowed halls of Cooperstown, like all those pleas for reassessment of ballplayers standing squarely on the cusp of greatness, may arguably reflect the narrow prejudices of the advocate as much as the considerable merits of the nominee. It could very well be countered that Luque, like Roger Maris or Brady Anderson, was a one-season aberration whose 1923 year in the sun far outstripped any of his other achievements. Or one might well take the position, as in the case of Brooklyn's Gil Hodges, that the Cuban right-hander was not even the best player on his own team at the time of his loftiest triumphs. But the numbers amassed across the full decade of the twenties — ten consecutive seasons of double-figure victory totals, three seasons pacing the senior circuit in shutouts, and a pair of ERA crowns — at least work in Luque's case to neutralize if not silence such naysaying. And when it comes to recognizing trailblazing pioneers among Latin ballplayers on the big league scene before Jackie Robinson, on that front alone Havana's Dolf Luque remains lodged in a class entirely by himself.

This was a pitcher, let it never be forgotten, whose numbers for decades stood unmatched by any of his countrymen, one who today still remarkably outstrips all Latino pitchers with singular exceptions of the immortal Marichal, the legendary Tiant, and the more contemporary Dennis Martínez, and possibly now the flamboyant Pedro Martínez. In the often-times falsely attributed phrase of the same Casey Stengel who was once an accidental recipient of one of Dolf Luque's most torrid knockout pitches — "You can look it up!"

References and Suggested Readings

Bjarkman, Peter C. *Diamonds around the Globe: The Encyclopedia of International Baseball.* Westport, CT: Greenwood Publishing Group, 2005. (cf. Chapter 1: Cuba — *Béisbol Paradiso*)

_____. *Baseball with a Latin Beat: A History of the Latin American Game.* McFarland: Jefferson, NC, and London, 1994.

González Echevarría, Roberto. *The Pride of Havana: A History of Cuban Baseball.* New York: Oxford University Press, 1999.

Gordon, Peter M. "Bob Gibson in 1968" in: *The Perfect Game* (A Collection of Facts, Figures, Stories and Characters from the Society for American Baseball Research). Edited by Mark Alvarez. Dallas: Taylor Publishing, 1993, 62–69.

Rathgeber, Bob. "A Latin Temper on the Mound — Adolfo Luque" in: *Cincinnati Reds Scrapbook.* Virginia Beach: JCP Corporation of Virginia, 1982, 54–55.

Rogosin, Donn. *Invisible Men: Life in Baseball's Negro Leagues.* New York: Atheneum Books, 1983.

Rucker, Mark, and Peter C. Bjarkman. *Smoke: The Romance and Lore of Cuban Baseball.* New York: Total Sports Illustrated, 1999.

Dolf Luque's Almost-Forgotten Major League Record

Year	Team	W–L	Pct.	ERA	G	GS	CG	IP	BB	SO	ShO
1914	BOS N	0–1	.000	4.15	2	1	1	8.2	4	1	0
1915	BOS N	0–0	.000	3.60	2	1	0	5.0	4	3	0
1918	CIN N	6–3	.667	3.80	12	10	9	83.0	32	26	1
1919	CIN N	10–3	.769	2.63	30	9	6	106.0	36	40	2
1920	CIN N	13–9	.591	2.51	37	23	10	207.2	60	72	1
1921	CIN N	17–19	.472	3.38	41	36	25	304.0	64	102	3
1922	CIN N	13–23	.361	3.31	39	32	18	261.0	72	79	0
1923	CIN N	27–8	<u>.771</u>	<u>1.93</u>	41	37	28	322.0	88	151	6
1924	CIN N	10–15	.400	3.16	31	28	13	219.1	53	86	2
1925	CIN N	16–18	.471	<u>2.63</u>	36	36	22	291.0	78	140	4
1926	CIN N	13–16	.448	3.43	34	30	16	233.2	77	83	1
1927	CIN N	13–12	.520	3.20	29	27	17	230.2	56	76	2
1928	CIN N	11–10	.524	3.57	33	29	11	234.1	84	72	1
1929	CIN N	5–16	.238	4.50	32	22	8	176.0	56	43	1
1930	BKN N	14–8	.636	4.30	31	24	16	199.0	58	62	2
1931	BKN N	7–6	.538	4.56	19	15	5	102.2	27	25	0
1932	NYG N	6–7	.462	4.01	38	5	1	110.0	32	32	0
1933	NYG N	8–2	.800	2.69	35	0	0	80.1	19	23	0
1934	NYG N	4–3	.571	3.83	26	0	0	42.1	17	12	0
1935	NYG N	1–0	1.000	0.00	2	0	0	3.2	1	2	0
Totals	**20 Years**	**194–179**	**.520**	**3.24**	**550**	**365**	**206**	**3220.1**	**918**	**1130**	**26**

Underscored = League Leader

World Series Record

Year	Team	Record	Pct.	ERA	G	GS	GC	IP	BB	SO	ShO
1919	CIN N	0–0	.000	0.00	2	0	0	5	0	6	0
1933	NYG N	1–0	1.000	0.00	1	0	0	4.1	2	5	0
Totals	2 Series	1–0	1.000	0.00	3	0	0	9.1	2	11	0

Hispanic Pitchers as Hitters

Among hard-hitting Hispanic pitchers, Adolfo Luque stands supreme, having led other Latinos in almost all lifetime batting categories, including runs scored, hits, triples, RBI and batting average. Sufficient proof that "The Pride of Havana" knew how to deftly wield his bat against more than just the raucous bench jockeys of the New York Giants dugout derives from the fact that Luque also won a Cuban League batting title in 1917 (.355 during a 25-game season) and compiled a lifetime .252 BA over 22 seasons of Cuban winter league play (with 671 career at-bats). A listing of top Latin-born heavy-hitting pitchers follows:

Pitcher	AB	Runs	Hits	2B	3B	HR	RBI	B.A.
Dolf Luque (1914–1935)	**1043**	**96**	**237**	**31**	**10**	**5**	**90**	**.227**
Camilo Pascual (1954–1971)	977	71	198	32	5	5	81	.203
Juan Pizarro (1957–1974)	658	72	133	18	2	8	66	.202
Rubén Gómez (1953–1967)	477	58	95	11	1	3	22	.199
Jesse Flores (1942–1950)	304	18	55	7	2	0	22	.181
Sandy Consuegra (1950–1957)	218	15	37	2	0	0	18	.170
Mike Fornieles (1952–1963)	308	25	52	7	1	1	16	.169
Juan Marichal (1960–1974)	1219	73	202	29	2	4	75	.165
Luis Tiant, Jr. (1964–1982)	495	36	81	12	1	5	40	.163

Note: Fernando Valenzuela also compiled a respectable career .200 BA (with 187 hits) over 17 seasons (1980–1997), but current statistical encyclopedias fail to provide complete numbers for Valenzuela in all major batting categories.

Dolf Luque's Winterball Statistics

The following Cuban winter league statistics for Dolf Luque are provided with assistance from reputable Cuban baseball scholar and journalist Severo Nieto and have previously appeared in their most complete form within Gabino Delgado and Severo Nieto's valuable and long out-of-print book, *Béisbol Cubano, Récords y Estadísticas* (Havana, 1955).

Year	Team	Dolf Luque Pitching Record GP	CG	W–L (Pct.)	Dolf Luque Batting Record G	AB	H	HR	BA
1912	Club Fe	7	2	0–3 (.000)	11	27	2	0	.071
1913	Club Fe	2	0	0–2 (.000)	16	52	15	0	.294
1913–14	Havana	6	3	2–3 (.400)	16	43	11	0	.256
1914–15	Almendares	16	6	7–4 (.636)	23	69	18	0	.261
1915–16	Almendares	20	11	12–5 (.706)	—	64	15	0	.234
1917	Orientales	9	6	4–4 (.500)	11	31	11	0	.355
1918–19	Did not play								
1919–20	Almendares	15	9	10–4 (.714)	19	45	6	0	.133
1920–21	Almendares	10	6	4–2 (.667)	15	46	6	0	.130
1921	Did not play								
1922–23	Havana	23	12	11–9 (.550)	31	73	20	1	.278
1923–24	Havana	11	5	7–2 (.778)	19	41	16	0	.390
1924–25	Almendares	3	3	3–0 (1.000)	3	10	3	0	.300
1925–26	Did not play								
1926–27	Alacranes (CT)	16	13	10–6 (.625)	—	54	15	0	.278
1927–28	Almendares	13	6	6–4 (.600)	16	36	6	0	.167
1928–29	Cuba-Havana	17	9	9–2 (.818)	—	37	8	0	.216
1929–30	Havana	15	7	4–8 (.333)	—	35	12	1	.343
1930–32	Did not play								
1932–33	Almendares	6	2	2–2 (.500)	8	18	4	0	.222
1933–34	Season cancelled								
1934–35	Almendares	10	6	6–2 (.750)	11	31	7	0	.226
1935–36	Almendares	7	5	4–2 (.667)	NA	NA	NA	NA	NA
1936–37	Almendares	7	1	2–2 (.500)	7	11	2	0	.190
1937–38	Almendares	1	0	0–1 (.000)	1	2	0	0	.000

(continued on page 51)

Year	Team	*Dolf Luque Pitching Record*			*Dolf Luque Batting Record*				
		GP	CG	W-L (Pct.)	G	AB	H	HR	BA
1938–39	Almendares	1	0	0–1 (.000)	1	0	0	0	.000
1945–46	Cienfuegos	1	0	0–0 (.000)	1	0	0	0	.000
Totals	**22 Seasons**	**210**	**99**	**93–62 (.600)**	**216**	**671**	**169**	**2**	**.252**

Note: It might be noted with interest that during approximately the same period (the 19 seasons between 1923 and 1947) Negro league all-star and Cooperstown Hall-of-Famer Martín Dihigo compiled a highly comparable pitching record within the Cuban Professional Baseball League, posting 262 games pitched, 120 complete games, and a slightly superior won-lost mark of 106–59 (a .642 winning percentage).

Latin America's Top Big-League Pitchers (20th Century)

Fifteen pitchers below comprise the select list of Latin American-born hurlers who have won a minimum of 100 big-league games through the 2000 season. This listing of all-time greats among Latino pitchers is arranged on the basis of total wins, with career leaders in other statistical categories indicated by underscoring. While the all-time runner-up (behind Dennis Martínez) in career losses, Dolf Luque ranks near the top in all other statistical categories, standing 4th overall in victories, 5th in ERA (trailing Marichal, Pedro Martínez, Cuéllar and Rijo), and 4th all-time in innings pitched (behind only Marichal, Tiant and Dennis Martínez).

Pitcher	Wins–Losses	Pct.	ERA	IP	SO	BB
Dennis Martínez (Nicaragua) 1976–1998	245–193	.559	3.70	3999	2149	1165
Juan Marichal (Dominican) 1960–1974	243–142	.631	2.89	3509	2303	709
Luis Tiant, Jr. (Cuba) 1964–1982	229–172	.571	3.30	3486	2416	1104
Dolf Luque (Cuba) 1914–1935	194–179	.520	3.24	3220	1130	918
Mike Cuéllar (Cuba) 1959–1977	185–130	.587	3.14	2808	1632	822
Camilo Pascual (Cuba) 1954–1971	174–170	.506	3.63	2930	2167	1069
Fernando Valenzuela (Mexico) 1980–1997	173–153	.531	3.54	2930	2074	1151
Ramón Martínez (Dominican) 1988–2000	135–86	.611	3.62	1880	1418	779
Juan Pizarro (Puerto Rico) 1957–1974	131–105	.555	3.43	2034	1522	888
Joaquín Andújar (Dominican) 1976–1988	127–118	.518	3.58	2154	1032	731
Pedro Martínez (1992–2000)	125–56	.691	2.68	1576	1818	442
Pedro Ramos (Cuba) 1955–1970	117–160	.422	4.08	1643	1415	629
Jaime Navarro (Puerto Rico) 1989–2000	116–126	.479	4.72	2055	1113	690
José Rijo (Dominican) 1984–1995	111–87	.561	3.16	1786	1556	634
Mario Soto (Dominican) 1977–1988	100–92	.521	3.47	1731	1449	657

3

Orestes Miñoso — The Cuban Comet

One of baseball's prize Horatio Alger tales is that of a player whose parents were so poor he didn't start school until he was ten, who had to quit four years later to go to work, cutting sugar cane with a machete.

— A.S. "Doc" Young (on Minnie Miñoso)

Orestes Miñoso ("The Cuban Comet") and Orlando Hernández ("El Duque") stand at two extreme poles of four decades demarcating Fidel Castro's ongoing socialist experiment in Cuba. The fleet-footed Miñoso epitomizes an era when Cuba first proudly launched its full-scale invasion of big-league diamonds; the fast-balling Hernández reflects an epoch in which government-sponsored Cuban national baseball strives to hide its most talented performers from prying eyes of U.S. professional scouts. Hernández and Miñoso — all such symbolizes aside — also easily remain the two most recognizable Cubans ever to carry the big league banner of the world's most baseball-crazed country.

Among 150-odd Cubans performing to date on big-league diamonds, it is Hernández and Miñoso who most sharply evoke the image of Cuban baseball for North American fans. "El Duque's" considerable notoriety during recent seasons has admittedly come largely from politically charged circumstances surrounding his daring flight from Castro's "evil empire" communist island. A four-season 45–33 pitching record (1998–2001) with the New York Yankees' perennial World Series entrants is, in itself, hardly the stuff of baseball legend. (By 2005 the 39-year-old veteran Hernández had revived his career for one last hurrah with the pennant bound Chicago White Sox.) Miñoso's reputation, by contrast, was always hard-earned on the field of play and had nothing at all to do with an ongoing forty-year saga of political tensions between the world's foremost ball-playing nations.

Miñoso is arguably the only Cuban born-and-bred ballplayer ever to attain legitimate big-league star status, though half-a-dozen others have also come tantalizingly close. Orlando Hernández and half-brother Liván Hernández have themselves enjoyed their moments of eye-popping performance, mostly in the World Series and postseason playoff spotlight. Both have earned cherished October MVP trophies for their efforts on championship clubs (1998 New York Yankees and 1997 Florida Marlins). But in both cases, celebrity status as bold escapees from Castro's island — purported heroes of the anti–Castro crusade, who each supposedly risked life and limb for the cherished freedom to play for countless millions of dol-

lars in corporate big league baseball — has seemed always to color the picture dramatically. At any rate, the once-polished celebrity stars of both Hernández brothers have already faded rather rapidly after a single autumn for each of performing brilliantly on the postseason center stage.

A quarter-century earlier, Luis ("Looie") Tiant was perhaps a more legitimate star-quality Cuban pitcher. Tiant won better than 225 games (mainly in Cleveland and Boston) and is unsurpassed in rank as the all-time Latin-born big league strikeout leader. But even Tiant, in the end, was always overshadowed by larger pitching luminaries during an epoch overflowing with quality mound stars — some of them fellow Latinos like Dominican Juan Marichal and fellow Cubans Camilo Pascual and Miguel (Mike) Cuéllar. Tiant ironically also earned his own most spectacular moment in the sun on the World Series stage, and again this all came about in circumstances relating rather directly to headline-grabbing Cuban-American cold war politics. The primary drama attached to Looie Tiant during the 1975 Boston-Cincinnati World Series showdown was seemingly the off-field events that surrounded an emotional reunion with his Negro-league-legend father, freed from Cuba for the solemn occasion by an opportunistic President Castro amidst much propagandistic journalistic hoopla.

Pascual was still another talented Cuban major leaguer emerging from the same era as Miñoso himself. Some might argue that Pascual was in the long haul a better big league hurler than Tiant, even if the record doesn't easily back up such a claim. Pascual was after all doomed to play for much of his 18-year career with a truly woeful team in Washington, and when he did finally approach true star status, it was while laboring for a transplanted Minnesota franchise that stirred preciously little national media attention. Cuban countrymen Tony Oliva (two-time American League batting champ and AL top rookie in 1964) and Zoilo Versalles (the first-ever Latino league MVP in 1965) suffered equally from the same Minnesota "small market" syndrome. Had Versalles earned an MVP trophy with the vaunted Yankees or had Oliva registered a pair of batting titles with the Dodgers or Cubs or even the Tigers, both might be celebrated today in much the same fashion as Clemente and Marichal. Certainly both were substantial players even if never serious hall-of-fame contenders. Yet neither ever quite earned superstar status on a national level.

Tony Pérez comes perhaps closest to earning the legitimate badge of Cuban big league headliner. But Pérez always lived in the distinct shadow of Big Red Machine teammates Pete Rose, Joe Morgan, and Johnny Bench. Today Pérez may finally enjoy adulation as a certified Cooperstown hall-of-famer, yet the Camagüey native was often little more than an afterthought in Cincinnati during the 1970s glory seasons of championship play under famed mentor Sparky Anderson. And Pérez is also robbed of full honors by a technicality that attaches equally to Oliva, Versalles, Oakland A's speedster Bert Campaneris, Cuéllar (a Cy Young winner in Baltimore who rivals Tiant as the best Cuban big-league hurler of the 1960s and seventies), and even others like Tony Taylor and Tony González with the 1960s-era Phillies, and more contemporary sluggers José Canseco and Rafael Palmeiro. Members of this considerable contingent were all born on Cuban soil, yet none ever played much baseball in their homeland before fleeing the onslaughts of the Communist Castro regime. Thus, these players fail to hold the same allure for fans back in Havana or Matanzas or Cienfuegos as did Dolf Luque or Mike González in the 1920s and 1930s, Miñoso and Willie Miranda throughout the 1950s, or even the high-profile political defectors and asylum-seekers of the late nineties. Miñoso's claim as the only true Cuban big leaguer of legitimate superstar proportions is based in large part on the fact that "The Cuban Comet" was both a top-ranking U.S. major leaguer plus a winter-season headliner back on his native island — at one and the same time.

Ironically, from the perspective of North American baseball boosters, the two greatest Cuban stars of the first half of the twentieth century both lived in relative obscurity for most North American fans, yet for starkly contrasting reasons. Martín Dihigo — the greatest all-around Cuban ballplayer and for some the greatest raw talent ever to step on a pro or amateur diamond in any league or any era — was permanently barred from baseball's biggest stage by his ebony skin color. Dolf Luque — playing in the same era, but blessed with more acceptable skin tone — knew the taste of big league action closed to Dihigo but was nonetheless also a sad victim of an equally insidious reigning prejudice. Luque fell casualty to a stereotype (the hot-blooded Latino warrior with limited command of the game's finer points) that attached to so many fiery Spanish-speaking ballplayers of an earlier era. Despite one of the greatest single-season performances in National League history (twenty-seven wins with the 1923 Cincinnati Reds) and a host of additional top-flight achievements (the first Latin to win twenty games in a single season or one hundred for a career), Luque was never taken very seriously in northern cities as a first-rate big leaguer like Ed Reulbach, Dizzy Dean, or Nap Rucker (all of whom won far less games).

Miñoso — despite his somewhat demeaning moniker (Minnie) and his flashy image — was never ignored like Dihigo

Minnie Miñoso with the Chicago White Sox in the mid-fifties (courtesy Transcendental Graphics).

nor dismissed like Luque. His status was as huge in Chicago (or nearly so), and sometimes in Cleveland, as it always was back in Havana. The batting and base-running star of the Paul Richards-managed "Go-Go" White Sox was one of the most popular diamond figures of his colorful era. The fan assessment of Miñoso was never that he was simply a one-dimensional player, a charge frequently leveled or a suspicion frequently held when discussing most Latin American ballplayers at mid-century. Rather, a league-wide consensus concerning Miñoso was more often than not an opinion that he never quite got his full and just due from fans and writers in the league's rival cities. This was never more true than at the end of his stellar debut season, when he was edged out on sportswriters' ballots by a clearly inferior (but New York Yankee owned) Gil McDougald for the American League's cherished top rookie honors.

But Miñoso was never altogether free from career-diminishing stereotypes, either. Part of the reason may have been the lack of a career-legitimizing postseason stage. Season after season Miñoso's teams were blocked from October baseball by Casey Stengel's dynasty Yankees outfits. If Miñoso lived under the shadow of New York's "M Boys" (Mantle and McDougald in the fifties) during hard-fought American League seasons, he was even more severely diminished by the Bronx Bombers' predictable presence whenever World Series play rolled into view.

And by a cruel trick of fate, when the Indians (1954) and White Sox (1959) did make their single World Series appearances of the decade, in both cases Miñoso had been robbed of his own opportunity by an untimely player trade; Cleveland unloaded him to Chicago three years before arising as American League champs, and the Chisox shipped him back to the Indians on the eve of their own long-postponed run at the Fall Classic. But there may have been an even more insidious reason for the remarkable Cuban's inability to reach the full-fledged stardom he deserved. The "Go-Go" image of flair and flash that was such a big part of Miñoso's impressive résumé was also in the end something of a career-inhibiting factor. It was precisely that flashy image (as was also the case with Puerto Rico's Vic Power) that may have diverted much attention from the true level of Miñoso's big league skills. And the late-ca-

reer publicity stunts that brought him back from retirement to appear in a fourth and fifth decade didn't help any either, serving only to cheapen Miñoso's already substantial image by clouding it with further elements of cheesy showmanship.

In the end Minnie Miñoso was perceived as more of an ebony-hued folk hero than a true diamond idol. At least this was the case for his substantial North American fans. Cubans back on his native island always cherished Miñoso as a legitimate star of the grandest proportions — one of the stellar exemplars of their deeply ingrained baseball heritage.

* * *

May 1st of 1951 was a date of great significance in the venerable history of a usually lackluster Chicago American League baseball franchise. For diehard Second City fans it was a rare moment of proud triumph for the ball club long known as Chuck Comiskey's ill-fated and much-cursed White Sox. But it would also be a date pregnant with considerable import for the history of professional baseball, Latin American style. May Day of 1951 would, unfortunately, also be a day robbed of a large chunk of its deep-seated significance by a rude twist of fate and a case of inexorably bad timing. It was the kind of terrible timing, in fact, that seemed to reoccur throughout the entire career of a flashy Cuban outfielder known by the adopted moniker of "Minnie" Miñoso.

On that very afternoon, in tradition-rich Comiskey Park, the twenty-nine-year-old jet-skinned rookie outfielder from Cuba was destined to become the first black ballplayer ever to don a White Sox uniform for official American League play. He was hardly a normal rookie, of course, given his advanced age and his two earlier trials — he had already played seventeen games with Cleveland, in 1949 and during the previous month of April 1951. Yet to the unrestrained joy of long-suffering supporters crammed into the Comiskey bleachers, as well as those glued to radios throughout the Windy City, this pioneering "rookie" was destined to debut with a bang and a flair rarely seen during the three dark decades of Chicago South Side baseball that had followed the curse of the 1919 Black Sox scandal. And the castoff freshman replacement certainly didn't disappoint. In his very first at-bat for his new Chicago team, Saturnino Orestes Armas Arrieta Miñoso ("Minnie" for short) pounded out a bullpen home run off Yankee ace Vic Raschi.

Yet the inescapable irony that plagued and often diminished almost every step of Miñoso's brilliant career was to saturate this glorious debut moment just as it would so many career moments that were to follow. Few baseball historians today would, a half-century later, think to point to May Day 1951 as the watershed date of baseball integration for Chicago. Another event would upstage the local heroics that day. Unfortunately for Miñoso and his fans, in the sixth inning of that same contest, future Hall of Famer and fifties legend Mickey Mantle would also blast his very first career round-tripper for the visiting New York Yankees. And to add further insult to injury, it would be Miñoso — stationed at third base — who would later let a Mantle grounder escape through his legs,

Young Minnie Miñoso in Havana, 1951, with his favorite tools.

thus handing the Yankees a lead which they would never relinquish that day. The error and the loss would soon enough disappear into baseball's endless cycles. It would be Mantle's own debut homer, however — not Miñoso's — that would etch this particular date into the bedrock of baseball history.

This knack for inadvertently playing second-fiddle on the baseball diamond would strangely become something of a hallmark of Miñoso's otherwise brilliant big league career. Miñoso was not only the first black to perform for a hometown club in Chicago — Sam Hairston would be the first North American black, debuting with the Sox in July, and Ernie Banks would eventually come along on the North Side two years later — he was also (and more significantly) the very first indisputably "black Cuban" and "black Latino" player to take his position on any big league diamond. There were indeed Cubans (Armando Marsans, Rafael Almeida, Mike González), Puerto Ricans (Hi Bithorn, Luis Olmo Rodríguez), and Venezuelans (Alex Carrasquel) well before him whose skin was dark enough to stir debate about violations of the odious "gentlemen's agreement" that continuously cheapened the national sport. But Miñoso was a "pure Negro" like Martín Dihigo and José Méndez (not a light-skinned *mestizo* like Bithorn or Olmo), and thus had only Jackie Robinson to thank for his belated "welcome" into the big leagues.

Yet it was nonetheless somewhat of a misfortune that the Cuban Comet's debut in 1949 should have been with the Cleveland Indians, a team already featuring two headline-hogging blacks named Larry Doby and Satchel Paige. Doby earned the lion's share of notoriety, of course, as the first American Leaguer to represent his race; and venerable Satchel Paige was a full-blown Negro leagues legend who, while far past his pitching prime, was still every bit as much a celebrity in Cleveland as he was everywhere else from Topeka to Tampico. Had Miñoso's debut been staged with any other junior circuit club it might thus have stirred far greater media and fan attention than it ever could have with Bill Veeck's already-integrated Cleveland Indians.

Miñoso's somewhat ill-timed debuts with both the Indians and White Sox were only two disheartening foreshadows of things yet to come. The Cuban sensation would parlay speed and daring on the base paths and in the outfield, along with power and clutch base hits at the plate, into a truly phenomenal rookie season. And yet it was a season doomed to be laced with little more than "second best" accolades. At year's end the colorful "colored" Chisox rookie would indeed be the league pacesetter in several lesser-noted categories such as stolen bases (31) and triples (14), but his brilliant batting mark of .326 (one of the highest ever for an "official" rookie) would fall eighteen points behind the average of Philadelphia's "Punch-and-Judy" hitting first sacker, Ferris Fain. His 112 runs scored also fell a single tally short of league leader Dom DiMaggio of the Boston Red Sox. But the biggest "near-miss" came at the ballot box. Although dubbed top rookie by *The Sporting News*, Miñoso would surprisingly finish only second in scribe voting for the more prestigious Baseball Writers Association American League Rookie of the Year award. Winner Gil McDougald of the eventual World Champion New York Yankees had not only trailed Miñoso in all the important offensive categories save homers (where McDougald had a slim fourteen to ten edge), but also finished a distant ninth in the same sportswriters poll for league MVP. Miñoso himself placed only fourth in tallying for the latter award, despite loud protests among diehard Chisox supporters, but he was nonetheless still five slots ahead of rookie rival McDougald.

It was the matter of pennant-winning, however, that provided the epitome of Miñoso's career-long timing problems. His brief debut with the 1949 Indians came but a single spring after the rare Cleveland pennant-winning season of 1948. Moving on to Chicago in a blockbuster trade that opened the 1951 campaign, Miñoso would next be found laboring in Chicago, and not in Cleveland, when the Indians soon charged to yet another league title three summers later. Then, a second headline-grabbing trade between the 1957 and 1958 seasons would shuttle Miñoso back to Cleveland, while at the same

Orestes Miñoso as a star outfielder with the Marianao Tigres during the 1950 winter league season.

time ironically providing the Chicago White Sox with their own missing pennant ingredient in the form of future Hall-of-Fame hurler Early "Gus" Wynn. Miñoso remained in a Cleveland uniform just long enough to miss out on the single Chicago pennant run in the final season of the decade.

In a final bitter touch of irony, at least from Miñoso's point of view, Cleveland GM Frank "Trader" Lane had apparently engineered a deal that would have returned the Cuban outfielder to the Windy City late in 1959 and just in time for the Comiskey Park pennant celebration party. But Miñoso went on an ill-timed hitting tear the very week the deal was quietly being negotiated, and this sudden upswing in performance made even the trade-happy Lane fearful of a fan rebellion in Cleveland if he pulled the trigger on any such deal. The ill-starred trade was postponed until the year-end league winter meetings, and then put off once again until after the opening of the new spring season.

The greatest irony of all surrounding Miñoso, of course, is the fact that his Go-Go White Sox ball club managed to transform the freewheeling baserunning style introduced originally by Miñoso himself into a serious pennant challenge only *after* the fleet-footed Cuban had already been sent packing. Bill Veeck — Miñoso's original boss in Cleveland and the new White Sox owner by 1959 — worked with Lane to rectify the situation (via the proposed mid–1959 re-trade), yet was un-

A jovial Miñoso in the Cerro Stadium dugout with the Marianao Tigres (c. 1951).

able to reel Miñoso back to Chicago until shortly after the American League pennant had already been hoisted above Comiskey Park. Veeck nonetheless would charitably recognize Minnie's earlier contributions to the ball club by presenting the newly re-acquired Miñoso, in the spring of 1960, with an honorary (and well deserved) World Series ring. But it was little consolation for the Cuban Comet, since his former team, the Chisox, had celebrated their 1959 World Series appearance while Miñoso was still an "also-ran," stuck in second place with Cleveland.

Miñoso's full career (one that stretched nearly thirty seasons in the majors, Cuba, and Mexico) would from beginning to end be marked by such tantalizing near-miss brushes with the highest levels of diamond fame — painfully close encounters with achievement and celebrity far greater than that which actually ever materialized. Here was the most colorful dark-skinned Cuban ballplayer of the post–Jackie Robinson integration years: His flashy and often dramatic style translated into huge efforts at doing precisely what was needed to win ball games for his team. He played with a reckless abandon aimed always at achieving nothing short of total victory; his on-field flair was indeed one saturated with a clear work ethic. He stole bases with the game on the line, harassed pitchers with daring base-running ploys, took extra bases and made impossible wall-crashing catches — a daring on-field style that was always appreciated by fans and teammates alike. Yet he was never quite so celebrated as his equally flashy Latino rival, Victor Power of Puerto Rico.

Power's flamboyance was tainted with staged showmanship, and usually a brand of showmanship that was more personal in performance and far less team-oriented in impact. Thus Power drew a fan club following from Kansas City to New York to Boston to Detroit, while Miñoso was far more quietly revered in mid–1950s Chicago. When today's middle-aged fans recall that fifties golden era of their lost youthful fandom, it is more likely to be Power than Miñoso who is first mentioned when the talk turns nostalgically to early examples of unbridled Latin American ball-playing enthusiasm on display for the first time in the big leagues.

In all this tendency to achieve much on the diamond, and yet always in the end suffer the ultimate humiliation of never receiving true credit due, Miñoso seemed only to be repeating a fate specially reserved for the earliest black-skinned ballplayers — those who poured from the Cuban cane fields and Puerto Rican barrios in the decades immediately before and after Jackie Robinson's debut with the Dodgers. Miñoso became the example that would motivate claims later voiced by Roberto Clemente: Black Hispanic ballplayers never received their full due from managers, writers, teammates, fans, owners, or anyone else in the revered baseball establishment.

Ace Negro leaguer Martín Dihigo was of course the earliest prototype, robbed altogether of a career in the big leagues by the simple matter of his skin color. José de la Caridad Méndez, Luis Tiant, Sr., Perucho Cepeda, Cuban sluggers Alejandro Oms and Cristóbal Torriente, and dozens of others before Miñoso suffered equal anonymity. Miñoso would perhaps most fully underscore the tradition, as would his friendly rival Vic Power (despite the latter's more evolved cult-figure stature in the mid-fifties and early 1960s). Down the road a small stretch, Clemente, Oliva, Versalles and Orlando Cepeda would soon enough be equal victims squashed under the heel of baseball's ongoing — if now more subtle — sugar-coated racism. Yet oftentimes, as with Minnie Miñoso of the Go-Go Chicago White Sox, it all seemed just a matter of exceedingly poor timing.

* * *

One measure of the Latin ballplayer's often-schizophrenic personality and ongoing identity crisis is the regrettable frequency with which his North American fans forget, misapprehend, or altogether butcher his proud family names. The greatest of Cuban players — Martín Dihigo — remained a name virtually unknown to stateside fans for all the years of his brilliant backwater career. Once Dihigo's name had been belatedly rescued from anonymity, it continued to be mispronounced by uninformed North American fans. The given first name of this Hall of Famer is still more often than not pronounced with incorrect stress on the first syllable, as if it were an English moniker. The family name, on the other hand, likely proves unpronounceable on first encounter. Such a state of affairs is not totally surprising in an environment where one of baseball's most beloved radio and television voices of the recent past, Harry Caray, made it his stock-in-trade to frequently stumble over Hispanic names like Vizcaino ("Vis-cane-oh" for Harry), Peña ("Pena"), Cedeño ("Cedeno"), Guillén (Caray never pronounced it the same way twice), and the like. Strangely enough, no one (even tongue-tied Harry Caray) ever had quite such difficulty with names like Yastrzemski, or DiMaggio, or Kluszewski, or even Lajoie.

While the name of Cuba's

Miñoso displays "Go-Go White Sox" flair at home plate beating the tag by Cleveland catcher Jim Hegan in April 1952 (courtesy Transcendental Graphics).

Three Cleveland Indians fifties-era Latino stars: Venezuela's Chico Carrasquel, Cuba's Miñoso, and Mexico's Beto Avila (left to right) (courtesy Transcendental Graphics).

greatest pre-integration diamond star seemed to have been altogether lost, two of the true greats among the first post–Jackie Robinson black Latin big leaguers suffered equal "name abuse" despite their new-found fame. Vic Power of Puerto Rico carried a false last name of "Power" because his earliest pro baseball contacts (scouts and managers), as well as local writers, could not properly decipher (and thus pronounce) his mother's true name — Pellot. And Pedro Oliva (known to American fans as "Tony" Oliva) bore a false first name for equally ludicrous reasons — the need to substitute a brother's birth certificate when signing a first pro baseball contract back in Cuba. Oliva had little wherewithal and less courage to correct the error in the months that followed. Thus, for both Victor Pellot (Pay-OAT) Pove (PO-VEY, butchered as *Power*) and Pedro Oliva, it was simply easier to assume a new name along with a new life in the big leagues than it was to stubbornly (and perhaps disrespectfully) insist that powerful strangers pay due respect to an old name and an old identity.

Marianao's prize outfielder, Orestes Miñoso, during the 1958-59 Havana winter league season.

Minnie Miñoso, by sad contrast, carried with him neither a proper first or last name when he arrived sensationally upon the big league scene in the early fifties. Born with the imposing title of Saturnino Orestes Arrieta Armas, Miñoso would much later volunteer in his entertaining autobiography (*Extra Innings: My Life in Baseball*, 1983) the true story behind his designation as "Miñoso" and not as (perhaps) Nino Armas. It was all a matter of mistaken identity back in boyhood Cuba. The young ballplayer's half brothers from his mother's first marriage, it turns out, were also his older teammates in earliest sandlot days in Matanzas, and it was they who were actually named Miñoso. Once the youngest member of the ballplaying family began attracting attention around his home village of Perico, and throughout the wider province of Matanzas, he was naturally referred to by fans, scouts and the press alike as Miñoso — an unavoidable confusion with his siblings. Once a reputation was earned it was foolish indeed to spurn it, and by the time he hooked up with a semi-pro factory team in Havana, the name had already stuck like glue. The budding young star quickly realized that to abandon his false name was also to abandon his small but vital ball-playing reputation and his diamond identity. Once the name was affixed in Cuba and among the big league scouts as well, the young and insecure prospect was not about to torpedo his own chances by abandoning it.

But what about the strange moniker "Minnie"? Here the surviving story seems to be altogether muddled; even Miñoso himself cannot seem to give an adequate accounting. First there is the story attributing the "handle" to Joe Gordon, the veteran Indians second sacker, who reputedly hung the designation on his rookie teammate during the 1949 Cleveland spring training camp. Others (though not Boudreau himself) contend that Lou Boudreau (Cleveland's manager) first used the alliterative nickname with his young Cuban third sacker. Some have suggested that it was used in the Cleveland training camp as a shorter and easier form of Miñoso; others that it referred to a smallish ballplayer who was under six feet in height. Then there is Miñoso's own shadowy story of a visit to a Chicago dentist's office. Miñoso suggests (in *Extra Innings*) that he heard his dentist calling to someone named "Minnie" and thought he was being addressed when it was actually the doctor's receptionist who was being hailed. Of course, this explanation does nothing to account for how the colorful name quickly spread among Chicago fans and Miñoso watchers everywhere around the league. As with the best of baseball legends, however, all parties seemed early on to have adopted a tacit conspiracy of silence on the matter. Whatever the truth, the fictions and fantasies seemed far better still. Whatever they called him, American League fans were soon falling in love with Saturnino Orestes Armas Arrieta "Minnie" Miñoso. Larry Doby, the American League's first black regular, possessed a stable temperament that made him far more like Jackie Robinson's teammate Roy Campanella — a quiet revolutionary determined to lead by strong silent slugging and soft-spoken clubhouse diplomacy. Miñoso — Doby's teammate for a brief spell in 1949 and then himself the first black to grace the roster of the Chicago White Sox when traded there two seasons later— burned instead with Robinson's own brand of dignified fire. The Cuban Comet also burned up the American League base paths with three consecutive stolen base titles (1951–1953) in an age when base speed was of little premium and rarely an offensive strategy of preference. The flashy style he brought to the game not only guaranteed that Miñoso's reputation would be solidified with fair-minded fans, it also ensured that the flames of hatred would burn hotter among those spectators and opponents who could not stand to see a self-possessed black man upstaging everyone else (especially home club heroes) on the field of play.

His career shortened by the color barrier which robbed him of perhaps five productive seasons, Miñoso's seventeen-year big league numbers are today seen by most as falling slightly below Hall of Fame standards. He won stolen base titles but never copped a hitting crown; he fell short of two thousand base hits (though only by a handful); his career batting average in the end was also a hair's-breadth under the magic .300-level measure of excellence. Yet Minnie might well stand as one of the greatest stars of his era if his total accumulated stats in organized baseball were ever summed into a single listing. That is in part because Miñoso's seemingly endless career continued on in Mexico for nearly ten more summers (well beyond age fifty) after his regular big league tenure had ended in 1964. The records earned in Mexican play and on winter circuits are rarely seen by today's students of big league history, but are themselves enough to nail down a measure of diamond immortality.

Refusing to admit the encroachment of natural aging, Miñoso appeared back in the big time once more in 1976 and again in 1980 for cameo appearances with the White Sox, making him both the second oldest big leaguer ever (Satchel Paige was probably fifty-nine when he took the mound for three innings with Kansas City in 1965) and only the second player (Nick Altrock was the first) to don a major league uniform in five distinct decades. In the second of his three 1976 game appearances, Miñoso, at age fifty-four, would collect his final big league hit— making him the oldest man to bat safely in a major league contest. Some might (with justification) belittle these late-career cameos as shameless publicity stunts. Even the ballplayers on the 1993 American League Western Division champion Chicago White Sox squad reportedly balked when rumors were once more circulated that the ageless Cuban (by then serving as a token front office goodwill ambassador) would achieve six-decade status with a late season pinch-hitting appearance at age seventy-one. Several

Marianao's Miñoso receives the Cuban League's MVP trophy at the finish of the 1952-53 winter league season in Havana (courtesy Transcendental Graphics).

White Sox players even commented to an eager press corps that any such appearance by the grandfatherly Miñoso would certainly weaken the game's integrity. In the spirit of team cooperation that always marked his every on-field and off-field move, Miñoso quickly informed club officials that he had no intention of tarnishing the image of the game he so deeply revered.

If Minnie Miñoso's recent baseball decades as White Sox front office public relations fixture have been filled with joyous enthusiasm and marked with an infectious spirit of international goodwill, his early lot in the majors was every bit as rough as the ones known by Robinson, Doby, Campanella, and numerous other black-skinned pioneers. Miñoso was an immediate favorite with hometown fans during debut seasons in Cleveland and Chicago, yet he was nonetheless taunted mercilessly by opposing rooters and rival dugouts. It has been

Minnie Miñoso's Composite Professional Batting Numbers

Leagues (Time Span)	G	AB	R	H	2B	3B	HR	RBI	B.A.
Majors (17 Seasons)	1830	6589	1136	1962	336	83	186	1023	.299
Minors (3 Seasons)	369	1349	265	429	77	18	47	217	.318
Mexico (9 Seasons)	931	2692	432	861	156	26	67	451	.320
Cuba (14 Seasons)	773	2992	494	838	125	51	66	392	.280
Totals (43 Seasons)	3903	13,622	2327	4090	694	178	366	2083	.300

widely reported (by Miñoso himself, as well as by former teammates) that opposing manager Jimmy Dykes of the Philadelphia Athletics regularly indulged a favored pastime of releasing a black dog onto the dugout steps each and every time the dark-skinned Miñoso appeared in the visiting team on-deck circle. And the vicious racial epithets that flew constantly from rival dugouts had to be endured with the same bravery as a life-threatening Bob Feller or Early Wynn fastball.

While Miñoso was often overlooked, overshadowed, and just plain underappreciated throughout his lengthy baseball career, he certainly left a mark that was difficult to ignore. In a career that seemed to stretch on and on without pause — on both sides of the Caribbean — Miñoso finally overwhelmed his critics and naysayers with mere longevity and the weight of his substantial ball-playing record. Combine his big league career with his service in Cuba and Mexico, and few ever played quite so long or quite so well.

But it is in the end for his remarkable rookie year that Miñoso is perhaps best remembered. Throughout a sensational debut summer the nearly middle-aged rookie tore up the American League, inspired a climb in the standings for the longtime doormat White Sox, and singlehandedly put Cuban baseball onto the big league map. By season's end he had defined a new age of hit-and-run daredevil baseball in the Windy City of Chicago, and revived a long-slumbering baseball franchise in the process. The Chicago White Sox were a sixth-place ball club in 1950, as they had been in 1949 and 1947 (they finished dead last in 1948); after Miñoso came on the scene with his rookie explosion of 1951, the same club climbed to fourth (their first time in the first division in a full decade), then nestled into a comfortable position as a pennant contender with five straight third-place finishes. If Minnie Miñoso was not there in the Chicago dugout to finish the pennant drive in 1959, he was clearly the one individual player who, more than any other, had launched the once-hapless ball club to full recovery after four decades of debilitating "Black Sox" swoon.

* * *

Minnie Miñoso is today most recognizable in our memories for his relentless style of down-and-dirty play. None ever hustled more in a big league uniform — not even Pepper Martin or Pete Rose. And none played with more dedication to the twin tasks of winning ball games and entertaining the paying fans. Minnie's motto always seemed to be "to hit or get hit" and he crowded into the batter's box determined never to give the slightest quarter. A pitch from Detroit's Frank Lary once cracked his jaw and loosened all his teeth, yet Miñoso would characteristically demand to finish out the inning as a lively baserunner. For six straight years from 1956 through 1961, it was Miñoso who would regularly pace the junior circuit in the number of times being hit by a pitch. If this was his most inglorious big league record, it was also a record that most accurately reflected the hell-bent and fearless style with which he always played each and every big league game.

But the flair of his style and the energy of his play seems always to be buried under an avalanche of press clippings concerning yet another aspect of Miñoso's storied career — his exceptional longevity. For if in one sense Miñoso was aptly dubbed "The Cuban Comet" — a daring meteor flashing across the base paths — he was hardly a momentary heavenly body when it comes to the continuing glow of his seemingly endless diamond career. Here, after all, is baseball's unique five-decade ballplayer. If Miñoso played legitimately in only slightly more than fifteen big league campaigns, it must be remembered that Cuban and Negro league tours, plus two full years in the Pacific Coast League preceded his American League debut; and at the end of his active major league career, a decade of Mexican League play still lay ahead. If one includes winter league seasons as well, Miñoso took the field for an amazing total of forty-three baseball campaigns. Never has a talented baseball player ever proven more durable.

Yet today, this longevity somehow tarnishes Miñoso in many fans' eyes. Weren't some of these lingering final appearances, after all, little more than outrageous Bill Veeck-engineered promotional gimmicks? Didn't the aging athlete — a mere shell of his dashing earlier self — take the field merely to pack grandstands with his popularity and shamelessly sell seats for a struggling franchise in trouble at the ticket counter? It is indeed unfortunate that the circus-like atmosphere surrounding some of these later "promotional" events has cast such a long shadow over the brilliance of Miñoso's tireless performance in the first decade of his big league sojourn.

Even so, Miñoso remains one of baseball's most beloved figures and finest goodwill ambassadors, especially within the dual-league city of Chicago. For years he has been a familiar face almost everywhere on the Chicago baseball scene. If Miñoso once sold White Sox ducats with his flashy base running and thunderous slugging, then later promoted the ball club in leaner days with the magnetism of his ageless presence, he now provides much-needed public relations with his infectious smile, endless baseball stories, and irrepressible love for the game of his youth and of his middle age. Annually he makes the rounds promoting the American League ball club, entertaining youth groups, senior citizens, and civic and business organizations throughout the Chicagoland area. Never was baseball more in need of just such an ambassador than in this present epoch, an era when big league players have been so distanced from rooters by astronomical salaries, the impersonal nature of televised baseball, and the inevitable commercialism which has descended upon America's national pastime. Minnie Miñoso never won a pennant for Chicago; yet like Ernie Banks on the city's North Side, he continues to provide a most priceless gift to the city's baseball-loving youth: love for the game itself, and for those who perform its magic.

In the end, Miñoso has never seemed to receive the full notice he so richly deserved. Thus, the meteoric ballplaying career of one of Cuba's greatest major leaguers has somehow been reduced to little more than a bright comet flashing through the star-filled baseball heavens. In this sense, then, one of baseball's most colorful nicknames remains doubly appropriate.

Before Nellie Fox was finally sanctioned a Hall of Famer in 1997, Chicago fans often and loudly bemoaned the second baseman's absence from Cooperstown as a grave injustice. But Miñoso arguably deserves to be there even more; the career numbers would certainly argue this way, especially when Fox's sixteen full seasons are compared with Miñoso's mere eleven Windy City campaigns. (Indeed, Fox and Miñoso boast lifetime stats — offensive and defensive — that are roughly comparable.) And while Fox was an excellent clutch player and standby of the Go-Go Sox during the Paul Richards and Al Lopez eras, he was hardly more of a fan favorite at the time, nor did be provide the very inspiration and hell bent style responsible for the team's lasting "Go-Go" reputation. Certainly when it comes to groundbreaking achievement or pioneering influence, Miñoso seemingly stands head and shoulders above Fox.

It is indeed ironic — yet not at all surprising — that Miñoso receives so little Hall of Fame support from Chicago fans while teammate Fox long drew so many cries of outrage each year that he was passed over by the Hall's Veterans Selection Committee. But this may be only the final injustice: None loved the game any more than the irrepressible Cuban who was Latin America's first black star on the big league scene. None gave the game more of himself. None was a more infectious and more ceaselessly joyful ambassador of the diamond sport. And perhaps none got back so little of the recognition he so richly deserved. Yet none could have been less concerned about the slights that have always been aimed his way. ("I never look for anything," Miñoso says today. "I only do my duty and offer my friendship to everyone.") If only there was a Hall of Fame for selfless champions of the game: Miñoso assuredly would own the first pedestal, directly inside Valhalla's main entry way.

References and Suggested Readings

Bjarkman, Peter C. *Baseball with a Latin Beat: A History of the Latin American Game.* Jefferson, N.C., and London: McFarland, 1994.

Fagen, Herb. "Go Minnie, Go — Minnie Miñoso's Six-Decade Career Keeps Going and Going and Going..." in *The Diamond — The Official Chronicle of Major League Baseball.* March-April 1994, 54–58.

Miñoso, Orestes "Minnie" (as told to Fernando Fernández and Robert Kleinfelder). *Extra Innings: My Life in Baseball.* Chicago: Regnery Gateway, 1983.

Mortenson, Tom. "Tom Mortenson on Minnie Miñoso" in *Cult Baseball Players — The Greats, the Flakes, the Weird, and the Wonderful.* Danny Peary, Editor. New York: Simon & Schuster (Fireside Books), 1990, 235–40.

Young, A.S. (Doc). "Comet from Cuba," in *Great Negro Baseball Stars (and how they made the major leagues).* New York: A.S. Barnes, 1953, 165–179.

Miñoso's Latin American and Winter League Batting Record

Mexican League (Summer Seasons)

Year	Club	G	AB	R	H	2B	3B	HR	RBI	B.A.
1965	Jalisco	134	469	106*	169	35*	10	14	82	.360
1966	Jalisco	107	376	70	131	18	1	6	45	.348
1967	Orizaba	36	100	20	35	7	3	5	19	.350
	Jalisco	13	37	5	9	1	2	0	3	.243
1968	Puerto Mexico	56	145	30	53	17	2	4	23	.366
	Jalisco	22	54	9	16	5	1	2	13	.296
1969	Puerto Mexico	74	193	33	58	10	2	2	32	.301
	Jalisco	36	103	18	33	3	1	2	14	.320
1970	Gómez Palacio	40	47	6	22	6	0	2	17	.468
1971	Gómez Palacio	112	336	37	106	15	2	6	57	.315
1972	Gómez Palacio	181	425	48	121	24	1	12	63	.285
1973	Gómez Palacio	120	407	50	108	15	1	12	83	.265
Totals:	**9 Seasons**	**931**	**2692**	**432**	**861**	**156**	**26**	**67**	**451**	**.320**

* = League Leader

Cuban League (Winter Seasons)

Year	Club	G	AB	R	H	2B	3B	HR	RBI	B.A.
1945–46	Marianao*	37	143	14	42	7	2	0	13	.294
1946–47	Marianao	64	253	36	63	9	5	0	20	.249
1947–48	Marianao	70	270	43	77	15	13**	1	36	.285
1948–49	Marianao	69	260	42	69	8	5	4	27	.263
1949–50	Did Not Play									
1950–51	Marianao	66	252	54	81	12	6	4	41	.321
1951–52	Marianao	42	144	19	39	6	1	2	10	.271
1952–53	Marianao	71	266	67**	87	9	5	13	42	.327
1953–54	Marianao	47	176	25	52	9	3	9	36	.295

(continued on page 62)

Year	Club	G	AB	R	H	2B	3B	HR	RBI	B.A.
1954–55	Did Not Play									
1955–56	Marianao	64	252	47	69	10	3	8	35	.274
1956–57	Marianao	50	218	40	68	13	3	7	38	.312
1957–58	Marianao	58	238	37	60	9	1	8	34	.252
1958–59	Marianao	55	223	33	60	8	1	5	25	.269
1959–60	Marianao	45	169	25	39	3	2	4	23	.231
1960–61	Marianao	35	128	12	32	7	1	1	12	.250
Totals:	**14 Seasons**	**773**	**2992**	**494**	**838**	**125**	**51**	**66**	**392**	**.280**

* = Rookie of the Year

** = Cuban League Record

4

The Baseball Half-Century of Conrado Marrero

Connie Marrero had a windup that looked like a cross between a windmill gone berserk and a mallard duck trying to fly backwards.

— Felipe Alou

A substantial majority of Cuba's most celebrated BC–era ("Before Castro") diamond heroes earned the bulk of their reputations while laboring skillfully from the pitcher's rubber. Yet theirs seemed always to be a diminished fame, and one very much muted outside the confines of island baseball culture. Cuban Blackball legends Martín Dihigo and José Méndez were, in the broader view, merely lamentable victims of the vicious racial politics defining their era. (That Dihigo starred year-in and year-out at eight different positions and that Méndez briefly mesmerized hordes of island-hopping big league batsmen went largely unnoticed in the lily-white American sporting press.) Cuba's acknowledged two greatest pitchers were both doomed to play out their entire unmatched careers largely hidden from view on barnstormers' dusty bush league diamonds — far from the din of big-league cheering — exhausting their unparalleled talents during strictly segregated North American summertime seasons. Unlike Pedro Martínez, Sammy Sosa, Roberto Alomar and most other Latin superstars by century's end, the earliest Cuban ball-playing legends were heroes nowhere but back in own their distant island homeland.

Blessed with a lighter skin, Adolfo Luque actually made it to the white man's top leagues and even starred brilliantly there for a brief spell. But for all his triumphs in Cincinnati and New York, Luque was no less a victim of the endemic stereotyping continually dogging Spanish-speaking athletes in the days before the second great world war. While Dihigo and Méndez were thus destined to remain entirely unknown to a wider American baseball public, Luque for his part was either repeatedly downplayed in the press or callously dismissed by unappreciative fans, despite his considerable National League achievements. (These included the best-ever single-season record in the glorious century-plus history of the Cincinnati franchise and a starring role in the 1933 World Series.) And the oppressive lot of Cuban-born big leaguers would be little mollified by long-overdue racial integration. On the eve of Cuba's mid-century communist revolution and only a handful of seasons after Jackie Robinson, yet another diminutive and equally under-appreciated island moundsman — this one named Conrado Marrero — was also predictably fated to re-main far more of a colorful cult figure and far less of a recognized big-league talent than actual diamond skills might otherwise dictate.

In Dihigo's tragic case, Latin America's greatest pre-integration-era ball-playing legend would ultimately have to sneak in the back door at Cooperstown without so much as a single inning of big-league service. Luque's even nastier fate — as Cuba's top big-league star of the first half of the 20th-century — was to become one of Cooperstown's most unjust and inexplicable post-dead-ball-era omissions. More lamentable still, the greatest Cuban pitcher of them all — the ebony-skinned and rubber-armed Méndez — was an even more total victim of the Jim Crow policies and practices that diminished nearly a half-century of North American "organized" baseball. Méndez never made it anywhere near Cooperstown and was ultimately destined to be prematurely sabotaged as much by physical injury as by despicable diamond politics.

When it comes to Cuba's fourth great pitching legend of pre-revolution days, however, Cooperstown was never much of an issue. The big-league résumé of Conrado Marrero — an always colorful if often clownish journeyman hurler employed by tight-wad owner Clark Griffith's also-ran Washington Senators — is admittedly anything but eye-popping. Few other big-leaguers, in fact, have ever gotten quite so much mileage and notoriety out of a mediocre lifetime ledger (39–40) or a ho-hum best-ever 11–8 campaign with one of the junior circuit's most pathetic cellar-dwelling ball clubs. Señor Marrero — affectionately dubbed "the hick from Laberinto" back home in Cuba — always seemed (away from his native soil, at least) something more of a sports world cartoon figure than a true big-league baseball icon. Of course, the fact that the seasoned Marrero had already been a living legend back in Cuba for more than a decade before facing a single batter in the "grand leagues" up north is a very significant footnote to the entire Marrero saga.

For North American fans whose memories stretch back a full half-century, it is nearly impossible to separate Marrero from nostalgic memories of one of the Fabulous Fifties' most charismatic yet inept teams. Marrero seemed, in fact, to epitomize Clark Griffith's entire stable of sad sack Washington Senators. There was plenty of raw talent to be sure in the magical arm of the fire-plug-shaped Cuban right-hander — as there was in those of fellow countrymen and Washington teammates Camilo Pascual and Pedro Ramos — but the more entertaining story for beat writers and their readers was always in the end his oversized Havana cigar, his laughter-provoking slaughtered–English phrases, and his whirling-dervish high-kicking delivery while launching the league's most tantalizing slider and curveball. The stogie, the thick Spanish accent and the elaborate windmill windup were trademark realities that merged rapidly into all-too-familiar stereotypes. In the large scheme of things Conrado Marrero was little more than a blip on the screen of baseball's golden age fifties so dominated by names like Mantle, Musial, Williams, Spahn, Mays and Banks. But from yet another perspective, the American League Washington Senators and the whole enterprise of big league baseball were themselves, in turn, but a mere blip in the baseball-playing career of the seemingly ageless and remarkably durable Conrado Marrero.

In the end it remains a lamentable legacy of Cuban baseball history throughout the years before Fidel's revolution that far more American fans today still boast more familiarity with a young Fidel Castro's bogus if highly advertised pitching tal-

ents than they do with the more legitimate Cooperstown-level achievements of Dihigo, the legendary strikeout feats of Méndez, or the remarkable several-decade-long sagas of the indefatigable Cuban big leaguers Luque and Marrero.

* * *

They were certainly one of the more forgettable big league outfits when it comes to tallying up league pennants won, Hall-of-Fame idols produced, or even first-division finishes clinched. "First in war, first in peace, and last in the American League" was always their backhanded epitaph. But when it came to local color and a cast of unforgettable diamond characters, they nonetheless had a niche all their own. They were the stumblebum Washington Senators (a.k.a. Washington Nationals) managed by redoubtable Bucky Harris (who served usually lackluster teams in the nation's capital for eighteen seasons spread over nearly four decades) and owned and operated by penny-pinching octogenarian Clark Griffith — a dinosaur among club owners who still made his living strictly on gate receipts. And they were also an outfit that gained considerable notoriety merely as the laughingstock depository for superscout Joe Cambria's irrepressible if talent-thin band of carefree and colorful imported "Cubanolas."

Erstwhile Baltimore laundryman and small-time minor league tycoon, Cambria turned to scouting for Griffith in the thirties and was soon filling his boss's low-budget big league and minor league rosters with a collection of both promising and mediocre low-salaried Cuban recruits. The Washington ball club once crammed its lineups with as many as forty-nine Cubans in a single season (1952, with four of them playing on the parent American League club), and it has been estimated that as many as four hundred Cubans had signed with the organization by the time it was spirited off to Minnesota in search of more lucrative gate receipts. Mid-century Washington baseball historian Morris Bealle once observed (in the pages of his underground classic, *The Washington Senators*, self-published in 1947) that "Papa Joe" had overall not done so badly as Clark Griffith's "one-man scouting force" but that he would soon do even better if he could somehow get over his apparent predilection for "Cubanolas" among the numerous recruits he signed — usually for a mere song and promise of a one-way ticket off the island.

The Cambria-Cuban connection reached its apogee at the century's midpoint. The first full-time bird dog to wander the sugarcane trail of the Caribbean islands, Cambria set up shop in Havana in the late thirties, held endless tryout camps on his adopted island for the next three decades, flailed the Cuban bushes for any raw talent that displayed a strong arm or quick bat and a willingness to sign for peanuts, and thus provided the cash-strapped Washington ball club with enough raw imports to keep expenses down, though hardly ever enough to challenge for the league pennant. Cambria's first notable recruit was a slugging Cuban third baseman named Roberto ("Bobby") Estalella who banged big league pitching well enough to hang out with the sad-sack Senators, Browns, and Athletics for nine seasons (he was a lifetime .282

Jovial 37-year-old Conrado Marrero in an Almendares uniform in 1948, two years before his belated big league debut in Washington.

hitter) but whose lead glove also meant he had to be eventually shifted to the outfield for his own physical safety.

Other Cambria island recruits of note would eventually include fifties-era mound stars Camilo Pascual and Pedro Ramos, plus stateside worthies Mickey Vernon, Early Wynn, Eddie Yost, and Gil Coan. The Cambria résumé is also filled with dozens of lesser Cubanolas — the most memorable being Sandalio "Sandy" Consuegra, Carlos Paula, Roberto Ortiz, Conrado Marrero, Julio Moreno, Raúl Sánchez, Juan Delís, Zoilo Versalles, Willie Miranda, José Valdivielso, and future big league skipper Preston (Pedro) Gómez, all of whom tasted various-sized cups of big league coffee in Washington and points north and west during the decade and a half following the nation's second great war. Cambria's most legendary recruit ironically turns out to be a mere myth, as there is no truth whatsoever to numerous popular accounts of Papa Joe's pursuit and near-signing of a fast-balling Havana prospect in the mid-forties named Fidel Castro (for details of the Castro pitching myth, see Chapter 9 below). The Cambria-Senators pipeline was indeed a tantalizing sidebar to baseball's golden age fifties. In retrospect it was also a tame foreshadow of the explosive stateside interest in Cuban baseball which would return with something of a vengeance a full half-century later.

Joe Cambria may have (in folk tale at least) missed out on one overblown phenom named Fidel Castro, but he hit the mark squarely when it came to the pursuit and signing of another colorful cigar-puffing mound legend whose heroic stature in today's Cuba is nearly as large as that of the Maximum Leader himself. Foremost on the local-color scale among Papa Joe's Fabulous Fifties Washington recruits was a junk-balling, stogie-smoking roly-poly known in his homeland by such poetic handles as El Guajiro de Laberinto (The Laberinto Peasant or Laberinto Hillbilly), El Premier (Grade A or Number One) and El Curveador (The Curveballer). Those Cuban nicknames were quickly matched by Washington's epithet-wielding sports hacks who came up with such beauties as Conrado the Conqueror, the Cuban Perfecto (referring to a popular cigar brand), or simply Chico — that most time-worn and degrading pseudonym for Latin ballplayers of almost any era. He pitched for only five seasons in the big time and lost more games (forty) than he won (thirty-nine). His reputation was that of a mystifying craftsman who tantalized hitters with offspeed deliveries and was always far more successful against less-talented junior circuit clubs. (Marrero outright owned Mr. Mack's weak-hitting Athletics, as well as the pathetic Browns in St. Louis and dysfunctional Tigers of Detroit.) And he bore the further reputation of a spunky artisan who proved most unhittable in early-season outings, when coming fresh off a full winter league season back home in Havana and thus seemingly several weeks if not months ahead of other still-rusty springtime hitters.

Conrado Marrero inevitably became simply "Connie" for Washington ball fans and beat writers (just as fellow Cubans Roberto Ortiz and Roberto Estalella inevitably became "Bobby" while Miguel Angel González and Miguel Guerra likewise were "Mike" to monolingual and condescending stateside sportswriters). Whatever the designation, it is today hardly a household name anywhere north of Miami. Yet for Cuban fans Marrero still remains the closest thing there is to a native big league legend. Indeed Adolfo Luque enjoyed greater big league successes back in the twenties and thirties with nearly two hundred National League victories and a dominant 1923 season for Cincinnati's second-place Reds. Blackball legend Martín Dihigo built a legacy in the Cuban and Mexican winter circuits and the U. S. Negro leagues sufficient to merit a permanent home in Cooperstown. Pascual, Ramos, Miñoso, Campaneris, and Versalles were all more accomplished major leaguers. And Cuban-born José Canseco and Rafael Palmeiro are modern-era stars of far loftier proportion. But none before or since has matched Conrado Marrero's combined fame in *Las Grandes Ligas* (the U. S. major leagues) and unsurpassed baseball stature on the island, for Marrero is the most celebrated and admired amateur pitcher in the century-long saga of Cuba's own national game.

Marrero's badge as a short-haul big leaguer was his advanced age and his irrepressibly colorful style. On-field he was a sneaky-fast curveballer known for his exceptional control and infallible mastery of the strike zone. Off the field he was a genuine homespun character who puffed monster cigars, wisecracked with reporters in broken English (which of course endeared him to fifties-era journalists whose portrayals often bordered on racist in tone), and seemed to love every spontaneous moment spent in the clubhouse spotlight.*

And there was of course always the mystery surrounding his advanced age. His 1953 Topps bubblegum card listed his birthplace and birth date as Las Villas on May 1, 1915, and the Washington Senators own yearbooks and published roster sheets of the period opted for May 1, 1917 (making Marrero just shy of thirty-three as a rookie); but reports that Marrero had pitched for as many as eighteen seasons in the Cuban amateur league before signing up with Joe Cambria and interning with the Senators' Havana affiliate in the Class B Florida-International League (beginning in 1947) fueled much speculation that he might be as much as a full decade older.

---

*Five decades after his big league debut the spry and puckish Marrero remains the same colorful character. One humorous incident, if slightly off-color, will illustrate the point. While leading a tour of Canadian and U.S. fans to the island during February 2001, this author had arranged an early-morning meeting of the group with Marrero at the downtown Havana Libre Hotel. I was scheduled to translate while my ancient friend entertained wide-eyed "aficionados" with answers to their many inquiries about his still crystal-clear baseball memories. The session opened with Marrero taking a large gulp of his favorite rum (which we had provided, despite the crisp breakfast hour) and a puff on his ever-present stogie, then turning to his audience of twenty-five for the first question. It was inevitably the standby query about his current age and health, asked by a handsome female in our group (she was a reporter for the Washington Post, traveling with us to write a story about the rare ballpark tour). Without missing a single beat Marrero tugged at his right appendage and boasted that his arm was as strong as it ever was while donning big league flannels fifty years ago; he then sheepishly pointed below his belt and wisecracked that the only current problem was that another of his appendages was unfortunately not quite as strong and lively now as it once had been. Pantomime gestures accompanying Marrero's words made his meaning all too obvious for the non-speakers of Spanish and thus saved this nervous translator from what had all the earmarks of a slightly embarrassing opening to an otherwise delightful session of diamond nostalgia.

Writing in *The Saturday Evening Post* in August 1952, journalist Collie Small stoked the controversy by reporting that the wily hurler had at various times reported that he was "positively thirty-five, absolutely thirty-seven, indisputably forty-three, and definitely forty-two"—yet when pressed for details always coyly admitted (with appropriate amounts of journalistically jumbled foreign idiom) only that "Me old enough, but me not too old."

Marrero was hardly the first Latin recruit to either add or subtract years from his résumé (a practice attaching to such current-era Cuban big leaguers as Orlando Hernández and Rey Ordóñez, who are both several years older than claimed by Miami agent Joe Cubas and late–1990s New York Yankees and New York Mets press guides). And the practice is not one limited to Caribbean diamond recruits; Dizzy Dean invented a rash of fanciful tales regarding his natal circumstances (both place and year) and also his given name (was it Jerome Herman or Jay Hanna?), feeding eager reporters precisely the scoops they were so anxious to hear. "Them ain't lies, them is scoops," bubbled the effusive Diz when pressed on the matter. For Marrero the true date of birth would eventually turn out to be May 1, 1911 (and the birthplace was Sagua La Grande), making him an even ninety in the second spring of the new millennium, a well-heeled thirty-one when he enjoyed his most glamorous career moment in the storied amateur world series showdown with Venezuela in 1941, and an absolutely ancient thirty-nine at the hour of his big league debut.

Connie Marrero's big league sojourn was always more a matter of homespun folklore than of Cooperstown legend. Here was a pitcher who often baffled enemy hitters with his herky-jerky motions and time-lapse deliveries, yet spent nearly as much time baffling fans and the local press with his garbled witticisms. Most of the amusing stories in the Washington newspapers and national sporting magazines may today—a full half-century later—be viewed as blatant racism of an all-too-familiar type that has dogged all Spanish-speaking ballplayers up to the recent hour (in August 2005 a San Francisco broadcaster was suspended for labeling the hometown Giants' band of Latino "airhead" free-swingers as responsible for that club's mid-season swoon). But even if stilted by their stylized lingo and the journalist's eagerness to make a humorous figure of his popular subject, the accounts of Marrero's lighter moments with the press still make delightful enough reading.

There is, for example, an account found in now-yellowing pages of *The Saturday Evening Post* featuring a typical Marrero response to a Dizzy Dean critique of the ancient Cuban's pitching style. When broadcaster Dean suggested over the airwaves that batters would be well advised to wait out the sawed-off Cuban because he had nothing more going than the ability to keep hitters off stride, Marrero had a bemused post-game response: "Deezy Dean, he good peetcher, hokay peetcher, but no more. Deezy he peetch too much. He peetch one day, Deezy brother Pablo peetch next day, Deezy peetch again. Cardinals win championsheep of pennant, but Deezy he no peetch now. Peetch too much. Me rest plenty. Me still peetch." (The sad attempt at Spanish-tinged mispronunciations here are the typical offerings of *Post* columnist Collie Small.)

There is also the likely more-or-less accurate quip regarding the belittling of his talents by big league skipper and Hall-of-Fame batsman Rogers Hornsby. When Marrero on one of his especially effective days whitewashed Hornsby's inept St. Louis Browns 2–0 on four harmless hits in the spring of 1951, the ex–.400-hitter groused that he had batting-practice pitchers in his entourage with more stuff than the exasperating Cuban could offer. Marrero is reported to have responded—when appraised of Hornsby's savage put-down—with typical playful calm: "Thees is good, maybe they should peetch in a game."

A slightly less endearing (if equally enduring) legend has the linguistically challenged Washington hurler snubbing a guileless fan who had offered a cheap cigar in exchange for the hurler's autograph. "Me sorry," the pint-sized moundsman reportedly complained, "but it take two thees kind ceegar for me to sign one time."

And of course there are the endless Ted Williams stories. My own favorite involves an account of the first time the undaunted Marrero faced the legendary Boston slugger. The face-off supposedly came in one 1950 spring training game (Marrero's big league rookie campaign, a few months shy of age thirty-nine) and is recounted frequently and with glamorous embellishment

Connie Marrero (Cuba) and Daniel "Chino" Canónico (Venezuela) pose before their legendary championship confrontation in Havana at the 1941 Amateur World Series.

to underscore the unflappable nature of the ancient rookie. Entering from the bullpen with the bases loaded and Williams wagging his lumber menacingly in the batter's box, the Cuban — at least as the legend now has it — called Nats receiver Al Evans to the hill, apparently intent on imparting some sign of his own over-brimming confidence. Assured by the befuddled backstop that this was indeed the great Williams about to take his cuts, Marrero pressed for still further reassurance on the point: "Eef eet eesn't him, I no geev him my best peetch." Instructed by his nervous catcher to deliver nothing but outside fastballs, the confident Cuban reportedly heaved only tantalizing curves and struck out Williams on four pitches. But Marrero himself only looked puzzled and amused when I recounted the famous tale to him in our face-to-face meeting in Havana in the early winter of 1999.

With the flesh-and-blood Marrero on the big-league scene, Roy Hobbs (protagonist of Bernard Malamud's novel *The Natural*, 1952) was thus certainly not the only improbable thirty-nine-year-old rookie sporting a mystery-wrapped past when he first arrived out of nowhere to tackle the big league wars. The difference between Bernard Malamud's popular fictional account of improbable stardom and Marrero's own baseball reality, of course, was that the cigar-chomping Cuban never worked any late-season pennant miracles fit for a Hollywood script (neither, of course, did Hobbs in Malamud's novel; only in the cinematic version does Roy save the season). Marrero did contribute mightily, alongside fellow Cubans Sandalio Consuegra and Julio Moreno, to a few memorable springtime runs at American League respectability — one in 1952 that even had Griffith's usually tame Senators contending inside the first division at the midsummer All-Star break. But late-season dips always left Bucky Harris and crew within a stone's throw of the league basement by early September; and during Marrero's tenure the club finished fifth three times, sixth once, and seventh once. And the Macmillan *Baseball Encyclopedia* entry next to the name of Conrado Marrero hardly suggests pure brilliance of talent, though the fine print does reveal a few marvels that might escape casual notice. These include three winning campaigns with a team that was twenty-eight games under the break-even point during that same stretch, one sub-3.00 ERA (among the league's top ten that particular year), and a consistently stingy walks-to-innings-pitched ratio (one walk every 2.95 innings across his full big league career).

It is the stories surrounding Marrero's clubhouse antics — not the numerical pitching lines — that have reached often legendary proportions. One Ted Williams tale featuring a Mar-

The Washington Senators' 39-year-old rookie sensation Conrado Marrero warming up at Yankee Stadium in June 1950 (courtesy Transcendental Graphics).

Conrado Marrero's Record with the Washington Senators (American League)

Year	G	IP	W	L	Pct.	H	SO	BB	ERA	Age
1950	27	152	6	10	.375	159	63	55	4.50	38–39
1951	25	187	11	9	.550	198	66	71	3.90	39–40
1952	22	184.1	11	8	.579	175	77	53	2.89	40–41
1953	22	145.2	8	7	.533	130	65	48	3.03	41–42
1954	22	66.1	3	6	.333	74	26	22	4.75	42–43
Totals (5 yrs)	118	735.1	39	40	.494	736	297	249	3.67	38–43

rero autograph request is perhaps the most memorable, even if it is more than likely the most apocryphal. It is a story Marrero himself loves to tell, though he usually admits that it never happened quite as reported. Marrero approached Williams before a game and requested the slugger's signature on a ball with which he had earlier fanned the Splendid Splinter. Williams grudgingly signed — the legend continues — but that same afternoon crushed a Marrero curve into the far reaches of the right field grandstand. As he rounded third base Williams glanced toward the mound and shouted out a biting reminder to the diminutive Washington hurler: "Why don't you see if you can find that one and I'll sign IT for you too!"

But the lasting image for most fans was one capsulated in a series of 1951 and 1952 magazine photos placed alongside accompanying stories that played up the paunchy Washington right-hander as a kind of carefree Cuban goodwill ambassador to the thriving "Golden Fifties" era big league scene. Most of the photos involve a rotund Marrero sandwiched between teammates Consuegra, Moreno, and Campos and enjoying some old-fashioned big league horseplay. A few illustrate an unorthodox pitching delivery which one scribe of the period described fittingly as resembling "an orangutan heaving a 16-pound shot put" and which El Curveador himself often characterized as an unsettling delivery in which he threw everything at the plate but his ever-present Havana stogie.

Marrero's right-handed delivery began with his left foot "stuck in the bucket"— slanted toward first base — and often featured a drawn-out cranking double or triple windmill windup (a la Satchel Paige) which on one occasion had Philadelphia Athletics' infielder Eddie Joost so steamed that he literally jumped up and down in the hitter's rectangle while screaming obscenities at his taunting mound opponent.

Marrero's Cuban teammates were often just as charismatic, and some of them also merited far more than the occasional tribute that was usually given them. Broad-shouldered Carlos Paula was perhaps the worst fielding flychaser of his generation, but the jet-black outfielder could nonetheless hit like few islanders before or since. Paula smashed AL pitching at a .299 clip during his one full season (1955) in Washington (115 games and 351 ABs) before atrocious fielding and hopeless baserunning (and also a reported penchant for hard living) quickly washed him out of the big time the following summer. Paula provided a classic antithesis to the old "good field, no hit" adage that seems surgically attached to Latin-born ballplayers of the fifties and sixties; he was also living proof that batting skills are not always a one-way ticket to major league glory. If Clark Griffith desperately needed base hits in his anemic lineup during those wasteland seasons that preceded Bob Allison and Harmon Killebrew, he also needed outfielders who didn't risk life and limb every time they pursued a routine can of corn.

The bulk of the Cuban imports during the Cambria era were tricky moundsmen — fence-busting Carlos Paula and glue-fingered infielder Willie Miranda aside. Camilo Pascual and Pedro Ramos would be best remembered by decade's end, in large part because they were the most talented of the lot. Ramos never had much luck attached to his raw talent; while his arm was as lively as any in the league, his penchant for giving up long balls (his homers-to-innings-pitched ratio is one of the highest in big league history) spelled an inevitable legacy of losing records. And like Marrero, Pistol Pete was just colorful enough (he made cameo appearances in Western movies, challenged Mickey Mantle to a footrace, and spent a long post-career stint behind bars for drug trafficking) for off-field events to always overshadow on-field accomplishments. Pascual was far luckier, and that luck came largely in the shape of three sluggers named Killebrew, Lemon, and Allison, and also thanks to a fortuitous franchise transfer to the northerly climes of Minnesota, where the Cuban curve-

Marrero (left) provides Spanish lessons for manager Bucky Harris while fellow Cuban teammate Julio "Jiquí" Moreno is an amused bystander (courtesy Transcendental Graphics).

ball ace eventually won twenty twice (1962 and 1963) and paced the circuit in strikeouts three seasons running in the early sixties.

But other Cuban hurlers made their marks as well. Miguel "Mike" Fornieles earned a rare distinction when he became the first Latin pitcher (and second American Leaguer) to toss a one-hitter in his debut major league outing (September 2, 1952). Sandy Consuegra flashed brilliance, especially after he escaped the curse of playing in Washington. Hard-throwing Julio Moreno was never the frontline star he was back home on the island (16–4 and a sensational 1.47 ERA with the 1950 Class B Havana Cubans), yet displayed talent enough to survive four partial seasons in the majors. Consuegra (a lanky 5'11" righty who cracked the Washington roster at age thirty-one) contributed three early-season mound victories to the Senators' fastest start in fifty years during the heady 1952 campaign; two years

Marrero (second from left) enjoys the comradeship of fellow Cuban teammates on the Washington bench (c. 1950) (courtesy Transcendental Graphics).

later with the better-supplied Chicago White Sox he produced the junior circuit's top winning percentage (16–3, .842), won eight in relief without defeat, and even enjoyed a brief All-Star Game outing. Moreno also came to the big time as a thirty-something rookie (along with Marrero in 1950) and won half of his eighteen decisions (with a solid 3.97 ERA) during the surprising 1952 Washington uprising.

Yet for engaging personality and even for mound effectiveness, the sawed-off Marrero stood tall above the rest of the Cubanolas who took up temporary residence with Bucky Harris and Clark Griffith in Washington. Pascual and Ramos would earn most of their substantial credentials away from the nation's capital, the former as staff ace of the Killebrew-led Twins resurrected by Clark Griffith's adopted son (Calvin Griffith) out in Minnesota, the latter as a briefly effective late-season Yankee bullpen replacement during the New York pennant dash of September 1964. Marrero was also a quality big league pitcher saddled — just like Pascual and Ramos — with a hopeless contingent of losers for teammates and also with his best years already trailing far behind him. His reputation was solid as a dependable starter who rarely defeated himself, and his mound feats (which included a 1951 one-hitter against Philadelphia, spoiled only by a Barney McCosky round-tripper) were often truly remarkable for a journeyman hurler of his advanced age.

But there is quite a bit more to the story. The Conrado Marrero known to American League fans in the inaugural seasons of the century's middle decade was only one slim chapter in a rather remarkable baseball life of six decades duration. For countless Cuban fans (and certainly for Marrero himself) the big league stopover was only icing on an already substantial cake. Connie Marrero had long been a legend in his homeland before he ever showed up in *Las Grandes Ligas*. And his seemingly endless baseball sojourn would turn perhaps even more remarkable once he returned to his native island just a handful of years before Fidel Castro's revolution sent Cuban baseball hurtling toward the dark side of the moon.

* * *

The showdown between the American League's Baltimore Orioles and Cuba's national team — staged in Havana's Estadio Latinoamericano in March 1999 — was truly a moment for the ages. Events surrounding the historic first visit in four decades of a Major League Baseball team to the island of Cuba left a number of indelible images. One was the teeming Havana ballpark crammed with wildly enthusiastic flag-waving Cuban fans. Another was Fidel Castro himself seated alongside a somber Bud Selig and seemingly moribund Peter Angelos. ("Hear no evil, see no evil, do no evil!") A return match in Baltimore a month later would capsule — with a single wire service front-page photograph of Cuban Andy Morales dancing joyfully around the base paths — two far different baseball worlds: one of seeming sandlot innocence and the other of sour professional arrogance.

But there was no moment attached to the long-anticipated and politically charged contest that was more poignant than the one which witnessed a still-fit eighty-eight-year-old ex–big league midget poised on the pitching rubber in Havana's March sunshine, determined to bridge the existing gulf of four decades of uneasy separation between two baseball-loving nations. Conrado Marrero took the mound for a celebratory game-opening ceremonial "pitch" and was not about to quickly release his moment of relived glory. Once handed the ball and back on familiar ground, Cuba's most famous living hurler was determined to make his presence felt and test an arm that had not seen serious action since the days when Fidel was still a budding young revolutionary and Washington and Havana were still hardball cronies.

A still-spry Marrero was determined to toss a pitch or two to big leaguer Brady Anderson, who apparently never quite grasped the tenor of the moment. The scene offered every bit the drama of the landmark game that was about to follow. Marrero lobbed three eephus balls plateward, each one a bit straighter and truer than the last. When it became clear that the old-timer would not relinquish the hill without a bullpen call, Cuban home plate umpire Nelson Díaz motioned Anderson into the box for one final serious toss. It was pure theater — the stuff baseball used to be made of.

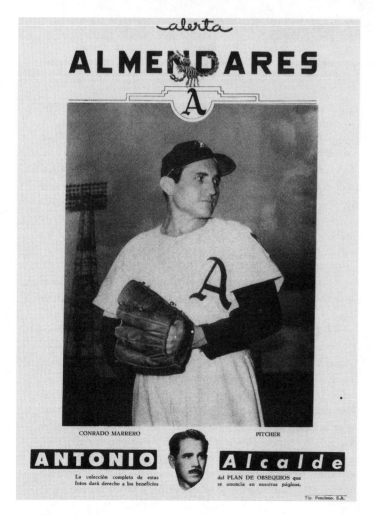

Conrado Marrero poses in an Almendares uniform in the early fifties.

While Marrero may have seemed a long-lost relic to stateside fans, he has been anything but a useless icon from a past era back on his own native island. Ensconced for the past four decades in "revolutionary" Cuban society, with its new brand of amateur baseball, the ex–big leaguer has remained a fixture of the game still played with undying passion on the home front. He had started late in life as both an amateur and professional ballplayer; he only reluctantly signed a pro contract after he was suspended from amateur competitions in the mid-forties for playing on two different teams (strictly against the rules of the time); then he hung around as a professional player and coach for almost as long as Satchel Paige. As the millennium approached and then passed, and as he faces his tenth decade on the planet, he is still hanging around, today coaching youngsters who are often seventy years his juniors.

Marrero's recent work has involved training some of the island's best young apprentice moundsmen. (He serves on a part-time basis with the Cuban League team representing Granma Province.) His most recent trainee of note is Ciro Silvino Licea, a raw talent who sprang on the international scene a couple of winters back when he mowed down Team USA batters for nine impressive innings in the semifinals of Intercontinental Cup play in Australia. The truly ancient part-time coach explains it as an easy form of labor for a ninety-year-old. "I never run, just chat a little, grab a baseball sometimes, even sometimes throw a toss or two. I tell them that you do it this way or that way. And I tell them about the psychological things. An arm is important, but you have to have a good head to be a pitcher."

Marrero has been most outspoken about the baseball now played on the island. Some of his comments were carried in a recent feature story (June 3, 1998) in the pages of *Granma* (official organ of the Cuban Communist Party), an interview which was billed as a tell-all account by the famed octogenarian pitcher. Marrero reminisced in that piece about seeing Mickey Mantle's most gigantic homer (the 565-foot bomb off Chuck Stobbs which Marrero witnessed from the Griffith Stadium dugout), about his frequent horseplay with Ted Williams, and about his adjustment to the big leagues at age thirty-nine, where the English language barrier seemed to prove even less unsettling than his first views of big league sluggers from out on the pitcher's rubber. Asked about his struggles with a torturous foreign tongue, Marrero (who to this day commands about two dozen words of English) simply laughed off the issue. "Everyone knows that in baseball there is only one language — strikes and balls" (translating here from Marrero's Spanish interview). "And when you have a manager like I had [Bucky Harris] who always speaks quite slow, you understand a lot." But whatever Marrero did or didn't understand, he always seemed to figure out how to work his way around most big league hitters.

If anyone can conjure comparisons of today's Cuban baseball with that of past epochs, it would have to be Conrado Marrero. As early as the late thirties — seven long decades ago, during the heyday of Lou Gehrig, a fading Babe Ruth, and a young Joe DiMaggio — Marrero was already making his lasting mark within Cuban amateur circles. He was a surprisingly late starter, even in the amateur ranks back home, signing on with the league team from Cienfuegos only after he had already turned twenty-seven and had been running his father's farm and toiling on Sundays with a local sandlot club called Los Piratas for nearly a full decade. And he recounts that he became a pitcher in the first place only because of an early unpleasant taste of the hazards of defensive play. A bad-hop grounder had once blackened his eye while playing third base for a local school team and quickly turned his preferences toward a seemingly safer perch on the pitcher's mound.

Pitching never dulled his interest in swinging the bat though. One of the most colorful tales about Marrero involves his hitting exploits in the Cuban League during the mid-fifties, where he once jumped into the wrong batter's box and still somehow laced out a crucial base hit. The story has it that with a runner on third, Marrero swaggered to the plate and shockingly decided on the spur of the moment to try his skill and luck from the left side of the dish. It was a moment that reportedly left manager Mike Guerra nearly catatonic in the Almendares dugout. Before his manager could react, however, Marrero somehow dumped a lucky run-producing blooper over the stunned opposition infield, saving the day and perhaps even his own skin.

Connie Marrero's greatest moments were those played on the amateur diamonds of World War II–era Cuba, and the most luminous hours came with a pair of celebrated international contests in the early forties. Marrero's personal career apex arguably arrived with the IBA world championships of those wartime seasons. First there was the tense championship match up with Team Venezuela in Havana's La Tropical Stadium on October 23, 1941. The diminutive Cuban right-hander squared off against Daniel "Chino" (Chinaman) Canónico in a classic duel that fell ultimately to the visitors 3–1 on three first-inning tallies. (Two walks by the usually control-happy Marrero fueled the rally.) But the Cuban ace would gain his sweet revenge and his country's grateful adulation a mere year later (October 4, 1942) when he returned to the hill to face a Venezuelan lineup sporting Luis Aparicio (father of the Cooperstown-inducted shortstop) at second base

A published box score commemorating Marrero's 1938 no-hitter for the Cienfuegos ball club in 1938 Amateur League play.

Conrado Marrero's Cuban Amateur League Pitching Record (1938–1945)

Year	Team	G	IP	W	L	Pct.	CG	SO	BB	ERA
1938	Cienfuegos	22*	170.0*	10	7	.588	16*	124*	63	2.54
1939	Cienfuegos	23*	173.1*	13*	4	.765	17*	120*	75*	1.92
1940	Cienfuegos	23*	178.0*	15*	4	.790	18*	117*	59	1.67*
1941	Cienfuegos	25*	196.1*	18	6	.750*	21	155	71	1.51
1942	Cienfuegos	27*	235.0*	22*	5	.815	26*	179	59	1.22*
1942	Desempate	1	9.0	0	1	.000	1	6	4	4.00
1943	Cienfuegos	10	79.2	7	1	.875	7	79	15	1.13
1944	Cienfuegos	30	240.0	21	8	.724	24*	183	89	1.76
1945	Cienfuegos	30	244.1	22	5	.815	24	218*	88	1.21
Totals (8 yrs)		191	1525.2	128	41	.757	154	1180	519	1.65

* = League Leader in this category

and the same tantalizing Canónico on the hill. This time around the masterful Marrero spun a memorable three-hitter of his own in the 8–0 victory which touched off wild island-wide celebrations.

The pro career of Cuba's most famous ball-playing *guajiro* (peasant) stretched both long before and long after his brief stay with the big league Senators. There were some remarkable years spent with the Havana Cubans, the island's first team in organized baseball. Thoroughly dominating minor league swingers with his assortment of wicked sliders, bouncing knucklers, and bending curves, the league's oldest player racked up three straight twenty-win campaigns (also tossing a masterful no-hitter) and some ERAs that were so

Marrero enjoys perusing the author's books (including McFarland's 1994 *Baseball with a Latin Beat,* on the table) during a December 1999 visit in Havana.

microscopic they stretch credulity, even for that basement level of pro ball. It was the veteran Cuban's ticket straight to the big time, where he debuted with six victories as a long-toothed rookie in 1950 and then celebrated the spring of his fortieth year (1951) by reeling off five straight cold-weather wins (the feat that earned him a full-blown spread in *Life* magazine) and checking in at 11–5 by mid–August before wilting in the late summer heat. The eleven victories were tops on that year's anemic Washington staff and he was also 11–7 that same winter with the Almendares Alacranes of the wintertime Cuban League. His Cuban League career (where he struck out 478 and only walked 295 during a decade of service) didn't wind down until 1955 (age forty-four) and two summers later he was still throwing an occasionally effective inning or two for the Havana-based AAA Cuban Sugar Kings.

Marrero was still a popular dugout and bullpen fixture throughout the mid-fifties with Havana's better-known Sugar Kings. This was a team that represented the last hurrah of Cuban professional baseball in the years immediately preceding the Cuban Revolution. The Sugar Kings (a top Cincinnati Reds affiliate from 1954–1960) would over a half-dozen seasons boast such local fixtures and future big leaguers as Orlando Peña, Mike Cuéllar, Leo Cárdenas, Juan Delís, Fermín Guerra, Ray Noble, Carlos Paula, and Cookie Rojas, as well as such notable imports as Owen Friend, Lou Skizas, Brooks Lawrence, Jim Pendleton, Luis Arroyo (Puerto Rico), and Pompeyo Davalillo (Venezuela). Here Marrero's role was much more muted. The aging right-hander posted a 7–3 record for the International League outfit in 1955 and was also 3–1 in spot duty for the 1956 Havana-based AAA club. Not much of a record at first glance perhaps, until it is pointed out that the veteran junk-baller was nearly five years older at the time than the club's veteran skipper, Reggie Otero, whose own brief big league playing career had opened and closed with the Chicago Cubs a full ten years earlier.

All told, Marrero pitched hundreds of games in dozens of leagues before he finally hug up his well-traveled glove on the eve of Fidel Castro's rise to political power. A career that began almost accidentally with Cienfuegos in the Cuban Amateur Athletic Union league at the ripe age of twenty-seven was nonetheless still durable enough — despite such a delayed start — to stretch for a full two decades. He would be the only pitcher to toss a pair of no-hitters in Cuban AAU Amateur League history, and in his first three pro seasons (in the Florida International circuit) his control was so outstanding that he struck out 586 while walking only 117. He became the first Cuban ever to defeat the USA in world amateur play (during the 1939 IBA world championships staged in Havana). He

Conrado Marrero's Record with Havana Cubans (Florida International League)

Year	G	IP	W	L	H	SO	BB	R	ERA	Age
1947	40	271	25	6	180	251	46	59	1.66	35–36
1948	35	264	20	11	206	168	24	55	1.67	36–37
1949	35	258	25	8	175	167	47	51	1.53	37–38
Totals (3 yrs)	**110**	**793**	**70**	**25**	**561**	**586**	**117**	**165**	**—**	**35–38**

was also a big leaguer who in his twilight years still contends that his fondest moments and greatest achievements came with his first team in Cienfuegos as a rank amateur. Not bad for a hydrant-shaped junkballer whom Bob Feller once described as "something you'd expect to find under a sombrero."

* * *

A stone-faced, cigar-chomping Conrado Marrero sat stoically in the sparsely furnished front room of his granddaughter's third-floor apartment in mid–January of 1999, a mere two months before his resurrection in front of American television cameras during the first Orioles-Cuba game at Estadio Latinoamericano. He fielded our questions (mine and those of photo researcher Mark Rucker) at first with considerable reserve, but soon with an increasing enthusiasm, frequently rising from his perch on a sparse wooden bench to demonstrate — sometimes haltingly — a favorite pitching stance, or to reenact a dramatic and precisely recalled moment of distant ballpark action. He wore a tattered blue cap of the Cuban national team (vintage early 1970s) and sucked an ever-present fine-quality cigar about half the size of a Louisville slugger. The latter — along with his thick *guajiro* (peasant) countryside accent — made his Spanish at times nearly indecipherable even for a practiced ear. But histrionic gestures and animated facial expressions always adequately clarified the points at hand.

Rucker and I were not the first American journalists to visit the ranking patriarch of Cuban baseball in recent years. Noted film writer Gerald Peary, for one, had paid a similar visit two decades earlier to pen a piece on Marrero for a classic book entitled *Cult Baseball Players* (a must read for fans of the old Washington Senators). But few Americans had called during the more recent years of the Helms-Burton embargo, and those Havana travelers who may have recently sought him out always found logistics to be most difficult. We ourselves had failed on two earlier trips. Marrero is not often to be found in Havana, still spending the bulk of his time ranching and coaching in the far reaches of the Cuban countryside, out in Granma Province on the eastern half of the island.

This time the way had been paved for us by our Havana friend Jorge Alfonso, a veteran magazine sports journalist (for *Bohemia*, a slick Cuban popular culture monthly) who would be our guide to Marrero's temporary Havana residence. At first the old man was cautious of our motives — was it autographs we were seeking? Or perhaps we only wished to extract some quotable nugget about baseball after Castro's revolution? But then unexpectedly a rare fortuitous moment of male bonding suddenly cleared the air. When I innocently posed the standard question (searching for an icebreaker) about his toughest outs as a big league hurler, the old-timer hesitated, then struggled to recall the name of a stocky Detroit first sacker from a half century earlier who always seemingly had his number. "Vic Wertz?" I hesitantly offered. Yes, Wertz!— these gringos went back in their baseball recollections as far as he did! From that moment on we were simply a bunch of compatible old-timers fondly recollecting our mutually shared baseball youths over tiny cups of too-strong Cuban coffee. The ex-

pitcher's middle-aged grandson entered and left several times before joining in for the final stages of what became nearly a four-hour visit. Most of the session was tape recorded, but a constantly barking neighborhood dog, and also Marrero's rapid-fire mumbled speech (muffled further by the ever-present cigar which never left his clenched teeth), conspired to render most of the resulting tapes utterly unusable.

An issue that needed immediate resolving was Marrero's true age. He chortled scornfully as if this were about the ten-thousandth time some Yankee journalist had dragged up that question. The old North American bubblegum cards were all wrong, Marrero cautioned. As discussed earlier, the date of his birth was May 1 (Topps bubblegum cards of his playing days were at least consistent on that fact) but the year was 1911, not 1915. Again, that meant he was nearly thirty-nine when he tossed his first big-league pitch, already in his late thirties when he starred with the Class B Havana Cubans, past thirty when he twice (1941 and 1942) enjoyed his greatest amateur moments against the Venezuelan challengers in Havana, and nearly forty-five when he finally shut down his winter league career. *Total Baseball* and the *Big Mac* now have the year cor-

Spry 88-year-old Marrero demonstrates his batting style during a December 1999 interview with the author at his granddaughter's Havana apartment (courtesy Transcendental Graphics).

Conrado Marrero's Pitching Record in the Cuban Winter League (1947–1955)

Year	Team	G	CG	W	L	IP	SO	BB	ERA	Age
1947	Oriente (FN)	18	5	8	5	102	77	30	2.24	35
1947	Almendares	4	1	1	0	14.1	6	5	1.88	35
1948	Almendares	22	17	12	2	184.2	99	55	1.12	36
1949	Almendares	15	4	6	4	77.2	27	19	3.48	37
1950	Almendares	15	5	7	3	81.1	38	20	2.26	38
1951	Almendares	27	9	11	7	159.2	58	32	2.37	39
1952	Almendares	21	6	6	9	115.2	51	40	3.50	40
1953	Almendares	22	8	8	8	135	48	47	2.60	41
1954	Almendares	22	3	7	5	107.1	46	28	3.27	42
1955	Almendares	21	1	2	3	58.2	28	19	2.61	43
Totals (9 years)		187	59	68	46	1036.1	478	295	— —	35–43

rect, it seems, but not the precise birth date (which both sources still list in their latest editions as April 25).

Marrero also had some most revealing insights to offer about that other tantalizing element of his pitching career — his diminutive size. I reminded him at one point of all the negative press once generated in the States by his less-than-athletic appearance. Much was made of his 5' 7" stature and soaking-wet 165-pound frame, his disproportionate legs which had some hitters complaining that it appeared as though he was buried up to his waist out on the mound, his bowlegged stance, tiny hands, knobby fingers, and even flat feet. In short, he didn't look at all like a pitcher, or like any kind of athlete for that matter.

Conrado was quick to offer a bemused defense. Yes, it may have been true that his throwing arm was slightly shorter than its partner ("but only because I was a bit hunchbacked from so much pitching over the years"), and his hands were admittedly small ("but I have seen hurlers with smaller mitts"). If his fingers were admittedly stubby, that came from many years of hard labor on the farm throughout his amateur pitching days. But he never had flat feet, he protested. That was surely a mistaken view. And it was also a misconception that he was 5'7" at the top of his career; he was actually only 5'5" when he reported to his first Washington training camp. It was the team doctor who measured him, Conrado chuckled, who actually stood a more lofty 5'7".

The old man was at his liveliest when reliving his moments on the hill facing the likes of "Teddy Ballgame" Williams, "Mad Jimmy" Piersall, Detroit's Vic Wertz, or the venerable DiMaggio. He was also quick to clarify the oft-told Williams autograph tale — obviously basking in its mere telling. "That's just a big tale," the old man chuckled (and I am paraphrasing here from a conversation held entirely in Spanish): "An old friend, Enrique Núñez Rodríquez — a real joker — planted that tale many years ago and it kind of caught on. But it wasn't that way. Williams horsed around a lot with me and was always joking when he saw me. He was a big kidder. But the story of the signed ball never actually happened that way at all."

Marrero is most opinionated when grilled about the state of current Cuban baseball or when asked to rank players from different epochs. He is high (even effusive) in his praise for the

level of contemporary Cuban play and hardly an apologist for his own bygone era of the thirties, forties, and fifties. He leaves little doubt about the high rank of modern stars like national team third baseman Omar Linares and glue-fingered Cuban League shortstop Germán Mesa. The stable of young strong-armed pitchers on today's Cuban scene is also Marrero's pride and joy, especially his protégé from the Granma team, lanky twenty-six-year-old right-hander Ciro Silvino Licea. (Silvino Licea mesmerized this writer in Havana in January 1999 with his ninety-five-mph-plus fastball, pinpoint control, and mound savvy beyond his years; he won seventy-eight games over his best past eight Cuban seasons [1993–2000] — half the length of big league campaigns — and dominated U.S. hitters in semifinal showdown action during the 1999 Intercontinental Cup tourney in Sydney.) And Marrero sees a clear-cut reason for improved play in the modern (post-revolution) era. He was quick to remind us that in his own era both amateur league and (pro) winter league games were only once a weekend affairs, a situation which left less opportunity for proper development of raw talents.

Some of Marrero's opinions in his rambling conversation with two Yankee writers were eerie echoes of his published *Granma* interview from several months back. If he was indeed spouting the Cuban version of baseball political correctness in his views regarding post-revolutionary island baseball, he was certainly consistent — almost to a fault. For Marrero there is something altogether more pure and admirable about *pelota* (literally "ball") when it is played on dusty amateur diamonds with a goal of defending hometown, regional, or even national honor, rather than in lavish professional stadiums for top-dollar paydays. This is not at all a surprising pronouncement from a six-decade ballpark veteran who spent ten-plus seasons as a local amateur nonpareil before signing on with the play-for-pay leagues at the twilight of his own career. The same Marrero who was always so consistent with his tantalizing assortment of breaking balls today remains equally consistent with his views that baseball is equally as enjoyable (if not more so) on the local sandlots as it is in packed urban stadiums.

Who stands forth as the best Cuban-born ballplayer in Marrero's well-seasoned view? Unquestionably Martín Dihigo, a Cooperstown legend whom Marrero himself actually once faced on local amateur diamonds during his own distant youth. The closest rival to Dihigo from among modern-era "peloteros"?—Omar Linares, again without the slightest hesitation. (Marrero's opinion of Linares was a most welcomed affirmation for the present author, who boldly counts the all-world third sacker among the half-dozen best natural ballplayers he has ever witnessed in a personal fandom stretching back to Williams, Mays, Aaron, and Mantle.)

When it comes to fielding prowess, Marrero is quick to second the view of many contemporary Cuban baseball watchers regarding recently retired Industriales shortstop and long-time national team star Germán Mesa. A few years back, at least, Mesa was as good as one could imagine and seemed to rate with even the position's greatest big leaguer, Ozzie Smith, whom Marrero claims to have seen on television a time or two. Mesa, of course, was perhaps a major reason for Rey Ordóñez's defection during the 1993 World University Games in Buffalo (since Mesa seemingly blocked any prospects Ordóñez might have had for gaining a starting shortstop position on the vaunted Cuban national squad). In Marrero's ancient eyes Willie Miranda (a 1950s-era Senators, Orioles, and Yankees defensive standout) was the best he ever played with or against, but even the "good-field, no-hit" Miranda was no match for the magical Germán Mesa.

At the time of my first interview with Marrero in January 1999, there were but a tiny handful of erstwhile Cuban big leaguers left on Castro's communist-controlled island. The inventory had dipped to but a scant three—Marrero, Juan Delís (once a bright infield prospect in Clark Griffith's sparse minor league chain who ultimately proved incapable of hitting top-notch pitching and thus logged a mere fifty-four career games in *Las Grandes Ligas*), and Ramón (Moín) García (a journeyman pitcher with but three 1948 stateside innings to his lasting credit). Delís and García would both succumb within the two following years. Conrado Marrero is thus the last of a vanishing breed. He is a seemingly indestructible baseball institution tucked away in a mysterious land were the Yankee national pastime also remains the most unchallenged of all Cuban institutions. If one needs any tangible evidence for the pervasive time warp that is inevitably presented by contemporary Communist Cuba, there is no finer specimen to clinch the argument than a living legend named Conrado Marrero.

On a more exclusively baseball-related note, Marrero drew his biggest laughs later in this same session when he explained that Mickey Grasso was always his favorite catcher in Washington because the two of them communicated so well and thus never had any language barriers. Marrero continued that he and Grasso used six distinctive signs for calling his pitches and that these were: one finger for "ehslider" (Spanish pronunciation of "slider"), two digits for a slider, three also for slider, four once more for slider, five of course for slider, and—you guessed it—six (a clenched fist) was for the famed and overworked slider.

References and Suggested Readings

Bjarkman, Peter C. "Covering the Latin Beat: Those Colorful Señores—Recalling the 1950s-Era Cuban Washington Senators," *Oldtyme Baseball News* 8:3 (March 1997), 22–24.

_____. "The Baseball Half-Century of Conrado Marrero" in: *Elysian Fields Quarterly* 17:1 (Winter 2000), 27–44.

Bealle, Morris A. *The Washington Senators: The Story of An Incurable Fandom.* Washington, D.C.: Columbia Publishing Company, 1947.

Nieto Fernández, Severo. *Conrado Marrero—El Premier.* Havana: Editorial Cientifico-Téchnica, 2000.

Peary, Gerald. "Gerald Peary on Conrado Marrero," *Cult Baseball Players—The Greats, the Flakes, the Weird, and the Wonderful.* Danny Peary, editor. New York: Simon & Schuster (Fireside Books), 1990, 231–34.

Rucker, Mark, and Peter C. Bjarkman. *Smoke—The Romance and Lore of Cuban Baseball.* New York: Total Sports Illustrated, 1999.

Silverman, Al. "Connie Marrero Throws a Cuban Curve," *Sport* XI (September 1951), 38–39.

Small, Collie. "Baseball's Improbable Imports," *The Saturday Evening Post* (August 2, 1952), 28–29, 88–90.

Smith, Marshall. "The Senators' Slow-Ball Señor," *Life* XXX (June 11, 1951), 81–82, 85–86, 89, 92.

Valdes, Rafael Pérez. "Conrado Marrero: Hay que tener cabeza para lanzar" ("You have to be smart to pitch"), *Granma: Organo Oficial del Partido Comunista de Cuba* (June 3, 1998). Digital internet edition (*www.granma.cubaweb*).

PART II

The Cuban Leagues

5

Myths and Legends of the
Cuban Professional League (1878–1961)

They were deities in knickered uniforms who hurled not thunderbolts but baseballs, Mercuries in spiked shoes, Thors who swung bats and not hammers; not statues but blood-carrying men sculpting their own figures inning by inning, game by game, year after year, until they were complete in memory and record book, hallowed and emblazoned.
— Donald Honig

Across the full three-quarter century history of Cuba's professional baseball enterprise a central theme would always remain the bitterly intense rivalry between the island's two oldest and most celebrated baseball nines. The red-clad Lions of Club Habana (which I will spell here with "b" as it is spelled in Spanish, to distinguish the ball team from the city) and the blue-vested Scorpions from Club Almendares (which I will consistently refer to as the *Alacranes*, the team's popular Spanish nickname) shared unrivaled primacy in every epoch of the Cuban professional baseball league. Both these teams would date their origins to the earliest years of ball-playing in the capital city. And from the era of the War for Independence (1895–98) onward they would eventually divide the city's and the entire country's fan loyalties almost exactly down the center. It was the rare Cuban rooter, indeed, during the last two decades of the 19th century and the first six decades of the 20th century, who did not owe a strong allegiance to one club or the other. And it was these two teams, of course, that would also split down the middle the great bulk of the championship seasons that were year-in and year-out contested against a handful of other shifting professional baseball clubs (some lasting but a year or two) mostly based in or near the city of Havana.

Matanzas and adjacent Villa Clara Province (namely the city of Santa Clara), both some miles to the east, from time to time had their occasional entrants in the Havana-based pro circuit, and a few teams carrying the banner and nameplate of Cienfuegos (sometimes only nominally, and occasionally quite literally) represented that seaport city on the island's south-central coast. But from start to finish Cuban professional baseball was almost exclusively a Havana-based phenomenon.

The first official Cuban League game ever contested was most fittingly a match between those two legendary "eternal rivals" of Cuban baseball lore — the Red Lions representing Habana and the Blue Scorpions of Almendares. That inaugural game transpired on December 29th of 1878 (all games but one of the inaugural championship tournament were played on Sunday afternoons), at a makeshift ball yard located in Vedado (on the southeast corner of H and 9th Streets, a mere stone's toss from the waterfront). The historic site is marked today not only by one of the city's largest maternity hospitals but also by a small bust of Emilo Sabourín, erected in 1953 to commemorate the pioneer rebel-ballplayer's "heroic" death in a Spanish colonial prison. The game itself was a high-scoring affair won by Habana, 21–20, largely on the strength of eight tallies in the final turn at bat; it was indeed a maiden outing hardly resembling the type of game known to modern-era followers of the sport.

This celebrated inaugural match between the soon-equally-popular Reds and Blues launched a first championship "season" that was in reality little more than a short round-robin-style tournament, each participating team scheduled to meet the other pair twice. Details of a first formal season had been worked out in mid–December, during a meeting of Habana and Almendares club officials on Havana's Obrapía Street; a third team from Matanzas (remnants of the same nine that hosted Habana in a famed December 1874 contest — reputedly but not actually the first game ever played on the island) sent a letter agreeing to abide by the adopted tournament conditions, which included round-robin matches, a winner's prize of a white silk banner, and individual medals for winning team players. Less than a week after the inaugural contest, Habana and Matanzas tied at 17 at the Matanzas club's Palmar del Junco grounds on New Year's Day, the winter's only non–Sunday match. Habana also won other games in January and February versus Matanzas by scores of 34–26 and 34–17. The first winter's championship matches between the nation's earliest three professional baseball clubs were thus hardly a baseball "season" of the more-familiar type — like the ones to unfold several winters down the road that had four, five or six clubs competing in dozens of games stretching out for several months' duration. Club Habana under the direction of captain (player-manager) Esteban "Steve" Bellán, veteran of brief years of professional play in the United States, would nonetheless walk off with the first official championship silk banner (plus the individual player medals) by virtue of an additional victory over Almendares (18–10, on February 2, in the lowest-scoring affair of the winter) and its two manhandlings (one being a makeup of the New Year's Day tie) of the third club representing the nearby seaport city of Matanzas.

For the first few winter renewals of what was initially called the *Liga de Base-Ball* (Cuban Baseball League), ballplayers taking part for the Habana, Almendares or Matanzas B.B.C.s (Base Ball Clubs) were still mostly gentleman amateurs performing for elite social clubs. They were not true professionals — salaried mercenaries playing for a fee or other financial considerations — in any sense of the word. They did not devote themselves exclusively to practice and play of the bat and ball sport, and they certainly did not draw their identities from the profession of fulltime ball-playing. (As explained in Chapter 10, many were affiliated with the rebellion against

Pedro Formental, slugging star with the Cuban League's Habana Leones during the decade of the fifties and one of that league's most popular figures. Formental was the Cuban pro league all-time career home run leader.

an unpopular occupying Spanish government and used baseball as a means to raise cash for underground rebel forces.) Games were part and parcel of Sunday afternoon club outings (modern-era church or fraternity picnics come most readily to mind) which included well-dressed female spectators, and elaborate post-game banquets and dances as a main focus of the afternoon's festivities. Such status of early ball-playing accounts for the small number of games constituting a "league season" and also for the lack of any early efforts at tabulating and recording individual ball-player statistics.

Parallels to early forms of ball-playing in United States towns and cities are quite obvious and instructive here. The hiring of full-time mercenary athletes to assure victories and thus advance club pride (as well as spike the interest and profit of those who wagered on such matches, or sold admissions to popular games) was still a decade or more in the future. In Havana, the more mercenary forms of baseball activity that could truly be called professional first emerged in the early 1890s, and the most visible outward signs of the recasting of the game as a "spectacle for profit" were the increased number of contests held, the first visits by teams of touring North American professionals, the recruitment of some of the latter to stay on the island and sign on with local clubs, and (perhaps most significantly) the gradual appearance of black-skinned Cuban ballplayers who at first had been barred from strictly social-club B.B.C. rosters.

The opening winter of a formal Cuban pro baseball circuit (December 29, 1878 through February 16, 1879) launched a rivalry between the island's two principal clubs (B.B.C.s) that would hold the Havana baseball scene in its firm grip for most of the remainder of the sport's professional life on the island. Families would often be divided by their loyalties to either the red-clad team (these were the *Habanistas*) or the outfit sporting blue (followers of Almendares and thus called *Almendaristas*). It was an inherited affliction among baseball fans or *aficionados* that easily matched big league versions between Yankees and Dodgers supporters, Yankees and Red Sox loyalists, or Cardinals and Cubs fanatics. For non–Cubans or for those now a half-century removed from the final Cuban pro season, it is perhaps difficult or even impossible to appreciate what *Habanista* and *Almendarista* loyalties meant to an island nation where there were few families that did not have at least some dedicated baseball followers in their midst.

In the most extensive English-language treatment of Cuban baseball fanaticism, Roberto González Echevarría (*The Pride of Havana*, Chapter 2) belabors the intensity of the Almendares-Habana rivalry with his detailed scene-setting surrounding a memorable pennant-deciding playoff game — one pitting the "eternal rivals" head-to-head in Havana's pristine Gran Stadium (Cerro Stadium) on February 25, 1947. Professor González Echevarría may be guilty of more than moderate revisionist history in labeling this single game as the apogee of Cuba's century-plus baseball history. (I will make the argument later in this chapter that Cuban pro baseball of the forties and fifties was much more a game in steep decline than it was a sport enjoying its ascendancy.) But the Yale professor and Cuban ex-patriot is nonetheless quite on target in portraying the fervor attached to a moment during which passions on the streets of Havana reached a boiling point and "the entire country paused for the epic struggle between Habana and Almendares" (*The Pride of Havana*, 18). What began in the 1880s and 1890s as a bitter competition between the capital city's two most prestigious high-society sporting clubs often reached such proportions over the years that fan league-wide support actually languished when neither of "the eternal rivals" fielded a particularly strong team. The entire Cuban League circuit frequently faced imminent collapse for lack of a third or fourth rival team which could demand even weak partisan support. An ongoing search by league officials for another strong fan-favored club would indeed remain a dominant theme throughout most of league history.

Club Habana was the older of the two outfits by a small stretch and actually preceded the 1878 Cuban League itself in its origins by a full decade. Among the numerous founders of the Habana B.B.C. were such giants of island baseball history as Emilio Sabourín, Ricardo Mora, Nemesio Guilló and the widely traveled "Steve" Bellán. Bellán remains the best known today if only because he owns the unique distinction of being the first Latin American to play for a team and league once considered part of the U.S. major leagues (see Chapter 10). Sabourín looms equally large in stature (in Cuba) as one of the ball-playing patriots who utilized popular Sunday-afternoon baseball games as a means for raising cash funds to support festering revolts against an oppressive and despised Spanish colonial government. Sabourín's own ball-playing would come to a premature end when he was arrested by ruling Spanish authorities (1896) and dispatched to a North African prison camp from which he never returned (Chapter 10). And Guilló (along with brother Ernesto, the first Habana B.B.C. secretary) is today credited with no less a feat than the very act of first transporting the game itself to his native island a mere four years before the prestigious group of young Havana enthusiasts met to form the club that would proudly wear the city's name.

Nemesio Guilló's precise role in introducing the popular new "American" sport to his homeland was clarified with a valuable interview published in Havana a few year's before his death. Quoted at length in *Diario de la Marina* (January 6, 1924), one of Cuba's legitimate baseball pioneers elaborated on his efforts in founding the Habana B.B.C. and also in launching informal games in his Vedado neighborhood a few years earlier. The published account unravels some of the tantalizing mysteries surrounding the true origins of baseball play in nineteenth-century Cuba. Guilló details an early club outing to Matanzas in the same year as the club's founding (1868) during which members enjoyed a rousing and victorious match against officers and crew of an American naval vessel anchored for repair. He recalls the banning of baseball games by Spanish governors during the subsequent winter, which forced the neophyte B.B.C. into mostly underground activities. And he recounts events of the club's resurfacing in 1878, when the Independence War concluded and the first league tournament

was arranged with a newborn Almendares team and the old rivals from Matanzas.

While the Habana B.B.C. thus came into existence in 1868, there was little notable activity under its banner before the birth of the first organized Latin American pro league exactly ten years later. The most colorful moment in the early annals of this pace-setting club from the capital city was its well-documented excursion in December 1874 to play a challenge match with the similar sports club already active in nearby Matanzas. The now-renowned game staged in Matanzas on December 27, 1874, was soon enough sanctioned to occupy the same mythic role for Cuban baseball history that Cooperstown and Abner Doubleday would long continue to fill for the home-grown American game. Baseball fans and even baseball historians in all quarters are seemingly enamored of illogical if inspired creation myths, which all have the na-

Almendares forties-era star Andrés Fleitas. Also a catcher for legendary national teams of the early forties and a mainstay with the International League Jersey City Giants, Fleitas signed with Jorge Pasquel's Mexican League in 1946, a move which cost him a likely shot at the majors.

tional game somehow springing forth full-blossomed, without any painstaking, chaotic, or difficult-to-track stages of piece-meal evolution. But as with the instance of General Double-day and Upstate New York in 1839, there was of course no ac-tual "miraculous conception" for baseball to be found in Cuba. The one-sided collision between the Habana B.B.C. and Matanzas B.B.C. in the final week of 1874 was indisputably the first game notably celebrated by the local press, but it cer-tainly could not have been the first game played. Guilló's pub-lished comments of 1924 (indicating an 1868 match with American sailors) have certainly put the lie to any remaining claims for the uniqueness of the December 1874 contest. Both clubs had undoubtedly honed their skills a good bit before the first inter-city challenge had been formally issued.

The historic baseball action unfolded on that late–1874 Sunday afternoon in Matanzas has been well chronicled (by others such as Roberto González Echevarría, as well as in Chapter 10 of this volume). Havana, led by Bellán and Sabourín, won a lopsided contest by a final 51–9 count that reflected the lack of defensive prowess found in most mid-nineteenth-century versions of the game. Bellán (two homers) was a batting hero and Sabourín is also mentioned in several existing press accounts. The location for the slugfest was the Palmar del Junco playing grounds, a site that would remain down to present a hallowed shrine for Cuban baseball. González Echevarría (*The Pride of Havana*, Chapter 4) has ex-posed many of the mythic elements surrounding the historic event and, in particular, has set straight the details of the venue's often mis-stated name (Palmar del Junco and not Pal-mar de Junco). I later return (in Chapter 10) to the significance of González Echevarría's debunking of mythologies attached to the celebrated Matanzas contest. The Palmar del Junco field not only still stands, in close approximation to its original ap-pearance (the original home plate area is now the right field corner), but it has continued off and on to be used as a site for amateur and even some professional matches down through the many intervening years. (And the historic flavor of the Matanzas grounds is only enhanced by the fact that the birth-places of three Cuban diamond legends — Martín Dihigo plus big leaguers José Cardenal and Leo Cárdenas — all stand within a hardball's heave from the park, on side streets in the surrounding neighborhood.)

The younger (by a decade) Almendares B.B.C. was soon formed under the primary leadership of another pair of ball-playing Havana brothers, Carlos and Teodoro Zaldo. The team named for an outlying distinct of the capital and the river that flowed through that district was assembled just in time for the first winter season of championship play in 1878–79. Two of the leading players on the club's "primary team" were the Zaldo brothers themselves. (Each amateur B.B.C. had several squads of ballplayers, the top "nine" for matches with rivals and the remainder for staging frequent intra-club contests.) The youngsters had attended New York's Fordham University (as had Bellán) where they picked up substantial ball-playing skills and even greater enthusiasms for the game. Carlos (the eldest) played shortstop on the earliest Almen-

dares teams and younger brother Teodoro was a pitcher who is sometimes credited with having thrown the first curveball on the island. Carlos has earned dubious credit in some quar-ters for having performed the first successful bunt in a Cuban baseball game on Christmas Day of 1879. The elder Zaldo re-putedly achieved the feat while facing the Hops Bitter club, the first American team to visit Cuba. González Echevarría (*The Pride of Havana*, 100) reports this visit as taking place in December 1878, which would place it before the first games of the inaugural "Cuban League" tournament. The event is usually placed a year later by competing accounts (Angel Tor-res offers the most detail in *La Leyenda del Béisbol Cubano*, 18). A conflicting version published in 1889 by historian-ballplayer Wenceslao Gálvez places the first bunt on Christmas Day of that same year (1879), but credits it to another Cuban player, Carlos Maciá, and suggests that it occurred during an actual Cuban League game. But the admittedly often unreliable Díez Muro history, with its year-by-year listings of line scores, chronicles no Cuban League game occurring on that date. Such is the mix of fact and legend in early Cuban baseball his-tory.

Most significant of all, perhaps, the two Zaldo brothers purchased land in the Almendares district on which they con-structed the famed park that would bear the club name and serve as primary league venue for several decades to come. Constructed just in time for games of the first season of the *Liga de Base-Ball* and located on Carlos III Boulevard, this spa-cious grounds would serve as one of the Cuban League's prin-ciple homes (along with the Habana B.B.C. grounds in Vedado and the Palmar del Junco park in Matanzas) for thirty-five years. Almendares Park I would finally be abandoned after the 1915–16 winter season and replaced by a new version occupy-ing the site of the current Havana Bus Terminal. Almendares Park II would be short-lived, however, destroyed by a brutal hurricane in 1926 and permanently replaced by La Tropical Stadium in 1930. It was Almendares Park, in its two manifes-tations, as well as the Almendares B.B.C. itself that were the Zaldo brother's ultimate legacy to ball-playing in their native city.

Founders of the two Havana baseball clubs turned their attentions to organizing a first championship or "league" round robin in time for the early weeks of 1879, shortly after the con-clusion of the devastating Ten Years' War. An organizational meeting transpired on December 22 of 1878 and was attended by representatives of Habana (Manuel Landa, Ricardo Mora, Beltrán Senarens) and Almendares (Joaquín Franke, Adolfo Nuño, Carlos de Zaldo). Matanzas B.B.C. representatives were not present but had already agreed to follow any plan adopted by the two rival clubs. Five agreements ratified were: that each team would play three games against each other with the over-all winner being the one that defeated each of its two rivals twice; that the winning club would receive the handsome prize of a silk banner emblazoned with the word "Championship" and paid for by the losers; that winning team members would receive individual medals of silver inscribed "Island of Cuba, Baseball Championship, 1878" again at the expense of the losers; that games would begin on December 29 and be played only on Sundays and holidays; and that the American *Spalding Baseball Guide* of 1878 would determine all rules and conditions of play. A week later the first game of the new "league" was staged and the first annual competition was under way. Habana won all of its games save one tie (with Matanzas on New Year's Day) and the first Cuban baseball champion was formally crowned by mid-February.

Almendares would not savor the immediate successes on the field enjoyed by its more powerful rival. Club Habana would dominate most of the 19th century league play and Almendares would in fact not capture a single championship banner during the first dozen winters of competitions. In those dozen years before

Cuban League action between Cienfuegos and Marianao at Havana's pristine Cerro Stadium during the mid-fifties.

the final independence war against the Spanish (1895–98) it was Habana that had most of the best ballplayers and thus also the best results. Steve Bellán gave way to Ricardo Mora, Francisco Saavedra and eventually Sabourín as the team manager. Adolfo Luján was a top pitcher for the Leones (winning all five of his outings in the short campaigns of both 1886 and 1887) and Antonio Maria García garnered numerous accolades (four hitting crowns included) as a crack batsman. Twice the Habana stranglehold was broken by Club Fe, which won a banner in 1888 and then again in 1891. Matanzas also broke through with a victory in 1893 when Habana was bested in a season-ending playoff. Only in the final championship played before the outbreak of war, which interrupted two seasons and cancelled outright two others, did Almendares finally finish on top of the Cuban League standings.

It is important to emphasize that 19th-century Cuban baseball had a most special character and was a sporting phenomenon far removed from the cutthroat game of baseball as it is played in modern times. Short seasons would make it difficult in later eras to compare players from the earliest Cuban "seasons" with those of the league's heyday in the winter campaigns held after the First World War, or even after the arrival of substantial numbers of itinerate black American ballplayers who began crowding Cuban League rosters at the turn of the twentieth century. In short, these were not seasons at all as we know them today. Instead they were round robin tournaments and they were played at first as much for recreation as for hardcore competition. The teams as already noted were still in large part social clubs during the 1880s and even into the 1890s, and the competition against rival "nines" was only a part (if a central part) of the scheduled Sunday after-

noon fare of baseball and social activities. It is true that even in the earliest seasons some of the native Cuban players—Steve Bellán for one—were full-fledged pros and paid regular if not tidy salaries. By the final decade of the nineteenth century a corner had been turned and almost all athletes with Habana, Almendares and other league clubs were being compensated for their services. But vestiges of appreciable social ritual still attached to Cuban baseball down to at least the year 1900, when the aftermath of the Spanish-American War brought both professionalism and racial integration to the Havana sporting scene. Cuban baseball historian Roberto González Echevarría (*The Pride of Havana*, Chapter 4) is at his best when he is reconstructing the atmosphere that surrounded this early phenomenon of genteel Cuban baseball.

Over its first two decades the Cuban League evidenced a slow if steady transition from amateur sporting event to full-scale entertainment spectacle. In the process there was much chaos and considerable upheaval—even the ever-present specter of imminent collapse for the entire operation. Seasons were rearranged and cancelled, often without any advanced notice. The second championship tournament (1882) came to an abrupt halt when Habana filed a protest after the fourth contest with Fe which officials failed to resolve; play was thus suspended without a championship trophy awarded. Sometimes there were only three teams (or two, as in 1882) and sometimes there were several more (five competed in 1885–86 and again in 1889 and 1890). Clubs that started the seasons often didn't last out the entire championship round: in the second year of competition neither Colón nor Progreso completed a full schedule of matches, and in 1887 Carmelita played only half as many contests (6) as the other three entrants. And the months of play sometimes varied as well: the tournament of 1885 was staged in March and April, while others of that decade were played in January and February. Add to these irregularities the added interruptions due to factors external to the league operations (e.g., seasons suspended as a result of the 1895–98 War for Independence) and the early history of Cuban baseball often becomes a true nightmare to decipher.

Nineteenth-century Cuban seasons boasted noteworthy individual performances as well as some odd features that uniquely marked island championship play. Most distinctive perhaps for the appearance of games was the fact that Cuban baseball from the outset was played with ten men to a side, the extra player being a fourth outfielder who usually took up a post in short right field. When visiting clubs arrived from the States in the 1890s they would contend with Cuban teams sporting an extra fielder in the lineup, but no one seemed to mind the imbalance and few in the contemporary press saw fit to comment. When it came to the record books, official statistics were not kept until the 1886 season. From the mid–1880s until the years immediately preceding the First World War, the sparse surviving records involve only a limited number of batting and pitching categories. Antonio Maria García would make his mark as a top batsman of the pre–1900 epoch mainly on the strength of a posted .448 B.A. for a 15-game 1888 campaign, plus three other leading averages over the next half-dozen tournaments. Adolfo Luján dominated the early pitching field by winning all of his decisions in 1886 and 1887 —five each winter. But such extremely short seasons and the sparse numbers they produced make the numerical accounts of early Cuban League play of spurious value at best.

The art of pitching, especially, had its notables before the turn of the century, even if pitching dominance was suggested mainly by eye-witness reports and few hard numbers exist to back up the anecdotal accounts. The first Cuban League no-hitter occurred on February 13, 1887, with Carlos Maciá winning by an unlikely lopsided 38–0 count. A second no-hit masterpiece was tossed in July 1889 by Progreso's Eugenio de Rosas, but this one would be the last for a full thirty-five years. While de Rosas's no-hitter occurred in a game with a more familiar-looking score than the one authored by Maciá, it nonetheless also featured an odd line score by modern standards: the losing Cárdenas club aided Progreso's cause with 14 errors. Another notable aspect of this epoch was an apparent anomaly that the best pitchers were also not infrequently the best hitters. Small rosters are enough to explain the phenomenon, as are the conditions of more primitive baseball (think of modern Little League play) when the best athletes are often the hardest throwers and thus the natural choices for mound duty. Yet even when teams carried more players this tradition of great hitting pitchers would continue as a Cuban League staple. Two decades later José Méndez, Eustaquio Pedroso and Cristóbal Torriente would double as masterful hurlers and fearsome batters; Martín Dihigo would extend the tradition in the 1920s and thirties. Robert González Echevarría and other commentators have noted that such versatility in early

Cuban League action demonstrated not only the exceptional talents of some of the native sons but also resulted from the economic conditions of the epoch, when barnstorming teams could hardly afford to carry inflated rosters.

The Cuban League's first formal contacts with baseball outside the island came as early as 1879 — on the eve of the second season of an organized baseball league in Havana. The Hops Bitter team, a club of U.S. semi-pros sponsored by a beverage company, visited that December and trounced the Almendares B.B.C. The second visit by American barnstormers seems to have been in 1885 when two teams called Providence and Athletic and stocked with players from the American Association (then considered a major league) toured Havana and played local clubs, one of which featured author-ballplayer Wenceslao Gálvez. The same Gálvez also reports that during the earliest seasons Habana B.B.C. began a practice of importing U.S. catchers to shore up play at that difficult position. González Echevarría (*The Pride of Havana*, 100) establishes that a character named Billy Taylor was one such American catcher brought to Havana, and also that the rotund backstop set a precedent for American ballplayers on the island when he developed more of a reputation for drinking than for handling lively tosses from his pitchers. It is also known that the Colón B.B.C. brought two Americans to the island for the 1879–80 tournament — a pitcher named Carpenter and a catcher named McCuller. The latter socked a homer in one of his earliest games and both were so talented by Cuban standards that various cries of protest arose from the remaining local clubs that winter. Perhaps the most memorable of all these early forays was the one of 1885, when the Americans' Athletic "nine" trounced both Habana and Almendares and a slugger known only as Crane belted a mighty homer over the distant racetrack in spacious Almendares Park. But the games were hardly a smash hit themselves and apparently few fans were drawn to such exhibition matches.

During the 1880s and 1890s struggle for independence from Spain American-style baseball played a pivotal role. It was a role, indeed, that would ultimately fuse an intimate and lasting bond between the new sport and emerging twentieth-century Cuban society as a whole. The practice of baseball playing from the first had been identified with anti–Spanish sentiments in Havana and elsewhere around the island. Seemingly all things American were increasingly seen as forward-looking, trendy, modern, and thus part of a new desired national identity. Spanish cultural practices —bullfighting in particular — were rejected as archaic and even barbaric. Ballplayers themselves often were patriots and many of them actually took up arms to fight in the guerilla-style warfare against the oppressors. Several —like Almendares pitching hero José M. Pastoriza and slugger Ricardo Cabaleiro — were killed in the conflict and others —like pioneering player and manager Emilio Sabourín — were captured and exiled to off-shore prison camps. The Spanish commanders eventually tried unsuccessfully to limit baseball play throughout the island and the Spanish Civil Governor of Havana cancelled one tournament (the 1895 post-season playoffs between Habana and Almendares, which ended in a full-blown riot) as threatening to the safety of the governing regime.

Throughout the final chaotic decade of the fading century commerce between the United States and Cuban versions of organized baseball continued to escalate. A team of exiled Cuban patriots from Key West had visited Havana in 1890 to play exhibitions, although the secret motive was to transfer funds raised in North America for the aid of anti–Spanish rebel forces. A year later an all-star team including three undistinguished big leaguers, one of whom was 17-year-old John McGraw, made an island tour but won only one of the half-dozen matches staged against locals. A handful of U.S. imports continued to play on Cuban teams in the late-nineties although all of these were white Americans. So far it was only a trickle that seeped from diamonds of the north to those of the tropics. But what started as a mere trickle would soon swell to a near floodtide of American visitors before Cuban baseball had moved very far into the new century that waited just around the corner.

* * *

The 1900 season was one of the most pivotal campaigns in Cuban baseball history, largely because this was the year that professional island baseball was for the first time racially integrated. It would also be — and the two facts are not unrelated — the turning-point season that witnessed league baseball beginning a rapid transition from the last vestiges of amateurism to a full-fledged professionalism. The campaign was still strictly a weekend affair and stretched from mid–May until late December. Habana's versatile Luis "Mulo" Padrón made most of the on-field headlines as champion pitcher (he won 13 of 17 decisions) and also the leader in base knocks (with 31 hits), yet the roster make-ups of two of the teams proved the most newsworthy items.

What historian Raúl Díez Muro labels in his 1907 volume only as "social reasons" led to the temporary disintegration of the Liga Nacional de Base-ball and the forming in its stead of the replacement Liga Cubana, consisting of four clubs: Habana, Almendarista, Cubano, and San Francisco. The real explanation, avoided by the politically correct Díez Muro, was that two of that year's entrants had decided to employ "men of race" to fill out their lineups. Integration thus arrived overnight with one entirely black ball club (San Francisco) and a second team (Cubano) that was racially mixed. There was also a special significance to be found in the names of two teams entering the 1900 championship fray. Almendarista ("followers of Almendares") was not the normal Almendares contingent; many of the same players (including mainstays Antonio María García and Miguel Prats) had returned under the club banner, but the altered name was obviously an effort to avoid legal problems with the sponsoring social club (Almendares B.B.C.) which still admitted white members only. And the name Cubano ("Cuba-No" on the front of the team jerseys) involves a still more interesting tale. When the owner of the club that had played as "Cuba" the previous season turned the team (and its uniforms) over to new managers Tinti

Molina and José Poyo, the latter pair decided to hire several blacks. The previous owner, Severino Solloso, demanded that the "Cuba" name not be used for the now integrated club; thus Molina and Poyo cleverly responded by having the letters "NO" sewn onto the existing jerseys. The implication in Spanish would of course be that this was not the familiar "Cuba" team.

It was also during the 1900 season that a future vital link between the Cuban League and the U.S. Negro leagues was initially forged. This came about when the highly successful stateside black outfit managed by E.B. Lamar, Jr. and called Cuban X Giants made their first barnstorming visit to the island that winter. The Havana press would drop the X from the club name when it announced that the renowned touring team would visit the island before the scheduled championship season for a series of ten matches with the four Cuban League clubs — Habana, Almendares, San Francisco and Cuba — as well as with all-stars patched together from local teams. Much was also made by local Havana writers in advance of the tour of the sterling record of the Negro leagues team, which reputedly had won more than three-quarters of its 400-odd matches during three previous years. After a rainout, the series finally began on February 25 with a 6–5 Giants victory over Habana, the top Cuban nine and defending league champs. The visitors continued to win while playing amateur clubs in the vicinity of the capital but eventually succumbed twice to a racially mixed all-star squad of Cuban leaguers called Criollo and managed by Valentín "Sirique" Gonzálcz. What was most significant about the visit was that the final games provided the first significant victories of Cuban teams over American visitors and thus gave some measure of the advancements taking place in the level of island baseball. Local pride must have also been stoked by the fact that these victories came against the backdrop of the first season played under the American occupation of the island that followed on the heels of the Spanish-American War and "liberation" from Spanish rule. But there would be many of these victories to come in the near future, and the savoring of such triumphs over the occupiers would soon become the highlight of many a Cuban baseball season.

The North American black barnstorming club visiting Cuba for the first time at the turn of the century had a most interesting origin that also provides an important chapter in early U.S. blackball history. The X Giants were a direct descendent of the first team that had seized on the marketability of an identification with Cuban baseball. Lamar's team had evolved from the "nine" originally organized by Frank P. Thompson in 1885 at the Argyle Hotel in Babylon, New York; more importantly, Lamar's troop was only one of dozens of Negro clubs at the turn of the century that carried various versions of the names Giants and Cubans as an important symbol of what had apparently already become a certain degree of romance and prestige attached to Cuban ball-playing and Cuban society throughout black communities up north. This may have had to do with circulating reports of a more racially tolerant atmosphere on the Caribbean island nation, or to the known fact that numerous blacks had staffed integrated rebel army units (*mambises*) during the 1868–78 rebellion known as the Cuban Ten Years' War. What is apparent is that American black teams calling themselves "Cubans" had a certain sizable cachet by the turn of the century.

The next important clasp in the link of the Cuban League and the Negro leagues would come with the 1907 and 1908 seasons when U.S. Negro leaguers would first show up on Cuban League playing rosters. Against the backdrop of an unwelcome American occupation, the importing of black stars from up north worked in a backhanded way to stimulate a good deal of patriotism among Havana fans, and it was nationality and not race which was the issue. The 1907 season witnessed an all–Cuban Almendares team win a league title over a Fe club stocked mostly with African-American imports from the Philadelphia Giants — Preston Hill, Rube Foster, Home Run Johnson, Charlie Grant, and Bill Monroe among them. It was a tight race throughout with Almendares, paced by Marsans and Almeida, managing to pull out the victory on the final day of the season before an enthusiastic overflowing crowd jamming Almendares Park. The 1907 season's emotional Almendares victory over Tinti Molina's import-laced team spurred a passion among fans for further Cuba versus United States match-ups that could test the strength of the local warriors and prove their merits against the best American clubs.

There are several major misunderstandings about the integration of baseball in Cuba. The first is an assumption that Cuba was something of a racial paradise in which blacks and whites were completely free to mix on the diamond as well as in other quarters of society. But it was only in the Havana-based pro league that integration existed during decades preceding and following the First World War, and then only after the turn of the century, when the game slowly transformed itself away from being strictly a social affair for upper-class gentlemen. There was also mixing of the races in semi-professional sugar mill baseball (see Chapter 7), but the amateur leagues on the island were strictly segregated with no black ballplayers allowed until the eve of World War II. And regarding the pro leagues there is another misnomer that Cuban blacks and U.S. Negro leaguers regularly tested their skills with the best professional whites during winter league action. Donn Rogosin states that "since the great white ballplayers, the Ty Cobbs and Babe Ruths, participated in the Cuban Leagues, the Negro leaguer knew after a few Cuban seasons whether or not he was a player of major-league caliber." (*Invisible Men*, 156) This is a highly misleading assessment of course. Some of the better major leaguers occasionally barnstormed against Cuban League clubs that boasted U.S. Negro leaguers on their rosters; both Cobb (1910) and Ruth (1920) made brief one-time visits to Havana. But none of the white major league stars ever played in the Cuban League in the 1910s, 1920s, or 1930s. The first white U.S. major leaguers showed up on Cuban League rosters in the forties and then they were marginal players like Rocky Nelson, Max Lanier, "Spook" Jacobs and a host of other career journeymen. Before that the white major leaguers on Habana, Almendares or other Cuban League rosters

during winter months were Cubans like Luque, Almeida, Marsans and Migel Angel González. It was the white Cubans and not many white Americans who mixed freely in Havana with top Cuban and U.S. blackball stars.

These years also brought a new feature to Cuban baseball that would be known widely as the "American season" (*temporada Americana*) and that often cemented the Havana circuit's financial solvency. Preceding each Cuban League campaign, usually in early fall, exhibitions were scheduled with visiting U.S.–based teams, usually barnstorming big leaguers or more often clubs from the outlaw Negro leagues. American teams would be pitted against Cuban League clubs (sometimes filled with U.S. Negro leaguers plying their winter trade in Havana), Cuban League all-star selections, top amateur outfits in the Havana area, and even themselves. The games, usually in Almendares Park, meant money in the coffers for Cuban League officials and Havana promoters. At the same time the matches fed the by-now considerable nationalistic sentiments of the time. The popularity of the so-called American season began with the visits of touring Negro leaguers in 1907 (a combined team of Philadelphia Giants and Brooklyn Royals Giants) and big leaguers in 1908 (the Cincinnati Reds, again accompanied by the Brooklyn Royal Giants). The Reds, New York Giants, Detroit Tigers and two Philadelphia big league clubs soon provided a steady stream of early fall "preseason" baseball entertainment. These increasingly popular American seasons would finally culminate with the celebrated visit of Babe Ruth and John McGraw in November 1920, a showcase event in which the touring big league club counted five future Cooperstown hall of famers in its entourage.

It was in this first decade of the new century that outstanding Cuban pitching first came to the fore on the international scene. What the Reds and McGraw's Giants and other big league clubs ran smack into in Havana in 1907 and 1908 were several dark-skinned Cuban moundsmen who could seemingly tame big-league hitters without fear. The strength of Cuban talent, especially pitching, was certainly a shock to the top white pros, even if the barnstorming U.S. clubs often featured lineups with more bench players than established regulars. From these landmark encounters grew some very large early Cuban baseball legends and none was any larger than that surrounding 21-year-old José de la Caridad Méndez, a surprise hero in 1908 who had only been discovered a few months earlier while laboring for regional teams near his native Cárdenas, in Matanzas Province. The story of how Méndez was discovered by star Cuban pitcher Bebé Royer is almost the stuff of fictional accounts. Royer was freelancing with Armando Marsans and other Almendares regulars at a provincial tournament when he spotted "a scrawny black kid playing short" who also threw a mean fastball and snappy curve in relief for a rival Remedios team. Royer's report caused the Blues manager Pájaro Cabrera to immediately sign up the 5–9, 150 pound untried prospect.

Méndez was one of those remarkable athletes who occasionally come along at just the right moment to take full advantage of chance fate and circumstance. It was precisely in the fall of 1908 — the exact moment of the winter league debut of the Matanzas phenom — that Cuban baseball truly became a national pastime. The novel experiment of a so-called American season was just now first catching the public fancy. An increasingly unpopular American occupation initiated two years earlier had adequately set the stage for the playing out of hostilities on the baseball diamond. Cubans — as in other periods in the future — would look to baseball as a level playing field to test themselves against the colonial power of the much-admired if also much-resented neighboring United States. And against this ideal backdrop the young Méndez would step to the forefront as a much needed national hero. After only a handful of American seasons Méndez would in fact emerge as the first genuine Cuban baseball hero to boast substantial island-wide fame.

Thus the greatest Cuban pitching legend of all would burst almost overnight onto the scene at the end of the first decade of a new century. José de la Caridad Méndez was the oversized star who would truly put Cuban baseball on the map, both at home and also outside the island, and especially in the big league cities of the American northeast where the press of New York, Cincinnati and Philadelphia would report his successes against often mesmerized big leaguers. In the process Méndez became not only a star but also a major national celebrity, outstripping such earlier native ballplaying heroes as Strike González, Bebé Royer and Mulo Padrón by a wide margin.

That celebrity would mainly be earned with a series of outstanding performances against the stream of big leaguers arriving on the Havana scene over the next couple of seasons. Over the course of four autumn sessions (1908–1911) the skinny kid from Matanzas faced five big league clubs in 18 games and won a total eight decisions, while dropping seven and tying one. On November 5, 1911, he blanked the Philadelphia Phillies on but three hits; in 1913 he also no-hit the Birmingham Southern Association club for good measure. With such eye-popping feats he became a lasting legend known forever in Cuba as "El Diamante Negro" and he was soon also being heralded back in the States as a treasure beyond the reach of the all-white major leagues. The most startling performance, perhaps, was a string of 45 scoreless innings that included 25 against major league lineups. But there were also other remarkable moments that nearly topped the astonishing shutout streak, and none sticks out more than his debut against Cincinnati on November 15, 1908, when he tossed a sterling one-hitter, won 1–0, and lost his "perfect game" with two outs in the ninth on a scratch single by future Yankees manager Miller Huggins.

Beating American big leaguers in Havana thrust Méndez into the national and even international spotlight, but his numerous victories in 1908 and 1909 over rival Cuban League clubs Habana and Fe — teams staffed with American Negro leaguers — worked just as heavily to cement his immediate national icon status. Performances in the American seasons were thus certainly matched if never quite altogether overshadowed by a string of equally noteworthy Cuban League outings. For his first four years in the league Méndez truly dominated rival hitters, including some of the era's best imported Negro leaguers like Clarence Winston, Preston Hill, George Johnson and Bruce Petway. Several seasons he won league pennants for Almendares almost single-handedly, posting more than half his team's victories. And like most Cuban stars of the era, he was a versatile ballplayer who could also perform with precision as a shortstop.

In the end injury would cut short a brilliant career and even provide a note of tragic outcome. Méndez performed equally as well as a Negro league hurler on the U.S. summer circuit as he did in winter venues, at least before arm troubles limited his effectiveness at the end of a half-dozen stellar seasons. With the Cuban Stars in 1909 he is estimated to have compiled a 44–2 record, one of the best pitching ledgers found anywhere in baseball history. Once injuries set in he would stay on with the Kansas City Monarchs as a part-time shortstop and highly skilled manager. He would star in the first-ever modern-era Negro leagues World Series in 1924, when he recovered some of his pre-injury mound magic and hurled a shutout and another victory in relief for the victorious Kansas City Monarch club he also managed. His Negro league performances have left rich descriptions of his pitching style among former rivals and latter-day historians. John Holway cites unnamed old-timers as claiming the Cuban threw "a fastball that looked like a pea" and "a curve that looked like it was falling off a pool table" (*Blackball Stars*, 50). James Riley repeats a probably apochrypal story that Méndez once killed a teammate by hitting him in the chest with a fastball during batting practice (*The Biographical Encyclopedia of the Negro Baseball Leagues*, 546). But tragedy was never far away from Méndez's doorstep. In late October 1928 — at age 41 and only two years removed from his final game with the Negro National League Monarchs — Méndez succumbed to a brief bout with bronchopneumonia back in his native Havana.

Méndez at times was nearly rivaled by Eustaquio "Bombín" Pedroso. Pedroso, playing variously with Fe, San Francisco and Almendares in the Cuban League, shared the mound duties with Méndez for the Alacranes in 1912 and 1913, pacing the circuit in losses the first of those years and in wins during the second; more importantly, he also spun his own brand of mastery over visiting big leaguers. The highlight moment for the hard-throwing black ace was a no-hitter he tossed at the Detroit Tigers on November 18, 1909, but there were other outstanding performances against both the Tigers and the New York Giants. Against a Detroit team that had Ty Cobb in tow in 1910 Pedroso split four decisions while yielding only 15 hits in 22 innings. Less noticed by the white press was his sterling career back in the States with the Cuban Stars (both East and West teams) which stretched for 21 seasons (1910 through 1930). He also proved nearly as large a star in the Cuban League itself, being judged in a 1924 poll as one of the four best-ever Cuban pitchers alongside Méndez, Luque, and Luis Padrón. A teammate of Méndez with Almendares for a large part of his Cuban career, Bombín twice led the circuit in total victories (11 in 1913, 10 in 1915). And like Méndez he was a

José de la Caridad Méndez's Cuban League Career Pitching Records

Note: Méndez was CL individual pitching champion in years indicated by **Boldface**

Year	Team	G	CG	W–L	Pct.	IP	SO	BB	Hits
1908	**Almendares**	**15**	**6**	**9–0**	**1.000**	**NA**	**58**	**38**	**NA**
1908–09	**Almendares**	**28**	**18**	**15–6**	**.714**	**NA**	**106**	**56**	**NA**
1910	**Almendares**	**7**	**7**	**7–0**	**1.000**	**66**	**51**	**16**	**39**
1910–11	**Almendares**	**18**	**12**	**11–2**	**.846**	**129**	**68**	**41**	**91**
1912	Almendares	19	NA	9–5	.643	138	92	36	115
1913	Almendares	7	2	1–4	.200	41	17	21	47
1913–14	**Almendares**	**12**	**7**	**10–0**	**1.000**	**85**	**38**	**25**	**67**
1914–15	Almendares	2	1	2–0	1.000	13	3	1	14
1915–16	Did Not Pitch								
1917	Did Not Pitch								
1918–19	Did Not Pitch								
1919–20	Did Not Pitch								
1920–21	Almendares	5	1	1–2	.333	NA	NA	NA	NA
1921	Did Not Pitch								
1922–23	Did Not Pitch								
1923–24	Santa Clara	9	1	3–1	.750	NA	NA	NA	NA
1924–25	SC–Matanzas	19	2	2–3	.400	NA	NA	NA	NA
1925–26	Havana	6	1	1–1	.500	32	5	8	34
1926–27	Alacranes	10	1	3–1	.750	NA	NA	NA	NA
Totals	**13 years**	**153**	**58**	**72–26**	**.735**	**(504)**	**(438)**	**(242)**	**(407)**

versatile ballplayer and feared hitter on top of his outstanding mound skills. Playing for both Almendares and San Francisco in 1915–16 and batting in the middle of the order even when pitching, the multi-talented Pedroso was the top Cuban batsman, smacking the ball at a .413 clip with over 100 official at-bats. Bombín Pedroso was perhaps not quite Méndez in either reputation or results, but he was certainly close enough in the eyes of both occasional barnstorming visitors and daily league rivals.

The opening decade of the new century also witnessed the first influx of top U.S. black stars as regular Cuban leaguers and not just visiting barnstormers. Soon rosters of Habana, Fe, and Colón in particular were filled with imports who had already established their worth up north. The immediate effect was indisputably a definite upgrade in the quality of the league as a whole. Sure-handed shortstop John Henry Lloyd and ace pitcher Rube Foster were the most notable of these invaders during the first handful of seasons after Cuban League integration. American Preston Hill dominated several hitting categories as early as 1908, and Grant (Home Run) Johnson was also drawing headlines by wearing out local pitching by the end of the century's first decade. Johnson captained Habana to a league title and was an outstanding performer for the Cuban club during 1910 exhibitions with the Detroit Tigers and New York Giants. That winter he outhit both Cobb and Sam Crawford with a .412 average over a dozen-game span: Pop Lloyd (.500) and Bruce Petway (.389) also outpaced the glamorous American duo during that same series. Preston "Pete" Hill, in turn, was the first visiting American to walk off with a Cuban League batting title when he posted a .365 average for Habana during the 1910–11 winter season.

Another result of the new imports — coming at the time of U.S. occupation of the island — was the stimulus it gave to burgeoning nationalistic pride, especially when local black and white players (mostly Almendares) were able to beat the teams composed mainly of Afro-Americans (Habana and Fe B.B.C.). The feeling attached to such league victories by the home-grown Almendares players was similar to that euphoria generated by successes of Cuban League squads against visiting big league clubs. An example of such unleashed patriotism came with the 1907 season, the first played with imported American Negro leaguers and also the second staged under a short-lived American military governor. That year the ethnically pure Alacranes outstripped Fe with Foster, Hill, Charlie Grant and Grant Johnson in the lineup, and Habana with George Johnson and Wilson in toe. A year later, buoyed by the perfect 9–0 pitching performance of Méndez, the Blues again swept their American-reinforced rivals. The notion of Cuban players competing head to head with the best Americans seemed even to be now outstripping the young rivalry between the top city teams, Habana and Almendares. A few years down the road this shift in fan priorities would continue to be a problem for Cuban baseball promoters, especially after Judge Landis cracked down on barnstorming big leaguers touring in Cuba. Such visits by the white clubs stopped after 1920, though big leaguers would still often play Havana spring training matches against each other throughout the thirties and early forties.

By decade's end — on the heels of runaway 1910 and 1911 pennant victories — Almendares was for the first time a legitimate match for the Habana club that had so dominated the first quarter-century of Cuban League action. With pitchers like Méndez and Pedroso in their stable, the Blues had added several pennants at the end of the decade to the two they had captured in the middle. For a few years Almendares actually had its toughest challenges from the Fe club and not from Habana which was in a temporary swoon before the importing of American black stars once again allowed the Lions to keep pace. But the rivalry had been rekindled by 1909 when Habana broke its five-year pennant dry spell despite the brilliant pitching of Méndez who won 15 games and completed eighteen.

Other outstanding players of the century's first decade included Strike González, Emilio Palmero, Julián Castillo, and Regino Garcia with his four batting titles. González earned fame as the preferred catcher for Méndez on the championship Almendares teams of the late 1900s and early 1910s, but "Streaky" was also a talented hitter as well as a wonder with the glove during an epoch of primitive fielding. Palmero was a light-skinned southpaw hurler, known as "El Rubio de Guanabacoa" in reference to his light hair and native barrio, who played briefly in the big leagues with the Giants, and also appeared in the Federal League. Manuel Cueto, Angel Aragón and José Rodríguez were other whites who starred in Cuba and tasted brief major league action: "Patato" Cueto logged 151 games in the outfield with the National League Reds and Federal League St. Louis club; Aragón became the first "Latino" to crack the Yankees roster in 1914; José Rodríguez bore the unusual nickname of "El Hombre de Goma" ("The Rubber Man") while briefly manning first and second part-time with McGraw's Giants (1916–18). Alfredo (Pájaro) Cabrera was a standout Almendares shortstop, named in one 1903 survey as the island's best player and earning his merit as a manager when he signed up the untried Méndez. Agustín Parpetti garnered his reputation as the island's top defensive first baseman while dark-skinned Julián Castillo was both a batting champ (.454 in 1901) and base-hits leader (37 in 1903). And there were others like mound ace Carlos Royer, sure-handed outfielder Helidoro Hidalgo, and eye-catching shortstop Luis Bustamante whose stars shown bright; Bustamante even gained some measure of fame up north playing independent ball in both black and white leagues. Two additional players named Armando Marsans and Rafael Almeida also came on the scene in these years and would gain a substantial measure of immortality in 1911 as the first Cuban National Leaguers.

The years between 1911 and 1920 brought increased contact between Cuba and U.S. professional baseball. Visitors to Havana included the Philadelphia Phillies (1911), New York Giants (1911), Lincoln Giants (1914), Indianapolis ABCs (1915), Pittsburgh Pirates (1919) and a 1919 big-league all-star contingent called All-Americans. In 1915 the Chicago American Giants took up winter residence in Havana and played a full Cuban League season under the banner of a club called San Francisco. While barnstorming tours continued to arrive in the

Cienfuegos star Silvio García (right), a North American Negro league mainstay and widely rumored to be one of Branch Rickey's earlier choices for Jackie Robinson's historic big league integration role. García was an accomplished pitcher and heavy-hitting infielder in both the Cuban League and U.S. Negro leagues.

fall, American players continued to swell the ranks of Cuban League teams in the winter. In 1912 Club Fe rebounded from a dismal 1911 campaign as league doormat by hiring Spotswood Poles, Judy Gans and Louis Santop from the Lincoln Giants and copping a pennant. Furthermore, some of the Cuban stars themselves were now playing in the major leagues: Marsans (1911), Almeida (1911), Mike González (1912), Merito Acosta (1913), Jack Calvo (1913), Angel Aragón (1914), Luque (1914), Emilio Palmero (1915), Joseíto Rodríguez (1916), Manolo Cueto (1917), Eusebio González (1918) and Oscar Tuero (1918) all debuted in the big time before the decade was played out.

The presence of Marsans, Almeida and Luque on the Cincinnati roster made the Reds a huge favorite back in Havana as Cuban fans and press now followed big league play with increased enthusiasm. Especially loved were "*Los Queridos Rojos*" ("The Beloved Reds") who could trace their island popularity in large part to Adolfo Luque and his 1919 World Series appearance. While Marsans, Almeida, Acosta, González, Luque and others cracked the big league barriers, the biggest names back on the island remained the top blacks too dark in skin-tone for organized baseball. The most often cited names in today's history books are those of Méndez and Pedroso and perhaps catcher Strike González, all the equals of any imported blacks from the north. But there were others who soon would make the Cuba-Negro leagues connection very much a balanced two-way street. None was more memorable than a Havana icon who would bear the unlike diamond sobriquet of "El Caballero" ("The Gentleman").

Alejandro Oms was both a remarkable fielder and a spectacular hitter, in the U.S. blackball leagues as well as in the hometown Cuban circuit. The chunky 5'9" lefty swinger is easily today the most overlooked Cuban blackball star of the epoch. A homegrown talent from the Santa Clara region, Oms was a left-handed swinger who possessed equal doses of raw natural power at the plate and blinding speed on the bases and in the outfield, seemingly lacking only in the area of a strong throwing arm. The large ballparks of the era allowed him to roam center making often-spectacular catches which were as eye-popping as his own extraordinary batting feats. Though he didn't begin his Cuban League career until the advanced age of 27, Oms made the most of his talents once he got to Havana, and he also hung around for a full decade and a half on the winter circuit. (Robert González Echevarría points out that his final few seasons in the forties on the Cienfuegos roster were largely the result of manager Luque's pity for a sick and destitute former all-star.) Highlight seasons came in 1929 and 1930 when he posted .432 and .380 marks to outdistance all rivals. A lifetime batting average in Cuba of .351 trailed only Torriente (by a single point) among native islanders and was fourth best in league history. And Oms was also remarkable for his gentlemanly deportment on and off the field of play, a facet of his career captured by his arresting nickname. Oms was said to never have been thrown out of a game and never even to have argued with an umpire over a close call at the plate or in the field.

Then there was the aforementioned Cristóbal Torriente — a slugger and defensive wizard the Pittsburgh *Courier* (in naming their all-time black all-stars in 1952) once labeled "a prodigious hitter, a rifle-arm thrower, and a tower of strength on defense" (quoted by John Holway in *Blackball Stars*, 125). In a period which saw the rise of numerous island nonpareils — a large percentage of them black — one alone is seemingly without peer when it comes to judging overall Negro league careers both north and south of the Florida Straits. Of all the players produced on the island during the teens and early twenties, perhaps only Méndez can rival the diverse talents displayed by Torriente. "The Cuban Strongboy" (as he is labeled by Holway) was almost as renowned for his flawless outfield play as for his heroic feats with the bat. But it was hitting that in the end set this light-skinned but kinky-haired paragon apart from the pack. Torriente was arguably the greatest Cuban-born hitter ever with his .350-plus winter league average and almost–.340 summer season mark up north. Torriente's feats in Chicago with Foster's American Giants have been catalogued and praised by Holway, Riley and a host of others. His achievements back in Cuba were just as noteworthy if not more so. Torriente would eventually claim two Cuban League batting titles playing for Almendares to go along with the less-well-documented crown he earned in the Negro leagues as a barnstormer. Cuban ballparks (especially Almendares Park) may have limited this slugger's towering long balls and turned many likely homers into long doubles and triples or even longer outs. But there are stories enough still existing about some of his prodigious pokes over faraway fences and into distant grandstands.

González Echevarría has reported on the many exaggerations surrounding the greatest day in the legendary career of Cristóbal Torriente, when he smacked three homers at Almendares Park in November 1920 and in the process overshadowed Babe Ruth and a group of touring New York Giants big leaguers (*The Pride of Havana*, 160–61). Standard reports by Holway and others overlook some of the most important facts: namely that the Giants pitcher serving up the Torriente blasts was an out-of-position first baseman, the New York players were all suffering from head-splitting hangovers, and none of the ballplayers on either side were trying especially hard that afternoon. But the myth surrounding Torriente's performance apparently fueled a popular need in Cuba at the time. Like the elaborate Havana welcome for Luque on the heels of his 1923 "career season" in Cincinnati, or the triumphs of Méndez and Pedroso in the American seasons 1908 and 1909, it fed the deep-seated need for a Cuban hero beating the best of the Americans. A good myth is rarely if ever diminished by the troublesome facts which might surround it.

Cristóbal Torriente's Cuban League Career Batting Record

Note: Torriente was Cuban League batting champion in years indicated by **Boldface**

Year	Team	G	AB	R	H	2B	3B	HR	BA
1913	Habana 28	102	11	27	1	3	1	6	.265
1913–14	Almendares	30	104	12	35	5	2	2	.337
1914–15	**Almendares**	**34**	**124**	**33**	**48**	**5**	**5**	**0**	**.387**
1915–16	Almendares	39	139	41	56	5	6	2	.402
1917	Did Not Play								
1918–19	Did Not Play								
1919–20	**Almendares**	**25**	**100**	**19**	**36**	**5**	**5**	**1**	**.360**
1920–21	Almendares	27	98	19	29	3	4	1	.296
1921	Habana	5	20	3	7	0	1	0	.350
1922–23	Habana	46	174	37	61	9	6	4	.350
1923–24	Habana-Marianao	43	162	28	56	9	1	2	.346
1924–25	Habana	46	163	30	62	13	2	4	.380
1925–26	Habana	32	122	17	43	7	4	1	.344
1926–27	Cuba-Almendares	3	8	1	3	0	0	0	.375
1926–27	Havana Red Sox	3	9	1	2	0	0	0	.222
Totals	**12 years**	**358**	**1316**	**251**	**463**	**62**	**39**	**18**	**.352**

There were substantial changes in the offering as Cuban baseball played out the string in the years surrounding the first great world war. At least one season (1917) was played with no Americans at all to be found anywhere on the three league rosters. But the largest changes came in the playing venues themselves. Old Almendares Park was finally replaced in 1918 by an impressive new facility that would enjoy its own legend-filled if rather short tenure. The old park at the long-used location was abandoned after the 1916 season simply because its grandstands were dilapidated and seemed a threat to public safety. The new Almendares Park opened two years later on adjacent grounds and would last barely a decade (it was done in by a 1926 hurricane), though a glorious decade by all accounts.

The new Almendares Park with its double-tiered grandstand and stately outside blue portals was a true marvel for its era. The size of both parks nonetheless revealed something significant about the game as it was still played in the shadows of World War I. Playing dimensions were huge and this meant that the old style of "dead ball" strategy would persist in Cuba even after the live ball-craze was introduced to American baseball in the early twenties by the slugging feats of Babe Ruth. Almendares Park II featured a left-field wall that loomed more than 500 feet from home plate, and there are no reports of any ball ever clearing that formidable barrier. Cuban ball fields had a definite impact on the Cuban style of play. There were often more triples than home runs and the home runs when they did occur were often inside-the-park events. Sluggers like Torriente and Oms and later Dihigo built their legends in Cuba without the benefit of inviting nearby outfield fences. It was another factor that fed the special nature of Cuba's favorite pastime during its initial Golden Age.

* * *

Three story lines seemingly dominated Cuban baseball throughout the sports-crazy 1920s — an era of increased affluence, rampant and even incautious optimism, and also an eventual collapse made all the more severe by its unforeseen suddenness. The first noteworthy event on the ball park scene was the arrival in the mid-twenties of the incomparable Martín Dihigo, a paragon of a player who across the next three decades would overhaul even Méndez as Cuba's grandest baseball legend. A second event of consequence was the brief but spectacular rise of a short-lived powerhouse team based in Santa Clara and built on the backs of the imported and native Negro leaguers now shoring up the winter league scene. And finally there was the revival of Club Habana under the long-time guidance of big-league fixture Miguel Angel González. By the end of the decade Habana's B.B.C. was both the pride of Cuban baseball and also a symbol of the hard times into which the league had fallen almost overnight in the face of the nation's burgeoning economic crisis.

Martín Dihigo ("*El Inmortal*") was easily the biggest individual star by the time the twenties were ready to close and Almendares Park II had given way to La Tropical Stadium. The only rival for the hearts of most Cuban rooters at the time was big league star Dolf Luque, especially after Luque's remarkable National League season of 1923, when he won a franchise-record 27 games. Dihigo was already a substantial fixture in the Habana lineup by the late-twenties and even walked off with the league's first-ever MVP trophy in 1928, when he batted .415, tallied a league-best hits total, and registered a 4–2 pitching ledger as backup to club ace Oscar Levis.

It was this kind of versatility that would become Dihigo's calling card in Mexico and on the U.S. blackball circuit across the subsequent thirties and forties. Especially as he grew older and concentrated more on pitching while at the same time maintaining his skills as a feared batsman. It is one of the two misfortunes of Dihigo's illustrious career, of course, that his peak seasons would come in the Depression and post–Depression years when the league itself was at its weakest, forcing Dihigo to earn most of his lasting reputation on the road in Mexico. The other misfortune, of course, was the fact that Dihigo's skin color closed the doors to the major leagues and what therefore might have been a much earlier and more celebrated enshrinement in Cooperstown. But by the end of the twenties Dihigo was nonetheless already one of the grandest talents on the scene in Cuba and elsewhere throughout the Caribbean.

Santa Clara's *Leopardos* team also wrote their lasting legend at the outset of the new decade on precisely the eve of Dihigo's own debut. Almost all of Santa Clara's claim on history was centered on a single season that began late in 1923 and then struggled to a bizarre conclusion early in the following spring. The 1923–24 league championship had opened with a joyous celebration staged to honor the triumphs of Dolf Luque that summer with the NL Reds (see Chapter 2). The pageant in Luque's honor was something of a orgy of local pride and nationalism, with the local press even crowing about how Luque ("The Pride of Havana") had outstripped an entire North American nation of stellar athletes (rather than merely besting National League hitters for a single season). It was a bright beginning nonetheless to the new league season, one full of an air of patriotism and a never-before-matched pride in the institution of Cuban baseball. But by mid-winter all the euphoria would quickly collapse in a spate of disorder and disappointment. The surface veneer of the Luque celebrations could not for long cover the substantial cracks now showing under the surface of the island's professional baseball.

Santa Clara boasted one of the strongest teams ever put upon the playing field in 1923–24 and it did so with a balance of native Cuban and itinerant North American black ballplayers. The unparalleled outfield that was the team's showcase feature boasted two Cubans — Oms and Champion Mesa — and one American, Oscar Charleston, whose talents forced Oms to play out of position in left rather than center. The team would quickly become one of Cuba's greatest baseball legends as it zoomed to the easiest pennant romp in league annals. Tinti Molina's outfit had debuted a season earlier and started well before dropping out in mid-stream and leaving the race to Marianao and the two "Eternal Rivals" by forfeiting its final 26 matches; Molina took his action after an earlier protested game won by the Leopards had been awarded to

Marianao. But the second time around Santa Clara would prove so dominant that the season would never be completed as actually scheduled. Play would be halted in mid–January with Santa Clara holding a 36–11 ledger and 11-game lead over Luque's Havana Reds. A bad situation would only then be made worse when league officials attempted a second truncated championship round staged in Havana and called the Gran Premio (Grand Prix); not only did disillusioned fans stay away but American blacks soon began abandoning the extended season to return to Negro league outfits up north.

Popular myth would long hold that the truncated 1924 campaign came about solely because a kind of "technical knockout" had been called in favor of the superior Santa Clara team; the real reasons for suspension of the original championship were obviously economic and had to do with little fan interest in a season that found Havana's favored Lions and Blues so far out of the money. One of the Cuban League's most glorious seasons on the surface had quickly exposed the financial problems always simmering behind the scenes. Things would only get considerably worse in coming winters.

There was also yet another failure of confidence and crisis of management confronting league moguls during that same memorable 1923–1924 winter tournament. Growing dissatisfaction among many native Cuban players with the avalanche of imports (who grabbed up roster slots previously available to locals) led to a minor rebellion of sorts. A group of disaffected players led by Miguel Angel González boycotted action in Almendares Park and Santa Clara's La Boulanger Park and headed for Matanzas to stage their own independent tournament at the venerable Palmar del Junco grounds. Much of the reason for the defection was indeed the crack Negro leaguers being imported by Abel Linares and Tinti Molina, but Miguel Angel and many of the Cuban minor leaguers who defected with him reportedly also feared rumors that big league commissioner Judge Landis was about to crack down on Cuban Leaguers as part of his new ban on barnstorming any later than November. Most significant about the games at Palmar del Junco, however, was the appearance there of a young Martín Dihigo, who had only briefly debuted with the Habana B.B.C. a season earlier and would now display his first glimmers of future stardom during the outlawed contests staged in Matanzas.

Miguel González and his Habana club seemed to own the league as the decade of the twenties roared to an end. Habana captured a string of pennants with super utility man Dihigo (from 1925 through 1929) and outfielder Oms (for 1928 and 1929) now both in its stable. In reality the strength of the Habana B.B.C. may have underscored the overall malaise being now suffered by the league as a whole. Habana's first pennant of the string in 1927 came after the new Cienfuegos entry folded with only a dozen games under its belt, while the Cuba and Almendares teams both posted losing records. A second pennant of the run found the Lions once more as the league's only team to put up a winning ledger. The following year Miguel Angel's crack nine outdistanced Almendares by a country mile (8.5 games in a 40-game season) and Cuba and Cien-

fuegos both again folded from the chase early. This resulted in Luque, the league's leading pitcher that season, joining Habana in mid-season.

Miguel Angel González himself was one of the true giants of early-century Cuban baseball legend and lore. Miguel Angel was never a headline-grabbing big leaguer even though he hung around in the majors in various capacities for three decades or more. He did have his moments up north both as a backup catcher and later a savvy and trusted coach. His biggest claim to fame came as a Cardinals third base coach when he waved home Enos Slaughter with the winning run of the 1946 World Series. But in Cuba González was a force both as a durable catcher and a legend as a tireless manager. In the latter capacity he served the Habana club with an unrivaled tenure that stretched from 1914 through the league's demise in 1961 — a remarkable four and a half decades. While he did not manage all of those seasons, his string at the helm of the club was nonetheless the longest in league annals. Had the Cuban Revolution not come about as it did in 1959 and had Cuban League baseball not faded from the scene only two years later, Miguel Angel González might have enjoyed a managerial tenure that outstretched even that of big league baseball's Grand Old Man, the venerable Connie Mack.

Throughout the Roaring Twenties the backstage roles of enterprising promoters and power-broker moguls named Abel Linares and Agustín "Tinti" Molina were two of the biggest behind-the-scenes stories of Cuban baseball. Linares, especially, played a role that did not seem always positive or even in the best interests of the growth of Cuban baseball. Linares became prominent on the Cuban League scene early in the 20th century when he served regularly as a league treasurer and was active in forming plans for luring visiting U.S. teams to the island. His role increased when he eventually gained ownership of the Habana B.B.C. in 1914, expanding his grip which had included Almendares, in partnership with the Zaldo brother, from at least the turn of the century. Once Linares had control of both "Eternal Rivals" he effectively pulled most of the strings for the entire league. Upon his death in 1930 his influence would stretch on even in his absence, once control of the two top teams and also the legal rights to their names, passed into the hands of his surviving widow.

If Linares was the Cuban League's top impresario for much of the Golden Age that was the teens and twenties, it was Agustín "Tinti" Molina who painstakingly built the crucial connections between Cuban baseball and the thriving if always somewhat chaotic Negro leagues to the north. Tinti Molina was a true patriot who saw action in the War for Independence and his roots thus stretched back to the very epoch when baseball was first cemented in Cuba as a national institution born out of the rebellion against Spanish overlords. An early connection with Cuban professional baseball came with Molina's participation on the roster of the Key West team that toured in Havana in 1890. Four years later he would debut as a league player (mostly a catcher) and compete for a dozen seasons on a half-dozen different ball clubs. Molina was not much of a hitter — compiling a lifetime batting average well below

.200 — and certainly not an outstanding player by much of any measure. But he would nonetheless earn a spot in the Cuban hall of fame for his role in managing the Cuban Stars barnstorming teams of the 1910s and '20s and also directing the 1923–24 Santa Clara nine considered almost universally to have been the best Cuban League outfit ever. It was Molina, also, who brought most of the top U.S. black stars to play winter seasons in the Cuban League during the heyday of separate but never quite equal North American black baseball.

A crowning jewel for both Linares and Molina was the final important "American season" staged at the end of 1920. In reality that fall saw two American seasons — the first being sold as a pre–American season — and they were collectively the biggest sensation that Cuban baseball had yet witnessed. The first short exhibition series was staged during the week be-

A trio of big league pitchers on the staff of the mid-fifties Cuban League club Cienfuegos Elefantes: Camilo Pascual (left), Pedro Ramos, and Raúl Sánchez.

ginning on October 9 and the action pitted black Cubans (Molina's Cuban Stars club) against white Cubans (a team called the All Leagues consisting of players light-skinned enough to play in organized baseball up north). The blacks won the best-of-three showdown which was plagued by rain, but the teams proved quite evenly matched. Then a week later, McGraw's (mostly) New York Giants arrived with Miguel Angel González already in tow and the sensational Babe Ruth (a Yankee not a Giant) reportedly on the way. Cuban players from the pre–American season were redistributed on the local rosters of Almendares and Habana for the upcoming heavily hyped exhibitions against the celebrity big leaguers.

George Herman Ruth had revolutionized American baseball with his almost incomprehensible 54-homer performance in the just-concluded big league season. The Babe would undoubtedly be the big attraction of the two-week barnstorming extravaganza. But there were other highlights even before the Babe landed a bit behind schedule in Havana harbor. Much hoopla surrounded the October 15 arrival by steamer of McGraw and his players, who would be housed in the Hotel Plaza (an establishment still operating on the *Parque Central* and maintaining much of its past appearance). The games were launched on October 17 and the big leaguers survived in a close 1–0 11-inning opening match. Local journalists were soon touting the Cubans as clear equals of the big leaguers. The Giants were short on pitching and had in tow only one of their three 20-game winners. The advantage seemed to swing back and forth and bad weather marred some games. One highlight came when Oscar Tuero (pitching for Habana but a St. Louis Cardinal in the summer) blanked the Giants 1–0 in a game in which the victorious locals only had a single

hit off of Giants ace Jesse Barnes. On October 24 there was a spectacular tie game which drew the biggest crowd of the tour.

Ruth made a most dramatic entrance into the series on October 30 when he arrived at the park directly from the docks — wife in tow — and promptly smacked a pair of long hits, a savage triple and booming double. Through the remaining games the Babe would put on considerably fewer such power displays. The huge playing expanse in Almendares Park worked against the Babe's long-ball heroics. There would, however, be one long Ruthian home run blast that was reported as one of the most prodigious ever seen on the island. The highlight for Cuban fans was undoubtedly the game of questionable seriousness when Torriente drew headlines with his three homers off low-quality pitching. But there were mostly disappointments surrounding the Babe himself. Ticket prices were raised upon his arrival to meet the $2000 he earned from each game. A result was that these games drew less attendance than the ones before Babe put in an appearance. The incorrigible big leaguer also gambled and drank away most of his earnings between games and was rarely in sufficient shape the afternoon after such binges for any serious play. The Giants team as a whole seemed to show the effects of constant partying for most of the games. And a final contest in which Ruth refused to take part turned into a fiasco when the Cuban all-stars took a page from the clowning big leaguers and stuck three local jai alai players (wearing their *cestas* rather than gloves) into the lineup at first, center and right. But on the whole it was all a most glorious month for Cuban baseball which — as a result of the visit by McGraw and his entourage — now seemed to have arrived on a somewhat grander stage.

Ruth's visit had still another less calculable impact. The

head-to-head battles between Cuban and American stars were an obvious crowd draw and it now seemed to make sense to attempt bringing an entire American ball club to the island to perform throughout a full Cuban League season. McGraw's big league Giants were thus quickly followed in December by the Bacharach Giants of the Negro leagues circuit. Again things didn't work quite as smoothly as Linares had hoped they might. The "Colored" Giants were certainly as loaded with talent as their big-league namesakes — perhaps even more so. Oscar Charleston, Louis Santop and Cannonball Redding headed a roster that also featured Dick Lundy, Pud Flournoy and Charles Blackwell. And these Giants had Cubans on the club that also toured with them regularly in the summer. It was assumed that fans would flood Almendares Park to see either Almendares Alacranes or Habana Leones battle the club that was American in name if not entirely in roster, even when the Eternal Rivals were not now facing each other. But the Giants did not provide much hoped-for opposition and therefore much interest for discerning patrons. They won but four games in the first round and Redding was bombed on several occasions. Things got even worse in the second half-season. By mid–January most of the Giants were returning piecemeal to the States and the league dropped the team altogether on January 13, again leaving Amendares and Habana in finish out the season by themselves.

From the mid-twenties on there were also a number of other failed seasons. The problem continued to be the inability of Linares and his partners to find a third and fourth team to stoke fan interest and balance the rivalry between Almendares and Habana. As we have seen, one imbalanced season (1923–24) was shortened due to a lopsided pennant race. Shifting teams and rosters, reshuffled schedules, and truncated seasons were a sad legacy under Abel Linares and his cronies throughout much of the decade of the twenties. Players were constantly shuffled from one roster to another in a manner that today seems to have foreshadowed the free-agency legacy of modern-era professional baseball. Top black players were sometimes brought to town in mid-season (like Pop Lloyd with Habana in 1923) or left before the schedule was played out (like Satchel Paige with Santa Clara the same year). From one season to the next the lineups for Almendares and Habana were never even close to the same and this fact alone had to hurt ball club loyalties and thus also box office profits. Luque and Dihigo showed up on different teams every couple of years. And the opposing teams that were lined up to battle the "Eternal Rivals" were never the same from winter to winter either.

One long-lasting effect of such juggling by Linares to solve the always-present third team situation would be the birth in the '20s of the newly minted Marianao and Cienfuegos ball clubs, two teams destined to become future fixtures in the league's stability a couple of decades down the road. Marianao took its first bow in the very season when Santa Clara also first came on the scene. The Marianao debut was every bit as much of a success that first season of 1922–23 as the Santa Clara entry was a disappointment; the former walked

off with an early surprise pennant while the latter dropped out early due to a dispute involving a single forfeited ballgame. The new Marianao club was located in the identically named neighborhood on the outskirts of Havana which was also the setting for Oriental Park — an aging venue that was used mostly as a horse racing track but could also double as a makeshift ballpark when needed. While Santa Clara would rely on Negro leagues imports recruited by Molina, Marianao under Baldomero Acosta would be stocked with homegrown Cuban talent. Headlining the Marianao roster was player-manager Merito Acosta, crack shortstop Pelayo Chacón, and respected catcher José María Fernández.

Marianao may well have been the bigger immediate hit with its final three-game victory margin over Habana. Yet a year later, when Santa Clara proved such a sudden powerhouse that the season was suspended in mid-stream, the Marianao entry suddenly appeared quite expendable. When the Gran Premio season was launched after an early halt to regular league action, the Marianao players were distributed on the rosters of other Havana teams. Marianao would subsequently suffer from an off-and-on status in the league across the next decade and on into the World War II years. But by the mid-forties, fortified by players like Miñoso, Julio Bécquer and Asdrúbal Baró, the previously luckless club would finally become a true staple of the annual Cuban League competitions.

Cienfuegos first came on the scene (in 1926–27) four winters after the debut of Marianao. This team, initially called *Petroleros* (Oil Drillers) before eventually adopting its more recognizable nickname of *Elefantes*, would at first be located in the coastal city of the same name and thus again served as part of Linares's ambitious plans to bring league action into the provinces to the east of the capital. The fortunes of the Cienfuegos B.B.C. were also at first tied to those of the earlier team in Santa Clara. It seemingly made sense to have two teams located in Las Villas Province, if only to facilitate the travel schedules of the Havana-based clubs. Molina was again assigned the task of building and directing this new entry, as he had with Santa Clara, and his approach would be largely the same. The team makeup would therefore also be eerily parallel and Negro league imports (Cool Papa Bell, Willie Wells, and homegrown Luis Tiant Senior) anchored the heart of the early Cienfuegos rosters.

Cienfuegos on-field and off-field fortunes at first largely paralleled those of the new Marianao ball club. Molina's new team won a pennant in only its third year while managed by Pelayo Chacón, one of the circuit's best shortstops of the twenties who was now reaching the end of an illustrious playing career. But Cienfuegos also was saddled with a small stadium and thus (like Santa Clara in quaint La Boulanger Park) suffered the handicap of ongoing attendance problems. Several seasons found the team starting a campaign but never finishing — a fate that befell the club only a year after its first pennant, when the entire league shut down early due to limited fan interest at Havana's new La Tropical Stadium. The debut season for the *Petroleros* was also a complete disaster as the team which began the 1926–27 campaign lasted a mere 13 games before crumbling in financial wreckage. By 1931 the ill-fated Cienfuegos club was dropped from the roster of teams altogether by panicky league management. When the team returned to the fray in the fall of 1939 it would represent the southern port city in name only since the reborn Cienfuegos *Elefantes* of the 1940s and 1950s played all their games in Havana, as for that matter did the entire league.

Abel Linares would suffer one of his biggest blows with the unfolding 1927 season. Miguel Angel González and Adolfo Luque — already two of the giants of the league — defected from the scene that year and staged their own tournament at the new stadium on the grounds of the University of Havana. The Campeonato Triangular actually turned out to be one of the most colorful seasons of this particular era of Cuban baseball. The new stadium was a unique structure with its unbalanced grandstand layout and sloping bleachers: the grandstand and both dugouts lined the first base side while steep temporary bleachers were erected on a hillside along the third base line. To avoid legal hassles the defecting ball clubs changed names and were known as Leones, Alacranes and Marianao, but the first two teams (those headed of González and Luque) did little else to hide their former identities and thus damage their widespread fan appeal. And fans knew that the teams playing on the university grounds under Miguel Angel and his rival Luque were in truth the real "Eternal Rivals" even if they sported disguised identities and had to dip into the island's extensive amateur ranks to fill out their rosters with new players. The substitute Habana club would also occasionally be called Havana Reds, using the English spelling because Linares maintained legal claim to the Habana B.B.C. If the rival championship did not represent enough of a disaster for Linares, this was also the year that the decade-old Almendares Park II was largely destroyed by natural disaster when a vicious hurricane struck in the midst of the regular Cuban League season (the "official" one being run by Linares). The wrecked park was hastily rebuilt in a matter of days but it was never the same venue during its final few seasons at the end of the decade.

By the beginning of the thirties the league had finally settled on the four-team structure it would more or less keep for the duration of its lifespan. The introduction of a team in Cienfuegos was an important innovation and a tentative step in the direction of the still-persistent dream of expanding a viable Cuban League beyond the limiting confines of the capital city. The Cienfuegos pennant triumph of 1930 indeed accomplished the short-term goal of spreading at least a degree of fandom's rooting interests outside of Habana proper. But it was a dream perhaps well ahead of its time in an era still faced with primitive transportation infrastructure and limited media access. Cienfuegos would therefore not be much of a success at the box office until all the teams' games were moved into Havana's larger playing venues. But for all that, Cienfuegos and Marianao were now a permanent part of the league picture. And especially the Cienfuegos ball club provided some of the best action and biggest stars of early thirties. One of the

Slugging Cienfuegos Elefantes catcher Rafael "Ray" (Sam) Noble, a native Cuban who also caught for the 1951 National League champion New York Giants.

league's most storied moments, in fact, took place when American Jimmy "Cool Papa" Bell smacked an unprecedented three homers on a single afternoon in the tiny Aída Park grounds located in the pristine coastal city.

Santa Clara enjoyed a sudden revival in the mid and late thirties with a trio of league pennants, the first under the guidance of Martín Dihigo who not only managed a pennant-winner in 1935–36 but also posted a unique triple-crown as the league's top batter and pitcher. Another future hall-of-fame, Lázaro Salazar, would manage the final two of these Santa Clara breakthroughs with runaway victories in 1938 and 1939, the first by a four-game margin over Almendares and the second by a five-game spread over Habana. The Santa Clara club was now known as "*Los Pilongos*" ("The Locals") and again was directed by a manager who doubled as a pitcher (3–0 in 1938) and position player (Salazar hit .318 as a first baseman in 1938 and paced the league in two-base knocks a season later.

Some have argued that the two teams organized under Salazar at the close of the 1930s could even match the phenomenal Santa Clara clubs of 1923 and 1924 and the argument is not altogether unreasonable. This team like those *Leopardos* clubs of Tinti Molina during an earlier decade were built largely on Negro league talent, both imported Americans and native Cubans. Ray "Jabao" Brown was the staff ace with a 12–5 mark in 1938 and an 11–7 ledger during the 1939 title run. Sam Bankhead anchored the infield at the shortstop post and dominated league hitters in 1938 with bests in average (.366), runs (47) and base hits (89). The outfield boasted Santos Amaro, Jacinto Roque, and once again a now-aging but still-agile Alejandro Oms. Bill "Cy" Perkins handled the catching duties in the first of these pinnacle seasons and was then replaced by the immortal Josh Gibson who tore up the league in 1939 as home run champion (11) and as the backbone of a fearsome batting order that also featured league leaders in av-

erage (Tony Castaño), base hits (Santos Amaro), doubles (Salazar) and RBI (Amaro).

Lázaro Salazar ("The Prince of Belén") himself would join the list of true Cuban immortals with his handful of strong seasons spread throughout the thirties in both Habana (winter) and Mexico (summer). Salazar, a lefty on offense and defense) was a truly versatile ballplayer like so many other Cuban stars before him. Like Méndez, Pedroso, Torriente, Oms, Dihigo or Cocaina García he was a talented hitter and infielder-outfielder as well as a crack pitcher. And he gained a considerable measure of fame as a manager when he wasn't turning heads as a star player. Nearly as effective in Mexico as on his native island, he won 112 games on the mound as a Mexican Leaguer and also compiled a .334 career batting average over fifteen seasons as a slick first sacker and durable if not overly swift fly chaser. It might be reasonable to contend that Lázaro Salazar was a true left-handed Dihigo, even if he was a bit less powerful at bat and more limited in his overall versatility as a southpaw thrower.

The Cuban League entered its final two decades during the war years of the early 1940s with an increasing presence of big leaguers on Havana-based team rosters. Once integration came to organized baseball in the shadows of World War II and the North American Negro leagues fell by the wayside, Cuban winter league baseball became more of a big league farm operation than an escape for unappreciated and barred black stars from up north. By the late forties names of imported Cuban leaguers would have been largely familiar to any big league fans perusing winter circuit box scores: Sal Maglie (Giants and Cienfuegos), Dick Sisler (Phillies and Habana), Max Lanier (Cardinals and Almendares), George Hausmann (Giants and Almendares), Hank Thompson (Giants and Habana), Canadian Paul Calvert (Indians and Marianao), Don Richmond (Phillies and Cienfuegos), Lou Klein (Cardinals and Habana) and Sam Jethroe (Braves and Almendares) among others.

Few imported North American ballplayers — especially those not tied to the Negro leagues — would ever enjoy a season in Havana like the one Dick Sisler experienced in the first winter after the close of the bloody World War. Angel Torres (*La Leyenda del Béisbol Cubano*, 132) refers to the 1945–46 season as "The Year of Dick Sisler" and that might not be an overstatement. Sisler, son of big league Hall of Famer George Sisler, paced the circuit that winter in only a single category, that of home runs. But he did bat over .300 for second-place Habana and posted other impressive numbers, including 44 hits, 27 runs scored, and an equal number driven home. The highlight for the lefty-swinging Sisler came with three gigantic homers in a single game against eventual champion Cienfuegos on January 24. The three round trippers and an additional single all came off deliveries of future big league ace Sal 'the Barber' Maglie. And Sisler might have had a fourth homer that day had not *Elefantes* manager Dolf Luque ordered a free pass for the slugging first sacker during his final trip to the plate. Sisler had to settle for a feat only accomplished once before in Cuban League action — more than a decade and a half

Lorenzo "Chiquitín" Cabrera, heavy-hitting Marianao first sacker who was also the champion batter during the 1949 Caribbean Series winter league championships staged in Havana's Cerro Stadium.

earlier by Negro Leaguer Cool Papa Bell. Sisler's greatest career moment certainly would always remain another homer which won a pennant for the Whiz Kid Phillies in Ebbets Field at the end of the 1950 National League season. But the day in Cuba in 1946 could not have ranked too far behind.

For Roberto González Echevarría, and likely for others, the season played throughout the winter months of 1946–47 (on the eve of Jackie Robinson's historic Brooklyn debut and on the heels of the tragic death of Alejandro Oms in a local hospital for the indigent) represents a true highpoint in the long saga of Cuban League battles. That winter indisputably witnessed one of the most dramatic two-team pennant races ever to grip the interests of island fans. And perhaps also of some of the more memorable individual performances, like Cocaina García winning ten games for a record fourth time. It was also the year that saw the debut of a sparkling new 30,000-seat stadium built in the central Cerro district and thus popularly referred to as El Cerro Stadium as well as Havana's Gran Stadium.

The inaugural game at the new venue came on October 25, 1946, and found Almendares overpowering Cienfuegos 9–1. Roberto Ortiz smacked the park's first homer, while Jorge Comellas bested Venezuelan Alejando Carrasquel in the pitching category. The historic match was quickly overshadowed, however, by an exceptionally exciting season — one spiced by the additional fact that it was played against the backdrop of a rival league that was now holding forth in the recently abandoned La Tropical Stadium and also a few other nearby venues. This second league called itself the Liga de la Federación and provided refuge for a contingent of Cuban big leaguers who were unwilling to risk their standing in organized baseball by playing alongside possible "ineligibles" from Jorge Pasquel's outlaw Mexican League. There were indeed many so-called "ineligibles" performing in El Cerro that first winter of the new ballpark. When an agreement was eventually inked between organized baseball and the Cuban League in June 1947 the banned players (those performing in Cerro Stadium in 1946–47) suddenly had no choice but to retreat to a separate league of their own in La Tropical the following winter. To clarify the obvious confusion, the "ineligibles" or banned players performed in the regular Cuban League in Gran (Cerro) Stadium in 1946–47, then fled to the alternative league at La Tropical for 1947–48. Eligible players (a small handful only) who had feared playing in Cerro Stadium in 1946–47 returned to the sanctioned Cuban League a year later when the banned ballplayers had all hastily retreated to La Tropical.

Against this confusion, the "official" Cuban League season which opened in October of 1946 soon was providing a true dilly of a pennant race. This was the season that historian González Echevarrá in *The Pride of Havana* would anoint as the best ever in league annals and a true apogee moment for the nation's sporting legacy. The significance of the season in the broad view can be debated — it is more likely that nothing has ever gripped the entire island quite the way that Olympic gold-medal performances by the national team would in 1990s and 2000s. But it was certainly an exciting

campaign nonetheless. In the end Almendares staged a furious rally at season's end behind the pitching of native lefty Agapito Major (quaintly dubbed "Triple Feo" or "Trice Ugly" for his homely visage) and big league southpaw Max Lanier. Lanier of the St. Louis Cardinals was one of the "ineligibles" who had performed for Pasquel's circuit in Mexico. Almendares captured 13 of its last 14 outings, including the final two over Habana behind brilliant outings by Mayor and Lanier. It was without doubt a breathtaking finish and one that spurred always near-the-boiling-point fan loyalties surrounding the two "Eternal Rivals" to a near-fever pitch.

While a most memorable season was taking place in the new Gran Stadium del Cerro, Cuban fans could also enjoy a most unusual rival campaign in the long-popular Tropical Stadium. Organized baseball's threat to ban Americans or Cubans who had participated in Pasquel's Mexican League (along with those who later competed against them) forced veteran Cuban players hoping to protect their professional eligibility back in the States to form a second league of their own. The new circuit opened with three teams, one representing Havana (called the Reds) and playing in the now empty former park near the banks of the Almendares River in the Marianao district, and two in outlying Matanzas and Santiago de Cuba. A fourth club was added in the provincial capital of Camagüey for the second half of the season. The bold venture was not very successful, despite the attempts to utilize the colors and logos of the "Eternal Rivals" by teams called the Habana Reds and Oriente (the Santiago Club), with the latter sporting Almendares Blue. There was also the selling point of the pastoral setting of La Tropical Stadium, of course, along with games played by the Matanzas club at the historic Palmar del Junco grounds. It was in fact Matanzas, under player-manager Silvio Garcia, that was the surprise of the circuit, taking the championship in a single playoff game at the end of December as the league put an early end to its sagging venture. The hastily added Cienfuegos team which entered for an announced but never-completed second "etapa" only lasted a few weeks and played only a dozen games.

A year later the Cuban ballplayers with organized baseball connections were back in the "official" winter league at Cerro Stadium, while it was the shunned Mexican Leaguers like Tomás de la Cruz, Adrián Zabala, Andrés Fleitas, and Americans Sal Maglie and Danny Gardella, who were seeking refuge at La Tropical in what was now called the Liga Nacional. But if the short-lived rebel Federación League of 1946–47 had an important role to play it was undoubtedly the fact that it served as stage for a winter league professional debut by long-time local amateur hero Conrado Marrero. Marrero hurled for the Santiago-based team and was the circuit's most successful pitcher with 8 wins and a microscopic 1.94 ERA. When the short-season "outlaw" circuit ended early, Marrero fled in January to the established league and signed on with Almendares. A year later the future big leaguer had already begun writing new legends with a 12–2 ledger and an even stinger 1.12 ERA.

Once the bulk of Cuba's major leaguers and minor

leaguers had returned to the league sanctioned by organized baseball, the bonds between Cuban and U.S. professional leagues had been firmly cemented, with the big league clubs now holding most of the regulatory powers. On the surface the Cuban League seemed to function as usual, featuring a tight race in which Mike González's Habana Leones edged the Almendares forces by a single game but also finishing only four up on Cienfuegos managed by former Yankees pitching great Lefty Gomez. It was again an unusual winter league scene in Havana, with attention once more divided by the second competition being staged in La Tropical Stadium and featuring players of star quality now banned by major League baseball for their participation in Jorge Pasquel's rebel Mexican League. And the separate Liga Nacional produced some exceptional performances while also featuring Luque and Nap Reyes as managers and some of the best-known Cuban players of the past decade: the list included, among others, Bobby Estalella, Carlos and Heberto Blanco, Natilla Jiménez, Sandy Consuegra, Santiago Ullrich, Adrián Zabala, and Roberto Ortiz. While America black star Harry Kimbro was setting a new record for base hits with 104 in the sanctioned league at El Cerro, homegrown Avelino Cañizares was knocking out 114 safeties in the "ineligibles" league at La Tropical.

A landmark event at the outset of the 1946 season had of course been the gala opening of a brand new stadium in downtown Havana. This structure would remain home to Cuban baseball for more than a half-century and is today still the nation's pride forty-five years after the revolution. With the demise of almost all pre–1950 big league venues, the venerable Havana ballpark becomes an increasing treasure with each passing season. The stadium today looks much as it did during its maiden days early in 1947 and throughout the final decade and a half of the professional Cuban League. The biggest change in appearance came in 1971 with the enclosure of the outfield and the construction of cement bleachers to increase capacity to above 55,000 fans. There was also a name change that accompanied the reconstruction on the eve of the November 1971 Amateur World Series matches. But today's visitor to what has for the past 35 years been known as Estadio Latinoamericano still feels he/she is sitting in a ball park that belongs more to an era now a half-century and more in the past.

* * *

The conflicts and upheavals surrounding the 1947–48 campaign and its two separate championships seemed to demonstrate beyond debate that the Cuban League was coming under the increasing control of U.S. organized baseball. For some — mainly those who harbored the dream of Havana as a potential big league outpost — this was perhaps altogether good news. But it was not a welcomed sight for those who may have valued the independent spectacle and native traditions that marked Cuba's own special version of a shared national pastime. Earlier the complaint always had been that too many Americans filled up Cuban League rosters. Now it was also clear that the entire Cuban season was being designed to serve

organized baseball and that the Americans were largely in control of what would and would not happen during each winter Cuban baseball season.

The Americanization of Cuban winter baseball was in one sense only part and parcel of the lust for all things American that came with the prosperity following the end of the world war, that boomed after the bloodless coup of 1952 that put Fulgencio Batista in power, and that led eventually, if ironically, to the Castro revolution and thus the death knell of Havana's professional baseball scene. Cuban League uniforms were upgraded to big league standards, Almendares began donning grey visitors' jersey that were almost exact replicas of those sported by the Philadelphia A's, and (more telling) the increased number of imported American big league farmhands included Triple A regulars and big leaguers with 45-days or less of service.

The campaigns of the 1950s, taken as a whole, constitute an era of steady decline for Cuban baseball. There was an inevitable drop-off in on-field heroics after the heyday of the glorious forties — just as the Golden Age of the teens and the early twenties was inevitably followed by cycles of decline throughout the late 1920s and early thirties. The larger-than-life bat-wielding and glove-toting Cuban heroes of the previous two generations were no longer in evidence. There were quality local stars to be sure — Miñoso, Marrero, Amoros, soon Pascual and Ramos — and with the lifting of the color barrier in organized baseball several of them were now playing in the majors. But Marrero for all his colorful antics was not a Méndez or a Luque, or even a Ramón Bragaña or Cocaina García. There was no match for Dihigo or Torriente or Oms or Champion Mesa. Pascual and Ramos were talented big leaguers by the late fifties but nonetheless didn't have the aura of the great Negro leaguers who once flooded the league. Attendance was now again on the slide after the peak seasons of the mid and late forties; perhaps this had in large part to do with an over-saturated market. Winter play and its associated American season were now being partially diluted by the existence of summertime minor league franchises in Havana, first in the form of the Class C-B Havana Cubans and later in the guise of the AAA International League Sugar Kings.

What Luque was for the Cuban winter baseball scene in the 1920s, Dihigo in the thirties, and the pair of Garcías (Silvio and Cocaina) in the early '40s, that was what Pedro (Perucho) Formental became for diehard Cuban fans throughout the late-forties and early-fifties. Formental was the best thing the Cuban League had going in the years immediately after the world war — at least in terms of a heaving-hitting offensive star. There were others on the scene like charismatic Nap Reyes and flamboyant Orestes Miñoso and muscle-bound Roberto Ortiz. Willie Miranda was a spectacular glove man at short as was Héctor Rodríguez at the hot corner. But Formental was the most luminous local star and the one who put up the biggest numbers and most talked-about individual performances. For old-timers, however, "Perico" Formental was far too much of a "postalita" or hotdog in his style of play. (He fed his own legend by boasting to the press of his potential as a big leaguer and by insisting he be called "Perico 300" in reference to his batting level.) That style did nonetheless produce some big results — a career line of 746 hits, 106 doubles, 47 triples and 56 homers during 13 seasons, mostly with Habana. He would eventually own the league's career home run mark for lefty-swingers. (The right-hander's record of 71 would set by future Giants catcher Ray Noble, a black Cuban whose name was pronounced "NO-blay.") Clearly the smaller-dimension ballpark and longer schedules of the 1940s and '50s were enough for mid-century batters to outstrip earlier stars in home run hitting. Perucho also tied Alejandro Crespo for the career RBI mark at 362, a standard Noble would also surpass a few years down the road.

The portly lefty with the pencil-thin moustache would star as well in Mexico (where he posted four .300-plus seasons for three clubs in the summer seasons of the mid-forties) and later with the AAA Sugar Kings. Pedro Formental was one of those ill-starred players a bit too old once integration finally came to have any chance of cracking the majors and thus making good on his boasts of big league fame. Yet from 1945 to 1955 he was the obvious choice for most baseball-crazed Havana youngsters looking for a home-grown idol on whom to hang their dreams.

A notable sidebar to the Cuban League action of the 1950s was the experimental Caribbean Series playoff between winter league champions that was held at the end of each season and on the eve of major league spring training. The inaugural competition was held in February 1949 and not surprisingly staged in Havana's showcase Cerro Stadium. It would prove, the first time around, to be an all–Cuban show, with Almendares under the direction of Fermín Guerra copping all six of its games and thus the first *Serie del Caribe* title. Fittingly enough a popular Cuban ballplayer would also prove the tournament's dominant individual star. Almendares easily outclassed the field with double victories over Cervecería Caracas (Venezuela), Spur Cola (Panama) and Mayagüez (Puerto Rico) and ran up such scores as 16–1 (over Cervecería Caracas behind the hurling of Marrero) and 11–4 (over Mayagüez behind Agapito Mayor). It was the veteran Mayor who seized upon this tournament to register the highlight moment of his brilliant winter season career. The veteran southpaw became the first and only hurler to win three games in a single tourney, with two victories coming in short relief and the third as a starter in the romp over Puerto Rico. For all his occasional brilliance in Cuba, Mayor would never taste a moment of major league action. Yet on this single occasion he proved invincible against the cream of the crop among winter league all-stars.

Two additional *Serie del Caribe* tournaments were held in Havana in 1953 and again in February 1957 and neither proved quite so successful for the home forces. These events were nonetheless again the scenes of some most memorable moments involving Cuban teams and Cuban ballplayers. The 1953 tournament offered something of a surprise as Puerto Rico's entry, the Santurce Crabbers, stole the show by reclaiming the title it had garnered two years earlier in Caracas. San-

One of the greatest southpaws in Cuban professional and amateur league history, Almendares ace Agapito Mayor bore the uncomplimentary nickname of "Triple Feo" (Thrice Ugly), a commentary on his facial features and not his mound style.

turce, with future big leaguers Junior Gilliam and Vic Power in the infield and former Negro leaguer Willard Brown smashing a record four homers, was only the second club to win all of its games at the event and the first winter league team to repeat as champion. Miguel Angel González's Habana team — fresh off its last Cuban league pennant — finished in second place and benefited from the .560 batting of Pedro Formental. Four years later Marianao managed by Nap Reyes would restore lost Cuban honor in the final Caribbean Series event staged on home turf in Havana. Miñoso would prove the batting star with seven clutch RBI and big-league import Jim Bunning would steal the show on the mound with victories in both his starts. Another big leaguer named Sammy Drake also made noise for the Cubans as batting champ with a stellar 10-for-20 performance.

Few could have imaged at the time that this would be the final hurrah for this prestigious event on Cuban soil, but the very fact that it was Marianao now carrying the Cuban banner might have signaled that storm clouds were forming on the horizon. All seemed well enough at the time, however, and Cuban leaguers took the next three tournament titles on foreign grounds in San Juan (Marianao), Caracas (Almendares) and Panama City (Cienfuegos).

Cuban forces would dominate in seven of the twelve Caribbean Series tournaments convened between 1949 and 1960. There has always been speculation about what this tournament might have become in subsequent decades had Cuba in fact remained a vital part of the year-end winter league playoff ritual. But that was not meant to be as the doors to professional baseball on the island would soon slam shut and the existing roster of four thriving winter circuits in the Caribbean Basin region would overnight be trimmed to three. (Panama would also lose its winter circuit in the early sixties, but replacements soon emerged with the Dominicans switching to winter sessions in 1955–56, and with Mexico's Pacific Coast League waiting in the wings throughout several name changes between the late fifties and late sixties.) One immediate result of the upcoming termination of professional play in Cuba was the sudden suspension of the Caribbean Series for a full decade. And when the event returned (February 1970 in Caracas, with the Dominicans and Mexicans joining the fold) it would no longer feature the showcase Cuban teams that had been its biggest boasting point for most of the fifties.

There were indeed highlights throughout the "Fabulous Fifties" decade, for all the upheaval off the field and all the signs of doom and gloom surrounding the league itself. Agapito Mayor not only performed brilliantly in the showcase 1949 Caribbean Series but also contributed on the mound for Almendares across several subsequent campaigns. "Triple Feo"

Infielder Napoleón "Nap" Reyes starred in the forties-era amateur league with the University of Havana, played in the Cuban League with Cienfuegos, briefly tasted the big leagues with the New York Giants, and managed the International League Cuban Sugar Kings after the AAA franchise was rudely relocated to Jersey City.

hung on until 1953, pitching 54 complete games in total, winning 68 of 132 decisions, and working artfully out of the bullpen at career's end. Camilo Pascual nearly outshone Mayor on the Caribbean Series scene when he logged a record five complete games in three different appearances; Pascual did outdistance Mayor's earlier achievements on home turf with back-to-back league MVP honors in 1956 and 1957. Minnie Miñoso (also a two-time MVP) returned each winter to play for Marianao while his major league fame spread during summer seasons up north.

Other Cuban big leaguers stoked local pride and were thus surefire drawing cards in Cerro Stadium. Pascual and sidekick Pete Ramos were the most notable among them as they paced Cienfuegos to a final pair of league titles. The duo also became front line pitchers with the Washington Senators and by 1961 seemed to be still approaching their destined big league potentials. Sandalio Consuegra also made a smash at home and abroad by hurling 162 innings for Marianao in 1950 and topping the American League in winning percentage for the Chisox four years later. Limonar Martínez hurled the final Cuban League no-hitter on February 15, 1950, for Marianao versus Almendares. And Sandy Amoros was a substantial hero in Havana — winning a batting title in 1953 — several years before emerging as a Brooklyn icon with his single momentous outfield defensive play to save the 1955 World Series finale at Yankee Stadium.

Interest was nonetheless rapidly waning on the Havana ballpark scene as the ongoing rebellion against Fulgencio Batista's increasingly repressive government finally approached its surprising climax. It also didn't help fortunes in the sagging league that Cienfuegos and Marianao now possessed the most talented and most successful teams. The Eternal Rivals were suddenly the weak sisters of winter play as Miguel Angel's club was a .500 or below outfit every season after 1955–56, and Almendares could only hoist one pennant during its final half-dozen campaigns, even if the Scorpions remained a bit more competitive. Marianao captured consecutive flags (1956, 1957) for the first time in club history under manager Nap Reyes, mainly thanks to slugging from imports Milt Smith and Solly Drake and natives Miñoso and Julio Bécquer. After one final hurrah by Almendares, Cienfuegos would next duplicate the feat during the league final two campaigns. Pascual was 15–5 on the hill in 1960 and Ramos next encored at 16–7 in 1961. At long last the tide had finally turned on the two popular teams that were rarely ever out of the money for more than a season or two at a time.

Habana didn't win another championship after 1953 and was only once a runner-up down the league's final eight-year home stretch. Miguel Angel González had briefly turned his club over to Luque in 1954, and then again to Fermín Guerra in 1959, as his own half-century league tenure creaked to a pathetic last-gasp windup. Cienfuegos boasted big leaguers Ramos, Pascual and Raúl Sánchez on the hill and thus owned the best pitching. While Formental was now over the hill and gone from the winter scene after 1955 (though he hung on with the summertime Sugar Kings), Miñoso had emerged as

Future big leaguer Julio Bécquer slides home safely for Marianao in mid-fifties Cuban League action versus Almendares at Havana Cerro Stadium.

a wildly popular star and he was still suiting up for Marianao until the league's final season. Miñoso's Tigers and the Pascual-Ramos-led Elephants were now ruling the roost and the old Habana-Almendares rivalry was unfortunately little more than tame nostalgia.

Once Fidel came to power the Cuban League entered a most tenuous period and the very future of the pro circuit suddenly seemed very much in doubt. The initial days after Fidel's forces entered Havana brought only minor disruption to the baseball scene; joyous celebrations and a bit of temporary chaos throughout the capital city resulted in suspension of a mere five days worth of games. In addition to the season that was in mid-course when Batista fled the island on New Years Day 1959, two more campaigns were destined to be played all the way to their scheduled conclusions. The first of these saw American and Canadian players with big league ties still performing on the island as usual, and among them were such names Rocky Nelson, Art Fowler, Marv Breeding,

George Altman and Tom Cheney. But by the time the 1960–61 season rolled around the Cuban League was strictly a local affair for the first time since the first decade of the century. The last season with no American ballplayers had been played way back in 1910 when there were only three clubs and a skimpy eighteen-game schedule. The handwriting was clearly on the wall, of course, before the final death-throes campaign of 1960–61. Increasingly tenuous relationships between Cuban baseball and organized baseball, arising in the face of Havana's political upheavals, would not be able to withstand the complete fracture between Washington and the new leftist-oriented Cuban government. But it also quickly became the stated goal of Fidel's new regime that sports should be a pillar of a reformed Cuban society, and also that those sports should be strictly of an amateur nature. The death knell had finally and perhaps even thankfully sounded for professional baseball in Cuba.

* * *

An important footnote to fading Cuban League glory was provided by two minor league franchises that spanned the fifteen seasons between World War II and the new regime destined to alter Cuban society, as well as Cuban baseball, once and for all. The Havana Cubans of the low-classification Florida International League, and Cuban (Havana) Sugar Kings of the AAA-class International League, together provide one of the final bittersweet chapters in the saga of Cuban professional baseball. Both teams enjoyed their brief successes and even pennant thrills when it came to championship-level play. The earlier club — the Class C and later Class B Havana Cubans — was the stronger representative of island baseball year-in and year-out over an eight-year span, even if it played at a lower classification. It was also the first mid-century club to re-ignite a long-standing island-held dream of a native Cuban team carrying the country's name and pride within the framework of professional organized baseball.

Cuba's entry into the world of organized baseball had a modest beginning in the middle forties with the Havana Cubans Class C ball club of the Florida International League. The team's debut came the summer before the completion of the new Cerro ballpark and the first season was played in the

Habana Leones southpaw ace Adrián Zabala warms up at Cerro Stadium in 1946. Zabala later had a big league cup of coffee with the National League New York Giants.

pastoral environs of La Tropical Stadium. Other league clubs included the Tampa Smokers, Miami Beach Flamingos, West Palm Beach Indians, Lakeland Pilots, Miami Sun Sox (the original franchises), plus later the St. Petersburg Saints, Ft. Lauderdale Braves (eventually the Key West Conchs), and re-named Miami Tourists. Operating as a C-level organization its first three summers, the expanded league moved up to B classification for the 1949 season.

It was a team stuffed full with local players and often a very good team indeed; playing in a park that could seat 35,000 and featuring such talent as future Washington Senators hurlers Conrado Marrero and Julio Moreno (1950 FIL ERA leader at 1.47), the Havana club of the late forties was more like a AAA outfit than a B-level club. Located in a major metropolis and enjoying radio coverage of their games on several Havana stations, the showcase franchise steadily drew 200,000-plus spectators, ran away with five straight (1946–1950) regular season banners under manager Oscar Rodríguez, and walked off with a pair of league post-season titles. Other native stalwarts with the Havana Cubans were infielder Gilberto Torres, outfielder Antonio Zardón, and shortstop Chino Hidalgo. Marrero was the team and league star for three seasons (1947–1949) when he ran up successive 20-win campaigns (25–6, 20–11, 25–8) and tossed a no-hitter in Cerro Stadium. Other top Cubans also played in the same league for other Florida-based franchises and included catcher Emilio Cabrera (Tampa), pitcher Octavio Rubert (West Palm Beach), 1946 home run champ Armando Valdés (West Palm Beach), and pitcher Ernesto "Chico" Morilla (Miami Beach). Havana's league domination slid dramatically after 1950, when Marrero and Moreno escaped to the big league club in Washington and Oscar Rodríguez abandoned the manager's seat on the bench. The operation nonetheless continued until it was set aside for the prospects of having a AAA franchise based in Havana in time for the 1954 International League season. The birth of the officially named Cuban Sugar Kings — the team was often labeled as Havana Sugar Kings in U.S. press accounts and later publications — coincided with the mid-season death of the lower-class FIL which could no longer survive once stripped of its showcase Havana franchise.

The Sugar Kings owned and operated by Bobby Maduro (who also had owned the Havana Cubans) sparked a dream — in the minds of some Cubans at least — that major league baseball in Havana was now only a small step away. Of course it was an entirely futile dream from the outset. A great baseball city indeed, Havana was nonetheless not a likely immediate choice as a big league venue during the decades before runaway major league expansion of the seventies and eighties and beyond. And the AAA club itself was only a moderate success, peaking with an average attendance of 4,067 (in a park that sat 33,000-plus) in its second season but plummeting to less than 1,100 by 1957 (while finishing sixth for a second straight season. The team on the field was not exceptionally strong for most of its seven years of existence and never finished higher than third place: twice third, twice fifth, once sixth and eighth in the nadir season of 1958. In brief, the Sugar Kings at times

Cuban Minor League Franchise History

HAVANA CUBANS (Florida International League)

Year	Record	Finish (Attendance)	Manager	Post-Season Results
Florida International League (Class C)				
1946	76–41 (.650)	First (202,875)*	Oscar Rodríguez	Round I (Lost to West Palm Beach 3 games to 2)
1947	105–45 (.700)	First (264,813)	Oscar Rodríguez	**Champions** over Tampa (4 games to 0)
1948	97–57 (.l630)	First (205,967)	Oscar Rodríguez	**Champions** over Tampa (4 games to 3)
Florida International League (Class B)				
1949	95–57 (.625)	First (226,293)	Oscar Rodríguez	Runner-up (Lost Finals to Tampa, 4 games to 0)
1950	101–49 (.673)	First (168,419)	Oscar Rodríguez	Runner-up (Lost Finals to Miami, 4 games to 1)
1951	68–71 (.489)	Fifth (83,051)	Adolfo Luque	Did Not Qualify
1952	76–77 (.497)	Fifth (81,463)	Fermín Guerra	Did Not Qualify
1953	63–69 (.477)	Fourth (23,460)	Armando Marsans	Did Not Qualify

CUBAN SUGAR KINGS (AAA International League)

Year	Record	Finish (Attendance)	Manager	Post-Season Results
International League (Class AAA)				
1954	78–77 (.503)	Fifth (295,453)	Reggie Otero	Did Not Qualify
1955	87–66 (.569)	Third (313,232)	Reggie Otero	Round I (Lost to Toronto, 4 games to 1)
1956	72–82 (.468)	Sixth (220,357)	Reggie Otero / Napoleón Reyes	Did Not Qualify
1957	72–82 (.468)	Sixth (84,320)	Napoleon Reyes	Did Not Qualify
1958	65–88 (.425)	Eighth (178,340)	Napoleón Reyes / Tony Pacheco	Did Not Qualify
1959	80–73 (.523)	Third (200,094)	Preston Gómez	**Champions** over Richmond (4 games to 2)**
1960	76–77 (.497)	Fifth (121,755)	Tony Castaño# / Napoleón Reyes	Did Not Qualify

*Attendance figures from Lloyd Johnson and Miles Wolff, *The Encyclopedia of Minor League Baseball*, Second Edition, 1997

**Also defeated American Association Champion Minneapolis Millers in Little World Series (4 games to 3)

#Franchise moved to Jersey City on July 13, 1960 (Napleón Reyes became manager at time of franchise relocation to Jersey)

Havana Minor League Franchise No-Hitters

May 12, 1946	Fernando Rodríguez (Havana Cubans) versus Miami (4–0, 7 innings)
July 12, 1947	Connie Marrero (Havana Cubans) versus Tampa (7–0)
May 28, 1949	Wilfred Roca (Havana Cubans) versus West Palm Beach (4–0)
August 17, 1958	Rudolfo Arias (Cuban Sugar Kings) versus Rochester (7–0, 7 innings)

seemingly couldn't draw flies even in one of Latin American baseball's hottest venues. Often the team played to a mostly empty grandstand despite numerous promotions aimed at propping up the team. One reason was likely that its two biggest native stars — Conrado Marrero and Pedro Formental — were well passed their peak seasons when they finally donned the uniform of the local minor league franchise.

Cuba's Sugar Kings would peak on the field of play if not at the gate in the very season when the opening stages of Fidel Castro's revolution against the Batista government came to its dramatic conclusion. The colorful but often lackluster Havana International League ball club would ironically make its only run towards a championship under manager Preston Gómez in the politically tense summer of 1959, on the heels of Batista's ouster and amidst considerable speculation about the future of professional baseball under the new regime. Against this backdrop a solid if unspectacular Sugar Kings lineup featuring Miguel Cuéllar and Raúl Sánchez on the hill, Elio Chacón and Cookie Rojas in the infield, and outfielders Tony González and Carlos Paula — all future big leaguers —

limped home in third place, nine games off the pace set by the front-running Buffalo Bisons. The Buffalo ball club ironically featured native Cuban Francisco "Panchón" Herrera, the league batting champion and MVP. But a surprising post-season spurt found the Havana club stoking island enthusiasms by first sweeping runner-up Columbus in the first playoff round and then gaining the International League title with a four-games-to-two triumph over the equally surprising fourth-place Richmond Virginians, a team managed by Steve Souchock and touting league pitcher-of-the-year Bill Short.

A dramatic Triple-A championship series — then known as the Junior World Series — would next unfold against the backdrop of the unsettled transition period that had brought Fidel Castro to power in Havana. The opponent, a Minneapolis Millers team managed by Gene Mauch and featuring future Red Sox notables Lu Clinton, Pumpsie Green and Carl Yastrzemski, had also been a surprise pennant-winner after finishing second in the American Association's Eastern Division. The championship round with Minneapolis took on a special character when cold weather up north caused relocation of games to Havana's favorable climate. Barely one thousand turned out under frigid conditions in Minnesota as the teams split the first two matches. Ninety-degree temperatures and a packed stadium (including as many as 3,000 armed Cuban infantry troops keeping order in the politically tense Cuban capital) greeted the teams for five final contests filled with more than their share of high drama. Two extra-inning wins place Havana on the verge of a championship before Minneapolis battled back in two straight to knot the series. The deciding seventh match went to the wire with Daniel Morejón's clutch single scoring pitcher Raúl Sánchez with the championship-clinching tally in the bottom of the ninth. A series opening in ice and snow in Minneapolis finished with fireworks in tropical Havana. It was indeed hot in the Cuban capital throughout the first week of October 1959, though much of the heat was not strictly a meteorological phenomenon.

Many stories of interference and intimidation of the American Association team would spread like wildfire in the U.S. press and continue for years to be part of the mythology of the dramatic Havana-Minneapolis showdown series. Certainly the dramatic seven-game series provided some of the most unusual if not outright bizarre moments of a Junior World Series saga that lasted from the early 1900s until the early seventies. Most of the tales attached to the Havana series were unfortunately mostly the stuff of exaggerations and even downright bending of the truth. Some have taken delight in calling this the only post-season baseball series in which submachine guns outnumbered bats. A favorite tale suggests that armed Castro troops stationed in the Havana dugout made slicing motions across their throats when Millers out-

fielder Tom Umphlett returned to the bench after an inning-ending catch. Gene Mauch would later claim his players feared for their lives if they won the deciding game. Good stories but little if any confirmation from local old-timers on the scene in the grandstands who have been (admittedly 45 years after the fact) interviewed by this author. What transpired indisputably was a dramatic on-field victory for the underdog Cubans. It was in retrospect also a fitting final swan song for professional baseball on the island of Cuba.

In the end the Sugar Kings were a final desperate gasp for professional baseball in a country now under control of Fidel Castro's communist-leaning government. Only half of the following International League season would unfold before organized baseball pulled the final plug on the six-year-old Havana franchise. The actual situation surrounding responsibility for the final dismantling of Bobby Maduro's Havana ball club remains clouded at best, and the final details may never be accurately sorted out. The bare facts are that the Havana club was spirited away (the official date was July 13, 1960) and placed in Jersey City while the club was on a mid-season road trip. A number of Cubans — including Raúl Sánchez, Orlando Peña, Leo Cárdenas and Mike Cuéllar — opted to remain in the States and pursue their promising professional careers; manager Tony Castaño (later a skipper in the new amateur league) and coach Reinaldo Cordeiro resigned and returned to their homeland. The loss of a prestigious baseball franchise was certainly a blow to Fidel and his neophyte government, but it seems to have had more to do with paranoia on the part of organized baseball than anything else. International League president Frank Shaughnessy reportedly had decided to move the club in mid-season "for the protection of the players" but there is also plenty of evidence (*The Pride of Havana*, 345–46) that the reaction by U.S. government and business officials to transitions gripping Havana in 1960 and 1961 was indeed a heavy-handed and largely miscalculated one.

A few months later the Cuban League, a winter staple for three-quarters of a century — would also take its final meek bow. The dream of Havana as a major league city, one that had unrealistically flowered only a few short years earlier, was now completely moribund. And with it a great era of Cuban baseball had also ended. It would not, however, mean a death knell for the sport on the island, since an equally glorious era lay just ahead. And with it another dream would soon awaken, this one having to do with a truly national baseball spreading everywhere across the baseball-crazy land known as the Pearl of the Caribbean.

Viewed from fifty years' distance, the saga of Cuban professional baseball

Lineup of 1954 International League Havana Sugar Kings includes two future unheralded Cuban big leaguers, pitcher Julio Moreno (second from left) and infielder Juan Delís (second from right).

remains a charming and engaging tale fleshed out with larger-than-life heroes, passionate pennant races, and a substantial dose of legendary on-field heroics. But it is also a tale infused by historians and aging fans alike with far more prominence than seemingly is its just due. Cuban old-timers, today residing in South Florida and cut off from their homeland for three decades or more, often look back fondly on the Havana teams and ball-playing heroes of their youth and cling to a shaky belief that Cuba's proud baseball traditions all fled the island in the same era which launched their own lives of exile.

But the facts regrettably dictate otherwise. Seventy-odd professional seasons preceding Cuba's mid-century socialist revolution were in truth but a minor chapter in the island's own rich baseball legacy, and they were also hardly more than an intriguing footnote in the larger chronicle of U.S. major league action. Cuban ballplayers reaching the majors during the half-century separating Almeida and Marsans from Fidel Castro were, on the whole, but second-rate journeymen; the Carlos Paulas, Tony Taylors, José Valdivielsos and Willie Mirandas were, as a lot, more noted for being colorful stereotypes than for providing significant contributions; perhaps only Luque (largely a single-season wonder for all his longevity), Miñoso (a colorful footnote to the fifties but a mere footnote nonetheless), and Pascual (who enjoyed his grandest big league seasons after the Cuban League folded) qualify as anything like big-league stars. The Cuban League itself attracted few front-line American big leaguers for anything more than brief barnstorming tours; Negro leaguers such as Oscar Charleston, Cool Papa Bell and Josh Gibson figure more prominently in Cuban League annals than do any notable major leaguers, and the Cuban circuit provided a steady stream of talent (Dihigo, Oms and Méndez come first to mind) for the renegade black circuits up north. But Negro league history of the 1920s, 30s and 40s was itself (justly or unjustly) a backwater of professional baseball interest. Even the most noted chronicler of Cuba's nineteenth and twentieth century professional game (Roberto González Echevarría writing in *The Pride of Havana*) readily acknowledges that for many of its seasons the Havana-based winter circuit remained little more than a second-rate shoe-string operation plagued by truncated schedules, a dwindling fan base, social and governmental instabilities, and an unhealthy amalgam of corrupt and incompetent club ownerships and league managements. In many of its heyday seasons the Cuban League was easily the number two baseball attraction around the island, widely trailing in popularity an endless stream of amateur, sugar mill and semi-professional ball clubs that boasted bigger fan followings and often also better lineups than the professional teams.

Cuba's early-twentieth-century pro league that finally limped to a complete halt in 1961 and was long celebrated for its population-splitting rivalry between legendary teams representing Almendares and Club Habana fails in the end to provide anything even resembling a center stage saga of Cuban baseball. More appropriately it might be viewed as an important prologue to the ultimate glories of the island's national pastime, which in large part unfolded in the final decades of the twentieth century. It was only after 1962 that the dream of a major island-wide baseball circuit was finally realized. It was across the same forty-year era that Cuba has enjoyed its long and unparalleled run atop the field in international amateur play. And it was in post-revolutionary Cuba that the island's top ballplayers finally shed their long-held image as mere journeyman big leaguers (an image inspired in the main by Connie Marrero, Willie Miranda and Pete Ramos) and replaced it with the far-more lustrous image (inspired with post-season heroics from Liván and El Duque Hernández and the equally stunning successes of Team Cuba versus the Baltimore Orioles) of highly prized aliens from a mysterious parallel baseball universe.

When the Cuban national team reached the finals of the World Baseball Classic it also demonstrated beyond debate that the organized league baseball produced for almost half a century after the revolution was of a far loftier level than that of the thirties, forties or fifties professional heyday. Even the most rabid supporter of old-time versions of the island national pastime could not reasonably imagine Cuban stars of the late Cuban pro league (Marrero, Formental, Bécquer, Miñoso, Ortiz, Amoros) besting all-stars from the majors (Mantle, Williams, Mays, Aaron, Ford). Such a fanciful dream would have to remain on hold for nearly fifty seasons, for the day when Paret, Gourriel, Cepeda, Urrutia and company would prove their considerable mettle against Dominican and Venezuelan all-stars the caliber of Albert Pujols, Bartolo Colón and Johann Santana, and in the process defeat two big league Cy Young winners en route to the WBC finals. Professional winter league baseball was never quite a center stage attraction of the lengthy Cuban baseball drama. But it was admittedly nonetheless an intriguing opening act for the more star-studded show to follow.

References and Suggested Readings

Díez Muro, Raúl. *Historia del base ball profesional de Cuba (Libro official de la Liga de Base Ball Profesional Cubana)*. Third Edition. Havana: no publisher indicated, 1949.

Gálvez y Delmonte, Wenceslao. *El base-ball en Cuba. Historia del base-ball en la Isla de Cuba, sin retratos de los principales jugadores y personas más caracterizadas en el juego citado, ni de ninguna otra.* Havana: Imprenta Mercantil de los Herederos de Santiago, S. Spencer, 1889.

González Echevarría, Roberto. *The Pride of Havana: A History of Cuban Baseball.* New York: Oxford University Press, 1999.

_____. "Peloteros cubanos: tres testimonios" in: *Nueva Sociedad* 154 (March-April 1998), 87–100.

_____. "The game in Matanzas: On the origins of Cuban baseball" in: *The Yale Review* 83:3 (1995), 62–91.

Holway, John B. *The Complete Book of Baseball's Negro Leagues: The Other Half of Baseball History.* Fern Park, Florida: Hastings House Publishers 2001.

_____. *Blackball Stars: Negro League Pioneers.* Westport, Connecticut: Meckler Books 1988.

Pérez, Louis A., Jr. "Between baseball and bullfighting: the quest for nationality in Cuba, 1868–1898" in: *The Journal of American History* 81:2 (September 1994), 493–517.

Riley, James A. *The Biographical Encyclopedia of the Negro Baseball Leagues*. New York: Carroll and Graf Publishers, 1994.

Rogosin Donn. *Invisible Men: Life in Baseball's Negro Leagues*. New York: Atheneum, 1983.

Rucker, Mark, and Peter C. Bjarkman. *Smoke: The Romance and Lore of Cuban Baseball*. New York: Total Sports Illustrated, 1999.

Torres, Angel. *Tres Siglos de Béisbol Cubano, 1878–2006*. Pico Rivera, CA: Best Litho, Inc. (self-published), 2006.

_____. *La Leyenda del Beisbol Cubano, 1878–1997*. Miami: Review Printers Inc. (self-published), 1996.

Season-by-Season Summaries of Professional Cuban League

Some of the season won-lost records for individual teams given below — especially for years of the 19th century — differ slightly from those provided in the standard handbook by Raúl Díez Muro entitled *Historia del Base Ball Profesional de Cuba* (Habana, 1949, Third Edition). The season-by-season accounts in Díez Muro's work do not account in many cases for tie games and have also been continuously revised/corrected by more recent research (including my own). Team records given here are in part based on the exhaustive but unpublished records compiled by the late dean of Cuban baseball historians, Severo Nieto (along with my own revisions of Nieto's work). For those years where the total number of wins and losses for league teams do not match it is often because Nieto's team records reflect some games played against opponents other than Cuban League teams.

1878–1879 (First Championship Season)

Habana captured the first "official" game on December 29, 1878, by the unlikely count of 21–20 over eventual longtime rival Almendares. Steve Bellán's club went on to win four contests without defeat, though a fifth match with Matanzas ended in a 17-all deadlock. In a far different baseball age, Habana won its other games by scores of 34–26 (Matanzas), 18–10 (Almendares) and 34–17 (Matanzas). The practice of using a short right fielder as a tenth man in the lineup was adopted for the opening tournament and would be retained throughout most of the remainder of the century. The Matanzas team played three of its four contests on the famed grounds at Palmar del Junco and additional playing sites were the grounds located in the Havana neighborhoods of Tulipán and Vedado.

Original League Name— Liga de Base Ball
Champion— Habana (4–0–1), Manager: Esteban Bellán
Other Teams— 2-Almendares (1–2), 3-Matanzas (0–3–1)
Individual Leaders— No official records kept

1879–1880 (Second Championship Season)

Habana again proved superior in the second season of weekly games stretched between November 16 (Almendares and Habana were rained out on that date) and March 7 (when details of game action between the same two clubs were never adequately or accurately reported). Noted ballplayer and author Wenceslao Gálvez (infielder with Almendares for two sea-

sons and batting champion in 1886) would later report in his 1889 book entitled *El Base Ball en Cuba* that the first apparent bunt for a base hit (rather than a sacrifice effort) was registered on Christmas Day 1879 by Carlos Maciá of the Almendares ball club. (This same Maciá would later pitch the very first Cuban no-hitter.) At the outset of the tournament a new rule was adopted — it had just gone into effect the previous summer in the National League — making all hitters/runners automatically out when struck by a batted ball. Previously baserunners would frequently kick ground balls away from infielders in an attempt to aid the batter in reaching first base safely. Another landmark of the 1879–1880 season was the hiring by Colón of two Americans — a pitcher named Carpenter and a catcher named McCuller — presumably the first Americans to suit up for any Cuban baseball team.

New League Name— Liga General de Base-Ball de la Isla de Cuba
Champion— Habana (5–2), Manager: Esteban Bellán
Other Teams— 2-Almendares (3–4), 3-Colón (2–0), 4-Progreso (Vibora) (0–4)
Individual Leaders— No official records kept

1880–1881

No championship tournament was held among Cuban teams but a club of barnstorming Americans visited the island in December 1880 under the leadership of big league manager Frank Bancroft. A few poorly attended exhibitions were apparently staged between Cuban and American players, but the tour was quickly abandoned due to lack of fan interest and the Americans soon sailed for home after enjoying the Christmas holidays on the streets of Havana.

1882

The first league games were played at the original Almendares Park, built and owned by the same Zaldo brothers instrumental in founding the Almendares B.B.C. Almendares did not complete in the tournament, however, which had only two entrants, Fe and Habana. The former team captured three of the four games played, but a "legal" protest by Habana after the fourth outing (won 8–7 by Club Fe) was never resolved by league officials and tournament play was finally declared suspended without any official champion being declared.

Teams and Records— Fe (3–1), Habana (1–3)
Individual Leaders— No official records kept

1882–1883 (Third Championship Season)

The third championship season was most notable for the debut of pitcher Adolfo Luján with the Almendares team, for whom he won two of his three outings on the mound. When play resumed two winters later Luján suited up in a Club Habana uniform, where he would remain for the final seven years of his Cuban hall-of-fame career that featured a lifetime 34–9 pitching record and four consecutive seasons as the league's top hurler. On the field in 1883 Habana and Almendares posted equal 5–1 records, but the former was declared champion when the latter forfeited a final showdown match.

Champion— Habana (5–1), Manager: Esteban Bellán
Other Teams— 2-Almendares (5–1), 3-Ultimátum (2–4), 4-Caridad (0–6)
Individual Leaders— No official records kept

1883–1884

No attempt was made to organize a baseball championship season in the winter of 1883 or the spring of 1884. Professional baseball activities were therefore on hold in Cuba for slightly more than two full years between the finale of the short 1883 winter season (February 11) and the opening of the springtime 1885 tournament (on March 22, 1885).

1885 (Fourth Championship Season)

Habana won the tournament for the fourth straight outing but this time around was managed by Ricardo Mora and not Steve Bellán. While "official" batting records were still one season away, outfielder Pablo Ronquillo appears to have posted the highest batting mark and also socked more triples than anyone in the tournament. The three-bagger remained the most dramatic blow of 19th-century Cuban baseball given the expansive outfield dimensions of old Almendares Park and other occasional playing venues like the Vedado Tennis Club grounds, both of which were used for the 1885 shortened season.

Champion— Habana (4–3), Manager: Ricardo Mora
Other Teams— 2-Fe (3–3), 3-Almendares (1–2)
Individual Leaders— **BA**: Pablo Ronquillo (F) .350

1885–1886 (Fifth Championship Season)

For the second time in five completed tournaments, Habana won all of its games to outdistance four rivals in a "season" that lasted barely two months. A notable innovation this winter was the first use of catchers' masks, an improvement that had been on the scene for more than ten years in North American baseball. This change in equipment was a natural outcome of the first importation of "foreign" players from the United States, the first several of whom were indeed catchers. One such import named Billy Taylor quickly earned his reputation in Habana based much more on epic drinking bouts than on any native baseball talents. This was also the first championship with recorded individual player statistics.

Champion— Habana (6–0), Manager: Francisco Saavedra
Other Teams— 2-Almendares (4–2), 3-Fe (2–3), 4-Boccacio (1–4), 5-Unión (0–4)
Individual Batting Leaders— **BA**: Wenceslao Gálvez (A) .345; **AB**: Ricardo Martínez (A), Carlos Maciá (A), Francisco Coca (A), Francisco Delebat (A) 30; **Hits**: Wenceslao Gálvez, Ricardo Martínez, Carlos Maciá 10.
Individual Pitching Leaders— **Pct**: Adolfo Luján (H) 5–0 (1.000); **G**: Adolfo Luján 5; **CG**: Adolfo Luján 5; **W**: Adolfo Luján 5; **L**: Enrique Soler (U) 3.

1887 (Sixth Championship Season)

Highlighting the year's play was a first-ever Cuban League no-hitter, a one-sided 38–0 whitewashing of Carmelita by Almendares ace Carlos Maciá. In one of the most lopsided contests in the entire history of baseball played in any nation, the Almendares club itself posted 32 base hits, surely the most ever by the beneficiaries of a no-hit performance from their own pitcher. Maciá was also the season's leader in games and complete games pitched and in victories recorded. A strange-sounding rule innovation of this season was the regulation requiring the umpire to immediately replace any lost ball. Earlier seasons had been played with a novel rule allowing players five minutes to search for a lost ball before a new one had to be produced.*

Champion— Habana (10–2), Manager: Francisco Saavedra
Other Teams— 2-Almendares (9–3), 3-Fe (2–10), 4-Carmelita (0–6)
Individual Batting Leaders— **BA**: Ricardo Martínez (A) .439; **AB**: Gustavo Aróstegui (H) 47; **Hits**: Ricardo Martínez 18.
Individual Pitching Leaders— **Pct**: Adolfo Luján (H) 5–0 (1.000); **G**: Carlos Maciá (A) 9; **CG**: Carlos Maciá 9; **W**: Carlos Maciá 7; **L**: Evaristo Cachurro (F) 6.
No-Hit Game— Carlos Maciá (February 13, 1887), Almendares defeated Carmelita (38–0)

1888 (Seventh Championship Season)

Club Fe finally broke the stranglehold of the Habana ball club that marked most of the seasons before the Cuban War for Independence at century's end. Games were played at three locations—the Vedado Tennis Club grounds, Palmar del Junco in Matanzas, and the Quinta de Oña grounds also located in Matanzas. The season was marked by two unusual rule modifications, the first allowing four strikes to the batter and the second marking bases on balls as hits (a fact that perhaps helps explain the lofty .448 batting average posted by league pacesetter Antonio María García). A less radical and more permanent rule modification awarded first base to any batter struck by a pitched ball.

Champion— Fe (12–3), Manager: Antonio P. Utrera
Other Teams— 2-Habana (11–4), 3-Matanzas (4–11), 4-Progreso (3–12)
Individual Batting Leaders— **BA**: Antonio María García (H) .448; **AB**: Evaristo Cachurro (F) 70; **Hits**: Antonio María García 26; **2B**: Antonio María García 6.
Individual Pitching Leaders— **Pct**: Francisco Hernández (F) 10–2 (.833); **G**: Adolfo Luján (H) 15; **CG**: Adolfo Luján 15; **W**: Adolfo Luján 11; **L**: Enrique Ovares (M), Moisés Quintero (P) 10.

1889 (Eighth Championship Season)

Habana was back on top of the heap and now captained by Emilio Sabourín, one of the acknowledged fathers of Cuban

---

*It perhaps now seems rather difficult to understand how balls actually could be lost, even under the most primitive of playing conditions.

baseball. The season was an eight-month affair stretching through the full summer and ending in early August. The year's most noteworthy game was a second Cuban League no-hit, no-run masterpiece by Progreso's Eugenio de Rosas, authored on July 14 against the forces of Cárdenas. Adolfo Luján continued his mastery of the league's hitters with ten victories for the league champions. Baseball continued to search for its place as the new national game while the Spanish governors of the island openly promoted soccer and bull fights as preferred forms of recreation and entertainment.

Champion— Habana (16–4–1), Manager: Emilio Sabourín

Other Teams— 2-Fe (15–5), 3-Cárdenas (7–13), 4-Matanzas (6–14), 5-Progreso (6–14–1)

Individual Batting Leaders—**BA**: Francisco Salabarría (F) .305; **AB**: Alfredo Arcaño (H) 87; **Hits**: Francisco Hernández (F) 24; **2B**: Pablo Ronquillo (H) 3; **3B**: Alfredo Arcaño 3.

Individual Pitching Leaders—**Pct**: Adolfo Luján (H) 10–3 (.769); **G**: Eugenio de Rosas (P) 20; **CG**: Eugenio de Rosas 18; **W**: Adolfo Luján 10; **L**: Eugenio de Rosas 14.

No-Hit Game— Eugenio de Rosas (July 14, 1889), Progreso defeated Cárdenas (8–0)

1889–1890 (Ninth Championship Season)

Club Habana made it eight victories in the nine championships contested in a once-a-week string of games that ran from December through June. Exiled Cuban baseball historian Angel Torres has reported in *La Leyenda del Béisbol Cubano* (Miami, 1996) that it was this spring and summer, in particular, when baseball demonstrated great growth of interest in both Havana proper and throughout the island as a whole. Dozens of adult and youth teams were founded in 1890 in such outposts as Sagua de Grande, Santa Clara and Santiago in Oriente Province. Further interest was stimulated by the visit of Club Cuba from Key West, a talented touring ball club founded a year earlier and composed largely of sons of Cuban exiles who had emigrated to Florida during ongoing independence struggles against Spanish colonial rule on the island. Carlos Royer, Agustín Molina, and Esteban Prats — all soon to be significant Cuban League figures — comprised part of the roster of this barnstorming Key West-based team. (More details of this visit are found below in Chapter 6.)

Champion— Habana (14–3), Manager: Emilio Sabourín

Other Teams— 2-Fe (12–5), 3-Progreso (8–9), 4-Almendares (3–14), 5-Cárdenas (1–7)

Individual Batting Leaders—**BA**: Antonio María García (F) .364; **AB**: Antonio María García, Francisco Hernández (F) 65; **Hits**: Antonio María García 24; **3B**: Antonio María García, Alfredo Arcaño (H) 4; **HR**: Antonio María García 1.

Individual Pitching Leaders—**Pct**: Miguel Prats (H) 11–2 (.846); **G**: José M. Pastoriza (F) 14; **CG**: José M. Pastoriza 14; **W**: Miguel Prats 11; **L**: Salvador Villegas (A) 6.

1890–1891 (Tenth Championship Season)

With a full stable of five clubs answering the opening bell, Fe was declared the eventual champion, but only as the result of a large assist from two forfeit victories over runner-up Almendares. José Pastoriza earned 10 of the 12 Fe victories but also suffered five of that club's six losses. Nineteenth-century Cuban pitching legend Carlos "Bebé" Royer debuted with Club Habana during this season, but performed only as an infielder. Another rookie of note was Valentín González, Habana outfielder, a eventual two-time batting champion who would also pace the circuit in homers, triples, doubles, and base hits at various times during his 19-year career. Both Royer and González joined the Habana roster when Emilio Sabourín rounded up players from a neighborhood Havana team called Columbia to replace several defectors (including Moises Quintero and Miguel Prats) who had been enticed to join the rival Almendares squad. This campaign also marked the swan song season for a second early-epoch Cuban moundsman of note, Adolfo Luján.

Champion— Fe (12–6), Manager: Luis Almoina y Meléndez

Other Teams— 2-Almendares (10–8–1), 3-Progreso (9–7–1), 4-Habana (7–9), 5-Matancista (4–12)

Individual Batting Leaders—**BA**: Alfredo Crespo (M) .375; **AB**: Alejandro Castillo (F) 70; **Hits**: Francisco Hernández (F) 23; **2B**: Valentín González (H) 2; **HR**: Antonio María García (F) and Ricardo Caballero (H) 1.

Individual Pitching Leaders—**Pct**: Miguel Prats (H) 9–4 (.692); **G**: José Castañer (P), José M. Pastoriza (F) 15; **CG**: José Castañer, José M. Pastoriza 12; **W**: José M. Pastoriza 10; **L**: José Castañer, Alfredo Crespo (M) 7.

1892 (Eleventh Championship Season)

During the year that would bring the first group of touring big leaguers to the island, championship play ran from January 31 through August 7 and resulted in a ninth crown for Club Habana, captained by patriot and baseball pioneer Emilio Sabourín. Batting champion Antonio María García accomplished the unusual feat of a third hitting crown in the service of a third different team (a year later García would make it four titles in four different uniforms). Alfredo Arcaño earned an early reputation for power hitting by blasting three home runs (as far as can be determined, all of the inside-the-park variety); Arcaño would continue as league leader in this category the next two seasons, in an era when two round-trippers during the campaign would likely outstrip all competition.

Champion— Habana (13–7), Manager: Emilio Sabourín

Other Teams— 2-Aguila de Oro (10–10), 3-Almendares (7–13)

Individual Batting Leaders—**BA**: Antonio María García (A) .362; **AB**: Francisco Hernández (H) 95; **Hits**: Francisco Hernández 34; **3B**: Alfredo Arcaño (H) 3; **HR**: Alfredo Arcaño 3.

Individual Pitching Leaders—**Pct**: Emilio Hernández (H) 4–1 (.800); **G**: José M. Pastoriza (A) 17; **CG**: José M. Pastoriza 15; **W**: Miguel Prats (H) 9; **L**: José M. Pastoriza 10.

1892–1893 (Twelfth Championship Season)

Matanzas recorded its only pennant in nine outings in the league, coming home the winner on the strength of two victories over Habana in a best-of-three tie-breaker. The season-deciding series was not held until the final week of July and first week of August in 1893, ringing to a close a weekly season that had opened way back in mid–December of 1892. Batting champion Antonio María García ("El Inglés") played his only season with the short-lived Aguila de Oro club; the versatile catcher and outfielder was widely considered the most talented 19th-century player Cuban baseball had to offer. García's nickname reportedly resulted from his fine, light-skinned features as well as his impeccable dress and mastery of the English language.

Champion— Matanzas (14–9), Manager: Luis Almoina y Meléndez

Other Teams— 2-Habana (11–12), 3-Aguila de Oro (8–12)

Individual Batting Leaders—**BA**: Antonio Maria García (AO) .385; **AB**: Francisco Hernández (H) 99; **Hits**: Valentín González (H) 36; **2B**: Alfredo Arcaño (H) 4; **3B**: Valentín González 5; **HR**: Antonio María García, Alfredo Arcaño 2.

Individual Pitching Leaders—**Pct**: Francisco Hernández (F) 4–1 (.800); **G**: Enrique García (M), Manuel Martínez (AO), Miguel Prats (H) 12; **CG**: Miguel Prats 8; **W**: Enrique García 6; **L**: Miguel Prats 9.

1893–1894 (Thirteenth Championship Season)

Almendares finished atop the championship standings for the first and only time during 19th century competitions, primarily due to the heroic pitching of veteran José Pastoriza who earned all but one of his team's victories and suffered all of its defeats. Pastoriza and other Cuban pitchers had to adapt in this season to an adjustment of the distance between home plate and the pitching box (mound) from an original 50 feet to the current distance of sixty feet and six inches.

Champion—Almendares (17–7–1), Manager: Ramón Gutiérrez

Other Teams— 2-Matanzas (15–9–1), 3-Habana (13–11), 4-Cárdenas (3–21)

Individual Batting Leaders—**BA**: Miguel Prats (H) .394; **AB**: Valentín González (H) 113; **Hits**: Miguel Prats 41; **3B**: Alfredo Arcaño (H) 4; **HR**: Alfredo Arcaño 2.

Individual Pitching Leaders—**Pct**: José M. Pastoriza (A) 16–7 (.695); **G**: José M. Pastoriza 23; **CG**: José M. Pastoriza 18; **W**: José M. Pastoriza 16; **L**: Francisco Llanes (C) 8.

1894–1895

Regular season play (November 1894 through May 1895) was completed but year-end playoffs were suspended while in progress due to the encroaching Independence War; thus the season was declared to have no official champion. Individual player statistics were recorded, however, making the campaign similar to one that transpired in the U.S. major leagues exactly a century later. A new rule this season counted foul bunts as strikes against the batter. Díez Muro reports that a playoff series between Habana and Almendares was actually in its third game (Habana winning the first and the second remaining tied) when a suspension caused by rain ignited full-scale riot-

ing among fans and resulted in further games immediately being cancelled by the Spanish Civil Governor of Havana.

Teams and Records— Habana (17–4), Almendares (13–8), Matanzas (1–19)

Individual Batting Leaders—**BA**: Alfredo Arcaño (H) .430; **AB**: Manuel López (A) 84; **Hits**: Valentín González (H) 32; **HR**: Valentín González 3.

Individual Pitching Leaders—**Pct**: Enrique García (H) 12–4 (.750); **G**: Enrique García 17; **CG**: Enrique García 15; **W**: Enrique García 12; **L**: José M. Pastoriza (A) 6.

1895–1896 and 1896–1897

For the next two seasons after 1895 the Cuban League championship campaign was cancelled due to the War for Independence (Spanish-American War) fought by Cuban rebels against occupying Spanish forces. Many Cuban ballplayers took part in the hostilities and a number gave their lives in the revolutionary cause. Important off-field events during these years were the adoption in U.S. professional baseball of new rules governing the "infield fly" as an automatic out and the counting of foul tips as strikes. Both changes would be adopted in Cuban League action when championship contests resumed in late 1897.

1897–1898

Championship play was cancelled before its conclusion due to the increased hostilities of the ongoing War for Independence. Feista (Fe) outdistanced Habanista (Habana) in the handful of games completed between December 1897 and April 1898. The only official statistics kept for individual performances were those for batting, where Habanista's Valentín González led all comers in three recorded categories.

Teams and Records— Feista (8–2), Habanista (4–5), Almendares (2–7)

Individual Batting Leaders—**BA**: Valentín González (H) .394; **AB**: Valentín González 33; **Hits**: Valentín González 13.

1898(–1899)
(Fourteenth Championship Season)

Again playing under the name Habanista, the forces of Club Habana continued domination of their rivals when league competition finally returned to normal. The last 19th-century championship came on the heels of two cancelled seasons, surrounded by two seasons in which league play was started but later suspended. All games were played on Sundays between late February and early July of 1898 and Habanista was the only one of the three teams to post a winning record. Valentín "Sirique" González was the league hitting star with 12 safeties and a .414 average compiled over the championship team's dozen games, while Habanista right-hander José Romero started nine, completed seven, and won five of his team's 12 contests.

Champion— Habanista (9–3–1), Manager: Alberto Azoy

Other Teams— 2-Almendarista (4–8), 3-Cuba (5–7–1)

Individual Batting Leaders—**BA**: Valentín González (H)

.414; **AB**: Esteban Prats (A) 36; **Hits**: José M. Baeza (C), Valentín González 12.

Individual Pitching Leaders—**Pct**: José Romero (H) 5–2 (.714); **G**: José Romero 9; **CG**: José Romero 7; **W**: José Romero 5; **L**: Salvador Rosado (A) 3.

1900 (FIFTEENTH CHAMPIONSHIP SEASON)

In a season that stretched from May to December (league games were played once a week on Sundays), San Francisco captured its only championship in five attempts. Habana's new southpaw pitching ace Luis "Mule" Padrón not only topped the circuit as a moundsman, with the most victories and best winning percentage, but also starred on offense as base hits leader. An early pioneer in changing his pitching speeds, Padrón would perform in the league for two decades (1900–1919), serving as a pitcher in eleven campaigns and posting a lifetime 39–23 record. The most significant development of this 1900 season, however, was the first appearance of black players, with San Francisco fielding a squad of almost all blacks while Cubano ("Cuba-No") was a fully integrated team. Also accompanying this social upheaval was a change of the formal league name from "Liga Nacional de Base-Ball" to "Liga Cubana" (effective for the following season) and the related decision of Almendares to play under the name Almendarista ("followers of Almendares").

Champion— San Francisco (17–10–1), Manager: Patricio Silverio

Other Teams— 2-Habana (13–12–1), 3-Cubano (11–13–2), 3-Almendarista (9–15–3)

Individual Batting Leaders—**BA**: Esteban Prats (H) .333; **AB**: Manuel Martínez (SF), Ramón Calzadilla (H) 33; **Hits**: Luis Padrón (H) 31; **3B**: Rogelio Valdés (SF), Alfredo Arcaño (H) 2.

Individual Pitching Leaders—**Pct**: Luis Padrón (H) 13–4 (.765); **G**: Salvador Rosado (SF) 20; **CG**: Luis Padrón, Salvador Rosado 17; **W**: Luis Padrón 13; **L**: Carlos Royer (C), José Muñoz (A) 7.

1901 (SIXTEENTH CHAMPIONSHIP SEASON)

Only the second of nine championships celebrated within a single calendar year produced another title for Habana and a new individual league batting mark set by San Francisco's Julián Castillo. Almendares Park played host on February 3, 1901, to what was recognized at the time as the first league game of the 20th century, with Habana's Carlos Royer besting Emilio Palomino and San Francisco by a 7–2 count. A notable game also occurred on March 10 when Almendares ran up a dozen runs in the seventh inning against the team still known as Cubano. With a second individual hitting crown, Julián Castillo (1901, 1903, 1909, 1910) took another step toward eventually joining Antonio María García (1888, 1890, 1892, 1893) and Regino García (1904, 1905, 1906, 1907) as the only trio of four-time Cuban League batting champions.

New League Name— Liga Cubana de Base-Ball

Champion— Habana (16–3–1), Manager: Alberto Azoy

Other Teams— Almendares (12–6–3), San Francisco (11–7–3), Cubano (4–14–1), Fe (3–16)

Individual Batting Leaders—**BA**: Julián Castillo (SF) .454; **AB**: Ramón Calzadilla (H) 90; **Hits**: Julián Castillo 30; **2B**: Julián Castillo 5; **3B**: Alfredo Arcaño (H) 1.

Individual Pitching Leaders—**Pct**: Carlos "Bebé" Royer (H) 12–3 (.800); **G**: Carlos Royer 15; **CG**: José Muñoz (A) 15; **W**: Carlos Royer 12; **L**: Angel D'Meza (C) 9.

1902 (SEVENTEENTH CHAMPIONSHIP SEASON)

Remarkable individual performances by Habana's duo of Carlos "Bebé" Royer and Luis "Mulo" Padrón highlighted the final season in which games were restricted to the once-a-week Sunday format. Royer pitched every inning for the undefeated but twice-tied Leones (Lions), thus posting the best one-year unblemished mark for a pitcher in Cuban annals. Padrón — also a top-flight pitcher in 11 of his 19 league seasons — rang up a .463 batting mark, a record that would never be surpassed on a Cuban League diamond. (Osmani Urrutia posted a .446 high-water mark at the beginning of the 21st century during post-revolution Cuban League action. Oscar Charleston also hit at a .471 clip in 1920–21 but did not earn enough plate appearances to qualify for a batting title, or to erase Luis Padrón's record figure.) The 1902 campaign was also notable for the debut with San Francisco of hall-of-fame catcher Gervasio "Strike" (pronounced "Streaky") González, who would a half-dozen seasons later earn the bulk of his reputation with Almendares as a favored receiver of legendary pitcher José de la Caridad ("El Diamante Negro") Méndez.

Champion— Habana (17–0–2), Manager: Alberto Azoy

Other Teams— 2-Almendares (9–9), 3-Fe (7–10–2), 4-San Francisco (2–16)

Individual Batting Leaders—**BA**: Luis Padrón (H) .463; **AB**: Ramón Calzadilla (H) 79; **Hits**: Valentín González (H) 24; **2B**: Valentín González, Carlos Royer (H) 2; **3B**: Luis Padrón 4; **HR**: Luis Padrón 2.

Individual Pitching Leaders—**Pct**: Carlos "Bebé" Royer (H) 17–0 (1.000); **G**: Carlos Royer 19; **CG**: Carlos Royer 17; **W**: Carlos Royer 17; **L**: José Muñoz (A), Salvador Rosado (F) 7.

1903 (EIGHTEENTH CHAMPIONSHIP SEASON)

Habana was again team champion, edging Fe at season's end with the necessary three victories in a decisive five-game playoff series. Hall-of-famer Carlos "Bebé" Royer was still at his mid-career peak and posted the top marks for games won (18) and games lost (10), while completing all 28 of his pitching starts. With three victories (plus two defeats) in the final playoff series, the workhorse Royer ran his year's victory total to 21, a number matched only one other time in Cuban League play, by U.S. blackball import Raymond "Jabao" Brown during the much-longer 1936–37 season.

Champion— Habana (21–13), Manager: Alberto Azoy

Other Teams— 2-Fe (21–14), 3-Almendares (6–21)

Individual Batting Leaders—**BA**: Julián Castillo (H) .330; **AB**: Ramón Govantes (F) 117; **Hits**: Julián Castillo 37; **2B**: Rogelio Valdés (H) 3; **3B:** Julián Castillo 4; **HR:** Julián Castillo 2.

Individual Pitching Leaders—**Pct:** Cándido Fontanals (F) 14–6 (.700); **G:** Carlos Royer (H) 28; **CG:** Carlos Royer 28; **W:** Carlos Royer 18; **L:** Carlos Royer 10.

1904 (Nineteenth Championship Season)

Habana ran its victory string to four straight under captain Alberto Azoy by capturing 16 of their 20 outings to easily outdistance the entries from San Francisco and Almendares. While one four-year string would come to an end with this season—which stretched from early February to early June—another would be launched when Regino García (currently playing for San Francisco) earned the first of his quartet of uninterrupted batting championships. Outside of Cuban League action, the All-Cubans made their initial appearance this summer in the U.S. Negro leagues (still a barnstorming circuit without organized league structure) and toured in the north with a racially mixed squad including Rafael Almeida, Antonio María García, Luis "Anguilla" Bustamante, Joseíto Muñoz, Julián Castillo, Emilio Palomino and other early-era Cuban stars.

New League Name—Liga Habanera de Base-Ball

Champion—Habana (16–4), Manager: Alberto Azoy

Other Teams—2-San Francisco (8–12), 3-Almendares (6–14)

Individual Batting Leaders—**BA:** Regino García (SF) .397; **AB:** Valentín González (H) 83; **Hits:** Regino García 31; **2B:** Regino García 3; **3B:** Julián Castillo (H) 5; **HR:** Valentín González (H) 2.

Individual Pitching Leaders—**Pct:** Carlos "Bebé" Royer (H) 13–3 (.813); **G:** Carlos Royer (H) 16; **CG:** Carlos Royer 16; **W:** Carlos Royer 13; **L:** Juan Violá (A) 7.

1905 (Twentieth Championship Season)

Almendares nested at the top of the small pack for only the second time in club history. The Alacranes (Scorpions) were captained by future league impresario Abel Linares and led on the field of battle by the batting of Regino García and the strong pitching arm of Angel D'Mesa. An irony of the season was the fact that hurler José Muñoz, who topped the league in both victories and defeats, hurled this particular season with Habana, the only campaign in 15 that he did not labor for the Alacranes. Between 1900 and 1914 Muñoz built a career record in Cuba of 81–57 and was viewed by many old-timers as the island's best pitcher before the 1908 arrival of José de la Caridad Méndez.

Champion—Almendares (19–11), Manager: Abel Linares

Other Teams—2-Habana (15–15), 3-Fe (11–19)

Individual Batting Leaders—**BA:** Regino García (A) .305; **AB:** Esteban Prats (A) 121; **Hits:** Valentín González (H) 32; **2B:** Regino García 5; **3B:** Julián Castillo 4.

Individual Pitching Leaders—**Pct:** Angel D'Meza (A) 10–4 (.714); **G:** José Muñoz (H) 20; **CG:** Luis González (F) 16; **W:** Angel D'Meza, José Muñoz 10; **L:** José Muñoz 9.

1905–1906 (Twenty-First Championship Season)

Club Fe returned to the winner's circle for the third time, but for manager/captain Alberto Azoy the 1906 championship represented the sixth of his career, the previous five (including four straight) all earned with league powerhouse Habana. While Habana's José Muñoz was crowned pitching champion with a sterling 8–1 record, it was Fe's Luis González who proved the league's workhorse hurler, starting 19 games and winning 10, which represented two-thirds of the champion club's total victories. Although the large-scale appearance of imported Negro leaguers was still a season away, star blackball pitcher Andrew "Rube" Foster (at the time with the Philadelphia Giants during the summer) made his Cuba debut with 15 complete game appearances. Regino García captured his third of four straight batting titles with the second lowest mark ever posted by the league's top batsman (.304, versus the .303 posted by Tony Taylor in 1959).

New League Name—Liga General de Base Ball de la Republia de Cuba

Champion—Fe (15–9–1), Manager: Alberto Azoy

Other Teams—2-Almendares (14–10–1), 3-Habana (7–17)

Individual Batting Leaders—**BA:** Regino García (A) .304; **AB:** Eliodoro Hidalgo (A) 95; **Hits:** Regino García 28; **2B:** Julián Castillo (F) 5.

Individual Pitching Leaders—**Pct:** José Muñoz (A) 8–1 (.889); **G:** Luis González (F) 19; **CG:** Andrew "Rube" Foster (F) 15; **W:** Luis González 10; **L:** Pedro Olave (H) 10.

1907 (Twenty-Second Championship Season)

The 1907 and 1908 seasons, played against the continued backdrop of American military occupation, proved of great historical significance, since the Almendares victories in these years over teams made up largely of visiting American Negro leaguers went a long way toward building rampant Cuban nationalism and thus toward cementing baseball as the true Cuban national game. This was the first campaign in which American blacks staffed Cuban rosters and a significant number flooded line-ups of both Habana (boasting George Johnson of the Philadelphia Giants, alongside several American whites including top pitcher George Mack and George "Pepper Wilson" Prentiss, once with the Boston Red Sox) and Fe (whose roster featured Negro league standouts Preston "Pete" Hill, Andrew "Rube" Foster, Bill Monroe, Grant "Home Run" Johnson and Charlie "Chief Tokahoma" Grant). The season played entirely in Almendares Park stretched from New Year's Day until April 14, and the Almendares team with its exclusively native Cuban flavor seemed to be making a strong political statement, which it underscored with a coveted championship banner.

Champion—Almendares (17–13–1), Manager: Eugenio Santa Cruz

Other Teams—2-Fe (16–14), 3-Habana (12–18–1)

Individual Batting Leaders—**BA:** Regino García (F) .324;

AB: Emilio Palomino (A) 118; **Hits**: Regino García 36; **2B**: Julián Castillo (F) 5; **3B**: Julián Castillo 4.

Individual Pitching Leaders — **Pct**: George Mack (H) 4–2 (.667); **G**: José Muñoz (A) 17; **CG**: Julián Pérez (H) 13; **W**: Andrew "Rube" Foster (F) 9; **L**: Luis González (F) 7.

1908 (TWENTY-THIRD CHAMPIONSHIP SEASON)

Matanzas fielded a team for the first time in the 20th century while Fe was again stocked by director Abel Linares with imported Negro leaguers, this time including Ashby Dunbar, Bruce Petway, Walter Ball, Sam Mongin and Nate Harris. Almendares was still the best club, despite the presence of the Americans, in no small part due to local black imports of its own. Previously unheralded José Méndez broke onto the Cuban League scene in spectacular fashion, debuting on February 2 in relief against Habana, starting his first game 17 days later against Matanzas and winning 8–3 with eight shutout innings, and capturing all nine of his season's decisions to pace Almendares to championship victory. In the fall months of that same year — on the eve of his second Cuban League outing — "El Diamante Negro" became a true national hero by twirling a near no-hitter against the visiting Cincinnati Reds (broken up in the ninth inning by a Miller Huggins single), recording 25 uninterrupted scoreless innings against the touring big leaguers, and pushing his overall scoreless innings streak to 45 before it was finally ended by Habana on Christmas Eve, in the first week of 1908–1909 league play.

Champion — Almendares (37–8–1), Manager: Dr. Juan L. Sánchez

Other Teams — 2-Habana (32–13–1), 3-Fe (11–34), 4-Matanzas (10–35)

Individual Batting Leaders — **BA**: Emilio Palomino (A) .350; **AB**: Clarence Winston (H) 171; **Runs**: Emilio Palomino, Preston Hill (H) 53; **Hits**: Preston Hill 60; **2B**: Julián Castillo (H) 6; **3B**: Preston Hill 5; **HR**: Luis Padrón (H) 3; **Steals**: Clarence Winston 33.

Individual Pitching Leaders — **Pct**: José Méndez (A) 9–0 (1.000); **G**: José Muñoz (A) 19; **CG**: Julián Pérez (H) 13; **W**: José Muñoz 13; **L**: Luis González (F) 11; **Shutouts**: José Muñoz 5.

1908–1909 (TWENTY-FOURTH CHAMPIONSHIP SEASON)

Biggest headlines were made during the "American Season" when Eustaquio "Bombín" Pedroso outdid the earlier heroics of José Méndez by tossing a no-hit, no-run game (11 innings) at the befuddled visiting big league Detroit Tigers. The league season that followed in late December found Méndez back in the individual spotlight for the Alacranes with his winningest-ever winter season (15–6) and 18 complete games tossed for the runner-up ball club. Habana nonetheless broke its longest dry spell to date (five years without a banner) and thus interrupted a string of Almendares pennants that would eventually stretch to four in five seasons. New rules prevented pitchers from marking, darkening or defacing the baseball and also permitted for the first time the use of catchers' shin guards.

Champion — Habana (33–13–1), Manager: Luis Someillán

Other Teams — 2-Almendares (30–15–1), 3-Fe (21–23), 4-Matanzas (3–36)

Individual Batting Leaders — **BA**: Julián Castillo (F) .315; **AB**: Rafael Almeida (A) 164; **Hits**: Julián Castillo, Grant Johnson (H) 46; **2B**: Julián Castillo 12.

Individual Pitching Leaders — **Pct**: José Méndez (A) 15–6 (.714); **G**: José Méndez 28; **CG**: José Méndez 18; **W**: José Méndez, Louis Haggerman (H) 15; **L**: Walter Ball (F) 7.

1910 (TWENTY-FIFTH CHAMPIONSHIP SEASON)

José Méndez posted his second undefeated season (7–0) in his three initial campaigns with Almendares, winning by himself more than half the club's 13 victories. It was enough to pace an easy championship for the Alacranes, who also boasted .400-plus hitter Julián Castillo and ace catcher Gervasio "Strike" González in their potent lineup. The brief season (January 27 thru April 3) was also notable, in retrospect, for the initial appearance of future big leaguer Miguel Angel González, who (like Luque two years later) debuted with Club Fe and posted a weak .190 batting average in only six games with the league's tail-end ball club.

Champion — Almendares (13–3–1), Manager: Dr. Juan L. Sánchez

Other Teams — 2-Habana (9–7), 3-Fe (2–14–1)

Individual Batting Leaders — **BA**: Julián Castillo (A) .408; **AB**: Armando Cabañas (A) 68; **Runs**: Gervasio "Strike" González (A) 18; **Hits**: Julián Castillo, Regino García (F) 20; **3B**: Regino García 4; **HR**: Rogelio Valdés (A) 1; **Steals**: Agustín Parpetti (H), Alfredo Cabrera (A) 10.

Individual Pitching Leaders — **Pct**: José Méndez (A) 7–0 (1.000); **G**: (first name unknown) Marlotica (F) 9; **CG**: Pastor Parera (H) 8; **W**: José Méndez 7; **L**: (first name unknown) Marlotica 6.

1910–1911 (TWENTY-SIXTH CHAMPIONSHIP SEASON)

Having wrapped up one championship banner during the previous summer months (January-April 1910), Almendares continued their momentum when play renewed in December for a longer winter season (December 1910 thru April 1911). José Méndez was again relied upon for half the team's victories while also dominating all the league's individual categories for moundsmanship (winning percentage, games pitched, complete games, victories). For the first time in Cuba, balls with cork centers were used for league play and Negro leaguer Preston Hill pounded the new sphere for a league-best .365 batting average. Another unusual feature of the season was the fact that games were held at Oriental Park (a venue also used for horse racing) rather than the usual site at Almendares Park. Three months after the Cuban season closed, Almendares infielders Armando Marsans and Rafael Almeida debuted with Cincinnati as the first Cuban big leaguers of the 20th century.

Champion — Almendares (21–6–3), Manager: Dr. Juan L. Sánchez

Other Teams— 2-Habana (18–9–3), 3-Fe (2–26–2)

Individual Batting Leaders—**BA:** Preston Hill (H) .365; **AB:** (first name unknown) Barber (F) 103; **Runs:** Armando Marsans (A) 22; **Hits:** Preston Hill 35; **Steals:** Armando Cabañas (A) 24.

Individual Pitching Leaders—**Pct:** José Méndez (A) 11–2 (.846); **G:** José Méndez 18; **CG:** José Méndez 12; **W:** José Méndez 11; **L:** Walter Ball (F) 8.

1912 (Twenty-Seventh Championship Season)

Adolfo (Papá Montero) Luque saw action for the first time in Cuban winter play, losing all three of his pitching decisions with last-place Club Fe. The championship banner earned by Habana was already its sixteenth, captured under its seventh different pennant-winning manager. The year's most exciting game was staged on March 25 and was memorable for two gigantic home runs by Fe's Julián Castillo, both socked off the famous "Diamante Negro" José Méndez and providing all the necessary scoring in a 2–1 Fe victory. One of the drives off Castillo's potent bat cleared the distant outfield fence of old Almendares Park and was long considered one of the longest blasts ever witnessed on the island.

Champion— Habana (22–12–1), Manager: Eduardo Laborde

Other Teams— 2-Almendares (17–17–1), 3-Fe (14–24)

Individual Batting Leaders—**BA:** Emilio Palomino (A) .440; **AB:** (first name unknown) Lyons (F) 118; **Runs:** Carlos Morán (H) 32; **Hits:** Grant Johnson (H) 43; **2B:** Julián Castillo (F) 8; **HR:** Julián Castillo 5; **Steals:** Bruce Petway (H) 20.

Individual Pitching Leaders—**Pct:** José Junco (H) 6–1 (.857); **G:** A. Joe "Cyclone" Williams (H) 21; **CG:** Joe "Cyclone" Williams, José Méndez (A) 13; **W:** Fred Wickware (F) 10; **L:** Eustaquio Pedroso (A) 10.

1913 (Twenty-Eighth Championship Season)

In a season of notable firsts and lasts, Club Fe captured its fourth and final banner while Agustín Molina registered his first pennant as a team manager. Tinti Molina, a Cuban hall-of-famer who had played twelve seasons (mostly in the century's first decade) with seven different teams, would gain later fame as manager of Cuba's greatest club, the legendary 1923–24 Santa Clara Leopardos (Leopards) featuring Oscar Charleston, Alejandro Oms and Champion Mesa. At season's end three Cubans — Merito Acosta, Alfredo "El Pájaro" Cabrera, and Jacinto Calvo — broke into big league action, thus joining Marsans, Almeida and Miguel Angel González on the big-time summer circuit. Fe boasted a lineup featuring such imported U.S. Negro leaguers as Spotswood Poles, Jude Gans, Cannonball Redding, and John Henry Lloyd, in addition to up-and-coming local pitcher Adolfo Luque. Almendares, with a strong season from Bombín Pedroso (11 wins) and an off-year from sore-armed José Méndez (1–4), lagged five games off the championship pace.

Champion— Fe (21–11–2), Manager: Agustín Molina

Other Teams— 2-Almendares (16–16–1), 3-Habana (11–21–1)

Individual Batting Leaders—**BA:** Armando Marsans (A) .400; **AB:** Spotswood Poles (F) 151; **Runs:** Spotwood Poles 40; **Hits:** Spotswood Poles 55; **HR:** Julián Castillo (A) 1; **Steals:** Jude Gans (F) 23.

Individual Pitching Leaders—**Pct:** Dick "Cannonball" Redding (F) 7–2 (.778); **G:** Eustaquio Pedroso (A) 22; **CG:** Eustaquio Pedroso 11; **W:** Eustaquio Pedroso 11; **L:** (first name unknown) Lazaga (H) 7.

1913–1914 (Twenty-Ninth Championship Season)

For the third time in its brief history, the Cuban League opened a winter season beginning on December 6, 1913, after having staged an earlier complete championship season within the same calendar year (January through March of 1913). José de la Caridad Méndez returned to the peak of his powers and re-emerged as the big story in Cuban baseball, posting ten victories without defeat. Without Méndez on the hill the Alacranes posted only 12 victories in their other 24 contests, a break-even record. On the heels of this particular season, Habana right-hander Adolfo Luque — destined to be Cuba's greatest big league hurler before his long career was finished — would make his quiet debut with the Boston National League club.

New League Name— Liga Nacional de Base Ball de la Republia de Cuba

Champion— Almendares (22–11–1), Manager: Eugenio Santa Cruz

Other Teams— 2-Fe (19–14–1), 3-Habana (8–24)

Individual Batting Leaders—**BA:** Manuel Villa (F) .351; **AB:** Manuel Villa, Pelayo Chacón (F) 129; **Runs:** Armando Marsans (A) 28; **Hits:** Manuel Villa 46; **Steals:** Armando Marsans 21.

Individual Pitching Leaders—**Pct:** José Méndez (A) 10–0 (1.000); **G:** Pastor Pareda (F) 21; **CG:** Pastor Pareda 12; **W:** Pastor Pareda 11; **L:** Pastor Pareda 9.

1914–1915 (Thirtieth Championship Season)

Miguel Angel González picked up the first of 14 league titles earned while managing the Habana team and it came on the heels of the twenty-five-year-old's first full season in the big leagues as a backup catcher with Cincinnati. Another important debut was Cristóbal Torriente's first appearance among the individual league leaders as batting champion. Miguel Angel spiced his managerial breakthrough with a solid season as the Leones' regular backstop, batting .284 and stealing 23 bases, a remarkable number for a catcher even in an age when base stealing was one of the game's primary weapons. González trailed only his own teammate, fleet outfielder Armando Marsans (30), in the thievery department. Marsans, the first Cuban big leaguer and an earlier teammate of González in Cincinnati, had switched his summertime employment in mid–1914 to the St. Louis team of the short-lived Federal League.

Champion— Habana (23–11), Manager: Miguel Angel González

Other Teams— 2-Almendares (22–12), 3-Fe (6–28)

Individual Batting Leaders—**BA**: Cristóbal Torriente (A) .387; **AB**: Cristóbal Torriente 124; **Runs**: Cristóbal Torriente 33; **Hits**: Cristóbal Torriente 48; **Steals**: Armando Marsans (H) 30.

Individual Pitching Leaders—**Pct**: José Acosta (H) 5–1 (.823); **G**: Eustaquio "Bombín" Pedroso (A) 20; **CG**: Eustaquio Pedroso 12; **W**: Eustaquio Pedroso 10; **L**: Pedro González (F) 9.

1915–1916 (THIRTY-FIRST CHAMPIONSHIP SEASON)

Old Almendares Park enjoyed its final season of play before being abandoned because of its deteriorating grandstands and now inadequate seating capacity. Construction had already begun on the replacement Almendares Park only several blocks distant. The Almendares team remained a success story with its second championship of the past three seasons. The emerging pattern of top Cuban pitchers who were also feared hitters (Luque, Méndez, Lázaro Salazar, Cocaina García) was underscored by Eustaquio "Bombín" Pedroso, who captured the individual batting championship and also lead all hurlers in mound appearances and complete games while pitching for two different teams.

New League Name— Asociación de Base Ball de la Republia de Cuba

Champion— Almendares (30–12–3), Manager: Alfredo Cabrera

Other Teams— 2-Habana (28–15–2), 3-San Francisco (6–37–1)

Individual Batting Leaders—**BA**: Eustaquio Pedroso (SF-A) .413; **AB**: Jacinto Calvo (H) 153; **Runs**: Cristóbal Torriente (A) 41; **Hits**: Cristóbal Torriente 56; **Steals**: Cristóbal Torriente 28.

Individual Pitching Leaders—**Pct**: José Acosta (H) 8–3 (.727); **G**: Eustaquio Pedroso (SF-A) 21; **CG**: Eustaquio Pedroso 12; **W**: Adolfo Luque (A) 12; **L**: Francisco Campos (SF-A) 8.

1917 (THIRTY-SECOND CHAMPIONSHIP SEASON)

This short season — played under the temporary name of the Liga Cubana-Americana de Base Ball — featured a trio of teams with unusual names and was held in Oriental Park, a horseracing facility located in Marianao. Construction meanwhile continued on the new Almendares Park, which would not debut until a season later. The champion Orientals guided by Armando Marsans drew their moniker from the facility where games were played, and the Red Sox and White Sox clubs apparently account for labeling this a Cuban-American league. No actual Americans played in the tournament, which was contested against the backdrop of an aborted revolt against U.S.–backed president García Menocal. Luque starred for the winners as both a hurler and batsman, winning the hitting title while splitting eight pitching decisions and leading the circuit in mound appearances.

New League Name— Liga Cubana-Americana de Base Ball

Champion— Orientals (8–6–1), Manager: Armando Marsans

Other Teams— 2-White Sox (6–7), 3-Red Sox (6–7–1)

Individual Batting Leaders—**BA**: Adolfo Luque (O) .355; **AB**: Tomás Romañach (O), Bartolo Portuondo (WS) 57; **Runs**: Miguel Angel González (RS) 9; **Hits**: José Maria Fernández (WS) 16; **Steals**: Jacinto Calvo (O) 6.

Individual Pitching Leaders—**Pct**: José Acosta (O) 2–1 (.667); **G**: Adolfo Luque (O) 9; **CG**: Adolfo Luque, Emilio Palmero (RS) 6; **W**: Adolfo Luque, Emilio Palmero 4; **L**: Adolfo Luque 4.

1918–1919 (THIRTY-THIRD CHAMPIONSHIP SEASON)

Novel features of the first season played at the impressive new Almendares Park included the appearance of Tinti Molina's summer Negro leagues team playing under its own name of Cuban Stars, as well as a rare unassisted triple play, plus the absence of both imported American players and local hero Dolf Luque, and an unusual year-end playoff schedule. The Cuban Stars substituted for usual entry Club Fe and were runners-up with a roster that included Bombín Pedroso, flashy shortstop Pelayo Chacón, and southpaw hurler Isidro Fabré. The triple killing was executed on December 2nd by Habana flychaser Merito Acosta, who made a shoestring catch in short center before running down two base runners to end the inning. All three clubs tied during the second half of the campaign, after Habana ran away with first-half proceedings, and a double-elimination playoff was utilized to determine a final champion. Habana prevailed with two straight wins after dropping a hard-fought opening contest to the Cuban Stars.

New League Name— Liga General de Base Ball de la Republia de Cuba

Champion— Habana (29–19), Manager: Miguel Angel González

Other Teams— 2-Cuban Stars (21–25–1), 3-Almendares (20–26–1)

Individual Batting Leaders—**BA**: Manuel Cueto (A) .344; **AB**: Marcelino Guerra (CS) 178; **Runs**: Baldomero Acosta (H) 30; **Hits**: Marcelino Guerra, Miguel Angel González (H) 52; **Steals**: Bienvenido Jiménez (CS) 30.

Individual Pitching Leaders—**Pct**: José Acosta (H) 16–10 (.615); **G**: José Acosta 34; **CG**: José Acosta 17; **W**: José Acosta 16; **L**: José Acosta, José Junco (CS) 10.

1919–1920 (THIRTY-FOURTH CHAMPIONSHIP SEASON)

In a season that began in late December and wrapped up by the end of February, Dolf Luque captured his first managerial championship starting a string that would eventually run to eight. Luque also pitched for Almendares and his victory ledger was almost half the winning total of the league's top team. Cuban Stars impresario Tinti Molina put most of his summertime roster on the field under the team name of América, but when his club had won only twice by early February and seemed to give up totally in a 21–7 routing by Almendares it was dropped from the competition, with its remaining games being forfeited. Batting champion Torriente smacked a tremendous homer February 14 that remained one of the most memorable in the history of the short-lived new Almendares Park.

Champion—Almendares (22–5–2), Manager: Adolfo Luque

Other Teams—2-Habana (17–10–3), 3-América (2–26–1)

Individual Batting Leaders—**BA**: Cristóbal Torriente (Almendares) .360; **AB**: Bernardo Baró (Almendares) 105; **Runs**: Bernardo Baró 21; **Hits**: Bernardo Baró 37; **HR**: Not Recorded (but most likely Cristóbal Torriente); **Steals**: Bartolo Portuondo (Almendares), Miguel Angel González (H) 10.

Individual Pitching Leaders—**Pct**: Emilio Palmero (Almendares) 5–1 (.833); **G**: José Acosta (H), Adolfo Luque (Almendares) 15; **CG**: José Acosta 11; **W**: Adolfo Luque 10; **L**: Oscaro Tuero (H), Lucas Boada (América), Juilo LaBlanc (América) 5.

1920–1921 (THIRTY-FIFTH CHAMPIONSHIP SEASON)

The three highly symbolic home runs smacked by Torriente on November 5 against the questionable efforts of the New York Giants provided the highlight for the "American season" and perhaps also the entire baseball winter. League play opened in late October of 1920 and finished up with a three-game Habana-Almendares playoff and a resulting Habana league championship in mid–February of the following year. Even though the Almendares-Giants game that bolstered Torriente's legend was more like batting practice according to contemporary press accounts, nonetheless Cuban fans romanticized the triumph of their hero over the biggest American star, Babe Ruth. The regular season that followed saw Torriente outslugged by Almendares teammate Pelayo Chacón while his team was nipped at the wire by a Habana nine featuring the superior pitching of José Acosta and Oscar Tuero. The most noteworthy feature of this season, however, was the fact that a visiting American Negro leagues team—the Bacharach Giants—competed as a unit and even played under their own name during the regular league championship campaign. This was a clear ploy to capitalize on growing interest among Cuban fans in competitions between the two countries, and the fact that the Giants won only four games and finished dead last behind the "Eternal Rivals" was another obvious boon to soaring nationalistic pride. The Bacharach Giants only completed their first half-season schedule before most of the American players (including Oscar Charleston, Louis Santop, Dick Lundy, Pud Flournoy and Cannonball Redding) departed Cuba and all 15 of their second-half games were thus forfeited.

Champion—Habana (21–9–5), Manager: Miguel Angel González

Other Teams—2-Almendares (20–10–6), 3-Bacharach Giants (4–26–1)

Individual Batting Leaders—**BA**: Pelayo Chacón (A) .344; **AB**: Rafael Almeida (H) 116; **Runs**: Manuel Cueto (H), Cristóbal Torriente (A) 19; **Hits**: Pelayo Chacón 32; **2B**:

Cristóbal Torriente, José Rodríguez (H) 4; **3B**: Jacinto Calvo (H), Bienvenido Jiménez (H) 3; **Steals**: Manuel Cueto 12.

Individual Pitching Leaders—**Pct**: José Hernández (A) 4–1 (.800); **G**: José Acosta (H), Oscar Tuero (H) 13; **CG**: Oscar Tuero 8; **W**: José Acosta 6; **L**: Dick "Cannonball" Redding (B), "Pud" Flournoy (B) 6.

1921 (THIRTY-SIXTH CHAMPIONSHIP SEASON)

As a result of worsening economic and political conditions, accompanied by plunging sugar prices, bank failures, and yet another intervention by the U.S. military to prevent civil unrest, this fall's Cuban season saw only two teams answer the bell. If the roster of teams was as small as allowable, so was the championship round robin as truncated as allowable, with only five games being played before the two teams packed it in and Habana was declared victor by default. The stabilizing of sugar prices and the continued rush of tourist to Havana, however, meant that a new season would open the following November under renewed hope and considerable optimism.

New League Name—Liga General de Base Ball

Champion—Habana (4–1), Manager: Miguel Angel González

Other Teams—Almendares (1–4)

Individual Batting Leaders—**BA**: Bienvenido Jiménez (H) .619; **AB**: Bienvenido Jiménez, Valentín Dreke (A), José Ramos (H), Rafael Almeida (H) 21; **Runs**: Bienvenido Jiménez 7; **Hits**: Bienvenido Jiménez 13; **HR**: Manuel Cueto (H) 1; **Steals**: Bienvenido Jiménez 3.

Individual Pitching Leaders—**Pct**: Julio LeBlanc (H) 2–0 (1.000); **G**: Emilio Palmero (A) 3; **CG**: Oscar Tuero (H) 2; **W**: Julio LeBlanc 2; **L**: Pilar Alonso (A) 2.

1922–1923 (THIRTY-SEVENTH CHAMPIONSHIP SEASON)

Significant debuts included those of the club representing Santa Clara, which finished dead last with but 14 victories; a new Marianao team, which launched play in more spectacular fashion by walking off with the championship banner; and a young second baseman named Martín Dihigo, who batted only 28 times and posted a lame .179 mark at the plate. Once the lanky and agile Dihigo learned to hit the curveball and also settled on pitching as his preferred vocation, the versatile youngster from Matanzas would quickly mature into the most talented among all Cuban ballplayers. Santa Clara was a much stronger team than the final record would indicate and actually stood at 14–14–1 in mid–January when club director and manager Tinti Molina decided to withdraw from competition after a protest by Marianao resulted in the Leopardos being stripped of an earlier victory (earned on January 10). Marianao, for its part, wore the nickname of Grey Monks (they would also later be called Tigers) and were managed by Baldomero Acosta in their highly successful bolt from the gate, winning primarily on the talented trio of pitching arms represented by Lucas Boada (10–4), Emilio Palmero (7–5) and Juanito Mirabel. Boada's dramatic win over Habana on the last day of the season clinched the surprise pennant for the upstart Marianao team.

New League Name— Liga de Base Ball Professional de la Republia

Champion— Marianao (35–19–1), Manager: Baldomero Acosta

Other Teams— 2-Habana (32–22–1), 3-Almendares (27–27–3), 4-Santa Clara (14–40–1)

Individual Batting Leaders— **BA**: Bernardo Baró (A) .401; **AB**: Valentín Dreke (A) 188; **Runs**: Cristóbal Torriente (H) 37; **Hits**: Bernardo Baró, Cristóbal Torriente 61; **HR**: Cristóbal Torriente 4; **Steals**: Cristóbal Torriente 15.

Individual Pitching Leaders— **Pct**: Lucas Boada (M) 10–4 (.714); **G**: Adolfo Luque (H) 23; **CG**: Adolfo Luque 12; **W**: Adolfo Luque 11; **L**: Adolfo Luque, Oscar Levis (A) 9.

1923–1924 (Thirty-Eighth Championship Season)

A truly memorable if somewhat tainted season unfolded for a powerful Santa Clara squad, which boasted one of the best teams ever put on the playing field — in any league or any year — and which was also destined to become the most fabled one-season outfit in all of Cuban League history. Such was the dominance of the Leopardos team and its roster of blackball superstars that league officials called an early halt in mid–January and simply handed the championship cup to Molina's club, which then held an 11-plus game lead after less than fifty contests. The official reason given for the suspension of action was the one-sided pennant race and the embarrassment to the three outclassed clubs, but a far more important economic reason may have been the continued poor attendance in Santa Clara, despite that team's winning ways. The shortened season was followed by a hastily organized Gran Premio tourney featuring Santa Clara, Habana and Almendares, with the two Havana teams now reinforced with players from Marianao. As players began abandoning the series in droves, Santa Clara held its diminished roster together just long enough to squeeze out another victory, edging Habana by a mere half-game. As a result of continued complaints about too many imported Americans taking up roster spots on Cuban League clubs, some native players led by Miguel Angel González held their own separate championship in Matanzas, playing a series of games at the famed Palmar del Junco site. A young infielder named Martín Dihigo also played in the Matanzas games, before then accompanying Miguel Angel back onto the Habana roster for the following league season.

New League Name— Liga General de Base Ball de la Republia

Champion: Santa Clara (36–11–1), Manager: Agustín "Tinti" Molina

Other Teams— 2-Habana (25–23–2), 3-Almendares (18–29–2), 4-Marianao (16–32–1)

Individual Batting Leaders— **BA**: Oliver Marcelle (SC) .393; **AB**: Clinton Thomas (A) 199; **Runs**: Oscar Charleston (SC) 59; **Hits**: Dobie Moore (SC) 71; **2B**: Chuck Dressen (M), Frank Warfield (SC) 15; **3B**: Dobie Moore 6;

HR: Bienvenido Jiménez (A-H) 4; **Steals**: Oscar Charleston 31.

Individual Pitching Leaders— **Pct**: Bill Holland (SC) 10–2 (.833); **G**: Isidro Fabré (A) 20; **CG**: Oscar Fuhr (A) 9; **W**: Bill Holland 10; **L**: Lucas Boada (A), Jack Ryan (M-SC) 8; **Shutouts**: Juanelo Mirabal (H) 2.

1924–1925 (Thirty-Ninth Championship Season)

During one of the few Cuban seasons that started with five teams, Almendares walked off with its first title in five years. At least some of the credit went to Adolfo Luque (later a successful Alacranes manager) who returned to the team after two campaigns with rival Habana and posted an unblemished 3–0 pitching mark. Counting largely on imported Negro leaguers, Almendares benefited heavily from a league-best 73 hits by "Pop" Lloyd, game-breaking baserunning by Dick Lundy, and nine pitching victories posted by Wilbur "Bullet" Rogan. Home-grown Negro leaguer Oscar Levis was the true mound ace for Joseíto Rodríguez's Blues and tied Rogan with nine wins while also logging a dozen complete games. Just as the previous season's schedule had been cut short due to the landslide victory by Santa Clara, again league officials called a formal halt to the one-sided action once Almendares had piled up an eight-and-a-half game margin over Habana by the end of January.

Champion— Almendares (33–16–1), Manager: Joseíto Rodríguez

Other Teams: 2-Habana (26–26–2), 3-Marianao (18–27–3), 4-Santa Clara (16–22–2), 5-Matanzas (5–7)

Individual Batting Leaders— **BA**: Alejandro Oms (SC) .393; **AB**: John "Pop" Lloyd (A) 196; **Runs**: Valentín Dreke (A) 45; **Hits**: John "Pop" Lloyd 73; **2B**: Alejandro Oms, Cristóbal Torriente (H) 13; **3B**: John "Pop" Lloyd 6; **HR**: Mayarí Montalvo (SC-M) 5; **Steals**: Dick Lundy (A) 11.

Individual Pitching Leaders— **Pct**: José Acosta (A) 4–1 (.800); **G**: Oscar Levis (H), Martín Dihigo (H) 20; **CG**: Oscar Levis 12; **W**: Oscar Levis, Wilbur "Bullet" Rogan (A) 9; **L**: Bill Holland (SC-M) 8; **Shutouts**: Arthur Henderson (H) 3.

No-Hit Game— Oscar Levis (October 11, 1924), Habana defeated Almendares (1–0)

1925–1926 (Fortieth Championship Season)

Three clubs started the campaign but only two finished. San José withdrew early and forfeited its final 25 matches (13 against Habana and an even dozen to Almendares). The deciding head-to-head contest between the evenly matched Reds and Blues was played on January 31 and witnessed Almendares' Isidro Fabré overcome Habana, 6–2, despite permitting 11 base hits. Valentín Dreke starred in the outfield for the Alacranes and posted a lofty .387 batting average, still a distant runner-up to the sterling .430 of Jud Wilson (the second highest Cuban League mark ever for a batter with 100 plate appearances). Another noteworthy performance with the bat was turned in by Negro leagues immortal John Henry "Pop" Lloyd (called "El Cuchara" or "The Shovel" for his defensive prowess at shortstop), who stroked the ball at an amazing .373 clip though already approaching the tender age of 42 and near the end of his second decade in the league.

New League Name— Liga General de Base Ball

Champion—Almendares (34–13–2), Manager: Joseíto Rodríguez

Other Teams— 2-Habana (32–15–2), 3-San José (3–41)

Individual Batting Leaders—**BA**: Jud "Johnny" Wilson (H) .430; **AB**: Valentín Dreke (A) 163; **Runs**: Johnny Wilson, Valentín Dreke 37; **Hits**: Johnny Wilson 64; **HR**: Johnny Wilson, John "Pop" Lloyd (A) 3; **Steals**: Johnny Wilson 10.

Individual Pitching Leaders—**Pct**: César Alvarez (A) 10–2 (.833); **G**: Oscar Levis (H) 15; **CG**: César Alvarez 9; **W**: César Alvarez 10; **L**: Jesse Winters (SJ-H), C.A. Dudley (SJ-A) 6.

1926–1927 (FORTY-FIRST CHAMPIONSHIP SEASON)

The search for a more balanced league continued with the addition of a Cienfuegos club (which lasted for only 13 games before folding) in Las Villas Province, and the revival of a team cleverly named Cuba. All this tinkering was an effort to find a third team capable of providing interest outside of fan-favorites Habana and Almendares. By labeling a team "Cuba" the league fathers were most likely counting on a certain patriotic appeal, but they also loaded this team with such stars as Dihigo, Alejandro Crespo, Bartolo Portuondo, Champion Mesa and Isidro Fabré. Cuba endured the next three seasons, with little on-field success, before being scuttled in favor of a resurrected Santa Clara team. Storm signals arose this season both figuratively and literally, however, and underscored the rapidly worsening conditions of the Cuban winter circuit. Luque and Miguel Angel González abandoned the Cuban League to form their own championship tournament (with teams called Alacranes, Leones and Marianao) played in the new University of Havana stadium and referred to as the Campeonato Triangular. A further severe blow for league mogul Abel Linares and his partners came in late October, when a vicious hurricane gutted the new Almendares Park, which was hastily rebuilt on a lesser scale and thus continued in use, yet was never quite the same magnificent venue thereafter.

New League Name— Liga General de Base Ball de la Republia de Cuba

Champion—Habana (20–11), Manager: Miguel Angel González

Other Teams— 2-Almendares (11–16), 3-Cuba (8–12–1), 4-Cienfuegos (6–6–1)

Individual Batting Leaders—**BA**: Manuel Cueto (H-Cuba) .398; **AB**: Oscar Estrada (H) 132; **Runs**: Paito Herrera (H) 24; **Hits**: Manuel Cueto 41; **2B**: Manuel Cueto 7; **3B**: Julio Rojo (H), Cuco Correa (Cuba-Cienfuegos) 4; **HR**: José Hernández (A) 4; **Steals**: Cando López (Cienfuegos-A) 15.

Individual Pitching Leaders—**Pct**: Juan Olmo (H) 3–0 (1.000); **G**: Raúl Alvarez (H) 15; **CG**: Raúl Alvarez 7; **W**: Pedro Dibut (H), Claude Grier (Cuba-H-Cienfuegos) 5; **L**: Bob McClure (Cienfuegos-H-Cuba) 8.

1927–1928 (FORTY-SECOND CHAMPIONSHIP SEASON)

The first award given for Most Valuable Player (Jugador Más Valioso) was presented to Martín Dihigo, who would later reclaim the honor on three additional occasions (1936, 1937, and 1942). While Dihigo inspired the champion Leones with a solid 4–2 pitching mark, plus a .415 batting average built upon a league-best 45 hits, teammate Jud (called "Johnny" in Cuba) Wilson was actually the circuit's top batsmen (.424) and Oscar Levis (also with Habana) paced all pitchers by claiming seven of his nine decisions. While only eight different batters ever topped the .400 mark in Cuban League play while posting more than 100 at-bats (Wilson did it twice), this was the only time two achieved the feat during the same league season. Campanita Bell also posted five pitching victories for the champion Habana club and the batting title earned by Wilson was his second in the short span of three years.

Champion—Habana (24–13), Manager: Miguel Angel González

Other Teams— 2-Almendares (17–23–1), 3-Cuba (16–21–1)

Individual Batting Leaders—**BA**: Jud "Johnny" Wilson (H) .424; **AB**: Cando López (C) 158; **Runs**: Johnny Wilson 36; **Hits**: Martín Dihigo (H) 54; **HR**: Oscar Charleston (C) 5; **Steals**: Oscar Charleston 11.

Individual Pitching Leaders—**Pct**: Oscar Levis (H) 7–2 (.778); **G**: Willie Powell (C) 18; **CG**: Willie Foster (C) 8; **W**: Oscar Levis 7; **L**: Willie Foster 8.

MVP— Martín Dihigo (H)

1928–1929 (FORTY-THIRD CHAMPIONSHIP SEASON)

The season's outstanding individual moment came when Negro leagues immortal Cool Papa Bell (known as "Jimmy" to Cuban fans) socked three homers in a single game at the tiny Aída Park baseball grounds in Cienfuegos. Known as a speedster and not a slugger, Bell's surprising trio of blasts came off three separate Habana pitchers, including Martín Dihigo and Campanita Bell. Cienfuegos brought up the rear in its second season in the league under manager Tinti Molina but nonetheless showed considerable promise on the field. Featured in the Cienfuegos line-up were home-grown southpaw hurler Luis Tiant and a stable of imported blackball stars that included Bell, flashy shortstop Willie Wells, slugger Mule Suttles, and standout Kansas City Monarchs catcher Frank Duncan, who a few seasons earlier had contributed heavily with Santa Clara. The .432 batting average recorded by Alejandro Oms was an all-time Cuban League high water mark among those batsmen who came to the plate at least one hundred times.

Champion—Habana (43–12–1), Manager: Miguel Angel González

Other Teams— 2-Almendares (31–27–1), 3-Cuba (17–34–1), 4-Cienfuegos (15–38–1)

Individual Batting Leaders—**BA**: Alejandro Oms (H) .432; **AB**: Alejandro Oms 176; **Runs**: Jimmy "Cool Papa" Bell (Cienfuegos) 44; **Hits**: Alejandro Oms 76; **2B**: Alejandro Oms 18; **3B**: Orville Riggins (A) 9; **HR**: Jimmy "Cool Papa" Bell 5; **Steals**: Jimmy "Cool Papa" Bell 17.

Individual Pitching Leaders—**Pct**: Adolfo Luque (Cuba-H) 9–2 (.818); **G**: Charles Williams (Cienfuegos) 19; **CG**: Cliff "Campanita" Bell (H) 11; **W**: Adolfo Luque, Cliff Bell 9; **L**: Charlie Williams 8.

MVP—Alejandro Oms (H)

1929–1930 (Forty-Fourth Championship Season)

In one of the few seasons that featured extensive action outside of Havana, Cienfuegos and Santa Clara both played home games in those respective cities. The addition of a Santa Clara team not only made road trips to Las Villas Province (to play Cienfuegos) more sensible for the two Havana clubs, but also set up a Santa Clara–Cienfuegos rivalry outside of the capital. Interest in the Cuban pro league was finally extended to the provinces with a Cienfuegos pennant victory under player-manager (and star shortstop) Pelayo Chacón. Notable players included local standbys Dihigo with Almendares and Luque with Habana, while Cienfuegos once more boasted Negro leaguers Willie Wells and Cool Papa Bell and Santa Clara brought back such luminaries from their early-twenties team as Marcelle, Warfield and Oms (the eventual batting champion). It was perhaps the last quality season for nearly a full decade, as the Cuban League would soon fall unfortunate victim to the country's deteriorating financial health.

New League Name—Liga General de Base Ball de la Republia

Champion—Cienfuegos (33–19–2), Manager: Pelayo Chacón

Other Teams—2-Almendares (23–26–3), 3-Santa Clara (21–21–2), 4-Habana (20–31–1)

Individual Batting Leaders—**BA**: Alejandro Oms (SC) .389; **AB**: Jimmy "Cool Papa" Bell (C) 220; **Runs**: Jimmy Bell 52; **Hits**: Chino Smith (H) 67; **2B**: Jimmy Bell 14; **3B**: Chino Smith 7; **HR**: George "Mulo" Suttles (SC) 7; **Steals**: Rap Nixon (A) 19.

Individual Pitching Leaders—**Pct**: Eliodoro "Yoyo" Diaz (C) 13–3 (.813); **G**: Cliff "Campanita" Bell (H) 23; **CG**: Eliodoro "Yoyo" Diaz 11; **W**: Yoyo Diaz 13; **L**: Cliff "Campanita" Bell, Adolfo Luque (H) 8; **Shutouts**: Johnny Allen (A) 2.

MVP—Willie Wells (Cienfuegos)

1930–1931

The first season's play scheduled for La Tropical Stadium barely got off the ground before it was called to a halt during the last week of October for lack of fan interest. A hastily arranged second championship called the "Campeonato Único" was then pasted together with reshuffled teams. For the second tournament Marianao was substituted for Santa Clara and Almendares took up the name (occasionally used in the past) of Almendarista. Almendares came out on top of both the suspended and "official" seasons, lead primarily by the solid pitching of a quartet of aces composed of Martín Dihigo, Cocaina García, Basilio "Brujo" Rosell and Isidro Fabré. A second solid ball club was the one fielded by Marianao which featured big leaguers Billy Herman and Claude Jonnard and blackball stars Oscar Charleston and Ramón Bragaña.

Cuban League Suspended Season

Teams and Records—Almendares (3–1), Habana (1–2–1), Cienfuegos (1–1–2), Santa Clara (0–1–1)

Individual Batting Leaders—**BA**: Tom Young (SC) .571; **AB**: John Kalton (A) 18; **Runs**: Pedro Arango (C) 6; **Hits**: José Rodríguez (A), Julio Rojo (H) 6; **2B**: Julio Rojo, Manual "Cocaina" García (A), José Maria Fernández (A), Manuel Cueto (SC) 2; **HR**: Pedro Arango, Rogelio Alonso (A), "Tetelo" Vargas (H) 1.

Individual Pitching Leaders—**Pct**: Manuel "Cocaina" García (A), Johnny Allen (A), Emilo Sarda (A), Chet Brewer (H) 1–0 (1.000); **G**: Cliff "Campanita" Bell (H) 3.

Campeonato Unico Extended Season

Teams and Records—Almendarista (9–4–1), Marianao (9–5), Habana (5–9), Cienfuegos (2–7–1), Santa Clara (3–3)

Individual Batting Leaders—**BA**: Oscar Charleston (M) .373; **AB**: Cando López (H) 61; **Runs**: Oscar Charleston 12; **Hits**: Oscar Charleston, Dick Lundy (A) 19; **2B**: Johnny Gill (M), Cheo Ramos (A) 4; **3B**: Oscar Charleston 5; **HR**: Ernest Smith (H), José Maria Fernández (A) 1; **Steals**: Chuck Dressen (H) 6.

Individual Pitching Leaders—**Pct**: Martín Dihigo (A) 2–0 (1.000); **G**: Claude Jonnard (M) 7; **CG**: Claude Jonnard 4; **W**: Claude Jonnard 5; **L**: Cliff "Campanita" Bell (H) 3.

1931–1932 (Forty-Fifth Championship Season)

Back in action after the previous year's interrupted season, the league featured but three teams and a one-sided race that fell in favor of the Scorpions of Almendares. Eight straight victories out of the shoot for the Blues over rival Habana (plus 13 of 15 overall) doomed the lackluster Leones to the league basement and also left Regla trailing in the dust behind the runaway champions. Despite their "off season" performance Miguel Angel González's Habana club did feature three stellar rookies — Silvio García, Roberto "Tarzan" Estalella, Jacinto "Battling Siki" Roque — all destined to be future league stars. Negro league standout Rodolfo Fernández established himself as one of Cuba's top pitchers (with the most complete games, wins and shutouts), but the brightest stars for Almendares were a pair of youngsters who peaked early and made little noise in coming seasons. One was catcher Ramón Couto, who salted away a batting title with a .400 average; the other was MVP outfielder Carlos Etchegoyen, who rang up the top RBI total.

New League Name—Liga General de Base Ball Profesional

Champion—Almendares (21–9–4), Manager: Joseíto Rodríguez

Other Teams— 2-Regla (15–15–3), 3-Habana (9–21–1)

Individual Batting Leaders—BA: Ramón Couto (A) .400; **AB**: Cando López (R) 120; **Runs**: Alejandro Oms (H) 28; **Hits**: Alejandro Oms 44; **2B**: Carlos Etchegoyen (A) 11; **3B**: Cando López, Pedro Arango (R), Ismael "Mulo" Morales (R) 3; **HR**: Alejandro Oms, Ismael Morales 3; **RBI**: Carlos Etchegoyen 28; **Steals**: Alejandro Oms 14.

Individual Pitching Leaders—Pct: Juan Eckelson (A) 5–1 (.833); **G**: Luis Tiant, Sr. (R) 19; **CG**: Rodolfo Fernández (A) 9; **W**: Rodolfo Fernández 8; **L**: Luis Tiant, Sr. 6; **IP**: Luis Tiant, Sr. 92.1; **SO**: Luis Tiant, Sr. 54; **BB**: Eliodoro "Yoyo" Diaz (R) 23; **Shutouts**: Rodolfo Fernández 2.

MVP— Carlos Etchegoyen (A)

1932–1933 (Forty-Sixth Championship Season)

Growing political upheavals in Havana brought the season to an abrupt end the first week in January (it had started in October) with Miguel Angel González's Leones and Luque's Alacranes locked in a dead-heat after only 22 games. A crucial late-inning home run slugged for Habana by Roberto "Tarzán" Estalella in the final game played gave the Leones a narrow 4–3 win and caused the frustrating deadlock between the "Eternal Rivals." The blow also gave Estalella the longball crown with a mere three. And the short season also accounted for Miguel Angel González's astronomical league-best batting mark, which had soared to a .432 level when play abruptly halted.

New League Name— Liga de Base Ball Professional de la Republia

Co-Champion— Habana (13–9), Manager: Miguel Angel González

Co-Champion— Almendares (13–9) Manager: Adolfo Luque

Other Teams— 3-Marianao (7–15)

Individual Batting Leaders—BA: Miguel Angel González (H) .432; **AB**: José Abreu (H), Ismael "Mulo" Morales (H-M) 92; **Runs**: José Abreu, Pedro Arango (A-M) 17; **Hits**: José Abreu, Lázaro Salazar (A) 30; **2B**: Alejandro Oms (H) 4; **3B**: Jacinto Roque (M), Eddy Gutiérrez (H) 3; **HR**: Roberto Estalella (H) 3; **RBI**: Ismael Morales, Lázaro Salazar, Carlos Etchegoyen (A) 15; **Steals**: Lázaro Salazar 13.

Individual Pitching Leaders—Pct: Jesús Lorenzo (A) 3–0 (1.000); **G**: Jesús Miralles (H) 6; **CG**: Jesús Miralles 6; **W**: Jesús Miralles 6; **L**: Jesús Miralles 5.

MVP— Not Selected

1933–1934

Political turmoil and civil unrest surrounding the first 20th-century Cuban revolution and the downfall of President Gerardo Machado not only cut short an ill-fated 1932–33 season but also resulted in cancellation of championship play altogether during the following winter. Almendares Park now lay in ruined abandon, overrun by decay and weeds, though it was only barely fifteen years old. A new playing venue would have to be unveiled when championship play resumed after the temporary suspension of professional baseball in the capital city.

1934–1935 (Forty-Seventh Championship Season)

With political rest still in the air, a new season was launched in La Tropical Stadium, a facility that had been built a half-dozen years earlier and inaugurated with the Second Central American Games staged in Havana in the spring of 1930. With the new park located in the Marianao district, the Marianao team was retained as the third league entry and managed to edge out Habana for the season's runner-up slot. Lázaro Salazar emerged as a superstar, beginning the campaign in Marianao but finishing it with the champions managed by Dolf Luque. The talented southpaw was champion batter with an average above .400 and won all but one of his seven mound decisions, teaming with Luque for an effective one-two, righty-lefty pitching punch. "The Pride of Havana" (Luque) himself posted a remarkable 1.27 ERA. It was not a proud season for the Cuban League, however, as all three league teams suffered embarrassing exhibition defeats at the hands of the independent semi-pro Rum Havana Club team (based in Cárdenas and featuring several ex–Cuban Leaguers plus future big leaguer Roberto Estalella) and some league games had to be played on the Vedado Tennis Club grounds, since soccer matches were still the feature event at La Tropical.

New League Name— Liga General de Base Ball de la Republia

Champion— Almendares (18–9–1), Manager: Adolfo Luque

Other Teams— 2-Marianao (12–16), 3-Habana (11–16–1)

Individual Batting Leaders—BA: Lázaro Salazar (M-A) .407; **AB**: Cando López (A) 125; **Runs**: Cando López 18; **Hits**: Cando López 36; **2B**: Alberto Alvarez (H) 7; **3B**: Lázaro Salazar 6; **RBI**: Alberto Alvarez 16; **Steals**: Helio Mirabal (M) 7.

Individual Pitching Leaders—Pct: Lázaro Salazar (M-A) 6–1 (.857); **G**: Gil Torres (H) 13; **CG**: Tommie de la Cruz (M) 7; **W**: Lázaro Salazar, Tommie de la Cruz, Adolfo Luque (A) 6; **L**: Jesús Miralles (H) 8 **IP**: Tommie de la Cruz 81; **ERA**: Adolfo Luque 1.27.

MVP— Lázaro Salazar (M-A)

1935–1936 (Forty-Eighth Championship Season)

Martín Dihigo reached another lofty peak in a career full of mountain tops when he duplicated a remarkable feat of versatility also later accomplished in the summer Mexican League — that of being both the league's winningest pitcher and batting champion at one and the same time. Cando López (Almendares) set a somewhat less noticeable record when he paced the circuit in plate appearances for the third time. The team title for Santa Clara was the second for that occasional club and some thought this edition was nearly as strong as the great 1923–24 team with Oscar Charleston. The up-beat season signaled a definite revival of league fortunes, although the successes of Los Leopardes did not mean much economic health for the circuit, since the champions still drew small crowds in their tiny La Boulanger Park in Santa Clara and also never replaced the "Eternal Rivals" as fan favorites in Habana.

New League Name— Liga de Base Ball Professional de la Republia

Champion— Santa Clara (34–14–1), Manager: Martín Dihigo

Other Teams— 2-Almendares (28–20–3), 3-Habana (18–29–1), 4-Marianao (15–32–3)

Individual Batting Leaders—**BA**: Martín Dihigo (SC) .358; **AB**: Cando López (A), Javier Pérez (A) 200; **Runs**: Martín Dihigo 42; **Hits**: Martín Dihigo, Willie Wells (SC) 63; **2B**: John Williams (H) 11; **3B**: Martín Dihigo 8; **HR**: Willie Wells, Jacinto Roque (A) 5; **RBI**: Martín Dihigo, Cy Perkins (SC) 38.

Individual Pitching Leaders—**Pct**: Martín Dihigo (SC) 11–2 (.846); **G**: Tommie de la Cruz (M) 23; **CG**: Martín Dihigo 13; **W**: Martín Dihigo 11; **L**: Luis Tiant, Sr. (H), Gilberto Torres (H) 10; **Shutouts**: Martín Dihigo 4.

MVP— Martín Dihigo (SC)

1936–1937 (FORTY-NINTH CHAMPIONSHIP SEASON)

Negro leaguer Ray Brown established a new standard for Cuban League pitchers with his 21–4 record in the service of Santa Clara, but it was the durable veteran Martín Dihigo who proved to be the league's most valuable pitcher as well as its most valuable all-around player. Dihigo was now managing and playing for Marianao which resulted in his winning back-to-back titles with different clubs, the first time this trick had been turned. Such American stars as Ray Brown, Buck Leonard, Dave "Showboat" Thomas, and Willie Wells also contributed heavily to the noticeably improved quality of league teams. Among the other accomplishments of Ray Brown (U.S. blackball star with the Homestead Grays) was included a November no-hitter in La Boulanger Park against Habana and its ace Tommie de la Cruz, plus a most remarkable December doubleheader in the same venue. In the latter, Brown pitched both games, allowed no earned runs in 20 innings, and shut out Habana in the nightcap, after losing 1–0 to Luis Tiant in the lid-lifter. When the Leopardos and Grey Monks finished in a dead heat, a best-of-three playoff settled the championship claims.

New League Name— Liga Nacional de Base Ball Profesional

Champion— Marianao (38–31–3), Manager: Martín Dihigo

Other Teams— 2-Santa Clara (36–30–1), 3-Almendares (31–36), 4-Habana (29–37–2)

Individual Batting Leaders—**BA**: Harry Williams (SC) .339; **AB**: Clyde Spearman (M), Huesito Vargas (SC) 261; **Runs**: Lázaro Salazar (A) 47; **Hits**: Clyde Spearman 84; **2B**: Harry Williams 18; **3B**: Cando López (M), Herman Andrews (H) 5; **HR**: Herman Andrews, Roberto Estalella (H) 5; **RBI**: Clyde Spearman 48; **Steals**: Harry Williams 15.

Individual Pitching Leaders—**Pct**: Raymond "Jabao"

Brown (SC) 21–4 (.840); **G**: Martín Dihgio (M) 30; **CG**: Raymond Brown 23; **W**: Raymond Brown 21; **L**: Luis Tiant, Sr. (H) 12.

No-Hit Game— Raymond "Jabao" Brown (November 7, 1936), Santa Clara defeated Habana (7–0)

MVP— Martín Dihigo (M)

1937–1938 (FIFTIETH CHAMPIONSHIP SEASON)

Lázaro Salazar emerged as a true star, managing Santa Clara (known this season as "Los Pilongos" or "Locals"— a nickname they had occasionally also worn in the early 1920s) to another pennant, winning three pitching decisions without defeat, batting a solid .318 while playing first base, and fittingly garnering MVP honors at season's end. Habana suffered through its worst season ever, losing 58 times, including 20 forfeits after the club disbanded in late January. When Habana left the fray the majority of its players went to either Almendares (infielder Gilberto Torres and pitcher Tommie de la Cruz) or Marianao (hurler Basilio Rosell), while the already solid Santa Clara team picked up only reserve Tony Castaño.

Champion— Santa Clara (44–18–4), Manager: Lázaro Salazar

Other Teams— 2-Almendares (40–23–3), 3-Marianao (35–28–4), 4-Habana (8–58–1)

Individual Batting Leaders—**BA**: Sam Bankhead (SC) .366; **AB**: Sam Bankhead 243; **Runs**: Sam Bankhead 47; **Hits**: Sam Bankhead 89; **2B**: Gilberto Torres (H-A) 11; **3B**: Sam Bankhead, Lázaro Salazar (SC) 5; **HR**: Raymond "Jabao" Brown (SC), Willie Wells (A), Roberto Estalella (A) 4; **RBI**: Sam Bankhead 34; **Steals**: Ray "Tatúla" Dandridge (A) 11.

Individual Pitching Leaders—**Pct**: Raymond "Jabao" Brown (SC) 12–5 (.706); **G**: Bob Griffith (SC) 24; **CG**: Raymond Brown 14; **W**: Raymond Brown, Bob Griffith 12; **L**: Basilio Rosell (H-M) 12; **Shutouts**: Bob Griffith 5.

MVP— Lázaro Salazar (SC)

1938–1939 (FIFTY-FIRST CHAMPIONSHIP SEASON)

Santa Clara finished first for the third time in four seasons, and the second straight winter under the leadership of Salazar, and again comparisons were made to the great Santa Clara team of the early 1920s. For all its strength with a lineup of pitchers Salazar, Cocaina García, Ray Brown, and Schoolboy Taylor and sluggers Josh Gibson, Sam Bankhead and Santos Amaro, Los Leopardos never completely outdistanced Habana, which had rebounded behind another outstanding pitching effort from Martín Dihigo. The year's most memorable moment perhaps came with a tremendous Josh Gibson homer slugged in La Boulanger Park off a delivery from Chino Fortes of Team Cuba. The towering drive quickly became a centerpiece of Gibson's growing (and even mythic) Negro league and winter league baseball legend.

Champion— Santa Clara (34–20–2), Manager: Lázaro Salazar

Other Teams— 2-Habana (29–25–2), 3-Cuba (25–29–2), 4-Almendares (20–34–2)

Individual Batting Leaders—**BA**: Tony Castaño (SC) .371;

AB: Alberto Alvarez (H) 228; **Runs**: Josh Gibson (SC) 50; **Hits**: Santos "Canguro" Amoro (SC) 78; **2B**: Lázaro Salazar (SC) 12; **3B**: Mantecado Linares (A) 5; **HR**: Josh Gibson (SC) 11; **RBI**: Santos Amaro 49; **Steals**: Jacinto Roque (C) 6.

Individual Pitching Leaders— **Pct**: Martín Dihigo (H) 14–2 (.875); **G**: Alejandro Carrasquel (C) 26; **CG**: Raymond "Jabao" Brown (SC) 16; **W**: Martín Dihigo 14; **L**: Theolic Smith (A) 9; **Shutouts**: Manual "Cocaina" Garcá (SC) 3.

MVP— Alejandro Carrasquel (C)

1939–1940 (FIFTY-SECOND CHAMPIONSHIP SEASON)

Almendares climbed back on top by a slim two-game margin in one of the most hotly contested seasons in years. Rodolfo Fernández proved the key hurler for Luque's club when he posted four straight wins in the final crucial weeks and also blanked Cienfuegos in the last match between the two leading clubs to seal the league title. An additional pair of Negro leaguers contributed heavily to the cause, with Ted "Double Duty" Radcliffe recording seven victories and three shutouts and shortstop Willie Wells earning MVP honors with fine all-around offensive and defensive play. Santa Clara's Tony Castaño (a future Sugar Kings manager) became the league's first back-to-back batting champion since Alejandro Oms turned the trick exactly one decade earlier.

New League Name— Liga Cubana de Base Ball Profesional

Champion— Almendares (28–23–1), Manager: Adolfo Luque

Other Teams— 2-Cienfuegos (26–25–1), 3-Santa Clara (24–27–1), 3-Habana (24–27–3)

Individual Batting Leaders— **BA**: Tony Castaño (SC) .340; **AB**: Sam Bankhead (SC), Frank Crespi (H) 209; **Runs**: Sam Bankhead 41; **Hits**: Sam Bankhead 67; **2B**: Gilberto Torres (H) 10; **3B**: Huesito Vargas (SC) 5; **HR**: George "Mulo" Suttles (C) 4; **RBI**: Tony Castaño 44; **Steals**: Harry Kimbro (A) 18.

Individual Pitching Leaders— **Pct**: Rodolfo Fernández (A) 7–4 (.636); **G**: Tommie de la Cruz (H) 31; **CG**: Barney Morris (C) 15; **W**: Barney Morris 13; **L**: Luis Tiant, Sr. (H), Barney Brown (H) 9; **Shutouts**: Barney Morris, Rodolfo Fernández, Ted "Double Duty" Radcliffe (A) 3.

MVP— Willie Wells (Almendares)

1940–1941 (FIFTY-THIRD CHAMPIONSHIP SEASON)

Habana put an end to its own eight-year championship dry spell during a season noted for such historical footnotes as the briefest game in league history, the final appearance of a team representing Santa Clara, and a ten-game suspension of famed veteran umpire Amado Maestri. The historic "shortest-ever" outing came on the season's final day (Santa Clara's last game ever) and saw Cienfuegos blank the Leopardos behind Vidal López 1–0, in a contest timed at only one hour and nine minutes. Maestri's forced vacation came after fans protested an overly quick suspension of a rain-plagued

game. Victory was wrapped up for the Leones with some shrewd moves by manager Miguel Angel González before the first pitch of the campaign was ever thrown. These included the signing of veteran Martín Dihigo (who would win eight games) to supplement the pitching corps, and the additional acquisition of hurler Rodolfo Fernández (who claimed seven more) from Almendares in exchange for Tommie de la Cruz. Almendares fell into the basement when manager Dolf Luque experienced ongoing disputes over salary with Negro leaguers Terris McDuffie (who demanded salary increases after each victory) and Sam Bankhead (who gained a raise and then showed up for a doubleheader so drunk he committed six errors during the afternoon's double action).

Champion— Habana (31–18–5), Manager: Miguel Angel González

Other Teams— 2-Santa Clara (25–26–1), 3-Cienfuegos (25–26–2), 4-Almendares (20–31–8)

Individual Batting Leaders— **BA**: Lázaro Salazar (A) .316; **AB**: Cuco Correa (A) 219; **Runs**: Pedro Pagés (C) 37; **Hits**: Helio Mirabal (C) 59; **2B**: Roberto "Tarzán" Estalella (H) 13; **3B**: Carlos Blanco (H), Silvio García (C) 5; **HR**: Alejandro Crespo (C) 3; **RBI**: Clemente "Sungo" Carrera (H) 30; **Steals**: Alejandro Crespo 13.

Individual Pitching Leaders— **Pct**: Gilberto Torres (H) 10–3 (.769); **G**: Gilberto Torres 27; **CG**: Vidal López (C) 16; **W**: Vidal López 12; **L**: Luis Tiant, Sr. (H), Armando "Indio" Torres (SC), Tommie de la Cruz (H-A) 7.

MVP— Gilberto Torres (Habana)

1941–1942 (FIFTY-FOURTH CHAMPIONSHIP SEASON)

With the league reduced to but three teams, Almendares returned to the winner's circle and Dolf Luque claimed his fifth managerial crown (adding to those already earned in 1920, 1933, 1935 and 1940, all under the banner of "Los Azules"). Righty Ramón Bragaña and southpaw Agapito Mayor posted 15 of the 25 Almendares victories between them and Bragaña rang up five shutouts (four in a row for a new record) among his own nine triumphs. A season's highlight outside of league play was a five-game exhibition series in March at La Tropical in which Cuban all-stars were victorious three times versus the defending National League champion Brooklyn Dodgers. The series was notable for a brilliant game-saving catch by outfielder Alejandro Crespo off a drive by Brooklyn's Peewee Reese, a play that turned the series in favor of the host Cubans.

Champion— Almendares (25–19–4), Manager: Adolfo Luque

Other Teams— 2-Habana (23–21–5), 3-Cienfuegos (18–26–3)

Individual Batting Leaders— **BA**: Silvio García (C) .351; **AB**: Napoleón Heredia (C) 191; **Runs**: Silvio García 24; **Hits**: Silvio García 60; **2B**: Alejandro Crespo (C) 12; **3B**: Roberto Estalella (H) 4; **HR**: Silvio García 4; **RBI**: Roberto Estalella 27; **Steals**: Clemente "Sungo" Carrera (H) 10.

Individual Pitching Leaders— **Pct**: Agapito Mayor (A),

Max Macon (C) 6–2 (.750); **G**: Ramón Bragaña (A) 21; **CG**: Ramón Bragaña, Martín Dihigo (H) 11; **W**: Ramón Bragaña 9; **L**: Steve Rachunok (C) 9; **Shutouts**: Ramón Bragaña 5.

MVP — Martín Dihigo (Habana)

1942–1943 (FIFTY-FIFTH CHAMPIONSHIP SEASON)

Almendares' second straight triumph under Luque and the club's seventeenth title overall came mainly on the strength of top offensive performances by outfielder Roberto Ortiz (the league home run and RBI pacesetter), MVP Antonio "El Pollo" Rodríguez (who posted the top marks for base hits and runs scored), and rookie sensation Héctor Rodríguez (later a crack big league third baseman in Chicago). Cocaina García of rival Habana shown brilliantly on the mound with the first of a pair of campaigns in which he was Cuba's winningest pitcher. Season's end was later surrounded with controversy when it was discovered that official scorer Julio Franquiz had erred in assigning one plate appearance too few to announced batting champion Alejandro Crespo (Cienfuegos), which allowed Crespo to own a title that should have belonged to Jacinto Roque (Almendares) by mere percentage points. Although the error was later acknowledged by league officials, it was never corrected in recorded league statistics and Crespo remained the tainted batting leader.

Champion — Almendares (28–20–1), Manager: Adolfo Luque

Other Teams — 2-Habana (24–24–2), 3-Cienfuegos (20–28–1)

Individual Batting Leaders — **BA**: Alejandro Crespo (C) .337; **AB**: Antonio Rodríguez (A) 210; **Runs**: Antonio Rodríguez 31; **Hits**: Alejandro Crespo 63; **2B**: Alejandro Crespo 12; **3B**: Carlos Colás (C) 8; **HR**: Roberto Ortiz (A), Sal Hernández (H) 2; **RBI**: Roberto Ortiz 36; **Steals**: Fermín Guerra (A) 8.

Individual Pitching Leaders — **Pct**: Manuel "Cocaina" García (H) 10–3 (.769); **G**: Ramón Bragaña (A), Adrián Zabala (C) 22; **CG**: Adrián Zabala 14; **W**: Manuel "Cocaina" García 10; **L**: Gilberto Torres (H) 9; **Shutouts**: Adrián Zabala 3.

Top Rookie — Héctor Rodríguez (A)
MVP — Antonio Rodríguez (A)

1943–1944 (FIFTY-SIXTH CHAMPIONSHIP SEASON)

Nearing the end of his brilliant career, Martín Dihigo posted the league's first "official" ERA title and also proved the league's dominant hurler with a near-perfect 8–1 won-lost record for champion Habana. The season got off to a notable start when a number of league mainstays (including Lázaro Salazar, Santos Amaro and future big-league Hall-of-Famer Roy Campanella) were stranded in Mexico, first by World War II flight restrictions and then by an ensuing hurricane which swept through Havana. Southpaw Cocaina García (12–4) provided Miguel Angel González and the Habana Leones with an invincible one-two pitching punch (teaming with right-

hander Dihigo) and highlighted the season early with a rare no-hit, no-run game.

Champion — Habana (32–16), Manager: Miguel Angel González

Other Teams — 2-Almendares (26–22), 3-Cienfuegos (25–23), 4-Marianao (13–35)

Individual Batting Leaders — **BA**: Roberto Ortiz (A) .337; **AB**: Alejandro Crespo (C) 208; **Runs**: Roberto Ortiz 41; **Hits**: Roberto Ortiz 64; **2B**: Alejandro Crespo 11; **3B**: Pedro Formental (C) 6; **HR**: Sal Hernández (H) 3; **RBI**: Pedro Pagés (C) 30; **Steals**: Agustín Bejerano (M) 14.

Individual Pitching Leaders — **Pct**: Martín Dihigo (H) 8–1 (.889); **G**: Coty Leal (M) 26; **CG**: Tommie de la Cruz (A) 10; **W**: Manuel "Cocaina" García (H), Santiago Ullrich (A) 12; **L**: Manolo Fortes (M) 12; **Shutouts**: Cocaina García 3; **ERA**: Martín Dihigo 2.23.

No-Hit Game — Manuel "Cocaina" García (December 11, 1943), Habana defeated Marianao (5–0)

Top Rookie — Conrado Pérez (M)
MVP — Antonio Rodríguez (A), Gilberto Torres (H)

1944–1945 (FIFTY-SEVENTH CHAMPIONSHIP SEASON)

This time around Almendares came out on top under the managerial leadership of Reinaldo Cordeiro, ending a string of five pennants (including two earlier in the decade) earned while being guided by the irrepressible Dolf Luque. Oliverio Ortiz (10–4), Agapito Mayor (7–3) and Tommie de la Cruz (9–4) posted strong seasons on the hill for an Alacranes team that outdistanced Habana by seven games. Tommie de la Cruz provided a season's highlight when he hug up the sixth no-hitter in league history, a 7–0 blanking of rival Habana on January 3, 1945, punctuated by the right-hander's own bases-loaded double that provided more than the needed margin of victory. The season's low point followed four days later when heavy-hitting Almendares outfielder Roberto Ortiz punched umpire Bernardino Rodríguez after a disputed ball-strike call, a regrettable incident that led to suspension and later public apologies from the journeyman major leaguer.

Champion — Almendares (32–16–6), Manager: Reinaldo Cordeiro

Other Teams — 2-Habana (25–23–1), 3-Cienfuegos (24–24–2), 4-Marianao (15–33–3)

Individual Batting Leaders — **BA**: Claro Duany (A-M) .340; **AB**: Héctor Rodríguez (A) 205; **Runs**: Héctor Rodríguez, Avelino Cañizares (A), Santos Amaro (A), Conrado Pérez (C) 29; **Hits**: Santos Amaro, Alejandro Crespo (C) 59; **2B**: Andrés Fleitas (A) 10; **3B**: Héctor Rodríguez 5; **HR**: Claro Duany 3; **RBI**: Alejandro Crespo, Andrés Fleitas 29; **Steals**: Antonio Rodríguez (A) 13.

Individual Pitching Leaders — **Pct**: Oliverio Ortíz (A) 10–4 (.714); **G**: Luis Tiant, Sr. (M) 29; **CG**: Manuel "Cocaina" García (M), Terris McDuffie (C) 9; **W**: Oliverio Ortíz 10; **L**: Daniel Ríos (M) 9; **SO**: Terris McDuffie 68; **Shutouts**: Tommie de la Cruz (A) 4; **ERA**: Tommie de la Cruz, Jorge Comellas (H) 2.30.

No-Hit Game—Tomás de la Cruz (January 3, 1945), Almendares defeated Habana (7–0)

Top Rookie—Leovigildo Xiqués (A)

MVP—Pedro Pagés (C)

1945–1946 (Fifty-Eighth Championship Season)

The last championship season played at La Tropical Stadium also marked the only campaign of the decade in which the league's pennant winner was not one of those "Eternal Rivals" wearing either red or blue uniforms. Cienfuegos (guided by the veteran manager Dolf Luque and still featuring Martín Dihigo in his penultimate season as an active pitcher) marched to victory primarily on the strength of front-line pitching from native southpaw Adrián Zabala (9–3) and imported right-hander Sal Maglie (9–6), while runner-up Habana strengthened its roster in mid-season with the additions of Americans Dick Sisler (9 homers), Lou Klein (.275 BA) and Fred Martin (2–3 pitching record). A season's highlight was three homers belted in a single game (January 24) by Sisler, all struck off deliveries from future New York Giants ace Sal Maglie.

Champion—Cienfuegos (37–23–4), Manager: Adolfo Luque

Other Teams—2-Habana (31–29–2), 3-Almendares (29–31–5), 4-Marianao (23–37–3)

Individual Batting Leaders—**BA**: Lloyd Davenport (H-A) .332; **AB**: Antonio Rodríguez (C) 250; **Runs**: Roland Gladu (C) 41; **Hits**: Alejandro Crespo (C) 72; **2B**: Andrés Fleitas (A), Barney Serrell (M) 14; **3B**: Cisco Campos (M), Napoleón Reyes (C) 6; **HR**: Dick Sisler (H) 9; **RBI**: Alejandro Crespo 35; **Steals**: Fermín Guerra (A), Avelino Cañizares (A) 6.

Individual Pitching Leaders—**Pct**: Adrián Zabala (C) 9–3 (.750); **G**: Natilla Jiménez (H) 32; **CG**: Natilla Jiménez, Jorge Comellas (H-A), Sal Maglie (C) 9; **W**: Natilla Jiménez 13; **L**: Agapito Mayor (A), Julio Moreno (M) 10; **Shutouts**: Jorge Comellas 4.

Top Rookie—Orestes Miñoso (M)

MVP—Alejandro Crespo (C)

1946–1947 (Fifty-Ninth Championship Season)

A new modern Havana Stadium (popularly named Cerro Stadium for the distinct in which it was located) was inaugurated with the season opener between Almendares (a 9–1 winner) and Cienfuegos on October 26, 1946. Immortals Dolf Luque (Almendares) and Martín Dihigo (Cienfuegos) fittingly managed the two clubs in the historical lidlifter that drew a throng estimated at over 31,000 fans. Almendares captured one of the most intense races in league history with a sizzling streak of 13 wins in the season's final 14 outings, overcoming a earlier Habana first-place lead of six and a half games. Victory was ultimately seized by the Alacranes with two dramatic final victories over Habana on the strength of brilliant pitching performances by Agapito Mayor and American Max Lanier, a pair of stellar southpaws. An exotic element to the 1946–47 winter season was provided by existence of a rival league (Liga de la Federación Nacional) staged in abandoned Tropical Stadium and also in outlying provinces. The four-team alternative league consisted of players under contract to organized baseball who feared jeopardizing their standing by playing with pros banned (by MLB commissioner A.B. "Happy" Chandler) for participation in Jorge Pasquel's rebel Mexican League. This new league featured teams named Habana Reds and Oriente (the Blues) that utilized colors and logos of the popular "Eternal Rivales" to gain fan support. Surprising Matanzas captured a shortened season title with its final decisive one-game playoff victory (4–3) over the Habana Reds on December 31. Conrado Marrero made his winter pro debut in the Federation League with Oriente, but later skipped to Almendares in January when the alternative league folded up its abbreviated session.

Champion—Almendares (42–24–2), Manager: Adolfo Luque

Other Teams—2-Habana (40–26–5), 3-Cienfuegos (25–41–1), 4-Marianao (25–41–4)

Individual Batting Leaders—**BA**: Lou Klein (H) .330; **AB**: Leonard (Lennox) Pearson (H) 265; **Runs**: Avelino Cañizares (A) 47; **Hits**: Andrés Fleitas (A) 83; **2B**: George Hausmann (A) 15; **3B**: Hank Thompson (H), Pedro Formental (H) 6; **HR**: Roberto Ortiz (A) 11; **RBI**: Lennie Pearson 45; **Steals**: Héctor Rodríguez (A) 15.

Individual Pitching Leaders—**Pct**: Cocaina García (H) 10–3 (.769); **G**: Sandalio "Sandy" Consuegra (M) 31; **CG**: Adrián Zabala (C) 14; **W**: Adrián Zabala 11; **L**: Sandalio "Sandy" Consuegra 11; **Shutouts**: Cocaina García, Paul Calvert (M), Jorge Comellas (A) 3; **ERA**: Cocaina García 2.03.

Top Rookie—Mario Arencibia (M)

MVP—Andrés Fleitas (A)

Liga de la Federación Nacional (Major League Baseball "Eligible" Players)

Teams and Final Standings—1-Matanzas (19–19–0), Manager: Silvio García; 2-Habana Reds (19–19–1), Manager: Gil Torres; 3-Oriente (Santiago de Cuba) (20–18–2), Manager: Fermín Guerra; 4-Camagüey (5–7–1), Manager: Antonio Rodríguez. *Matanzas won one-game championship playoff versus Habana.

Individual Leaders—**Batting**: Claro Duany (H) .368; **Pitching**: Conrado Marrero (O), 8–5, 2.24 ERA. *Camagüey team was added for second half of season, but planned post-season playoff against champion of third pro league located in Oriente Province (Contramaestre, Santiago, Holguín, Camagüey) was abandoned when season ended early.

1947–1948 (Sixtieth Championship Season)

Perhaps the most unusual winter in Cuban professional baseball history resulted from major league baseball's suspension of both Cuban and American ballplayers who had jumped in 1945 and 1946 to Jorge Pasquel's rebel Mexican League. The result was two separate Cuban winter leagues running parallel campaigns, with banned players competing in La

Tropical in what was called La Liga Nacional de la Federación (i.e., Liga Nacional, not to be confused with Liga de la Federación of the previous season). Habana clubs won both titles, edging Almendares by a single game in the sanctioned league and outpacing two teams named Cuba and the Alacranes (featuring ineligibles from Almendares) in the "Outlaw League" race. Habana's Harry Kimbro, with a new league record for base hits, was the top Cuban League batsman and Connie Marrero (12–2, 1.12 ERA) walked off with top pitching honors. In the "ineligibles" league, Avelino Cañizares (Alacranes) smacked 114 base hits, ten better than Kimbro's newly posted and "official" Cuban League record total.

Champion— Habana (39–33–9), Manager: Miguel Angel González

Other Teams— 2-Almendares (38–34–7), 3-Cienfuegos (35–37–2), 4-Marianao (32–40–4)

Individual Batting Leaders—**BA**: Harry Kimbro (H) .346; **AB**: Leonard (Lennox) Pearson (H) 338; **Runs**: Sam Jethroe (A) 53; **Hits**: Harry Kimbro 104; **2B**: Claro Duany (M) 21; **3B**: Orestes Miñoso (M) 13; **HR**: Chanquilón Diaz (M) 7; **RBI**: Hank Thompson (H) 50; **Steals**: Sam Jethroe 22.

Individual Pitching Leaders—**Pct**: Conrado Marrero (A) 12–2 (.857); **G**: Steve Gerkin (M-H) 33; **CG**: Alex Patterson (H) 18; **W**: Conrado Marrero, Alex Patterson 12; **L**: Alex Patterson 9; **IP**: Alex Patterson 211.2; **SO**: Dave Barnhill (M) 122; **BB**: Alex Patterson 72; **ERA**: Conrado Marrero 1.12.

Top Rookie— Francisco Gallardo (A)

MVP— Conrado Marrero (A)

Liga Nacional (Major League Baseball "Ineligible" Players)

Teams and Final Standings—1-Havana Leones (50–41), Manager: Salvador Hernández; 2-Cuba (46–45–1), Manager: Napoleón Reyes; 3-Alacranes (no record available), Manager: Dolf Luque; 4-Santiago de Cuba (no record available), Manager: Lázaro Salazar. *Santiago withdrew from competition before the season came to early conclusion.

Individual League Batting Leaders—**BA**: Raymond Gladu (C) .330; **Runs**: Avelino Cañizares (A) 53; **Hits**: Avelino Cañizares 114; **HR**: Danny Gardella (C) 10; **RBI**: Roberto Ortiz (A) 55.

Individual League Pitching Leaders— **Pct**: Adrián Zabala (A) 13–7 (.650); **CG**: Sal Maglie (C) 20; **W**: Sal Maglie 14.

MVP— Luis Rodríguez Olmo (H)

1948–1949 (Sixty-First Championship Season)

The pennant parade for Almendares was anchored by a half-dozen top pitching performances from Octavio Rubert (8–1), Morrie Martin (9–2), Agapito Mayor (4–2), Jorge Comellas (4–2), René Solis (7–4) and Conrado Marrero (6–4). Also wearing Almendares colors was the league's top rookie, Willie Miranda, widely considered the best fielding Cuban shortstop before the amateur era following the 1959 revolution. Manager Fermín Guerra's Alacranes would also move on after the season's finale to capture a second championship during the first-ever Caribbean Series, staged at Havana's new ballpark (El Cerro Stadium) between league champions from Cuba (Almendares), Puerto Rico (Mayagüez), Venezuela (Cervecería Caracas) and Panama (Spur Cola). Marianao star outfielder Orestes "Minnie" Miñoso would also break into the big leagues with Cleveland only weeks after the close of the Cuban League season.

Champion— Almendares (47–25), Manager: Fermín Guerra

Other Teams— 2-Habana (39–33–1), 3-Marianao (29–42–1), 4-Cienfuegos (28–43)

Individual Batting Leaders—**BA**: Alejandro Crespo (C) .326; **AB**: Lennie Pearson (H) 301; **Runs**: Hank Thompson (H) 60; **Hits**: Hank Thompson 85; **2B**: Don Richmond (C) 17; **3B**: Hank Thompson 8; **HR**: Monte Irvin (A) 10; **RBI**: Lennie Pearson 54; **Steals**: Sam Jethroe (A) 32.

Individual Pitching Leaders—**Pct**: Octavio Rubert (A) 8–1 (.889); **G**: Max Surkont (C) 31; **CG**: Dave Barnhill (M) 13; **W**: Dave Barnhill 13; **L**: Max Manning (C) 12; **Shutouts**: Morrie Martin (A) 4; **ERA**: Octavio Rubert 1.63.

Top Rookie— Willie Miranda (A)

MVP— Morrie Martin (A)

1949–1950 (Sixty-Second Championship Season)

A repeat title for Almendares and manager Fermín Guerra came despite one of the closest league races in many years. Marianao (with the circuit's workhorse hurler, Sandy Consuegra) and Habana (boasting Pedro Formental, the batting champion) finished deadlocked in the cellar only three games off the pace of the victorious Alacranes, and only a single game behind the runner-up Cienfuegos Elefantes (featuring Tommie Fine, the league's winningest pitcher). The individual race for a batting championship was equally tight with Formental finally edging a dozen other .300-plus hitters. The season's biggest single highlight, however, was a mid–February no-hitter tossed by Marianao's Limonar Martínez, a masterful 6–0 white-washing of the league champions.

Champion— Almendares (38–34–4), Manager: Fermín Guerra

Other Teams— 2-Cienfuegos (36–36–1), 3-Marianao (35–37–2), 4-Habana (35–37–3)

Individual Batting Leaders—**BA**: Pedro Formental (H) .336; **AB**: Ray Dandridge (M) 318; **Runs**: Pedro Formental 51; **Hits**: Pedro Formental 99; **2B**: Lennie Pearson (H) 19; **3B**: Héctor Rodríguez (A) 9; **HR**: Roberto Ortiz (A), Don Lenhardt (H) 15; **RBI**: Lennie Pearson 55; **Steals**: Jack Cassini (C) 12.

Individual Pitching Leaders—**Pct**: Octavio Rubert (A) 5–1 (.833); **G**: Tommie Fine (C) 35; **CG**: Albert Gerheauser (H) 11; **W**: Tommie Fine 16; **L**: Sandalio "Sandy" Consuegra (M) 12; **IP**: Sandalio "Sandy" Consuegra 162.1; **SO**: Albert Gerheauser 74; **BB**: Ray Shore (C) 67; **ERA**: Conrado Marrero (A) 2.62.

No-Hit Game— Rogelio "Limonar" Martínez (February 15, 1950), Marianao defeated Almendares (6–0)

Top Rookie— Carlos de Souza (A)

MVP— Fermín García (A)

1950–1951 (SIXTY-THIRD CHAMPIONSHIP SEASON)

On the eve of Bobby Thomson's famed "shot-heard-round-the-world" to decide the most famous ever major league pennant playoff between the National League Giants and Dodgers, "Los Eternal Rivales" also finished in a year-end dead heat and thus staged their own historic playoff showdown. A further curiosity of the remarkable 1951 season was that the leading batsman on the championship club — rookie Sandy Amoros — ranked only tenth overall in the circuit. This season also featured a dramatic curtain call by MVP Silvio García, who won a surprise batting title with a hefty late-career performance for also-ran Cienfuegos.

Champion— Habana (41–32–1), Manager: Miguel Angel González

Other Teams— 2-Almendares (40–33), 3-Marianao (36–36–1), 4-Cienfuegos (28–44)

Individual Batting Leaders—**BA**: Silvio García (C) .347; **AB**: Héctor Rodríguez (A) 289; **Runs**: Orestes Miñoso (M) 54; **Hits**: Lorenzo "Chiquitín" Cabrera (M) 88; **2B**: Steve Bilko (H) 15; **3B**: Regino Otero (C) 7; **HR**: Pedro Formental (H), Ed Mierkowics (H), Charles Grant (C), Bert Haas (H) 8; **RBI**: Héctor Rodríguez 50; **Steals**: Silvio García 17.

Individual Pitching Leaders—**Pct**: Vicente López (A) 7–3 (.700); **G**: Red Barrett (M) 32; **CG**: Bill Ayers (H), Hoyt Wilhelm (H) 10; **W**: Conrado Marrero (A) 11; **L**: Bill Ayers 9; **IP**: Conrado Marrero 159.2; **SO**: Hoyt Wilhelm 72; **BB**: Jim Hughes (M) 83; **ERA**: Hoyt Wilhelm 2.36.

Top Rookie— Edmundo "Sandy" Amorós (H)
MVP— Adrián Zabala (H) and Silvio García (C)

1951–1952 (SIXTY-FOURTH CHAMPIONSHIP SEASON)

Habana's repeat pennant was sparked by the offensive contributions of Americans Johnny Jorgensen (85 hits) and Bert Haas (.323 BA), and Cubans Sandy Amoros (.333 BA in part-time play) and Pedro Formental (league leader in RBI, homers and runs scored). Hurler Joe Black of Cienfuegos foreshadowed his exceptional 1952 National League rookie season in Brooklyn as easily the most effective (2.42 ERA) and productive (15 wins) Cuban League moundsman. The runner-up Cienfuegos ball club was managed a second straight winter by Cooperstown Hall of Famer Billy Herman, while Habana manager Miguel Angel González walked off with the twelfth of his record thirteen Cuban League titles.

Champion— Habana (41–30–1), Manager: Miguel Angel González

Other Teams— 2-Cienfuegos (39–32), 3-Marianao (32–39–1), 4-Almendares (30–41)

Individual Batting Leaders—**BA**: Bert Haas (H) .323; **AB**: Johnny Jorgensen (H) 293; **Runs**: Pedro Formental (H) 47; **Hits**: Johnny Jorgensen 85; **2B**: Marvin Rickert (A) 17; **3B**: Héctor Rodríguez (A), Regino Otero (C) 6; **HR**: Pedro Formental, Jim Basso (C-M) 9; **RBI**: Pedro Formental 46; **Steals**: Jack Cassini (C) 15.

Individual Pitching Leaders—**Pct**: Joe Black (C) 15–6 (.714); **G**: Tommie Fine (M) 30; **CG**: Red Barrett (M), Bill Ayers (H) 12; **W**: Joe Black 15; **L**: Tommie Fine, John Yuhas (M) 11; **SO**: Joe Black 78; **BB**: John Yuhas 63; **ERA**: Joe Black 2.42.

Top Rookie— Oscar Sierra (C)
MVP— Bert Haas (H)

1952–1953 (SIXTY-FIFTH CHAMPIONSHIP SEASON)

For the first time since the late 1920s the Habana Leones ran their string of consecutive pennants to three. This was also destined to be the last flag ever earned by the league's all-time leader in pennant victories. The three major individual batting crowns also all fell to Habana, with Amoros the runaway pacesetter in batting average, Formental the best run producer with 57 RBI, and Lou Klein of the St. Louis Cardinals authoring a new home run standard with 16 circuit blasts. Big league outfielder Walt Moryn, playing with outmanned Cienfuegos, also entered the record book by banging home eight runs in a single contest.

Champion— Habana (43–29–1), Manager: Miguel Angel González

Other Teams— 2-Almendares (37–35–1), 3-Marianao (37–35–1), 4-Cienfuegos (27–45–1)

Individual Batting Leaders—**BA**: Edmundo "Sandy" Amoros (H) .373; **Runs**: Orestes Miñoso (M) 67; **Hits**: Paul Smith (A) 93; **2B**: Pedro Formental (H) 18; **3B**: Orestes Miñoso, Héctor Rodríguez (A), Felipe Montemayor (C) 5; **HR**: Lou Klein (H) 16; **RBI**: Pedro Formental 57; **Steals**: Orestes Miñoso 13.

Individual Pitching Leaders—**Pct**: Bob Alexander (H) 10–3 (.769); **G**: Hal Erickson (A) 33; **CG**: Al Gettel (C) 13; **W**: Al Gettel, Mario Picone (H) 13; **L**: Al Gettel, Ed Roebuck (A) 11; **IP**: Al Gettel 174.1; **SO**: Julio Moreno (H) 106; **BB**: Clarence Iott (M) 100; **ERA**: Miguel "Mike" Fornieles (M) 2.33.

Top Rookie— Miguel "Mike" Fornieles (M)
MVP— Orestes Miñoso (M)

1953–1954 (SIXTY-SIXTH CHAMPIONSHIP SEASON)

North American minor league standouts Rocky Nelson (.352 BA), Vern Rapp (10 HRs and 51 RBI) and righthander Cliff Fannin (13–4 with 1.45 ERA) provided the biggest individual numbers as manager Bobby Bragan's Almendares Scorpions glided to an easy first-place finish. Lefty-swinging Nelson walked off with his only Cuban batting title, while Rapp was at or near the top in several hitting categories, and Fannin was the undisputed staff and league ace during his best-ever winter season. Imported U.S. pitchers paced every important league individual category with a single exception of total runs allowed. Marianao ace Mike Fornieles walked off with the latter rather dubious distinction.

Champion— Almendares (44–28–1), Manager: Bobby Bragan

Other Teams— 2-Cienfuegos (36–36–1), 3-Habana (35–37–3), 4-Marianao (29–43–5)

*Individual Batting Leaders—***BA:** Rocky Nelson (A) .352; **AB:** Forrest "Spook" Jacobs (A) 295; **Runs:** Forrest Jacobs 58; **Hits:** Forrest Jacobs 94; **2B:** Chuck Diering (C) 20; **3B:** Chuck Diering, Julio Bécquer (M), Amado Ibanez (A-H), Lloyd Merriman (C), Bob Boring (M-C) 5; **HR:** Earl Rapp (A), Rafael Noble (C) 10; **RBI:** Earl Rapp 51; **Steals:** Humberto "Chico" Fernández (C), Angel Scull (A) 14.

*Individual Pitching Leaders—***Pct:** Cliff Fannin (A) 13–4 (.765); **G:** Joe Coleman (H) 44; **CG:** Dick Littlefield (C), Al Sima (M) 12; **W:** Cliff Fannin, Dick Littlefield 13; **L:** Jim Davis (C) 11; **IP:** Al Sima 193.2; **SO:** Dick Littlefield 132; **BB:** Bob Darnell (C) 107; **ERA:** Cliff Fannin 1.45

Top Rookie— Juan Delís (M)

MVP— Cliff Fannin (A)

1954–1955 (SIXTY-SEVENTH CHAMPIONSHIP SEASON)

For the second straight season American skipper Bobby Bragan and his Almendares Scorpions sat firmly atop the final league standings. Diminutive outfielder Angel Scull (a talented Cuban prospect owned by the Washington Senators who never reached the majors due to injury) was Bragan's leading offensive star and paced the league in hitting, ahead of a dozen other .300-plus batsmen. Righthander Joe Hatten, also toiling with Almendares, was the most effective hurler of the winter with 13 victories, while Marianao's Connie Johnson proved the workhorse by logging 174-plus innings on the mound. A new RBI mark was established by lefty fence-buster Rocky Nelson, as were new team records for RBI (Habana with 360) and also runs scored (again second-place Habana with 394). Hatten was the second straight Almendares pitcher (following Cliff Fannin) to earn special honors as league MVP.

Champion— Almendares (44–25–2), Manager: Bobby Bragan

Other Teams— 2-Habana (36–33–2), 3-Marianao (31–38), 4-Cienfuegos (27–42–2)

*Individual Batting Leaders—***BA:** Angel Scull (A) .370; **AB:** Humberto "Chico" Fernández (C), Bob Boyd (C) 288; **Runs:** Rocky Nelson (A) 60; **Hits:** Bob Boyd 88; **2B:** Julio Bécquer (M) 22; **3B:** Don Blasingame (H) 6; **HR:** Rocky Nelson 13; **RBI:** Rocky Nelson 57; **Steals:** Angel Scull 12.

*Individual Pitching Leaders—***Pct:** Joe Hatten (A) 13–5 (.722); **G:** Jim Melton (C) 38; **CG:** Ed Roebuck (H) 12; **W:** Joe Hatten, Ed Roebuck 13; **L:** Floyd Woolridge (H-C) 12; **IP:** Connie Johnson (M) 174.2; **SO:** Connie Johnson 123; **BB:** Connie Johnson 84; **ERA:** George "Red" Munger (A) 2.85.

Top Rookie— Vicente Amor (H)

MVP— Joe Hatten (A)

1955–1956 (SIXTY-EIGHTH CHAMPIONSHIP SEASON)

St. Louis Cardinals veteran lefthander Wilmer "Vinegar Bend" Mizell wrote the biggest headlines with a new league single-season strikeout standard of 206, surpassing a record by Carlos Royer that had stood since 1903 and busting the old mark with 11 Ks against Marianao in the final contest of the campaign. A nine-year run of pennants split between "The Eternal Rivals" was finally brought to an end when Cienfuegos hung up its first banner in a decade, mainly on the strength of the one-two pitching punch of Washington Senators aces Pete Ramos (13–5 record) and Camilo Pascual (league-best 1.91 ERA). Mizell also tied Negro leaguer Dave Barnhill's 1948 mark of fifteen to equal the record for single-game strikeouts by pitchers in the 20th century.

Champion— Cienfuegos (40–29–1), Manager: Oscar Rodríguez

Other Teams— 2-Habana (34–35–1), 2-Marianao (34–35–2), 4-Almendares (30–39)

*Individual Batting Leaders—***BA:** Forrest "Spook" Jacobs (H) .321; **AB:** Humberto "Chico" Fernández (C) 292; **Runs:** Orestes Miñoso (M) 47; **Hits:** Forrest Jacobs 91; **2B:** Humberto Fernández 17; **3B:** Milton Smith (C), Curt Roberts (C) 6; **HR:** Ultus Alvarez (C) 10; **RBI:** Julio Bécquer (M) 49; **Steals:** Angel Scull (A) 12.

*Individual Pitching Leaders—***Pct:** Pedro Ramos (C) 13–5 (.722); **G:** Ben Wade (A) 38; **CG:** Wilmer Mizell (H) 13; **W:** Pedro Ramos 13; **L:** Vicente Amor (H), Mike Fornieles (M), Ben Wade (A) 10; **IP:** Wilmer Mizell 179; **SO:** Wilmer Mizell 206; **BB:** Wilmer Mizell 102; **ERA:** Camilo Pascual (C) 1.91.

Top Rookies— Ultus Alvarez (C) and Pedro Ramos (C)

MVP— Camilo Pascual (C)

1956–1957 (SIXTY-NINTH CHAMPIONSHIP SEASON)

Napoleón "Nap" Reyes posted his first-ever managerial victory as often cellar-bound Marianao captured its first pennant in two full decades. Tigers outfielder Orestes Miñoso, league batting champion, was one of only three hitters in the entire circuit to top the coveted .300 mark (Chiquitín Cabrera and Asdrúbal Baró were the others) in a winter completely dominated by masterful pitching. Big league aces Jim Bunning (with 11 wins for Marianao) and Camilo Pascual (15–5 for Cienfuegos) topped the parade of successful moundsmen, with Pascual tossing six shutouts and ringing up an eye-catching ERA of 2.04 (earning his second straight league title in that department).

Champion— Marianao (40–28–1), Manager: Napoleon Reyes

Other Teams— 2-Cienfuegos (36–33–3), 3-Habana (34–34–3), 4-Almendares (27–42–3)

*Individual Batting Leaders—***BA:** Orestes Miñoso (M) .312; **AB:** Curt Roberts (C) 292; **Runs:** Solly Drake (M) 52; **Hits:** Archie Wilson (C) 76; **2B:** Solly Drake 14; **3B:** Bob Skinner (A) 7; **HR:** Archie Wilson 11; **RBI:** Archie Wilson 39; **Steals:** Solly Drake 12.

*Individual Pitching Leaders—***Pct:** Camilo Pascual (C) 15–5 (.750); **G:** Joe Hatten (A), Lynn Lovenguth (H) 33; **CG:** Camilo Pascual 16; **W:** Camilo Pascual 15; **L:** Hank Aguirre (A) 11; **IP:** Camilo Pascual 176.2; **SO:** Camilo Pascual 153; **Shutouts:** Camilo Pascual 6; **ERA:** Camilo Pascual 2.04.

Top Rookie— Daniel Morejón (A)

MVP— Camilo Pascual (C) and Orestes Miñoso (M)

1957–1958 (SEVENTIETH CHAMPIONSHIP SEASON)

The season's highlight came early in the campaign (November 23) when Tony Díaz (Cienfuegos) authored an eighth and final Cuban League no-hitter, a 2–0 whitewash of Club Habana. Veteran Nap Reyes directed Marianao to a comfortable year-end four-game lead over second-place Almendares, managed for the final time by Bobby Bragan. American pitchers enjoyed a banner year with Billy O'Dell pacing the circuit in winning percentage and Bob Shaw (also the complete games leader) and Dick Brodowski racking up the most victories. The U.S. individual pacesetters also included Billy Muffett in pitching defeats, Milt Smith as league batting champ, and Norm Larker and Brooks Robinson, who tied for the long ball title.

Champion— Marianao (43–32–1) Manager: Napoleon Reyes

Other Teams— 2-Almendares (39–36–1), 3-Habana (38–37–2), 4-Cienfuegos (30–45–2)

Individual Batting Leaders— **BA**: Milton Smith (M) .320; **AB**: Héctor Rodríguez (A) 291; **Runs**: Milton Smith 46; **Hits**: Tony Taylor (A) 83; **2B**: Casey Wise (M) 14; **3B**: Tony Taylor 7; **HR**: Daniel Morejón (A), Ponchón Herrera (C), Brooks Robinson (C), Norm Larker (H) 9; **RBI**: Román Mejías (H) 43; **Steals**: Solly Drake (M), Julio Bécquer (M) 11.

Individual Pitching Leaders— **Pct**: Billy O'Dell (A) 7–2 (.778); **G**: Orlando Peña (A) 37; **CG**: Bob Shaw (M) 12; **W**: Dick Brodowski (A), Bob Shaw 14; **L**: Billy Muffett (H) 10; **IP**: Bob Shaw 176; **SO**: Pedro Ramos (C) 103; **BB**: Billy Muffett 67; **ERA**: Bob Shaw 1.48.

No-Hit Game— Antonio "Tony" Díaz (November 23, 1957), Cienfuegos defeated Habana (2–0)

Top Rookie— Antonio Díaz (M)

MVP— Bob Shaw (M)

1958–1959 (SEVENTY-FIRST CHAMPIONSHIP SEASON)

Almendares registered their 24th and final championship triumph, coasting to a eight-game cushion over the Marianao Tigers. Future Cooperstown hall-of-fame manager Tom Lasorda enjoyed a career highlight season as an active moundsman with an 8–3 season's mark for the Alacranes, but Cincinnati Reds property Orlando Peña (formerly with the Sugar Kings) was the Almendares staff ace as well as the league's best hurler. Another future big-league fixture, Cuban infielder Tony Taylor, walked off with the batting title in his second strong winter season, although Taylor posted a mark barely above the .300-level of distinction.

Champion— Almendares (46–26–6), Managers: Oscar Rodríguez and Clemente Carrera

Other Teams— 2-Marianao (38–34–3), 3-Cienfuegos (29–43–3), 4-Habana (29–43–3)

Individual Batting Leaders— **BA**: Tony Taylor (A) .303; **AB**: Humberto "Chico" Fernández (C-H) 291; **Runs**: Rocky Nelson (A) 37; **Hits**: Tony Taylor 88; **2B**: Prentice Brown (H), Dick Drown (A) 13; **3B**: Edmundo Amoros (A) 6; **HR**: Jim Baxes (A) 9; **RBI**: Prentice Brown 37; **Steals**: Angel Scull (A) 18.

Individual Pitching Leaders— **Pct**: Orlando Peña (A) 13–5 (.750); **G**: René "Látigo" Gutiérrez (H) 45; **CG**: Orlando Peña 15; **W**: Orlando Peña 15; **L**: Vicente Amor (A), Pedro Ramos (C) 13; **IP**: Pedro Ramos 189.2; **SO**: Camilo Pascual (C) 108; **BB**: Al Cicotte (M) 60; **ERA**: Al Cicotte 1.38.

Top Rookie— Cándido Andrade (C)

MVP— Orlando Peña (A)

1959–1960 (SEVENTY-SECOND CHAMPIONSHIP SEASON)

Defeating each of its rivals exactly 16 times, Cienfuegos walked off with the first of two final league pennants under summertime AAA Sugar Kings skipper Tony Castaño. In the process the Elefantes broke the league record for victories (Almendares, 47) that had stood since 1949. Cienfuegos also posted a new league mark for homers by socking 72 (as did the entire league with a total of 209). A final high-water mark was the champion's 12-game victory margin over runner-up Marianao.

Champion— Cienfuegos (48–24), Manager: Tony Castaño

Other Teams— 2-Marianao (36–36–2), 3-Habana (35–37), 4-Almendares (25–47–2)

Individual Batting Leaders— **BA**: Tony González (C) .310; **AB**: Román Mejías (C) 281; **Runs**: Marv Breeding (H), George Altman (C) 41; **Hits**: Román Mejías 79; **2B**: Román Mejías 15; **3B**: Tony Taylor (A) 5; **HR**: Ponchón Herrera (H) 15; **RBI**: Ponchón Herrera 50; **Steals**: Angel Scull (A) 15.

Individual Pitching Leaders— **Pct**: Camilo Pascual (C) 15–5 (.750), Raúl Sánchez (C) 12–4 (.750); **G**: Manuel Montejo (M) 40; **CG**: Camilo Pascual 13; **W**: Camilo Pascual 15; **L**: Jim Archer (H) 11; **IP**: Pedro Ramos (C) 163; **SO**: Camilo Pascual 163; **BB**: Tom Cheney (H) 78; **ERA**: Raúl Sánchez 1.64.

Top Rookie— Hilario Valdespino (H)

MVP— Raúl Sánchez (C)

1960–1961 (SEVENTY-THIRD CHAMPIONSHIP SEASON)

The final downbeat season of the Cuban League featured a close race with Cienfuegos on top and only four games separating the four teams in the final standings. The season's notable feature was that only Cuban players were used for the first time since the 19th century. Future big league infield regulars Cookie Rojas (.322 BA) and Julio Bécquer (15 homers) were the batting stars, but Washington Senators fire-balling Pete Ramos (16 wins and 17 complete games) was the league's runaway MVP. Ramos dominated most of the individual pitching categories as well as claiming nearly half of the victories for the champion Elefantes.

Champion— Cienfuegos (35–31–1), Manager: Tony Castaño

Other Teams— 2-Almendares (34–32–2), 3-Habana (32–34–3), 4-Marianao (31–35)

Individual Batting Leaders—**BA**: Octavio "Cookie" Rojas (H) .322; **AB**: José Tartabull (M) 265; **Runs**: Tony González (C) 42; **Hits**: Cookie Rojas 85; **2B**: Daniel Morejón (H) 17; **3B**: Tony Taylor (A), José Tartabull 6; **HR**: Julio Bécquer (M) 15; **RBI**: Julio Bécquer 50; **Steals**: Tony Taylor 22.

Individual Pitching Leaders—**Pct**: Pedro Ramos (C) 16–7 (.696); **G**: Manuel Montejo (M) 36; **CG**: Pedro Ramos 17; **W**: Pedro Ramos 16; **L**: Andrés Ayón (A) 12; **IP**: Pedro Ramos 218; **SO**: Pedro Ramos 150; **BB**: Luis Tiant, Jr. (H) 90; **ERA**: Julio Moreno (H) 2.03.

Top Rookie— Luis Tiant, Jr. (H)

MVP— Pedro Ramos (C)

CUBAN LEAGUE CHAMPIONSHIPS (TEAM-BY-TEAM)

Habana Leones (aka "Los Rojos" and also played under name of Habanista in 1897–98 and 1898–99) (29 championships)—1878–79, 1879–80, 1882–83, 1885, 1885–86, 1886–87, 1888–89, 1889–90, 1892, 1898–99 (Habanista), 1901, 1902, 1903, 1904, 1908–09, 1912, 1914–15, 1918–19, 1920–21, 1921, 1926–27, 1927–28, 1928–1929, 1940–41, 1943–44, 1947–48, 1950–51, 1951–52, 1952–53 (**1608–1346–99, .544 Pct.** overall record for 77 total league seasons)

Almendares Alcranes (aka "Los Azules" and also played with name Almendarista in 1897–98, 1898–99 and 1931) (24 championships)—1893–94, 1905, 1907, 1908, 1910, 1910–11, 1913–14, 1915–16, 1919–20, 1924–25, 1925–26, 1931–32, 1932–33, 1934–35, 1939–40, 1941–42, 1942–43, 1944–45, 1946–47, 1948–49, 1949–50, 1953–54, 1954–55, 1958–59 (**1568–1308–115, .545 Pct.** overall record for 73 league seasons)

Cienfuegos Elefantes (5 championships)—1929–30, 1945–46, 1955–56, 1959–60, 1960–61 (**731–807–38, .475 Pct.** overall record for 27 total league seasons)

Marianao Tigres (aka "The Grey Monks") (4 championships)—1922–23, 1936–37, 1956–57, 1957–58 (**744–861–49, .464 Pct.** overall record for 28 total league seasons)

Santa Clara Leopardos (aka "Los Pilongos") (4 championships)—1923–24, 1935–36, 1937–38, 1938–39 (287–233–17, .552 Pct. overall record for 11 total league seasons)

Fé (4 championships)—1887–88, 1890–91, 1906, 1913 (232–266–9, .466 Pct. overall record for 22 total league seasons)

San Francisco (1 championship)—1900 (44–82–5, .349 Pct. overall record for 5 total league seasons)

Matanzas (1 championship)—1892–93 (63–135–2, .318 Pct. overall record for 10 total league seasons)

Orientals (1 championship)—1917 (8–6–1, .571 Pct. overall record for one league season)

ADDITIONAL TEAMS WITHOUT LEAGUE CHAMPIONSHIPS

Cuba (132–175–10, .430 Pct. overall record for 8 league seasons)

Colón (2–0–0, 1.000 Pct. overall record for one league season)

Progreso (Vibora) (0–4–0, .000 Pct. overall record for one league season)

Progreso (Matanzas) (26–42–2, .382 Pct. overall record for 4 league seasons)

Ultimátum (2–4–0, .333 Pct. overall record for one league season)

Caridad (0–6–0, .000 Pct. overall record for one league season)

Boccacio (1–4–0, .200 Pct. overall record for one league season)

Unión (0–4–0, .000 Pct. overall record for one league season)

Carmelita (0–6–0, .000 Pct. overall record for one league season)

Cárdenas (11–41–0, .211 Pct. overall record for 3 league seasons)

Aguila de Oro (18–22–0, .450 Pct. overall record for 2 league seasons)

Red Sox (6–7–1, .462 Pct. overall record for one league season)

White Sox (6–7–0, .462 Pct. overall record for one league season)

Cuban Stars (21–25–1, .457 Pct. overall record for one league season)

América (2–26–1, .071 Pct. overall record for one league season)

Bacharach Giants (4–26–1, .133 Pct. overall record for one league season)

San José (3–41–0, .068 Pct. overall record for one league season)

Regla (15–15–3, .500 Pct. overall record for one league season)

Explanatory Note: Totals of all-time won-and-lost records for each and every league team provided above represent corrections to previous inconsistent or inaccurate records offered in numerous published sources, especially the volumes by Díez Muro (notoriously inaccurate in its data on the earliest league seasons) and Angel Torres (who draws heavily on Díez Muro), as well as the unpublished record-keeping of Havana's tireless Severo Nieto. While errors and inconsistencies likely still exist above — given the inaccuracies hopelessly rampant in existing contemporary newspaper accounts of most Cuban League seasons before 1940 — the summaries of team records offered here at least approach the most accurate reconstruction of Cuban League data currently possible.

Nearly all previously published Cuban League statistics blithely reproduce the Díez Muro year-by-year standings without noting that for many seasons the totals Díez Muro tallies for individual team victories and defeats simply don't add up (just as his box scores for individual games do not properly scan to provide correct final scores, and his team rosters are also often horribly incomplete and generally inconsistent). A good deal of guesswork is sometimes involved in summing the wins and losses of clubs in most 19th century Cuban League seasons; one pitfall is that hastily arranged unscheduled year-end tying-breaking playoffs were sometimes counted in published standings and other times not included. Records compiled for this chapter attempt to include all games actually played, including numerous ties, and this approach was equally applied for the many short seasons that were suspended without champions crowned and without planned schedules completed. It must be said that for much of its history the Cuban League was at best as much a shameful record keeper's nightmare as it was a true fan's delight.

6

Cuban Blackball's Doubleheaders on the Dark Side of the Moon

From its outset in the 1870s Cuban baseball served as an unparalleled racial proving ground. This was just as true of the league championship season beginning late each autumn as it was of the exhibition tours by visiting Negro league and big league teams that normally preceded it. If there was a testing ground hidden away someplace in the hinterlands — a land where great ballplayers cursed with a single flaw of swarthy skin color could nonetheless prove their merit against the best diamond all-stars the white baseball world had to offer — then that proving ground was surely to be found in the sultry environs of early 20th-century Havana.

It is also a fact of considerable significance that the period between 1900 — the year of integration in the Cuban League and also the winter of the first island visit by black barnstormers from the north — and the end of World War II, with its simultaneous integration of U.S. organized baseball and death-knell for North American Negro league circuits, was the true apogee stretch for Cuban baseball. It was in these five decades, exclusively, that island ball clubs regularly competed head-to-head with the very best ballplayers the world had to offer. The spectacle of visiting blackball aces and major league barnstormers mixing with integrated Cuban squads during so-called "American Season" fall exhibitions, especially in the first two decades of the 20th century, plus the exotic blend of top black and white stars in Cuban winter league games, all meant that the showcase display of unsurpassed talent outstripped even what was available in the big leagues themselves. For the big leagues at that time remained without names like Pop Lloyd and Smoky Joe Williams and Josh Gibson, and thus without at least half of the game's truest superstars.

Before blacks and whites first intermixed in Havana's original Almendares Park in 1900 and 1901, the baseball played in Cuba reflected little more than the first glimmerings of a mature professional sport. After Jackie Robinson entered the majors (1947) and the Negro leagues dissipated (late forties and early fifties), the raw number of outstanding black players took an immediate dip both in Cuba and across the United States. (If between 1947 and 1952 there were suddenly dozens of black big leaguers, there were also hundreds fewer roster spots on all-black professional clubs.) And after the 1959 Castro revolution, talented Cuban players of both races were again stripped of any chance — this time by international politics and not social injustices — to match talents with the best athletes of the major leagues. More than anything else, it was the rare mix of Cubans, Negro leaguers and big leaguers displaying their wares in Havana in the 1910s, 1920s and 1930s that justifies Cuban baseball historian Robert González Echevarría (*The Pride of Havana*, Chapter 5) in labeling this epoch as the true Golden Age for Cuban baseball.

Connections between Cubans (white and black and mulatto) and African-Americans on the baseball diamond hold deep-seated historical and sociological roots. For both Cuban islanders and North American blacks baseball was always more than mere sport; as scholars Lisa Brock and Bijan Bayne best explain it, baseball for late-nineteenth-century Afro-Americans and Afro-Cubans was "a natural site in which both racism and imperialism could be effectively mediated." The playing fields hosting amateur and professional games — in Chicago, New York, Pittsburgh or Havana — were locations of huge and lasting symbolism — "a metaphor for nationhood." In the second half of the nineteenth century emancipated slaves in North America saw their hopes for economic and social liberty already being dashed by post–Civil War white reentrenchment. Reconstruction in the Deep South quickly closed doors of prejudice and discrimination earlier cracked open by the battlefield victories of Union troops. But baseball left a small if valuable arena to counter such racism and neutralize prevailing myths of black male unmanliness. For Cubans, the fleeting dreams of emancipation from their Spanish overlords were also soon enough undercut by a vicious U.S. imperialism on the heels of the misnamed Spanish-American War. Cubans (of all races) and American blacks alike were thrown into despair at century's end by a complex of events that threatened to hold them in symbolic if not virtual servitude. If baseball provided racial pride for U.S. blacks, it also and in similar fashion fostered national pride for Cubans of all colors and racial mixtures.

Baseball in Cuba, from the first, had been directly tied to nationalism, and especially to the late-nineteenth-century struggle for independence from hated Spanish overlords. The game first arrived in Havana environs with returning native Cubans who had been students in the United States, and not as a gift from Yankee marines or merchant seaman as legend oft-times has it. Nemesio Guilló (assisted by brother Ernesto and companion Enrique Porto) was the game's true "Cuban father" when he brought balls, bats and rules back to Havana in 1864, after a brief tenure at Springhill College in Mobile, Alabama. The full story of these origins is related elsewhere in these pages (Chapter 10) and has only passing interest here. Most important and relevant at the moment is an observation that Cubans themselves imported and fostered the game on their native soil. And, like the Japanese on the other side of the globe, they quickly made the sport of bats and balls something entirely of their own imagining.*

Not only did the Cubans themselves beat their North American role models to the punch in bringing ball games to their own native island, but they also outpaced the proselytizing Yankees in spreading the emerging North American game around the rest of the Caribbean island realm. It was Cubans who over the next several decades took baseball to the shores of the Dominican island, where in the 1870s thousands of *Cubano* refugees settled in coastal towns and villages, fleeing a destructive ten-year-long war for independence from ruling Spanish overlords, and bringing their sugar plantations as well as their new ball-playing passions along with them. It was also Cubans who spread the sport farther afield to Puerto Rico, where the first reported game in 1897 included a "nine" named Almendares after the already thriving Havana club. This Cuban baseball mission would soon extend to the mainland of South America (in 1895 Havana ballplayer Emilio Cramer and his touring contingent of itinerant pros reportedly first demonstrated the heretofore unknown game to curious spectators in metropolitan Caracas), as well as to the eastern shores of Mexico (where in 1890 the Spanish war vessel *Ciudad Condal* deposited a Cuban exile family toting bats and balls in a Yucatán port town). All the existing records affirm that the Cubans were baseball's undisputed apostles almost everywhere throughout the Caribbean basin.†

Baseball had started out as a gentleman's game in Cuba, played by true "clubs" and not by organized and highly competitive teams, just as it had a few decades earlier in the towns and cities of the American northeast. The evolution of ball-playing as a recreational pastime was indeed strikingly similar in both locations. Early games staged by Havana-area social clubs were elaborate society events — far more like "picnic" outings than league matches. They were played on weekends (usually Sunday afternoons) and normally tied to banquets and dances that were the true highlight of an afternoon's pleasurable match (Chapter 5). Once professionalism began to creep onto the scene in the late 1870s and early 1880s the club

traditions of amateurism and recreation would undergo drastic change yet hardly be dissipated overnight. Teams representing elite social clubs (Almendares BBC, Havana BBC, Regla BBC, Matanzas BBC, Vedado Tennis Club, etc.) became increasingly competitive and concentrated somewhat more strenuously on the pride of winning championship prize trophies. But the amateur tradition of sport played purely for recreation, rather than profit or staged entertainment, remained strong if not any longer universal.

Thus baseball in Cuba developed on two distinct fronts after 1878 and the founding of a "Liga General de Base-Ball de la Isla de Cuba" (Cuban Baseball League). While games sold as professional entertainment (with admission fees charged) soon enough became increasingly cutthroat affairs and often involved widespread gambling among patrons, who wagered on the outcomes or even on individual plays, the most popular form of the sport on the island long remained the matches contested between teams sponsored by upper-crust social clubs (Vedado Tennis Club, Sociedad Marianao, Habana Yacht Club, Clío BBC, Fortuna Sports Club) and eventually also sugar mills (Hershey Central, Central Resulta, Central Constancia) and even public and private companies (Teléfonos, Casa Bacardí, Ferroviario, Policía, Aduanas) spread in and around Havana in western Cuba and Santiago on the island's eastern end.

The arrival of a pro circuit in Havana in the late seventies and early eighties was inevitably followed (in 1890) by Afro-Cuban players, alongside whites or mestizos of a lower class status, appearing on teams like Club Habana and Club Almendares. Professional league play had broken down the leisure-oriented gentlemen's grip on ball-playing in the U.S. as early as the late 1860s, with the appearance of such mercenary teams as the salaried Cincinnati Redstockings of Harry Wright and east coast clubs like the New York Excelsiors and the Brooklyn Atlantics. Cuba would witness similar patterns, as teams raced to hire on the most talented athletes available, players who might guarantee both victories and a marketable entertainment spectacle. In Havana, such an evolution meant that for the first time black as well as white Cuban ballplayers would soon be filling the city's handful of ball fields. The sporting arena was one of the few places where blacks — often among the city's most impoverish residents — could find economic opportunities unavailable to those without educational advantages or social connections. While the Havana pro league after 1900 became increasing black in tone, the parallel amateur leagues spread throughout the island continued for most of the next half century to field white players exclusively (since the clubs sponsoring many of the teams didn't allow black members).

Cuba's winter league, by the turn of the century, quickly became a magnet for both black and white professional

---

For details on the parallel and contrasting adoptions of baseball as a national game in both Cuba and Japan, the reader is directed to the author's more elaborate discussion in a forthcoming article presented at the April 2006 Michigan State University Conference on Japanese and Asian Baseball (see bibliography on page 150 for details).   .

†*For details concerning the extensive role of Cubans as baseball's nineteenth-century apostles throughout the Caribbean region, readers are directed to the individual histories of baseball's founding in each of the Latin American countries (including Cuba) as outlined in my volume* Diamonds around the Globe.

ballplayers willing to pick up some "off-season" cash and at the same time test their skills in a more racially tolerant ballpark environment than anything found north of Key West or the Rio Grande. The Cubans had mastered the game quickly after their first contacts with touring U.S. professionals in the 1880s and nineties. There was little question about the high quality of Cuban pro games in the early years of the new century, especially when the first pro clubs from the north began arriving on tour and suffering more than an occasional defeat at the hands of the locals. But far more important still was the fact that race seemingly mattered far less in most quarters of a newly independent Cuba (one free from Spanish rule if not American influence) and this was especially true on the nation's increasingly popular baseball diamonds.

Touring clubs began appearing on Cuban shores almost as soon as a Cuban professional league came into existence. The earliest documented visits were by "nines" of white pros from the north, mostly either rag-tag outfits of Cuban exiles or loosely knit groups of major and minor leaguers. These pioneering visits can be dated back as far as December 1879, when the Hops Bitter club representing a soft drink company

Legendary "Diamante Negro" ("Black Diamond") José de la Caridad Méndez, Cuba's greatest pitching icon and a recent entrant into Cooperstown's Hall of Fame.

defeated the newly founded Almendares BBC. More regular tours began in 1890 and 1891 and at least some had direct connections to the revolutionary struggle against an established Spanish colonial government. In 1890 a team composed of the sons of Cuban exiles and calling itself Club Cuba of Key West made a brief stop, though there are no records of actual games played or existing results for those early matches. It is known, however, that Club Cuba had been staging matches a full year earlier in Key West to raise funds for the Havana-based anti-colonial revolutionary forces, and also that the visiting nine of 1890 included Agustín "Tinti" Molina, later a Cuban League catcher and eventually the "white" business and field manager of the Cuban Stars West Negro leagues outfit. Britisher Al Lawson, a full-time self-promoter and part-time pitcher in Baltimore, brought a small contingent of his Orioles teammates (including a young John McGraw, and two others with big league experience) and various hangers-on, for a whirlwind January 1891 tour that drew few fans but provided a string of wins for the surprisingly prepared local teams.

Even a team made up entirely of U.S. blacks was found traveling in Cuba in 1900, when the New Jersey–based and curiously named Cuban X Giants played 18 games, against both regular teams and all-stars of the new Cuban pro league, and won all but three. Three years later the same U.S. Negro club returned for yet another tour, still devoid of any actual Cubans in the line-up, but this time accompanied by a second Negro league team, the All-Cubans, stocked with such local blacks and whites as Rafael Almeida, José Borges, Luis "Anguilla" Bustamante, Mamelo García, Julián Castillo, Antonio María García ("El Indio") and Emilio Palomino. Celebrated Andrew "Rube" Foster, legendary pitcher and eventual founder of the first U.S. Negro professional league in 1920, was a member of the Cuban X Giants on at least one of its tours of the island, the 1903 nine-game visit to Havana which preceded Foster's incredible 54–1 pitching record with the X Giants in barnstorming play that same summer. While white ball clubs and some black clubs were heading to the islands, teams of black Cubans also began to appear on the already thriving if disorganized blackball summer circuit in the States. The first such teams to bear Cuban names (Cuban Giants, Cuban X Giants, Famous Cuban Giants) rarely had any native Cubans on their rosters. E.B. Lamar's Cuban X Giants, who first toured Havana in 1900, were one notable example of such a contingent playing boldly on the name-recognition or exotic cachet that Cuban baseball already seemingly had in black communities up north. By the first decade of the new century Cuban baseball and Cuban ballplayers obviously already had a certain marketable attraction back on the U.S. mainland.

These pioneering teams can also be credited with establishing another trend which would later become a more prominent if not always popular feature of black barnstorming ball clubs. It was the Cuban Giants of the 1890s (supposedly the first salaried all-black ball club) that also introduced on-field slapstick comedy routines, outrageous "showboating" displays, and even vaudeville-style costumes as a supplement to on-field baseball entertainment. Throughout the late 1880s the misnamed Cuban Giants remained something of a sensation on the growing black baseball circuit and played well-enough — despite occasional vaudeville antics — to claim somewhat dubious titles as "Colored Champions" in 1887 and 1888 and nearly beat the 1887 National League champion Detroit Tigers. Their attractive name as both "Cuban" and "Giants" also marked a trend that was to become equally popular in blackball circles. But sham Cuban teams quickly enough began to give way to the real thing as baseball commerce continued to thrive between Afro-Americans and Afro-Cubans. The first genuine Cuban outfit to come north was a club known significantly and fittingly as the All-Cubans; this team is documented to have toured on the summer blackball circuit as early as 1904, the same year they appeared in Havana as part of the November tours by barnstormers. Sketchy evidence even suggests that black U.S. clubs were playing Cuban revolutionary clubs (sent to raise funds for the anti–Spanish liberation movement back home) in such American port cities as New Orleans, New York, Key West, Tampa and Philadelphia as early as the 1880s and 1890s.

While the first genuine Cuban ball club featuring recognized professionals to travel north can be placed as early as Summer 1904, it is also established that individual Cuban ballplayers were also wending their way north for Negro league play no more than a single summer later. Angel Torres reports three Negro league outfits employing Cuban League veterans in the summer of 1905, but only five individual islanders on black U.S. rosters during the subsequent 1906 campaign. None of these Spanish-speaking "rookies" in 1905 were to be found on the roster of the Famous Cuban Giants (operated by the infamous white entrepreneur J.M. Bright), which remained an all–Yankee black outfit. But Rogelio Valdés played with the Cuban X Giants, after beginning the summer with the All-Cubans, a team packed with both black and white native Cubans. Fourteen Cubans besides Valdés played on the latter team, and the roster included future big leaguers Marsans, Almeida and Palomino. The explanation for the diminished native Cuban presence on the 1906 U.S. blackball circuit (only Valdés, Palomino, Antonio María García, Joseito Muñoz and Julián "Fallenca" Pérez are known to have played with the Cuban X Giants) was the fact that the All-Cubans dropped from sight that summer, before returning a year later with a new designation as the Havana Cuban Stars.

If American visits of Cuban barnstormers in the final decade of the 19th century hardly ever featured top-flight Cuban ballplayers, those occurring in the first decade of the new century certainly did. In 1910, their only season, the Stars of Cuba ball club with a near-major-league-quality lineup that included Joseito Muñoz, Luis Bustamante and Armando Cabañas was a small sensation while touring the American Midwest. This team also featured José Méndez and Pelayo Chacón, two of the most reputable and beloved island stars. A summer later in 1911 both the All-Cubans and Cuban Stars were back on the U.S. circuit with talented but racially mixed rosters that could only play on the blackball circuit. Noticeably absent from the Cuban black lineups, however, were

Alejandro Oms poses in a Habana Leones uniform late in his illustrious Cuban League career (c. 1930).

Marsans and Almeida, both acquired in mid-summer by the National League Cincinnati Reds. In subsequent years a regular lineup of Cuban teams played as units in the pioneering Negro league summer circuits in the American midwest and south and on the east coast. Robert Peterson, among other authorities, speculates that there were two or more genuine Cuban teams (clubs with at least a spattering of native Cubans rather that imposters) touring North America every summer between 1904 and 1947. The 1904 barnstormers christened the All-Cubans undoubtedly chose their name to demonstrate that they were indeed the genuine item. But by the time Rube Foster had converted the black summer circuit into a form of stability with his Negro National League, Cubans were a substantial part of the North American blackball universe. The Cuban Stars East and Cuban Stars West were among the handful of mainstays during two decades of twenties and thirties-era Negro league seasons.

The most successful of all the pseudo–Cuban teams that toured the U.S. or hitched its star more-or-less permanently to a North American Negro league circuit was the outfit known in the mid and late 1930s as the New York Cubans. This team briefly featured the great Martín Dihigo, who suited up for the apex seasons of 1935 and 1936, then again took the field in the Polo Grounds for one final go-round in 1945, when the then-weakened team limped in with the worst record in the Negro National League. And there were others like Luis Tiant, the elder, who spent eight intermittent summers with the outfit between 1935 and 1947 and enjoyed a remarkable 10–0 ledger while pacing the club to a 1947 N.N.L. pennant and Black World Series triumph over the Cleveland Buckeyes. Resurrected from Alex Pompez's Cuban Stars of an earlier period, the mid-thirties team played out of the Polo Grounds and became a championship contender for the first time in 1935 (winning the second-half title but dropping the playoff championship to Josh Gibson's Pittsburgh Crawfords). Four summers later Pompez's Cubans would once more be resurrected as one of the best teams on the blackball circuit, again the second-half champs, but this time falling to Gibson's Homestead Grays in the post-season finale. Cuban teams in the U.S. Negro leagues were also accompanied by Cuban freelancers who sometimes played with largely Cuban clubs (like the Cubans Stars East and West) but also took the field with mostly African-American teams, or even performed within the white man's "organized" baseball circuits.‡

Dolf Luque was one who appeared briefly with a black club (Long Branch) and then showed up (in Luque's case for 20 seasons) in the major leagues. Pitcher José Acosta and outfielder Jacinto Calvo were two more who crossed back and forth over the gulf separating baseball's chasm-like racial divide. Between Rafael Almeida at the turn of the century and Francisco Campos in the aftermath of Jackie Robinson's 1947 triumph, a total of fifteen native Cubans set foot for at least a brief spell in both the white man's and black man's leagues.

One troubling issue permeating the interactions between Afro-Cuban and Afro-American ballplayers before 1947 was the occasional tension over the issue of "passing" as white in the major leagues. American and Cuban blacks played side by

CUBANS APPEARING IN WHITE MAJOR LEAGUES AND BLACK NEGRO LEAGUES

Rafael Almeida
MLB: Cincinnati Reds (1911–1913)
NL: All-Cubans (1904–1905)

Armando Marsans
MLB: Cincinnati Reds, New York Yankees (1911–1918)
NL: All Cubans, Cuban Stars East (1905, 1923)

Mike González
MLB: Boston (N), Cincinnati (N), St. Louis (N), New York (N), Chicago (N) (1912–1932)
NL: Cuban Stars, Long Branch Cubans, New York Lincoln Stars (1911–1914, 1916)

Jacinto (Jack) Calvo
MLB: Washington Senators (1913, 1920)
NL: Long Branch Cubans (1913, 1915)

Angel Aragón
MLB: New York Yankees (1914–1917)
NL: Long Branch Cubans (1913)

Adolfo Luque
MLB: Boston (N), Cincinnati Reds, Brooklyn (N), New York Giants (1914–1935)
NL: Cuban Stars, Long Branch Cubans (1912–1913)

Emilio Palmero
MLB: New York (N), St. Louis (A), Washington (A), Boston (N) (1915–16–21–26–28)
NL: All Cubans (1904–1905)

José Acosta
MLB: Washington Senators, Chicago White Sox (1920–1922)
NL: Long Branch Cubans (1915)

Pedro Dibut
MLB: Cincinnati Reds (1924–1925)
NL: Cuban Stars West (1923)

Ramón (Mike) Herrera
MLB: Boston Red Sox (1925–1926)
NL: Jersey City Cubans, Long Branch Cubans, Cuban Stars West (1916, 1920–21, 1925–26)

Oscar Estrada
MLB: St. Louis Browns (1929)
NL: Cuban Stars East, Cuban House of David (1924–1925, 1931)

Sal (Chico) Hernández
MLB: Chicago Cubs (1942–1943)
NL: Indianapolis Clowns (1945)

Orestes Miñoso
MLB: Cleveland Indians, Chicago White Sox, Washington (AL), St. Louis (NL) (1949–1980)
NL: New York Cubans (1945–1948)

Rafael (Sam) Noble
MLB: New York Giants (1951–1953)
NL: New York Cubans (1945–1947)

Francisco Campos
MLB: Washington Senators (1951–1953)
NL: New York Cubans (1946)

Ricardo Torres
MLB: Washington Senators (1920–1922)
NL: Long Branch Cubans (1914–1916)

‡ A compete listing of U.S. Negro leagues stars who competed in Cuban League winter baseball (also containing partially complete career Cuban statistics) is found in Appendix B. The same appendix also provides a year-by-year list of genuine Cuban teams and individual Cuban players who performed in the U.S. Negro leagues between 1904 and the 1947 season of major league integration.

side with Cuban whites on the winter circuit and it is not implausible that some of the American Negro leaguers resented the success of light-skinned (but probably mulatto) Cubans who were able to sneak across boundaries that kept American blacks out of organized baseball. Such tensions were likely voiced — however occasionally — even if they never became a source of widespread animosity. And if American blacks on the Cuban winter circuit were sometimes upset by the major league privileges of, say, Dolf Luque, José Acosta or Mike González (later Bobby Estalella and Frankie Campos), there was also a reverse form of tension between teammates on Havana-based winter clubs. Native Cubans were usually saddled with salaries in their homeland that could not match those of top American stars imported from Negro circuits in the States. Nonetheless, Cuban League play by all accounts remained a scene relatively free from outward displays of any such potentially simmering hostilities.

There certainly was, nonetheless, an all-too-apparent feeling — widespread in the Afro-American community — that Cubans and other non–African U.S. "blacks" or "Indians" were always treated differently (i.e. better) by established American institutions. Some in stateside black communities were visibly angered simply because such "passing" was seen as denying one's racial heritage. The case of such advantageous bypassing of restrictions seemingly aimed more at American "blacks" than at blacks from other lands seemed to be a lightning-rod issue especially in the shared national game of baseball. It appeared perhaps as though narrow-minded whites judged "Cubans" or "Indians" as less threatening to white supremacy than African-Americans. If non–Afro-Americans with nonetheless swarthy skin did not pour across baseball's racial barriers, a select few did sneak through. And the fact that such a possibility and its injustices were widely commented upon in the North American black community is itself evidence of a popular perception (among American blacks) of special privilege being accorded to non-white foreigners.

The myth of Spanish-speaking dusky Cubans passing as whites eventually became a fixed part of Negro league lore. There are many tales (most apocryphal) of white scouts or managers attempting to convince coveted American black players to learn Spanish and adopt the guise of a Cuban "foreigner" who was something other than a despised "nigger." Quincy Trouppe, a cup of coffee major leaguer in 1952 after integration came on the scene, figures in one such tale. Trouppe (quoted by Brock and Bayne) claims that a big league scout approached him in the early thirties with the suggestion that he disappear into a Caribbean country for a few years and then return speaking Spanish. The movie version of William Brashler's *The Bingo Long Traveling All-Stars and Motor Kings* exploits this fanciful theme, and there are numerous variations to be found in popular novels. (One of the prime examples is the character of catcher Joe Louis "José" Brown in Paul Hemphill's hilarious *Long Gone*, a 1979 satire portraying the mythical Class D Alabama-Florida League.) Such examples of "passing" by the ruse of Latin birthright were widely exaggerated, to be sure, yet like so many apocryphal legends, there was

Legendary Cuban blackball outfielder Alejandro "El Caballero" ("Gentleman") Oms was known as much for his exquisite manners and gentle deportment as for his graceful offense and defense play.

likely a small grain of truth to be found somewhere in the mountain of sand.

Brock and Bayne argue insightfully that manipulating the color line was tolerated in organized baseball (especially major league baseball) as long as it helped the team doing the manipulating. One perfect example is the case of Cuban World War II–era pitcher Tommy de la Cruz who appeared for a single 1944 season with the Cincinnati Reds. Bronze-skinned Tomás de la Cruz, a native of Marianao and winter league ace with Almendares, performed well with a break-even record and 18 decisions but was nonetheless quietly dismissed after only one wartime campaign in the Queen City. Even with Almeida and Marsans three decades earlier, the heat in Cincinnati would eventually become too much to comfortably tolerate ballplayers whose racial roots might be open to question. Other Latinos with possible mixed bloodlines like Venezuelan Alex Carrasquel with the 1940s Senators, and Cárdenas native Roberto Estalella, who also played mostly in Washington, were subject to continuous racial slurs from fans and press alike. The immortal Luque himself was not above such continuous racial taunts across his two decade National League tenure in Cincinnati, Brooklyn and New York's Polo Grounds. Even as white a Cuban as future Padres, Astros and Cubs manager Preston Gómez felt the cold shoulder and heated tongue of fellow ballplayers during his 1944 cup of coffee in Griffith Stadium. In the case of de la Cruz, a well-timed return of pre-war regulars gave a ready-made excuse for dumping the too-dark Cuban hurler.

One footnote of interest to the saga of racial confusion surrounding Cuban ballplayers is the fact that Cuban blacks continued to be passed off wherever possible as "whites" (or at least as tolerated "foreigners") even years after the arrival of full-fledged big-league integration. For years it was claimed in all the baseball history books touching on big-league integration that John Kennedy (a North American black) had first crossed the line in 1959 for the Philadelphia Phillies, the final National League ball club to allow racial mixing on its roster. But the reality is that Humberto "Chico" Fernández, a light-toned Cuban with Negro bloodlines, had broken the starting lineup in Philadelphia several games earlier than Kennedy (see Chapter 10). Fernández was simply passed off as "Cuban" at the time by a Philadelphia press corps that wished to skirt the black ballplayer issue as long as possible. Chico Fernández had of course also been cast as a Cuban (thus officially white or at least not officially Negro) by his first big league team in Brooklyn. The Dodgers, nervous about too many blacks suddenly arriving on Robinson's heels supposedly had tried to bury Roberto Clemente in Montreal in 1954, and then shipped Fernández to Philadelphia on the eve of the 1959 season. (Closer examination of box scores for Montreal games during the 1954 summer doesn't seem to justify the prevailing notion that Clemente was indeed held from action so that other teams might not notice his talents.) Fernández later claimed bitterness (in personal correspondence with the author) about being robbed of the distinction as a racial pioneer during his debut year with the Phillies. After all, Chico complains, he was considered black enough off the field to have only been able to obtain housing in the city's rundown Negro ghetto neighborhood.

Cubans too dark for U.S. white baseball were often included on established Negro league clubs. Méndez became a fixture with the Kansas City Monarchs, first as ace pitcher and later as infielder and playing manager. Torriente followed a similar path with the Chicago American Giants and a host of lesser clubs once alcoholism began eroding his skills. Pablo Mesa was briefly a notable star in the American outlaw leagues during the twenties with the Cuban Stars East in the Eastern Colored League. If these talents were an impossible dream for the managers of big league clubs like John McGraw — who reportedly announced in 1911 he would fork over $50,000 apiece for José Méndez and Mike González (who turned up a year later with the Boston Braves anyway) if only the pair were white — they were a salvation for black managers and club owners like Rube Foster and Alessandro Pompéz. Thus Cubans in the Negro leagues remained as big a summertime story as were U.S. Negro leaguers during winter play back on the island.

* * *

It was the celebrated barnstorming tours of the glamorous big league clubs during the early decades of the past century, however, that grabbed the largest headlines back north (especially in the white press) and also the biggest crowds in Cuba itself. The historic first visit of a team from the "Grandes Ligas" to do combatant with Cuban leaguers came in January 1891 when an outfit called the "All Americans" managed by Al Lawson and featuring, among others, John McGraw of the American Association Baltimore Orioles celebrated a five game tour.* The American team arrived shorthanded and had to borrow several Cuban players to fill out their lineup. Star batsman Antonio María García was one of the athletes on loan and

Cristóbal Torriente once outslugged Babe Ruth in a legendary 1920 Havana exhibition and would have been a sure-fire big leaguer had he been born two decades later.

---

*Roberto González Echevarría (*The Pride of Havana*, 100) claims that John McGraw first visited Havana in 1889, but the details of McGraw's biography as carefully laid out by Charles C. Alexander (*John McGraw*, 1988) establish indisputably that the initial appearance on the island by the future New York Giants manager was the January 1891 barnstorming tour accompanying Al Lawson's "All-Americans" club.

a story persists that it was during this visit that McGraw was tutored by García in the novel art of tactical bunting. The series, swept by the North Americans, was one filled with errors, though it must be noted that scoring rules were quite different at the time. Cuban baseball in 19th century was played with ten men on a side, the extra athlete being a roving fourth outfielder similar to the one used in some modern versions of industrial league softball. But more importantly from a scoring standpoint, all infield grounders that permitted runners to reach first safely were scored as errors, whether the ball was misplayed or not. And if McGraw picked up some bunting skills, it was obvious that it was most likely the Cubans who learned the most about techniques from the somewhat superior visitors.

Almost twenty years would pass before more big leaguers would pour onto the island for wintertime barnstorming tours. And when the practice was renewed it would come at a most significant time for the evolution of Cuban League history. The end of the first decade of the new century witnessed a three-year period (1906–1909) of American occupation of the island and thus a period when nationalistic fervor predictably reached something of a fever pitch. It was also precisely the moment when a new hero fortuitously had arisen on the local baseball scene just in time to capitalize on the growing patriotic passions. José Méndez, a native of the coastal village of Cárdenas in Matanzas Province, made his first Cuban League appearance on February 2, 1908. It was a relief outing against Habana, to be subsequently followed by a successful start, an 8–3 win, versus Matanzas three week later. The frail-appearing fastballer became an overnight success — as Roberto González Echevarría notes, the first Cuban Leaguer to enjoy true island-wide fame — and by season's end had lead Almendares to a pennant while posting a perfect 9–0 rookie pitching ledger.

But young Méndez's greatest triumphs were still down the road, though only a handful of months away. Against the annoying backdrop of American occupation, promoter Eugenio Jiménez (who leased Almendares Park to stage baseball matches and other public spectacles) invited the National League Cincinnati Reds to visit Havana in the fall of 1908 for what was already being called the "American season" of pre-winter-league exhibitions. The big leaguers would arrive along with the touring Brooklyn Royal Giants, a crack club from the barnstorming Negro circuit. There would be numerous eventual consequences of the Reds first Cuba visit, including the soon-realized recruitment of Luque, Marsans and Almeida for big-league play in Cincinnati. But the most pronounced and immediate fallout was the overnight stardom of Méndez, both at home and abroad, as well as the launching of a seemingly indelible romantic image of Cuban baseball throughout both major league and Negro league circles to the north.

The most memorable feature of the Cincinnati club's arduous tour of Havana was destined to be the remarkable hurling by Méndez. Over the final two weeks of November and the first week of December the previously unknown Cuban ace hurled 25 consecutive shutout innings at the embarrassed National League club. The string was launched with a marvelous one-hitter on November 15, with a no-hitter being spoiled only by a ninth-inning scratch single off the bat of future Yankee manager Miller Huggins. Méndez himself fielded the weak roller that resulted in the only safety. The artistic 1–0 win for Almendares came with a first inning tally when future Reds' outfielder Armando Marsans was driven home on a single by Méndez's favorite receiver, Strike (pronounced "Streaky") González. Two more brilliant games by "El Diamante Negro" would soon follow. After a week-long series recess in late November, Cincinnati (having already defeated Habana three times, but now owning a pair of losses to Almendares, and having also suffering a one-sided humiliation by the Royal Giants) was finally able to defeat the Almendares club, 3–2. But in that hard-fought contest the wily Méndez relieved starter Bebé Royer in the third and shut down Reds bats for seven more frames. And on December 3 Méndez was back in the box as a starter to miraculously blank the big leaguers yet once more, this time to the happy tune of 3–0.

If Cuba's "Black Diamond" ("El Diamante Negro") became an instant hero by so efficiently taming white big league bats, and in the process proving that native islanders could hold their own against the best the overlord Americans could offer, he was only lighting the first flames of a smoldering legend about to spread like wildfire. Within two weeks of handcuffing the visiting big leaguers, Méndez again mesmerized a barnstorming club of Americans and Cubans (black and white) playing under the banner "Key West" — this time by a 4–0 count. The same clubs met for a renewal with the Almendares players sailing to Key West for the rematch; this time around Méndez didn't allow a base hit, let alone a run, to mar still another superb outing. The string would finally be snapped at 45 shutout innings when the Habana Reds eventually broke through in the third frame, during the opening game of 1908–09 regular-season Cuban League action.

If the Reds from Cincinnati departed the island of Cuba with their tails between their legs in the early winter of 1908–09, it would not be long before they would have company in their misery, in the form of the soon-to-be-equally-embarrassed American League champion Detroit Tigers. The Tigers would be next to venture into Cuba, only a week after suffering their 1909 World Series defeat at the hands of the Pittsburgh Pirates. Still inflated by their successes against the Cincinnatis twelve months earlier, Cuba's top-flight Almendares club was primed to deliver another kayo punch to the much-ballyhooed but clearly not superior big league visitors. In a near repeat of the previous year's tour opener, the big leaguers were quickly again dazzled by superior Almendares pitching. This time, however, it was another unknown Cuban black moundsman, Eustaquio "Bombín" Pedroso, who surprisingly did José de la Caridad Méndez one better. Pedroso tossed a sparkling no-hitter against the baffled Tiger lineup (which lacked stars Cobb and Crawford but included starters Matty McIntyre (OF), George Moriarty (3B), Boss Schmidt (C), and George Mullin (OF), the latter an ace pitcher here playing out of position) in a 2–1 triumph that stretched out for extra innings and featured some wild and truly unpredictable action. Hitless Detroit knotted the game in the seventh when McIntyre circled the bases on an infield roller, after Chino Cabañas threw wild to first and a fan assisted catcher Strike González in retrieving the errant toss. Almendares triumphed in the eleventh, when the same Cabañas atoned with a perfect squeeze play after another wild heave left the Cubans with a runner perched on third.

Pedroso's remarkable victory over Detroit was another cause for joyous celebration by a Cuban population chaffing under U.S. military occupation. Fans immediately passed a hat through the grandstands to reward Pedroso for his feat and contributors included President José Miguel Gómez and several members of the Detroit team. The two-week Detroit tour as a whole also featured a number of other noteworthy sidelights. Tigers stalwarts Ty Cobb and Sam Crawford were regrettably absent from the Detroit roster, though recognized names like outfielder McIntyre, third-sacker Moriarty, and 29-game winner Mullin were present and accounted for. Detroit played a dozen games in all in Havana, winning four of

Powerful Claro Duany won Cuban League batting and home run crowns in 1944–45 while performing for Marianao. Duany also played two Negro league seasons as an outfielder with the New York Cubans during the mid-forties.

the first five, but then dropping seven straight including the rare no-hitter which came in the seventh contest. After the luckless Tigers departed another barnstorming all-star unit of big-leaguers appeared on the scene and also dropped three of five to a select squad of Cuban hosts. With Fred Merkle (Giants), Sherry Magee (Phillies), and Germany Schaefer (Tigers) in the field and Addie Joss (Indians), Three-Finger Brown (Cubs) and Howie Camnitz (Pirates) on the mound, this club was likely stronger than most previous visiting big league nines. In the highlight contest of this second series of the early winter, Pittsburgh World Series ace Howie Camnitz was bested 3–1 by a still-potent José Méndez.

The next couple of winter seasons would witness continued pitched battles in Havana between visiting big-league clubs and Cuban nines that would prove every bit the equals of all-white rivals from the top echelons of organized baseball. In 1910 the Tigers would return and taste a bit more success by winning seven of their dozen contests, with one ending in a extra-inning deadlock. Manager Hugh Jennings this time had Cobb in the lineup for part of the series, as well as top stars Crawford and Schaefer, which certainly strengthened the Detroit cause. But Cobb was in the end actually outplayed by a trio of black stars, two Americans and one native Cuban. Pop Lloyd, starting shortstops with the Havana Reds, shown brilliantly for the locals in the games staged this time around in Oriental Park (a converted racetrack). Black catchers Bruce Petway (American) and Strike González (Cuban) both earned further notoriety by gunning down the frustrated Cobb on the base paths; one report has it that Petway threw out Cobb three times in one game, though other versions have González as the Cobb nemesis and existing newspaper accounts indicate that Cobb in reality made only one unsuccessful base-stealing attempt.

This second Detroit visit, in December 1910, was part of a lengthy series which also featured the touring Philadelphia Athletics of manager Connie Mack. Mack's team was fresh off a World Series victory over the Chicago Cubs and posted a most impressive pitching quartet of Coombs, Bender, Morgan and Plank. Coombs managed to defeat Pedroso 2–1 in a nip-and-tuck affair, but Chief Bender lost his first two outings in Havana and Plank was bested by the still-marvelous Méndez. Despite the presence of their $100,000 infield the World Champions were manhandled in the series by the Cuban leaguers — dropping six of ten — and left the island muttering about the peskiness of the superior Cuban athletes.

Four consecutive years of high-spirited competition between big leaguers and Cuban leaguers was capped in November-December 1911 with the island visits of three teams: the New Britain club of the Connecticut League, along with the Philadelphia Phillies and John McGraw's New York Giants. The confrontations this time around took on something of a special flavor since the just-concluded big league season had witnessed the historic debut of pioneering Cubans Marsans and Almeida with the National League club in Cincinnati. The minor league outfit from New Britain enjoyed little success against Cuban all-stars, posting only four victories in

18 mostly one-sided outings. The fourth-place National League Phillies (without star pitcher Grover Cleveland Alexander) captured five of their own nine outings but quickly proved to be another big-league outfit that would suffer considerable exasperation at the hands of Cuban black ace José Méndez. El Diamante Negro slugged a triple in his 3–1 victory over George "Dut" Chalmers and then hurled a shutout at the big leaguers while besting journeyman Eddie Stack. The Philadelphia club finally gained a measure of revenge when Dut Chalmers was redeemed with an 8–1 cakewalk over the for-once surprisingly ineffective Méndez in the series finale.

The highlight of the 1911 American Season, however, was the arrival of McGraw's Giants, fresh of a World Series licking by Connie Mack's Athletics. It was the diminutive McGraw's first visit to Cuba since his appearance as a 17-year-old novice ballplayer two decades earlier with the barnstorming all-star team cobbled together by Al Lawson. In the interim the fiery McGraw had established his reputation as a top manager and one of the most volatile personalities in the game. McGraw's charges seemed to be in for the same kind of drudgery that had faced several earlier big league nines in Cuba when they dropped the first three contests and were seemingly overmatched by the three top Cuban aces, Méndez, Pedroso, and future big leaguer Adolfo Luque. Méndez turned in the most memorable performance when he defeated the immortal Christy Mathewson 4–3 in ten nail-biting frames. But the Giants bounced back after a severe scolding by their diminutive skipper and raced through the final nine matches unbeaten. It was the most successful run to date by a big league outfit in Cuba and featured a 4–0 shutout by Mathewson over the durable Méndez. McGraw left Cuba victorious but he also left with indelible and covetous impressions of the Cuban ace Méndez, who he compared quite favorably with his own top gun, Mathewson.

It would be another full decade before McGraw again returned to Cuban soil with his touring National League club. On the eve of the 1920–21 Cuban League season the New York Giants paid a second visit to Havana to square off in a series of late-autumn games with Cuban League teams, all staged in the now-revamped Almendares Park. One irony here was that McGraw's second-string catcher in New York was now Miguel Angel González, the winter league manager for Habana. This time McGraw would not be the sole headline attraction, however, since Cuban promoter Abel Linares had netted an even bigger fish in the figure of Yankees slugging sensation George Herman Ruth. Ruth was reportedly paid a sensational $1,000 per contest to suit up with McGraw's Giants and hopefully demonstrate his remarkable and innovative home run stroke, one that had just reshaped the major league game with an almost unimaginable total of 54 homers. As it turned out, Ruth would draw most of his headlines with his escapades off the field of play rather than his fence-bashing at Almendares Park. Ruth and his wife didn't arrive at the Hotel Plaza until two weeks of the Giants' tour had already elapsed; after entertaining Havana partisans in several contests, the Babe decided not to play in the last scheduled match because Cuban promoters

refused to meet his demand for a still larger paycheck; in the end the incorrigible Ruth apparently lost almost all of his considerable take while gambling on jai alai matches during frolicking evening hours. The actual home run heroics of the tour would surprisingly be authored not by Babe Ruth but instead by an "unheralded" Cuban about to build his own lasting reputation (at least with the white American press) mostly on a single Havana encounter against touted but not altogether serious big league all-stars.

Matched with teams representing both Habana and Almendares, Ruth had a rough time against Cuban competition right from the start. He smacked both a single and triple in the opening game with Club Habana, yet was struck out three consecutive times by José Acosta in the second contest of the series. But it was the third memorable outing, against Almendares on November 5, 1920, that would find a permanent spot in winter baseball lore. It was this game in which the powerful Negro leaguer Cristóbal Torriente would smack three towering homers and thus provided heroics more Ruthian than anything offered by the original Babe himself.

Both a substantial U.S. Negro leagues career with the Chicago American Giants and a respectable tenure in the Cuban League have long been altogether overshadowed by the amplified accounts of Torriente's heroics against Ruth and the Giants in Almendares Park. The record clearly shows that the Cuban slugger smashed three mammoth round-trippers during his most renowned outing. But Roberto González Echevarría has largely put the lie to the mythic status of Torriente's famous one-day slugging feat. Three long balls (apparently of the inside-the-park variety) hit by the "Cuban Strongboy" that afternoon came against Highpockets Kelly, regularly a Giants first baseman who pitched that day on something of a lark. Torriente did sock a double against Ruth, but not his third homer as often reported by the enhancers of the myth. And a local press account of the game in *Diario de la Marina* suggests that Giants pitchers were not taking the game very seriously, were lobbing "batting practice tosses" at the Almendares hitters, and were at any rate still feeling the effects of excessive parting which took place the previous night.

The tour by Ruth and the Giants in November 1920 was not only an apogee but also something of a denouement. After a decade and a half of less than equal competition with teams composed in large part of Afro-Cubans and Afro-Americans, the psychic distress caused by repeated losses to black all-stars became less and less bearable for big league moguls up north. Such regular beatings at the hands of Cubans and American blacks may also have worn somewhat thin on the big leaguers themselves, despite the consolations of some hefty extra winter paychecks and the bonuses provided by the dazzling climate and exotic nightlife Havana had to offer. Judge Landis put an end to the encounters with a ruling in 1923 that barred intact major league clubs from facing black nines on barnstorming tours in Cuba or elsewhere. Big leaguers certainly continued their individual (if not team) presence in Havana after the mid-twenties and that presence would increase dramatically once integration came upon the big league scene in the late forties. Some white major leaguers played on integrated Cuban winter teams in the years preceding the Rickey-Robinson experiment. Max Lanier and Rocky Nelson (with Almendares) and Steve Bilko and Dick Sisler (with Habana) were several who starred in the late-forties and early-fifties. But white Americans were rare (almost non-existent) on Cuban League teams between the world wars. It was the Negro leaguers who continued to perform alongside Cuban whites and blacks for Almendares, Havana, Marianao or Santa Clara. When white major league clubs did visit between the wars it was for exhibitions against each other (1930) or against white amateur ball clubs from the island operating outside of the Cuban professional league.

One notable example of the latter phenomenon came in March 1941, on the heels of Cuba's exciting triumph the previous fall during Havana's hosting of a second Amateur World Series in La Tropical Stadium. With largely the same lineup of amateur league stars that had brought home the gold medal

Rodolfo "Rudy" Fernández pitched with the Cuban Stars East, Cuban Stars and New York Cubans during 1930s and 1940s Negro leagues seasons up north.

only months earlier, a Cuban all-star selection triumphed over the Boston Red Sox who were making a brief spring training stop on Cuban shores. Juanito Decall, a small-stature lefty who never played professionally, authored a brilliant 5-hit 2–1 conquest of a Boston team boasting Bobby Doerr, Jimmie Foxx, Dom DiMaggio and Joe Cronin (but absent Ted Williams). This game served as another indicator that Cubans (even Cuban amateurs) could hold their own with the best American Leaguers or National Leaguers.

Cuban League teams after the year 1900 were always racially mixed, containing some blacks, some whites, and some of mixed African and Caucasian blood. And when they traveled north for summer play they were always viewed as "black" clubs within the prevailing context of North American race relations. The one-drop rule (one drop of Negro blood certifying a man as an African descendent) applied to full teams as it did to individual dark-skinned ballplayers in the eyes of both North American fans and North American baseball administrators. Racially mixed teams, like the Long Branch Cubans in 1914 (with Luque and Acosta on the roster), were forced to play on the black circuit only and were never welcomed anywhere within the numerous minor leagues of organized baseball.

The notorious 1920 Havana tour by Ruth and McGraw was the last significant appearance on Cuban shores of a major league outfit before Judge Landis struck his edict in 1923, effectively freezing the embarrassing encounters between big league teams and predominantly black or even integrated clubs. The series of startling defeats in Cuba over the years had been an embarrassment to the big league enterprise as a whole. Such losses were certainly a most severe blow against the reigning concept behind segregated baseball — the one that claimed blacks were not up to competing with top white professionals. And although the big leaguers clearly held their own against the Cubans and faired no worse than in stateside exhibitions with Negro league outfits, they hardly struck a blow for the superiority of white-only ball clubs. One further spin-off of these tours was that they served to create larger-than-life legends out of dark-skinned Cuban stars for fans who read about them up north, in a land where black ballplayers were still by and large an outlawed breed.

* * *

The rather shocking triumphs (to the big leaguers at least) of Bombín Pedroso and the legendary feats of José Méndez and Cristobal Torriente were certainly a climactic hour for both Cuban League teams and the integrated baseball of which they were a showcase feature. In future years Eustaquio Pedroso would remain the least recognized of the trio; Cuba's "big brute" was touted in 1924 by the Cuban press as one of the three best island pitchers of all-time (with Méndez and Luis Padrón), yet today he is rarely mentioned in reviews of top Cuban blackball stars from the century's early decades. His blackball legacy was, nonetheless, considerable and his future triumphs would be memorable: he once led the Cuban League in batting (.413 in 1915–16), and in 1913 (11) and again in 1915

(10) he paced the Havana circuit in pitching victories. Pedroso, in the end, would boast a sterling 21-year career on the Negro league circuit that would stretch all the way to 1930, though by the mid-twenties he played mostly as a first baseman and even a catcher, and his hitting skills had by then largely eroded.

The career of Méndez, by contrast, would turn out in the long run to be even more personally tragic than athletically spectacular, and the eye-popping triumphs of 1908 and the three following winters were an early career zenith that the young hurler would never be able to sustain. And yet the celebrated triumphs of Cuba's greatest natural pitcher were certainly not limited to the often-retold victories over visiting big leaguers in Havana. There was also a brilliant Negro league record in North America, as well as considerable achievement as a manager, position player, and part-time hurler after bad luck sabotaged Méndez's pitching career and before illness also prematurely cut short his life. Tragically, the great Black Diamond was doomed by a string of unexplained arm injuries never to become the true immortal he might well have been.

If there was any blackball star — emerging out of Cuba and roaming the byways of the Negro leagues during the heyday of barnstorming baseball — that was truly the stuff of inflated legend, then it was certainly the magical Méndez. When he first arrived in the United States in 1908, only months before his shocking performance against the Cincinnati Reds in Havana later that fall, he was already recognized as an exceptional talent. A lean and rangy right-hander with long fingers that allowed him to apply extra spin to his fastball, Méndez was also a crafty artist who mixed his blazer with a sharp curve and dazzling change of pace. Hurling for the Brooklyn Royals Giants his first summer in the north, the fluid Cuban was victorious three times without defeat. A summer later, fresh from his stunning performances against big leaguers, Méndez catapulted to major stardom with the Cuban Stars, reputedly winning 44 of 46 decisions and pitching a ten-inning perfect game masterpiece. While he dazzled at home in the wintertime during his peak years of 1908–1912, he was equally sensational with the Cuban Stars and Stars of Cuba over the same stretch of dual summer and winter seasons. The four following years he toiled with Wilkinson's All Nations club but soon began experiencing troublesome arm problems which by 1917 eventually ended all too early his value as a top flight pitching ace. Méndez already owned a 62–17 winter league ledger by 1914, when he first reported debilitating arm pain; his lifetime Cuban won-lost mark would eventually rest at 72–26 (a .736 winning percentage), but two-thirds of his defeats were suffered after his unprecedented opening four-year spurt for Almendares.

Arm-problems aside, Méndez remained a Negro league regular as a shortstop with Rube Foster's Chicago American Giants in 1918 and 1919 and then switched to the Kansas City Monarchs where he continued to man the shortstop position and also serve as playing-manager for a club that walked off with Negro American League pennants in 1923, 1924 and 1925. Méndez even still pitched occasionally with Kansas City,

American Ray "Talúa" Dandridge earned a small portion of his Cooperstown Hall of Fame credentials playing for the fifties-era Cuban League Marianao Tigres. For all his prowess, Dandridge never paced the Cuban circuit in any major batting categories, but did lead once in steals and once in official times at bat.

recovering his one-time magic long enough to post an 8–2 mark in the first of the Monarchs' three pennant seasons and finish with a 20–4 ledger over his seven late-career seasons for owner J.L. Wilkinson in Kansas City. A final hurrah on the mound came in the 1924 Colored World Series against Eastern Colored League champion Hilldale, where the still wily Méndez toss a complete-game shutout and picked up two mound victories. The final season for "El Diamante Negro" was 1926 in Kansas City. Only two years later he succumbed in Havana to the ravages of tuberculosis (the official cause of death was bronchopneumonia), having barely passed his fortieth birthday.

The power-packed image of muscle-bound outfielder Cristóbal Torriente also rests on more that a single-game encounter with the legendary Babe Ruth. Torriente would soon build a reputation in the world of black baseball as a slugging star for Rube Foster's Chicago American Giants between 1918 and 1925 and was known as much for his strong throwing arm and great range as he was for his fence-bashing at the plate. Most of Torriente's reputation nonetheless rests upon seemingly fanciful tales of power-hitting feats which sometimes read more like the stuff of fairy tales that of sports page history. There is one account (attributed to teammate Jelly Gardner) of a vicious line drive he hit high off the wall in Indianapolis that caromed so sharply to a waiting fielder that he was thrown out at first. John Holway (*Blackball Stars*) quotes another Negro leagues old-timer reporting the Cuban strongman smashing a scoreboard clock 17 feet above an outfield fence in Kansas City ("the hands just started going round and round") and legging out a mere double. Yet where there are raw numbers available (Holway provides some of these) they suggest that whatever exaggerations surrounded Torriente's phenomenal hitting, they more than likely amplified rather than distorted his remarkable batting talents. And it should not pass unnoticed that Torriente was apparently also a pitcher of rather exceptional talent and one historian (James Riley, *The Biographical Encyclopedia of the Negro Baseball Leagues*) reports a 15–7 mound record during Torriente's early seasons with the Chicago American Giants (1918–1920). In this latter respect he paralleled Dihigo, though Dihigo was foremost a pitcher who also hit and fielded remarkably well, while Torriente was a natural-born outfielder and slugger with an arm strong and talented enough to also allow some noteworthy pitching performances.

But Torriente, like Méndez, would be also doomed to fall short of a still more remarkable career that might well have been. In this case it was personal demons not injury and accident that would cut short seemingly unlimited potential. A fondness for nightlife and alcoholic spirits took enough of a toll on the star outfielder by mid-career that he was traded from Foster's Chicago club to the Kansas City Monarchs in 1926 (at age 31), then quickly ran afoul of Monarchs' management for surly behavior despite a .381 batting average. Outside of some sporadic heavy hitting for the Detroit Stars in two subsequent summer seasons, Torriente's career began to wane in the early thirties, perhaps due in large part to an inability to control his excessive drinking. After stints with several lesser clubs (Cleveland Cubs, Union Giants, Atlanta Black Crackers) in the mid–1930s, the slugger mysteriously dropped out of sight and his final years remain something of an unresolved mystery. He was reported to have lived in poverty in Tampa's Ybor City for a brief spell, and unconfirmed rumor has it that he died in New York City (probably in 1938), a victim of tuberculosis. Holway (without providing specifics or anything in the way of documentation) reports the cause of Torriente's demise to have been his alcoholism. Available Cuban sources remain uncharacteristically silent on the matter.

A handful of additional Cuban blacks also made their not unsubstantial marks on the blackball scene before the Second World War, with its death knell for segregated play. The incomparable Martín Dihigo (see Chapter 1) earned Cuban League, Mexican League and Negro league reputations that carried universal acknowledgement as the most versatile athlete ever to play the game of professional baseball. Dihigo's three-decade achievements (outlined in a separate chapter of this book) stretched beyond his glory as a pitcher and infielder to include noteworthy post-playing-career service as umpire and broadcaster, as well as one of the most memorable managers in Cuban League annals. Some latter-day blackball historians (John Holway for one, in private correspondence with the author) have recently questioned Dihigo's lofty reputation by pointing to more impressive offensive statistics for sluggers like Torriente and Alejandro Oms. Yet it is here that Dihigo seems to be hurt somewhat by his uncanny and unrivalled versatility. He was after all primarily a pitcher, for all the plaudits he received while manning other positions. That he was so talented with the bat (once a champion hitter in Mexico) while earning his board primary on the mound is itself the measure of his true legacy. Dihigo was the first Cuban and only the sixth blackball star to find enshrinement (1977) in the Valhalla built at Cooperstown. He is also the only ballplayer in the game's history to find homes in the hallowed halls of fame established by three (USA, Mexico, Cuba) separate baseball playing nations.

In the firmament of Cuban blackball stars a special place must also be reserved for outfielder Pablo "Champion" Mesa, a defensive wizard who once teamed with fellow Cuban Alejandro Oms and American Oscar Charleston to form one of the legendary outfields of baseball history. The immortal trio of skilled fly chasers was the anchor of a Santa Clara team that ran away with the 1923–24 winter league season and has long remained one of the most fabled nines in the island's top-heavy baseball lore. Mesa also performed in a second all-everything outfield with Oms and Dihigo, this time on the American blackball circuit with the Cuban Stars ball club of the early twenties. Often overshadowed by the latter two stars, Mesa was nonetheless a complete ballplayer who combined excellent all-around hitting, raw power and bunting skills with speedy base running and a reputation as one of the most dependable black defensive outfielders of his generation. Mesa's peak individual year came in 1927: that final winter season he played in Havana for a club called "Cuba" and posted a league-best .407 batting mark yet didn't claim an "official" batting crown for lack of sufficient plate appearances. But his lasting reputation was built on the outfield trio he anchored in 1923–24 with the memorable Santa Clara club, as well as his service alongside Dihigo and Oms up north.

A bit of mystery also surrounds Mesa's brief six-season career on the Cuban winter circuit and his parallel six summers with American blackball clubs. After his heavy-hitting 1927 season Mesa's name disappears overnight from rosters in the Havana-based league, and there is also no further trace of him on subsequent Negro league rosters either. His whereabouts after the late twenties have somehow fallen into the dustbin of history.

Alejandro Oms, outfield teammate of Dihigo and Mesa — and also earlier of Bernardo Baró and Mesa on the same Eastern Colored League club known as the Cuban Stars — may in the end have been the greatest Cuban hitter of them all, unless that distinction is given, but only by a slim nod, to Torriente. Oms is most often now recalled by Negro league historians as integral part of a sterling outfield defensive trio, whether that trio was the one in Santa Clara in 1923 (Oms, Mesa and Charleston) or the one which terrorized the Eastern Colored League throughout the decade of the 20s (Oms, Mesa and first Baró, then later Dihigo). But Oms in his own heyday was first and foremost celebrated for such strictly individual attributes as his powerful and consistent bat, as well as his colorful showmanship while manning the outfield pastures. His lifetime batting average in Cuba (15 seasons) was a lofty .351, he hit over .300 eleven different times, eight of those coming in a row. Up north he never posted a mark lower than .308 in a half-dozen Eastern Colored League seasons and in the early 1920s once reportedly smashed 40-plus homers during a single summer barnstorming and league season. Oms' hall-of-fame Cuban League career was also marked by three batting titles (1925, 1929, 1930), two league-leading marks in slugging (1929, 1930) and one in stolen bases (1932), plus spots on four league championship rosters. Following a common practice of comparing Negro leagues to big leaguers, James Riley once dubbed Alejandro Oms the "Black Paul Waner" in an effort to adequately underscore the Cuban star's remarkable combination of offensive and defensive skills.

There were dozens of others who filled the Cuban talent pool to overflowing across the glorious decades of black professional baseball that separated the century's two world wars. Bartolo Portuondo (father of Buena Vista Social Club singing legend Omara Portuondo) was an often overlooked headliner at third base with Alessandro Pompez's Eastern Colored League Cuban Stars of the early and mid-twenties. Pelayo Chacón (father of Venezuela-born big leaguer Elio Chacón), in his own heyday of the teens and twenties, sported a reputation as one of the best shortstops in baseball, white or black. Diminutive light-skinned pitcher José Acosta owned the rare distinction of performing admirably in both the black Negro leagues (as ace of the 1915 Long Branch Cubans) and the white major leagues (where he split 20 decisions with the Senators and White Sox in the early 1920s). In the forties, on the eve of integration, Alejandro Crespo enjoyed a brief sojourn as a clean-up hitter with the New York Cubans before fashioning an outstanding career in Mexican summer league play. And another power-packed outfielder of the same late blackball era, Claro Duany, slugged away in the middle of the order for the 1947 Negro National League champion New York Cubans outfit. Both Cubans appeared in early-forties Negro league East-West all-star games.

Bernardo Baró was a brilliant Cuban outfielder who made most defensive plays look easy but also earned an unfortunate reputation as a "show off" during 17 seasons in the U.S. Negro leagues. Baró, as noted, teamed with Oms and Mesa with the Cuban Stars of the Eastern Colored League in 1924 for still another of the classic all-everything Cuban outfields of black baseball lore. Back home also he starred with Almendares as first a pitcher and later an outfielder who also slugged with au-

MAX MANNING — PITCHER

American Negro leaguer Max Manning pitched four seasons (1946–1950) with the Habana Leones, compiling a 26–33 record in 88 outings.

thority and ran the bases with abandon. Baro's career ended with a sudden and tragic twist at the end of the 1920s when he suffered a mental collapse while performing for the Cuban Stars East (1929) and had to be temporarily restrained with a straightjacket. Returning briefly the following year, he played only a partial season with the Kansas City Monarchs, then dropped out of sight in Cuba; the sad late-career saga came to a tragic conclusion when Baró died suddenly, shortly after his less-than-joyous return to his homeland. An eerie parallel to the sudden collapse of Baró was found in the case of another stellar Cuban outfielder of the epoch who also burned up the northern circuits during the same decade. Speedy outfielder Valentín Dreke hit .353 for the Cuban Stars West in the inaugural season (1920) of the Negro National League and also shone as a stellar lead-off batter with the Cuban Stars of Havana barnstorming outfit. Back home, he also manned the outfield during eight seasons with Almendares and hit over .300 for that entire stretch, as well as reigning as a base-stealing champion. But Dreke also died suddenly at the peak of his career, succumbing to a mysterious infection in Havana a mere year before the demise of the ill-starred Baró. Both men hardly had their best on-field years behind them at the time of their twin tragic deaths.

The island of Cuba supplied the prime setting for the world's best baseball between the opening of the modern major league era in 1903 and the closing of segregated organized baseball in 1947. Here were found the only playing fields where the very best ballplayers of both races matched head-to-head in epic battles for diamond superiority. And much of the very best diamond talent was also native to the island of Cuba during this epoch. For nearly five decades Havana remained at the very epicenter of the baseball universe, even if this fact was too often ignored by both the white press and the all-white organized baseball circuit that had so long maintained such a one-dimensional view of the true baseball universe.

Had there been no odious "gentleman's agreement" tainting the North American version of the shared national pastime between the 1880s and 1940s, would organized baseball have gutted the Cuban League long before its eventual demise with the arrival of the Cuban revolution? It is not unreasonable to jump to the conclusion that this would have been highly unlikely. Even if they were blasting long balls and blazing fastballs for the white man's leagues at Yankee Stadium, or Shibe Park, or in Cleveland's League Park, the best of the swarthiest Cubans would almost certainly have been back home playing for Almendares or Club Habana or Santa Clara or some other Cuban League outfit during the "off-season" winter months. Ballplayer salaries in the epoch between the wars were never sufficient to support a professional athlete throughout an entire year, and it is likely that top Negro stars made as much summer cash as most big leagues at any account. White Cubans—like Luque and "Iron Mike" González — who went north to the Giants or Cardinals or other big league clubs for the summer months always returned to Havana to renew their trade each winter. Their black teammates like Oms, Pagés, Chacón, Pedroso and Méndez would most certainly have done exactly the same.

Today there is much speculation concerning what top-flight Cuban ballplayers might have filled major league rosters in the 1970s, 80s and 90s, were it not for the frigid political relations separating the world's two foremost baseball-playing nations. But what might the big leagues have been like in the more distant era of Ruth and Gehrig and Mathewson and Walter Johnson if, say, Martín Dihigo had been a regular in the Yankees lineup, if Méndez had squared off against Mathewson on a regular basis in the Polo Grounds rather than on only two isolated occasions in Havana, or if Torriente and Oms and Pablo Mesa regularly roamed National League or American League outfields and took their cuts at the best big league pitching? Or perhaps if an elder Louie Tiant (the southpaw version) had hurled for the Red Sox or Indians a generation earlier than his colorful mustachioed son? One conclusion only can likely be reached on this count. And that is that it would have been a far, far richer brand of major league baseball indeed.

*   *   *

As impressive as native Cuban blacks might have been on the diamonds in and around Havana, they often got a substantial run for their money on the island from "foreign" black stars that were soon being imported in significant numbers from up north. The first American-born black professionals had reached Cuban shores as a unit, in the guise of a touring team ironically dubbed Cuban X-Giants, in the pivotal year of 1900. The first season of the new century (or was it the last of the old, depending on the view of whether centuries are launched in the year '00 or '01) was a turning point campaign for blackball ballplayers in Cuba. The "Liga Nacional de Base-Ball" now stretched from mid–May to late–November, with each team playing a shade less than 30 weekend games. Far more importantly, this was the year that the Cuban League itself was first integrated by the San Francisco club (with a roster almost entirely of blacks) and the "Cubano" team (also partially integrated and spelling its name *Cuba-No* on team jerseys to suggest that its inclusion of blacks was a departure from racist views held by the club's previous owners). Perhaps not unworthy of mention is the fact that this was also the very first Cuban season played under American military occupation that followed the Spanish-American War (1895–1898). It was simultaneously the year of the first visit by a touring U.S. black team, and that event would be one destined to build considerable confidence among the native Cuban ballplayers.

The story of the pioneering American blackball team known as Cuban X-Giants is well known among present-day Negro leagues *aficionados* who have read celebrated accounts by Peterson, Holway, Riley, Rogosin and other prominent blackball historians. This club claimed an indirect link to the original "Cuban Giants" outfit that evolved from Frank P. Thompson's Long Island (Babylon) Argyle Hotel team of 1885. James Riley, among latter-day historians, and Sol White, among pioneering blackball chroniclers, outline the evolution of the Argyle club, which claimed pre-eminence as the first professional black baseball team. Frank Thompson, headwaiter at the Argyle, formed his original nine among the Babylon resort's wait staff, ostensibly to entertain affluent hotel guests; soon he was hiring known pros as waiter-ballplayers and challenging better competition during the hotel's off-season. Thompson reportedly added crack players from the Philadelphia Orions and Washington, DC, Manhattans to form a re-christened Cuban Giants that toured in 1886 as the first black professional squad. It was only when the ball club later moved to Trenton, New Jersey, and fell under the leadership of S.K. Govern and the financial control of Walter Cook, however, that they made their lasting mark on the emerging Negro baseball scene. Such was their popularity that it would later account for the high currency of both the names "Giants" and "Cubans" among numerous black U.S.-based touring clubs. Among the most prominent imitators was a group of defectors from the original squad which called themselves the Cuban X-Giants, with "X" translating as "ex–Giants" to indicate the team's historic roots. Under E.B. Lamar this team had already laid claim to several summertime Negro "championships" (including the first challenge playoff series between East and West clubs in 1899) before it headed to Havana in the late winter of 1900.

The Cuban X Giants were the first to link Afro-American and Afro-Cuban ball-playing traditions and their turn-of-the-century foray into Cuba would foreshadow a later autumn "American season" which fell between the end of the big league campaign (the major league World Series) and the opening of Cuban winter league play; after 1908 this so-called American Season would find various Cuban League squads warming up by competing with U.S. major, minor and blackball league clubs. Thus the tradition Lamar's visiting Negro leaguers launched would soon become the backbone of Cuban League successes for much of the following five decades. It was first announced in early February, 1900, in the pages of Havana's *Diario de la Marina*, that E.B. Lamar was bringing his already renowned Cuban X Giants (they were simply called "Cuban Giants" by the Cuban press) to Havana for a much-anticipated barnstorming tour. On tap would be a ten-game series which had the blackball stars matched against each of the four Cuban League clubs — San Francisco, Habana, Cubano, Almendarista — and also against some pseudo-all-star squads comprised of ballplayers drawn from all league teams. The first newspaper accounts could not make enough of the quality of the visiting Afro-American nine (333 wins against only 96 defeats were reported for a recent three-year span) and the U.S. club was claimed to be the strongest found anywhere outside of the prestigious National League.

González Echevarría (*The Pride of Havana*, 121) provides the best English-language account available to modern readers of this historic encounter. After an opening match with Cubano was washed away by a typical winter downpour, the Americans won the lidlifter 6–5 over Habana, who reportedly gifted the game to the visitors with sloppy fielding even though the American blackballers (stifled by Habana's ace José Romero) didn't bat exceptionally well. It was perhaps significant that the Cuban press continually referred to the team as the Cuban Giants without the X attached; the labeling of these visiting Americans as "Cubans" had to be confusing enough on its own merit. The tour also involved some exhibitions against independent Havana-area teams like Regla's Libertad squad, which accounted themselves well before dropping a 15–11 slugfest. But the highlight was a pair of culminating games between the Giants and a league all-star squad dubbed "Criollo" and featuring Carlos "Bebé" Royer on the mound and other Cuban stars in the field. Cuban victories in both matches sent the signal that Cuban League baseball had perhaps "arrived" on a par with the best very baseball being played up north.

Individual players were quick to follow the first touring black teams. Black U.S. players were heading to Cuba for winter employment as early as 1907, with Grant "Home Run" Johnson, Rube Foster, Bill Monroe, Charles (alias "Chief Tokahoma") Grant, and Preston "Pete" Hill all showing up on the Fe team roster that winter. Black players and their agents

Cuban outfielder Pedro "El Gamo" Pagés appeared two seasons with the Negro league New York Cubans (1939, 1947) and also paced the Cuban League in runs scored in 1941 while with Cienfuegos.

apparently had been made sufficiently aware of the enticements of Cuba by the visits of the Cuban X Giants and the Philadelphia Giants over the several preceding winters. The Americans' impact was immediate as Fe finished in second place behind Almendares, with their U.S.–flavored roster, and George "Chappie" Johnson of the Philadelphia Giants also cracked the starting lineup for the league's third club, Habana. A season later the influx continued with Preston Hill (now with Habana) pacing the circuit in runs, hits and triples, and Clarence Winston (also with Habana) stealing 33 bases. Almost immediately the imported blacks were contributing to strengthening the teams that recruited them and were also appearing among the leaders in individual league batting and pitching performance. Rube Foster won a league-best nine games for Fe in 1907, while Grant Johnson was a pacesetter in base hits in 1909.

By 1910 John Henry "Pop" Lloyd was also a legitimate star

on the Havana winter scene, performing for more than a decade with the Habana, Fe and Almendares ball clubs and earning his memorable nickname "El Cuchara" ("The Shovel") for unparalleled if unorthodox shortstop play. (Lloyd reportedly scooped up handfuls of dirt when he grabbed infield rollers.) If the immortal Lloyd ("The Black Wagner" for Negro league historians) didn't tear up the Cuban League during his dozen winters in Havana, he did put his stamp on the American Season matches versus big league barnstormers. In December 1910 he out hit Ty Cobb (.500 to .367) in a five-game set with the visiting Detroit Tigers, also wearing cast-iron shin guards to protect his legs against Cobb's spikes-first slides on base-stealing attempts; a week later Lloyd batted .356 for an all-star nine of Cuban leaguers during a ten game series with the visiting world champion Philadelphia Athletics.

Ironically this arrival of U.S. blacks on the Cuban winter league scene coincided precisely with the very seasons in which the first large-scale tours of big league clubs occurred. And more ironic still, they overlapped with the years in which Cuba was chaffing under a most unpopular intrusion of U.S. imperialism. Finally, they overlapped as well with the dramatic debuts of two of the greatest black Cuban stars, hurlers José Méndez and Eustaquio Pedroso, phenoms whose overnight reputations were certainly enhanced by their string of victories over visiting American clubs. With U.S. marines occupying the island between 1906 and 1909, games between Cuban League squads and visiting American teams most certainly took on added patriotic overtones for local fans and players alike. American administration of the island (under military governors William Howard Taft and Charles Magoon) also likely contributed to the increasing willingness of U.S. black and white players to visit in the first place. If the first waves of Negro leaguers (both teams and individual ballplayers signing on for duty with Cuban clubs) injected new life into the island's winter baseball scene before the end of the century's first decade, this significant trickle would eventually become a substantial flood tide. For larger numbers and bigger names would soon follow.

The honor roll of Negro league stars in wintertime Cuban baseball during the pre and post World War I years is extensive and altogether rich. Grant "Home Run" Johnson outhit both the venerable Ty Cobb and the imposing Wahoo Sam Crawford while dressing with Club Habana (alongside Preston Hill, that year's Cuban League batting champ) in 1910 exhibitions games versus the visiting Detroit Tigers. Johnson would hit over .400 in 1912 while again playing with Habana; he also earlier suited up with Club Fe, the most active importer of North American Negro leaguers. Preston "Pete" Hill, a hard-swinging lefty outfielder who drew frequent comparisons with Cobb, starred alongside Rube Foster both on Cuban tours and for the American Giants in Chicago. In addition to the 1910–11 batting title posted by the speedy Hill (he hit .365 and also paced the circuit in base knocks and triples), some sources credit him with a largely unverifiable .307 career average over a half-dozen winters in Havana. Both Hill (.400 in 1915–16) and Johnson (.410 in 1912, with too few at-bats to take the hit-

ting crown) rang up single .400-plus seasons on the Cuban winter circuit. And another remarkable southpaw basher, Chino Smith ("built along the lines of Lloyd Waner," according to Robert Peterson), also reached his peak as a slugger during his seasons in the Cuban League. The compact outfielder and second baseman paced the Havana circuit in base hits (67) in 1929–30, although he was bested for the batting title by local star Alejandro Oms. Charles Smith's half-dozen or so seasons with Habana produced a batting average reported by James Riley as .335, though again such numbers appear to be more estimates than hard data.

Oscar Charleston may have been the greatest all-around player in baseball history — black, white or mixed. He and Cuba's own native Martín Dihigo today seem the only rivals for that elevated mythical title. The bulk of the barrel-chested slugger's seasons in the teens, twenties and thirties on the Negro league circuit with the Indianapolis ABCs and a host of other clubs (the Homestead Grays and Pittsburgh Crawfords most prominently) generated endless comparisons with a similarly built white legend named Babe Ruth. A younger and slimmer Charleston had also once been labeled as a clone for Ty Cobb; and his style of shallow center-field play drew further comparisons with Hall-of-Famer Tris Speaker. No other player of any color has ever been seriously mentioned after this fashion in the same breath with both of organized baseball's top unrivaled twentieth-century offensive stars.

Oscar Charleston debuted in Cuba with also-ran Santa Clara during the 1922–23 season, a year before that team became the most dominant ball club on the winter circuit. It was a sensational coming-out-party by almost any stretch as the Indianapolis native stroked the ball at a lofty .446 pace (with 41 safeties in 92 trips to the plate); he did not win the batting crown, however, as reported by John Holway in *Blackball Stars*, since his less than 100 at-bats were insufficient to qualify for the official crown (captured by Bernardo Baró of Almendares, who slugged at a paltry .401 clip). His two top Caribbean seasons were the next two campaigns, first with the suddenly invincible *Leopardos* of 1924 and then with Almendares the following winter. During the follow-up four years Charleston continued to return regularly to Cuba to play with Habana in 1926, the Habana Red Sox club of 1927, and a team called "Cuba" for the 1928 and 1929 seasons. His batting average never dipped below the .322 standard of his final season in Havana, and he posted a .366 overall mark during ten Cuban winter outings. Charleston's greatest single day north or south of the Straits of Florida came with a six-for-six barrage on January 10, 1924, versus Marianao in Havana's picturesque Almendares Park.

Beyond the astronomical numbers, Charleston also spun quite a legend in his numerous winter months in Cuba and that legend arose mainly from the remarkable season of 1923–24 and the unparalleled Santa Clara team that dominated all comers that particular year. For one remarkable stretch Charleston anchored an outfield that few could debate was the greatest fly-chasing trio ever assembled. Oms manned right and slugged away at a .381 clip; Charleston was in center and banged the ball to the tune of .375; Pablo "Champion" Mesa anchored left and batted a seemingly anemic .328. The same lineup boasted the league pacesetter in batting (not Oms or Charleston but rather American Negro leaguer Oliver Marcelle), hits (Dobie Moore, another star-quality U.S. import), doubles (American blackballer Frank Warfield), and triples (once again Moore). Charleston himself had to settle for honors as league champion in runs scored and in stolen bases.

The phenomenal Santa Clara Leopards (also called *Pilongos*) of 1923–24, with their star-studded outfield and noteworthy overall season, were unquestionably one of the more remarkable single chapters of Cuba's pre-revolution baseball history, legend or lore. The margin of runaway victory that season achieved by the *Leopardos* ball club was the largest in league annals; the final gap was 11.5 games over runner-up Habana, with Almendares and newcomer Marianao bunched at 18 and 20.5 games in the rear. The *Pilongos* team has often been compared in their domination to the 1927 New York Yankees squad of Murderer's Row fame. And certainly the Santa Clara lineup of that season was a true Murderer's Row by any imaginable standard inside or outside of the big leagues. There is also a remarkable story surrounding how this team was brought together — mainly through the efforts of Tinti Molina with his numerous U.S. Negro leagues connections, and as part and parcel of impresario Abel Linares's continuing desperate search for a third rival to challenge Habana and Almendaers — and how it was so quickly once again dismantled as star players (including Charleston) fled back to the stateside Negro circuit before season's end. It is a story researched in great detail in recent years by blackball historian David Skinner and told in fine detail in an article first published obscurely in the 2000 SABR convention handbook (see bibliography at chapter's end).

Two other top blackball figures of the 1920s and '30s, James Bell and Willie Wells, also rang up legendary seasons and indelible moments on the Havana baseball scene. "Cool Papa" Bell — reputedly the fastest man ever to set foot on a baseball diamond — expanded his lofty slugging and base running reputations on the island's winter circuit for several seasons of the late twenties. Ironically, Bell is best remembered in Cuba for a remarkable day of long-ball slugging which seemed a bit out of character with his normal reputation for advancing on the bases largely by blinding stealth or base-running savvy. On January 1, 1929 Bell (known as "Jimmy" Bell in Cuba) became the first Cuban Leaguer to sock three homers in a single game. Three homers during a game had been achieved twice before in Cuba, by Bellán in the famed 1874 "first game" at Matanzas, and by Torriente in the 1920 exhibition showdown with Ruth. But those in truth were not Cuban League contests per se. Bell's feat came in Aida Park, in Cienfuegos, against the Habana ball club and involved three distinct pitchers, Oscar Levis, James "Campanita" Bell (further irony), and the immortal Martín Dihigo. Bell was batting in the leadoff slot for Cienfuegos that day and all three smashes were of the inside-the-park variety on a field with no outfield wall. To supplement the rare slugging outburst, Bell was also the league's leader that very season in his more usual forte of stolen bases.

Willie Wells — a premier blackball shortstop between the mid-twenties and mid-forties — played on the same Cienfuegos team with Papa Bell in 1929; and a season later when Cienfuegos captured a league pennant, Wells was honored with his first of two Cuban MVP awards. The second such honor came a full decade later when "El Diablo" toiled with the more popular *Alacranes* of Almendares. While playing for yet a third club, Santa Clara in 1936, Wells tied Dihigo for the league leadership in base hits. For his seven Cuban winter seasons Wells posted a most respectable .320 cumulative batting average. His value to the league was underscored in his farewell season of 1940 when he hit .328 to pace Almendares to a championship, its first in five seasons, thus earning a spot on the league all-star team as well as his second MVP honors, despite failing to lead the circuit in a single notable offensive category. .

Other North American blacks also wrote lively legends throughout the so-called Golden Age of Cuban baseball. Henry Kimbro, an outfielder known more for producing runs with his bat than for saving them with his glove, became an island fixture in the 1940s. Jimbo Kimbro peaked with a 1947–48 batting title (.346) while in uniform with Habana; still earlier (1939–40) he copped a stolen base title (18) as a fixture in the Almendares lineup. John Henry Lloyd, dubbed "El Cuchara" ("The Scoop") by Havana partisans as early as 1910, starred with Havana's most popular team, the Club Habana outfit that embarrassed the visiting Detroit American Leaguers in 1909 (without Ty Cobb in the lineup) and again in 1910 (despite an appearance by the intimidating Cobb). "The Black Wagner" enjoyed one of his many career highlights when he not only outhit Cobb in Havana but also teamed with African-American catcher Bruce Petway to shut down the flashy big leaguer at his specialty of pilfering bases. Bill Foster was an outstanding lefty pitcher with Cienfuegos in the late 1920s and considered by some the top blackball southpaw of his era. Foster would later credit turn-of-the-century Habana ace Luis Padrón with teaching him the deadly change-up delivery while he labored with the 1927–28 Cienfuegos team. If Cuban stars unquestionably flavored the Negro leagues up north, African-Americans were returning the favor with substantial interest in Cuba's *béisbol paradiso* during each and every winter season.

A final chapter of Cuba's blackball legacy would be written in the years immediately preceding big league integration. Havana would of course play a not-insignificant role in the unfolding drama surrounding Branch Rickey's 1946–1947 scheme for launching Jackie Robinson onto the major league scene. It was — not surprisingly, given the decades of African-American and Cuban interactions on the diamond — a much-heralded Cuban ballplayer that emerged as one of the earliest candidates in Rickey's plotting for the role that Robinson would eventually fill. And big league integration would soon have almost as much of a negative impact on the integrity and stature of the Cuban winter circuit as it would also have on the ill-fated U.S. Negro leagues themselves.

Colorful Cuban League shortstop and all-around diamond nonpareil Silvio García was destined to play a somewhat mysterious but nonetheless significant role in the intriguing plot surrounding Branch Rickey and Jackie Robinson. Much has been written about Rickey's elaborate smoke screen designed to camouflage backroom manipulations crucial to the Mahatma's carefully orchestrated movements toward breaking the "gentleman's agreement" in the aftermath of the Second World War. Rickey histrionically set up the sham United States Colored League as a blatant cover operation and put a short-lived Brooklyn Brown Dodgers team managed by Oscar Charleston into Ebbets Field. It was an especially effective cover for scouting available black talent for the inevitable integration experiment once it came. The Mahatma was beyond doubt motivated as more by business acumen and on-field baseball considerations (a belief that any influx of black talent could help his Dodgers win pennants) than he was by mere altruism,

Cienfuegos slugger Alejandro Crespo was at various times a Cuban League leader in homers, batting average and RBI during the early and mid-forties. Crespo twice played for the New York Cubans (1940, 1946) during forties-era Negro league seasons. Miami sportswriter and Havana native Fausto Miranda once labeled Crespo the greatest Cuban outfielder ever.

a fact much discussed in the literature. (Robert Peterson's treatment in Chapter 14 of *Only the Ball Was White* is as good a starting point on this issue as any.) Rickey nonetheless had to have precisely the right man to cross the racial barrier first. That man had to be a very talented ballplayer and one who also owned personal characteristics easing the way toward his acceptance by fans, teammates and opponents alike. But that brave pioneer also had to be quite a bit more than just a sound ballplayer. Perhaps the frequently raised issue of seemingly greater tolerance for Cubans as potential big leaguers (they were "foreigners" not "Niggers") as distinct from taboo African-Americans may have also soon entered the considerations.

It was not so surprising, then, that it was a Cuban who was near the top of the list of those quietly considered for Rickey's bold experiment. Major League Baseball (as well as Rickey himself) would obviously want integration to come, if it did, strictly on organized baseball's own narrow terms. That meant that black players might eventually be tolerated, but only under conditions that meant continued total white domination of the business of baseball. This is precisely the way the scenario would play out, of course. There would be a trickle of black players led by Robinson, but there would be no black owners or black administrators or black managers trailing along with them. Integration, after all, was only grudgingly considered in the mid-forties when continued successes in the Negro leagues (especially continued victories by black team during winter barnstorming clashes, often in Cuba) demonstrated that top black stars meant ticket sales at the box offices as well as victories for the teams that had them. But the dreams of black owners like Newark's Effa Manley for a true partnership between Negro leagues and white "organized leagues" or the absorption of complete black teams and their ownerships were idle dreams indeed.

All this meant that the first black players — especially the very first — had to carry the right attitude and project an acceptable image. And it was the story surrounding Silvio García that dramatically underscored Rickey's seriousness on this issue. The mainstream tale about the Dodgers' approaches to the super-talented Cuban infielder may be largely apocryphal. There are conflicting versions that seem nonetheless to reveal a grain of truth somewhere in the telling. Rickey, as the popular version goes, approached García with a point-black question about the Cuban's potential reactions in the face of challenges to his blackness and his manhood. The response García reportedly gave Rickey regarding the fate of his challengers ("I would kill them!") abruptly ended all considerations, not only for Silvio but probably for all other Cubans also. There is no proper documentation for this delightful and almost-too-perfect tale about Rickey and his first Cuban prospect. (Brooklyn did, soon after integration, sign the likes of Sandy Amoros, Chico Fernández and René Valdéz and bring them all to the parent club in the mid-fifties.) There are elements here of old stereotypes about Cuban ballplayers that cast considerable doubt on authenticity. There are also further tales about teetotaler Rickey being appalled by reports of García's widely rumored problems battling the demon alcohol.

Silvio García was — for all the rumors concerning a mean streak of rebelliousness and a potential for dissipation — a most talented natural ballplayer. García was indeed one of the best the Cuban circuit had to offer in the final decade before the century's midpoint. He began as a pitcher of great promise by blasting out of the box with a 10–2 mark for league champion Marianao under manager Martín Dihigo. The budding mound career was cut short in the early 1940s by a line drive which struck him on the arm while he was sitting in the dugout. For three years before that accident Silvio García rang up impressive mound performances in Cuba with Marianao (though he was only 3–10 overall outside the peak 1937 season) and also in the Puerto Rican winter league, where he registering an impressive 1.32 ERA for Ponce (1939–40) while also batting .298 as part-time infielder. After converting to an infield slot the 5'1" right-hander posted impressive batting marks (.319 and .324 in 1946, 1947) for several years up north with the New York Cubans club operated by Alex Pompez. It was widely acknowledged that García was a complete ballplayer who excelled with the bat and glove and also had baserunning talent far beyond the norm. Dodgers' farmhand Tommy Lasorda pitched against him in Cuba late in García's career and labeled him among the best hitters who never played in the majors. Another Dodgers manager, Leo Durocher, was also effusive about his fielding abilities, which may have played a small role in calling García to the attention of Branch Rickey and the Dodgers organization on the eve of the great integration experiment.

Another García (no relation) who headlined among a previous generation of Cuban Leaguers was an equivalent symbol of the depth of island talent in the pre-integration years. Manual García was a stocky, hard-throwing lefty who also mixed stellar pitching with big-league quality performances at just about every other position on the diamond — including catcher. Manuel García was known universally in Cuba and also on the Negro league circuit by the colorful nickname of "Cocaina" (cocaine), though the moniker had nothing at all to do with his own recreational use of chemical substances but rather with an impression that his fastball, drop-ball and exceptional curveball seemed to have the effect of literally mesmerizing batters and inducing an appearance of intoxication in the batter's box. "Cocaina" devoted a full ten seasons to Negro league play and ultimately reached a level of respect that meant classification alongside Satchel Paige and Martín Dihigo as the top mound trio in the Negro National League. In addition to performing with the Cuban Stars (1926–1933) and New York Cubans (1935–1936), he also put in appearances in Santo Domingo during the famed 1937 "Trujillo season" and in the Mexican League throughout the entire decade of the 1940s. Three different campaigns (1943, 1944, 1947) he paced the Cuban League in victories for Club Habana, and two of these campaigns came back-to-back, one featuring a rare no-hitter versus Marianao. "Cocaina" (85–61 for his full career as a Cuban League hurler) is today remembered by old-timers as one of the true legends of Cuban professional baseball; accomplished as a hurler in three quality leagues (Cuba, Mexico,

NNL), he was also as colorful a figure as island baseball has ever produced.

Among the most luminous links establishing Negro league and Cuban League symbiosis, another Havana-bred pitcher also stands out as the near equal in legendary stature to the figures of Manuel García, Silvio García, and the ever-present Dihigo. Ramón Bragaña starred for a handful of Cuban Negro league contingents in the late '20s and across the '30s and '40s (Cuban Stars East, Stars of Cuba, New York Cubans) and yet, like Dihigo, earned his lasting reputation on other winter league fronts in Venezuela and especially Mexico. There are those in Cuba who would still rank Bragaña alongside the immortal Dihigo and the fiery Luque as the three most memorable if not also most talented Cuban pitchers of any touted era. In 1937, in Havana, Ramón Bragaña pitched Almendares to victory in an encounter with the touring defending National League champion New York Giants. He enjoyed several stellar seasons as a league-leader in Cuba, winning nine games in a short winter season on three different occasions. A lanky right-hander owning a 90-plus-mph fastball and devastating curve, along with a considerable inventory of other deceptive tosses, "El Professor" only made token appearances in a handful of Negro league seasons, the last with the Cleveland Buckeyes in 1947. But in Mexico Bragaña was truly a living legend over an extended career that stretched from the mid-thirties all the way to the mid-fifties. His peak perhaps came in 1944 with a remarkable 30–8 season. It was the best year for a Cuban in Mexico outside of Dihigo's top summer — the one in 1938 when he doubled as batting champ and triple-crown pitcher. Bragaña enjoyed still other solid years in Jorge Pasquel's circuit and also enjoyed some controversy over well-publicized disputes with his Veracruz manager Mickey Owen, whom the star hurler once accused of blatant prejudice against black ballplayers, then later replaced as field boss for the Pasquel-owned Veracruz ball club.

It was perhaps the fact that Bragaña earned most of his claims on immortality on the Mexican League circuit that has somewhat dimmed his reputation in the Cuban League and also in U.S. blackball circles. But few native Cuban pitchers (perhaps only the younger Tiant can join the list, alongside Bragaña, Luque and Dihigo) have been so dominant on the mound for such a long stretch of years while performing exclusively in professional baseball's highest echelons.

The epilogue for black baseball's glorious run was also destined to be written on the Cuban landscape, when the Dodgers planted their spring training camp in Havana on the eve of Jackie Robinson's rookie season. The Dodgers had already trained several winters in Havana before the tense spring of Jackie Robinson's final grooming for big league action and a fateful date with American cultural history. They had recently prepped for the 1942 National League season in La Tropical, for example, and a decade earlier in 1931, when they still carried the name Robins not Dodgers, they had visited the same facility with 39 roster hopefuls including future Cooperstown hall of famer Al Lopez behind the plate and Havana icon Dolf Luque on the mound. But for Rickey's post-war integration scheme the relaxed racial atmosphere of Havana and the prospect of a spring training session away from the glare of the U.S. press corps was an almost inevitable choice. So it was on the fields of Havana and in the new stadium in El Cerro where Robinson took his final warm-ups for the Brooklyn debut in April that would alter the landscape of organized baseball forever.

The legacy of early and mid-century barnstorming in Havana is indelible. As social historians Brock and Bayne ("Not Just Black: African-Americans, Cubans and Baseball") have established, by the time the NNL was formed in 1920, African-Americans and Cubans already shared forty-plus years of intimacy through their baseball commerce. After big-league segregation fell by the wayside in 1947, it was big league baseball that opened a window on Cuba for North American fans. The island's passion for the sport was briefly revealed by flashy major league imports of the 1950s and '60s like Miñoso, Willie Miranda, Pascual, Ramos, Cuéllar, Oliva and Tony Pérez. Several decades later it would be Fidel Castro's Cold War manipulations of baseball on an amateur stage that would thrust Cuban baseball tradition back into North American headlines. North American interests in the Cuban national game would eventually peak with the short-lived détente represented by the Orioles–Team Cuba matches of spring 1999 and then finally with the MLB–sponsored World Baseball Classic tournament of March 2006.

Yet for more than a half-century before Robinson and Miñoso Cuban-American baseball relations were almost exclusively a blackball and winterball affair. North American Negro stars rejected by the racially pure white leagues annually enriched Cuban diamonds over the winter months. Cuban stars too dark for the Yankees or Cardinals or McGraw's Giants built legends with other "Giants" nines on the outlaw summertime Negro leagues circuit. Before 1947 and again after 1962 the greatest Cuban stars have always lived on the periphery of U.S. professional baseball. And both baseball-loving nations have been the ultimate losers because of this fact.

References and Suggested Readings

Alfonso, Jorge Chacón. "La Leyenda del Diamante Negro (José de la Caridad Méndez)" in: *Bohemia* 93:2 (2001), 17–18.

Bjarkman, Peter C. "American Baseball Imperialism, Clashing National Cultures, and the Future of Samurai *Besuboru*" in: *Baseball and Besuboru: Passion and Diplomacy Between the Baselines.* Proceedings of the Michigan State University Asian Studies Center Conference on Japanese and Asian Baseball (April 1, 2006), to appear.

_____. *Diamonds around the Globe: The Encyclopedia of International Baseball.* Westport, CT: Greenwood Press, 2005.

_____. "History's Many Shades — Tracking Jackie's Latino Predecessors" in: *Primera Fila* (The New York *Daily News*). Volume 2:2 (October 1997), 12, 14.

_____. *Baseball with a Latin Beat: A History of the Latin American Game.* Jefferson, NC, and London: McFarland, 1994.

_____. "Introduction" for: *The Bingo Long Traveling All-Stars & Motor Kings* (a novel by William Brashler). Chicago and Urbana: University of Illinois Press, 1993, xvii–xxxiii.

_____. "Cuban Blacks in the Majors Before Jackie Robinson" in: *The Inter-National Pastime: A Review of Baseball History.* Volume 12 (1992): 86–95. Society for American Baseball Research.

Brock, Lisa, and Bijan Bayne. "Not Just Black: African-Americans, Cubans and Baseball" in: *Between Race and Empire: African-Americans and Cubans before the Cuban Revolution.* Edited by Lisa Brock and Digna Casteñeda Fuentes. Philadelphia: Temple University Press 1998.

Burgos, Adrian, Jr. "Jugando en el Norte: Caribbean Players in the Negro Leagues 1910–1950" in: *Centro: Journal of the Center for Puerto Rican Studies.* Volume 8:1 and 8:2 (1996): 129–149.

Clark, Dick, and Larry Lester (Editors). *The Negro Leagues Book.* Cleveland: Society for American Baseball Research, 1994.

Dixon, Phil (with Patrick J. Hannigan). *The Negro Baseball Leagues: A Photographic History.* Mattituck, New York: Amereon House, 1992.

González Echevarría, Roberto. *The Pride of Havana: A History of Cuban Baseball.* New York: Oxford University Press, 1999.

Holway, John B. *Blackball Stars: Negro League Pioneers.* Westport, Connecticut: Meckler Books 1988.

_____. *The Complete Book of Baseball's Negro Leagues: The Other Half of Baseball History.* Fern Park, Florida: Hastings House 2001.

Nieto Fernández, Severo. *José Méndez — El Diamante Negro.* Havana: Editorial Científico-Técnica (Colección Deportes), 2004.

Peterson, Robert. *Only the Ball Was White: A History of Legendary Black Players and All-Black Professional Teams.* Englewood Cliffs, New Jersey: Prentice-Hall, 1970.

Riley, James A. *The Biographical Encyclopedia of the Negro Baseball Leagues.* New York: Carroll & Graf, 1994.

Rogosin Donn. *Invisible Men: Life in Baseball's Negro Leagues.* New York: Atheneum, 1983.

Rucker, Mark, and Peter C. Bjarkman. *Smoke: The Romance and Lore of Cuban Baseball.* New York: Total Sports Illustrated, 1999.

Skinner, David C. "Twice Champions: The 1923–24 Santa Clara Leopardos" in: *Road Trips: A Truckload of Articles from Two Decades of Convention Journals.* Cleveland: The Society for American Baseball Research, 2004, 97–103.

Torres, Angel. *La Leyenda del Beisbol Cubano, 1878–1997.* Miami: Review Printers (self-published), 1996.

7

Havana as Amateur Baseball
Capital of the World

Cuba's amateur leagues and frontline amateur ballplayers have always been a showcase feature of island baseball. This is a thriving scenario that stretches far back before Fidel Castro and his mid-century socialist revolution. Since the 1959 communist takeover it has been the world's primer amateur circuit — the 50-to-90-game National Series — that has been both sole stage for Cuba's national pastime and launching pad for a remarkable string of world championship victories; those victories have received, for the most part, little notice in the United States, while nonetheless remaining the envy of other baseball-playing nations throughout Asia, the Pacific Rim and the entire Caribbean Basin. Critics of Cuban socialist sport under the Castro regime may well argue that those in charge of the Cuban national game (foremost the Maximum Leader himself) have only exploited baseball to score meaningless propaganda victories over inferior competition; the companion complaint is that INDER officials at the same time deprive their star athletes of the recognitions and lifestyles that would inevitably come with exposure to free-market professional salaries found in North American–style organized baseball. But at the very least the Cuban government has remained steadfastly consistent for forty-plus years in its deep-seated and frequently espoused belief that baseball should not be viewed as an exploitative capitalist venture. The strictly amateur flavor of the Cuban national sport is anything but a late product of Castro-era governmental meddling.

In maintaining its policy of amateur dedication ("love of the game") above professional business enterprise (exhibitions staged for profit), Cuba's government-controlled baseball management has forged strong links with the country's earliest baseball history. Recall that ball-playing was launched in Cuba in the mid–nineteenth-century as a recreational activity for the socially privileged, performed as avocational "pastime" among members of exclusive Havana social clubs. Weekly ballgames among these pioneering Havana club teams (complete with parades, concerts and even post-game picnics) were popular recreational events where social intercourse had primacy over mere spectacle or the thrills of cutthroat competition, and where any commercializing of the sport was seen as a distasteful form of crass exploitation. This is not too far removed, of course, from similar origins of the national pastime in nineteenth-century North America. As traced at the outset of Chapter 5, the early history of professional play in Cuba during the 1880s–1890s involves an inevitable if surprisingly rapid transfer of the emerging national game from the hands of upper-crust recreational athletes (largely white Spanish Creoles) to those of less socially elite ballplayers (often black and sometimes imported from North America) who were soon flocking to the burgeoning sport as a means of professional livelihood.

But baseball evolution would soon follow a unique course in Cuba. While professional league games took a first toehold on the island with the early decades of the Cuban winter league, amateur play also continued to maintain an equally strong grip on the nation's baseball passions. And this purer form of "recreational baseball" also came in several distinct manifestations. There were numerous amateur leagues, usually local in flavor but occasionally competing on an island-wide scale, most launched by the second decade of the twentieth century and many still thriving during the social and political upheavals of the late fifties. Equally ubiquitous were the competitive semipro teams and circuits found in many corners of the island and boasting equally early roots, plus the numerous sugarmill-sponsored teams (and even entire sugarmill leagues) that throughout the first half of the century provided many of the island's most talented and celebrated players. Ironically, there was often a solid living to be made from "amateur" play, which usually involved associated off-season factory jobs, plenty of prize money and countless other hefty perks. Away from Havana there was also far more celebrity to be earned by playing on such local teams during baseball's pre-radio days, an era when professional games restricted to the capital city received little exposure in the outlying provinces. Many of the island's top baseball players thus repeatedly shunned the pro circuits right up to the time of the Second World War and Cuba's own ventures into U.S. organized baseball with the Class B Havana Cubans (Florida International League) of the late forties and Class AAA Sugar Kings (International League) of the early fifties.

In the baseball heyday of the 1930s and forties it was thus

the amateur game and not the celebrated professional version that by almost any standard represented the highest level of competition being staged anywhere on the island. Some of the best Cubans (bulldog pitcher Conrado Marrero and flashy shortstop Antonio "Quilla" Valdés, to cite but two outstanding cases) rejected pro contracts, in part because the pay wasn't good enough to be much of an enticement (being far less rewarding than cushy off-field jobs usually provided by social club contacts or company teams), and also because the pro circuit was widely seen as a cheap promotion-oriented spectacle run and staffed by Cubans (often black Cubans) of lesser social rank. And there was also little perceived difference in level of talent: Cuban amateur and semipro ball clubs usually held their own and often even whipped clubs comprised of touring big leaguers or imported Negro leaguers, as well as all-star contingents of pro Cuban Leaguers.

Sugarmill-based teams (like the powerful Hershey Sports Club) often availed themselves of the same visiting American recruits or local black stars that graced Cuban League rosters, hiring such headline attractions as Oscar Charleston or Martín Dihigo or Pablo Mesa on a mercenary basis for crucial games against touring pro clubs or other "amateur" tournament rivals. Unfettered by racial restrictions attached to Amateur Athletic Union teams, company-sponsored semi-pro outfits like Casa Bacardí, Cuban Mining Company and Nicaro Nickel Company also followed the practice of importing such paid ringers, and often names like Oliver Marcelle, Dick Lundy, Oscar Charleston and Frank Duncan would grace their equally impressive rosters. It was evident to all that such imports sold their services and where thus performing as thinly disguised professionals. But it was also common knowledge that local sugarmill or amateur league teams (especially those nines sponsored by rum or tobacco factories and mining companies rather than the old-style social clubs) were often equal if not superior to ball clubs in the vaunted Cuban winter league, which itself (as detailed in Chapter 5) nearly collapsed on more than one occasion during the chaotic and financially troubled 1930s and early forties.

And not only did amateur or semipro clubs boast many of the country's best and brightest players, but the amateur game also corralled greatest attention both at home and abroad once annual world championship tournaments began being staged regularly in Havana and elsewhere around the Caribbean during the years encompassing and following World War II. Amateur Cuban baseball thus indisputably stoked the greatest degree of raw national pride. And it was also the most purely Cuban in flavor, despite occasional imported mercenaries. Havana's pro circuit, by clear contrast, relied heavily on foreign imports (mostly major leaguers and Negro leaguers from the United States, but also occasional Mexicans like José "Chili" Gómez and Dominicans like Juan "Tetelo" Vargas) for much of its own top-level talent.

Failure to apprehend this strong amateur focus of Cuban baseball history has led to repeated misinterpretations. Not only are there those outside the island (including many native Cubans who fled Castro's authority in the sixties) who believe that the entire enterprise of Cuban baseball can be reduced to the professional league operating in Havana between 1878 and 1961, but also those in the States who believe that Cubans only turned to amateur versions of the national sport after these where rudely thrust upon them by the communist conspiracies of the Castro regime.

One stark example of such misinterpretation involves the celebration outside of Cuba of the island's most memorable past-era stars. A recent chapter by author William McNeil (*Baseball's Other All-Stars*, 2000) provides us with one particularly egregious sample of blindness to true Cuban baseball history. Bent on demonstrating that all the world's great ballplayers have not been restricted to major league rosters (an admirable enough thesis at face value), McNeil devotes his chapter on Cuba entirely to celebrations of players between the two world wars (mostly black Cubans) who performed in Havana's pro league. He labors to call up statistics from Cuban League and blackball records that make José Méndez, Alejandro Oms, Cristóbal Torriente and others appear to be the equal of white major leaguers of the same era. But there is no mention of the great amateur stars like "Quilla" Valdés, Juan Ealo, Natilla Jiménez, Conrado Marrero and numerous others (Agapito Mayor, Antonio "Loco" Ruíz, Chito Quicutis, Rogelio "Limonar" Martínez, Julio Moreno) who were the grandest ball-playing heroes on the entire island during this precise epoch. McNeil, one believes, has read all the requisite books on the Negro leagues but none of the less-readily-available accounts of Cuban baseball. In focusing as he does on the professionals alone McNeil also stumbles on yet another count. He portrays (as is common practice) Cuba as a racial paradise in which blacks and whites performed on equal footing, while ignoring the other half of the Cuban story — the substantial racism on the island which kept Cuban blacks off all the amateur league rosters and for the most part also off the rosters of the world champion Cuban national squads until the epoch of Jackie Robinson.

Segregation in Cuban amateur league baseball was part and parcel of a complex social and economic fabric constituting early 20th-century Cuban culture. Amateur baseball (baseball as a whole) began in Cuba in the 1860s and 1870s as a sporting phenomenon carrying heavy overtones of class consciousness. This history is outlined in rich detail with Robert González Echevarría's excellent chapters in *The Pride of Havana* (1999). By the first substantial flowering of amateur league baseball in the 1920s and 1930s the strictly amateur teams were indisputably much less "upper crust" in make-up than during the *belle époque* (1880s–1890s) struggle for national independence. Social club and sugarmill teams alike sought ballplayers for their athletic talent alone, and then blatantly compensated them for producing prestigious victories. Far fewer players (likely only a small minority) were by then drawn from elite-class Creole (Spanish lineage but island-born) backgrounds. But even in the Roaring Twenties epoch true professional baseball, despite its wide fan following in Havana, maintained a largely negative stigma in many quarters. The amateur game was seemingly far nobler in spirit and

An unidentified USA runner scores against Cuba during the first Amateur World Series (World Cup II) held in Havana's La Tropical Stadium, August 1939.

perceived by true devotees as more passionately played. It was also more accessible everywhere around the island, where teams and loosely formed leagues abounded and fired local pride (while also providing affordable local entertainment). This all changed drastically in the 1940s and 1950s, once radio for the first time brought Cuban League games being played almost exclusively in the capital (or occasionally in Matanzas or Cienfuegos) into every village of the island. The Cuban League of course featured numerous native black players, if only because blacks were most often of humble origins and thus could not afford to play with amateur outfits even if they were not barred by harsh racial barriers. Playing for mere recreation — even for national glory — was a luxury not available to those from the bottom social rungs. Cuban League rosters were also filled up with imported American athletes, both black and white, even before the formalized agreements with U.S. organized baseball in the mid-forties that would turn the Havana-based four-team league exclusively into a feeder system for major league teams. Cuban national teams competing in the high profile amateur world tournaments during the World War II years

were, by contrast, composed of all amateurs and thus also almost exclusively of whites.

If the Cuban amateur leagues (along with numerous semipro and sugar-mill leagues) were the more mainstream attraction in Cuba in the '30s and '40s, nevertheless amateur baseball seemed destined eventually to be killed off by the professional version once the country's economic landscape shifted drastically in the aftermath of World War Two. Integration throughout organized baseball also played a central role in the irreversible changes. With opportunities suddenly emerging for Cuban blacks to play professionally, wholesale scouting and signings by Joe Cambria and other cash-carrying big league bird dogs quickly depleted amateur league rosters in the peacetime afterglow of World War II. Radio broadcasts (as mentioned) suddenly made the now-revived Cuban League of the 1940s a more prominent drawing card in distant corners of the island far removed from Havana. But the bottom line remained the fact that increased opportunities for a wider segment of Cuban players to earn living wages playing in professional baseball up north was soon undercutting the long-time attraction of amateur league action back home. When Joe Cambria and Bobby Maduro formed the Florida International League in 1946 even more siphoning of amateur league talent quickly followed. The future did not bode well for baseball in Cuba once the loftiest dream of skilled young Cuban ballplayers was to escape the home turf for greater riches promised on foreign soil. And while amateur talent disappeared under the pressures of pro signings, the Cuban League itself withered under big league administrators whose motive was to suck talent off the island as fast as possible. Those who so loudly bemoan the death-knell given to Cuban League baseball by Fidel Castro (in tandem with Washington officials who pulled the plug on the Havana International League franchise) ignore a significant fact that what was overnight killed off by the Cuban revolution was already largely a moribund enterprise.

Fifty years later an eerie parallel now seems once more to loom on the near horizon. Rapidly worsening economic conditions resulting from Cuba's sagging socialist system today appear to foreshadow eventual movement in the direction of some approximation of a more capitalist-oriented free-enterprise system. Some pundits predict this will bring at least limited contact with major league baseball and its rapacious hunger for purchasing Cuban talent. Yet it is not unreasonable to assume that if organized baseball (in the form of the major leagues) is once more able to exploit changing political and economic conditions in Cuba by signing up both veteran Cuban stars and promising Cuban prospects for major and minor league duty, then the results will likely be yet another death-knell for the showcase national game in Cuba. It has been nearly six decades since the avarice of major league owners last pulled the plug on a half-century of thriving amateur Cuban baseball. But the cycle now seems poised to repeat itself.

In a truly ironic instance of the self-repeating lessons of history, the vibrant amateur league that forty years back supplanted a dying professional circuit during Fidel Castro's first months in power is now itself standing on the doorstep of an all-too-similar fate. The island-wide amateur National Series, which has gripped fans in Cuba for forty-five years, will most likely languish and die once the bulk of Cuban Leaguers don major or minor league uniforms in New York, Chicago, Chattanooga and Pittsfield. Wholesale recruitment of Cuban players into U.S. organized baseball will inevitably once more mark the overnight extinction of talent-rich island amateur teams. It will be an old story, oft-repeated, and a truly sad one for all baseball fans in Cuba, despite whatever economic liberation it might bring to heretofore lightly compensated Cuban ballplayers themselves.

If this seems an overstatement of the case, one has only to examine today's pro winter circuits languishing in the Dominican Republic and on the island protectorate of Puerto Rico. Standing in vivid contrast to the thriving leagues of the 1940s and fifties — once crammed with top big-league imports plus all the most recognizable homegrown stars — early 21st-century island circuits feature virtually no frontline imported pros and also few of the local heroes who have already reached major league rosters. The explanation is more than obvious:

there is no longer any economic incentive for today's big leaguers to toil during winter months. Local heroes — once enamored of showcasing their talent for faithful hometown boosters — are even barred from winter circuit competitions by restrictive contract clauses or by management's fear of unnecessary off-season, career-slowing injuries. Stadiums in Santo Domingo, Santiago, Mayagüez and San Juan now sit half empty and former winter league excitement throughout the Caribbean Basin has now been replaced by epidemic island baseball ennui and by stale memories of a long-faded Golden Era representing past island baseball glories.

There is another blunter way of stating the case. Those — both on and off the island — who long for the eventual and (as they see it) inevitable truce between Cuban amateur baseball and professional organized baseball also unwittingly celebrate the dismantling of everything that has represented the uniqueness and the glory of the island's national sport — both before Castro's 1959 revolution and certainly after. Once its amateur heritage is again ignored the Cuban pastime will once again be transformed as it was at mid-century into still another productive plantation site for the plucking of cheap major league talent by the literal barrel full. The process will leave few rewards for the fans back home on the island, who will eventually and inevitably see their cherished baseball fare reduced to far-away televised games beamed home from foreign fields. The very charm of the isolated Cuban League has for four decades resided in its existence as an alternative universe outside the commercial spectacle represented by major league baseball. The death knell is now nonetheless tolling for this final remaining frontier beyond organized baseball's ever-extending monopoly. Some Cuban players will certainly prosper once doors are flung open on big league dollars; many more will find no place to play on the limited rosters in North American leagues, and at the same time no thriving league left for them at home. Their fate will be akin to the hundreds of black ballplayers of the 1940s who — being less talented than Robinson or Doby or Satchel Paige — found their lifeblood earned on the diamonds of black baseball suddenly stripped from them. It will be the heart-rending saga of the mid-century Negro leagues played out in its full tragic scope yet one more time.

It has been on the amateur fields and not in the professional ballparks that Cuba has written the proudest pages of its baseball legacy — from the first third of the 20th century on down to the present hour. Once those amateur ballplaying fields are silenced (or at least robbed of their main luster) Cuba will, in baseball terms at least, be little more than yet another Dominican Republic, Puerto Rico or Venezuela. That which was for more than a century a true "baseball paradise" will transform overnight into yet another third-world baseball wasteland. The Cuban baseball legacy will then once more unfortunately lie almost entirely in the unrecoverable past.

*   *   *

From the first tossed balls and cracked bats in the streets of Havana in 1864 down to the fateful and far-reaching deci-

The Cuban team that lost the legendary Amateur World Series gold medal battle to Venezuela's Daniel Canónico at La Tropical Stadium, October 23, 1941. Losing pitcher Conrado Marrero stands fifth from the right in the back row.

sions of the Castro government in 1960 regarding the status of amateur and professional sport in Cuba — the spread of approximately a full century — the island's baseball was always played on four distinctive and equally glorious stages. There was the pro circuit that performed in Havana (mostly) during winter months and imported American ballplayers (mostly black) to fill out rosters alongside local talent. There was an informal network of semipro teams spread across the island and most notably consisting of the teams representing sugarmills and sometimes grouped into rag-tag leagues. There were the strictly amateur leagues built with crack teams representing elite social clubs like the Vedado Tennis Club and also eventually including some sugarmill teams like Central Hershey (playing in numerous amateur leagues and tournaments under the guise of the Hershey Sports Club). And there were the national teams selected annually to carry national honor, first in the Amateur World Series competitions and annual or occasional tournaments like the Central American Games, and much later (after 1951) the newly founded Pan American Games.

Of the four levels, only the first has been exhaustively or even adequately documented. There is no shortage of data on the history of Cuban professional baseball, even if some of the details of the first couple of 19th century decades remain at times murky. But what happened through the years on amateur and semi-professional fields often was recorded only in the memories of fans who might have witnessed the action.

Roberto González Echevarría (*The Pride of Havana*, Chapter 6) has reopened this branch for today's readers in his chapter laced with interviews with surviving participants. Some statistics from early years in the professional league are scarce or non-existent and often the Cuban Leagues stats of even the thirties and forties are inconsistent and contradictory from one source to another. But the Amateur League has little reliable recorded history at all (what exists in the way of season standings and individual leaders is provided at the end of this current chapter). And when it comes to historical records, the sugarmill baseball (the *ligas azucareras*) of Cuba remains a vast wasteland.

Sugarmill baseball, despite its ephemeral documentation, was arguably the highest-quality baseball on the island outside of the Havana-based professional Cuban League, and at times it was arguably the highest level of all, pro winter leagues included. Many Cuban Leaguers and notable American pros played from time to time as hired mercenaries signed on for single games or full tournaments by various sugarmill teams, and the action on these diamonds has left impressive eyewitness accounts if not an accurate or well-documented history. There are still circulating stories of truly legendary encounters involving natives like Dihigo and Oms and imports like Oscar Charleston and Oliver Marcelle showing up on rural diamonds to do occasional battle for the likes of Central Resulta, Central España (where Miñoso played as a novice), and Central Senado (which once employed future big leaguer Roberto Ortiz).

There were also other patchwork tournaments on the island that were contested outside of the sugarmill competitions and the loosely organized sugarmill leagues. Here another source of Cuban baseball legend emerges from the shadows and tantalizes with its poorly recorded events stretching over the first half of the twentieth century. Often the pros performing in Havana left — sometimes in mid-season — to participate in such hastily arranged local tournaments and some of the events of these competitions are still traceable. González Echevarría cites accounts from his own father who played in the thirties for Central San Agustín, a sugarmill club near Sagua la Grande in the environs of Matanzas; these reports suggest that local sandlot players often tested their skills in trials by fire against seasoned pros on the tough barnstorming circuits.

But the true foundation of Cuban baseball down through the years remained the confederations of teams that have come generally to be known as the amateur leagues (here for convenience lumped together under the rubric of Cuba's Amateur League). Like the Negro leagues of North America, these were loose confederations and sometimes not exactly formal leagues at all. But the cover term applies to the system of baseball that Cubans over the years referred to as "los amateurs" and to the extensive network of competitions that provided many of the island's eventual pro stars. Baseball as played across the island between the 1910s and 1940s by "los amateurs" was always "an event of the moment" (to adopt the phrase provided by González Echevarría). With no fixed league seasons or structured pennant chases to unfold in an ordered manner over the course of a full campaign, and with no statistics or records documented in press accounts, focus was always on the thrilling encounters of a single memorable afternoon frozen in time. Each game was a special festival which long after continued to live in legendary proportions within the minds of those few fans who might have witnessed it first hand.

Cuban baseball, recall, began in the 1860s as a strictly amateur affair, just as the game in North American also boasts amateur club sporting traditions at its roots. Habana B.C.C. and Almendares B.B.C. debuted as amateur baseball nines that were essentially social clubs (replete with a full agenda of recreational and social rituals) and thus only in part interested in baseball play as an independent pursuit. González Echevarría has best traced the history of these origins in painstaking detail. *The Pride of Havana*, among existing documents, provides the most complete and insightful portrait found anywhere of what social club baseball of the late nineteenth-century was truly like. (We have also traced this evolution at the heart of the early Cuban pro winter league in an earlier chapter.) But over its first few decades — the 1880s and 1890s — the original Cuban League evolved quickly from an amateur confederation to a full-scale professional league. At the heart of this transformation was no small amount of controversy as debate raged over the issue of maintaining the purity of games played for recreation and not strictly for commerce and profit.

As baseball inevitably became a public entertainment spectacle rather than a private social club event, the nature of the ballplayers themselves would also change. Many of the earliest athletes on the transforming professional circuit came from working class backgrounds, and after the turn of the new century many were black as well as economically disadvantaged. In the final two decades of the nineteenth century Cuban pro baseball was already being driven by clear-cut economic interests (including heavy waging on the results of contests) and also by economic necessity (the need to sell admissions and fill grandstand seats). Even for the numerous amateur teams which continued as white-only segregated clubs, such "organized" league baseball eventually became a form of entertainment business and a source of healthy revenues. Games drew paying customers, and if players on amateur league teams (such as Central Hershey or Vedado Tennis Club) were not paid salaries directly for their diamond work, they were instead compensated with comfortable salaried positions (usually requiring a minimum of labor) provided by club officials and team supporters. Amateur league players were thus retained (and compensated) for their diamond skills which could produce cherished victories during heated weekend club matches.

What was left outside of the professional winter league was the system of social clubs (Amateur League) and industry-sponsored teams (sugarmill and semipros) that continued to play increasingly high levels of competitive baseball in the capital city and also in the outlying provinces. Some of Cuba's greatest performances and peak moments on the baseball diamond over the final two decades of the 19th century and first five decades of the 20th century came on these amateur diamonds. But these fields also housed one of the great blights and persisting shames of Cuba's burgeoning national pastime. For amateur baseball throughout most of the first half of the century remained closed to all but the whitest among Cubans.

The popularity of sugarmill and industry-sponsored teams did nonetheless produce something of positive note, especially outside of the games played by excessively white social clubs. This was the emergence of the Oriente (the eastern provinces) as a secondary hotbed of the island's always expanding baseball culture. With the spread of sugarmills eastward beyond Matanzas and Camagüey around 1910, Oriente Province began to spawn stellar ballplayers of its own, which in succeeding decades would include the likes of Pedro Formental, Napleón Reyes, Preston Gómez, Carlos and Heriberto Blanco and other eventual stars of the Havana professional circuit. The region not only formed talented sugarmill clubs (such as Central Contramaestra) but also powerhouse industry-sponsored teams like Casa Bacardí, Cuban Mining Company and Nicaro Nickel Company. And even the white amateur leagues by the second and third decades of the century were spreading their popularity eastward outside the grip of Havana Province. While white Amateur League teams (Vedado Tennis Club, for example) did not field colored ballplayers on their own rosters, they did nonetheless frequently play against semipro or sugarmill outfits that were racially mixed, although they usually did not do so on their own club-owned playing fields. In brief, the lines separating sugarmill, semipro and Amateur League baseball were never very strictly drawn.

There are several explanations for the racial exclusiveness found in Cuban amateur baseball before the 1959 revolution. The main one, of course, was the nature of the exclusive social clubs that sponsored these teams. Club affiliation for prospective ballplayers would have to entail full club membership rights — including access to Sunday banquets, weekend picnics and post-game dances — and for clubs like the Vedado Tennis Club or the Havana Yacht Club such privileges for black Cubans would not have been thinkable at the time. But there was also the fact that Afro-Cubans, almost exclusively members of the lower social and economic strata, simply could not afford to play baseball as recreational amateurs. For them sport needed to remain a profession and not an avocation, a way of earning a living and not just an excuse for leisure-time entertainment during idle weekend hours. The first evidence of skilled if economically disadvantaged black athletes being paid to play on semiprofessional clubs comes in the final decades of the nineteenth century with the Havana-based Liga de los Torcedores (Tobaccomakers' League), a highly competitive circuit made up of clubs sponsored by the city's various cigar factories.

The several amateur leagues — as rivals to the *ligas azucareras* and various fluid semipro circuits and ball clubs — long remained a source of the highest quality baseball on the island. These numerous clubs provided the rosters for national teams that represented the country in international competitions as early as the thirties. Amateur League teams, as noted, often played against the professionals and semi-professionals and even occasionally against touring U.S. Negro leaguers and visiting major leagues pro outfits. For many Cubans the amateur teams were far from being viewed as inferior in talent but instead were seen as the crown jewel of the nation's pastime. At the same time the professional league operating in Havana was judged by many dedicated baseball followers, and by much of the general public at large, as little more than cheap public entertainment and thus not much elevated above such spectacles as the circus or traveling carnivals. There was little preferred social status attached to being a professional ballplayer, and life was often considerably harder for the pro than for the pampered and privileged amateur. As a result most top white players chose amateur competition over pro careers. Examples of some of the island's best players who shunned the pro circuit as both socially unacceptable and economically unprofitable included Juan Ealo (a slugging first baseman for Fortuna Sports Club who bulging Popeye-like forearms earned him the nickname "Espinacas" or "Spinach"), Quilla Valdés (Hershey shortstop still considered by some the best-ever at that position), and pitcher Narciso Picazo (tiny lefthander who starred for the Cuban Telephone Company team of the late 1920s). The choice to remain amateur was well founded at the time. The pro athlete laboring on the Havana circuit with Almendares or Habana B.B.C. would have to play more games; often he was not nearly as well compensated (as amateurs provided with cushy weekday jobs requiring little labor and providing substantial remuneration), and he usually had to head north (or to Mexico) in the summers to continuing plying his

trade and thus likely suffer racial humiliation and face tedious language barriers. This was true even if he was deemed white in skin tone by looser Cuban racial standards.

There are many outstanding legends surrounding Cuban Amateur League play. There were great individual teams, such as the Rum Havana Club outfit from Cárdenas that on one occasion (1934–35) humiliated all three Cuban League pro clubs (Marianao, Almendares and Habana). Some of the top stars of the island were nurtured in these venues and first starred on amateur teams, there earning their earliest and most lasting reputations. One was future big leaguer Roberto "Tarzán" Estalella, who first bolstered the lineup of the Havana Rum squad that embarrassed the Cuban Leaguers. Another was Connie Marrero who compiled 123 victories (mostly for Cienfuegos) as an amateur leaguer and (as we saw in Chapter 4) during the forties became one of the island's most adorned national team icons. A third was Agapito Mayor, a pitcher of legendary status in Havana even though he never made it as far as the U.S. majors. Still another was eventual big league infielder and Cuban Sugar Kings manager Nap Reyes, who originally earned his stripes on the University of Havana baseball team (an Amateur League club) before claiming all-star status in numerous pro circuits.

A comprehensive history for the formal seasons of amateur play between the teens and the forties is unfortunately not very well recorded. There are nonetheless many existing and at least partially documented legends, as well as numerous fascinating journalistic accounts. González Echevarría in *The Pride of Havana* provides us with the seminal English language summary of this facet of the Cuban game. The earliest major circuit was launched in 1914 and was known officially as the Liga Nacional de Baseball Amateur (National Amateur Baseball League). This league is what is usually meant when referring to Amateur League baseball in Cuba from the onset of the first world war until the years immediately preceding the Castro-led revolution.

The Amateur League (Liga Nacional) was comprised at first of such teams as the Vedado Tennis Club, Instituto de la Habana, Sociedad de Marianao, and Club Atlético de Cuba. An unofficial organization during its first three seasons, the circuit achieved legal status in time for the 1917 campaign, when it became the country's first "official" athletic organization with government sanction. Strong entries in later years were Fortuna, Hershey, Deportivo Matanzas, Teléfonos (representing the national telephone company), Cubanaleco (electric company), Regla, Artemisa, Havana Yacht Club, Círculo Militar and Círculo de Artesanos. Seasons varied in length from as few games as eleven in 1917 to more than thirty games in the early fifties. The league would fall under the jurisdiction of the Unión Atlética Amateur de Cuba after 1922. Some of Cuba's most talented individual players of the first three-quarters of a century (most notably Pedro Dibut, Marrero, Jiqui Moreno, Limonar Martínez, Sandalio Consuegra, Nap Reyes, Mayor, Ealo and Quilla Valdés) played initially if not exclusively in this constantly evolving league, and the circuit also attracted notable names as managers (Rafael Almeida with

Vedado Tennis Club, Reinaldo Cordeiro with Fortuna, and León Rojas, with Club Atlético de Cuba). Among the most pronounced Amateur League stars the bulk were pitchers, a fact accounted for largely by the schedule which provided weekly Sunday games only. Thus a star pitcher like Marrero with Cienfuegos, Isidro León with Círculo Mititar, or Moreno with Círculo de Artesanos could literally carry a ball club through an entire campaign without missing a single turn on the mound.

There were several other leagues that comprised the top level of Cuban amateur baseball. A pioneering circuit called the Asociación Atlética was formed as early as 1905 by the Vedado Tennis Club and the University of Havana B.B.C. Additional teams named Columbia and Clio competed in subsequent years in this pioneering circuit that was soon superceded by the Liga Nacional in 1914. There was later a Liga Social (1931–1939) and also a short-lived Liga Intersocial that came into being in 1927 and featured the first strong Cuban Telephone Company team. The latter league lasted only four short years and over that brief span a championship playoff known as the *Serie Co-Criolla* was staged between the Liga Intersocial and Liga Nacional championship teams. One highlight of the brief Co-Criolla inter-league championship series was a deciding game played in November 1928 between Teléfonos and the Vedado Tennis Club. In the final match of this first best-of-three showdown between the established National League winner and the upstart Intersocial League challenger, Narciso Picazo's shutout effort for the newcomers earned Teléfonos its first of three straight national amateur championships at the end of the first truly remarkable decade of Cuban amateur league action.

Among the strongest amateur teams the first place of honor has to lie with the Vedado Tennis Club, which traced its history back to 1905 and was a mainstay of two different leagues. Vedado's crack club captured the first three championships (1914–1916) of the Liga Nacional behind ace pitcher Ramón Goizueta (who produced the first league no-hitter on June 16, 1915) and also again reigned supreme in the mid-twenties (1925–1928) when Antonio Casuso was the top mound ace. Fortuna Sports Club was another strong club with a most colorful history; Fortuna captured its first league crowns in 1921 and 1922 and remained a strong contender for nearly two decades. Fortuna (managed by Reinaldo Cordeiro) and Hershey (a sugarmill-sponsored team played under the amateur banner of the Hershey Sports Club) also dominated the true glory years of the amateurs throughout the thirties and forties, but received frequent stiff challenges from Cienfuegos (with Marrero), Deportivo Matanzas (with its triple-threat mound corps composed of Limonar Martínez, Sandalio Consuegra, and Catayo González), and Círculo de Artesanos (with Julio Moreno). The Fortuna club (boasting ace pitcher Silvino Ruiz in the twenties and Agapito Mayor a decade later) sported classic uniforms, featuring striking black piping and a Gothic letter F, that were often pictured in the pages of *Carteles* magazine. Teams representing the Cuban Telephone Company and Cuban Electric Company were the centerpiece nines of the

Amateur League during the final decade of the fifties, each claiming three league titles, including the final pennant won by Teléfonos in 1960.

Games and seasons of the Amateur League were followed enthusiastically by fans across the country, and the top-drawing stars of this league and its teams were often the biggest baseball names on the island. The amateurs frequently had it all over the Cuban League professionals in terms of name recognition and drawing power, especially in the thirties when the struggling pro league slipped into a steady if temporary decline. Phenoms from the Amateur League were also the celebrated heroes of Team Cuba at the end of the thirties and outset of the forties. It was in the Amateur World Series at the dawn of the forties, most particularly, where the all-star amateurs earned their greatest recognition and wrote their most memorable legends.

The sparsely preserved history of the Liga Nacional or Cuban Amateur League is arguably a main chapter in the evolving history of Cuba's national pastime, for all its scarcity of detail. No treatment of Cuba's great teams or top players can overlook this league, which often ranked in popularity a full step or two above the now more celebrated professional winter league operating in Havana and stuffed with better known (at least outside the island) U.S. and Cuban blackball stars. My interest throughout the bulk of this long chapter, however, will be the amateur baseball played not within the numerous island leagues, but rather the amateur baseball (pre-revolution and post-revolution) played by teams representing Cuba in celebrated international competitions. It was in the later arenas that Cuba eventually earned an indelible baseball reputation reaching far outside of the island's narrow boundaries. And it is this latter realm of the amateur baseball saga that has also been far better documented over the years and thus far more readily lends itself to cogent historical accounts.

* * *

Cuba began making its significant mark as an amateur baseball power at least three decades before the sudden rise to political power of the island's most famous "amateur" baseball pitcher — Fidel Castro. Throughout the twenties, thirties and forties amateur league action was the preferred venue for most Cuban fans. It was also the preferred venue for many of the best Cuban players — especially white players of elevated social standing. And a considerable Cuban international diamond reputation was also already being forged by these same players with the earliest "world tournaments" that were soon being staged, mainly through the efforts of the Cubans themselves, in the late thirties and early forties.

Amateur baseball supremacy for Cuba thus dates back to an era long before Castro's 1959 revolution. Cuba was in fact winning world tournaments on a regular basis at least two full decades before Castro's July 26 Movement grabbed power from the increasingly corrupt government of U.S.–backed strongman Fulgencio Batista. Cuba's first inroads in world amateur play actually came as early as 1930, with a resounding victory during the second-ever Central American and Caribbean

Games staged before enthusiastic home crowds in Havana. But it was only with the second edition of the Amateur World Series championships, again housed on Cuban soil, that the island's long run of international success would be more firmly launched. Cuban teams would eventually capture 15 of 24 Amateur World Series tournaments held between 1939 and 1978 (and then 10 of 11 after 1980) and in the process create a host of diamond legends virtually unknown to the followers of North American big league action. Among the many heroes of Cuban amateur play in the years before Castro, none stands any taller than Conrado Marrero, the fiery right-hander who built an indelible legend back in his homeland by winning island-gripping world cup matches more than a decade before his journeyman labors with Clark Griffith's Washington Senators.

The first international baseball tournament of any legitimacy was staged in Mexico City in 1926 under the auspices of the inaugural Central American Games. Only three countries entered, with the Cubans and Guatemalans traveling to Mexico City to do battle with the host nation in a collection of events that would include track and field, soccer, swimming and tennis as well as the team sport of baseball. Guatemala did not send a baseball team, however, reducing the matches in that featured sport to a head-to-head two team series. Cuba swept Mexico in three straight games by lopsided scores of 13–0, 10–3 and 8–2. Lalo Rodríguez of the Amateur League's Police Club tossed the opening shutout, while Vedado Tennis Club outfielder Joaquín de Calvo batted above .700 for the three winning outings. So strong was the Cuban entrant, in fact, that it upended an all-star squad from the Cuban winter league in a single tune-up match before leaving Havana. Cuba's long-standing rank as the true cream of international amateur play was thus established right from the opening bell, however modest the initial field of participants might have been.

Four years later (March 1930) would witness a second Central American Games, and this time the showcase venue would be Havana itself. For the festive occasion a new stadium was hastily erected on the grounds of the local beer factory, as the government of Gerardo Machado — facing increasing unrest and even terrorist opposition in the wake of the 1929 market crash — sought some form of legitimacy with the staging of an attention-diverting athletic spectacle. Stadium Cerveza Tropical would serve as host venue for all the field sports during the three-week event, and it would prove an especially attractive venue for the featured baseball matches. La Tropical would long remain a scene for track and field and soccer contests in the future (it is still used for these sports today). But it also served for the next decade and a half as a showcase baseball field (a celebrated shrine for the pro Cuban League itself), and its sparkling debut came with these first Havana-based Central American Games competitions.

Cuba again romped through the limited opposition in 1930 as it had four years earlier. This time the Cubans would lose but a single game, a 2–1 heartbreaker to Mexico. The crowds were sparse and the games on the whole were a gigantic failure as only nine countries attended and only five sent

baseball squads. Even the baseball matches drew slim crowds despite the winning performance of the host team. The bulk of the victorious Cuban roster was drawn from the Vedado Tennis Club and Teléfonos amateur squads and featured such standouts as pitchers Narciso Picazo and Manuel Domínguez (loser of the upset setback with Mexico). Most of the games were routs, even those that didn't feature the crack Cuban team, which slaughtered Panama 15–4 and Guatemala 15–1. Mexico finished second (with a 4–2 ledger) and Panama seized the bronze medal with a .500 record.

On the heels of two Central American championships, amateur baseball would continue to thrive throughout the island and also across the next full decade after the hasty construction of *La Tropical* Stadium. The game's popularity continued despite some inevitable setbacks in both amateur and pro venues as a result of ongoing political unrest and the eventual toppling of Machado. Much of the game action was now centered in the new venue in Havana, but the full country also took part since sugarmill games and semipro tournaments remained popular across the island. Many new stars came onto the scene as amateur play slowly evolved into a unifying social phenomenon. The better teams by the third decade of the century were now the ones representing more working class roots and not the upper-class social clubs that had earlier dominated recreational matches. Some Afro-Cubans with lighter skin were now also jumping into the amateur league competitions. Roberto Estalella debuted with Rum Havana Club and then made his mark with both Deportivo Cárdenas and Hershey Sports Club before slipping to the pros. Another Afro-Cuban appearing in Amateur League action was future big leaguer Tomás de la Cruz, who practiced his trade with Hershey before signing in 1934 with Marianao of the pro winter league. And there were others who trained for later roles as Cuban Leaguers and even major leaguers. Gilberto Torres of Regla's amateur nine was versatile enough as an infielder and pitcher to draw comparisons with Martín Dihigo, before following his father Ricardo into the pro ranks and thus providing the first Cuban father-son duo in the major leagues up north.

The surge of Cuban amateur league baseball to its greatest heights coincided with the assumption of political power by Fulgencio Batista's forces during the late thirties and early forties. This would later prove something of an irony, of course, once the Castro government unseated Batista and took amateur baseball, of quite another form, in entirely new directions and to new heights as an organized island-wide league competition. The Batista-era surge of the less-structured and less-centralized amateur leagues came in part with the formation of the DGND (*Dirección General Nacional de Deportes*, later simply the DGD or *Dirección General de Deportes*) in June 1938. This branch of the Cuban government, initially under the command of Batista's associate Colonel Jaime Mariné, would play a significant role not only in formalizing play on the home front but also in organizing ambitious international tournament competitions that would prove a great success only a few years down the road.

The biggest individual star of the amateur ranks in the thirties was a lefty pitcher named Agapito Mayor who would later also impress in the pro leagues, though he didn't make the majors, and even figure prominently in some legendary Cuban League games of the mid and late forties. But like Marrero, who would overhaul him in reputation in the forties, Mayor's professional achievements never outstripped or even approached his near-mythical amateur performances. The most legendary of those heroics would take place in 1938 in Panama, during the fourth go-round of Central American Games, when the tireless southpaw earned four victories as both a starter and reliever. But Mayor was already a scourge in the amateur leagues at home for several years before turning pro and by his own claim he likely both tossed and won more games at all levels on Cuban soil than any of the island's numerous other talented hurlers. And he also enjoyed other stellar performances in foreign arenas: eleven years after his one-man-show outing in Panama, Mayor duplicated the effort in the first professional Caribbean Series staged in Havana in February 1949. Carrying his Almendares club to victory over teams from Venezuela, Panama and Puerto Rico, Mayor became the only pitcher to win three games in a single edition of an event which is still played today among winter league champions from the Caribbean nations.

The rapid growth of the homespun "Amateur League" was arguably the biggest story of the thirties. But there were also two additional important victories outside the island in the continuation of the Central American Games and these also occupied headlines back home. The next Central American Games (the third edition) were convened in El Salvador and unfortunately marred by considerable bickering among delegations over an issue of the professional status of many athletes entered; especially egregious was the known pro-league affiliations of certain Mexican baseball players. The Cuba delegation protested vehemently about a number of Mexican ballplayers who had faced such Cubans as Dihigo, Bragaña and Tiant during summer Mexican League games, with a resulting withdrawal of the Mexican team. The tournament also got off to a rather bad start on yet another count. Hurricane damage worked to delay the opening of the games for almost a full year. When play did commence in late March of 1935 the superior Cuban amateurs (who were amateurs indeed) walked away with an easy victory in the baseball matches, posting an 8–1 record and receiving excellent pitching and hitting from Manuel Fortes. A few winters later "Chino" Fortes would earn another less honorable page in island lore when as a pro he surrendered a mammoth homer to American Negro leaguer Josh Gibson in Santa Clara's spacious La Boulanger Park, a blast which legend contends traveled nearly 700 feet.

A fourth edition of the Central American Games were staged in Panama in February 1938, and while there was more fan interest in Panama City on the heels of the 1936 Berlin Olympics there was also more controversy surrounding the baseball events. The Cubans were again unsettled by the appearance of known Mexican pros and also recognized professionals on several other teams. The delegation was prompted to request assurances that their own athletes would not jeopardize their amateur status by competing with such imposters. But professionals or no, the rest of the competition was no match for Cuban pitcher Agapito Mayor. Mayor was known affectionately if cruelly throughout his career as "Triple Feo" — but there was nothing ugly about his performances in Panama. As mentioned, the tournament was one of Mayor's several career highlights. He captured four fifths of the club's victories, a couple as a starter and a couple out of the bull pen. There have been few solo performances in international play that were any more impressive than this one by the unflappable Mayor.

The mild success of the 1938 Central American Games was destined to have a big payoff since it cracked open the door and planted the seed for a newly imagined event that would be ambitiously labeled the Amateur World Series. Although the competition for the first few "world series" matches didn't come close to representing a wide spectrum of the world's nations — even the few most prominent baseball-playing countries — the first few outings staged in Havana were nonetheless much more of a true international showdown than anything the professional versions of the game had to offer. Roberto González Echevarría (*The Pride of Havana*, Chapter 6) suggests that a convergence of world politics, nationalism and sports (in this case baseball) that was surging in the years between the two world wars made the atmosphere ripe for the birth of international tournament challenges on something more than a mere barnstorming exhibition level. In Havana, where the spark was first lit by Colonel Mariné and his newly founded DGND, the movement now also fostered the growth and development of amateur baseball competitions, both home and abroad, as the sport's strongest and most vibrant branch.

But the initial "world cup" baseball idea was not entirely a Cuban invention, even if it was soon to be recognized as largely a Cuban creation. The first attempt at a world tournament featuring some of the globe's baseball-playing nations was in reality a championship event in name only. Staged in London in August 1938, this was actually a two-team five-game playoff of clubs featuring visiting American military personnel stationed on bases throughout Europe, along with a smattering of native British baseballers from an earlier experimental and short-lived British professional league that operated in the mid-thirties around Manchester. The one-time event was a brainchild of American businessman Leslie Mann who wished to celebrate the sport's small inroads in the cricket-crazed British Isles. Mann presented "The John Moore Trophy" (honoring the founder of the English Baseball Federation) to a winning squad wearing uniforms with "England" emblazoned across their jerseys. Some diehard enthusiasts of the "American sport" in the British Isles still point with pride to their country's somewhat dubious distinction as the game's first amateur tournament world champion.

When more realistic if still modest competitions began in Latin America a year later at the devising of the enterprising Cubans, the English baseballers, if there truly were any, were nowhere to be seen. Cuban officials explained this by announcing that the baseball season in England (does one truly believe there was one?) would prevent a British team from traveling to the second world championships which the Cubans themselves (seizing upon a good idea) had arranged for Havana exactly one year later. What transpired in the way of a second "world cup" match in the Cuban capital during two weeks of August 1939 represented a painfully erratic start to an eventual world class event. But the earliest years of Amateur World Series matches devised under Cuban leadership would nonetheless soon boast their own considerable lore and foster their own considerable baseball legends.

Buoyed by the earlier success of a Cuban Amateur League throughout the 1930s and the Central American Games competitions that had been staged in 1926 (Mexico City), 1930 (Havana), 1935 (San Salvador), and 1938 (Panama City), Cuban sports Czar Colonel Jaime Mariné had decided by late 1938 on a far more ambitious project with the staging of a second world amateur tournament (this one hopefully more legitimate) at Havana's picturesque La Tropical Stadium (built originally for the second Central American Games in 1930 and still in use today as a serviceable track and field facility and soccer pitch). Thirteen countries were invited to participate, but only the USA and Nicaragua answered the bell. Mariné's tournament was hardly a world series by any stretch, though it did promise better and fuller competitions than those earlier staged in London. This time around at least some trained baseballers were involved.

Cuba won all six of its games and was never even mildly challenged on the field. Nicaragua brought a few good hitters, especially Stanley Cayasso and Jonathan Robinson (a pair of muscular blacks) who slugged the only homers. But the Nicaraguans won only three games, and those only because the rag-tag USA squad was so inept. The Americans (weekend amateurs with not a pro or even collegiate prospect among them) lost all three to the Cubans (13–3, 8–3, 12–7) and all three to the Nicaraguans (2–0, 7–3, 7–2). They batted a collective .187 and featured a pitcher named Frank Webb (4.42 ERA) as their only competitive hurler. There was one close game with Nicaragua edged 3–2 by the hosts, and a handful of Nicaraguan players — especially Cayasso who stroked a mammoth round tripper — won the local crowd's respect. More important, there were some big gates at La Tropical topping 16,000 and the event was thus a wild success for that practical reason alone.

The Havana tournament of August 1939 was also a launching pad of sorts for two future legends of Cuban baseball. Both Conrado Marrero (a big leaguer with Washington by the early fifties) and Natilla Jiménez (an unparalleled Cuban amateur league headliner) here first captured the widespread adoration of the expansive Cuban baseball fandom. Jiménez won a pair of games, including a 4–3 extra-inning thriller against a crack Nicaraguan ace who was probably a seasoned professional. Marrero also captured his only decision in the first of his many legendary international appearances. Marrero's win came in a 13–3 romp over Team USA on August 13,

in an historic first-ever international tournament match-up of two future heated traditional rivals.

The first legitimate world series round-robin among amateurs did not quite meet the high expectations laid out by Cuban amateur baseball officials. Only three of thirteen invitees made the effort to reach Havana and with three entrants this was not a big improvement over the London inaugural. It was nonetheless an on-field success by any measure, with the home forces going undefeated and thus easily outdistancing a mediocre Nicaragua nine and a very weak entry from the United States. An existing team photo reveals that two unmistakable blacks (probably Clemente González and Esteban Maciques) suited up for the Cuban team and this was a noteworthy event in itself. But the big story was that Conrado Marrero and Natilla Jiménez became so popular after the tourney that they were now the biggest diamond stars on the island and were sure to outdraw the pros whenever they appeared. Amateur leagues and teams were now the centerpiece of the Cuban baseball scene and it would remain this way throughout the early forties and even until the end of the prosperous war years.

The third world title tournament was again staged in Havana a year later. This time the Cubans were once more dominant although they did not run through the field undefeated. The USA (with future big league lefty Stubby Overmire) and Nicaragua (with heavy-hitting Stanley Cayasso) were the strongest challengers, and the team representing Hawaii featured a contingent of surprisingly talented Japanese players who could run the bases with skill even if they were not strong batsmen. Both the USA and Nicaragua managed to beat the Cubans once and both finished at 9–3, a game behind the host team. This event was clearly a step up in scope with seven clubs entered (Venezuela, Mexico and Puerto Rico rounded out the field) and each team taking to the diamond a dozen times. Cuba's manager was Reinaldo Cordeiro, the long time skipper of the Amateur League powerhouse Fortuna club. Jonathan Robinson of Nicaragua smacked the only homer of the tournament and proved the best all-around hitter with a hefty .444 average.

There was a most interesting aspect to the first two Amateur World Series tournaments played in Havana's sprawling La Tropical Stadium and it is a feature that only continued a long Cuban baseball tradition. It was masterful pitching that lent the excitement and not the slugging of home runs or any untoward displays of onslaught scoring. Only two homers were smashed in the first tourney and but one in the second, and Nicaragua's Cayasso and Robinson were the only hitters to reach the fences — though in fact they never did reach the fences since all three long belts remained within the confines of the playing grounds. This had a lot to do with the layout and dimensions of Tropical Stadium, of course. But it also had to do with the stellar pitching talent that marked amateur baseball of the era.

That there were again some blacks on the Cuban national team in 1940 was an important signal that things were changing in amateur baseball on the island. The starting catcher —

a crucial position on any team — was a black named Carlos Colás. Colás split the receiving duties with Kiko Gutiérrez and together they handled the skilled staff of Marrero, Jiménez, Eliecer Alvarez, lefty sensation Daniel Parra from Fortuna, and Antonio Ruiz from Club Hershey. A second black played a more limited role but one with historic overtones nonetheless. Pedro ("Charolito" meaning "Patent Leather") Orta was a backup third baseman from the far western province of Pinar del Río. He would later play professionally with Marianao and also in the Mexican League, and his son Jorge Orta (born in Mexico) would one day be a distinguished major leaguer.

The Cuban team fielded for the 1940 Havana tournament was a fearsome powerhouse, especially when it came to the pitching staff. Marrero won three games but also suffered both defeats. He posted a 1.15 ERA that was only slightly better than several of his teammates. Hechevarría logged in at 1.16,

One of Cuba's top amateur pitchers of the forties, Rogelio "Limonar" Martínez was anchor of the Deportiva Matanzas mound staff and the early–1940s Cuban national team before entering the pro Cuban League with Marianao. The unusual nickname was a reference to the small town in Matanzas Province where Martínez began his career.

Ruiz at 1.29, and Jiménez at 1.91. Parra held the poorest mark on the staff and that was a more-than-solid 2.77. And there were also some heavy hitters in the Cuban lineup. Future big leaguer and winter league manager Nap Reyes played on this club, as did fifties-era Almendares shortstop Manuel "Chino" Hidalgo. Mario Fajo, a holdover from the previous year's tournament, batted .341, and Virgilio Arteaga was a slugging first baseman from the Círculo Militar y Naval amateur club. It was again an unbeatable combination.

Spring and summer of 1941 brought as much excitement as Cuban amateur baseball had yet witnessed and might ever witness again. Given the stellar tradition already existing and the steady growth of popularity for the amateur game in the thirties this is not any small claim. In the spring Havana-area fans witnessed a legendary pitching performance that would take its place alongside those of Méndez against the Cincinnati Reds and Pedroso versus the Pittsburgh Pirates, glorious memories from thirty years in the past. Amateur hurler Juan Decall stunned the baseball world, both north and south, when he paced a select Cuban nine of fellow amateurs in a 2–1 victory over the Boston Red Sox, visiting Havana on a spring training junket. Decall's five-hitter came against a Bosox lineup that didn't have Ted Williams but that did boast the likes of Foxx, Doerr, Cronin and Dom DiMaggio.

The domestic Amateur League season that followed was one of the most intense in collective memory. Fans followed the action packed in the stands and entranced by the radio, and cheered to the pitching exploits of Natilla Jiménez with Hershey, Rogelio "Limonar" Martínez with Matanzas, and Marrero with Cienfuegos. Many claim with justification that the Matanzas staff of Martínez, Catayo González and Sandalio Consuegra was the best amateur trio festooned in the same uniform in island history. And there were also the exploits of Julio Moreno, a slender right hander and future modest big leaguer who struck out 160 and drew reasonable comparisons with Cleveland's rising star Bob Feller. The season's deciding game was fittingly a pitching duel between Marrero for Cienfuegos and Isidoro León (the winner) for Círculo Militar. The showdown was part of a doubleheader on September 27 which opened the intensely advertised world championships that once more had returned to Havana and La Tropical Stadium. Between Decall's masterpiece, the summer amateur pennant race, and the third Havana-based tournament for a world title that was about to unfold, 1941 was arguably the most intense baseball year ever witnessed in Cuba.

A pair of true highlight moments for Cuban baseball history emerged with the Amateur World Series matches celebrated in Havana during autumn 1941 and autumn 1942. Soon to transpire were two remarkable head-to-head match-ups between Cuba and Venezuela, the nonpareils of that era's international play. Front and center would be the legendary pitching feats of the two nation's greatest amateur pitching legends, Connie "Chico" Marrero and Daniel "Chino" Canónico.

Local interest was at a fever pitch in Havana when the fourth Amateur World Series kicked off in the lush surroundings of La Tropical Stadium on September 27, 1941, mere months before a fateful attack on Pearl Harbor by Japanese bombers would embroil the United States in a widening Second World War. The tournament included nine countries — Venezuela, Mexico, Panama, the Dominican Republic, the USA, Nicaragua, Puerto Rico, El Salvador and the host Cubans — and the level of competition was expected to be the highest yet seen for such international games. Mexico had a veteran team and the Venezuelans featured a roster that had played well in exhibitions against the Cuban champions a year earlier. Panama boasted pitcher Patricio Scantlebury, a Cuban League regular and future major leaguer, and the Dominican team reflected the baseball progress being made on that neighboring island. But the Cuban team was again the showcase with a pitching staff that was truly without peer. On that staff were the best hurlers (Julio Moreno, Conrado Marrero, Limonar Martínez, Natilla Jiménez, Ramón Roger and Daniel Parra) from the exciting Amateur League season that had just wound down as one of the best ever in Cuba.

The series itself was a closely matched affair that went right down to the wire as both Cuba and Venezuela finished with seven victories in eight matches, the tie resulting when Venezuela ace Canónico shut down the home team in the crucial finale that brought the series to its scheduled conclusion. Righty Canónico was a pesky junk-ball pitcher who specialized in throwing a wicked knuckleball. The Cuban hitters consequently found him a most difficult opponent to crack. Venezuela was undoubtedly more satisfied with their deadlock at the end of regulation games, but the host Cubans were seemingly unwilling to have their party spoiled by anything but outright victory. The Cubans thus demanded an unscheduled tiebreaker, a proposal at which the Venezuelans first balked. They had no pitcher to turn to but their ace, and he had just thrown the final match and could not reasonably return to action without rest. The Cubans agreed to a short delay and the showdown was scheduled for October 23, with the Venezuelans allowed a tune-up game in the interim.

It all turned out to be a fatal mistake for the overconfident Cubans and one with great consequences for sporting pride in both countries. Marrero and Canónico squared off for all the marbles with Cuban fans and officials still supremely confident of merely postponed victory. But Marrero had one of his all-too-characteristic slow starts in the showdown and the visitors jumped to an early insurmountable three-run first-inning lead. It was sloppy play that did in the Cubans during the opening inning, with centerfielder Guajiro Rodríguez and third sacker Mosquito Ordeñana both guilty of bonehead plays. Natilla Jiménez was promptly brought on the scene by manager Joaquín Viego and Natilla successfully shut down the visitor's attack. But it was already too late for the devastated home club. When the final out was recorded in the 3–1 loss the Cuban crowd, in a remarkable display of both sportsmanship and pure appreciation of the sport's artistry, swarmed the field and hoisted the opposing victorious hurler to their shoulders for an improbable victory lap around the Tropical Stadium infield.

The unlikely victory by Canónico and his teammates would remain down through the years perhaps the greatest hour in the history of Venezuelan baseball — certainly Venezuelan amateur baseball. Wild celebrations were set off at home by the team's first international title. Even the Cubans were most gracious in defeat, despite whatever major disappointments might have been harbored by both fans and (perhaps even more so) by officials at the head of Cuban amateur baseball hierarchy. Marrero's temporary embarrassment would, of course, be quickly enough rectified a few short months down the road and certainly overshadowed by his career as a whole. The loss did little over the long haul to shatter the already ballooning image of Cuban dominance in Latin American baseball. If anything the game became one of the most cherished moments of the island's baseball lore. Cuban fans appreciate great diamond displays, even when the heroes are wearing the uniform of the visitors.

Amateur baseball on both the national and international scale had reached its apogee with the exciting climax to the fourth Amateur World Series that wrapped up in late October of 1941. Only a few weeks later the infamous bombing of Pearl Harbor would occur and the world inside and outside of Cuba would undergo drastic change. Cuba did not have any large scale direct involvement in the war, of course, and for Cuban fans and officials alike the highest priority remained the next world tournament and a chance for revenge against Venezuela and also for recapturing global amateur baseball supremacy. That would all happen soon enough to be sure. But during the lean war years the teams competing in world play would now be reduced, and the focus of much of the rest of the world was now clearly elsewhere. In Cuba itself, after the war, the professional game would again enjoy an important upsurge. Some of Cuba's greatest amateur triumphs still lay ahead. But an era of early supremacy had also been rung to a close.

*   *   *

There was no bigger star in the pre-revolution era of amateur baseball than Conrado Marrero. Marrero became an island icon as a result of his ballyhooed international matchups — especially with Canónico and Venezuela — at the outset of the forties. But as we have seen here and in an earlier chapter, The Premier had already fashioned a substantial legend by the late thirties on the amateur fields throughout the island with his seasons of service for the Amateur League team in Cienfuegos.

Another rousing success marked the 1942 Amateur League season, which was again highlighted by a host of stellar pitchers spread across the island. León, Marrero and Jiqui Moreno were the most celebrated trio of top winners. Isidro León posted a 19–4 mark with a stellar 1.75 ERA that was enough to lead Círculo Militar y Naval (which was 22–5 overall) to a narrow victory over Moreno's Círculo de Artesanos ball club. Moreno's own ERA was a near-identical 1.76 and his won-lost record weighed in at 20–5; his strikeouts totaled an unmatched 213. Not to be outdone, Marrero had a better record still (22–5) and also the top ERA mark at an even more eye-popping 1.22. There was so much individual talent and so much interest in the next edition of the Cuban national team that *Carteles* seized upon the momentum by running a survey by which fans could handpick the all-star starting nine. Marrero was — not surprisingly — the top vote-getter with more than 7,000 and was joined on the final selection by the likes of Ealo at first, Quilla at short, Fleitas behind the plate, Quicutis in center, the league's leading hitter Pedro Echevarría in right, and Moreno, León, Coco del Monte and Fortuna's ace southpaw Daniel Parra rounding out the more-than-impressive starting pitching rotation.

Amateur World Series number five was again slated for La Tropical from late September through late October of 1942 and expectations were understandably high throughout Cuba for a redeeming rematch with the Venezuelan forces. The atmosphere elsewhere, off the island itself, had now of course

JULIO MORENO   PITCHER

La colección completa de estas fotos dará derecho a los beneficios

del PLAN DE OBSEQUIOS que se anuncia en nuestras páginas.

Tip. Ponciano, S.A.

Julio "Jiquí" Moreno labored on memorable Amateur World Series Cuban mound staffs of the early forties, alongside Conrado Marrero and Limonar Martínez, before enjoying a substantial pro career which included a brief stretch with the Washington Senators.

begun to sour. Global war was now raging in Europe, Northern Africa and the Asian Pacific and, despite Cuba's attempts at exerting pressure on U.S. officials to ease war-time travel restrictions, it was a much reduced field of but five teams that showed up to do battle this time around. The Americans did send a contingent — perhaps somewhat surprisingly, given the war preoccupations at home — but then withdrew before competition was completed.

Cuba wouldn't have to wait very long for its own sweet savoring of revenge. This came early and almost too easily. Venezuela had arrived with its crack pitching staff and lineup in tact, featuring Canónico, Colmenares, Fonseca, Bracho and other familiar faces. They also now boasted a sensational shortstop named Luis Aparicio, whose son would one day earn stripes as the country's first ballplayer destined for enshrinement in Cooperstown. When the two clubs squared off in the second week of play it proved a one-sided match, Marrero going the route and yielding but three hits while Canónico was anything but spell-binding this time, being crushed for ten hits and eight runs in the middle innings. The game was highlighted by a titanic home run blast over the distant scoreboard (approximately 500 feet) stroked off of Canónico by Artemisa outfielder Chito Quicutis. With the 8–0 whitewashing under their belts the Cubans cruised to a 10–2 record, followed by the Dominican Republic a game behind, Venezuela in the middle if the pack, and the unenthusiastic Mexicans and Americans with 10 defeats each, the last four for the U.S. coming as a result of forfeits. The senior Aparicio was brilliant in the field and won a game against the Americans with a well-timed clutch base hit. But it was the Cuban pitching that stole the show. Despite Marrero's celebrated win over Canónico, it was Moreno and León who were the true limelight mound stars, and Andrés Fleitas not only handled the unmatched mound corps but himself hit .405 and walked off with an MVP trophy. For icing on the cake, Cuba thrashed the USA twice to the tunes of 20–0 and 17–0. It didn't get much better than this.

There was, unfortunately, one ugly incident devaluing the 1942 Amateur World Series and it involved the better-than-expected runner-up team from the Dominican Republic. The Dominican club managed by the popular Ernesto "Burrolote" Rodríguez might have taken the Cubans to the wire had they not been upset 3–1 by the lowly Americans in a contest that remained for years the calling card of this particular tournament. Throughout the tense game the partisan Cuban crowd at La Tropical had boisterously backed the American squad, since a USA victory would obviously help the Cuban cause. Almost from the opening frame the fans had kept up a endless sing-song chant of "Bu-rro-lo-te" in reference to the infamous nickname ("Big Donkey"). Such heated heckling of manager Rodríguez eventually led to a most uncharacteristic explosion by the Dominican skipper, one involving a bat thrown into the crowd and an ensuing riot in which fans stormed the field in pursuit of the Dominican manager and ballplayers. All eventually ended well and "Burrolote" (in large part due to the manager's later intelligent and well spoken responses to the incident on Havana radio) subsequently remained a popular figure in Cuba. The incident also was destined to long occupy an indelible spot in Cuban baseball lore.

By tournament's end politics and jingoism also entered the picture as the prized first-place trophy was now given a hometown Cuban flavor. What had so far been the Moore Cup was now renamed the "Copa Presidente Batista" by DGND officials who had largely made the world tournament their own in recent years. But such Cuban dominance on and off the field was about to end and end rather abruptly. The Batista government still had fifteen-plus years ahead of it before its own destiny would run out in the face of Castro's insurgency. The surge in Cuban amateur baseball, however, was on a much shorter time schedule and about to experience a much shorter lifespan. DGND administrators and Amateur League officials were about to launch an overambitious crackdown on assumed "professionalism" that would leave the Cuban baseball world and its showcase national team both reeling.

Insulated Cuba—which had itself finally declared war against Germany—found that its own internal baseball wars were little impacted by the more savage global hostilities that followed Pearl Harbor and Hitler's advances across the face of Europe. The 1943 amateur season on the island was yet another resounding triumph. This time around the year's top headlines were being written by a stellar pitching trio for Deportivo Matanzas that had spent several previous seasons in the long shadows of Marrero, Moreno, León, Parra and others among the island's substantial core of top pitching stars. It was a breakout year for the one-two-three punch of Limonar Martínez, Catayo González and Sandalio (Sandy) Consuegra; the combo paced Matanzas to the title in a nip-and-tuck battle with defending champion Círculo Militar y Naval, a club still featuring Isidro León. Star pitchers still dominated the circuit from top to bottom and most were the old and familiar faces. In a league where pitchers could count on a week's rest between outings it was not so surprising that hitters were always at a rather large disadvantage.

The next edition of the world championship tournament was again on tap for Havana in the late fall and it came off as scheduled even though the competitive field was now reduced by wartime travel restrictions to a barely adequate coterie of four teams. Panama and the Dominican Republic would likely provide the only serious opposition, but that was not expected to be much of a challenge against the vaunted Cuban pitchers. The biggest story surrounding the Cuban team itself was the suspension of Marrero for supposedly receiving payment for one or more amateur league games. It all seemed an overreaction by the DGND whose officials were seemingly becoming obsessive about protecting the amateur status of their own teams, even though opponents often harbored known professionals. Mexico was the fourth entrant, and determined to improve on past weak showings the Aztecas arrived (rather ironically, given the fate suffered by Conrado Marrero) with several known Mexican League professionals on their roster.

With Marrero finally out of the limelight it would now be Moreno's time to shine as the number one Cuban amateur star. Jiqui (Julio) Moreno was a fearsome little right-hander who had been steadily building a reputation for his strikeout artistry both inside Cuba and in past world tournaments. But ironically the future big leaguer was destined to earn his biggest headlines (as had Marrero versus Canónico a couple of years earlier) by losing (not winning) a classic match-up with a surprising upstart rival. This time it was Mexico that pulled the shocker, besting Moreno in a 14-inning thriller that stands alongside the 1941 Cuba-Venezuela tiebreaker match as one of the showcase games of 20th-century Latin American baseball history. It was always the biggest news when the Cubans lost, even in the earliest days of Amateur World Series play.

It was only a momentary stumble and this time at least it didn't come in a game that cost a gold medal. Cuba won nine of its dozen games and Moreno rebounded to shine as the tournament star just as expected. Mexico could do no better that split its twelve matches and Panama and the Dominican Republic finished further back still. Pitchers for all four teams displayed their dominance over hitters in the overly spacious La Tropical ballpark. With his one loss to go with three victories Moreno had posted an ERA of less than a run per game (0.70) and another Cuban pitcher, Natilla Jiménez, also starred as both a starter and reliever and thus emerged as the upset MVP choice. It was a fitting way to ring down the curtain on five straight winters of brilliant world tournament play in the baseball-crazy city of Havana. Few at the time had any inkling that another important epoch for Cuban baseball was now rapidly drawing to an inevitable close.

There would be one more fateful encounter before the war years were actually over and it would prove to be one of the most truly unforgettable if most embarrassing hours in the entire history of world amateur baseball competitions. Change was now coming to Cuba faster in the political area than on the baseball diamonds, and the loss of 1944 elections by Batista's handpicked successor led to a new national government that downplayed sport and thus weakened the hand of a now largely revamped DGND. Colonel Jaime Mariné, who had nurtured La Tropical tournaments after 1939, was suddenly gone from the scene. There would now be no push for another new tournament in Havana and the role thus fell to Venezuela to host the next round of amateur baseball competitions. The Cubans would of course send a team and that team would have Marrero back in the fold, as well as a stronger showing of black players—heavy-hitter Pablo García and slick infielder Amado Ibáñez being the most notable—than ever before. But a number of the stars of the past were now missing, since the better amateurs had increasingly been turning to the professional ranks in recent months. Top past stars now lost to the pro league included catching mainstay Andrés Fleitas, heavy-hitting infielder Napoleón Reyes and Chito Quicutis, a fly-chaser who also pitched and had been a huge amateur league star with Artemisa.

The seventh Amateur World Series was staged with a definite upgrade in participants even though wartime travel re-

Cuban stalwart Luis Casanova is greeted at home plate after slugging a homer during an Intercontinental Cup V (Edmonton, Canada) match versus Australia.

strictions were still a burden and this time affected the Cuban contingent itself, which first had to travel by rail to Camagüey in order to board a KLM flight en route to Caracas. Mexico (featuring eventual Cleveland Indians star Beto Avila), Panama and Puerto Rico would all show up with strong rosters for the month-long 1944 tournament renewal. Nicaragua and especially the Dominican team, still under Burrolote Rodríguez, both promised to be serious contenders. The host Venezuelans were as imposing as their entries from a couple of years past, though Canónico and some of the other old faces were no longer around. Chino Canónico and the elder Luis Aparicio had both turned to the professional ranks, like some of their Cuban counterparts. Mexico, Cuba and the host Venezuelans all limped to the finish in a dead heat and a tie-breaking playoff would therefore be necessary. But there was already trouble aplenty brewing even before the final string of showdown games had gotten underway.

The difficulties resulted from a crew of tournament umpires supplied by the host country that were quite obviously

not up to the challenge of full impartiality. The first flare-up came when a playoff match-up between the Dominicans and host Venezuelans ended in bitter controversy. The Venezuelan umpire ruled the contest suspended by darkness in the middle of the final inning, wiping out several Venezuelan tallies in the top of the ninth and handing a victory to the Dominicans (who were the home team for that contest). The offending umpire was promptly removed from further games by Venezuelan officials. Then came a pivotal game that resulted in Cuba's hasty and angry withdrawal from the field of play. The substitute official who worked the Venezuela-Cuba game a day latter had been serving as a coach for the Venezuelan club before his unorthodox switch of assignments — an ominous recipe for built-in disaster.

It was a truly bizarre play that brought Cuba's stay at the tournament to an unpredicted end. With a man on first, a Cuban batter was involved in a close play at first in which the pitcher covering the bag dropped the toss from his fellow infielder. The errant heave was surprisingly retrieved by a photographer positioned on the field near first base, and he immediately tossed it to the first sacker, who then relayed to third to nail the original Cuban runner coming around from first. When Cuban manager Pipo de la Noval next justifiably protested the unorthodox event he was shockingly informed that photographers were legitimate "baseball persons" and thus allowed to intervene in on-field action. Noval angrily withdrew his forces from the competition at the end of the day's play and Mexico next followed suit after another disputed decision a day later. The tournament thus never reached completion, though Venezuela claimed forfeits by both the Cubans and Mexicans and ceremoniously declared themselves controversial champions.

After the 1944 debacle in Caracas the fortunes of the Cuban amateur juggernaut began to fade somewhat on the world stage. Cuba would not return to the Amateur World Series until 1950, although three intervening tournaments were held in Venezuela, Colombia and Nicaragua. The 1950 entry did claim another first place finish, but that team was considerably reduced in talent compared to its predecessors. The reason was simply that the pendulum had shifted, the professional Cuban League was now again in ascendancy, and as a result many of the best players on the island were now turning pro at the earliest possible opportunity. The amateur ranks were for the first time in decades no longer the most popular among competing island baseball venues. After the war and Brooklyn's Jackie Robinson, the major leagues had also opened up to Cubans of all colors and pro scouting had thus increased many fold on the island. And Cuba also now had its own teams in organized baseball, first at the B level in the Florida International League with the Havana Cubans, and then at the top minor league level with the International League Cuban Sugar Kings.

There were nonetheless a few proud moments in the last decade leading up to the cataclysmic 1959 revolution. Luis (Lindo) Suárez pitched a heroic game in Venezuela in 1953 as Cuba captured an Amateur World Series title for only the second time on foreign soil. Suárez tossed a shutout after giving up an early double to Luis Aparicio Junior, a name destined for eventual Cooperstown greatness. A year earlier the tourney had even returned to Havana for the first time in a decade and the Cubans racked up another title on their home grounds. Two notable future big leaguers also made head-turning appearances in the only slightly less prestigious venue of the quarter-century-old Central American Games. Willie Miranda, a budding amateur star with Club Teléfonos between 1942 and 1947, flashed his fielding talents on an international scene for the first time in 1946 in Barranquilla, Colombia. And future Brooklyn Dodgers World Series hero Edmundo "Sandy" Amoros clouted a surprising six homers in 1950 at the same event, in a bandbox stadium in Guatemala.

By the end of the decade and with the 1958–1959 collapse of the Batista government the stature of amateur baseball on the island was also in finally freefall. In the country's first appearance on the stage of world amateur baseball after Fidel's revolutionary government had taken the reins of power in Havana, there was a huge embarrassment in the form of an eighth-place finish at the Pan American Games competition. What made the collapse of the uncharacteristically weak Cuban team all the more of an embarrassment was the fact that the ignominious performance had occurred in the Americans' own backyard, in Chicago's Comiskey Park. It was unquestionably a low point for Cuban baseball — perhaps the lowest point in more than half a century. But if the dip was sudden and painful it was also destined to be exceptionally brief and impermanent. For nothing quite like this would ever again be witnessed with a Cuban national team over the next full half-century.

Braudilio Vinent performed brilliantly in dozens of international matches throughout the seventies and eighties, making a record 96 game appearances. Vinent's blue-ribbon outing came during 1972 Amateur World Series play in Managua, where he not only captured all four tournament appearances with a microscopic 0.62 ERA but also tossed a spectacular eight-hit complete game whitewashing against a squad of multi-national all-stars.

* * *

Once the decision was made to eradicate all vestiges of professionalism in all domestic island sporting events and thus to convert to amateur baseball exclusively, it didn't take long to completely overhaul the shape of formalized baseball play all across the island. Nor did it take very long for Cuban all-star teams to establish renewed dominance on the world amateur tournament stage. Professional baseball was now — overnight and without any ceremony — consigned straight to the junk heap. But a new socialist Cuba in the process would hardly disappear from its preferred place among the world's leading baseball-playing nations.

The projected vision of Fidel's revolutionary government in the early sixties was clearly a sports program that would faithfully serve the goals of the revolution; it would promote health and recreation for citizens on the home front, provide continued domestic entertainment via the national pastime in its renewed and purified format, and hopefully produce teams and athletes capable of demonstrating the achievements of the socialist system on a broadening stage of international athletic matches. There was thus to be a radically new set of goals for sports, and particularly for baseball, as the game was re-institutionalized on the home front. Another set of goals would also now emerge for baseball as it was played on the international front. Foremost among these would of course be to beat the now demonized "Yankees" at their own self-proclaimed national game, and in the process to demonstrate to the world at large that the purity of amateur baseball enterprises was to be much valued over the self-serving capitalized enterprise represented by America's professional organized baseball. Over the years it would sometimes prove a bit difficult to keep the twin objectives of the new Cuban baseball in proper balance; at times it seemed as though gaining propaganda points with Olympic or World Cup wins on the road was elevated over the interests of maintaining competitive and entertaining national series championship seasons at home.

On the home front a new league format was up and running in the first few years of the new regime. The task was handled by a new government agency put in place in February 1961, almost at the same time the last Cuban League professional season wound to a halt. Few Cuban fans probably imagined at the time how extensive would be the changes that were now taking place. INDER immediately decreed the abolishing of the professional version of the game and set in motion a tournament that was hopefully a first step toward the long-held fantasy of a truly national baseball competition. It was perhaps a piece of remarkable good fortune that the team hastily patched together and sent to compete in an Amateur World Series in Costa Rica in the first two months of INDER's existence not only won in impressive style but did so at a pivotal moment in the island's political and military history. The baseball team battled in Costa Rica for national honor at the very hour that Fidel's hardscrabble military repulsed an April 1961 American-backed invasion by counter-revolutionary forces at the Bay of Pigs. There seemed a natural and inevitable link between the two events — one a symbolic battle and the other an all-too-real military campaign. When the first National Series of only four teams started up in the spring of that following year (January-March 1962) there was already a good deal of momentum in place for the new style of amateur baseball.

The new national series started off modestly enough (as related in detail in Chapter 8). This was amateur baseball of a very different form, of course, from that of previous decades. The teams had been created from scratch and none of the old affiliations — amateur or professional — could now be relied upon to draw potential fans. The "Habana" team of the first season was renamed "Industriales" for the second season, and it has been speculated that the name and team colors (blue and white) were an attempt to appeal to the ingrained popularity of fan-favored Almendares from the erstwhile pro circuit. But there were few other connections outside of the familiar venue of El Cerro Stadium and the raw talent of many new Cuban players. It would not be the same amateur baseball scene as in the glory years of the 1940s, but it would be a baseball that relied on some of the same principles. The overriding goal was to build a strong national team and also to provide much-needed diversionary entertainment at home. In the broad view, then, the aim of the Castro government in maintaining baseball as a public institution and crowd-pleasing diversion was not all that different from a goal once held by the Batista forces themselves.

From the outset the revamped National Series baseball season instituted by Fidel's new revolutionary government in January 1962 was designed with international competitions as a primary focus. Baseball could now again be used as a political weapon, just as it had been used by Cuban governments so often in the past. Baseball had been born out of the rebellion against the Spanish, as recounted in Chapter 5. The Cuban League had first flourished in the 1910s and twenties when fans could be drawn to Almendares Park to see Cuban all-stars battle teams of American blacks or barnstorming major leaguers in what was popularly referred to as the pre-league "American season." The most popular national baseball of all had been the Amateur League play of the early forties and the teams that it produced to contest for national honors at the earliest (usually Havana-based) versions of the fledgling Amateur World Series.

Before the decade of the sixties was played out Cuba was once again making its indelible mark on the international scene. The Cuban program had recovered quickly enough under the new organizational structure to score a couple of early if only mildly impressive comeback victories. First there was the gold medal win in the amateur world tournament in Costa Rica in April 1961, played as mentioned against the backdrop of the Bay of Pigs invasion by U.S.-encouraged exile forces launched from Miami. Pedro Chávez — who had performed in the old Amateur League (winning a triple crown there in 1957) and would soon star in the new National Series — was a key player on the first team to bring home an international triumph after the revolution.

A first signal was soon sent forth to the outside world that the experiment to revamp Cuban baseball in accordance with the needs of the revolution was headed for surprising successes. Within two years there was an upset over the United States team at the Pan American Games in Brazil. Pitching stars (Aquino Abreu, Manuel Alarcón, Modesto Verdura) and batting stars (Urbano González, Pedro Chávez, Antonio González) from the first two National Series seasons sparked an impressive 7–1 record and paced 13–1 and 3–1 wins over Team USA. Gold in Brazil was at least a partial redemption for the Pan American Games debacle in Chicago four years earlier, even if the United States team in São Paulo was not an overly strong one. And of course, after the worsening of political relations between the two countries in 1961, the USA versus Cuba matches now suddenly had a more intensified significance on both sides of the Straits of Florida.

So good and so dominant was the Cuban team throughout most of the 1970s, 1980s and 1990s — and even most of the 1960s — that the games and tournaments most remembered would inevitably be the ones the Cubans managed somehow to lose. Not only did they rarely ever lose tournament titles, but in reality the Cuban teams very rarely ever lost any individual games. Of 22 major international tournaments (World Cup, Intercontinental Cup, Pan American Games, Central American Games) contested between 1961 and 1982 in which Cuba entered, there were 11 in which the Castro forces went undefeated and six others in which they lost but a single pre-championship-round contest. Over that stretch the number of gold medals was an astounding 18, with three silvers added to the count; in brief, Cuba won gold or silver in every outing except the 1962 Central American Games. When it comes to individual games played the twenty-year ledger stood at 192–19, a .910 winning percentage. And the onslaught would only become even more one-sided in the final two decades of the twentieth century. Nothing found in baseball history approaches such uncluttered domination.

After a surprise 1961 Amateur World Series XV success in San José, Cold War tensions would enter the fray and Cuban contingents would experience considerable difficulties in just getting into world and hemisphere competitions over the next several years. Political pressures kept the Cubans out of the next Amateur World Series which was not held until the final year of the decade. On that occasion the Colombian government (under pressure from the OAS and the United States) refused visas to the Cuban athletes and coaches.

Trouble peaked at the Tenth Central American and Caribbean games held in June 1966 at San Juan, Puerto Rico. The Cubans again found it difficult enough just arriving at the competitions and taking the field of play for baseball and other scheduled events. The Cuban delegation was delayed by red tape from disembarking from the cargo vessel that had brought them and most Cuban athletes missed out on the opening ceremonies. There was stress thrust on Cuban athletes in all sports, and baseball was an exception only in degree. Games were played before hostile crowds and the Cuban team was subjected to continuous taunts (and worse) from anti–Castro

exiles. Aquino Abreu, Gaspar Pérez and Rigoberto Betancourt all pitched brilliantly in a series of close games under this kind of excruciating pressure. The Cubans and Puerto Ricans ultimately tied at identical 5–1 ledgers and a playoff contest was needed to decide the tournament. The club managed by Gilberto Torres in the end came away with a heroic 6–2 victory that stands as one of the milestone moments of post-revolution Cuban baseball. (Ironically, the pitching star of this dramatic tournament — Rigoberto Betancourt — would be the lone member of the Cuban contingent to seek political asylum 33 years later when the national team made its much celebrated visit to Camden Yards in Baltimore.)

There was a temporary setback a year later that should have served as sufficient warning against complacency. The disaster came with the renewal of the Pan American Games, this time staged far to the north in Winnipeg, Manitoba, Canada. A surprisingly strong entry from the United States hung with the Cubans in the opening round, though the Cubans took both head-to-head matches (by 4–3 and 9–2 scores). But in the best-of-three finals the Americans came out on top twice, in the first (8–3) and third (2–1) games, to walk off with the championship. It was the first time that Team USA had ever beaten the Cuban team for an international championship. And it would also remain the only Pan American Games title Team USA has registered to date. In the exciting deciding game rain delayed the ninth frame of a 1–1 tie, adding to the considerable drama. The sudden downpour almost washed the game out entirely with the USA waiting to bat in the bottom of the ninth. Manuel Alarcón had pitched brilliantly for eight frames, but after the delay Alarcón had lost his edge and loaded the bases by surrendering two walks followed by a single. George Greer then delivered the clutch hit, another single past a drawn-in infield that scored Ray Blosse with the game-winner. It was a shocking loss for the seasoned Cubans, since Team USA consisted of two United States Army officers and 18 college players, including Mark Marquess who would later coach both Stanford University and the 1988 U.S. Olympic Team.

One of the strongest Cuban teams ever took the field for the seventeenth renewal of the Amateur World Series convened in the Dominican Republic during the final year of the sixties. Recalling San Juan a few years earlier, the atmosphere in Santo Domingo would also hold a high political charge. But this time it was not the Cubans who were designated as targets for the wrath that spewed from the grandstands. Considerable anti–American feeling lingered in the wake of a U.S. military invasion of the island only four years earlier. Ironically the United States was fielding a team for the first time since the 1942 tournament in Havana, when the slapstick American entrant had been anything but a representative or even competitive squad. This time the Americans would prove reasonably strong, especially in the pitching department, and both the Cubans and Team USA reached the finals with only a single loss. The hometown Dominicans were also a solid ball club and finished only a game behind the two pacesetters. In the showdown finale the hero for Cuba was pitcher Gaspar

Pérez, a seasoned veteran who not only performed brilliantly in relief but also managed to knock home the game's winning run. This victory was perhaps the biggest of the near-decade since the Castro communist takeover. The showcase championship game, and indeed the tournament as a whole, seemed

a major turning point for Cuban fortunes. Over the next three decades island teams would only rarely be challenged by the Americans, or by anyone else attending international competitions.

The decade of the seventies saw Team Cuba entrench its dominance on the international scene under replacement manager Servio Borges. Borges was the first of a new school of coaches who had been trained entirely in the revolutionary baseball that had followed Castro's sweeping reforms. This new managerial crop (Borges and then Pedro Chávez and José M. Pineda) would preside over the transition to aluminum bats (mid-seventies) and guide the national team across an entire decade which was to prove a high water mark of post-revolution Cuban baseball. Most of the major international tournaments of this ten-year span were played at home on Cuban soil, in a newly revamped and expanded Latin American Stadium. Against the backdrop of increasing economic hard times the Havana citizenry could again enjoy witnessing their team's repeated triumphs largely first hand. Roberto González Echevarría draws a parallel with the similar uses of baseball as diversionary tactic for dulling social upheaval by Fulgencio Batista (with Amateur World Series matches in Havana in the early 1940s), and still earlier by President Machado (with the 1930 Central American Games). By any measure, and despite the possible political overtones of the national sport, it was indeed a glorious baseball decade for the residents of Havana. And most of the highlights all seemed to be packed into the first three years.

The biggest breakthrough came with the 1970 Amateur World Championships staged in Cartegena, Colombia. The highlight would be a single showcase game that would long live on in both collective Cuban memory and also elsewhere in the lore attached to world amateur baseball competitions. Excitement began with a brilliant performance by a touted American prospect named Burt Hooton who tossed a 3–1 gem at the Cubans. Then came the inevitable rematch duel between Hooton, the American ace, and a top

Antonio Muñoz was hero of World Cup XXV (Italy) with a record eight homers and runaway MVP honors.

Cuban pitcher, José Huelga. Huelga was destined to be victorious in two games of the finals and would be rewarded by Fidel himself with designation as the "Hero of Cartagena" for his gutsy performances. In the match-up with Hooton, Huelga pitched brilliantly for 11 innings and earned a mirror-image 3–1 victory. The second match in the best-of-three was delayed by rain for several days. When the game was finally held Cuba's other ace, Changa Mederos, faced future big leaguer Richard Troedson of the American squad. Cuba prevailed once more, sealing the sweep, this time on the strength of masterful relief from both Manuel Alarcón and the same dependable José Huelga.

José Huelga would star for several seasons in the Cuban League before being erased by untimely tragedy only four years later. But the career highlight moment for one of Cuba's best-ever pitchers came with his two clutch victories on Colombia's world championship stage. The game featuring Hooten versus Huelga was easily one of the most memorable in amateur tournament annals. The Cartagena tournament in the end also proved a crucial crossroads for both Cuban and USA international baseball fortunes. Hooten's opening-round masterpiece would ultimately prove to be a final U.S. victory over the irrepressible Cubans during the entire decade of the seventies, a decade which was only just beginning.

Significant tourneys were played in Cuba itself in both 1971 and 1973, with games held all over the island as well as in the showcase ballpark in Havana. Quarter-century old Cerro Stadium — henceforth known as Latin American Stadium — was significantly rebuilt and expanded for the first of these events, with enclosing outfield grandstands being the main improvement. It was the first time that an Amateur World Series had been staged in Havana in almost two full decades and the occasion was one of national celebration and festive atmosphere both on and off the field of play. Since Cold War tensions were now peaking with Washington, no USA team came to Havana in 1971 and the host nation easily swept the field with nine straight wins, the closest a 2–0 thriller versus Nicaragua. Rodolfo Puente and Elipidio Mancebo supplied much of the offense and Changa Mederos pitched brilliantly in both his outings. Several of Cuba's big guns (especially Armando Capiró) uncharacteristically faltered at the plate. But the Cuban pitching could not be challenged, resulting in six shutouts, including the final five contests for the winners.

Another world championship encounter was celebrated on the island only two years later. It was more of the same, with the bullying Cubans remaining undefeated and untested and with Puerto Rico finishing a distant second. Armando Capiró returned to the slugging form that was missing two years earlier and he was supported by newcomer Agustín Marquetti and by veteran Félix Isasi. Julio Romero and unheralded Luis Barreiro turned in the top pitching performances with three victories apiece. Cuba had also claimed another world championship title in November-December 1972 in Managua, during a tournament sandwiched between the two events staged in Havana. The Americans were back in the fold in Nicaragua — where they were not exiled by cold war politics —

and they did offer something of a challenge, as did the surprise team from Nicaragua. But the Cubans won 14 of 15 games and featured once more the brilliant pitching needed to defend their championship laurels. The top pitchers this time around were the veteran Huelga (in his final international event) and the striking newcomer Braudilio Vinent.

The heady decade was fittingly capped in 1979 with the fourth Intercontinental Cup, also held on home grounds in Havana. This outing — Cuba's debut in Intercontinental Cup action — provided something of a personal showcase for a new Cuban slugger named Pedro José Rodríguez, one of the most proficient home run hitters in the sport's annals. Rodríguez was the unchallenged star of an eleven-day affair extending through Christmas week with his phenomenal home run slugging (7) and run production (totaling 17 RBI in only 40 trips to the plate). The Cuban press would make much of the fact that Cheíto's home run ration (ratio of home runs to times at bat) was at this point in his career superior to that registered by any of the legendary major league sluggers, including Ruth, Aaron, Mays or Ralph Kiner. (In February 2001 I would witness the son of Cheíto — also named Pedro José Rodríguez — stroke one of the longest homers I have ever eye-balled, a blast propelled clear over the roof of the left field grandstand at spacious "Fifth of September" ballpark in Cienfuegos.)

The 1979 games in Havana were noteworthy for yet another reason. The USA delegation represented the first American amateur team to visit the island in thirty-seven years. With his Intercontinental Cup victory manager Servio Borges ended the decade undefeated in world tournaments and thus established himself as one of the most successful Cuban managers ever. By the end of the seventies Cuba had still further established its total dominance in world baseball, just as it once had in the early forties. The Cubans had captured the first place prize in all three of the Central American Games competitions of the decade — all three held on foreign soil. They had won the top prize in all the Amateur World Series competitions except the one they had not entered (1973 in Managua). It was a knockout performance that would be hard to match in the coming years — though matched it would be.

The new decade of the eighties would hardly seem to be any kind of slump, however, as the Cuban juggernaut continued to roll relentlessly through tournament after tournament. The decade opened with the Amateur World Series being played for the first time in Japan. Servio Borges was still the manager, Wilfredo Sánchez and Cheíto Rodríguez were still in the batting order, Braudilio Vinent and Julio Romero were still taking the mound, and the results, unsurprisingly, were still the same. Cuba breezed through eleven games again without tasting defeat and first baseman Antonio Muñoz walked off with a second straight MVP. Several of the Cuban wins were of the knockout variety, with the 10-run mercy rule terminating one-sided slaughters over Puerto Rico (23–1) and Colombia (25–0). Lourdes Gourriel, a new star on the Cuban horizon, would collect the biggest hit against the biggest rival when he stroked a game-winning smash to decide a 5–4 thriller with the United States.

A new venue of importance was now the Intercontinental Cup championship series. This tournament had been launched in Italy in 1973 at the time of a breakup of the FIBA into two short-lived rival governing bodies for international baseball. There were renewals of the tournament in Canada in 1975 and again two years later in Managua. Cuba was not a participant in any of the first three events. But by the end of the decade FIBA and FEMBA had reunited and Cuba had also joined the tournament fold. The first Cuban appearance had been with the event staged in Havana in 1979 and won by the host nation in a customary rout. The Intercontinental Cup tournament was soon to be the scene of a surprising — even stunning — loss once the fifth competitions were held in mid–August 1981 at Edmonton, Canada. Just as in Winnipeg in 1967, the Cubans would now suffer a surprise setback that should have provided another important wakeup call against easy complacency. In the long run a true wake-up call was exactly what it proved to be.

Pedro Chávez starred in Cuba's first post-revolution Amateur World Series triumph at San José, Costa Rica, in April 1961. The victory came in the shadows of the infamous Bay of Pigs invasion and launched Cuba's remarkable four-decade dominance of international baseball.

The Cuban team for Edmonton had been selected from an early summer Selective Series season that was considered one of the very best campaigns the Cuban League had staged in its first twenty years of competitions. That team included such heavy hitters as Luis Casanova, Antonio Muñoz, Pedro Medina, Pedro Jova, and Lourdes Gourriel. The stellar pitching staff was anchored by Rogelio García (Cuba's all-time strikeout king), Braudilio Vinent (the Cuban League's top winner when he retired), Julio Romero and José Luis Alemán. The Cubans would crush the Americans in their first match before dropping a surprising pair of games to Canada and the Dominican Republic. The showdown game with Team USA proved to be a full-fledged disaster, however. García opened against future big leaguer Ed Vosberg and was relieved subsequently by Vinent, who was working with only a single day's rest. Pedro Medina almost saved the afternoon with a game-tying homer in the late going. But the affair was finally lost to an American rally in the tenth frame. It would remain the most painful single defeat of Braudilio Vinent's illustrious national team career.

Amateur World Series XXVIII was again staged in Havana in mid–October 1984, the first time the event was held on Cuban soil in slightly more than a decade. After two straight world championship events in Asia, the return to the Caribbean was accompanied by much festivity as well as the inevitable political trappings. Fidel attended the opening game in the company of visiting West German president Willy Brandt while venerable Conrado Marrero — star of these games in Havana four decades earlier — was on hand to toss out the obligatory ceremonial first pitch. Long-forgotten nineteenth century stars were celebrated during pre-game rituals in an obvious attempt to link post-revolution baseball and society to the ancient Cuban struggle for independence from Spain. Cuba's socialist government was now not only admitting the pre-revolutionary history of the entrenched national game but even exploiting it in order to underscore the uninterrupted continuity of patriotism and nationalism.

On the field of play the tournament also brought with it yet another in the handful of memorable losses or near-losses that always seemingly provided necessary impetus for getting the Cuban juggernaut back on track from each and every temporary derailment. This time the shocker came in the opening game, in the form of a near-upset loss at the hands of a less-than-noteworthy team from Italy. Trailing in the final frame, the Cubans were saved by some ninth-inning hitting heroics from Alfonso Urquiola and always-dependable Lourdes Gourriel. In the next outing things didn't get much better when the hometown favorites were whipped 5–4 by Puerto Rico. There was predictable grousing by the Havana faithful, of course, especially over the late-inning pitching moves by manager Pedro Chávez. The ship was eventually righted, however, mainly on the strength of heavy hitting from outfielders Victor Mesa and Luis Casanova and a pair of game-winning homers from first baseman Antonio Muñoz. Five Cubans (Urquiola, Muñoz, Pacheco, Victor Mesa and catcher Juan Castro) completed the tournament with .400-plus batting averages and Julio Romero and Jorge Luis Valdés both posted perfect 3–0 pitching records. The USA team that finished well back in the third medal slot featured a 19-year-old future Cooperstown Hall-of-Famer named Barry Bonds.

The then-wispy Bonds was typical of the improved line-ups that Team USA was now beginning to put on the field for international competitions. If amateur baseball was not taken anywhere near as seriously in North America as it was in Cuba, at least USA teams were now offering a stiffer challenge. Three of the most memorable showdowns between the Cuban juggernaut and improving USA teams came in the final years of the eighties, and one was even staged on United States soil. The first of these clashes occurred at the 1987 Pan American Games competitions in America's heartland city of Indianapolis. Here the Cubans were able to score a most dramatic victory over the Americans in their own backyard, coming from behind in the gold medal game with two runs in the eighth and three more in the ninth against overused reliever Cris Carpenter. An early round loss to the Americans — on a dramatic late homer by Ty Griffin — made the ultimate 13–9 victory in the finals all the sweeter and also all the more dramatic.

An important footnote to the Indianapolis tournament was the arrival of a young Omar Linares who played flawless defense at third and paced the Cuban hit parade with a stellar .520 batting mark. The oldest son of 1960s-era National Series star Fidel Linares, Omar was a true baseball prodigy who arrived on the scene at age 14 during a Juveniles tournament in Venezuela, where he batted above .300 and displayed awesome power. Two seasons later, still under sixteen, he had blasted eight homers and hit above .500 at another Juveniles event in Canada. The summer before Indianapolis the young phenom had debuted with the senior national team at the Central American Games in Santo Domingo (where he batted .497 but was out-slugged by another youthful prospect named Orestes Kindelán) and the Amateur World Series in Holland (where he hit .457 and tied Pacheco for the base hits leadership of the tournament). Over the next fifteen years Linares would post phenomenal statistics in international play (see Chapter 11), establishing a reputation as the best ballplayer of the late 20th century who was not performing in the majors. In Indianapolis, Linares first showed American observers that he was truly "for real" with his eye-popping offensive displays and rocket-launching arm at third. At the time he was not yet twenty. And he had already captured two Cuban League batting titles with lofty marks above .400.

The strength of Team USA opposition now being thrown at the Cubans had already been revealed to Havana fans in July when a USA team scheduled to perform in Indianapolis a month later visited for a tightly-contested exhibition series in Estadio Latinoamericano. Playing for the Americans were such future professional stars as Frank Thomas, Cris Carpenter, Gregg Olson. Ed Sprague, Tino Martinez, Scott Servais, and one-armed pitcher Jim Abbott; Abbott defeated the Cubans in a stellar outing and in the process become a huge fan favorite on the island. In October of that same year another strong field of teams assembled back in Havana for yet another

Intercontinental Cup shootout, and this time the Americans sent an entirely new roster (with catcher Scott Servais the only holdover) that was nonetheless bent on avenging the late-inning Pan Am Games loss to their arch-rivals. Crack teams from South Korea, Japan and Taiwan also upped the competition a notch over Indianapolis. But the Cubans back on their home grounds simply demolished the field with a 101–9 advantage in runs over the opposition in preliminary games and a 37–10 edge in the playoff round. An extra-inning 3–2 defeat of Taiwan was the only game that even came close to blemishing the Cuban's record. And to demonstrate that he was no flash-in-the-pan in Indianapolis, young Linares stroked a remarkable 11 homers in the 13 games his team played.

The Red Tide rolled on and on in seemingly endless fashion. The following year (August 1988) another world championship was staged, this time on neutral European soil in Italy. The stage was set for still another dramatic victory to close out one of most successful decades of amateur baseball history. The 1988 world championships in Parma and Rimini fell in the same year as a Cuban boycott of Olympic matches in Seoul, Korea. The Korean Olympics would feature an "unofficial" or "demonstration" tournament, an event widely anticipated as a showdown between the relentless Cubans and perhaps the most powerful USA roster in years — one again featuring Jim Abbott, Robin Ventura (who had played in Havana in the Intercontinental Cup matches a year earlier), and such sterling pitching prospects as Charles Nagy, Ben McDonald and Andy Benes.

The Cubans and Americans did lock horns earlier in the summer in Millington, Tennessee and the Cubans took four straight after an opening loss. But the final showdown would have to occur in Italy in late summer and not in Seoul during the fall as hoped. Whatever the venue, Team Cuba would maintain their momentum and their remarkable luck as well, beating the Americans twice with mirror-image ninth-inning rallies. The highlight event was the championship match in which Abbott held the Cubans to three hits and owned a 3–1 advantage for eight innings. But a disputed call at first in the ninth opened the floodgates. Gourriel smacked a dramatic homer to knot the game; then Lázaro Vargas stroked a pop-fly single off Benes that provided the winning margin. Antonio Pacheco was the top star of this tournament with stellar offensive and defensive play. And in the championship game two future early defectors would play crucial roles. René Arocha started against Abbott and Euclides Rojas was the untouchable reliever who picked up a championship victory.

What didn't occur in Seoul in 1988 would nonetheless inevitably unfold four years later. The 1990s would finally witness the birth of true Olympic baseball as a crown jewel of international competitions, and with Cuba not very surprisingly at the very forefront of the unfolding Olympic baseball saga. The Barcelona Olympic baseball competitions would prove anything but a big deal here in the United States. The Americans sent another highly undervalued team — one loaded with plenty of big-leaguers-in-grooming (Nomar Garciaparra, Jason Giambi, Michael Tucker, Jeffrey Hammonds) but no big-league household names — and, quite predictably, preciously few Americans were interested or even aware of the diamond action unfolding at the Olympic venues. Baseball would not be part of the U.S. network television coverage of the games; NBC would instead feature only events (track sprints, diving and swim races) more suited to the short time-span actions of the commercial airwaves. But the Olympics were indeed very much a big deal in Cuba, as international competitions — especially in baseball — had always been. The Barcelona Olympic baseball tournament — a footnote to the Olympiad just about everywhere else in the world — was the unrivaled crown jewel of the competitions for fans back home in Cuba.

The handwriting was on the wall for both the USA and Cuban squads by mid-summer when Team USA visited the island for a series of tune-up exhibition games in Holguín and was thoroughly embarrassed by a powerhouse Cuban nine that again featured the slugging of Linares, Kindelán, Pacheco and Victor Mesa. Two of three games in Holguín (where the Cuban national team had never played before) ended in 16–1 and 17–6 scores. No one was surprised, then, in September when the Cubans romped through the field in Barcelona. Falling behind the Americans 5–0 in the first frame of their pool play match, the Red Machine rallied for an easy 9–6 win. USA coach Ron Fraser observed that the Cubans were so good that they often got bored and didn't really try until the late innings. A rematch between Cuba and Team USA in the semifinals ended 6–1, with Osvaldo Fernández as the winning hurler, Kindelán and Victor Mesa slugging homers, and Linares predictably going three-for-three at the plate. The gold medal game was an 11–1 rout of Chinese Taipei with Giorgi Díaz tossing a four-hitter. The most memorable image of the tournament was that of Victor Mesa wrapped in the Cuban flag leading a victory lap around the infield after the final out of the gold medal contest.

Among the Cuban stars in the first Olympic gold medal victory run were some names to be heard from in the future. Orlando Hernández, Rolando Arrojo and Osvaldo Fernández all posted victories on the mound for the team managed by Jorge Fuentes. All three would eventually get their belated chance to pitch in the major leagues. Antonio Pacheco would play most of his career in the shadows of Victor Mesa, Kindelán, and especially Omar Linares. But in Barcelona, Pacheco enjoyed his grandest moments on an international stage. Pacheco, of course, would eventually emerge as the all-time Cuban League leader in base hits before he was retired to Japan's industrial leagues at the end of the 2002 National Series season.

Four years down the road U.S. fans would not find it quite so as easy to ignore Olympic baseball. The games would this time around be played right in the Americans' own backyard, in a major league stadium and during the middle of summertime baseball season. And the "official" games were also preceded by another intriguing tour by the Cuban national team that seemed guaranteed to peak the interest of those American fans whose passions rarely ran beyond the major

leagues. The Atlanta Olympics would finally focus at least some North American eyes on the marvelous spectacle that quietly masqueraded as international amateur baseball. And these games would also serve to expose the Cuban national team to a far wider audience in the States, where Castro-era Cuban baseball had long remained little more than an occasional rumor.

For the Cubans themselves, however, Atlanta would prove to be a tough proving ground. Sportswriters on the island underscored from time to time the pressures that always surrounded Cuban teams in international competitions. On the eve of the earlier Barcelona Olympiad a *New York Times* reporter had quoted one Cuban journalist as admitted: "It is almost unfair the burden that [our players] are carrying. They are the best in the world and are not expected to lose to anyone." There would again be much pressure for the Castro revolution to shine through its baseball team, especially on a grand stage in the United States. And that proving ground this time would be close to Miami, deep in the American southeast where most of the often hostile North American Cuban exile community resided. There would also presumably be tough competition from the retooled Americans, Japanese and Koreans. And the defection of top pitcher Rolando Arrojo on the eve of the Olympic competition also seemed an ominous sign for the Cuban team, coming as it did before the first pitch was ever thrown.

* * *

American baseball had fallen on exceedingly hard times in the aftermath of the strike-ruined season of 1994 — the second time in little more than a dozen seasons that contract disputes between players and owners had sabotaged a substantial portion of a big-league schedule. Recent summers for the national pastime had seemed more like baseball's winter of discontent. Attendance was down in big league parks from Atlanta to Los Angeles to all points between and beyond; owners and players continued to squabble over slaughtering their sacred cash cow while fan interest waned; pennant races had been turned into wild-card tournaments and ballparks converted to shopping malls and high-tech entertainment complexes; World Series play was no longer as inevitable as the first leaves of autumn (as the 1994 debacle proved) and our onetime idolized diamond heroes vanished somewhere along the line and were seemingly replaced by thin-skinned spoiled brats and ego-driven media celebrities. Beyond the wasteland of big league parks the once teeming sandlots also stood largely empty as American youngsters increasingly turned to video games, rap music, and bouncing basketballs for their leisure-time activities.

And if the news wasn't already bad enough for fans of America's pastime, July 1996 brought another sobering dose of reality arising from Atlanta's Fulton County Stadium in the form of one more laughably easy Gold Medal run for Cuba's "Wonder Team" of seemingly invincible international stars. The Cubans dominated that summer's "Real World Series" (Olympic baseball, after all, is global in more than name alone) with as much pizzazz as they had dominated all such international competitions in the recent past. And for the second straight "official" Olympic baseball festival (medal play was inaugurated in Barcelona four years earlier) Team USA — stocked with highly touted collegiate stars and top big league draft picks like Kris Benson, Mark Kotsey and Jacque Jones — collapsed against Japan in semifinal action. Despite $5 million in training and travel expenses and a crack team that toured together for two summers of intense preparation, coach Skip Bertman's squad simply could not capture must-win games (against Cuba and Japan) once they presented themselves. A bronze medal victory over surprising Nicaragua was the sad consolation for a disappointing USA squad; the sport's self-proclaimed originators had to sit helplessly on the sidelines while Cuba and Japan battled it out before a crowd of 44,221 mostly American spectators for the pride of world baseball domination.

Several lessons seemed to emerge from two exciting weeks of Olympic round robin action in Atlanta's Fulton County Stadium. Foremost was the striking fact that Cuba's juggernaut was apparently far less susceptible to the threats of ballplayer defections, inevitable aging, or improved USA and Japanese talent than had been so widely predicted in months leading up to a second baseball Olympiad. Despite a suspect and often shaky pitching staff anchored by 31-year-old southpaw Omar Ajete (hero of Cuba's Gold Medal romp in Barcelona) and 23-year-old Pedro Luis Lazo (who saved both the 10–8 victory over Team USA and the title game with Japan), the Cubans effectively exploited long-ball hitting (slugging 30 of the 133 homers banged out during 32 games played) and often brilliant infield defense (especially from diminutive 24-year-old shortstop Eduardo Paret) to leave the rest of the field in the dust. On the heels of their 13–9 championship pasting of Japan — sparked by three round trippers from Omar Linares, who demonstrated time and again why he might well be the best third sacker on the planet — Cuba's unbeaten string in international competitions had been run up to an incredible 143 consecutive games. Rey Ordóñez may have fled Castro's communist island for the New York Mets and former star pitchers like Osvaldo Fernández and Liván Hernández might also now be major league properties, but Cuba's diamond dynasty was alive and very well indeed — occasional defections and all.

A second lesson, painful for American boosters, was that the United States simply no longer measured up in international competitions in the very game it has so long boasted as its very own. No whining was needed here about Castro sending professionals: if national heroes like Linares and slugging star Orestes Kindelán received state-support, it was nonetheless likely that they suffered a lifestyle several notches below that of most of our own collegiate ballplayers. And it seemed disingenuous to start screaming about the need for a baseball "Dream Team" composed of Griffey Jr., Bonds, Maddox, Roger Clemens and the like. After all, such a maneuver (which would finally come to fruition a decade later with the MLB World Baseball Classic) was as likely as anything else to put

Heavy-hitting infielder Lázaro Vargas starred on showcase Cuban national teams throughout the 1990s, including gold medal winners at the Barcelona and Atlanta Olympics.

either Puerto Rico or the Dominican Republic squarely at the head of the gold medal chase. The simple fact here was that a nation which once lived, ate and slept the diamond sport ought still to find talent enough on thousands of heartland sandlots to challenge the hand-picked few from Castro's poverty-wracked island of barely 11.5 million inhabitants. That this was no longer the case was clearly the sharpest indicator of the demise of Doubleday's bat-and-ball sport as a genuine American pastime.

There were other stark lessons emerging from Atlanta. One was a realization that the spectacle of big-league-level baseball played with aluminum bats in major league parks is indeed an excitement-packed affair (not at all the sham that traditionalists have long descried) and might in fact be just the antidote needed to rescue a sport that modern fans find too slow-paced and too low-scoring for an era worshipping instant gratification and constant stimulation. Cuban sluggers Linares (8 homers) and Kindelán (9 circuit clouts, including two exceeding 500 feet) opened a rare window on the future and gave rapt bleacherites a momentary preview of what the thrill-a-minute aluminum-charged game might indeed be like once

Nineties-era star Victor Mesa (center, with arms raised) leads a gold medal victory celebration at the 1992 Barcelona Olympics, the first official Olympic baseball tournament.

metal war clubs were put into the hands of the likes of Mark McGwire, Albert Belle, Juan González and Fred McGriff. It was an idle dream, of course, as this was destined to be the final Olympics without pro-style wooden bats. Hemming in the Cuban sluggers, however, would be a different matter.

Finally, baseball as staged by Atlanta's Olympic organizers — replete with eerily silent scoreboards that flashed only lineups and line scores and offered neither rock music nor video blooper-highlights from MLB Productions, nor endless spates of blaring noisome commercials — was indeed once again a source of quiet joy very much in tune with those rhythms that have always moved the summer game. Here was amble evidence that the game itself could still generate sufficient excitement and joy without superfluous trappings a new generation of owners and promoters have tried relentlessly to foist upon today's fans-turned-consumers. One highly exciting rally-filled Cuba–USA game — played on a brilliant Sunday afternoon before a throng of 50,000 fans feeding on nothing but the raw energy of the game itself–could not help but recall for middle-aged fanatics the long-lost spectacle of a Giants-Dodgers slugfest of 1950s. And if there was something unsettling about a constant ping of aluminum lumber, there was nonetheless a clear signal to be found here that at the Olympics, at least, America's greatest game was still alive and well. For those who sat in Fulton County Stadium in the

sunshine of late July rather than the arc-lights of late October (when the Yankees and Braves squared off in MLB's version of a "world series") there was also present something of an unabashed glee in knowing that they themselves — not those corporate high rollers who would arrive three months hence for the big league's now-much-tarnished finale — had indeed stumbled upon baseball's Real World Series.

* * *

Cuba's celebration of an unexpectedly easy Olympic triumph on U.S. turf would not leave room for resting on past laurels. To defend its Olympic title at Sydney in late 2000 Team Cuba would have to earn its way back with a first or second place finish in the qualifying matches staged at the July-August 1999 Pan American Games in Winnipeg, Canada. It wouldn't be an easy task, given the signs of disintegration that were surrounding the Cuban League and the Cuban team by late winter and early spring of 1999, less than three years after the highs of Atlanta. Omar Linares had been injured much of the year and had only reappeared at season's end in time for two gutsy exhibition performances against the Orioles. Kindelán and Pacheco were also aging and also injured. Both Paret and Germán Mesa had lost time to suspension and Michel Enríquez did not yet seem ready to step in as an adequate replacement. The Cuban pitching had also faltered in the past few years in international play, especially in a shocking Intercontinental Cup loss in late-summer 1997 in Spain. Even if Linares and Kindelán were healthy, there was a necessary adjustment to wooden bats now to be made. And professionals Japanese leaguers and minor leaguers appearing on the scene had strengthened all of the top rivals.

The tournament in Winnipeg played out in the end as one of the most exciting weeks of baseball in the long history of international amateur competitions. What happened in July and August 1999 in central Canada merits extensive coverage here, for this tournament above all others appeared to be a major turning point in the recent fortunes of Cuban baseball.

For the moderate-sized collection of MLB scouts, curious local fans, and skeptical press pundits who were all shoehorned into a spanking new Can West Global Park, 1999's Pan Am Games baseball tournament was a week-long orgy of constant surprises, all leading to the most predictable of final results. When the dust cleared on a 5–1 Cuban gold medal conquest of Team USA, the juggernaut Cubans were once more qualifiers for Olympic play, as was universally expected, and the MLB-stocked USA roster had also achieved the vital goal of a Sydney Olympic berth. For Cuba it was a face-saving performance back home that was watched most critically by an entire nation; for the Americans it was still another blow (losing again to Cuba) to national sporting pride on the diamond which went largely unnoticed back home in a country that pays little attention to Olympic sporting spectacles that are not sold as prime-time television fare. But the road that led to such a predictable outcome was full of numerous potholes and a collection of shocking surprises at almost every turn.

The biggest surprise, of course, was the difficult struggle experienced by the heavily-favored Cuban team on its path to yet another international triumph. For a full half-century (starting more than a decade before Castro) the Cubans had dominated world amateur baseball play; the Cuban tally in previous Pan Am Games tourneys alone (before Winnipeg '99) stood at ten gold medals (the last eight uninterrupted) and one silver (1967) in only a dozen tries (the Cubans sat out the 1955 competition in Mexico). Since a 1987 Pan Am preliminary-round loss to Team USA in Indianapolis (before rebounding to win gold) the Cuban juggernaut had lost but a single game (one game!) in senior-level tournament competition (the 1997 Intercontinental Cup finals match with Japan) in over 150 outings! And after demonstrating themselves to be on near-equal footing with major leaguers in two spring exhibitions against the Baltimore Orioles the Cuban national squad again looked to be more than ready to handle a souped-up field of hemisphere rivals in the Winnipeg Olympic-qualifying tournament, despite the promised presence of a bevy of AAA and AA prospects dotting the USA, Canadian, Mexican and Dominican team rosters. Cuba's road to Sydney had been made perhaps only ever-so-slightly easier by an eleventh-hour decision by Venezuela and Puerto Rico to drop from the competition.

Yet in opening-round pool play the vaunted Cubans — perhaps turned complacent by their impressive showing against the Orioles — looked anything like the invincible powerhouse nine whose praises have been so lavishly sung in the past by veteran international baseball watchers. After unimpressive (even lazy) victories over Mexico (5–1) and Brazil (10–1), the Cubans fell flat in their pool play first-week matches against both Canada (an clear-cut 8–1 drubbing) and Team USA (a sloppy 10–5 loss on the strength of a 5-run USA ninth-inning rally). The loss to the Americans was a mild surprise but not an outright shock, since the otherwise close game turned on but one series of late-inning events. Touted 19-year-old prospect Maels Rodríguez blew up in the ninth with two walks, four hits and a gopher ball (to Marcus Jensen); the Cubans crumbled via a single disastrous and thus uncharacteristic frame. Canada, by contrast, dominated the defending champions behind the 3-hit (7 innings) pitching of Steve Green and a 14-hit attack paced by Andy Stewart (3), Todd Betts (2), Jeremy Ware (2), and Troy Fortin (2) — hardly a cluster of top-flight big-league prospects.

Cuban pitching (somewhat suspect as well during the Atlanta Olympics, though more than impressive versus the Orioles) was roundly rocked in these early games by American and Canadian minor league hitters who were clearly a cut above the usual international rosters faced by the overconfident Cubans in past international venues. In Atlanta and Barcelona (1992 Olympics) Cuban pitchers and hitters (especially) could seemingly coast in most games and always count on a single late rally to inevitably turn the tide against inferior opponents.

In Winnipeg it was the legendary Cuban batsmen that were the biggest surprise: proven veteran sluggers slumped badly against talented but nonetheless rather low-profile minor-league moundsmen. Especially disarming were the tentative performances of Orestes Kindelán (Atlanta's home run hero who now hit .188 in four first-week pool-play games without an extra-base rap), Omar Linares (a .400-plus lifetime hitter in international play who stood at .133 after the opening round, with but a single longball blast), Danel Castro (who stroked two triples in Baltimore but was so lackluster in Winnipeg, with one single in nine trips, that he was benched after three games), Yobal Dueñas (1999 Cuban League batting champ who was hitting an even .200 and struggling defensively, as well, while playing out of position in center field) and Robelquis Videaux (1998 Cuban batting champ whose zero for six in the opening two games included three strikeouts).

Was it the wooden bats or just a mystifying slump of the kind which is baseball's regular fare? Or was this a clear indication of just how overrated the Cubans had always been against U.S. collegians and Dominican or Japanese amateur stars? To make matters worse for boosters of the Cuban program, some veteran players like Linares and Kindelán and Mesa (a surprise presence on the Cuban roster) seemed to be doing little more at the plate or in the field than merely going through the motions. Mesa missed ground balls he easily tracked in past seasons and Kindelán on several occasions even failed to run out fly balls or infield grounders off his own slumping bat.

Numerous rumors filled the air and the newspaper press

accounts in Winnipeg concerning the early Cuban slump. There was even one outrageous story making the rounds that top Cuban stars had not been given promised rewards and perks back home in Havana after the victory in Baltimore and were therefore goldbricking rather than hunting gold. There was also speculation that the media circus and constant press taunting about defections was rattling the Cuban delegation. The Cubans themselves were reported in the media to have complained about American player agents and MLB scouts harassing their cloistered ballplayers at the athletes' village.

The real explanations for an early Cuban slump at the plate and on the mound seemed to be obvious enough to Cuban baseball insiders. There was an obvious difficulty in adjusting to wooden bats, which several of the starters (especially batsmen like Gabriel Pierre, Germán Mesa and Isaac Martínez who didn't play in the two-game Orioles series) had never yet used. AAA-packed USA and Canadian rosters were also unquestionably far more talented than past opponents and clearly more motivated than the spoiled big-leaguers wearing Baltimore uniforms. But a crucial overlooked fact was the reality that the Cuban season had now been over for three months and the Cuban players were essentially in their first week of spring training. Not having played a pre-tournament exhibition schedule (Team USA held a half-dozen such exhibitions in both Arizona and Winnipeg) had definitely put the Cuban players behind the eight ball against seasoned (if still young) minor league professionals all competing in mid-season form and midseason groove.

USA and Canadian rosters, along with the crack Dominican lineup, were much tougher than similar batting orders thrown at the Cubans in past Olympics or in an assortment of other international tournaments. Team USA in Atlanta during the summer of 1996 had been a mere collection of untested if talented college stars. Despite some promising young pitchers (Kris Benson and Jim Parque were soon both card-carrying big league starters), that outfit was not a pressure-tested or representative USA team.

The roster trucked to Winnipeg by former big-league manager Buddy Bell and supervised as well by MLB overseers Pat Gillick and Bob Watson was a far more potent and better-drilled contingent. And these players were now coming straight from the minor league wars in mid-season fitness. The USA team had preciously little power, but it did boast raw speed and defense. Shawn Gilbert (Mets and Dodgers), Jon Zuber (Phillies) and Craig Paquette (New York Mets) were already big league veterans. There were legitimate prospects in Milton Bradley (an acrobatic outfielder prepping for the Montreal Expos at AA Harrisburg), swift infielder Adam Kennedy (AAA Memphis) and speedy fly chaser Dave Roberts (AAA Buffalo). All would soon be major league fixtures. And the pitching was especially potent and deep with righties John Patterson (AA El Paso), Brad Penny (AA Portland), Derek Wallace (AAA Norfolk), Dan Wheeler (AAA Durham), and Todd Williams (AAA Indianapolis), plus Tampa Bay Devil Rays crack southpaw prospect Bobby Seay and fellow lefties Mark Mulder

(AAA Vancouver) and Puerto Rican team refugee J.C. Romero (AA New Britain).

The Canadians could also boast their share of big-leaguers in waiting. Lee Delfino was a promising college prospect (East Carolina) plucked in the fifth round of the 1998 draft by the Toronto Blue Jays but never signed. Andy Stewart (a defensive backstop with AAA and AA experience in Reading and Omaha), Troy Fortin (another catcher training with the independent Northern League's hometown Winnipeg Goldeyes and thus a local crowd favorite) and Seattle Mariner outfielder Ryan Radmanovich (at the time slugging at a .289 clip with AAA Tacoma) all carried lofty credentials. And then there were the Dominicans with potential MLB stars of the future like rangy shortstop Pablo Ozuna and long-legged outfielder Israel Alcantara.

The Cubans, in turn, presented a lineup that trumpeted international experience and was largely a duplication of the roster that had twice faced Baltimore earlier in the spring, but there were also a few mild surprises. One unanticipated entry was legendary shortstop Germán Mesa (often compared in Cuba with Ozzie Smith) who had recently returned from two-year suspension and was previously reported to be still barred from any international travel. Mesa's presence alone suggested the seriousness of Cuba's approach to this Olympic-qualifier tournament. Additional eye-openers on the Cuban roster were a trio of young pitchers — Ciro Silvino Licea, Maels Rodríguez and Danys Báez — none of whom had taken part in the history-making Orioles series. Rodríguez possessed blazing speed (he threw in the mid-90s with outstanding movement) and was considered the country's hottest prospect — at least back in Cuba. Lanky righty Silvino Licea owned the most impressive arm seen by this author in recent winters on the Cuban circuit. And untested Báez impressed scouts in his one brief Winnipeg outing, though he was buried in the Pinar del Río rotation back home, as number four starter on one of the top CL teams.

A particularly sour note arose from the Canada-Cuba vital semifinal match. An event that had remained largely free of politics (despite stirring of the waters by a Canadian press that wrote ceaselessly about groundless defection rumors) suddenly took a turn toward the bizarre when an anti–Castro protester ran onto the field just before the game's final out. It was an unfortunate repeat of the similar scene in Camden Yards months earlier, with the same individual protester reportedly evolved. The embarrassing moment nearly disrupted a crucial game and almost unsettled the Cubans at a most telling juncture — with an Olympic qualifying spot hanging in the balance and one vital final out still unsecured. When the protester made a threatening move toward pitcher José Ibar, Cuba's bench rushed onto the field and pummeled the hapless intruder. A shaken Ibar was quickly removed from the scene with the Canadians still threatening in the top of the ninth of a one-run game. But in most heroic style, dependable bullpen stopper Pedro Lazo rushed to the mound and saved the day for the embattled Cubans with two swift final strikeouts.

Cuba's performance on the last three days was enough to

Atlanta Olympics hero Orestes Kindelán (Cuban League all-time home run king) is greeted at home plate by Antonio Pacheco (Cuba's career hits leader) and Omar Linares (Cuban League lifetime batting champion) after one of his tournament-leading nine round-trippers (courtesy Transcendental Graphics).

turn the heads of even the most hardened skeptics. Facing a do-or-die scenario against a talented Dominican team on Saturday morning in the quarterfinals, the embarrassed but seemingly unshaken Cubans got just enough pitching out of ace José Contreras to survive for the important semifinal match. There were questions and speculations around why Cuban manager Alfonso Urquiola had started his best live arm against the Dominicans with Canadian and U.S. challengers still on the horizon. But this was after all the most crucial game at the moment: only a berth in the gold medal finals would clinch a coveted spot in the Sydney Olympics. Cuba had already put itself in a bad spot, and the Dominicans had not helped matters much when they stumbled against Nicaragua on the final night of pool play and thus slipped into the final playoff spot against the defending champions.

The tournament's most celebrated contest was the Cuba-Canada semifinal match-up. Few, after all, expected the USA to fail against Mexico in the other Olympic-qualifying semifinal. The drama and storyline of the first semifinal match, however, was packed with almost unbearable tensions. Cuba

needed a win to salvage prestige abroad and save face at home. The careers of team management (bench boss Urquiola and commissioner Carlos Rodríguez, in particular) were squarely on the line, as were renewed national team appointments for many veterans. Commander Fidel and the nation at large were watching every pitch back home. The embattled Cubans had been forced to use Norge Vera in this mean-everything game and Vera had been untested in his single outing against Brazil. Vera had admittedly shone well against the Orioles in Baltimore but to date had never handled a big tournament assignment. And Vera was shaky in the early going, giving up an early lead by yielding single runs in the second and third frames. In the end Linares saved the day with a single clutch blow in the bottom of third, when he laced a grooved fastball from single-A starter Mike Meyers over the left field fence. And brilliant relief performances by Ibar and Lazo also saved face for Cuba.

A surreal experience for this author occurred in the moments leading up to the gold medal showdown game between Cuba and Team USA. Owner of a press pass that permitted access to the photographers well alongside the dugouts but not to the playing field, I had taken up a position alongside the Cuban dugout an hour before game time with hopes of exchanging a brief greeting with Cuban League commissioner Carlitos Rodríguez, head of the Cuban delegation and a long-time personal acquaintance. When the Cuban team arrived and Carlitos emerged on the field he immediately spotted me and signaled that he would approach the restricted area to converse after his team had begun batting practice. When Rodríguez and I did take up our brief conversation moments later we were interrupted by a ringing on the commissioner's cell phone. His expression turned a bit somber and he excused himself and retreated to the dugout steps, out of my hearing range, engaging in a brief one-sided conversation to which he contributed little beyond head nods. I would later learn, as I expected at the time, that this call was from the top team manager — Commandante Fidel Castro himself — who was checking with his top lieutenant to offer final instructions regarding the team batting order. It was direct and firsthand confirmation for me that all the stories were indeed true about how Cuba's commander and chief does indeed continue to micro-manage even the minutest details of Cuban baseball.

The finale seemed to a foregone conclusion from the start, although team USA stayed close for awhile. But it was now Kindelán's turn to come to life in huge measure with two rocket homers that provided sufficient margin for victory. A longtime national team backup third sacker to Linares, Gabriel Pierre, also blasted his second homer of the week to provide a measure of insurance. And Contreras — even on one day's rest — had AAA and AA USA hitters completely overmatched from the start, fanning a baker's dozen, walking but a pair, and allowing only a single tally in eight dominating frames. Canada salvaged some local pride by taking the anticlimactic earlier game from Mexico for bronze medal honors.

A dozen or so ballplayers in particular seemed to stand above the crowd when the ledger finally closed on a week of entertaining hemisphere diamond clashes. These were the stars that had written their names yet again in the pages of international baseball legend and lore. Omar Linares and Orestes Kindelán were once more the slugging heroes when national pride and Olympic gold was squarely on the line. Both struggled throughout the tournament and writers and scouts seeing them for the first time scratched their heads about the seemingly overblown reputations of the two touted Cuban batsmen. Linares, especially, seemed only a shadow of his reported stature, now facing healthier arms and armed himself with wood rather than aluminum. But before the week was out the Cuban hero justified his lofty reputation with a single crushing blow (a line-drive semifinal homer that produced the night's only three runs for the winners) that saved Cuba's international reputation and salvaged its anticipated spot in Sydney. Linares always seemed somehow to come through in do-or-die clutch situations, as he had done so often in big-pressure international tournaments, and as he did in both exhibition tussles with the Baltimore Orioles.

Kindelán authored a similar last-minute heroic performance to obliterate his week of tame hitting and generally lackluster performance. Kindelán was the hero of the gold medal night with two crushing blasts, the second a 425-foot sixth-inning opposite-field shot that iced a gold medal victory. Throughout the week the hefty first baseman had been more than mortal as he failed repeatedly with runners on base and his team desperately needing clutch hits. But in the end it was long-ball business as usual for both of Cuba's biggest slugging stars.

But it was clearly pitching and not slugging that saved Cuba in the end, and the true tournament MVPs were a trio of outstanding right arms that had pro scouts drooling throughout the medal round. José Contreras authored a marvelous performance that surpassed and also punctuated his long relief outing against the Orioles in Havana. His 13-strikeout effort in the finale versus Team USA would have been brilliant enough out of context; but given the fact that it was performed on but one day's rest provided the highlight moment of the week. Pedro Luis Lazo (a legitimate Lee Smith clone) took up where he had left off in Atlanta, relieving in several crucial situations and slamming the door on the Canadians in what was arguably Cuba's biggest international win of recent memory. And veteran José Ibar was perhaps the most impressive of the Cuban tandem. Hard-throwing Ibar had been almost unbeatable across two recent Cuban League seasons. It was thus fitting and not surprising that his winning bullpen performance in the huge semifinal contest (5.1 innings, 2 hits, 5 strikeouts, 0 runs) was ultimately the one that put Cuba squarely back in the Olympic gold medal hunt for Sydney.

And there were other lesser heroes. Isaac Martínez (.391 BA, one round-tripper) and Gabriel Pierre (.286 BA, two dingers) surprised by swinging potent bats in the early going while Linares and Kindelán struggled. Thirty-year-old veteran Luis Ulacia (.308 BA) once more proved a thorny competitor with timely lead-off hitting when given his usual spot in the Cuban lineup as the team's veteran leader. But scouts buzzed most over the vaporizing live fastball of 19-year-old prodigy Maels Rodríguez, and one favored pastime among fans and media types was speculating on Rodríguez's potential market value on the current big-league scene. And Danys Báez (the single Cuban ballplayer to seek political asylum) was the eventual darling of a Canadian press that seemed much more enamored with potential headlines about defection than with the impressive athletic saga unfolding with each day's stellar diamond play.

In the end the thrill-packed Winnipeg tournament demonstrated just how far international baseball had come during the recent decade. There was of course a huge assist here from major league baseball, with its decision to provide seasoned professionals to enliven competitions, challenge the Cuban juggernaut, and balance out the playing field against Fidel Castro's always-loaded quasi-amateurs. The beauty of this tournament was precisely the balance struck between minor league talent and the non-commercial spirit of true Olympic-style play. The stage had now been set for an exciting showdown between the Americans and Cubans around the corner in Sydney. Yet for all the freshness of what transpired in Winnipeg a dark cloud now hovered ominously in the background. This cloud assumed the form of renewed efforts among major league baseball officials to seize control — and thus also to alter directions — of international versions of the "American" sport by sponsoring a revenue-producing (read here "television-friendly") world-cup-style event as immediate replacement for the current Olympic baseball scene. It would take a half-dozen more years before the scheme turned into the World Baseball Classic. But as activities shut down in Winnipeg it was already a topic of lively discussion.

It is not so much the latent desire to "win against the Cubans at any cost" that seems troublesome about major league baseball's threats to seize the reins of international baseball. It is instead the prospect of losing forever that delightful small-scale ambiance and flag-waving enthusiasm which surrounded the Winnipeg tournament and which will certainly be the first casualty of a perhaps inevitable exchange for a high-profile, commercial-drenched "made for television" spectacle which big-league executives were now already conjuring up in their own image.

* * *

Last-gasp gold medal victory in Winnipeg was both an apex and a turning point for Cuban baseball under the 40-year-old revolutionary regime. On the heals of a resounding triumph against the poorly motivated big-league Orioles, the Fidel Castro's national team had further proven their merit against crack professional minor leaguers in Winnipeg's Olympic-qualifying Pan American Games showdown. A major hurdle had thus been cleared and the Cubans would now indeed be able to defend their Olympic crown in Sydney at the outset of a new century.

There were also, however, signs of dangerous transition to be found everywhere in the Cuban baseball program. The vaunted national all-stars were now confronting seasoned professionals and not collegiate amateurs at each and every international outing. They were now also using wooden bats for the first time in a quarter-century and thus entering a level playing field with North American professionals. And old standbys on the national team roster were suddenly also giving way to a clear-cut youth movement of somewhat major proportions.

The first signs of that youth movement had already been displayed in Winnipeg with the appearance of pitchers like 19-year-old flamethrower Maels (pronounced as "Miles") Rodríguez and 23-year-old control artist Ciro Silvino Licea. But it had nonetheless been the veterans who bailed the team out against other nations' seasoned pros. It was José Contreras and Ibar and Lazo who had been the medal-round saviors, with a boost from the standby bats of Linares (game-winning homer in the semifinals with Canada) and Kindelán (two vital circuit blasts during the gold medal showdown with the arch-rival Americans). Youth did seem poised to take their long-awaited turn, however, especially when Maels Rodríguez and not Lazo or Ibar closed out the gold medal victory against the talented USA minor leaguers.

Jorge Fuentes managed Cuban gold medal champions at both the Barcelona (1992) and Atlanta (1996) Olympic Games.

Dramatic changes continued throughout late summer months preceding a new Cuban League season — one which would mark the 39th National Series since amateurs replaced pros on the heals of Fidel's revolution. The Cubans had taken their lumps in the opening rounds of Pan Am competition in Winnipeg and Linares and Kindelán had struggled mightily with the new lumber that had replaced aluminum war clubs. Young stars like Dueñas, Videaux and Danel Castro were a major disappointment and the most promising young pitchers like Maels Rodríguez and Ciro Silvino Licea also struggled against more seasoned pro hitters from Canada and the USA. More recently a second-level national team that journeyed to Panama in October had suffered even greater embarrassment in the form of three straight one-sided losses.

And there was still some international baseball to be played before the onset of Y2K and those games would prove to be crammed with surprises of an even higher order. A 1999 Intercontinental Cup tournament scheduled for Sydney was, for the host-nation Australians, a rare chance to showcase readiness (both on and off the field) for the now fast-approaching Olympics. For more traditional baseball powerhouses like Cuba, the United States, Japan and Korea, however, this tournament didn't seem to merit much serious preparation. At least not to judge from several of the teams that were sent to Sydney in November. The disinterested Americans compiled a roster of independent leaguers, a full-circle retreat from the AAA team put on the field in Winnipeg. And Cuba pulled a major surprise by entering a squad missing almost all the familiar stars of the past decade.

Cuban fans were obviously unsettled by losses to the USA and Canada in Winnipeg and to Panama and Nicaragua later in the year. They had to be even more startled by the lineup announced in early November for a national team picked for travel to Sydney and for recapturing the Intercontinental Cup lost two years earlier to Japan in Barcelona. For the first time in a decade and a half Omar Linares would not be the anchor of a ballclub representing the island's honor. But Linares was not the only veteran star left home. Kindelán and Mesa and Padilla would not play in Sydney either, and the pitching contingent would feature names like Faustino Corrales and Ciro Silvino Licea but would be missing standbys Ibar, Contreras and Lazo. And the team manager would be Granma's inexperienced Carlos Martí and not Pinar del Río's Winnipeg-tested Alfonso Urquiola as universally expected.

The Cuban roster was a huge bow to untested youth. It stood out more for the faces (like Linares, Kindelán, Pacheco and Ibar) that were absent than for those present. Some roster names were representative of the country's best or nearbest, especially Dueñas, Castro, Pestano and Isaac Martínez. But novice youngsters were now being given the chance to wear the national colors, especially on the mound. Was this for purposes of seasoning youth for the 2000 Olympic Games? Were there other more hidden motives? Were some rookies placed on the team to keep them in the country and in the league? (A decade earlier Rey Ordóñez had skipped out on the national team largely because his path to a starting roster spot was blocked by Germán Mesa.) It is easy to speculate about numerous competing scenarios. But even if names on this team were mystifying to non–Cubans, this was still a powerhouse Cuban League team. And this was also a roster dotted with top prospects like Yobal Dueñas (a recent .400 hitter), Isaac Martínez (a timely slugger in Winnipeg) and Gabriel Pierre Lazo (preferred back home by some *fanáticos* as a better all-around hot-corner prospect than Linares).

An opening loss by the narrowest of margins may have sparked immediate second-guessing of the Cuban youth movement both at home and abroad. The opener with South Korea was frittered away on late inning defensive lapses after the Cubans had held a 3–1 advantage in the eighth frame behind ace Ciro Silvino Licea. But as the week unfolded the Cubans looked as strong as ever with five straight victories, including a two-hitter by veteran southpaw Faustino Corrales versus Taiwan, and a 4–1 pasting of defending champion Japan (upset winners over the Cubans during the 1997 gold medal match in Spain). The faces may thus have been somewhat different, but not the results. Meanwhile Australia proved a strong entrant by winning five of six, including a 12–2 pounding of the American team featuring a hodge-podge of independent leaguers. Team USA also posted a pair of impressive

victories over The Netherlands (with minor league mound ace Rob Cordemans) and Japan, despite an unrepresentative team that was patchwork at best.

The Cubans did fall again against Australia at the end of pool-play round matches, but this seemed at the time to be a game which the islanders blew off as largely unimportant. The Cuban lineup featured several players who had not yet seen action in the week-long round robin. But the game did hold some significance since it represented the first victory over Cuba in major tournament play by any team other than one representing the USA, Japan, Korea or Canada. The USA squad also had to struggle on the final day of pool-round play in order to qualify for medal round action. The Americans avoided another international embarrassment by edging Taiwan 5–2 on the strength of solid 5-hit, 8-inning hurling by Milwaukee farmhand Steve Faltesiek.

The highlight of the tournament for Cuba and the lowlight for Team USA obviously came with the 7–0 Cuban whitewashing of the Americans in the Saturday semifinal match-up. The issue was never in doubt as the Cuban arms (of starter Silvino Licea and two relievers) and bats (Michel Enríquez and Oscar Macías) completely took over in middleinning action. The game was in the end an international coming-out ceremony for the highly touted Ciro Silvino Licea, one of the finest among many young arms on the island. Silvino Licea was also now redeemed against the USA bats for a rather lackluster performance at Winnipeg earlier in the summer (where he hurled 4-plus innings, posted a gigantic 12.46 ERA, and blew up in early innings of an opening-round outing with host Canada). Australia overtook Japan 2–0 in the other semifinal, a game which assured that an expected rematch of the 1997 Barcelona finalists would not now be in the offering. The finals proved a spirited ballgame, one in which the Cuban youth brigade was not quite up to a hoped-for championship rebound effort. A late outfield error by young Industriales standout Yasser Gómez proved fatal during an extra-inning 4–3 loss to the host Australian club stacked with pros and paced by Milwaukee Brewers catcher Dave Nilsson, whose overall 11 RBI and timely slugging earned tournament MVP accolades.

For the second straight time Cuba had slumped in the Intercontinental Cup final round, with this year's loss echoing the gold medal rout by Japan in Barcelona two summers earlier. And for only the second time in more than two decades Cuba failed to carry home a gold medal in a major international tournament. The Australian upset victory provided a major boost for the sport in the country that was now poised to host the following summer's gala Olympic contests against what would assuredly be strengthened U.S. and Cuban contingents. Cuba perhaps had not seemed to take the off-year cup play all that seriously; nor had the USA whose slapped-together lineup did not even score a single run in either of its crucial medal-round games. But one nonetheless had to speculate about the possible repercussions of this loss back home in Cuba — especially for those young players and a new team manager (Carlos Martí) who had been entrusted with defending the national honor and had failed to deliver. A similar slip in Barcelona in 1997 had, after all, spelled a career end for both team manager Jorge Fuentes and also the league commissioner and much of his staff.

* * *

It stretches the most fertile imagination that Harry Wright's legendary 1869 Cincinnati Red Stockings could have won nearly a hundred games without a single defeat during the sport's infant years. It boggles the mind still more that Cuba's modern-era national team between 1987 and 1997 captured double that many within the more pressure-packed settings of increasingly competitive world amateur baseball competition.

Cuban teams have dominated international competitions from the earliest Castro years, racking up a long string of world senior and junior titles across the '60s and '70s and then turning heads with an undefeated exhibition tour against Mexican AAA pro teams in 1978. But it has been particularly in the years following a dramatic comeback gold medal victory at the 1987 Pan American Games in Indianapolis that the present-day Cuban juggernaut has written a story of nearly unimaginable diamond successes. With a one-time string of 149 straight single-game victories in tournament play, back-to-back undefeated gold medal sweeps in Barcelona and Atlanta, a current string of nine straight World Cup titles stretching back across a quarter-century, appearances in the championship game of what is now a string of 38 straight major tournaments, and a seemingly endless supply of stars (Omar Linares foremost among them and Yulieski Gourriel and Osmani Urrutia the latest exemplars) boasting big-league credentials, Cuban baseball has perhaps now reached its proudest hour in the afterglow of the March 2006 inaugural World Baseball Classic.

It was especially the decade of the 1990s that set the tone for this remarkable winning streak. The string that began in Indianapolis in 1987 had finally run out in 1997 in Barcelona. There, Cuba's defending Gold Medal Olympic squad would finally feel the sting of defeat against a talented and revenge-minded Japanese ball club that was filled with hardened returnees. This was largely the same Japanese squad that had lost to essentially the same Cuban roster in the Olympic finals in Atlanta's Fulton County Stadium only twelve months earlier. The Cubans played well enough to win as usual, at least until they reached the gold medal showdown. Early games brought the accustomed one-sided breathers: 14–0 and 15–0 over soft France and Spain, and closer but never very tense matches with the USA (4–1) and Japan (7–3). But against the Japanese a second time around the tables were suddenly turned. Several rocky innings at the start put Cuba in an early hole from which even seasoned veterans could not recover; Kohji Uehara (destined to be a star nine years later in the first World Baseball Classic) proved unhittable once the Nippon outfit built a comfortable lead. This was a Cuban team, after all, due to lose at some point, to someone; nobody wins forever in baseball. But for the fans and officials back home the loss would be taken hard and there would obviously be shakeups after Barcelona throughout the Cuban baseball hierarchy.

There were soon further defeats to be absorbed, as the rest of the world slowly caught up with the Cuban juggernaut. The introduction of professional players representing other nations changed the playing field after Atlanta. The 1999 Pan American tournament in Winnipeg, which doubled as an Olympic qualifier for Sydney, demonstrated that the Cubans might still win with their edge in talent and experience, but it would not be quite so easy as before. In the Intercontinental Cup in Sydney only three months after Winnipeg the Cubans would again blow a gold medal game with an uncharacteristic letdown in the final frames. This time the loss was to an even less potent opponent and certainly one with spotty international credentials. The host Australians caught the Cubans on another bad day, but were nevertheless still fortunate to win, thanks to a rare defensive lapse (a dropped fly ball in the eleventh). It could be claimed as at least a partial excuse that this edition of the Cuban national team was hardly up to the standards of recent tournaments. Old standbys like Linares and Kindelán and Germán Mesa were not on hand in the fall of 1999 in Sydney to do battle with an ever-improving collection of rivals. But the Cubans should have won anyway since their pitching rotation of Maels Rodríguez, Faustino Corrales, Carlos Yanes and Ciro Silvino Licea approximated a major league staff. The armor was apparently chipped and cracking.

Ironically, such increasing vulnerability on the world amateur stage came at the very time when Cuban League baseball rose to unexpected prominence on the U.S. scene due mainly to a pair of landmark exhibitions with the major league Baltimore Orioles. The 12–6 laugher which fell Cuba's way in Baltimore might well have been Fidel's greatest single propaganda victory in decades. Perhaps the Orioles were only going through the motions after their hard-fought earlier win in Havana. (The U.S. press was not entirely unjustified in underscoring the disdain of Baltimore players for an early-season exhibition scheduled on what was originally a rare day off from competition.) But beating a major league team in its own stadium certainly now seriously undercut any argument that the vaunted Cubans always won because they played only wet-behind-the-ear amateurs.

Yet the Baltimore triumph at the time may also have seemed like temporary refuge in the midst of a brewing storm front. The biggest blow to Cuban pride would be reserved for a second showdown in Sydney, this one in the first year of the new millennium. Cuba entered the September 2000 defense of its Atlanta Olympic crown with numerous questions surrounding a veteran national team that struggled in Winnipeg, peaked in Baltimore, rested at home while second-liners squandered the 1999 Intercontinental Cup, and now hardly seemed any longer invincible. These doubts persisted despite a respectable showing the previous year against major leaguers and a strong last-ditch effort against pros in the Pan American competitions a few months later. The defending champs from Atlanta, with the heart of their squad intact, had to be considered the odds-on favorite in Sydney. But a strong chal-

An enthusiastic Cuban crowd packs Havana's Estadio Latinoamericano during October 2003 World Cup tournament action.

lenge was expected from an improved USA team, now coached by Hall-of-Fame manager Tommy Lasorda. The Japanese and Koreans would also be sending their pros and the Japanese had trounced the Americans and scared the Cubans in the medal round in Atlanta. And even Australia appeared ready to become a major player after their surprising victory a year earlier on this same field in Sydney.

The seriousness of the Sydney challenge was to be met by a Cuba team stacked with a mix of seasoned veteran stars and promising prospects. Linares, Pacheco and Kindelán were again in the lineup and Contreras and Norge Vera would anchor the pitching corps. But novices like Yasser Gómez, Yobal Dueñas and Ariel Pestano would now be counted on to play major roles despite slim international experience. Perhaps there were fears of defections that seemingly led to selection of players based more on proven trustworthiness than raw talent alone, but this was likely a factor overplayed in the defection-enamored American press. The Cuban roster hardly seemed shaped by a fear of defection with promising youngsters like

Gómez and Pestano in the mix, though it was true that 20-year-old National Series batting champion Yorelvis Charles and emerging prospect Osmani Urrutia were left behind in favor of such veterans as Luis Ulacia and Gabriel Pierre. The much larger fear than potential escapees had to be the improved professional pitching staffs of most top rival teams.

The first week of preliminaries in Sydney brought immediate shockwaves in the form of one of the biggest upsets of recent amateur baseball history. It came in the form of a Dutch victory over a stunned Cuban club earned on the strength of a single four-run inning and a stretch of strong pitching by an unheralded former U.S. pro hurler, Rob Cordemans. The loss to the unimposing Dutch spawned a reaction of absolute shock for fans back in Havana, as did the team's scramble for runs in less-than-impressive wins against Australia (1–0), Japan (6–2) and Korea (6–5). Such a loss and such offensive woes (Kindelán and Linares were both demonstrating considerable dips in bat speed) did not bode well for any chance to reclaim the gold medal. The 4–2 shocker with Holland also represented the first time the Cubans had ever lost a single Olympic ball game, let alone a full tournament.

Such a rude upset at the hands of the unheralded Dutch squad also brought immediate and predictable assumptions in the American press that the seemingly endless stretch of glory days for Castro's baseballers were suddenly a thing of the past. Tom Dodd of *USA Today* was quick to declare the Americans the clear-cut favorites for gold, even if the USA team had itself only escaped by gifts and miracles in several of its own first round outings. But the Cuban ship would be quickly righted when José Contreras again proved the stopper with a shutout masterpiece against Australia. And then José Ibar mastered the Americans in a game which could only suggest that U.S. minor leaguers were still no match for the seasoned Cuban mound corps. The 6–1 victory was shown on tape delay back in the States and the final three innings were dropped with the Cubans safely ahead. American viewers (however few there might have been for the early morning broadcast) never got to see a sixth-inning outfield grab by Yasser Gómez that was one of the most remarkable defensive gems in amateur baseball annals.

The medal round would now feature precisely the four teams everyone thought would eventually be there. In a rematch with Japan the Cubans breezed again behind Contreras. And the Americans were again able to pull a miracle out of a hat against South Korea, in a virtual repeat of the thriller played by the same two teams in the preliminaries. By pitching Contreras in the semifinal match, however, manager Servio Borges had taken a huge calculated risk. Perhaps Ibar would now have to face seasoned American pros that were seeing him for the second time in five days. Or Pedro Lazo would have to assume the role of a starter, a role he has not normally maintained for the national team in international play. In the end it proved to be the latter scenario which would seal the fate of the defending champions. Using up top ace Contreras in the semifinals was a move that would be long second-guessed by fans back in Havana. It would also be a move destined to end the illustrious career of Borges as national team manager.

The luck and the clutch performances that had so long accompanied the Cuban national team all ran dry in the showcase gold medal game. This time around it would be the American pitching that would have the upper hand from the opening inning. Ben Sheets of the Milwaukee Brewers proved too tough for the usually hard-hitting Cubans as he dominated the action in Homebush Stadium with a 103-pitch complete game in which he struck out five, walked only one, and allowed but three tame safeties. Sheets threw the game of his lifetime in blanking the arch-rival Cubans, and he was still reaching 96 mph with his sizzling fastball late in the one-sided contest. It was the first time in several decades that Team USA was able to beat Cuba when it really counted; the Americans had lost 25 of the last 28 tournament matches between the two intense rivals. Lazo and Ibar, in relief, both pitched well, but with the Cubans not scoring a single run or mustering a single offensive threat it was all for naught. For the third time in two years the Cuban juggernaut had surprisingly run out of gas in the most important game of all.

There are numerous ways to assess the surprising Cuban loss in the final-round Sydney showdown with the Americans. Perhaps the most reasonable is to suggest that this was nothing more than a normal baseball development. Even the top teams in this sport don't go on winning forever and winning at even a sixty percent rate is usually the mark of a champion. Time and circumstance as much as anything else was on the side of Team USA which had beaten the perennial champions only once, during the 1999 Pan American Games, over the past thirteen years and two dozen meetings. There are inevitably also those who will argue that this Sydney game was more than just a case of baseball luck. This group will make the strong case that the leveling of the playing field by pro baseballers has now suggested once more that earlier Cuban domination was more than anything a matter of inferior opposition, especially from the USA and its college-staffed Pan American and Olympic squads of 1992 and 1996.

It is hard not to speculate that the Sydney Olympic loss — like those in Intercontinental Cup action at Barcelona in 1997 and again Sydney in 1999 — was indeed a strong indication that Cuba's baseball machinery was now finally coming apart at the hinges. Milton Jamail had written extensively about the crisis of recent Cuban baseball and I take up Jamail's assessments here in my final chapter below. Jamail's view seems to be that the current Cuban system of treating ballplayers as state servants could only have disastrous consequences somewhere down the road. That the Sydney games were any true indication of a full-scale Cuban collapse would have seemed a more reasonable reading of the situation, of course, had the squad headed by veterans Linares, Kindelán and Pacheco been shut out of the medal round altogether, beaten perhaps by the Japanese or Koreans, or even defeated more than twice in the nine contests they played. Except for one uncharacteristic loss to the Dutch in a meaningless opening round face-off, the Cubans instead had seemed every bit as strong as ever, despite the improved opposition they were facing. It is likely more proper to assume that the rivalry between the world's two great baseball countries has simply now tightened up a bit and thus awaited another showdown round to prove actual superiority.

The question remained, however, about the degree of negative fallout the gold medal loss in Sydney might have on the baseball scene back on the island. A 1997 humiliation in Barcelona brought a major overhaul in league structure and national team coaching personnel. Perhaps another such overreaction by INDER officials would now be in the immediate offering. It wasn't long before at least one change was indeed made, with Santiago manager Higinio Vélez hastily installed as new field boss in yet another shift of national team managers. But the rest of the baseball administration outside of deposed head coach Servio Borges hung on to their jobs, however tenuously. The determination merely to regroup seemingly outweighed any possible panic in the Cuban baseball camp.

The fallout from Sydney had to be mitigated to at least some degree by the results unfolded in Taiwan fourteen months later. Not only did Cuba's national team under Vélez

The Cuban team celebrates their October 2003 World Cup championship moments after the final out of the deciding game with Panama. Norge Vera (center, number 20) gained the pitching victories in both the semifinal and final matches.

rebound and recoup much of its lost prestige during the 34th World Cup Championships of November 2001, but the veteran Cuban team did so with the same kind of gutsy style exhibited in Winnipeg three years earlier. The showdown matches in Taipei were again with the two foremost rivals — Japan and the defending Olympic champion Americans. It was noteworthy that this time around the Japanese presented a demonstrably stronger roster than the one they had brought to Sydney, whereas the American squad was clearly not up to the high standards set by the one managed in Australia by hall of famer Tom Lasorda. But even if the American team had slipped a notch, nonetheless the Cuban back-to-the-wall performance in the championship round was impressive for the third straight time against teams made up largely of professionals from the Japanese leagues and experienced minor leaguers from the deep wells of organized baseball.

The victory over Japan was the showcase event of the tournament. Again the Cubans elected to rely on José Contreras to get them to the finals, and again they were not to be disappointed by the stellar performance of their ace stopper.

Contreras once again came up with a true championship caliber outing under the extreme pressures of high expectations back home in Havana. The masterpiece Contreras unleashed against Japan was of the same quality as his playoff-round performances in Winnipeg and Sydney, this time an extra-inning complete game won in the top of the eleventh on key hits by Linares and Yobal Dueñas. Contreras permitted a single run in the opening frame when future White Sox big leaguer Tadahito Iguchi singled through a drawn-in infield with two outs. The hard-throwing Cuban right-hander had now run his international record to an amazing 13 victories without a single defeat. And four of those wins had been under the most extreme circumstances imaginable, all coming in semi-final matches that held the keys to expected appearances in gold medal final games.

The resulting rematch with the USA team — the gold medal again hanging on the outcome — once more saw José Ibar take the mound with all the marbles on the line. Ibar was not as sharp against the American pros as he had once been in the preliminary round in Sydney. But the USA had no Ben

Sheets this time around, either, and the Cubans had their hitting shoes on as they had so many times in the past. In the end it was veteran Germán Mesa — known mainly for his stellar defense — who delivered the decisive victory-producing base hit, a single to right in the eighth that plated the two deciding tallies. But the game turned primarily on a surprising top-notch bullpen performance from an altogether unanticipated source. Camagüey's largely untested Vicyohandri Odelín endured a baptism by fire with four stellar innings of shutout relief that in the end saved the day.

Whatever the fallout from the 2000 Olympic loss in Sydney (and no matter how much chest-thumping there might be in the USA about shutting down Cuban dominance after the Ben Sheets performance), one fact remained indelible. In the overall series of head-to-head meetings in major international tournament competitions during the past two decades, the record now stood 25–3 (in individual games) in favor of the Cubans. The issue of Cuba's dominance on the world amateur stage was still quite indisputable. And that dominance was now once more being demonstrated with the first international competitions of the new millennium. It was perhaps a Cuban national team with its backs to the wall and many doubts hanging over its head that had showed up in Taipei for the thirty-fourth renewal of the once-amateur world championships. But by the time the dust had settled the impressive Cubans had not only dusted off their armor and repaired their sagging image, but they had gained some sweet revenge in the process.

It was again Cuban pitching that proved the difference against insufficient opposition in Taipei. But hefty hitting from some familiar veterans would also play a key role in another impressive Cuban international triumph. Luis Ulacia was the tournament's surprise hero with a remarkable performance at the plate, where he pounded the ball at better than a .500 clip. This was a marvelous swan song outing for one of the most durable and dependable national team performers of the past decade. But there were other heroes as well during the steam-roller-like ride over the world's best mixture of amateur and professional challengers. Odelín was the biggest surprise, perhaps, since he was at the time only emerging as a regular in the Camagüey rotation during National Series matches. But for all the continued luster there was also a good deal of sadness for fans back home in the aftermath of this impressive victory. For it was certain that this was the final time the national team would boast a lineup of Linares, Kindelán, Germán Mesa, Pacheco and Ulacia. Like so many times in the past, the old guard of the nineties was now about to be replaced by the emerging stars of the future.

Cuba's rather easy victory in Taipei had seemed to set things right again back home in Havana. There seemed a greater likelihood now of long-accustomed stability returning to the world of Cuban baseball. But the international baseball scene itself was now rapidly evolving. And dramatic changes were therefore in the wind for Cuba as a direct result of this uncontrollable external evolution. One domestic fallout of the victory in Taipei would be a small tweaking of the National

Series schedule — the short second season, now recast as the Super League, would be put back on the docket for June 2002. And there were also more significant changes in the wind regarding Cuba's role in international baseball. First there was an agreement with the professional league in Mexico to play a series of exhibitions between the capital city Mexico City Reds and the winning club from the National Series midseason All-Star Game. The immediate result was an interruption of National Series XLI (2001–2002) play on the eve of post-season playoffs in order to accommodate the last-minute Mexican exhibition matches that were to be split between Mexico City and Havana. And by season's end there was some even more startling news. Several of the top Cuban stars were not only slated for official retirement from the league and the national team, but a select group was now being earmarked to play professionally in Japan.

This unprecedented loaning of top veteran players to the Japanese leagues was perhaps the biggest story surrounding Cuban baseball at the outset of a new millennium. Cuban veterans have "retired" from league play in the past before their abilities had completely diminished, and then been rewarded with one or two years of service on industrial league teams in Japan, or have been shipped to amateur leagues in Colombia, Nicaragua or Italy. The opportunity to live outside the country and received salaries and travel allowances was a huge perk for former stars, even if eighty percent of the salary might be earmarked for INDER rather than for the individual ballplayer. But now for the first time there would be a Cuban star sold directly to the Japanese pro circuits as a commercials venture. Hard on the heals of the 2002 Cuban League season it was announced that 20-year veteran Omar Linares would report immediately to the Chunichi Dragons of the Japanese Central League, while Orestes Kindelán and Antonio Pacheco were reporting to the amateur-status industrial league Sidas ball club. The remarkable announcement carried in the small sports section of the government newspaper *Granma* also indicated that star shortstop Germán Mesa and Amateur World Series 2001 MVP Luis Ulacia would begin immediate assignments in Japan as industrial league coaches.

It is far too early, perhaps, to read the signals being sent by the new Cuban agreements with professional leagues in Japan and Mexico. Linares's career in the Central League was short-lived and surprisingly unproductive. The 2002 Mexico series has so far proven a one-time event. Pacheco and Kindelán were back in Santiago, as manager and coach respectively, with the former league time in time for the 2004–2005 National Series. Were the tentative steps of 2002 indicative of a new openness toward an eventual trafficking with the U.S. major leagues? Did they represent cautious preparations for an eventual, and perhaps inevitable, pro-style baseball world cup supplanting the one-time "amateur" Olympics — an event owned and operated by the capitalist baseball forces to the north? Or were they a mere aberration? International baseball was now clearly evolving from an amateur to a professional sport, as witnessed by the number of athletes from organized baseball filling Olympic rosters in

Cuba's 2003 World Cup champions after the deciding contest in Havana. Manager Higinio Vélez (center) hoists the championship trophy, representing Cuba's eighth straight world title dating back to 1984.

Sydney and Athens. By March 2006 and the emergence of Major League Baseball's first-ever World Baseball Classic it seemed more certain than ever that the amateur and professional branches of international baseball were now on a crash course toward some form of uneasy merger.

The impact of all this evolution on Cuban baseball — the enclosed Cuban League universe as it has stood throughout the Castro years — likely will be quite severe and perhaps even fatal in the long haul. But for all the storm clouds, the isolated National Series and the talented national teams it produces, five years into the new century, was still proving remarkably adaptable and surprisingly resilient. If the efforts by MLB to replace Olympic tournaments with the new-fangled professional World Baseball Classic were even in small part motivated by a subtle plan to end Cuba's long-time domination of international tournaments, then the events of March 2006 must be unsettling to MLB moguls at the very least. Invited to participate (despite roadblocks presented by the Bush ad-

ministration's continued enforcement of an economic boycott), Cuba seized upon the tournament and its own shocking run to the championship game as a perfect stage to prove its unrivalled dominance. In the wake of the first WBC, Cuba stood unseated as the kingpin of world tournament play, no matter what the quality of professional opposition. On the heels of the inaugural World Baseball Classic it would become more evident than ever that nothing was about to erase a Cuban legacy that remains the untainted banner story of nearly seventy years of international baseball competitions.

What Cuba had begun in the second half of the twentieth century, with its almost inexplicable domination on the international baseball scene, would only be amplified and even taken to another level in the first half-dozen years of the new millennium. By 2000 the playing field had been more then leveled by the introduction of top minor league professionals — if not yet many major leaguers — on the rosters of most international rivals. Any notion that Cuba only won the big tournaments year-in and year-out because USA, Japanese and Puerto Rican forces were rarely more than university clubs or low-level minor leaguers quickly proved to be another of baseball's endless string of indefensible myths. The USA Olympic team in Sydney was loaded with major league veterans (Pat Borders, Doug Mientkiewicz, Ernie Young) and top emerging pro prospects (Ben Sheets, Adam Everett, Brad Wilkerson) and the Cubans more than held there own. And in a pair of upcoming World Cup matches as well as the 2004 Athens Olympics the increased presence of USA, Japanese, Canadian or Australian professionals did almost nothing to slow the onrushing Cuban gold medal express.

The Taipei games had been only a tame preview of what was to come. At the 2003 World Cup renewal in Havana the Cubans were nearly upset in the quarterfinals by overachieving Brazil — rescued only by a dramatic ninth inning homer off the bat of future defector Kendry Morales — but recovered to gain another title with convincing back-to-back wins over Chinese Taipei (which had eliminated Team USA) and Panama (which had scuttled a crack squad of Japanese university all-stars). If the USA had not sent its top club to Havana in October 2003, electing to save a more potent lineup managed by Frank Robinson for the Olympic Qualifier in Panama City a month later, the ploy only proved yet another American disaster. The American team led by Twins minor league player of the year Joe Mauer was rudely ousted by upstart Mexico (and the surprise pitching performance of ex–big-leaguer Rigo Beltrán), while Cuba and Canada eventually advanced to Athens.

At the 2004 Olympics the Japanese mounted a stiff challenge by entering their top Central League and Pacific League all-stars for the first time; but the Nippon all-stars failed to reach the finals, where the Cubans copped yet one more crown by edging Australia with former big leaguers Dave Nilsson, John Stephens, Adrian Burnside and Graeme Lloyd. The most convincing display of Cuban invincibility to date would come in the 2005 World Cup (Netherlands) when one of the most talented red-clad outfits ever — buoyed with such new sluggers as Yulieski Gourriel, Osmani Urrutia and Frederich Cepeda — crushed an American AAA all-star lineup and top Mets prospect Brian Bannister in the quarterfinals on the way to an unblemished record. Detailed summaries of these tournaments are found in the year-by-year tournament recaps at chapter's end. By the time the record closed on Cuba's ninth straight World Cup victory in Rotterdam in September 2005 the stage had been set for the biggest shock of all. That, of course, would come when the major leagues opened its own doors to international competition with its March 2006 World Baseball Classic, where Cuba miraculously rose up yet again to prove that its national team was every bit the equal of any of big league baseball's most potent all-star forces.

References and Suggested Readings

Bjarkman, Peter C. *Diamonds around the Globe: A Reference Guide to International Baseball.* Westport, CT: Greenwood Publishing Group, 2005.

_____. "The Real World Series: Cubans again dominate Olympic action" in: *The Baseball Research Journal 26* (1997). Cleveland, OH: Society of American Baseball Research, 28–29.

_____. "The Baseball Half-Century of Conrado Marrero" in: *Elysian Fields Quarterly* 17:1 (Winter 2000), 27–44.

Casas, Edel, Jorge Alfonso, and Alberto Pestana. *Viva y en juego.* Havana: Editorial Científico-Techníca, 1986.

González Echevarría, Roberto. *The Pride of Havana: A History of Cuban Baseball.* New York: Oxford University Press, 1999.

Pestana, Alberto. *Memoria de los Campeonatos Mundiales de Béisbol Aficionado.* Havana: Ediciones Deportivas, 1971.

_____. *Breve Historial de las Series Mundiales de Béisbol Amateur.* Havana: Periodico Juventud Rebelde, 1965.

Rucker, Mark, and Peter C. Bjarkman. *Smoke: The Romance and Lore of Cuban Baseball.* New York: Total Sports Illustrated, 1999.

Pre-Revolution Cuban Amateur League Baseball Championships (1914–1960)

CUBAN NATIONAL AMATEUR BASEBALL LEAGUE (LIGA NACIONAL DE BASEBALL AMATEUR)

Twentieth-century Cuban amateur baseball begins in large part with the Clío B.B.C. team composed of Havana high society youth and founded sometime in 1901, and the similarly staffed Vedado Tennis Club team founded in June 1902 (and managed in the 1920s by former big leaguer Rafael Almeida). Both clubs played informally arranged games throughout the early years of the century. But league play only became successfully established with the Asociación Atlética, organized by the Vedado Tennis Club and University of Havana teams in 1905 and also eventually including the Clío B.B.C. and various clubs named Columbia, Atlético de Cuba, and Sociedad Marianao, among others. The short-lived Asociación Atlética (Athletic Association) was supplanted in 1914 by a more stable Liga Nacional (Unión Atlética Amateur) that for the entire first half of the 20th Century was synonymous with Cuban amateur baseball.

Year-by-Year Results

1914 — **Champion**: Vedado Tennis Club (13–3, .813), Manager: Gustavo de Zaldo; **Final Standings**: Vedado Tennis Club (13–3), Instituto (10–6), Marianao (7–10), Atlético de Cuba (3–14); **Batting Leader**: M. Lara (Atlético de Cuba) .455; **Pitching Leader**: G. Portela (Vedado Tennis Club).

1915 — **Champion**: Vedado Tennis Club (12–4, .750), Manager: Gustavo de Zaldo; **Final Standings**: Vedado Tennis Club, Progreso, Universidad de Habana, Atlético de Cuba; **Batting Leader**: Daniel Blanco (Universidad de Habana) .404; **Pitching Leader**: Ramón Goizueta (Vedado Tennis Club). **No-Hit Game**: Ramón Goizueta (Vedado Tennis Club) vs. Atléticos de Cuba (2–0 score) on June 16, 1915.

1916 — **Champion**: Vedado Tennis Club (16–4, .800), Manager: Ignacio Zayas; **Final Standings**: Vedado Tennis Club, Progreso, Universidad de Habana, Atlético de Cuba, Club Lawton; **Batting Leader**: F. Ríos (Club Atlético de Cuba) .444; **Pitching Leader**: G. Portelo (Vedado Tennis Club).

1917 — **Champion**: Atlético de Cuba (9–2, .818), Manager: Gustavo Gutiérrez; **Final Standings**: Atlético de Cuba, Vedado Tennis Club, Club Lawton, Universidad de Habana, Loma Tennis Club; **Batting Leader**: C. Seigle (Club Loma) .500; **Pitching Leader**: A. Sansirena (Atlético de Cuba).

1918 — **Champion**: Club Bellamar de Matanzas (13–3, .813), Manager: E. González; **Final Standings**: Bellamar de Matanzas, Ferroviario, Atlético de Cuba, CAC, Medina Sport Club, Club Lawton; **Batting Leader**: L. Alfonso (Ferroviario) .478; **Pitching Leader**: Adrian Alonso (Bellamar de Matanzas).

1919 — **Champion**: Atlético de Cuba (18–4, .818), Manager: Gustavo Gutiérrez; **Final Standings**: Atlético de Cuba, Aduanas, Federales de Heredia, Medina Sport Club, Víboro Social Club; **Batting Leader**: A. de Juan (Aduanas) .358; **Pitching Leader**: A. Sansirena (Atlético de Cuba).

1920 — **Champion**: Cienfuegos Sports Club (19–4, .826), Manager: C. Esquivel; **Final Standings**: Cienfuegos Sports Club, Sagua de la Grande, Fortuna Sports Club, Universidad de Habana, Deportivo Matanzas, Atlético de Cuba, Aduanas; **Batting Leader**: L. García (Cienfuegos) .409; **Pitching Leader**: Pedro Dibut (Cienfuegos).

1921 — **Champion**: Fortuna Sports Club (15–3–1, .833), Manager: Juan Albear; **Final Standings**: Fortuna Sports Club, Atlético, Aduanas, Cienfuegos, Santiago de las Vegas, Universidad de Habana; **Batting Leader**: F. Espiñeira (Atlético de Cuba) .436; **Pitching Leader**: Silvino Ruiz (Fortuna Sports Club). **No-Hit Game**: Silvino Ruiz (Fortuna Sports Club) vs. Santiago de las Vega (4–0 score) on May 15, 1921.

1922 — **Champion**: Fortuna Sports Club (14–5, .737), Manager: Alfonso Peña; **Final Standings**: Fortuna SC, Santiago de las Vegas, Atlético, Policía, Aduanas, Atlético de Cuba, Liceo de Regla; **Batting Leader**: J. Oteiza (Fortuna Sports Club) .433; **Pitching Leader**: Silvino Ruiz (Fortuna Sports Club).

1923 — **Champion**: Universidad de Habana Caribes (16–1–2, .941), Manager: G. Kendrigan; **Final Standings**: Universidad de Habana, Policía, Loma Tennis Club, Atlético de Cuba, American Steel, Fortuna Sports Club, Aduanas, Liceo de Regla, Santiago de las Vegas, Ferroviario, Club La Salle; **Batting Leader**: M. Sotomayor (Atlético de Cuba) .491; **Pitching Leader**: I. Ruiz (Policía).

1924 — **Champion**: Atlético de la Policía (14–4, .778), Manager: Horacio Alonso; **Final Standings**: Policía, Aduanas, Ferroviario, Vedado Tennis Club, Loma Tennis Club, Atlético, Fortuna Sports Club; **Batting Leader**: P. Palmero (Loma Tennis Club) .459; **Pitching Leader**: Adrian Alonso (Ferroviario).

1925 — **Champion**: Vedado Tennis Club (17–5–2, .773), Manager: Rafael Almeida; **Final Standings**: Vedado Tennis Club, Loma Tennis Club, Ferroviario, Policía, Atlético, Habana Yacht Club, Club La Salle; **Batting Leader**: P.A. Flores (Ferroviario) .400; **Pitching Leader**: Not recorded.

1926 — **Champion**: Vedado Tennis Club (20–7–1, .741), Manager: Rafael Almeida; **Final Standings**: Vedado Tennis Club, Policía, Habana Yacht Club, Universidad de Habana, Atlético de Cuba, Ferroviario, Fortuna Sports Club, Loma Tennis Club; **Batting Leader**: Gustavo Alfonso (Vedado Tennis Club) .382; **Pitching Leader**: Antonio Casuso (Vedado Tennis Club).

1927 — **Champion**: Vedado Tennis Club (16–5, .764), Manager: Rafael Almeida; **Final Standings**: Vedado Tennis Club, Policía, Universidad de Habana, Fortuna Sports Club, Habana Yacht Club, Atlético de Cuba, Loma Tennis Club, Ferroviario; **Batting Leader**: Cándido Hernández (Policía) .386; **Pitching Leader**: Not recorded.

1928 — **Champion**: Vedado Tennis Club (17–4, .810), Manager: Rafael Almeida; **Final Standings**: Vedado Tennis Club, Atlético de la Policía, Universidad de Habana, Fortuna Sports Club, Habana Yacht Club, Atlético de Cuba, Loma Tennis Club, Ferroviario, Deportiva Cárdenas* (*Cárdenas didn't complete the full season); **Batting Leader**: Ramiro Seigle (Vedado Tennis Club) .400; **Pitching Leader**: J. Ravena (Vedado Tennis Club).

1929 — **Champion**: Universidad de Habana Caribes (23–5, .821), Manager: Oscar Ortiz; **Final Standings**: Universidad de Habana, Policía, Vedado Tennis Club, Fortuna Sports Club, Habana Yacht Club, Atlético de Cuba, Loma Tennis Club, Ferroviario; **Batting Leader**: G. Macías (Universidad de Habana); **Pitching Leader**: Juan Mendizabel (Universidad de Habana).

1930 — **Champion**: Universidad de Habana Caribes* (12–3, .800), Manager: Oscar Ortiz; tied with Club Teléfonos (12–3, .880) *Universidad won playoff for championship; **Final Standings**: Universidad de Habana, Club Teléfonos, six other teams (details now lost); **Batting Leader**: Gustavo Alfonso (Vedado Tennis Club) .424; **Pitching Leader**: Not recorded.

1931 — **Champion**: Club Teléfonos (18–3–1, .856), Manager: Octavio Diviñó; **Final Standings**: Club Teléfonos, Hershey, ADC, Regla, Ferroviario, Círculo de Artesanos, Víbora Tennis Club, Fortuna Sports Club, YMCA, Atlético de Cuba; **Batting Leader**: Conrado Martínez (Víbora Tennis Club) .426; **Pitching Leader**: Manuel Domínguez (Club Teléfonos) 4–1.

1932 — **Champion**: Hershey Sports Club (18–2–1, .900), Manager: Joaquín Viego; **Final Standings**: Hershey, Regla, Teléfonos, Cubaneleco, ADC, Fortuna, Deportivo Cárdenas, Yara, Ferroviario; **Batting Leader**: E. García (Deportivo Cárdenas) .559; **Pitching Leader**: Juan Mendizábal (Regla) 8–0, Tomás de la Cruz (Hershey) 8–1.

1933 — **Champion**: Regla B.B.C. (15–7–1, .682), Manager: Joaquín López; **Final Standings**: Regla, Yara, Fortuna Sports Club, Cubaneleco, Club Teléfonos, Vedado Tennis Club; **Batting Leader**: Gustavo Alfonso (Cubaneleco) .410; **Pitching Leader**: Adrián Zabala (Fortuna Sports Club) 6–0.

1934 — **Champion**: Hershey Sports Club (17–3, .850), Manager: Joaquín Viego; **Final Standings**: Hershey, Regla, Fortuna Sports Club, Yara, Cubaneleco, Vedado Tennis Club; **Batting Leader**: E. García (Hershey) .413; **Pitching Leader**: Manuel (Manolo) "Chino" Fortes (Hershey) 10–1.

1935 — **Champion**: Hershey Sports Club (20–5, .800), Manager: Joaquín Viego; **Final Standings**: Hershey, Regla,

Fortuna, Cubaneleco, Club Teléfonos, Atlético de Cuba, Vedado Tennis Club; **Batting Leader:** Antonio "Quilla" Valdés (Hershey) .379; **Pitching Leader:** Manuel "Chino" Fortes (Hershey) 4–0. **No-Hit Game:** José Mercadefe (Club Teléfonos) vs. Cubaneleco (9–0 score) on June 2, 1935.

1936—**Champion:** Fortuna Sports Club (14–5–2, .737), Manager: Reinaldo Cordeiro; **Final Standings** Fortuna Sports Club, Cubaneleco, Hershey, Regla, Vedado Tennis Club, Club Teléfonos, Atlético de Cuba, Yara: **Batting Leader:** Segundo "Guajiro" Rodríguez (Fortuna Sports Club) .403; **Pitching Leader:** M. Tamayo Saco (Fortuna Sports Club), 4–0, 1.33 ERA.

1937—**Champion:** Fortuna Sports Club (13–6–1, .684), Manager: Reinaldo Cordeiro; **Final Standings:** Fortuna Sports Club, Hershey, Club Naval, Regla, Atlético de Cuba, Club Teléfonos, ADC, Universidad de Habana, Yara, Cubaneleco; **Batting Leader:** Antonio "Quilla" Valdés (Hershey) .395; **Pitching Leader:** Agapito Mayor (Hershey) 1.13 ERA, Pedro "Natilla" Jiménez (Hershey) 1.70 ERA.

1938—**Champion:** Hershey Sports Club (21–3, .875), Manager: Joaquín Viego; **Final Standings:** Hershey, Regla, Fortuna Sports Club, Cienfuegos Casa Stany, Club Teléfonos, Universidad de Habana, Cubaneleco, Club Naval, Deportivo Cárdenas, ADC, Sociedad de Pilar, Yara, Vedado Tennis Club; **Batting Leader:** Gustavo Ubieta (Universidad de Habana) .444; **Pitching Leader:** Pedro "Natilla" Jiménez (Hershey) 15–1. **No-Hit Games:** Conrado Marrero (Cienfuegos) vs. Universidad de Habana (4–0 score) on September 11, 1938; Pedro "Natilla" Jiménez (Hershey) vs. Deportivo Cárdenas (12–0 score) on September 23, 1938.

1939—**Champion:** Hershey Sports Club (21–5–1, .800), Manager: Joaquín Viego; **First Half-Season Standings:** Hershey (13–3, .813), CAC, Cienfuegos, Club Naval, Regla, Club Teléfonos, Círculo de Artesanos, Cubaneleco, Fortuna Sports Club, Deportivo Cárdenas, Yara, Vedado Tennis Club, Artemisa, Universidad de Habana, Loma Tennis Club, ADC, Sociedad de Pilar; **Second Half-Season Standings:** Hershey (21–5, .813), Cienfuegos, Club Naval, Círculo de Artesanos, Fortuna Sports Club, Regla, Club Teléfonos, CAC, Cubaneleco, Deportivo Cárdenas, Vedado Tennis Club, Yara; **Batting Leader:** Segundo "Guajiro" Rodríguez (Fortuna Sports Club) .424; **Pitching Leader:** Pedro "Natilla" Jiménez (Hershey) 11–1.

1940—**Champion:** Hershey Sports Club (20–5, .800), Manager: Joaquín Viego; **First Division Standings:** Hershey, Fortuna Sports Club, Cienfuegos, ADC, Naval, Círculo de Artesanos, Club Teléfonos, Regla, Deportivo Matanzas; **Second Division Standings:** Universidad de Habana, Artemisa, Sociedad de Pilar, Loma Tennis Club, Cubaneleco, Atlético de Cuba, Yara, Deportivo Cádenas, Vedado Tennis Club; **Batting Leader:** Mario Fajo (Círculo Militar) .442; **Pitching Leader:** Antonio "Loco" Ruíz (Hershey Sports Club) 12–0.

1941—**Champion:** Cienfuegos (18–6–1, .750), Manager: Candido González; **First Division Standings:** Cienfuegos, Hershey SC, Deportivo Matanzas, Universidad de Habana, Club Teléfonos, Círculo de Artesanos, Fortuna Sports Club,

Regla, Santiago de las Vegas; **Second Division Standings:** Círculo Militar, Artemisa, Atlético de Cuba, ADC, Cubaneleco, Deportivo Cárdenas, Yara, Sociedad de Pilar, Loma Tennis Club; **Batting Leader:** M. Díaz (Deportivo Cárdenas) .460; **RBI:** Napoleón "Nap" Reyes (Universidad de Habana) 23; **Pitching Leader:** Conrado Marrero (Cienfuegos) 18–6.

1942—**Champion:** Círculo Militar* (22–5, .815), Manager: E. Miranda; tied with Cienfuegos (22–5, .815) *Circular Militar won playoff for championship; **First Division Standings:** Círculo Militar, Cienfuegos, Círculo de Artesanos, Deportivo Matanzas, Fortuna Sports Club, Universidad de Habana, Hershey, Regla; **Second Division Standings:** Atlético de Cuba, Vedado Tennis Club, Artemisa, Teléfonos, Aduanas, ADC, Deporivo Cárdenas, Cubaneleco; **Batting Leader:** Pedro Echevarría (Hershey) .408; **RBI:** Chito Quicutis (Artemisa) 27; **SB:** Pedro Echevarría (Hershey) 22; **Pitching Leader:** Rogelio "Limonar" Martínez (Deportivo Matanzas) 7–0. **No-Hit Games:** Conrado Marrero (Cienfuegos) vs. Vedado Tennis Club (4–0 score) on May 24, 1942; Daniel Parra (Fortuna Sports Club) vs. Círculo Militar y Naval (4–0 score) on August 16, 1942.

1943—**Champion:** Deportivo Matanzas (23–5–2, .821), Manager: Tomás de la Noval; **First Division Standings:** Deportivo Matanzas, Círculo de Artesanos, Fortuna Sports Club, Círculo Militar, Regla B.B.C., Atlético de Santiago, Hershey Sports Club, Vedado Tennis Club, Artemisa, Deportivo Cárdenas; **Second Division Standings:** Cienfuegos, Universidad de Habana, Club Teléfonos, Sociedad de Pilar, Yara, Cubaneleco, Deportivo Rosario, Loma Tennis Club, Asociación Deportiva de Cuba, Casino Español; **Batting Leader:** Hiram González (Universidad de Habana Caribes) .424; **Pitching Leader:** Pedrito Ruíz (Yara) 6–0.

1944—**Champion:** Círculo de Artesanos (26–3–1, .897), Manager: José R. Castañeda; **First Division Standings:** Círculo de Artesanos, Círculo Militar, Deportivo Matanzas, Cienfuegos, Atlético de Santiago, Regla B.B.C., Artemisa B.B.C., Club Teléfonos; **Second Division Standings:** Vedado Tennis Club, Hershey Sports Club, Fortuna Sports Club, Cubaneleco, Casino Español, Casino Deportivo, Deportivo Cárdenas, Yara Sports Club; **Batting Leader:** Juan Ealo (Fortuna Sports Club) .500; **Runs Scored:** Orlando Moreno (Artemisa) 32; **Pitching Leader:** Julio Moreno (Círculo de Artesanos) 26–3. **No-Hit Games:** Julio "Jiqui" Moreno (Círculo de Artesanos) vs. Santiago de Las Vegas (4–0 score) on March 19, 1944; Rigoberto Villarnovo (Vedado Tennis Club) vs. Habana Deportivo (3–0 score) on April 23, 1944.

1945—**Champion:** Deportivo Matanzas (27–4–2, .871), Manager: Tomás de la Noval; **First Division Standings:** Deportivo Matanzas, Cienfuegos, Regla, Artemisa, Deportivo Rosario, Universidad de Habana, Círculo de Artesanos, Fortuna Sports Club, Atlético de Santiago; **Second Division Standings:** Club Teléfonos, Atlético de Cuba, Vedado Tennis Club, Asociación Deportiva de Cuba, Casino Español, Círculo Militar, Casino Deportivo, Hershey, Deportivo Cárdenas; **Batting Leader:** Angel Torres (Círculo de Artesanos) .396; **Pitching Leader:** Antonio Suárez (Regla) 10–0.

1946—**Champion**: Universidad de Habana Caribes (26–5–2, .831), Manager: Victor Muñoz; **First Division Standings**: Universidad de Habana, Deportivo Matanzas, Deportivo Rosario, Regla, Club Teléfonos, Aduanas, Deportivo Cárdenas, Círculo Artesanos, Casino Español; **Second Division Standings**: Asociación Deportiva de Cuba, Atlético de Cuba, Santiago de las Vegas, Hershey, Juventud Sociedad de Marianao, Círculo Militar, Miramar Yacht Club, Loma Tennis Club, Fortuna Sports Club; **Batting Leader**: Hiram González (Universidad de la Habana) .452; **Pitching Leader**: Eloy Ramentol (Universidad de Habana) 11–1, Catayo González (Deportivo Rosario) 24–5. **No-Hit Games**: Manuel Paula (Universidad de Habana) vs. Deportivo Rosario (4–0 score) on June 18, 1946; J.A. González (Deportivo Rosario) vs. Cubaneleco (8–0 score) on August 4, 1946.

1947—**Champion**: Deportivo Rosario (23–3, .885), Manager: Luis Fernández; **First Division Standings**: Deportivo Rosario, Club Hershey, Universidad de Habana, Círculo de Artesanos, Deportivo Matanzas, Club Teléfonos, Regla; **Second Division Standings**: Atlético de Cuba, Aduanas, Casino Español, Pinar del Río, Víbora Tennis Club, Club Santiago, Juventud Sociedad de Marianao; **Batting Leader**: Santiago Mariño (Pinar del Río) .475, Quilla Valdés (Hershey) .439; **Pitching Leader**: René "Tata" Solís (Deportivo Rosario) 18–1. **No-Hit Games**: Juan Suárez (Deportivo Matanzas) vs. Santiago de las Vegas (5–0 score) on June 8, 1947; Marcelo Fernández (Hershey Sports Club) vs. Casino Deportivo (4–0 score) on July 13, 1947.

1948—**Champion**: Hershey Sports Club (17–4–2, .810), Manager: Joaquín Viego; **First Division Standings**: Hershey SC, Universidad de Habana, Regla, Club Teléfonos, Cubaneleco, Atlético de Cuba, Deportivo Matanzas, Círculo de Artesanos, Víbora Tennis Club; **Second Division Standings**: Miramar Yacht Club, Atlético de Santiago, Víbora Tennis Club, Asociación Deportiva de Cuba; **Batting Leader**: Eduardo Vázquez (Víbora Tennis Club) .451, Juan Mir (Círculo de Artesanos) .397; **Pitching Leader**: Roberto Kaiser (Miramar Yacht Club) 4–0. **No-Hit Game**: Lorenzo Fernández (Cubaneleco) vs. Deportivo Matanzas (2–0 score) on July 13, 1948.

1949—**Champion**: Universidad de Habana Caribes (20–4, .833), Manager: Victor Muñoz; **First Division Standings**: Universidad de Habana Caribes, Club Teléfonos, Regla, Juventud de Pinar del Río, Deportivo Matanzas, Miramar Yacht Club, Santiago Sports Club, Cubaneleco; **Second Division Standings**: Club Hershey, Atlético de Cuba, Aduanas, Círculo de Artesanos, Víbora Tennis Club, Asociación Deportiva de Cuba, Loma Tennis Club, Artemisa; **Batting Leader**: Antonio "Pancho" Villa Armas (Club Teléfonos) .453; **Pitching Leader**: Gerardito Pérez (Club Teléfonos) 8–0.

1950—**Champion**: Club Teléfonos (20–3–1, .870), Manager: Oscar Reyes; **First Division Standings**: Club Teléfonos, Círculo de Artesanos, Atlético de Santiago, Cubaneleco, Vedado Tennis Club, Hershey, Miramar Yacht Club, Víbora Tennis Club; **Second Division Standings**: Aduanas, Regla, Atléticos, Juventud Sociedad de Marianao, Universidad de Habana, Artemisa, Liceo de Guanabacoa, Juventud de Pinar

del Río; **Batting Leader**: Juan Mir (Círculo de Artesanos) .403; **Pitching Leader**: Gerardito Pérez (Club Teléfonos) 6–0.

1951—**Champion**: Club Telefónos (20–3, .870), Manager: Oscar Reyes; **First Division Standings**: Club Teléfonos, Universidad de Habana, Regla B.B.C., Hershey, Círculo de Artesanos, Deportivo Matanzas, Santiago de las Vegas; **Second Division Standings**: Cubaneleco, Juventud Sociedad de Marianao, Asociación Deportiva de Cuba, Deportivo Cárdenas, Víbora Tennis Club, Liceo de Güines, Miramar Yacht Club; **Batting Leader**: Derubin Jácome (Deportivo Matanzas) .484; **Pitching Leader**: Chein García (Club Teléfonos) 14–2.

1952—**Champion**: Cubaneleco (20–4–1, .833), Manager: Manuel Lafuente; **First Division Standings**: Cubaneleco, Liceo de Regla, Teléfonos, Deportivo Matanzas, Círculo de Artesanos, Regla; **Second Division Standings**: Santiago SC, Artemisa, Vedado Tennis Club, Casino Español, Liceo de Guanabacoa, Universidad de Habana; **Batting Leader**: Manolito García (Matanzas) .424; **Pitching Leader**: J.R. "Bacardi" Tabares (Cubaneleco) 13–2; **No-Hit Game**: J.R. Tabares (Cubaneleco) vs. Víbora Tennis Club (9–0 score) on May 11, 1952.

1953—**Champion**: Cubaneleco (25–5; .833), Manager: Manuel Lafuente; **First Division Standings**: Cubaneleco, Deportivo Matanzas, Liceo de Regla, Atlético de Santiago, Universidad de Habana, Fortuna Sports Club, Liceo de Guanabacoa, Miramar Yacht Club; **Second Division Standings**: Club Teléfonos, Círculo de Artesanos, Hershey, Club San Carlos, Regla, Artemisa, Vedado Tennis Club, Juventud Sociedad de Marianao; **Batting Leader**: Gustavo Cárdenas (Universidad de Habana) .389; **Pitching Leader**: J.R. Blanco (Deportivo Matanzas) 8–0. **No-Hit Games**: Alejandro Eiriz (Regla) vs. Club Atlético de Cuba (4–0 score) on March 29, 1953; Luis Díaz (Club Atlético de Cuba) vs. Asociación Deportiva de Cuba (7–0 score) on July 4, 1953.

1954—**Champion**: Cubaneleco (24–7–1, .774), Manager: Manuel Lafuente; **First Division Standings**: Cubaneleco, Liceo de Regla, Club Teléfonos, Fortuna Sports Club, Regla, Hershey, Liceo de Guanabacoa, Vedado Tennis Club; **Second Division Standings**: Círculo de Artesanos, Artemisa, Santiago de las Vegas, Asociación Deportiva de Cuba, Víbora Tennis Club, Universidad de Habana, Union Club de Catalina, Sociedad Martí de Wajay; **Batting Leader**: Rafael Mori (Liceo de Guanabacoa) .458; **Pitching Leader**: José Francisco Oramas (Club Teléfonos) 7–0; **No-Hit Game**: Miguel Oliver* (Sociedad Martí de Wajay) vs. Club Ferroviario (0–1 score) on August 7, 1954; *Oliver pitched 9-inning no-hitter but lost in tenth, giving up one hit.

1955—**Champion**: Liceo de Regla (9–1–1, .900), Manager: Jesús Mera; **First Division Standings**: Liceo de Regla, Club Teléfonos, Atlético de Santiago, Fortuna, Hershey, Círculo de Artesansos, Regla, Cubaneleco, Universidad de Habana, Liceo de Guanabacoa, Asociación Deportiva de Cuba, Casino Español de Güines; **Second Division Standings**: Liceo de Madruga, Artemisa, Aduanas, Sociedad Martí de Wajay, Vedado Tennis Club, Liceo de Güines, Atlético de Cuba, Club San Carlos, Víbora Tennis Club, Ferroviario, Union Club de

Catalina; **Batting Leader:** Jesús Gutiérrez (Sociedad Martí de Wajay) .434, Rubén Piloto (Liceo de Madruga) .417; **Pitching Leader:** Luis Cárdenas (ADC) 6–0.

1956—**Champion:** Atlético Santiago de las Vegas (26–2–1, .929), Manager: Oscar del Calvo; **First Division Standings:** Santiago de las Vegas, Cubaneleco, Hershey SC, Círculo de Artesanos, Artemisa, Vedado Tennis Club, Regla, Fortuna Sports Club; **Second Division Standings:** Casino Español, Liceo de Madruga, Club Teléfonos, Union Club de Catalina, Liceo de Güines, Ferroviario, Víbora Tennis Club, Sociedad Martí de Wajay; **Batting Leader:** Angel Acosta (Artemisa) .417; **Pitching Leader:** Yuyo Rojas (Santiago de la Vegas) 10–1, 1.38 ERA; **No-Hit Games:** Oscar Miranda** (Santiago de las Vegas) vs. Professional All-Stars (9–0 score) on March 18, 1956 (**Miranda pitched perfect game); Rolando Pastor (Círculo de Artisanos) vs. Club San Carlos (10–0 score) on August 5, 1956.

1957—**Champion:** Artemisa (20–5–1, .800), Manager: A. Gómez; **Final Standings:** League standings not recorded; **Batting Leader:** E. Cruz (Teléfonos); **Pitching Leader:** Rolando Pastor (Círculo de Artesanos). No further league statistics available.

1958—**Champion:** Regla (19–5–1, .791), Manager: Antonio Suárez; **Final Standings:** League standings not recorded; **Batting Leader:** Juan Torres (Liceo de Madruga): **Pitching Leader:** Eduardo Suárez (Regla). No further league statistics available.

1959—**Champion:** Artemisa (20–3–1, .870), Manager: Francisco Quicutis. *No additional accurate records or statistics survive for the 1959 league season.

1960—**Champion:** Club Teléfonos (15–2–1, .882), Manager: Orlando Garmandia; **Final Standings:** League standings not recorded; **Batting Leader:** Antonio Pérez (Artemisa); **Pitching Leader:** Alfredo Street (Club Teléfonos). No further league statistics available.

ADDITIONAL CUBAN AMATEUR LEAGUES

More than a dozen Cuban amateur leagues of varying degrees of fan interest and talent level existed across the first half of the 20th Century. Championship teams for the more prominent among these leagues are provided here, as well as a complete listing of all other Cuban amateur leagues and their operating seasons.

Liga Inter-Municipal de Quivicán (Havana Province)

This Havana-based winter league spawned a number of post-revolution Cuban League stars and other fifties-era and sixties-era players of note, among them Pedro Chávez (winner of a triple crown in the Pedro Betancourt League and 1964 National Series batting champion), Urbano González (base hits leader in the inaugural post-revolution Cuban League National Series season of 1962), Antonio Crespo, Julio Alvarez, Eduardo Cárdenas, and Alberto Castillo. Team champions were the following:

1953–54: Quivicán
1954–55: Círculo Familiar de la Salud

1955–56: Club Atlético de Santiago de las Vegas
1956–57: Guira de Melena
1957–58: Alquisar
1958–59: Quivicán
1959–60: San José de Las Lajas

Liga de Pedro Betancourt (Matanzas Province)

One of two leagues (this one in the Matanzas area) along with the Liga de Quivicán (Havana) created in the 1940s specifically to counter the racism still found in the more established National Amateur League. Some black players debuting in this popular league who later gained widespread fame as professionals in the U.S. included Edmundo "Sandy" Amoros, Román Mejias, Antonio "Tony" Taylor, Daniel Morejón, José Tartabull, Zoilo Versalles, Miguel de la Hoz, Leo Cárdenas, Diego Segui and Antanasio "Tany" Pérez.

1944: Club Navajas (Manager: Nicolas de Armas)
1945: Central Dolores (Manager: Aurelio Mendoza)
1946: Central España (Manager: Miguel Mosquera)
1947: Casino Español (Manager: Luis Mazán)
1948: Central España (Manager: Elverio Granada)
1949: Tarafá (Manager: Gonzalo Barral)
1950: Tarafá Cuba (Manager: Gonzalo Barral)
1951: Calimete (Manager: Nicolas Chávez)
1952: Central Porfierza (Manager: Pascual Terry)
1953: Central Porfierza (Manager: Pascual Terry)
1954: Tarafá (Manager: Eduardo Oteda)
1955: Central España (Manager: Antonio Delgado)
1956: Central España (Manager: Antonio Delgado)
1957: Departamento Grani (Manager: Antonio Pacheco)
1958: Central Tinguaro (Manager: José Nakamura)
1959: Central Tinguaro (Manager: José Nakamura)
1960: Central Cuba (Manager: Gonzalo Barral)

Social League of Amateurs (Liga Social de Amateurs)

The Social League existed through the 1930s alongside the better-known National Amateur League. The Social League also replaced the Intersocial League for the 1936 Co-Criollos Series. This league (with both winter and summer sessions) held separate junior category championships for the 1935 and 1936 seasons.

1931–32 (Winter): Shell Mex de Cuba (Batting Leader: V. Muñoz)
1932 (Summer): Club Paramount (Batting Leader: Luis de la Noval)
1932–33 (Winter): Asociación Cubana de Beneficencia (Batting Leader: Pedro Navarrete)
1933 (Summer): Havana Electric (Batting Leader: J. Vasquez)
1933–34 (Winter): Asociación Cubana de Beneficencia (Batting Leader: A. Alvarez)
1934 (Summer): Asociación de Empleados de Whiz (Batting Leader: A. Alvarez)
1934–35 (Winter): Asociación Deportiva de Cuba (Batting Leader: G. Davila)

1935 (Summer): Acción Republicana (Batting Leader: F. de Cárdenas)

1936 (Summer): Escuela de Comercio (Batting Leader: J. López)

1937 (Summer): Regla Yacht Club (Batting Leader: I. Rodríguez)

1937–38 (Winter): Regla Yacht Club (Batting Leader: I. Rodríguez)

1938 (Summer): Esso Sports Club (Batting Leader: Not recorded)

1938–39 (Winter): Círcilo Militar (Batting Leader: Not recorded)

1939 (Summer): Guanabacoa (Batting Leader: Not recorded)

Co-Criollas Series (Series Co-Criollas)

From 1928 to 1930 a championship playoff was held annually between winners of the National Amateur League and Intersocial League. This series was played for a fourth time in 1936, then finally disbanded.

1928: Club Teléfonos (Intersocial League) defeated Vedado Tennis Club (National League)

1929: Club Teléfonos (Intersocial League) defeated University of Havana (National League)

1930: Club Teléfonos (National League) defeated Círculo de Artesanos (Intersocial League)

1936: Fortuna Sports Club (National League) defeated Escuela de Comerico (Social League)

Amateur Sports Organization (Organización Deportiva Amateurs)

Four seasons were played in the late 1930s and early 1940s by a group of "independent" amateurs forming a confederation called the Amateur Sports Organization. The following league champions were crowned:

1936: Bella Unión
1937: Bella Unión
1938: Unión Fraternal
1940: Havana Electric

Amateur Intersocial League (Liga Intersocial de Amateurs)

This league celebrated four championships between 1927 and 1930 and was a top quality circuit whose best champion (Club Teléfonos) twice (1928 and 1929) defeated representatives from the more prestigious National Amateur League in annual Co-Criollos playoff matches. Winners of the short-lived league were:

1927: Maristas
1928: Club Teléfonos
1929: Club Teléfonos
1930: Círculo de Artesanos

Campeonatos de las Fuerzas Armadas (Cuban Armed Forces Championships)

This short-lived series of championships produced numerous island semi-professional, professional and amateur

players of note, most especially Yuyo Ruiz who hurled for the Cuban national team and played minor league baseball in Milwaukee in 1943 and 1944.

1935: Regimiento No.6 (Batting Leader: A. Calderón, Regimiento No.6)

1936: Marina Constitucional (Batting Leader: R. Linares, Regimiento No.7)

1937: Marina Constitucional (Batting Leader: R. Heredia, Regimiento No.6)

Complete Listing of Cuban Amateur Leagues with Operating Seasons

A complete listing of Cuban amateur leagues and amateur tournaments operating during the 20th century would include all of the below events, listed chronologically by starting date. Those leagues and/or tournaments that came into existence after the 1959 revolution and thus comprise contemporary Cuban baseball are marked with an asterisk (*) and those in boldface are discussed in other chapters of this book.

Unión Atlética Amateur de Cuba (1914–1960)
Liga Intersocial de Amateurs (1927–1930)
Liga Social de Amateurs (1931–1939)
Campeonatos de las Fuerzas Armadas (1935–1937)
Organización Deportiva Amateurs (1936–1940)
Campeonatos Obreros (Workers League) (1940–1947)
Liga de Pedro Betancourt (1944–1960)
Campeonatos Nacionales Juveniles (Junior National Championships) (1949–2002)
Liga Inter-Municipal de Quivicán (1953–1960)
*Series Nacionales (1962–2006)
*Juego de la Estrellas (1963–2006)
*Serie de las Estrellas (1968–1997)
*Serie de Los "10 Millones" (1970)
*Series Selectivas (1975–1995)
*Liga Azucarera (Sugar Workers League) (1981–2002)
*Liga de Desarrollo (1992–1998)
*Torneo de Club Campeones (1992–2002)
*José Huelga International Invitational Tournament (1983–1994)
*Copas de la Revolución (1996–1999)

Summaries of World Amateur Baseball Championships

Readers attempting to capture some coherent sense of Cuba's performance over a 75-year span in international amateur tournaments by reading Robert González Echevarría's *The Pride of Havana* (the only book in English even touching upon this subject) are quickly lost in a morass of disjointed and sometimes contradictory detail. González's narrative style often successfully captures the flavor of many individual tournaments — especially those played at the outset of the forties. But numerous important international tournaments are ignored altogether or mentioned with little supporting detail. (González focuses largely on the first eight Amateur World

Series (1938–1945) and on the major showdowns between Cuban and USA teams in international events after the 1959 revolution.)

More distracting to one genuinely interested in this aspect of Cuban baseball is the amount of error and inconsistency in Professor González's treatment. He refers throughout his chapters on amateur baseball (Chapter 6) and post-revolution baseball (Chapter 9) to something he calls International Cup tournaments, which in reality are the **Intercontinental** Cup tournaments. The Second Central American Games staged to inaugurate La Tropical Stadium in 1930 are referred to more than once erroneously as the Pan American Games (an event which did not begin until 1951). Amateur World Series #19 is placed in February 1972 by González instead of December 1971 (the 1972 tournament was staged in Managua in November–December and was #20); Amateur World Series #17 (1969) is discussed incorrectly as the sixteenth reunion of that event; Amateur World Series #26 in Japan (1980) is labeled by González as #21 of the series. And finally, there are no detailed listings of most of the Cuban team rosters for these events (although such rosters are painstakingly supplied by González for most Cuban League professional seasons).

Provided below are the most extensive and complete summaries yet available on year-by-year international amateur tournaments. The rosters of Cuban teams are as complete as existing data permits and individual statistical leaders as well as final team standings are here offered for all years and for all five major tournaments: Amateur World Series, Olympic Games, Intercontinental Cup, Pan American Games and Central American Games (in that order). These extensive summaries parallel those also provided for the pre-revolution National Amateur League (immediately above), and for both the Cuban professional league (Chapter 5) and the amateur Cuban League National Series (Chapter 8) that followed the 1959 revolution.

WORLD CUP CHAMPIONSHIPS (AMATEUR WORLD SERIES), 1938–2005

Cuba's Overall Performance: Tournaments (25 of 28 Tournament titles won, plus one second place and one third place); Games (280 Won and 28 Lost, .909 Pct.)

Country-by-Country Championships Won: Cuba (25 of 28 tournaments entered), Venezuela (3), Colombia (2), Dominican Republic (1), Puerto Rico (1), South Korea (1), USA (1) and England (1)

Note: In 1944 (World Championship VII held at Caracas) Cuba (7–4) withdrew in the final round and forfeited its final game (Mexico also withdrew from the championship round). In 1976 (World Championship XXIV held at Cartagena) Cuba was declared champion when Puerto Rico withdrew and thus forfeited an earlier win against the Cubans. Cuba did not participate in the following eight events: 1938 (England), 1945 (Venezuela), 1947 (Colombia), 1948 (Colombia), 1965 (Colombia), 1973 (Managua, Nicaragua), 1974 (St. Petersburg, Florida), and 1982 (South Korea). This tourney

was known for years as the Amateur World Series but is now officially named the IBAF Baseball World Cup.

1938 Amateur World Series I (London, England, August 13–18)

World championship play is inaugurated with a two-team and five-game series that is the brainchild of American businessman Leslie Mann. "The John Moore Trophy" (honoring the founder of the English Baseball Association) is presented to a winning squad representing England, but both teams in reality consist of American soldiers currently on duty at European military bases.

Champion: England

Teams and Final Standings: England (4–1), USA (1–4)

Individual Statistical Leaders: No statistics are available for this tournament (Game Scores: England beat USA 3–0, England beat USA 8–6), USA beat England 5–0, England beat USA 4–0, England beat USA 5–3.

Cuba Did Not Participate

1939 Amateur World Series II (Havana, Cuba) (August 12–26)

The pastoral setting of Havana's La Tropical Stadium hosts the first "legitimate" international tournament consisting of amateurs representing three countries. Outfielder Juan Torres paces undefeated Cuba with a decisive game-winning hit in the opening match versus Nicaragua. Nicaragua boasts heavy hitting by black stars Stanley Cayasso and Jonathan Robinson who slug the only two homers of the week-long event. A winless USA team is exceptionally weak and only serves to round out the three-team field.

Champion: Cuba (6–0)

Teams and Final Standings: Gold: Cuba (6–0), Silver: Nicaragua (3–3), Bronze: USA (0–6)

Individual Statistical Leaders: **BA**: Sam Garth (NIC) .500; **Runs**: Esteban Maciques (CUB) 7; **Hits**: Sam Garth (NIC), G. Toyo (CUB) 9; **2B**: Ernesto Estévez (CUB), Stanley Cayasso (NIC) 2; **3B**: Wenceslao González (CUB), Bernardo Cuervo (CUB) 2; **HR**: Stanley Cayasso (NIC), Jonathan Robinson (NIC) 1; **RBI**: Bernardo Cuervo (CUB) 6; **SB**: C. Newell (NIC) 4; **Wins**: Pedro "Natilla" Jiménez (CUB) 2–0; **MVP**: Juan J. Torres (CUB).

Cuba Roster: **Manager**: León Rojas. **Batting** (AB–H–BA): Wenceslao González (6–3–.500), Conrado Marrero (4–2–.500), Eliecer Alvarez (4–2–.500), Ernesto Estévez (18–7–.389), G. Toyo (27–9–.333), A. González (6–2–.333), M. Tamayo Saco (3–1–.333), Kiko Gutiérrez (7–2–.286), Clemente González (15–4–.267), Esteban Maciques (16–4–.259), L. Minsal (22–5–.227), Bernardo Cuervo (20–4–.200), Mario Fajo (10–2–.400), Juan J. Torres (23–4–.174), Andres Fleitas (12–2–.167), Natilla Jiménez (7–1–.143), D. Pérez (2–0–.000), N. Corbo (0–0–.000). **Pitching** (W–L–ERA): Pedro "Natilla" Jiménez (2–0–0.95), Wenceslao González (2–0–5.14), Eliecer Alvarez (1–0–2.00), Conrado Marrero (1–0–3.00), M. Tamayo Saco (0–0–0.00).

Cuba Game Scores Round Robin: Cuba beat Nicaragua

4–3 (11), Cuba beat USA 13–3, Cuba beat Nicaragua 3–2, Cuba beat USA 8–3, Cuba beat Nicaragua 9–1, Cuba beat USA 12–7.

1940 Amateur World Series III (Havana, Cuba) (September 14–October 6)

The field increases to seven teams, including distant Hawaii (featuring several Japanese players), but Cuba is again dominant despite more balanced competition and a more representative USA entrant. Robinson and Cayasso repeat their heavy-hitting displays for Nicaragua; but Cuba's pitching — especially Marrero, Jiménez and Parra — is the deciding factor. Two notable players appearing in this tournament are USA pitcher Stubby Overmire (later a ten-year major leaguer with Detroit) and Cuban black infielder Pedro "Charolito" Orta, father of Mexican-born future major leaguer Jorge Orta.

Champion: Cuba (10–2)

Teams and Final Standings: Gold: Cuba (10–2), Silver: Nicaragua (9–3), Bronze: United States (9–3), Venezuela (5–7), Hawaii (5–7), Mexico (2–10), Puerto Rico (2–10)

Individual Statistical Leaders: **BA**: Jonathan Robinson (NIC) .444; **Runs**: Jonathan Robinson (NIC) 14; **Hits**: Stanley Cayasso (NIC) 19; **2B**: José Pérez (VEN), J.N. Vallecino (NIC) 4; **3B**: José Pérez (VEN) 3; **HR**: Jonathan Robinson (NIC) 1; **RBI**: J.N. Vallecino (NIC) 10; **SB**: L. Kunihisha (HAW) 7; **Wins**: José "Chino" Meléndez (NIC) 3–0; **MVP**: Conrado Marrero (CUB).

Cuba Roster: **Manager**: Reinaldo Cordeiro. **Batting** (AB–H–BA): Eliecer Alvarez (4–3–.750), Segundo "Guajiro" Rodríguez (30–13–.433), Natilla Jiménez (12–5–.417), Tomás Hechevarría (10–4–.400), Antonio Ruiz (43–16–.372), Mario Fajo (41–14–.341), Manuel "Chino" Hidalgo (38–12–.316), Napoleón Reyes (37–11–.297), Virgilio Arteaga (45–13–.289), Pedro Orta (39–11–.282), Pedro "Kiko" Gutiérrez (18–5–.278), C. Ramos (30–7–.233), F. Sánchez (22–5–.227), Esteban Maciques (19–4–.211), Conrado Marrero (12–2–.167), Carlos Colás (32–5–.156), J.R. López (22–3–.136), Daniel Parra (4–0–.000). **Pitching** (W–L–ERA): Conrado Marrero (3–2–1.15), Tomás Hechevarría (2–0–1.16), Eliecer Alvarez (1–0–1.26), Antonio "Loco" Ruiz (1–0–1.29), Natilla Jiménez (2–0–1.91), Daniel Parra (1–0–2.77).

Cuba Game Scores Double Round Robin: Cuba beat Hawaii 3–1, Cuba beat Mexico 6–0, Cuba beat Nicaragua 8–5, Cuba beat Venezuela 11–1, Cuba beat Puerto Rico 10–4, Cuba beat Hawaii 6–5, USA beat Cuba 2–1, Cuba beat USA 3–2, Cuba beat Puerto Rico 19–3, Cuba beat Venezuela 7–1, Cuba beat Mexico 6–2, Nicaragua beat Cuba 5–4.

1941 Amateur World Series IV (Havana, Cuba) (September 27–October 22)

One of the most hotly contested and highly memorable tournaments of international baseball history is again staged in La Tropical Stadium. Cuba and Venezuela deadlock with 7–1 records and an unscheduled deciding match is thus a last-minute addition. Allowed extra days of rest for their ace pitcher Daniel "Chino" Canónico, Venezuela surprises favored Cuba with three first-inning runs against Marrero in the dramatic finale. Venezuela behind Canónico holds on to win despite superb seven-inning relief from Cuban southpaw Natilla Jiménez and a ninth-inning rally by the home club that falls two runs short of victory.

Champion: Venezuela (8–1)

Teams and Final Standings: Gold: Venezuela (8–1), Silver: Cuba (7–2), Bronze: Mexico (6–2), Panama (5–3), Dominican Republic (5–3), USA (2–6), Nicaragua (2–6), Puerto Rico (1–7), El Salvador (1–7). *Venezuela defeated Cuba 3–1 in tie-breaking single play-off game for championship.

Individual Statistical Leaders: **BA**: G. Prieto (MEX) .545; **Runs**: Antonio "Mosquito" Ordeñana (CUB) 14; **Hits**: Clemente González (CUB) 17; **2B**: Víctor Manuel Canales (MEX) 5; **3B**: Héctor Romero Benitez (VEN) 3; **HR**: Leon Kellman (PAN) 1; **RBI**: Bernardo Cuervo (CUB) 10; **SB**: Carlos "Pinchón" Navas (NIC) 6; **Wins**: Daniel Canónico (VEN) 4–0; **MVP**: José Casanova (VEN).

Cuba Roster: **Manager**: Joaquín Viego. **Batting** (AB–H–BA): Bernardo Cuervo (30–12–.400), Clemente González (43–17–.395), Andres Fleitas (37–14–.378), Nap Reyes (35–12–.343), D. Galvez (6–2–.333), Conrado Marrero (6–2–.333), Segundo "Guajiro" Rodríguez (31–10–.323), Carlos Pérez (37–10–.270), Antonio Ordeñana (43–11–.256), Rafael Cabrera (32–5–.156), Rogelio "Limonar" Martínez (12–0–.000), Julio Moreno (7–0–.000), Natilla Jiménez (6–0–.000), Ramón Roger (3–0–.000), Tomás Hechevarría (4–0–.000), P.A. Fernández (0–0–.000), Rouget Avalos (0–0–.000), Daniel Parra (0–0–.000). **Pitching** (W–L–ERA): Rogelio "Limonar" Martínez (2–0–0.00), Natilla Jiménez (0–0–0.00), Conrado Marrero (3–0–0.46), Tomás Hechevarría (1–0–1.00), Julio "Jiqui" Moreno (1–1–1.29), Ramón Roger (0–0–2.08). (*Team Cuba stats do not include extra playoff game)

Cuba Game Scores Round Robin: Cuba beat El Salvador 16–0, Cuba beat Dominican Republic 4–2, Cuba beat USA 5–4, Cuba beat Nicaragua 7–0, Cuba beat Panama 9–0, Cuba beat Puerto Rico 7–0, Cuba beat Mexico 11–1, Venezuela beat Cuba 4–1. Playoff: Venezuela beat Cuba 3–1.

1942 Amateur World Series V (Havana, Cuba) (September 26–October 20)

Cuba revenges the disappointing loss of a year earlier, with Marrero this time besting Canónico 8–0 in a one-sided opening-round rematch. Cuban catcher Andres Fleitas enjoys a career highlight as tourney MVP and batting leader and both Julio Moreno and Isidoro León post 3–0 pitching records and sub-2.00 ERAs. The tournament trophy is now designated as the "Copa Presidente Batista" and wartime restrictions limit the field to five teams (with the USA team pulling out early and forfeiting several matches). A memorable moment involves a near grandstand riot inspired by the antics of colorful Dominican Republic manager Burrolote ("Big Donkey") Rodríguez. Luis Aparicio, Sr. (father of the future Cooperstown hall-of-famer), plays at shortstop for Venezuela.

Champion: Cuba (10–2)

Teams and Final Standings: Gold: Cuba (10–2), Silver:

Dominican Republic (9–3), Bronze: Venezuela (7–5), Mexico (3–9), USA* (1–11) *USA withdrew before tournament's completion and lost four games by forfeit.

Individual Statistical Leaders: **BA**: Andrés Fleitas (CUB) .405; **Runs**: Carlos Pérez (CUB) 20; **Hits**: Antonio "Quilla" Valdés (CUB) 16; **2B**: Juan Ealo (CUB) 4; **3B**: Pedro Echevarría (CUB), Carlos Pérez (CUB) 1; **HR**: Francisco "Chito" Quicutis (CUB), Carlos Pérez (CUB), Quilla Valdés (CUB) 2; **RBI**: Quilla Valdés (CUB) 14; **SB**: Carlos Pérez (CUB) 4; **Wins**: Julio Moreno (CUB), Isidoro León (CUB) 3–0; **MVP**: Andrés Fleitas (CUB).

Cuba Roster: **Manager**: León Rojas. **Batting** (AB–H–BA): Luis Suárez (19–11–.579), José R. Hernández (25–12–.480), Villa Cabrera (14–6–.429), Andrés Fleitas (37–15–.405), Juan Ealo (40–15–.375), Pedro Echevarría (35–13–.371), F.P. Sánchez (15–5–.333), Conrado Marrero (3–1–.333), Antonio "Quilla" Valdés (53–16–.302), Carlos Pérez (52–15–.288), José Luis García (26–7–.269), Eraso del Monte (13–3–.231), Remigio Vega (25–5–.200), Daniel Parra (5–1–.200), Julio Moreno (16–3–.188), Chito Quicutis (34–6–.176), Mario Fajo (32–4–.125), Isidoro León (9–1–.111). **Pitching** (W–L–ERA): Erasmo "Coco" del Monte (2–1–0.94), Julio Moreno (3–0–1.36), Isidoro León (3–0–1.93), Daniel Parra (1–0–2.38), Conrado Marrero (1–1–3.09).

Cuba Game Scores Multiple Round Robin: Dominican Republic beat Cuba 7–6, Cuba beat Dominican Republic 5–2, Cuba beat USA 11–1, Cuba beat Venezuela 8–0, Cuba beat USA 20–0, Cuba beat Mexico 8–0, Cuba beat USA 17–0, Cuba beat Venezuela 9–2, Cuba beat Mexico 11–3, Cuba beat Venezuela 11–4, Dominican Republic beat Cuba 4–3, Cuba beat Mexico 7–6.

1943 Amateur World Series VI (Havana, Cuba) (September 25–October 19)

Cuba wins for the fourth time during five-straight tournaments played in Havana. Pitching dominates during event that saw no home runs hit during 24 games in Tropical Stadium. Julio Moreno with three victories and Natilla Jiménez with no earned runs allowed in two outings are the top pitching stars, with Jiménez chosen as tourney MVP. Unheralded infielder Angel Fleitas (brother of catcher Andrés Fleitas) is Cuba's offensive hero and the tournament's batting champion. Conrado Marrero sat out this tournament having been temporarily stripped of his amateur status by the Cuban Baseball Federation.

Champion: Cuba (9–3)

Teams and Final Standings: Gold: Cuba (9–3), Silver: Mexico (6–6), Bronze: Dominican Republic (5–7), Panama (4–8)

Individual Statistical Leaders: **BA**: Angel Fleitas (CUB) .371; **Runs**: Gil Garrido (PAN) 10; **Hits**: Luis Suárez (CUB) 17; **2B**: José Luna (MEX) 5; **3B**: Luis Suárez (CUB), Luis Báez (DOM) 2; **HR**: None; **RBI**: Luis Suárez (CUB) 9; **SB**: Luis Báez (DOM) 7; **Wins**: Julio Moreno (CUB) 3–1; **MVP**: Pedro "Natilla" Jiménez (CUB).

Cuba Roster: **Manager**: León Rojas. **Batting** (AB–H–BA): Angel Fleitas (35–13–.371), Luis Suárez (48–17–.354),

Rouget Avalos (15–5–.333), Alberto Morera (41–12–.292), Sandalio Consuegra (7–2–.286), Ernesto Estévez (43–13–.279), Rogelio Valdés (23–5–.217), Antonio "Quilla" Valdés (50–10–.200), Pedro "Natilla" Jiménez (15–3–.200), Félix del Cristo (28–5–.179), Virgilio Arteaga (41–6–.146), Julio Moreno (14–2–.143), Rogelio Martínez (8–1–.125), Chito Quicutis (33–2–.061), Armando "Jojo" Báez (11–1–.091), Leandro Pazos (11–1–.091), Bautista Aristondo (1–0–.000), Isidoro León (5–0–.000), Agustín Cordeiro (1–0–.000). **Pitching** (W–L–ERA): Pedro "Natilla" Jiménez (1–1–0.00), Isidoro León (1–0–0.00), Julio "Jiqui" Moreno (3–1–0.70), Rogelio "Limonar" Martínez (3–0–0.96), Sandalio Consuegra (1–1–3.44).

Cuba Game Scores Multiple Round Robin: Mexico beat Cuba 2–1, Cuba beat Mexico 3–2, Dominican Republic beat Cuba 1–0, Cuba beat Panama 2–1, Cuba beat Dominican Republic 5–4, Cuba beat Panama 5–3, Cuba beat Mexico 7–0, Cuba beat Dominican Republic 3–0, Cuba beat Panama 5–3, Cuba beat Dominican Republic 3–0, Cuba beat Mexico 6–0, Panama beat Cuba 7–0.

1944 Amateur World Series VII (Caracas, Venezuela) (October 12–November 18)

The first legitimate Amateur World Series (later to be called the World Cup) held outside of Havana turned into a nightmare of controversy and lasting ill will when incompetent and overly partial umpiring in three late-round games resulted in acrimonious withdrawal by both Cuban and Mexican teams. Hometown umpires cost host Venezuela one victory when a game was unaccountably suspended by darkness after a late Venezuelan rally, the game thus reverting to an earlier inning with the Dominicans declared winners. The next contest saw the Cubans leaving the field in protest after a Cuban base runner was thrown out with an assist from a sideline photographer who interfered with on-field play. A similar dispute also sent Mexico packing several days later. The final suspended playoff match between Mexico and Venezuela was ruled a forfeit and the host team declared a much-disputed victory in its own favor.

Champion: Venezuela (7–3)

Elimination-Round Teams and Final Standings: Gold: Venezuela (2–1), Silver: Mexico* (2–1), Bronze: Cuba* (2–1), Panama (0–3) *Cuba and Mexico both withdraw in protests over umpiring and host Venezuela then declares its own team to be champion.

Qualifying-Round Teams and Final Standings: Mexico (6–1), Panama (5–2), Venezuela (5–2), Cuba (4–3), Dominican Republic (4–3), Colombia (2–5), Nicaragua (1–6), Puerto Rico (1–6)

Individual Statistical Leaders: **BA**: Leonard Roberts (PAN) .478; **Runs**: Guillermo Vento (VEN) 14; **Hits**: Antonio Briñez (VEN) 19; **2B**: Stanley Cayasso (NIC), Guillermo Vento (VEN) 5; **3B**: P. Miranda (COL), P. García (CUB) 2; **HR**: A. González (VEN), B. López (MEX), J. Diaz (MEX) 2; **RBI**: Dalmiro Finol (VEN) 15; **SB**: José Araujo (COL) 4; **Wins**: Mirno Zuloaga (VEN), F. Alcaraz (MEX) 3–0.

Cuba Roster: **Manager**: Pipo de la Noval. **Batting** (AB–H–BA): A. Rodríguez (11–6–.545), Félix del Cristo (12–6–.500), Sandalio Consuegra (2–1–.500), Angel Fleitas (38–13–.342), Rogelio "Limonar" Martínez (3–1–.333), Carlos Pérez (37–11–.297), J.L. García (34–10–.294), Pablo García (36–10–.278), F. Fernández (11–3–.273), Antonio "Quilla" Valdés (24–6–.250), Amado Ibáñes (12–3–.250), Julio Moreno (12–3–.250), Juan Ealo (34–7–.206), Conrado Marrero (10–2–.200), Angel Torres (17–3–.176), Tango Suárez (18–3–.167), Isidoro León (6–1–.167), Rouget Avalos (15–1–.067), Antonio Estrella (0–0–.000), A. Gallart (0–0–.00). **Pitching** (W–L–ERA): Sandalio Consuegra (1–0–1.00), Conrado Marrero (2–1–2.20), Isidoro León (1–0–2.70), Antonio Estrella (0–0–3.00), Julio Moreno (2–2–3.80), Rogelio "Limonar" Martínez (0–1–3.86).

Cuba Game Scores Qualifying Round: Cuba beat Puerto Rico 6–0, Cuba beat Colombia 4–0, Cuba beat Nicaragua 6–3, Panama beat Cuba 6–3, Mexico beat Cuba 2–0, Cuba beat Dominican Republic 2–1, Venezuela beat Cuba 7–2. Playoffs: Cuba beat Dominican Republic 3–2. Finals: Cuba beat Panama 8–0, Cuba beat Venezuela 9–7, Mexico beat Cuba 4–1.

1945 Amateur World Series VIII (Caracas, Venezuela) (October 27–November 18)

With Cuba and Mexico still sitting on the sidelines after the previous year's debacle in Caracas, Venezuela stages a less controversial defense of its tainted championship by cruising through a depleted six-team field. Héctor Benitez is the heavy hitter for undefeated Venezuela, batting over .500, knocking in 16 runs, and scoring another 16 himself. Mirno Zuloaga wins four pitching decisions for the victors but trails teammate Benitez in the MVP voting. Mexico and Puerto Rico will return for the next tournament (1947) and the Dominican Republic will re-enter and also win in 1948, but Cuba will remain on the sidelines until the beginning of the next decade.

Champion: Venezuela (10–0)

Teams and Final Standings: Gold: Venezuela (10–0), Silver: Colombia (7–3), Bronze: Panama (6–4), Nicaragua (5–5), El Salvador (1–9), Costa Rica (1–9)

Individual Statistical Leaders: **BA**: Héctor Benitez (VEN) .526; **Runs**: Héctor Benitez (VEN) 16; **Hits**: Ramón Fernández (VEN) 21; **HR**: L. Kellman (PAN) 2; **RBI**: Héctor Benitez (VEN) 16; **SB**: Luis Romero Petit (VEN) 9; **Wins**: Mirno Zuloaga (VEN) 4–0; **MVP**: Héctor Benitez (VEN). No additional statistics available.

Cuba Did Not Participate

1947 Amateur World Series IX (Baranquilla, Colombia) (November 29–December 20)

With Cuba again a notable absentee, host Colombia bests Puerto Rico and Nicaragua in the playoff round to capture its only title. Stanley Cayasso is still a slugging presence for Nicaragua and captures the RBI crown. This is Colombia's second consecutive strong showing and comes with balanced team play, as the Colombians have only one player in 1945 or 1947 who leads in any individual statistical category (Armando Crizón with 14 steals in 1947). Timoteo Mena earns three pitching victories for third-place Nicaragua.

Champion: Colombia (7–2)

Teams and Final Standings: Gold: Colombia (6–2), Silver: Puerto Rico (6–2), Bronze: Nicaragua (6–2), Mexico (5–3), Venezuela (5–3), Panama (3–5), El Salvador (2–6), Costa Rica (2–6), Guatemala (1–7). *In final playoff round, Puerto Rico eliminated Nicaragua (6–1 score) and Colombia defeated Puerto Rico (6–5 score) to decide cup championship.

Individual Statistical Leaders: **BA**: Fausto Fuenmeyer (VEN) .483; **Runs**: Eduardo Green (NIC), J. Hernández (NIC) 14; **3B**: O. Lara (SAL) 3; **HR**: E. Pessuey (PAN) 2; **RBI**: Stanley Cayasso (NIC) 12; **SB**: Armando Crizón (COL) 6; **Wins**: Timoteo Mena (NIC) 3–0. No additional statistics available.

Cuba Did Not Participate

1948 Amateur World Series X (Managua, Nicaragua) (November 20–December 12)

Cuba stays on the sidelines for the third straight tournament, with most of the country's top amateur players now holding pro contracts. Cuba's Juan Ealo does direct the host Nicaragua team but is fired by Nicaraguan dictator Anastasio Somoza after a close loss to Mexico. Somoza himself then manages the Nicaragua squad that not surprisingly still finishes far out of the running. The Dominicans edge Puerto Rico in a brief playoff series to capture their first and only world title. Ramón del Monte of the DR posts a perfect 4–0 pitching record as the tournament MVP.

Champion: Dominican Republic (8–1)

Teams and Final Standings: Gold: Dominican Republic* (6–1), Silver: Puerto Rico (6–1), Bronze: Colombia (5–2), Mexico (5–2), Panama (3–4), Guatemala (2–5), Nicaragua (1–6), El Salvador (0–7). *In playoff round, Dominican Republic defeated Puerto Rico (11–1 and 2–1) in first two games of best-of-three series.

Individual Statistical Leaders: **BA**: Manuel Caceres (DOM), Luis Morales (COL) .522; **Runs**: Elias Farias (DOM) 9; **Hits**: Manuel Caceres (DOM), Luis Morales (COL), Miguel Corrales (MEX) 12; **2B**: F. Arrieta (MEX), M. Ruiz (PRI) 4; **3B**: R. Baldiris (COL), B. Arias (DOM), M. Ruiz (PRI) 2; **HR**: Miguel Corrales (MEX) 3; **RBI**: Eduardo Green (NIC) 11; **SB**: Nugent Josephs (PAN) 9; **Wins**: Ramón del Monte (DOM) 4–0; **ERA**: Ramón del Monte (DOM) 0.34; **MVP**: Ramón del Monte (DOM).

Cuba Did Not Participate

1950 Amateur World Series XI (Managua, Nicaragua) (November 18–December 10)

In another tournament wrapped in controversy, Cuba finishes in a three-way tie with the Dominican Republic and Venezuela and enters a round-robin playoff that is finally won by the Dominicans. This playoff is annulled the following October in a special FIBA meeting which names Cuba champion, by virtue of disqualifying Puerto Rico for using professional players. An opening round 13–11 loss to Puerto Rico is thus changed to a Cuban victory, amending the team's record from 9–2 to 10–1. Several outstanding individual performances highlight an event from which most statistical records unfortunately have been lost. Cuba's Juan Izaguirre set tournament (21) and game (7) marks for runs batted in, Cecilio Miller of Panama stole 14 bases, and Mexico's Nicolas Genestas posted a perfect 4–0 pitching ledger.

Champion: Cuba (10–1) (including forfeit victory over Puerto Rico)

Teams and Final Standings: Gold: Cuba* (9–2), Silver: Dominican Republic (9–2), Bronze: Venezuela (9–2), Panama (8–3), Nicaragua (7–4), Colombia (6–5), Mexico (6–5), Puerto Rico (5–6), El Salvador (3–8), Guatemala (2–9), Costa Rica (2–9), Honduras (0–11). *Cuba declared champion when Puerto Rico is sanctioned for using professional players and Puerto Rico's victory over Cuba is changed to forfeit win for the Cubans, breaking a tie between Cuba, Dominican Republic and Venezuela.

Individual Statistical Leaders: **BA**: Eduardo Green (NIC) .487; **Runs**: Juan Izaguirre (CUB) 16; **Hits**: Eduardo Green (NIC) 19; **2B**: Candelario Guevara (VEN), Eduardo Green (NIC) 7; **3B**: Fernando García (MEX) 2; **HR**: Juan Izaguirre (CUB) 4; **RBI**: Juan Izaguirre (CUB) 21; **SB**: Cecilio Miller (PAN) 14; **Wins**: Nicolas Genestas (MEX) 4–0; **ERA**: Nicolas Genestas (MEX) 1.13.

Cuba Partial Roster: **Position Players**: Juan Izaguirre (4 HR, 21 RBI, 16 R), L. Seijo, D. Domínguez, Gilberto Soto, E. Muñoz, A. Armas, Juan Mir. **Pitchers** (W–L): Erasmo "Coco" del Monte (2–1), C. Cossio (3–1), Juan Ravelo (2–0), Marcelo Fernández (2–0). No additional roster names or statistics available.

Cuba Game Scores Round Robin: Cuba beat Costa Rica 9–7, Cuba beat Venezuela 7–1, Cuba beat Honduras 26–0, Cuba beat El Salvador 9–5, Cuba beat Panama 5–4, Cuba beat Guatemala 5–0, Puerto Rico beat Cuba 13–11 (Cuba later declared forfeit winner, 9–0), Mexico beat Cuba 5–1, Cuba beat Colombia 7–1, Cuba beat Nicaragua 7–2, Cuba beat Dominican Republic 11–2.

1951 Amateur World Series XII (Mexico City, Mexico) (November 1–19)

After matching Venezuela with a 9–1 record and first-place standing in preliminary round play, an undistinguished Cuba team dropped a pair of one-run decisions to Venezuela and Puerto Rico in the playoffs and limped home in third place. Statistical records from the only Amateur World Series ever played in Mexico are hopelessly sparse, although a complete listing of game scores does survive. This is only the third time (in eight tournaments attended) that Cuba does not claim first place. Nicaragua's unheralded Bert Bradford was the top hitter while playing for a team that did not make the final round. After this debacle in Mexico, Cuba would proceed to win each and every renewal of the World Amateur Series it attended over the next half-century (which would amount to 18 of the 22 tournaments staged).

Champion: Puerto Rico (10–3)

Final Round Teams and Standings: Gold: Puerto Rico (3–0), Silver: Venezuela (2–1), Bronze: Cuba (1–2), Dominican Republic (0–3)

Preliminary Round Teams and Standings: Cuba (9–1), Venezuela (9–1), Puerto Rico (7–3), Dominican Republic (7–3), Nicaragua (6–4), Costa Rica (5–5), Panama (5–5), Colombia (4–6), Mexico (2–8), Guatemala (1–9), El Salvador (0–10)

Individual Statistical Leaders: **BA**: Bert Bradford (NIC) .481; **Runs**: Sotero Ortiz (PRI) 21; **Hits**: Bert Bradford (NIC) 25; **2B**: Ramón Maldonado (PRI) 8; **3B**: Reinaldo Grenald (PAN) 4; **HR**: Walter James (DOM) 3; **SB**: Sotero Ortiz (PRI) 10. No additional statistics available.

Cuba Final Round Scores: Cuba defeated Dominican Republic 14–1 (WP: Puentes); Venezuela defeated Cuba 7–6 (LP: García); Puerto Rico defeated Cuba 7–6 (LP: Naranjo).

Cuba Preliminary Round Scores: Puerto Rico defeated Cuba 13–12 (LP: Naranjo); Cuba defeated Panama 8–2 (WP: Puentes); Cuba defeated Dominican Republic 8–7 (WP: García); Cuba defeated Venezuela 6–2 (WP: Brull); Cuba defeated Mexico 5–5 (WP: Puentes); Cuba defeated Guatemala by forfeit; Cuba defeated Colombia 5–0 (WP: Naranjo); Cuba defeated Nicaragua 5–4 (WP: García); Cuba defeated El Salvador 4–0 (WP: Erasmo del Monte); Cuba defeated Costa Rica 6–1 (WP: Isidro Brull).

Cuba Roster: **Pitchers** (W–L): Naranjo (1–2), Puentes (3–0), García (2–1), Isidro Brull (2–0), Erasmo del Monte (1–0). No further data or statistics available for Cuban player roster in this tournament.

Cuba Game Scores Preliminary Round: Puerto Rico beat Cuba 13–12, Cuba beat Panama 8–2, Cuba beat Dominican Republic 8–7, Cuba beat Venezuela 6–2, Cuba beat Mexico 5–4, Cuba beat Guatemala 9–0 (forfeit game), Cuba beat Colombia 5–0, Cuba beat Nicaragua 5–4, Cuba beat El Salvador 4–0, Cuba beat Costa Rica 6–1. Finals: Cuba beat Dominican Republic 14–1, Venezuela beat Cuba 7–6, Puerto Rico beat Cuba 7–6.

1952 Amateur World Series XIII (Havana, Cuba) (September 6–26)

Cuba's iron-clad fifty-year grip on amateur world championships began in Havana in September 1952, six months after strongman Fulgencio Batista grabbed power (March 10) and suspended constitutional government. No Cubans appear in the list of individual statistical leaders, but the pitching of Isidro Brull, Alejandro Eiriz and J. Suárez in the final round sustained crucial wins over Panama (10–9), the Dominican Republic (9–5), Nicaragua (6–2) and Venezuela (5–4) to wrap up a gold medal. Existing team photographs reveal that black ballplayers now held five slots on the Cuban team roster as the slow process of amateur baseball racial integration continued.

Champion: Cuba (9–2)

Final Round Standings: Gold: Cuba (4–1), Silver: Dominican Republic (3–2), Bronze: Puerto Rico (2–2), Panama (2–2), Nicaragua (2–3), Venezuela (1–4)

Group A Preliminary Standings: Cuba (5–1), Puerto Rico (5–1), Nicaragua (4–2), Mexico (3–3), Dutch Antilles (2–4), El Salvador (2–4), Honduras (0–6)

Group B Preliminary Standings: Venezuela (4–1), Dominican Republic (4–1), Panama (4–1), Colombia (2–3), Costa Rica (1–4), Guatemala (0–5)

Individual Statistical Leaders: **BA**: E. Marte (DOM) .436; **Runs**: A. Martínez (DOM), Sotero Ortiz (PRI) 13; **Hits**: E. Marte (DOM) 17; **2B**: J. Ortiz (NIC), Sotero Ortiz (PRI) 4; **3B**: W. Figueredo (PRI) 3; **HR**: J.R. García (PRI) 2; **RBI**: O. Hardy (PAN) 12; **SB**: J.R. García (PRI) 7; **Wins**: E. Evangelista (DOM) 4–1. No additional statistics available.

Cuba Roster: **Manager**: Clemente "Sungo" Carreras. **Batting** (AB–H–BA): Alejandro Eiriz (4–2–.500), R. Navarrete (5–2–.400), Juan Mir (15–5–.333), L. Estrada (22–7.318), A. Armas (34–10–.294), Antonio Suárez (7–2–.286), J. Barrios (7–2–.286), C. González (37–10–.270), Rouget Avalos (37–10–.270), E. Ferrer (34–9–.265), E. Marcos (27–7–.259), J. Suárez (4–1–.250), L. Olivares (13–3–.231), Manolo García (10–2–.200), Alfonso Suárez (35–6–.167), Isidro Brull (8–1–.125), I. Rodríguez (9–0–.000), G. Pérez (3–0–.000). **Pitching** (W–L): Isidro Brull (2–0), Alejandro Eiriz (2–0), R. Navarrete (1–0), Antonio Suárez (1–0), J. Suárez (3–1), G. Pérez (0–1).

Cuba Game Scores Preliminary Round Robin: Cuba beat Mexico 2–1, Cuba beat Dutch Antilles 8–1, Cuba beat El Salvador 11–3, Cuba beat Puerto Rico 7–4, Nicaragua beat Cuba 6–2, Cuba beat Honduras 6–0. Finals: Cuba beat Dominican Republic 9–5, Puerto Rico beat Cuba 7–1, Cuba beat Panama 10–9, Cuba beat Nicaragua 6–2, Cuba beat Venezuela 5–4. .

1953 Amateur World Series XIV (Caracas, Venezuela) (September 12–October 9)

Cuba defended its 1952 title by sweeping Venezuela in the best-of-three final-round playoffs. Despite owning the most balanced team (with Alfonso Suárez and Manolo García both hitting above .400 and Antonio Suárez, along with Alejandro Eiriz, again providing formidable pitching), Cuba once more had no individual statistical pacesetters. The only loss for the champions came in the tournament's most exciting opening-round game, a 3–2 pitchers' duel between Antonio Suárez and Venezuela's tournament MVP Andrés Quintero.

Champion: Cuba (11–1)

Teams and Final Standings: Gold: Cuba (9–1), Silver: Venezuela (9–1), Bronze: Nicaragua (7–3), Dominican Republic (7–3), Panama (6–4), Puerto Rico (5–5), Colombia (3–7), Guatemala (3–7), Mexico (3–7), Dutch Antilles (2–8), El Salvador (1–9). *Cuba defeated Venezuela (4–3 and 4–0) in first two games of best-of-three championship playoffs.

Individual Statistical Leaders: **BA**: Domingo Vargas (DOM) .455; **Runs**: L. Cumberbatch (PAN), Dario Rubenstein (VEN) 16; **Hits**: O. Alvarado (NIC) 18; **2B**: Juan A. Pérez (ANT) 4; **3B**: A. Castillo (PAN) 4; **HR**: Conrado Griffith (PAN) 2; **RBI**: F. Torres (PRI) 15; **SB**: Dario Rubenstein (VEN) 10; **Wins**: Andrés Quintero (VEN) 4–0; **ERA**: M. Estrada (MEX) 0.00; **MVP**: Andrés Quintero (VEN).

Cuba Roster: **Manager**: Osvardo Castellanos. **Batting** (AB–H–BA): Alfonso Suárez (36–15–.417), Manolo García (37–15–.405), M. González (33–11–.333), J. M. Fernández (33–10–.303), C. Cordova (30–9–.300), L. Olivares (42–11–.262), A. López (Not Available), F. Foyo (NA), G. de Cárdenas (NA), J. Figarola (NA), L. Seijo (NA), E. Cruz (NA), Antonio Suárez (NA). **Pitching** (W–L–ERA): Antonio Suárez (2–1–0.87), L. Fiuza (3–0–1.78), J. Suárez (2–0–2.35), Alejandro Eiriz (1–0), Ricardo Diaz (1–0), C. Pérez (0–0). No additional statistics available.

Cuba Game Scores Preliminary Round: Cuba beat Puerto Rico 3–2, Cuba beat Dominican Republic 8–4, Venezuela beat Cuba 3–2, Cuba beat Dutch Antilles 9–1, Cuba beat Nicaragua 1–0, Cuba beat Mexico 3–1, Cuba beat El Salvador 6–2, Cuba beat Colombia 1–0, Cuba beat Guatemala 5–0, Cuba beat Panama 10–7. Playoffs: Cuba beat Venezuela 4–2. Cuba beat Venezuela 4–0.

1961 Amateur World Series XV (San José, Costa Rica) (April 7–21)

Mass tryouts in Havana produced an exceptionally strong Cuban team for the first international competition after the installation of Fidel's revolutionary government. In a quirk of fortuitous timing the Cuban entry ran roughshod over five other participating teams at precisely the same moment when Fidel's army was repulsing a USA-backed home-front invasion at the Bay of Pigs. Alfredo Street, a lanky black right-hander from Oriente Province and holdover from the National Amateur League of the final years of the Batista era, won three games without defeat and José M. Pineda (2–0) allowed only one earned run in 18 innings of work. Pedro Chávez, another key transitional figure in the transfer from pre-revolution to post-revolution amateur leagues, provided most of the team's heavy hitting with tournament-best figures in both RBI and base hits.

Champion: Cuba (9–0)

Final Round Standings: Gold: Cuba (5–0), Silver: Mexico (4–1), Bronze: Venezuela (3–2), Panama (2–3), Costa Rica (1–4), Guatemala (0–5)

Group A Preliminary Standings: Panama (4–0), Venezuela (3–1), Costa Rica (2–2), Honduras (1–3), El Salvador (0–4)

Group B Preliminary Standings: Cuba (4–0), Mexico (3–1), Guatemala (1–3), Nicaragua (1–3), Dutch Antilles (1–3)

Individual Statistical Leaders: **BA**: Mario González (CUB) .500; **Runs**: J. Fernández (CUB) 20; **Hits**: Pedro Chávez (CUB), J. Fernández (CUB) 17; **2B**: José Parcero (MEX) 5; **3B**: eight players with one each; **HR**: Williams Proutt (PAN) 6; **RBI**: Pedro Chávez (CUB) 19; **SB**: J. Fernández (CUB) 5; **Wins**: Luis García (MEX) 4; **ERA**: José M. Pineda (CUB), 0.50.

Cuba Roster: **Manager**: Clemente "Sungo" Carreras. **Batting** (AB–H–BA): Mario González (32–16–.500), Jorge Trigoura (23–11–.478), Pedro Chávez (37–17–.459), Eladio Sauquet (18–8–.444), J. Fernández (41–17–.415), René Díaz (25–10–.400), Angel Fuentes (33–12–.364), Raúl Ortega (30–8–.267), Antonio González (12–3–.250), Urbano González

(28–7–.250), Ricardo Lazo (27–6–.222), D. Blanco (10–2–.200), José M. Pineda (9–3–.333), Santiago Pérez (3–1–.333), Alfredo Street (10–3–.300), Rolando Pastor (7–1–.143), Ricardo Díaz (8–1–.125), Jacinto Blanco (2–0–.000). **Pitching** (W–L–ERA): Jacinto Blanco (0–0–0.00), José M. Pineda (2–0–0.50), Ricardo Díaz (1–0–0.72), Alfredo Street (3–0–1.15), Rolando Pastor (2–0–1.50), Santiago Pérez (1–0–3.60).

Cuba Game Scores Preliminary Round: Cuba beat Dutch Antilles 18–0, Cuba beat Nicaragua 16–0, Cuba beat Guatemala 25–0, Cuba beat Mexico 11–1. Finals: Cuba beat Panama 12–3, Cuba beat Guatemala 13–2, Cuba beat Mexico 13–1, Cuba beat Costa Rica 12–2, Cuba beat Venezuela 9–3.

1965 Amateur World Series XVI (Cartagena, Colombia) (February 12–27)

Colombia's right-wing government denied visas to the favored Cuban contingent, striking a Cold War blow against the new communist island government and leaving the powerhouse defending champions sitting at home on the sidelines. Colombia and Mexico finished in a dead heat in the playdown round, necessitating a championship series swept by the hosts in two straight. Two notable pitching feats marked this tournament: a perfect game (and the first Amateur World Series no-hitter) by Mexican hurler David García against Guatemala (February 14) and a single-game World Series strikeout record by Puerto Rico's Efraín Contreras (19 Ks) versus the Dutch Antilles (February 22).

Champion: Colombia (9–2)

Teams and Final Standings: Gold: Colombia* (7–1), Silver: Mexico (7–1), Bronze: Puerto Rico (5–3), Panama (4–4), Nicaragua (4–4), Guatemala (3–5), Dutch Antilles (2–6), El Salvador (0–8). *After losing opening playoff game (4–2), Colombia defeated Mexico twice (11–5 and 4–0) in best-of-three championship finals round.

Individual Statistical Leaders: **BA**: Andres Cruz (PRI) .485; **Runs**: Luis de Arcos (COL) 12; **Hits**: Andres Cruz (PRI) 16; **2B**: José Parcero (MEX) 4; **3B**: seven players with 2 each; **HR**: five players with one each; **RBI**: Andres Cruz (PRI) 8; **SB**: Urbano Camarena (PAN) 5; **Wins**: Arturo Hudson (NIC), David García (MEX) 3; **ERA**: Arturo Hudson (NIC) 0.00.

Cuba Did Not Participate

1969 Amateur World Series XVII (Santo Domingo, Dominican Republic) (August 15–26)

Played under considerable political tension in Santo Domingo (due to strong anti–American feeling spawned by the U.S. invasion of the Dominican Republic four years earlier), the 1969 World Cup Series was a landmark event for post-revolutionary Cuban baseball. Cuba returned after their 1965 banishment from Colombia, and the USA fielded a team for the first time since their debacle performance of 1942: both teams moved undefeated through the field and squared off in a dramatic gold medal showdown. Gaspar Pérez was the hero of the finale, pitching brilliantly in relief, driving in the crucial tying run, and also scoring the eventual winning tally.

The 2–1 Cuban victory was witnessed by 20,000 pro-Cuba spectators, of whom almost one third were reported to be armed soldiers and military police on hand to control potential anti–American hostilities.

Champion: Cuba (10–0)

Teams and Final Standings: Gold: Cuba (10–0), Silver: USA (9–1), Bronze: Dominican Republic (7–2), Venezuela (7–3), Panama (4–6), Puerto Rico (4–6), Colombia (4–6), Nicaragua (4–6), Mexico (2–7), Guatemala (1–8), Dutch Antilles (1–8)

Individual Statistical Leaders: **BA**: Owen Blandino (CUB) .371; **Runs**: Owen Blandino (CUB) 13; **Hits**: Owen Blandino (CUB) 20; **2B**: Luis Mercado (PRI) 6; **3B**: Fermín Laffita (CUB), E. Ruiz (MEX), Luis Mercado (PRI) 3; **HR**: Fermín Laffita (CUB) 3; **RBI**: Fermín Laffita (CUB) 16; **SB**: Carlos Urriola (VEN) 5; **Wins**: Gaspar Pérez (CUB) 4–0; **ERA**: G. Rodríguez (DOM) 0.00; **MVP**: Gaspar Pérez (CUB).

Cuba Roster: **Manager**: Servio Borges. **Batting** (AB–H–BA): Owen Blandino (40–20–.500), Luis Pérez (25–12–.480), Fermín Laffita (43–19–.442), Féliz Isasi (21–9–.429), Felipe Sarduy (38–16–.421), Rigoberto Rosique (14–5–.357), Agustín Marquetti (32–11–.344), Andres Telemaco (27–9–.333), Antonio González (11–3–.273), Silvio Montejo (45–12–.267), Rodolfo Puente (24–4–.167), Ramón Hechavarría (13–2–.154), Gaspar Pérez (11–6–.545), Lázaro Santana (6–2–.333), Rolando Macías (7–2–.286), José Antonio Huelga (4–1–.250), Roberto Valdés (5–1–.200), Santiago "Changa" Mederos (5–1–.200). **Pitching** (W–L–ERA): Santiago "Changa" Mederos (1–0–1.00), Gaspar Pérez (4–0–0.35), José Antonio Huelga (1–0–0.75), Roberto Valdés (1–0–0.96), Rolando Macías (1–0–2.20), Lázaro Santana (2–0–2.45).

Cuba Game Scores Round Robin: Cuba beat Venezuela 9–0, Cuba beat Nicaragua 10–1, Cuba beat Panama 8–0, Cuba beat Guatemala 17–0, Cuba beat Dominican Republic 10–3, Cuba beat Colombia 9–3, Cuba beat Puerto Rico 9–1, Cuba beat Mexico 5–3, Cuba beat Dutch Antilles 12–1, Cuba beat USA 2–1.

1970 Amateur World Series XVIII (Cartagena, Colombia) (November 18–December 4)

The 1970s are arguably the showcase decade for post-revolution Cuban amateur baseball, and the era opened with a truly spectacular international tournament win. Cuba's only opening round loss came at the hands of an exceptionally strong USA club and the knuckle-ball pitching of future big league stalwart Burt Hooton. When the same two teams opened a best-of-three championship round, Hooton was matched up against young Cuban ace José Antonio Huelga in a classic mound duel which finally fell to the Cubans 3–1 after 11 hard-fought innings. Cuban southpaw ace Santiago "Changa" Mederos started the second playoff game and received stellar relief support from Manuel Alarcón — and once again from José Antonio Huelga — in the 5–3 win that clinched Cuba's tenth world championship crown.

Champion: Cuba (12–1)

Teams and Final Standings: Gold: Cuba (10–1), Silver:

USA (10–1), Bronze: Puerto Rico (9–2), Colombia (8–3), Venezuela (7–4), Dominican Republic (6–5), Nicaragua (4–7), Dutch Antilles (3–8), Italy (1–9), Canada (1–9), Netherlands (1–10). *Cuba wins championship cup with two straight wins (3–1 and 5–3) over USA in best-of-three championship round.

Individual Statistical Leaders: **BA**: Abel Leal (COL) .477; **Runs**: Félix Isasi (CUB), Wilfredo Sánchez (CUB), Abel Leal (COL), W. Pérez (DOM) 12; **Hits**: Abel Leal (COL) 21; **2B**: Luis Hernández (VEN), Luis Gaviria (COL) 5; **3B**: five players with two each; **HR**: Ramón Ortiz (PRI) 3; **RBI**: Félix Isasi (CUB) 15; **SB**: Orlando Ramírez (COL) 8; **Wins**: five pitchers with three each; **IP**: A. Jaramillo (COL) 32.2; **Strikeouts**: Burt Hooton (USA) 44; **ERA**: Burt Hooton (USA) 0.00. **MVP**: Abel Leal (COL).

Cuba Roster: **Manager**: Servio Borges. **Batting** (AB–H–BA): Felipe Sarduy (28–12–.429), Wilfredo Sánchez (46–19–.413), Félix Isasi (48–19–.396), Fermín Laffita (39–14–.359), Vicente Diaz (27–9–.333), Rigoberto Rosique (31–10–.323), Ramón Hechevarría (19–6–.316), Rodolfo Puente (27–8–.296), Urbano González (27–8–.296), Luis Pérez (18–4–.222), Armando Capiró (21–4–.190), Agustín Marquetti (18–3–.167), Antonio González (12–2–.167), Raul Reyes (8–1–.125), José Antonio Huelga (3–2–.667), Oscar Romero (8–3–.375), Emilio Salgado (6–2–.333), Manuel Hurtado (5–0–.000), Santiago "Changa" Mederos (6–0–.000), Gaspar Legón (9–0–.000). **Pitching** (W–L–ERA): Emilio Salgado (2–0–0.00), Manuel Hurtado (2–0–0.00), José Antonio Huelga (1–0–0.00), Gaspar Legón (3–0–0.43), Oscar Romero (2–0–0.50), Santiago "Changa" Mederos (2–1–1.59).

Cuba Game Scores Preliminary Round: Cuba beat Canada 12–0, Cuba beat Puerto Rico 10–0, Cuba beat Dominican Republic 11–1, Cuba beat Italy 9–1, Cuba beat Netherlands 10–1, Cuba beat Venezuela 8–1, Cuba beat Dutch Antilles 7–0, USA beat Cuba 3–1, Cuba beat Guatemala 4–0, Cuba beat Nicaragua 10–0, Cuba beat Colombia 6–0. Playoffs: Cuba beat USA 3–1, Cuba beat USA 5–3.

1971 Amateur World Series XIX (Havana, Cuba) (November 21–December 4)

World Cup Series action returned to Havana in December with games played all around the island and the hosts easily sweeping a weakened field that had no USA representative. Rodolfo Puente (batting champion and MVP) and Elpidio Mancebo were the hitting stars for Cuba, while Armando Capiró (that year's National Series RBI champion) and Rigoberto Rosique (National Series batting leader) both slumped badly throughout the nine-game tournament. Nelson García of Colombia tossed the second-ever World Cup no-hitter when he shut down Italy 7–0 in Pinar del Río. Santiago "Changa" Mederos pitched flawlessly for Cuba while Antonio Jiménez, Oscar Romero and José Antonio Huelga also each won a pair of games. Huelga tossed a 2-hit shutout in Cuba's 6–0 win over a tournament all-star squad in the event finale.

Champion: Cuba (9–0)

Teams and Final Standings: Gold: Cuba (9–0), Silver: Colombia (7–2), Bronze: Nicaragua (6–3), Puerto Rico (6–3), Panama (5–4), Dominican Republic (4–5), Canada (4–5), Italy (2–7), Mexico (2–7), Dutch Antilles (0–9)

Individual Statistical Leaders: **BA**: Rodolfo Puente (CUB) .429; **Runs**: Elpidio Mancedo (CUB) 12; **Hits**: Ruperto Cooper (PAN) 14; **2B**: Ramón Greene (DOM, Alvin Fleming (ANT), Eduardo Ruiz (MEX) 5; **3B**: A.T. Wester (ANT), Ramón Greene (DOM), Luis Gaviria (COL) 2; **HR**: Luis Escoba (COL), Rick Cruise (CAN) 7; **RBI**: Ruperto Cooper (PAN) 11; **SB**: Orlando Ramírez (COL) 7; **Wins**: Carlos Lowell (PRI) 3; **ERA**: Santiago "Changa" Mederos (CUB) 0.00; **MVP**: Rodolfo Puente (CUB).

Cuba Roster: **Manager**: Servio Borges. **Batting** (AB–H–BA): Rodolfo Puente (21–9–.429), Luis Pérez (27–11–.407), Eulogio Osorio (5–2–.400), Elpidio Mancebo (34–13–.382), Wilfredo Sánchez (33–12–.364), Raul Reyes (18–6–.333), Owen Blandino (16–5–.313), Félix Isasi (33–9–.273), Urbano González (11–3–.273), Antonio González (4–1–.250), Rigoberto Rosique (33–8–.242), Armando Capiró (23–5–.217), Ramón Hechevarría (6–1–.167), Vicente Diaz (17–2–.118), José Antonio Huelga (5–2–.400), Roberto Valdés (3–1–.333), Antonio Jiménez (8–2–.250), Santiago "Changa" Mederos (6–1–.167), Oscar Romero (6–0–.000), Rolando Macías (0–0–.000). **Pitching** (W–L–ERA): Santiago "Changa" Mederos (2–0–0.00), Roberto Valdés (1–0–0.00), Antonio Jiménez (2–0–0.51), Oscar Romero (2–0–0.53), José Antonio Huelga (2–0–0.75), Rolando Macías (0–0–2.70).

Cuba Game Scores Round Robin: Cuba beat Dominican Republic 16–2, Cuba beat Canada 4–0, Cuba beat Mexico 4–1, Cuba beat Panama 5–1, Cuba beat Puerto Rico 7–0, Cuba beat Nicaragua 2–0, Cuba beat Dutch Antilles 9–0, Cuba beat Italy 16–0, Cuba beat Colombia 3–0.

1972 Amateur World Series XX (Managua, Nicaragua) (November 15–December 5)

Cuba wins for a fourth straight time over the largest field to date, with 16 nations competing in November at Managua. Braudilio Vinent was the pitching star with a perfect 4–0 slate (0.62 ERA) while Wilfredo Sánchez slugged at a .414 clip and Armando Capiró (making up for his slump a year earlier) knocked home 21 runs. Cuba's 5–3 victory over the USA accounted for the difference in the standings between the top two teams. The only loss suffered by the champions was a 2–0 whitewashing at the hands of Nicaragua. In an additional all-star contest matching the champion Cubans with top stars drawn from other participating nations, Cuba was again victorious, 6–0, with Vinent pitching an 8-hit complete-game victory and Armando Capiró slugging a three-run first-inning homer. The tournament also featured no-hitters by Puerto Rico's Sandalio Quiñonez (versus Costa Rica) and Panama's Ronaldo Montero (versus Germany).

Champion: Cuba (14–1)

Teams and Final Standings: Gold: Cuba (14–1), Silver: USA (13–2), Bronze: Nicaragua (13–2), Japan (11–4), Panama (10–5), Dominican Republic (9–6), Puerto Rico (9–6), Taiwan (9–6), Canada (8–7), Guatemala (5–10), Honduras

(4–11), Brazil (4–11), Costa Rica (4–11), El Salvador (4–11), Italy (2–12), German Federal Republic (0–15)

All-Star Game (December 5, 1972): Cuba 6, World Cup All-Stars 0 (WP: Braudilio Vinent)

Individual Statistical Leaders: **BA**: Masaru Oba (JAP) .415; **Runs**: Wilfredo Sánchez (CUB) 22; **Hits**: Wilfredo Sánchez (CUB) 29; **2B**: Félix Isasi (CUB) 8; **3B**: Wilfredo Sánchez (CUB), Armando Capiró (CUB), Manuel Estrada (USA) 3; **HR**: René Mena (GUA) 4; **RBI**: Armando Capiró (CUB) 21; **SB**: Masaru Oba (JAP) 4; **Wins**: Jay Smith (USA), Richard Smith (USA), Braudilio Vinent (CUB) 4; **IP**: Tan Shing-Ming (TAI) 51.1; **Strikeouts**: Tan Shing-Ming (TAI) 53; **ERA**: Zengo Ikeda (JAP) 0.00.

Cuba Roster: **Manager**: Servio Borges. **Batting** (AB–H–BA): Evelio Hernández (20–10–.500), Wilfredo Sánchez (77–29–.414), Lázaro Pérez (34–14–.412), Armando Capiró (61–23–.377), Arturo Linares (14–5–.357), Félix Isasi (55–19–.345), Urbano González (38–12–.316), Rodolfo Puente (42–13–.310), Fermín Laffita (43–13–.302), Rigoberto Rosique (31–9–.290), Owen Blandino (33–8–.240), Agustín Marquetti (54–15–.278), Agustín Arias (19–7–.368), Braudilio Vinent (8–4–.500), Oscar Romero (4–2–.500), Orlando Figueredo (10–4–.400), Antonio Jiménez (8–1–.125), Bernardo González (1–0–0.00), Santiago "Changa" Mederos (1–0–.000), José Antonio Huelga (10–1–.100). **Pitching** (W–L–ERA): Bernardo González (1–0–0.00), Santiago "Changa" Mederos (0–0–0.00), Braudilio Vinent (4–0–0.62), José Antonio Huelga (3–1–0.79), Orlando Figueredo (3–0–0.86), Oscar Romero (3–0–1.17), Antonio Jiménez (1–0–1.35).

Cuba Game Scores Round Robin: Cuba beat Germany 10–0, Cuba beat Panama 13–2, Cuba beat Costa Rica 19–0, Cuba beat Brazil 13–3, Cuba beat Japan 2–0, Cuba beat Honduras 3–0, Cuba beat El Salvador 16–0, Cuba beat Puerto Rico 4–2, Cuba beat Chinese Taipei 10–1, Cuba beat Dominican Republic 14–0, Cuba beat Italy 19–1, Cuba beat Canada 5–1, Cuba beat USA 5–3, Cuba beat Guatemala 7–2, Nicaragua beat Cuba 2–0.

1973 Amateur World Series XXI (Havana, Cuba) (November 25–December 9)

Another undefeated Cuban squad was one of the strongest ever in World Cup play, featuring a pitching staff that logged 110 consecutive innings without allowing a single earned run. (Cuba was scored upon in only three of its 14 outings!) One highlight moment of this stellar two-week pitching performance came when Juan Pérez tossed a no-hitter against Venezuela, the first ever "perfecto" for Cuba in World Cup play. On the hitting front, Fermín Laffita smacked two homers in the same inning against Mexico, Marquetti collected the most base hits of the tournament, and three Cubans shared home run hitting honors. Despite these remarkable performances by Laffita and Pérez, it was the consistent Marquetti who walked off with the tournament MVP honors.

Champion: Cuba (14–0)

Teams and Final Standings: Gold: Cuba (14–0), Silver: Puerto Rico (10–3), Bronze: Venezuela (10–4), Dominican Republic (7–6), Panama (6–8), Mexico (5–9), Dutch Antilles (3–11), Netherlands (0–14)

Individual Statistical Leaders: **BA**: J. Fontánez (PRI) .432; **Runs**: Félix Isasi (CUB) 20; **Hits**: Agustín Marquetti (CUB) 25; **2B**: F. Rodríguez (MEX) 6; **HR**: Evelio Hernández (CUB), Armando Capiró (CUB), Félix Isasi (CUB) 3; **RBI**: Agustín Marquetti (CUB) 21; **SB**: Wilfredo Sánchez (CUB) 9; **Wins**: Julio Romero (CUB), Luis Barreiro (CUB), E. Ovalles (VEN) 3–0; **IP**: E. Ovalles (VEN) 27.0; **Strikeouts**: Luis Barreiro (CUB) 34; **ERA**: Julio Romero (CUB) 0.00; **MVP**: Agustín Marquetti (CUB).

Cuba Roster: **Manager**: Servio Borges. **Batting** (AB–H–BA): Evelio Hernández (21–11–.524), Rigoberto Rosique (10–5–.500), Agustín Marquetti (60–25–.417), Rodolfo Puente (48–17–.354), Armando Capiró (57–21–.368), Lázaro Pérez (28–9–.321), Wilfredo Sánchez (55–20–.364), Félix Isasi (52–17–.327), Julian Villar (21–6–.286), Alfonso Urquiola (14–4–.286), Ubaldo Alvarez (10–2–.200), Alfredo García (7–1–.143), Luis Barreiro (13–3–.231), Julio Romero (13–1–.077), Mario Fernández (4–0–.000), Antonio Jiménez (5–0–.000), Juan Pérez Pérez (5–0–.000), Braudilio Vinent (2–0–.000). **Pitching** (W–L–ERA): Julio Romero (3–0–0.00), Alfredo García (2–0–0.00), Antonio Jiménez (2–0–0.00), Luis Barreiro (3–0–0.00), Mario Fernández (2–0–0.00), Braudilio Vinent (1–0–0.00), Juan Pérez Pérez (1–0–0.95).

Cuba Game Scores Round Robin: Cuba beat Dominican Republic 8–2, Cuba beat Mexico 7–0, Cuba beat Dutch Antilles 8–1, Cuba beat Netherlands 14–0, Cuba beat Venezuela 4–0 (no-hitter by Juan Pérez), Cuba beat Dominican Republic 11–0, Cuba beat Puerto Rico 10–0, Cuba beat Panama 8–0, Cuba beat Mexico 13–0, Cuba beat Dutch Antilles 7–0, Cuba beat Netherlands 7–0, Cuba beat Venezuela 6–0, Cuba beat Puerto Rico 3–2, Cuba beat Panama 13–0.

1973 Amateur World Series (FEMBA) XXII (Managua, Nicaragua) (November 22–December 5)

Political infighting among members of amateur baseball's governing body (FIBA, International Baseball Federation) leads to a meeting in Bologna, Italy, where delegates from 24 countries announce a rival organization (FEMBA, World Federation of Amateur Baseball). While FIBA holds its own 1973 tournament as scheduled in Havana, FEMBA also orchestrates a rival event in earthquake-devastated Nicaragua with eleven countries participating. Team USA claims the FEMBA title, followed by Nicaragua in the runner-up slot. In the final game Team USA clinches the trophy in a thrilling 1–0 pitchers' duel between two future big leaguers, USA's Dick Wortham and Nicaragua's Dennis Martínez.

Champion: USA (10–0)

Teams and Final Standings: Gold: USA (10–0), Silver: Nicaragua (8–2), Bronze: Puerto Rico (8–2), Colombia (7–3), Taiwan (7–3), Canada (4–6), Honduras (4–6), Costa Rica (3–7), Guatemala (3–7), Mexico (1–9), Germany (0–10)

Individual Statistical Leaders: No statistics are available from this tournament. (Gold Medal winner USA Game Scores: USA beat Mexico 4–0, USA beat Germany 4–0, USA beat Chinese Taipei 4–2, USA beat Guatemala 4–0, USA beat Colombia 7–1, USA beat Canada 8–1, USA beat Puerto Rico 7–0, USA beat Costa Rica 9–0, USA beat Honduras 8–0, USA beat Nicaragua 1–0).

Cuba Did Not Participate

1974 Amateur World Series (FEMBA) XXIII (St. Petersburg, Florida USA) (September 13–23)

FEMBA member countries attempt a second alternative Amateur World Series (World Cup), this time staged in the United States, with the Americans again claiming a championship. Cuba remains on the sidelines until the next FIBA event scheduled for 1976 at Cartagena, Colombia. Subsequent World Cup tournaments sponsored by FIBA will recognize the two FEMBA tournaments as World Cup XXII and World Cup XXIII in order to preserve the consecutive numbering system already in use.

Champion: USA (9–1)

Teams and Final Standings: Gold: USA (7–0), Silver: Nicaragua (7–0), Bronze: Colombia (5–3), Canada (3–5), Italy (3–5), Chinese Taipei (3–5), Dominican Republic (3–5), Puerto Rico (3–5), South Africa (1–7). *USA defeated Nicaragua twice (5–4 and 9–2) in best-of-three championship playoff round.

Individual Statistical Leaders: **BA**: J. Cuaresma (COL) .470; **HR**: P. Llamas (COL), D. Comm (USA) 3; **RBI**: C. Jarquin (NIC) 10; **Wins**: Six pitchers with two wins each; **ERA**: P. Altamirano (NIC) 0.50. No additional player data or statistics are available. All other records appear to be lost. (Note: Spelling of names for non–Latin American players also are questionable.)

Cuba Did Not Participate

1976 Amateur World Series XXIV (Cartagena, Colombia) (December 3–19)

Semi-normalcy returns to the world of amateur international baseball as FEMBA disbands and FIBA renews its series of tournaments held in alternate years. FIBA will henceforth be known as AINBA or IBA (International Association of Amateur Baseball). Normality also reigns on the playing field with Cuba again a walk-away champion, although Cuba and Puerto Rico actually finish with identical 8–2 records and victory comes to the defending champs when Puerto Rico withdraws and forfeits its playoff-round contests. Armando Capiró and Agustín Marquetti are the big guns in the Cuban lineup and Omar Carrero logs four pitching victories.

Champion: Cuba (10–2)

Teams and Final Standings: Gold: Cuba (8–2), Silver: Puerto Rico (8–2), Bronze: Japan (7–3), Nicaragua (7–3), South Korea (5–5), Taiwan (5–5), Dominican Republic (5–5), Colombia (4–6), Panama (3–7), Mexico (2–8), Netherlands (1–9). *Cuba awarded gold medal with two forfeit victories over Puerto Rico in playoffs.

Individual Statistical Leaders: **BA**: Manuel Cabrejas (DOM) .521; **Runs**: Armando Capiró (CUB) 17; **Hits**: Manuel Cabrejas (DOM) 25; **2B**: Agustín Marquetti (CUB) 7; **3B**: Douglas Moody (NIC) 4; **HR**: Armando Capiró (CUB) 5; **RBI**: Agustín Marquetti (CUB) 20; **SB**: A. Rosario (DOM) 5; **Wins**: Omar Carrero (CUB) 4–0; **IP**: Omar Carrero (CUB) 29.2; **Strikeouts**: Kuo Yuan Chin (TAI) 41; **ERA**: J.L. de León (PRI) 0.00.

Cuba Roster: **Manager**: Servio Borges. **Batting** (AB–H–BA): Elpidio Osorio (9–6–.667), Evelio Hernández (9–9–.667), Agustín Marquetti (42–21–.500), Rodolfo Puente (39–18–.462), Armando Capiró (45–19–.422), Lázaro Pérez (31–12–.387), Wilfredo Sánchez (44–17–.381), Pedro Jova (6–2–.333), Bárbaro Garbey (18–6–.333), Félix Isasi (16–5–.313), Antonio Muñoz (26–8–.308), Fermín Laffita (32–9–.281), Rey Anglada (22–5–.227), Pedro José Rodríguez (44–9–.205). **Pitching** (W–L–ERA): Omar Carrero (4–0–0.61), Santiago "Changa" Mederos (1–0–1.80), Rogelio García (0–1–1.80), Braudilio Vinent (2–1–.2.84), Oscar Romero (0–0–5.00), Julio Romero (1–0–6.75).

Cuba Game Scores Round Robin: Cuba beat Netherlands 27–1, Cuba beat Mexico 15–1, Dominican Republic beat Cuba 13–12, Cuba beat Panama 7–3, Cuba beat Chinese Taipei 6–2, Cuba beat South Korea 13–2, Cuba beat Japan 4–0, Nicaragua beat Cuba 5–0, Cuba beat Puerto Rico 8–1, Cuba beat Colombia 7–5.

1978 Amateur World Series XXV (Parma, Bologna and Rimini, Italy) (August 25–September 6)

World Cup play returns to Europe for the first time since the initial two-team event of 1938 and Cuba once more outdistances the field, winning the crucial showdown match with Team USA. A pair of no-hitters are authored by César Monge of Nicaragua (against Belgium) and Yasuyuki Yamamoto of Japan (versus the same hapless Belgians) and both transpire in seven innings via the ten-run knockout rule. Australia and Belgium participate for the first time and finish in the final two spots in the standings. Antonio Muñoz establishes a new tournament record for home runs with eight and not surprisingly wears the crown as tournament MVP.

Champion: Cuba (10–0)

Teams and Final Standings: Gold: Cuba (10–0), Silver: USA (9–1), Bronze: South Korea (8–2), Japan (7–3), Nicaragua (5–5), Italy (5–5), Netherlands (4–6), Mexico (3–7), Canada (2–8), Australia (2–8), Belgium (0–10)

Individual Statistical Leaders: **BA**: Roberto Espino (NIC) .500; **Runs**: Antonio Muñoz (CUB), T. Wallace (USA) 14; **Hits**: Roberto Espino (NIC), Fernando Sánchez (CUB) 16; **2B**: Fernando Sánchez (CUB) 5; **3B**: J. Simon (USA), Terry Francona (USA) 2; **HR**: Antonio Muñoz (CUB) 8; **RBI**: Antonio Muñoz (CUB) 18; **SB**: M. Kobayashi (JAP) 13; **Wins**: Mori Shigekazu (JAP), D. Wong Choi (KOR) 4; **IP**: D. Wong Choi (KOR) 33.1; **Strikeouts**: D. Wong Choi (KOR) 44; **ERA**: M. Thurman (USA) 0.00; **MVP**: Antonio Muñoz (CUB).

Cuba Roster: **Manager**: Servio Borges. **Batting** (AB–H–BA): Agustín Marquetti (20–9–.450), Luis Casanova (36–16–

.444), Fernando Sánchez (37–16–.432), Pedro Jova (19–8–.421), Antonio Muñoz (32–13–.406), Pedro Medina (19–6–.316), Rodolfo Puente (36–13–.361), Alfonso Urquiola (37–11–.297), Armando Capiró (28–9–.321), Wilfredo Sánchez (17–4–.235), Pedro José Rodríguez (37–8–.216), Alfonso Martínez (13–2–.154), Rey Anglada (1–0–.000). **Pitching** (W–L–ERA): Rogelio García (1–0–0.00), Juan Carlos Oliva (2–0–0.00), Omar Carrero (0–0–0.00), Lázaro Santana (2–0–0.69), Julio Romero (1–0–1.00), Braudilio Vinent (3–0–1.80), Félix Pino (1–0–2.70).

Cuba Game Scores Round Robin: Cuba beat Italy 6–0, Cuba beat Japan 3–2, Cuba beat Australia 10–3, Cuba beat Nicaragua 7–2, Cuba beat Canada 5–1, Cuba beat Netherlands 12–1, Cuba beat USA 5–3, Cuba beat Mexico 11–1, Cuba beat Belgium 16–0, Cuba beat South Korea 11–0.

1980 Amateur World Series XXVI (Tokyo, Japan) (August 22–September 5)

Servio Borges serves as World Cup winning manager for the eighth time (without defeat), a record that will likely stand for decades. Lourdes Gourriel again proved his mettle during international competition with a game-winning hit in the showdown with Team USA, but the Cubans were rarely challenged in sweeping through eleven games without defeat. This was the first tournament staged in Asia and Japanese fans had plenty to cheer with the host country and Korea both winning nine games apiece. Antonio Muñoz again hit over .400 and again locked up MVP honors, tying teammate Gourriel for the home run crown. Braudilio Vinent anchored the pitching corps with three more victories in his penultimate World Cup tournament appearance.

Champion: Cuba (11–0)

Teams and Final Standings: Gold: Cuba (11–0), Silver: South Korea (9–2), Japan (9–2), USA (8–3), Canada (6–5), Italy (5–6), Venezuela (4–7), Puerto Rico (4–7), Colombia (4–7), Australia (4–7), Mexico (1–10), Netherlands (1–10)

Individual Statistical Leaders: **BA**: Eusebio Moreno (COL) .448; **Runs**: Kim Kwon (KOR) 18; **Hits**: Fernando Sánchez (CUB) 21; **2B**: Stan Edmonds (USA) 6; **3B**: A. Romero (USA) 3; **HR**: Antonio Muñoz (CUB), Luis Casanova (CUB) 7; **RBI**: Antonio Muñoz (CUB) 19; **SB**: Kim Kwon (KOR) 18; **Wins**: Lee Sung Hee (KOR) 4; **IP**: Lee Sung Hee (KOR) 40.1; **Strikeouts**: Choi Dong Won (KOR) 43; **ERA**: José Luis Alemán (CUB) 0.00; **MVP**: Antonio Muñoz (CUB).

Cuba Roster: **Manager**: Servio Borges. **Batting** (AB–H–BA): Alfonso Martínez (9–7–.778), Carmelo Pedroso (12–6–.500), Lourdes Gourriel (42–19–.452), Pedro Medina (31–14–.452), Fernando Sánchez (47–21–.447), Alfonso Urquiola (32–13–.406), Antonio Muñoz (45–18–.400), Luis Casanova (47–17–.362), Rodolfo Puente (36–13–.361), Héctor Olivera (26–9–.346), Pedro Jova (18–6–.333), Pedro José Rodríguez (46–13–.263), Wilfredo Sánchez (8–2–.250). **Pitching** (W–L–ERA): José Luis Alemán (2–0–0.00), Félix Pino (0–0–0.00), Jesús Guerra (1–0–1.33), Braudilio Vinent (3–0–1.38), José Darcourt (2–0–2.16), Julio Romero (1–0–2.45), Juan Carlos Oliva (2–0–3.24).

Cuba Game Scores Round Robin: Cuba beat Italy 10–2, Cuba beat Puerto Rico 23–1, Cuba beat Australia 3–1, Cuba beat Colombia 25–0, Cuba beat Canada 15–1, Cuba beat Venezuela 11–3, Cuba beat South Korea 9–3, Cuba beat Mexico 10–0, Cuba beat Netherlands 8–0, Cuba beat Japan 1–0, Cuba beat USA 5–4.

1982 Amateur World Series XXVII (Seoul, South Korea) (August)

Cuba remains on the sidelines while South Korea hosts and wins the second straight World Cup staged in the Orient. Japanese, Taiwanese and Korean hitters and pitchers also thoroughly dominate the individual tournament leaders lists. For only the third time in thirty years (not counting the two FEMBA events) a team other than Cuba celebrates a championship; and Cuba will henceforth win all the remaining World Cup tournaments of the 20th Century (eight straight beginning in 1984 and extending through 2003).

Champion: South Korea (8–1)

Teams and Final Standings: Gold: South Korea (8–1), Silver: Japan (7–2), Bronze: USA (6–3), Chinese Taipei (6–3), Canada (5–4), Netherlands (3–6), Panama (3–6), Dominican Republic (3–6), Italy (2–7), Australia (2–7)

Individual Statistical Leaders: **BA**: Chen Sin Chang (TAI) .531; **Runs**: R. Cobb (USA) 10; **Hits**: Chen Sin Chang (TAI) 17; **2B**: Chen Sin Chang (TAI) 7; **3B**: four players with three each; **HR**: K. Takssue (JAP) 4; **RBI**: K. Takssue (JAP) 18; **SB**: M. Kobayashi (JAP) 7; **ERA**: Sun Dong Yul (KOR) 0.00; **MVP**: Sun Dong Yul (KOR). No additional player data or statistics are available. All other records appear to be lost. (Note: Spelling of names for non–Latin American players are also questionable.)

Cuba Did Not Participate

1984 Amateur World Series XXVIII (Havana, Cuba) (October 14–28)

The first World Cup Series held in Cuba in eleven years is surrounded with expected propaganda and pageantry as Fidel Castro visits opening game festivities with West German president Willie Brandt. Ceremonies honor Cuba's legendary nineteenth-century players, and 1950s' era star Connie Marrero throws a ceremonial first pitch to postrevolution Cuban League legend Rodolfo Puente. Key hits by Lourdes Gourriel and Alfonso Urquiola avoid a potentially embarrassing opening round loss to Italy and Cuba then rolls to its seventeenth world title and first of what will eventually become the current string of seven straight. Victor Mesa was the MVP and early shaky pitching was quickly corrected with Romero, Costa and Valdés all posting perfect 3–0 records. Future major league home run king Barry Bonds played for the third-place USA squad as a skinny nineteen-year-old outfielder.

Champion: Cuba (11–2)

Teams and Final Standings: Gold: Cuba (11–2), Silver: Chinese Taipei (7–5), Bronze: USA (8–4), Japan (8–5), Panama (7–5), Venezuela (6–4), Puerto Rico (6–7), South Korea

(5–7), Nicaragua (5–8), Dutch Antilles (4–6), Dominican Republic (3–6), Italy (3–7), Netherlands (1–8)

Individual Statistical Leaders: **BA**: Victor Mesa (NIC) .475; **Runs**: Victor Mesa (CUB) 17; **Hits**: Victor Mesa (CUB) 28; **2B**: Lourdes Gourriel (CUB) 7; **3B**: four players with two each; **HR**: Pedro José Rodríguez (CUB), Luis Casanova (CUB) 6; **RBI**: Lourdes Gourriel (CUB), Barry Bonds (USA) 16; **SB**: Victor Mesa (CUB) 8; **Wins**: H. Nagatomi (JAP), J. Moya (NIC) 4; **ERA**: S. Deng Ryeul (KOR) 0.00; **MVP**: Victor Mesa (CUB).

Cuba Roster: **Manager**: Pedro Chávez. **Batting** (AB–H–BA): Juan Castro (31–14–.452), Alfonso Martínez (16–4–.250), Pedro Medina (25–5–.200), Alfonso Urquiola (49–22–.449), Antonio Muñoz (33–14–.424), Pedro José Rodríguez (49–11–.229), Antonio Pacheco (35–15–.429), Pedro Jova (25–6–.240), Rolando Verde (4–0–.000), Lourdes Gourriel (55–17–.309), Victor Mesa (59–28–.475), Luis Casanova (55–20–.364), Lázaro Junco (40–15–.375). **Pitching** (W–L–ERA): Julio Romero (3–0–2.03), Rogelio García (0–1–4.61), Reinaldo Costa (3–0–1.65), Jorge Luis Valdés (3–0–2.21), Braudilio Vinent (1–0–6.97), José Sánchez (0–0–16.00), Angel Leocadio Diaz (1–1–2.89).

Cuba Game Scores Qualifying Round: Cuba beat Italy 6–5, Puerto Rico beat Cuba 5–4, Cuba beat Venezuela 13–0, Cuba beat Dutch Antilles 9–2, Cuba beat Nicaragua 10–0, Cuba beat Japan 3–1. Finals: Cuba beat Panama 10–6, Cuba beat South Korea 5–0, Cuba beat Japan 14–4, Cuba beat Nicaragua 16–7, Chinese Taipei beat Cuba 7–4, Cuba beat Puerto Rico 7–5, Cuba beat USA 10–1.

1986 Amateur World Series XXIX (Haarlem and Rotterdam, The Netherlands) (July 19–August 2)

Nineties-era heroes Linares and Kindelán appear in their first World Cup with this transitional Cuban team that also features Victor Mesa and Luis Casanova, two celebrated Cuban sluggers of the mid-eighties. This is the final national team managed by Pedro Chávez before Jorge Fuentes arrives on the scene. Casanova captures his second of three straight home run crowns in the "Mundiales" while Mesa, Pacheco and Linares all bat above .500 for the tournament. Pablo Miguel Abreu is the Cuban ace with three wins, and future big leaguer René Arocha also pockets two victories.

Champion: Cuba (10–1)

Teams and Final Standings: Gold: Cuba (10–1), Silver: South Korea (8–3), Bronze: Chinese Taipei (8–3), USA (7–4), Japan (6–5), Italy (6–5), Puerto Rico (5–6), Venezuela (5–6), Netherlands (5–6), Colombia (3–8), Dutch Antilles (2–9), Belgium (1–10)

Individual Statistical Leaders: **BA**: G. Carelli (ITA) .478; **Runs**: R. Biachi (ITA) 18; **Hits**: G. Carelli (ITA) 22; **2B**: R. Chung (KOR) 8; **3B**: M. Fujoshi (JAP) 3; **HR**: Luis Casanova (CUB) 6; **SB**: R. Santana (PRI) 6; **Wins**: Pablo Miguel Abreu (CUB), P. Dong Hec (KOR) 3; **ERA**: K. Ming Shan (TAI) 0.35. No additional statistics available.

Cuba Roster: **Manager**: Pedro Chávez. **Batting** (AB–H–BA): Victor Mesa (44–18–.409), Antonio Pacheco (46–21–.457), Omar Linares (46–21–.457), Orestes Kindelán (46–18–.391), Luis Casanova (44–18–.409), Lourdes Gourriel (42–15–.357), Antonio Muñoz (39–15–.385), Juan Castro (23–7–.304), Luis Ulacia (39–13–.333), Pedro Medina (8–2–.250), Jorge García (2–1–.500), Juan Padilla (3–2–.667), Lázaro Vargas (3–1–.333). **Pitching** (W–L–ERA): Pablo Miguel Abreu (3–1–1.55), Omar Carrero (1–0–0.00), Félix Nuñez (1–0–3.68), Jorge Luis Valdés (1–0–0.00), René Arocha (2–0–2.13), Luis Tissert (1–0–1.35), Rogelio García (1–0–2.25).

Cuba Game Scores Round Robin: Cuba beat Puerto Rico 11–1, Cuba beat Dutch Antilles 15–3, Cuba beat Colombia 11–0, Cuba beat USA 11–0, Cuba beat Netherlands 12–1, Cuba beat Venezuela 9–3, Cuba beat Belgium 21–3, Cuba beat South Korea 10–2, Cuba beat Italy 15–5, Cuba beat Japan 4–2, Chinese Taipei beat Cuba 4–3.

*1988 Baseball World Cup XXX (Parma and Rimini, Italy) (August 23–September 7)

Future MLB all-star Robin Ventura swung a big bat for the USA and led the field in several power-hitting categories. Another future big leaguer of note, Tino Martínez, also swung a heavy stick for the Americans, and Ben McDonald (a rookie with the Orioles the next spring) was the tournament's most outstanding pitcher. Jim Abbott was another hurler on one of the strongest-ever USA contingents. But Cuba remains undefeated with a gold medal victory over talent-laden Team USA. Despite the likes of Ventura and Martínez, it is Antonio Pacheco of Cuba who turns the most heads by leading in hitting and earning a selection as the tourney's top defensive performer. Cuba would avoid another showdown with nearly the same USA squad by conveniently boycotting the demonstration baseball tournament held at the Olympic Games in Seoul, South Korea, later this same year.

Champion: Cuba (13–0)

Finals: Cuba beat USA 4–3 (Gold Medal), Chinese Taipei beat Japan 4–2 (Bronze Medal)

Semifinals: Cuba beat Japan 7–3, USA beat Chinese Taipei 6–3

Preliminary Round Standings: Cuba (11–0), USA (10–1), Chinese Taipei (8–3), Japan (7–4), Canada (7–4), Puerto Rico (6–5), Nicaragua (5–6), South Korea (5–6), Italy (4–7), Netherlands (2–9), Dutch Antilles (1–10), Spain (0–11)

Individual Statistical Leaders: **BA**: Antonio Pacheco (CUB) .500; **Runs**: Omar Linares (CUB), T. Griffith (USA) 17; **Hits**: Antonio Pacheco (CUB) 21; **2B**: Robin Ventura (USA) 8; **3B**: J. Kokas (CAN), T. Kajima (JAP) 3; **HR**: Luis Casanova (CUB) 7; **RBI**: Robin Ventura (USA) 28; **SB**: J. Medina (NIC), K. Tmashino (JAP) 6; **Wins**: four pitchers with three each; **ERA**: Ben McDonald (USA) 0.00; **MVP**: Tino Martínez (USA).

Cuba Roster: **Manager**: Jorge Fuentes. **Batting** (AB–H–BA): Antonio Pacheco (42–21–.500), Lourdes Gourriel

(26–13–.500), Luis Casanova (43–18–.419), Luis Ulacia (37–14–.378), Omar Linares (47–17–.362), Victor Mesa (40–14–.350), Ermidelio Urrutia (30–10–.333), Alejo O'Reilly (35–11–.314), Orestes Kindelán (44–13–.295), Pedro Luis Rodríguez (26–13–.500), Juan Castro (13–3–.231), Juan Padilla (6–1–.167), Lázaro Vargas (15–4–.267). **Pitching** (W–L–ERA): Lázaro Valle (2–0–1.50), Omar Ajete (1–0–2.07), Jorge Luis Valdés (1–0–4.36), José Luis Aleman (2–0–2.59), René Arocha (1–0–6.56), Orlando Hernández (1–0–5.19), Euclides Rojas (3–0–0.93).

Cuba Game Scores Preliminary Round: Cuba beat Italy 11–1, Cuba beat South Korea 9–5, Cuba beat Canada 18–0, Cuba beat Chinese Taipei 7–3, Cuba beat Spain 11–0, Cuba beat Puerto Rico 7–6, Cuba beat Dutch Antilles 10–3, Cuba beat Japan 3–2, Cuba beat Nicaragua 11–1, Cuba beat Netherlands 15–5, Cuba beat USA 10–9. Playoffs: Cuba beat Dominican Republic 3–2. Semifinals: Cuba beat Japan 7–3. Finals: Cuba beat USA 4–3.

1990 Baseball World Cup XXXI (Edmonton, Canada) (August 4–19)

Orestes Kindelán was the tournament's hitting star as he rang up a triple crown with the leadership in homers and RBI and also a spot as champion batter. An easy team victory was the fourth straight World Cup Series success for Team Cuba in a string that now stretches through seven tournaments dating back to 1984 (a period in which Cuba has lost only four individual games of 77 played). This was perhaps Cuba's easiest international victory ever, with runner-up Nicaragua winning only half as many games and with little serious challenge from usual rivals Puerto Rico, Japan and Team USA. A dozen Cuban players bat above .333 and Lázaro Valle is virtually unhittable in his three tournament pitching starts.

Champion: Cuba (10–0)
Teams and Final Standings: Gold: Cuba (10–0), Silver: Nicaragua (5–5), Bronze: South Korea (5–4), Puerto Rico (7–2), Japan (6–3), USA (5–4), Chinese Taipei (4–5), Netherlands (3–5), Italy (3–5), Mexico (2–6), Canada (2–7), Venezuela (1–7)

Individual Statistical Leaders: **BA**: Orestes Kindelán (CUB) .581; **Runs**: Orestes Kindelán (CUB) 23; **Hits**: Orestes Kindelán (CUB) 25; **2B**: Orestes Kindelán (CUB) 7; **3B**: five players with three each; **HR**: Orestes Kindelán (CUB) 9; **RBI**: Orestes Kindelán (CUB) 25; **SB**: M. Naito (JAP) 6; **Wins**: Lee Chien Fu (TAI) 4; **ERA**: Lázro Valle (CUB) 0.00; **MVP**: Orestes Kindelán (CUB).

Cuba Roster: **Manager**: Jorge Fuentes. **Batting** (AB–H–BA): Pedro Luis Rodríguez (29–10–.345), Alberto Hernández (3–1–.333), Antonio Pacheco (37–13–.351), Omar Linares (32–18–.563), Luis Ulacia (8–2–.250), Juan Padilla (2–1–.500), Germán Mesa (32–16–.500), Orestes Kindelán (34–20–.588), Lourdes Gourriel (33–17–.515), Victor Mesa (33–13–.394), Javier Méndez (23–8–.348), Luis Casanova (13–6–.462), Ermidelio Urrutia (23–9–.391). **Pitching** (W–L–ERA): Jorge Luis Valdés (2–0–3.95), Omar Ajete (2–0–0.64), Osvaldo Fernández Rodríguez (2–0–0.95),

Lázaro Valle (3–0–0.00), Orlando Hernández (0–0–0.00), Euclides Rojas (1–0–0.00), Reinaldo Santana (0–0–4.50).

Cuba Game Scores Qualifying Round: Cuba beat Italy 18–2, Cuba beat Nicaragua 7–3, Cuba beat South Korea 26–1, Cuba beat Mexico 11–0, Cuba beat Japan 8–2, Cuba beat Chinese Taipei 16–3, Cuba beat South Korea 5–1, Cuba beat USA 23–1. Playoffs: Cuba beat Nicaragua 14–0, Cuba beat Nicaragua 11–5.

1994 Baseball World Cup XXXII (Managua, Nicaragua) (August 3–14)

Again Cuba finishes undefeated and largely unchallenged in a tournament featuring the hitting of Lourdes Gourriel, Ermidelio Urrutia, Kindelán and Pacheco and the pitching of a balanced staff that included four future major leaguers (Liván Hernández, Orlando Hernández, Osvaldo Fernández and Rolando Arrojo). It was the third World Series title for manager Jorge Fuentes and the fourth straight for Cuban teams boasting Linares and Kindelán in the lineup. At the halfway point between the Barcelona and Atlanta Olympics the Cubans again looked as invincible as ever. They had now not lost a single World Cup ballgame since eight years earlier in Haarlem.

Champion: Cuba (10–0)
Finals: Cuba beat South Korea 6–1 (Gold Medal), Japan beat Nicaragua 8–1 (Bronze Medal)
Semifinals: Cuba beat Nicaragua 13–1, South Korea beat Japan 9–0
Quarterfinals: Cuba beat USA 15–2, Japan beat Chinese Taipei 6–5, Nicaragua beat Panama 10–4, South Korea beat Italy 13–2
Group A Preliminary Round: Cuba (7–0), Nicaragua (6–1), Italy (4–3), Chinese Taipei (4–3), Australia (3–4), Colombia (2–5), Dominican Republic (2–5), France (0–7)
Group B Preliminary Round: Japan (6–1), South Korea (5–2), Panama (5–2), USA (4–3), Netherlands (3–4), Puerto Rico (3–4), Sweden (1–6), Canada (1–6)
Individual Statistical Leaders: **BA**: Ermidelio Urrutia (CUB) .667; **Runs**: Lourdes Gourriel (CUB) 13; **Hits**: Lourdes Gourriel (CUB), Omar Linares (CUB), D. López (COL) 15; **2B**: G. Jenkins (USA), H. Park (KOR), H.M. Matsumoto (JAP) 4; **3B**: I. Ho (TAI), Lourdes Gourriel (CUB), R. Hunter (NIC) 2; **HR**: Orestes Kindelán (CUB) 5; **RBI**: Antonio Pacheco (CUB) 13; **SB**: S. Moreno (NIC) 5; **Wins**: several pitchers with two each; **ERA**: M. Santana (DOM), 0.00; **MVP**: Lourdes Gourriel (CUB).

Cuba Roster: **Manager**: Jorge Fuentes. **Batting** (AB–H–BA): Alberto Hernández (21–6–.286), Antonio Pacheco (31–11–.355), Eduardo Paret (1–0–.000), Ermidelio Urrutia (21–14–.667), Germán Mesa (24–10–.417), Jorge Luis Toca (3–2–.667), José Estrada (26–8–.308), Juan Carlos Linares (8–1–.125), Juan Manrique (2–0–.000), Juan Padilla (1–0–.000), Lourdes Gourriel (30–15–.500), Omar Linares (30–15–.500), Orestes Kindelán (26–11–.423), Pedro Luis Rodríguez (4–2–.500), Victor Mesa (32–7–.219). **Pitching** (W–L–ERA): Faustino Corrales (1–0–1.80), Lázaro Valle

(1–0–0.00), Liván Hernández (1–0–0.00), Omar Ajete (0–0–0.00), Orlando Hernández (1–0–0.00), Osvaldo Fernández Rodríguez (2–0–1.50), Luis Rolando Arrojo (1–0–1.80).

Cuba Game Scores Preliminary Round: Cuba beat France 24–0, Cuba beat Colombia 7–1, Cuba beat Italy 14–1, Cuba beat Dominican Republic 12–0, Cuba beat Chinese Taipei 7–1, Cuba beat Nicaragua 12–1, Cuba beat Australia 7–3. Quarterfinals: Cuba beat USA 15–2. Semifinals: Cuba beat Nicaragua 13–1. Finals: Cuba beat South Korea 6–1.

1998 Baseball World Cup XXXIII (Parma and Rome, Italy) (July 22–August 2)

Cuba captured its 22nd overall world title and sixth in a row by breezing undefeated through ten games in Italy in late July. The victory string also stretched out to 41 straight games for the Cubans, who have now not lost a single World Cup Series contest since the 1986 event in Holland. This time the victim in the gold medal game was South Korea by a lopsided 7–1 score. José Contreras (who didn't allow a single earned run during his two outings) went the distance in the finale, striking out thirteen and tossing a five-hitter. The other medal-round contests were even more lopsided routs for the champions: 14–2 over Nicaragua in the semifinals and 12–1 over The Netherlands in the quarterfinals match-up. While this World Cup tournament was open to professional ballplayers for the first time, no major leaguers performed and the only competing teams with professionals (minor leaguers in this case) on their rosters were Panama and the Dominican Republic.

Champion: Cuba (10–0)

Finals: Cuba beat South Korea 7–1 (Gold Medal), Nicaragua beat Italy 5–1 (Bronze Medal)

Semifinals: Cuba beat Nicaragua 14–2, South Korea beat Italy 8–2

Quarterfinals: Cuba beat Netherlands 12–1, Italy beat Australia 9–8, Nicaragua beat Dominican Republic 12–4, South Korea beat Japan 8–5

Group A Preliminary Round: Cuba (7–0), Japan (6–1), Dominican Republic (5–2), Italy (3–4), Panama (3–4), Spain (2–5), China (2–5), South Africa (0–7)

Group B Preliminary Round: Nicaragua (5–2), Australia (5–2), South Korea (4–3), USA (4–3), Netherlands (4–3), Chinese Taipei (3–4), Canada (3–4), Russia (0–7)

Individual Statistical Leaders: **BA**: Orestes Kindelán (CUB) .560; **Runs**: Robelquis Videaux (CUB) 15; **Hits**: Robelquis Videaux (CUB), R. Padilla (NIC) 15; **2B**: R. Padilla (NIC), Sh. Abe (JAP) 5; **3B**: G. Cibati (ITA) 3; **HR**: F. Chon Chin (TAI) 5; **RBI**: Antonio Pacheco (CUB) 14; **SB**: D. Rigol (ITA) 5; **Wins**: several pitchers with two each; **IP**: E. Yano (JAP) 18.0; **ERA**: José Ariel Contreras (CUB), D. Ricci (ITA) 0.00.

Cuba Roster: **Manager**: Alfonso Urquiola. **Batting** (AB–H–BA): Ariel Benavides (8–2–.250), Robelquis Videaux (31–15–.484), Danel Castro (21–9–.429), Loidel Chapelli (27–12–.444), Orestes Kindelán (25–14–.560), Omar Linares (22–11–.500), Oscar Machado (24–10–.417), Oscar Macías

(3–0–.000), Yosvany Madera (10–4–.400), Juan Manrique (17–9–.529), Javier Méndez (3–1–.333), Juan Carlos Moreno (7–2–.286), Antonio Pacheco (25–11–.440), Gabriel Pierre (8–3–.375), Carlos Tabares (30–10–.333). **Pitching** (W–L–ERA): Yovani Aragón (2–0–1.13), José Ariel Contreras (2–0–0.00), José Ibar (2–0–2.25), Pedro Luis Lazo (2–0–0.00), Omar Luis (1–0–1.08), Walberto Quesada (0–0–0.00), Norge Vera (1–0–4.70).

Cuba Game Scores Preliminary Round: Cuba beat Spain 14–2, Cuba beat South Africa 14–1, Cuba beat Italy 20–0, Cuba beat Japan 9–0, Cuba beat China 10–0, Cuba beat Dominican Republic 9–2, Cuba beat Panama 8–5. Quarterfinals: Cuba beat Netherlands 12–1. Semifinals: Cuba beat Nicaragua 14–2. Finals: Cuba beat South Korea 7–1.

2001 Baseball World Cup XXXIV (Taipei, Taiwan) (November 6–17)

The uninterrupted string of World Cup victories continued for Cuba with their seventh straight crown and twenty-third title in twenty-six tournaments entered. Veteran outfielder Luis Ulacia — likely making his final appearance for Team Cuba — was the undisputed series hero with a remarkable .512 batting average and tourney MVP honors to his credit. Championship victory came with an emotional 5–3 defeat of Team USA in the gold medal showdown, with unheralded Camagüeyano Vicyohandri Odelín pitching brilliantly in relief of starter José Ibar. This was the second championship victory in three years against USA squads using major league and minor league professional players. Again (as in the Sydney Olympics) José Contreras was selected for the crucial semifinal outing versus Japan and fanned eleven in a tight 11-inning 3–1 victory. Norge Vera and Ciro Silvino Licea pitched brilliantly as well in two outings apiece. Veteran stars Omar Linares, Antonio Pacheco, Orestes Kindelán and Germán Mesa also most likely appeared for the final time in international tournament play.

Champion: Cuba (9–1)

Finals: Cuba beat USA 5–3 (Gold Medal), Chinese Taipei beat Japan 3–0 (Bronze Medal)

Semifinals: Cuba beat Japan 3–1 (11 innings), USA beat Chinese Taipei 4–1

Quarterfinals: Cuba beat Dominican Republic 3–1, USA beat Panama 7–2, Chinese Taipei beat Netherlands 2–0, Japan beat South Korea 3–1

Group A Preliminary Round: Chinese Taipei (6–1), South Korea (5–2), USA (5–2), Dominican Republic (5–2), Nicaragua (4–3), Italy (2–5), South Africa (1–6), France (0–7)

Group B Preliminary Round: Japan (7–0), Cuba (6–1), Panama (5–2), Netherlands (4–3), Australia (3–4), Canada (2–5), Russia (1–6), Philippines (0–7)

Individual Statistical Leaders: **BA**: Luis Ulacia (CUB) .512; **Runs**: Yoshinobu Takahashi (JAP) 10; **Hits**: Luis Ulacia (CUB) 18; **2B**: Hae Young Ma (KOR) 5; **3B**: Chin Feng Cheng (TAI) 4; **HR**: Evert-Jan T. Hoen (NET) 3; **RBI**: Chin Feng Cheng (TAI), Jayane Valera (DOM) 11; **SB**: Ralph Milliard (NET) 7; **Wins**: Chin Chia Chang (TAI) 3–0; **ERA**:

Samuel Meaurant (FRA) 0.00; **MVP**: Luis Ulacia (CUB). Statistics do not include medal round games.

Cuba Roster: **Manager**: Higinio Vélez. **Batting** (AB–H–BA): Luis Ulacia (43–22–.512), Antonio Scull (8–4–.500), Orestes Kindelán (33–12–.364), Michel Enríquez (28–10–.357), Antonio Pacheco (34–12–.353), Giorvis Duvergel (6–2–.333), Yobal Dueñas (21–7–.333), Omar Linares (25–8–.320), Rolando Meriño (13–4–.308), Yasser Gómez (25–6–.240), Ariel Pestano (21–5–.238), Eduardo Paret (13–3–.231), Germán Mesa (19–4–.211), Oscar Macías (29–6–.207), José Estrada (6–1–.167), Osmani Urrutia (13–1–.077). **Pitching** (W–L–ERA): Ciro Silvino Licea (2–0–0.00), José Ariel Contreras (2–0–0.00), Norge Vera (2–0–0.47), Vicyohandri Odelín (1–0–0.79), Pedro Luis Lazo (2–0–1.08), Lamey de la Rosa (0–0–4.50), Maels Rodríguez (0–0–4.66), José Ibar (0–1–6.75).

Cuba Game Scores Preliminary Round: Cuba beat Canada 1–0, Cuba beat Philippines 17–0, Cuba beat Australia 9–5, Japan beat Cuba 5–3, Cuba beat Panama 8–0, Cuba beat Netherlands 6–2, Cuba beat Russia 11–1. Quarterfinals: Cuba beat Dominican Republic 3–1. Semifinals: Cuba beat Japan 3–1 (11 innings). Finals: Cuba beat USA 5–3.

2003 Baseball World Cup XXXV (Havana, Cuba) (October 12–25)

Back on home turf for the first time since 1984, Cuba's impressive juggernaut ran its record of uninterrupted World Cup titles to eight straight, posting a fifth unblemished record over that stretch. The impressive home field performance came against a backdrop of defections by a pair of top Team Cuba stars — fastballing pitcher Maels Rodríguez and slugging outfielder Yobal Dueñas. Tournament highlight moments were a dramatic game-saving ninth-inning homer by Kendry Morales during the quarterfinal round, a pair of important solo round trippers by Frederich Cepeda in the title showdown with Panama, and the record-setting clutch pitching of veteran ace Norge Vera. Morales's blast saved Cuba from disaster against upstart Brazil and its ace pitcher Kleber Tomita. Cepeda starred alongside youngsters Morales and Yulieski Gourriel in a Cuban line-up that averaged but 22-years-of-age. Vera became the first pitcher in World Cup history to post wins (with two stellar seven-inning outings) in both the semifinal and final games. With Pan American and Asia Pre-Olympic Qualifying tournaments scheduled for the following week, traditional powerhouses Japan, South Korea, Canada, and the USA sent B-level squads to Havana; nevertheless Cuba's victory in the finals came against a Panama team that featured seven players in its lineup boasting previous major league experience.

Champion: Cuba (9–0)

Finals: Cuba beat Panama 4–2 (Gold Medal), Japan beat Chinese Taipei 7–3 (Bronze Medal)

Semifinals: Cuba beat Chinese Taipei 6–3, Panama beat Japan 4–1

Quarterfinals: Cuba beat Brazil 4–3, Chinese Taipei beat USA 2–1, Panama beat Nicaragua 5–0, Japan beat Korea 2–0

Group A Preliminary Round: Cuba (6–0), Nicaragua (4–2), Chinese Taipei (3–3), South Korea (3–3), Canada (3–3), Italy (1–5), Russia (1–5)

Group B Preliminary Round: Japan (7–0), USA (5–1), Panama (5–2), Brazil (4–3), Netherlands (3–3), Mexico (2–5), China (1–6), France (0–7)

Individual Statistical Leaders: **BA**: Michel Enríquez (CUB) .571; **Runs**: Omar Moreno (PAN) 11; **Hits**: Michel Enríquez (CUB) 12; **2B**: Akihide Shimuzu (JAP) 5; **3B**: 15 players with 1 each; **HR**: Takashi Yoshiura (JAP) 5; **RBI**: Takashi Yishiura (JAP) 16; **SB**: Eduardo Paret (CUB) 7; **Wins**: 7 pitchers with 2 each; **ERA**: Vicyohandri Odelín (CUB) 0.00; **MVP**: Takashi Yoshiura (JAP). Statistics do not include medal round games.

Cuba Roster: **Manager**: Higinio Vélez. **Batting** (AB–H–BA): Ariel Pestano (23–4–.174), Roger Machado (5–1–.200), Eriel Sánchez (1–0–.000), Joan Carlos Pedroso (2–1–.500), Kendry Morales (34–9–.265), Yulieski Gourriel (38–14–.368), Eduadro Paret (30–10–.333), Danel Castro (25–7–.280), Michel Enríquez (33–14–.424), Yorelvis Charles (1–0–.000), Ariel Benavides (3–1–.333), Osmani Urrutia (23–7–.304), Carlos Tabares (23–11–.478), Robelquis Videaux (16–1–.063), Frederich Cepeda (32–13–.406). **Pitching** (W–L–ERA): Adiel Palma (1–0–0.00), Vicyohandri Odelín (1–0–2.12), Yadel Martí (0–0–3.46), Norge Vera (3–0–1.22), Ormari Romero (1–0–1.10), Yovani Aragón (0–0–2.25), Jonder Martínez (2–0–1.29), Ifredi Coss (0–0–0.00), Pedro Luis Lazo (1–0–1.13).

Cuba Game Scores Preliminary Round: Cuba beat Chinese Taipei 6–3, Cuba beat Korea 4–0, Cuba beat Russia 20–1, Cuba beat Italy 7–0, Cuba beat Canada 8–0, Cuba beat Nicaragua 7–1. Quarterfinals: Cuba beat Brazil 4–3. Semifinals: Cuba beat Chinese Taipei 6–3. Finals: Cuba beat Panama 4–2.

2005 Baseball World Cup XXXVI (Rotterdam and Haarlem, The Netherlands) (September 2–18)

Critics of international baseball often claim that the Cubans repeatedly win because they play only inferior competition. But such complaints are largely a distortion. Team USA's entry in Holland sported a cast of stellar AAA prospects including Mets top pitching prospect Brian Bannister, Devil Rays infielder Josh Phelps, and Diamondbacks southpaw Chris Michalak. But the American squad under manager Davey Johnson under-performed from the opening bell. Team USA was crushed 11–3 by the heavy-hitting Cubans in the quarterfinals and limped home a disappointing seventh. Cuba, behind new mound sensation Dany Betancourt, edged South Korea 3–0 in the gold medal contest at Rotterdam's Neptunus Stadium to cap another unbeaten run. Panama, featuring ex–big-leaguer Rafael Medina and minor leaguers Freddy Herrera, Earl Agnoly and Jonathan Vega, edged a Netherlands team of Dutch Antillean stars 7–6 in the bronze medal game staged in Haarlem. The outstanding individual performer of World Cup 36 was veteran Cuban shortstop Eduardo Paret, who batted .632 before falling to injury late in the pool-play opening round. Despite losing team-captain Paret for the playoff round, Cuba emerged victorious this time around with one of its strongest national teams ever. A new generation of stars had now emerged despite all the attention given in the North American press to a handful of defections by veterans like José Contreras and Kendry Morales. Fresh Cuban headliners boasting unquestioned major league abilities were third baseman Yulieski Gourriel, who slugged a leading eight homers, and DH/infielder Michael Enríquez, the tournament's top hitter and RBI producer. Once again Cuban fans and sports officials had much to crow about after another surprisingly easy victory in a showcase event of international baseball that the red-clad islanders have thoroughly dominated since their earliest entries way back on the eve of World War II.

Champion: Cuba (11–0)

Finals: Cuba beat South Korea 3–0 (Gold Medal), Panama beat Netherlands 7–6 (Bronze Medal)

Semifinals: Cuba beat Panama 15–2, South Korea beat Netherlands 7–0

Quarterfinals: Cuba beat USA 11–3, Netherlands beat Puerto Rico 10–0, South Korea beat Japan 5–1, Panama beat Nicaragua 2–1

Group A Preliminary Round: Cuba (8–0), Netherlands (7–1), Panama (6–2), South Korea (5–3), Canada (4–4), China (3–5), Brazil (2–6), Sweden (1–7), South Africa (0–8)

Group B Preliminary Round: Japan (7–1), Nicaragua (6–2), Puerto Rico (6–2), USA (6–2), Australia (4–4), Chinese Taipei (3–5), Spain (2–6), Colombia (2–6), Czech Republic (0–8)

Individual Statistical Leaders: **BA**: Michel Enríquez (CUB) .500; **Runs**: Eduardo Paret (CUB), Yohei Kaneko (JAP) 12; **Hits**: Michel Enríquez (CUB) 23; **2B**: Percy Isenia (NED) 5; **3B**: Yufeng Zhang (CHN), William Hernández (COL), Harvey Monte (NED) 2; **HR**: Yulieski Gourriel (CUB) 8; **RBI**: Michel Enríquez (CUB) 20; **SB**: Eduardo Paret (CUB) 7; **Wins**: Shinsuke Saito (JAP), Yulieski González (CUB), Diegomar Maxwell (NED) 3; **SO**: Dae Sung Choi (KOR) 37; **ERA**: Dae Woo Kim (SOR), Sung Kwui Yun (KOR) 0.00; **MVP**: Eduardo Paret (CUB). Statistics do not include medal round games.

Cuba Roster: **Manager**: Higinio Vélez. **Batting** (AB–H–BA): Alexei Ramírez (17–6–.353), Ariel Pestano (41–12–.293), Carlos Tabares (28–8–.286), Eduardo Paret (19–12–.632), Eriel Sánchez (28–8–.286), Frederich Cepeda (38–7–.184), Joan Carlos Pedroso (16–1–.063), Juan Carlos Moreno (14–6–.429), Leslie Anderson (3–1–.333), Michel Enríquez (46–23–.500), Osmani Urrutia (31–12–.387), Roger Machado (2–1–.500), Rudy Reyes (38–12–.316), Yoandry Urgelles (1–0–.000), Yulieski Gourriel (47–15–.319). **Pitching** (W–L–ERA): Adiel Palma (2–0–3.38), Dany Betancourt (2–0–1.84), Frank Montieth (1–0–0.00), Norberto González (0–0–4.50), Ormari Romero (1–0–0.00), Pedro Luis Lazo (2–0–0.54), Yadier Pedroso (1–0–7.71), Yulieski González (3–0–1.62), Yunieski Maya (0–0–1.23).

Cuba Game Scores Preliminary Round: Cuba beat South Africa 12–2 (7), Cuba beat Panama 6–2, Cuba beat Brazil 11–1 (7), Cuba beat Sweden 15–0 (7), Cuba beat China 12–8, Cuba beat South Korea 4–1, Cuba beat Canada 7–0, Cuba beat Netherlands 3–1. Quarterfinals: Cuba beat USA 11–3. Semifinals: Cuba beat Panama 15–2 (7). Finals: Cuba beat South Korea 3–0.

OLYMPIC GAMES BASEBALL CHAMPIONSHIPS, 1992–2004

Cuba's Overall Performance: Tournaments (3 gold medals and one silver medal in four Olympic tournaments held); Games (33 Won and 3 Lost, .917 Pct.)

Country-by-Country Championships Won: Cuba (3 of 4 tournaments entered), and USA (1)

Note: Cuba has lost only three games total in Olympic competition: to The Netherlands (4–2) in preliminary round at Sydney 2000 and to USA (4–0) in gold medal game at Sydney 2000, also to Japan 6–3 in opening round in Athens.

1992 Olympic Baseball Championships (Barcelona, Spain) (July 26–August 5)

Cuba establishes the same dominance over the first-ever Olympic Games field it has traditionally held in all other international tournaments. A showdown semifinal game between Cuba and Team USA (featuring future big league stars Nomar Garciaparra, Jason Giambi, Michael Tucker, Charles Johnson, Darren Dreifort and Jeffrey Hammonds) fell to the Cubans 4–1 with Victor Mesa driving home all four tallies for the proud winners. Giorge Díaz hurled a 4-hit complete-game masterpiece in the finale, aided by three Cuban homers to spice the 11–1 routing of Chinese Taipei. Cuba scored in seven of nine innings during the gold medal match. Victor Mesa and Omar Linares were overall batting stars and future defector (and big leaguer) Osvaldo Fernández was the tournament's most effective pitcher.

Champion: Cuba (9–0) (Silver Medal: Chinese Taipei and Bronze Medal: Japan)

Finals: Cuba beat Chinese Taipei 11–1 (Gold Medal), Japan beat USA 8–3 (Bronze Medal)

Semifinals: Cuba beat USA 4–1, Chinese Taipei beat Japan 5–2

Preliminary Round Standings: Cuba (7–0), Chinese Taipei (5–2), Japan (5–2), USA (5–2), Puerto Rico (2–5), Dominican Republic (2–5), Italy (1–6), Spain (1–6)

Individual Statistical Leaders: **BA**: Victor Mesa (CUB) .545*; **Runs**: Omar Linares (CUB) 13; **Hits**: Omar Linares (CUB) 16; **2B**: Ermidelio Urrutia (CUB) 5; **3B**: 17 players with one each; **HR**: Koji Tokunaga (JAP) 4; **RBI**: Koji Tokunaga (JAP) 13; **SB**: Calvin Murray (USA) 9; **Wins**: four pitchers with two each; **IP**: Lee Chien-Fu Kuo (TAP) 20; **ERA**: Osvaldo Fernández (CUB) 0.00. *Mesa's batting title (plus all other stats here) based on preliminary round only and does not include medal-round games.

Cuba Roster: **Manager**: Jorge Fuentes. **Batting** (AB–H–BA): José Raúl Delgado (8–3–.375), Alberto Hernández (26–8–.308), Lourdes Gourriel (39–16–.410), Antonio Pacheco (40–14–.350), Omar Linares (40–20–.500), Germán

Mesa (26–10–.385), Juan Padilla (5–3–.600), Lázaro Vargas (37–17–.459), Luis Ulacia (5–0–.000), Orestes Kindelán (30–11–.367), Victor Mesa (30–15–.500), Ermidelio Urrutia (36–14–.389), José Estrada (5–1–.200). **Pitching** (W–L–ERA): Jorge Luis Valdés (1–0–5.14), Omar Ajete (1–0–0.00), Orlando "El Duque" Hernández (1–0–5.40), Osvaldo Fernández Rodríguez (2–0–0.57), Rolando Arrojo (1–0–0.00), Juan Carlos Pérez (1–0–1.04), Giorge Díaz (2–0–1.00).

Cuba Game Scores Preliminary Round: Cuba beat Dominican Republic 8–0, Cuba beat Italy 18–1, Cuba beat Japan 8–2, Cuba beat USA 9–6, Cuba beat Spain 18–0, Cuba beat Puerto Rico 9–4, Cuba beat Chinese Taipei 8–1. Semifinals: Cuba beat USA 4–1. Finals: Cuba beat Chinese Taipei 11–1.

1996 Olympic Baseball Championships (Atlanta, Georgia USA) (July 20–August 2)

Omar Linares's three homers in the gold medal slugfest with Japan was the tournament highlight as Cuba defended its Barcelona title and remained seemingly invincible, despite considerable signs of vulnerability in the usually brilliant Cuban pitching corps. Defection by Rolando Arrojo on the eve of the tournament may have added to the Cuban pitching jitters, but remaining aces José Contreras and Omar Ajete were soundly spanked by opposing hitters. Orestes Kindelán supplemented the slugging of Linares with tournament-high totals in both homers and RBI. Kindelán also shared the leadership in base hits with Linares. Team USA proved a disappointment before enthusiastic home crowds, losing a hard-fought preliminary round match with the Cubans (10–8) and dropping the semifinal game versus Japan (11–2). Cuba's overall Olympic record would now stand at 18 games won without a single defeat.

Champion: Cuba (9–0) (Silver Medal: Japan and Bronze Medal: USA)

Finals: Cuba beat Japan 13–9 (Gold Medal), USA beat Nicaragua 10–3 (Bronze Medal)

Semifinals: Cuba beat Nicaragua 8–1, Japan beat USA 11–2

Preliminary Round Standings: Cuba (7–0), USA (6–1), Japan (4–3), Nicaragua (4–3), Netherlands (2–5), Italy (2–5), Australia (2–5), South Korea (1–6).

Individual Statistical Leaders: **BA**: L. Carroza (ITA) .571; **Runs**: Omar Linares (CUB) 17; **Hits**: Omar Linares (CUB), Orestes Kindelán (CUB) 16; **2B**: F. Casolari (ITA) 5; **3B**: Jacque Jones (USA), T. Igustzi (JAP) 2; **HR**: Orestes Kindelán (CUB) 7; **RBI**: Orestes Kindelán (CUB) 14; **SB**: Luis Ulacia (CUB) 3; **Wins**: Omar Luis (CUB) 3; **IP**: R. Cabalisti (ITA) 19.2; **ERA**: P. Nanne (ITA) 0.00.

Cuba Roster: **Manager**: Jorge Fuentes. **Batting** (AB–H–BA): Miguel Caldés (34–11–.324), José Estrada (44–13–.295), Alberto Hernández (9–2–.222), Rey Isaac (14–9–.643), Orestes Kindelán (43–19–.442), Omar Linares (42–20–.476), Juan Manrique (26–11–.423), Antonio Pacheco (39–14–.359), Juan Padilla (1–1–1.000), Eduardo Paret (32–12–.375), Antonio Scull (5–2–.400), Luis Ulacia (27–15–.556), Lázaro Vargas (35–12–.343). **Pitching** (W–L–ERA): Omar Ajete (0–0–4.00), José Ariel Contreras (1–0–6.23), Jorge Fumero (1–0–8.53), Pedro Luis Lazo (1–0–5.40), Eliecer Montes de Oca (1–0–10.13), Omar Luis (3–0–5.71), Ormari Romero (2–0–7.11).

Cuba Game Scores Preliminary Round: Cuba beat Australia 19–8, Cuba beat Japan 8–7, Cuba beat Netherlands 18–2, Cuba beat South Korea 14–11, Cuba beat Italy 20–6, Cuba beat USA 10–8, Cuba beat Nicaragua 8–7. Semifinals: Cuba beat Nicaragua 8–1. Finals: Cuba beat Japan 13–9.

2000 Olympic Baseball Championships (Sydney, Australia) (September 17–27)

Legendary veteran national team manager Servio Borges returns to the helm for the first time in several years and receives considerable second-guessing from many quarters after he uses ace José Contreras in a semifinal match with Japan, thus expending his best hurler before the gold medal showdown with improved Team USA. USA (under major league hall of fame manager Tommy Lasorda) pulls off the championship upset when big leaguer Ben Sheets blanks the stunned Cubans on but three hits in the finale. Cuba had dominated the USA squad in a preliminary round match 5–1 behind masterful pitching from José Ibar. Cuba's first-ever defeat in an Olympic Games outing also came in the preliminary round with a stunning 4–2 loss to unheralded Holland.

Champion: USA (8–1) (Silver Medal: Cuba and Bronze Medal: South Korea)

Finals: USA beat Cuba 4–0 (Gold Medal), South Korea beat Japan 3–1 (Bronze Medal)

Semifinals: Cuba beat Japan 3–0, USA beat South Korea 3–2

Preliminary Round Standings: Cuba (6–1), USA (6–1), South Korea (4–3), Japan (4–3), Netherlands (3–4), Italy (2–5), Australia (2–5), South Africa (1–6). *USA beat Cuba (4–0) in gold medal game and South Korea beat Japan (3–1) in bronze medal game.

Individual Statistical Leaders: **BA**: Dave Nilsson (AUS) .565; **Runs**: Miguel Caldés (CUB), Omar Linares (CUB), Mike Neill (USA) 8; **Hits**: Dave Nilsson (AUS), So Taguchi (JAP), Bill Abernathy (USA) 13; **2B**: Bill Abernathy (USA) 5; **3B**: several players with one each; **HR**: eight players with two each; **RBI**: Danilo Sheldon (ITA), Orestes Kindelán (CUB), Norihiro Nakamura (JAP) 8; **SB**: J. Soo-Keun (KOR) 5; **Wins**: Robert Frankly (USA) 3; **IP**: Daisuke Matsuzaka (JAP) 19; **ERA**: José Ibar (CUB) 0.00. *Statistics based on preliminary round and not medal-round games.

Cuba Roster: **Manager**: Servio Borges. **Batting** (AB–H–BA): Ariel Pestano (19–4–.211), Juan Manrique (10–2–.200), Orestes Kindelán (34–12–.353), Antonio Scull (9–3–.333), Antonio Pacheco (26–10–.385), Oscar Macías (29–10–.345), Omar Linares (33–11–.333), Gabriel Pierre (1–0–.000), Germán Mesa (22–8–.364), Daniel Castro (5–1–.200), Javier Méndez (3–1–.333), Luis Ulacia (36–11–.306), Yobal Dueñas (18–6–.333), Yasser Gómez (24–6–.250), Miguel Caldés (30–10–.333), Rolando Meriño (DNP). **Pitching** (W–L–ERA): José Ariel Contreras (2–0–.0.86), Pedro Luis Lazo

(1–1–4.26), Omar Ajete (0–0–2.45), José Ibar (2–0–1.69), Lázaro Valle (1–0–0.00), Yovani Aragón (0–0–7.50), Maels Rodríguez (0–0–0.00), Norge Vera (1–1–1.23).

Cuba Game Scores Preliminary Round: Cuba beat South Africa 16–0, Cuba beat Italy 13–5, Cuba beat South Korea 6–5, Netherlands beat Cuba 4–2, Cuba beat Australia 1–0, Cuba beat USA 6–1, Cuba beat Japan 6–2. Semifinals: Cuba beat Japan 3–0. Finals: USA beat Cuba 4–0.

2003 Pan American Pre-Olympic Qualifying Tournament (Panama City, Panama) (October 30–November 10)

Defending Olympic champion Team USA is shocked in its quarterfinal game by Mexico (0–3 in the qualifying round) and thus loses a chance to defend its 2000 title in Athens. But a young and seemingly invincible Cuban squad, fresh off its World Cup victory one week earlier in Havana, continues to roll with another unblemished ledger and three straight shut-out victories (behind starters Norge Vera, Vicyohandri Odelín and Adiel Palma) during medal round competitions. Yulieski Gourriel and Frederich Cepeda again supply the long-ball action in a 5–0 quarterfinal win over Brazil, Puerto Rico is eliminated with a surprising 10–0, 7-inning knockout victory, and a two-run round tripper by first sacker Joan Carlos Pedroso alongside a two-run triple by veteran catcher Ariel Pestano provide the muscle in gold medal action versus Canada. Cuba is now again poised to win back its Olympic Gold Medal embarrassingly lost in 2000 at Sydney.

Champion: Cuba (6–0) (Silver Medal: Canada and Bronze Medal: Mexico)

Finals: Cuba beat Canada 5–0 (Gold Medal), Mexico beat Puerto Rico 10–1 (Bronze Medal)

Semifinals: Cuba beat Puerto Rico 10–0, Canada beat Mexico 11–1

Quarterfinals: Cuba beat Brazil 5–0, Canada beat Colombia 14–6, Puerto Rico beat Panama 5–3, Mexico beat USA 2–1

Group A Preliminary Round: Cuba (3–0), Canada (2–1), Puerto Rico (1–2), Mexico (0–3)

Group B Preliminary Round: USA (3–0), Panama (3–1), Colombia (2–2), Brazil (1–2), Nicaragua (0–4)

Individual Statistical Leaders: **BA**: Eriel Sánchez (CUB) .571, Angel Pagán (PUR) .500, Omar García (PUR) .500, Eduardo Paret (CUB) .500, Ariel Pestano (CUB) .500, Ernest Young (USA) .500; **ERA**: Claudio Yamada (BRA) 0.00 (9.0 innings), Jason Stanford (USA) 0.00 (7.0 innings), Rafael Medina (PAN) 0.00 (6.0 innings), Isidro Márquez (MEX) 0.00 (5.0 innings), Ryan Madson (USA) 0.00 (5.0 innings), Horacio Ramirez (USA) 0.00 (5.0 innings). *Statistics based on preliminary round and do not include medal-round games.

Cuba Roster: **Manager**: Higinio Vélez. **Position Players**: Eduardo Paret (SS), Michel Enríquez (3B), Yulieski Gourriel (2B), Eriel Sánchez (DH, C), Frederich Cepeda (OF), Ariel Pestano (C), Robelquis Videaux (OF), Joan Carlos Pedroso (1B), Danel Castro (SS), Carlos Tabares (OF), Roger Machado (C), Yorelvis Charles (IF), Ariel Benavides (OF, DH), Osmani Urrutia (OF). **Pitchers**: Adiel Palma (L), Yovani Aragón (R),

Jonder Martínez (R), Norge Vera (R), Pedro Luis Lazo (R), Vicyohandri Odelín (R), Yadel Martí (R), Ifredi Coss (R), Ormari Romero (R).

Cuba Game Scores Preliminary Round: Cuba beat Puerto Rico 4–2, Cuba beat Mexico 5–4, Cuba beat Canada 7–2. Quarterfinals: Cuba beat Brazil 5–0. Semifinals: Cuba beat Puerto Rico 10–0. Finals: Cuba beat Canada 5–0.

2004 Olympic Baseball Championships (Athens, Greece) (August 15–25)

Athens 2004 was a tournament marked by seemingly endless surprises, not the least of which was the fact that no team took the field representing the USA. Cuba, despite fielding its youngest and perhaps weakest team yet for Olympic competitions, again proved too much for the field and remained unscathed in the end, suffering only a single opening round defeat at the hands of pre-tourney favorite Japan. The Japanese arrived with a stellar team of pro league all-stars and swept everything in sight but the Australians, tumbling from contention with a shocking 1–0 semifinal loss to the Aussies. Canada held up well with its roster of minor league veterans and made it to the medal round. Chinese Taipei somehow managed to drop a game to the otherwise winless Italians, an unaccountable loss which kept the Taiwanese on the sidelines for medal round action. And Australia was the biggest surprise of all, rebounding from a disastrous tourney four years earlier in Sydney to reach the gold medal contest. Cuba's victory was highlighted by the hitting of veteran catcher Ariel Pestano, brilliant pitching from rising star Adiel Palma, and a miraculous eighth-inning six-run comeback against Team Canada in the semifinal. The gold medal showdown was marred by an egregious umpiring call on a fly ball "caught" by outfielder Carlos Tabares to squelch an early Aussie rally; but in the end the blown call was a mere footnote that had little impact on yet another impressive Cuban championship victory.

Champion: Cuba (8–1) (Silver Medal: Australia; Bronze Medal: Japan)

Finals: Cuba beat Australia 6–2 (Gold Medal), Japan beat Canada 11–2 (Bronze Medal).

Semifinals: Cuba beat Canada 8–5, Australia beat Japan 1–0.

Preliminary Round Standings: Cuba (6–1), Japan (6–1), Canada (5–2), Australia (4–3), Chinese Taipei (3–4), Netherlands (2–5), Greece (1–6), Italy (1–6). *Cuba beat Australia (6–2) in gold medal game and Japan beat Canada (11–2) in bronze medal game.

Individual Statistical Leaders: **BA**: Ariel Pestano (CUB) .512; **Runs**: Kosuke Fukudome (JAP) 11; **Hits**: Ariel Pestano (CUB), Shinya Miyamoto (JAP) 18; **2B**: Ariel Pestano (CUB), Kenji Jojima (JAP) 5; **3B**: several players with one each; **HR**: four players with three each; **RBI**: Ariel Pestano (CUB) 14; **SB**: Cheng-min Peng (TAP) 5; **Wins**: Adiel Palma (CUB) 3; **IP**: Adiel Palma (CUB) 19.1; **ERA**: Chris Oxspring (AUS), Hiroki Kuroda (JAP) 0.00. *Statistics based both preliminary round and medal-round games.

Cuba Roster: **Manager**: Higinio Vélez. **Batting** (AB, H,

BA): Frederich Cepeda (33, 15, .455), Michel Enríquez (38, 10, .263), Yulieski Gourriel (35, 12, .343), Danny Miranda (16, 3, .188), Eduardo Paret (34, 10, .294), Ariel Pestano (35, 18, .514), Alexei Ramírez (18, 5, .278), Carlos Tabares (25, 4, .160), Osmani Urrutia (33, 11, .333), Yorelvis Charles (3, 0, .000), Roger Machado (0, 0, .000), Eriel Sánchez (25, 9, .360), Antonio Scull (17, 3, .176), Yoandri Urgelles (3, 1, .333). **Pitching** (W, L, ERA): Pedro Luis Lazo (0, 0, 4.92), Jonder Martínez (0, 0, 27.00), Adiel Palma (3, 0, 1.40), Danny Betancourt (1, 0, 3.46), Norge Luis Vera (1, 0, 0.69), Norberto González (1, 0, 0.75), Vicyohandri Odelín (0, 1, 6.75), Manuel Alberto Vega (0, 0, 2.70), Luis Borroto (2, 0, 0.00), Frank Andy Montieth (0, 0, 0.00).

Cuba Game Scores Preliminary Round: Cuba beat Australia 4–1, Cuba beat Greece 5–4, Japan beat Cuba 6–3, Cuba beat Chinese Taipei 10–2, Cuba beat Netherlands 9–2, Cuba beat Canada 5–2, Cuba beat Italy 5–0. Semifinals: Cuba beat Canada 8–5. Finals: Cuba beat Australia 6–2.

INTERCONTINENTAL CUP BASEBALL CHAMPIONSHIPS, 1973–2002

Cuba's Overall Performance: Tournaments (9 of 12 Tournament titles won, plus three second place finishes); Games (107 Won and 11 Lost, .907 Pct.)

Country-by-Country Championships Won: Cuba (9 of 12 tournaments entered), Japan (2), USA (2), South Korea (1), and Australia (1)

Note: Cuba did not participate in the following three tournaments: 1973 (Italy), 1975 (Canada), and 1977 (Nicaragua)

1973 Intercontinental Cup Championship I (Parma and Rimini, Italy) (September 1–8)

Squabbling within amateur baseball's governing body (FIBA, International Baseball Federation) reaches a climax at the group's annual meeting in Bologna, Italy, with the resulting formation of a rival organization (FEMBA, World Federation of Amateur Baseball) boasting 24 member countries. This meeting in late August coincides with the first Intercontinental Cup baseball championships organized by Italy's FIBA delegation and featuring national teams from eight countries representing Europe (Italy), Asia (Japan and Taiwan) and the Americas (Puerto Rico, USA, Nicaragua, Canada and Argentina). Japan claims the first title of the FEMBA event that was initially planned for alternate years.

Champion: Japan (6–1)

Teams and Final Standings: Gold: Japan (6–1), Silver: Puerto Rico (5–2), Bronze: USA (5–2), Nicaragua (4–3), Canada (4–3), Italy (4–3), Chinese Taipei (1–6), Argentina (0–7)

Individual Statistical Leaders: **BA**: J. Ortiz (PRI) .417; **Runs**: D. Simon (CAN) 8; **Hits**: N. Morales (PRI) 11; **2B**: P. Lepage (CAN) 4; **3B**: Y. Hosaya (JAP) 2; **HR**: N. Morales (PRI) 4; **RBI**: N. Morales (PRI) 12; **SB**: H. Naito (JAP) 8; **Wins**: four pitchers with two each; **ERA**: Kojiro Ikegaya (JAP) 0.00.

Cuba Did Not Participate

1975 Intercontinental Cup Championship II (Montreal, Canada) (August 14–31)

FEMBA sponsors a second Intercontinental Cup competition — this time located in Montreal, Canada — and the USA earns the championship trophy while Cuba once again sits on the sidelines. South Korea and Colombia replace Taiwan and Nicaragua in the eight-team field. Team USA features future major leaguer catcher Ron Hassey as its top slugger and breezes through its nine games undefeated, with defending champion Japan, a two-time loser, in the runner-up slot. Only the top two teams record winning records.

Champion: USA (9–0)

Teams and Final Standings: Gold: USA (9–0), Silver: Japan (7–2), Bronze: Nicaragua (4–5), Canada (4–5), Puerto Rico (3–4), South Korea (3–4), Italy (2–5), Colombia (0–7)

Individual Statistical Leaders: **BA**: T. Mirakami (JAP) .588; **Runs**: Ron Hassey (USA) 9; **Hits**: Ron Hassey (USA), Y. Mackawa (JAP) 14; **2B**: J. Mondalto (USA) 4; **3B**: C. Jarquín (NIC) 2; **HR**: Y. Mackawa (JAP) 3; **RBI**: Y. Mackawa (JAP) 11; **SB**: L. Mc. Chong (KOR) 4; **Wins**: S. Anderson (USA), I. Osborne (CAN) 2–0; **IP**: K. Ho Joong (KOR) 26.0; **ERA**: S. Anderson (USA) 0.60.

Cuba Did Not Participate

1977 Intercontinental Cup Championship III (Managua, Nicaragua) (November 10–20)

The field is expanded to nine teams for the third IC championship tournament in Managua and a preliminary round and championship round format is adopted. South Korea edges the USA in a thrilling tie-breaker to claim the first-place trophy. The FIBA-FEMBA split has now been resolved and this and all remaining tournaments are held under the auspices of AINBA (International Amateur Baseball Association). For the third and final time Cuba sits out the IC event which it will soon come to dominate.

Champion: South Korea (10–4)

Championship Round Final Standings: Gold: South Korea (4–1), Silver: USA (4–1), Bronze: Japan (3–2), Nicaragua (3–2), Colombia (1–4), Puerto Rico (0–5). *South Korea beat USA (5–4) in tie-breaking playoff game.

Preliminary Round Standings: USA (8–0), South Korea (5–3), Japan (4–4), Nicaragua (4–4), Colombia (4–4), Puerto Rico (3–5), Chinese Taipei (3–5), Canada (3–5), Venezuela (2–6). *Top six teams qualified for final round.

Individual Statistical Leaders: **BA**: Kim Jae Bak (KOR) .426; **Runs**: E. López (NIC) 12; **Hits**: Kim Jae Bak (KOR) 23; **2B**: E. Moreno (COL), Pablo Juárez (NIC) 6; **3B**: T. Bogenez (USA), Kim Jae Bak (KOR), W. Taylor (NIC) 2; **HR**: J. Cuaresma (NIC), E. López (NIC) 5; **RBI**: L. Percey (USA), J. Cuaresma (NIC) 12; **SB**: N. Kobayashi (JAP) 11; **Wins**: Shicekazu Mori (JAP) 4–0; **IP**: Sun Hee Lee (KOR) 48.2; **ERA**: Jack Lazorko (USA) 0.00.

Cuba Did Not Participate

1979 Intercontinental Cup Championship IV (Havana, Cuba) (December 15–26)

The fourth Intercontinental Cup tournament heralds its fourth different champion as Cuba hosts the event for the first time and charges through the field undefeated. Japan earns a silver medal with Team USA collecting the bronze. Team USA's appearance marks the first visit of an American amateur team to Cuban soil in 37 years. Cuban third sacker Pedro José "Cheíto" Rodríguez turns this tournament into his own personal showcase with his .450 BA, 1.000 slugging average (more total bases than times at bat), 17 RBI and seven circuit blasts. Manager Servio Borges again leads the Cuban forces and this tournament marks for Borges ten years of uninterrupted international victories.

Champion: Cuba (10–0)

Teams and Final Standings: Gold: Cuba (10–0), Silver: Japan (8–2), Bronze: USA (6–4), Nicaragua (3–7), Puerto Rico (3–7), Panama (0–10)

Individual Statistical Leaders: **BA**: Pedro Medina (CUB) .462; **Runs**: Pedro José Rodríguez (CUB) 15; **Hits**: Pedro José Rodríguez (CUB) 18; **2B**: P. Dobson (USA) 6; **3B**: Alfonso Urquiola (CUB) 2; **HR**: Pedro José Rodríguez (CUB) 7; **RBI**: Pedro José Rodríguez (CUB) 17; **SB**: M. Kobayashi (JAP) 7; **Wins**: seven pitchers with two each; **IP**: I. Kido (JAP) 22.2; **ERA**: José Luis Aleman (CUB) 0.00.

Cuba Roster: **Manager**: Servio Borges. **Batting** (AB–H–BA): Pedro Medina (26–12–.462), Alfonso Martínez (8–5–.624), Antonio Muñoz (38–7–.184), Agustín Marquetti (33–5–.152), Alfonso Urquiola (42–14–.333), Rodolfo Puente (30–11–.367), Pedro Jova (27–4–.148), Pedro José "Cheíto" Rodríguez (40–18–.450), Leonardo Goire (2–1–.500), Fernando Sánchez (29–10–.345), Luis Casanova (40–15–.375), Lourdes Gourriel (34–10–.294), Wilfredo Sánchez (15–5–.333). **Pitching** (W–L–ERA): Braudilio Vinent (2–0–2.18), Jesús Guerra (2–0–2.51), Carlos Mesa (0–0–0.00), José Luis Alemán (2–0–0.00), Rogelio García (1–0–0.90), Juan Carlos Oliva (2–0–0.75), Rafael Castillo (1–0–0.82).

Cuba Game Scores Double Round Robin: Cuba beat Japan 7–1, Cuba beat Puerto Rico 7–1, Cuba beat Nicaragua 4–0, Cuba beat Panama 16–0, Cuba beat USA 6–4, Cuba beat Japan 4–1, Cuba beat Puerto Rico 9–1, Cuba beat Nicaragua 10–1, Cuba beat Panama 6–1, Cuba beat USA 7–4.

1981 Intercontinental Cup Championship V (Edmonton, Canada) (August 6–16)

Luis Casanova enjoys his finest international tournament, walking off with the batting triple crown as the home run, RBI and batting champion. But the over-confident Cuban squad managed by Servio Borges suffers a humiliating and eye-opening defeat when Team USA captures its second and final Intercontinental Cup (both won in Canada). After the strong Cuban contingent led by the bats of Casanova, Muñoz, Fernando Sánchez and Victor Mesa crushed the USA in opening round action, two unaccountable setbacks were suffered at the hands of Canada and the Dominicans. Rogelio García matched up with future big leaguer Ed Vosberg in the title

game; Braudilio Vinent pitched heroically in relief on one day's rest; and veteran Pedro Medina's clutch homer tied the contest in late innings. But Team USA nonetheless pulled out a tense 6–5 victory in the tenth frame.

Champion: USA (7–2)

Finals: USA beat Cuba 6–5 (10 innings) (Gold Medal), Dominican Republic beat South Korea 4–3 (15 innings) (Bronze Medal)

Semifinals: Cuba beat South Korea 9–1, USA beat Dominican Republic 5–3

Preliminary Round Standings: USA (5–2), Cuba (5–2), South Korea (5–2), Dominican Republic (4–3), Canada (4–3), Japan (3–4), Panama (1–6), Australia (1–6)

Individual Statistical Leaders: **BA**: Luis Casanova (CUB) .517; **Runs**: Luis Casanova (CUB) 12; **Hits**: Luis Casanova (CUB) 15; **2B**: J. Gerbar (DOM) 5; **3B**: twelve players with one each; **HR**: Luis Casanova (CUB) 6; **RBI**: Luis Casanova (CUB) 19; **SB**: M. Kobayashi (JAP) 8; **Wins**: Dong Won Choi (KOR) 2–0; **IP**: Dong Won Choi (KOR) 27.1; **ERA**: P. Lychak (CAN) 0.66.

Cuba Roster: **Manager**: Servio Borges. **Batting** (AB–H–BA): Carmelo Pedroso (0–0–.000), Francisco Javier Carbonell (0–0–.000), Alfonso Martínez (16–7–.438), Luis Casanova (37–19–.514), Antonio Muñoz (35–15–.429), Pedro Jova (37–12–.324), Victor Mesa (7–3–.429), Pedro Medina (14–5–.357), Lourdes Gourriel (37–11–.297), Alfonso Urquiola (41–11–.268), Héctor Olivera (35–11–.314), Fernando Sánchez (32–11–.344), Rodolfo Puente (35–7–.200). **Pitching** (W–L): Julio Romero (2–0), Rogelio García (0–0), Juan Carlos Oliva (0–0), Braudilio Vinent (3–1), José Darcourt (1–1), José Luis Alemán (0–0), Rafael Castillo (0–1).

Cuba Game Scores Preliminary Round: Cuba beat Australia 5–0, Cuba beat Japan 10–8, Canada beat Cuba 2–1, Dominican Republic beat Cuba 8–4, Cuba beat South Korea 8–0, Cuba beat Panama 23–12, Cuba beat USA 14–3. Semifinals: Cuba beat South Korea 9–1. Finals: USA beat Cuba 6–5 (10).

1983 Intercontinental Cup Championship VI (Brussels, Belgium) (July 13–25)

Cuba reclaims the Intercontinental Cup championship lost two years earlier in Edmonton, winning mainly on the strength of offensive displays provided by slugging outfielder Victor Mesa. Mesa was tournament leader in most major offensive categories (including BA, hits, runs scored, and home runs). Veterans Antonio Muñoz (with 14 RBI), Lourdes Gourriel (with a .400-plus BA) and Antonio Pacheco (batting .378) also swung potent bats and Rogelio García (3) and Braudilio Vinent (2) claimed the bulk of the pitching victories. Former national team pitching star José Pineda took over for Servio Borges as manager and claimed the first of what would eventually be seven straight Cuban first-place finishes in this event.

Champion: Cuba (8–2)

Championship Round Standings: Cuba (1–0), USA (1–1), Chinese Taipei (0–1)

Playoff Round Standings: Cuba (2–1), USA (2–1), Chinese Taipei (2–1), Netherlands (0–3)

Elimination Round Standings: Cuba (5–1), USA (5–1), Chinese Taipei (3–3), Netherlands (3–3), South Korea (3–3), Nicaragua (1–5), Canada (1–5)

Individual Statistical Leaders: **BA**: Victor Mesa (CUB) .567; **Runs**: Victor Mesa (CUB) 13; **Hits**: Victor Mesa (CUB) 17; **2B**: Lourdes Gourriel (CUB) 4; **3B**: Antonio Pacheco (CUB) 2; **HR**: Victor Mesa (CUB), Eric Foxx (USA) 5; **RBI**: Antonio Muñoz (CUB) 14; **SB**: W. Fu Lien (KOR) 4; **Wins**: Chen Chiu (TAI) 3–0; **IP**: Zon Dong Liu (KOR) 31.0; **ERA**: Bill Swift (USA) 0.00.

Cuba Roster: **Manager**: José M. Pineda. **Batting** (AB–H–BA): Victor Mesa (42–20–.476), Pedro Jova (41–17–.415), Antonio Muñoz (44–17–.386), Lourdes Gourriel (42–18–.429), Pedro José Rodríguez (45–17–.378), Fernando Sánchez (39–15–.385), Fernando Hernández (18–5–.278), Antonio Pacheco (37–14–.378), Anselmo Martínez (31–7–.389), Luis Casanova (18–7–.389), Pedro Medina (11–5–.455), Alfonso Urquiola (4–1–.250), Leonardo Goire (6–3–.500). **Pitching** (W–L–ERA): Rogelio García (3–1–3.32), Braudilio Vinent (2–1–4.36), Lázaro de la Torre (0–0–6.24), Mario Veliz (1–0–6.24), Jorge Luis Valdés (0–0–7.60), Anselmo Martínez (0–0–37.95), Julio Romero (2–0–0.50).

Cuba Game Scores Preliminary Round: Cuba beat South Korea 17–2, Cuba beat USA 6–1, Cuba beat Netherlands 17–7, Cuba beat Chinese Taipei 12–3, Canada beat Cuba 12–11, Cuba beat Nicaragua 8–4. Playoffs: Cuba beat Netherlands 11–0, Chinese Taipei beat Cuba 13–1, Cuba beat USA 4–1. Finals: Cuba beat USA 8–4.

1985 Intercontinental Cup Championship VII (Edmonton, Canada) (August 8–18)

Eighteen-year-old Omar Linares made his first Intercontinental Cup appearance and batted .467 as the starting third baseman. Established stars Lourdes Gourriel and Luis Casanova provided the biggest bats in the Cuban lineup, however, with Gourriel hitting over .400 and Casanova blasting six homers. Veteran righthander José Luis Alemán earned victories in relief in both playoff games (over South Korea and Chinese Taipei) and was fittingly named tournament MVP. This was the first international tournament in which the dependable trio of Linares, Kindelán and Pacheco (who would together dominate world tournaments for the next 15-plus years) appeared together in the same Cuban lineup.

Champion: Cuba (8–1)

Finals: Cuba beat South Korea 4–3 (Gold Medal), Japan beat Chinese Taipei 4–2 (Bronze Medal)

Semifinals: Cuba beat Chinese Taipei 8–7, South Korea beat Japan 4–3

Preliminary Round Standings: Cuba (6–1), Japan (6–1), South Korea (5–2), Chinese Taipei (5–2), Canada (2–5), USA (2–5), Nicaragua (1–6), Australia (1–6).

Individual Statistical Leaders: **BA**: Ch. Tai Chuang (TAI) .531; **Runs**: Ch. Tai Chuang (TAI) 12; **Hits**: Ch. Tai Chuang (TAI) 17; **2B**: P. Meyers (USA), Antonio Muñoz (CUB) 6; **3B**:

six players with two each; **HR**: Luis Casanova (CUB) 6; **RBI**: Luis Casanova (CUB) 14; **SB**: T. Hirose (JAP) 3; **Wins**: K. Bum Kim (KOR), H. Nagatomi (JAP) 3–0; **IP**: K. Bum Kim (KOR) 20.1; **ERA**: Reinaldo Costa (CUB) 0.00; **MVP**: José Luis Alemán (CUB).

Cuba Roster: **Manager**: José M. Pineda. **Batting** (AB–H–BA): Juan Castro (17–5–.294), Orestes Kindelán (6–2–.333), Antonio Pacheco (29–11–.379), Antonio Muñoz (28–11–.393), Rolando Verde (4–0–.000), Pedro Jova (31–7–.226), Lázaro Vargas (1–0–.000), Omar Linares (30–14–.467), Lourdes Gourriel (29–12–.414), Fernando Sánchez (10–1–.100), Lázaro Contreras (26–10–.385), Luis Casanova (28–12–.429), Fernando Hernández (10–3–.300). **Pitching** (W–L–ERA): Luis Tissert (2–0–2.57), Julio Romero (1–0–3.24), Jorge Luis Valdés (1–0–2.00), Reinaldo Costa (1–0–0.00), Lázaro de la Torre (0–0–3.00), José Luis Alemán (3–0–1.00), José Ramón Riscart (0–1–6.75).

Cuba Game Scores Preliminary Round: Cuba beat Nicaragua 17–3, Cuba beat Chinese Taipei 8–4, Japan beat Cuba 3–2, Cuba beat Australia 9–2, Cuba beat Canada 11–4, Cuba beat South Korea 7–1, Cuba beat USA 3–2. Semifinals: Cuba beat Chinese Taipei 8–7. Finals: Cuba beat South Korea 4–3.

1987 Intercontinental Cup Championship VIII (Havana, Cuba) (October 10–18)

Tournament play is staged in Havana for a second time (first in 1979) and Cuba scores one of its most lopsided victories, winning 13 games without defeat. Future major leaguers Chuck Knoblauch and Mickey Morandini play on Team USA, which finishes in the runner-up slot. Linares slugs 11 homers for an IC tournament record and walks off with MVP honors. Jorge Fuentes debuts as Cuban manager while a trio of pitchers (Jorge Luis Valdés, Rogelio García, and future big-leaguer René Arocha) win three games apiece.

Champion: Cuba (13–0)

Teams and Final Standings: Gold: Cuba (13–0), Silver: USA (8–5), Bronze: Japan (10–3), Chinese Taipei (8–5), Canada (4–9), South Korea (6–7), Nicaragua (2–6), Mexico (2–6), Italy (1–7), Aruba (1–7)

Individual Statistical Leaders: **BA**: Alejo O'Reilly (CUB) .553; **Runs**: Omar Linares (CUB) 22; **Hits**: L. Chu Ming (TAI) 25; **2B**: Mickey Morandini (USA) 3; **3B**: Antonio Pacheco (CUB) 3; **HR**: Omar Linares (CUB) 11; **RBI**: Omar Linares (CUB) 26; **SB**: Chuck Knoblauch (USA) 7; **Wins**: Rogelio García (CUB), Jorge Luis Valdés (CUB) 3–0; **IP**: H. Ping Yang (TAI) 30.1; **ERA**: Pablo Miguel Abreu (CUB) 0.00.

Cuba Roster: **Manager**: Jorge Fuentes. **Batting** (AB–H–BA): Orestes Kindelán (47–23–.469), Juan Castro (20–1–.050), Pedro Luis Rodríguez (9–2–.222), Alejo O'Reilly (38–21–.553), Antonio Muñoz (7–1–.143), Antonio Pacheco (48–19–.396), Omar Linares (51–23–.451), Lázaro Vargas (27–10–.370), Luis Ulacia (45–13–.289), Lourdes Gourriel (49–16–.327), Ermidelio Urrutia (18–8–.444). **Pitching** (W–L–ERA): Jorge Luis Valdés (3–0–1.29), Omar Ajete (1–0–0.69), Luis Tissert (1–0–0.75), Pablo Miguel Abreu

(2–0–0.00), Rogelio García (3–0–0.81), René Arocha (3–0–1.64).

Cuba Game Scores Multiple Round Robin: Cuba beat Mexico 10–0, Cuba beat Italy 4–1, Cuba beat Canada 28–2, Cuba beat South Korea 12–1, Cuba beat Mexico 14–1, Cuba beat Canada 10–0, Cuba beat Italy 15–3, Cuba beat South Korea 8–1, Cuba beat Japan 11–5, Cuba beat South Korea 7–2, Cuba beat Canada 11–1 Cuba beat USA 5–0, Cuba beat Chinese Taipei 3–2.

1989 Intercontinental Cup Championship IX (San Juan, Puerto Rico) August 16–27)

Cuba rings up an 8–2 victory over Japan in the title game to claim a fourth straight cup and also finishes its second consecutive tournament with an undefeated ledger. Lourdes Gourriel hits .435 (with a .913 slugging percentage) to walk off with MVP honors, punctuating his performance with four RBI in the final contest. Cuba's semifinal victory was a 14–0 rout of South Korea behind five hits (including a triple and a homer) by outfielder Luis Ulacia. The highlight of this tournament, however, came in the opening round when Lázaro Valle pitched an eight-inning perfect game (ended at 11–0 by the ten-run mercy rule) over South Korea, striking out 13 of the 24 batters he faced.

Champion: Cuba (8–0)

Finals: Cuba beat Japan 8–2 (Gold Medal), Puerto Rico beat South Korea 3–2 (Bronze Medal)

Semifinals: Cuba beat South Korea 14–0, Japan beat Puerto Rico 5–4

Preliminary Round Standings: Cuba (6–0), Japan (4–2), Puerto Rico (3–3), South Korea (3–3), Chinese Taipei (3–3), USA (1–5), Italy (1–5)

Individual Statistical Leaders: **BA**: T. Matsui (JAP) .500; **Runs**: Orestes Kindelán (CUB) 10; **Hits**: T. Matsui (JAP) 13; **2B**: M. Mieske (USA) 4; **3B**: Ch. Tai Chuang (TAI) 2; **HR**: Orestes Kindelán (CUB) 5; **RBI**: Orestes Kindelán (CUB) 11; **SB**: H. Son Lee (KOR) 2; **Wins**: T. Yoda (JAP) 2–0; **IP**: D. Sung Gu (KOR) 18.2; **ERA**: Lázaro Valle (CUB) 0.00. **MVP**: Lourdes Gourriel (CUB).

Cuba Roster: **Manager**: Jorge Fuentes. **Batting** (AB–H–BA): Pedro Luis Rodríguez (15–3–.200), José Raul Delgado (5–1–.200), Alejo O'Reilly (15–5–.333), Antonio Pacheco (24–8–.333), Juan Padilla (2–0–.000), Omar Linares (23–11–.478), Germán Mesa (10–1–.100), Victor Mesa (22–9–.409), Luis Ulacia (13–5–.385), Ermidelio Urrutia (5–2–.400), Orestes Kindelán (20–9–.450), Lourdes Gourriel (23–10–.435), Ivan Rojas (20–8–.400). **Pitching** (W–L–ERA): Lázaro Valle (2–0–0.00), José Luis Aleman (1–0–1.29), Jorge Luis Valdés (1–0–0.00), Pablo Miguel Abreu (1–0–3.00), Euclides Rojas (1–0–2.16), Osvaldo Duvergel (0–0–0.00), Omar Ajete (0–0–2.70).

Cuba Game Scores Preliminary Round: Cuba beat Italy 16–0, Cuba beat Chinese Taipei 7–3, Cuba beat USA 13–2, Cuba beat South Korea 11–0, Cuba beat Japan 4–2, Cuba beat Puerto Rico 12–4. Semifinals: Cuba beat South Korea 14–0. Finals: Cuba beat Japan 8–2.

1991 Intercontinental Cup Championship X (Barcelona, Spain) (July 2–13)

Team Cuba now makes it five Intercontinental Cup titles in a row with an exciting extra-inning defeat of the strong challengers from Japan in the tournament finale. Southpaw ace Omar Ajete made an early exit from the championship game after two homers sent Cuba's starter to the showers in the fourth inning. Hiroshi Shintani held Cuba to a single run until the ninth frame when two runs knotted the score. Japan tallied again in the tenth but a bases-loaded single by catcher José Delgado brought home the Cuban victory. Ajete shut out Japan in the preliminary round on the strength of two homers by second baseman Juan Padilla. Site for the tournament was Hospitalet Stadium on the grounds prepared for the upcoming 1992 Barcelona Olympics.

Champion: Cuba (10–1)

Finals: Cuba beat Japan 5–4 (Gold Medal), Nicaragua beat Chinese Taipei 4–3 (Bronze Medal)

Semifinals: Cuba beat Chinese Taipei 2–1, Japan beat Nicaragua 4–3

Preliminary Round Standings: Cuba (8–1), Japan (7–2), Nicaragua (6–3), Chinese Taipei (6–3), South Korea (6–3), Mexico (5–4), Italy (4–5), Spain (2–7), Russia (1–8), France (0–9)

Individual Statistical Leaders: **BA**: Y. Yamoda (JAP) .500; **Runs**: José Estrada (CUB) 16; **Hits**: Carlos Manrique (MEX) 17; **2B**: H. Roa (NIC), R. Blandi (ITA), Y. Yamoda (JAP) 6; **3B**: seven players with two each; **HR**: Ramón Padilla (NIC), Luis Casanova (CUB) 4; **RBI**: Carlos Manrique (MEX) 17; **SB**: Y. Teing Chang (TAI) 10; **Wins**: D.S. Gu (KOR) 3–0; **IP**: Epifanio Pérez (NIC) 23.2; **ERA**: Omar Ajete (CUB), R. Sánchez (NIC) 0.00. Statistics based on preliminary round only.

Cuba Roster: **Manager**: Gerardo Junco. **Batting** (AB–H–BA): Evenecer Godinez (30–9–.300), Juan Padilla (32–10–.313), Gabriel Pierre (29–9–.310), Luis Casanova (26–10–.385), Miguel Zayas (4–0–.000), Carlos Kindelán (5–2–.400), Victor Bejerano (13–2–.154), Lázaro Madera (21–10–.476), Lázaro Junco (34–14–.353), José Raul Delgado (26–7–.269), Manuel Morales (5–0–.000), Julio Germán Fernández (34–13–.382), José Estrada (34–14–.412). **Pitching** (W–L–ERA): Osvaldo Duvergel (1–0–4.00), Leonardo Tamayo (2–0–1.13), Ariel Cutiño (1–0–1.29), Wilson López (1–0–1.69), Felipe Fernández (0–0–13.50), Omar Ajete (2–0–0.00), Jorge Martínez (1–1–5.06).

Cuba Game Scores Preliminary Round: Cuba beat France 10–0, Cuba beat South Korea 7–4, Cuba beat Japan 3–0, Cuba beat Italy 13–1, Cuba beat Chinese Taipei 4–2, Cuba beat Russia 11–1, Cuba beat Mexico 15–0, Cuba beat Spain 12–2, Nicaragua beat Cuba 10–5. Semifinals: Cuba beat Chinese Taipei 2–1. Finals: Cuba beat Japan 5–4.

1993 Intercontinental Cup Championship XI (Northern Italy) (June 23–July 4)

Cuba ran its string of consecutive Intercontinental Cup titles to six by defeating top rival Team USA 9–4 in the gold medal contest. Japan whitewashed Nicaragua 9–0 in the bronze medal game. Play was hosted in several northern Italian cities: Macerata, Rimini, Bologna, Verona, Navara, Modena, Reggio Emilia and Parma. A crucial early-round game saw Cuba defeating Japan 4–3 in ten innings after a game-tying late-inning homer by Japan's Hidenori Taniguchi. Team USA also pushed the Cubans to the limit before losing 5–2 in an early-round meeting of the eventual finalists. Omar Linares clubbed six homers for the winners while Orestes Kindelán walked off with the individual RBI crown and Linares again was the batting champion.

Champion: Cuba (11–0)

Finals: Cuba beat USA 9–4 (Gold Medal), Japan beat Nicaragua 9–0 (Bronze Medal)

Semifinals: Cuba beat Nicaragua 10–1, USA beat Japan 6–3

Preliminary Round Standings: Cuba (9–0), Japan (8–1), USA (6–3), Nicaragua (5–4), South Korea (5–4), Australia (5–4), Mexico (3–6), Italy (2–7), Spain (2–7), France (0–9)

Individual Statistical Leaders: **BA**: Omar Linares (CUB) .576; **Runs**: Omar Linares (CUB) 16; **Hits**: Omar Linares (CUB) 19; **2B**: Ermidelio Urrutia (CUB), H. Kokibo (JAP), Todd Walker (USA) 5; **3B**: A. Fau (FRA) 3; **HR**: Omar Linares (CUB) 6; **RBI**: Orestes Kindelán (CUB), Hidenori Taniguchi (JAP) 16; **SB**: T. Ido (JAP), T. Nishi (JAP) 5; **Wins**: H. Watanabe (JAP) 2–0; IP: J. Woong Shin (KOR) 26.0; ERA: H. Watanabe (JAP) 0.00.

Cuba Roster: **Manager**: Jorge Fuentes. **Batting** (AB–H–BA): José Estrada (43–18–.419), Antonio Pacheco (44–17–.386), Omar Linares (40–22–.550), Orestes Kindelán (42–16–.381), Lourdes Gourriel (42–16–.381), Victor Mesa (44–16–.364), Ermidelio Urrutia (44–18–.409), Adrian Hernández (25–8–.320), Germán Mesa (34–15–.441), Juan Padilla (1–0–.000), Miguel Caldés (1–0–.000), Juan Carlos Bruzón (2–1–.500), Daniel Lazo (3–3–1.000), Juan Manrique (3–1–.333), José Raul Delgado (9–1–.111). **Pitching** (W–L–ERA): Orlando "El Duque" Hernández (1–0–2.08), Giorge Díaz (2–0–0.00), Lázaro Valle (1–0–1.93), Omar Ajete (1–0–1.17), Luis Rolando Arrojo (2–0–0.82), Jorge Luis Valdés (1–0–0.00), Osvaldo Fernández Rodríguez (1–0–1.93).

Cuba Game Scores Preliminary Round: Cuba beat Australia 12–2, Cuba beat South Korea 11–0, Cuba beat Italy 12–0, Cuba beat Mexico 10–0, Cuba beat USA 5–2, Cuba beat Japan 4–3, Cuba beat Spain 8–0, Cuba beat France 14–2, Cuba beat Nicaragua 6–1. Playoffs: Cuba beat Dominican Republic 3–2. Semifinals: Cuba beat Nicaragua 10–1. Finals: Cuba beat USA 9–4.

1995 Intercontinental Cup Championship XII (Havana, Cuba) (October 26–November 5)

Cuba plays host for the third time, a record number of twelve teams participate in preliminary and playoff rounds, and Team Cuba runs its string of IC championships to seven straight (the final two without losing a single game). This will be the last Cuban championship triumph in this event for the 1990s. An irony of this tournament is that Cuba does not boast a single leader in individual statistics but does get strong performances from pitcher Omar Luis (3–0, 0.86 ERA) and sluggers Omar Linares, Rey Isaac, and José Estrada, who all bat over .400 for the nine-game stretch.

Champion: Cuba (9–0)

Finals: Cuba beat Japan 4–1 (Gold Medal), Nicaragua beat South Korea 10–5 (Bronze Medal)

Playoffs: Cuba beat South Korea 6–5, Japan beat Nicaragua 4–2, Cuba beat Nicaragua 7–6, Japan beat South Korea 16–3, Cuba beat Japan 7–6, South Korea beat Nicaragua 10–2

Group A Preliminary Round Standings: Cuba (5–0), Nicaragua (4–1), Netherlands (2–3), Chinese Taipei (2–3), Brazil (2–3), Spain (0–5)

Group B Preliminary Round Standings: Japan (5–0), South Korea (4–1), Puerto Rico (3–2), South Africa (1–4), Mexico (1–4), Italy (1–4)

Individual Statistical Leaders: **BA**: S. Yusuyuki (JAP) .692; **Runs**: O. Hideaki (JAP) 8; **Hits**: C. Jeffrey (NET) 11; **2B**: O.R. Hidemi (BRA) 6; **3B**: thirteen players with one each; **HR**: J.C. Rodríguez (PRI) 4; **RBI**: M. Nobuhike (JAP) 11; **SB**: L. Byoung Kyu (KOR) 6; **Wins**: D. Miranda (NIC) 2–0; **IP**: D. Miranda (NIC) 16.0; **ERA**: R. Rivera (PRI) 0.00.

Cuba Roster: **Manager**: Jorge Fuentes. **Batting** (AB–H–BA): Adrian Hernández (24–9–.375), Juan Manrique (4–1–.250), Jorge Luis Toca (36–11–.306), Orestes Kindelán (35–11–.314), Antonio Pacheco (27–7–.259), Omar Linares (37–17–.459), Germán Mesa (36–10–.278), Juan Padilla (12–2–.167), Eduardo Paret (1–0–.000), Lourdes Gourriel (1–0–.000), Victor Mesa (36–10–.278), Rey Isaac (29–13–.448), José Estrada (39–16–.410), Luis Piloto (5–1–.200), Michel Perdomo (DNP). **Pitching** (W–L–ERA): José Ibar (2–0–3.75), José Ariel Contreras (0–0–0.00), Lázaro Valle (0–0–2.84), Rolando Arrojo (1–0–3.27), Orlando Hernández (2–0–4.00), Pedro Luis Lazo (1–0–1.23), Omar Luis (3–0–0.86).

Cuba Game Scores Preliminary Round: Cuba beat Netherlands 12–2, Cuba beat Nicaragua 4–3, Cuba beat Chinese Taipei 6–1, Cuba beat Brazil 12–2, Cuba beat Spain 10–0. Playoffs: Cuba beat South Korea 6–5, Cuba beat Nicaragua 7–6, Cuba beat Japan 7–6. Finals: Cuba beat Japan 4–1.

1997 Intercontinental Cup Championship XIII (Barcelona, Spain) (August 1–10)

A string of seven straight Intercontinental Cup titles for Cuba finally comes to an end with a shocking 11–2 defeat at the hands of Japan during the finals in Barcelona. Kohji Uehara is the winner for Japan in a contest put well out of reach by three runs in the first frame and three more in the second. The title game defeat would be the first single game loss in international tournament play for the Cubans since an early-round defeat during the 1991 Intercontinental Cup, also staged in Barcelona. Shockwaves from this defeat would cause immediate shakeups throughout Cuban baseball that result in firings of national team manager Jorge Fuentes and national team technical director Miguel Valdés.

Champion: Japan (6–3)

Finals: Japan beat Cuba 11–2 (Gold Medal), Australia beat USA 7–6 (Bronze Medal)

Semifinals: Cuba beat USA 7–1, Japan beat Australia 10–5

Preliminary Round Standings: Cuba (7–0), Australia (6–1), Japan (4–3), USA (4–3), Nicaragua (4–3), Italy (2–5), France (1–6), Spain (0–7)

Individual Statistical Leaders: **BA**: Paul Gonzalez (AUS) .588; **Runs**: Orestes Kindelán (CUB) 10; **Hits**: J. Tyner (USA) 13; **2B**: five players with four each; **3B**: José Estrada (CUB), Y. Takahashi (JAP) 2; **HR**: Orestes Kindelán (CUB) 6; **RBI**: Paul Gonzalez (AUS) 14; **SB**: Luis Ulacia (CUB) 3; **Wins**: José Ariel Contreras (CB), A. Shiamizu (JAP) 2–0; **IP**: S. Meurant (FRA) 15.0; **ERA**: Kohji Uehara (JAP) 0.00.

Cuba Roster: **Manager**: Jorge Fuentes. **Batting** (AB–H–BA): José Estrada (34–10–.294), Luis Ulacia (35–12–.343), Omar Linares (30–11–.367), Orestes Kindelán (32–11–.344), Antonio Pacheco (33–12–.364), Yobal Dueñas (29–8–.276), Gabriel Pierre (29–12–.414), Juan Manrique (24–8–.333), Miguel Caldés (32–10–.313), Danel Castro (3–0–.000), Lázaro Vargas (6–2–.333), Juan Carlos Linares (2–1–.500), Yosvany Madera (1–0–.000), Rey Isaac (2–1–.500). **Pitching** (W–L–ERA): José Ariel Contreras (2–0–2.61), Pedro Luis Lazo (2–0–1.23), Oscar Romero (1–0–10.29), Lázaro Garro (0–0–0.00), Ciro Silvino Licea (1–1–2.92), Wilson López (0–0–0.00), Leonides Turcás (0–0–1.80), Abel Madera (2–0–0.00).

Cuba Game Scores Preliminary Round: Cuba beat France 14–0, Cuba beat Australia 9–6, Cuba beat Spain 15–0, Cuba beat USA 4–1, Cuba beat Nicaragua 6–0, Cuba beat Italy 6–3, Cuba beat Japan 7–3. Semifinals: Cuba beat USA 7–1. Finals: Japan beat Cuba 11–2.

1999 Intercontinental Cup Championship XIV (Sydney, Australia) (November 3–14)

Cuba lost its second consecutive Intercontinental Cup with a sub-par gold medal game performance, this time falling to host Australia in extra innings on a misplayed fly ball by outfielder Yasser Gómez in the eleventh frame. Australia was paced by Milwaukee Brewers catcher Dave Nilsson, whose timely slugging and eleven RBI earned tournament MVP honors. Cuban selections for the all-tournament team were veteran pitcher Faustino Corrales, second baseman Oscar Macías, shortstop Danel Castro, and outfielder Yobal Dueñas. Veteran stars like Linares, Kindelán, Pacheco, Contreras and Germán Mesa were left off this slightly sub-par Cuban roster in favor of youngsters like Gómez, Dueñas, Ciro Silvino Licea, and catcher Ariel Pestano.

Champion: Australia (8–1)

Finals: Australia Beat Cuba 4–3 (11 innings) (Gold Medal), Japan beat USA 6–0 (Bronze Medal)

Semifinals: Cuba beat USA 7–0, Australia beat Japan 2–0

Preliminary Round Standings: Australia (6–1), Cuba (5–2), Japan (5–2), USA (5–2), Chinese Taipei (3–4), South Korea (2–5), Italy (2–5), Netherlands (0–7).

Individual Statistical Leaders: **BA**: A. Wamura (JAP) .483; **Runs**: A. Burton (AUS) 8; **Hits**: A. Wamura (JAP) 14; **2B**: Dave Nilsson (AUS), Danel Castro (CUB) 4; **3B**: C. Pan

(TAI) 3; **HR**: Oscar Macías (CUB) 3; **RBI**: Dave Nilsson (AUS) 11; **SB**: Y. Hyung Ahn (KOR), B. Ralph (USA) 4; **Wins**: seven pitchers tied with two each; **IP**: T. Chong (KOR) 18.1; **ERA**: T. Fujita (JAP) 0.00; **MVP**: Dave Nilsson (AUS).

Cuba Roster: **Manager**: Carlos Martí. **Batting** (AB–H–BA): Ariel Pestano (25–7–.280), Oscar Machado (2–2–1.000), Michel Abreu (4–0–.000), Loidel Chapelli (23–7–.304), Danel Castro (28–8–.286), J.C. Moreno (1–1–1.000), Oscar Macías (25–6–.240), Michel Enríquez (30–10–.333), Gabriel Pierre (24–5–.208), Michel Perdomo (21–2–.095), Yobal Dueñas (26–10–.385), Robelquis Videaux (12–3–.250), Yasser Gómez (1–0–.000), Isaac Martínez (12–4–.333). **Pitching** (W–L–ERA): Yosvani Pérez (1–0–1.00), Faustino Corrales (2–0–0.00), Maels Rodríguez (0–0–13.50), Carlos Yanes (0–1–1.59), Leonides Turcás (1–0–1.42), Jorge Luis Machado (0–0–0.00), Ciro Silvino Licea (2–0–3.46), Yoide Castillo (0–1–5.40).

Cuba Game Scores Preliminary Round: South Korea beat Cuba 4–3, Cuba beat Chinese Taipei 1–0, Cuba beat Netherlands 7–2, Cuba beat Japan 4–1, Cuba beat Italy 14–2, Cuba beat USA 5–1, Australia beat Cuba 5–1. Semifinals: Cuba beat USA 7–0. Finals: Australia beat Cuba 4–3 (11).

2002 Intercontinental Cup Championship XV (Havana, Cuba) (November 8–20)

Not surprisingly, Cuba regained its Intercontinental Cup supremacy when play returned to island home turf in a tournament staged in both Matanzas and Havana and featuring the youngest Cuban international squad in more than two decades. The host team races through its opposition largely untested in both the preliminary (five-game round robin) and championship rounds (double-elimination), after the USA fails to send a team to Cuba for largely political reasons. Yobal Dueñas is ultimately the hitting star with a mammoth seventh-inning two-run homer to decide a hard-fought 2–1 gold medal victory over South Korea (Cuba's only severe test). New third-base star Michel Enríquez proves an adequate replacement for Omar Linares as the tourney's leading hitter and veteran hurler José Ibar proves largely unhittable in two 8-inning outings. The successful tournament also sets the stage for AWS competition scheduled to return to Havana in November 2003.

Champion: Cuba (10–0) (Silver Medal: South Korea and Bronze Medal: Dominican Republic)

Playoff Finals Phase: Cuba beat South Korea 2–1, South Korea beat Panama 8–0, Cuba beat Dominican Republic 11–0

Playoff Semifinals Phase: Cuba (3–0), South Korea (2–1), Dominican Republic (2–1), Panama (2–1), Venezuela (1–2), Japan (1–2), Chinese Taipei (1–2), Italy (0–3)

Group A Elimination Round: Cuba (5–0), Venezuela (3–2), Japan (3–2), Dominican Republic (2–3), Netherlands (2–3), China (0–5).

Group B Elimination Round: South Korea (4–1), Chinese Taipei (4–1), Panama (3–2), Italy (2–3), Brazil (1–4), Mexico (1–4).

Individual Statistical Leaders: **BA**: Michel Enríquez (CUB) .526; **Runs**: Frederich Cepeda (CUB), Michel Enríquez (CUB) 7; **Hits**: Luis Iglesias (PAN) 11; **2B**: Carlos Muñoz (PAN) 5; **3B**: Germain Chirinos (VEN) 2; **HR**: Katsuaki Furuki (JAP), Feng-An Tsai (TPE) 4; **RBI**: Yobal Dueñas (CUB), Feng-An Tsai (TPE) 10; **SB**: Daniel Matsumoto (BRA) 3; **Wins**: Ifreidi Coss Gómez (CUB) 2; **IP**: Chi-Hsien Ho (TPE) 12.2; **ERA**: José Ibar (CUB) 0.00; **MVP**: Bárbaro Cañizares (CUB). *Official tournament statistics include preliminary round qualification games only.

Cuba Roster: **Manager**: Héctor Hernández. **Batting** (AB–H–BA): Michel Enríquez (34–17.500), Yasser Gómez (26–7–.269), Eduardo Paret (31–11–.355), Frederich Cepeda (26–6–.231), Bárbaro Cañizares (34–14–.412), Kendry Morales (37–10–.270), Oscar Macías (7–1–.143), Amaury Casañas (26–11–.423), Ariel Pestano (32–7–.219), Robelquis Videaux (7–1–.143), Yobal Dueñas (32–11–.344), Yunieski Gourriel (3–0–.000), Yorelvis Charles (5–2–.400), Giorvis Duvergel (7–1–.143), Roger Machado (5–0–.000). **Pitching** (W–L–ERA): José Ibar (2–0–0.46), Pedro Luis Lazo (0–0–2.84), Yicyohandri Odelín (1–0–4.97), Orelvis Avila (1–0–0.00), Yadel Martí (2–0–2.25), Norge Vera (1–0–1.42), Ifreidi Coss Gómez (2–0–0.00), Maels Rodríguez (1–0–1.42), Yosvani Pérez (0–0–9.00). *Cuba roster statistics complete for preliminary round and medal round games.

Cuba Game Scores Elimination Round: Cuba beat Netherlands 5–0, Cuba beat Japan 8–7, Cuba beat Venezuela 15–2, Cuba beat Dominican Republic 14–5, Cuba beat China 12–1. Semifinals Phase: Cuba beat Dominican Republic 3–2. Semifinals: Cuba beat Japan 5–0, Cuba beat Italy 11–0, Cuba beat Panama 7–1. Finals Phase: Cuba beat Dominican Republic 11–0, Cuba beat South Korea 2–1.

PAN AMERICAN GAMES BASEBALL CHAMPIONSHIPS, 1951–2003

Cuba's Overall Performance: Tournaments (11 of 13 Tournament titles won, plus one second place and one fourth place); Games (91 Won and 13 Lost, .875 Pct.)

Country-by-Country Championships Won: Cuba (11 of 13 tournaments entered), Venezuela (1), Dominican Republic (1), and USA (1)

Note: Cuba finished in fourth place in 1959 tournament at Chicago (USA); it was Cuba's only non-medal finish in 13 tournaments attended. Cuba did not participate in 1955 Pan American Games (held in Mexico City, Mexico)

1951 Pan American Games Championship I (Buenos Aires, Argentina) (February 27–March 6)

Cuba captures the first-ever Pan Am Games baseball title by defeating a surprisingly strong USA college contingent from Wake Forest University in the final round-robin game by an 8–1 score. Mexico matched the Americans' overall record but fell to the USA in their head-to-head match-up. Violent windstorms delayed the opening of the Games and adversely affected playing-field conditions. Standing-room-only crowds of four to five thousand attended every game, with 8,000 packed into the host stadium (most of them standing) for the Cuba-USA showdown. Future minor leaguer Angel Scull was

the hitting star for Cuba and tied for the home run lead with USA slugger Frank Wehner.

Champion: Cuba (6–1) (Silver Medal: USA and Bronze Medal: Mexico)

Teams and Final Standings: Gold: Cuba (6–1), Silver: USA (5–2), Bronze: Mexico (5–2), Nicaragua (4–3), Venezuela (4–3), Colombia (3–4), Brazil (1–6), Argentina (0–7). Note: USA defeated Mexico (9–3) during round-robin play to earn silver medal.

Individual Statistical Leaders: **BA**: Fernando García (MEX) .423; **Runs**: Frank Wehner (USA) 13; **Hits**: Juan Izaguirre (CUB), Israel Arredondo (VEN) 13; **2B**: Israel Arredondo (VEN) 5; **3B**: five players with two each; **HR**: Angel Scull (CUB), Frank Wehner (USA) 3; **RBI**: Angel Scull (CUB) 14; **SB**: Angel Scull (CUB) 4; **Wins**: Stanley Johnson (USA) 3–0; **Strikeouts**: Stanley Johnson (USA) 25; **IP**: Stanley Johnson (USA) 30; **ERA**: Juan Ravelo (CUB), 0.00.

Cuba Roster: **Manager**: Fabio de la Torre. **Position Players**: M. Díaz, A. Brito, Juan Izaguirre (13 H), D. Jácome, O. Orgelles, J. Silva, L. Feijo, G. Delgado, Angel Scull (3 HR, 11 RBI, 4 SB), Juan Vistuer, A. Herrera. **Pitchers** (W–L): N. Campbell (1–0), G. Martínez (1–0), L. Fiuza (2–0), Juan Ravelo (1–0), C. Oviedo (1–1). No additional data or player statistics are available.

Cuba Game Scores Round Robin: Cuba beat Mexico 3–0, Cuba beat Colombia 5–2, Cuba beat Nicaragua 6–5, Venezuela beat Cuba 4–3, Cuba beat Argentina 18–0, Cuba beat USA 8–1, Cuba beat Brazil 24–3.

1955 Pan American Games Championship II (Mexico City, Mexico) (March 13–24)

Action took place at the 30,000-seat Social Security Baseball Park in downtown Mexico City and featured a double round-robin format involving five teams. The surprising Dominican squad (which included future big leaguer Felipe Alou) lost once in the opening round to Team USA and again in the second round to Mexico, but held on to edge the USA (which lost three straight in the second round) by a single game in the standings. Cuba sat on the sidelines, the bulk of its best amateur talent recently having been funneled off to the Class B Havana Cubans (1946–1953), Class A Cuban Sugar Kings (after 1954), and minor league clubs in the United States.

Champion: Dominican Republic (6–2) (Silver Medal: USA and Bronze Medal: Venezuela)

Teams and Final Standings: Dominican Republic (6–2), USA (5–3), Venezuela (4–4), Mexico (4–4), Dutch Antilles (1–7). Note: Venezuela defeated Mexico (8–2) in playoff game for bronze medal.

Individual Statistical Leaders: **BA**: Domingo Vargas (DOM) .453; **Runs**: Pablo Tineo (DOM) 13; **Hits**: Domingo Vargas (DOM) 16; **2B**: J. Faillo (DOM), J. Matos (VEN), James Temp (USA) 4; **3B**: four players with three each; **HR**: J. Schoolmaker (USA) 3; **RBI**: James Temp (USA) 14; **SB**: Pablo Tineo (DOM), J. Chico (MEX) 5; **Wins**: Rafael Quesada (DOM) 3–0; **Strikeouts**: R. Quesada (DOM), Paul Ebert

(USA) 18; **IP**: Juan Julián (ANT) 23; **ERA**: F. Barranca (MEX), 1.59.

Cuba Did Not Participate

1959 Pan American Games Championship III (Chicago, Illinois USA) (August 27–September 7)

Cuba returns to action but suffers a disappointing fourth-place finish, mustering only two opening-round wins and losing three straight in championship play. Nine teams took part in the event staged in Comiskey Park and the large field necessitated a "two group" structure for opening round games. A final-round 3–2 USA victory over Cuba clinched a bronze medal for the winners. Southwest Conference batting champion and future major league hall of fame hero Lou Brock garnered only a single base hit in ten at-bats. Future post-revolution Cuban Leaguers Pedro Cháves and Urbano González led an uneven Cuban line-up that boasted few other recognizable names or all-star performers.

Champion: Venezuela (6–1) (Silver Medal: Puerto Rico and Bronze Medal: USA)

Teams and Final Standings: Gold: Venezuela (6–1), Silver: Puerto Rico (5–1), Bronze: USA (4–3), Cuba (2–4), Mexico (3–2), Costa Rica (3–3), Nicaragua (2–4), Dominican Republic (2–3), Brazil (0–6). Note: Cuba qualified for four-team medal round as second-place finisher in preliminary round Pool A.

Individual Statistical Leaders: **BA**: Irmo Figueroa (PRI) .500; **Hits**: Carlos Pizarro (PRI) 12; **2B**: Roberto Coto (MEX) 5; **3B**: José Flores (VEN) 3; **HR**: R. Vázquez (PRI), A. Hall (USA) 2; **RBI**: R. Vázquez (PRI) 10; **Wins**: M. Ruiz (MEX), M. Pérez (VEN), L. Peñalver (VEN) 2–0; **ERA**: Charles Davis (USA) 0.69.

Cuba Roster: **Manager**: M. de la Fuente. **Batting** (AB–H–BA): R. Bringas (12–3–.250), Pedro Carvajal (21–4–.181), A. Castillo (19–2–.105), A. Crespo (25–7–.280), Pedro Chávez (9–5–.556), R. Díaz (9–2–.222), Urbano González (11–4–.363), Antonio Jiménez (12–4–.333), M. González (18–3–.167), P. Moret (15–3–.200), T. Ramos (2–1–.500), J. Torres (10–3–.300), O. Flores (16–4–.250), O. Albelo (6–2–.333), R. Pérez (4–0–.000), A. Rodríguez (3–0–.000), F. Sanfeliz (4–2–.500), Alfredo Street (4–1–.250). **Pitching** (W-L): R. Pérez (1–0), O. Albelo (0–1), A. Rodríguez (1–0), F. Sanfeliz (0–2), Alfredo Street (0–1).

Cuba Game Scores Preliminary Round: Cuba beat Dominican Republic 9–3, Puerto Rico beat Cuba 9–1, Cuba beat Nicaragua 5–4. Finals Phase: Venezuela beat Cuba 6–5, Puerto Rico beat Cuba 4–3, USA beat Cuba 3–2.

1963 Pan American Games Championship IV (San Paulo, Brazil) (April 21–May 1)

Paced by a pitching staff of veteran Cuban Leaguers Aquino Abreu, Manuel Alarcón and Modesto Verdura, plus the booming bats of Urbano González, Pedro Cháves and Antonio González, Cuba climbed back to the top of the heap by winning seven of eight contests. Team USA lost twice to the champions by 13–1 and 3–1 counts. Alarcón, Verdura and Abreu each registered two pitching wins while Cuban hitters paced most individual batting categories (all but doubles, triples and stolen bases). Only one member of the strong Cuban pitching staff registered an ERA as high as 3.00.

Champion: Cuba (7–1) (Silver Medal: USA and Bronze Medal: Mexico)

Teams and Final Standings: Gold: Cuba (7–1), Silver: USA (5–3), Bronze: Mexico (4–4), Venezuela (2–6), Brazil (2–6)

Individual Statistical Leaders: **BA**: Urbano González (CUB) .485; **Runs**: Antonio González (CUB) 13; **Hits**: Urbano González (CUB) 16; **2B**: Archie Moore (USA), Wilson Parma (USA) 4; **3B**: Angel Méndez (VEN) 4; **HR**: Miguel Cuevas (CUB) 3; **RBI**: Pedro Chávez (CUB) 13; **SB**: Alan de Jardin (USA) 4; **Wins**: Manuel Alarcón (CUB), Modesto Verdura (CUB), Aquino Abreu (CUB) 2–0; **Strikeouts**: Oscar Ogassawara (BRA) 19; **IP**: Luis García (MEX) 27.1; **ERA**: Aquino Abreu (CUB) 0.50.

Cuba Roster: **Manager**: Gilberto Torres. **Batting** (AB–H–BA): Miguel Cuevas (17–9–.529), Urbano González (33–16–.485), Pedro Chávez (32–14–.438), Daniel Hernández (31–11–.355), Ramón Hechavarría (18–6–.333), Raul Ortega (6–2–.333), Ricardo Lazo (16–5–.313), Jorge Trigoura (32–9–.281), Fidel Linares (30–7–.233), Lázaro Pérez (19–4–.211), Santiago Scott (11–2–.182), Antonio González (28–5–.179). **Pitching** (W–L–ERA): Aquino Abreu (2–0–0.50), Modesto Verdura (2–0–1.00), Antonio Rubio (0–1–1.42), Manuel Alarcón (2–0–1.50), Rolando Pastor (0–0–2.25), Franklyn Aspillaga (1–0–3.00).

Cuba Game Scores Double Round Robin: Cuba beat USA 13–1, Cuba beat Brazil 11–2, Mexico beat Cuba 5–2, Cuba beat Venezuela 13–3, Cuba beat USA 3–1, Cuba beat Brazil 17–3, Cuba beat Mexico 7–3, Cuba beat Venezuela 6–4.

1967 Pan American Games Championship V (Winnipeg, Canada) (July 23–August 6)

In a break-out year for USA amateur baseball interests the Americans captured their only Pan Am Games title, defeating defending champion Cuba in the first and third games of a showdown final series. The only two USA losses in the preliminaries also came at the heads of the Cubans. High drama marked the final game when rain showers delayed the top of the ninth frame of a 1–1 tie, setting the stage for a clutch two-run game-winning single by George Greer off Cuban ace Manuel Alarcón. For the first time Team USA was the Pan Am champion, but it would also be the final time. Across the next three decades and eight tournaments, Cuba would come home winners each and every time.

Champion: USA (8–3) (Silver Medal: Cuba and Bronze Medal: Puerto Rico)

Playoffs: USA beat Cuba 8–3, Cuba beat USA 7–5, USA beat Cuba 2–1

Preliminary Round Standings: Cuba (7–1), USA (6–2), Puerto Rico (4–4), Mexico (2–6), Canada (1–7).

Individual Statistical Leaders: **BA**: Allan Robertson (CAN) .467; **Runs**: Steve Sogge (USA) 11; **Hits**: Allan Robertson (CAN) 14; **2B**: George Greer (USA) 6; **3B**: José Báez (PRI) 2; **HR**: Steve Sogge (USA) 3; **RBI**: Félix Isasi (CUB) 10; **SB**: Fermín Laffita (CUB) 5; **Wins**: Rigoberto Betancourt (CUB), Roberto Valdés (CUB), T. Plodinet (USA) 2–0; **Strikeouts**: Joe Sanderfield (USA), R. Stead (CAN) 23; **IP**: R. Stead (CAN) 23.1; **ERA**: Joe Sanderfield (USA) 0.75.

Cuba Roster: **Manager**: Roberto Ledo. **Batting** (AB–H–BA): Elpidio Mancebo (17–6–.353), Felipe Sarduy (26–9–.346), Fermín Laffita (42–14–.333), Antonio González (36–11–.306), Félix Rosa (7–2–.286), Ricardo Lazo (21–6–.286), Urbano González (36–10–.278), Féliz Isasi (46–10–.217), Pedro Chávez (46–10–.217), Miguel Cuevas (16–3–.188), Antonio Jiménez (22–4–.182), Lázaro Pérez (19–2–.105). **Pitching** (W–L–ERA): Rigoberto Betancourt (2–0–2.45), Roberto Valdés (2–0–2.81), Jesús Torriente (2–0–1.17), Manuel Alarcón (1–2–2.33), Gaspar Pérez (0–0–2.70), Felipe Sarduy (0–0–3.60), Alfredo Street (1–1–6.14).

Cuba Game Scores Preliminary Round: Cuba beat USA 4–3, Cuba beat Mexico 4–1, Cuba beat Puerto Rico 3–0, Cuba beat Canada 6–4, Cuba beat USA 9–2, Cuba beat Mexico 6–5, Cuba beat Puerto Rico 6–5, Canada beat Cuba 10–9. Playoffs: USA beat Cuba 8–3, Cuba beat USA 7–5, USA beat Cuba 2–1.

1971 Pan American Games Championship VI (Cali, Colombia) (July 31–August 9)

The defending champion Americans took their title defense quite seriously in 1971 and played a 30-game exhibition schedule before arriving in Cali with a team that included future major leaguers Fred Lynn and Alan Bannister. A key match-up was the third opening round game in which the confident Americans lost to Cuba 4–3, despite solo home runs by outfielders Fred Lynn and Jerry Mims and first baseman Jerry Tabb. An SRO crown of 11,000 watched this headline contest, which provided the only close call for the undefeated Cuban team. Cuba's victory accomplished the first of a string of eight straight Pan American Games gold medals that extends down to the present moment.

Champion: Cuba (8–0) (Silver Medal: USA and Bronze Medal: Colombia)

Teams and Final Standings: Gold: Cuba (8–0), Silver: USA (6–2), Bronze: Colombia (4–4), Canada (4–4), Puerto Rico (3–5), Venezuela (3–5), Dominican Republic (3–5), Nicaragua (3–5), Mexico (2–6). Note: Colombia defeated Canada (7–6) during round-robin play to claim bronze medal.

Individual Statistical Leaders: **BA**: Luis Escobar (COL) .552; **Runs**: six players with eight each; **Hits**: Luis Mercado (PRI) 16; **2B**: Félix Isasi (CUB) 6; **3B**: Wilfredo Sánchez (CUB), C. Errington (NIC) 2; **HR**: Fred Lynn (USA) 4; **RBI**: Wilfredo Sánchez (CUB), Armando Capiró (CUB) 10; **SB**: Miguel Dilone (DOM) 3; **Wins**: six players with two each; **Strikeouts**: J. Smith (USA) 21; **IP**: J.J. Tineo (DOM) 20.1; **ERA**: Antonio Herradora (NIC) 0.00. **MVP**: Alan Bannister (USA).

Cuba Roster: **Manager**: Servio Borges. **Batting** (AB–H–

BA): Lázaro Martínez (2–1–.500), Rigoberto Rosique (20–10–.455), Lázaro Pérez (32–14–.438), Urbano González (7–3–.429), Agustín Marquetti (31–12–.387), Féliz Isasi (34–13–.382), Wilfredo Sánchez (39–13–.333), Rodolfo Puente (27–9–.333), Armando Capiró (35–11–.314), Vicente Díaz (25–7–.280), Silvio Montejo (8–1–.125). **Pitching** (W–L–ERA): Rolando Macías (2–0–0.59), Emilio Salgado (1–0–0.90), Braudilio Vinent (1–0–1.35), José Antonio Huelga (2–0–1.72), Walfrido Ruiz (1–0–7.45), Oscar Romero (1–0–0.00).

Cuba Game Scores Round Robin: Cuba beat Dominican Republic 4–0, Cuba beat Puerto Rico 15–1, Cuba beat Nicaragua 4–1, Cuba beat USA 4–3, Cuba beat Canada 7–4, Cuba beat Venezuela 6–0, Cuba beat Mexico 6–2, Cuba beat Colombia 10–4.

1975 Pan American Games Championship VII (Mexico City, Mexico) (October 13–24)

Cuba's successful and undefeated title defense came largely on the strength of a stellar pitching staff that included Braudilio Vinent, Juan Pérez, Santiago "Changa" Mederos, Julio Romero, Oscar Romero and Omar Carrero. Four of the Cuban triumphs (half their tournament total) were shutouts. Cuba assured its victory in the final two games with a come-from-behind 4–3 conquest of the Americans and a 3–0 white-washing of host Mexico. Runner-up USA also boasted a stellar mound corps with future big leaguers Bob Owchinko, Pete Redfern, Rich Wortham, Scott Sanderson and Mike Scott, all still collegians at the time. The USA roster also featured additional big league prospects Ron Hassey (catcher), Wayne Krenchicki (infielder) and Steve Kemp (outfielder).

Champion: Cuba (8–0) (Silver Medal: USA and Bronze Medal: Venezuela)

Teams and Final Standings: Gold: Cuba (8–0), Silver: USA (6–2), Bronze: Venezuela (5–3), Dominican Republic (5–3), Mexico (5–3), Colombia (3–5), Canada (2–6), Puerto Rico (2–6), El Salvador (0–8). Note: Venezuela defeated Mexico (8–2) and Dominican Republic (9–3) in round-robin series to determine bronze medal.

Individual Statistical Leaders: **BA**: Luis Mercado (PRI) .500; **Runs**: Luis Bravo (VEN), David Stegman (USA) 8; **Hits**: J. Hernández (VEN) 14; **2B**: Gustavo Bastardo (VEN), Agustín Marquetti (CUB) 4; **3B**: Osvaldo Oliva (CUB) 3; **HR**: nine players with one each; **RBI**: Ron Hassey (USA) 9; **SB**: J. Hernández (VEN) 6; **Wins**: Bob Owchinko (USA) 3–0; **Strikeouts**: Bob Owchinko (USA) 28; **IP**: V. Cruz (DOM) 26; **ERA**: Juan Pérez (CUB) 0.00.

Cuba Roster: **Manager**: Servio Borges. **Batting** (AB–H–BA): Pedro José Rodríguez (5–3–.600), Félix Isasi (10–5–.500), Agustín Marquetti (25–12–.480), Evelio Hernández (26–12–.462), Osvaldo Oliva (29–13–.448), Fermín Laffita (24–9–.375), Alfonso Urquiola (287–9–.333), Rodolfo Puente (24–8–.333), Fernando Sánchez (6–2–.333), Armando Capiró (32–10–.323), Lázaro Pérez (4–1–.250), Agustín Arias (2–0–.000), Antonio Muñoz (20–4–.200), Wilfredo Sánchez (21–4–.190). **Pitching** (W–L–ERA): Braudilio Vinent (2–0–3.44), Juan Pérez (2–0–0.00), Santiago "Changa"

Mederos (1–0–1.38), Julio Romero (1–0–2.08), Omar Carrero (0–0–2.16), Oscar Romero (2–0–1.80).

Cuba Game Scores Round Robin: Cuba beat Canada 9–8, Cuba beat Dominican Republic 4–3, Cuba beat Puerto Rico 6–3, Cuba beat El Salvador 6–0, Cuba beat Venezuela 2–0, Cuba beat Colombia 12–0, Cuba beat USA 4–3, Cuba beat Mexico 3–0.

1979 Pan American Games Championship VIII (San Juan, Puerto Rico) (July 2–11)

Team USA was shut out of a Pan Am baseball medal for the first time in eight tries while the Cubans rang up their third gold medallion in a row and fifth overall. One of the best USA teams ever — featuring future big league pitchers Tim Leary and Craig Lefferts and solid hitters Terry Francona and Mike Gallego — slumped in the late going and finished in fourth slot. Vinent again led the Cuban pitching with four victories (and 0.44 ERA) and Pedro José (Cheíto) Rodríguez continued his slugging onslaught from earlier Intercontinental Cup matches in Havana with five more round trippers. Cheíto and Armando Capiró also both hit an even .500 to pace the tournament in batting.

Champion: Cuba (8–0) (Silver Medal: Dominican Republic and Bronze Medal: Puerto Rico)

Teams and Final Standings: Gold: Cuba (8–0), Silver: Dominican Republic (7–1), Bronze: Puerto Rico (6–2), USA (5–3), Bahamas (3–5), Venezuela (3–5), Colombia (2–6), Canada (1–7), Mexico (1–7)

Individual Statistical Leaders: **BA**: Pedro José Rodríguez (CUB), Armando Capiró (CUB) .500; **Runs**: Fernando Sánchez (CUB) 11; **Hits**: Luis Casanova (CUB), Agustín Marquetti (CUB), Terry Francona (USA) 13; **2B**: J. Cazáeez (MEX) 5; **3B**: Luis Casanova (CUB), Terry Francona (USA) 3; **HR**: Pedro José Rodríguez (CUB) 5; **RBI**: Agustín Marquetti (CUB) 13; **SB**: A. Romero (DOM), Y.A. Morrillo (VEN) 3; **Wins**: Braudilio Vinent (CUB) 4–0; **Strikeouts**: J. Feliciano (PRI) 22; **IP**: Braudilio Vinent (CUB), R. Seymour (BAH) 20.1; **ERA**: O. de León (DOM) 0.00.

Cuba Roster: **Manager**: Servio Borges. **Batting** (AB–H–BA): Armando Capiró (22–11–.500), Pedro José Rodríguez (22–11–.500), Alfonso Urquiola (2–1–.500), Rey Anglada (31–9–.290), Pedro Jova (18–5–.278), Luis Casanova (35–13–.371), Agustín Marquetti (32–13–.406), Antonio Muñoz (35–11–.314), Fernando Sánchez (30–12–.400), Fernando Hernández (5–1–.200), Pedro Medina (24–9–.375), Rodolfo Puente (27–10–.370), Wilfredo Sánchez (13–3–.231), Alberto Martínez (1–0–.000). **Pitching** (W–L–ERA): Braudilio Vinent (4–0–0.44), Jesús Guerra (2–0–2.45), Rogelio García (0–0–5.40), Juan Carlos Oliva (1–0–3.00), Lázaro Santana (0–0–6.23), Rafael Castillo (1–0–2.70).

Cuba Game Scores Round Robin: Cuba beat Dominican Republic 9–0, Cuba beat Bahamas 12–0, Cuba beat Colombia 12–1, Cuba beat Mexico 9–6, Cuba beat Canada 9–8, Cuba beat Venezuela 8–7, Cuba beat USA 7–1, Cuba beat Puerto Rico 11–3.

1983 Pan American Games Championship IX (Caracas, Venezuela) (August 15–26)

For the fourth straight time Cuba blasted through the Pan American tournament field undefeated and it was beginning to look like the Cubans might never lose another game to hemisphere opponents. Team USA — with future big leaguers Jeff Ballard, Tim Belcher, Mark McGwire and B.J. Surhoff — also cruised undefeated through the first round before stumbling against Nicaragua and then being blitzed 8–1 by Cuba with the title squarely on the line. The Cuba-USA game saw a precarious 1–0 American lead through six, before catcher Juan Castro's homer ignited a Cuban rally in the late innings. Cuba's Pedro Medina posted a scorching .667 batting average to claim the individual hitting title.

Champion: Cuba (9–0) (Silver Medal: Nicaragua and Bronze Medal: USA)

Finals Round Standings: Cuba (5–0), Nicaragua (3–2), USA (3–2), Dominican Republic (2–3), Venezuela (2–3), Panama (0–5). Note: Nicaragua beat USA 9–5 in Finals Round to determine Silver Medal and Bronze Medal

Pool A Preliminary Round: USA (5–0), Nicaragua (3–2), Dominican Republic (3–2), Canada (3–2), Puerto Rico (1–4), Brazil (0–5)

Pool B Preliminary Round: Cuba (4–0), Venezuela (2–1), Panama (2–1), Colombia (1–3), Dutch Antilles (0–4)

Individual Statistical Leaders: **BA**: Pedro Medina (CUB) .667; **Runs**: Pedro Medina (CUB) 9; **Hits**: Tom Nelson (CAN) 12; **2B**: Luis Fontanez (PRI) 5; **3B**: six players with 1 each; **HR**: Pedro Medina (CUB), Mark McGwire (USA) 4; **RBI**: B.J. Surhoff (USA) 11; **SB**: John Ivan (USA), A. Delgado (NIC), C. García (NIC) 2; **Wins**: Julio Moya (NIC) 2–0; **Strikeouts**: Julio Moya (NIC) 12; **IP**: Julio Moya (NIC) 18; **ERA**: John Hoover (USA) 0.00.

Cuba Roster: **Manager**: José M. Pineda. **Batting** (AB–H–BA): Amado Zamora (7–1–.143), Pedro Jova (1–0–.000), Victor Mesa (17–5–.294), Antonio Muñoz (16–3–.167), Lourdes Gourriel (19–10–.526), Pedro Medina (15–10–.667), Ramón Otamendi (16–8–.500), Antonio Pacheco (16–8–.500), Juan Castro (10–7–.700), Fernando Hernández (10–4–.400), Alfonso Urquiola (18–4–.222), Alberto Martínez (6–2–.333), Leonardo Goire (1–0–.000). **Pitching** (W–L–ERA): Braudilio Vinent (2–0–0.00), Rogelio García (3–0–0.00), Julio Romero (0–0–4.50), Jorge Luis Valdés (3–0–13.51), Félix Nuñez (1–1–3.44), Mario Veliz (1–0–0.00), Lázaro de la Torre (DNP).

Cuba Game Scores Preliminary Round: Cuba beat Dutch Antilles 12–2, Cuba beat Venezuela 5–4, Cuba beat Panama 5–0, Cuba beat Colombia 24–5. Finals Round: Cuba beat Nicaragua 8–3, Cuba beat Dominican Republic 15–3, Cuba beat Panama 11–0, Cuba beat Venezuela 13–3, Cuba beat USA 8–1.

1987 Pan American Games Championship X (Indianapolis, Indiana USA) (August 9–22)

Cuba finally lost a single game but remained nonetheless invincible by again winning a clutch contest head-to-head with Team USA. The Cuban loss was at the hands of an American team (on a dramatic homer by Ty Griffin) that breezed undefeated through the preliminary round. An August 22nd showdown for the top prize matched the tournament's two perennial powerhouses and found the Americans leading 9–8 in the sixth inning with Cris Carpenter suddenly being called upon to protect a late lead for the second day in a row. Two Cuban runs in the eighth and three more in the ninth against the overworked Carpenter provided the final victory margin for the defending champions.

Champion: CUBA (8–1) (Silver Medal: USA and Bronze Medal: Puerto Rico)

Finals: Cuba beat USA 13–9 (Gold Medal), Puerto Rico beat Canada 12–2 (Bronze Medal)

Semifinals: Cuba beat Puerto Rico 6–5, USA beat Canada 7–6

Elimination Round Standings: USA (7–0), Cuba (6–1), Puerto Rico (5–2), Canada (4–3), Nicaragua (3–4), Aruba (1–6), Venezuela (1–6), Dutch Antilles (1–6)

Individual Statistical Leaders: **BA**: Efrain García (PRI) .533; **Runs**: Ty Griffin (USA) 14; **Hits**: Efrain García (PRI) 16; **2B**: Bill Byckowski (CAN) 6; **3B**: Omar Linares (CUB), Greg Duce (CAN) 2; **HR**: Orestes Kindelán (CUB) 7; **RBI**: Orestes Kindelán (CUB), Tino Martínez (USA) 19; **SB**: Rick Hirstenstener (USA) 5; **Wins**: Cris Carpenter (USA) 3–0; **ERA**: Cris Carpenter (USA) 0.00. *Statistics do not include metal round games.

Cuba Roster: **Manager**: Higinio Vélez. **Batting** (AB–H–BA): Luis Casanova (21–9–.429), Juan Castro (22–4–.181), Jorge García (13–2–.153), Giraldo González (2–0–.000), Lourdes Gourriel (28–9–.321), Orestes Kindelán (28–14–.500), Omar Linares (25–13–.520), Pedro Medina (6–2–.333), Victor Mesa (24–7–.281), Alejo O'Reilly (10–6–.600), Antonio Pacheco (26–12–.481), Luis Ulacia (23–12–.521), Lázaro Vargas (6–4–.667). **Pitching** (W–L–ERA): Pablo Miguel Abreu (2–1–1.08), Omar Ajete (2–0–0.00), Rogelio García (1–0–2.84), Euclides Rojas (0–0–0.00), Luis Tissert (0–0–0.00), Jorge Luis Valdés (2–0–5.40), Lázaro de la Torre (DNP).

Cuba Game Scores Elimination Round: Cuba beat Dutch Antilles 12–1, Cuba beat Puerto Rico 1–0, Cuba beat Aruba 13–2, Cuba beat Venezuela 13–1, USA beat Cuba 6–4, Cuba beat Nicaragua 17–1, Cuba beat Canada 15–4. Semifinals: Cuba beat Puerto Rico 6–5. Finals: Cuba beat USA 13–9.

1991 Pan American Games Championship XI (Havana, Cuba) (August 4–17)

Cuba was again champion and again undefeated in the eleventh Pan American Games venue staged once more in Havana. The new batch of Cuban slugging stars — Pacheco, Victor Mesa, Linares, Kindelán and Gourriel — dominated the statistics in almost all categories. Cuba appeared weakened before the tourney with an injury to starter Lázaro Valle (reportedly a blood clot in his pitching arm) and the defection of top hurler René Arocha. But in reality the Cubans were stronger than ever, thrashing Puerto Rico 18–3 in the finale (with three homers by Ermidelio Urrutia). Cuba scored 136

runs and batted .400 as a team over the ten-game stretch; five of Cuba's ten victories came with the 10-run knockout rule. Jorge Luis Valdés also pitched the first no-hit no-run game in Pan American Games history, blanking Canada 14–0 and striking out 12 in the mercy-rule-shortened 7-inning contest.

Champion: Cuba (10–0) (Silver Medal: Puerto Rico and Bronze Medal: USA)

Finals: Cuba beat Puerto Rico 18–3 (Gold Medal), USA beat Dominican Republic 2–1 (Bronze Medal)

Semifinals: Cuba beat Dominican Republic 14–5, Puerto Rico beat USA 7–1

Elimination Round Standings: Cuba (8–0), USA (7–1), Puerto Rico (5–3), Dominican Republic (5–3), Nicaragua (4–4), Mexico (3–5), Aruba (2–6), Canada (1–7), Dutch Antilles (1–7)

Individual Statistical Leaders: **BA**: Antonio Pacheco (CUB) .545; **Runs**: Victor Mesa (CUB), Antonio Pacheco (CUB), Omar Linares (CUB), Germán Mesa (CUB) 13; **Hits**: Antonio Pacheco (CUB) 18; **2B**: four players with five each; **3B**: 14 players with one each; **HR**: Lourdes Gourriel (CUB), Orestes Kindelán (CUB), Chris Roberts (USA) 4; **RBI**: Antonio Pacheco (CUB) 15; **SB**: Chris Wimmer (USA) 8; **Wins**: Félix Nova (DOM) 3–0; **Strikeouts**: Félix Nova (DOM) 23; **ERA**: Jorge Luis Valdés (CUB) 0.73. **MVP**: Antonio Pacheco (CUB).

Cuba Roster: **Manager**: Jorge Fuentes. **Batting** (AB–H–BA): Alberto Hernández (9–1–.111), José Raúl Delgado (20–10–.500), Omar Linares (29–12–.414), Lourdes Gourriel (31–13–.419), Antonio Pacheco (33–18–.545), Lázaro Vargas (8–4–.500), Germán Mesa (27–11–.407), Luis Ulacia (24–12–.500), Victor Mesa (27–11–.407), Orestes Kindelán (31–11–.355), Ermidelio Urrutia (15–5–.333), Romelio Martínez (22–9–.409), Pedro Luis Rodríguez (DNP). **Pitching** (W–L–ERA): Jorge Luis Valdés (3–0–0.73), Euclides Rojas (0–0–9.82), Osvaldo Fernández Guerra (1–0–3.27), Osvaldo Duvergel (1–0–4.50), Leonardo Tamayo (2–0–0.90), Omar Ajete (2–0–3.86), Osvaldo Fernández Rodríguez (1–0–0.82).

Cuba Game Scores Elimination Round: Cuba beat Nicaragua 14–6, Cuba beat Mexico 22–0, Cuba beat Canada 14–0, Cuba beat Dutch Antilles 8–3, Cuba beat Puerto Rico 16–2, Cuba beat Aruba 20–1, Cuba beat USA 3–2, Cuba beat Dominican Republic 16–5. Semifinals: Cuba beat Dominican Republic 14–5. Finals: Cuba beat Puerto Rico 18–3.

1995 Pan American Games Championship XII (Mar del Plata, Argentina) (March 11–24)

Another undefeated Cuban championship squad featured a pitching staff (Osvaldo Fernández, Omar Ajete, Rolando Arrojo, Orlando "El Duque" Hernández, José Ibar, Eliecer Montes de Oca and Pedro Luis Lazo) with no single ERA as high as one run per nine-inning game. If previous Cuban entries rarely lost a single game, this one rarely gave up an earned run. Montes de Oca earned the ERA title with most innings pitched and the top hitters for Cuba were Lourdes Gourriel (.464 BA), José Estrada (the tournament leader in hits, runs and home runs) and Victor Mesa (the top RBI producer).

Champion: Cuba (9–0) (Silver Medal: Nicaragua and Bronze Medal: Puerto Rico)

Finals Round Standings: Cuba (5–0), Nicaragua (4–1), Puerto Rico (2–3), Mexico (2–3), Panama (1–4), Argentina (1–4). Note: Puerto Rico earned bronze medal by defeating Mexico during medal-round play.

Group A Preliminary Round: Mexico (4–0), Argentina (3–1), Puerto Rico (2–2), Guatemala (1–3), USA (0–4)

Group B Preliminary Round: Cuba (4–0), Panama (3–1), Nicaragua (2–2), Brazil (1–3), Dutch Antilles (0–4)

Individual Statistical Leaders: **BA**: Lourdes Gourriel (CUB) .464; **Runs**: José Estrada (CUB) 14; **Hits**: José Estrada (CUB) 18; **2B**: Alonso Reyes (MEX) 5; **3B**: Omar Linares (CUB), Jaime Roque (PRI) 4; **HR**: José Estrada (CUB) 2; **RBI**: Victor Mesa (CUB) 16; **SB**: Mariano Cadiz (ARG) 3; **Wins**: Elicer Montes de Ocha (CUB), Luis Miranda (NIC) 3–0; **ERA**: Elicer Montes de Ocha (CUB) 0.00.

Cuba Roster: **Manager**: Jorge Fuentes. **Batting** (AB–H–BA): Pedro Luis Rodríguez (4–0–.000), Juan Manrique (29–12–.414), Orestes Kindelán (32–10–.313), Lourdes Gourriel (28–13–.464), Jorge Luis Toca (8–3–.375), Antonio Pacheco (32–14–.438), Juan Padilla (4–1–.250), Germán Mesa (25–11–.440), Eduardo Paret (6–1–.167), Omar Linares (32–12–.375), Victor Mesa (33–13–.394), Ermidelio Urrutia (38–13–.342), José Estrada (30–18–.462), Luis Ulacia (4–2–.500), Daniel Lazo (5–0–.000). **Pitching** (W–L–ERA): Osvaldo Fernández Rodríguez (2–0–0.00), Omar Ajete (0–0–0.50), Luis Rolando Arrojo (2–0–0.69), Orlando "El Duque" Hernández (2–0–0.00), José Ibar (0–0–0.00), Elicer Montes de Oca (3–0–0.00), Pedro Luis Lazo (0–0–0.00).

Cuba Game Scores Preliminary Round: Cuba beat Panama 16–6, Cuba beat Brazil 22–4, Cuba beat Dutch Antilles 9–0, Cuba beat Nicaragua 11–0. Finals Round: Cuba beat Panama 11–0, Cuba beat Argentina 10–0, Cuba beat Puerto Rico 6–1, Cuba beat Nicaragua 6–1, Cuba beat Mexico 8–0.

1999 Pan American Games Championship XIII (Winnipeg, Canada) (July 25–August 2)

One of the best-played and hardest fought international tournaments on record resulted from the first such event in which teams (with the exception of Cuba) drew their rosters from AA and AAA minor leaguer players representing organized baseball. Also for the first time in more than two decades wooden bats were reintroduced for international tournament matches. Cuba surprisingly lost to both Team USA and Team Canada in the preliminary round and seemed on the verge of blowing an expected trip to the 2000 Sydney Olympics (only the two finalists would qualify for Sydney). The veteran Cuban team came alive in the medal round, however, largely on brilliant pitching by José Ariel Contreras in the quarterfinal match with the Dominican Republic, and again in the gold medal collision (two days later) versus Team USA. José Ibar (with Pedro Luis Lazo in ninth-inning relief) also shut down Canada in the crucial semifinal match that assured an Olympic berth. Little-used and previously unheralded reliever Danys Báez defected from the Cuban contingent in Winnipeg and would

emerge several years later as a big league regular in Cleveland, Tampa Bay and Los Angeles.

Champion: Cuba (5–2) (Silver Medal: USA and Bronze Medal: Canada)

Finals: Cuba beat USA 5–1 (Gold Medal), Canada beat Mexico 9–2 (Bronze Medal)

Semifinals: Cuba beat Canada 3–2, USA beat Mexico 2–1. Note: Semifinal winners (Cuba, USA) both qualify for 2000 Olympic Games Tournament.

Quarterfinals: Cuba beat Dominican Republic 3–1, Canada beat Guatemala 12–2, Mexico beat Nicaragua 5–1, USA beat Panama 5–2

Group A Elimination Round: Canada (4–0), USA (3–1), Cuba (2–2), Mexico (1–3), Brazil (0–4)

Group B Elimination Round: Dominican Republic (2–1), Nicaragua (2–1), Panama (2–1), Guatemala (0–3)

Individual Statistical Leaders: **BA**: Héctor Alvarez (MEX) .625; **Runs**: Andy Stewart (CAN) 8; **Hits**: Andy Stewart (CAN) 12; **2B**: Jeromy Ware (CAN) 4; **3B**: Lee Delfino (CAN), Orlando Miller (PAN) 1; **HR**: Andy Stewart (CAN), Marcus Jensen (USA) 3; **RBI**: Andy Stewart (CAN) 12; **SB**: David Roberts (USA), Félix Martínez (DOM) 3; **Wins**: Yan Lachapelle (CAN) 2; **ERA**: Steve Green (USA), 0.00.

Cuba Roster: **Manager**: Alfonso Urquiola. **Batting** (AB–H–BA): Ariel Pestano (21–7–.333), Juan Manrique (0–0–.000), Orestes Kindelán (28–6–.214), Germán Mesa (17–3–.176), Danel Castro (9–1–.111), Omar Linares (25–4–.160), Gabriel Pierre (14–4–.286), Michel Enriquez (3–1–.333), Javier Méndez (6–1–.167), Yobal Dueñas (18–4–.222), Daniel Lazo (6–1–.167), Robelquis Videaux (11–0–.000), Luis Ulacia (26–8–.308), Isaac Martínez (22–9–.409). **Pitching** (W–L–ERA): José Ariel Contreras (2–0–0.98), Pedro Luis Lazo (0–0–1.13), Norge Vera (1–0–2.25), José Ibar (1–0–1.74), Maels Rodríguez (1–1–8.53), Ciro Silvino Licea (0–1–12.47), Ormari Romero (0–0–7.73), Faustino Corrales (0–0–3.38), Danys Báez (0–0–0.00).

Cuba Game Scores Elimination Round: Cuba beat Mexico 5–1, Cuba beat Brazil 10–1, USA beat Cuba 10–5, Canada beat Cuba 8–1. Quarterfinals: Cuba beat Dominican Republic 3–1. Semifinals: Cuba beat Canada 3–2. Finals: Cuba beat USA 5–1.

2003 Pan American Games Championship XIV (Santo Domingo, Dominican Republic) (August 2–12)

Surviving a shocking preliminary round 7–1 pasting by Mexico, a young Cuban squad bounced back to sweep the Dominican Republic, Nicaragua and Team USA in medal play and thus capture the country's eleventh Pan Am gold medal in only thirteen outing. The victory also ran Cuba's overall Pan Am Games ledger to 91 victories in 104 total contests. Veteran mound ace Norge Vera was the gold medal hero with his brilliant complete-game two-hit shutout versus an American roster laced with minor league professional players. Catcher Ariel Pestano provided the offensive punch in the deciding game, stroking a double and a homer and knocking home two of

Cuba's three tallies. Another sterling pitching performance was provided in the semifinal match with Nicaragua by Vicyohandri Odelín who logged 8.1 shutout innings after relieving starting Yovani Aragón in the opening frame. Nineteen-year-old second baseman Yulieski Gourriel and outfielder Osmani Urrutia represented the champion Cubans on the tournament all-star squad.

Champion: Cuba (5–1) (Silver Medal: USA and Bronze Medal: Mexico)

Finals: Cuba beat USA 3–1 (Gold Medal), Mexico beat Nicaragua 6–2 (Bronze Medal)

Semifinals: Cuba beat Nicaragua 2–1, USA tied Mexico 2–2 (13 innings). Note: USA earns Championship Finals on basis of better Preliminary Round record.

Quarterfinals: Cuba beat Dominican Republic 10–0, Nicaragua beat Panama 5–2, Mexico beat Guatemala 6–0, USA beat Brazil 7–0

Group A Preliminary Round: Cuba (2–1), Mexico (2–1), Brazil (1–2), Panama (1–2)

Group B Preliminary Round: Nicaragua (4–0), USA (3–1), Dominican Republic (2–2), Guatemala (1–3), Bahamas (0–4)

Individual Statistical Leaders: **BA**: Mario Santana (MEX) .571; **Runs**: Jesús Taváres (DOM), Eric Patterson (USA) 6; **Hits**: Jim González (NIC) 9; **2B**: Ramón Martínez (MEX), Osmani Urrutia (CUB), Daniel Putnam (USA) 3; **3B**: Luis García (MEX) 2; **HR**: Roberto Saucedo (MEX), Jonathan Vega (PAN), Eduardo Romero (NIC), Jim Greene (USA) 1; **RBI**: Eduardo Romero (NIC) 6; **SB**: Amilcar Estrada (GUT) 3; **Pitching Strikeouts**: Yosvani Aragón (CUB) 9; **ERA**: Cairo Murillo (NIC) 0.00 (9.0 innings).

Cuba Roster: **Manager**: Higinio Vélez. **Batting** (AB-H-BA): Ariel Benavides (1–1–1.000), Frederich Cepeda (12–1–.083), Michel Enríquez (12–1–.083), Yulieski Gourriel (10–5–.500), Roger Machado (4–1–.250), Javier Méndez (11–3–.273), Eduardo Paret (10–3–.300), Joan Carlos Pedroso (12–3–.250), Ariel Pestano (6–2–.333), Alexander Ramos (0–0–.000), Carlos Tabares (11–3–.273), Osmani Urrutia (12–5–.417), Robelquis Videaux (0–0–.000). **Pitching** (W-L-ERA): Yovani Aragón (1–0–0.00), Orelvis Avila (0–0–0.00), Yadel Martí (0–0–2.57), Vicyohandri Odelín (0–1–6.00), Norge Vera (1–0–0.00). Note: Statistics for Preliminary Round games only.

Cuba Game Scores Preliminary Round: Cuba beat Panama 5–0, Cuba beat Brazil 4–0, Mexico beat Cuba 7–1. Quarterfinals: Cuba beat Dominican Republic 10–0. Semifinals: Cuba beat Nicaragua 2–1. Finals: Cuba beat USA 3–1.

CENTRAL AMERICAN AND CARIBBEAN GAMES CHAMPIONSHIPS, 1926–2002

Cuba's Overall Performance: Tournaments (13 of 16 Tournament titles won, plus one second place and one third place); Games (100 Won and 14 Lost, .877 Pct.)

Country-by-Country Championships Won: Cuba (13, out of 16 tournaments entered), Dominican Republic (2), Puerto Rico (2), Venezuela (1), and Colombia (1)

Note: Cuba finished in fourth place (2–3 record) in 1962

tournament at Kingston (Jamaica), for Cuba's only non-medal finish in 16 tournaments attended. Cuba did not participate in the 1954 Central American Games (held in Mexico City), 1959 Central American Games (held in Caracas, Venezuela), nor 2002 Central American Games (held in El Salvador)

1926 Central American Games Championship I (Mexico City, Mexico) (October 12–November 2)

The first Central American Games also marked both Cuba's first participation in amateur international baseball competition and also its first championship in what would soon be a regular floodtide of world amateur baseball crowns. The games in Mexico City attracted only three participants and Guatemala arrived without a baseball team. In the three-game set with Mexico for the baseball medal the Cubans were unchallenged and blanked the Mexicans 13–0 in the opener behind Lalo Rodríguez. The Cuban squad contained mostly players from the amateur league powerhouse Vedado Tennis Club team, including star pitcher Antonio Casuso, who had earlier whitewashed a pro outfit in Cuba during a pre-tournament warm-up match. Players from the Police Club, Havana Yacht Club, Loma Tennis Club and the University of Havana filled out Team Cuba's rag-tag roster.

Champion: Cuba (3–0)

Teams and Final Standings: Cuba (3–0), Mexico (0–3)

Individual Statistical Leaders: **BA**: Joaquín del Calvo (CUB) .714; **Runs**: C. Hernández (CUB) 6; **Hits**: Joaquín del Calvo (CUB) 5; **HR**: J. Echarri (CUB) and C. Hernández (CUB) 1. No additional stats available for this tournament.

Cuba Roster: **Manager**: Horacio Alfonso. **Batting** (BA): Miguel Aguilera (.000), Gustavo Alonso (.333), Joaquín del Calvo (.714), Antonio Castro (.571), R. Puig (.181), P. Ruíz (.333), C. Vietti (.400), Gustavo Consuegra (.500), J. Echarri (.333), Jorge Consuegra (.500), Cándido Hernández (.300), Rafael Inclán (.429), Porfirio Espinosa (.400). **Pitching** (W-L): Tomás Minguillón (1–0), Bernardo (Lalo) Rodríguez (1–0), Antonio Casuso (1–0).

Cuba Game Scores Round Robin: Cuba beat Mexico 13–0, Cuba beat Mexico 10–3, Cuba beat Mexico 8–2.

1930 Central American Games Championship II (Havana, Cuba) (March 15–April 5)

Strongman president Gerardo Machado organized a second Central American Games in Havana to divert attention from growing domestic unrest on the island. These games also took on significance as the maiden event staged in the new Cerveza La Tropical Stadium, a facility built specifically for the occasion. A significant appearance was made by Cuba's first National Leaguer, Rafael Almeida, who served as Team Cuba manager. The only loss for the host team was a 2–1 nail-biter with Mexico, and most of the five wins were laughable routs (including 15–1 over Guatemala). University of Havana outfielder Porfirio Espinosa hit .429 and also won the javelin throw competition, while Cuban pitcher Juan Mendizábel earned a track & field gold medal in the shot put. Narciso Picazo, star hurler with the National Amateur League powerhouse Club Teléfonos, was the tournament's most effective pitcher.

Champion: Cuba (5–1) (Silver Medal: Mexico and Bronze Medal: Panama)

Teams and Final Standings: Cuba (5–1), Mexico (4–2), Panama (3–3), Guatemala (0–3), El Salvador (0–3)

Individual Statistical Leaders: **BA**: M. Chávez Méndez (MEX) .500; **Runs**: R.E. Ruiz (PAN) 8; **Hits**: P. Espinosa (CUB) 8; **HR**: J.A. Antadilla (PAN) 3; **SB**: F. Torrijos (MEX), J. Torrijos (MEX) 5; **Wins**: Narciso Picazo (CUB) 2–0.

Cuba Roster: **Manager**: Rafael Almeida. **Batting** (BA): Gustavo Consuegra (.500), Carlos Fleites (.500), Porfirio Espinosa (.429), Francisco Espiñeira (.429), M. Morera (.333), Gustavo Alfonso (.278), A. Paituni (.250), Cándido Hernández (.250), Miguel Aguilera (.238), Jorge Consuegra (.235), A. Arredondo (.143), Luis Romero (.090), Oscar Reyes (.000), Juan Montero (.000). **Pitching** (W–L): Narciso Picazo (1–0), Juan Mendizábal (1–0), Juan Montero (1–0), Manuel Domínguez (1–1), F. Clavel (0–0).

Cuba Game Scores Round Robin: Cuba beat Mexico 7–3, Cuba beat Panama 2–1, Cuba beat Guatemala 15–1, Cuba beat El Salvador 9–0 (forfeit), Mexico beat Cuba 2–1, Cuba beat Panama 15–4.

1935 Central American Games Championship III (San Salvador, El Salvador) (March 24–April 7)

Hurricane damage delayed the opening of the next games nearly a full year and built anticipation for a Cuba-Mexico showdown on neutral grounds. But when Cuba protested that the Mexican baseball roster was filled with professionals the Mexicans hastily withdrew. Teams from Panama and Nicaragua (both also accused by the Cubans of using pros, some actually being themselves Cubans playing under assumed names) offered the main opposition. Used to playing seasoned professionals at home, Team Cuba with National Amateur League pitching stars Manuel Fortes (also a heavy hitter) and Naciso Picazo breezed through the field almost unchallenged.

Champion: Cuba (8–1) (Silver Medal: Panama and Nicaragua, with no bronze medal)

Championship Round Final Standings: Cuba (3–1), Panama (1–2), Nicaragua (1–2)

Opening Round Teams and Final Standings: Cuba (5–0), Panama (4–1), Nicaragua (3–2), El Salvador (2–3), Guatemala (1–4), Honduras (0–5)

Individual Statistical Leaders: **BA**: F. Hernández (CUB) .444; **Runs**: José Luis García (CUB) 13; **HR**: José Luis García (CUB), H. Carter (NIC) 5; **SB**: José Luis García (CUB) 6; **Wins**: Manuel Fortes (CUB) 3–0. No additional statistics available for this tournament.

Cuba Roster: **Manager**: León Rojas. **Batting** (BA): Lenguita Fernández (.154), Carlos Fleites (.211), Manuel (Manolo) "Chino" Fortes (.357), E. García (.359), José Luis García (.395), F. Hernández (.444), Esteban Maciques (.316), Conrado Morales (.187), F. López (.338), M. López (.400), A. Izquierdo (.297), Antonio Palencia (.269), Jorge Santacruz (.364). **Pitching** (W–L): Narciso Picazo (2–0), Rafael (Felo)

Suárez (0–1), Adrián Zabala (1–0), Manuel (Manolo) "Chino" Fortes (3–0), Lenguita Fernández (2–0).

Cuba Game Scores Opening Round: Cuba beat Panama 12–2, Cuba beat Nicaragua 13–7, Cuba beat El Salvador 9–3, Cuba beat Guatemala 16–2, Cuba beat Honduras 13–4. Championship Round: Panama beat Cuba 3–1, Cuba beat Nicaragua 6–2, Cuba beat Panama 10–5, Cuba beat Nicaragua 8–3.

1938 Central American Games Championship IV (Panama City, Panama) (February 11–23)

Mexico returned to the baseball wars, still using at least some of its Mexican League pros, and Puerto Rico and Venezuela entered for the first time. Club Atlético's manager León Rojas directed Team Cuba for the second time and fielded a formidable squad headed by the pitching of Agapito Mayor (Fortuna), Juan Decall (Vedado Tennis Club) and Natilla Jiménez (Hershey). Mayor was almost the whole story, winning four games in a combination of starting and relief appearances, a feat not duplicated before or since in this long-standing tournament. The deciding game saw Natilla Jiménez blank hapless El Salvador and also smack a mammoth homer to cap his own winning performance.

Champion: Cuba (5–1) (Silver Medal: Panama and Bronze Medal: Nicaragua)

Teams and Final Standings: Cuba (5–1), Panama (4–2), Nicaragua (4–2), Puerto Rico (4–2), Mexico (3–3), Venezuela (1–5), El Salvador (0–6). *Panama, Nicaragua and Puerto Rico played extra round-robin series to determine second through fourth place.

Individual Statistical Leaders: **BA**: E. Lanuza (PAN) .556; **HR**: O. Arleuwite (PAN) 2; **Wins**: Agapito Mayor (CUB) 4–0. No additional statistics available from this tournament.

Cuba Roster: **Manager**: León Rojas. **Batting** (BA): M. Fajo (1.000), Carlos Fleites (.174), A. Gómez (.174), Esteban Maciques (.275), J. Nápoles (.200), R. Ortiz (.000), Antonio Palencia (.087), David Pérez (.294), Segundo "Guajiro" Rodríguez (.200), Jorge Santacruz (.370), José Luis "Cocoliso" Torres (.200), Antonio "Quilla" Valdés (.333), Remigio Vega (.318). **Pitching** (W–L): Agapito Mayor (4–0), Pedro "Natilla" Jiménez (1–0), Juanito Decall (0–1), J. Valdés (0–0), E. Aguirre (DNP).

Cuba Game Scores Round Robin: Cuba beat Panama 6–2, Cuba beat Nicaragua 2–0, Puerto Rico beat Cuba 6–2, Cuba beat Mexico 7–2, Cuba beat Venezuela 5–4, Cuba beat El Salvador 4–0.

1946 Central American Games Championship V (Baranquilla, Colombia) (December 9–28)

Future Cuban League great and slick-fielding big league shortstop Willie Miranda (later of the New York Yankees and Baltimore Orioles) made his first appearance on Team Cuba in these games staged in Baranquilla. Miranda's Cuban career began in 1942–47 as an amateur star with powerhouse Club Teléfonos. With little hitting and less than their usual pitching strength, Cuba dropped both final-round games, to

Colombia and the Dominicans, and failed to defend its Central American crown for the first time. It was the beginning of what would prove a brief dry spell in Cuban amateur play, brought on largely by increased pro signings of amateur stars in the wake of the 1946–1947 racial integration of organized baseball in the United States.

Champion: Colombia (8–1) (Silver Medal: Dominican Republic and Bronze Medal: Cuba)

Championship Round Final Standings: Colombia (2–0), Dominican Republic (1–1), Cuba (0–2)

Preliminary Round Final Standings: Colombia (6–1), Cuba (6–1), Dominican Republic (4–3), Venezuela (3–3), Puerto Rico (3–3), Mexico (2–5), Costa Rica (0–7)

Individual Statistical Leaders: **BA**: C. González (PRI) .478; **HR**: five players tied with one each; **Wins**: R. Rodríguez (COL) 3–0. No additional statistics available from this tournament.

Cuba Roster: **Manager**: Vitico Muñoz. **Batting** (BA): Rouget Avalos (.091), Bernardo Cuervo (.200), Julio Delgado (.000), Mario Díaz (.250), A. Domínguez (.130), Galate Gómez (.441), Hiram González (.200), José Luis García (.207), Guillermo "Willie" Miranda (.250), Mario Pérez (.211), Ramiro Ramírez (.320), Gilberto Soto (.143). **Pitching** (W-L): Manuel Chacón (0–0), Ignacio Ferrer (1–0), Angel "Catayo" González (1–2), Miguel Montiel (1–0), René "Tata" Solis (1–1), Curricán "Generoso" Stable (2–0).

Cuba Game Scores Round Robin: Colombia beat Cuba 1–0, Cuba beat Dominican Republic 2–1, Cuba beat Venezuela 3–0, Cuba beat Puerto Rico 4–3, Cuba beat Mexico 8–2, Cuba beat Costa Rica 5–2. Championship Round: Colombia beat Cuba 2–0, Dominican Republic beat Cuba 3–2.

1950 Central American Games Championship VI (Guatemala City) (February 25–March 12)

Cuba reversed its brief slump and reclaimed the Central American Games baseball title lost four years earlier in Colombia. Another eye-popping debut occurred when future Brooklyn Dodgers World Series hero Edmundo "Sandy" Amorós, a recent product of the Juveniles (the youth leagues), slammed six homers in seven games to thoroughly dominate tournament headlines. Amorós and pitcher Justiniano Garay were two token blacks carried on Team Cuba's roster as racial integration slowly and quietly arrived within Cuban amateur baseball circles.

Champion: Cuba (7–0) (Silver Medal: Mexico and Bronze Medal: Nicaragua)

Teams and Final Standings: Cuba (7–0), Mexico (6–1), Nicaragua (4–3), Colombia (4–3), Costa Rica (3–4), El Salvador (2–5), Honduras (1–6), Guatemala (1–6). *Nicaragua beat Colombia during round-robin match-up to earn third place.

Individual Statistical Leaders: **BA**: M. Jacques (MEX) .474; **HR**: Edmundo Amorós (CUB) 6; **Wins**: D. Reatiga (MEX) 3–0. No additional statistics available from this tournament.

Cuba Roster: **Manager**: Oscar Reyes. **Batting** (BA):

Derubin Jácome (.423), Edmundo Amorós (.370), E. Ballester (.370), Angel Scull (.344), E. Tamayo (.308), Antonio González (1.000), Alfonso Suárez (1.000), L. Seijo (.500), M. Hernández (.333), L. Estrada (.333), C. Balvidares (.222). **Pitching** (W-L): Erasmo del Monte (2–0), Luis Fiuza (2–0), Justiniano Garay (2–0), G. Martínez (0–0), Roque Contreras (1–0).

Cuba Game Scores Round Robin: Cuba beat Mexico 8–0, Cuba beat Nicaragua 11–3, Cuba beat Colombia 2–1, Cuba beat Costa Rica 11–2, Cuba beat El Salvador 5–4, Cuba beat Honduras 12–0, Cuba beat Guatemala 12–2.

1954 Central American and Games Championship VII (Mexico City, Mexico) (March 6–20)

With Cuban amateur baseball now in a precarious state (due to mass signings of young players by professional teams both in Cuba and abroad), Team Cuba is absent from the Central American Games for the very first time. Venezuela seizes the opportunity and edges host Mexico for first-place honors. The four-team field is the smallest since the first edition of the tournament back in 1926. Nicaragua is the only entrant that wins neither a medal nor a single game.

Champion: Venezuela (5–1) (Silver Medal: Mexico and Bronze Medal: Dominican Republic)

Teams and Final Standings: Venezuela (5–1), Mexico (4–2), Dominican Republic (3–3), Nicaragua (0–6)

Individual Statistical Leaders: **BA**: J. Matos (VEN) .455; **Runs**: J. Matos (VEN), D. Rubenstein (VEN), E. Reveron (VEN), A. Ríos (MEX) 9; **HR**: C. Duarte (MEX) 3; **RBI**: R. Caballero (MEX), J. Matos (VEN), E. Reveron (VEN) 10; **SB**: P. Colina (VEN) 4; **Wins**: Angel Guillen (VEN) 3–0; **ERA**: Angel Guillen (VEN) 1.29. No additional statistics available.

Cuba Did Not Participate

1959 Central American Games Championship VIII (Caracas, Venezuela) (January 6–18)

With political turmoil back home during the month when Fidel Castro and Che Guevara's Sierra Maestra-based rebels finally seize government authority from President Fulgencio Batista, Cuba is absent from the tournament for a second straight session. Puerto Rico thus emerges as champions of the still-small five-team field, with the host country losing in the crucial tie-breaking title game. This is the last time in the 20th Century Cuba misses this tournament and in forty years that follow the Cubans will be outright champions eight times and runners-up on one of the other two occasions.

Champion: Puerto Rico (8–1) (Silver Medal: Venezuela and Bronze Medal: Panama)

Teams and Final Standings: Puerto Rico (7–1), Venezuela (7–1), Panama (4–4), Mexico (2–6), Dutch Antilles (0–8). *Puerto Rico defeated Venezuela in tie-breaker playoff game to earn gold medal game.

Individual Statistical Leaders: **BA**: L. Sanjur (PAN) .500; **Runs**: M. Mendible (VEN) 13; **HR**: four tied with one each; **RBI**: F. Sánchez (PAN) 11; **SB**: B. Hoftjzer (ANT) 5; **Wins**: F. Castilleros (PAN), J.E. Marrero (PRI), R. Molina (PRI), P.

Higuerey (VEN), J. Pérez (VEN) 2–0; **ERA:** P. Pérez (PRI) 0.00. No additional statistics available.

Cuba Did Not Participate

1962 Central American Games Championship IX (Kingston, Jamaica) (August 11–26)

Cuba returns to action and finishes out of medal contention for the only time in sixteen visits to the Central American Games. This would be largely the same Cuban team that would score a major triumph in the 1963 Pan Am Games — a selection of all-stars from the new National Series that would include manager Gilberto Torres, infielders Urbano González and Jorge Trigoura, outfielders Fidel Linares and Erwin Walter, and pitchers Aquino Abreu, Modesto Verdura, Alfredo Street and Manuel Alarcón. Several heart-breaking losses plagued a team that had not yet fully jelled.

Champion: Dominican Republic (4–1) (Silver Medal: Puerto Rico and Bronze Medal: Mexico)

Teams and Final Standings: Dominican Republic (4–1), Puerto Rico (3–2), Mexico (3–2), Cuba (2–3), Venezuela (2–3), Colombia (1–4). *Puerto Rico defeated Mexico in round-robin play and thus awarded second place.

Individual Statistical Leaders: **BA:** A. Méndez (VEN) .500; **HR:** four players tied with one each; **Wins:** S. Vázquez (MEX) 2–0; **ERA:** S. Vázquez (MEX) 0.00. No additional statistics available from this tournament.

Cuba Roster: **Manager:** Gilberto Torres. **Batting (AB–H–BA):** Urbano González (24–10–.417), Fidel Linares (13–5–.385), Jorge Trigoura (21–8–.381), Ricardo Lazo (16–6–.375), Daniel Hernández (18–6–.333), Ramón Hechavarría (3–1–.333), Julio Bécquer (8–2–.250), Mario González (18–4–.222), Erwin Walter (20–5–.250), Juan Emilio Pacheco (23–3–.130), Miguel Cuevas (5–0–.000), Antonio González (1–0–.000), Aquino Abreu (2–2–1.000), Modesto Verdura (2–1–.500), Manuel Alarcón (5–2–.400), Alfredo Street (3–1–.333), A. Rubio (3–0–.000). **Pitching (W–L–ERA):** Aquino Abreu (0–0–1.50), Alfredo Street (1–0–1.80), Modesto Verdura (0–1–2.70), Manuel Alarcón (1–1–2.25), Antonio Rubio (0–1–2.57), Francisco Salcedo (DNP).

Cuba Game Scores Round Robin: Dominican Republic beat Cuba 3–2, Puerto Rico beat Cuba 4–3, Mexico beat Cuba 2–1, Cuba beat Venezuela 12–1, Cuba beat Colombia 4–2.

1966 Central American Games Championship X (San Juan, Puerto Rico) (June 11–25)

Post-revolution political troubles surrounding Cuban sports were again in evidence as the cargo ship *Cerro Pelado* carrying Cuban athletes was detaining in entering San Juan harbor and most of the Cuban delegation missed opening ceremonies. Anti-Castro exiles threw stones at Cuban ballplayers during several matches and tensions remained high. A series of dramatic close games included Aquino Abreu's 5–2 opening day win over Puerto Rico, Gaspar Pérez's heartbreaking 1–0 loss to Venezuela (resulting from his own fielding error), and a 1–0 blanking of the Dominicans won with Miguel Cuevas's clutch double. Southpaw Rigoberto Betancourt, top

pitcher of this tournament, would eventually become a celebrated defector thirty-three years later during the Cuba-Orioles exhibition match staged in Baltimore.

Champion: Cuba (6–1) (Silver Medal: Puerto Rico and Bronze Medal: Panama)

Teams and Final Standings: Cuba (5–1), Puerto Rico (5–1), Panama (4–2), Dominican Republic (3–3), Venezuela (3–3), Mexico (1–5), Dutch Antilles (0–6). *Cuba beat Puerto Rico (6–2) in extra playoff game for gold medal.

Individual Statistical Leaders: **BA:** Pedro Chávez (CUB) .444; **Runs:** six players tied with five each; **Hits:** Pedro Chávez (CUB) 12; **2B:** R. Ortiz (PRI) 5; **3B:** nine players tied with one each; **HR:** four players tied with one each; **RBI:** Pedro Chávez (CUB) 6; **SB:** Antonio González (CUB), J. Santos (PRI) 5; **Wins:** E. Castillo (PAN) 2; **Strikeouts:** Rigoberto Betancourt (CUB) 18; **ERA:** A. Villamil (VEN) 0.00.

Cuba Roster: **Manager:** Gilberto Torres. **Batting (AB–H–BA):** Ramón Hechavarría (5–3–.600), Pedro Chávez (27–12–.444), Miguel Cuevas (23–10–.435), Urbano González (29–8–.276), Lino Betancourt (27–7–.259), Ricardo Lazo (21–5–.238), Felipe Sarduy (19–4–.211), Antonio González (28–6–.214), Rafael Herrera (26–5–.192), Antonio Jiménez (7–1–.143), Rigoberto Betancourt (2–1–.500), Aquino Abreu (5–2–.400), Jesús Torriente (4–1–.250), Gaspar Pérez (5–1–.200), Alfredo Street (4–0–.000), Raúl López (2–0–.000), Agustín Arias (0–0–.000). **Pitching (W–L–ERA):** Gaspar Pérez (1–1–0.00), Jesús Torriente (1–0–0.00), Alfredo Street (1–0–0.00), Raúl López (1–0–0.00), Rigoberto Betancourt (1–0–1.80). Aquino Abreu (1–0–3.29).

Cuba Game Scores Round Robin: Cuba beat Puerto Rico 5–2, Cuba beat Panama 7–0, Cuba beat Dominican Republic 1–0, Venezuela beat Cuba 1–0, Cuba beat Mexico 4–3, Cuba beat Dutch Antilles 6–0, Cuba beat Puerto Rico 6–2 (Championship Game).

1970 Central American Games Championship XI (Panama City, Panama) (February 28–March 14)

The Cubans successfully defended their title under new manager Servio Borges. This victory was preliminary to the more dramatic Amateur World Series showdown near year's end with Team USA in Colombia. As in Cartagena in December, young phenom José Antonio Huelga was the pitching star with two nearly perfect outings. Wilfredo Sánchez, Rodolfo Puente, Silvio Montejo, and Félix Isasi all chipped in with batting averages above .350, but Fermín Laffita was the biggest offensive hero with top tournament marks for RBI, homers and stolen bases.

Champion: Cuba (7–1) (Silver Medal: Dominican Republic and Bronze Medal: Mexico)

Teams and Final Standings: Cuba (7–1), Dominican Republic (6–2), Mexico (6–2), Colombia (5–3), Venezuela (4–4), Panama (4–4), Puerto Rico (3–5), Nicaragua (1–7), Dutch Antilles (0–8). *Dominican Republic defeated Mexico in round-robin play to earn silver medal.

Individual Statistical Leaders: **BA:** W. Pietersz (ANT) .560; **Runs:** T. Moreno (COL) 11; **Hits:** W. Pietersz (ANT) 14;

2B: T. Moreno (COL) 6; 3B: C. Rosales (NIC) 3; HR: Fermín Laffita (CUB), Urbano González (CUB) 2; RBI: Fermín Laffita (CUB) 11; SB: Fermín Laffita (CUB), Wilfredo Sánchez (CUB), Félix Isasi (CUB) 5; Wins: O. García (COL) 3–0; ERA: José Antonio Huelga (CUB) 0.00.

Cuba Roster: Manager: Servio Borges. Batting (AB–H–BA): Armando Capiró (15–10–.667), Wilfredo Sánchez (33–13–.394), Rodolfo Puente (23–9–.391), Silvio Montejo (29–11–.379), Fermín Laffita (32–12–.375), Félix Isasi (28–10–.357), Urbano González (23–7–.304), Owen Blandino (13–4–.308), Felipe Sarduy (30–9–.300), Ramón Hechavarría (10–3–.300), Agustín Arias (11–2–.182), L. Pérez (18–3–.167), José Antonio Huelga (6–3–.500), Santiago Mederos (6–0–.000), Braudilio Vinent (5–0–.000), Gaspar Pérez (4–0–.000), Manuel Hurtado (2–0–.000), Gregorio Pérez (2–0–.000). Pitching (W–L–ERA): José Antonio Huelga (2–0–0.00), Manuel Hurtado (1–0–0.00), Santiago "Changa" Mederos (2–0–0.50), Gaspar Pérez (1–0–0.96), Braudilio Vinent (1–1–3.48), Gregorio Pérez (0–0–5.40).

Cuba Game Scores Round Robin: Dominican Republic beat Cuba 7–4, Cuba beat Mexico 7–1, Cuba beat Colombia 8–2, Cuba beat Venezuela 1–0, Cuba beat Panama 7–0, Cuba beat Puerto Rico 10–0, Cuba beat Nicaragua 11–0, Cuba beat Dutch Antilles 14–1.

1974 Central American Games Championship XII (Santo Domingo, Dominican Republic) (February 27–March 12)

A new generation of sluggers named Antonio Muñoz, Agustín Marquetti, and Armando Capiró joined Rodolfo Puente and Wilfredo Sánchez to spark the potent offense of yet another unbeatable Servio Borges-managed Cuban team. The predictable result was a third straight Central American Games title with only a single opening round defeat in nine total games. Juan Pérez was the anchor of a pitching staff that also featured a young Braudilio Vinent. The latter would be heard from in many international tournaments of the future, though he didn't earn a decision here in his fifth national team outing.

Champion: Cuba (9–1) (Silver Medal: Dominican Republic and Bronze Medal: Puerto Rico)

Teams and Final Standings: Cuba (9–1), Dominican Republic (8–2), Puerto Rico (6–4), Venezuela (4–5), El Salvador (1–8), Virgin Islands (1–9). *One game between Venezuela and El Salvador was cancelled.

Individual Statistical Leaders: BA: Rodolfo Puente (CUB) .500; Runs: A. Louis (DOM) 13; Hits: A. Louis (DOM) 20; 2B: Agustín Marquetti (CUB), J. Guerrero (DOM) 4; 3B: Armando Capiró (CUB) 3; HR: A. Louis (DOM), E. Maldonado (PRI), A. López (PRI) 1; RBI: Armando Capiró (CUB) 15; SB: Wilfredo Sánchez (CUB), J. Hernández (VEN), P. Avila (VEN) 4; Wins: Juan Pérez (CUB), H. Flores (PRI) 3; Strikeouts: S. Martínez (DOM) 29; ERA: Juan Pérez (CUB) 0.00.

Cuba Roster: Manager: Servio Borges. Batting (AB–H–BA): Rodolfo Puente (28–14–.500), Ubaldo Alvarez (10–5–.500), Lázaro Pérez (14–6–.429), Alfonso Urquiola (24–10–.417), Evelio Hernández (30–11–.357), Fermín Laffita (24–8–.333), Agustín Arias (12–4–.333), Armando Capiró (37–12–.324), Agustín Marquetti (38–12–.316), Germán Aguila (34–10–.294), Félix Isasi (14–4–.286), Wifredo Sánchez (40–11–.275), Julian Villar (16–4–.250), Rigoberto Rosique (18–3–.167), Luis Barreiro (8–5–.625), Alfredo García (6–3–.500), Juan Pérez Pérez (8–1–.125), Mario Fernández (4–0–.000), Julio Romero (2–0–.000). Pitching (W–L–ERA): Juan Pérez (3–0–0.00), Luis Barreiro (2–0–0.00), Mario Fernández (2–0–.061), Alfredo García (2–0–0.73), Braudilio Vinent (0–0–2.00), Julio Romero (0–1–2.08).

Cuba Game Scores Round Robin: Cuba beat Dominican Republic 9–0, Puerto Rico beat Cuba 3–2, Cuba beat Venezuela 2–0, Cuba beat El Salvador 7–0, Cuba beat Virgin Islands 12–0, Cuba beat Virgin Islands 13–0, Cuba beat El Salvador 26–0, Cuba beat Venezuela 7–3, Cuba beat Puerto Rico 6–1, Cuba beat Dominican Republic 7–0.

1978 Central American Games Championship XIII (Medellín, Colombia) (July 6–22)

Cuba dominates the field to make it four straight Central American Games titles. The Cubans had an offensive field day in their opening round victory over Puerto Rico, setting numerous offensive team records (31 runs, 32 hits, 30 RBI, 7 doubles, 11 home runs, 19 extra base hits). First baseman Antonio Muñoz posted 20 hits in 28 appearances for a hefty .714 BA during the full ten games, while outfielders Armando Capiró (.614) and Luis Casanova (.606) also both logged stratospheric .600-plus batting averages. Third baseman Pedro José Rodríguez added to the onslaught with a tournament record 15 round-trippers while Rogelio García and Juan Carlos Oliva both rang up unblemished 3–0 pitching marks. Cuba's unstoppable offensive machine also ran up knockout scores against the Dominicans (21–9) and Venezuelans (21–2).

Champion: Cuba (10–0) (Silver Medal: Nicaragua and Bronze Medal: Puerto Rico)

Second Round Team Standings: Cuba (5–0), Puerto Rico (4–2), Nicaragua (4–2), Dominican Republic (3–3), Venezuela (2–4), Dutch Antilles (1–4), Colombia (1–5). *Cuba and Dutch Antilles did not play each other in second round.

First Round Team Standings: Cuba (5–0), Nicaragua (5–1), Puerto Rico (3–3), Venezuela (3–3), Dominican Republic (2–4), Colombia (2–4), Dutch Antilles (0–5). *Cuba vs. Dutch Antilles rained out and not rescheduled.

Individual Statistical Leaders: BA: Antonio Muñoz (CUB) .714*; Runs: Pedro José Rodríguez (CUB), Armando Capiró (CUB) 23*; Hits: Armando Capiró (CUB) 27*; 2B: Luis Casanova (CUB), A. Llenas (DOM) 5; 3B: G. Villegas (COL), D. Abrahams (ANT), M. González (VEN) 2; HR: Pedro José Rodríguez (CUB) 15*; RBI: Pedro José Rodríguez (CUB) 37*; SB: H. Jones (ANT) 3; Wins: Rogelio García (CUB), Juan Carlos Oliva (CUB) 3–0; Strikeouts: O. Valentín (PRI), IP: R. Colin (VEN) 27, ERA: J. Moya (NIC) 0.75. *Starred items are tournament records.

Cuba Roster: Manager: Servio Borges. Batting (AB–H–

BA): Antonio Muñoz (28–20–.714), Armando Capiró (44–27–.614), Luis Casanova (33–20–.606), Pedro José Rodríguez (45–25–.556), Pedro Jova (32–16–.500), Alfonso Urquiola (11–5–.455), Fernando Sánchez (47–21–.447), Agustín Marquetti (42–18–.429), Pedro Medina (39–15–.385), Rey Anglada (34–12–.353), Alberto Martínez (3–1–.333), Wilfredo Sánchez (21–6–.286), Rodolfo Puente (21–6–.286). **Pitching** (W–L–ERA): Félix Pino (1–0–0.00), Juan Carlos Oliva (3–0–2.25), Rogelio García (3–0–4.50), Braudilio Vinent (2–0–4.95), Lázaro Santana (1–0–5.40), Gaspar Legón (0–0–7.71), Santiago "Changa" Mederos (0–0–22.50).

Cuba Game Scores Opening Round: Cuba beat Nicaragua 12–0, Cuba beat Puerto Rico 18–4, Cuba beat Venezuela 15–5, Cuba beat Dominican Republic 16–3, Cuba beat Colombia 11–5, Cuba versus Dutch Antilles (Rain). Championship Round: Cuba beat Puerto Rico 31–2, Cuba beat Nicaragua 14–11, Cuba beat Dominican Republic 21–9, Cuba beat Venezuela 21–2, Cuba beat Colombia 11–2.

1982 Central American Games Championship XIV (Havana, Cuba)

This disappointing runner-up outing interrupted two separate streaks of four consecutive Central American Games titles. Young Lázaro de la Torre would share top pitching honors for Cuba with veteran Braudilio Vinent; the pair would latter emerge as two of only four Cuban League pitchers with 200 career National Series victories. (A third 200-game winner, Jorge Luis Valdés, was also a member of this same Cuban pitching staff.) Cuba would not lose another championship in this event over the next twenty-year stretch.

Champion: Dominican Republic (5–1) (Silver Medal: Cuba and Bronze Medal: Panama)

Teams and Final Standings: Dominican Republic (5–1), Cuba (4–2), Panama (3–3), Dutch Antilles (3–3), Nicaragua (2–4), Puerto Rico (2–4), Venezuela (2–4).

Individual Statistical Leaders: **BA**: J. Cartagena (VEN) .523; **Runs**: Antonio Muñoz (CUB), R. Valbuena (VEN) 6; **Hits**: J. Cartagena (VEN) 11; **2B**: Antonio Muñoz (CUB) 4; **3B**: six players tied with one each; **HR**: Pedro José Rodríguez (CUB), R. Machado (PRI), A. Cruz (NIC) 2; **RBI**: Pedro José Rodríguez (CUB), Lourdes Gourriel (CUB) 6; **SB**: O. Cuarrero (DOM) 6; **Wins**: M. Quiñones (PRI), O. Torres (VEN) 2–0; **ERA**: Lázaro de la Torre (CUB), 0.00.

Cuba Roster: **Manager**: Servio Borges. **Batting** (AB–H–BA): Pedro Medina (8–3–.375), Juan Castro (16–2–.125), Antonio Muñoz (24–8–.333), Juan Luis Baró (11–5–.455), Pedro Jova (23–8–.348), Pedro José Rodríguez (21–4–.190), Agustín Arias (5–2–.400), Wilfredo Hernández (0–0–.000), Giraldo González (18–4–.222), Victor Mesa (28–7–.250), Fernándo Hernández (25–8–.320), Lázaro Junco (1–0–.000), Fernándo Sánchez (14–5–.357), Lourdes Gourriel (23–5–.217). **Pitching** (W–L–ERA): Félix Pino (0–1–3.00), Braudilio Vinent (2–0–0.54), Lázaro de la Torre (2–0–0.00), Octavio Galvez (0–0–10.13), Alfonso Ilivanes (0–0–3.00), Jorge Luis Valdés (0–1–2.25).

Cuba Game Scores Round Robin: Cuba beat Dominican

Republic 4–1, Panama beat Cuba 2–1, Cuba beat Dutch Antilles 10–0, Cuba beat Nicaragua 5–2, Puerto Rico beat Cuba 3–2, Cuba beat Venezuela 10–4.

1986 Central American Games Championship XV (Santiago de los Caballeros, Dominican Republic)

Cuba regained its winning touch under new manager Pedro Chávez and left the field far behind with a perfect seven-game record. Orestes Kindelán emerged as yet another Cuban international slugging star with a .533 batting average and the top spot in the tournament for homers and RBI as well as base hits. Omar Linares also fell a single base hit shy of a .500 BA and Lourdes Gourriel and Luis Casanova also weighed in as .500 hitters. An unheralded team from the Dutch Antilles provided a major surprise with their silver medal finish ahead of such traditional baseball powers as Venezuela, Puerto Rico, Nicaragua, and the host Dominicans.

Champion: Cuba (7–0) (Silver Medal: Dutch Antilles and Bronze Medal: Venezuela)

Teams and Final Standings: Cuba (7–0), Dutch Antilles (4–3), Venezuela (4–3), Puerto Rico (4–3), Nicaragua (3–4), Dominican Republic (2–5), Colombia (2–5), Panama (2–5).

Individual Statistical Leaders: **BA**: C. Rodríguez (COL) .556; **Runs**: Luis Casanova (CUB) 16; **Hits**: Orestes Kindelán (CUB) 16; **2B**: Luis Ulacia (CUB) 5; **3B**: L. Tavera (DOM) 3; **HR**: Orestes Kindelán (CUB) 7; **RBI**: Orestes Kindelán (CUB) 20; **SB**: several players with one each; **Wins**: D. Raudez (NIC) 3–0; **ERA**: Omar Carrero (CUB) 0.00.

Cuba Roster: **Manager**: Pedro Chávez. **Batting** (AB–H–BA): Juan Castro (9–3–.333), Orestes Kindelán (30–16–.533), Pedro Medina (18–6–.333), Antonio Muñoz (24–9–.375), Antonio Pacheco (29–13–.440), Omar Linares (27–11–.497), Luis Ulacia (32–15–.469), Lázaro Vargas (5–3–.600), Juan Padilla (2–1–.500), Lourdes Gourriel (21–11–.524), Luis Casanova (26–13–.500), Victor Mesa (33–12–.364), Jorge García (1–1–1.000). **Pitching** (W–L–ERA): Omar Carrero (1–0–0.00), Rogelio García (2–0–4.50), Pablo Abreu (1–0–2.16), René Arocha (1–0–1.13), Jorge Luis Valdés (0–0–4.50), Félix Nuñez (1–0–0.90), Luis Tissert (1–0–1.00).

Cuba Game Scores Round Robin: Cuba beat Dutch Antilles 6–1, Cuba beat Venezuela 7–1, Cuba beat Puerto Rico 17–5, Cuba beat Nicaragua 17–0, Cuba beat Dominican Republic 17–1, Cuba beat Colombia 12–2, Cuba beat Panama 11–1.

1990 Central American Games Championship XVI (Mexico City, Mexico)

Cuba defends its 1986 title with yet another perfect record in Mexico during November, while Orestes Kindelán puts on a one-man power show as first-ever Central American Games triple crown winner (7 homers, 18 RBI, .533 batting average). Servio Borges returns as manager of the Cuban national team, making his fifth Central American Games appearance in that capacity. Veteran southpaw Jorge Luis Valdés (soon to be a 200-game winner in National Series action) is the tournament pitching star, throwing three consecutive shutouts and not allowing a single earned run in his trio of super-successful starts.

Champion: Cuba (8–0) (Silver Medal: Puerto Rico and Bronze Medal: Dominican Republic)

Final Round Team Standings: Cuba (2–0), Puerto Rico (1–1), Dominican Republic (1–1), Mexico (0–2)

Preliminary Round Team Standings: Cuba (6–0), Puerto Rico (4–2), Mexico (4–2), Dominican Republic (3–3), Dutch Antilles (3–3), El Salvador (1–5)

Individual Statistical Leaders: **BA**: Orestes Kindelán (CUB) .533; **Runs**: Orestes Kindelán (CUB) 12; **Hits**: Orestes Kindelán (CUB), Antonio Pacheco (CUB) 16; **2B**: C. Rostran (SAL) 4; **3B**: J. Vera (DOM) 3; **HR**: Orestes Kindelán (CUB) 7; **RBI**: Orestes Kindelán (CUB) 18; **SB**: S. Andriano (ANT) 3; **Wins**: Jorge Luis Valdés (CUB) 3–0; **ERA**: A. Bonavacia (ANT) 0.00.

Cuba Roster: **Manager**: Servio Borges. **Batting** (AB–H–BA): Germán Mesa (31–7–.226), Antonio Pacheco (33–16–.485), Omar Linares (32–11–.344), Orestes Kindelán (30–16–.533), Lourdes Gourriel (28–12–.429), Javier Méndez (25–5–.200), Ermidelio Urrutia (31–13–.419), Pedro Luis Rodríguez (27–11–.407), Victor Mesa (30–11–.368), Lázaro López (3–0–.000), Juan Carlos Millán (4–3–.750), Luis Ulacia (6–1–.167), José Raúl Delgado (3–0–.000). **Pitchers** (W–L–ERA): Ivan Alvarez (1–0–1.04), Eucildes Rojas (0–0–0.96), Osvaldo Fernández Rodríguez (0–0–4.50), Lázaro Valle (1–0–3.00), Jorge Luis Valdés (3–0–0.00), Omar Ajete (2–0–1.32), René Arocha (1–0–0.82).

Cuba Game Scores Preliminary Round: Cuba beat Puerto Rico 12–2, Cuba beat Mexico 6–1, Cuba beat Dominican Republic 9–2, Cuba beat Dutch Antilles 16–1, Cuba beat El Salvador 10–0, Cuba beat Puerto Rico 9–0. Championship Round: Cuba beat Puerto Rico 9–2, Cuba beat Dominican Republic 10–0.

1993 Central American Games Championship XVII (Ponce, Puerto Rico)

Another undefeated victory for the Cubans, this one under the directorship of replacement national team manager Jorge Fuentes. Future major leagues Rolando Arrojo (Tampa Bay and Boston), Osvaldo Fernández (Giants and Reds) and Orlando "El Duque" Hernández (New York Yankees) headline a brilliant Cuban pitching staff, along with second-tier aces Omar Ajete, Lázaro Valle and Ernesto Guevara. Position players Antonio Pacheco, Lourdes Gourriel and Omar Linares all bat over .400 to pace the expected Cuban hit parade.

Champion: Cuba (7–0) (Silver Medal: Mexico and Bronze Medal: Puerto Rico)

Teams and Final Standings: Cuba (7–0), Nicaragua (5–2), Puerto Rico (4–3), Mexico (4–3), Panama (2–5), Venezuela (2–5), Aruba (2–5), Dutch Antilles (2–5).

Individual Statistical Leaders: **BA**: Rigoberto Aparicio (PAN) .579; **Runs**: Antonio Pacheco (CUB) 10; **Hits**: Lourdes Gourriel (CUB) 12; **2B**: Omar Linares (CUB) 4; **3B**: seven players tied with one each; **HR**: Antonio Pacheco (CUB), Orestes Kindelán (CUB) 3; **RBI**: J.R. Padilla (NIC) 9; **SB**: S.

Moreno (NIC), R. Aparicio (PAN) 5; **Wins**: Rolando Arrojo (CUB), R. Santiago (PRI), J. Huazequi (MEX) 2; **ERA**: M.J. Zelaya (NIC) 0.00.

Cuba Roster: **Manager**: Jorge Fuentes. **Batting** (AB–H–BA): Alberto Hernández (21–2–0.95), Angel López (2–1–.500), José Raúl Delgado (2–2–1.000), Orestes Kindelán (26–8–.308), Lourdes Gourriel (27–12–.444), Antonio Pacheco (25–10–.400), Juan Padilla (1–0–0.00), Omar Linares (28–12–.429), Gabriel Pierre (1–0–.000), Germán Mesa (25–10–.400), Eduardo Paret (1–0–.000), Victor Mesa (30–9–.300), Ermidelio Urrutia (28–10–.333), Juan Carlos Linares (3–1–.333). **Pitchers** (W–L–ERA): Omar Ajete (1–0–0.00), Jorge Luis Valdés (0–0–2.70), Osvaldo Fernández Rodríguez (1–0–0.00), Luis Rolando Arrojo (2–0–0.00), Lázaro Valle (1–0–0.00), Ernesto Guevara (1–0–0.00), Orlando "El Duque" Hernández (1–0–0.00).

Cuba Game Scores Round Robin: Cuba beat Nicaragua 16–0, Cuba beat Puerto Rico 9–4, Cuba beat Mexico 1–0, Cuba beat Panama 10–0, Cuba beat Venezuela 10–0, Cuba beat Aruba 10–0, Cuba beat Dutch Antilles 4–3.

1998 Central American Games Championship XVIII (Maracaibo, Venezuela)

Cuba wins a fourth consecutive Central American Games title during the late–August event and extends its individual-game unbeaten streak through four consecutive tournaments. Former national team star infielder Alfonso Urquiola becomes the third Cuban manager to capture a team title in this event during the decade of the nineties. First baseman Orestes Kindelán (.588 BA), catcher Juan Manrique (the surprise home run and RBI leader) and outfielder Loidel Chapelli (pacesetter in homers, along with Manrique, and also in runs scored) provide the major offense, while mound stars Omar Luis and José Contreras each capture two pitching victories.

Champion: Cuba (6–0) (Silver Medal: Nicaragua and Bronze Medal: Venezuela)

Teams and Final Standings: Cuba (6–0), Nicaragua (5–1), Venezuela (4–2), Panama (4–2), Dominican Republic (3–3), Puerto Rico (2–4), Dutch Antilles (1–5), Colombia (1–5), Virgin Islands (0–4). *Cuba beat Nicaragua (13–3) in gold medal game and Venezuela beat Panama (5–4) in bronze medal game.

Individual Statistical Leaders: **BA**: Orestes Kindelán (CUB) .588; **Runs**: Loidel Chapelli (CUB) 13; **Hits**: J. Solis (PAN) 13; **HR**: Juan Manrique (CUB), Loidel Chapelli (CUB), J. León (COL) 3; **RBI**: Juan Manrique (CUB), E. Agnoly (PAN) 12; **SB**: A. Rodríguez (PRI), S. Martínez (DOM) 3; **Wins**: I. Avila (VEN), Omar Luis (CUB), José Ariel Contreras (CUB) 2–0; **Strikeouts**: J. Avila (VEN) 19, **IP**: O. Clemencia (ANT), J. Avila (VEN) 21.1, **ERA**: J. Viñas (DOM) 1.04.

Cuba Roster: **Manager**: Alfonso Urquiola. **Batting** (AB–H–BA): Ariel Benavides (3–2–.667), Danel Castro (21–8–.381), Loidel Chapelli (20–10–.500), Orestes Kindelán (17–10–.588), Omar Linares (14–6–.429), Oscar Machado (18–3–.167), Oscar Macías (6–4–.667), Yosvani Madera (2–0–.000), Juan Manrique (21–7–.333), Javier Méndez

(6–4–.667), Juan Carlos Moreno (3–0–.000), Antonio Pacheco (15–4–.267), Gabriel Pierre (5–1–.200), Carlos Taberas (23–9–.391), Robelquis Videaux (25–12–.480). **Pitchers** (W–L–ERA): Yovani Aragón (1–0–1.13), José Ariel Contreras (2–0–4.61), José Ibar (0–0–2.70), Pedro Luis Lazo (1–0–1.35), Omar Luis (2–0–1.38).

Cuba Game Scores Round Robin: Cuba beat Nicaragua 13–3, Cuba beat Venezuela 12–2, Cuba beat Panama 11–7, Cuba beat Puerto Rico 9–4, Cuba beat Dutch Antilles 11–0, Cuba beat Virgin Islands 11–1.

2002 Central American Games Championship XIX (San Salvador, El Salvador) (November 27–December 7)

For the first time since the 1959 games in Caracas, Venezuela, Cuba skipped this tournament, claiming that the Salvadoran government would not issue sufficient guarantees for the security of the Cuban team and delegation. With the perennial champions out of the picture, Puerto Rico swept to its second-ever championship, its first since Cuba's last absence. Ten countries participated and Panama and the Dominican Republic also posted strong showings.

Champion: Puerto Rico (6–1) (Silver Medal: Panama and Bronze Medal: Dominican Republic)

Team and Final Standings: Puerto Rico (6–1), Panama (5–2), Dominican Republic (6–1), Nicaragua (4–3), Mexico (3–4), Dutch Antilles (2–5), El Salvador (2–4), Venezuela (3–3), Honduras (0–4), Guatemala (0–4).

Cuba Did Not Participate

World Professional Baseball Championships

MLB's inaugural World Baseball Classic was a resounding success by almost any measure, despite much debate among fans about the early-spring timing of the event and much carping from big league owners unhappy with stars missing from Florida and Arizona training camps. MLB was a clear winner in the spectacle — despite an unpredictable turn of events on the field of play that saw teams boasting top big league stars eliminated in the early rounds and MLB rivals Japan and Cuba left standing for the championship match. The stated goal of spreading a message that baseball is truly an international sport was indisputably accomplished, especially given the successes of the two Asian teams and two Caribbean teams that reached the championship round. Merchandize was sold in record numbers and stadiums were jam packed for all six tournament venues (Tokyo, Phoenix, Orlando, San Juan, Anaheim, San Diego). All-important television ratings exceeded all expectations, despite the rather underwhelming underperformance of a star-studded Team USA. Fans tuned in to televised games beamed from San Diego's Petco Park intrigued by the "no-name teams"(Korea, Japan, Cuba) that had reached the pinnacle of international baseball success. The atmosphere was truly electric for second round matches in San Juan's Hiram Bithorn

Stadium, where four Latin American powers faced off in the first true "Caribbean Series" matching the Cuban juggernaut against top big leaguers from Venezuela, the Dominican and host Puerto Rico. And most importantly, a huge North American television audience had its eyes rudely opened to the undeniable fact that top flight baseball is not restricted to the United States and the Dominican Republic.

WBC success came in a form very different from the one MLB honchos and ESPN television executives had likely envisioned. Plans for a showdown final in San Diego between ballyhooed Team USA and star-studded big league lineups of Venezuelans or Dominicans — a game title whose appeal lay in the appearance of Derek Jeter, Roger Clemens, Alex Rodríguez, Albert Pujols and other household names — did not materialize. The only star big leaguers to make it to San Diego other than Japan's Ichiro were the Dominicans, who themselves were not around for the grand finale. Japan, Korea and Cuba were able to demonstrate to a nation of American skeptics that the most successful baseball winning style was one largely eschewed in the big league camps. What could possibly have been a better scenario for marketing international baseball — at least everywhere outside the USA — than a final featuring the two top non–USA league all-stars? The tournament in the end showcased baseball in the two prime outposts of the sport's ever-expanding international universe.

WORLD BASEBALL CLASSIC (PROFESSIONAL WORLD SERIES), 2006

2006 World Baseball Classic I (San Diego, San Juan, Anaheim, Phoenix, and Orlando) (March 2–20)

Cuba's entrant in the inaugural MLB–sponsored World Baseball Classic reached the championship game in San Diego, in the process keeping alive a remarkable streak of either gaining a championship or at least reaching the gold medal game of every major international tournament entered since the 1959 Pan American Games (did not medal) and every world championship event since the 1951 World Cup in Mexico City (Bronze Medal). The Cubans had first been denied permission by the U.S. Treasury to compete in this first fully professional (major league caliber) world tournament and were late entries only after agreeing to donate all prize money to Hurricane Katrina relief efforts. Rumors then persisted that the Cubans would send an inferior team (fearing player defections) or that Cuban stars would defect in large numbers once the Cubans reached San Juan. The results were entirely the opposite, and despite a title-match defeat by Japan the Cubans were clearly the surprise of the event. Defeating big-league all-star lineups of three Caribbean rivals — Venezuela, Puerto Rico and the Dominican Republic, Cuba's juggernaut put to rest once and for all the long-standing assumptions that the island team had dominated international play for more than half a century only because it always played against rank amateurs or inferior professionals. A silver medal finish demonstrated to the world that Cuban League all-stars could compete successfully head-to-head with the top major league professionals. Individual tournament stars were Yoandry Garlobo (WBC all-star DH who lead the club in batting during his first national team outing), Pedro Luis Lazo (with outstanding relief efforts to close out victories over Venezuela in Round 2 and the Dominicans in the semifinals), Yadel Martí (who won one game, saved two, and led the tournament with a 0.00 ERA in 12.2 innings of work), and Frederich Cepeda (whose dramatic three-run homer iced a crucial victory versus Venezuela and whose second round-tripper briefly put Cuba in contention in the finals). Cuba's eight WBC games were followed on the island with unparalleled intensity and the three victories over rival Caribbean big leaguers were arguable the three greatest victories in Cuba's long and stored baseball history.

Champion: Japan (5–3); Runner-Up: Cuba (5–3)

Finals (San Diego): Japan beat Cuba 10–6 (Gold Medal and Silver Medal)

Semifinals (San Diego): Cuba beat Dominican Republic 3–1, Japan beat Korea 6–0.

Round 2, Pool 1 (Anaheim): Korea (3–0), Japan (1–2),* Mexico (1–2), USA (1–2) *Japan wins tie-breaker (defensive runs allowed divided by defensive innings played)

Round 2, Pool 2 (San Juan): Dominican Republic (2–1), Cuba (2–1), Venezuela (1–2), Puerto Rico (1–2)

Round 1, Group A (Tokyo): Korea (3–0), Japan (2–1), Chinese Taipei (1–2), China (0–3)

Round 1, Group B (Phoenix): Mexico (2–1), USA (2–1), Canada (2–1),* South Africa (0–3) *Canada loses tie-breaker (defensive runs allowed divided by defensive innings played)

Round 1, Group C (Orlando): Dominican Republic (3–0), Venezuela (2–1), Italy (1–2), Australia (0–3)

Round 1, Group D (San Juan): Puerto Rico (3–0), Cuba (2–1), Netherlands (1–2), Panama (0–3)

Tournament All-Star Team: Catcher: Tomoya Satozaki (Japan); First Base: Seung Yeop Lee (Korea); Second Base: Yulieski Gourriel (Cuba); Shortstop: Derek Jeter (USA); Third Base: Adrian Beltre (Dominican); Outfield: Ken Griffey, Jr. (USA); Outfield: Ichiro Suzuki (Japan); Outfield: Jong Beom Lee (Korea); DH: Yoandry Garlobo (Cuba); Pitcher: Daisuke Matsuzaka (Japan); Pitcher: Chan Ho Park (Korea); Pitcher: Yadel Martí (Cuba).

No-Hit Game: Sharion Martis (Netherlands) versus Panama, 10–0 (7 Innings) *65-pitch-count limit (March 10, 2006).

Individual Statistical Leaders: **BA**: Adam Stern (Canada) .667; **Runs**: Nobuhiko Matsunaka (Japan) 11; **Hits**: Nobuhilo Matsunaka (Japan) 13; **2B**: Jong Beom Lee (Korea) 6; **3B**: fifteen players tied 2; **HR**: Seong-Yeop Lee (Korea) 5; **RBI**: Ken Griffey, Jr. (USA, Seung-Yeop Lee (Korea) 10; **SB**: Tsuyoshi Nishioka (Japan) 5; **Wins**: Daisuke Matsuzaka (Japan) 3; **SO**: Koji Uehara (Japan) 16; **ERA**: Yadel Martí (Cuba) 0.00 (12.2 Inn); **MVP**: Daisuke Matsuzaka (Japan).

Cuba Roster: **Manager**: Higinio Vélez. **Batting** (AB–H–BA): Leslie Anderson (5–0–.000), Ariel Borrero (22–7–.318), Frederich Cepeda (26–10–.385), Michel Enríquez (31–6–.194), Yoandry Garlobo (25–12–.480), Yulieski Gourriel (33–9–.273), Juan Carlos Moreno (0–0–.000), Eduardo Paret (35–8–.229), Joan Carlos Pedroso (9–1–.111), Ariel Pestano (31–6–.194), Alexei Ramírez (16–6–.375), Rudy Reyes (1–0–.000), Eriel Sánchez (3–1–.333), Carlos Tabares (13–3–.231), Osmani Urrutia (29–10–.345), Roger Machado (DNP). **Pitching** (W–L–ERA): Luis Borroto (0–1–10.80), Maikel Folch (0–0–0.00), Norberto González (0–0–3.86), Yulieski González (0–0–0.00), Pedro Luis Lazo (1–0–2.45), Yadel Martí (1–0–0.00), Jonder Martínez (0–0–9.82), Yunieski Maya (1–0–0.00), Adiel Palma (0–0–6.14), Yadier Pedroso (0–0–3.60), Yosvani Pérez (0–0–27.00), Ormari Romero (2–1–4.15), Vicyohandri Odelín (0–1–6.48), Deinys Suárez (0–0–0.00).

Cuba Game Scores First Round: Cuba beat Panama 8–6 (11), Cuba beat Netherlands 11–2, Puerto Rico beat Cuba 12–2. Second Round: Cuba beat Venezuela 7–2, Dominican Republic best Cuba 7–3, Cuba beat Puerto Rico 4–3. Semifinals: Cuba beat Dominican Republic 3–1. Finals: Japan beat Cuba 10–6.

Note: Appendix D at the end of this volume provides complete Cuban League career batting and pitching records for all individual players appearing on National Team rosters during the post-revolution period (1962–2002). Composite international tournament career batting and pitching records for a handful of selected stars are also found in Chapter 11.

Cuba's Composite Record in International Baseball Championships

Tournaments	Championships Entered	Won	Games Won–Lost (Pct)	Shutout Victories	Shutout Losses
MLB World Baseball Classic	1	0	5–3 (.625)	0	0
World Cup Championships	28	25	280–28 (.909)	90	5
Olympic Games	4	3	33–3 (.917)	6	1
Pre-Olympics (Pan American)	1	1	6–0 (1.000)	3	0
Intercontinental Cup	12	9	107–11 (.907)	25	0
Pan American Games	13	11	91–13 (.875)	22	0
Central American Games	16	13	100–14 (.877)	35	3
University World Cup	1	1	7–0 (1.000)	6	0
TOTALS	**76**	**63**	**629–72 (.897)**	**187**	**9**

8

Cuba's Revolutionary Baseball (1962–2005)

Cuba unfolds as a genuine ballpark paradise for any tradition-loving North American baseball fan. The quaint stadiums of Havana, Camagüey, Matanzas, Cienfuegos and other cities around the 16-team Cuban League are largely reminiscent of those found stateside in the forties, fifties or sixties. Cuban League talent is consistently top-notch and grandstands overflow with highly knowledgeable and passionate partisans. There is, as might only be expected, a notable absence of any hint of capitalist commercialism in ballparks on the communist island. No fence-plastered billboards hawking beer, burgers or life insurance; no shrill scoreboard videos hyping sponsors' merchandise or orchestrating grandstand cheers; no ear-splitting rock concerts or noisy commercial jingles — only an occasional muted patriotic slogan painted upon an outfield wall or adorning crude canvas banners stretched between light-tower stanchions. In short, big-time ballgames in Cuba are laced with diamond purity and hence showcase a prelapsarian innocence that has long-since evaporated on the North American ballpark scene.

Such nostalgic trappings are also at times something of a misleading veneer covering up the considerable warts likewise ever-present on the Cuban baseball scene. The national sport on Fidel Castro's island bastion has suffered its fair share of crises of late and this has been especially apparent over the past eight or nine seasons. Several dozen disloyal athletes have weakened the nation's showcase program since 1991 (René Arocha was the first) by fleeing to the cash-rich majors. Possible overreaction by INDER officials (including the banning of several stars considered to be future defection threats) has soured ballplayer morale and alienated loyal fans — especially in the capital city where two local teams (Industriales and Metropolitanos) have been recently stripped of much valuable talent.

And beyond defections of key players, the overall talent pool seems also to have leveled off rather noticeably — though new phenoms like infielder Yulieski Gourriel, outfielder Frederich Cepeda and hurler Yunieski Maya are now promising once more to enflame island passions. Recently retired stars boasting the stature of Omar Linares, Orestes Kindelán and Germán Mesa are in no immediate danger of being quickly overshadowed by new prospects like Osmani Urrutia (a five-time batting champ), Yasser Gómez (Havana's current fan fa-

vorite) or Michel Enríquez (currently the most potent national team slugger). During a recent 2002 National Series two unheralded teams from Holguín and Sancti Spíritus won their way into the championship finals during a season marked by numerous stoppages of play and other unseemly interruptions. Postseason playoff games were suspended once for a spur-of-the-moment series between the Cuban All-Star Game champions and AAA–level Mexico City Reds, again for a surprise visit by former U.S. president Jimmy Carter (and resulting pair of staged exhibitions held in Carter's honor), and a third time for impromptu national patriotic holidays of five-days duration occasioned by window-dressing revamping of Cuba's 40-year-old socialist constitution. All such stoppages of course came at the sole whim of the island's top baseball fan and micro-manager — Maximum Leader Fidel Castro.

Attendance has also been on the wane in Cuban ballparks during recent campaigns. At least this was true before a sudden revival of fan interest near the end of an exciting 1999 season — a reawakening fueled by an unexpected pennant challenge from Havana's wildly popular Industriales team and an even-more surprising exhibition-game visit to Havana by the major league Baltimore Orioles. But even renewed contact with the major leagues after forty long years of total isolation (a span covering two distinct generations of Cuban fans) was not seemingly enough to stem a perceptible slide that witnessed the vaunted Cuban national team — invincible for most of three-plus decades — being unaccountably upset in not one but several prestigious international tournaments.

For the first time in more than a century baseball seems to be losing some of its luster for Cuban fans and thus also some of its ironclad grip on the national psyche. Basketball tournaments occasionally outdrew Cuban League games in Havana over the past several winters. And the nation's few daily sports pages published in *Granma* and *Trabajadores* have devoted increasing coverage to the island's crack women's volleyball program, or to provincial *fútbol* (soccer) matches or the perennial favorite sport of amateur boxing. (Baseball alone outranks boxing on the Cuban sports scene, and this has been true for much of the past century.) During June 2002 — with popular powerhouse teams like Pinar del Río, Industriales and cross-island rival Santiago de Cuba all on the sidelines, while hinterland teams representing Holguín and Sancti Spíritus surprisingly met for the league trophy — there appeared to be almost more fan interest generated among crowds in Havana bars and on Havana street corners by televised World Cup soccer matches beamed in from Asia, even if there was no Cuban team to cheer for.

Yet despite numerous ills spawned by the island's recent severe economic woes, it is still baseball — from topnotch league games to ragtag sandlot contests among Havana street urchins — that nonetheless remains unchallenged king of Cuba's considerable sports culture. And recent uplifting national team victories in two World Cup tournaments (one at home in Havana) and the Athens Olympics have done much to rekindle the flame.

Baseball's pre-eminent rank as heart and soul of Cuban culture stretches back more than a full century. The Cuban League (CL here for easy reference) in its current guise, however, boasts a history less than a third that long. For three and a half decades under the Castro regime baseball has built a bold new tradition and followed a brave new path. Most of the current ballparks were erected in the 1960s and early 1970s and feature cantilevered single-tier grandstands, towering concrete light stanchions, and single-deck seating in the 20,000–35,000 range. The showcase park, however, remains Estadio Latinoamericano (Latin American Stadium), located in the central Havana neighborhood of El Cerro, which today features 55,000 unobstructed-view seats after its large-scale 1971 renovation. The former Gran Estadio del Cerro (as it was known when it debuted in 1946) has thus taken on a radical new look since the early seventies, with its expanded outfield bleacher sections and stark pale-green revolutionary paint scheme. And this new look has spread everywhere else across the 900-mile-long island. There is not a single fan-distancing upper-deck structure to be found anywhere among Cuba's fan-friendly ballpark venues. Cuban ballparks are without exception intimate if dimly lit, and since there are few food concessions or electronic sideshows it is always the action on the diamond that remains the only entertainment offered to stadium patrons.

Today's showcase CL arose phoenix-like in 1962 from the ashes of professional baseball, which suffered a most sudden and inglorious death on the island in the revolution-scarred summer months of 1960. Pro ball in Cuba had peaked during the previous decade, both with a "golden age" era of top winter league play in Havana (featuring four renowned teams — Almendares, Habana, Cienfuegos and Marianao) and a mildly successful seven-year run of Bobby Maduro's Cuban Sugar Kings International League franchise. But in the wake of deteriorating relations between Washington and Castro's intractable socialist-leaning government the International League had overnight pulled the plug on its Havana AAA franchise in mid-season of 1960. The Havana ballclub was abruptly relocated to distant Jersey City, and a considerable collection of *cubanos* on its roster (including Leo Cárdenas, Elio Chacón, Miguel Cuéllar, Orlando Peña, Raúl Sánchez and Octavio "Cookie" Rojas) almost to the man fled the island to pursue North American professional careers. The net result was that often leaky valves were screwed tightly shut on a once productive pipeline of Cuban talent flowing directly onto big league rosters.

But Cuban diamonds did not lie dormant for very long. Under the guiding influence of Fidel Castro himself and a hand-picked coterie of sports advisers — which included Negro league legend and multi-country hall of famer Martín Dihigo as a technical assistant, and fellow Sierra Maestra "Barbudos" veteran Felipe Guerra Matos as newly tapped national sports director — a brand new Cuban baseball establishment was molded during the first few seasons of the sixties. And it was a revisionist baseball world with considerable and even quite remarkable differences. Professionalism was banned outright as being contrary to revolutionary principles, ballpark admissions were suddenly free of charge, wooden Louisville Sluggers were eventually traded in for Japanese-made aluminum models (this change being introduced in 1976, in time for National Series XVI), modest state-of-the-art stadiums were constructed mostly with volunteer communist youth corps labor, and home-stitched Batos-brand baseballs became the new trade tools of Cuban batters and hurlers.

From the outset the CL has thus showcased its altogether unique features. One is the strict regional structure featuring provincial-level teams representing each of the island's major political divisions. Cuban teams are geographically fixed with players being drawn only from each team's immediate locale (viz., from the local province, which approximates a U.S. state). Players thus never switch willy-nilly from roster to roster as in North America's professional scheme; they never sign contracts with individual teams but are instead owned by the league itself. Special dispensation is sometimes granted a player with good enough reason (such as family relocation, which is rare in Cuba) to shift his employment. But there are no player trades or free-agent signings in Cuban baseball. This practice is consistent with reigning socialist notions that athletes are never mere chattel, or just so much team property to be bought and sold at a clubowner's whim or fancy.

Fan loyalties run very deep due to this regional organization, as do the heated intersectional rivalries. Favorite players are guaranteed to be remain with the local club for season after season and any league game is truly "our guys" versus "their guys" in a most literal sense. (Not like in the big leagues, where an Arizona D-Backs fan might crow to a New York Yankees booster after the 2001 World Series that "our Dominican imports finally beat your Dominican imports.") The current CL setup now includes four divisions of four teams each, further divided into western and eastern zones. The CL postseason tournament featuring four division winners and four runners-up is thus similar to the big league LCS (League Championship Series) format and the final series (as in the majors) is a best-of-seven affair.

League structure has occasionally altered somewhat over the years and so has seasonal pennant-race organization. But the basic scheme has remained largely intact since 1962 (ironically the same year that the U.S. majors took on their own present look of divisional alignment with multi-tiered playoffs). The CL season also provides a means for selecting national teams for international competitions at the senior or Olympic level. Traditionally (until the past decade) there have been two separate seasons in Cuba, a provincial round of play (normally 39 games) followed by a super-provincial round (usually around 54 games). The super-provincial season always involves collapsing several adjacent provinces into one team (e.g., Matanzas, Cienfuegos, Camagüey and Sancti Spíritus forming "Centrales") and thus restructuring the CL into larger geographical chunks.

Under this two-seasons-a-year format, then, the National Series (2005–2006 marks National Series XLV) or inter-province schedule was for years followed immediately by a sectional (super-provincial) round robin known as the Selective Series, with 16 CL teams collapsed to either half or a quarter that many and their rosters selectively reduced. *Series Selectiva* competition was thus between four larger zones (typically called Occidentales, Habana, Centrales and Orientales) and the combined rosters of one hundred top players represented a further winnowing of talent in the direction of final selection of A-level and B-level national teams for late summer of early fall international competitions. CL play commences each year in the late autumn and continues through the late spring. With the 1998 (National Series XXXVII) schedule, however, the two-season format was finally scrapped and replaced by a much longer 90-game schedule stretching from early November to late April. But this format was once again revised in 2002 with a new short season "Super League" again scheduled between mid July and early August.

Another unique feature of contemporary Cuban baseball is the strange-sounding team names, which currently (with three exceptions) are the names of provinces represented by each ballclub. Habana (often called Habana Province) refers to the provincial team that plays its home games in San José de la Lajas and not in the capital city, which is instead represented by two teams named Industriales and Metropolitanos. Villa Clara is the team of that province, which plays most home games in the provincial capital of Santa Clara. Camagüey, Granma, Santiago de Cuba and Sancti Spíritus are similarly provincial teams. The club called Isla de la Juventud represents a political sub-division that is technically a "special municipality" and not strictly a province.

Cuban ballclubs uniquely lack official or formal team nicknames. Industriales is simply Industriales and not the Industriales Tigers, Industriales Redbirds, Industriales Rum Distillers or what-have-you. But from time to time nicknames have in fact been employed, at least informally by creative fans and in some press accounts. For the 1981 National Series season, for example, the following set of nicknames (in parentheses) were semi-officially recognized for league teams: Vegueros (*Tabaqueros*—"Tobacco Workers"), Forestales (*Madereros*—"Wood Workers"), Habana (*Agricultores*—"Farmers"), Isla de la Juventud (*Toronjeros*—"Grapefruit Harvesters"), Metropolitanos (*Cerrajeros*—"Locksmiths"), Henequeneros (*Hilacheros*—"Spinners" or "Threaders"), Industriales (*Azules*—"The Blues"), Citricultores (*Naranjeros*—"Orange Pickers"),

Cuban League Team Names (after 2003)

CL teams for years had no official symbolic names (Cubs, Yankees, Red Stockings) but only their provincial designations. Over the years "unofficial" nicknames (even occasional mascots) were attached by local boosters or media accounts, and such names are now increasingly found in the Cuban press. But these remain popular labels only since there are no "franchises" seeking commercial promotions, and more than one team nickname may co-exist simultaneously.

Group A

Pinar del Río = *Pativerdes* (Green Feet) or *Vegueros* (Tobacco Growers)
Havana Metros = *Los Metros* or *Guerreros* (Warriors)
Isla de la Juventud = *Isleños* or *Pineros* (Pine Cutters)
Matanzas = *Rojos* (Reds)

Group B

Habana Province = *Vaqueros* (Cowboys)
Cienfuegos = *Camaroneros* (Shrimpers) or *Sureños* (Southerners)
Sancti Spíritus = *Gallos* (Roosters)
Havana Industriales = *Azules* (Blues) or *Leones Azules* (Blue Lions)

Group C

Camagüey = *Tinajoneros* (Clay Pot Makers or Potters)
Ciego de Avila = *Avileños* or *Tigres*
Las Tunas = *Tuneros* (Cactus Growers) or *Magos* (Magicians)
Villa Clara = *Azucareros* (Sugar Growers) or *Naranjas* (Orangemen)

Group D

Guantanamo = *Indios del Guaso* (Guaso Indians)
Holguín = *Perros* (Dogs)
Granma = *Alazanes* (Stallions)
Santiago de Cuba = *Avispas* (Wasps)

Villa Clara (*Azucareros*—"Sugarcane Cutters"), Cienfuegos (*Camaroneros*—"Shrimp Fishers"), Sancti Spíritus (*Vaqueros*—"Cowboys"), Ciego de Avila (*Piñeros*—"Pineapple Growers"), Camagüey (*Tinajoneros*—"Potters"), Granma (*Arroceros*—"Rice Growers"), Guantánamo (*Los Cósmicos*—"The Cosmics") and Santiago de Cuba (*Montañeses*—"Highlanders"). It can also be noted from this 1981 team list that in many past National Series and Selective Series some if not most of the teams — while province-based — did not carry names that were identical to the recognized province name.

Ballparks themselves also represent a special feature of Cuban baseball at the end of the twentieth century and outset of the new millennium. A majority of the current parks were erected in the first or second decade after the revolution — in the sixties or early seventies — and as a result are quaint if sparse by North American big league standards. Scoreboards are electronic (containing linescores and lineups) but altogether stark in their appearance. Grandstands are colorless concrete structures, though a few of the parks feature fresh paint schemes (usually green or grey or yellow). There is no attention paid to concession areas and the baseball-viewing atmosphere is intimate in the extreme. Seating capacity is usually in the 15,000–30,000 range with grandstands crowding close to the foul lines. The single exception is Havana's grandiose Latin American Stadium that dates back (minus only outfield grandstands) to the pre-revolution era.

The primary home stadium of each provincial team is lo-

Four managers of Cuba's first post-revolution National Series baseball season (1962): José Maria Fernández (Habana), Fermín Guerra (Occidentales), Antonio Castaño (Azucareros), and Pedro "Natilla" Jiménez (Orientales).

cated in the capital city of that region, but most teams also play occasional games in a number of secondary parks that are smaller in size but far from shoddy in structure. Several of the Cuban ballparks boast attention-grabbing features or carry intriguing histories. There is for starters the unusual name of the ballpark in Guantánamo (Nguyen Van Troi, in honor of a North Vietnamese war hero). There are also patriotic tales behind other names, as in Pinar del Río (Captain San Luis, martyred hero of the revolution), Cienfuegos (Fifth of September, a revolution patriotic holiday) and Matanzas (Victory at Girón, commemorating the infamous 1961 Bay of Pigs invasion).

The most elaborate history, of course, attaches itself to Estadio Latinoamericano, which in its guise as Gran Stadium hosted the final two decades of professional winter league action and also housed the International League Sugar Kings (also called the Havana Cubanos). By contrast, the tiny and almost crude ballpark located in Nueva Gerona and housing the Isla de la Juventud (Isle of Youth) team may indeed be the

most unusual ballpark structure used by a big-time baseball league anywhere in the world. At Estadio Cristóbal Lara, the third base foul line is a mere five feet from a concrete wall (stretching from the backstop all the way to the foul poll) and both dugouts, along with the only covered grandstand and a cramped press box all occupy the first base side of the field. The charm of intimate and old-style Cuban ballparks is indeed one of the primary attractions of today's island baseball scene. (This park was replaced in January of 2006.)

As with the U.S. major leagues, the CL has also boasted enormous stars and landmark performances down through its forty-odd years of colorful history. Each decade has in turn witnessed its own memorable batting and hurling paragons and thus given rise to its own unparalleled on-field achievements. But because Cuba has long focused on winning world amateur tournaments and not on flooding big league rosters, and since international baseball was largely downplayed in North America (at least before the 1992 Barcelona Olympics),

Primary Home Ballparks of Cuban League Teams

Province Name	Stadium Name	City Name	Team Name
Pinar del Río	Capitán San Luis	Pinar del Río	Pinar del Río
Havana	Nelson Fernández	San José de las Lajas	Habana
(Ciudad de la Havana)	Latinoamericano	Havana	Industriales
(Ciudad de la Havana)	Latinoamericano	Havana	Metropolitanos (Metros)
(Isla de la Juventud)	Cristóbal Lara	Nueva Gerona	Isla de la Juventud
Matanzas	Victoria de Girón	Matanzas	Matanzas
Cienfuegos	5 de Septiembre	Cienfuegos	Cienfuegos
Villa Clara	Augusto C. Sandino	Santa Clara	Villa Clara
Sancti Spíritus	José Antonio Huelga	Sancti Spíritus	Sancti Spíritus
Ciego de Avila	José Ramón Cepero	Ciego de Avila	Ciego de Avila
Camagüey	Cándido Gónzalez	Camagüey	Camagüey
Las Tunas	Julio Antonio Mella	Las Tunas	Las Tunas
Holguín	Calixto García	Holguín	Holguín
Granma	Mártires de Barbados	Bayamo	Granma
Guantánamo	Nguyen Van Troi	Guantánamo	Guantánamo
Santiago de Cuba	Guillermón Moncada	Santiago de Cuba	Santiago de Cuba

Cuba's biggest stars have remained totally unknown to the average U.S. fan. Almost nothing has been heard or read north of Miami of either Antonio Muñoz (1967–90) or his twenty-plus years of fence-rattling slugging. There is almost no stateside awareness of primer batsmen like Agustín Marquetti (1968–89, who smacked homers of Ruthian proportions), Wilfredo Sánchez (1967–84, who captured six batting titles) or Pedro José Rodríguez (1974–88, who once hit .446 for a 54-game season) — though the equally foreign-sounding name of Japanese slugger Sadaharu Oh (who slugged more homers than either Babe Ruth or Hank Aaron) does have considerable currency with U.S. fans. Stellar pitchers like Braudilio Vinent (1969–88), Aquino Abreu (1962–70), José Antonio Huelga (1967–1974) and Jesús Guerra (1980–91) have performed heroically on the restricted island stage with only a smattering of international fame. Abreu was especially brilliant when he matched big-leaguer Johnny Vander Meer's incomparable June 1938 feat of back-to-back no-hitters in January 1966 — performing what likely stands as international baseball's most surprisingly overlooked individual pitching feat.

The biggest Cuban stars have arguably been Marquetti, Muñoz, Sánchez, Pedro José Rodríguez, Omar Linares, and the flamethrowing Braudilio Vinent. Agustín Marquetti, a southpaw-swinging Havana first sacker, banged out prodigious round-trippers in the early 1970s, while Antonio Muñoz, also a first baseman with Las Villas, still holds league records for games played and runs scored, as well as for doubles, RBI and total bases. Veteran *Sports Illustrated* writer Ron Fimrite, upon seeing Muñoz up close in 1977, dubbed him a lefthanded Tony Pérez. Another portside swinger, Wilfredo Sánchez was the first CL player to reach 2,000 base hits (2,174) and with that feat appropriately earned a most colorful and memorable moniker among his countrymen as "El Hombre Hit" (The Hitman). Pedro José Rodríguez (known popularly as "Cheíto" or "Little Che") was the supreme Cuban slugger before current stars Linares and Kindelán arrived in the late eighties, and his career with Cienfuegos boasted a record for home run frequency (one digger for every 14.5 at-bats) that challenges any

of the top bashers housed in Cooperstown. Braudilio Vinent, a righthander who pitched for 20 full seasons, possesses lifetime CL mileposts for pitching starts, innings hurled, complete games, losses (167, versus his 221 victories), and shutouts, and was also the CL's first 200-game winner.

More recently there has been muscular Omar Linares, who more than a few scouts and writers have hailed enthusiastically (some would say over-enthusiastically) as the best third baseman (at least outside the majors) found anywhere on the planet. Linares has several times batted above .400 and has also impressed with his range and rifle arm in the infield. His lifetime average hovers above .370 after twenty seasons, and his 400-plus CL homers are topped only by Orestes Kindelán. Linares arrived on the international scene at age 14 (in 1981 at the world junior championships in Venezuela) with a .500-plus BA in his first world tourney; then became the youngest-ever CL full-timer a season later, after barely turning fifteen. His Olympic performance in Atlanta (three homers in the gold medal game with Japan) demonstrated to skeptical American fans that all the hype surrounding Linares was not necessarily excessive. The Japanese Central League, the world's top pro circuit outside the majors, reportedly once made an offer of $10 million cash for the services of Linares, along with Olympic slugger Orestes Kindelán and ace CL pitcher Pedro Luis Lazo. If not for the controversial Helms-Burton legislation with its on-going economic embargo of Castro's communist government, more than one big league club would probably long ago have offered considerably more.

Top names dominating Cuban baseball over the final decade of the 20th century, besides Linares, were a pair of equally talented Mesas — speedy Villa Clara outfielder Victor and glue-fingered Industriales shortstop Germán — along with Orestes Kindelán (Cuba's all-time home run champion), Pedro Luis Lazo (pitching ace for 1997 and 1998 champion Pinar del Río), Eduardo Paret (flashy shortstop for Atlanta's Olympic squad), and once-promising Matanzas flychaser José Estrada (1997 CL batting champion). Victor Mesa emerged in the late '80s as one of the island's unmatched sluggers and base stealers, pilfering 577 bases in his dozen-year career. He was also colorful enough and free-spirited enough to earn the moniker of "El Loco" among Cuban press and fans; Mesa played with an all-out reckless style quite uncharacteristic of Cuban baseball, which normally frowns upon the *postalita* or hotdog. Germán Mesa (unrelated to Victor) was once such a sterling gloveman that future big leaguer Rey Ordóñez chose defection from the national junior team largely because of slim hopes for supplanting Mesa on Team Cuba, or even in the

Azucareros pitcher Jorge Santín is hoisted on teammates' shoulders after winning the first game ever played in the Cuban National Series, January 14, 1962.

hometown Industriales lineup. Villa Clara's Eduardo Paret later flashed enough mid-field brilliance in Atlanta to actually supplant Germán Mesa, but only after the stellar veteran was temporarily booted from the national squad for reportedly conversing with big league scouts. And Estrada appeared to be the best young slugger on the island a few years back, then slumped badly once he seemingly lost motivation after capturing an Atlanta Olympic gold medal.

Defectors (a term always disparaged within Cuba itself) like Osvaldo Fernández, René Arocha, Ariel Prieto, and Liván and Orlando (El Duque) Hernández (all of them top-line pitchers) were significant members of the national team in the mid–'90s, yet never ultimately established themselves in the top echelons of CL stardom. Infield tyro Rey Ordóñez fled his homeland in July 1993 while still only an up-and-coming CL prospect (a rookie backup to entrenched Germán Mesa), while Fernández, Liván and "El Duque" were all established but second-tier CL stars when they finally abandoned Cuba. Tampa Bay 1998 rookie hurler Rolando Arrojo (already in his mid-thirties) also enjoyed a measure of success back home as a Team Cuba mainstay alongside strapping righty Giorge Díaz and bulky southpaw Omar Ajete (both of whom would later suffer career-shortening injuries) on the 1992 Barcelona Olympic gold medal squad.

But none of the 1990s-era defectors were ever as brilliant on native soil as the half-dozen or more top hurlers who remained behind. Burly Pedro Luis Lazo's many highlights in international competitions include a sterling no-hitter featuring 17 Ks against Team USA in the semifinal round of 1995's World University Games. Norge Vera has slowly but steadily — despite some career-slowing injuries — zeroed in on El Duque's record CL career winning percentage; Vera also mesmerized Taipei and Panama in unprecedented back-to-back 2003 World Cup victories (semifinals and finals). Lazo's Pinar del Río teammate José Ariel Contreras (who finally did flee in October 2002) was even more spectacular in Olympic venues, winning crucial semifinals games in the 1999 Winnipeg Olympic qualifier, 2000 Sydney Olympics, and 2001 Taipei World Cup; Contreras eventually owned a perfect 13–0 record in international tournaments and earned his stripes by pitching the bulk of Cuba's key games over the final seasons of his CL tenure.

Recently retired Lázaro Valle (star of 1990 World Cup action in Canada) hurled an eight-inning perfect game versus Korea during 1989 Intercontinental Cup matches, striking out 13 of 24 batters faced. José Ibar emerged as a major CL force in 1998 by authoring the first 20-victory season in Cuban history and then dazzled Team USA in an Olympics preliminary round match at Sydney. The aforementioned Norge Vera (now almost 35 and clearly, with Lazo, the top Cuban pitching star to resist defection) has not only been the most durable CL pitcher of the past five or six seasons, but proved big league potential with seven memorable innings of brilliant relief work versus the Orioles in Baltimore. More recently, 20-year-old fastball phenom Maels Rodríguez (righthander with Sancti Spíritus, and finally a defector after career-ending arm problems in October 2003) obliterated CL strikeout records, displayed a 100-plus game-measured fastball, and authored two CL no-hitters (one a perfect game and the other hurled during the 2002 inaugural Super League championship series).

While numerous Cuban Leaguers — from Vinent in the eighties, to Linares in the nineties, and Contreras in the new century — have been of unquestioned major league quality, the CL itself has always taken on a look that has been anything but major league. Aluminum bats were the standard offensive weapons between 1976 and 1999. CL uniforms and caps are primitive at best and some years have looked more like what might be expected in an industrial softball league. CL stadiums are often impressive while (except for Havana) a good deal smaller than big league counterparts, and several (especially Camagüey's Estadio Cándido González with its crumbling light stanchions) now stand in sad disrepair. The showcase Cuban ballyards are those found in Holguín and Santiago de Cuba, as well as the older and more mammoth Estadio Latinoamericano. Even in Havana there are no five-story-high electronic entertainment centers substituting for fence-topping scoreboards. Fans — especially youngsters — often flood fields after league games to romp the basepaths and interact with their diamond heroes. Glowing electric-light foul poles add a bizarre touch to night game action. And the non-commercial settings for Cuban ballgames — sans concession stands, roving beer vendors, or ubiquitous outfield billboards — is anything but reminiscent of our own big-league-style entertainments.

In Cuba the baseball game as a community entertainment spectacle still stands entirely on its own — without the aid of promotional trappings — and the diamond sport is thus exclusively one for unabashed purists. After four decades under Fidel Castro's guidance, Cuban baseball fans fortunately are all still such died-in-the-wool purists, down to the last man, woman and child.

*   *   *

One thing was crystal clear at the outset of the amateur baseball experiment launched by the Castro government in January 1962. Cuba's own national pastime was already too deeply ingrained within the national psyche ever to be eliminated altogether by any social revolution, especially to be supplanted by some less–American or less-capitalistic sports spectacle like European soccer. Not only would the decision therefore have to be made to focus anew upon baseball as the national sport, but the idea quickly arose in government circles to take full advantage of another long cherished Cuban dream and at the same time institute what pre–1961 professional baseball always sorely lacked — a true coast-to-coast na-

tional competition in the guise of an island-wide championship tournament.

Events surrounding the transition from professional to amateur status in Cuba's top baseball league unfolded rapidly in the spring and summer of 1961, slightly more than two years after Fidel's rise to power. As Robert González Echevarría (*The Pride of Havana*, 354–55) sees it, the revolutionary government was improvising under pressure and this might indeed be a fair analysis. González Echevarría notes that it was one thing for the revolutionary government to wipe away memories of Cuba's political history (of which most citizens may not have been well versed at any rate) but yet quite another to supplant the island's cherished cultural traditions (and thus also its deep-seated collective memories) surrounding the institutions of amateur and professional baseball.

The first step was the creation in February 1961 of INDER (*Instituto Nacional de Deportes, Educación Física y Recreación*) to assume the role of Batista's old DGND (*Dirección General Nacional de Deportes*) and oversee all of Cuba's sports activities. (The detailed history of INDER's birth is best told by Paula Pettavino and Geralyn Pye in their book *Sport in Cuba*, published in 1994.) A mere month later INDER (translated as "National Institute of Sports, Physical Education and Recreation") had legislated with its National Degree Number 936 what amounted to a total ban on all professional sports competitions, including most prominently the once-popular winter league affiliated with U.S. organized baseball, and also announced plans for an annual amateur national championship to begin within the coming year.

At almost the same moment an ironic event would occur which played directly into the unfolding schemes of this revolutionary transition. Another IBAF Amateur World Series was fortuitously scheduled for San José, in Costa Rica, that very April (a mere month after the fateful INDER decree). It would be the first such *Serie Mundial* since 1953 and thus the first for Cuba in nearly a decade. A hastily assembled Cuban team unaccountably proved to be hugely talented and ran through all opposition with ease during the very week when a landmark Bay of Pigs invasion staged by U.S.–supported counter-revolutionaries was being successfully repulsed by Fidel's militia back on the homefront.

It was inevitable perhaps, under such ideal circumstances, that an idea would now be floated to link baseball competitions to the island's past amateur traditions (as opposed to professional glories of bygone eras) and also simultaneously to the heroic military defense of the homeland. This was an old connection, of course, a linking of baseball and patriotism as venerable as the former Cuban Republic itself. Baseball had been born with just such an association during the late 19th-century struggle for independence from the hated Spanish overlords. In the 1880s and 1890s the motive had been to identify with baseball playing as both modern-looking and uncompromisingly American — thus as the antithesis of all that was old-fashioned and distastefully Spanish. Now in 1961 the immerging idea would be to beat the American imperialists (quite literally it was hoped) at their own revered national game. And that game was of course by now equally well established as the Cuban national game, with every bit the same lasting grip on Havana natives as it had on natives of New York or Pittsburgh or Boston.

By January 1962 plans had fully materialized for the new national amateur tournament. The opening game was celebrated in Gran Stadium on January 14, 1962, with the chief commander himself striding boldly to home plate in military fatigues to take the official "first cuts" of a new season. What followed was a brief one-sided pennant race captured by the western province all-stars (the Occidentales) managed by former big leaguer Fermín Guerra. Fidel repeated his staged performance a year latter for the opening of National Series II in Gran Stadium, this time taking his stance in the batter's box against ace hurler Modesto Verdura of the Azucareros team, who apparently lobbed some very friendly tosses toward the chief *commandante*. A 1963 *Official Cuban Baseball Guide* features photos of Fidel taking warmup swings, squaring off against Vedura, and finally enjoying a celebratory laugh with

the star pitcher moments later along the sidelines. The *Guide* reports that Fidel fouled away the first delivery and then connected with a roller into center field for the first successful hit launching a new season. If there were plenty of staged theatrics here, they were certainly matched by the more genuine theatrics which followed during a most exciting 30-game season, decided only on the final day in favor of local Havana favorites, a team for the first time called Industriales.

Four teams competed in the inaugural National Series of 1962 that featured a 27-game January–March schedule. Some sense of partial continuity with the Cuban baseball of old was retained with the four managers of the competing clubs. Fermín Guerra headed the champion Occidentales team, although the veteran pro catcher would soon fall from favor and be forced to flee the country. Star amateur pitcher of yesteryear, Pedro "Natilla" Jiménez, took up the reins of the Orientales club and held them for the first three seasons. Tony Castaño, who had elected to remain in Cuba when the Sugar Kings were transferred to New Jersey, was tabbed as skipper

Manager Fermín Guerra (center) and Occidentales players celebrate the first-ever championship of the 1962 inaugural National Series season.

for the Azucareros. And the final manager (with Habana) was José Maria Fernández, one-time star catcher and long-time professional fixture in Mexico as well as at home on the Cuban winter circuit. Fernández was also a more immediate link with the moribund Havana pro circuit, since he had only recently served as the final field boss for the 1961 Marianao Tigers. With the second National Series season, still another veteran of pro baseball returned to the scene when Gilberto Torres assumed the manager's slot for Occidentales. The teams and league games were all situated in Havana — as had been the case for most seasons with the now defunct pro league — but this time the players were native Cubans only (no more U.S. imports or mercenaries from other Caribbean countries) and they came from all of the island's six provinces (Pinar del Río, La Habana, Matanzas, Las Villas, Camagüey and Oriente). Occidentales ("Westerners") captured the initial pennant in National Series I, an opening season which Fidel himself would call "the triumph of free baseball over slave baseball."

There was also continuity between amateur baseball of pre-revolution and post-revolution eras to be found with a handful of the players who suited up for the inaugural National Series campaign. Squat but muscular outfielder/infielder Pedro Chávez was probably the most luminous carryover. Chávez had loomed large during the emotional national team victory in Costa Rica in April, batting .459 and posting the top tournament numbers for both base hits and runs batted home. The future Team Cuba and Industriales manager would log eight seasons (the remainder of the sixties) in the CL as a popular and dependable .287 hitter, mostly with Industriales. Twice Chávez won league batting titles, first with Occidentales (NS III) and later with Industriales (NS VI). Pedro Chávez had already made his mark in the late-fifties on the Cuban amateur circuit: with Círculo de Artesanos in the popular National Amateur League he was a regular in 1956 and 1957, and he also played simultaneously in the lesser Pedro Betancourt League (where he won a triple crown in 1957 with Araújo) and the Quivicán League (in 1961 with Aeropuerto).

Third sacker Jorge Trigoura, second baseman Urbano González and outfielder-shortstop Antonio Gonzalez were other heroic performers in Costa Rica who proceeded to earn additional fame in the CL throughout the sixties. Trigoura was a league homerun and RBI champion for Industriales in NS III and labored through the 1967 season. Urbano González, champion batter for Cuba in the 1963 Brazil Pan American Games, was a pesky lefthanded spray hitter who stood atop several batting categories in the inaugural NS (leading in hits and runs scored) and picked up a CL batting title three seasons later. And Antonio González was runaway batting champion of NS II while wearing the colors of Occidentales. Yet another familiar name in the NS of the first few years was merely a deception, however. The Julio Bécquer playing outfield for Azucareros was no relation to his notorious namesake, who had starred at first base with Marianao in the pre-revolution winter league and was by the sixties performing in the majors with the Minnesota Twins.

On the pitching side, Habana's top moundsman in the inaugural National Series had also been the National Amateur League's most notable hurler with the champion Teléfonos squad during NAL swan song years in 1959 and 1960. Tall and powerful righty Alfredo Street had thrown a no-hitter for Club Teléfonos at Gran Stadium in 1960, was yet another anchor of the IBAF world championship team performing in Costa Rica the previous April, and had turned down several pro offers after earning champion pitcher honors during the 1960 NAL season. Despite a poor performance at the 1959 Pan American Games in Chicago, Street was nonetheless still a much-admired pitcher throughout Cuba when he became a mainstay with first Habana (1962) and then both Occidentales and Industriales (where he was ERA champion in 1966) in the new post-revolution amateur league.

The first National Series was a small affair involving only a handful of teams and as such hardly looked like the true national championship tournament that had been envisioned. There were only four teams and the single venue for league games was the Gran Stadium; the capital city thus remained the sole league host, just as it had been throughout the previous decade with the professional Cuban League. In fact, with but four teams competing and with Gran Stadium as the single stage, it might have appeared at first that only the names of the ballclubs had changed, not at all an unfamiliar practice in Cuban baseball if one looked back at earlier decades. One of the teams the first year was even still called Habana; and when Industriales replaced Habana in NS II a new parallel in name and team colors (royal blue) with ancient Almendares was not lost on most Cuban fans. Of course most of the familiar players who had built lasting legends in the winter professional circuit were now toiling for healthy salaries in the majors or minors of U.S. organized baseball, or in Mexico, and were thus notably absent from the revamped scene.

If the new league did not at first have teams placed in every province, the players were nonetheless drawn from cities and villages all across the island. The names of the four teams were thus significant in this regard. The 27-game season saw Occidentales (Westerners) win by a five-game spread over both the Azucareros (Sugar Growers) and Orientales (Easterners). Habana, which would be rechristened Industriales a mere year later, brought up the rear. And there were some new stars to root for. Erwin Walters (also spelled Walter in the Cuba guidebooks), a jet-black outfielder of lanky stature, was the first batting champion, playing for Fermín Guerra's first-place outfit, and Urbano González proved an equally exciting hitter in the same lineup. By the second season Modesto Verdura, another black stalwart, emerged as one of the best Cuban pitchers of the entire decade.

But if it was new and even appropriately revolutionary in concept, the first season or two of amateur baseball under Fidel's replacement government did still feature a number of old faces and a healthy contingent of quite familiar baseball figures. These were not the standby ballplayers (Miñoso, Bécquer, Ramos, or Pascual) who had starred in a previous decade. But there were still some valued household names involved. To start with there was Fermín Guerra who served briefly as manager for Occidentales (nominally representing the western sector of the island). There were also, as mentioned, Alfredo Street and Pedro Cháves, who honed their reputations in amateur ballplaying even before the revolution. Tony Castaño (Azucareros) was managing in the new league after winning the final two professional league pennants with Cienfuegos and directing summer-season fortunes for the AAA Sugar Kings. Gilberto Torres, who replaced Guerra as skipper of Occidentales for NS II, had long been a fixture in Cuban baseball of an earlier era. *El Jabarito* carried the Cuban banner during four forties-era seasons with the Washington Senators as a big-league utility man and also logged 18 Cuban pro seasons, mostly with Habana but also in the uniforms of Almendares and Marianao.

A dozen-year period that stretching from 1963 through 1975 constituted the years of maximum growth for the young Cuban League. The four-team structure lasted only four seasons and Industriales with three pennants was inarguably the strongest club in this early stretch. A fifth and sixth national series were played with six teams, exactly equaling the number of provinces, and the total number of games had been upped significantly to 65 by the mid-sixties. The biggest organizational overhaul came in 1967–68 when the league roster was bumped up to 12 teams, doubling league size from one season to the next. Two more teams would be added by 1972–73 and that number (14) would remain consistent through 1977, the year of National Series XVI. One new ballclub added with large-scale 1968 league expansion was once more christened Club Habana, giving the capital city two hometown squads for the first time. But by the end of the first dozen years most teams still didn't carry provincial names as such (or strict provincial affiliations either) and expansion toward baseball in every province was still only partially complete. A few teams now sported colorful identifying tags (such as Constructores, Serranos, Granjeros, and the still present Azucareros), a practice that was to be dropped in later years.

One truly noteworthy moment came early in league history — during National Series V — when a diminutive junkballing righthander named Aquino Abreu matched the unique big-league feat of Johnny Vander Meer by tossing a pair of consecutive no-hit, no-run games. Abreu toiled for the last-place Centrales in 1965–66 and his masterpieces were authored against Occidentals, to the tune of a lopsided 11–0 score, and Industriales, by a 7–0 count. Three years later it was the hitters who gabbed most of the headlines when Raúl Reyes (Azucareros) knocked in 11 runs during a single game (including three homers, one a grand slam), Agustín Marquetti slammed a record 19 roundtrippers for the expanded 99-game winter season, and Wilfredo Sánchez stroked a long-standing record 140 base hits.

Three significant changes had also modified the face of Cuban baseball during this first dozen-year stretch. One was a full face-lifting and expansion for venerable Gran Stadium, which would henceforth be known as Estadio Latinoamericano (Latin American Stadium). The drastic renovation took place in mid-1971 when seating capacity was expanded from

Diminutive right-hander Aquino Abreu duplicated Johnny Vander Meer's unique big league feat with back-to-back no-hitters during the 1965 National Series season.

30,000 to 55,000 in time for hosting the 19th edition of the ever-expanding Amateur World Series. Repairs and additions to the ballpark (in the form of a massive concrete outfield grandstand and towering electronic center field scoreboard) were to be the last of any significance until the visit of the big league Baltimore Orioles nearly thirty years later. Estadio Latinoamericano, after 1971, looked almost precisely as it still looks today. A second modification was an introduction of aluminum bats that appeared in time for the 1976–1977 season; with Cuba's increasing isolation from U.S. markets this change was one dictated largely by economics. The third change of note was the league size itself. By the end of the sixties the CL was already much larger in membership than the Cuban professional circuit had ever become at any time in its 75-year history.

Another novel look came to Cuban baseball in 1975 when the winter season was split in two and the National Series was supplemented with a new second-season format called the Selective Series, which would now be tacked on after the regular-season campaign had ended. In subsequent years the National Series would remain the heart of Cuban baseball, and this is the portion of the year's play that most Cubans have in mind when they talk about Cuban League seasons. But the Selective Series now would be part of a more ambitious program to select players for the national team. The National Series was soon contracted from 78 games to only 39 games. At the end of this reduced National Series, rosters of the fourteen teams were further whittled down to seven squads that would play an additional 54 games under the format of the Selective Series.

The Selective Series emphasized once more that the goal of each season's play was not merely to entertain fans at home but also to train and select new talent for national teams capable of winning top honors at international competitions. Each league season — now actually two seasons — was an ongoing six-month tryout camp of grandest proportions. Top players from youth and municipals teams would be selected annually for about 400 roster spots in the National Series. But first they would have to play in a "development league" (the *Serie de Desarrollo*) in which each National Series team had a "farm club" of reserves (another 416 total players). National Series players, after 1975, were then winnowed further for prestigious Selective Series rosters. Finally a national team roster — often both an A team (25 players) and B team (25 players) — would be selected at year's end, with international tournaments customarily scheduled during late summer or early fall, which is the off-season for domestic Cuban League baseball.

But where did the 400-odd athletes come from in the first place? How were they scouted and recruited for the top-level teams? The answer was a system of training academies and baseball schools best described by University of Texas researcher Milton Jamail (*Full Count: Inside Cuban Baseball*, 2000). Jamail's details will not be painstakingly repeated here; a bare-bones outline of the system will be sufficient. Talented youngsters are hand-picked early for training in the various sports at elementary-level boarding schools known as the EIDE (*Escuelas de Iniciación Deportiva*) or Sports Initiation

Manuel Alarcón was an ace pitcher in the decade of the sixties and registered 200 strikeouts during the 1968 National Series #7.

Schools. The age-range for such institutions is 13–16 and the curriculum provides a half-day session of academic subjects and another half-day of sports training. From these lower level academies top prospects in each sport move on to secondary-level institutions called the ESPA (*Escuelas Superior de Perfeccionamiento Atlético*) or Advanced Schools for Athletic Perfection. The student-athletes again train in their chosen sport (in this case baseball) with intensive daily morning drills. In afternoon classroom sessions they receive traditional academic instruction. The hoped-for result with this structured Soviet-style training routine is efficient selection of the very best players for provincial teams in the Development League. Those who do not make the strenuous final cut look forward to respectable careers as physical education teachers or perhaps as coaches and academy athletic trainers.

The Selective Series would remain an important focus of CL seasons for more than two decades. The number of games would be expanded to 60 in 1979, then scaled back again for some later campaigns. There were 43 games for each team in 1984 and 45 in the season following. Down through the years Pinar del Río would capture the most Selective series championships with six. The final season of play transpired in 1995, with a team called Orientales capturing the ultimate title. Along the way there would also be several other tournaments folded into the year's play, though most suffered short life spans. For two years following 1995 suspension of Selective Series play a 30-game "Cup of the Revolution" tournament was staged. One year (1970) witnessed a marathon 89-game season labeled the "Series of the Ten Million" and won by Las Villas province. This unique name resulted from the projected (but not realized) size of sugar cane harvests that year and from Fidel's personal decision to provide an extra "season" to reward patriotic sugar workers for hoped-for productivity. The ten million tons of sugar that Fidel had aimed for never materialized, but there were nonetheless numerous public events throughout 1970 displaying the "Ten Million" label — even some popular salsa songs and a proliferation of witticisms that played on the ubiquitous term. In the end less than five million tons were reached in the cane fields, but the baseball tournament at least turned out to be a grand one, with Las Villas barely edging Habana for the pennant, Wilfredo Sánchez enjoying one of his most productive campaigns as a legendary slugger, and José Huelga briefly peaking as one of the best Cuban pitchers of all time.

The sum total of all these compacted and protracted seasons, often several with in a given calendar year, made the amorphous structure of post-revolutionary CL baseball at times confusing and always somewhat difficult to follow. Seeming instability among teams, leagues, seasons and schedules was nothing new to Cuban baseball, as earlier accounts of pre-revolution professional (Chapter 5) and amateur (Chapter 7) Cuban circuits have already revealed. But to any outsider the landscape of island baseball is often confusing territory indeed, more akin perhaps to haphazard Negro league structures than to the relatively stable landscape defining even 19th-century major league play.

Another significant landmark in CL structure would arise from the 1983–84 season, the first in which National Series pennant races would be divided into two-division affairs. For a period stretching from the late eighties until the present, however, league structure has remained quite stable. With the end of the two-year Revolution Cup tournament there was once more only a National Series to constitute the Cuban League season. The league has for a decade and more consisted of four divisions (called Groups) and these contain four teams each. Each province boasts a team that plays most of its games in the capital city of that region, and a few home contests in smaller outlying ballparks (normally one per week or one per homestand). One team is located on Isla de La Juventud, a so-called "special municipality" that is not technically a province but essentially functions like one. The capital city of Havana, by contrast, has two teams — Industriales and Metropolitanos. The postseason involves both quarter-final rounds (best of five format) and semifinal rounds (best of seven), along with a seven-game championship showdown between surviving teams from the eastern provinces (Groups C and D) and western provinces (Groups A and B).

Many of the greatest sluggers of CL baseball emerged from a period encompassing the mid-seventies to mid-eighties and thus overlapping the first decade of Selective Series action. Agustín Marquetti, Antonio Muñoz ("The Escambray Giant") and Wilfredo "El Hombre Hit" Sánchez provided the most legendary trio of southpaw swingers. But there were other only slightly less memorable bashers who also hammered their reputations across this identical period. Pedro José Rodríguez ("Cheíto") — mighty Cienfuegos third baseman — was one of the most noteworthy among them, boasting four straight home run crowns and pair of RBI titles thrown in for good measure. Cheíto was especially devastating in the batter's box when it came to high-pressure international tournaments, and with his peak performance in 1979 Rodríguez converted the Havana-based Intercontinental Cup tourney into his own personal showcase by cracking seven homers in but ten games and remarkably registering more total bases than official times at-bat.

Pitchers held their own during this first decade of aluminum bats filled with so many talented sluggers. Among the immortal hurlers of the 1970s none was more talented than Oriente-born righthander Braudilio Vinent ("The Meteor from La Maya"). Laboring with Mineros, Oriente and Santiago de Cuba, Vinent established numerous records that have withstood the true test of time. His international ledger (a remarkable 56–4 won-lost mark posted with 36 different Cuban national teams), like Cheíto's, was especially impressive. But on domestic diamonds alone Vinent remained a National Series and Selective Series mainstay across a full twenty seasons.

Three contemporaries of Vinent also proved rather remarkable CL hurlers. José Antonio Huelga is remembered in Cuba and abroad for his 1970 showdown in Cartegena, Colombia, with future LA Dodger ace Burt Hooton (see Chapter 11) and thus is the only one of the stellar trio with any currency (however small) in U.S. baseball circles. But Huelga for seven seasons also rang up outstanding CL numbers — sometimes even spectacular numbers — before an untimely death that cut off what might otherwise have been an unequalled career. Huelga is today memorialized by the name gracing the CL stadium of his home province, Sancti Spíritus. Santiago "Changa" Mederos was a devastating southpaw who piled up strikeout totals (including the single-season top mark of 208) that stood untouched until Maels Rodríguez rewrote all the record books nearly three decades later. Sadly and shockingly, Mederos suffered a similar tragic fate (again killed in a fiery auto wreck) only five short years after Huelga. A third figure among the memorable trio was Rogelio García, who might be remembered by serious international baseball followers as a lead player in one of Cuba's most disastrous international defeats. García started the gold medal game of the 1981 Intercontinental Cup in Edmonton that saw the Cuban nine fall victim to both the Americans and their own disastrous complacency. (García pitched ineffectively but was not the pitcher of record in the devastating extra-inning upset loss.) But in the Cuban League for 16 arduous seasons García (202–100 with 201 complete games) rang up totals that still place him among the top five in a half-dozen or more lifetime pitching categories.

As might only be expected, the modern-era Cuban League has remained relatively free from ballplayer scandals involving drug or alcohol abuse or any distasteful game-fixing. Not completely free of taint, nonetheless, despite the rarity of such abhorrent immorality in wider post-revolution Cuban society. There was one dark and poorly reported series of incidents in the late 1970s and early 1980s that did involve implications of some apparent run-shaving and game-tampering. A prominent figure in this inglorious moment turned out to be none other than the first post-revolution Cuban ballplayer to show up in the major leagues, flashy 1970s Industriales outfielder and occasional national team designated hitter Bárbaro Garbey. Suspended and ultimately jailed in 1979 and then allowed to flee to Florida with Mariel ex-patriots a year latter, Garbey was signed by the Detroit Tigers despite his shady Cuban past. Current Industriales manager Rey Anglada (back in the good graces of INDER officials in 2002 after a decades of CL exile) also had his promising career cut short in 1982 by implications of betting improprieties.

A new crop of equally outstanding ballplayers emerged in the mid and late eighties. Most noteworthy by far was Omar Linares. Before Linares fully matured, Matanzas outfielder Lázaro Junco also wrote a

Current Cuban League Divisional Structure

Group A (West)	Group B (West)	Group C (East)	Group D (East)
Pinar del Río	La Habana (Province)	Villa Clara	Santiago de Cuba
Isla de la Juventud	Industriales (Havana)	Ciego de Avila	Holguín
Metros (Havana)	Sancti Spíritus	Camagüey	Granma
Matanzas	Cienfuegos	Las Tunas	Guantánamo

lesser legend with his string of individual home run titles only recently matched by Santiago's Orestes Kindelán. Victor Mesa, in turn, became one of the most colorful and popular players of Cuba's modern era by combining exceptional talents as a dangerous slugger, reckless baserunner and daring outfielder. Mesa earned his nickname "El Loco" with a flashy style somewhat out of step with the usually more conservative Cuban approaches to slick on-field performance. Mesa's most infamous and embarrassing moment came with a show-boating home run trot against Team USA in Brussels (1983 Intercontinental Cup) that resulted in his immediate and unprecedented ejection from the field of play. (A half-inning later "El Loco" was seated proudly in the Cuban radio play-by-play booth excusing his actions to millions of fans back home.) And by the early 1990s another Mesa (Germán) was drawing rave comparisons as a shortstop wizard parallel in artistry to both Willie Miranda of island fame and Ozzie Smith on the big league scene. Pitchers were not scarce either as "El Duque" Hernández would carve out a new standard for consistent winning in the late eighties and early nineties — before his sudden flight to major league fame — and Jorge Luis Valdés would approach Vinent's

Fidel Linares was a multi-talented outfielder with several clubs during the first nine National Series, but his greatest gift to Cuban baseball was his son, the legendary Omar Linares.

once-seemingly-safe records for appearances, starts, wins and losses. Industriales stalwart Lázaro Valle (with a career winning percentage only a shade below El Duque's, plus brilliant international performances) also hewed a resume perhaps only rivaled by Vinent or Huelga or Rogelio García.

The biggest changes in more than two decades refreshed Cuban baseball in the final few seasons of the nineties. This was a revamping desperately needed to counter growing dissatisfaction among long-suffering fans, who had began to stay away from ballparks in increasing numbers, and who had especially abandoned Estadio Latinoamericano in the capital. The CL season was lengthened to ninety games with the simultaneously return to a single November-to-May series each winter and spring. Highly unpopular INDER practices like player suspensions (usually for suspected disloyalty) and forced retirements or overseas assignments for favored aging veterans were suddenly eliminated. (A few officially disgraced stars like Germán Mesa and Eduardo Paret were even reinstated.) And most dramatic of all, wooden bats were finally reintroduced into league play after a quarter-century of using only aluminum war clubs. The latter development was a direct result of the celebrated May 1999 visit of Baltimore's Orioles for a rare, unanticipated, and long-overdue moment of baseball détente with the professional major leagues.

González Echevarría advances an argument (*The Pride of Havana*, Chapter 9) that the present-day Cuban League is actually a professional league by all reasonable standards and thus not technically an example of amateur baseball as so vociferous claimed by the Cubans themselves. The argument hinges on an assumption that any sport in which athletes receive monetary compensation (however limited), or partake full-time in their sport without other primary employment, thus qualifies as professional in the strictest sense. González Echevarría's claim is essentially that Cuban ballplayers form a highly-compensated elite who enjoy a privileged status on their own island. (Here it is popular to cite the cases of a handful of stars like Omar Linares, or heavyweight boxer Félix Savón, who have received luxury automobiles or modest private houses from Commandante Castro to reward outstanding international performances.) The argument only holds, of course, from the narrowest of possible perspectives. Cuban ballplayers are compensated at a level that is only laughable by the standards of even small-scale college sports here in North America. The standard Cuban ballplayer salary approximates $135 monthly and furthermore is paid in Cuban pesos and not U.S. dollars (or new dollar-equivalent CUCs). Cuban Leaguers not infrequently pedal rickety bicycles (or more likely walk) to their home ballpark; often they picnic on the outfield grass with friends, neighbors and family after daylight games have ended; while on road trips they sleep in dingy hotels sometimes built directly under the ballpark grandstands; and they travel only by bus and only for the past several seasons (since 2000) by comfortable air-conditioned, TV-equipped buses.

But more important still, the Cuban ballplayer is at a sharp disadvantage within the current Cuban economy precisely because he is paid only in Cuban pesos and not with the dollars available to anyone employed in the island's tourist industry. Here Milton Jamail (*Full Count*) comes much closer to the mark in describing the life and status of the Cuban Leaguers than does the skeptical author of *The Pride of Havana*. American pro ballplayers share elite privilege alongside rock stars and corporate CEOs. Cuban ballplayers, even at the highest levels, suffer inferior economic status when compared with any Cuban earning dollars on the black market or in the legitimate tourist trade, by working as a shopkeeper or bartender or table server. Professionalism for Cuban athletes extends only to their remarkable skill level and noticeable on-field pride in performance, never to their level of material compensation. This seems obvious, despite any trumpeted reports of government support and privileged treatment for Linares and company.

There is a more relevant intended sense in which Cuban baseball is strictly amateur. The notion of a league in which players work other jobs and play in the evenings as a hobby (González Echevarría's apparent notion of "amateur") would never be possible for a top-level league involving traveling teams and almost daily games. Indeed, CL players must be full-time athletes and must receive some level of compensation. The players are not farmers or university students who play merely for health and recreation. Cuba's is a government-run league with a mission of entertaining ticket-buying fans. The sense in which the Cuban League is *not* professional involves the ownership of teams and the league administrative structure. Ballclubs are not franchises operated by capitalistic owners bent primarily if not exclusively on turning a year-end profit. The league itself, not capitalist moguls, owns all player contracts. Players are not sold and traded and they do not shift teams except in the rarest of cases. Nor is the game a spectacle staged primarily to sell souvenir merchandise, alcohol and fast food on the sidelines.

This may have its distinct disadvantages: there are still regrettable exploitations — especially of players (who earn little) and sometimes of fans (who are taken just as much for granted as in the major leagues). But for lovers of baseball as pure spectacle there are huge plusses that seem to overshade all drawbacks. Players stay put and team loyalties are sacrosanct. Games are affordable (for a long while they were even free). Players relate intimately to fans and vice versa. The drawback from the capitalistic perspective is that players are not free to become millionaires and earn their unlimited wealth by holding fans and club owners hostage at the end of each contract extension. And billionaire franchise moguls are not granted the privilege of exploiting sports entertainment for ruthless profiteering. Cuban baseball is decidedly un–American. From the fan's standpoint this is a small sacrifice for quality baseball.

Despite the numerous structural changes, today's Cuban League relentlessly displays its original mission and its original guiding spirit. Seasons have the same dual purpose: top-level baseball entertainment all across the island leading to an annual national champion, set alongside an efficient year-long

selection process designed to produce an invincible national team for world amateur competitions abroad. Little has altered since 1962 and the ever-present "retro" appearance of Cuban baseball extends quite far beyond archaic uniforms and rustic stadiums. The Cuban League indeed remains alive and well.

* * *

The final several Cuban League seasons of the 20th century witnessed some landmark highs and lows for island baseball. These were produced both in the public glare of high-profile international tournaments as well as in the relative obscurity of National Series action on the homefront. Of late it has been both the "best of times" and "worst of times" for Cuba's national pastime. A runaway Olympic Games gold medal victory at Atlanta in August 1996 displayed Castroland's baseball juggernaut at its invincible best. Yet a mere twelve months later the vaunted Cuban nine seemingly collapsed during a championship round of Intercontinental Cup competitions in Barcelona. And the 1996–97 CL National Series season that separated those two international outings was itself laced with disappointments and ominous signals for Cuba's beleaguered baseball establishment.

While Cuba's international stature may have peaked with Olympic triumphs in first Barcelona (1992) and then Atlanta (1996) — where the Red Machine swept 18 total games without a single defeat — league play on the island itself was indeed falling on some hard times by the mid and late 1990s. Defections by a dozen or more established or potential stars (including Rey Ordóñez, René Arocha, Osvaldo Fernández and Liván Hernández) from various junior or senior-level national teams, plus continued perceived threats of further such escapes by valuable young talent at the core of the showcase national team, cast a considerable pall over the island and its baseball operations. In addition to the half-dozen front-line "defectors" in the nineties who quickly made it to the majors, there were a score or more additional "baseball traitors" who eventually reached U.S. shores only to see their big league dreams wither quickly in the low-level minors, plus others who never snared a pro contract or even a legitimate tryout. Among the later group were pitcher Iván Alvarez, infielder Osmani Estrada, and outfielder Alexis Cabreja — promising members of Havana's Industriales club — who abandoned flag and teammates during a low-profile September 1992 tournament in Mérida, Mexico.

One immediate result of such talent drain was the adoption of several policies and administrative actions that were perhaps not altogether well advised. Most visible were the swift suspensions of several top CL and national team stars allegedly guilty of "contact" with foreign talent scouts. National team shortstop Germán Mesa and his Atlanta replacement Eduardo Paret were the most visible among notable Cuban ballplayers put on the shelf by such political intrigues. Orlando "El Duque" Hernández (suspended from CL play as both punishment and precaution when half-brother Liván jumped ship) was soon the cause of additional adverse publicity in the U.S., especially after Liván stirred an underground buzz among

Havana fans with a stellar 1997 World Series MVP performance. American and Canadian press coverage of Cuban baseball defections was especially intense when El Duque himself fled the island during Christmas week of 1997 — reportedly on a flimsy raft, which later turned out to be a comfortable luxury yacht conveniently provided by a future U.S.–based agent.

In addition to the publicized suspensions there were also "retirements" and "transfers" of other regulars (popular ace pitcher Lázaro Valle was one) who found themselves moved to lesser semi-pro or industrial circuits in Italy, Colombia, Nicaragua and also Japan. Players shuttled to Japan were not bartered to the Japanese pro leagues for huge salaries and eye-popping sale prices, but rather loaned (as player-coaches) to the Japanese industrial leagues for perhaps a fraction of their true marketplace worth. Valle, for example, was ignominiously retired from Havana's Industriales team in the middle of the 1997 CL postseason playoffs. And popular outfielder Victor Mesa of Villa Clara — a colorful folk hero and the league's all-time basestealing champion — was another headliner who disappeared seemingly overnight from the local baseball scene.

There seemed to be a dual motive for transactions that shipped fading stars off to Japan and Italy and cleared rosters spots for up-and-coming but less fan-familiar prospects. It

Occidentales outfielder Erwin Walter was the first National Series batting champion in 1962.

was a way of rewarding veterans who had contributed mightily to international triumphs with a few years of hard-cash salaries outside of Cuba and also a means of garnering needed revenues for the national coffers (since like all Cuban workers abroad, ballplayers saw much of their salary paid directly into the government treasury). But the transactions also had a still more subtle role in INDER's ongoing battle against potential player defections. Clearing out some of the tenured veterans opened up roster spots for hot prospects like pitcher Maels Rodríguez, infielder Michel Enríquez and outfielder Yasser Gómez, who might otherwise have quickly grown frustrated (as had Rey Ordóñez) while waiting months or even years for a shot at national team recognition.

By shipping veteran players to Japanese industrial league clubs rather than peddling them for top dollar to the Japanese pros, or perhaps even to the majors, INDER officials seemed to be saving face with the decades-old hard-line notion that communist baseball would not traffic with professional leagues whatever the penalties might be for failing to do so. One result was an obvious failure to exploit the country's best "natural resource" (talented ballplayers) and thus prop up a faltering national economy. (Cuba workers placed overseas send 75% of their earned salary home in government taxes, and high-income-bracket athletes would be no exception.) Another inevitable consequence was a noticeable slide in morale among many young ballplayers who had preciously few future prospects (like advancing salary) to look forward to as their careers droned on.

Elite Santiago third sacker Gabriel Pierre posted huge offensive numbers across a half-dozen seasons for one of the island's best teams yet was nonetheless shut out of international play as long as Omar Linares was still around. Eduardo Paret only earned a shot in Atlanta when Mesa unexpectedly fell into disfavor. And Matanzas outfielder and Olympic team veteran José Estrada seemed another prime example. After starring in Atlanta and then walking off with the 1997 CL batting title (.391), Estrada seemingly sleepwalked through the first half of the 1998 National Series before barely climbing back above .300 by season's end.

And finally there was the growing frustration among Cuban fans who secretly (and sometimes not so secretly) wished to see their stars shine on a grander (perhaps even big league) stage. Rumors frequently swept through Havana in the mid-nineties about huge offers for Linares from the Japanese League. Cuban luminaries in other sports like women's volleyball and men's soccer were permitted to move to pro leagues elsewhere and were pointed to with pride back home simply for being able to do so. But baseball remained ideologically pure and thus baseball — so intimately tied to the fading ideals of Fidel's ongoing socialist revolution — remained always somehow intrinsically different. At the same time Cuban baseball seemed now to be wilting in the process.

It might be interjected here that baseball in Cuba — or Japan, Korea and Taiwan for that matter — is not merely a potential U.S. big league supermarket — whatever lusting agents and always-vigilant MLB birddogs might be conditioned to surmise. If Cuban fans take natural pride in big league victories by José Contreras, Liván or El Duque, this is not to be interpreted as suggesting that Havana partisans simply long for the day when all their top stars are swept away to big league ballparks.

Unfortunately a "gold rush" mentality is all too often MLB's own myopic view of all international programs — including those found in Canada, Australia, Venezuela, the Orient, Mexico, the Dominican Republic, and anywhere else on the planet where a cheap prospect or two might be found. The sport maintains its own distinctive (often quite idiosyncratic) life in each of its far-flung international outposts. It always serves its own native functions of patriotism, tradition and cultural ritual and these usually have little if anything to do with an American version of the game. Columnist Joe Clark eloquently stated the case regarding Australia in the pages of *International Baseball Rundown* (September 1998) by responding to Atlanta Braves superscout Bill Clark's views of how the Aussie pro league might be successfully revamped to better serve talent-searching efforts by North American organized baseball. Columnist Clark scolded scout Clark that Aussie baseball was anything but "a common consumer item being examined by discriminating big league shoppers" bent on bleeding another country's talent dry. Australians (like Koreans, Japanese and Taiwanese) take pride in their native game no matter what the successes or failures of its occasional big-league recruits. The case is even more clearcut with Cuba, where baseball is not only a century-old national treasure but has for several decades also evolved (again as it has in both Korea and Taiwan) into a most potent instrument for scoring crucial image-building international triumphs.

One alarm bell for Cuban baseball was the lack of fan interest observed during the post–Olympics 1996–97 National Series. Fresh from their gold medal triumph, Cuban national team stars seemingly failed to inspire the usual hoopla back home. Attendance was bleak especially in Havana for CL games featuring the locals, Industriales and Metros. The two Havana-based teams had suddenly fallen on hard times and seemed to suffer even more than other squads from the new rash of player transfers: Industriales (without side-lined Germán Mesa) outpaced three rivals in Group B yet barely posted a winning record; the Metropolitanos came home second in Group A and won ten more games than the wildly popular Blues. Subsequent 1997 postseason playoffs — including a brief semifinal series between Pinar del Río (with Linares and the league's best pitchers, Contreras and Pedro Lazo) and Industriales — drew meager crowds. Neither game of the Pinar-Industriales showdown played in Estadio Latinoamericano hosted 10,000 spectators. Olympic stars Linares, Contreras and Lazo (plus Olympic manager Jorge Fuentes) paced Pinar to resounding back-to-back playoff sweeps over Industriales (semifinals) and eastern sector champion Santiago (featuring additional Olympians Orestes Kindelán, Rey Isaac, Ormari Romero and Antonio Pacheco). But fans were not impressed and stayed away from local stadiums in droves.

One plausible explanation for these sudden attendance

Urbano González was base hits leader in the National Series I (1962) and National Series V (1966), and also batting champion of the National Series IV (1965). González also starred on the first post-revolution Amateur World Series champion team, crowned in Costa Rica in 1961 during the USA-backed Bay of Pigs invasion.

lapses at Cuban ballparks — especially at cavernous Estadio Latinoamericano — was the island's dire economic crisis, especially in the capital city. Cubans were perhaps understandably too preoccupied with daily hand-to-mouth survival by 1997 to expend much energy or a few hard-earned pesos on public entertainments — even baseball. There was now also an admission charge (one peso or about five U.S. cents) for games that had been free for decades. And it was challenging to find public transportation to and from Havana's Cerro neighborhood ballpark. (Cubans don't own vehicles in most cases, beyond rickety bicycles; and for the handful with cars, gasoline is a scarce and expensive black market commodity.) Busses didn't run regularly (again because of the gasoline shortages). Taxis (even ramshackle peso taxis) were too much of a luxury on a Cuban salary, and at any rate taxis didn't linger in the ballpark environs anyway, clustering instead in the Havana Vieja (Old Havana) tourist distinct.

But there was general disillusionment among fans with

the game itself. Enthusiastic baseball rooters — members of the renowned informal *esquina caliente* or "hot corner" baseball debating society — still gathered in Havana's Parque Central for heated daily discussions of diamond events both past and present. But these local experts now regularly lamented the state of the current league and most stayed away from the local ballpark. Most interest suddenly seemed to be focused on the achievements of 1997 World Series phenom Liván Hernández and other countrymen (Ariel Prieto with the Athletics, Osvaldo Fernández of the Giants, and Rey Ordóñez with the Mets) who had found their way into big league parks. While radio and television reports in Cuba focus exclusively on CL games and officially ignore the distant majors, fans nonetheless find ways to keep abreast of MLB stars and pennant race action. One source is a small but steady stream of current baseball publications trucked to Havana by the small army of American travelers, especially ex-patriot relatives visiting from Miami.

There were also loud complaints echoing from Central Park about the makeup of recent editions of the Cuban national team — even the one that was undefeated and unchallenged in Atlanta. There was grumbling from local "fanaticos" on Havana street corners about certain players who seemed to have made Team Cuba's roster merely because they were "politically safe" (not a risk to jump the team outside the country) or were in full favor with INDER officials for their progovernment ideologies. Younger, more exciting stars (1996 Revolution Cup batting champ Yobal Dueñas, for example) were seemingly being bypassed for entrenched but fading veterans like 34-year-old light-sticking Camagüey outfielder Luis Ulacia or 33-year-old steady if unspectacular Industriales utility infielder Lázaro Vargas. The rumor was that some younger phenoms were considered risks to defect, though this may well have been largely groundless speculation.

Trouble fomenting on the Cuban baseball scene first bubbled to the surface when INDER officials suddenly cancelled a scheduled July tour of U.S. cities. On the docket had been eight scheduled games versus Team USA as tune-ups for the 1997 Intercontinental Cup showdowns in Spain later in the month. The tour was merely a renewal of similar past exhibition junkets in North America and seemingly a valuable preparation for the upcoming Barcelona games. INDER cited potential security risks for its players and this charge may have held at least some validity. Gone were the days when Team Cuba would visit the USA national team in small backwoods outposts like Millington, Tennessee, and when few stateside fans or press took note of such high-powered encounters. Games were now scheduled for more accessible venues like Indianapolis, Trenton, and Wichita. Demonstrations, harassments and agitations by Miami-based anti–Castro forces might well be expected to shadow the series and potentially unsettle the visitors. Whatever the true reasons (American media speculated Cubans merely feared more player defections), INDER pulled the plug with little advanced notice and in the process disappointed both American fans (hopeful of witnessing an exciting return engagement on U.S. soil featuring Olympic stal-

warts like Linares, Lazo, Estrada and Kindelán) and the Cuban faithful (anticipating still another shellacking of the rival Yankees).

Less than a month later Cuba suffered humiliation with a gold medal Intercontinental Cup loss to virtually the same Japanese team they had beaten (but not easily) in Atlanta. The defeat (11–2, with Japan scoring six times in the first two innings) was perhaps only a single game of a single tournament. But for the defending champs who had won nine of ten Intercontinental Cups and eight in a row, losing was barely tolerable. The shocking defeat brought a sudden end to longstanding dominance on the world baseball stage, during which Cuban squads were rarely challenged for the better part of a decade.

Inevitable fallout was swift and severe back home in Havana. Administration of the Cuban national team, as well as the entire CL, was abruptly overhauled. National team manager Jorge Fuentes and Cuban Baseball Federation head (league commissioner) Domingo Zabala were suddenly out of work. (Fuentes also lost his post with league champion Pinar del Río, but he would eventually resurface as Pinar bench boss and later as visiting national team coach in Nicaragua.) Miguel Valdés was also canned as *Equipo Cuba* technical director (general manager). A new format was soon announced for the 1998 CL season which would constitute National Series XXXVII. Gone overnight was the short-season Selective Series that had followed each traditional National Series in years past. If panic did not yet reign among island baseball officialdom, confusion and desperation certainly did now seem to have the upper hand.

Cuba's subsequent 1998 league season didn't display very many obvious indicators of anticipated revival during the opening months of November and December. During our own December visit fellow author Mark Rucker and I attended several games in Havana with crowds that numbered in the mere hundreds of fans and not the usual tens of thousands. Rooting spirit seemed somewhat healthier in the outlying cities of Camagüey, Holguín and Santiago when we also visited there. (The explanation may well still have been a sagging economy; it is easier to walk to the ballpark in the smaller outlying cities, and community pride is also more entrenched there.) But new CL commissioner Carlos ("Carlitos") Rodríguez was only guardedly optimistic during our personal interviews with him (December 1997) as he laid out plans for further modifications (an all-star game, new selection methods for the national team, and other similar fine tunings) and also spoke of the desperate need to bring "spectacle" back into Cuba's national pastime.

There would be one immediate step in the direction of improved *spectacle*. A CL all-star game was hastily added to the agenda for March 1998, resurrecting an institution that had remained dormant for ten seasons. Staged in centrally located Ciego de Avila Province, the showcase exhibition match — complete with home run hitting, base-running and distance throwing contests — proved a resounding success. A full weekend of events were billed as a national celebration of Cuban

A typical Cuban League ballpark is Holguín's stately single-decked 30,000-seat Calixto García Stadium.

baseball and included beach outings and block parties with all-star players as honored guests. National Series XXXVII regular-season action unveiled plenty of "spectacle" of its own, with sterling new performers like Metropolitanos teenaged rookie center fielder Yasser Gómez (who ran and threw like a small Clemente and hit .358 with over 300 at-bats) and third-year Santiago hurler Norge Luis Vera (14–4, 1.82 ERA) stirring renewed fan passions at both ends of the island. The league also caught fire around veteran Havana hurler José Ibar who took advantage of a new longer-season format to rewrite Cuban record books with 20 victories (against two defeats). And it didn't hurt fan enthusiasms that Ibar toiled for the Havana Province team located conveniently on the fringes of the capital city.

The two Havana-based teams also again showed welcomed improvement, both posting winning records, second-place division finishes, and coveted playoff appearances. By late-season the large and enthusiastic crowds of earlier eras were back, even in Havana's echo-filled Estadio Latinoamericano. More uplifting still for Cuba's baseball directors (with their eyes always on future world tournaments) was the fact that former national team pitchers Giorge Díaz (13–4 for Guantánamo) and Omar Luis (13–5 with Camagüey) had apparently bounced back from lengthy battles with career-slowing injuries.

Another factor elevating spirits among Havana fans and elsewhere around the league was a surprising late-spring bulletin in *Granma* that revised policies were being instituted re-

garding "retirements" and "suspensions" of disgraced league players. Germán Mesa and Eduardo Paret apparently would be allowed to play again during the summer of 1998 (both would work out their kinks in summertime development league games). And the policy of marketing veteran players to foreign leagues was also being temporarily suspended. There was almost nothing but good news on the CL front by the time Pinar del Río (which had not skipped a beat under new manager Alfonso Urquiola) wrapped up a second straight postseason championship in late April by closing out cross-island rival Santiago in five games. Pedro Lazo was again the pitching ace of the National Series finals, just as Havana's José Ibar (first 20-game winner in CL history) had been the top luminary during regular season action.

One final fallout of the 1998 season was an early-summer announcement of a revamped national team containing both familiar and fresh faces. Among the returnees from Atlanta and Barcelona were catcher Juan Manrique (Matanzas), outfielder Javier Méndez (Industriales), and pitchers Ibar, Vera and Contreras — along with the standby regulars Kindelán, Linares and Pacheco — enough experience and continuity to provide the carryover stability so necessary to winning ballclubs. New faces included first sacker Loidel Chapelli (Camagüey), and outfielders Oscar Machado (Villa Clara) and Robelquis Videaux (Guantánamo). This latter trio augured a continuing bright future for Cuba in the international arena. Selection of the likes of Machado and Videaux also silenced recent grumblings about roster spots occupied by safe but

Perhaps Cuba's most pastoral baseball setting is offered by Santiago's 25,000-seat Guillermon Moncada Stadium.

no-longer-productive veterans. The new national team manager was a former long-time all-star second baseman, Alfonso Urquiola, taking over for the deposed Jorge Fuentes following a terrific debut season at the helm with league champion Pinar del Río.

This partially revamped team moved undeafeated (6–0) and barely challenged (they were extended to 10 innings by Australia in the title game) through a stiff July tuneup provided by the always-challenging Harleem Baseball Week staged annually on the outskirts of Amsterdam. A full redemption was soon gained at the IBAF world championships (known since 1988 as the Baseball World Cup) held in Italy during late July and early August. Again Cuba ran the schedule undefeated, spanking Holland (12–1) in the quarterfinals and Nicaragua (14–2) in the equally one-sided semifinals. It was mostly old faces that carried the team, with José Contreras going the distance with a five-hitter in the title match, and Kindelán (.560 BA), Linares (also over .500), and Pacheco (14 RBI) providing much of the offensive onslaught. But there were some new heroes as well in the guises of heavy-hitting newcomers Machado (.417), Videaux (.484) and Danel Castro (.429). (Nine Cuban regulars batted above .400 for the tournament's duration.) In the anticlimactic finals South Korea was brushed aside with a lopsided 7–1 score and the uninterrupted Cuban winning streak in World Cup action was now

upped to 43 straight games, stretching back to the 1988 event also played in the same Italian venues.

The Big Red Menace had now taken home the cherished gold medal at every IBAF world championship event it had entered since 1952, a mind-numbing total of 22 trophies won in 25 tournaments played. (After renewals in Taipei 2001, Havana 2003 and Holland 2005, the string would be run to 25 of 28 and an overall individual-game mark of 280 victories and but 28 defeats.) Cuba's 1998 national team unquestionably established that Fidel Castro's socialist baseball (Fidel still called it "la pelota libre") had indeed fully rebounded from its recent temporary setbacks. If the domestic Cuban League had not yet completely recovered from its recent temporary malaise, at least it had now arrived at a new and promising crossroads. Once a new millennium dawned, things would quickly get even better.

* * *

Liván Hernández never had an especially big impact on CL baseball when he suited up as a raw prospect for three National Series and two Selective Series seasons of the early nineties (1992–1995). Exiled as an 18-year-old from his home in Havana Province to the Isla de Juventud squad (the one that draws recruits from locations all over the island), the strapping 6–2, 206-pounder (at the time) won 27 games (lost 16), with a hefty 4.57 ERA and a strikeout ratio of one for every 2⅔ innings. After his September 1995 Mexican flight to greener pastures, it was nonetheless surprisingly Liván Hernández who single-handedly revived U.S. fan interest in the shadowy world of Cuban baseball, doing so with eye-catching 1997 Fall Classic performances for the equally surprising Florida Marlins.

In the NLCS versus Atlanta Liván began his string of postseason miracles by posting two victories and a sterling 0.84 ERA over 10.2 innings; his second outing featured a record 15 strikeouts in a masterful three-hit shutout that earned NLCS MVP honors. Two World Series wins (sufficient for a second postseason MVP trophy) included eight-plus innings during a pivotal fifth game in Cleveland. A much-publicized, scene-stealing off-field sideshowed featured Fidel Castro himself granting eleventh-hour permission for Liván's Havana-based mother to obtain a fast-track visa, thus allowing her to join her son for the final series game in Miami. The scene was an eerie reprise of the memorable 1975 Series starring another refugee Cuban hurler, Luis Tiant, who also benefited from a high-profile family reunion (with his father, the former Negro leagues great) at the largess of master media manipulator Fidel Castro. But this time around the melodramatic exiled Cuban pitcher saga featured all the trappings of post–Cold War international political intrigue thrown in for good measure.

Cuba has always been perhaps more renowned for its colorful mound magicians than for its hefty fence bashers (like Puerto Rico) or its glue-fingered infield magicians (like the Dominican Republic). Near the dawn of 20th-century big-league history fiery Dolf Luque stood in the vanguard of Latino big-league invaders, logging the first-ever World Series appearance by a Latin American (during the infamous Black Sox Series of 1919) as well as posting nearly 200 notches in the career victory column. Black stars José Méndez and Eustaquio "Bombín" Pedroso also mystified touring big-leaguers with their unhittable arsenal at the end of the same century's first decade. Martín Dihigo today remains perhaps the most durable Negro league legend — north or south — and may have been the best all-around ballplayer of any color, despite his still-shadowy image in Cooperstown. Tragically never allowed to set foot on any big league diamond, Dihigo once led the Mexican League in both pitching (wins and ERA) and hitting (batting average) in the same season, and tossed that top-flight league's first-ever no-hitter for good measure.

A Cuban invasion of big-league parks (especially Washington's Griffith Stadium) in the fifties and sixties was again led primarily by pitchers — Pascual and Ramos in the 1950s and Tiant and Cuéllar a decade later. And among the Cuban defectors who have grabbed so many muted headlines in the past handful of years, almost all have likewise been pitchers: Arocha, Prieto, Osvaldo Fernández, Liván and "El Duque" Hernández, 30-something 1998 rookie sensation Rolando Arrojo, and latest and loudest, José Contreras. Only recently retired New York Mets and Tampa Devil Rays acrobatic (but hitless) shortstop Rey Ordóñez among the spotlight '90s-era "defectors" was a non-pitcher.

And only a trio of defectors after 2000 seemed to offer any realistic prospect of breaking the seeming taboo on Cuban position players. The most heralded has been Yuniesky Betancourt (.281 hitter for Villa Clara over four seasons), surprise rookie shortstop with the 2005 Seattle Mariners who at times showcases the defensive flash of Ordóñez. Kendry Morales, who slugged 22 homers and batted .315 during AA and A minor league apprenticeships with the LA Angels, excites promise as a DH, even if his defensive prowess falls short of big-league standards. And 24-year-old Brayan Peña (who never played in Cuba before leaving as a pubescent teenager) may yet turn out to be a starting catcher for the Atlanta Braves.

Yet there are huge negatives attached to Cuban pitching which often work to cancel out exaggerated reputations attached to island hurlers. Pascual and Ramos were the best of their countrymen in the majors at the century's dividing point, but neither were especially dominant in the big-time (with the single exception of two consecutive 20-win Minnesota seasons for Pascual). Dolf Luque (as we have seen in Chapter 2) earned more of a reputation for his explosive personality than his flaming fastball; Luque's kayo of Casey Stengel in the Giants dugout is more often recounted than his successful 1919 and 1933 World Series appearances, and "The Pride of Havana" never became "The Pride of Cincinnati" despite the best single-season in Reds franchise history. Achievements by blackball stars like Dihigo or Méndez were never accomplished on a level playing field where they could be adequately judged against big-league standards. While Tiant and Cuéllar were far more than short-lived sensations — the former peaking in five of his 19 seasons and the latter breaking the 20-victory circle for three years running — they were hardly comparable in their own era to Koufax or Drysdale or even Marichal.

In more modern times Cuban national teams appear to have won international tournaments more with their slugging (recently Omar Linares and Orestes Kindelán, earlier Antonio Muñoz and Cheíto Rodríguez) than with truly dominant pitching, despite some memorable performances across the years in individual games by Lázaro Valle, José Contreras, Pedro Lazo, Braudilio Vinent, José Antonio Huelga and many others. At any rate, the use of aluminum bats in Cuba long put pitchers at a distinct disadvantage and both encouraged and rewarded junk-ballers rather than fast-ballers. And despite sensational October encores by the Brothers Hernández during the late nineties and Contreras in 2005, the overall performance of recent defectors has been far closer to strictly average than to eye-popping or record-setting. All-in-all, numerous questions (both historical and contemporary) can legitimately be raised about the overall effectiveness of island pitchers.

Liván Hernández was only the vanguard member of a small but noteworthy onslaught of pitchers recently escaping from Castro's Cuba to bolster big league starting rotations and bullpen corps. Liván's half-brother El Duque made only a slightly less remarkable debut with the New York Yankees a single season later, improving on Liván's 9–3 rookie ledger with a 12–4 mark of his own. Together the Hernández siblings

Honor Roll of Pre-Revolution Cuban Pitching Aces

Cuban Pre–1980 Big League Aces

Pitcher	MLB Statistics	Claim to Fame
Adolfo Luque	(1914–35) 194–179, 3.24 ERA	First Latino in World Series and first Latino 100-game winner
Conrado Marrero	(1950–54) 39–40, 3.67 ERA	Colorful junkballer of early 1950s; AL rookie at age 39 (1949)
Camilo Pascual	(1954–71) 174–170, 3.63 ERA	Top big-league curveball of the 1950s; AL 20-game winner
Pedro Ramos	(1955–70) 117–160, 4.08 ERA	Owns highest HR/innings ratio in major league history
Sandy Consuegra	(1950–57) 51–32, 3.37 ERA	AL's top winning percentage (16–3, .842) in 1954
Mike Fornieles	(1952–63) 63–64, 3.96 ERA	Pitched one-hitter for Washington in major league debut
Miguel Cuéllar	(1959–77) 185–130, 3.14 ERA	First Latin American Cy Young Award winner
Luis Tiant, Jr.	(1964–82) 229–172, 3.30 ERA	Most colorful Latin big-league hurler of 1960s and 1970s

Cuban Blackball Aces

Pitcher	Notable Statistics	Claim to Fame
José Méndez	74–25 Cuban lifetime W–L record	One-hitter against barnstorming Cincinnati Reds in 1908
Bombín Pedroso	10–2 record in 1915 Cuban League	No-hitter against touring Detroit Tigers in 1909
Martín Dihigo	497–221 overall career W–L record	Led Mexican League in both pitching and hitting in 1938
Ramón Bragaña	30–8 record in 1944 Mexican League	Star pitcher of Mexican League throughout 1940s
Luis Tiant, Sr.	10–0 record in 1947 Negro leagues	Pitched in two Negro league East-West Games (1935, 1947)

pulled off the improbable feat of starring for World Series winners, as over-achieving rookies, in back-to-back seasons. For his own part "El Duque" (with a boost from playing for the number one team, the Yankees, in the number one media capital, New York) overnight became the sport's most celebrated *nouveau riche* capitalist posterboy. Meanwhile El Duque's rookie campaign with the champion New Yorkers was matched in the record books if not in the headlines by the near rookie-of-the-year performance of Tampa Bay's Rolando Arrojo (14–12, 3.56 ERA). Arrojo had defected on the eve of the Atlanta Olympics and — barely a year older than the Yankees' Hernández — was himself first cracking the big-league scene at the ripe age of nearly thirty-three.

There were other polished CL-veterans-turned-MLB-rookies who in the mid-nineties soon raised expectations about a new recruiting gold mine. Osvaldo Fernández (who had fled from the national team in Tennessee in 1995 and entered the majors less than six months later) and Ariel Prieto (defected in 1994 and also became a major leaguer within a year) struggled for limited success with the west coast Giants and A's respectively; Fernández almost immediately suffered a serious spring training arm injury (reinjuring a wing previously damaged in Cuba) which put him on the shelf for the entire 1998 season while similar arm miseries limited Prieto to a single 1998 decision. By 2000 Prieto was finished as a big leaguer, while Arrojo (after two seasons and a mildly impressive 21–24 ledger in Tampa Bay) first stumbled with Colorado as a part-time starter, then moved over to Boston where he struggled to revive his unraveling career as a mop-up reliever. Hard-throwing young southpaw Vladimir Núñez (who had defected in 1995 at age 20) arrived on the scene with the Arizona Diamondbacks amid glowing scouting reports, but within months was barely managing to hang on with the Florida Marlins after earning only 11 victories in his first 32 decisions. Pinar del Río refugee Danys Báez followed a fast track to the majors after leaving the 1999 Pan Am Games national team in

Winnipeg and by early 2002 had seemingly established himself as Cleveland's likely future bullpen closer. Báez, who claimed but 6 career wins with Pinar, subsequently shifted allegiances to Tampa Bay, where he garnered 71 saves across 2004–2005 before a third move to the LA Dodgers. Twenty-three-year-old lefty Michael Tejera flashed considerable promise during his brief debut with the Florida Marlins (1999), before just as quickly dropping back into obscurity in the minors. By late 2004 Tejera belonged to the Texas Rangers, where he spent most of the 2005 season as a spot reliever for AAA Oklahoma City.

Only Contreras — after abandoning Cuba in October 2002 to debut with the Yankees in March 2003 — established himself as a quality big leaguer. Yet even Contreras struggled considerably in New York, despite a 7–2 rookie campaign (perhaps because his talents were first squandered in a part-time bullpen mop-up role), before gaining new life as staff ace with the 2005 world champion Chicago White Sox.

The onslaught of rags-to-riches Cuban defectors in the big league pitching ranks raises numerous intriguing questions. Foremost, why have so many among the small core of defectors been moundsmen? Are pitchers really that far advanced over bat-wielding sluggers in the modern-day Cuban League? (All pre–2000 defectors who pitched in the CL faced aluminum for most or all of their careers; ash bats only made their way back to Cuba for the 1999 playoffs.) Olympic results in Atlanta as early as 1996, and again in Athens as late as 2004, certainly didn't seem to suggest any notable dominance by Cuba's touted starters and relievers. At Fulton County Stadium (1996) the Cuban heroes where in fact all home run bashers like Omar Linares and Orestes Kindelán, or sure-handed fielders like shortstop Eduardo Paret and flychasers Miguel Caldés and Luis Ulacia. Top red-clad moundsmen like Pedro Luis Lazo and Omar Luis barely survived against American, Nicaraguan, Japanese and even Italian sluggers, and the Cubans gave up 7-plus runs a game (with an astronomical 6.71 staff ERA) in Atlanta, yielding nine runs in the gold medal shootout alone, yet remained undefeated by scoring at an average pace of 14 runs per game themselves. The final Olympic tournament with aluminum bats was decidedly not a pitchers' showcase.

Cuban hurling improved in Sydney (2000 Olympics) but it certainly didn't overwhelm, allowing five runs to both the Koreans and Italians in opening round matches. In Athens (2004 Olympics) the Cuban pitchers were strong (especially Lazo and Dany Betancourt out of the bullpen, and Vera and Adiel Palma as starters) when they needed to be in the clutch, but a new crop of young hitters led by Michel Enríquez and Yulieski Gourriel were the team's dominant weapon. Beyond Contreras, Cuba didn't win with mound mastery between 1999 and 2003, though some of its aces were indeed impressive in short stints. This was certainly true of Ibar in his first Sydney outing against the Americans, when he shut down AAA-level American hitters with 10 Ks and a single earned run over seven strong frames. Lazo stood at the top of the heap, but mainly in his role as a hard-throwing closer. Back home in the CL he was a most effective (even dominant) starter.

Another question likely to be raised in the minds of big league fans having preciously little familiarity with Cuban baseball might have to do with the status of pitchers like Liván, El Duque, Arrojo, Prieto or René Arocha (the first defector, in 1991, who lasted four years with the Cardinals and won 18 games, more than half of them his rookie campaign) back home in Castroland. Have the majors — with an assist from Miami-based agent Joe Cubas — already stripped Cuba of the cream of its top pitching talent? Were Liván and company the best Cuban moundsmen, or is there a larger talent font of flamethrowers still waiting to be siphoned off once the iron curtain around Cuban baseball is finally cracked wide open? What were the records or rankings of these defectors when they played for CL clubs and also on the vaunted Cuban national team?

And what about rumored phenoms over the past decade like Lazo, Ibar, Omar Ajete, Omar Luis, Lázaro Valle, Ormari Romero, Yovani Aragón, Maels Rodríguez and Norge Vera? Are the best Cuban moundsmen still languishing back home? Is Lazo (as some of us who have seen him under postseason or Olympic pressures would contend) a cut above Duque or Liván, or certainly René Arocha and Osvaldo Fernández? The closest true physical comparison for the gigantic Pinar del Río righthander — who is equally at home as staff ace or as intimidating closer — seems in my view to be Cooperstown-bound Lee Smith, author of 478 big league saves.

When it comes to such evaluations of defectors compared with Cuban League loyalists the most difficult case for judgment is probably that of Liván Hernández. Liván left Cuba far too early to make much of a mark there, as did shortstops Rey Ordóñez in 1993 and Yunieski Betancourt exactly a decade later. Liván Hernández did manage 26 wins in three brief CL seasons and went 10–4 (3.59 ERA) with the Isla de la Juventud (Isle of Youth) team in 1994 as a mere 19-year-old second-year sensation. Former Diamondback and Florida Marlin Vladimir Núñez presents a similar case, defecting while still a

Powerful first sacker Antonio Muñoz (seen here in Estadio Latinoamericano action) was a headliner of National Series and Selective Series seasons from the early 1970s through the mid-eighties.

budding star with the national junior team (but nonetheless having a notable 14–7 CL 1994 season to his credit as a still-wet-behind-the-ears 18-year-old prospect).

There is little question that some of the best among the Cuban pitchers are those who have remained behind, putting patriotism, family, and fan adulation ahead of the lure of American dollars. It is not a judgment that can be nailed down with any certainty, since it is hard to evaluate a Pedro Lazo or Omar Luis or Omar Ajete or Lázaro Valle against aluminum bats back home, against the lesser (perhaps AA-level) sluggers filling most CL lineup slots, or against often subpar international talent on the Olympic scene. Perhaps a better handle can be had on a newer crop of Cuban arms like righties Yunieski Maya (Pinar del Río) and Dany Betancourt (Santiago), or southpaws Yulieski González (Habana Province) and Adiel Palma (Cienfuegos). This promising quartet has regularly faced wooden bats and a horde of new Cuban sluggers (national team stars Michel Enríquez and Yulieski Gourriel, plus .400-hitter Osmani Urrutia, for starters) as good as or better than Linares and company of the 1990s. And they have also faced heftier contingents of USA, Dominican and Panamanian pros at the Olympic and World Cup level. Palma slammed the door on an American roster of AAA stars during a recent 11–3 quarterfinal romp at the 2005 Rotterdam World Cup, and Betancourt was even more brilliant against South Korea in the 3–0 finale of the same event.

Pedro Lazo appears to be the most talented of the current lot of Cuban pitchers (barely edging out Norge Vera and the now-departed Contreras and Maels Rodríguez) and thus the CLer most likely to make any professional scout that sees him salivate. Lazo has time and again proven invincible in big games during the past several Cuban seasons, although he often sleepwalks through non-vital mid-season outings. De-

A pitching change during a National Series XXI (1982) game between Vegueros (that year's champion) and Isla de la Juventud. Future national team manager Jorge Fuentes is the Vegueros coach standing at the far left.

spite a mediocre 1998 league record of 9–7 Lazo would out-duel Ormari Romero of Santiago 2–1 in the deciding game of the championship series in late April. And he played a major role on the national team that year despite the less than spectacular regular-season performance. (The next two years he was 15–4 and 14–5 with ERAs of 2.34 and 1.85). The 6–3, 227 pound Pinar native dominated foreign hitters both out of the bullpen and as a starter during the July 1998 Haarlem Baseball Week in Amsterdam and again at the IBAF world championships in Italy during the latter half of the same month. In the Italian games he won both starts and didn't allow a single earned run in either outing. And seven years later he seems better than ever — especially in Rotterdam last September when he was flawless in the final innings of both the quarter-finals (USA, where he got the win in relief, allowing one earned run in 5.2 innings) and finals (South Korea, where he wiped out the last six batsmen as the untouchable closer).

There were others in the 1990s with obvious major league talent. Lázaro Valle by 1996 was at the tail end of a career that flashed brilliance from the mid-eighties onward. But in his peak years Valle (who was first "officially retired" during the 1997 playoffs and rumored bound for the Italian League, before reappearing with the national team at the Sydney Olympics) was a consistent force on Team Cuba and with In-

dustriales in the annual National Series. The chunky 6–1 righthander's top career outing, a perfect game gem (8 innings, 11–0 versus South Korea) in the IX Intercontinental Cup tourney in San Juan, ironically came on the very same day as Nolan Ryan's celebrated 5,000th career strikeout (August 22, 1989). José Ibar also blossomed in the final seasons of the nineties with his assortment of masterful breaking balls, though he had already enjoyed an accomplished career for more than a decade that earlier included 70 victories before his explosive reinvigoration following the Atlanta Olympics. The bulldog Habana Province ace owned an 11-year career mark that stood at a solid but not spectacular 109–84 before his 20-game outburst in 1998 and his 18 wins a season later. Ibar's record-shattering 20 victories in National Series #37 was to some extent an aberration due to a new lengthened 90-game season, but it was an impressive and unparalleled performance nonetheless.

By 2001 Norge Vera and Maels Rodríguez were the top stories in domestic Cuban pitching. Rodríguez after 2000 became the new darling of the National Series and enjoyed a heady if all-too-brief peak that lasted for but three seasons. In 2000 the strapping freckle-faced righty hurled the first perfect game in league history and also became the first to throw at 100 mph in an official league game. He also finished the subsequent season with a year-long strikeout performance that predicted a truly brilliant future. Maels singlehandedly owned the 2001 National Series: he obliterated a long-standing strikeout mark of Changa Mederos that was one of the league's most cherished milestones. He also paced the circuit in walks (76), but he did so with more than three times as many strikeouts (263). Such a feat is almost unthinkable in the major leagues. The following winter Maels again crossed the 200 strikeout plateau, ringing up a 219 total that again nearly tripled his league-leading 85 walks. He also led his team to a surprise berth in the postseason, their first in 25 years. But at year's end Maels seemed to falter from his load of 165 innings pitched and additional appearances in several late-season exhibitions sandwiched around the stressful playoffs. By late July, however, he would rebound by tossing a second no-hitter during the Super League short series that was reintroduced that summer as Cuba's new second season.

Vera (whose first name is a distortion of the once-popular USA–made refrigerator brand, yet is pronounced NOR-gay) has been nearly as good, except when slowed by injuries (such as the tired arm which limited him to four appearances and but one win in National Series #42, on the eve of his remarkable Havana World Cup performances). It was Vera who so impressed Baltimore fans with a stellar victory-clinching relief outing against the big leaguers. The Santiago ace also has a January 2001 no-hitter to his credit and a few seasons back he was "pitcher of the year" with an outstanding ERA (0.97 in 157 innings) in what was truly Cuba's "year of the pitcher." (A remarkable 22 pitchers finished the 2000 campaign with ERAs below 2.00 during the first full season in decades played exclusively with wooden bats.) Vera has also been a most reliable stopper in international play, ringing up records of 2–0 (0.47 ERA) at the Taipei World Cup and 1–1 (1.23 ERA) at

the Sydney Olympics. He peaked with back-to-back victories in the semis (7 innings against Chinese Taipei as a starter) and finals (7 innings of relief vs. Panama) during Havana-based World Cup 2003, the second (gold medal game) outing ironically coming on the very night Maels Rodríguez fled the island as a defector. Vera outstripped Maels when it came to international efforts and eventually held second slot in the rotation for the Cuban Olympic team behind first José Contreras (Sydney) and later Adiel Palma (Athens). An unfortunate hamstring injury at the 2000 All-Star Game (where he opposed none other than Maels) slowed the second half of Vera's peak CL season yet didn't prevent Santiago from breezing to a second straight National Series crown and the top campaign in ball club history.

When it comes to the bulk of the defectors, most did indeed make a considerable mark in Cuba before departing. El Duque's career was only reaching its midpoint at the time of his surprise suspension on the eve of the 1996 Atlanta Olympics. But he had already performed brilliantly enough in the CL to own the all-time career winning percentage. Osvaldo Fernández and Rolando Arrojo also enjoyed individual seasons on the top of the Cuban League pitching heap. Fernández was twice CL ERA champ in the early 1990s (1992 and 1994) while hurling for his hometown Holguín club. Arrojo (Luis Rolando Arrojo in Cuba) duplicated the honor with an ERA title of his own, toiling for Villa Clara in 1995. Both hurlers in their best seasons posted ERAs below 2.00 in close to (or over) 100 innings of work, and this feat was accomplished against whip-like aluminum bats.

One question surrounding Cuban pitching involves the overuse of star moundsmen on the island, a practice leading directly to career-shortening arm injuries. This is not a problem unique to Cuba, of course — it has always been a down-

Honor Roll of Post-Revolution Cuban Pitching Aces

Amateur Cuban League Aces

Pitcher	Notable Statistics	Claim to Fame
Maels Rodríguez	65–45 CL career record (1998–2003)	CL single-season strikeout record with 263 (2001 NS#40)
Norge Vera	Second-best CL career W–L Pct. (.711)	7 shutout innings versus Baltimore Orioles in Baltimore (1999)
José Contreras	13–0 W–L record in international play	8 shutout innings versus Baltimore Orioles in Havana (1999)
Braudilio Vinent	Pitched in 20 Cuban League seasons	Holder of numerous Cuban League career pitching records
Jorge Luis Valdés	234 Cuban League career victories	Cuban League career record for victories (234) and starts (414)
Lázaro Valle	1.93 ERA in 1989 National Series #28	Pitched perfect game vs. South Korea in 1989 International Cup
Pedro Luis Lazo	14–5 2000 Cuban League W–L record	Ace of repeat CL champions (Pinar del Río, 1997–1998)
José Ibar	20–2 1998 Cuban League W–L record	First modern Cuban League 20-game winner (1998)
Aquino Abreu	Surprising 57–61 lifetime losing record	Consecutive no-hitters in 1966 Cuban League season

Top Cuban Big-League Defectors

Pitcher	MLB Statistics	Claim to Fame
José Contreras	(2003–05) 35–18, 3.30 ERA	Ace of 2005 Chicago White Sox World Champions
René Arocha	(1993–97) 18–17, 4.11 ERA	First Castro-era big league defector (July 1991)
Ariel Prieto	(1995–01) 15–24, 4.85 ERA	First defector to sign $1 million big league contract (1995)
Osvaldo Fernández	(1996–01) 19–26, 4.93 ERA	1992 and 1994 Cuban League ERA leader
Liván Hernández	(1997–05) 110–104, 4.22 ERA	1997 World Series MVP (Florida Marlins)
Duque Hernández	(1998–05) 70–49, 4.04 ERA	1998 wins in ALCS and World Series (New York Yankees)
Rolando Arrojo	(1998–02) 40–42, 4.55 ERA	Top 1998 American League rookie pitcher with Tampa Bay
Danys Báez	(2001–05) 26–31, 3.92 ERA, 102 Saves	Cuban career leader in ML saves (41 for Tampa Bay in 2005)

side of Japanese League pitching philosophy — yet there have been a number of top CL hurlers whose careers have been prematurely sidetracked. Pablo Miguel Abreu, Giorge Díaz, Juan Carlos Pérez, Leonardo Tamayo, and Omar Ajete head the list, and all without suffering the pressures of a 162-game big league season. Omar Ajete was 1992 Olympic team ace in Barcelona, but only a shadow of his former self by the time the 1996 Atlanta Games rolled around only four seasons later. Giorge Díaz is another former Olympic team star who was wiped out by serious arm problems shortly after a four-hit masterpiece in the Barcelona gold medal game. And Osvaldo Fernández saw his promised brilliance in the majors slowed by similar problems involving a tired arm and dating back to his CL career (where he topped the circuit in complete games in 1991 and 1992 before abandoning the island in the mid-nineties). The practice does not seem about to abate in Cuba. Sancti Spíritus phenom Maels Rodríguez was used almost daily in the 2002 National Series semifinals with Pinar del Río — as both starter and reliever — and again in the finals versus Holguín (where he lost all three decisions on late inning mistakes, despite numerous moments of brilliance).

The Cuban League of recent years has hardly been a pitcher-friendly circuit. The ballparks are of average dimensions, but aluminum bats (as long as they were being used) certainly lent a large advantage to the offense. Even more damaging to Cuban pitchers' psyches were the Batos-manufactured Cuban baseballs. Scarce materials (especially cow hides) by the early-nineties meant an altered "pelota" with enlarged core constructed of softer synthetic material. Not only was the Cuban ball livelier, but the synthetic non-leather surface allowed for poor gripping and thus ineffective breaking balls. Since Cuban pitchers have often been handicapped by the ball itself many have naturally given up finesse pitching and have simply tried to throw the sphere past enemy hitters, either getting clubbed regularly or injuring their arms in the process.

A popular pitching model to combat the free swinging brought on by aluminum "lumber" and juiced horsehide has been the junk ball pitcher, a Cuban prototype today represented by Adiel Palma and earlier by Havana ace José Ibar. (Reported improvements in the ball's surface at the end of the nineties may have partially explained Ibar's sudden success.) Past-era mound greats like Braudilio Vinent (CL career leader in many categories including complete games, starts, and innings pitched) and Aquino Abreu (back-to-back no-hitters in

A Pinar del Río team meeting at the mound in Estadio Latinoamericano during the National Series XX (1981) match. Future national team manager Alfonso Urquiola is the Pinar infielder standing at the center (glove under arm, white wrist band).

1966) have also been cut squarely in this mold. A third such prototype is svelte southpaw Jorge Luis Valdés who in the late–1990s overhauled Vinent's record for career victories.

The strongarmed Cuban flamethrower cut in the mold of Liván, El Duque, Arrojo and Osvaldo Fernández, in the majors, or Pedro Lazo, José Contreras (before 2002) or Maels, back on the island, seems the exception rather than the generalized rule. If the Cuban League has its more obvious shortcomings the most glaring flaws seem to be on the defensive side of the game. The Cuban fielders are often quite brilliant (as anyone who saw shortstop Eduardo Paret at the Atlanta Olympics will attest), but they are hardly polished and routinely inconsistent. Flash seems today to be much valued over fundamentals in all CL fielding. This is also of course a standard complaint about the current major league scene. But it is complicated in Cuba by years of coaching isolation and lack of intimate contact with baseball played off the island. And it was already a problem keenly noted by *Sports Illustrated* writer Ron Fimrite on a visit to the CL scene three full decades ago.

Fimrite wrote back in 1977 that "the most baffling aspect of the Cuban game is a propensity for the bonehead play" and this is an element that still often shocks Americans visiting Cuban League venues. I myself witnessed a weird unassisted triple play in Estadio Latinoamericano (November 1998) performed by Villa Clara third sacker Rafael Acebey only because Industriales batter Juan Padilla and three baserunners all suffered a moment of simultaneous brain lock. Padilla stood in the batter's arguing a tipped roller (which he thought was foul, but which ended in Acebey's glove) while the savvy defender strolled around the infield tagging out everyone in sight.

Next in line among shortcomings is the lack of pitching depth. Again this is admittedly a rather universal problem in baseball stretching from Tokyo to Toronto, and to all points between. Cuba's pitching per se, however, is not what usually wins gold medals during international tournaments. Why then such an overwhelming preponderance of pitchers among the Cuban defectors? It may be mere circumstance, of course, or perhaps the fact that hurlers are simply more rebellious or adventurous souls. But it likely has far more to do with the longer period of adjustment for infielders and batters attempting to learn the U.S.-style professional game (and also before 2000 to acclimate to wooden bats). Non-pitchers have defected in numbers equally large. Roberto Colinas (a 30-year-old 10-year CL veteran first sacker when he escaped Cuba and was signed back in 1997) struggled with Tampa Bay and batted only .248 at Class A St. Petersburg (Florida) his first professional season. Rey Ordóñez was carried into the New York Mets starting lineup by his brilliant glove rather than his overall game. Andy Morales (a .328 batter for eight seasons with Habana Province) failed to make the grade in lengthy spring training trials with both the New York Yankees and the Boston Red Sox. On the eve of the 2006 MLB season, Yunieski Betancourt (surprise rookie shortstop in Seattle) and Kendry Morales (coming off a summer of top AA and AAA power numbers in the Angels system) now finally offer hope that the drought of defecting position players may finally be ending.

Of two young late-nineties defectors signed by the Arizona Diamondbacks (Larry Rodríguez was the second), 6–3 righty Vladimir Núñez enjoyed the quickest route to the pitching-starved majors. The three-time selectee on the Cuban national junior team reached Phoenix for a 1998 September cup of coffee that produced no decisions and only a few innings of mop-up work. Núñez managed to hang with the Florida Marlins for several seasons, though he never had a breakthrough year and won only slightly more than half as many (20) as he has lost (32). Núñez's 2002 Topps bubblegum card announces that his recent successes as a middle reliever in Miami have come once "he stopped diddling with arm angles and trick pitches and just trusted his exceptional hard stuff." Danys Báez wasted little time reaching the majors with Cleveland and has been surprisingly effective as first a regular-rotation starter (2001) and later an intimidating closer (after 2002, in Cleveland and Tampa Bay). Báez and Núñez together have demonstrated yet again what a half-dozen of their fellow defectors had already illustrated a few seasons earlier. A healthy, live arm is the quickest ticket to the big time anywhere in the game of baseball.

* * *

Baseball traditionalists shrink in horror from the concept of aluminum bats (especially the newer "high-tech" metal alloy lightweight bats) almost as readily as they carp about the designated hitter rule or are repulsed by stadiums adorned with plastic grass. Evidence has been presented and debated in various forums for the manner and degree to which metal bats have transformed the game into something other than it has always been — a delicate balance between the trickery of pitching (changing speeds and shifting locations) and the refined art of batting (hitting a round ball with a round stick). And the standard complaint has to do with safety — the obvious dangers posed by such offensive weapons which seem to put at great risk the health and livelihood of pitchers standing only 60 feet away from free-swinging assassins wielding aluminum wands.

One excellent study in the little-seen journal *International Baseball Rundown* (May 1998, penned by Amherst College head coach Bill Thurston) eloquently sounded an alarm bell concerning the deleterious effects of aluminum bats, especially the very real dangers of injury that these instruments appear to represent. The conjecture is everywhere heard that no matter what the demands of economics may be in the foreseeable future, aluminum Louisville Sluggers (or metallic Easton mallets) will never be possible in major league play — or even high-level minor league play — since pitchers throwing 90-plus-mph fastballs will be immediately thrust into almost certain life-threatening situations. American colleges, long the prime market for these high tech offensive instruments, are now themselves moving swiftly in the direction of a return to traditional wooden war clubs, or at least a wholesale conversion to technologically refined aluminum bats that perform after the fashion of wood.

Yet anyone watching CL action for much of the nineties (before wooden bats returned with the 2000 National Series) can't help wondering if— all the scientific studies aside — this is not just a good bit of excessive wolf crying. Metal "lumber" has been employed by the baseball-savvy Cubans since 1976 (when world tournament standards as well as the country's own depressed dollar-poor economy and embargo-limited markets mandated such change) without so much as a single reported serious injury as the direct result. Also without any CL moundsmen reported as being either assassinated or maimed in the line of duty.

The counterargument might be that Cuban baseball simply doesn't feature the kind of flamethrowers found in the majors or top U.S. colleges, and while this may be true to some extent, it does not explain away recent CL hurlers like Pedro Lazo (who throws invisible peas in the mid–90 mph-range) and Mael Rodríguez (clocked at speeds matching or outstripping Randy Johnson), or big-league refugees Liván Hernández, Orlando Hernández, Osvaldo Fernández, Luis Rolando Arrojo and Ariel Prieto. Some pretty fair Cuban fastballers (as well as junkballers like José Ibar and sidearmer Jorge Fumero)

José Luis Alemán (1969–1994), eighth winningest pitcher (174 career victories) in Cuban League history.

have not only survived against such monster swingers as Omar Linares, Orestés Kindelán, Lázaro Junco and Victor Mesa over the past decade, but they have even managed to get them out on a more-or-less consistent basis.

Aluminum bats certainly had their noticeable effect on the game's balance of power across the years between the mid-seventies and late-nineties. For one thing they altered the popular pitching styles in Cuba. Knuckleballers and screwballers have been a mainstay now for several decades and Cuban pitchers of the '70s and '80s were also aided in their war against souped-up war clubs by discolored and scuffed baseballs often left in play (an economic factor) for innings at a time. Throughout much of the early 1990s inferior Cuban-manufactured balls (produced by the domestic Batos company) with overly slick surfaces made gripping the "pelota" and thus throwing effective breaking balls quite difficult (the problem has been corrected in recent seasons). It was thus balls and not bats that seemed to work most strongly against CL hurlers and in favor of CL sluggers.

Anyone watching international baseball at its highest levels of competition in recent years (Cuban League, Olympics, Pan American Games, IBAF World Cup tournaments, etc.) might reasonably conclude that it is indeed a most entertaining spectacle and one that provides high-quality competition and manages to maintain more than mere semblance of the traditional balance between offensive banging and the pitcher's clever deceptions of timing, speed and ball movement. Baseball in the Olympic Games or Intercontinental Cup matches might be a bit more aesthetic (certainly lower scoring) if played with 19th-century-style wooden war clubs. (In truth, introduction of wooden bats for Sydney 2000 and Athens 2004 had almost no impact on the number of runs scored during Olympic tournaments.) But for this observer, at least, the steel bats didn't spoil the earlier Olympic sport anywhere near as much as familiar big league staples like plastic outfield carpets, roofed shopping mall stadia, and ear-splitting fifteen story entertainment centers which substitute for what once were merely bleacher-backdrop scoreboards.

What the aluminum war clubs did accomplish — as far as the high-level Cuban circuit is concerned — was to make it a bit difficult at times to project the talents and achievements of top Cuban batsmen like Linares, Kindelán, Victor Mesa or José Estrada onto the U.S. professional scene. How good actually were/are these touted Cuban hitters? Would either Linares or Kindelán have slugged against major league hurlers the way they pounded U.S. collegians Jim Parque or Kris Benson (big leaguers in training) in Atlanta? And would some of the mammoth upper deck homers that Kindelán launched at Fulton County Stadium in July 1996 have been possible if his bats had been of the standard ash construction? We can, of course, only speculate on both points. But the first bit of helpful evidence perhaps has been the fact that in Winnipeg (1999 Pan Am Games), Sydney (2000 Olympics), Taipei (2001 World Cup), Athens (2004 Olympic), and Rotterdam (2005 World Cup) the Cubans have continued their heavy hitting (beating the Americans 11–3 and the Panamanians 15–2 in the championship round of the latter event)—despite any changes in lumber or any improvements in U.S. pitching (now that legitimate pros have entered the scene for Team USA and other national squads).

I have elsewhere in this volume contended that overall player quality in the CL is probably about AA level by U.S. professional standards; but the strong caveat here is that major league baseball is itself arguably only about AAA by the standards of previous decades. (Does anyone really believe that Mark McGwire and Sammy Sosa—or Juan González and Barry Bonds—are truly that far ahead of Ruth, Mantle or Mays?) Certainly today's MLB pitching is—on average—diluted, and if Clemens or Randy Johnson or Pedro Martínez are among the all-time greats, many of today's big league hurlers would not have made it out of the Three-I League in the pre-expansion era. There are obviously top-level players coming out of the CL (and even some coming out of Cuba before they ever make it to the top levels there) who have legitimate big-league credentials. Liván Hernández, El Duque, Rolando Arrojo (MLB's top 1998 rookie pitcher) and the Mets' flashy shortstop Rey Ordóñez have all proven this beyond any shadow of a doubt.

The CL is admittedly in essence a hitters' league, despite a number of top pitchers and some sterling mound performances over the years (Braudilio Vinent in the '60s and '70s, Lázaro Valle in the 1980s, and Pedro Lazo and El Duque in the nineties). Cuban national teams have time and again won in the big international tournaments much more with their clutch slugging than with their often inconsistent pitching. Lazo and Omar Ajete and Omar Luis all stumbled in Atlanta in 1996 (by giving up 8 runs against Team USA, another 8 versus the unheralded Australians, 11 to Korea and 7 to Nicaragua, and finally 9 in the gold medal showdown with Japan), but bashers like Linares (8 homers including three in the title match), Kindelán (9 mammoth round trippers), Estrada (one of the team's eight clutch longballs in the slugfest versus Japan) and veteran outfielder Luis Ulacia (clutch hitting throughout the tournament) certainly did not. Cuba's pitching weaknesses a decade ago in Atlanta have only shown modest improvement in two subsequent Olympic tournaments, and then largely due only to the overpowering arms of José Contreras (since departed) and Pedro Lazo (whose big-league closer skills have saved many a shaky Cuban starter).

In short, the pitchers gave up tons of runs in Atlanta, even to inexperienced sluggers from Italy, The Netherlands and Australia. At the end of pre-medal play (seven games for each team) the Cubans (7–0) stood fourth in team pitching stats with a 6.71 ERA; Nicaragua was tops and the USA second. But Cuban hitters more than compensated, posting the heftiest team numbers by wide margins for slugging (.785), B.A, (.405), runs (97), total bases (219) and RBI (95). Almost every player (pitchers excepted) on each recent Cuban national team is a clutch batsman; even defensive wizards like shortstop Eduardo Paret (his homer broke open the semifinal game with Nicaragua) and outfielder Miguel Caldés (1995 CL home run champion) swung potent bats in Fulton County Stadium. A

decade later—at the recent Rotterdam World Cup—the Cuban batting order was so strong from top to bottom that perhaps for the first time in baseball history a .400-hitter (four seasons running) named Osmani Urrutia occupied the seventh slot in the lineup.

Some of Cuba's biggest international victories of the past decade have come on late longball heroics—Omar Linares in Atlanta's gold medal game with his trio of long balls, Orestes Kindelán in a dramatic extra-inning win over Japan earlier the same week with his game-ending third-deck blast of more than 500 feet, and outfielder Lourdes Gourriel a decade back with an MVP performance at the 1989 Intercontinental Cup which included the game-winning homer and four RBI in the title victory versus Japan. At the 1999 Pan Am Games (Winnipeg) that served as a Sydney Olympic qualifier, Linares' dramatic homer saved the semifinal win and a blast by Kindelán locked up the gold medal contest.

Across the years Cuban batsmen have posted some extremely impressive numbers: in nine straight seasons between 1985 and 1993 the CL batting leader posted .400 or better. Since 2000 portly Las Tunas outfielder Osmani Urrutia has hit .400 so regularly (four of the past five seasons) that he has seemed almost to be a second coming of Cooperstown's Rogers Hornsby. The yearly home run and RBI totals usually don't look like much (27 HRs by Lázaro Junco in 1993 was the National Series one-year best until matched in 2005 by Urrutia's teammate Joan Carlos Pedroso); that is, until one checks out the lengths of Cuban seasons, sees firsthand the often spacious stadiums, and observes that much of the Cuban pitching against aluminum bats was (and still is) of a tantalizing off-speed variety. Cuban batters don't get many ready-made home run balls thrown their way. This is quite obviously self-defense on the part of island pitchers.

A substantial quintet of sixties-seventies-eighties-era legends virtually unknown off the island featured Wilfredo Sánchez, Agustín Marquetti, Antonio Muñoz, Lázaro Junco and Armando Capiró. All possessed impressive batting credentials that must have turned heads of the few scouts who might have secretly witnessed their exploits during Intercontinental Cup or World Cup matches in Europe or Canada. Sánchez was the celebrated "Hombre Hit" who reached new milestones for hit totals and captured five CL batting titles, including the first back-to-back pair (1969 and 1970). Today his lifetime mark (.331) still ranks in the top ten, even if it now falls far short of contemporary bashers like Linares (.367, and the CL's first-ever National Series .400 hitter), Urrutia (.360, with a record four .400-plus campaigns), and Michel Enríquez (.358, and the most feared bat on recent editions of the Cuban national squad). Marquetti and Muñoz, a pair of awesome lefty swingers, both caught the eye of touring *Sports Illustrated* writer Ron Fimrite, who branded the latter (known among Cuban *fanaticos* as "El Gigante of Escambray") as "a left-handed Tony Pérez." Muñoz, in turn, may have been the most potent Cuban slugger ever and still stands near the top of the country's (amateur era) career list for RBI production (second to Kindelán) and total bases (fourth behind Kindelán, Linares and Antonio Pacheco). Junco (1978–95), a lithe but muscular lefty, set most of the league home run marks (including single season and career standards) which have in recent seasons been overhauled by Atlanta Olympic hero Orestes Kindelán.

Perhaps the most colorful Cuban batsman in the lost-era of the '60s and '70s was a righty flychaser sporting number 18 for Havana's Industriales who drew constant comparisons in Caribbean circles to Roberto Clemente. Armando Capiró (Cop-ear-OH) is subject of colorful tales concerning a celebrated throwing contest that ultimately never took place. So potent and legendary was the arm of the left-field star on the Cuban national team that both Cuban and Nicaraguan fans clamored for a showcase throwing exhibition during the 1972 amateur world championships (World Cup XX) between Nicaraguan hotshot David Green (a future mediocre big leaguer), Capiró with the gold medal–winning Cubans, and the celebrated Clemente, who was also in Nicaragua at the time to manage Puerto Rico's entry in the tournament.

The much-anticipated event collapsed when Clemente refused to enter such a competition with mere amateurs that might distract from his important role as team manager. But if Capiró did not have the chance to demonstrate his arm against the famed Clemente, he did audition his bat the following winter versus his own countrymen by pacing the island league in base hits, RBI and home runs (as first to slug more than 20 in a single National Series). And he did so in the era before introduction of power-packed aluminum bats.

In the modern-day era of the past three decades none can compare of course with Linares — unless perhaps the case is made for Urrutia and his 2000–2005 streak of .400-plus batting. But Linares had a flair and balance of all-around talent that Urrutia seemingly lacks. The powerpacked third sacker (6'0" and 200 lbs of coiled muscle) might be the most complete player ever to rise from Cuban soil (excepting perhaps Negro league legend Martín Dihigo, who could play every position but catcher). And this includes big leaguers Miñoso, Oliva and Pérez as well as all other Cuban professionals of bygone pre–Castro decades. Linares — to count mere raw talent alone and leave aside the issues of fine tuning gained from years of big-league experience — is the equal of any international tournament player and almost any major leaguer (exempting perhaps Mays, Mantle, Clemente and Ted Williams) this writer has ever watched over the course of a half-century of avid baseball watching.

Aluminum bats and short seasons admitted, Linares' career numbers are still truly mind-boggling: five CL batting titles, all earned with .400-plus averages, and an endless string of international tournament showcase performances beginning at the raw age of 17 and continuing through the 2001 IBAF world championships in Taipei. During his final five seasons Linares' star faded considerably on the home front and he would not pace the CL in hitting for nearly a half-dozen-plus seasons at career's end. The legendary Pinareño appeared to be inexcusably overweight and even a little lethargic his final handful of winters, suffered several nagging injuries (most severe was a damaged shoulder), and consequently spent part of the 1998 CL season on leave touring for exhibitions and clinics in Japan. At the end of National Series #41 in 2002, approaching age 35, Linares' CL career and national team tenure were finally over after he departed (with government assistance) for a career-capping pro stint in the top-flight Japanese Central League. There (used by Chunichi as part-time pinch hitter and posting BAs as low as .174 in 2003), he was but a mere shadow of his former self, like so many big leaguers (Joe Pepitone, Don Blasingame, Warren Cromartie, Larry Doby, Don Newcome, etc.) who slipped quietly into Japan only after once-glorious major league days were thoroughly exhausted.

If Linares finally got his crack at the pros in Japan, no single talented hitter has yet fled Castro's baseball paradise to make a loud splash (or even a minor ripple) in organized professional baseball. (Kendry Morales seems poised at the opening of the 2006 MLB season to end that curious drought.) Castro-era refugees to the big league scene have almost exclusively been pitchers, as already observed; the only non-pitching defector currently playing regularly in the big leagues (Yunieski Betancourt in Seattle) made the grade on his defensive prowess and not his batting eye. Detroit Tigers two-season washout Bárbaro Garbey once flashed brief promise in the mid-eighties (1984–1985) of being precisely that long-awaited Cuban hitter with legitimate pro credentials, but Garbey all-too-quickly fizzled. And in the process he became nothing more than the answer to an obscure trivia question about the first post–1962 CL refugee to don a big league uniform.

Garbey had paced the Cuban circuit in RBI in 1978, then was booted from the league along with 24 countrymen for involvement in an alleged game-fixing scandal. The Industriales outfielder was sent packing to U.S. shores by the Castro government during the Mariel "Freedom Flotilla" of spring 1980, soon signing on with the Detroit Tigers who debuted him with Class A Lakeland (Florida State League). When news of Garbey's Cuban antics reached U.S. shores (in 1983 while he was with the Tigers' AAA team in Evansville) he suffered a brief second suspension from minor league action which in the end was only an apparent "formal" slap on the wrist from sanctimonious officials of organized baseball.

Garbey had actually admitted his game fixing (in closed interviews with minor league president John Johnson) and yet paid no greater price than a brief suspension while the entire matter was reputedly under evaluation. Returning to play that same 1983 season Garbey eventually made the Detroit Tigers roster (for 1984 and 1985). Although he was respectable as a batsman (hitting .287 in 110 games as a rookie) he was inconsistent in the field and anything but a model big league citizen. Several on-field altercations led to yet other suspensions and ultimately a trade to the Texas Rangers. During a handful of seasons Garbey rapidly played his way out of professional baseball. A half-dozen years later he reappeared briefly as a 37-year-old union-busting "replacement player" for Cincinnati during 1995's lockout-year spring training sessions.

The rather laughable minor-league suspension of Bábaro Garbey is indeed remarkable, given his blanket admission of game-throwing in Cuba. Such untoward behavior would surely have been dealt with more severely if it had occurred anywhere but in an enemy state. Instead, there were only statements from U.S. baseball officials with seemingly strong political overtones. Evansville manager Gord MacKenzie even proudly excused Garbey's Cuban game fixing as "an economic necessity" and suggested "reporters should talk to people who live down there to find out what it's like." The Garbey situation, along with more recent revelations that El Duque's December 1997 departure from Cuba was not quite the daring and unassisted scramble for freedom it first appeared to be, both work to justify legitimate fears of Cuban baseball officials that their players are targets of underhanded recruitment practices by talent-starved organized baseball. Such flights from the island by Cuban stars will likely always be unfairly romanticized in the United States for narrow purposes of scoring needed political propaganda victories. The use of baseball and ballplayers as Cold War pawns is hardly a practice restricted solely to government officials or baseball moguls plying their disreputable trade in Communist Cuba.

Hernández, it turns out, did not risk life and limb on a flimsy raft as romanticized in the U.S. press (*Sports Illustrated* broke the unadorned details in November 1998) but received a somewhat more luxurious pre-arranged boat ride off the island facilitated by the ballplayer's Miami-based handlers. The revised El Duque saga is enough to suggest that Cuban players will inevitably be made to look like heroes in the American press no matter what the circumstances of their departures from Cuba. But the Bárbaro Garbey scandal had already demonstrated that to be the case a full decade and a half earlier.

Garbey was no Liván Hernández or Orlando Hernández in terms of either his MLB impact or his latent diamond talents. But merely a week or two of watching such talented swingers of the 1990s or 2000s as Linares, Kindelán, Osmani Urrutia, Juan Carlos Pedroso (2005's HR leader with a record-tying 27 in 90 games), Yulieski Gourriel or Michel Enríquez (a .358 career hitter after eight seasons and clean-up slugger in the potent national team lineup) on today's Cuban League scene quickly suggests that lack to date of any true impact slugger among Cuban ex-patriots is hardly a signal that such phenoms don't actually exist back home on the world's most baseball-crazy island.

* * *

Team Cuba's long-awaited showdown with vaunted big leaguers on their home grounds in May 1999 was arguably the apogee of Cuba's post-revolution baseball saga. Game two of the Cuba-Orioles series would provide not only a unique collision of distinct baseball universes, but also an unparalleled single moment of drama, one to be savored — stateside as well as in Havana — by all fans hankering for a more innocent version of America's revered national pastime. Designated hitter Andy Morales had just blasted a titanic homer into the center field bleachers of Orioles Park at Camden Yards, in the process capping a game-clinching 5-run ninth-inning outburst against touted big league pitching by an underdog but undaunted

lineup of CL all-stars. With unrestrained joy the Cuban slugger next enacted a scene that remains the single indelible image from the highly publicized showdown series: Morales tiptoed over three bases with his arms lifted toward the heavens, hugged the sky as he rounded second, then gleefully jumped atop home plate as he finally reached a mob of awaiting celebratory teammates.

Orioles veteran B.J. Surhoff later expressed typical big league sourness when he quipped in a post-game interview that "no one appreciates the guy running around like an idiot!" For the big leaguers, Morales's display of childlike joy was merely "a bush-league ploy" to be scorned and resented. It was not at all a "professional" reaction to victory of a kind everywhere today expected among elite play-for-pay athletes who seem long ago to have cashed in spontaneous joys of playing this boys' game in the process of earning their high-profile celebrity status, luxury lifestyles, and bulging investment portfolios.

Morales's timely circuit blast not only added an exclamation point to Cuba's resounding 12–6 drubbing of the Orioles in Baltimore but also capsulized a stark difference in flavor between international amateur baseball and the troubled big-league professional version of the sport. While Cuban ballplayers danced in the dugout and around home plate after both Danel Castro's rally-inspiring triple in the second frame and Morales's power blast in the ninth, Baltimore's representatives sleepwalked through a contest that for the big leaguers apparently meant only a much-resented usurpation of an originally scheduled open date. Disenchanted franchise star Albert Belle — in stark contrast to the energized Cubans — twice stood disinterested at home plate while taking called third strikes, then on a third occasion jogged half-heartedly toward first and was tagged out easily on an errant throw that had pulled Cuban first sacker Orestes Kindelán several feet off the bag.

With the lackluster big leaguers there was no evidence of playing for national pride, no displays of competitive sporting spirit, no battle for personal honor or even any apparent appreciation of the pure joys of top-flight ballplaying. Thus the contrast couldn't have been any more obvious or more compelling between two conflicting baseball universes.

The difference in attitude between Cuban and American ballplayers was even further highlighted with a pre-game press conference in which veteran Cuban stars Omar Linares and Luis Ulacia were peppered with inevitable questions about their apparent unwillingness to defect from Cuba for the chance to follow Orlando Hernández (New York Yankees) or Rolando Arroyo (Tampa Bay Devil Rays) into the high-salaried big leagues. Apparently seeing the game as a meaningless exhibition, U.S. writers were digging for any more colorful story laced with hot-button political implications. Linares and Ulacia together reiterated their firm commitments to remaining in the land of their birth, while at the same time expressing natural interest in testing big league waters — provided, of course, they could retain the privilege of spending winters and maintaining citizenship in their homeland. Ulacia wryly observed that the main obstacle for a non-defecting

Cuban would seem to be a U.S. economic embargo that would apparently block his receiving a big-league salary as long as he remained a Cuban resident.

Ulacia then (not altogether unseriously) dismissed the issue as not being all that difficult in the end, since he and his teammates would certainly be "quite willing and ready to play in the big leagues for free." With such a rankly uncapitalist attitude Cuban stars would likely find, of course, that their biggest obstacle would in truth not be the U.S. Treasury Department at all, but rather Donald Fehr and the major league baseball players' union.

The May 1999 drubbing of the lackluster Orioles on foreign soil in Camden Yards represented a resounding moral victory for Cuban baseballers and also for their nation of baseball-crazed fans back home. Overjoyed partisans in Havana weren't at all interested in frequent caveats that this was the very worst among big league clubs and that Orioles players had less motivation to prove anything than did the Cuban

Wilfredo "El Hombre Hit" Sánchez, seventies-era Cuban League hitting nonpareil and fifth on the National Series/ Selective Series career hits list.

amateur leaguers. Island enthusiasms for a long-awaited showdown with storied big-leaguers had already peaked in March, during the historic debut of baseball détente, and had been sustained unrelentingly through the May rematch. So many black and white TV sets blared out the signal from the state-run broadcast of the game back in Havana that it was possible to simply stroll the streets of the capital city and not miss a single exciting pitch.

Writer Milton Jamail has since groused in the pages of *Full Count* that Cuban fans were unfairly shut out from viewing the opening game of the series at Latin American Stadium by Fidel's unsavory ticket distribution plan: invitations went only to party loyalists (among them many nonfans), school children and hosts of INDER officials, in order to provide (as Jamail sees it) the kind a staid and well comported crowd desired by the Maximum Leader. But when have major league baseball officials recently handed out treasured tickets to man-in-the-street fans for World Series sessions, All-Star Games, or league championship matches? Ducets for "special events" in big league parks are also reserved mainly for well-connected high rollers who arrive to be part of the media event and not in search of any purified baseball fix.

If major league officials could contend that the Orioles were neither the most-talented nor most motivated of opponents, the Cubans could counter with equal justification that a top contingent of their own team's most talented performers — ace pitcher Ciro Silvino Licea, batting champion Yobal Dueñas, and winged-footed young flychaser Yasser Gómez, for starters — had been left back in Havana to prepare for crucial upcoming Pan American Games competitions that would determine Olympic qualifiers for the year 2000. At the first meeting in Havana the Cuban team was again without leading stars like Kindelán, Pacheco and Germán Mesa, whose teams were still involved in CL postseason playoffs.

There were admittedly some negatives to the Camden Yards game, though most of these involved matters other than on-field baseball play. The game was nearly cancelled at the eleventh hour when Cuba's oversized delegation of nearly a hundred athletes, officials, and assorted dignitaries encountered U.S. visa problems before departing Havana. Game-night action on the field was also delayed for an hour and a half by a first-inning field-soaking downpour. And a second brief interruption of baseball play came in the fourth frame when four anti–Castro protesters ran onto the outfield grass to interject a dose of blatant political posturing into the evening's intended sporting spectacle.

An inning later the scene turned ugly when a fifth sign-waving protester was body-slammed to the turf near second base by Cuban umpire César Valdés. (Cuban umpires distinguished themselves in both games of the series, since big league arbiters refused to work these exhibitions without additional compensation.) It was all part of an expected spate of histrionic outrage from Miami-Cuban forces and anti–Cuban sympathizers who viewed the entertainment as an unacceptable compromise with Fidel Castro's communist government. And stateside media jumped all over the story of a single defection from the Cuban delegation by Rigoberto Betancourt Herrera, widely but falsely reported by the U.S. press to be a leading national team pitching coach and a former star hurler in Cuban League play. Betancourt had in reality been only an above-average pitcher in the 1960s, with a 38–25 lifetime record compiled over eight seasons; he had traveled to Baltimore with the Cuban delegation as one of the dozens of former CL players being honored by inclusion in the excursion. Betancourt in point of fact had no official connection with the national team. Yet despite such lamentable political overtones, for the bulk of the 47,490 in attendance the game itself in the end was quite evidently a resounding display of the depth of long-hidden Cuban baseball talent.

Pedro José "Cheíto" Rodríguez tore up Cuban League pitching for fifteen seasons of National Series play (1974–1988).

The inaugural March game of the home-and-home baseball détente series was arguably both a more gripping baseball display and also a more successful international goodwill enterprise. There were of course no rowdy or ill-mannered fan outbursts in Havana's Estadio Latinoamericano. Cuban police certainly would not have tolerated them; and it is a fair assessment that the Cuban fans would never have considered them either. Baltimore won the tightly played contest 3–2 in extra frames with a dramatic run-producing 11th-inning single by Harold Baines finally deciding the outcome. Veteran national team star Omar Linares fittingly provided the hometown excitement with a game-tying single in the eighth. But perhaps the most shocking event of the pageantry-filled afternoon (for the big-league hitters at any rate) was the sterling two-hit, eight-inning relief performance by Cuban right-hander José Ariel Contreras. Aging flychaser Luis Ulacia (surprise member of the Cuban roster after showing little offense in recent CL seasons) also again proved his value in international competitions with three clutch base hits.

One further surprise of the opening game in Havana was a definite lack of long-ball power (there was but one homer, by Orioles catcher Charles Johnson), a factor which Baltimore GM Frank Wren blamed on inferior "soft" Cuban baseballs. Yet if the big leaguers were handicapped by mushy Cuban "pelotas" this advantage was likely more than neutralized by the fact that the Cubans were forced to hit with wooden bats after only a couple weeks of practice using the new lumber (aluminum warclubs having been used in Cuba exclusively since the mid-seventies).

In the end the series as a whole was an excellent showcase for the current state of CL baseball. It was clearly a glorious triumph for some aging Cuban stars like Linares (4 for 4 in Baltimore and author of the key Cuban hit in Havana) and Ulacia (five for ten in the two contests) who had missed their chance to shine in the more prestigious majors. And also the games clearly provided an emphatic statement about the quality of much-maligned Cuban pitching. The overall quality of hurlers produced by the CL had been open to legitimate

question if not derision in recent years in light of the sometimes mediocre performances by a handful of big league defectors such as Ariel Prieto, Osvaldo Fernández, Vladimir Núñez, and the flashy yet inconsistent half-brothers, Orlando and Liván Hernández. The frequent mantra by Cuban baseball insiders that the best talent was still back home on the island now suddenly gained a huge shot of veracity with the dominating performance from José Contreras in Havana and an equally shinny relief stint from Santiago's 27-year-old ace Norge Vera (7 innings, 3 hits, 3 runs) in Baltimore.

Many questions nonetheless remained in the afterglow of the Orioles-Cuba series. Would there now be more such games the following spring or in any future springs? One might now expect the Yankees or Mets or Orioles or Dodgers to next lobby for a week-long series of spring training games in Havana. And how did one now assess the Cuban talent in the light of the national team's ability to more than hold its own with a big league representative? It might be true that the 1999 Orioles (losers of 84) were not the 1998 Yankees (winners of 114) and that any big league all-star contingent might well beat the Cubans with easy regularity. But the Cubans had proved beyond any remaining doubt their ability to play respectably on the major league level. It was necessary to remember that if the Orioles were not the best of possible major league representatives, the top Cuban talent was also not always on display during this series. Remarkable shortstop Germán Mesa had now returned to CL action but was still not eligible for a national team slot due to the terms of his earlier suspension. Stellar second baseman Yobal Dueñas, who hit .418 during the year, was left off the squad that visited Baltimore in deference to long-time star Antonio Pacheco. Perhaps the best among young Cuban pitchers — Granma's lithe fast-balling righty Ciro Silino Licea — was also held back in preparation for the Olympic qualifier in Winnipeg. (It was rumored in Havana that Cuban officials didn't want U.S. scouts to get an eyeful of Licea or another young prospect named Maels Rodríguez.) And, finally, it had to be asked what the motives were on both sides for entering into such a showdown showcase series? Were the big leaguers (in this case the Orioles) primarily motivated by a first crack at the cornucopia of Cuban talent? And were the Cuban baseball lords themselves preparing the way for some eventual fire sale of top CL talent as the quick fix for a sagging national economy? Such intriguing speculations were equally as interesting as the colorful ballgames themselves.

As speculation raged about baseball détente, back in Havana and Santiago and Pinar del Río (and elsewhere all around the island), another National Series (number 38 in the sequence) was providing its own expected thrills and encouragements for Cuban ballpark watchers. What unfolded from November 1998 to March 1999 was one of the most exciting Cuban seasons in decades — both on and off the field of play. A tense pennant race featured a revived Havana-based Indus-

Cuban League legend Omar Linares displays his MVP trophy after the International Baseball Federation all-star game in Tokyo Dome. Linares completed his Cuban League career with a lifetime .368 BA (all-time best, .008 ahead of Osmani Urrutia) and 404 round-trippers (third all-time).

triales team as well as surprise challenges in Eastern provinces by the usually also-ran Guantánamo, Granma and Holguín ballclubs. With Linares (Pinar del Río), Kindelán and Pacheco (the latter two with Santiago) all withering on the disabled list for much of the campaign, usual powerhouse teams struggled early in the season. In the end, however, Santiago emerged as CL playoff champion (by defeating Industriales in a seven-game finale) after several seasons of trailing pitching-rich Pinar del Río.

An ironic twist to final postseason action was the staging of playoff games simultaneous with the Orioles' late–March visit to Havana, and also the sudden switch to wooden bats during post-season play (after a donation of lumber from Major League Baseball as part and parcel of the Orioles-Cuba matches). Excitement surrounding the Orioles visit on March 28 was nearly topped by two final CL semifinal shootouts the same week between Industriales and top rival Isla de la Juventud. The last of these thrilling games, played to an exuberant overflowing throng in Estadio Latinoamericano on the eve of the much-anticipated Saturday afternoon Orioles exhibition, propelled the local hometown favorites into the National Series finals for the first time in four long years.

National Series XXXVIII was also headlined by the dramatic return of suspended star Germán Mesa, perhaps the country's most popular individual player at the close of the nineties. Unknown in the U.S., Mesa was a living island legend seriously compared by international scouts with the likes of Ozzie Smith and Omar Vizquel. It is hard to judge Mesa on such a different field of play as that represented by the "retro" Cuban League. And admittedly I never saw the flashy infielder during his prime seasons before his suspension. But what I did eventually observe during the 1999 and 2000 campaigns was enough to suggest that Cubans who had watched his earlier year-in and year-out development were not exaggerating about Mesa's unique talents.

The 5–7 Mesa is nothing short of the flashiest fielder in CL history and perhaps the best shortstop of any era and any level of play. Astute observers of the Cuban scene certainly seem to think so. Mesa's brilliant career was short-circuited on the eve of the Atlanta Olympics when he was suspended (along with Orlando Hernández and promising catcher Alberto Hernández) for allegedly accepting cash gifts from a visiting undercover scout with MLB connections. In October 1996 the trio was "banned for life" for their actions; but while El Duque and Alberto Hernández subsequently chose to flee the country, Mesa quietly accepted his fate and began behind-the-scenes rehabilitation. Even staid oldtimers on the Cuban scene were convinced of Mesa's unparalleled defensive brilliance. Conrado Marrero — 88-year-old ex-big-leaguer who served as part-time pitching coach for Granma's CL team — told this writer in Havana in January 1999 that Mesa surpassed in defensive wizardry such Cuban notables as Willie Miranda and Héctor Rodríguez (fifties-era big leaguers) or anyone else Marrero had observed during his own amateur and professional playing and coaching career — a career reaching back well into the mid-thirties.

To tout Mesa as Cuba's best shortstop is no small claim in view of big-league escapee Rey Ordóñez and the host of skilled performers still residing on the island. The depth of Cuban middle-infield talent was heavily underscored especially during the unique Orioles series. With Mesa and 1996 Olympic stalwart Eduardo Paret (Villa Clara) both under suspension from national team play, 23-year-old Danel Castro — arguably only the fourth best at his position in the current CL — flashed enough brilliance to turn the heads of numerous big-league scouts. Subbing for starter Juan Carlos Moreno (Isla de la Juventud) in the opening game of the home-and-home series, Castro (infield anchor for Las Tunas) slashed a base hit in his single plate appearance. In Baltimore, Castro was that game's top hitting star, going 4 for 5, legging out two booming triples, rapping in 2 runs, and scoring himself four times. (The brilliance of Cuban shortstop play was further exhibited at the 2005 Holland-based World Cup when team captain Eduardo Paret went down with a leg injury at the end of pool-round play and a now-matured Juan Carlos Moreno took up the slack with flawless performances in both the middle infield and batter's box.)

Biggest news in Cuban baseball circles during National Series #38 — at least on the home front — was Mesa's emotional return to action in an Industriales uniform (see Chapter 11). But there were other headline stories as the season unfolded. Young outfield phenom Yasser Gómez (1998 top rookie with Metros) continued to shine for a second season after he was switched to the more popular Industriales team. Yobal Dueñas (who outslugged Gómez for the batting title) emerged as a legitimate star with Pinar del Río, substituting in that role for injured Omar Linares who spent much of the campaign on the sidelines. José Ibar also enjoyed another phenomenal campaign on the mound, nearly winning 20 (he finished with 18 after a late-year slump) for a second straight year. And a novice pitching star emerged in the figure of Granma ace Ciro Silvino Licea, a righty boasting a dancing fastball in the high nineties. Licea was league pacesetter in complete games pitched (16, with a 16–4 record); the following year he would also post the CL's top totals for games started (25) and innings pitched (194.2). Silvino Licea for a brief span would indeed appear unmatched among the young Cuban arms and was widely expected to have major impact on both the CL and the national team. After 2000, however, there would be a disturbing leveling off in Licea's CL and international tournament performances.

Recent winter seasons have also spawned a handful of oddities on the Cuban baseball scene. Tops was an unprecedented unassisted triple play completed by a third baseman (Villa Clara's Rafael Orlando Acebey), a feat believed to be unequalled anywhere in U.S. professional baseball. And there was also the rare feat of three triples (in consecutive at-bats) within a single game by Yasser Gómez. (This author actually witnessed both events firsthand.) Even more unusual still was a home run during a crucial 2002 playoff game that was wiped out when a Sancti Spíritus runner passed his teammate on the basepaths, not only costing the losers a single run but also

ending a potential big inning. It was the kind of slapstick bush league play one hardly expects to encounter with a league championship squarely on the line.

But when it comes to truly unusual plays the CL has never lacked for more than typical doses of the unpredictable and even the highly bizarre. One of the most remarkable and unprecedented plays in baseball annals occurred a number of seasons back in the CL and involved one of the circuit's biggest stars. Playing for Matanzas at the time, Wilfredo Sánchez made a spectacular diving outfield catch which came with the bases loaded and none out. Runners on both first and second had strayed far from their respective sacks on the sinking liner into right center and were easily doubled and tripled off their bases when Sánchez pegged the ball back to waiting and alert infielders. But here the plot thickens: the third base runner had also retreated and tagged up at the hot corner, then sprinted toward the plate, which he crossed well before the third out was called. Since the third and final out at first base was not a force play, the run apparently counted and thus put Matanzas behind on the scoreboard, 3–2.

But still further complications soon arose. The Matanzas manager was quick to appeal the strange play, claiming that the third base runner had left the bag a fraction too early, and one umpire immediately agreed and signaled a rare fourth out. (Although only three outs can be recorded in the scorebook, the runner at third would have to be technically "out" as well to nullify his run, due to the infraction of early departure from the base.) In the end the call was overruled by the umpiring crew chief, the sacrifice fly and thus the run were allowed, and the spectacular triple play actually cost Matanzas (which never scored again) the ball game. Wilfredo Sánchez almost (but not quite) initiated an unprecedented quadruple play. What he did take part in, however, was an equally bizarre triple play that drove in the opposing team's winning run. One of the great defensive gems of Cuban baseball turned out to be a play likely never witnessed in any other diamond venue.

There are other mysterious elements about Cuban League baseball to provoke the fancy of any fan. One burning issue surrounding the big league impacts of escaping CL stars like Liván Hernández and "El Duque" Hernández has been the verifiable ages of such renegade Cuban imports. While Miami-based agent Joe Cubas has often fudged stories about dramatic escapes from the island, he has also often peddled his Cuban talents as athletes considerably younger (and thus with potentially more market value) than they actually are. El Duque was early reported to be in his late 20s although those familiar with his CL and Cuban national team histories knew such a claim simply didn't accord with the facts. Any Cuba watcher also knows that Rey Ordóñez was a shade older than reported in MLB media accounts, and that Rolando Arrojo who enjoyed a sensational rookie season with Tampa Bay in 1998 likely had many fewer potential innings left in his flamethrowing arm than Devil Rays officials must have been led to believe.

Cuban League records reveal accurate birthdates for Ordóñez, El Duque, Rolando Arrojo, more recently signed Mets first base prospect Jorge Luis Toca, and one-time Tampa Bay minor league journeyman Roberto Colina, all of whom were repeatedly reported in stateside accounts as being several years younger than they actually were. Accurate birthdates follow: Rey Ordóñez (b. Havana, 1–11–1970, not November 11, 1972, as indicated in New York Mets media guides); Orlando "El Duque" Hernández (b. Boyoros, Havana, 10–11–1965, 33 years old when signed by New York, not 29 as announced by Joe Cubas); Rolando Arroyo (b. Las Villas, Villa Clara, 5–29–1964, 37 years old and not 33 as listed in *Total Baseball* 2001); Jorge Luis Toca (b. Remedios, Villa Clara, 1–7–1971, 31 years old at the time of his Mets debut); Roberto Colina (b. Havana, 9–5–1966, 36 years old when he washed out with Tampa Bay). These "official" birth dates are readily available in CL publications and thus there is no reason to doubt they are anything but accurate. Also, they are consistent with all earlier published data on past Cuban national teams.

Pinar del Río infielder-outfielder Yobal Dueñas was National Series #38 (1999) batting champion (with .418 BA) and 2002 Intercontinental Cup gold medal game hero before defecting to U.S. professional baseball, where he languished in the minor leagues.

* * *

Century-final competitions and celebrations had direct impact on the last CL season of the millennium, especially on its opening weeks. To accommodate Intercontinental Cup action in Sydney — an event featuring the Cuban national team — opening day for National Series XXXIX was delayed a full calendar month. With league action not opening in Havana until November 28, postseason playoffs would have to be pushed back until mid–May (with the regular season rescheduled to end May 15). And while seemingly every North American scribe or sports media outlet (print publications as well as the broadcast networks) was pushing an all-century all-star team of one sort or another for major league baseball, the Cuban press was busy with its own version. In this case it was an all-decade listing of top hitters and hurlers selected and defended by veteran baseball writer Sigfredo Barros of *Granma*, the official Communist Party daily in Havana.

The Barros Cuban all-star team was not a typical position-by-position affair but rather a statistics-based analysis of top batsmen (13 individuals) and mound aces (an even dozen) from the fourth full decade of CL action. What writer Barros provided was also in the main a fair selection of Cuba's twenty-five or so best performers from the century's final ten-year span. There are noteworthy omissions, of course, especially among position players known more for their defensive prowess than for heavy bats. Germán Mesa — the brilliant fielding shortstop — could find no place on a listing that celebrated batting averages above fielding percentages (or above spectacular highlight-film action, all but non-existent in Cuba). Flashy outfielder and renowned base thief Victor Mesa also didn't make the Barros numerical cut, although admittedly some of the latter Mesa's best play occurred in the '80s and not the '90s. And for not-so-surprising reasons there was no mention either of Orlando Hernández, even though the then-current New York Yankees ace did indeed pitch in his homeland during the first half of the nineties (until suspended at mid-decade) and still owned a top CL career winning percentage (.728, 126–47).

But there was little else to be disputed on the Barros published all-star list. It featured a mix of veteran players on their way out by decade's end with some recently celebrated novice stars that just now (in 1999) seemed to be peaking. Barros's entertaining survey began with the league's proven all-star batsmen. And, as expected, the illustrious Omar Linares sat at or near the top of the heap by just about every statistical measure.

Individual players require some additional commentary for those who haven't followed the CL scene religiously (thus most of the readers of this volume). Raw numbers quickly demonstrate that all-world third sacker Omar Linares boasts the most effective combination of pure power and speed in recent seasons of Cuban baseball. His .368 lifetime batting mark (through retirement in 2003) was constructed on the shoulders of five individual batting titles (four featuring .400-plus averages), though two of these fell in the '80s and the last was earned a decade before hanging up his spikes. In the nineties alone Linares boasted a .381 batting mark and was also the decade-long league pacesetter in walks with 434 and slugging average at .679 (neither category indicated in the table below). With the single exception of the last season of the nineties (when, at age 31, he was limited to 25 games by a nagging leg injury and thus registered only .287) Linares never saw his lofty batting average dip below a heady .351 mark.

Linares remains in a class by himself, whether one judges artistic merit or considers pure sabermetrics (i.e. statistical profile). Alexander Ramos (veteran second baseman with Isla de La Juventud) was perhaps the least likely entry on the Barros all-star list, since the talented keystone fireplug had never played on a national team despite a dozen-year .338 batting mark and 1305 career base hits, along with a nineties-era batting mark (.348) that trailed only Linares. (Ramos would retire in mid-season 2005 boasting the sixth-longest consecutive game playing streak in international baseball history and outpaced only by Linareas, Urrutia and Michel Enríquez on the CL career BA list.) Despite outdistancing such other outstanding batsmen as Kindelán and Pacheco (third at .334 for the full decade) and recent batting champs Yobal Dueñas (1999), Robelquis Videaux (pronounced as "Vee-due") (1998)

and José Estrada (1997), Ramos (also the decade pacesetter in games played, at-bats and base hits) had remarkably never captured an individual league batting title. Pacheco (a 20-season veteran widely considered to have few peers outside of Juan Padilla as all-time best defensive second baseman in league annals) and Kindelán (eventual lifetime CL home run king with 487) were veteran standbys who had built impressive numbers over the years. And Dueñas (who hit .418 for 86 games in 1999 with Pinar del Río) and Javier Méndez (still another 20-year veteran, playing for Industriales, who only recently had burst upon the tournament scene during the 1999 Pan American Games) were also rising international stars by decade's end.

Barros's list of pitchers offered an even less recognizable cache of buried treasure for non-specialists in Cuban baseball. Few of the names — outside of perhaps Ibar, Contreras and Lazo — have stirred much notice among pro scouts unwelcome on the island. The top ranking statistical ace of the past ten campaigns — Pinar del Río southpaw Faustino Corrales — was (above all others) a name unfamiliar to all but the most dedicated outside observers of island winter play, despite the fact that the 36-year-old (known for his 90-plus fastball and spectacular dropping curve) had already logged 19 seasons, captured 145 career victories (against 110 losses), and recently cracked the all-time top-ten in CL lifetime starts.

Corrales is a name especially unfamiliar to those world baseball *aficionados* who judge Cuban League talent strictly by national team rosters. The shifty southpaw was virtually uninitiated in international play before the century's final Pan Am Games tournament in Winnipeg, where he also saw only modest action (2.2 innings and a 3.37 ERA). But at the Sydney Intercontinental Cup Games a mere four months later Corrales was suddenly the staff ace, hurling the bulk of an impressive 5–1 victory over Team USA during pool-play (lasting five innings, allowing but a single earned run, and fanning six). Corrales was also the inspirational victor with a complete-game two-hitter in the opening 1–0 Cuban win over Chinese Taiwan, and for these efforts he made the all-tourney team roster as the top left-handed starter. His surprising performance in Olympic tune-up action thus signaled yet another

Best Thirteen Cuban League Hitters of the Nineties

*Statistics for these batters are for 10-season-period between 1990–99 only, and are not lifetime stats.

Player (Team)	BA	AB	R	H	2B	3B	HR	RBI
Omar Linares (Pinar del Río)	**.381**	1361	419	518	82	12	100	341
Alexander Ramos (Isla Juventud)	.348	**2388**	417	**830**	113	15	69	321
Antonio Pacheco (Santiago)	.334	1557	293	520	80	9	74	344
Javier Méndez (Industriales)	.333	1609	278	536	94	10	52	338
Yobal Dueñas (Pinar del Río)	.332	2127	380	707	**130**	16	48	328
José Estrada (Matanzas)	.331	2375	**464**	787	124	**36**	48	269
Reemberto Rosell (Cienfuegos)	.330	2369	313	782	83	22	8	152
Oscar Macías (Habana)	.328	2089	389	686	99	14	**111**	**406**
Eduardo Cárdenas (Matanzas)	.326	2245	363	732	108	5	14	233
Juan Padilla (Industriales)	.322	1945	315	626	99	12	52	316
Luis Ulacia (Camagüey)	.322	1743	320	562	69	15	40	199
Lázaro Vargas (Industriales)	.313	1695	301	531	85	6	30	257
Orestes Kindelán (Santiago)	.312	1460	318	456	84	9	107	363

Best Dozen Cuban League Pitchers of the Nineties

*Statistics for these pitchers are for decade between 1990–1999 only, and are not their lifetime stats.

Name (Team)	ERA	W–L	Pct.	E-Runs	Inn	SO	BB	OBA
Faustino Corrales (Pinar del Río)	**2.88**	55–19	.743	**204**	638	628	288	**.211**
Pedro Luis Lazo (Pinar del Río)	2.94	78–36	.684	308	944	754	349	.231
José Ibar (Habana)	3.13	**96–35**	.733	387	**1114**	**812**	323	.240
José Contreras (Pinar del Río)	3.16	67–32	.677	296	844	721	308	.235
Ernesto Guevara (Granma)	3.29	68–47	.591	348	952	634	244	.265
Oscar Gil (Holguín)	3.37	77–53	.592	362	968	665	323	.260
Ormari Romero (Santiago)	3.49	61–41	.598	337	870	392	**225**	.270
Omar Luis (Camagüey)	3.51	51–43	.543	301	772	806	381	.221
José M. Báez (Las Tunas)	3.71	66–58	.532	404	981	504	289	.262
Ciro Silvino Licea (Granma)	3.81	53–39	.576	335	792	517	247	.258
Lázaro Garro (Matanzas)	4.21	47–42	.528	353	754	372	307	.283
Carlos Yanes (Isla Juventud)	4.24	75–51	.595	503	1068	584	361	.280

hefty cannon still available in the amazing Cuban mound arsenal.

Lanky if spindly 25-year-old righthander Ciro Silvino Licea has been this writer's favorite prospect ever since I first saw him several winters back, during a breakout season (his sixth, in 1999) in which he posted a 16–4 won-lost mark and a brilliant league-best 1.85 ERA (across 185 innings) pitching for a Granma team that posted the best league record in the Eastern sector of the island. Licea's follow-up performance during 1999 Sydney Intercontinental Cup semifinals (13 Ks, 0 walks, and but 5 harmless hits allowed in a dominating 7–0 whitewashing of Team USA) seemed to signal his undisputed arrival as international mound star. And additional achievements during the same 1998–99 campaign — including 136 strikeouts against only 40 free passes — were enough to suggest almost certain future stardom. Licea would slip somewhat during the early 2000s, then suddenly revive his career with a dozen wins and a league best four shutouts in National Series XLIII (2004).

The list of top Cuban pitchers of the decade perhaps merits individual comments for the entire dozen selectees. Faustino Corrales has built a substantial reputation and some impressive numbers largely on the basis of a phenomenal curveball; that wrinkled pitch kept the veteran southpaw at the top of the CL 1990s list for mound stinginess, both in terms of scoring allowed (ERA) and opponents' aggregate batting average. Pedro Luis Lazo — the Lee Smith doppelgänger — posted the second highest winning total of the decade as well as the second-best ERA, and only a penchant for free passes kept Lazo out of the top spot in the latter category. Notably a switch to wooden bats at first appeared at work toward resolving the latter shortcoming as Lazo's ERA slid to 1.85 in 2000; but the improvement was only temporary as the mark leaped back to 4.33 in 2001 and 3.32 in 2002 (despite Lazo's sterling 11–4 and 15–5 winning records the same two seasons).

Soon-to-defect José Contreras was a relative newcomer among top Cuban aces in the late nineties and his career would only skyrocket after the decade had closed. Despite the somewhat advanced age of 30 by September 2001, Contreras would post 36 of his 94 wins in the trio of seasons (1999–2001) that marked the crossing of the millennium. Ibar made notable headlines near decade's end with the only 20-win campaign in island history and then proceeded to lump together the best consecutive seasons (1998–1999) in league annals: 38 wins (with but 4 defeats), a remarkable 1.90 ERA, and 347 strikeouts (against only 103 walks). Oft-injured righty Omar Luis was a talented national team veteran who causes writer Barros to puzzle aloud about a decade of inconsistent performances: how can the country's most effective strikeout ace (9.75 Ks per nine innings) who also allowed but three runs per every nine frames and a mere one hit for every five batters faced still manage to win only 51 games across a ten-year stretch?

Ernesto Guevara was perhaps the most surprising entrant among the top-dozen ranked pitchers: after two straight injury-riddle seasons with but six total wins this "Che" namesake rebounded for a 13–5 mark in 1999 which featured an ERA a shade under three runs per nine innings. Oscar Gil was yet another non-household name, even among veteran Cuban baseball watchers; Gil (pronounced "Hill") was a dedicated workhorse who managed to post the decade's third highest victory total despite laboring for a Holguín team (before its sudden resurgence in 2002) both lax on defense and notoriously weak on offense.

Ciro Silvino Licea (alongside then-teenager Maels Rodríguez in Sancti Spíritus) was the country's fastest rising nebula by the time of Barros's selections. Ormari Romero, in turn, remained perhaps Cuba's most consistent mound ace at 61–41 for the 1990s, although his luster had always been somewhat dimmed by lack of any single superior season. José M. Báez (with Las Tunas, 1999's losingest team at 30–60) was another hurler whose luster had been tarnished by his spot on an inferior roster: his National Series XXXVIII record was only 5–10 (3.71 ERA) but his decade-long ledger still remained slightly above sea level. Lázaro Garro burst on the scene only late in the decade's final season after a number of rather mediocre campaigns, registering 9 saves in 1999 and an overall 8–3 mark earned mostly in solid relief. If Matanzas could only have found an adequate closer, Garro might well have proven one of the most effective middle relievers in CL history. And while Báez and Silvino Licea (like Maels Rodríguez) were plagued by less-than-stellar support from teammates, Carlos Yanes (often spelled Llanes in CL guidebooks and press accounts) was regularly victimized by an inferior ballpark (at least from a pitching perspective), laboring for more than half his career starts in Nueva Gerona's tiny, eccentric and hit-happy Cristóbal Lara Stadium.

As Cuban baseball welcomed a new decade and a new century, the island appeared to be teeming with as much raw talent as ever. A trio of top young hurlers — Ciro Silvino Licea (Granma), Norge Vera (Santiago de Cuba), and Maels Rodríguez (Sancti Spiritus) seemed set to inherit the mantle from phemons of the past decade like José Contrares (Pinar del Río), José Ibar (Habana) and Lázaro Valle (Industriales). What had every indication of being an exciting (perhaps even a much-revived) National Series thus loomed on the horizon in November 1999, with Santiago de Cuba, despite an aging roster, seemingly prepared to defend its league title in grandiose style.

Santiago immediately reeled off 15 straight wins in the early weeks of the season and quickly made a shambles of any hoped-for pennant race. Kindelán and Pacheco and company would post 62 victories by season's end, the highest total since Habana rang up a 69–30 mark during an elongated National Series VIII at the tail end of the sixties. Manager Higinio Vélez and his crack club next swept through Camagüey, Granma and Pinar in eleven straight for an undefeated postseason. The 1999–2000 campaign also spurred more genuine fan interest on the island than any National Series of the past decade — due to the advent of wooden bats, the resulting overnight transition from hitters' to pitchers' circuit, and a seemingly palpable promise of renewed island visits in the spring from major league ballclubs. (The latter speculation of course provided a false dream.) And despite a disappointing gold medal extra-inning loss to the upstart Australians during November's Intercontinental Cup matches, the upcoming Olympic sessions in Sydney also promised to witness the vaunted Cubans once more installed as odds-on favorites for Olympic gold.

While "retro"-style ballparks disguised as lavish shopping malls — along with multi-million-dollar free-agent contracts and resulting musical-chairs rosters, plus expanded inter-league and postseason schedules — all finally conspired to render U.S. pro baseball almost totally unrecognizable for more tradition-minded fans, a far less commercialized international baseball scene seemed — at the dawn of a new millennium — still to be normal business as usual. Wooden bats were back on the scene for the first time in a full quarter-century. And the crimson-clad Cuban national team was still the prohibitive favorite in just about any senior-level or even junior-level world championship event. The more things changed, it seemed the more they only stayed the same.

But changes in island baseball, however gradual, are rarely predictable or even easily explicable. At the outset of the 1999 fall season the Cuban scene was literally rocked by 20-year-old Sancti Spíritus pitching sensation Maels Rodríguez. Rodríguez, barely recovered from off-season injury that kept him sidelined during the opening weeks of National Series XXXIX, opened eyes by hurling the first perfect game in CL history, handcuffing Las Tunas on December 22 in Estadio José Huelga. The stocky righthander (hurling for one of the circuit's less potent teams and thus posting a mere 7–11 mark the previous year, despite a brilliant 2.22 ERA) authored his masterpiece against admittedly the weakest lineup of the entire circuit. This rarest of diamond events nonetheless offered an appropriate exclamation point for opening-month CL action in which Cuban batters armed with less lively wooden bats were already experiencing considerable difficulty in catching up to superior league pitching. Earlier in the same month (ironically in the same ballpark and against the same Las Tunas club) Rodríguez had already made headlines by tossing the first-ever "officially measured" 100-plus mph pitch in nearly forty years of league action.

Easily the biggest story surrounding opening seasons of the new millennium was the sensational hurling of Maels Rodríguez. Maels had yet to distinguish himself on the international scene after the fashion of Linares or Kindelán (or pitchers Contreras, Lazo, and Ibar). But no single player in years had stirred more fan enthusiasm during National Series action than the fireballing righthander from Sancti Spíritus. Just as sluggers McGwire and Sosa seemed to rescue big league baseball from its doldrums a few seasons earlier, Maels would now play a similar role in Cuba. Maels would indeed be a short-lived comet in the heavens of Cuban baseball, crashing to earth with a damaged arm after only two sensational campaigns (200-plus strikeouts in both 2001 and 2002) and then fleeing his homeland when stripped of a spot on the natural team roster (an inevitable fallout when his crippled fastball fell below 85 mph). But while he lasted, Maels was as genuine a hero as any phenom from the preceding four decades of post-revolution baseball.

Orlando "El Duque" Hernández was the Cuban League all-time leader in winning percentage before his travels took him to the big leagues. El Duque's Cuban career mark with Industriales stood at 126–47 (.728 Pct.).

Anyone questioning the health of Cuban baseball needs only to look as far as the fortieth edition of the National Series completed in late May of 2001. The overall season was perhaps the best in Cuban annals and the supply of superstars once again seems unabated. Maels Rodríguez provided heroics uplifting the sagging Cuban League that were equal to those of McGwire and Sosa in their 1998 impact on the majors. A bevy of additional records were also broken: Maels himself encored with a new single-season strikeout mark and whiffed nearly half the batters he retired. Santiago de Cuba would distinguished itself during early seasons of the new century as perhaps the strongest team in league history, and yet pennant races and post-season playoffs during the same span were anything but lopsided runaways. Santiago's reign ended abruptly in 2002 when upstart Holguín not only claimed its first-ever title but reached the title round for the first time in its quarter-century history. With the emergence of surprise teams like Holguín and Sancti Spíritus (also in the finals in 2002) and with so many young hitting stars like Frederich

Cepeda, Yasser Gómez, and Osmani Urrutia — to say nothing of showcase pitchers like Norge Vera and Silvino Licea — the promise for coming National Series was indeed bright. And in Cuba there are no labor problems (overpaid megastars demanding more of the pie or capitalist owners hoping to hoard profits in their own coffers) to sully the game for its faithful fans. On the horizon lay a continued string of international championship to be topped by yet another Olympic title in Athens (September 2004). The Cuban League is by all accounts indeed very much alive and well.

Sancti Spíritus phenom right-hander Maels Rodríguez burned up Cuban League record books at the beginning of the 21st century with a single-season strikeout record (263 in a 90-game schedule), a 100-plus mph radar clocking, and the Cuban League's first-ever perfect game. An early arm injury and subsequent defection prematurely ended the career of Cuba's top mound prospect.

References and Suggested Readings

Bjarkman, Peter C. "Lifting the Iron Curtain of Cuban Baseball" in: *The National Pastime: A Review of Baseball History* 17 (1997), 31–35. Cleveland: Society for American Baseball Research.

Brown, Bruce. "Cuban Baseball" in: *Atlantic Monthly* (June 1984), 109–114.

Casas, Edel, with Jorge Alfonso, and Alberto Pestana. *Viva y en juego.* Havana: Editorial Científico-Technica, 1986.

Clark, Joe. "Australia is proud of its home-grown baseball talent" in: *International Baseball Rundown* 7:8 (September 1998), 12.

Fimrite, Ron. "In Cuba, It's Viva El Grande Old Game" in: *Sports Illustrated* (June 6, 1977), 69–80.

González Echevarría, Roberto. *The Pride of Havana: A History of Cuban Baseball.* New York: Oxford University Press, 1999.

Jamail, Milton. *Full Count: Inside Cuban Baseball.* Carbondale and Edwardsville: Southern Illinois University Press, 2000.

Padura, Leonardo, and Raúl Arce. *Estrellas del Béisbol — El Alma en El Terreno.* Havana: Editorial Abril, 1989.

Pettavino, Paula, and Geralyn Pye. *Sport in Cuba: The Diamond in the Rough.* Pittsburgh and London: University of Pittsburgh Press, 1994.

Rucker, Mark, and Peter C. Bjarkman. *Smoke: The Romance and Lore of Cuban Baseball.* New York: Total Sports Illustrated, 1999.

Thurston, Bill. "It's a Different Game" in: *International Baseball Rundown* 7:4 (May 1998), 4, 25.

Cuba's Post-Revolution Baseball Seasons

SEASON-BY-SEASON SUMMARIES OF
CUBAN NATIONAL SERIES, CUBAN SELECTIVE SERIES,
REVOLUTION CUPS, SUPER LEAGUE SERIES, AND
OTHER PROVINCIAL AND SUPER-PROVINCIAL
NATIONAL BASEBALL SERIES (1962–2005)

1962 National Series I

A remarkable over-night conversion from professional to amateur baseball structure is celebrated with the first National Series, including four teams each playing 27 scheduled games. Players for this first season are drawn from all provinces on the island. A central venue is Havana's 16-year-old Cerro Stadium (aka Gran Stadium), soon to be fittingly renamed Estadio Latinoamericano by Fidel Castro's revolutionary government. Long-time Cuban professional and amateur league star and former part-time major league catcher Fermín Guerra manages the Occidentales (Western) team to the first Cuban League (National Series) championship. Occidentales outfielder Erwin Walters (often Erwin Walter in league record books) captures the first batting title while Manuel Hernández (also Occidentales) is the top overall pitcher. Urbano González (Occidentales) establishes a pair of early individual marks with five hits and four runs scored in a single game versus Habana (February 17, 1962).

Champion — Occidentales (18–9) Manager: Fermín Guerra

Standings — Occidentales (18–9), Azucareros (13–14), Orientales (13–14), Habana (10–17)

Batting Leaders — **BA**: Erwin Walters (OCC) .367; **H**: Urbano González (OCC) 40; **R**: Urbano González 19; **2B**:

Tomás Soto (OCC) 10; **3B**: Daniel Hernández (OTE) 3; **HR**: Rolando Valdéz (OTE) 3; **RBI**: Tomás Soto, Pedro Carvajal (OCC), Ramón Hecheverría (OTE) 19; **SB**: Everildo Hernández (OTE) 10.

Pitching Leaders—**Pct**.: Rolando Pastor (OCC), Julio Morales (HAB) 3–1 (.750); **G**: Jorge Santin (AZU), Julio Morales (HAB) 13; **CG**: Manuel Hernández (OCC) 7; **Wins**: Manuel Hernández 6; **IP**: Manuel Hernández 76.2; **SO**: Manuel Hernández 94; **ERA**: Antonio Rubio (OCC) 1.39.

No-Hit/No-Run Games— None

1962–1963 National Series II

Havana-based Industriales — an early league powerhouse and long-reigning fan-favorite in future seasons — captures its first of four consecutive titles, edging Orientales in a special tie-breaker three-game playoff. The league's base-hits leader, Fidel Linares (Occidentales), is destined soon to father of a pair of future stars, Omar and Juan Carlos Linares (who will both debut in the 1980s). Early successes and strengths of the new Cuban League as a mechanism for selecting national team players are underscored by Cuba's surprise gold medal victory over the USA in the fourth Pan American Games staged in Brazil in late April.

Champion— Industriales (16–14) Manager: Ramón Carneado

Playoffs— Industriales over Orientales, 2–1 (Playoff series to break regular-season tie)

Standings— Industriales (16–14), Orientales (16–14), Occidentales (15–15), Azucareros (13–17)

Batting Leaders—**BA**: Raúl González (OCC) .348; **H**: Fidel Linares (OCC) 36; **R**: Antonio González (OCC) 24; **2B**: Jorge Trigoura (IND), Rolando Valdés (OTE) 7; **3B**: Antonio Jiménez (IND) 5; **HR**: Rolando Valdéz, Miguel Cuevas (OTE) 3; **RBI**: Jorge Trigoura 20; **SB**: Antonio Jiménez 8.

Pitching Leaders—**Pct**.: Modesto Verdura (AZU) 7–1 (.875); **G**: Rolando Pastor (IND) 15; **CG**: Modesto Verdura, Manuel Alarcón (OTE) 6; **Wins**: Modesto Verdura, Manuel Alarcón 3; **IP**: Modesto Verdura 79.2; **SO**: Modesto Verdura 55; **ERA**: Modesto Verdura 1.58.

No-Hit/No-Run Games— None

1963–1964 National Series III

Industriales under manager Ramón Carneado makes it two consecutive championships by posting the season's only winning record in a one-sided pennant chase. In a memorable game played at the historic Palmar del Junco ballpark in Matanzas (October 3, 1964), Industriales and Occidentales set a league record with 33 total runs scored. Industriales, 19–14 winner in this slugfest, also establishes a second mark by recording eight consecutive base hits in a single inning. Pedro Cháves, one of the decades' top performers, establishes an early league record with his modest 12-game hitting streak. Cháves is also the season-long batting star with a healthy .333 average, holding as well the league leadership in triples and runs batted in. Orlando Rubio (Industriales) becomes the first pitcher in league history (there will eventually be 14 more) to

top the circuit with an ERA of less than one-run per nine-inning game. For the first time tied games are counted as official games and thus recorded in the final league standings.

Champion— Industriales (22–13) Manager: Ramón Carneado

Standings— Industriales (22–13–0), Occidentales (18–18–2), Azucareros (17–19–1), Orientales (14–21–1)

Batting Leaders—**BA**: Pedro Chávez (OCC) .333; **H**: Miguel Cuevas (OTE) 44; **R**: Rigoberto Rosique (OCC) 34; **2B**: Eulogio Osorio (IND), Fidel Linares (OCC) 8; **3B**: Pedro Chávez 7; **HR**: Jorge Trigoura (IND) 3; **RBI**: Pedro Chávez 27; **SB**: Féliz Isasi (OCC) 15.

Pitching Leaders—**Pct**.: Isidoro Borrego (OCC) 4–0 (1.000); **G**: Roman Aguila (AZU) 22; **CG**: Rolando Pastor (OCC), Manuel Alarcón (OTE) 5; **Wins**: Roman Aguila, Manuel Hurtado (IND) 6; **IP**: Aquino Abreu (AZU) 102.2; **SO**: Rolando Pastor 97; **ERA**: Orlando Rubio (IND) 0.63.

No-Hit/No-Run Games— None

1964–1965 National Series IV

Industriales runs its championship streak to three straight while outfielder Urbano González — the team's top batsman — ends the three-year run of batting titles claimed by Occidentales ballplayers (Erwin Walter, Raúl González, Pedro Cháves). Antonio Jiménez wins the second of his eventual six stolen base titles, earned with three different league teams. Manuel Alarcón is the first pitcher to strike out more than 100 in a league season, accomplishing the feat in 94.2 innings. This is the last season played with only four teams and also the last before the major schedule expansion to a 65-game season. On October 11, 1965, Orlando "El Duque" Hernández (son of journeyman Industriales pitcher Arnaldo Hernández) is born in Havana, between the fourth and fifth National Series seasons.

Champion— Industriales (25–14) Manager: Ramón Carneado

Standings— Industriales (25–14), Occidentales (21–18), Granjeros (18–21), Orientales (14–25)

Batting Leaders—**BA**: Urbano González (IND) .359; **H**: Lino Betancourt (IND) 56; **R**: Antonio Jiménez (OCC) 30; **2B**: Lino Betancourt 6; **3B**: Rolando Valdés (GRA) 5; **HR**: Miguel Cuevas (GRA) 5; **RBI**: Miguel Cuevas 28; **SB**: Antonio Jiménez (OCC) 16.

Pitching Leaders—**Pct**.: Alfredo Street (OCC) 2–0 (1.000); **G**: Ernesto Alfonso (IND), Roman Aguila (AZU) 20; **CG**: Florentino Alfonso (GRA) 5; **Wins**: Maximiliano Reyes (IND), Gaspar Pérez (OCC) 6; **IP**: Manuel Alarcón (OTE) 94.2; **SO**: Manuel Alarcón (OTE) 101; **ERA**: Maximiliano Reyes 1.57.

No-Hit/No-Run Games— None

1965–1966 National Series V

Top stories are a fourth consecutive title for Industriales (this time narrow winners over both Orientales and Henequeneros) and the remarkable no-hit hurling of diminutive Aquino Abreu, laboring for the last-place Centrales ball club.

Crafty righthander Abreu matches the unique major league feat of Cincinnati's Johnny Vander Meer (1939) by tossing consecutive no-hitters and in the process establishes a yet-unbroken Cuban record with 19 consecutive hitless innings. Outside of league play the Cubans launch a resurrection of their long-dormant status as an international baseball power by capturing first place at the 10th Central American Games tournament staged in San Juan, Puerto Rico.

Champion— Industriales (40–25) Manager: Ramón Carneado

Standings— Industriales (40–25), Orientales (38–27), Henequeneros (37–28), Occidentales (29–35), Granjeros (26–38), Centrales (23–40)

Batting Leaders—**BA**: Miguel Cuevas (GRA) .325; **H**: Urbano González (IND) 76; **R**: Félix Isasi (HEN) 44; **2B**: Andrés Telémaco (OTE) 12; **3B**: Agustín Marquetti (IND) 5; **HR**: Lino Betancourt (HEN) 9; **RBI**: Lino Betancourt 45; **SB**: Félix Isasi 24.

Pitching Leaders—**Pct.**: Justino Gavilan (OTE) 6–1 (.875); **G**: Lázaro Santana (OTE), Raúl López (OCC) 28; **CG**: Alberto Reyes (GRA) 7; **Wins**: Gaspar Pérez (HEN) 11; **IP**: Carlos Galvez (CEN) 115.0; **SO**: Rigoberto Betancourt (OCC) 103; **ERA**: Alfredo Street (IND) 1.09.

No-Hit/No-Run Games—**Aquino Abreu** (Centrales 10–11–1, Occidentals 0–0–6, 1–16–66); **Aquino Abreu** (Centrales 7–8–0, Industriales 0–0–2, 1–25–66*) *Back-to-back no-hitters in consecutive starts for Abreu.

1966–1967 National Series VI

Orientales — behind the slugging of Miguel Cuevas (the league's RBI leader) and the pitching of Manuel Alarcón and Roberto Valdés — ends the Industriales pennant string with a narrow one-game margin over the defending champions. Valdés tosses the league's third no-hitter in a lopsided 12–0 whitewashing of the Granjeros in mid–February. Another remarkable pitching feat is the league-best 8–1 record of Román Aguila who hurled for a break-even Centrales team. Ihosvany Gallego (Occidentales) allows but six earned runs while pitching 67.2 innings. This is the last season with six teams and also the last year of the 65-game schedule. It was also during this season that admission charges for Cuban League baseball games (as well as for all other sporting events held on the island) were eliminated.

Champion— Orientales (36–29) Manager: Roberto Ledo

Standings— Orientales (36–29), Industriales (35–30), Occidentales (34–31), Centrales (33–32), Las Villas (30–35), Granjeros (27–38)

Batting Leaders—**BA**: Pedro Chávez (IND) .318; **H**: Pedro Chávez 78; **R**: Félix Isasi (CEN) 39; **2B**: Felipe Sarduy (GRA) 14; **3B**: Silvio Montejo (LVS) 8; **HR**: Erwin Walters (CEN) 7; **RBI**: Miguel Cuevas (OTE) 38; **SB**: Félix Isasi 31.

Pitching Leaders—**Pct.**: Roman Aguila (CEN) 8–1 (.889); **G**: Raúl López (IND) 30; **CG**: Manuel Alarcón (OTE) 11; **Wins**: Rigoberto Betancourt (OCC), Rolando Macías (LVS) 10; **IP**: Florentino Alfonso (GRA) 126.1; **SO**: Rigoberto Betancourt 126; **ERA**: Ihosvany Gallego (OCC) 0.80.

No-Hit/No-Run Game—**Roberto Valdés** (Orientales 12–16–0, Granjeros 0–0–6, 2–14–67)

1967–1968 National Series VII

In a remarkable season of no-hit performances five different pitchers throw masterpieces in a mere three-month stretch, the first two coming on the same day and ironically involving both Havana-based teams. Habana, under manager, Juan Gómez captures its first pennant and establishes a still-unbroken record for victories in the extended 99-game season. In this apparent "year of pitchers" Braudilio Vinent breaks onto the scene with his first ERA title and Modesto Verdura at 11–0 posts the best record for a league pitcher to date. Habana's Julio Rojo enters the league record books with 18 pitching victories, yet another aberration of a lengthy season. Also benefiting from the increased schedule, Eulogio Osorio is the first batter to register more than 100 base hits (with 129). Raúl Reyes (Industriales) provides still another "first" in the history of the post-revolution Cuban League by smacking three homers in a single game (versus the Azucareros on January 18, 1968); the performance also includes two grand slams and 11 runs batted in. Pinar del Río establishes an unenviable record with the most losses ever during a National Series season.

Champion— Habana (74–25) Manager: Juan Gómez

Standings— Habana (74–25–0), Industriales (69–30–0), Azucareros (63–35–0), Mineros (61–38–0), Las Villas (57–41–1), Henequeneros (57–42–0), Granjeros (49–49–0), Orientales (48–51–0), Camagüeyanos (37–62–0), Matanzas (36–63–0), Vegueros (33–65–1), Pinar del Río (12–85–2)

Batting Leaders—**BA**: José Pérez (AZU) .328; **H**: Eulogio Osorio (HAB) 129; **R**: Antonio Jiménez (IND) 72; **2B**: Eulogio Osorio 24; **3B**: Fermín Laffita (MIN) 8; **HR**: Felipe Sarduy (GRA) 13; **RBI**: Miguel Cuevas (GRA) 86; **SB**: Juan Díaz Olmo (LVS) 52.

Pitching Leaders—**Pct.**: Modesto Verdura (LVS) 11–0 (1.000); **G**: Raúl López (IND) 41; **CG**: Gaspar Pérez (MTZ) 18; **Wins**: Julio Rojo (HAB) 18; **IP**: Gaspar Pérez 212.2; **SO**: Manuel Alarcón (MIN) 200; **ERA**: Braudilio Vinent (MIN) 1.03.

No-Hit/No-Run Games—**Leopoldo Valdés** (Habana 5–12–0, Pinar del Río 0–0–0, 1–7–68); **Jesús Pérez** (Industriales 5–9–2, Vegueros 0–0–4, 1–7–68); **José Huelga** (Azucareros 1–7–1, Granjeros 0–0–1, 1–14–68); **Orlando Figueredo** (Oriente 1–2–1, Azucareros 0–0–1, 1–25–68); **Florentino González** (Camagüeyanos 1–8–0, Matanzas 0–0–2, 4–4–68)

1968 All-Star Series I

Champion— Orientales (5–3–1) Manager: Pedro Jiménez

Standings— Orientales (5–3–1), Occidentales (3–5–1)

Batting Leaders—**BA**: Pedro Cháves (OCC) .357; **H**: Pedro Cháves, Felipe Sarduy (OTE), Eulogio Osorio (OCC) 10; **R**: Felipe Sarduy 7; **2B**: Eulogio Osorio, Elpidio Mancebo (OTE), 3; **3B**: Felipe Sarduy 2; **HR**: Felipe Sarduy 2; **SB**: Felipe Sarduy 2.

Pitching Leaders—**CG**: José Huelga (OTE), Manuel Alarcón (OTE) 2; **Wins**: José Huelga 2; **IP**: José Huelga 38.1; **SO**: José Huelga 21; **BB**: José Huelga 15; **ERA**: Andrés Liaño (OCC) 0.36.

No-Hit/No-Run Games— None

1968–1969 National Series VIII

Santiago "Changa" Mederos (Habana) emerges as the league's new pitching phenom with a single-season record of 208 strikeouts, plus a record-breaking 20 Ks in a single contest (versus Camagüey on January 30, 1969). Mederos's 208 Ks will not be bested for another three decades, standing until 20-year-old Maels Rodríguez (Sancti Spíritus) establishes a new standard in 2001. The spate of no-hit and no-run games also continues with three more "perfectos" being rung up by Raúl Alvarez, Andrés Liaños and Alfredo García. Yet another new league star debuts when lefthanded swinger Wilfredo Sánchez claims his first of five eventual National Series batting crowns and raises the single-season base-hits record to 140. Habana slugger Agustín Marquetti captures his first home run crown with a record 19 roundtrippers. Three years after his remarkable double-no-hitter performance, Aquino Abreu enjoys his "career" season by posting a sterling 10–1 record for the Azucareros. For the second straight year a brief All-Star Series follows regular-season action.

Champion— Azucareros (69–30) Manager: Servio Borges

Standings— Azucareros (69–30), Industriales (68–31), Habana (68–31), Mineros (62–37), Granjeros (57–42), Henequeneros (55–43), Las Villas (45–53), Pinar del Río (43–56), Matanzas (35–64), Oriente (33–66), Vegueros (32–67), Camagüey (26–73)

*Batting Leaders—***BA**: Wilfredo Sánchez (HEN) .354; **H**: Wilfredo Sánchez 140; **R**: Antonio Jiménez (IND) 84; **2B**: Elpidio Mancebo (MIN) 26; **3B**: Wilfredo Sánchez 13; **HR**: Agustín Marquetti (HAB) 19; **RBI**: Agustín Marquetti 85; **SB**: Antonio Jiménez 49.

*Pitching Leaders—***Pct.**: Aquino Abreu (AZU) 10–1 (.909); **G**: Lázaro Santana (GRA) 43; **CG**: Roberto Valdés (MIN), Emilio Salgado (VEG) 20; **Wins**: Santiago "Changa" Mederos (HAB), Rolando Macías (AZU) 17; **IP**: Emilio Salgado 230.1; **SO**: Santiago Mederos 208; **ERA**: Roberto Valdés 1.03.

*No-Hit/No-Run Games—***Raúl Alvarez** (Pinar del Río 9–10–1, Camagüey 0–0–8, 12–10–68); **Andrés Liaño** (Industriales 8–8–1, Pinar del Río 0–0–6, 2–4–69); **Alfredo García** (Henequeneros 1–5–3, Azucareros 0–0–0, 4–6–69)

1969 All-Star Series II

Champion— Orientales (5–4) Manager: Servio Borges

Standings— Orientales (5–4), Occidentales (4–5)

*Batting Leaders—***BA**: Rigoberto Rosique (OCC) .389; **H**: Rigoberto Rosique 14; **R**: Andrés Telemaco (OTE) 9; **2B**: Elpidio Mancebo (OTE) 4; **3B**: Andrés Telemaco, Rigoberto Rosique 1; **HR**: Miguel Cuevas (OTE) 3; **RBI**: Rigoberto Rosique 9; **SB**: Felipe Sarduy (OTE), Wilfredo Sánchez (OCC), Félix Isasi (OCC) 2.

*Pitching Leaders—***CG**: Santiago Mederos (OCC), Manuel Hurtado (OCC), Andrés Liaño (OCC) 1; **Wins**:

Roberto Valdés (OTE) 2; **IP**: Santiago Mederos 18.2; **SO**: Santiago Mederos 17; **BB**: Orlando Figueredo (OTE) 11; **ERA**: Rolando Macías (OTE) 0.82.

No-Hit/No-Run Games— None

1969–1970 National Series IX

The final season of the league's first decade features a pioneering attempt at staging a late-spring and early-summer "second season" dubbed the "Series of the Ten Million" (the name refers to Fidel's goal of ten million tons for that year's sugar harvest, with the tournament promoted as entertainment for the sugar industry workers). Sixty-six games of the National Series are thus followed by a still-longer campaign with each team playing 89 times. Henequeneros is victorious for the first time in the National Series and posts the best team won-lost percentage to date (it will remain the eighth-best ever). Wilfredo "El Hombre Hit" Sánchez dominates individual hitting statistics as league-leader in batting average, runs scored and base hits for both championship seasons. It is the second National Series batting title in a row for Sánchez, who will remain Cuba's top hitter for most of the coming decade. Tie games (there were three) were counted in the official league standings.

Champion— Henequeneros (50–16) Manager: Miguel Domínguez

Standings— Henequeneros (50–16–0), Mineros (48–17–0), Azucareros (46–20–0), Industriales (43–22–1), Habana (35–31–0), Granjeros (33–32–1), Pinar del Río (29–36–0), Las Villas (27–38–0), Matanzas (26–36–2), Camagüey (19–47–0), Oriente (18–47–1), Vegueros (16–48–1)

*Batting Leaders—***BA**: Wilfredo Sánchez (HEN) .351; **H**: Wilfredo Sánchez 98; **R**: Wilfredo Sánchez 46; **2B**: Miguel Telemaco (OTE) 16; **3B**: Armando Sánchez (HEN) 6; **HR**: Raúl Reyes (IND) 10; **RBI**: Fermin Laffita (MIN) 44; **SB**: Wilfredo Sánchez 34.

*Pitching Leaders—***Pct.**: Rolando Macías (AZU) 6–0 (1.000); **G**: Oscar Romero (GRA) 28; **CG**: Santiago Mederos (IND) 13; **Wins**: Gregorio Pérez (GRA), Alfredo García (HEN) 12; **IP**: Santiago Mederos 136.2; **SO**: Santiago Mederos 143; **ERA**: Rolando Castillo (MIN) 0.60.

*No-Hit/No-Run Game—***Rigoberto Betancourt** (Industriales 1–3–2, Oriente 0–0–1, 1–7–70)

1970 Series of the Ten Million

Champion— Las Villas (56–33) Manager: Servio Borges

Standings— Las Villas (56–33), Habana (54–35), Camagüey (44–43), Oriente (40–46), Matanzas (39–48), Pinar del Río (30–58)

*Batting Leaders—***BA**: Wilfredo Sánchez (MTZ) .367; **H**: Wilfredo Sánchez 116; **R**: Wilfredo Sánchez 47; **2B**: Vicente Díaz (CMG) 20; **3B**: Antonio Muñoz (LVS) 9; **HR**: Agustín Marquetti (HAB) 12; **RBI**: Miguel Cuevas (CMG) 51; **SB**: Antonio Jiménez (HAB) 27.

*Pitching Leaders—***Pct.**: José Huelga (LVS) 11–1 (.917); **G**: Ernesto Alfonso (MTZ) 39; **CG**: Santiago Mederos (HAB), Roberto Valdés (OTE), Alfredo García (MTZ) 9; **Wins**: Oscar

Romero (CAM) 13; **IP**: Alfredo García 161.1; **SO**: Alfredo García 129; **ERA**: Rolando Macías (LVS) 0.69.

No-Hit/No-Run Games— None

1970–1971 National Series X

On the eve of a tenth Cuban League season José Antonio Huelga becomes a national hero with his brilliant mound performance at the Amateur World Series XVIII tournament staged in Cartagena and Baranquilla, Colombia. Fresh off an 11–1 performance for Las Villas in the previous summer's "Series of Ten Million" in Havana, Huelga twice defeats Team USA in the championship round, one victory coming over future big-league headliner Burt Hooten. In league play, the Azucareros capture their second title under manager Servio Borges in a three-year span. Industriales ace Manuel Hurtado posts the lowest ERA in Cuban League history by a pitcher logging more than 100 innings. At season's end Estadio Latinoamericano (now renamed) is remodeled and expanded to a seating capacity of 55,000 in preparation for the late-summer Amateur World Championships XIX scheduled for Havana.

Champion— Azucareros (49–16) Manager: Pedro Delgado

Standings— Azucareros (49–16–0), Habana (48–18–0), Industriales (47–19–0), Granjeros (47–19–0), Mineros (40–26–0), Henequeneros (40–26–0), Vegueros (29–36–0), Oriente (23–42–1), Las Villas (22–43–1), Camagüey (20–46–0), Matanzas (18–48–0), Pinar del Río (11–55–0)

*Batting Leaders—***BA**: Rigoberto Rosique (HEN) .352; **H**: Elpidio Mancebo (MIN) 77; **R**: Antonio Jiménez (HAB) 53; **2B**: Antonio Muñoz (AZU) 19; **3B**: Antonio Jiménez, Pedro Cruz (GRA) 6; **HR**: Miguel Cuevas (GRA) 10; **RBI**: Armando Capiró (IND) 51; **SB**: Antonio Jiménez 43.

*Pitching Leaders—***Pct.**: Antonio Jiménez (IND) 14–1 (.933); **G**: Eduardo de la Torre (MTZ) 24; **CG**: Rodoberto Pan (LVS) 14; **Wins**: Antonio Jiménez 14; **IP**: Rodoberto Pan 143.1; **SO**: Braudilio Vinent (MIN) 112; **ERA**: Manuel Hurtado (IND) 0.67.

*No-Hit/No-Run Games—***Walfrido Ruíz** (winner) and **Elpidio Paez** (Habana 10–9–2, Camagüeyanos 0–0–6, 1–16–71); **Aniceto Montes de Oca** (Azucareros 5–10–1, Pinar del Río 0–0–3, 1–21–71)

1971 All-Star Series III

Champion— Occidentales (6–3) Manager: Pedro Cháves
Standings— Occidentales (6–3), Orientales (3–6)
*Batting Leaders—***BA**: Juan Díaz (OTE) .455; **H**: Juan Díaz, Félix Isasi (OCC) 10; **R**: Elpidio Mancedo (OTE), Vicente Díaz (OTE) 4; **2B**: Félix Isasi, Agustín Marquetti (OCC) 3; **HR**: Eusebio Cruz (OTE) 2; **RBI**: Armando Capiró (OCC) 5.

*Pitching Leaders—***CG**: Roberto Valdés (OTE), Juan Pérez (OTE), Walfrido Ruíz (OCC), Santiago Mederos (OCC) 1; **Wins**: Walfrido Ruíz 2; **IP**: José Huelga (OTE) 21.2; **SO**: Walfrido Ruíz 13; **BB**: Emilio Salgado (OCC) 11; **ERA**: Walfrido Ruíz 0.57.

No-Hit/No-Run Games— None

1971–1972 National Series XI

Despite a managerial change, the Azucareros make it three titles in four years by nipping Mineros two-games-to-one in the tie-breaking championship playoff. Two of the top sluggers of the 1970s shine as Agustín Marquetti recaptures the home run and RBI crowns and Antonio Muñoz paces the circuit in runs scored. Hurling for Industriales, Ihosvany Gallego allows only three earned runs in 72-plus innings to ring up the lowest recorded ERA in league annals. In postseason international play Cuba captures the 20th Amateur World Series title, partially on the strength of a dramatic home run slugged by Marquetti in the deciding game versus the archrival USA squad in Managua. In this same tournament two other Cuban League stars also played crucial roles: Wilfredo Sánchez batted at a hefty .414 clip and fellow outfielder Armando Capiró knocked home a tournament-best 21 runs.

Champion— Azucareros (52–14) Manager: Servio Borges
Playoffs— Azucareros over Mineros, 2–1 (Finals)
Standings— Azucareros (52–14), Mineros (52–14), Industriales (51–15), Granjeros (49–17), Henequeneros (40–26), Habana (32–34), Vegueros (29–37), Oriente (24–42), Camagüey (19–47), Las Villas (18–48), Pinar del Río (17–49), Matanzas (13–53)

*Batting Leaders—***BA**: Elpidio Mancebo (MIN) .327; **H**: Wilfredo Sánchez (HEN) 90; **R**: Antonio Muñoz (AZU) 51; **2B**: Felipe Sarduy (GRA) 16; **3B**: Pablo Espinoza (OTE) 5; **HR**: Agustín Marquetti (IND) 11; **RBI**: Agustín Marquetti 53; **SB**: Antonio Jiménez (HAB) 28.

*Pitching Leaders—***Pct.**: Roberto Valdés (MIN) 12–0 (1.000); **G**: Domingo Pérez (VEG) 29; **CG**: Mario Fernández (OTE) 13; **Wins**: Orlando Figueredo (MIN) 14; **IP**: Mario Fernández 151.1; **SO**: Braudilio Vinent (MIN) 127; **ERA**: Ihosvany Gallego (IND) 0.37.

No-Hit/No-Run Games— None

1972 All-Star Series IV

Champion— Orientales (9–6) Manager: Servio Borges
Standings— Orientales (9–6), Occidentales (6–9)
*Batting Leaders—***BA**: Agustín Arias (OTE) .378; **H**: Pedro Jova (OTE) 18; **R**: Agustín Arias, Pedro Jova, Germán Aguila (OCC) 7; **2B**: Arturo Linares (OCC) 4; **3B**: Pedro Jova 3; **RBI**: Félix Isasi (OCC) 9; **SB**: Wilfredo Sánchez (OCC) 5.

*Pitching Leaders—***CG**: Rodovaldo Esquivel (OCC) 2; **Wins**: Rodovaldo Esquivel 3; **IP**: Rodovaldo Esquivel 26.2; **SO**: Braudilio Vinent (OTE), Bernardo González (OCC) 16; **BB**: Rodovaldo Esquivel 10; **ERA**: Rodovaldo Esquivel 0.68.

No-Hit/No-Run Games— None

1972–1973 National Series XII

With his 19 victories Braudilio Vinent establishes a winning standard that will not be surpassed for nearly three decades, the record finally falling only in 1997–98 when José Ibar becomes the first National Series pitcher to capture 20 wins in a season. Industriales returns to the victory circle after a lengthy seven-year drought, edging rival Habana by a margin of only three games. Armando Capiró smashes the existing home run record of Agustín Marquetti by banging 22 roundtrippers in 74 contests. The overwhelming strength of Cuban pitching is demonstrated at the 21st World Championships in Havana when the home staff tosses 110 whitewash innings and eleven straight shutouts throughout tournament play. Julio Romero is the ace of the Cuban staff at the tournament, delivering 26 innings without yielding a single earned run.

Champion— Industriales (53–25) Manager: Pedro Chávez

Standings— Industriales (53–25–0), Habana (50–28–0), Azucareros (46–28–1), Constructores (46–31–0), Camagüey (44–33–0), Oriente (42–35–1), Serranos (42–36–0), Granjeros (40–38–0), Vegueros (38–40–0), Matanzas (34–44–0), Mineros (32–45–0), Las Villas (32–46–0), Pinar del Río (28–47–0), Henequeneros (13–64–0)

Batting Leaders—**BA**: Eusebio Cruz (CMG) .341; **H**: Wilfredo Sánchez (MTZ) 95; **R**: Elpidio Mancebo (OTE) 56; **2B**: Arturo Linares (IND) 20; **3B**: René Moya (CMG) 7; **HR**: Armando Capiró (HAB) 22; **RBI**: Armando Capiró 74; **SB**: Antonio Jiménez (IND) 36.

Pitching Leaders—**Pct.**: Juan Chávez (IND) 6–1 (.875); **G**: Andres Layva (LVS), Elpidio Paez (IND) 32; **CG**: Braudilio Vinent (SER), Orlando Figueredo (OTE) 17; **Wins**: Braudilio Vinent 19; **IP**: Orlando Figueredo (OTE) 199.2; **SO**: Alfredo García (HEN) 160; **ERA**: Braudilio Vinent 0.85.

No-Hit/No-Run Game—**Juan Pérez Pérez** (Camagüey 7–10–0, Serranos 0–0–3, 2–22–73)

1973 All-Star Series V

Champion— Selección (8–4) Manager: Servio Borges
Standings— Selección (8–4), Industriales (4–8)
Batting Leaders—**BA**: Ubaldo Alvarez (SEL) .467; **H**: Wilfredo Sánchez (SEL) 12; **R**: Antonio Muñoz (SEL) 6; **2B**: Armando Capiró (IND) 2; **3B**: Antonio Muñoz, Leonardo Vilá (IND) 1; **HR**: Armando Capiró 3; **RBI**: Armando Capiró 6.

Pitching Leaders—**Wins**: Angel García (SEL) 2; **ERA**: Luis Barreiro (IND) 0.00.

No-Hit/No-Run Games— None

1973–1974 National Series XIII

This is the last season for two decades in which the National Series will hold center stage alone as the showpiece of the Cuban baseball season. Antonio Muñoz captures his first of two National Series home run titles, matching the 19 socked by Marquetti five seasons earlier, and is also the RBI pacesetter. Muñoz would soon prove the top Cuban slugger of the late 1970s with an additional six home run championships earned in the longer Selective Series seasons that were soon to begin. Habana meanwhile earns its second pennant on the strength of 11–2 pitching by Oscar Martínez and balanced overall offensive and pitching performances from a team without superstars. Juan Pérez pitches a no-hitter for the second straight season (the string will run to three a year later). Tie games are once again counted in league standings.

Champion— Habana (52–26) Manager: Jorge Trigoura
Standings— Habana (52–26–0), Constructores (47–31–0), Azucareros (46–32–0), Granjeros (44–34–0), Serranos (42–35–1), Camagüey (41–35–1), Pinar del Río (39–39–0), Vegueros (39–39–0), Industriales (39–39–0), Oriente (39–39–0), Las Villas (32–46–0), Matanzas (28–49–0), Henequeneros (28–50–0), Mineros (28–50–0)

Batting Leaders—**BA**: Rigoberto Rosique (HEN) .347; **H**: Lázaro Cabrera (PRI) 99; **R**: Antonio Muñoz (AZU) 54; **2B**: Eusebio Cruz (CAM) 17; **3B**: Sandalio Hernández (GRA) 9; **HR**: Antonio Muñoz (AZU) 19; **RBI**: Antonio Muñoz 68; **SB**: Reinaldo Linares (CON) 18.

Pitching Leaders—**Pct.**: Oscar Martínez (HAB) 11–2 (.846); **G**: Elpidio Paez (IND) 36; **CG**: Braudilio Vinent (SER), Alfredo García (HEN) 16; **Wins**: Braudilio Vinent (SER), Rafael Castillo (SER) 14; **IP**: Braudilio Vinent 191.2; **SO**: Julio Romero (VEG) 160; **ERA**: Juan Pérez Pérez (CAM) 1.13.

No-Hit/No-Run Game—**Juan Pérez Pérez** (Camagüey 1–10–1, Oriente 0–0–1, 4–25–74)

1974 All-Star Series VI

Champion— Habana (4–2) Manager: Jorge Trigoura
Standings— Habana (4–2), Selección (2–4)
Batting Leaders—**BA**: Reinaldo Linares (HAB) .348; **H**: Sandalio Hernández (SEL) 9; **R**: Antonio Muñoz (SEL) 6; **2B**: Reinaldo Linares 2; **HR**: Armando Capiró (HAB) 2; **RBI**: Armando Capiró 4; **SB**: Rodolfo Salazar (HAB), Reinaldo Linares 2.

Pitching Leaders—**Wins**: Bernardo González (HAB) 3; **ERA**: Braudilio Vinent (SEL) 0.00.

No-Hit/No-Run Games— None

1974–1975 National Series XIV (Provincial)

The National Series is scaled back from 78 to 39 games, with a second Selective Series and a third Special Series both tacked on in spring and early summer. This change comes in conjunction with redivision of Cuba into 14 provinces in May 1975 and is motivated by a desire in INDER for a higher-level tournament to select national team players. Fourteen National Series teams are collapsed into half that number for the longer Selective Series competitions. Oriente (representing the eastern provinces) edges Camagüeyanos by a single game to claim an inaugural Selective Series championship. Future national team manager Alfonso Urquiola is the first Selective Series batting champion and Armando Caprió and Antonio Muñoz share a home run crown. José Antonio Huelga, star pitcher in the 1970 Amateur World Series, is killed in a tragic July automobile accident. Huelga was still active in his seventh season with a 73–32 lifetime mound record at the point of his untimely death.

Champion— Agricultores (24–15) Manager: Orlando Leroux

Standings— Agricultores (24–15), Constructores (23–16), Vegueros (23–16), Citricultores (22–17), Granjeros (22–17), Metropolitanos (21–17), Cafetaleros (21–18), Ganaderos

(20–18), Serranos (18–21), Mineros (18–21), Azucareros (17–22), Forestales (17–22), Arroceros (13–26), Henequeneros (13–26)

Batting Leaders—**BA**: Fermín Lafitta (CAF) .396; **H**: Eulogio Osorio (AGR) 58; **R**: Anselmo Hernández (GRA) 29; **2B**: Arturo Linares (AGR), Raúl Reyes (CON) 11; **3B**: Julian Villar (AGR) 5; **HR**: Fernando Sánchez (HEN) 6; **RBI**: Armando Capiró (MET) 27; **SB**: Wilfredo Sánchez (CIT) 14.

Pitching Leaders—**Pct.**: Walfrido Ruíz (AGR) 9–0 (1.000); **G**: Ramón Villabrille (MET) 18; **CG**: Omar Carrero (GAN), Gregorio Pérez (CAF) 8; **Wins**: Walfrido Ruíz 9; **IP**: Santiago Mederos (AGR) 91.2; **SO**: Santiago Mederos 92; **ERA**: Walfrido Ruíz 0.62.

No-Hit/No-Run Game—**Juan Pérez Pérez** (Ganaderos 2–7–0, Citricultores 0–0–0, 1–19–75)

1974–75 Special Series (Super-Provincial)

Champion—Vegueros (32–22) Manager: José Pineda
Standings—Vegueros (32–22), Constructores (32–22), Serranos (31–23), Mineros (26–26), Granjeros (26–27), Henequeneros (20–33), Azucareros (20–34)
Batting Leaders—**BA**: Rogelio Montes de Oca (CON) .348; **H**: Rogelio Montes de Oca 73; **R**: José Sierra (CON) 47; **2B**: Romilio Romero (SER) 17; **3B**: José Sierra 11; **HR**: Jorge Francis (SER) 11; **RBI**: Jorge Francis 46; **SB**: José Sierra 24.
Pitching Leaders—**Wins**: José Brizuela (SER), Manuel Alvarez (GRA) 8; **SO**: Manuel Alvarez 84; **ERA**: Gilberto Rodríguez (CON) 1.08.

No-Hit/No-Run Games—None

1975 Selective Series I (Super-Provincial)

Champion—Oriente (33–21) Manager: José Carrillo
Standings—Oriente (33–21), Camagüeyanos (32–22), Habana (32–22), Pinar del Río (30–24), Las Villas (26–28), Matanzas (19–35), Industriales (17–37)
Batting Leaders—**BA**: Alfonso Urquiola (PRI) .358; **H**: Fernando Sánchez (MTZ), Eusebio Cruz (CMG) 66; **R**: Armando Capiró (HAB) 44; **2B**: Eusebio Cruz 15; **3B**: Agustín Arias (OTE) 6; **HR**: Armando Capiró, Antonio Muñoz (LVS) 12; **RBI**: Fernando Sánchez 42; **SB**: Félix Isasi (MTZ) 14.
Pitching Leaders—**Pct.**: Eduardo Terry (MTZ) 5–0 (1.000); **G**: Ramón Villabrille (HAB) 20; **CG**: Santiago Mederos (HAB) 10; **Wins**: Omar Carrero (CMG) 10; **IP**: Santiago Mederos 119.2; **SO**: Julio Romero (PRI) 85; **ERA**: Gregorio Pérez (OTE) 1.04.
No-Hit/No-Run Game—**Oscar Romero** (Camagüeyanos 4–11–1, Industriales 0–0–4, 5–4–75)

1975–1976 National Series XV (Provincial)

Antonio Muñoz — playing first for the Azucareros and then Las Villas — is the home run champion of both the National Series and Selective Series, slugging a combined 25 roundtrippers in 93 games. Wilfredo Sánchez (Citricultores and Matanzas) is also the base hits leader for both campaigns, but Sánchez is edged in tight narrow race for the Selective Series batting crown by Bárbaro Garbey, a future cup-of-coffee

major leaguer. Garbey would soon be expelled for rumored game-fixing and later sent to the U.S. during the 1980 Mariel boatlift, thus becoming the first post-revolution Cuban Leaguer to appear in the U.S. major leagues. Braudilio Vinent continues as the country's top-ranked pitcher, dominating the bulk of individual statistical categories (winning percentage, victories, innings pitched, complete games) during Selective Series play.

Champion—Ganaderos (29–9) Manager: Carlos Gómez
Standings—Ganaderos (29–9–0), Metropolitanos (24–15–0), Vegueros (23–16–0), Constructores (22–16–0), Azucareros (22–17–0), Agricultores (20–17–1), Forestales (18–20–1), Cafetaleros (17–20–1), Granjeros (17–20–0), Serranos (17–21–1), Henequeneros (16–22–0), Citricultores (16–23–0), Arroceros (15–24–0), Mineros (11–27–0)
Batting Leaders—**BA**: Wilfredo Sánchez (CIT) .365; **H**: Wilfredo Sánchez 62; **R**: Diego Mena (VEG) 32; **2B**: Eulogio Osorio (AGR) 12; **3B**: Héctor Olivera (ACC), Manuel González (MET) 4; **HR**: Antonio Muñoz (AZU) 13; **RBI**: Antonio Muñoz 35; **SB**: Wilfredo Sánchez 12.
Pitching Leaders—**Pct.**: Omar Carrero (GAN) 8–0 (1.000); **G**: Ramón Villabrille (MET), Jesús Plasencia (HEN) 17; **CG**: Lázaro Santana (GRA) 9; **Wins**: Omar Carrero (GAN), Lázaro Santana (GRA) 8; **IP**: Lázaro Santana (GRA) 99.0; **SO**: Omar Carrero 94; **ERA**: Omar Carrero 0.46.
No-Hit/No-Run Games—None

1976 Selective Series II (Super-Provincial)

Champion—Habana (34–20) Manager: Roberto Ledo
Standings—Habana (34–20), Orientales (33–21), Camagüeyanos (32–22), Las Villas (32–22), Pinar del Río (24–30), Matanzas (18–36), Industriales (16–38)
Batting Leaders—**BA**: Bárbaro Garbey (IND) .328; **H**: Wilfredo Sánchez (MTZ) 66; **R**: Antonio Muñoz (LVS) 45; **2B**: Antonio Muñoz, Armando Capiró (HAB) 12; **3B**: Wilfredo Sánchez 6; **HR**: Antonio Muñoz 12; **RBI**: Pedro José Rodríguez (LVS) 43; **SB**: Wilfredo Sánchez 18.
Pitching Leaders—**Pct.**: Braudilio Vinent (OTE) 12–2 (.857); **G**: Isidro Pérez (LVS) 25; **CG**: Braudilio Vinent 12; **Wins**: Braudilio Vinent 12; **IP**: Braudilio Vinent 127.0; **SO**: Rogelio García (PRI) 97; **ERA**: Omar Carrero (CMG) 0.62.
No-Hit/No-Run Games—None

1976–1977 National Series XVI (Provincial)

Aluminum bats (manufactured in the United States but purchased through third-party Central American nations) are introduced for the first time and will remain an identifying characteristic of the Cuban League until the 1999 return of wooden war clubs. The Citricultores are National Series champions for the first time ever by a slim game-and-a-half margin over Vegueros, while the Camagüeyanos win the longer Selective Series season by a more comfortable four-game spread over Las Villas. Pedro José Rodríguez emerges as a new slugging star with the first of four consecutive National Series home run titles. Rodríguez is also the longball champion of the Selective Series season.

Champion— Citricultores (26–12) Manager: Juan Bregio
Standings— Citricultores (26–12), Vegueros (25–14), Metros (24–15), Azucareros (23–16), Ganaderos (23–16), Forestales (21–18), Agricultores (20–18), Granjeros (20–19), Arroceros (20–19), Serranos (17–20), Henequeneros (14–23), Mineros (14–25), Constructores (12–27), Cafetaleros (11–28)

Batting Leaders— **BA**: Eulogio Osorio (AGR) .359; **H**: Armando Capiró (MET) 52; **R**: Valentín León (AZU) 32; **2B**: Pedro Medina (MET) 14; **3B**: Armando Capiró 7; **HR**: Pedro José Rodríguez (AZU) 9; **RBI**: Pedro José Rodríguez 45; **SB**: Gerardo Rionda (HEN) 9.

Pitching Leaders— **Pct.**: Gaspar Legón (GAN), Rafael Rodríguez (CIT), Isidro Pérez (AZU) 8–1 (.889); **G**: Manuel Rivero (CON) 15; **CG**: Lázaro Santana (GRA) 10; **Wins**: Gaspar Legón, Rafael Rodríguez, Isidro Pérez 8; **IP**: Lázaro Sananta (GRA) 93.1; **SO**: Rogelio García (VEG) 97; **ERA**: Isidro Pérez 0.90.

No-Hit/No-Run Games— None

1977 Selective Series III (Super-Provincial)

Champion— Camagüeyanos (36–18) Manager: Carlos Gómez
Standings— Camagüeyanos (36–18), Las Villas (33–21), Pinar del Río (30–24), Habana (28–26), Orientales (25–29), Matanzas (18–36)

Batting Leaders— **BA**: Wilfredo Sánchez (MTZ) .381; **H**: Wilfredo Sánchez 85; **R**: Pedro Jova (LVS) 49; **2B**: Elpidio Mancebo (OTE) 16; **3B**: Ubaldo Alvarez (IND), Giraldo Iglesias (PRI) 6; **HR**: Pedro José Rodríguez (LVS) 16; **RBI**: Pedro José Rodríguez 56; **SB**: Rey Anglada (HAB) 18.

Pitching Leaders— **Pct.**: Ariel Martínez (OTE) 3–0 (1.000); **G**: Eladio Iglesias (HAB), Rafael Rodríguez (MTZ) 20; **CG**: Braudilio Vinent (OTE) 10; **Wins**: Lázaro Santana (CMG) 10; **IP**: Braudilio Vinent 124.1; **SO**: Rogelio García (PRI) 122; **ERA**: Félix Pino (PRI) 1.28.

No-Hit/No-Run Games— None

1977–1978 National Series XVII (Provincial)

Another important rule change introduces the designated hitter to Cuban League play, an innovation that came to the major leagues four seasons earlier. The first DH on Cuban soil is Lázaro Mádam, who occupies the new lineup slot in a pre-season exhibition game played between the CDR and MININT Havana amateur clubs. Future big leaguer Bárbaro Garbey (Industriales) paces the National Series in runs batted in. In the Selective Series, Santiago "Changa" Mederos returns to the pitching spotlight with the best won-lost percentage. Pedro José Rodríguez again earns the home run title in both Series and his 28 (60 games) in the Selective Series tournament is the most in any post-revolution championship season. His mammoth timely homer also decides the Selective Series playoff round between Las Villas and Pinar del Río. The season also marks the completion of one hundred years of championship baseball played in Cuba.

Champion— Vegueros (36–14) Manager: José Pineda
Standings— Vegueros (36–14–0), Industriales (35–16–0),

Camagüey (30–21–0), Forestales (29–21–0), Villa Clara (28–21–0) Metropolitanos (28–21–0), Cienfuegos (29–22–0), Guantánamo (28–22–0), Ciego de Avila (26–23–0), Citricultores (27–24–0), Granma (25–25–0), Santiago de Cuba (25–25–0), Habana (21–26–1), Holguín (22–28–1), Sancto Spíritus (20–30–1), Henequeneros (16–30–1), Las Tunas (12–37–2), Isla de la Juventud (10–41–0)

Batting Leaders— **BA**: Fernando Sánchez (HEN) .394; **H**: Julian Villar (IND) 72; **R**: Rey Anglada (IND) 43; **2B**: Agustín Marquetti (MET) 14; **3B**: Juan Navarro (GRA) 8; **HR**: Pedro José Rodríguez (CFG) 13; **RBI**: Bárbaro Garbey (IND) 40; **SB**: Rey Anglada 29.

Pitching Leaders— **Pct.**: Adalberto Herrera (VEG) 6–0 (1.000); **G**: Isidro Pérez (VCL) 17; **CG**: José Pedroso (HAB) 10; **Wins**: José Pedroso, Servando Medina (CFG), Maximiliano Gutierrez (VEG) 9; **IP**: Gaspar Legón (CMG) 105.0; **SO**: Rogelio García (VEG) 120; **ERA**: José Riveira (VCL) 0.82.

No-Hit/No-Run Game— **Porfirio Pérez** (Forestales 3–7–1, Provincia Habana 0–0–1, 12–27–77)

1978 Selective Series IV (Super-Provincial)

Champion— Las Villas (35–25) Manager: Eduardo Martín
Playoffs— Las Villas over Pinar del Río, 3–2 (Finals)
Standings— Las Villas (35–25), Pinar del Río (35–25), Habana (33–27), Camagüeyanos (32–28), Matanzas (24–36), Orientales (21–39)

Batting Leaders— **BA**: Pedro Jova (LVS) .372; **H**: Pedro Jova 92; **R**: Antonio Muñoz (LVS) 55; **2B**: Pedro Medina (HAB) 15; **3B**: Geraldo Iglesias (PRI) 5; **HR**: Pedro José Rodríguez (LVS) 28; **RBI**: Pedro José Rodríguez 75; **SB**: Sixto Hernández (LVS) 13.

Pitching Leaders— **Pct.**: Santiago Mederos (HAB) 7–2 (.778); **G**: Roberto Ramos (LVS) 23; **CG**: Rogelio García (PRI) 11; **Wins**: Rogelio García 10; **IP**: Rogelio García 134.1; **SO**: Rogelio García 111; **ERA**: Rogelio García 2.21.

No-Hit/No-Run Games— None

1978–1979 National Series XVIII (Provincial)

Sancti Spíritus boasts a championship team for the only time while Wilfredo Sánchez claims yet another National Series batting title, his fourth overall. The hitting crown for Sánchez culminates the closest batting race in Cuban League history — the title being decided by four decimal places with Sánchez edging Agustín Arias. Pedro José Rodríguez captures another home run title in the National Series, but Antonio Muñoz is back on top in that department in the longer Selective Series. A rare multi-pitcher no-hitter occurs late in the National Series campaign with Juan Gómez, Pablo Castro and José Brizuela of Granma tossing the combined blanking at the team from Ciego de Avila. Nivaldo Pérez (Villa Clara) is easily the most brilliant National Series pitcher with an undefeated record (nine decisions) and a sub–1.00 ERA. Pérez also authors the only no-hitter of the follow-up Selective Series season.

Champion— Sancti Spíritus (39–12) Manager: Candido Andrade

Standings— Sancti Spíritus (39–12–0), Villa Clara (36–14–1), Vegueros (35–14–1), Cienfuegos (31–20–0), Forestales (30–20–0), Camagüey (28–21–1), Granma (27–21–1), Citricultores (28–23–0), Ciego de Avila (26–25–0), Metropolitanos (25–25–1), Santiago de Cuba (23–28–0), Industriales (22–27–0), Henequeneros (22–29–0), Guantánamo (21–29–0), Holguín (19–32–0), Las Tunas (15–35–1), Habana (14–36–0), Isla de la Juventud (10–40–0)

Batting Leaders—**BA**: Wilfredo Sánchez (CIT) .377; **H**: Wilfredo Sánchez 80; **R**: Pedro José Rodríguez (CFG) 42; **2B**: Armando Capiró (IND), Lourdes Gourriel (SSP) 12; **3B**: Sixto Hernández (CFG) 6; **HR**: Pedro José Rodríguez 19; **RBI**: Pedro José Rodríguez 53; **SB**: Victor Mesa (VCL) 20.

Pitching Leaders—**Pct.**: Nivaldo Pérez (VCL) 9–0 (1.000); **G**: Eduardo Rodríguez (MET) 20; **CG**: Rogelio García (VEG) 12; **Wins**: Gaspar Legón (CMG) 12; **IP**: Juan Gómez (GRA) 122.0; **SO**: Rogelio García 102; **ERA**: Nivaldo Pérez 0.86.

No-Hit/No-Run Game—**Juan Gómez** (winner), **Pablo Castro** and **José Brizuela** (Granma 14–18–3, Ciego de Avila 0–0–2, 2–18–79)

1979 Selective Series V (Super-Provincial)

Champion— Pinar del Río (40–20) Manager: José Pineda
Standings— Pinar del Río (40–20), Orientales (33–26), Habana (31–29), Matanzas (27–33), Camagüeyanos (25–35), Las Villas (23–36)

Batting Leaders—**BA**: Sixto Hernández (LVS) .368; **H**: Wilfredo Sánchez (MTZ) 81; **R**: Antonio Muñoz (LVS) 52; **2B**: Felipe Sarduy (CAM), Reinaldo Fernández (CMG) 13; **3B**: Luis Crespo (PRI) 9; **HR**: Antonio Muñoz 25; **RBI**: Antonio Muñoz 67; **SB**: Alfonso Urquiola (PRI) 12.

Pitching Leaders—**Pct.**: Lázaro de la Torre (HAB) 7–0 (1.000); **G**: Lázaro de la Torre 21; **CG**: Braudilio Vinent (OTE) 15; **Wins**: Rafael Rodríguez (MTZ) 11; **IP**: Braudilio Vinent 137.0; **SO**: Braudilio Vinent 105; **ERA**: Juan Oliva (PRI) 1.97.

No-Hit/No-Run Game—**Nivaldo Pérez** (Las Villas 4–9–0, Camagüeyanos 0–0–1, 3–28–79)

1979 All-Star Series VII

Champion— Selección (2–0) Manager: Servio Borges
Standings— Selección (2–0), Oriente (0–2)
Batting Leaders—**BA**: Rodolfo Puente (SEL) .500; **H**: Rodolfo Puente 4; **R**: Rodolfo Puente, Armando Capiró (SEL) 2; **3B**: Agustín Marquetti (SEL), Jorge Francis (OTE) 1; **HR**: Antonio Muñoz (SEL), Fidel García (OTE), Elpidio Mancebo (OTE) 1; **RBI**: Antonio Muñoz, Armando Capiró, Elpidio Mancebo, Pedro José Rodríguez (SEL) 2; **SB**: Jesús Guerra (SEL), Fermín Laffita (OTE) 1.

Pitching Leaders—**IP**: Jesús Guerra (SEL) 8.1; **SO**: Santiago Mederos (SEL) 8; **ERA**: Mario Fernández (OTE) 0.00.

No-Hit/No-Run Games— None

1979–1980 National Series XIX (Provincial)

Present-day powerhouse clubs Santiago de Cuba and Pinar del Río share the limelight for the very first time, with Santiago capturing its first-ever banner in the National Series

and Pinar ringing up a second straight Selective Series championship. Luis Casanova emerges as a new slugging star in Pinar del Río, tying Pedro José Rodríguez for the National Series home run crown. Braudilio Vinent paces the National Series in pitching victories for the final time, while Victor Mesa captures his second of six eventual base-stealing titles. Top performance of the year, however, is manufactured by Héctor Olivera in the Selective Series season; the righthanded Las Villas outfielder finishes with a .459 batting average in 146 at-bats, the highest Cuban League mark ever recorded.

Champion— Santiago de Cuba (35–16) Manager: Manuel Miyar

Standings— Santiago de Cuba (35–16), Villa Clara (34–17), Vegueros (33–18), Forestales (33–18), Sancti Spíritus (31–20), Industriales (31–20), Metropolitanos (30–20), Holguín (28–21), Henequeneros (28–21), Cienfuegos (26–25), Citricultores (25–24), Granma (22–29), Camagüeyanos (21–30), Ciego de Avila (18–33), Guantánamo (18–33), Provincia Habana (17–32), Las Tunas (12–38), Isla de la Juventud (12–39)

Batting Leaders—**BA**: Rodolfo Puente (MET) .394; **H**: Lourdes Gourriel (SSP) 77; **R**: Luis Casanova (VEG) 64; **2B**: Victor Mesa (VCL) 17; **3B**: Joaquin Martínez (HAB) 7; **HR**: Luis Casanova, Pedro José Rodríguez (CFG) 18; **RBI**: Pedro José Rodríguez 55; **SB**: Victor Mesa (VCL) 19.

Pitching Leaders—**Pct.**: Reinaldo López (IND) 6–0 (1.000); **G**: José Perulena (IJV), Alfonso Ilivanes (GTM), Leonardo Hernández (HEN) 19; **CG**: José Darcourt (MET), Braudilio Vinent (SCU) 13; **Wins**: Braudilio Vinent 12; **IP**: Braudilio Vinent 124.0; **SO**: Rogelio García (VEG) 132; **ERA**: José Sánchez (CMG) 0.76.

No-Hit/No-Run Games— None

1980 Selective Series VI (Super-Provincial)

Champion— Pinar del Río (39–20) Manager: José Pineda
Standings— Pinar del Río (39–20), Habana (33–27), Camagüeyanos (31–28), Las Villas (30–30), Matanzas (27–33), Orientales (19–41)

Batting Leaders—**BA**: Héctor Olivera (LVS) .459; **H**: Wilfredo Sánchez (MTZ) 88; **R**: Pedro Jova (LVS) 56; **2B**: Agustín Marquetti (HAB) 17; **3B**: Rogelio García (PRI), Luis Crespo (PRI) 5; **HR**: Antonio Muñoz (LVS) 18; **RBI**: Antonio Muñoz 67; **SB**: Rey Anglada (HAB) 17.

Pitching Leaders—**Pct.**: Juan Oliva (PRI) 8–1 (.889); **G**: Dagoberto Rodríguez (CMG) 21; **CG**: Julio Romero (PRI) 10; **Wins**: Rogelio García (PRI) 9; **IP**: José Darcourt (HAB) 114.2; **SO**: José Darcourt 91; **ERA**: Omar Carrero (CAM) 1.87.

No-Hit/No-Run Games— None

1980–1981 National Series XX (Provincial)

Felipe Sarduy becomes the first to compete in 20 National Series before retiring after the 1982 National Series with a total of twenty-one campaigns played. Omar Carrero pitches the first no-hitter of the decade and 22nd overall since the revolution. Vegueros captures its second of three National Series championships in a five-year stretch. Braudilio Vinent is strikeout king in the National Series for the final time in his career, breaking a four-year domination in that department by Vegueros ace Rogelio García. Vinent also paces the Selective Series in complete games and total innings pitched in his final super season. Future all-time base hits leader Antonio Pacheco plays in his first National Series with Santiago de Cuba.

Champion—Vegueros (36–15) Manager: José Pineda

Standings—Vegueros (36–15), Villa Clara (33–18), Citricultores (33–18), Industriales (32–19), Forestales (31–20), Cienfuegos (30–21), Sancti Spíritus (28–23), Guantánamo (26–25), Henequeneros (25–26), Santiago de Cuba (25–26), Granma (24–27), Metropolitanos (23–28), Camagüey (23–28), Holguín (22–29), Isla de la Juventud (20–31), Ciego de Avila (19–32), Habana (18–33), Las Tunas (11–40)

Batting Leaders—**BA**: Amado Zamora (VCL) .394; **H**: Pablo Pérez (IJV) 76; **R**: Victor Mesa (VCL) 60; **2B**: Juan Baró (CIT) 16; **3B**: Lázaro Junco (CIT) 6; **HR**: Agustín Lescaille (GTM) 15; **RBI**: Alejo O'Reilly (VCL) 69; **SB**: Rey Anglada (MET) 24.

Pitching Leaders—**Pct.**: Maximiliano Gutiérrez (VEG) 8–2 (.800); **G**: Alberto Cabreja (HOL), Miguel Isla (SSP), Anselmo Martínez (CIT), José Perulena (IJV) 18; **CG**: Rogelio García (VEG) 12; **Wins**: Rogelio García, Alfonso Ilivanes (GTM) 10; **IP**: Alfonso Ilivanes 118.2; **SO**: Braudilio Vinent (SCU) 90; **ERA**: Rogelio García 1.31.

No-Hit/No-Run Game—**Omar Carrero** (Ciego de Avila 13–16–1, Las Tunas 0–0–4, 1–27–81)

1981 Selective Series VII (Super-Provincial)

Champion—Orientales (38–22) Manager: Carlos Marti

Standings—Orientales (38–22), Las Villas (37–23), Habana (35–25), Pinar del Río (32–27), Matanzas (23–36), Camagüeyanos (13–46)

Batting Leaders—**BA**: Luis Casanova (PRI) .363; **H**: Antonio Muñoz (LVS) 82; **R**: Antonio Muñoz 51; **2B**: Antonio Muñoz 26; **3B**: Juan Baró (MTZ), Pablo Pérez (HAB), Oscar Rodríguez (OTE), Luis Casanova (PRI), Francisco Costa (PRI) 4; **HR**: Antonio Muñoz 18; **RBI**: Antonio Muñoz 64; **SB**: Rey Anglada (HAB) 17.

Pitching Leaders—**Pct.**: Angel Díaz (HAB) 9–2 (.818); **G**: Tomás Creo (CMG) 24; **CG**: Braudilio Vinent (OTE) 13; **Wins**: Rafael Castillo (OTE) 13; **IP**: Braudilio Vinent 138.0; **SO**: Rogelio García (PRI) 114; **ERA**: José Alemán (OTE) 2.41.

No-Hit/No-Run Games— None

1981–1982 National Series XXI (Provincial)

Vegueros wins once again in the National Series, then duplicates the feat under the name of Pinar del Río in the Selective Series. Future national team manager Jorge Fuentes thus becomes first skipper to claim both National Series and Selective Series titles in the same season. Fuentes would repeat this feat during the 1988 NS/SS seasons. Lázaro Junco captures the first (tied with Reynaldo Fernández) of his record total ten home run crowns that would make him the island's primer longball slugger until eventually outstripped by Orestes Kindelán. Kindelán ironically makes his own National Series

debut this very same season with also-ran Santiago de Cuba. Agustín Arias — loser of the closest batting race in Cuban history, to Wilfredo Sánchez three seasons earlier — rebounds with a .404 average in the Selective Series.

Champion—Vegueros (36–15) Manager: Jorge Fuentes

Standings—Vegueros (36–15), Citricultores (35–16), Metros (34–17), Forestales (33–18), Cienfuegos (29–22), Henequeneros (28–23), Industriales (27–24), Granma (26–25), Guantánamo (26–25), Villa Clara (24–27), Camagüey (23–28), Provincia Habana (22–29), Ciego de Avila (22–29), Sancti Spíritus (21–30), Isla de la Juventud (21–30), Santiago de Cuba (21–30), Holguín (17–34), Las Tunas (14–37)

Batting Leaders—**BA**: Fernando Hernández (VEG) .376; **H**: Fernando Hernández 77; **R**: Fernando Hernández 40; **2B**: Lázaro Junco (CIT), Reynaldo Fernández (CMG) 16; **3B**: Pablo Bejerano (GRA) 8; **HR**: Lázaro Junco, Reynaldo Fernández 17; **RBI**: Lázaro Junco 51; **SB**: Wilfredo Sánchez (CIT) 15.

Pitching Leaders—**Pct.**: Oscar Martínez (HAB) 6–0 (1.000); **G**: Isidro Pérez (VCL) 22; **CG**: Julio Romero (FOR), José Darcourt (MET), Pablo Martínez (GRA) 12; **Wins**: José Darcourt 12; **IP**: Pablo Martínez (GRA) 130.0; **SO**: Rogelio García (VEG) 144; **ERA**: Julio Romero (FOR) 1.45.

No-Hit/No-Run Games—**Angel Leocadio Díaz** (Industriales 2–6–3, Holguín 0–0–1, 1–16–82); **Carlos Mesa** (Citricultores 6–9–0, Provincia Habana 0–0–3, 2–11–82)

1982 Selective Series VIII (Super-Provincial)

Champion—Pinar del Río (35–22) Manager: Jorge Fuentes

Standings—Pinar del Río (35–22), Matanzas (30–27), Orientales (30–27), Las Villas (29–27), Habana (29–28), Camagüeyanos (18–40)

Batting Leaders—**BA**: Agustín Arias (OTE) .404; **H**: Agustín Arias 82; **R**: Luis Casanova (PRI) 49; **2B**: Roberto Pérez (CMG) 15; **3B**: Luis Casanova, Sixto Hernández (LVS), Amado Zamora (LVS), Pablo Hernández (MTZ) 4; **HR**: Lázaro Junco (MTZ) 19; **RBI**: Lázaro Junco 45; **SB**: Alfonso Urquiola (PRI) 14.

Pitching Leaders—**Pct.**: Julio Romero (PRI) 11–2 (.846); **G**: Lázaro de la Torre (HAB) 21; **CG**: Tomás Creo (CMG) 11; **Wins**: Julio Romero 11; **IP**: Lázaro de la Torre 126.0; **SO**: Rogelio García (PRI) 116; **ERA**: Rogelio García 1.70.

No-Hit/No-Run Game—**José Pedroso** (Habana 1–5–0, Camagüeyanos 0–0–1, 5–18–82)

1982–1983 National Series XXII (Provincial)

Slugging infielder Omar Linares debuts with Vegueros team (based in Pinar del Río) at the tender age of 16, making the future all-around sensation one of the youngest players ever in the National Series. The province of Villa Clara (under the name Las Villas in the Selective Series) captures both championships, allowing Eduardo Martín to duplicate Jorge Fuentes's rare managerial double of one season earlier. Villa Clara's José Riviera posts a perfect 6–0 mound record and also the second-lowest ERA in National Series record books. Rogelio García picks up his sixth National Series strikeout crown in the last seven seasons. In the Selective Series Antonio Muñoz is both home run champion and RBI leader for the final time of his brilliant career.

Champion— Villa Clara (41–8) Manager: Eduardo Martín

Standings— Villa Clara (41–8), Citricultores (35–16), Camagüey (35–16), Industriales (31–16), Vegueros (33–18), Henequeneros (28–20), Forestales (25–24), Ciego de Avila (25–26), Santiago de Cuba (24–25), Habana (23–26), Guantánamo (22–29), Cienfuegos (20–28), Sancti Spíritus (21–30), Granma (19–32), Isla de la Juventud (19–32), Metropolitanos (16–33), Holguín (16–33), Las Tunas (15–36)

Batting Leaders—**BA**: Juan Hernández (FOR) .367; **H**: Oscar Rodríguez (GTM) 71; **R**: Victor Mesa (VCL) 39; **2B**: Alejo O'Reilly (VCL) 15; **3B**: Antonio Pacheco (SCU), Pedro Luis Rodríguez (HAB) 6; **HR**: Lázaro Junco (CIT) 15; **RBI**: Alejo O'Reilly, Lázaro Junco 38; **SB**: Victor Mesa 21.

Pitching Leaders—**Pct.**: José Riveira (VCL) 6–0 (1.000); **G**: Luis Batista (HEN), Alberto Cabreja (HOL), Andres Sanabria (IND) 18; **CG**: Félix Núñez (LTU) 14; **Wins**: Jorge Luis Valdés (HEN) 10; **IP**: Félix Núñez 136.0; **SO**: Rogelio García (VEG) 119; **ERA**: José Riveira 0.63.

No-Hit/No-Run Game—**Mario Veliz** (Villa Clara 3–11–1, Citricultores 0–0–2, 12–30–82)

1983 Selective Series IX (Super-Provincial)

Champion— Las Villas (42–18) Manager: Eduardo Martín

Standings— Las Villas (42–18), Orientales (33–27), Matanzas (31–29), Habana (30–30), Pinar del Río (25–35), Camagüeyanos (19–41)

Batting Leaders—**BA**: Gerardo Simon (OTE) .350; **H**: Antonio Muñoz (LVS) 77; **R**: Victor Mesa (LVS) 47; **2B**: Sergio Quesada (CMG) 15; **3B**: José Sarduy (CMG) 6; **HR**: Antonio Muñoz 14; **RBI**: Antonio Muñoz 65; **SB**: Victor Mesa 21.

Pitching Leaders—**Pct.**: Octavio Gálvez (LVS) 6–1 (.857); **G**: Raúl González (PRI), Lázaro de la Torre (HAB) 19; **CG**: Braudilio Vinent (OTE) 10; **Wins**: Jorge Luis Valdés (MTZ) 11; **IP**: Jorge Luis Valdés 130.2; **SO**: Julio Romero (PRI) 109; **ERA**: Julio Romero 1.67.

No-Hit/No-Run Game—**Julio Romero** (Pinar del Río 2–9–0, Camagüeyanos 0–0–1, 3–9–83)

1983–1984 National Series XXIII (Provincial)

Future career home run record holder Orestes Kindelán wins his first individual longball title, tying for the most circuit blasts in the Selective Series. Lázaro Junco — the only another Cuban Leaguer with 400-plus career roundtrippers (until Omar Linares in 2002) — ties for the National Series lead with twenty. Wilfredo Sánchez is National Series batting leader for the final time. Victor Mesa (Villa Clara) continues to dominate National Series basestealing with a career-high 34 total. Future Cuban League leader in pitching victories, Jorge Luis Valdés, tosses no-hitter in National Series play for the Henequeneros. Pinar's Reinaldo Costa paces every major in-

dividual pitching category during the Selective Series with the single exception of game appearances.

Champion— Citricultores (52–23) Manager: Tomás Soto

First Division— Citricultores (52–23), Industriales (49–25), Villa Clara (48–27), Camagüeyanos (46–27), Santiago de Cuba (47–28), Vegueros (44–31), Henequeneros (36–36), Holguín (36–39), Sancti Spíritus (30–45)

Second Division— Forestales (40–35), Habana (37–38), Cienfuegos (34–40), Granma (34–41), Guantánamo (34–41), Metropolitanos (30–43), Isla de la Juventud (28–46), Ciego de Avila (25–48), Las Tunas (19–56)

Batting Leaders—**BA**: Wilfredo Sánchez (CIT) .385; **H**: Lázaro Vargas (IND) 102; **R**: Lázaro Madera (VEG) 64; **2B**: Sixto Hernández (CFG), Luis Casanova (VEG) 19; **3B**: Evenecer Godinez (SCU), Rolando Verde (IND) 8; **HR**: Luis Casanova, Lázaro Junco (CIT) 20; **RBI**: Luis Casanova 67; **SB**: Victor Mesa (VCL) 34.

Pitching Leaders—**Pct.**: Eduardo Terry (CIT) 13–1 (.929); **G**: José Salazar (MET) 27; **CG**: Félix Núñez (LTU), Luis Armenteros (IJV), Alfonso Ilivanes (GTM) 15; **Wins**: José Sánchez (CMG) 15; **IP**: Ulises Infiesta (SSP) 160.0; **SO**: Faustino Corrales (FOR) 143; **ERA**: Manuel Alvarez (CAV) 1.17.

No-Hit/No-Run Game—**Jorge Luis Valdés** (Henequeneros 1–2–1, Villa Clara 0–0–3, 1–31–84)

1984 Selective Series X (Super-Provincial)

Champion— Pinar del Río (28–15) Manager: Jorge Fuentes

Standings— Pinar del Río (28–15), Las Villas (24–19), Matanzas (24–21), Habana (22–23), Camagüeyanos (18–27), Orientales (17–26)

Batting Leaders—**BA**: Luis Casanova (PRI) .391; **H**: Lázaro Madera (PRI) 63; **R**: Victor Mesa (LVS) 38; **2B**: Pedro José Rodríguez (LVS), Javier Méndez (HAB) 12; **3B**: Oscar Rodríguez (OTE) 12; **HR**: Orestes Kindelán (OTE), Alejo O'Reilly (LVS) 12; **RBI**: Pedro José Rodríguez, Lázaro Madera (PRI) 38; **SB**: Victor Mesa 14.

Pitching Leaders—**Pct.**: Reinaldo Costa (PRI) 12–1 (.923); **G**: José Sánchez (CMG) 16; **CG**: Reinaldo Costa 9; **Wins**: Reinaldo Costa 12; **IP**: Reinaldo Costa 113.0; **SO**: Reinaldo Costa 60; **ERA**: Reinaldo Costa 1.67.

No-Hit/No-Run Games— None

1984–1985 National Series XXIV (Provincial)

Nineteen-year-old Omar Linares bats .400-plus and wins his first of five batting championships in the National Series, pacing Vegueros to yet another team title. Linares is also league leader in runs scored and triples. Linares's Pinar del Río club surprisingly finishes last in the Selective Series playdown, won by Las Villas with its own several-times batting champion, Amado Zamora (and this season's base-hits pacesetter). Noteworthy in the Selective Series season is the pitching performance of youngster Lázaro de la Torre, laboring for runner-up Habana Province. The durable hard-throwing righthander would pace the circuit in game appearances, innings pitched and victories. A full decade and a half later — at age 40, in the

2001 season — Lázaro de la Torre would become only the fourth Cuban League pitcher to post 200-plus career pitching victories.

Champion— Vegueros (57–18) Manager: Jorge Fuentes

First Division— Vegueros (57–18), Camagüey (50–25), Habana (46–29), Villa Clara (46–29), Santiago de Cuba (45–30), Industriales (44–31), Citricultores (43–32), Guantánamo (42–33), Cienfuegos (32–43)

Second Division— Forestales (34–36), Henequeneros (37–38), Sancti Spíritus (32–42), Ciego de Avila (31–44), Granma (31–44), Metropolitanos (30–44), Las Tunas (24–51), Isla de la Juventud (23–52), Holguín (22–53)

Batting Leaders—**BA**: Omar Linares (VEG) .409; **H**: Amado Zamora (VCL) 115; **R**: Omar Linares 65; **2B**: Fernando Hernández (VEG), Pedro Luis Rodríguez (HAB) 20; **3B**: Omar Linares, Amado Zamora 9; **HR**: Lázaro Junco (CIT) 24; **RBI**: Lázaro Junco 72; **SB**: Lázaro Madera (VEG) 37.

Pitching Leaders—**Pct.**: Ramón Espinosa (CMG) 6–0 (1.000); **G**: Fidencio Serrano (HOL) 31; **CG**: Félix Núñez (LTU) 15; **Wins**: Reinaldo Costa (VEG) 14; **IP**: Félix Núñez 170.1; **SO**: Félix Núñez 138; **ERA**: Andrés Luis (CAM) 1.67.

No-Hit/No-Run Games— None

1985 Selective Series XI (Super-Provincial)

Champion— Las Villas (26–19) Manager: Eduardo Martín

Standings— Las Villas (26–19), Habana (25–20), Matanzas (24–21), Orientales (20–25), Camagüeyanos (20–25), Pinar del Río (20–25)

Batting Leaders—**BA**: Amado Zamora (LVS) .361; **H**: Antonio Pacheco (OTE), Fernando Sánchez (MTZ) 60; **R**: Pedro Medina (HAB) 35; **2B**: Fernando Sánchez (MTZ) 12; **3B**: Antonio Pacheco 4; **HR**: Pedro Medina 13; **RBI**: Fernando Sánchez 36; **SB**: Victor Mesa (LVS) 12.

Pitching Leaders—**Pct.**: José Pedroso (HAB) 4–0 (1.000); **G**: Lázaro de la Torre (HAB) 18; **CG**: Reinaldo Costa (PRI) 6; **Wins**: Lázaro de la Torre 9; **IP**: Lázaro de la Torre 109.2; **SO**: José Riveira (LVS) 63; **ERA**: Manuel Alvarez (CAM) 1.98.

No-Hit/No-Run Games— None

1985–1986 National Series XXV (Provincial)

Havana fan-favorite Industriales — now under managerial leadership of sixties-era hitting star Pedro Chávez — earns its first National Series title in thirteen years. This is first season of a regularly scheduled round-robin playoff series to determine National Series champion. Omar Linares repeats as NS batting champion while Jorge Luis Valdés, Lázaro de la Torre and newcomer Omar Ajete prove the most outstanding individual NS pitchers. In the Selective Series Orestes Kindelán crunches 30 homers for the champion Serranos, the highest total in any Cuban League season. Kindelán's 84 RBI are also a Selective Series record and fall just short of the earlier NS highwater marks of 86 (Miguel Cuevas, 1968) and 85 (Agustín Marquetti, 1969).

Champion— Industriales (37–11, 6–0) Manager: Pedro Chávez

Playoffs— Industriales (6–0), Vegueros (4–2), Villa Clara (1–5), Santiago de Cuba (1–5) (Six-game round-robin playoff tournament)

Standings— Industriales (37–11), Villa Clara (35–13), Vegueros (33–15), Henequeneros (33–15), Santiago de Cuba (32–16), Camagüey (32–16), Citricultores (26–22), Ciego de Avila (24–24), Metropolitanos (21–26), Sancti Spíritus (21–27), Granma (21–27), Forestales (18–30), Guantánamo (19–29), Habana (18–30), Las Tunas (16–32), Cienfuegos (15–32), Holguín (14–34), Isla de la Juventud (14–34)

Batting Leaders—**BA**: Omar Linares (VEG) .426; **H**: Lázaro Vargas (IND) 75; **R**: Lázaro Vargas (IND) 48; **2B**: Pablo Pérez (IJV) 16; **3B**: José Lombillo (HAB) 5; **HR**: Reynaldo Fernández (CMG) 18; **RBI**: Julio Fernández (HEN) 52; **SB**: Antonio González (IND) 21.

Pitching Leaders—**Pct.**: Omar Ajete (VEG) 5–0 (1.000); **G**: Osvaldo Duvergel (GTM) 24; **CG**: Jorge Luis Valdés (HEN) 11; **Wins**: Luis Tissert (SCU), José Riveira (VCL), Lázaro de la Torre (IND) 11; **IP**: Jorge Luis Valdés 115.1; **SO**: Pablo Abreu (IND) 97; **ERA**: Jorge Luis Valdés 1.56.

No-Hit/No-Run Games— None

1986 Selective Series XII (Super-Provincial)

Champion— Serranos (41–22) Manager: Frangel Reynaldo

Standings— Serranos (41–22), Habana (39–25), Pinar del Río (36–27), Camagüeyanos (34–29), Las Villas (29–34), Matanzas (27–36), Agropecuarios (24–39), Mineros (22–41)

Batting Leaders—**BA**: Amado Zamora (LVS) .392; **H**: Jorge García (SER) 96; **R**: Orestes Kindelán (SER) 63; **2B**: Rolando Verde (HAB) 18; **3B**: Evenecer Godinez (SER) 9; **HR**: Orestes Kindelán 30; **RBI**: Orestes Kindelán 84; **SB**: Jorge García 30.

Pitching Leaders—**Pct.**: Jesus Bosmenier (PRI) 5–0 (1.000); **G**: Fidencio Serrano (MIN) 27; **CG**: Lázaro de la Torre (HAB) 11; **Wins**: Luis Tissert (SER) 12; **IP**: Enrique Cutiño (SER) 128.2; **SO**: Enrique Cutiño 111; **ERA**: Buenafe Napoles (CMG) 2.36.

No-Hit/No-Run Games— None

1986–1987 National Series XXVI (Provincial)

The Vegueros are National Series champions for fifth time and the Serranos repeat as Selective Series winners. Popular longtime Industriales outfielder Javier Méndez wins his only batting title with a .408 National Series average. Orestes Kindelán is National Series home run leader for the first time and future major leaguer René Arocha is NS ERA pacesetter. Pinar del Río (and Vegueros) mound ace Rogelio García enjoys brilliant curtain call performance during the Selective Series season, tossing a pair of no-hit games in a three-week span and also outdistancing all rivals with his 1.25 ERA.

Champion— Vegueros (34–13, 5–1) Manager: Jorge Fuentes

Playoffs— Vegueros (5–1), Santiago de Cuba (3–3), Villa Clara (2–4), Industriales (2–4) (Six-game round-robin playoff tournament)

Standings— Santiago de Cuba (35–13), Vegueros (34–13), Villa Clara (33–14), Industriales (30–17), Granma (29–19), Metropolitanos (28–20), Ciudad Habana (26–20), Ciego de Avila (26–22), Camagüey (24–23), Cienfuegos (24–23), Citricultores (23–22), Henequeneros (20–28), Las Tunas (19–29), Holguín (17–31), Guantánamo (16–32), Sancti Spíritus (16–32), Forestales (16–32), Isla de la Juventud (10–36)

Batting Leaders—**BA:** Javier Méndez (IND) .408; **H:** Reemberto Rosell (CFG), Luis Alvarez (LTU) 66; **R:** Omar Linares (VEG), Antonio Pacheco (SCU) 40; **2B:** Luis Alvarez, Pablo Bejerano (GRA) 16; **3B:** Pedro Luis Rodríguez (HAB) 5; **HR:** Orestes Kindelán (SCU) 17; **RBI:** Lázaro Madera (VEG) 40; **SB:** Enrique Díaz (MET) 22.

Pitching Leaders—**Pct.:** Wilson Hawthorne (SCU) 10–0 (1.000); **G:** Fidencio Serrano (HOL) 20; **CG:** Luis Tissert (SCU) 13; **Wins:** Luis Tissert 13; **IP:** Luis Tissert 132.0; **SO:** Juan Ramírez (SSP) 91; **ERA:** René Arocha (MET) 1.31.

No-Hit/No-Run Games— None

1987 Selective Series XIII (Super-Provincial)

Champion— Serranos (42–21) Manager: Higinio Vélez

Standings— Serranos (42–21), Habana (41–22), Pinar del Río (36–27), Las Villas (32–31), Matanzas (27–36), Agropecuarios (25–38), Mineros (25–38), Camagüeyanos (24–39)

Batting Leaders—**BA:** Luis Ulacia (CMG) .384; **H:** Antonio Pacheco (SER) 88; **R:** Jorge García (SER) 54; **2B:** Antonio Pacheco, Orestes Kindelán (SER), Pedro Luis Rodríguez (AGR), Miguel Valiente (AGR) 16; **3B:** Jorge Garcá 8; **HR:** Orestes Kindelán, Reinaldo Fernández (CAM) 16; **RBI:** Orestes Kindelán 60; **SB:** Victor Mesa (LVS) 30.

Pitching Leaders—**Pct.:** Osvaldo Duvergel (SER) 13–2 (.867); **G:** Ramón Espinosa (CMG) 25; **CG:** Luis Tissert (SER) 17; **Wins:** Luis Tissert, Osvaldo Duvergel 13; **IP:** Luis Tissert 169.0; **SO:** Pablo Abreu (HAB) 114; **ERA:** Rogelio García (PRI) 1.25.

No-Hit/No-Run Games—**Rogelio García** (Pinar del Río 10–11–0, Camagüeyanos 0–0–1, 3–1–87); **Rogelio García** (Pinar del Río 3–5–2, Serranos 0–0–1, 3–22–87)

1987–1988 National Series XXVII (Provincial)

Vegueros repeats its championship in the National Series, then wins again in the Selective Series (under the province name of Pinar del Río). Jorge Fuentes thus becomes the Cuban League's only two-time double-champion manager. For the first time the National Series standings are divided into Eastern and Western zones (nine teams in each division), providing the equivalent of two National Series pennant races instead of only one. Habana's Pedro Luis Rodríguez is the hitting star of the National Series (leading in BA, hits, runs scored and doubles) and Lourdes Gourriel (with a .430 BA) earns similar honors in the Selective Series. Rogelio García picks up a final ERA title in the National Series while future big league headliner Orlando "El Duque" Hernández duplicates the feat during the Selective Series. Kindelán smacks 28 homers in the second and longer season. Two future National Team stars also make an early mark in National Series play when Camagüey's

Luis Ulacia (with 26) edges Industriales' Germán Mesa (with 25) for the stolen base title.

Champion— Vegueros (39–9, 5–1) Manager: Jorge Fuentes

Playoffs— Vegueros (5–1), Santiago de Cuba (3–3), Habana (3–3), Camagüey (1–5) (Six-game round-robin playoff tournament)

Zona Occidental— Vegueros (39–9), Habana (35–13), Industriales (34–14), Henequeneros (26–22), Metros (22–26), Cienfuegos (22–26), Forestales (18–30), Isla de la Juventud (10–38), Citricultores (10–38)

Zona Oriental— Santiago de Cuba (40–8), Granma (29–19), Camagüey (29–19), Villa Clara (25–23), Las Tunas (22–26), Ciego de Avila (20–28), Sancti Spíritus (20–28), Holguín (17–31), Guantánamo (14–34)

Batting Leaders—**BA:** Pedro Luis Rodríguez (HAB) .446; **H:** Pedro Luis Rodríguez 87; **R:** Pedro Luis Rodríguez 59; **2B:** Pedro Luis Rodríguez, Rafael Acebey (VCL) 17; **3B:** Aldo Villar (CFG) 7; **HR:** Lázaro Junco (HEN) 25; **RBI:** Juan Padilla (IND) 63; **SB:** Luis Ulacia (CMG) 26.

Pitching Leaders—**Pct.:** Angel Díaz (IND) 4–0 (1.000); **G:** Justo López (IJV) 23; **CG:** José Luis Alemán (SCU) 8; **Wins:** Mario Veliz (HAB) 11; **IP:** Rafael Rodríguez (HEN) 99.2; **SO:** Buenafe Napoles (CMG) 96; **ERA:** Rogelio García (VEG) 2.21.

No-Hit/No-Run Games— None

1988 Selective Series XIV (Super-Provincial)

Champion— Pinar del Río (40–23) Manager: Jorge Fuentes

Standings— Pinar del Río (40–23), Habana (39–24), Serranos (36–27), Las Villas (35–28), Mineros (27–35), Camagüeyanos (26–37), Matanzas (25–37), Agropecuarios (23–40)

Batting Leaders—**BA:** Lourdes Gourriel (LVS) .430; **H:** Germán Mesa (HAB) 91; **R:** Orestes Kindelán (SER) 69; **2B:** Luis Alvarez (MIN) 22; **3B:** Germán Mesa 6; **HR:** Orestes Kindelán 28; **RBI:** Omar Linares (PRI) 68; **SB:** Victor Mesa (LVS) 35.

Pitching Leaders—**Pct.:** José Alemán (SER) 9–2 (.818); **G:** Enrique Cutiño (SER) 32; **CG:** René Arocha (HAB) 10; **Wins:** Lázaro Valle (HAB) 10; **IP:** Enrique Cutiño 134.1; **SO:** René Arocha 106; **ERA:** Orlando Hernández (HAB) 3.18.

No-Hit/No-Run Games— None

1988–1989 National Series XXVIII (Provincial)

Orlando Hernández posts a perfect 7–0 National Series pitching record for Industriales and is now well on his way to establishing the league's career record for winning percentage. Behind the slugging of Kindelán (24 home runs) and the brilliant pitching of José Luis Alemán, Santiago de Cuba captures its second NS pennant and first in nine seasons. Emerging pitching star Lázaro Valle — top rival to Orlando Hernández as league best for much of the early nineties — garners a National Series ERA title for Industriales and then posts a perfect 10–0 won-lost Selective Series mark for Habana.

Champion— Santiago de Cuba (29–19, 5–1) Manager: Higinio Vélez

Playoffs— Santiago de Cuba (5–1), Industriales (4–2), Granma (2–4), Henequeneros (1–5) (Six-game round-robin playoff tournament)

Zona Occidental— Industriales (38–10), Henequeneros (36–12), Habana (31–16), Vegueros (31–17), Metros (25–22), Cienfuegos (18–29), Isla de la Juventud (14–34), Forestales (12–36), Citricultores (9–38)

Zona Oriental— Santiago de Cuba (29–19), Granma (29–19), Camagüey (29–19), Ciego de Avila (26–22), Guantánamo (25–23), Sancti Spíritus (20–28), Las Tunas (19–29), Holguín (13–35)

Batting Leaders—**BA:** Juan Bravo (IND) .414; **H:** Luis Guerra (VEG) 78; **R:** Orestes Kindelán (SCU) 57; **2B:** Lázaro Madera (VEG) 15; **3B:** Reemberto Rosell (CFG) 7; **HR:** Orestes Kindelán 24; **RBI:** Juan Millan (HAB) 59; **SB:** Victor Mesa (VCL) 26.

Pitching Leaders—**Pct.:** Orlando Hernández (IND) 7–0 (1.000); **G:** Reinaldo Santana (VCL) 27; **CG:** José Luis Alemán (SCU) 11; **Wins:** Mario Veliz (HAB), Jorge Luis Valdés (HEN) 11; **IP:** José Luis Alemán 105.1; **SO:** José Luis Alemán, Domingo Ordaz (VEG) 87; **ERA:** Lázaro Valle (IND) 1.93.

No-Hit/No-Run Game—**Osvaldo Fernández Guerra** (Metros 6–9–3, Citricultores 0–0–0, 12–10–88)

1989 Selective Series XV (Super-Provincial)

Champion— Las Villas (45–18, 2–0) Manager: Abelardo Triana

Playoffs— Las Villas over Habana, 2–0 (Finals)

Standings— Las Villas (45–18), Habana (45–18), Serranos (33–30), Camagüeyanos (32–31), Pinar del Río (30–33), Mineros (27–36), Agropecuarios (24–37), Matanzas (14–47)

Batting Leaders—**BA:** Amado Zamora (LVS) .413; **H:** Eddy Rojas (LVS) 100; **R:** Eddy Rojas 72; **2B:** Gabriel Pierre (SER) 28; **3B:** Aldo Suarez del Villar (LVS) 8; **HR:** Eddy Rojas 25; **RBI:** Eddy Rojas 76; **SB:** Luis Ulacia (CMG) 21.

Pitching Leaders—**Pct.:** Lázaro Valle (HAB) 10–0 (1.000); **G:** Reinaldo Santana (LVS) 26; **CG:** Osvaldo Duvergel (SER) 10; **Wins:** Lázaro Valle, Osvaldo Duvergel, Reinaldo Santana (LV), René Arocha (HAB) 10; **IP:** José Baez (MIN) 111.0; **SO:** Buenafe Napoles (CMG) 98; **ERA:** Fidel Azcuy (PRI) 2.85.

No-Hit/No-Run Games— None

1989–1990 National Series XXIX (Provincial)

Omar Linares captures a third National Series batting title with lofty .442 mark and also tops the Selective Series in the base-hits category with an even ninety. Lázaro Valle and Orlando Hernández continue their domination of Cuban pitching: Valle (Industriales) has a league-best 8–1 record during the National Series and Hernández (Habana) leads the Selective Series with an even better 10–1 ledger. One of El Duque's ten Selective Series victories comes with his only Cuban League no-hitter, an 11–0 seven-inning (mercy rule) whitewashing of Matanzas.

Champion— Henequeneros (37–11, 4–2) Manager: Gerardo Junco

Playoffs— Henequeneros over Santiago de Cuba, 4–2

(First-Place Series); Industriales over Granma, 3–0 (Third-Place Consolation Series)

Zona Occidental— Henequeneros (37–11), Industriales (33–15), Vegueros (33–15), Metropolitanos (31–17), Habana (27–21), Cienfuegos (18–30), Citricultores (15–33), Isla de la Juventud (14–34), Forestales (8–40)

Zona Oriental— Santiago de Cuba (36–12), Granma (28–20), Holguín (26–22), Villa Clara (26–22), Las Tunas (25–23), Camagüey (24–24), Sancti Spíritus (18–30), Ciego de Avila (17–31), Guantánamo (16–32)

Batting Leaders—**BA:** Omar Linares (VEG) .442; **H:** José Estrada (HEN) 77; **R:** Santiago Bejerano (GRA) 54; **2B:** Victor Mesa (VCL) 17; **3B:** Dioel Reyes (IJV), Enrique Díaz (MET) 5; **HR:** Ermidelio Urrutia (LTU) 20; **RBI:** Pablo Bejerano (GRA) 58; **SB:** Enrique Díaz (MET) 31.

Pitching Leaders—**Pct.:** Lázaro Valle (IND) 8–1 (.889); **G:** Dessy Lomba (CFG) 21; **CG:** Osvaldo Fernández Guerra (MET) 12; **Wins:** Osvaldo Fernández Guerra 12; **IP:** Osvaldo Fernández Guerra 119.2; **SO:** Osvaldo Fernández Guerra 118; **ERA:** Jorge Fumero (MET) 1.44.

No-Hit/No-Run Game—**Héctor Domínguez** (Citricultores 2–3–1, Isla de la Juventud 0–0–1, 12–13–89)

1990 Selective Series XVI (Super-Provincial)

Champion— Ciudad Habana (46–17) Manager: Servio Borges

Standings— Ciudad Habana (46–17), Pinar del Río (41–22), Agropecuarios (38–25), Las Villas (31–32), Mineros (25–38), Matanzas (24–37), Serranos (23–40), Camagüeyanos (22–39)

Batting Leaders—**BA:** Antonio González (HAB) .416; **H:** Omar Linares (PRI) 90; **R:** Gerardo Miranda (AGR) 63; **2B:** Ermidelio Urrutia (MIN) 24; **3B:** Juan Bruzón (MIN) 5; **HR:** Leonel Moa (CMG) 23; **RBI:** Romelio Martínez (AGR) 64; **SB:** Victor Mesa (LVS) 22.

Pitching Leaders—**Pct.:** Orlando Hernández (HAB) 10–1 (.909); **G:** Emiliano Diament (SER) 24; **CG:** José Ibar (AGR), Remigio Leal (PR), Jorge Luis Valdés (MTZ), Omar Ajete (PRI) 9; **Wins:** Omar Ajete 14; **IP:** Omar Ajete 134.0; **SO:** Omar Ajete 106; **ERA:** José Ibar (AGR) 2.20.

No-Hit/No-Run Game—**Orlando Hernández** (Ciudad Habana 11–15–0, Matanzas 0–0–4, 4–7–90)

1990–1991 National Series XXX (Provincial)

Lázaro Valle duplicates El Duque's 10–1 Selective Series record for Habana, posted one season earlier. Henequeneros repeats as National Series champions and Pinar del Río is back on top for a record sixth time in the Selective Series. Lázaro Junco is still biggest slugger for the NS champions and comes out on top of the home run race for an eighth time. Victor Mesa captures another stolen base title in the Selective Series but brilliant Industriales shortstop Germán Mesa pilfers the most bases in the National Series. At season's end René Arocha (NS leader in complete games with Industriales) becomes the first major defection to the United States from the Cuban national team.

Champion— Henequeneros (33–15, 6–1) Manager: Gerardo Junco

Playoffs— Henequeneros over Camagüey, 4–1 (Series Finals); Henequeneros over Santiago de Cuba, 2–0 (Semifinals); Camagüey over Habana, 2–1 (Semifinals)

Zona Occidental— Habana (34–13), Henequeneros (33–15), Vegueros (33–15), Industriales (29–19), Metros (24–23), Isla de la Juventud (20–28), Cienfuegos (16–32), Forestales (13–35), Citricultores (13–35)

Zona Oriental— Santiago de Cuba (33–15), Camagüey (29–19), Villa Clara (27–21), Holguín (26–22), Las Tunas (24–24), Granma (22–26), Guantánamo (21–27), Ciego de Avila (20–28), Sancti Spíritus (14–34)

*Batting Leaders—***BA**: Lázaro Madera (VEG) .400; **H**: Eddy Rojas (VCL) 66; **R**: Luis González (HAB) 49; **2B**: Alcides Maso (CMG) 15; **3B**: Jorge García (MET), Alexis Cabrejas (IND), Juan Millan (HAB), Yobal Dueñas (VEG) 4; **HR**: Lázaro Junco (HEN) 17; **RBI**: Oscar Machado (VCL) 51; **SB**: Germán Mesa (IND) 22.

*Pitching Leaders—***Pct.**: Rolando Hernández (HEN 4–0 (1.000); **G**: Giorge Díaz (GTM), Angel Tumbarell (GTM) 22; **CG**: René Arocha (IND), Adiel Palma (CFG), Lázaro de la Torre (MET) 9; **Wins**: Ariel Cutiño (SCU), Jorge Luis Valdés (HEN) 9; **IP**: Juan Pérez (LTU) 106.2; **SO**: Juan Pérez 107; **ERA**: José Riscart (VCL) 1.51.

No-Hit/No-Run Games— None

1991 Selective Series XVII (Super-Provincial)

Champion— Pinar del Río (41–22) Manager: Jorge Fuentes

Standings— Pinar del Río (41–22), Habana (39–24), Matanzas (35–28), Serranos (30–33), Agropecuarios (29–34), Mineros (28–35), Las Villas (27–36), Camagüeyanos (23–40)

*Batting Leaders—***BA**: Pedro Luis Rodríguez (AGR) .380; **H**: Victor Mesa (LVS) 86; **R**: Omar Linares (PRI) 66; **2B**: Julio Fernández (MTZ) 19; **3B**: Jorge García (SER) 7; **HR**: Romelio Martínez (AGR) 20; **RBI**: Romelio Martínez 57; **SB**: Victor Mesa 30.

*Pitching Leaders—***Pct.**: Lázaro Valle (HAB) 10–1 (.909); **G**: Francisco Despaigne (HAB) 23; **CG**: Omar Ajete (PRI), Jorge Luis Valdés (MTZ) 9; **Wins**: Omar Ajete 11; **IP**: Omar Ajete 131.0; **SO**: Omar Ajete 104; **ERA**: Osvaldo Fernández Guerra (HAB) 2.09.

No-Hit/No-Run Games— None

1991–1992 National Series XXXI (Provincial)

Industriales is back on top in the National Series and Habana posts the best record in the Selective Series before dropping a seven-game championship round to the Serranos. Future career victories leader Jorge Luis Valdés produced a brilliant 12–0 NS record for Henequeneros, while Orlando Hernández is nearly as dominating (10–2 with a league-best 2.23 ERA) for Habana during the Selective Series. Omar Linares is once again National Series batting champion and also captures his only home run crown during the follow-up Selective Series. Southpaw Faustino Corrales authors the year's only no-hit, no-run game for Vegueros.

Champion— Industriales (36–12, 7–1) Manager: Jorge Trigoura

Playoffs— Industriales over Henequeneros, 4–1 (Finals); Industriales over Granma, 3–0 (Semifinals); Henequeneros over Camagüey, 3–0 (Semifinals)

Zona Occidental— Industriales (36–12), Henequeneros (31–17), Ciudad Habana (31–17), Vegueros (30–18), Metropolitanos (28–20), Cienfuegos (20–28), Isla de la Juventud (16–32), Forestales (14–34), Citricultores (10–38)

Zona Oriental— Camagüey (29–19), Granma (28–20), Holguín (27–21), Las Tunas (26–21), Santiago de Cuba (26–22), Villa Clara (25–23), Ciego de Avila (21–26), Guantánamo (18–30), Sancti Spíritus (15–33)

*Batting Leaders—***BA**: Omar Linares (VEG) .396; **H**: Luis González (HAB) 71; **R**: Luis González 52; **2B**: Juan Millan (HAB), Enrique Suárez (GTM) 17; **3B**: Juan Valle (CIT), Diego Fonseca (HOL) 4; **HR**: Romelio Martínez (HOL) 19; **RBI**: Oscar Macías (HAB) 45; **SB**: José Estrada (HEN) 32.

*Pitching Leaders—***Pct.**: Jorge Luis Valdés (HEN) 12–0 (1.000); **G**: Jorge Tissert (SCU), Ruben Rodríguez (SCU), Felipe Fernández (CMG) 20; **CG**: Osvaldo Fernández Rodríguez (HOL) 11; **Wins**: Jorge Luis Valdés 12; **IP**: Juan Pérez (LTU) 119.2; **SO**: Juan C. Pérez 134; **ERA**: Francisco Despaigne (IND) 0.92.

*No-Hit/No-Run Game—***Faustino Corrales** (Vegueros 7–10–1, Isla de la Juventud 0–0–1, 11–19–91)

1992 Selective Series XVIII (Super-Provincial)

Champion— Serranos (36–27) Manager: Higinio Vélez

Playoffs— Serranos over Ciudad Habana, 4–3 (Finals)

Zona Occidental— Habana (41–21), Pinar del Río (37–26), Matanzas (28–34), Agropecuarios (27–36)

Zona Oriental— Serranos (36–27), Las Villas (30–32), Camagüeyanos (27–35), Mineros (24–39)

*Batting Leaders—***BA**: Omar Linares (PRI) .398; **H**: Reemberto Rosell (LVS) 96; **R**: Omar Linares 65; **2B**: Pedro Luis Rodríguez (AGR) 19; **3B**: Reemberto Rosell 7; **HR**: Omar Linares 23; **RBI**: Omar Linares 58; **SB**: Victor Mesa (LVS) 52.

*Pitching Leaders—***Pct.**: Orlando Hernández (HAB) 10–2 (.833); **G**: Jesús Bosmenier (PRI) 25; **CG**: Luis Rolando Arrojo (LVS) 10; **Wins**: Orlando Hernández 10; **IP**: Osvaldo Fernández Rodríguez (MIN) 116.1; **SO**: Faustino Corrales (PRI) 89; **ERA**: Orlando Hernández 2.23.

No-Hit/No-Run Games— None

1992–1993 National Series XXXII (Provincial)

Omar Linares equals Pedro Luis Rodríguez's single-season National Series batting mark (.446 in 1988) while capturing his own fifth individual hitting crown. Linares's Pinar del Río club posts the season's best record but nonetheless falls to Villa Clara in the playoff finals. For Villa Clara it is only the beginning of a rare three-year run atop the National Series standings. Lázaro Junco's 27 roundtrippers for Matanzas are a National Series record, as are the 55 stolen bases achieved by Enrique Díaz. Speedster Díaz (playing for Metropolitanos) will reign in the stolen bases department for the next three seasons and also four of the next five. Future national team defector and big league starter Osvaldo Fernández (San Francisco Giants and Cincinnati Reds) hurls one of the season's two no-hit, no-run games. For the first time the National Series is divided into four divisions with four teams each, once more doubling the number of fan-gripping season-long pennant races.

Champion— Villa Clara (42–23, 8–3) Manager: Pedro Jova

Playoffs— Villa Clara over Pinar del Río 4–2 (Finals); Villa Clara over Santiago de Cuba, 4–1 (Semifinals); Pinar del Río over Industriales, 4–0 (Semifinals)

Group A— Pinar del Río (47–18), Matanzas (35–30), Metropolitanos (32–33), Isla de la Juventud (16–49)

Group B— Industriales (45–20), Habana (31–34), Sancti Spíritus (26–39), Cienfuegos (25–40)

Group C— Villa Clara (42–23), Camagüey (33–32), Las Tunas (28–37), Ciego de Avila (20–45)

Group D— Santiago de Cuba (41–24), Granma (39–26), Holguín (39–26), Guantánamo (21–44)

Batting Leaders—**BA**: Omar Linares (PRI) .446; **H**: Reemberto Rosell (CFG) 100; **R**: Omar Linares (PRI) 63; **2B**: Jorge Salfran (MET) 20; **3B**: Pedro Luis Rodríguez (HAB), José Estrada (MTZ) 5; **HR**: Lázaro Junco (MTZ) 27; **RBI**: Gabriel Pierre (SCU) 65; **SB**: Enrique Díaz (MET) 55.

Pitching Leaders—**Pct.**: Jorge Pérez (VCL) 10–1 (.909); **G**: Felipe Fernández (CMG) 28; **CG**: José Baez (LTU) 13; **Wins**: Ernesto Guevara (GRA) 13; **IP**: José Baez 153.1; **SO**: Ernesto Guevara 117; **ERA**: Jorge Pérez 1.74.

No-Hit/No-Run Games—**Osvaldo Fernández Rodríguez** (Holguín 10–11–0, Metropolitanos 0–0–2, 11–29–92); **Ernesto Guevara** (Granma 2–7–1, Industriales 0–0–0, 12–8–92)

1993 Selective Series XIX (Super-Provincial)

Champion— Orientales (25–20) Manager: Frangel Reynaldo

Standings— Orientales (25–20), Habana (24–21), Occidentales (23–22), Agropecuarios (18–27)

Batting Leaders—**BA**: Gerardo Miranda (OCC) .390; **H**: Juan Carlos Linares (OCC) 64; **R**: Germán Mesa (HAB) 40; **2B**: Juan Carlos Linares 16; **3B**: Miguel Caldés (AGR), Lázaro López (AGR) 3; **HR**: Orestes Kindelán (OTE) 14; **RBI**: Orestes Kindelán 46; **SB**: Victor Mesa (AGR) 15.

Pitching Leaders—**Pct.**: Ormari Romero (OTE) 3–1 (.750); **G**: Felipe Fernández (AGR) 19; **CG**: Rolando Arrojo (AGR), José Riscart (AGR), Rafael Gómez (HAB), Omar Ajete (OCC), Faustino Corrales (OCC) 4; **Wins**: Ernesto Guevara (OTE) 7; **IP**: Ernesto Guevara 78.0; **SO**: Osvaldo Fernández Guerra (HAB) 58; **ERA**: Omar Ajete 2.33.

No-Hit/No-Run Games— None

1993–1994 National Series XXXIII (Provincial)

Old stars begin to fade while new ones arrive on the scene. Lázaro Junco paces the league in homers for the tenth and last time; Lourdes Gourriel enjoys a final late-career batting title; and Orlando Hernández and Liván Hernández both star on the mound. Liván will soon defect and Orlando will be suspended in the wake of his half-brother's unsanctioned departure. Gourriel and Junco are on the doorstep of retirement, as is longtime basestealing king Victor Mesa with Villa Clara. By contrast, future batting champion Osmani Urrutia debuts in the outfield with Las Tunas. Villa Clara and Industriales share top billing with the best overall season's records and then battle to a near standoff in evenly matched playoff finals that the defending champions ultimately capture in seven games.

Champion— Villa Clara (43–22, 8–5) Manager: Pedro Jova

Playoffs— Villa Clara over Industriales, 4–3 (Finals); Villa Clara over Santiago de Cuba, 4–2 (Semifinals); Industriales over Pinar del Río, 4–2 (Semifinals)

Group A— Pinar del Río (39–23), Matanzas (36–26), Isla de la Juventud (35–30), Metropolitanos (22–43)

Group B— Industriales (43–22), Sancti Spíritus (36–29), Habana (35–30), Cienfuegos (20–45)

Group C— Villa Clara (43–22), Camagüey (35–30), Las Tunas (28–37), Ciego de Avila (18–44)

Group D— Santiago de Cuba (43–22), Holguín (33–32), Granma (32–33), Guantánamo (16–49)

Batting Leaders—**BA**: Lourdes Gourriel (SSP) .395; **H**: Pedro Luis Rodríguez (HAB) 100; **R**: Eduardo Paret (VCL) 59; **2B**: Lourdes Gourriel 19; **3B**: Pedro Luis Rodríguez, Jorge Díaz (VCL), José Estrada (MTZ) 6; **HR**: Lázaro Junco (MTZ) 21; **RBI**: Fausto Alvarez (SCU), Daniel Lazo (PRI) 63; **SB**: Enrique Díaz (MET) 53.

Pitching Leaders—**Pct.**: Jorge Fumero (IND) 9–0 (1.000); **G**: René Espin (MET) 30; **CG**: Liván Hernández (IJV) 13; **Wins**: Orlando Hernández (IND) 11; **IP**: Carlos Yanes (IJV) 125.1; **SO**: Liván Hernández 132; **ERA**: Osvaldo Fernández Rodríguez (HOL) 1.62.

No-Hit/No-Run Games— None

1994 Selective Series XX (Super-Provincial)

Champion— Occidentales (27–18) Manager: Jorge Fuentes

Standings— Occidentales (27–18), Centrales (26–19), Habana (19–26), Orientales (18–27)

Batting Leaders—**BA**: Juan Carlos Linares (OCC) .429; **H**: Juan Carlos Linares 70; **R**: José Estrada (OCC) 46; **2B**: Pedro Luis Rodríguez (HAB) 13; **3B**: Juan Padilla (HAB), Jorge Díaz (CEN) 4; **HR**: Romelio Martínez (HAB) 10; **RBI**: Juan Carlos Linares 42; **SB**: Eduardo Paret (CEN) 16.

Pitching Leaders—**Pct.**: Jorge Martínez (OCC) 4–0 (1.000); **G**: Miguel Pérez (OTE), Carlos Yanes (OCC) 16; **CG**: Liván Hernández (OCC), Rolando Arrojo (CEN) 5; **Wins**: Omar Ajete (OCC) 7; **IP**: José Baez (OTE) 68.0; **SO**: Omar Ajete 55; **ERA**: Eliecer de Oca (CEN) 2.40.

No-Hit/No-Run Games— None

1994–1995 National Series XXXIV (Provincial)

Villa Clara wins in the National Series for the third time running while Orientales captures what will prove to be the final Selective Series tournament. Rolando Arrojo establishes himself as the new Cuban ace with a perfect 11–0 pitching record for the National Series champions from Villa Clara. Pedro Luis Lazo and José Ariel Contreras, both lanky fireballing righthanders, show considerable future promise for Pinar del Río during the penultimate Selective Series season. Former heavy-hitting star Pedro Jova (.315 lifetime average with 1598 career hits) becomes first manager to capture three consecutive NS titles since Ramón Carneado turned the trick and posted four straight with Industriales during the early and mid-sixties.

Champion— Villa Clara (44–18, 8–2) Manager: Pedro Jova

Playoffs— Villa Clara over Pinar del Río, 4–2 (Finals); Villa Clara over Holguín, 4–0 (Semifinals); Pinar del Río over Habana, 4–0 (Semifinals)

Group A— Pinar del Río (41–24), Matanzas (37–27), Metropolitanos (29–36), Isla de la Juventud (23–39)

Group B— Habana (46–18), Industriales (35–28), Cienfuegos (33–31), Sancti Spíritus (23–41)

Group C— Villa Clara (44–18), Camagüey (27–38), Las Tunas (27–38), Ciego de Avila (18–47)

Group D— Holguín (37–28), Granma (37–28), Santiago de Cuba (37–28), Guantánamo (20–45)

Batting Leaders—**BA**: Amado Zamora (VCL) .395; **H**: Alexander Ramos (IJV) 100; **R**: Omar Linares (PRI) 63; **2B**: Antonio Scull (MET) 28; **3B**: Juan García (CAV), José Estrada (MTZ) 7; **HR**: Miguel Caldés (CMG) 20; **RBI**: Oscar Machado (VCL) 64; **SB**: Enrique Díaz (MET) 22.

Pitching Leaders—**Pct.**: Rolando Arrojo (VCL) 11–0 (1.000); **G**: Ruben Rodríguez (SCU) 30; **CG**: Pedro Luis Lazo (PRI) 11; **Wins**: José Ibar (HAB) 14; **IP**: Adiel Palma (CFG) 126.2; **SO**: Omar Luis (CMG) 108; **ERA**: Rolando Arroyo 1.88.

No-Hit/No-Run Games— None

1995 Selective Series XXI (Super-Provincial)

Champion— Orientales (29–16) Manager: Higinio Vélez

Standings— Orientales (29–16), Occidentales (26–18), Habana (29–16), Centrales (15–29)

Batting Leaders—**BA**: Rey Isaac (OTE) .424; **H**: Alexander Ramos (OCC) 72; **R**: Gabriel Pierre (OTE) 56; **2B**: Fausto Alvarez (OTE) 19; **3B**: Orlis Díaz (OCC) 6; **HR**: Romelio Martínez (HAB) 16; **RBI**: Fausto Alvarez 52; **SB**: Manuel Benavides (OTE) 9.

Pitching Leaders—**Pct.**: Pedro Luis Lazo (OCC) 3–0 (1.000); **G**: José Contreras (OCC) 15; **CG**: Lázaro Valle (HAB) 6; **Wins**: Ormari Romero (OTE) 6; **IP**: Lázaro Valle 81.1; **SO**: Lázaro Valle 53; **ERA**: Ernesto Guevara (OTE) 3.63.

No-Hit/No-Run Games— None

1995–1996 National Series XXXV

Industriales breaks three-year National Series championship grip of Villa Clara in season leading up to 1996 Atlanta Olympics. Veteran Camagüey outfielder Luis Ulacia captures the batting title with a lofty .421 mark before starring as leadoff hitter on the undefeated Olympic team. In a somewhat con-troversial move, Germán Mesa — considered the best Cuban shortstop ever — is left off Cuba's Olympic squad, but his replacement Eduardo Paret is one of the true stars on the field in Atlanta. Mesa is later in the year suspended from league action under suspicion of conversing with big league player agents. Rolando Arrojo defects from national team just before the opening of Olympic competition in Atlanta, but the loss again seems to do little damage to Cuban gold medal prospects or to team morale. A newly designed *Copa de La Revolution* "second season" is tried out as replacement for the suspended Selective Series and Pinar del Río and Santiago de Cuba lock horns in the short-season championship finals.

Champion— Industriales (41–22, 8–2) Manager: Pedro Medina

Playoffs— Industriales over Villa Clara, 4–2 (Finals); Industriales over Pinar del Río, 4–0 (Semifinals); Villa Clara over Santiago de Cuba, 4–2 (Semifinals)

Group A— Pinar del Río (41–23), Matanzas (37–27), Metropolitanos (32–32), Isla de la Juventud (29–35)

Group B— Industriales (41–22), Habana (37–27), Cienfuegos (28–37), Sancti Spíritus (21–44)

Group C— Villa Clara (48–17), Camagüey (38–27), Las Tunas (19–45), Ciego de Avila (19–46)

Group D— Santiago de Cuba (40–25), Granma (33–32), Holguín (30–35), Guantánamo (23–42)

Batting Leaders—**BA**: Luis Ulacia (CMG) .421; **H**: Reemberto Rosell (CFG), Jorge Salfran (MET) 106; **R**: Juan Manrique (MTZ), Enrique Díaz (MET) 76; **2B**: Jorge Luis Toca (VCL) 26; **3B**: Enrique Díaz 8; **HR**: Ariel Benavides (GTM) 25; **RBI**: Juan Manrique (MTZ) 79; **SB**: Enrique Díaz 35.

Pitching Leaders—**Pct.**: Luis González (IND) 5–0 (1.000); **G**: Jorge Fumero (IND), Rafael Delgado (MTZ) 27; **CG**: Faustino Corrales (PRI) 11; **Wins**: Oscar Gil (HOL) 11; **IP**: Oscar Gil (HOL) 118.1; **SO**: Faustino Corrales 128; **ERA**: Jorge Fumero 1.94.

No-Hit/No-Run Games— None

1996 Copa de la Revolucion I

Champion— Santiago de Cuba (23–7, 4–1) Manager: Higinio Vélez

Playoffs— Santiago de Cuba over Pinar del Río, 4–1 (Finals)

Zona Occidental— Pinar del Río (18–12), Industriales (14–16), Matanzas (13–17), Habana (12–18)

Zona Oriental— Santiago de Cuba (23–7), Villa Clara (20–10), Camagüey (11–19), Granma (9–21)

Batting Leaders—**BA**: Yobal Dueñas (PRI) .475; **H**: Juan Bruzón (GRA) 52; **R**: Enrique Díaz (GRA) 38; **2B**: Andy Morales (HAB) 17; **3B**: Marino Moreno (GRA) 6; **HR**: Daniel Lazo (PRI) 14; **RBI**: Daniel Lazo 42; **SB**: Enrique Díaz 12.

Pitching Leaders—**Pct.**: Ormari Romero (SCU) 8–0 (1.000); **G**: Jorge Fumero (IND), Ciro Silvino Licea (GRA) 15; **CG**: Ormari Romero 5; **Wins**: Ormari Romero 8; **IP**: Ormari Romero 53.1; **SO**: Pedro Luis Lazo (PRI) 55; **ERA**: Ormari Romero 2.19.

No-Hit/No-Run Games— None

1996–1997 National Series XXXVI

Pinar del Río is the runaway league champion, but only after equally strong Santiago de Cuba is upset by Villa Clara in the league semifinals. José Estrada of Matanzas is the year's equally surprising hitting star and José Contreras (in his seventh season) emerges as a new pitching phenom for Pinar del Río. This season on the surface is thus something of a successful celebration of a gold medal victory at the Atlanta Olympics the previous summer. But worsening economic conditions in Cuba and the continued policy of forced retirements of veteran players (some being sent to industrial league teams in Japan and Italy) dulls interest—especially in Havana—and many games are played before woefully small crowds, most often in Estadio Latinoamericano. The 30-game Revolution Cup season is played for the second and last time and again won by the team representing Santiago de Cuba.

Champion— Pinar del Río (50–15, 8–0) Manager: Jorge Fuentes

Playoffs— Pinar del Río over Villa Clara, 4–0 (Finals); Pinar del Río over Industriales, 4–0 (Semifinals); Villa Clara over Santiago de Cuba, 4–2 (Semifinals)

Grupo A— Pinar del Río (50–15), Metropolitanos (42–23), Matanzas (39–26), Isla de la Juventud (31–34)

Grupo B— Industriales (33–30), Habana (30–35), Cienfuegos (25–40), Sancti Spíritus (16–49)

Grupo C— Villa Clara (37–27), Camagüey (33–32), Las Tunas (28–37), Ciego de Avila (20–45)

Grupo D— Santiago de Cuba (49–16), Holguín (34–31), Granma (28–37), Guantánamo (23–41)

Batting Leaders—**BA**: José Estrada (MTZ) .391; **H**: José Estrada 104; **R**: José Estrada (MTZ) 60; **2B**: Oscar Valdés (MET) 23; **3B**: Enrique Díaz (MET) 9; **HR**: Julio Fernández (MTZ) 15; **RBI**: Julio Fernández 60; **SB**: Eduardo Paret (VCL) 43.

Pitching Leaders—**Pct.**: Osnel Bocourt (IND) 6–0 (1.000); **G**: Juan Pérez (HOL) 15; **CG**: Ormari Romero (SCU) 12; **Wins**: José Contreras (PRI) 14; **IP**: José Ibar (HAB) 132.2; **SO**: José Contreras 135; **ERA**: Pedro Luis Lazo (PRI) 1.15.

No-Hit/No-Run Games— None

1997 Copa de la Revolution II

Champion— Santiago de Cuba (22–8, 4–2) Manager: Higinio Vélez

Playoffs— Santiago de Cuba over Pinar del Río, 4–2 (Finals)

Zona Occidental— Pinar del Río (21–9), Industriales (16–14), Habana (13–17), Metropolitanos (9–21)

Zona Oriental— Santiago de Cuba (22–8), Villa Clara (20–10), Camagüey (12–18), Holguín (7–23)

Batting Leaders—**BA**: Javier Méndez (IND) .462; **H**: Juan Carlos Linares (PRI) 46; **R**: Orestes Kindelán (SCU) 28; **2B**: Ariel Pestano (VCL) 11; **3B**: Yobal Dueñas (PRI) 5; **HR**: Gabriel Pierre (SCU) 12; **RBI**: Gabriel Pierre 33; **SB**: Eduardo Paret (VCL) 13.

Pitching Leaders—**Pct.**: Ormari Romero (SCU), Pedro Luis Lazo (PRI) 6–0 (1.000); **G**: Juan Pérez (HOL) 15; **CG**:

Ormari Romero, Pedro Luis Lazo, Ciro Silvino Liceo (GRA), Ariel Tapanes (PRI), Carlos Yanes (IND) 3; **Wins**: Ormari Romero, Pedro Luis Lazo 6; **IP**: Ormari Romero 53.1; **SO**: Pedro Luis Lazo 42; **ERA**: Abel Madera (PRI) 0.70.

No-Hit/No-Run Games— None

1997–1998 National Series XXXVII

Cuban League action is again overhauled with a return to a single National Series season and the expansion of National Series action to a larger 90-game format. Oscar Machado establishes a new single-season RBI mark and Yasser Gómez debuts as brilliant young outfielder for Metropolitanos (soon to be shifted to Industriales). On the team front, Pinar del Río repeats as champion, despite a managerial switch from Jorge Fuentes to former star player Alfonso Urquiola. The surprise move by INDER officials comes on the heels of previous summer's disappointing Intercontinental Cup final-round loss to Japan in Barcelona. But the year's biggest story is veteran pitcher José Ibar of Habana Province, who becomes the first hurler in league history to register as many as 20 victories in a single season. Ibar is also the league's pacesetter in ERA, winning percentage, strikeouts and innings pitched. Another format change involves the introduction of a mid-season All-Star Game held in early March in Ciego de Avila.

Champion— Pinar del Río (56–34, 11–5) Manager: Alfonso Urquiola

Playoffs— Pinar del Río over Santiago de Cuba, 4–1 (Finals); Pinar del Río over Habana, 4–3 (Semifinals); Santiago de Cuba over Camagüey, 4–3 (Semifinals); Pinar del Río over Industriales, 3–1 (Quarterfinals); Habana over Metropolitanos, 3–2 (Quarterfinals); Camagüey over Ciego de Avila, 3–0 (Quarterfinals), Santiago de Cuba over Guantánamo, 3–0 (Quarterfinals)

Group A— Pinar del Río (56–34), Metropolitanos (52–38), Isla de la Juventud (46–44), Matanzas (39–51)

Group B— Habana (54–36), Industriales (47–43), Cienfuegos (27–63), Sancti Spíritus (27–63)

Group C— Camagüey (57–33), Ciego de Avila (57–33), Villa Clara (47–43), Las Tunas (32–58)

Group D— Santiago de Cuba (61–28), Guantánamo (52–38), Holguín (34–55), Granma (31–59)

Batting Leaders—**BA**: Robelquis Videaux (GTM) .393; **H**: Reemberto Rosell (CFG) 132; **R**: Oscar Machado (VCL) 65; **2B**: Loidel Chapelli (CMG) 32; **3B**: Daniel Castro (LTU) 11; **HR**: Oscar Machado (VCL) 24; **RBI**: Oscar Machado 87; **SB**: Enrique Díaz (MET) 38.

Pitching Leaders—**Pct.**: José Ibar (HAB) 20–2 (.909); **G**: Raúl Reyes (CMG) 35; **CG**: Giorge Díaz (GTM) 16; **Wins**: José Ibar 20; **IP**: José Ibar 196.1; **SO**: José Ibar 189; **ERA**: José Ibar 1.51.

No-Hit/No-Run Games—**Modesto Luis** (Las Tunas 7–9–1, Granma 0–0–0, 11–18–97); **Geovanis Castañeda** (Guantánamo 8–9–2, Las Tunas 0–0–2, 11–22–97)

Cuban League All-Star Game I— Location: Ciego de Avila (Estadio José Ramón Cepero), March 8, 1998. Score: Orientales 5, Occidentales 2

1998–1999 National Series XXXVIII

Santiago de Cuba surprises during the postseason, overhauling favored Industriales in the seven-game championship finals after first dropping the opening three games; Santiago thus proved the best among playoff challengers after finishing the regular campaign only two games above the break-even point. Postseason play is interrupted by the celebrated visit of the big-league Baltimore Orioles for an historic showdown with the vaunted Cuban national team (minus players such as Germán Mesa of Industriales and Orestes Kindelán and Antonio Pacheco of Santiago, still active in playoff action). Wooden bats donated by Major League Baseball are introduced in the middle of the playoffs for use in the semifinal and final series. Omar Linares misses most of the regular season with leg injuries but returns to star against the Orioles in both Havana and Baltimore and also in the Pan Am Games in Winnipeg. A highpoint for Cuban League baseball comes with surprising 12–6 romp over the professional Orioles in early May at Baltimore.

Champion— Santiago de Cuba (46–44, 11–7) Manager: Higinio Vélez

Playoffs— Santiago de Cuba over Industriales, 4–3 (Finals); Santiago de Cuba over Guantánamo, 4–2 (Semifinals); Industriales over Isla de la Juventud, 4–3 (Semifinals); Santiago de Cuba over Granma, 3–2 (Quarterfinals); Industriales over Habana, 3–0 (Quarterfinals); Isla de la Juventud over Pinar del Río, 3–2 (Quarterfinals); Guantánamo over Villa Clara, 3–1 (Quarterfinals)

Group A— Pinar del Río (53–37), Isla de la Juventud (52–38), Matanzas (40–50), Metropolitanos (34–56)

Group B— Industriales (58–32), Habana (51–39), Cienfuegos (42–48), Sancti Spíritus (33–57)

Group C— Villa Clara (51–39), Ciego de Avila (41–49), Camagüey (40–50), Las Tunas (30–60)

Group D— Granma (56–34), Guantánamo (50–40), Santiago de Cuba (46–44), Holguín (43–47)

Batting Leaders— **BA**: Yobal Dueñas (PRI) .418; **H**: Michel Enríquez (IJV) 152; **R**: Michel Enríquez 81; **2B**: Michel Enríquez 35; **3B**: Yasser Gómez (IND) 12; **HR**: Daniel Lazo (PRI) 18; **RBI**: Oscar Macías (HAB) 81; **SB**: Eduardo Paret (VCL) 46.

Pitching Leaders— **Pct.**: Jorge Machado (IND) 13–1 (.929); **G**: Amaury Sanit (IND) 39; **CG**: Ciro Silvino Licea (GRA) 16; **Wins**: José Ibar (HAB) 18; **IP**: José Ibar 193.0; **SO**: José Ibar 158; **ERA**: Ciro Silvino Licea 1.85.

No-Hit/No-Run Game— **José Baez** (Las Tunas 6–8–1, Metropolitanos 0–0–2, 11–17–98)

Cuban League All-Star Game II— Location: Güines (Estadio Héroes de Mayabeque), February 18, 1999. Score: Orientales 1, Occidentales 0.

1999–2000 National Series XXXIX

Sensational 19-year-old flamethrower Maels Rodríguez makes most of the year's headlines while pitching for one of the league's most inept team. Maels is first Cuban Leaguer officially clocked at above 100 mph during National Series action; several weeks later he tosses the first-ever perfect game in league annals in front of 4500 fans in Sancti Spíritus. Santiago proves to have one of the most dominant clubs in years and cruises to easy championship with 62 regular-season wins (third most ever) and perfect postseason ledger. The first season with wooden bats since 1976–77 (National Series XVI and Selective Series III) proves the "year of the pitcher" to no one's surprise. Hitting is depressed and home runner leader Ivan Correa boasts a mere 10, the lowest total since 1977. At one point late in the season five starters own ERAs under 1.00 and Norge Vera eventually finishes on top of the pack at 0.97. Sancti Spíritus twin aces Maels Rodríguez and Yovani Aragón tie for the strikeout leadership (with 177 each, but Maels hurls fewer innings).

Champion— Santiago de Cuba (62–28, 11–0) Manager: Higinio Vélez

Playoffs— Santiago de Cuba over Pinar del Río, 4–0 (Finals); Santiago de Cuba over Granma, 4–0 (Semifinals); Pinar del Río over Industriales, 4–3 (Semifinals); Santiago de Cuba over Camagüey, 3–0 (Quarterfinals); Pinar del Río over Isla de la Juventud, 3–1 (Quarterfinals); Granma over Villa Clara, 3–0 (Quarterfinals); Industriales over Metropolitanos, 3–2 (Quarterfinals)

Group A— Pinar del Río (59–31), Metropolitanos (46–44), Isla de la Juventud (42–48), Matanzas (39–51)

Group B— Industriales (57–33), Sancti Spíritus (39–51), Habana (35–55), Cienfuegos (34–56)

Group C— Villa Clara (53–37), Camagüey (52–38), Ciego de Avila (46–44), Las Tunas (32–58)

Group D— Santiago de Cuba (62–28), Granma (53–37), Holguín (40–50), Guantánamo (31–59)

Batting Leaders— **BA**: Yorelvis Charles (CAV) .353; **H**: Orlis Díaz (IJV) 117; **R**: Enrique Díaz (MET) 59; **2B**: Ariel Borrero (VCL) 27; **3B**: Nguyen Boulet (MTZ) 9; **HR**: Ivan Correa (IND) 10; **RBI**: Antonio Scull (IND) 65; **SB**: Enrique Díaz 35.

Pitching Leaders— **Pct.**: Aleydis García (IJV) 9–1 (.900); **G**: Roidel Enríquez (VCL) 39; **CG**: Gervasio Miguel (IJV), Yovani Aragón (SSP) 14; **Wins**: Norge Vera (SCU) 17; **IP**: Ciro Silvino Licea (GRA) 194.2; **SO**: Yovani Aragón, Maels Rodríguez (SSP) 177; **ERA**: Norge Vera 0.97.

No-Hit/No-Run Games— **Maels Rodríguez** (Sancti Spíritus 1–9–0, Las Tunas 0–0–2, 12–22–99*) *First and only "Perfect Game" in 40-year Cuban League history; **Adiel Palma** (Cienfuegos 4–8–1, Las Tunas 0–0–2, 12–25–99); **Carlos Yanes** (Isla de la Juventud 6–11–0, Villa Clara 0–0–1, 5–3–00)

Cuban League All-Star Game III— Location: Sancti Spíritus (Estadio José Antonio Huelga), February 27, 2000. Score: Orientales 4, Occidentales 1

2000–2001 National Series XL

The first season of the new millennium was literally one for the record books with a raft of new marks set during this campaign. Maels Rodríguez provided the top story, obliterating the single-season strikeout record by Santiago "Changa" Mederos (208 in 1969) that had stood unchallenged for three-plus decades. Also on the pitching front, Industriales veteran Lázaro de la Torre (at 40 years of age) became only the fourth Cuban pitcher to reach 200 career victories. Alexander Ramos (Isla) lifted his consecutive-games-played record to 712 straight by season's end; Osmani Urrutia became the first league batting champion to wear the uniform of Las Tunas; and Orlis Díaz tied the NS RBI record set several years back by Oscar Machado. Villa Clara shortstop Eduardo Paret also got into the act with 99 runs scored for yet another new NS record. Meanwhile Santiago finished strong, overhauling both Pinar and Villa Clara (co-leaders in wins) in postseason to capture a third straight title and claim the first pennant of the new century. Season ends on a dramatic note with grand slam homer by Antonio Pacheco determining the final playoff game.

Champion—Santiago de Cuba (55–35, 11–4) Manager: Higinio Vélez

Playoffs—Santiago de Cuba over Pinar del Río, 4–1 (Finals); Pinar del Río over Habana, 4–0 (Semifinals); Santiago de Cuba over Camagüey, 4–2 (Semifinals); Pinar del Río over Industriales, 3–2 (Quarterfinals); Camagüey over Villa Clara, 3–1 (Quarterfinals); Santiago de Cuba over Granma, 3–1 (Quarterfinals); Habana over Isla de la Juventud, 3–1 (Quarterfinals)

Group A—Pinar del Río (59–31), Isla de la Juventud (53–37), Metropolitanos (40–50), Matanzas (36–54)

Group B—Habana (50–40), Industriales (50–40), Sancti Spíritus (38–52), Cienfuegos (28–62)

Group C—Villa Clara (59–31), Camagüey (53–37), Ciego de Avila (35–55), Las Tunas (25–65)

Group D—Santiago de Cuba (55–35), Granma (55–35), Guantánamo (43–47), Holguín (41–49)

Batting Leaders—**BA**: Osmani Urrutia (LTU) .431; **H**: Alexander Ramos (IJV) 147; **R**: Eduardo Paret (VCL) 99; **2B**: Leslie Anderson (CMG) 28; **3B**: Ariel Borrero (VCL) 10; **HR**: Oscar Macías (HAB), Robelquis Videaux (GTM) 23; **RBI**: Orlis Díaz (PRI) 87; **SB**: Enrique Díaz (MET) 44.

Pitching Leaders—**Pct.**: Lemay de la Rosa (HAB) 14–1 (.933); **G**: Duniel Ibarra (HAB) 45; **CG**: Norge Vera (SCU) 12; **Wins**: Maels Rodríguez (SSP), Eliecer Montes de Oca (VCL) 15; **IP**: Maels Rodríguez 178.1; **SO**: Maels Rodríguez 263; **ERA**: Maels Rodríguez 1.77.

No-Hit/No-Run Game—**Norge Vera** (Santiago de Cuba 3-5-1, Habana 0-0-1, 1-21-01)

Cuban League All-Star Game IV—Location: Pinar del Río (Estadio Capitán San Luis), February 11, 2001. Score: Occidentales 5, Orientales 2

2001–2002 National Series XLI (Provincial)

The most surprising season in several decades witnesses Sancti Spíritus ride the stellar pitching trio of Maels Rodríguez (14–3, 2.13 ERA), Yovani Aragón (12–8, 3.46) and Ifreidi Coss (10–3, 1.94) to improve fifteen games in the standings and wrest the top spot in the western sector from a powerhouse Pinar del Río squad (featuring its own stellar pitching combo of league victories leader Pedro Lazo and ERA champ José Contreras). Equally shocking is the emergence of Holguín

under manager Héctor Hernández, upset winners over defending champion Santiago and emerging powerhouse Villa Clara in the eastern provinces. The result is a gripping if not always well-played championship showdown between two teams that owned one previous final-round appearance between them. Pinar del Río (celebrating the return of former national team manager Jorge Fuentes at the helm) rang up the year's best overall record, nine games better than postseason champion Holguín. Las Tunas outfielder Osmani Urrutia wins batting honors for a second year running and Maels Rodríguez again tops Changa Mederos's once-invincible strikeout mark. The year's sensational rookie is switch-hitting Industriales infielder/outfielder Kendry Morales, who posts a new freshman mark with 21 homers. In July and early August a revived experimental second season now called Super League I features four regional teams and a 27-game schedule. Habaneros defeats Centrales in a final playoff series that is highlighted by a second career no-hit, no-run game for Maels Rodríguez.

Champion—Holguín (55–35, 11–6) Manager: Héctor Hernández

Playoffs—Holguín over Sancti Spíritus, 4–3 (Finals); Sancti Spíritus over Pinar del Río, 4–2 (Semifinals); Holguín over Villa Clara, 4–2 (Semifinals); Pinar del Río over Industriales, 3–1 (Quarterfinals); Sancti Spíritus over Isla de la Juventud, 3–2 (Quarterfinals); Villa Clara over Santiago de Cuba, 3–0 (Quarterfinals); Holguín over Camagüey, 3–1 (Quarterfinals)

Group A—Pinar del Río (64–26), Isla de la Juventud (51–39), Matanzas (48–42), Metropolitanos (31–59)

Group B—Sancti Spíritus (53–37), Industriales (49–41), Habana (45–45), Cienfuegos (33–57)

Group C—Villa Clara (54–36), Camagüey (44–46), Ciego de Avila (42–48), Las Tunas (23–67)

Group D—Holguín (55–35), Santiago de Cuba (54–36), Granma (38–52), Guantánamo (36–54)

Batting Leaders—**BA**: Osmani Urrutia (LTU) .408; **H**: Luis Felipe Rivera (IJV) 136; **R**: Michel Abreu (MTZ) 78; **2B**: Michel Enríquez (IJV) 29; **3B**: Danny Miranda (CAV), Manuel Benavides (SCU), Yunieski Betancourt (VCL) 8; **HR**: Michael Abreu 23; **RBI**: Daniel Lazo (PRI) 89; **SB**: Eduardo Paret (VCL) 34.

Pitching Leaders—**Pct.**: Vladimir Hernández (VCL), 11–2 (.846); Maels Rodríguez (SSP) 14–3 (.824); **G**: Orestes González (PRI) 50; **CG**: Norge Vera (SCU) 11; **Wins**: Pedro Luis Lazo (PRI) 15; **IP**: Ciro Silvino Licea (GRA) 167.1; **SO**: Maels Rodríguez 219; **ERA**: José Contreras (PRI) 1.76.

No-Hit/No-Run Games—None

Cuban League All-Star Game V—Location: Holguín (Estadio Calixto García), March 17, 2002. Score: Occidentales 8, Orientales 1

2002 Super League I (Super-Provincial)

Champion—Habaneros (16–11, 2–1) Manager: Armando Johnson

Championship Playoff Results and Scores: Habaneros defeated Centrales in best-of-three series (2–1). Centrales over

Habaneros (1–0), Habaneros over Centrales (3–2), Habaneros over Centrales (5–2)

Final Standings— Habaneros (16–11), Centrales (16–11), Occidentales (12–15), Orientales (10–17)

Batting Leaders—**BA**: Andy Zamora (CEN) .391; **H**: Frederich Cepeda (CEN), Juan Carlos Linares (OCC) 35; **R**: Frederich Cepeda 24; **2B**: Frederich Cepeda 11; **3B**: Yasser Gómez (HAB) 3; **HR**: Frederich Cepeda 7; **RBI**: Bábaro Cañizares (HAB), Ariel Borrero (CEN), Frederich Cepeda 19.

Pitching Leaders—**Pct.**: Orestes González (OCC) 4–0 (1.000); **G**: Orestes González 12; **Wins**: Vicyohandri Odelín (HAB), Yadel Martí (HAB), Orestes González 4; **IP**: Ciro Silvino Licea (OTL) 43.1; **SO**: Maels Rodríguez (CEN) 41; **ERA**: Orestes González 1.13.

No-Hit/No-Run Game—**Maels Rodríguez** (Centrales 1–4–0, Habaneros 0–0–0, 8–21–02)

2002–2003 National Series XLII (Provincial)

Things seemed back to normal for the rabid fans in Havana as Industriales gelled under second year manager Rey Anglada to win 66 games (third highest total in league history) and sweep Villa Clara in the post-season finals, thus claiming their ninth National Series crown and first in seven years. Most of the Industriales power came from the slugging of young switch-hitter Kendry Morales (second best hitter in the league at .391), the basepath speed of Enríque Díaz (circuit pacesetter in both stolen bases and runs scored), and the pitching prowess of Yadel Martí (sporting the best won-lost mark of the year with 10–2). Best individual stories of the season were several new single-season and career marks which spiked the exciting pennant race: Enríque Díaz moved into the top slot in career stolen bases while also overhauling Eduardo Paret's earlier mark (set back in 2001) with 100 runs scored; powerful Joan Carlos Pedroso erased Lázaro Junco's long-standing milestone with 28 roundtrippers; and Industriales sentimental favorite Javier Méndez capped his stellar 22-season career by moving into the top career slot in doubles (381) and the number eight all-time position in base hits (2,101). Las Tunas outfielder Osmani Urrutia again walked off with individual batting honors for a third straight winter by posting another .400-plus mark (also his third in a row). The second-season Super League short-schedule tournament during May failed to spark much fan interest but nonetheless showcased the talents of two of the Cuban League's brightest young batsmen: Centrales teammates Frederich Cepeda (tops in homers, runs, RBI and BA) and Yulieski Gourriel (leader in doubles and triples) took up were they left off in National Series games as emerging superstars with Sancti Spíritus.

Champion— Industriales (66–23, 11–2) Manager: Rey Anglada

Playoffs— Industriales over Villa Clara, 4–0 (Finals); Industriales over Pinar del Río, 4–1 (Semifinals); Villa Clara over Granma, 4–2 (Semifinals); Industriales over Habana, 3–1 (Quarterfinals); Villa Clara over Santiago de Cuba, 3–2 (Quarterfinals); Granma over Camagüey, 3–1 (Quarterfinals); Pinar del Río over Cienguegos, 3–2 (Quarterfinals)

Group A— Pinar del Río (56–34), Isla de la Juventud (41–48), Matanzas (41–49), Metropolitanos (41–49)

Group B— Industriales (66–23), Cienfuegos (52–38), Habana (51–39), Sancti Spíritus (49–41)

Group C— Villa Clara (56–34), Camagüey (44–46), Ciego de Avila (37–53), Las Tunas (25–65)

Group D— Granma (45–45), Santiago de Cuba (44–46), Holguín (43–47), Guantánamo (28–62)

Batting Leaders—**BA**: Osmani Urrutia (LTU) .421; **H**: Alexei Ramírez (PRI) 131; **R**: Enríque Díaz (IND) 100; **2B**: Luis Piloto (HAB) 28; **3B**: Marino Luis (CMG), Andres Quiala (LTU) 8; **HR**: Joan Carlos Pedroso (LTU) 28; **RBI**: Javier Méndez (IND) 92; **SB**: Enríque Díaz 28.

Pitching Leaders—**Pct.**: Yadel Martí (IND), 10–2 (.833); **G**: Jorge Martínez (MTZ) 41; **CG**: Ciro Silvino Licea (GRA), Luis Rodríguez (HOL), Yovani Aragón (SSP) 10; **Wins**: Adiel Palma (CFG) 14; **IP**: Yovani Aragón 164.0; **SO**: Adiel Palma 179; **ERA**: Alain Soler (PRI) 2.01.

No-Hit/No-Run Games— None

Cuban League All-Star Game VI— Location: Cienfuegos (Estadio Cinco de Septiembre), February 23, 2003. Score: Orientales 8, Occidentales 6

2003 Super League II (Super-Provincial)

Champion— Centrales (13–7, 2–1) Manager: Lourdes Gourriel

Championship Playoff Results and Scores: Centrales defeated Occidentales in best-of-three series (2–1). Centrales over Occidentales (8–3), Occidentales over Centrales (6–3), Centrales over Occidentales (7–2)

Final Standings— Centrales (13–7), Occidentales (11–10), Orientales (11–10), Habaneros (6–14)

Batting Leaders—**BA**: Frederich Cepeda (CEN) .435; **H**: Luis Rivera (OCC), Michel Enríquez (OCC) 32; **R**: Frederich Cepeda 21; **2B**: Yulieski Gourriel (CEN), Yunieski Betancourt (CEN) 6; **3B**: Yulieski Gourriel, Frederich Cepeda 2; **HR**: Frederich Cepeda 7; **RBI**: Frederich Cepeda 20.

Pitching Leaders—**Pct.**: Yovani Aragón (CEN) 4–0 (1.000); **G**: Alexander Quintero (CEN) 10; **Wins**: Yovani Aragón 4; **IP**: Jonder Martínez (HAB) 30.1; **SO**: Norberto González (CEN) 21; **ERA**: Luis Rodríguez (OTE) 1.21.

No-Hit/No-Run Game— None

2003–2004 National Series XLIII (Provincial)

Some newsworthy defections, further amazing hitting by the phenomenal Osmani Urrutia, and a second straight pennant win for fan-favorite Industriales marked a National Series season that stretched between Team Cuba's October 2003 repeat World Cup title (Havana) and its August 2004 Olympic championship comeback (Athens). Industriales struggled early under manager Rey Anglada and trailed Pinar del Río by 2.5 games during the regular season Group B title race. But during the post-season Anglada's Blue Lions edged Sancti Spíritus in the quarterfinals (3 games to 2), next streaked past Pinar in the semis (4–2), and then rolled over Villa Clara in four straight as momentum built during the finals. The season's final contest ended in most dramatic fashion when shortstop Enrique Díaz doubled home the tying and winning runs in the bottom of the ninth against stellar Villa Clara reliever Eliecer Montes de Oca. Villa Clara starter Luis Borroto was the year's biggest pitching star with a 12–3 ledger and league bests in both strikeouts and ERA. For an encore Borroto (1.25 ERA) also shone brilliantly in the short-season Super League. But the individual hero of NS #43 was again Urrutia who ran his amazing string of .400-plus seasons to four straight, this time posting a league-record .469 BA, tying for the RBI crown, and missing the home run title (and triple crown) by only three round-trippers. Cuban baseball had suffered some notable losses when Maels Rodríguez and Yobal Dueñas left the country in October 2003 at the conclusion of the Havana World Cup. Kendry Morales was soon to follow in the spring, after being sent home for disciplinary reasons from the November 2003 Olympic Qualifier in Panama. But all three former national team stars were already out of the national team picture and the victorious roster in Athens showed enough youthful talent to make the losses insignificant. Both Michel Enríquez (league's third-best .385 BA) and Yulieski Gourriel (second in slugging behind Urrutia at .614) shone as brightly at home as they would a few months later in Athens.

Champion— Industriales (52–38, 11–4) Manager: Rey Anglada

Playoffs— Industriales over Villa Clara, 4–0 (Finals); Industriales over Pinar del Río, 4–2 (Semifinals); Villa Clara over Santiago de Cuba, 4–3 (Semifinals); Villa Clara over Granma, 3–0 (Quarterfinals); Pinar del Río over Isla de la Juventud, 3–0 (Quarterfinals); Industriales over Sancti Spíritus, 3–2 (Quarterfinals); Santiago de Cuba over Ciego de Avila, 3–0 (Quarterfinals)

Group A— Pinar del Río (57–33), Isla de la Juventud (46–43), Metropolitanos (43–47), Matanzas (27–63)

Group B— Sancti Spíritus (54–35), Industriales (52–38), Habana (38–51), Cienfuegos (27–62)

Group C— Villa Clara (57–33), Ciego de Avila (55–34), Las Tunas (44–46), Camagüey (38–52)

Group D— Santiago de Cuba (53–37), Granma (49–41), Holguín (42–48), Guantánamo (35–54)

Batting Leaders— **BA**: Osmani Urrutia (LTU) .469; **H**: Yordanis Scull (LTU) 131; **R**: Yordanis Scull 74; **2B**: Andy Zamora (VCL) 33; **3B**: Marino Luis (CMG) 9; **HR**: Reinier Yero (SSP) 19; **RBI**: Osmani Urrutia, Loidel Chapelli (CMG) 67; **SB**: Enríque Díaz (IND), Yusquiel García (CMG) 20.

Pitching Leaders— **Pct.**: Ifredi Coss (SSP), 10–2 (.833); **G**: Yolexis Ulacia (VCL) 45; **CG**: Carlos Yanes (IJV) 12; **Wins**: Carlos Yanes 13; **IP**: Carlos Yanes 167.0; **SO**: Luis Borroto (VCL) 135; **ERA**: Luis Borroto 1.49.

No-Hit/No-Run Games— None

Cuban League All-Star Game VII— Location: Santa Clara (Estadio Augusto Sandino), January 24, 2004. Score: Orientales 4, Occidentales 3

2004 Super League III (Super-Provincial)

Champion— Orientales (13–7, 2–0) Manager: Higinio Vélez

Championship Playoff Results and Scores: Orientales defeated Industriales in best-of-three series (2–0). Orientales over Industriales (10–5), Orientales over Industriales (6–5)

Final Standings— Industriales (10–5), Orientales (7–8), Occidentales (7–8), Centrales (6–9)

Batting Leaders— **BA**: Rudy Reyes (IND) .417; **H**: Alexei Ramírez (OCC) 25; **R**: Yasser Gómez (IND), Yoandi Garlobo (OCC) 14; **2B**: Antonio Scull (IND) 7; **3B**: Rudy Reyes, Enríque Díaz (IND) 2; **HR**: Eduardo Paret (CEN) 5; **RBI**: Amaury Casayas (OCC) 15.

Pitching Leaders— **Pct.**: Deinys Suárez Arag (IND), Vicyohandri Odelín (OTE) 2–0 (1.000); **G**: Orestes González (OCC) 9; **Wins**: nine tied with 2; **IP**: Yulieski González (OCC) 24.0; **SO**: Yovani Aragón (CEN) 15; **ERA**: Luis Borroto (CEN) 1.25.

No-Hit/No-Run Games— None

2004–2005 National Series XLIV (Provincial)

National Series #44 proved one of the most competitive of recent years, even if the 2005 domestic Cuban League was also one filled with considerable surprises. A three-year championship run by Havana favorite Industriales was unceremoniously ended when the island's fan-favorites were quickly eliminated by Sancti Spíritus in the opening playoff round, despite posting the most regular-season victories. Santiago de Cuba, now managed by career base-hits leader Antonio Pacheco, rolled over upstart Habana Province during the six-game championship finale. The top story was again national team right-fielder Osmani Urrutia who failed in his dramatic effort to continue one remarkable streak but succeeded in protecting another. Urrutia lost his bid for a fifth straight .400-plus season, but did walk off with his fifth straight batting title in the 90-game National Series. Urrutia's teammate Joan Carlos Pedroso (27) captured the league home run crown, edging Sancti Spíritus teammates Eriel Sánchez (25) and Yulieski Gourriel (23). On the pitching front, Industriales right-hander Yadel Marti was the most effective starter (11–2) while Pinar del Río righty Yunieski Maya posted the stingiest ERA (1.61 in 89.2 innings). Granma veteran Ciro Silvino Licea resurrected a faltering career as the league-leader in victories (13). Sancti Spíritus bullpen ace Dany González was saves leader (17) but only edged Pinar's Orestes González by a mere pair. Short-season Super League play again proved a failure with Cuban fans not identify with such all-star teams lacking provincial affiliations. Occidentales took team honors sweeping Centrales in a two-game final, though Centrales (16–10) posted the best record.

Champion— Santiago de Cuba (55–35, 11–2) Manager: Antonio Pacheco

Playoffs— Santiago de Cuba over Habana Province, 4–2 (Finals); Santiago de Cuba over Villa Clara, 4–0 (Semifinals); Habana Province over Sancti Spíritus, 4–2 (Semifinals); Habana Province over Pinar del Río, 3–1 (Quarterfinals); Sancti

Spíritus over Industriales, 3–1 (Quarterfinals); Villa Clara over Ciego de Avila, 3–0 (Quarterfinals); Santiago de Cuba over Granma, 3–0 (Quarterfinals)

Group A— Pinar del Río (55–34), Isla de la Juventud (42–48), Metropolitanos (33–57), Matanzas (28–61)

Group B— Industriales (59–30), Habana Province (54–35), Sancti Spíritus (54–36), Cienfuegos (31–59)

Group C— Ciego de Avila (54–36), Villa Clara (51–39), Las Tunas (47–43), Camagüey (35–55)

Group D— Santiago de Cuba (55–35), Granma (50–40), Holguín (37–53), Guantánamo (33–57)

Batting Leaders—**BA:** Osmani Urrutia (LTU) .385; **H:** Yulieski Gourriel (SSP) 126; **R:** Yulieski Gourriel 80; **2B:** Michel Enríquez (IJV) 30; **3B:** Adriano García (CFG) 12; **HR:** Joan Carlos Pedroso (LTU) 27; **RBI:** Eriel Sánchez (SSP), Antonio Scull (IND) 87; **SB:** Yordanis Scull (LTU) 35.

Pitching Leaders—**Pct.:** Yadel Martí (IND), 11–2 (.846); **G:** Yolexis Ulacia (VCL) 42; **CG:** Carlos Yanes (IJV) 12; **Wins:** Ciro Silvino Licea (GRA), Pedro Luis Lazo (PRI) 13; **IP:** Luis Rodríguez (HOL) 159.0; **SO:** Adiel Palma (CFG) 143; **ERA:** Yunieski Maya (PRI) 1.61.

No-Hit/No-Run Games— None

Cuban League All-Star Game VIII— Location: Las Tunas (Estadio Julio Antonio Mella), February 26, 2005. Score: Occidentales 4, Orientales 1

2005 Super League IV (Super-Provincial)

Champion— Occidentales (15–13, 2–0) Manager: Rey Anglada

Championship Playoff Results and Scores: Occidentales defeated Centrales in best-of-three series (2–0). Occidentales over Centrales (11–2), Occidentales over Centrales (9–3)

Final Standings— Centrales (16–10), Occidentales (15–13), Santiago de Cuba (14–13), Orientales (12–16), Habaneros (11–16)

Batting Leaders—**BA:** Roger Poll (CEN) .437; **H:** Alexei Ramírez (OCC) 46; **R:** Yulieski Gourriel (CEN) 30; **2B:** Alexei Ramírez, Rafael Orta (HAB) 10; **3B:** Juan Carlos Linares (HAB) 3; **HR:** Joan Carlos Pedroso (SCU) 14; **RBI:** Yulieski Gourriel 40.

Pitching Leaders—**Pct.:** Adiel Palma (CEN) 4–0 (1.000),

Norge Vera (SCU) 2–0 (1.000); **G:** Yolexis Ulacia (CEN) 15; **Wins:** Pedro Luis Lazo (OCC), Alberto Bicet (SCU) 5; **IP:** Pedro Luis Lazo 48.2; **SO:** Kenny Rodríguez (HAB) 36; **ERA:** Adiel Palma 2.10.

No-Hit/No-Run Games— None

Cuban League National Series Championships
(Team-by-Team)

Industriales (10 championships)—1963, 1964, 1965, 1966, 1973, 1986, 1992, 1996, 2003, 2004

Santiago de Cuba (6 championships)—1980, 1989, 1999, 2000, 2001, 2005

Vegueros (6 championships)—1978, 1981, 1982, 1985, 1987, 1988

Villa Clara (4 championships)—1983 1993, 1994, 1995

Henequeneros (3 championships)—1970, 1990, 1991

Azucareros (3 championships)—1969, 1971, 1972

Pinar del Río (2 championships)—1997, 1998

Habana (2 championships)—1968, 1974

Citricultores (2 championships)—1977, 1984

Occidentales (1 championship)—1962

Orientales (1 championship)—1967

Agricultores (1 championship)—1975

Ganaderos (1 championship)—1976

Sancti Spíritus (1 championship)—1979

Holguín (1 championship)— 2002

Cuban League Selective Series Championships
(Team-by-Team)

Pinar del Río (6 championships)—1979, 1980, 1982, 1984, 1988, 1991

Las Villas (4 championships)—1978, 1983, 1985, 1989

Orientales (4 championships)—1981, 1993, 1995, 2004 (Super League)

Serranos (3 championships)—1986, 1987, 1992

Occidentals (2 championships)—1994, 2005 (Super League)

Oriente (1 championship)—1975

Habana (1 championship)—1976

Camagüeyanos (1 championship)—1977

Ciudad Habana (1 championship)—1990

Habaneros (1 championship)— 2002 (Super League)

Centrales (1 championship)— 2003 (Super League)

Cuban League East (Oriente) vs. West (Occidentals)
All-Star Game Chronology

First Phase (ORI=Oriente and OCC=Occidentales) (Series: Occidentales 4–1, Oriente 1–4)

Year — Location	Line Score (W/L Pitchers)	Home Runs
1963 — Havana	ORI 5–9–1 (Florentino Alfonso), OCC 0–5–3 (Juan Medina)	None
1964 — Havana	OCC 5–5–1 (Antonio Rubio), ORI 1–3–4 (Emilio Vargas)	None
1965 — Havana	OCC 6–10–1 (Manuel Hurtado), ORI 5–12–1 (Manuel Alacrón)	None
1966 — Havana	OCC 3–8–2 (Berto Betancourt), ORI 1–6–2 (Aquino Abreu)	None
1967 — Havana	OCC 3–11–1 (Carlos Gálvez), ORI 2–5–3 (Justino Galiván)	None

Second Phase (ORI=Oriente and OCC=Occidentales) (Series: Oriente 4–3, Occidentales 3–4)

Year — Location	Line Score (W/L Pitchers)	Home Runs
1981 — Havana	ORI 4–8–2 (Roberto Ramos), Occ 3–9–1 (Pablo Pérez)	None
1982 — Havana	ORI 6–11–1 (Alfonso Ilivanes), OCC 3–8–1 (Rogelio García)	None

Year — Location	Line Score (W/L Pitchers)	Home Runs
1983 — Havana	OCC 4–8–0 (Félix Pino), ORI 0–6–0 (Omar Carrero)	None
1984 — Havana	OCC 7–14–0 (Julio Romero), ORI 0–2–1 (Braudilio Vinent)	None
1985 — Havana	OCC 5–7–0 (Reinaldo Costa), ORI 1–7–3 (Andrés Luis)	None
1986 — Havana	ORI 4–6–0 (Regino Robaina), OCC 0–5–2 (Pablo Miguel Abreu)	None
1987 — Havana	ORI 4–9–2 (José Riviera), OCC 3–9–2 (Pablo Miguel Abreu)	None

Third Phase (ORI=Oriente and OCC=Occidentales) (Series: Oriente 5–3, Occidentales 3–5)

Year — Location	Line Score (W/L Pitchers)	Home Runs
1998 — C. de Avila	ORI 5–6–2 (Oscar Gil), OCC 2–5–3 (Adrian Hernández)	None
1999 — Güines	ORI 1–5–0 (Walberto Quesada) OCC 0–4–1 (Carlos Yanes)	Danel Castro
2000 — S. Spíritus	ORI 4–10–1 (Norge Luis Vera), OCC 1–9–1 (Maels Roldríguez)	None
2001 — Pinar del Río	OCC 5–7–1 (Raúl Valdés), ORI 2–8–1 (Eliecer Montes de Oca)	None
2002 — Holguín	OCC 8–14–1 (Carlos Yanes), ORI 1–7–0 (Vladimir Hernández)	None
2003 — Cienfuergos	ORI 8–14–2 (Yolexis Ulacia), OCC 6–10–0 (Orestes González)	None
2004 — Santa Clara	ORI 4–10–1 (Yolexis Ulacia), OCC 3–7–0 (Carlos Yanes)	Reinier Yero, Danel Castro
2005 — Las Tunas	OCC 4–7–1 (Yunieski Maya), ORI 1–7–0 (Valeri García)	None

PART III

The Cuban Legacy

9

The Myth of Fidel Castro, Barbudos Ballplayer

His fastball has long since died. He still has a few curveballs which he throws at us routinely.
— Nicholas Burns, United States State Department Spokesman

We baseball fans tend to take our idle ballpark pastimes far too seriously. On momentary reflection, even a diehard rooter would have to admit that big league baseball's most significant historical figures — say, Mantle, Cobb, Barry Bonds, Walter Johnson, even Babe Ruth himself— are only mere blips on the larger canvas of world events. After all, 95 percent (perhaps more) of the globe's population has little or no interest whatsoever in what transpires on North American ballpark diamonds. Babe Ruth may well have been one of the grandest icons of American popular culture, but little in the direction of world events would have been in the slightest degree altered if the flamboyant Babe had never escaped the rustic grounds of St. Mary's School for Boys in Baltimore.

Such is certainly not the case with Cuba's most notorious pitching legend turned communist revolutionary leader. Although Fidel Castro's reputed blazing fastball (novelist Tim Wendel suggests in *Castro's Curveball* that he lived by a tantalizing crooked pitch) never earned him a spot on a big league roster, the amateur ex-hurler who once tested the baseball waters in a Washington Senators tryout camp would nevertheless one day emerge among the past century's most significant political leaders. Castro has now outlasted nine U.S. presidents and survived four decades of an ill-starred socialist revolution he in large part personally created. Cuba's Maximum Leader today greets the new millennium still entrenched as one of the most beloved (in some quarters, mostly third world) or hated (in others, mostly North American) of the world's charismatic political figures. Certainly no other ex-baseballer has ever stepped more dramatically from the schoolboy diamond into a role that would so radically affect the lives and fortunes of so many millions throughout the Western Hemisphere and beyond.

Castro remains the most dominant self-perpetuating myth of the second half of the twentieth century, and this claim is equally valid when it comes to the Cuban leader's longtime personal association with North America's self-proclaimed national game. Rare indeed is the ball fan who has not heard some version of the well-worn Castro baseball tale: that Fidel once owned a blazing fastball as a teenage prospect and was once offered big league contracts by several eager

scouts, slipshod bird dogs (especially one named Joe Cambria working for Clark Griffith's Washington Senators) whose failures to ink the young Cuban prospect sealed a coming half-century of Cold War political and economic intrigue.

The New York Yankees and Pittsburgh Pirates also somehow frequently make their way into the story. And in a scandalous article in the May 1989 issue of *Harper's Magazine*, journalist David Truby provides perhaps the most egregious elaboration of the myth by adding the New York Giants to the list of purported Castro suitors. (Truby's piece was actually a reprint, lifted from his monthly column in the short-lived journal *Sports History*.) Truby reports that Horace Stoneham was also hot on the trail of the young Castro, a "star pitcher for the Havana University baseball team," and quotes from supposedly extant Giants scouting reports (that no one else has apparently ever seen) as his proof. Yet Truby is not alone in falling for (or in this case manufacturing) the delightful story. Reputable baseball scholars, general sports historians, numerous network news broadcasters (and even former U.S. Senator Eugene McCarthy in an obscure 1995 journal article) have been taken in by the myth of Castro as a genuine major league prospect.

A charming related tale is also found in the June 1964 pages of *Sport* magazine, where ex–big-leaguer Don Hoak (aided by journalist Myron Cope) recounts a distant Havana day (reputedly during the 1950–51 winter season) when rebellious anti–Batista students interrupted Cuban League play while a young law student named Castro seized the hill and delivered several unscheduled pitches to Hoak himself. Detailed evidence deflates both the bogus Hoak rendition (easily proven to be historically impossible on numerous counts) and also the numerous associated accounts of Castro's pitching prowess. It turns out that Fidel the ballplayer is even more of a marvelous propaganda creation than Fidel the lionized revolutionary hero. But this is only a small part of the fascinating Fidel Castro baseball story.

One thing is ruthlessly clear about Castro the baseball player. The oft-presented tale of his prowess as a potential big league hurler simply isn't true as normally told. It is an altogether attractive supposition — one we can hardly resist — that baseball scouts might well have changed world history by better attending to Fidel's fastball. It makes perfect filler for Bob Costas during a tense World Series TV moment when Liván Hernández or "El Duque" Hernández mans the October mound. It makes great fiction in sportswriter Tim Wendel's fast-paced novel (*Castro's Curveball*, 1999), but fiction it nonetheless remains. As Bob Costas once pointedly reminded this author in personal correspondence, in this case the full-blown fiction is far too delectable ever to be abandoned by media types voluntarily.

Yet if Fidel was not a genuine pitching prospect he was nevertheless an undeniable influence on baseball's recent history within his own island nation. (And also perhaps on the big league scene, once his 1959 revolution closed the escape hatches for numerous Cuban League stars and potential sixties and seventies-era MLB prospects like Agustín Marquetti, Antonio Muñoz and Armando Capiró). Castro's personal role

Cuba's number one pitcher warms up for his "Los Barbudos" exhibition debut at Cerro Stadium, July 24, 1959. Note well Fidel's unprofessional style of demonstrating his pitching grip to any potential batter.

in killing off Cuban professional baseball has been long overstated, even overhyped. (Organized baseball figures like Cincinnati GM Gabe Paul and International League President Frank Shaughnessy — plus a bevy of Washington politicos — seemingly played a far larger role than Fidel in the dismantling of the AAA Havana Sugar Kings franchise in 1960.) At the same time, the Cuban president's active involvement during the dozen or more years after seizing political power, both in inspiring and also legislating a prosperous amateur version of the Cuban national sport, has equally been ignored by a generation or two of stateside baseball historians.

Is Fidel Castro in the end a contemptible baseball villain (responsible for pulling the plug on the island's pro leagues) or a certified baseball hero (architect of a nobler flag-waving rather than dollar-waving version of the bat-and-ball sport)? The answer — as with almost all elements of the Cuban Revolution — may well be a matter of one's own personal historical and political perspective.

It is undeniable that the presence of Castro's communist revolution ended once and for all professional baseball in Cuba. But that is only the prologue to the recent Cuban baseball saga. Castro and his policies would also be largely responsible during the 1960s and seventies for rebuilding Doubleday's and Cartwright's sport on the island into a showcase for patriotic amateur competitions. The direct result throughout those two decades and two more to follow would be one of the world's most fascinating baseball circuits (tense annual National Series competitions leading to yearly selections of powerhouse Cuban national teams) and by far the most success-filled saga in the entire history of the world amateur and Olympic baseball movements.

If modern-era professional baseball leaves a sour aftertaste for many North American fans fed up with out-of-control spendthrift owners and today's gold-digging (even steroid enhanced) big leaguers, Cuban League action as played under Castro's communist government has long provided an attractive alternative to baseball as a free-market enterprise. In brief, the future Maximum Leader who was never enough of a fastballing phenom to turn the eye of scouting legend Papa Joe Cambria was nonetheless destined to play out a small part of his controversial legacy as the most significant off-field figure found anywhere in the sporting history of the world's second-ranking baseball power.

* * *

Don Hoak didn't exactly create the myth of Fidel Castro the baseball pitcher. Nonetheless the light-hitting infielder did contribute rather mightily to the spread of one of balldom's most elaborate historical hoaxes. The journeyman baseball career of the former Dodgers, Cubs, Reds, Pirates, and Phillies third baseman is in fact almost solely renowned for two disastrous wild tosses — one on the diamond and the other in the interview room. In the first instance, Hoak unleashed the wild peg from third base on May 26, 1959, which ended Harvey Haddix's twelve innings of pitching perfection in Milwaukee's County Stadium (and in the process baseball's longest big-

El Comandante poses with Minneapolis Millers players during 1959 Little World Series at Cerro Stadium in Havana.

league perfect game). In the latter case, he teamed with a notoriety-seeking sportswriter to spin an elaborate false yarn about facing the future Cuban revolutionary leader in a highly improbable batter-versus-hurler confrontation laced with romance and dripping with patriotic fervor.

The fabricated story of Hoak's memorable square-off against one of the most famous political leaders of the 20th century did little to immortalize the ex–big-leaguer himself. Yet it was destined to become yet another piece of the circulating printed and oral record that worked overtime to establish Fidel Castro's own seemingly impressive baseball credentials.

Hoak conspired with journalist Myron Cope and the editors of *Sport* magazine to craft his fictionalized tale in June 1964 (only weeks after his career-ending release by the Philadelphia Phillies), thus launching one of the most widely swallowed baseball hoaxes of the modern era. As Hoak tells the story, his unlikely and unscheduled at-bat against young Castro came during his own single season of Cuban winter league play, which the ex–big-leaguer conveniently misremembers as the off-season of 1950–51. Hoak's account involves a Cuban League game between his own Cienfuegos ball club and the

Marianao team featuring legendary Havana outfielder Pedro Formental. The convenient backdrop was political unrest surrounding the increasingly unpopular government of military strongman Fulgencio Batista. During the fifth inning and with Hoak occupying the batter's box, a spontaneous anti–Batista student demonstration suddenly broke out (Hoak reported such uprisings as all-too-regular occurrences during that particular 1951 season) with horns blaring, firecrackers exploding, and anti–Batista forces streaming directly onto the field of play.

Hoak's account continues with the student leader — the charismatic Castro — marching to the mound, seizing the ball from an unresisting Marianao pitcher, and tossing several warm-up heaves to catcher Mike Guerra (a Washington Senators big-league veteran). Castro then barks orders for Hoak to assume his batting stance, the famed Cuban umpire Amado Maestri shrugs agreement, the American fouls off several wild but hard fastballs, the batter and umpire suddenly tire of the charade, and the bold Maestri finally orders the military police ("who were lazily enjoying the fun from the grandstand") to brandish their riot clubs and drive the student rabble from the field. Castro left the scene "like an impudent boy who has been cuffed by the teacher and sent to stand in the corner."

Hoak's wild tale underpinned a myth that was soon to take on a ballooning life of its own. The Hoak-narrated details are perhaps charming but highly suspicious from the opening sentence. Misspellings and misapprehensions of names, plus confusion of the baseball details, immediately destroy any credibility the account might have ever had. The star Cuban outfielder is Formental (not "Formanthael" as Hoak and Cope have it spelled) and Formental was actually a Club Havana outfielder and not a member of the Marianao team during the early '50s (he had played for Cienfuegos a decade earlier, before being traded to Havana for Gil Torres in the mid–40s); the umpire is Maestri (not Cope's spelling of "Miastri"); backstop Fermín (as he was always known in Cuba) Guerra would have been managing the Almendares team at the time and not catching for the ball club playing under the banner of Marianao.

Fidel unleashes a high hard one during his single famous and misunderstood public pitching performance.

To add to the implausibility of the account, the reported events themselves are entirely out of character with the several personalities allegedly involved, especially those details concerning umpire Maestri. Amado Maestri was the island's best mid-century arbiter, a bastion of respectability, and a man who had once even ejected Mexican League mogul Jorge Pasquel from the stadium grounds in Mexico City. This was not a spineless umpire who would have tamely ceded control of the playing field for even a split instant to troublemaking grandstand refugees of any known ilk — especially to rabble-rousing anti-government forces. In short, the details are so scrambled and outrageously inaccurate as to suggest that Hoak had indeed related his tale with tongue firmly planted in cheek, and also with a clear aim of tipping off any informed reader as to his elaborate literary joke.

Amateur baseball historian and Cuban native Everardo Santamarina has already pointed out (in SABR's *The National Pastime*, Volume 14, 1994) the rampant inconsistencies and overall illegitimacy of the farfetched Hoak account. Santamarina does so largely by stressing the contradictions related to Hoak's own winter league career (botched dates, incorrect Cuban ballplayer names, an inaccurate portrayal of umpire Maestri). Santamarina is right on target by again emphasizing the total implausibility of the umpire's role in the tale. And Santamarina astutely concludes that "not even Babe Ruth's 'Called Shot' ever got such a free ride."

There are also available facts from the Castro side of the ledger (largely unnoted by Santamarina) that are just as persuasive in putting the lie to Hoak's fabricated account. An even looser playing with the historical details than with the baseball data is apparent to any reader even vaguely familiar with legitimate accounts of the Cuban Revolution. For starters, Pedro Formental was a well-known Batista supporter and thus not likely "a great pal of Castro" and Fidel's "daily companion at the ballpark" as Hoak reports. While Fidel had in truth just received his University of Havana law degree in 1950 as Hoak accurately announces, Batista for his part was not then in power (he would only reassume the presidency with a coup d'etat in March 1952); the student movement against Batista led by Castro was thus still several years away. Most damaging of all, of course, is the fact that Hoak himself was not even in Cuba the year he claims he was, nor did he ever play for the team he cites before the winter season of 1953–54, on the eve of his rookie big-league season in Brooklyn. By the time Hoak did make his way onto the Cienfuegos roster, Castro was no longer in Havana but rather was spending time in jail on the Isle of Pines, serving a two-year lock-up for his part in the Moncada Rebellion of July 1953, an incarceration from which he would not be released until May (Mother's Day) 1955.

It might be noted here that there was in truth an actual event somewhat similar to the one Hoak fictionalizes, and this occurrence may indeed have contained the fertile seeds for the story conveniently dreamed up with ghostwriter Myron Cope. Cuban students did in fact interrupt a ballgame in Havana's El Cerro Stadium (also called Gran Stadium at the time) in early-winter 1955, leading to a swift intervention by Batista's militia and not by the game's beleaguered umpire. Castro at the time was already released from prison, but was now safely ensconced in Mexico.

But in this case, as in most others, historical facts rarely stand in the way of good baseball folklore. The Hoak-Cope tale would soon gain superficial legitimacy with its frequent revivals. Journalist Charles Einstein placed his own stamp of authority with an unquestioning and unaltered reprint in *The Third Fireside Book of Baseball* (1968), and then again in his *Fireside Baseball Reader* (1984). Noted baseball historian John Thorn follows suit in *The Armchair Book of Baseball* (1985), adding a clever legitimizing header above the story which reads: "*Incredible but true. And how history might have altered if Fidel had gone on to become a New York Yanqui, or a Washington Senator, or even a Cincinnati Red.*" A Tom Jozwik review of the Thorn anthology (*SABR Review of Books*, 1986) stresses with naïve amazement that the subject of the "autobiographical" piece is indeed Cuba's Fidel Castro and not major league washout Bill Castro.

Hoak's entertaining if bogus fantasy is admittedly full of foreshadowing, even if it is genuinely flimsy and fabricated. While neither Castro nor Hoak were simultaneously in Havana at the time the future political leader reputedly challenged the future big-league hitter (Hoak wasn't there in 1951 and Castro wasn't there in 1954), what is most remarkable about the clearly apocryphal tale is the degree to which its easy acceptance over the years parallels dozens of other accounts concerning Fidel as a serious moundsman — even a talented pitching prospect of big-league proportions. Legions of fans have run across the Fidel Castro baseball legend in one or another of its many familiar formats.

The story usually paints Fidel as a promising pitching talent who was scouted in the late '40s or early '50s (details are always sketchy) and nearly signed by a number of big league clubs. The widely circulated version is the one that involves famed Clark Griffith "bird-dog" Joe Cambria and the Washington Senators. But the New York Giants, New York Yankees and Pittsburgh Pirates (as already noted) often get at least a passing mention. It is just too grand a story and thus has been swallowed hook, line and fastball. If only scouts had been more persistent — or if only Fidel's fastball had a wee bit more pop and his curveball a bit more bend — the entire history of Western Hemisphere politics over the past half-century would likely have been drastically reshaped. Kevin Kerrane quotes Phillies Latin America scouting supervisor Rubén Amaro (a Mexican-raised ex–big leaguer whose own father was Cuban League legend Santos Amaro) on this familiar theme. Amaro (repeating that Cambria twice rejected Castro for a contract) deduces that "Cambria could have changed history if he remembered that some pitchers mature late." It is a fantasy devoutly to be wished and thus quite irresistible in the telling.

Even highly reputable baseball scholars, general sports historians, and network news broadcasters have often been taken in by the charming tale. Kevin Kerrane reports the Castro tryout story in his landmark book on scouting (*Dollar Sign*

on the Muscle, 1984) by noting (somewhat accurately if incompletely) that "at tryout camps Cambria twice rejected a young pitcher named Fidel Castro." Others have done the same and often with considerably less restraint. Michael and Mary Oleksak (*Béisbol: Latin Americans and the Grand Old Game*, 1991) quote both Clark Griffith and Ruben Amaro on the legend of Fidel and Papa Joe without much helpful detail but with the implication that it is more fact than fiction. John Thorn and John Holway (*The Pitcher*, 1987) pursue a more cautious route in citing Tampa-based Cuban baseball historian Jorge Figueredo's rebuttal that "there is no truth to the oft-repeated story."

The most unrestrained recounting of the myth occurs in Truby's *Harper's* reprint. Author Truby repeats the well-worn saw that a Castro signing might have truly changed history. He also reports that Horace Stoneham had his New York Giants hot on the trail of young Castro, who was "a star pitcher for the University of Havana baseball team," and even quotes scouting reports from Pittsburgh's Howie Haak ("a good prospect because he could throw and think at the same time"), Giants Caribbean scout Alex Pompez ("throws a good ball, not always hard, but smart ... he has good control and should be considered seriously"), and Cambria ("his fastball is not great but passable ... he uses good curve variety ... he also uses his head and can win that way for us, too"). The trouble here (and it is considerable trouble indeed) is that no other known source ever reports on such existing or once-available scouting reports. (It might also be noted that the lines quoted hardly sound like serious assessments from legitimate scouts — trained

"The Supreme Leader" warms up on the sidelines for the cameras before taking the mound for his brief mound debut with **"Los Barbudos"** squad.

talent hounds far more likely to report radar gun readings than impressions of quick-wittedness.)

All additional commentary (especially that coming from Castro's many biographers and from within Cuba itself) indicates that as a schoolboy pitcher Fidel threw hard but wildly (the exact opposite of Truby's quotes). And Castro in reality never made the University of Havana team (let alone being the team's star performer); his schoolboy baseball playing was restricted to 1945, as a high school senior. Truby caps his account with a report (supposedly from Stoneham's lips) that Pompez was authorized to offer a $5,000 bonus for signing (a ridiculous figure in itself, since no Latin prospects were offered that kind of cash in 1950, most especially one who would have been 22 or 23 at the time) which Castro stunned Giants officials by rejecting. The biggest curveball in the *Harper's* account is quite obviously the one being tossed by David Truby himself.

With the recent explosion of interest in Latin American

Cuba's number one batsman squares off against Cuban League hurler Modesto Verdura to receive the ceremonial first pitch launching a second National Series in 1962. The predictable result was a clean line-drive base hit.

ballplaying talent (and thus also in the history of the game played in Caribbean nations), the Castro baseball legend has inevitably taken on a commercial tone as well. One producer of replica Caribbean league hats and jerseys recounts the glories of Fidel the pitcher (in its catalogs and on its website) and manages in the process to expand the story by trumpeting Fidel as a regular pitcher in the Cuban winter leagues. The Blue Marlin Corporation website reports that their promotional photo of Castro is actually a portrait of the dictator pitching for his famed military team ("The Barbudos") in the Cuban League, whereas in reality the exhibition outing was nothing more than a staged one-time affair preceding a Havana Sugar Kings International League game. ESPN has also recently produced a handsome promotional flyer that uses Fidel's baseball "history" as part of the hook to sell its own televised games. The 1994 ESPN poster promoting Sunday night and Wednesday night telecasts features the same familiar 1959 photo of Fidel delivering a pitch in his Barbudos uniform, here superimposed with the bold-print headline "The All-American Game That Once Recruited Fidel Castro."

One of the more interesting promotions of the Fidel ballplayer myth comes with a Eugene McCarthy essay distributed in the journal *Elysian Fields Quarterly* (Volume 14:2, 1995) and reprinted from an earlier editorial column in *USA Today* (March 14, 1994). Here the ex-senator and former presidential candidate stumps (half seriously one presumes) for Fidel as the much-needed big-league baseball commissioner ("what baseball most needs — an experienced dictator"). While McCarthy may deliver his proposals tongue-in-cheek when it comes to the commissioner campaign, he nonetheless apparently buys into the myth of Fidel's ball-playing background. Thus: "Another prospect eyed by the Senators was a pitcher named Fidel Castro, who was rejected because scouts reported he didn't have a major-league fastball." Equally sold were *EFQ* editors, who commissioned artist Andy Nelson to create a volume-cover fantasy 1953 Topps baseball card of a bearded Castro in Washington uniform as pitcher for the Clark Griffith–era Washington Senators.

Andy Nelson's fantasy Topps 1953 ballcard inevitably features some immediate signals of historical anachronism for perceptive or wary readers. A 1953 Topps card neatly fits the artist's purpose, since in that particular year the Topps Chewing Gum Company indeed used just such artists drawings of ballplayers (mostly consisting of head portraits only) and Nelson's pen-and-ink portrait thus has a special feeling of reality about it. But of course Castro in early-season 1953 was still a non-bearded student about to launch his revolutionary career (not his ballplaying one) with an ill-fated attack on the Moncada military barracks in Santiago.

Despite all this, the entire Castro pitching legend is in the end just as much unsubstantial myth as was Hoak's published account of facing the revolutionary hurler back in 1951 (or 1954, or whatever season it might have been). Fidel was never a serious pitching prospect who might demand a $5,000 bonus or even a serious contract offer. He was never pursued by big league scouts or specifically by Joe Cambria. (Recall here that

Cambria's *modus operandi* was to sign up every kid in Cuba with even passing promise and then let the Washington spring training camp sort them out later; if Fidel Castro had any legitimate big league talent, Cambria could hardly have missed him.) Fidel was never on his way to the big leagues in Washington or New York or any points between, no matter how perfect might be the circulating story that (but for a trick of cruel fate or a misjudgment by Papa Joe) he could have been serving up smoking fastballs against fifties-era Washington American League opponents, instead of launching political curveballs against sixties-era Washington bureaucrats.

What then are the true facts surrounding Castro and baseball, especially those touching on Fidel's own ballplaying endeavors? Close examination of the historical and biographical records makes a number of points indisputably clear. First, the young Fidel did indeed have a passion for the popular sport of baseball, one that was apparent in his earliest years in Cuba's eastern province of Oriente. Biographer Robert Quirk (*Fidel Castro*, 1993) reports on the youngster's apparent fascination with the Cuban national game, and especially his attraction to its central position of pitcher ("the man always in control"). But it is also obvious from widely available biographical accounts that young Fidel was mostly enamored of his own abilities to dominate in the sporting arena (as in all other schoolboy arenas) and not with the lure of the game itself. He organized an informal team as a youngster in his hometown of Birán when his wealthy landowner father provided the needed supplies of bats, balls and gloves (Szulc, *Fidel: A Critical Portrait*, 1986). And when he and his team didn't win he simply packed up his father's equipment and went home. Fidel from the start apparently was never a team player or much of a true sportsman.

Fidel's baseball fantasies were (like those of so many of us) never to be matched by any remarkable batting or throwing talent. As a high school student Fidel maintained his early passion for sports and played on the basketball team at Belén, the private Havana Catholic secondary school he attended during the years 1942–1945. He also pitched on the baseball squad as a senior, as well as being a star at track and field (middle distances and high jumping) and also a Ping Pong champion.

Later efforts of Castro's inner circle (though seemingly never of Fidel himself) to promote his well-rounded image by fanning the rumors of athletic prowess are already apparent in connection with schoolboy days. Biographer Quirk (whose exhaustive study is the most recent and one of the most scholarly in a long list of Fidel biographies published in both Spanish and English) reports on uncovering numerous unsubstantiated accounts that Fidel was selected Havana's schoolboy athlete of the year for 1945. Yet when Quirk tirelessly poured over every single daily issue of the Havana sports pages (in *Diario de la Marina*) for that particular year he could find not a single mention of Castro's name. In a footnote to his account Quirk ironically demonstrates his own carelessness of historical details when he notes that the actual outstanding schoolboy star of that 1945 season was reported by *Diario* to be Con-

rado Marrero, an amateur pitching hero who would himself become legendary on Cuban diamonds of the late '40s and early '50s and who actually did make it onto the Washington Senators major league roster. What Quirk overlooks is the fact that Marrero was already 34 in 1945 and had long been established as a top star on the Cuban national team since the late thirties.

Yet there does turn out to be a source after all in the Belén high school years for the essence of the Castro baseball legend. Biographer Quirk falsely assumed Fidel's recognition as a top schoolboy athlete to be based on his senior season, when in actuality the recognition came a year earlier in 1943–44. Another Fidel chronicler, Peter G. Bourne (*Fidel*, 1988), indeed acknowledges Castro's status as a top basketball player at Belén, and also his recognition as Havana's top schoolboy sportsman during that earlier winter. Bourne also emphasizes Fidel's penchant for using athletics (as he also used academics, the debate society, and student politics) as a convenient method for proving he could excel in almost any endeavor imaginable. Fidel was so driven in this way that he once wagered a school chum he could ride his bicycle full speed into a brick wall. He succeeded, but the attempt landed him in the school infirmary for several weeks.

It is the Belén athletic successes that in the end contain the hidden key to the legend of Fidel the baseball prospect. By the mid-forties Joe Cambria had been for some time running his Washington Senators scouting activities from a Havana hotel room (also his part-time residence) and also holding regular open tryout camps for the legions of eager Havana prospects, as well as beating the bushes around the rest of the island to seek out cheap Cuban talent. Fidel is reported (by Bourne) to have showed up uninvited at two of these camps between his junior and senior years, largely to prove to school chums that he might indeed be good enough to earn a pro contract offer. Castro, in other words, sought out Cambria and the pro scouts and not vice versa.

Nonetheless, no contract was ever offered to the hard-throwing but wild prospect. And as biographer Bourne stresses, any offer would almost certainly have been rejected at any rate. Fidel was a privileged youth from a wealthy family and thus had other prospects looming on the horizon (a lucrative career in law and politics) far more promising than pro baseball. Ball-playing as an occupation would actually have been a step down for any prospective law student of that decade. There were no big bonus deals in the 1940s, especially in Cuba where Cambria's mission for the penny-pinching Clark Griffith was to find dirt-cheap talent among lower-class athletes desperate to sign for next-to-nothing. Fidel's own promising future was already assured in the lucrative fields of law and politics. His reported fascination with baseball could never have been more than the compulsive showoff's momentary diversion — an endeavor devoid of captivating dreams of escape into big-league glories or elusive promises of big-league riches.

When he next put in his time as a student at the University of Havana, Fidel's ball-playing fantasies were apparently not yet entirely squelched and he did play freshman basket-

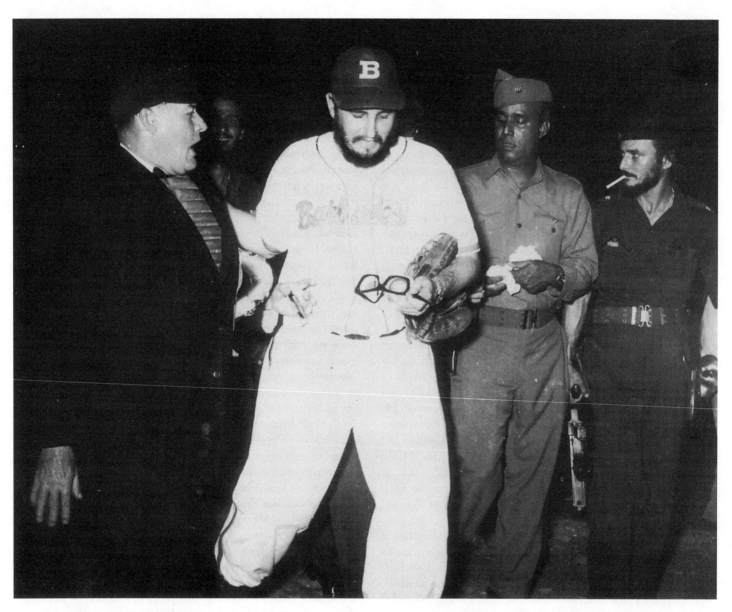

A triumphant Fidel leaves the mound at the conclusion of his successful single career Barbudos mound outing.

ball and also try out — although unsuccessfully — for the college varsity baseball team.* But as biographer Quirk notes, ballplayers in Cuba (as well as top athletes in other sports) were already by the late '40s coming mostly from poorer African descendents among the populace, not from the upper crust of privileged students like Fidel. The future politician displayed an abiding fascination for ball-playing (especially basketball and soccer, as later interviews would reveal) that would remain with him in future years. But it was unquestionably evident even to Fidel during college days that he had little serious talent as a baseball moundsman. Furthermore, political activities preoccupied the ambitious law student from 1948 onward and

left almost no available time for any serious practice on the baseball field. While his numerous biographers cover every aspect of his life in painstaking detail, none mention any further tryouts for baseball scouts, any serious playing on organized teams, indeed any baseball activity at all until his eventual renewed passion for the game as a dedicated fan. And the latter came only after the successful rise to political power in January 1959. Quirk and Bourne alone among Castro biographers emphasize Fidel's ball-playing, and then only to report that baseball never quite measured up to basketball or track and field as an arena for displaying athletic skill or for releasing an obsessive drive for unlimited personal success.

*Note: If Fidel was not a pitcher for the University of Havana varsity nine, as so often reported, he did apparently do some actual pitching while on the university campus. El Mundo for 28 November 1946 carries a game report and box score for the university's intramural championship contest between the faculties (schools) of Commercial Sciences and Law, in which one F. Castro hurled for the latter squad. The full box score (reproduced on pages 313–314) may be the only existing evidence containing game statistics for Fidel Castro's very abbreviated collegiate baseball career. As the losing hurler, Fidel struck out 4, walked 7, yielded 5 hits and 5 runs, and hit one batter in his complete-game losing effort.

Fidel's most notable chronicler (Tad Szulc) does, however, mention one later event that sheds considerable light on Castro's sublimated athletic interests. Szulc reports an interview in which Fidel suddenly and unexpectedly began to expound on the important symbolic values of his favored schoolboy sport, basketball. Basketball, Fidel would observe, could provide valuable indirect training for revolutionary activity. It was a game requiring strategic and tactical planning and overall cunning, plus speed and agility, the true elements of guerrilla warfare. Baseball, Fidel further noted, held no such promise for a future revolutionary. Most significantly, Szulc points out that Fidel's comments on this occasion came during a candid response in which he "emphatically denied" the reported rumors that he once envisioned a career for himself as a professional pitcher in the major leagues.

* * *

The true impetus for stories of Fidel as serious ballplayer seems also to follow as much from the Maximum Leader's post-revolution associations with the game as from bloated reports concerning an erstwhile schoolboy prospect. Central here are oft-recounted (but rarely accurately portrayed) exhibition-game appearances at stadiums in Havana and elsewhere across the island during the first decade following the 1959–1960 communist takeover. The most renowned single event, of course, was Fidel's onetime appearance on the mound in El Cerro Stadium (home of the Havana/Cuban Sugar Kings) wearing the uniform of his own pickup nine, aptly christened "Los Barbudos" ("The Bearded Ones"). Rarely, however, have the North American press or stateside baseball historians ever gotten the "Barbudos" story entirely straight.

The celebrated but little-understood Barbudos game took place in Havana on July 24, 1959, before a crowd of 25,000 "fanaticos" (26,532 to be precise), as a preliminary contest to a scheduled International League clash between the Rochester Red Wings and Havana Sugar Kings. A single pithy newspaper account from the Rochester (New York) *Democrat and Chronicle* provides the source for most details of the evening's events and also for a familiar Castro action photo that would later accompany most Fidel pitching tales. Fidel is reported (by *Democrat and Chronicle* writer George Beahon) to have practiced all day in his hotel room for his two-inning stint with the Cuban Army pick-up team which faced a squad of military police. (He is also reported in Beahon's account to have been a onetime high-school pitcher and to have "tried out" for the college team, but no mention is made of any collegiate competition* or of any interest among scouts in his moderate throwing talents.) Castro would pitch both pre-game exhibition innings and would be captured on the mound in the several action photos (he wore number 19) that would later become the only widely seen images of Cuba's Maximum Leader turned baseball pitcher. The entire latter-day public impression of Fidel as moundsman (in the U.S. at least) is indeed built largely if not exclusively upon the existing photographic images culled from this single evening's events.

Fidel would strike out two members of the opposing military team (one with the aid of a friendly umpire, on a call that had Fidel dashing toward the batter's box to shake hands with the cooperative arbiter). He is reported to have "needlessly but admirably" covered first on an infield grounder, to have bounced to short in his only turn at bat (captured by a photo in the next afternoon's Havana daily), and to have demonstrated surprisingly good mound style — "wild but fast, and with good motions." But the most memorable moment of the evening was reserved for still another military hero of the revolution, Major Camilo Cienfuegos, who was originally scheduled to hurl for the opposing MP team. "I never oppose Fidel in anything, including baseball," quipped the astute Cienfuegos, who then donned catcher's gear and went behind the plate for Fidel's Barbudos army squad.

If Major Cienfuegos would not risk upstaging Comandante Castro, the activities of lesser-known henchmen soon enough would. A single evening later transpired one of the most infamous and portentous events of Cuban baseball history — the oft-reported shooting incident in which Rochester third base coach Frank Verdi and Havana shortstop Leo Cárdenas were apparently nicked by stray bullets launched by revolutionary zealots who had crowded into El Cerro Stadium to celebrate the first Cuban Independence Day since Castro's rise to power.

The volatile occasion for mixing baseball with revelry was a much anticipated first "July 26th Celebration" of the revolutionary era, and baseball and local politics were thus about to collide head-on. Fulgencio Batista had fled the island on January 1, 1959, allowing Castro-led rebels to seize effective control of the entire country. The July 26th date commemorated a 1953 failed attack by 125 Castro-led student rebels against the Moncada army barracks in Santiago, an event that subsequently lent its name to the entire Castro-inspired revolutionary movement. (Fidel's rebel army was itself officially known as the July 26 Brigade.) The events of the moment had been further spiced by Fidel's dramatic resignation as prime minister only nine days earlier in a power struggle with soon-to-be-ousted President Manuel Urritia; Fidel would reassume the top government post at the conclusion of this very weekend's dramatic patriotic celebrations.

What followed that night in El Cerro Stadium was as much a comedy of errors as it was a tragedy of misunderstanding. And once more the facts surrounding the shooting itself — and the stadium frenzy that both preceded and followed — rarely get told correctly.

Beleaguered Rochester Red Wings manager, Ellis "Cot" Deal, would three decades later painstakingly recount the memorable events in his self-published autobiography (*Fifty Years in Baseball — or, "Cot" in the Act*, 1992), a rare first-hand version subsequently verified in interviews with the present author. In a stadium jammed-packed with *guajiros* (peasants from the Cuban countryside) and *barbudos* (Castro's soldiers, who like his military team of the previous evening, drew their moniker from the thick beards worn by most) — all on hand for a planned midnight "July 26" celebration — the two International League teams initially finished a suspended game,

Fidel demonstrates his mound form during an obvious photo opportunity (notice that the ball has not been released) with fellow revolutionaries.

then waded through the explosive atmosphere and intense tropical heat to a 3–3 tie at the end of regulation innings in the regularly-scheduled affair. The preliminary contest was the completion of a scoreless seven-inning game from the Red Wings' previous trip into town a month earlier.

Manager Deal suspected early on that the night would be long and eventful, especially when the umps and rival skippers (Deal and Sugar Kings boss Preston Gómez) met at the plate to discuss (in lieu of customary ground rules) what would transpire in the highly likely case of serious fan interference. Havana scored in the bottom of the eighth to win the preliminary and thus the festive stadium mood was further enlivened.

Veteran big-leaguer Bob Keegan had mopped up the preliminary game (since he had also been the starter of the suspended game in June) and was once more on tap by accident of the pitching rotation to start the regularly scheduled affair to follow. Keegan pitched courageously despite the oppressive heat and held a 3–1 lead into the bottom of the eighth when sweltering humidity finally sapped his energy and Deal resignedly changed hurlers. Tom Hurd closed the door in the eighth, but a walk and a homer by Cuban slugger Borrego Alvarez in the bottom of the ninth spelled dreaded extra innings.

Next came the dramatic patriotic interruption. With the crowd — an overflow throng which topped 35,000 — now at fever pitch, the regulation game was halted at the stroke of midnight, stadium lights were quickly extinguished, a spotlight focused on a giant Cuban flag in center field, and the Cuban anthem was played slowly and reverently. As soon as stadium lighting was rekindled, however, all hell broke loose and the air was suddenly filled with spasms of celebratory gunfire launched from both inside and outside the ballpark. A close Havana friend of the author, in attendance that night, today recounts how a patron seated next to him near the visiting team dugout emptied several rounds from his pistol directly into the on-deck circle. Deal also vividly recalls one overzealous Cuban soldier (perhaps the selfsame individual) unloading an automatic pistol into the ground directly in front of the Red Wings dugout.

Play resumed with further sporadic gunfire occasionally punctuating the diamond actions. Infielder Billy Harrell homered in the top of the 11th to give Rochester the momentary lead, but in the bottom of the frame the home club would rally and the crowd would thus again reach new heights of delirium. When Sugar Kings catcher Jesse Gonder (an American) led off the bottom of the frame with a hit slapped down the left field line and raced toward second, he seemed (at least to Deal) to skip over the first base sack while rounding the bag, an event unnoticed by the rooting throng but one that predictably sent manager Deal racing onfield to argue with umpires stationed at both first and home.

Naturally fearing an imminent riot if they now called anything controversial against the rallying home club, neither umpire was disposed toward hearing Deal's protests, which under calmer circumstances might have seemed valid. (Deal thought that first base ump Frank Guzetta had turned too quickly to follow the runner to second, in case a play was made there, and therefore missed Gonder's sidestepping of first; he merely wanted the home plate ump to help out on the play.) Guzetta ignored Deal's pleas and moments later the Rochester skipper was ejected for continuing his vehement protests. Gonder would soon score the lone run of the inning and the contest

Cuba's top fan celebrates a Cuban Sugar Kings victory in the 1959 minor league Little World Series at Cerro Stadium. Next to Fidel is ballplayer Daniel Morejón (center) and immediately behind Morejón is manager Preston Gómez.

would continue into the twelfth once more knotted at four apiece. Having already been banished to the clubhouse, Deal himself would not be on hand to witness firsthand the further drama that next unfolded.

In the moments that followed, Deal's ejection would ironically prove to be a significant event. As a chagrined Deal later recounted the circumstances of that "heave-ho" from the field of play, he would have to admit that umpire Frank Guzetta had reacted more out of deep wisdom than out of shallow self-defense. In the heat of the argument Deal had grabbed his own throat, giving a universal "choke" sign that led instantaneously to another universally understood gesture — the "thumb" which is Spanish for "adios" and English for "take a shower." Deal in hindsight would be much more sympathetic to the umps' plight and would realize that any attempt to reverse the decision on Gonder's baserunning might well have further ignited an already rowdy (and heavily armed) grandstand throng with quite disastrous consequences.

Back on the field, fate and happenstance were once more about to intervene. More random shots were fired as play opened in the twelfth, and stray bullets simultaneously grazed both third base coach Frank Verdi and Sugar Kings shortstop Leo Cárdenas. By now the frightened umps and ballplayers had seen enough. The game was immediately suspended by the umpires as Verdi, still dazed, was hastily carried by ashen teammates toward the Rochester locker room, followed closely by a wild swarm of escaping ballplayers. Apparently a falling spent shell had struck Verdi's cap (which fortuitously contained a protective batting liner) and merely stunned him. Deal (oblivious to on-field events) had just stepped from the shower when

his panic-stricken team burst into the clubhouse carrying the barely conscious Frank Verdi. The runway outside the Red Wings dressing room was pure chaos as the umpires and ballplayers from both clubs scrambled for safety within the bowels of the ballpark. An immediately apparent irony was the fact that the wounded Verdi had that very inning substituted for the ejected manager Deal in the third base coach's box, and while Verdi always wore a plastic liner in his cap, the fortune-blessed Deal never used such a protective device. Thus Deal's ejection from the field had likely saved the fate-blessed manager's life.

While umpires next desperately tried to phone league president Frank Shaughnessy back in New York for a ruling on the chaotic situation, manager Deal and his general manager, George Sisler, Jr., had already decided on their own immediate course of action. It was to get their team safely back to the downtown Hotel Nacional and then swiftly onto the next available plane routed for Rochester (or at least Miami). But some Cuban fans in attendance at the packed El Cerro Stadium that night (a few have been recently interviewed by the author in Havana) today hold very different memories of the event, perhaps colored by the changing perspective or fading recollections of several passing decades. They remember few shots, little that was hostile in the crowd's festive response to both the patriotic celebration and the exciting ballgame, and hardly any sense of danger to either the ballplayers or the celebrants themselves. And Cuban baseball officials at the time also had a slightly different interpretation, vociferously denying that the situation was ever truly out of control and pressing the Rochester manager and general manager to continue the suspended contest and attend the regularly scheduled game on tap for the following afternoon.

Captain Felipe Guerra Matos, newly appointed director of Cuban sports, would one week later cable Rochester team officials with a formal and truly heart-felt apology, assuring Red Wings' brass that Havana was entirely safe for baseball and that the team (and all other International League ball clubs) would be guaranteed the utmost security on all future trips to the island. Guerra Matos saw the events of the evening only as a spontaneous outpouring of nationalistic joy and revolutionary fervor by emotional Cuban soldiers and enthusiastic if unruly peasants, and thus a celebration of freedom no more unseemly perhaps than many stateside Fourth of July celebrations.

But Deal and Sisler at the time persisted, despite the pressures and threats of Cuban officials which continued throughout the night and subsequent morning. After a tense Sunday, sequestered at the waterfront Hotel Nacional and with the revolutionary revels continuing in the streets around them, the Rochester ball club was finally able to obtain safe passage from José Martí Airport before another nightfall.

Deal today gives an entertaining account of the labored efforts of Cuban officials to get his team to complete the weekend series, including the previous night's suspended match as well as the scheduled Sunday afternoon affair. While a World War II vintage bomber strafed an abandoned barge in Havana harbor as part of the ongoing revolutionary revelries, Deal and his general manager met with a pair of Cuban government officials in Sisler's hotel room, fortified only by strong cups of black Cuban coffee. The Cuban government spokesmen — in Deal's account — pleaded, cajoled and then finally even threat-ened boisterously in their efforts to convince the Americans to resume the afternoon's baseball venue. Deal and Sisler held fast in their refusals and eventually the government bureaucrats departed in a barely controlled fit of anger. Deal sensed that the failed Sunday morning meeting would be most difficult for their hosts to explain to their government superiors (and perhaps even to Fidel himself).

The bottom-line result of the eventful weekend — which first saw Fidel take the mound and later witnessed chaos overtake the ballpark — was the beginning of the end for International League baseball on the communist-controlled island. But the death knell would be slow to peal for the Havana franchise. The International League's Governors' Cup championship playoffs (with surprising third-place finisher Havana defeating the fourth-place Richmond Vees) and a Little World Series showdown with the Minneapolis Millers of the American Association (featuring a hot prospect named Carl Yastrzemski) would both transpire in Havana later that same fall. And Fidel the baseball fan was of course a fixture at both events, although frequent reports of *Comandante* Castro and his comrades toting firearms, strolling uninvited inside and atop the dugouts, and even intimidating first Richmond and later Minneapolis ballplayers with threats of violent intervention have likely been wildly exaggerated.

By mid-season of 1960 Castro's expropriations (both actual and threatened) of U.S. business interests on the island, as well as violent outbursts of anti-government political resistance ("terrorism") on the streets of Havana (numerous reported destructive explosions spread throughout the city), convinced International League officials and their Washington backers finally to pull the plug on the eight-year reign of the league's increasingly beleaguered Havana franchise. On July 13, 1960 (while on a road trip in Miami), the proud Sugar Kings (now managed by Tony Castaño and featuring future big leaguers Mike Cuéllar, Orlando Peña and Cookie Rojas) were closed down by the league's reigning fathers and relocated literally overnight to the northern wastelands of Jersey City.

*   *   *

Fidel's appearance with the Barbudos team was strictly a onetime event. "El Jefe" did not pitch regularly with any team in any version of the "Cuban League" — a distortion erroneously reported by several stateside sources, most infamously by San Francisco's Blue Marlin Corporation and by ESPN gurus as a featured centerpiece of calculated commercial advertising campaigns. Fidel did continue over the next decade and more to play informally in frequent pickup games with his inner circle of revolutionary colleagues. Biographer Quirk reports that Camilo Cienfuegos was able to maintain

Fidel poses with Minneapolis Millers manager Gene Mauch during the 1959 Little World Series in Cerro Stadium.

favor with Fidel for a time largely because of his ballplaying skills. (The ever-popular Major Cienfuegos became a liability, however, within a year of the revolutionary takeover and soon disappeared under mysterious circumstances on a solo flight between Camagüey and Havana in late 1959.) Even Che Guevara (an Argentine, who preferred soccer) and brother Raúl (who showed little raw athletic skill or sporting interest to match Fidel's) were occasionally photographed in military fatigues or T-shirts and jeans taking their enthusiastic "cuts" during batting exhibitions before Cuban League games of the early sixties. Fidel himself made numerous such exhibition appearances in Havana, Santa Clara, Cienfuegos, Matanzas, and elsewhere around the island.

Fidel's influence on Cuban baseball would nonetheless remain enormous after the successful military takeover by his July 26 Movement in January 1959. It was the already deteriorating relationships between Washington and the Cuban government during that very year, and the one that followed, that more than anything would lead to the sudden relocation of the Cuban International League franchise in July 1960 from Havana to Jersey City. In turn, that decision to strip Cuba of its professional baseball franchise may — as much as anything else in the early stages of the Cuban Revolutionary regime — have worked to sour Fidel Castro on the United States and its blatant imperialist policies. After the folding of the Havana professional ball club Fidel would reestablish baseball on the island (in 1962) as a strictly amateur affair, and under his revolutionary government a new "anti-professional" baseball spirit would soon come to dominate throughout Cuba.

And during coming decades under Fidel's leadership, the Cuban regime would ironically find in baseball its one proven arena for international triumphs. For thirty-five years (beginning with the 1969 IBAF World Championship in Santo Domingo) Cuban teams have dominated world amateur competitions, and few (if any) other achievements of the Cuban Revolution have provided nearly as hefty a source for either national identity or international successes. In the astute phrasing of one noted U.S.–based Cuban cultural historian (Louis A. Pérez, Jr., from the University of North Carolina), under Fidel Castro's regime, baseball — the quintessential American game — has most fully served the Cuban Revolution — the quintessential anti–American embodiment.

Perhaps the most balanced view of Fidel's ball-playing comes in a sixties-era book produced by American photojournalist Lee Lockwood (*Castro's Cuba, Cuba's Fidel*, 1967). Lock-

El Comandante ready to throw a ceremonial first pitch at an early National Series game in Havana. The Henequeneros uniform behind Fidel indicates this is no earlier than National Series V (1965–1966).

wood's groundbreaking portrait of Castro is drawn through hours of in-depth interviews (transcribed in careful detail) on far-ranging topics (viz., his assessments of his island nation, his own enigmatic personality, and the world at large), as well as a collage of the journalist's rare candid photographs. The single reference to baseball in this entire 300-page tome is a two-page spread featuring photos of Raúl batting ("a competent second baseman, he is the better hitter") and Fidel pitching ("Fidel has good control but not much stuff"). Both men are captured by Lockwood's lens in ball caps and informal ball-playing gear. In an interview segment several pages later Fidel comments effusively on his life-long love for sport, emphasizing basketball, chess, deep-sea diving and soccer as his lasting favorites. He stresses his high school prowess in basketball and track and field ("I never became a champion ... but

Rare photo of Fidel showing visiting Mexican ballplayers how to pitch in the streets of Havana, sometime during the sixties.

I didn't practice much."). But there is nary a mention of the national game of baseball.

It is clear from historical records that Fidel was an accomplished and enthusiastic athlete as a precocious youngster. His biographers underscore his repeated use of schoolboy athletics (especially basketball, track and baseball) to excel among fellow students. But Fidel's consuming interest and latent talent was never foremost in baseball itself. His strong identification with the game after the 1959 Revolution — he followed the Sugar Kings as dedicated fan, staged exhibitions before Cuban League games, and played frequent pickup games with numerous close comrades — was more than anything else, perhaps, an inevitable acknowledgment of his country's national sport and its widespread hold on the Cuban citizenry. It was also a calculated step toward utilizing baseball as a means of besting the hated imperialists at their own game. And baseball was early on also seen by the Maximum Leader as an instrument of revolutionary politics — a means to build revolutionary spirit at home and to construct ongoing (and headline-grabbing) international propaganda triumphs abroad. Fidel may not have exercised much control over his fastball in

long-lost schoolboy days. But he would eventually prove a natural-born expert at controlling baseball (the institution) as a highly useful instrument for carefully building his revolutionary society and also for maintaining his propaganda leverage in worldwide Cold War politics.

Fidel and baseball would remain inevitably linked across the next forty-five years of Castro's rule in Revolutionary Cuba, and the Maximum Leader would inevitably change the face and focus of the island's baseball fortunes just as he would dramatically change all else that constituted Cuban society. But it was only as political figurehead and Maximum Leader — not as legitimate ballplayer — that Fidel Castro would emerge as one of the most remarkable figures found anywhere in Cuban baseball history. As a pitcher he was perhaps never more than the smoky essence of unrelenting myth. He certainly wasn't Cuba's hidden Walter Johnson or Christy Mathewson, or even its latter-day Dolf Luque or Conrado Marrero; his role was destined to be much more akin to the shadowy and insubstantial Abner Doubleday, or perhaps even the promotion-wise and always market-savvy A.G. Spalding.

Cooperstown Hall-of-Famer Monte Irvin, who played

for Almendares in the 1948–49 Havana winter league, once quipped that if he and other Cuban leaguers of the late forties had known that the young student who hung around Havana ballparks had designs on being an autocratic dictator, they would have been well served to make him an umpire. Perhaps former U.S. Senator Eugene McCarthy (*EFQ*, Volume 14:2) had the more appropriate role in mind — that of baseball czar and big league commissioner. Without ever launching a serious fastball or ever swinging a potent bat, Fidel was nonetheless destined — like Judge Landis north of the border a generation earlier — to have a far greater impact on his nation's pastime then several whole generations of leather-pounding or lumber-toting on-field diamond stars. As McCarthy so astutely observed, an aspiring pitcher with a long memory, once spurned, can indeed be a dangerous man.

Fidel (left) with his Barbudos catcher, the ill-starred revolutionary hero Camilo Cienfuegos. Legend has it that Camilo was supposed to hurl for the rival military team before uttering the famous excuse that "I don't oppose Fidel in anything, even baseball."

References and Suggested Readings

Bjarkman, Peter C. "Baseball and Fidel Castro" in: *The National Pastime: A Review of Baseball History*, Volume 18 (1998), 64–68.

_____. "Fidel on the Mound: Baseball Myth and History in Castro's Cuba" in: *Elysian Fields Quarterly* 17:1 (Summer 1999), 31–41.

Bourne, Peter G. *Fidel: A Biography of Fidel Castro*. New York: Dodd, Mead and Company, 1988.

Castro, Fidel. *Fidel Sobre El Deporte (Fidel on Sports)*. Havana: INDER (National Institute for Sports, Physical Education and Recreation), 1975 (excerpts from speeches and publications by the Maximum Leader, providing the most comprehensive source on Fidel's own comments regarding sports and athletics in socialist society).

Deal, Ellis F. ("Cot"). *Fifty Years in Baseball — or, "Cot" in the Act*. Oklahoma City, OK: self-published, 1992.

Hoak, Don, with Myron Cope. "The Day I Batted Against Castro" in: *The Armchair Book of Baseball*. Edited by John Thorn. New York: Charles Scribner's Sons, 1985, 161–164 (originally appeared in *Sport*, June 1964).

Krich, John. *A Totally Free Man — An Unauthorized Autobiography of Fidel Castro (A Novel)*. Berkeley, CA: Creative Arts Books, 1981 (fiction filled with unsubstantiated references to Castro's ball-playing episodes).

Lockwood, Lee. *Castro's Cuba, Cuba's Fidel*. New York: Vintage Books, 1969 (best English source for Fidel's personal comments on sports and athletics in socialist society).

McCarthy, Eugene J. "Diamond Diplomacy" in: *Elysian Fields Quarterly 14:2* (1995), 12–15.

Quirk, Robert. *Fidel Castro*. New York and London: W.W. Norton and Company, 1993 (paperback edition, 1995).

Rucker, Mark, and Peter C. Bjarkman. *Smoke — The Romance and Lore of Cuban Baseball*. New York: Total Sports Illustrated, 1999 (especially pp. 182–204).

Santamarina, Everardo J. "The Hoak Hoax" in: *The National Pastime 14*. Cleveland, OH: Society for American Baseball Research, 29–30.

Senzel, Howard. *Baseball and the Cold War — Being a Soliloquy on the Necessity of Baseball in the Life of a Serious Student of Marx and Hegel From Rochester, New York*. New York and London: Harcourt Brace Jovanovich, 1977 (engaging if largely fictionalized account of July 26, 1959, Havana ballpark episode and its full aftermath).

Szulc, Tad. *Fidel: A Critical Portrait*. New York: William Morrow and Company, 1986.

Truby, J. David. "Castro's Curveball" in: *Harper's Magazine* (May 1989), 32, 34.

Wendel, Tim. *Castro's Curveball: A Novel*. New York: Ballantine, 1999 (the most free-ranging treatment of the fictional Fidel Castro pitching legend).

Wednesday, 27 November 1946, Havana University Stadium

Game Line Score	*123*	*456*	*789*	*R–H–E*
Derecho (Law)	000	011	011	4–7–2
Ciéncias Comerciales (Business)	310	000	10x	5–5–4

DERECHO (Law)

Player/Position	*AB*	*Runs*	*Hits*	*PO*	*Assists*	*Errors*
Quevedo, cf	5	2	2	3	0	0
García, ss	3	0	1	2	2	0
Granados, rf	2	0	0	1	0	0
Jiménez, lf	5	0	1	2	0	0
Villaescusa, cf-2b	2	0	0	1	0	1
Iglesias, 1b	5	0	0	7	1	0
Valdés, 2b-3b	4	2	1	2	1	0

Player/Position	AB	Runs	Hits	PO	Assists	Errors
Pedrasa, c	4	0	2	3	2	0
Castro, p	4	0	0	1	2	1
Freixas, 3b	1	0	0	2	1	0
Totals	**35**	**4**	**7**	**24**	**9**	**2**

CIENCIAS COMERCIALES (Commercial Sciences/Business)

Player/Position	AB	Runs	Hits	PO	Assists	Errors
Guerra, lf	2	2	0	1	0	0
Delgado, cf	2	1	2	2	0	0
Cuevas, 1b-rf	2	2	1	4	0	0
Ruíz, 1b-p	4	0	2	13	1	0
Jayo, c	3	0	0	3	0	1
Mosquera, 3b	4	0	0	2	7	2
Marroquin, ss	3	0	0	0	4	0
Alvarez, 2b	2	0	0	2	2	0
Cabrejas, p-rf	3	0	0	0	1	1
Ortega, 2b	2	0	0	0	0	0
Escobedo, cf	0	0	0	0	0	0
Totals	**27**	**5**	**5**	**27**	**15**	**4**

Pitching Summary: Cabrejas, Ruíz (9), F. Castro. 2B: Ruíz. SB: Guerra 2, Delgado 2, García 2, Villaecusa, Quevedo 3, Freixas, Valdés, Cuevas. Strikeouts: F. Castro 4, Cabrejas 1, Ruíz 1. Walks: F. Castro 7, Cabrejas 6, Ruíz 0. Hit-by-Pitch: Marroquin (by Castro), García (by Cabrejas). Hits off of pitchers: Cabrejas 7, Castro 5. Winner: Canrejas. Loser: F. Castro. Time: 2:20. Umpires: Izquierdo (HP), Cangas (Bases). Official Scorer: Quezada.

10

Tarzán, Minnie, Zorro and El Duque — Cubans in the Major Leagues

If colored meant being nonwhite, then Rafael Almeida and Armando Marsans, who played for the Cincinnati Reds 36 years before Jackie Robinson came along, should be credited with crashing the color barrier.

— Felipe Alou

The saga of colorful Cubans performing in the North American major leagues unfolds neatly in three distinct and formidable chapters. First — chronologically at least, if not by measure of historical primacy — comes the near half-century of racist-inspired segregated U.S. leagues. Both the senior and junior big-league circuits would witness only a small handful of Cubans slipping through the narrow doors of organized baseball* as somewhat marginal if nonetheless acceptable "whites." Some of these pioneering Cubans — those with dusky but not entirely swarthy skin tones — were routinely passed off as mere "foreigners" and thus never fully recognized as "niggers" and therefore outright outcasts. Others suffered substantial heckling and hostilities — both from teammates and opponents, as well as from raucous grandstand partisans — a plight that lasted throughout their entire shadowy careers on baseball's grandest stage.

The vast majority among those mere thirty-eight Cubans who preceded Jackie Robinson and Branch Rickey's integration experiment enjoyed little more than brief cups of coffee with eleven different big league clubs that employed them.† Only Dolf Luque (a.k.a. "The Pride of Havana") was a legitimate headliner, and even Luque was always much more of a flashy and even slightly comical stereotype for North American imaginations than he was a true diamond idol. This despite one of the top seasons ever enjoyed by a National League pitcher (with the Cincinnati Reds in 1923) plus a heroic late-career World Series performance (for the New York Giants in 1933). More typical by far was Baldomero "Merito" Acosta, a thoroughly forgettable fill-in outfielder with both Washington and Philadelphia who hung out in the majors for five partial seasons (1913–18), averaging about 35 game appearances annually and batting .209 in the one summer (1915) when he played nearly half his total career games. Equally representative was Yankees outfield part-timer Angel "Pete" Aragón,

whose mere 32 games spread over three seasons (1914–17) and included exactly one extra-base hit, a single lame two-base smash.

A barely hidden subplot of this first phase of the Cuban big league story is thus the somewhat sordid tale of a dozen or more players (among the total 38 Cubans) carrying partial or substantial African bloodlines. They were unheralded pioneers who were able to sneak across the odious color barrier* for brief appearances in the majors precisely because they were able to hide behind their spurious identities as exotic sun-tanned Cubans. For the "Lords of Baseball" (owners and front office decision-makers ruling the game) as well as a majority of fans, these swarthy intruders from the Caribbean were merely sideshow "foreigners" and thus somehow less objectionable than those banned "Negroes" of true native-grown African-American stock.

The second installment in Cuba's big league history comprises a dozen-year breakout period stretching from April 1947 — memorable for a Brooklyn diamond debut by Jackie Robinson — to January 1959 — marked by the Havana political triumphs of Fidel Castro. During this all-too-brief era it was the Cubans who were suddenly (thanks largely if indirectly to Robinson and Rickey) in the vanguard of a first substantial Latin American big-league immigration. Baseball's initial Hispanic invasion was admittedly quite tiny when compared with the second wave of Latin imports that washed on big-league shores a quarter-century later. The influx of anything beyond a mere handful of Latin ballplayers had only become a possibility once Robinson and Rickey had officially broken down the iron-clad color barrier; now for the first time all Latin American and Caribbean stars and journeymen were finally eligible for lucrative big league careers, regardless of their tropical skin tones or even the rumored African roots buried within their ethnic heritage.

*Organized baseball (oftentimes capitalized, but not here) is a reigning euphemism for U.S. professional baseball, including both the major leagues and all recognized minor leagues affiliated with major league baseball.
†The full list of pre-1947 Cuban-born big leaguers is found in Appendix C, included at volume's end.

Seemingly overnight in the late forties and early fifties Latinos formed an ever-increasing presence on big-league rosters. Many were light-swinging middle infielders who filled a popular new stereotype of glue-fingered but anemic-hitting utility men and who jabbered unintelligible Spanish while also exuding irresistible hustle and untold charisma. Others were flame-throwing pitchers cut in the mold of Luque, or swift and muscular outfielders following in the tradition of shadowy Negro league icons like Dihigo, Oms and Torriente. Ebony-skinned Orestes Miñoso (starring with the Indians and White Sox) and lighter-complexioned hurlers Pascual and Ramos (toiling with the hapless Senators) became the earliest headliners among Cubans leading the Latin charge; but this foremost trio of Cubans was only the advance guard of what quickly became a small groundswell. In a mere ten years between Robinson's debut in Brooklyn and Roberto Clemente's surge to superstardom in Pittsburgh, the roster of Cuban major leaguers equaled that of the entire previous half-century. Clark Griffith's lowly Washington Senators by themselves seemed to import an almost endless supply of marginal Cuban-born talent, though little of it ever appeared to improve in the slightest the team's woeful on-field performances as perennial second-division tail-enders.

A third and final chapter of the Cuban big league saga involves even steeper challenges for island-born athletes seeking to play in organized baseball than those barriers encountered during the pre-integration era. After Fidel Castro's sudden rise to power in 1958–1959 and the resulting rapid disintegration in USA–Cuba relations which immediately followed, there transpired four-plus long (and still ongoing) decades during which major league doors have been effectively slammed shut to most Cuban-born ballplayers.

There was a small trickle of islanders onto big league teams throughout the sixties, mostly consisting of the final few refugees of Cuban professional baseball who had escaped Havana during transitional years under the new leftist-leaning Castro regime. Some would mature into substantial stars in coming seasons. "Tony" Oliva (whose legal first name was Pedro) and Tony Pérez (whose actual nickname was "Tany"— from Antanasio) were the most notable, and indeed Oliva and Pérez today still retain prominence as arguably the loftiest Cuban-born idols ever to grace organized professional baseball.

Others, including seventies-era World Series stars Mike Cuéllar, Bert (Dagoberto) Campaneris and Luis Tiant (Junior), also carved substantial careers after fleeing their homeland in the aftermath of Cuba's communist revolution. Yet as this older post-revolution generation rapidly faded, the Cuban big league presence would just as rapidly become nearly extinct. Only four native Cubans entered the big leagues in the entire decade of the seventies; by 1984 Bobby Ramos, Tany Pérez and recent Castroland-escapee Bárbaro Garbey (expelled from the Cuban League and also from the island itself in wake of an infamous game-throwing incident) were the only Cuban big-leaguers remaining. Sluggers José Canseco (1985 debut) and Rafael Palmeiro (1986 debut)—both natives of Havana

Province—emerged in the late eighties as hitting paragons parallel to Oliva and Pérez, but these were technically both Cubans by mere accident of birthright alone. Whisked out of their native country during their first year of life, neither could claim much of an island baseball heritage.

Contrary to popular stateside notions, baseball in Havana, Matanzas, and Santiago had not dried up under Castro in the seventies and eighties. But all the top island-born and island-bred stars were now playing out their substantial careers back home in the shadows of an outlawed amateur league hidden away from North American eyes behind the Sugar Cane Curtain erected by late–20th-century Cold War politics. The irony here is quite palpable. Cuba's greatest pre–1947 stars were doomed by their race to hiding out in the little-noticed North American blackball leagues. Post-1959 Cuban stars in turn have been exiled from North American diamonds just as effectively by a clash between incompatible political systems and the posturing of Fidel Castro and his nine successive rival American presidents.

Of late, the final few seasons of the old millennium and the first few campaigns of the new century have nonetheless witnessed a small if noisy renewal of the long-dormant Cuban major league presence. Some of the late arrivals have been sons and even grandsons of Cold War-era Cuban exiles native mostly to Miami, some of them actually veteran ballplayers themselves. These are the Cuban-Americans who fled their island homeland during the earliest years of the Castro government and subsequently built new lives and raised new families in a thriving ex-patriot community centered largely in South Florida. Eduardo Pérez (son of Tany Pérez), David Seguí (son of Diego Seguí), Rubén Amaro (son of the elder Rubén Amaro and grandson of crack Negro leaguer Santos Amaro), Eli Marrero (grandnephew of Connie Marrero), Danny Tartabull (son of José Tartabull), Bobby Estalella (grandnephew of Roberto "Tarzán" Estalella)—along with first-generation big-leaguers Alex González, Fernando Viña, Alex Fernández, Jorge Posada and Mike Lowell—all count among this latest generation of Cuban-American ballplayers whose diamond heritage is legitimately stamped as Cuban even if their birth certificates are not.

But even more substantial in numbers (and perhaps also in talent) has been the new wave of island-bred Cuban athletes who have "defected" (a popular term for North American journalists but a disreputable one everywhere in island circles) from the top-flight Cuban amateur baseball system during the past decade, often risking extreme personal dangers or at least painful family disruptions to pursue dreams of fame and fortune in U.S. professional baseball. René Arocha, Rey Ordóñez, Rolando Arrojo, Osvaldo Fernández, Danys Báez, half-brothers Liván Hernández and Orlando "El Duque" Hernández, and José Ariel Contreras (all but one being pitchers, it might to be noted) have on the whole provided far more vacuous thunder than legitimate lightning with their somewhat uneven pro-league performances over the past decade. A few highly publicized achievements (particularly Liván's surprise 1997 NLCS and World Series MVP trophies and El

Photographer Mark Rucker (right) and the author pose in front of the current entrance to the historic Palmar del Junco ballbark in Matanzas, site of the first reported Cuban baseball game of December 27, 1874 (courtesy Transcendental Graphics).

Duque's strong debut with the 1998 Yankees) and notable failures (losing career records for all but Liván and El Duque, and most recently also for Contreras) by these Cuban big league "defectors" have so far offered more strictly political or propaganda currency than purely baseball interest for a jingoistic American press corps.

José Contreras, the most effective Cuban national team pitcher in international competitions before his October 2002 defection in Mexico, has of late proven the most accomplished among these renegade Cubans while fronting the stellar mound staff of the 2005 World Champion Chicago White Sox. Beyond Contreras — who seems to have revived a Cuban League career that once threatened many modern era National Series records — and also the Hernández brothers (Liván has been one of the most effective NL starters of the past two campaigns), the overall impact of Cuban defectors in the late-1990s and early-2000s has failed to constitute much more than a noisy sidebar on the big league scene. Nonetheless, the tale of these latter-day Cuban big leaguers provides a separate if equally substantial drama that demands its own detailed treatment (Chapter 12) later in this volume.

* * *

If Cubans have been a small presence in the North American big leagues, it is certainly not for any lack of ball-play-

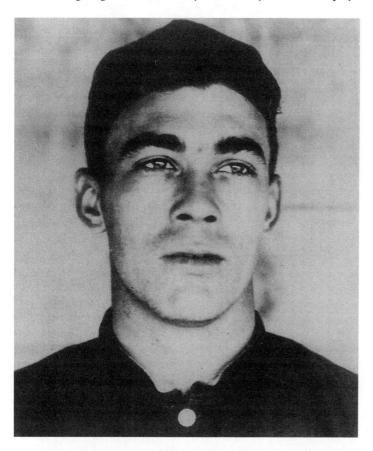

Armando Marsans, one of the first two Cuban big leaguers of the 20th century who debuted under a cloud of racial controversy with the 1911 National League Cincinnati Reds.

ing tradition within their own native homeland. As already recounted, Cuba was sporting its own popular professional games staged in Havana and surrounding towns at the very time when the venerable National League — major league baseball's granddaddy among pro circuits — was itself only first gaining a toehold with boosters and fanatics in post–Civil War North America.

Baseball had reputedly been transported to the island of Cuba as early as the end of the U.S. Civil War and was already thriving there only a handful of years later. Bats, balls, leather gloves — also rules for playing the new North American pastime — were all carried to Havana by a pair of brothers named Nemesio and Ernesto Guilló (along with an intimate friend, Enrique Porto) when the teenagers returned from a half-decade of secondary schooling at Alabama's Spring Hill College in 1864. Within mere days the siblings were organizing rudimentary play among companions in and around their crowded Vedado (central Havana) neighborhood; less than four years later the Guilló brothers and these same companions, now thoroughly dedicated to the novel ball-playing passion, had formed the Habana Base Ball Club — the same outfit that would travel to Matanzas in December 1874 for a celebrated landmark "first game" of Cuba's recorded baseball history. That notable Matanzas game — so often taken by later-era historians as the precise moment of baseball's spontaneous birth in Cuba — had in reality climaxed a full decade of exploding baseball interest throughout the city of Havana and all around the neighboring villages of the future Habana Province. And it was the local Guilló brothers who had first launched that interest and then painstakingly nurtured it to its first full flowerings.

Nemesio Guilló — at eleven the youngest of the trio of Havana teens shipped to Alabama in 1858 — would be treated most favorably in later historical accounts, often being tapped as a founding father of the national sport while the equally involved Ernesto Guilló and Enrique Porto were all but forgotten by succeeding generations. The reason, in large part, was a surviving interview with Nemesio, published decades later in the Havana popular press (*Diario de la Marina*, January 6, 1924). It is there that Nemesio Guilló recounts in detail the early organization of neighborhood play in Vedado in late 1864; the founding of the Habana Base Ball Club in 1868; the club's first excursion that same year to Matanzas, where they encountered a friendly pick-up game against crewman from an American schooner anchored in harbor for repairs; the eventual total ban on ball playing by Spanish authorities a mere year later with the outbreak of the savage Ten Years' War; the game's rapid reestablishment after the war's ending in 1878; and the subsequent inaugural league tournament that same winter, also involving the newly founded Almendares ball club and the already existing Matanzas nine.

Today Nemesio and Ernesto Guilló (along with other founders of the Habana Base Ball Club, including Leopoldo de Sola, Enrique Canal, Alfredo Maruri, Ricardo Mora, and Francisco and Rafael Saavedra) have faded to near obscurity in the annals of Cuba's baseball origins. Together they have seemingly little if any recognized claim on the parentage of the popular Cuban national game. Such are often the accidents and injustices in the recorded history of sporting events or other trappings of popular culture. Two other more prominent names, nonetheless, do remain before us to vie for the mythical honor of "Father of Cuban Baseball" and each seemingly boasts legitimate-enough claims on the ephemeral title. Again, in both cases, the baseball-playing careers of each of these men actually begin (as with Nemesio and Ernesto Guilló) during teenage school days spent on the road up north, in the baseball cradle of the United States.

One such Cuban visitor to American campuses in the 1860s was Havana native Esteban Enríque Bellán. Today buried among the sport's second tier of nineteenth-century notables, Bellán was destined to become not only a pioneering importer of baseball back home in Cuba but also, as chance would have it, Latin America's first official representative to the world of North American professional baseball. Dark-skinned "Steve" Bellán was perhaps the most accomplished athlete of the several dozen or more original Cuban converts who simultaneously received both formal classroom education and ballplaying indoctrination deep in Yankee territory. Bellán, more important still, was destined to become technically the first Latin American big leaguer, signing on with the NAPBBP (National Association of Professional Baseball Players) Troy Haymakers fresh off the campus of Fordham University in 1871, and later also playing a handful of games with the New York Mutuals of the same ground-breaking North American league. (A weak confederation controlled by ballplayers themselves rather than mogul owners, the National Association comprised a varying number of franchises and played an irregular schedule of games between 1871 and 1875; today it is accepted by most historians of the sport as the first legitimate attempt to construct a "major" professional league.)

Bellán is sometimes reported to have actually begun his brief sojourn in organized baseball back in 1868, with the Unions of Morrisania (while apparently still a Fordham student), and a year later had transferred to the Unions of Lansingburgh (today popularly known as the Troy Haymakers). That team's entry into the National Association at the outset of the 1871 campaign (before subsequently folding in midseason 1872) staked the Cuban import's claim as the first Latin big-leaguer. After only seven games with the Mutuals between April and June of 1873 Bellán returned permanently to his native soil. His short professional career was thus hardly distinguished: it consisted of parts of three seasons, 59 games with but 288 official at-bats, 68 hits, a lame "dead-ball"-era batting average of only .236, and 85 errors (remember that this was the era of bare-handed play and thus ragged fielding) at three infield positions. But the fact that he played with the

North American professionals was enough in later years to advance Bellán's cause as the true pioneer when it came to launching Cuban baseball.

Precious little is known of Bellán's non-athletic life beyond the bare facts that he was born in Havana city (likely sometime in 1850) and also died there on August 8, 1932. But Cuban *fanáticos* would long remember him for a much more significant pioneering role as acknowledged organizer of the now famous first formal island game, an event which transpired when Steve Bellán led his own already well-established Habana club (the one launched by Nemesio Guilló among others) to the nearby port city of Matanzas to face a lesser team of club enthusiasts on December 27th of 1874. Bellán would also earn an additional distinction that day as the first Cuban to connect for two home runs during the one-sided contest in which Habana was easily victorious over Matanzas by a lopsided count of 51–9. The match was staged on a local expanse of ground known then as Palmar **de** Junco (Junco's Palm Groves) but later referred to with the more poetic label of Palmar **del** Junco ("Palm Grove of the Reed") once a permanent ball field (surprisingly still in existence today) was built upon the historic site.* As one silver-tongued historian has since phrased it, if Guilló (Nemesio) actually introduced the diamond sport to island culture, it was seemingly Bellán in December of 1874 who performed the true marriage between baseball and the Cuban people.

The fame and import of the 1874 Matanzas game rests mostly on the fact that it was the first contest on the island to be written about, even if it could certainly not have been the first ever played by clubs that were clearly formed several years earlier. The oft-cited report on which the game's renown rests was penned by Enrique Fontanils (under the pseudonym "Henry") and appeared four days after the contest in the theater journal *El Artista*. Fontanils details the afternoon's onfield events, including a wild dispute about the manner in which the Matanzas moundsman was "throwing" his pitches rather than "tossing" them in the prescribed manner of the day. When Habana hurler Ricardo Mora was also allowed by the umpire to throw overhand, he so baffled the Matanzas hitters that they scored but nine tallies in a contest called by darkness at 5:35 P.M. Bellán's homers (hit deep into surrounding pastures but not over any fence) were supplemented by another from pitcher Mora himself. What has not been reported in other existing histories is that an earlier article with complete box score and game summary actually appeared only two days after the match (thus two days before the Fontanils account) on the back page of the single-sheet Matanzas weekly newspaper known as the *Aurora del Yumuri*. A tattered copy of this rare historical document is now housed in the restoration room of the tiny Matanzas public library building where it is today

---

*The most detailed, accurate and explanatory account of Cuba's first "reported" baseball game, staged at Matanzas in December 1874 — along with commentary on the controversy surrounding the proper name for the local grounds on which that notable game was played — is found in Chapter 4 of Roberto González Echevarría's The Pride of Havana. González eloquently defines the symbolic significance of Cuba's reputed (but not actual) first ballgame and also elaborates on the mythic trappings the event now carries. He also discusses the literary journal article penned by Enrique Fontanils (and published in El Artista four days after the match) which establishes the Matanzas game as "the first about which an article was written" in Cuba; but González apparently knew nothing about the even earlier printed account of this celebrated Matanzas match, one that actually appeared two days before Fontanils' piece (on Tuesday, December 29) in Aurora del Yumuri, a local Matanzas periodical treating primarily political and economic topics.

being belatedly even if amateurishly restored, and where this author and companion Mark Rucker examined it and even photocopied it in March 2002.

Bellán's main rival for Doubleday-type status in the early years of Cuban baseball was fellow Havana native Emilio Sabourín. Scant evidence suggests that young Sabourín, like Bellán and both Guilló brothers, was also educated for a brief spell on North American soil and that his education, similar to theirs, included ballplaying mixed in with more formal academic pursuits. What is now known about Sabourín's life can also be summarized quickly enough. He was born in Havana on September 2, 1853, to a French engineer (Claudio Esteban Sabourín) and a native Cuban mother (née Emilia de Villar); at an early age he was dispatched to the United States for his formal schooling, and eventually he studied economics at the prestigious French Academy in Washington, D.C. Reported to be a serious and talented student, Sabourín could speak fluent English and French by the time he returned to his native Havana, probably already in his late teens. He is also

Base Ball.

Almeida.
C. 21.

Marsans' fellow "Bar of Castilian Soap" in Cincinnati, Havana infielder Rafael Almeida. Almeida's spotty big league tenure never lived up to that of the moderately more successful Marsans.

reported in several early Havana newspaper accounts to have proselytized enthusiastically for the new American game of baseball upon his return to Havana, and he apparently himself played the sport with sufficient skill to man a regular outfield post on the Habana Club roster of the late 1870s. Guilló's aforementioned 1924 newspaper interview (cited by Roberto González Echevarría in his *The Pride of Havana*) credits Sabourín with being one of fourteen 1868 founders of the Habana Base Ball Club, but Emilio would have been only fifteen at the time and would most likely, by then, have not yet returned from his secondary school studies in Washington, D.C.

Sabourín was less doubtfully a participant ten years later, when it came to organizing a first professional tournament on the island, universally referred to as the first "season" of the Cuban Professional Baseball League (detailed above in Chapter 5). Without question he played as an outfielder/infielder on the Habana Base Ball Club that was managed by Bellán and competed in January and February 1879 against Almendares and Matanzas. A surviving primitive box score for the tournament's inaugural game (dated December 29, 1878) lists Sabourín as the Habana second baseman with Bellán as the catcher. California-based (but Cuban-born) journalist Angel Torres (in his self-published book entitled *La Leyenda de Beísbol Cubano*) rebuts a common misunderstanding that Sabourín was either manager or captain for Club Habana during that first 1878–79 season, arguing the record is clear that Sabourín did not assume such an elevated position with the team until approximately ten years later. But Torres mistakenly also suggests that Sabourín was barely eighteen during the first tournament season, while in reality he was already twenty-five. Nevertheless, Torres is likely quite correct in asserting that Sabourín did not manage until 1888–89, and also that his role as a founder of both Club Habana and the "Liga de Base Ball" (official name for the first six-game championship year) has been much exaggerated by legions of later chroniclers and historians. One such over-enthusiastic scribe is Rob Ruck, author of a summary essay on "Caribbean Baseball" for the 4th Edition of *Total Baseball*; Ruck severely exaggerates Sabourín's pioneering role by celebrating him as Cuba's equivalent to A.G. Spalding.

Also akin to Bellán, Sabourín contributed heavily as a player, whatever his role may or may not have been as league organizer or as a club manager during pioneering years of Cuban organized baseball. Sabourín also took the field for that first historic game at Palmar del Junco in December of 1874. Bellán caught, blasted his pair of long homers and scored seven runs for the winners; Sabourín played in the victorious Habana outfield (left field, according to the box score in *El Artista*) and tallied eight markers himself. Emilio Sabourín would eventually manage, once professional playing began in earnest in Cuba a mere four years hence (even if this role came somewhat later than often credited), again duplicating his teammate Bellán. It might be emphasized that at this early stage in league history the so-called manager was more akin to a team captain, guiding and inspiring his teammates while occupying his own position in the field and not while directing strategy from a seat along the sidelines (like most 20th century managers). While Bellán steered the Habana club to championships during the first three seasons of league play, Sabourín would also later claim three titles as the nominal leader for the same Habana ball club (1889, 1890, 1892). Set aside Bellán's brief North American pro career a decade earlier and their résumés are nearly identical.

Sabourín did claim one small but significant moment as pioneering manager that by itself cements his role as an innovator among early diamond strategists. During a league game in mid-winter 1891 he outmaneuvered the veteran-filled Progreso ball club in Matanzas by calling for three consecutive successful tenth-inning bunts, the final one being a game-winning "squeeze play" never previously seen on Cuban soil.

Championships and pioneering strategies aside, it was Sabourín's final years at century's end that most glorified his role in the formative era of Cuban baseball, and they did so with a series of dramatic events transpiring far from any baseball diamond. Married in 1883 (to a socialite named Martina de Poo y Pierra) and also soon established in the bureaucratic labor force as a dockside customs official (since baseball was never full-time employment in nineteenth-century Havana), the popular captain/manager of Club Habana was also by the late 1880s and early 1890s devoting considerable time and energy to patriotic revolutionary causes, once insurrection against hated Spanish colonial rule had again flamed up everywhere across the island. First and foremost Sabourín acted as rebel fund-raiser, funneling cash profits from his ball club into dangerous anti–Spanish causes. In his role as zealous patriot, Sabourín also fatefully provided secret refuge at his Havana residence for a popular rebel general, José Lacret Morlot, during early December 1895; soon thereafter his home was raided by a contingent of Spanish soldiers searching for weapons rumored to be stashed on the premises by the rebel forces. Sabourín was quickly arrested, immediately imprisoned in Havana, and in February 1896 formally tried for his anti-government activities and his bold acts of outright treason. The resulting sentence was twenty years of forced detention in the dreaded Moroccan dungeons at far-off Ceuta. After ten months delay the ballplayer-turned-insurrectionist was finally transported with a shipload of fellow rebel prisoners to the infamous North African prison camp, where he was subsequently confined under most inhuman conditions until his death on July 15, 1897. Precise cause of death was reported in circulating Havana newspaper accounts as a severe pneumonia brought on by general overall physical deterioration.

Bellán's foremost ball-playing and managerial rival was thus in the end a heroic patriotic figure whose private life away from baseball diamonds was deeply entangled in a savage independence struggle against occupying Spain overlords. Cuba's Ten Years' War for independence waged against the Spanish colonial government had brought continued chaos to the island between 1868 and 1878, and that struggle had only ceased with a temporary truce in the very winter when Sabourín, Bellán and their companions among high-society *criollo* youth

launched their first professional league tournament. From 1895 to 1898 the rebellion once more exploded upon Havana and its environs and baseball once more subsided in the aftermath of revolutionary hostilities (with three years of championships suspended by government degree). Evidence that ballplaying and politics were already as inseparable in Cuba in the late nineteenth century as they have remained throughout the late twentieth century is found in the fact that revenues from the 1879 championship and all others staged during the following decade and a half were being surreptitiously channeled directly into the hands of those patriots carrying on desperate guerrilla rebellions against the despised Spanish overseers.

Sabourín would pay the supreme price for as own involvement in revolt against unwanted Spanish rule. Several of his ball-playing compatriots were similar victims of this deadly mixture of baseball and revolution. One was José Manuel Pastoriza (a champion pitcher instrumental in leading Almendares to the 1894 league title) who was dragged from his home and publicly executed in Guanabacoa, a Havana suburb, by a Spanish firing squad during December 1896; yet another was Ricardo Cabaleiro (famed for smacking three homers, two doubles and a single in eight trips to the plate during one memorable February 1893 game) who also fell heroically with his outnumbered rebel battalion in September 1897 on the outskirts of Pinar del Río. Of these three athlete-heroes, Sabourín, especially, would be rewarded handsomely in the pages of Cuban history for his courageous role as baseball-loving patriot.

In the end Sabourín's contributions of baseball revenues to the anti–Spanish independence movement fronted by José Martí (alongside the conspiracies of others, like fellow Cuban hall-of-famers Pastoriza and Cabaleiro) not only cost these baseball-crazed patriots their personal freedoms but also caused a short-lived Spanish ban on the new sport enforced across much of the island colony. Throughout three final decades of military and economic control in Cuba (1870s through 1890s), Spanish colonial authorities had always deeply distrusted rebellious Cuban students and likely assumed that bats and balls used in the popular pastime of "*pelota Americana*" were merely cleverly disguised implements for rebel warfare. Sabourín himself was easy enough to eliminate with imprisonment — as were Pastoriza and Cabaleiro with firing squad and cavalry assault — but the new sporting passion of the local masses in the end proved far more difficult to eradicate permanently.

Sabourín's claim on the parentage of Cuban baseball was destined to rest heavily upon his adjunct status as revolutionary hero — both at the dawn of the past century and especially again during fervent patriotic days that would follow Fidel Castro's ascension to power a half-century later. Although prominent player and manager in his own country, Sabourín had never performed in any professional or amateur league in the United States and was thus more clearly a champion than an importer of the beloved North American pastime. Sabourín's position as baseball founder in Havana is hardly as tenuous as that of Abner Doubleday in Cooperstown; nonetheless it is a far stretch to see Bellán as the Cuban version of Alexander Cartwright or Sabourín as either the Cuban Henry Chadwick or (following Rob Ruck) an island resurrection of Albert Spalding. Both men indeed played significant roles in stabilizing and popularizing early Cuban professional baseball, yet neither could claim to have single-handedly launched the sport, nor to have personally lifted it to prominence as recognized corner piece of an emerging Cuban national identity.

But there is of course one count on which Bellán's fame is almost certain to outlast Sabourín's, even within Cuba itself. This is the simple if substantial fact that Bellán remains the first link between Cuba and the U.S. major leagues to the north. It was a link that alone would etch Cuban ballplayers into the North American consciousness. Great ballplaying feats back on the island would rarely if ever reach North American eyes or ears. Black Cubans traveling northward were never any more widely known to white stateside fans than were obscure Negro leaguers of native U.S. origins. Few American fans ever heard of Martín Dihigo, easily Cuba's supreme diamond idol. They knew nothing at all of the powerful Torriente, the unparalleled black slugger touring big leaguers had glimpsed in Havana and compared immediately to Babe Ruth, or of the incomparable fast-balling pitcher José Méndez that John McGraw considered a fair rival to his own crack ace Christy Mathewson. It was instead only the journeyman big leaguers like Adolfo Luque, Miguel "Mike" González and Armando Marsans who for more than half-a-century built all the reigning stereotypes attached to exotic Cuban ballplayers. Cubans were visible to Americans through the big leagues and not the winter leagues, and it was there that Steve Bellán had blazed his most significant trails.

* * *

For a while I thought that Hi Bithorn, a Puerto Rican who pitched for the Cubs, 1942–43 and 1946, and for the White Sox in 1947, might be entitled to be called the first black player to appear in a big league uniform.
— Fred Lieb, *Baseball As I Have Known It*

Organized baseball's half-century of racial segregation was built upon a pastiche of bald lies, each one pasted into the last. First there was the fabrication that black men simply didn't have the physical or mental tools to perform on a par with white athletes. That a black man could never play the game at the highest levels was long a commonplace wisdom. It was also a myth put quickly to the lie by Cuban League winter seasons of the 1920s, '30s and '40s, where North American and Cuban blacks not only achieved equally but also often dominated white-skinned big leaguers; yet few fans, sportswriters or club owners paid any heed to that fact up north. Then once the odious barriers were finally toppled with Jackie Robinson's spectacular debut in Brooklyn, a new and equally dark myth was conveniently propagated. Americans — ball-fans and non-fans alike — bought into the further untruth that no black man before Robinson had ever stepped upon a big-league diamond and, furthermore, that the entire weight and glory of busting baseball segregation had fallen to the lot of a single, specially anointed hero. It was perhaps a myth necessary for assuaging the guilt of a nation that had so long tolerated and even openly sanctioned bigotry in its national game. But it was a quaint legend crammed with numerous distortions nonetheless.

The bare truth was of course far more complex, as it always seemingly is. A total ban on black ballplayers known as "the gentlemen's agreement" had in reality never been an edict aimed broadly at men with dark African skin in general, but more specifically it was one levied mainly on native-born African-Americans. How else does one account for the occasional appearances in big league uniforms of assorted brown Cubans, Puerto Ricans, Mexicans or Venezuelans down through the years, men whose skin tone or physiognomy was barely if at all distinguishable from black men native to Alabama or Mississippi? Isolated Cubans (as far back as Armando Marsans and Rafael Almeida in 1911, or "Iron Mike" González in 1914) had already crossed 20th-century big league racial borders, however tentatively and with however little fanfare, decades before Robinson and Rickey gripped a nation or garnered headlines with the National League Dodgers in Brooklyn. That they could be dismissed as merely "foreigners" of questionable ethnic and racial background and thus tolerated on the field (even if usually vilified in the clubhouse or grandstands) only underscores the point about loosely drawn racial restrictions. These pioneering Latin blacks (and many if not all did most assuredly have indisputable African bloodlines) simply went unnoticed, and in the process also lost their substantial place in history.

We should hasten to affirm that the big league presence of an occasional Cuban black in the 1920s or '30s does absolutely nothing to diminish Jackie Robinson's desperate on-the-field struggles of 1947, or to cloud in the least Robinson's considerable legacy for baseball history. But it does nonetheless serve to cast the entire saga in a different and less "revisionist" light. Revisionist history from the second half of the last century may not have given Robinson more stature than he legitimately deserves. But it did nevertheless further extends untruths that somewhat cheapen the neatly packaged and popularly swallowed legend about one brave and isolated man's solo pioneering crusade against human injustice.

It was not Jackie Robinson's African blood per se that made him unique on a baseball diamond in 1947; a handful of Spanish-speaking imports in the big leagues before him could also trace their family origins to the despicable North American or Caribbean slave trade. It was rather Robinson's Georgia birthplace and California upbringing that made his black skin both unique and (for many Americans) unacceptable on the ball diamonds of Brooklyn's Ebbets Field or Philadelphia's Shibe Park or the New York Polo Grounds. In short, Jackie Robinson was North America's first modern-era black-skinned major leaguer; assorted Cubans, Puerto Ricans, Venezuelans and other Spanish-speaking sons of Africa had unarguably gotten their first.

The list of those who successfully leaped organized baseball's racial bar only because they could be dismissed as exotic "foreigners" included mostly Cubans — Mike González, Tommy de la Cruz, Roberto (a.k.a. "Tarzán") Estalella, and José Acosta are convenient examples. But there were also the Venezuelan Alejandro "Alex" Carrasquel, the Mexican Mel Almada, and the Puerto Rican Hiram Bithorn to raise howls of protest among those loudest-mouthed bigots who objected to the looseness of racial restrictions when it came to swarthy Caribbean islanders. Bithorn, who debuted five years ahead of Robinson and lasted (as did most of the Cubans also) only a handful of seasons, provides a typical case. Perhaps the greatest difference in the end between Jackie Robinson — acknowledged pioneer of baseball's integration — and Hiram Bithorn — forgotten journeyman pitcher for the lowly wartime Chicago Cubs — was in the "color" of their linguistic inflections, the distinctive rhythms of their native speech patterns; Robinson spoke English and Bithorn Spanish. There was perhaps little enough to set apart the shading of their skin tones or the heritage of their respective racial gene pools. There was, of course, also a matter of considerable and obvious raw athletic talent. Jackie Robinson of the Brooklyn Dodgers was a full-blown National League star; Hiram Bithorn with the also-ran Chicago Cubs was never much more than a cup-of-coffee journeyman fill-in. Yet to baseball's rough-hewn country ballplayer stock and its gentlemanly establishment of team owners (a great majority of whom were still bigoted Southerners at the close of World War II) — as well as to its hordes of ticket-buying patrons — one man (Robinson) remained an anathema, an upstart descendant of African slave stock who dared challenge baseball's long cherished and imbedded "gentlemen's agreement." The other (Bithorn) was merely something of a quaint distraction, another quirky "foreigner" of suspicious appearance and discordant language who lurked on the fringes of the sport and who thus could not be taken too seriously. And therein lies one of baseball's darkest and heretofore untold tales.

It is a revealing if somewhat whimsical indictment of our American national character that we North American "Yanks" like our national history to be tainted with a strong dose of patriotic myth. In the arenas of social history and politics, if not elsewhere, this axiom has held fast for generations of American school kids as well as for the serious-minded adult readers some of those youngsters would one day become. A mid-century American generation nurtured on World War II and then weaned on the four-decade Cold War thus all-too-eagerly adopted Esther Forbes's fanciful *Johnny Tremain* as its most vivid image of the Revolutionary War epoch (despite that novel's spurious historical treatment and thinly veiled flag-waving thesis: that colonial patriots had genuinely uncovered an American ideal worth fighting and dying for). More recently, social historian Michael Kammen has argued deftly with his *Mystic Chords of Memory* (1991) that in the end almost all our American popular history is but a contrived and depoliticized version of events and as such always carries a doctrinaire message — our popular history texts offer "revisionist history" written with a clear and heavy-handed social lesson in mind. American "history" as most of us know it is but the

Outfielder Jack (Jacinto) Calvo logged 34 brief games in the outfield with the 1913–14 Washington Senators as the sixth 20th century Cuban big leaguer.

meek servant of didactic purposes and thus never quite the true reflection of documented reality. And it is precisely in this respect, perhaps, that our national character is most perfectly — if ironically — reflected by our considerable passions for the national game of baseball.

Dedicated baseball fans are likely the most historically aware of all sports fans — our undiminished love for the game of our childhood feeds as much upon the memory of past events and past-era heroes as it does upon the thrill of contemporary contests. Baseball's reigning lords and the propaganda engines they employ — especially the partner-in-crime television industry — have now become painful aware of this fact, one result being that most of big league baseball's nostalgia trappings today exude the smell of heavy-handed marketing campaigns and not at all the flavor of spontaneous fan reactions. Network television executives have repeatedly twisted Cal Ripken's iron man streak or Barry Bonds' and Mark McGwire's home run feats into highly profitable commercial clichés aimed at jacking viewer ratings and thus cementing advertising dollars. And yet the most cherished historical memories sustaining the sport for its collective fandom (Ruth's gigantic home run blows or Walter Johnson's blazing fastballs) are quite often merely embellished fictions — at the very least elaborately woven legends tapping the very roots of fiction.

What fan (among past-generation boosters at least) has not heard, for example, that Abner Doubleday invented baseball in the pastures of nineteenth-century Cooperstown; that Jackie Robinson broke the odious color barrier as big league baseball's first 20th-century ballplayer from the Negro race; that Fred Merkle's boneheaded failure to touch second base instantaneously cost New York's Giants a guaranteed 1908 NL pennant; that Merkle's equally ill-fated teammate Fred Snod-

Roberto "Tarzán" Estalella was an adequate hitter if brutal fielder during nine American League seasons (1935–1949) in Washington, St. Louis and Philadelphia. Many thought Estalella, like most pre-integration Cubans, showed obvious traces of African heritage.

grass soon outdid his fellow "bonehead" by personally losing the 1912 World Series with his infamous ninth-inning dropped fly ball; that Joe Jackson and his 1919 White Sox cronies nearly ruined the nation's sporting spirit by successfully conspiring with shameless gamblers to fix that season's World Series against an inferior Cincinnati ball club; and that revolutionary home run bashing by Babe Ruth and others at the outset of the Roaring Twenties is easily accounted for by a blatant conspiracy among club owners and A.G. Spalding's factory workers to "juice up" manufactured league balls in order simultaneously to jack both slugging action and resulting ticket receipts? (We might also add here the quaint undying tale of young Fidel Castro's reported pitching prowess, which informed the previous chapter.) And what more careful and astute historian of the national game will not also know that each and every one of these sacred baseball legends is, in bare fact, not exactly true as it is almost always related? Each, instead, is an elaborately embellished myth, and each promotes at least one, and often more, significant historical distortions. Several — especially Jackie Robinson's fortuitous role in organized baseball's integration and Joe Jackson's onerous role during the 1919 Black Sox World Series — are patently incorrect in significant detail when clothed in the form in which they are traditionally reported.

It is the Jackie Robinson legend, in particular, that is so often glossed over with a rosy hue of romanticism and muddled with the inaccuracies of oftentimes sloppy (sometimes even shoddy) journalism. The idea that Robinson was a lonely crusader who boldly set the very first black foot on any professional baseball diamond — that with his dashing style of play Robinson single-handedly swept aside all final vestiges of prejudice and racial hatred on America's athletic fields — is as firmly ingrained in the popular psyche as, say, the notion that Abner Doubleday concocted the rules of baseball out of thin air in 1839 in the pastures of Cooperstown, or that Babe Ruth did indeed point to the exact spot in the bleachers where he would seconds later deposit a memorable 1932 World Series round-tripper, or that Fred Merkle irrationally threw away a Giants' pennant victory in 1908 with a thoughtless bonehead play. Ruth did not point (at least not at any intended spot for his next blast); Merkle neither committed an atrocity of judgment nor lost a pennant of his own accord; and Robinson was assuredly *not* the first Negro big league ballplayer and *not* the sole standard barrier for his downtrodden race. Nineteenth-century Afro-Americans (as is now well known) and early twentieth-century mixed-blood Cubans (as is still not well known) trod earlier paths toward hard-won integration of the sport. And once Robinson's debut in Brooklyn effectively ended blatant rejection of North American blacks (those who couldn't sneak by as mere "foreigners") the victory was still not complete for years to come.

This is not at all to belittle the enormity of the Rickey-Robinson experiment in Brooklyn in 1947, nor to discount Robinson's legitimate Hall-of-Fame career, nor to suggest for a single moment that Robinson was not *perceived* by his peers and by National League fans as a genuine racial pioneer and thus subjected to unimaginable pressures, harassment and abuse. It is simply to suggest — and this is quite a different matter — that the circumstances and events of Robinson's debut in the National League in 1947 have from the first been muddled, and that, furthermore, the full story of baseball's gradual and fitful racial integration has rarely been accurately told in mainstream accounts, nor popularly accepted when it has.

Much has already been accomplished by a handful of serious scholars of Negro baseball in hopes of setting the records straight regarding Branch Rickey's plan for integrating the majors at the close of the nation's second great world war. Most controversial in the Robinson-Rickey emancipation story is the true motive and hidden method of Branch Rickey's seemingly altruistic integration plan. And nowhere is this story and other aspects of the integration saga more accurately and entertainingly told than within Jules Tygiel's landmark study entitled *Baseball's Great Experiment — Jackie Robinson and His Legacy* (1983). Professor Tygiel recounts in exacting detail how Rickey's earthshaking moves not only opened big league fields to black players, but also had devastating effects upon the Negro leagues themselves, and thus also upon those black communities that had long sustained Negro baseball (just as black baseball had in equal part long sustained those communities). In Tygiel's view, something quite vital and distinctively American died with the passing of the black baseball leagues. The Negro leagues had once represented a thriving $2 million-per-annum empire, largely controlled by blacks, employing blacks, and providing crucial forms of cultural identification for millions of minority fans. After Robinson, more blacks were playing in the big leagues and none would have had it any other way; yet fewer African-Americans were making their living at baseball following 1947, and black communities had lost an important life force that could never again be replaced. And Tygiel, along with prolific baseball chronicler John Thorn, has also more recently presented persuasive new evidence that Branch Rickey in point of fact intended originally to bring three or more black stars to the big leagues simultaneously — a plan stymied by a convoluted course of events which Tygiel and Thorn have now finally unraveled ("Jackie Robinson's Signing" published in *The National Pastime 10*, 1990). It was apparently but an accident of history, then, that Robinson has long held the spotlight of racial integration so exclusively to himself.

But there is still another aspect of the Jackie Robinson legend that to this day not only remains under-reported (if not altogether unreported) but also, in doing so, continues to crowd out the legitimate historical record. This is the persistent notion that Robinson was the first black of any ethnic or national background to don the uniform of a big league ball club. The notion is, of course, patently false on at least several counts. Any devotee of ancient baseball lore worth his weight in dusty volumes of Putnam team histories or Macmillan encyclopedias knows that a Negro catcher named Moses Fleetwood Walker, alumnus of Oberlin College in Ohio, was a regular backstop with the Toledo club when it first gained

admittance to the American Association (then a legitimate big-league circuit) in 1884; the same Fleet Walker also later formed a colored tandem with pitcher George Stovey on the International League's Newark club in 1887, the very season when Chicago manager Cap Anson (already well on his way to instituting the "gentlemen's agreement" that would bar "coloreds" from the senior circuit and all other corners of organized baseball) staged his boycott of a scheduled exhibition match with the Newark team and its dark-skinned battery. Moses Fleetwood Walker was, for over sixty years, the proper answer to a pair of obscure trivia questions: Who was the first black major leaguer? And who was the last?

Reams have been also written about the odd plight of Cuban ballplayers between the two great wars, especially by such eloquent spokespersons on "colored baseball history" as John B. Holway, Jerry Malloy, Rob Ruck, and again Jules Tygiel. While fair-skinned Havana hurler Adolfo Luque was able to "pass" unchallenged (though certainly not without harassment) through the unwritten U.S. racial barrier and become the first legitimate Latino big league star — appearing in the 1919 and 1933 World Series matches, compiling a record 27 victories during his fabulous 1923 campaign, and gaining nearly 200 career wins over twenty seasons with the National League Reds, Dodgers and Giants — dark-skinned legend Martín Dihigo (born a decade and a half later and raised less than fifty miles from the home of Havana-born Luque) was doomed by his indelible racial markings to suffer a far different fate. Allowed no more than a hardscrabble barnstorming career that would lead him through backwater winter league campaigns stretching across three-plus decades and eventually into hallowed baseball halls of fame in both his native Cuba and Mexico — as well as to posthumous honors in Cooperstown after Negro leaguers finally developed a belated cachet — Dihigo remained nonetheless a celebrated outcast, virtually unknown to big league fans of both his own and subsequent generations. Like Martín Dihigo, numerous other bronze-toned Cuban and Puerto Rican stars were simply unacceptable to big league teams, whose beleaguered managers could thus only salivate privately upon seeing the likes of Cristóbal Torriente, Pancho Coimbre, Perucho Cepeda, the elder Luis Tiant, and fireballing José de la Caridad Méndez performing brilliantly during barnstorming off-season exhibitions with island and black-league all-star squads.

Meanwhile another scenario was being played out in the clubhouses and front offices of some of baseball's less successful and less glamorous big league ball clubs. Readers of Paul Hemphill's entertaining novel *Long Gone* (1979) might recall the bold gamble of fictional Sally League manager Stud Cantrell, who bolsters his weak-hitting Graceville Oilers with slugging Negro catcher Joe Brown and then passes off the "unacceptable" black as José Guitterez Brown, just off the banana boat from Venezuela. To management and fans starved for winning baseball, a little flirtation with the "gentlemen's agreement" might indeed be okay, provided that the swarthy ballplayer in question could pass as a "foreigner" and hit well enough to distract attention from an objectionable brown hue on his face and arms. On more than one occasion to be sure (as with Bill Veeck's midget pinch batter Eddie Gaedel in St. Louis, for instance) baseball reality has followed meekly a full step behind baseball fiction. The history of our national pastime between closure of the dead-ball era (after World War I) and the demise of the "gentlemen's agreement" (after World War II) is replete with more than one incident of big league management passing off dark-skinned Latinos as an excusable "Cuban" or marginal "Castilian"— thus severely bending but not quite breaking organized baseball's intractable racial stance.

The practice began with the once celebrated if now largely forgotten saga of two olive-skinned fly chasers first discovered in the lost outposts of the backwater minor leagues by Cincinnati Reds manager Clark Griffith. Cuban outfielders Armando Marsans and Rafael Almeida were destined to enjoy only short-lived yet nonetheless historically significant careers with the Cincinnati National Leaguers of the immediate pre–World War I era. Reds management (Clark Griffith himself reportedly) had stumbled upon the exotic duo during an off-day scouting mission and manager Griffith offered a tryout to one of the touted Cubans (Almeida) who had been playing with Class B New Britain (Connecticut League) in the spring of 1911. Almeida apparently spoke little English and thus brought along his countryman and teammate as his interpreter; the teammate (Marsans) impressed Griffith as much if not even more than the original invitee, and both were soon ensconced in the outfield with the big club back at Cincinnati's Redland Field.

By the time of their fortuitous signings with Cincinnati, 24-year-old Marsans (a Matanzas native) and the similar-aged Almeida (born in Havana) were already seasoned veterans of Cuba's winter circuit: Marsans had debuted with Almendares in 1905 and Almeida with rival Club Habana a single year earlier. Both had also appeared on the roster of a "mixed" Negro barnstorming ball club known as the All-Cubans that had toured stateside during the summer months of 1905. Angel Torres (*La Leyenda del Béisbol Cubano*, 1996) explains that "white Cubans" like Almeida and Marsans were permitted slots on all-black teams by a Negro league establishment up north that held to far looser racial standards. In reality, Cubans were widely recognized by owners of Negro teams in the U.S. and back home on the island as, in most cases, having likely bloodline connections with both races. Almeida was a light-colored mulatto whose paternal ancestors also claimed roots in the Spanish province of Galicia. Marsans possessed a Catalan surname, but nonetheless displayed skin tones a full shade darker than a significant portion of American-born African-Americans gracing early Negro team rosters. From the outset, at least in the big leagues, racial categories — especially for Caribbean islanders — were somewhat a matter of one's personal or cultural perceptions.

Almeida would hit a mere .270 over three short seasons of National League action (102 games, all with Cincinnati), while Marsans stretched out his own heftier career through 1918, compiling only a .269 lifetime average but bashing the ball at a .317 clip during a stellar single 1912 season. Playing also with the Browns and Yankees of the American League and the St. Louis Federal League outfit, Marsans developed a reputation as one of the league's toughest strikeout victims, fanning but 117 times in 2,273 official big-league trips to the plate. Yet if their on-field careers were less than remarkable by almost every measure, both were nonetheless immediate touchstones for considerable controversy, all resulting from their prominent and dubious olive-tinted skin. Within days of their joint signings and simultaneous debuts at Chicago on (ironically) July 4, a worried Cincinnati management was forced by mounting pressure of public opinion to contact Havana officials for documents designed to certify beyond doubt that the two imports owned verifiable Castilian bloodlines and not questionable Negro heritage.

Cincinnati baseball historians Lonnie Wheeler and John Baskin (*The Cincinnati Game*, 1988) report that even manager Griffith experienced mild concern when first hearing of club president Garry Herrmann's plans actually to sign up the Cuban prospects he had casually scouted ("We will not pay any Hans Wagner price for a pair of dark-skinned islanders"); and when Herrmann arranged to retrieve the two Latin imports upon their arrival at the Cincinnati train depot, he himself apparently suffered near heart-seizure when a couple of brown-skinned Pullman porters disembarked moments ahead of the expected ballplayers. Soon enough, however, Cincinnati newspapers were boasting that the two dark-skinned Cubans were "two of the purest bars of Castilian soap ever floated to these shores"— once the much-needed documentation, in form of a letter from Cuban baseball officials back in Havana, had arrived at club offices in the Queen City.

Serious doubts would persist nevertheless. Writing during the same season as Robinson's cataclysmic debut, Lee Allen, the dean of Cincinnati baseball historians, would put the whole matter in perspective by suggesting the tensions surrounding the Cubans' arrival in town: "Today [in 1947] it is almost impossible to realize what a furor the signing of two Cubans caused in 1911" (*The Cincinnati Reds*, 1948, 96). Lee Allen was penning his baseball history during a far different age, of course, and thus offers little speculation concerning what it was that so disturbed league fans about these "foreigners" of swarthy skin color. In brief, certain weighty sociological questions apparently simply did not yet get asked in popular-press sports books like Allen's Putnam Series team history of the Cincinnati franchise.

If Marsans and Almeida first stirred something of an uproar in the conservative mid-western frontier town of Cincinnati, there were soon similar upheavals on professional diamonds elsewhere — the nation's capital included. Racial tensions also greeted the brief major league appearances of two additional Cubans of the same era — outfielder Jacinto "Jack" Calvo and pitcher José Acosta. Calvo, a reputed speedster, appeared briefly with the Washington Senators in 1913 and then again in 1920 (logging 33 total games, posting an anemic .161 BA, and cracking a single home run); Acosta hurled for the same big league club, as well as for the Chicago

White Sox, between 1920 and 1922 (splitting 20 decisions with a modest 4.51 ERA). While Almeida and Marsans were apparently light-skinned enough to find brief acceptance in the majors (though not without comment and controversy) as well as dark enough to hitch on with barnstorming black outfits, the same was true of Calvo and Acosta. The pair teamed on both the Long Beach Cubans and New Jersey Cubans for 1915 Negro league stints sandwiched between their several big-league tours; and during a 1920 winter season exhibition game back in Cuba, Acosta is also reported to have fanned the mighty Babe Ruth not once but three times.

In addition to the pair performing with Cincinnati and the duo seeing brief service with Washington, the list of Cuban big leaguers who also suited up at one point or another for Negro league games would eventually include Luque, Miguel Angel (Mike) González, Angel (Pete) Aragón, Emilio Palmero, Joseito Rodríguez, Pedro Dibut, Ramón Herrera, and Oscar Estrada. The roster of those who crossed in and out of the white and black majors thus consists of more than a third of the Cuban big leaguers performing in the teens, twenties and thirties. Even for those Cubans who never appeared with black or "mixed" teams of the era there is room for speculation about mixed racial status. If the appearance of Jack Calvo and José Acosta in full-fledged Negro league play seems to give one pause concerning the percentage of Negro blood each man carried within his veins, one might also speculate about the racial status of the latter ballplayer's brother, Mérito Acosta, who also appeared briefly (175 games between 1913 and 1918) in the outfield of both the Washington Senators and Philadelphia Athletics.

Jack Calvo and José Acosta were not the only dusky-skinned Washington Senators to walk perilously on a racial tightrope across the American League during the decades after ragtime music and Shoeless Joe Jackson and before wartime rations and one-armed Pete Gray. They were followed a decade later on the same Washington ball club (which was now flooding its roster with low-salaried and often marginally talented Cubans and other Latinos) by a Venezuelan pitcher who stirred every bit as much doubt and as much consternation around the cities of the junior circuit. Venezuelan hurler Alejandro "Patron" Carrasquel was signed up for Clark Griffith's Senators by super scout Joe Cambria and apparently passed only tolerably well for a sanctioned "white" player from 1939 down through 1945, winning 50 games overall for the cellar-anchored Nationals (nee Senators) ball club. Seemingly the nation's capital was an at-least-slightly-less-hostile environment for "border-line whites" than were the heartlands of southern Ohio. Yet Carrasquel was nonetheless heckled for his dark complexion (as was even the more pale-skinned Dolf Luque) by fans and opponents alike, and when he tried to avoid attention by Anglicizing his name to Alex Alexandra, the beat writers around the league were not easily taken in by such a ploy and never flagged from calling the exotic foreigner simply "Carrasquel the Venezuelan"!

If the cataclysms of World War II would eventually throw open heretofore bolted big-league doors to the nation's black

Tomás de la Cruz enjoyed a single productive World War II–era campaign on the mound in Cincinnati before disappearing into Jorge Pasquel's Mexican League. No lesser authority than writer Fred Lieb claimed that De la Cruz likely broke baseball's color line without fanfare several seasons before Jackie Robinson.

athletes, it was that same damnable war that would also crack those doors for racially questionable Cubans, Venezuelans, Puerto Ricans and other assorted Caribbean athletes; and it would do so even sooner. Nats boss Clark Griffith (the same Griffith who as a young manager signed both Marsans and Almeida in Cincinnati) for one continued his policies of penny pinching in Washington, policies which leaned heavily upon Cuban scouting by former Baltimore laundryman Joe Cambria. So effective and narrowly focused was Cambria's Caribbean recruiting program that Washington baseball historian Morris Bealle carpingly claimed "he would do even better if he could get over his predilection for Cubanolas" (*The Washington Senators*, 1947, 162). In the two decades following 1935, Griffith and Cambria imported a full 31 naive Cubans into Griffith Stadium — most for only predictably brief big-league appearances — and in spring 1940 Cambria reportedly trucked so many Cubans into camp that Griffith "had to find a special farm for them in Williamsport, Pa." (*The Washington Senators*, 163). The sparse pool of wartime baseball talent made Cuban athletes all the more attractive, of course—for one thing they were not subject to the military draft, for another they demanded small wages—and a floodtide (18 players in all between 1940 and 1945) would appear in the uniforms of big league clubs during the first half of the 1940s. At least two of these imports were—just like Calvo and Carrasquel in Washington during previous decades—of highly dubious racial stock. Tommy de la Cruz (1944) apparently stirred almost as much ballpark undercurrent in Cincinnati as Marsans and Almeida had years earlier, though a patriotic spirit pervading wartime America seemingly kept most of the strongest disapproval out of that city's press. And up in Chicago there was also the case of Hiram Gabriel Bithorn (1942), a hefty and only run-of-the-mill right-handed journeyman hurler from the island commonwealth of Puerto Rico.

Tommy de la Cruz was a work-horse pitcher of distinctly mediocre talents who would experience both the triumphs and traumas of a single abnormal big-league season in Cincinnati's Crosley Field during the penultimate war-ruined campaign of 1944. As baseball's oldest and most traditional franchise, Cincinnati's venerable Redlegs are celebrated universally among baseball's numerous historians for their unmatched string of rare diamond firsts: such pioneering moments as the nation's first professional team (1869), the first uniformed manager (1869), first fielder's and catcher's mitts (1869 and 1890), first National League left-handed pitcher (1877), inaugural farm system (1887), first Ladies Day (1886), first big league night game (1935), first all-synthetic playing surface (Riverfront Stadium in 1970), and dozens more such footnotes sustaining baseball's cherished esoterica. And yet perhaps the most explosive "first" in club annals today remains buried from sight by the selective blindness of our revisionist history. The wartime Cincinnati summer of 1944 is today enthusiastically remembered for a rare if unimportant pitching debut—the two-thirds of an inning hurled by 15-year-old high schooler Joe Nuxhall, baseball's youngest all-time performer. Another landmark mound debut occurring that same summer has surprising received almost no notice, despite its truly unparalleled groundbreaking nature. Ebony-hued Cuban right-hander Tommy de la Cruz took the hill for manager Bill McKecknie's Reds thirty-four times during his single big-league campaign and fashioned a record of nine-and-nine across 191 innings of valiant season-long labor. The Reds steadfastly insisted that their Cuban journeyman was merely "Hispanic" and surely not black, yet enough doubt seemingly existed among rival club owners that young Tommy de la Cruz was never to be invited back for a second season's swing around the league. He would show up instead the following spring toiling in Jorge Pasquel's rebel Mexican League, one of the handful of big-leaguers Pasquel was able to lure "south of the border" during his ill-fated effort to launch full-scale economic competition with the big league outfits up north. That race and not mound talent was a motivating force in Cincinnati's release of Tommy de la Cruz is perhaps hinted at least in part by the fact that

the pitching-thin Cincinnati club (despite wartime returnees) would boast only three 10-game winners during the following campaign; De la Cruz for his own part was soon thriving on tacos and semi-tropical heat as he posted a 17–11 ledger and solid 2.26 ERA while toiling for the 1945 Mexico City Reds.

Others around organized baseball were most certainly aware that Tommy de la Cruz was something of a threat to the game's sanctioned racial purity. Veteran Pittsburgh Pirates scout Howie Haak, who followed Joe Cambria all across Cuba in the 1940s and 1950s, reports sarcastically on the policy of having Cuban ballplayers of that era sign phony forms claiming that their own ancestry was unquestionably Hispanic and thus acceptably white. Nonetheless, concludes the insightful Haak, "Hell, Tommy de la Cruz (for one) was as black as they came!" (quoted by John Krich in *El Béisbol*, 1989, 157).

It can also be noted here that if Tommy de la Cruz never received appropriate recognition as one of baseball's early modern-era black-skinned pioneers, he only set an unfortunate precedent that would die hard in backwater Cincinnati. A full decade and a half later an ex-University of Toledo basketball hero named Chuck Harmon would appear on opening day of 1954 as a token pinch hitter and thus officially claim the distinction in popular histories (and thus in the memories of local fans) as the first "black" Cincinnati Reds ballplayer. Ironically, however, Harmon was preceded in the batting order (by exactly one batter) by another pinch hitter who better deserved this history-making accolade. Saturnino (Nino) Escalera—native of Santurce, Puerto Rico—launched his own one-year big-league career with a pinch-hit single only moments *before* Harmon, who followed him in the lineup by tamely popping out. Nino Escalera was labeled by local writers at the time as being merely "a Puerto Rican" import, despite the fact that his Latino skin was visibly as dusky-toned as Chuck Harmon's.

A bold claim for Tommy de la Cruz as baseball's trailblazing first 20th-century black was belatedly made before a national television audience by producers of a special documentary on the history of Latin American ballplayers (entitled "Baseball with a Latin Beat" and aired by WNBC-TV, New York, October 1989). The claim was probably moot, however, not so much in light of Robinson's celebrated career, but rather in view of Hi Bithorn's equally obscure sojourn on the big league diamond in Chicago. Another Latino pitcher of quite modest talents, Bithorn preceded De la Cruz by three full seasons and then outlasted him by exactly the same number. The Puerto Rican fastballer showed promise with a 9–14 (3.68 ERA) 1942 rookie campaign, was staff ace (18–12, 2.60 ERA) for the fifth-place Cubbies during a war-cheapened season of 1943 (pacing the senior circuit in shutouts that year), then lost two seasons to wartime naval service (Puerto Ricans, unlike Cubans, were not draft exempt). Once feted on U.S. Navy chow Bithorn unfortunately ballooned to 225 pounds, developed a sore arm, and thus kissed goodbye to a promising big league career. Perhaps the most noteworthy events defining the baseball life of Hiram Bithorn were the fact that he teamed with Cuban backstop Sal Hernández to provide the 1942 Cubs with baseball's first all–Latino battery, and also the distressing fact that he was gunned down under mysterious circumstances by a police officer in Mexico City on New Year's Day of 1952. Yet not many fans or baseball historians ever noticed either obscure event.

One reputable historian and scribe did lift his comfortable racial blinders long enough to take note, however, and that scribe was one of the game's most celebrated and most respected — none other than the venerable Fred Lieb. Pausing in his entertaining 1977 autobiography to comment on baseball's rich ethnic mix, Lieb recalls a personal puzzle he once faced regarding the case of the swarthy Puerto Rican pitcher with the wartime Chicago Cubs. Lieb's full account is arresting for its candor:

> Late in the winter of 1946–7, when I was working in St. Louis, I was invited to see a performance of Katherine Durham's all-black dance troupe. I did not know the man who had arranged for me to sit in the wings throughout the performance. During the intermission he brought over one of the women dancers and introduced her to me. "She is a first cousin to Hi Bithorn, the pitcher," he explained to make conversation. "Yes," the girl volunteered immediately. "My mother and his mother are sisters."

Lieb then continues his narrative by speculating that perhaps the conversation had been after all arranged "to tell me something" (given his advantageous position in the baseball press), reporting that "it had been rumored among baseball writers and in clubhouses when Bithorn came up in 1942 that he was part black" (*Baseball As I Have Known It*, 1977, 260). Lieb, for all his candor, was still a company man, however, and what baseball scribe of his generation was not? He could only conclude that "I have been assured by a Puerto Rican baseball authority that Hi Bithorn was *not* black, despite my curious experience."

If the greatest among Cuban black ballplayers who sprung forth in the decades between the two wars were fated to live out their often glorious careers in the relative obscurity of island winter ball and outlaw Negro league play, at least their images were not altogether obliterated by the winds of cruel fate. Méndez, Torriente, Dihigo, Oms and a few others would one day emerge — tardy as it may have been — among the game's lasting legends, thanks in the main to persistent labor by literary champions like John Holway and Jules Tygiel. It is undeniable, despite such belated plaudits, that Dihigo and Torriente and Luis Tiant, Sr., and so many others of immortal stature within their own native Cuba or Puerto Rico were robbed by long delays of reputations that might easily have rivaled Cobb's or Mathewson's or Walter Johnson's. And their eventual enshrinements regrettably came far too late for their own personal savoring.

But it was those among their dark-skinned compatriots — due perhaps to lesser talents as much as anything — who snuck briefly and quietly past baseball's loose racial barriers, who also in the end suffered what now seems an even crueler fate. Why is it that Robinson was first vilified then deified while Hi Bithorn and Jack Calvo and Alex Carrasquel provoked more

Owner of a legendary curveball, Camilio Pascual was easily Cuba's greatest major league pitcher between Adolfo Luque and the younger Luis Tiant. After a slow start with a hapless Washington franchise, Pascual posted back-to-back 20-victory seasons in Minnesota and led the junior circuit in strikeouts three seasons running.

of mild amusement and stifled yawns than any threats or banishments? Is it merely that the latter were mysterious swarthy island princes while the former was an upstart and disrespectful "son of a slave" who didn't know his proper place? Was it that those black Cubans who enjoyed brief cups of espresso in the big time were simply never quite good enough as ballplayers to receive much notice in the first place? Was it only that fans and owners alike — perhaps mirroring the characters in Hemphill's novel — were actually fooled by protestations of local management that these dark-skinned "foreigners" weren't really true black men with unacceptable bloodlines nearly identical to Georgia or Mississippi or Alabama Negroes? Likely in the end it was some complex combination of all the above regrettable factors.

If any claim that Jackie Robinson's integration of the big league scene was neither unprecedented nor unanticipated seems too outrageous, it should be pointed out here that plenty of respectable voices have also earlier suggested as much. Renowned black sports writer and editor Art Rust, Jr., was one of the earliest to question such a well-established historical myth: "I have always been convinced that Jackie Robinson was not the first black man in the modern major leagues," wrote Rust; "The Washington Senators in the mid-thirties and forties were loaded with Latin players of darker hue, who because they spoke Spanish got away with it" (quoted by Rogosin, *Invisible Men*, 159). Negro league historian Donn Rogosin himself struck a similar note by suggesting that big league scouts bypassed the "Black Babe Ruth"—Cristóbal Torriente (a rather light-skinned Cuban black)—only on account of his unacceptably kinky hair and a flat African nose; and furthermore that Negro leaguer Quincy Trouppe was once told by scouts that he might well be signable if only he would learn some Spanish so he might pass for a "foreigner" instead of an American black.

Rogosin cites further examples as well: Art Rust once referred in print to Miguel Angel González (a Cuban who briefly managed the Cardinals in 1938 and 1940) as "a light-skinned black man" while Washington outfielder John Welau also admitted that the bulk of his teammates in the 1940s considered Cuban Bobby Estalella as a black man pure and simple; Negro leaguer Willie Wells who played under Mike González on the Almendares winter league team reported that his skipper's mother was surprisingly completely black.

But perhaps the most enlightening testimony comes from the most surprising source of all—Jackie Robinson's partner in the great integration experiment, Branch Rickey. In his outstanding book on black leagues history Rogosin reports that Rickey was dismayed when Clark Griffith, boss of the Senators, objected to Brooklyn's 1947 integration efforts (which, of course, promised to destroy the existing Negro leagues and thus Griffith's own lucrative business arrangement with the Homestead Grays, part-time tenants of Griffith's Washington ballpark). According to Rogosin it was a beleaguered Rickey who snickered to famed sportswriter Red Smith that Clark Griffith was hardly one to object to Jackie Robinson, given his own known propensity for hiring Cuban blacks. Smith later reported that the comments of Mr. Rickey indeed "seemed to imply that there was a Senegambian somewhere in the Cuban bat pile where Senator timber is seasoned" (*Invisible Men*, 159).

No legitimate baseball historian would dare to contend that Brooklyn's Jackie Robinson does not deserve every fragment of his huge and still-growing legend as a remarkable athlete of unmatched grace, skill and magnetism; and also as bold racial pioneer of incomparable courage and integrity. It should not be forgotten that once Robinson left the playing field he carried on a second all-consuming crusade (one that most likely cost him his health and his life) against racial bigotry everywhere across the land, dedicating himself to the battle with an intensity shown by few Americans of any color or creed. During the course of his decade-long big league career Robinson enjoyed the perfect forum for his conquest of sport's inexcusable racist traditions; he triumphed in large part by playing in New York's acknowledged baseball capital, wearing the uniform of the colorful Dodgers, and dancing his magic upon the base paths at the very moment when television's magical eye first captured images of the World Series. With the notoriety and exposure he enjoyed, Robinson took upon his lonely shoulders the full burden of the nation's ingrained racial hatred and the full weight of the desperate integration struggle; as a result he enjoyed in large measure the exclusive (and thus perhaps somewhat unmerited) credit for alone dismantling baseball's most unforgivable tradition. While Robinson wore his rebellion on his sleeve, other quiet pioneers like Campanella, Doby and Newcombe undoubtedly did nearly as much for the Negro cause simply by sustaining their cheerful and infectious enthusiasms for the nation's most cherished sport.

Yet in a contemporary era when baseball's dedicated historians (especially those wearing the label of *sabermetricians*) quibble *ad nauseam* over such matters as whether fine-tuned adjustments in rule interpretation or record keeping might or might not justify taking away a batting title earned four decades ago, or devote their labors to adjusting the statistical measures of some long bygone player's relative impact upon the game, it would seem only appropriate that factual inaccuracies of more far-reaching

Camilo Pascual's Washington sidekick, Pedro Ramos, was one of the most generous servers of the home run ball in major league history. He also was a talented hitter and one of the fleetest runners in the American League (courtesy Transcendental Graphics).

consequence for baseball's sociological history would also need to be set straight. A price must be paid, of course, in admitting that some of the truest heroes of America's usurped national game were not after all even Americans. Yet should there not be a place in our narratives to recognize the historical significance of a handful of forgotten men of color who crossed baseball's odious racial barrier (however tentatively and however obscurely) even before Jackie Robinson?

* * *

The Mick, the Sheeney, the Wop, the Dutch and the Chink, the Cuban, the Indian, the Jap or the so-called Anglo-Saxon — his "nationality" is never a matter of moment if he can pitch, or hit, or field.

— The Sporting News (1923)

Leave the latter-day Pirates (Clemente), Dodgers (Valenzuela), and Giants (Marichal, Cepeda, Pagán and a trio of Alous) all aside. It was the forgettable and even regrettable Washington Senators ball clubs of the late 1940s and early 1950s — "first in war and peace yet always last in the American League" — that also first exploited the rich mother lode of Caribbean and South American baseball talent. A backdoor Cuban recruiting tradition fitfully spawned in the last century's second decade with dark-skinned Cincinnati fly chasers Armando Marsans and Rafael Almeida (1911), then enhanced with flamboyant hurler Adolfo Luque (first attached to the Reds in 1918) on the eve of the Black Sox scandal, was even more notably pursued several decades later by the sad sack Senators and their legendary super scout named Joe Cambria.

Cambria ("Papa Joe" to the grateful Cubans who eventually adopted him as a full-blown local legend) pioneered at opening up the "Cuban Connection" for Clark Griffith's lowly Senators (alias Nationals) in the immediate postwar epoch. Yet it was Griffith himself who remained a motivating force behind Cambria's now legendary expeditions into strongman Fulgencio Batista's pre-revolution Cuba. A young Clark Griffith had become enamored of Cuban talent more than two decades earlier while finishing out a short stint as manager of the National League Cincinnati Reds, and Griffith took his own pioneering steps when he inked Armando Marsans and Rafael Almeida for the sluggish Redlegs in 1911. Griffith was already gone from Cincinnati by 1912, having departed to launch a remarkable half-century career as first Washington's intrepid bench manager and later its club owner and franchise icon. It would be a mild assertion to say that things did not always run smoothly for Griffith in his subsequent years as owner of a languishing second-division ball club in the nation's capital. When the Great Depression set in with full-force after a rare Washington pennant climb in 1933, the always tight-pocketed Griffith found himself especially strapped for player resources and much-needed gate receipts. Cambria (who had worked his way from sandlot ballplayer in his native Massachusetts, to controversial minor league club owner in Albany, New York, and finally to Griffith's unlikely back-room assistant in Washington) was soon dispatched to distant Cuban shores in search of some inexpensive but hopefully serviceable franchise-saving prospects.

Griffith could not have been entirely disappointed with Cambria's initial efforts. Papa Joe's first notable signee, Bobby "Tarzán" Estalella, a legendary long-ball slugger in the winter leagues of his native Cuba, was an immediate fan-favorite who cracked the door for further island imports. Estalella was in reality a lead-fingered third sacker who managed but 44 round trippers (alongside 41 errors) and a barely respectable .282 BA over parts of nine big league campaigns (half of those spent with Connie Mack's Philadelphia Athletics during the upcoming talent-thin war years). But Washington fans of the late thirties had so much fun watching the gritty Estalella knock down enemy grounders with every part of his anatomy save his glove hand that they often phoned the park in advance to find out if the handsome swarthy Cuban was in the lineup before making the trek out to the usually sparsely populated Griffith Stadium grandstands.

The scheme launched by Clark Griffith under gathering storm clouds foreshadowing a Second World War would eventually be scuttled, barely two decades later, by Fidel Castro's standoff with Washington (the U.S. government and not the A.L. ball club) at the launching of a soon-to-follow Cold War. The results of owner Griffith's forays into Cuba were quite mixed. By the time Griffith's tireless bird dog, Joe Cambria, was forced to close up camp in Havana — after signing over 70 young Cuban prospects during the quarter century stretching between 1934 and 1959 — the Senators surprisingly still maintained only six farm clubs and three full-time scouts (by far the lowest totals in the majors) and the ball club still chose to recruit seriously only along the eastern seaboard region and throughout the nearby Caribbean basin. And while Clark Griffith's penny-pinching plan for garnering cheap talent won preciously few ball games for the hapless Nats of the Golden Fifties, an influx of colorful Latino players like Camilo Pascual, Pete Ramos, José Valdivielso, Julio Bécquer, Carlos Paula, Sandalio Consuegra, Miguel Fornieles, and dozens more, not only salvaged the ailing Washington franchise but also opened the eyes of most competing general managers to a rich and untapped pool of Latin America player talent seemingly quite ripe for easy picking.

Latin American (particular Cuban) ballplayers began appearing in force on Washington rosters in the years immediately preceding the Second World War. Mexican Mel Almada was among the first, as full-time center fielder with a .309 BA in 1937; Almada (not a Cambia recruit) had already logged five campaigns with Boston before he was traded to Washington. Estalella (who first joined the club in 1935) was also both an infield and outfield fixture of this same era, while charismatic Venezuelan right-hander Alex (Alejandro) Carrasquel (winner of 50 games in eight big-league seasons) posted 103 mound appearances with the Senators before the raids on Pearl Harbor. Carrasquel — uncle to fifties shortstop sensation "Chico" Carrasquel — carried the colorful nickname "Bigfoot" (Patón) and was the first big leaguer from continental South America. Other notable Latino players wearing Senators colors in the late 1940s and early 1950s included René Monteagudo (Cuban pitcher whose son, Aurelio, would also pitch seven major league seasons during the 1960s), Gilberto Torres (Cuban-born third baseman), Roberto Ortiz (Cuban outfielder), Baby Ortiz (pitcher and brother of Roberto Ortiz), Pedro (Preston) Gómez (Cuban infielder and later big-league manager), Chile (José) Gómez (Mexican infielder), and Fermín Guerra (Cuban catcher).

The onset of wartime conditions soon worked to dramatically increase Clark Griffith's growing stockpile of Latin players. The fact that such non-citizens (unlike Puerto Ricans) were altogether free from wartime draft board call must have held a certain appeal for the financially strapped and minor-league-thin Senators owner (although Cubans also would become draft-eligible by the final stages of the war). A smattering of Latin-born players on the big league roster actually worked to improve Senators' fortunes ever-so-slightly in the early forties. While other teams inevitably faded under

the exodus of top talent drained off by the war effort, Washington slid past normally stronger clubs like Boston, New York, and Cleveland for two surprising second-place finishes during 1943 and 1945. The 1945 edition — with Gil Torres handling shortstop and topping the junior circuit in putouts among the middle infielders, and Alex Carrasquel posting seven victories as a part-time starter — actually won 87 games and finished within a whisker of an American League pennant by closing to within a final game and a half of league champion Detroit. Notably, that same 1945 campaign also had fans cheering extra loud back in Havana for Bobby Estalella, sent packing by Griffith only two seasons earlier, who also enjoyed a career outing with Mr. Mack's Athletics and finished a surprising fourth in batting, a mere ten points behind the league leader.

It was a sudden giddy rise in league stature that would not be long maintained by such an imbalanced franchise. A return to peacetime conditions saw the Griffithmen slump back to a more comfortable nest near the league basement. Penurious by nature and reeling from the inevitable wartime fall-off in ballpark attendance, Clark Griffith had trimmed the Senators' already inadequate farm system to a mere six affiliates before even two more seasons had passed. In what seemed to be a direct result of such drastic cutbacks, by the late 1940s the Washington Senators had been reduced to scouting the Caribbean region almost exclusively. Griffith maintained only three full-time scouts during 1947 and 1948 and restricted his skeleton crew of bird dogs to a narrow beat along the nation's eastern seaboard, in tropical climes of Havana, and throughout other mostly unfrequented (by other big league teams at least) nearby Caribbean ports of call.

Motivation for Griffith's pioneering interests in Latin America as a primary source of player talent appears, therefore, to have been almost exclusively financial from the outset. Even when decade-long improvement in the farm system was finally launched with a 1947 appointment of former manager Ossie Bluege as minor league operations director, maverick scout Joe Cambria (finally named official scout for Cuba and Puerto Rico in 1949, then also for the West Indies and South America in 1954) continued to comb Latin American soil for potential big leaguers to serve his boss Clark Griffith in Washington. "Papa Joe" (as he was widely known by Havana locals, who even named a popular cigar brand after him) stirred little attention outside the nation's capital for all his work in tramping the back roads of virgin recruiting territory; much later he would be ironically and inaccurately remembered in most journalistic circles for supposedly first noticing and nearly signing a promising young Havana pitching prospect of the early 1940s (see the previous chapter) named Fidel Castro.

If Cambria's lasting legacy was unfortunately destined to be the runaway legend of a mythical prospect never actually scouted, the factual legacy of Papa Joe was not so unsubstantial. The following considerable cache of Cambria signees all made eventually appearances for the Senators during the early 1950s, performing with varying degrees of big-league success:

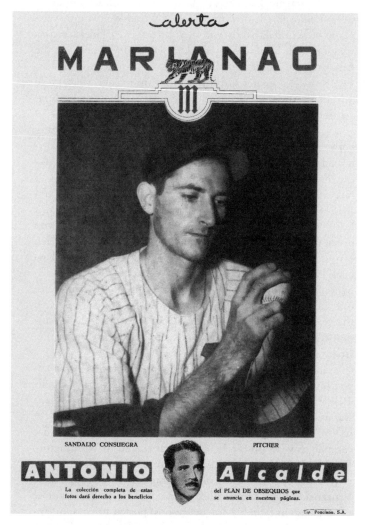

Oddly named Sandalio Consuegra parlayed a robust career as a Cuban amateur leaguer into eight big league seasons with Washington, Chicago and Baltimore. The lanky right-hander enjoyed a most memorable 1954 American League season when he paced the circuit in winning percentage (16–3, .842).

pitchers Sandalio Consuegra (Cuba), Miguel Fornieles (Cuba), Conrado Marrero (Cuba), Julio "Jiquí" Moreno (Cuba), Camilo Pascual (Cuba), Carlos Pascual (Camilo's older brother), and Pedro Ramos (Cuba); outfielders Francisco Campos (Cuba), Pompeyo Davalillo (Venezuela), Juan Delís (Cuba), and Carlos Paula (Cuba); infielders Osvaldo "Ossie" Alvarez (Cuba), Julio Bécquer (Cuba), Willie Miranda (Cuba), and José Valdivielso (Cuba). If Cambria's now legendary scouting activity did not in the end transform Clark Griffith's ball club into instant winners (or even eventual challengers), it did corral a steady cheap supply of adequate big league talent sufficient to keep the often floundering franchise just barely afloat.

The considerable honor role of Latin American ballplayers toiling in Washington in the 1950s begins, of course, with the always solid pitching of Pedro (Pete) Ramos (67–92 for the Senators between 1955 and 1960) and Camilo Pascual (53–77 record over the same period). Other strong-armed Cuban pitchers rounded out the bulk of the Senators always-undermanned staff throughout the late fifties: Sandalio (Sandy) Consuegra was 20–16 across three seasons before being dealt off to the Chicago White Sox in 1953; Conrado (Connie) Marrero compiled a 39–40 career mark in the first half-dozen seasons of the decade after debuting as a 39-year-old rookie; Miguel (Mike) Fornieles registered an impressive rookie 1.37 ERA in 1952 action before being perhaps too hastily peddled to the White Sox (in a nonetheless fortuitous exchange which nabbed eventual Washington ace lefthander Chuck Stobbs). And then there were less luminous utility players like journeyman middle infielder José Valdivielso, somewhat inept fly chaser Carlos Paula, and light-sticking first sacker Julio Bécquer. In all, better than two dozen native Cubans appeared in big league action for the Senators during the cellar-dwelling ball club's final topsy-turvy decade-plus residence in the nation's capital.

Griffith's Senators of the post–World War II era also assisted in launching a tradition of sure-fingered but light-sticking Spanish-speaking big league shortstops, a small handful of whom first blossomed at the outset of the fifties and thus branded the decade with an image of memorable and flashy infield play. The entire stretch of years was distinguished by such paragons of defense as Chico Carrasquel (White Sox, Indians, A's, Orioles), Luis Aparicio (White Sox, Orioles, Red Sox), Willie Miranda (Senators, White Sox, Browns, Yankees, Orioles), and José Valdivielso (Senators, Twins) — American Leaguers all, and ball hawks who revolutionized the entire concept of glove work around the second base post. While Cubans Miranda and Valdivielso were never much more than mere role players on a handful of also-ran clubs, Venezuelans Aparicio and Carrasquel enjoyed far more distinguished fates. Carrasquel (who as late as the end of the century still handled play-by-play broadcasts for the Chicago White Sox Spanish-language radio network) was the first of the flamboyant Latinos to appear in a big league All-Star Game, earning a choice spot in the Briggs Stadium (Detroit) mid-summer classic during his sophomore 1951 season. Aparicio, supplanting Chico Carrasquel as White Sox shortstop in 1956, would eventually earn a still greater slice of immortality as only the third-ever Latin big leaguer enshrined in Cooperstown (in 1984), the second after Marichal (1983) to earn election through normal induction procedures (since standard election rules had been waived by consensus for Roberto Clemente following the Puerto Rican star's tragic premature death in 1972).

Willie Miranda and José Valdivielso in the nation's capital were hardly ever a match for Aparicio and Carrasquel in the Windy City of Chicago. By the time the gut-wrenching Senators had donned new flannels as the fence-busting Twins of Minneapolis and St. Paul, however, Clark Griffith's franchise (by then in the hands of adopted son Calvin) had indeed finally come up with a Spanish-speaking shortstop good enough to dazzle his way through American League cities and unparalleled by any other keystone defender in the junior circuit. Marianao native Zoilo "Zorro" Versalles arrived in Griffith Stadium from the baseball-rich shores of Cuba in mid-summer 1959, the same summer when Fidel Castro was first launching a government transition back home that would soon turn off for good the once-rich pipeline of Cuban diamond talent. One of the very last of Papa Joe Cambria's promising imports would ironically prove also to be one of the very best.

Versalles' debut was nonetheless not particularly auspicious. Two early summers in Griffith Stadium provided only part-time play (44 games, 15 hits, and an anemic .142 BA) and offered little showcase for the flashy Cuban prospect who would down the road prove a de-

Honor Roll of Cuban-Born Washington Senators Pitchers

Name	Threw	Years	W–L*	ERA	IP	Games
Sandalio Consuegra	Right	1950–1957	51–32	3.37	809	248
Mike Fornieles	Right	1952–1963	63–64	3.96	1156	432
Ramón García#	Right	1948	0–0	17.18	3	4
Julio González#	Right	1949	0–0	4.72	34	13
Wenceslao González#	Left	1955	0–0	27.00	2	1
Evelio Hernández#	Right	1956–1957	1–1	4.45	58	18
Conrado Marrero#	Right	1950–1954	39–40	3.67	735	118
Rogelio Martínez#	Right	1950	0–1	2.25	1	2
René Monteagudo	Left	1938–1944	3–7	6.42	168	46
Julio (Jiqui) Moreno#	Right	1950–1953	18–22	4.25	336	73
Baby Ortiz#	Right	1944	0–2	6.23	13	2
Camilo Pascual	Right	1954–1971	174–170	3.63	2930	529
Carlos Pascual#	Right	1950	1–1	2.12	17	2
Pedro (Pete) Ramos	Right	1955–1970	117–160	4.08	2355	582
Armando Roche#	Right	1945	0–0	6.00	6	2
Raúl Sánchez	Right	1952–1960	5–3	4.62	89	49

* = **Complete record, with Washington and all other ball clubs (# = Played for Washington only)**

fensive rival for Cooperstown-bound Luis Aparicio. By 1965, however, Zorro Versalles was already transformed into a major star within a minor baseball market. In one truly glorious campaign he sparked the revamped team Calvin Griffith had inherited to its first pennant since the Joe Cronin era thirty-two years earlier, in the process copping AL MVP honors and leading the junior circuit with 45 doubles, 12 triples, 126 runs scored, and 666 at-bats. There would be other memorable moments for Versalles of almost equal achievement: a Gold Glove in 1963 and another in 1965, two American League All-Star selections, and even a notorious single vote for league MVP in 1967 that blocked Carl Yastrzemski's much-deserved unanimous selection for the coveted best-player award. Yet this fiery catalyst of the Minnesota baseball revival was also plagued by crippling back problems before the decade was out and Versalles soon slipped below the radar into the backwater Mexican League after barely a decade of big-league stardom. There was one final unsuccessful comeback stint with the transplanted Atlanta Braves in 1971, but it hardly seemed a just swan song for a wiry overachiever who had earlier beaten out hall-of-famers Clemente (by one year) and Cepeda (by two) as the first Latin American ever to salt away a big league MVP trophy.

Regrettably for long-suffering fans in the nation's baseball-poor capital, Ramos, Pascual, and Versalles — easily the best of the Cambria discoveries — never hit their stride until the former had long departed for greener pastures (with the Indians and Yankees) and the latter two had moved on with the likes of sluggers Harmon Killebrew and Jim Lemon to distant Minneapolis. Usually comical infield exploits by Bobby Estalella and equally savage outfield antics by a lumbering slugger named Carlos Paula instead provided the bulk of Washington's mid-century Cuban legacy. The unfortunate image that would remain most vivid for a generation of fans when it came to Griffith's and Cambria's "Senators Señores" was essentially one captured decades later by writers Brendan Boyd and Fred Harris (*The Great American Baseball Card Flipping, Trading and Bubble Gum Book*, 1973) in their indelible

portrait of one of the fifties' most endearing diamond clowns. From the baseball of their youth, for Boyd and Harris there was no image of the hapless Senators more vivid than that of a lumbering jet-black Cuban import who once pounded the baseball at a fraction under a .300 clip for most of the 1955 season and yet still quickly earned a permanent ticket back to the minors due to such atrocious fielding that he seemed to endanger his own life on almost any fly ball hit in his general direction. The Boyd and Harris portrait of Paula is simply too good not to reproduce verbatim:

> Carlos Paula's ability to hit the baseball (.314 lifetime minor league batting average) could never quite make up for his inability to catch it. Washington fans would shutter whenever the ball was hit his way. I myself was once witness to his mishandling of three consecutive fly balls in one inning, two of which fell for extra base hits. Carlos had good speed, excellent range, and he usually got a pretty good jump on the ball, but he could never quite seem to get the hang of catching the damn thing, and in an outfielder this can be a disheartening weakness.

The intent of this take on cup-of-coffee Cuban outfielder Carlos Paula is quite obviously to provoke as much humor as nostalgia; but humor in the end was oftentimes the best approach to an otherwise usually dreary saga of the Washington Senators' two-decade-long Cuban major league connection.

* * *

The decade discounted as the Turbulent Sixties was truly major league baseball's lost decade, and one important if infrequently noted residual of this unfortunate reality was the fact that a first significant wave of Latin American big league immigration was also largely lost to our collective baseball consciousness. Americans simply weren't paying as much attention to their national pastime during a chaotic epoch of national turmoil that fostered both the Vietnam War and related tidal waves of political and social upheaval on the home front.

More in tune with an unpopular Southeast Asian war, as well as the distancing realities of television and rampant societal violence defining the times, American football (especially professional football) had suddenly assumed pre-eminence as the nation's newest sporting passion. For the first and perhaps only significant span during the entire past century, professional baseball — for a brief spell at least — was pushed far to the back of the nation's collective awareness.

Public disinterest aside, the 1960s did launch the

Honor Roll of Cuban-Born Washington Senators Fielders

Name	Position	Years	BA*	Games	HR	RBI	Hits
Oswaldo Alvarez	Infielder	1958–1959	.212	95	0	5	42
Julio Bécquer	First Base	1955–1963	.244	488	12	114	238
Francisco Campos#	Outfielder	1951–1953	.279	71	0	13	41
Juan Delís#	Infielder	1955	.189	54	0	11	25
Roberto Estalella	Infielder	1935–1949	.282	680	44	308	620
Angel Fleitas#	Shortstop	1948	.077	15	0	1	1
Preston Gómez#	Infielder	1944	.286	8	0	2	2
Mike (Fermín) Guerra	Catcher	1937–1951	.242	565	9	168	382
Willie Miranda	Shortstop	1951–1959	.221	824	6	132	423
Carlos Paula#	Outfielder	1954–1956	.271	157	9	60	124
Luis Suárez#	Third Base	1944	.000	1	0	0	0
Gil Torres#	Shortstop	1940–1946	.252	346	0	119	320
Rogelio (Roy) Valdés#	Pinch Hitter	1944	.000	1	0	0	0
José Valdivielso	Infielder	1955–1961	.219	401	9	85	213
Zoilo Versalles	Shortstop	1959–1971	.242	1400	95	471	1246

* = Complete record, with Washington and all other ball clubs (# = Played for Washington only)

two most eminent Latino stars onto America's baseball diamonds — Puerto Rico's Roberto Clemente and "The Dominican Dandy" Juan Marichal — however little attention we may have paid them both at the time. There had been earlier noteworthy Latin sluggers and hurlers, to be sure. Luque (Chapter 2) had performed in a memorable 1919 World Series and had even enjoyed a single spectacular National League season (1923) during the heyday of Ruth and Hornsby. Mexico's pesky Bobby Avila was the first Latino to capture a league batting title when he paced the 1954 American League with a .341 average (trailed at considerable distance, ironically, by another Spanish-speaking phenom named Miñoso). But Luque was sporadic and always branded (however unfairly) as a hopeless hot-head. And Avila was as unspectacular as he was steady, barely reaching .300 in only two other AL campaigns, as well as being upstaged on his own power-laden Cleveland team by legitimate superstars like Larry Doby, Al Rosen and the fence-bashing Rocco Colavito.

Clemente and Marichal were admittedly a different breed of Latino ballplayer altogether. Roberto shook off an early-career mixed reputation as a notorious bad-ball hacker suddenly to emerge in Pittsburgh after 1960 as the most flamboyant and athletic right fielder the sport had yet witnessed. Having topped .300 at the plate only once in five tries during the 1950s, Clemente suddenly staked out the sixties as more or less his own personal stage with eight consecutive .300-plus seasons and a permanent perch at the top among NL batsmen; at the same time he wowed fans, writers and rivals alike with his amazing displays of Willie Mays–like outfield prowess. And if it were not for a single rival named Koufax in Los Angeles, Marichal for his part would have assuredly remained the dominant pitcher in all of baseball for at least a full decade after his 18–11 coming-out campaign of summer 1962 in San Francisco.

And there were now numerous other bold diamond pioneers spilling out of the barrios of Puerto Rico and sun-drenched sugar plantations of Dictator Rafael Trujillo's Dominican Republic. Dominicans, for example — today so noticeable at the vanguard of baseball's Latin invasion — were already making their first widespread appearance during the decade of the Beatles, flower children, nation-shattering political assassinations, and the divisive antiwar movement. Rico Carty barely missed out on both an NL batting title and rookie-of-the-year honors with a sensational 1964 Milwaukee debut. Wildly popular Orlando Cepeda superseded Willie Mays as local hero for Horace Stoneham's transplanted West Coast Giants, mainly because quirky San Francisco fans never warmed to Mays since he was not their own but a holdover from New York. Venezuela's Aparicio added to four straight stolen base crowns capping the fifties with five more in a row across the first half of the next decade; when Aparicio finally slowed on the base paths he was replaced by Cuba's Bert Campaneris, who secured the AL stolen base crown as a Latino specialty for six of the next eight years. Clemente's own four batting titles in the 1960s were supplemented with two more earned by Cuban Tony Oliva and one each for Dominican

Román Mejías logged more than 600 games (1955–64) with Pittsburgh, Houston and Boston, mostly as a utility outfielder. His peak season came with the expansion Houston club in 1962, when he bashed 24 homers, hit .286, and cracked the lineup in 146 games (courtesy Transcendental Graphics).

Matty Alou (1966) and the Panamanian novice Rod Carew (1969). The sixties also featured stellar Latino pitching performances outside of those annually registered by Marichal: Miguel Fornieles (Cuba), Luis Arroyo (Puerto Rico) and Minnie Rojas (Cuba) all claimed "relief pitcher of the year" awards during the decade; Cuba's Luis Tiant (the younger) captured an AL ERA crown a year earlier than Marichal turned the trick in the senior circuit; Mike Cuéllar distinguished self and country (Cuba) as the first-ever Latino Cy Young winner; Camilo Pascual (twice) and Tiant also both broke through as prestigious 20-game winners.

The Cubans were very much in the vanguard of this considerable Latin American talent flood now being unleashed on the big leagues in the wake of Jackie Robinson. Miñoso (Chapter 3) was already an established star in both Chicago and then Cleveland during the mid-fifties and in 1960 he peaked one final time as junior circuit pacesetter in base hits after returning for a second stint in the Windy City. Camilo Pascual was recognized as one of the American League's top hurlers despite his yearly losing records with a doormat team in the nation's capital (1954–1960), then came of age as the AL's biggest winner with the transplanted Twins of 1962 and 1963. There had been few flasher shortstops around in the 1950s than journeyman Willie Miranda, despite the Havana-native's almost nonexistent skills with a bat; though Miranda had already washed out before 1960, Minnesota's Versalles was soon putting a lie to the popular image of Latin middle infielders as strictly "good field, no hit" prototypes.

It was more than a little ironic, nonetheless, that by the time the brunt of a first Latino invasion had peaked near the end of the 1950s, Cuban ballplayers were inexplicably becoming suddenly scarcer than they had been in decades. It was not just the slamming of the doors to professional baseball in Havana after Fidel Castro's sudden rise to power. Already in the forties and fifties the Cuban talent stream had begun to thin out if not give signs of drying up altogether. Super skilled black players cut in the image of Dihigo, Oms or Méndez were surprisingly no longer there in the same numbers as only a few decades earlier. Back in the Cuban winter circuit annual batting titles had recently been claimed by such undistinguished American imports as Bert Haas (1952), Rocky Nelson (1954), Forrest "Spook" Jacobs (1956), and Milt Smith (1958); Cuban winter ball appeared to be sinking to all-time lows sev-

Cuba's charismatic Luis "Looie" Tiant rivals "The Dominican Dandy" Juan Marichal and Nicaragua's Dennis Martínez as Latin America's all-time most productive big league hurler (courtesy Transcendental Graphics).

eral years before the Castro revolution had arrived on the scene. It was all a matter of unfortunate timing for the Cubans: Robinson had flung the doors open to Latino black stars like Miñoso, Vic Power and Roberto Clemente at precisely the moment when Cuba's diamond heyday already seemed to have passed. But the Cubans were not altogether silent even if their presence had been notably muted.

Camilo ("Little Potato") Pascual and Pedro ("Pistol Pete") Ramos — a pair of lively Cuban flamethrowers long shipwrecked in Washington — were among the earliest imports to turn the heads of numerous appreciative North American fans. Yet the spotty careers of these two largely underrated hurlers were unfortunately as checkered as they were diverse and disparate. Pascual suffered humiliation as the league's most ineffectual hurler for half a decade (late 1950s) before he suddenly and surprisingly dominated the same circuit for a second half-decade (early 1960s). And Ramos eventually supplanted his career traumas as welcomed target for rival league sluggers with a larger dose of real-world trauma — a postcareer stretch stuck in Miami prisons after convictions for such egregious offenses as pistol-toting and drug dealing.

One of my favorite baseball historians (Donald Dewey in *The Biographical History of Baseball*, 1995) once stumbled upon a perfect turn of phrase for capturing the plight of pitchers like Ramos and Pascual when he wrote tongue-in-cheek of anemic toothpick companies (weak-hitting lineups) collapsing wholesale under otherwise respectable pitching staffs, while hefty lumber companies (rosters of potent sluggers) were often enough to shore up even the feeblest mound corps during the 1950s reign of mostly erratic clubs like the Pirates, Phillies, Red Sox, Cardinals and Senators. Such was certainly the fate of Pascual and Ramos as the erstwhile Senators of Washington transformed themselves overnight into the potent Twins of Minneapolis and St. Paul.

Pascual or Ramos were never helped, of course, by the fact that they first earned their meager major league paychecks with Clark and Calvin Griffith's basement-dwelling Washington Senators. Although Pascual would eventually develop a wicked sidearm curve, making him nearly unhittable in the early 1960s, such was not the case at the outset. Few hurlers have survived a rocker debut in the big time and then rebounded to earn pitching fame and fortune. (Sandy Koufax might come immediately to mind, but Koufax's early trials in Brooklyn resulted more from youthful wildness and lack of work than from any lack of support by lame teammates.) "Little Potato" (his brother Carlos was branded as "Big Potato" during an earlier brief big league trial) seemed at first to own exclusive rights to the loser's column in morning newspaper box scores, posting an embarrassing 28–66 ledger over his first five summers. No one could boast a more solid claim to the title of "best losing pitcher" in the junior circuit between 1954 and 1958.

Ramos fared even worse. Pistol Pete always appeared more skilled on the base paths and in the batter's box than on the hurler's hill, where his only remarkable achievement was leading the league in losses four straight seasons (1958–1961).

Ramos often announced he was the fastest man afoot in the entire American League — a rare boast for a pitcher — and he reportedly challenged Yankees speedster Mickey Mantle to pre-game foot races on several occasions without ever being granted a trial. And as a better-than-average hitter (he was frequently used as a pinch batter) Ramos could boast of fifteen lifetime homers, a performance that did little to compensate for the fact that as a moundsman he generously surrendered a league-record (since eclipsed) 43 circuit blasts to the opposition.

Pete Ramos did later experience a remarkable career upsurge when he moved over to the powerhouse Yankees during the pennant stretch run of 1964, but only after his arm had already logged almost all of its ordained allotment of lifetime innings. And Pascual would finally enjoy a reputable team behind him when the younger Griffith relocated his lackluster franchise to Minnesota. But what if this ill-starred pair had enjoyed a lineup consisting of the mature Killebrew, the flashy Versalles, and a clutch-hitting Earl Battey batting and fielding behind them only half a decade earlier? Would Camilo Pascual, with his sidewinder curve and smoking straight ball, not have won 200, perhaps even 300 games? Would not Pete Ramos perhaps have been the Luis Tiant or Juan Marichal of the American League during the era of Casey Stengel's Damn Yankees?

Pascual was a prototype workhorse who labored ceaselessly with a mediocre Washington team, then belatedly blossomed with an equally exceptional Minnesota club. Each ten-year span of the past half-century has unexpectedly showcased some single dominant Latin American hurler: Marichal in the sixties, Tiant in the 1970s, Fernando Valenzuela in the 1980s, Pedro Martínez in the nineties. And each of these pitching imports has in turn reflected the special ambiance of his own particular decade. The fifties thus featured the yeoman-like Camilo Pascual, who labored nobly in pursuit of a confidence-shattering .297 winning percentage (1954–1959) strapped to a hapless Washington team that could neither knock out base hits from the batter's box or knock them down in the outfield. Despite his fabulously futile record, Pascual was nonetheless respected by league fans and ballplayers alike as one of the most fearsome right-handers on the circuit. Once the lowly Senators donned a new disguise as the much-improved Minnesota Twins, Camilo Pascual performed a chameleon act almost unmatched in baseball history. Newly ensconced in the Twin Cities and revived by a legitimate pennant contender, the once hapless Pascual turned in sterling 20–11 (1962) and 21–9 (1963) campaigns, also leading the league in strikeouts for three straight seasons (1961–1963).

Had Pascual labored in Yankee Stadium rather than Griffith Stadium during the epoch of Yogi Berra and Mickey Mantle, his name and not Marichal's might well have been toasted regularly in hot-stove discussions of Latin America's original pitching hero — to say nothing of likely enshrinement in Cooperstown. Equally snake-bit teammate Pedro Ramos presented quite another somber saga, however. While Pascual's career coalesced with the arrival of a more talented sup-porting cast in Minnesota, Ramos drew new blood from a late-career transition into the bullpen. In the end, nevertheless, Cuba's second best power pitcher of the 1950s, despite his similar potential, somehow never quite escaped the treacherous pitfalls always built into the joyride of sudden athletic fame.

If the maturing of Killebrew and company had saved Pascual, it was the trade wire that eventually salvaged life in the big leagues for Pete Ramos. Only briefly did Ramos savor his single shot at true glory with the front-running Yankees, and handed such a rare career break so late in his baseball life, the Cuban Cowboy performed admirably well. By the time he had arrived in Yankee Stadium, however, both he and the invincible Bronx Bombers were dangerously near the end of a fragile prosperity. Acquired by manager Yogi Berra's Yanks at considerable cost (Ralph Terry, Bud Daley and $75,000 cash), Ramos initially proved well worth the investment, especially during the pennant dash of September 1964. Ramos shored up a sagging New York staff by posting a sterling 1.25 ERA along with eight crucial saves. The "Ramos Revival" could not have been better timed for Berra's outfit since a record-tying fifth-straight pennant was squarely on the line for the New Yorkers. Two final seasons in New York would also bring 32 additional saves from the Cuban Cowboy Ramos, yet the Bronx Bombers' sudden tumble from contention after 1964 soon made their aging relief ace quite expendable.

Once his brief joyride was over in New York, Ramos nosedived rapidly into almost total obscurity (drifting from Philadelphia to Pittsburgh to Cincinnati and back to Washington in three unsuccessful swan song seasons). And post-baseball life brought only an endless spell of further downward spiral. A lengthy string of arrests in the late 1970s and early 1980s for such egregious offenses as carrying concealed weapons, possessing and dealing marijuana and cocaine, aggravated assault, and drunken driving along with parole violation eventually landed a three-year term at a Florida federal correction center. Life itself had at long last knocked Pete Ramos from the box even more effectively than had a decade or more of uncooperative American League hitters.

If Pete Ramos was not nearly so effective over his total career as his Washington sidekick Camilo Pascual, winning nearly 60 games fewer and never approaching a 20-victory season, he was every bit as unforgettable. What is most memorable about Ramos — off-field antics aside — was his personal contribution to baseball's long-ball slugging of the offense-happy 1950s. Indeed, few pitchers in baseball history have yielded more home runs to rival batters and in more charitable fashion.

A chart cataloguing the game's most generous providers of the long ball (adapted from unpublished research by Raymond González) suggests the Cuban Cowboy's uniqueness as a home run dispenser. Ramos, owner of the highest number of homers allowed per innings pitched (one homer in every 7.48 frames), stands at the furthest end of the spectrum from dead-ball ace Big Ed Walsh. Working in the pre–Ruthian era and owning a truly "heavy" fastball, Walsh dispensed only about half as many round-trippers (24) across a full 14-year career as Ramos provided for Mantle, Williams, Zernial, Colavito and company during the 1957 season alone. Almost outdoing himself with a career-high 48 gopher balls in 1957, Ramos matched or surpassed Walsh's career totals in each of eight straight seasons (1956–1963) during one of baseball's most homer-happy epochs. Ramos pitched the bulk of this period in two of the league's most spacious arenas at Washington and Cleveland. Cozy ballparks around the rest of the circuit (Fenway Park and Yankee Stadium were two) may have brightened up the decade for sluggers like Mantle, Berra, Zernial or Ted Williams, but no more than did a generous Washington hurler named Pistol Pete Ramos.

Pascual and Ramos — Washington's *Cubano* twin towers of strength — were not the only front-line Cuban pitchers in the big leagues throughout the century's middle decades. Mike Fornieles suddenly peaked for Boston with a career performance (as league leader with 70 appearances and 14 saves) during his ninth big league season (1960); his overall career was nonetheless quite spotty, with an 18–31 mark as a starter and an overall 63–64 break-even ledger. Sandy Consuegra was also something of a one-year wonder, posting a 16–3 record for Chicago in 1954, winning all eight relief decisions, and hurling in that season's All-Star Game in Cleveland. Orlando Peña would prove a competent performer for several years (across the 1960s) with eight different teams; but his most notable "achievement" was the less-than-admirable feat of losing 20 games in 1963 with Kansas City during the first of his two campaigns as a regular starter. And Luis Tiant (son the renowned Negro league star of the same name) was already being heard from before the 1960s had quite reached their tumultuous peak against a backdrop of late-decade national chaos; Tiant's lasting mark would not be made, however, until he labored with Boston for eight seasons, spanning most of the quieter decade to follow.

If there was any island-bred rival in stature to Pascual and Ramos before 1970 it had to be still another stellar alumnus of the Havana-based Cuban Sugar Kings (AAA–level International League farm club where Fornieles, Consuegra and Peña all served brief apprenticeships). Miguel Cuéllar first flashed brilliance with Havana's Sugar Kings, where he struck out seven straight in his initial game and posted a 2.44 ERA for his debut season. Perhaps the best-ever Cuban southpaw arrived on the big league scene with cups of coffee in Cincinnati (where he pitched only two games in 1959) and St. Louis (where five wins in 1964 played a small role in the Cardinals' successful pennant drive). There was also a more successful stop in Houston, before Cuéllar made a much bigger impact over in the American League. During his first full big league season with the Astros (1966) the Cuban ace rang up the year's second best NL ERA (behind Koufax); a summer later he fanned 203 and established a then-franchise-record with 16 victories. But it was a fateful one-sided trade to Baltimore for promising slugger Curt Blefary (1965 AL rookie of the year) during the 1968 off-season that opened the doors wide on one of the biggest impact careers ever enjoyed by a Latin American major league pitcher.

Southpaw Miguel Cuéllar was not only a full cut above most of the Cuban journeyman pitchers who had preceded him to the big time, but he also claims one distinction that can be matched by no other Cuban hurler. He is the only island ace ever to take possession of a prestigious Cy Young Award, the supreme modern-era measure of big league pitching excellence. The honor was shared with Detroit's Denny McLain and was earned with a sensational 23–11 debut season for the American League champion Orioles. (He was also the only Oriole to beat the Miracle Mets during that October's surprising World Series.) Cuéllar's Cy Young-winning year was hardly, however, a single summer of unmatchable over-achievement. What was launched in Baltimore during the last gasp of the sixties continued on unabated for a half-dozen more campaigns that never witnessed less than 18 victories for the talented Cuban; indeed few southpaws, native or foreign-born, were quite as dominant in the American League at any time during the decade of the seventies. A second Baltimore season (1970) witnessed the most wins (24) and complete games (21) in the junior circuit. Cuéllar was one of four Baltimore 20-game winners in 1971; his 22 wins in 1974 were also accompanied by the league's top winning percentage; and the all-around natural athlete was even able to belt a crucial wind-blown grand slam flour-bagger off Minnesota's Jim Perry during the 1970 ALCS post-season showdown.

There is little argument that Camilo Pascual's sudden successes in Minnesota resulted from increased offensive support for his steady pitching efforts, and yet that support came as much from one of his own newly arrived countryman as it did from the Ruthian bats of Killebrew and fellow North American behemoths like Jim Lemon and Bob Allison. Another chunky Cuban youngster with little advanced billing debuted in Minnesota in the early

20th Century's Most Generous Home Run Pitchers

Pitcher	HRs Allowed	Innings	Innings/HR Allowed
Pedro Ramos (1955–1970)	315	2355	7.48
Denny McLain (1963–1972)	242	1886	7.79
Jim "Mudcat" Grant (1958–1971)	292	2442	8.36
Don Newcombe (1949–1960)	252	2155	8.55
Jim "Catfish" Hunter (1965–1979)	374	3449	9.22
Ferguson Jenkins (1965–1983)	484	4501	9.30
Robin Roberts (1948–1966)	505	4689	9.29
Preacher Roe (1938–1954)	199	1914	9.62
Jack Morris (1977–1994)	389	3824	9.83
Luis Tiant (1964–1982)	346	3486	10.1
Jim Bunning (1955–1969)	372	3760	10.1
Murry Dickson (1939–1959)	302	3052	10.1
Least Generous Home Run Pitcher			
"Big Ed" Walsh (1904–1917)	24	2964	123.5

sixties and was almost overnight recognized throughout the baseball world as a rare natural hitting wonder. Just about everyone had misjudged Pedro (Tony) Oliva before his rookie-year breakout, despite brief .400-hitting trials with the Twins in 1962 (nine games) and 1963 (seven games), but no one made a more misguided judgment than *Baseball Digest* editors when they published the following succinct scouting report: "Fair hitter, can make somebody a good utility outfielder."

If the decade of Vietnam hostilities obscured Latino baseball stars, a subsequent decade of Watergate scandals finally exposed them in all their glory. The 1970s belatedly and thankfully replaced time-worn stereotypes with a celebrated class of colorful Latino diamond heroes. The mere number of new bat-and-glove-toting immigrants from "south of the border" now assured much greater impact than was possible in any previous era. While Clemente, Cepeda, Marichal and Camilo Pascual stood head-and-shoulders above perhaps several dozen of their utility-role countrymen in the six-

"Papa Joe" Cambria, Clark Griffith's legendary Cuban bird dog, flanked here by a trio of non–Cuban Senators (Eddie Yost, left, Mickey Vernon, and Herbie Plews) (courtesy Transcendental Graphics).

ties, the field was indeed more crowded with Spanish-speaking "franchise players" by the mid-seventies. At the forefront of this new invasion were two dominant hitters on the same Minnesota team—Tony Oliva and Rod Carew. Oliva (native of Pinar del Río) had already arrived with a bang in the mid–1960s, of course, wresting two batting titles and leading the junior circuit in base hits four times during his initial big league decade. But by the early 1970s Tony Oliva was a well-established star, earning a third AL hitting title in 1971 and knocking out a league-best 204 safeties a year earlier at the dawn of the new decade. Over the long haul, however, Oliva would be largely overlooked by stateside fans and media and thus would experience some of the same form of silent rejection that had shadowed Orlando Cepeda in west coast San Francisco and heartland St. Louis. If Pete Ramos was Latin baseball's biggest disappointment of the 1950s, and if Cepeda would have a legitimate claim on that dubious distinction in the 1960s, Oliva owned it outright across the decade that followed.

The painful fact is that while Oliva streaked into Minneapolis like a flaming comet he would also soon feature in one of the era's saddest tales of unremitting overachievement and sustained under-recognition. Perhaps no rookie of any epoch has ever burst on the scene with more intensity and more offensive firepower than did Cuba's unassuming all-star big league outfielder. Here is the only athlete in a century of American League play to lay claim to batting titles in each of his first two campaigns. For at least half a decade after his record-

setting rookie campaign of 1964 Oliva looked like the next great hitting superstar, a magical batsman cut in the mold of Ty Cobb, Joe DiMaggio, even Ted Williams. Cooperstown seemed an iron-clad certainty for a seeming lefty-swinging version of Clemente. But Oliva was all-too-soon perhaps unfairly dimmed by other bright comets and also tarnished by his own personal handicaps with the electronic media during baseball's newly emerging television age. Poor command of English in the long run jettisoned a proud slugger's career far more than enemy pitching ever could. Eventually it was teammate Rod Carew (with seven batting titles of his own) who ironically also took a huge bite out of Oliva's diminishing star both in Minnesota and elsewhere around the league.

Tony Oliva was also yet another Cuban pioneer who experienced especially hard times in the wintry climates of a frigid North American big league city—this time Minneapolis. For Oliva, who was released from his first minor league try-out camp just months after the failed Bay of Pigs invasion, a return to Cuba after 1960 was unthinkable. Given a second chance to remain on U.S. soil, the talented youngster quickly delivered, posting a .410 average with Wytheville of the Appalachian League, a feat which brought him a Silver Louisville Slugger as top hitter in professional baseball for 1961 and, more importantly, a guaranteed spot with the Minnesota Twins organization. Yet at times the world of big league baseball must have appeared as complex and frightening as the politics of Oliva's own unsettled and revolution-wracked Cuban homeland. Oliva today speaks eloquently of the loneliness and pain of his earliest major league days. Knowing little English and frightened by an unfamiliar and often seemingly hostile environment, Oliva would walk the dozen or so miles each day from his apartment to the suburban Bloomington ballpark where the Twins played. A fearless ballplayer who held his own against wicked enemy fastballs, the youngster was nonetheless deathly afraid of a bus ride on which he might become hopelessly lost without any English skills to aid him in navigating a strange landscape. And he was also simply too poorly paid as a 1962 rookie to afford the luxury of daily cab fare. One of the hottest prospects of the American League would walk almost everywhere he went, undoubtedly strengthening his already powerful legs in the process. It was just one more case of how the irrepressible Tony Oliva always managed to extract a positive value from even the most negative of his early baseball experiences.

Today Oliva bitterly complains in rare interviews that he did everything that could be expected for earning Cooperstown immortality — a 15-year lifetime .300 batting average, rookie-of-the-year honors and eight-time league All-Star selection, multiple-year batting champion and league hits leader on five different occasions, and consistent Gold Glove outfielder. Only an MVP season (he was second to Brooks Robinson during his rookie campaign) and serious hall-of-fame consideration escaped this brilliant Cuban batsman who ranks second only to Rod Carew as the all-time Minnesota franchise leader in nearly every important hitting category outside of long-ball production.

Language much more than race scuttled Oliva's dreams of a smooth route to fame and fortune on foreign soil. For others it was quite the reverse. A tiny handful of early black Latins of the 1950s were also the first to integrate their teams, and with these brave integration roles inevitably came even larger burdens of being exiled strangers in a most hostile big league world. Saturnino Escalera, an undistinguished one-season Puerto Rican outfielder-infielder, played the odious role in Cincinnati and yet stirred preciously little excitement with his

landmark achievement. Unfortunately for Nino Escalera a black North American teammate would crack the Reds' lineup on the very same day. Ironically, many accounts of Cincinnati baseball history have assigned the integration credit to the man who batted in the lineup immediately *behind* Escalera on the precise day in 1954 (April 17) when racial barriers tumbled in the oldest National League city. Chuck Harmon (not Nino Escalera) is often cited as the first black Cincinnati Redleg; the reason for the oversight is that Harmon was a North American of African descent, and thus not eligible for being passed off as some kind of racial or ethnic technical exception. Escalera was more often than not in most subsequent accounts of Reds history simply discounted as a mere "foreigner" who had briefly (and more or less invisibly) intruded upon the Queen City baseball scene.

Another Latin American black who received even less credit for his pioneering role than Escalera was Cuban shortstop Humberto "Chico" Fernández. Fernández first appeared in the majors with little fanfare in Brooklyn, a place where black players were already commonplace by the time the Havana native debuted in mid–July 1956. With slim hopes for unseating hall-of-famer Pee Wee Reese from the middle infield slot at Ebbets Field, the brown-skinned rookie had no future with Walter Alston's Dodgers; he was a hot enough prospect, nonetheless, for the Phillies to peddle five players in order to obtain his services for the 1957 season. Departing Brooklyn for hopefully greener pastures, Fernández would once more miss out — through an oversight much like the one in Cincinnati — on a spot in the history books as the first black ballplayer for the Philadelphia National League team. The distinction this time wrongfully went to another shortstop named John Kennedy, purchased that same spring from the Kansas City Monarchs and thus the last player to jump directly from the Negro leagues to the majors. Yet fate was in the end finally on the side of Chico Fernández. Kennedy would injure his shoulder after only two big league at-bats and never again appear in a major league uniform. Before the month was out Fernández took

First Blacks, Latins and Cubans on Original 16 Big League Clubs

Ball Club	First Black Ballplayer (Latinos in Bold Italics)	First Latin Ballplayer (Blacks in Bold Italics)	First Cuban Ballplayer (Blacks in Bold Italics)
Brooklyn Dodgers	Jackie Robinson (4–15–47)	Adolfo Luque (1930)	Adolfo Luque (1930)
Cleveland Indians	Larry Doby (7-5 -47)	*Minnie Miñoso* (1949)	*Minnie Miñoso* (1949)
St. Louis Browns	Hank Thompson (7–17–47)	Oscar Estrada (1929)	Oscar Estrada (1929)
New York Giants	Hank Thompson (7–8–49)	Emilio Palmero (1915)	Emilio Palmero (1915)
Boston Braves	Sam Jethroe (4–18–50)	Mike González (1912)	Mike González (1912)
Chicago White Sox	*Minnie Miñoso* (5–1–51)	Chico Carrasquel (1950)	Witto (Luis) Aloma (1950)
Philadelphia Athletics	Bob Trice (9–13–53)	Luis Castro (1902)	*Bobby Estalella* (1943)
Chicago Cubs	Ernie Banks (9–17–53)	Hiram Bithorn (1942)	Sal Hernández (1942)
Pittsburgh Pirates	Curt Roberts (4–13–54)	Mosquito Ordeñana (1943)	Mosquito Ordeñana (1943)
St. Louis Cardinals	Tom Alston (4–13–54)	Oscar Tuero (1918)	Oscar Tuero (1918)
Cincinnati Reds	*Nino Escalera* (4–17–54)	Armando Marsans (1911)	Armando Marsans (1911)
Washington Senators	*Carlos Paula* (9–6–54)	Mérito Acosta (1913)	Mérito Acosta (1913)
New York Yankees	Elston Howard (4–14–55)	Angel Aragón (1914)	Angel Aragón (1914)
Philadelphia Phillies	*Chico Fernández* (4–16–57)	Chili Gómez (1935)	Sid (Isidoro) León (1945)
Detroit Tigers	*Ozzie Virgil* (6–6–58)	*Ozzie Virgil* (1958)	*Chico Fernández* (1960)
Boston Red Sox	Pumpsie Green (7–21–59)	Eusebio González (1918)	Eusebio González (1918)

Two of Cuba's small army of early-fifties cup-of-coffee Washington recruits — outfielder Francisco Campos (far left) and pitcher Raúl Sánchez (far right) — flank a collection of equally undistinguished Senators teammates (courtesy Transcendental Graphics).

over as the first black regular in the Phillies' lineup, and the Cuban would retain the club's crucial shortstop position until he slumped badly at the plate midway through the 1959 campaign.

There is still more to the story. Kennedy is to this day still often cited as the first Phillies black ballplayer after his April 22 debut, but Chico Fernández had already cracked the same lineup six days earlier, on Opening Night and on the hometown field. Fernández filled the shortstop slot during the 1957 lid-lifter in Connie Mack Stadium versus his old Brooklyn club and stroked three base hits to spice the evening's action. The Phils at the time were the only remaining all-white outfit in the senior circuit and the local press, mindful of this uncomfortable racial status quo, was successful in dismissing the new swarthy infielder as a "Cuban newcomer" without so much as mentioning the taboo integration question. A week later African-American John Kennedy unjustly earned pre-

dictable headlines in the City of Brotherly Love as purportedly the first intrepid Negro athlete to cross racial barriers for the heel-dragging Phillies.

The normally mild-mannered Fernández for years remained bitter about this historical oversight in Philly. "I was forced to live in the black section of town," Fernández later complained in a personal letter to this author, "but I never got my full due as a black ballplayer when I stepped onto the field." And the unfortunate slight still retains its currency in some quarters at least: an Associated Press wire story by Hal Brock in 1997, celebrating Jackie Robinson's Golden Anniversary, correctly listed Escalera as the first black in Cincinnati and Miñoso as the pioneer in Chicago (it was not Sam Hairston as many have wrongly claimed), yet still improperly credited John Kennedy and ignored Fernández when it came to racial pioneering in Philadelphia.

Fernández finally moved on yet again, to Detroit, just in

time for still another near-miss, this time as the first black ballplayer in the Motor City. While the Phillies had been the last National League ball club to drag their lead feet across the integration border, the Tigers edged in only ahead of the Boston Red Sox in this regrettable department among American League franchises. It was the Dominican-born and New York–raised Ozzie Virgil who would actually integrate the Tigers in 1958 as the club's first "official" barrier-busting black. But Virgil's Detroit stopover would be limited to 49 games in 1959 and 62 more in 1960, mostly as a utility player and late-inning defensive fill-in. Fernández, by contrast, would be handed the starting shortstop slot in Detroit for the 1960 campaign, thus becoming the first-ever black regular for a second big league club. The pioneering sojourn would again last only a couple of seasons yet would include a surprising power display with 20 homers during the 1962 pennant chase. But all record of the role of Chico Fernández as a pioneering black-skinned big leaguer has been conveniently expunged from the short memories of Motor City fans, just as it has been equally lost for two-plus generations of history-blind Phillies fanatics.

Fernández was but one of a number of sure-handed pioneering shortstops who stood out among Cuban imports of the post-war era. Guillermo "Willie" Miranda was perhaps the most noteworthy of the lot when it came to pure skill at one of the diamond's most demanding defensive positions. Miranda stirred faint ripples in 1953 when he departed the Washington Senators to become the first Cuban with the New York Yankees since Armando Marsans back in 1918; after a celebrated eighteen-player trade moved him to Baltimore he made an even bigger splash in 1955 by leading AL shortstops in every defensive category outside of fielding average (mostly because he occasionally muffed balls that most infielders could never have gotten anywhere near in the first place). Venerable old-timers in Cuba still actively debate the greatest Cuban glove man — Miranda for Almendares in the 1950s or modern-day paragon Germán Mesa with Industriales; for big league fans first discovering the exotic Cubans in the shadows of World War II Miranda's non-existent bat (he managed to hit an anemic .192 in 616 at-bats over his final three big-league campaigns) and unparalleled glove made him a primary prototype of what Miguel Angel González had once dismissed as "good field, no-hit" South American imports.

Not far behind Miranda as a defensive nonpareil (and also as a near automatic out in the batting order) was lifetime .219 hitter José Valdivielso, another one-dimensional infielder also earning his paycheck with Washington (and later with Minnesota). "Joe" Valdivielso earned an immortal niche in the sport's numerous trivia volumes by being accidentally featured, along with Pedro Ramos and first baseman Julio Bécquer, in one of baseball's all-time most bizarre infield plays. On the afternoon of July 23, 1960, journeyman Kansas City outfielder Whitey Herzog smashed a frozen rope liner which Ramos speared, then tossed to Bécquer who quickly relayed on to Valdivielso to finish off what diehards in Havana still proudly point to as the big leagues' only all–Cuban triple play.

One of the most fortuitous finds by scouts mining Cuban territory at mid-century was Matanzas native Dagoberto (Bert) Campaneris, inked to an Kansas City A's contract by scout Felix Delgado for a mere $500 bonus. Campaneris will likely always be best remembered for the rare stunt he performed in September 1965 when he single-handedly and consecutively (occupying a new post each inning) manned all nine defensive positions on the diamond. During his unprecedented trip around the ballpark "Campy" committed a single error (while in right field), allowed one run and two hits from the mound, and was kayoed while catching the final frame by a home-plate collision with hefty Los Angeles Angels runner Ed Kirkpatrick. Two ironies would attach themselves to this ultimate utility display, as well as to Campy's opening four-season stint in Kansas City. When Latino infielder César Tovar duplicated the nine-position feat for Minnesota versus Oakland three seasons later, Campaneris himself would fittingly be the initial batter to face Tovar during the Venezuelan's own first-inning turn on the mound. And four years to the day after the all––Cuban triple play in Kansas City, Campaneris (on July 23, 1964) debuted in the same ballpark and made some significant history of his own as only the third player ever to stroke a pair of homers (one on the very first big league pitch he ever saw) in his initial big league ballgame.

Campaneris's side-show nine-position performance — some might call it grandstanding — marked the first time this feat had ever been attempted on a big league diamond; it was the kind of outrageous publicity stunt that marked the Kansas City Athletics teams under rebellious owner Charles Finley. But Campaneris was much more than just a clever stunt man during his 19 years (2,328 games) on the scene with both Kansas City and Oakland (and later also with Texas, California and the Yankees). Before he was done Campy had established credentials that made him perhaps the best all-around Cuban big-league shortstop of them all. Among his achievements were three World Series championship rings (earned in the starting lineup with Oakland in 1972, 1973, 1974), six American League stolen base crowns, six All-Star Game picks, 2,249 career base hits, and a 1968 AL–leading base hits total of 177 posted during the A's first west coast season in Oakland.

Yet another Cuban transplant was soon carving out personal baseball fame for himself against the backdrop of the political upheavals besetting his abandoned island homeland. Luis Tiant — a strapping right-hander with a quirky twisting windup that featured a dozen different release points for his assortment of baffling curves and off-speed deliveries — came to the big leagues in 1964 with Cleveland's Indians, carrying with him a largely lost (for North American ballpark fans) if nonetheless impressive family baseball heritage. Luis Tiant, Sr., had once been a substantial hero for an earlier generation of Cuban rooters during the heyday of Dihigo, Lázaro Salazar, Alejandro Crespo and other Cuban giants of blackball renown. The little lefty with the same name as the latter big leaguer had carved out his own niche in black league and winter league play between the early 1930s and the close of the Second World War. Tiant, the elder, peaked with appearances in two East-

West Negro league all-star games (Chicago) spaced twelve summers apart; in 1935 he earned selection as staff ace for perhaps the best-ever New York Cubans outfit; in 1947 he was tabbed in the midst of a perfect 10–0 season with the same club. Like others of his race, Papa Tiant was banned from the white man's ballparks but was nonetheless able to grab at least a small slice of immortality with his reputation as a blackball and winter-ball master practitioner of the art of junk-ball tosses. The best story surrounding the elder Tiant's substantial career is one involving his legendary pick-off technique; once a befuddled rival batsman reputedly swung when a ball was delivered to first rather than toward the plate, an embarrassing mistake that brought but little sympathy from a grizzled home plate umpire. "If you're dumb enough to swing it's still a strike," bellowed the sarcastic arbiter. Tiant Sr. (also known as Lefty and Señor Skinny) was destined to be remembered by generations of Latino and blackball fans as the perfect prototype of the junk-ball hurler, a master of changing-speed deliveries, justly famed for his herky-jerky motions and those lethal pick-off tosses toward first base. But the name Tiant meant preciously little if anything at all to mainstream white fans of the big leagues up north before it began appearing regularly a quarter-century later in American League box scores featuring ball clubs in first Cleveland and later Boston.

Across the sixties it was, of course, Juan Marichal who reigned supreme, outstripped perhaps only by Koufax and Bob Gibson for an undisputed mythical title of "number one" during one of pitching's brightest eras. The 1980s was in turn the decade for Fernandomania as the Mexican phenom mowed down NL batsmen from one end of the decade (as the first combined Cy Young winner and Rookie-of-the-Year in 1981) to the other (with 200-plus innings and a no-hitter in 1990); and the final ten-year span of the millennium would be claimed on one end by Nicaraguan veteran Dennis Martínez (who retired in 1998 after passing Marichal as the all-time winningest Latin American) and Dominican newcomer Pedro Martínez (with a Cy Young-caliber 23–4 1999 season plus a pair of additional stellar sub–2.00 ERA campaigns). But as much as The Dominican Dandy owned the 1960s and Fernando Valenzuela would dominate in the 1980s, so too did Cuban Luis Tiant, Jr., seize the 1970s as his very own stage for individual excellence.

"Looie" Tiant's pitching career was seemingly sealed by birthright and family heritage, yet marked at the same time by an agonizingly slow start and then dogged even after retirement by an unfortunate set of continuing ironies. The younger Tiant flashed early brilliance much like his ill-fated father had decades earlier. Inked to a first professional contract with the Mexican League's Mexico City Tigers by former Cleveland Indians batting star Beto Avila, Tiant toiled two seasons "south of the border" before Cleveland acquired his rights for $35,000. Following strong minor league stints at Jacksonville (International League), Charleston (Eastern League), and Burlington (Carolina League, where he hurled a no-hitter in 1963), the promising Cuban made his first big splash at Portland where he set a Pacific Coast League record for winning

Cuba's Tony Taylor logged 2,195 games across 19 seasons in the majors, the most of any countryman outside of Tony Pérez, Bert Campaneris and Rafael Palmeiro (courtesy Transcendental Graphics).

percentage (15–1, .938). The AAA performance was a springboard to the majors, where he joined the parent club midway through the 1964 American League season. His big league debuts in Cleveland and Minnesota were largely a woeful tale of unfulfilled potential, however; Tiant won 20 games only one time with the floundering Indians franchise (in 1968, when he also paced the AL with a brilliant 1.60 ERA), but he also lost 20 the following summer and was peddled off to Minnesota as a result. Thus after only a half-dozen seasons in the majors Tiant had already duplicated a dubious feat also claimed by his best known Cuban predecessor. Dolf Luque had ironically also posted back-to-back 20-won and 20-lost seasons in his fifth and sixth campaigns as a big league regular; although Luque most fortuitously had turned the trick in the reverse (more satisfying) order.

Then came a fateful stop at venerable Fenway Park, a fortuitous career detour which led to exploding nationwide stardom and a niche as one of the fabled Boston franchise's most popular all-time players. Tiant was assured a firm place in diamond history by his heady 1972 and 1975 seasons alone. During the former campaign the flamboyant cigar-puffing Cuban again reigned as AL ERA champ, fashioning an eye-catching 1.91 standard this time around; during the latter summer he paced the pennant-bound Red Sox with 18 victories and then earned a crucial Series-tying complete-game win in Game Four of the Fall Classic. Tiant was also immortalized (like only Stengel and Berra before him) by his colorful mangling of the English language ("Ees great to be weeth a weiner") and his eccentric non-stop off-the-field cigar puffing — albeit in Tiant's case the eccentric images most assuredly carried strong racial and ethnic overtones. Branded by a twisting mound delivery that recalled and even rivaled his father's, and continuously puffing on his huge black Havana cigars (even in the clubhouse whirlpool or shower), Luis Tiant, Jr., was an all-too-perfect reflection of an imagined outlandish figure on which most dominant myths about eccentric Latino ballplayers had always seemed to thrive.

Once his active playing days ended, Luis Tiant, Jr., settled back to endure an arduous wait for Cooperstown recognition earlier denied his under-appreciated father. But that wait would turn into a lengthy and seemingly unjust ordeal. The timing, for one thing, was all wrong. When Cuba's most successful big-league hurler (with his 229 wins and 2,416 career strikeouts) first became eligible for Cooperstown election in 1988 he received only 47 votes from a panel seemingly far more disposed in recent winters toward balloting for long-ball slugging heroes than polling for dominant pitching aces. And in the stretch of years that followed, Tiant would have to contend as well with a glut of eligible pitching immortals (first Palmer, Perry, and Jenkins, and later Seaver, Carlton, Niekro, Fingers and Sutton) stacked up for Cooperstown consideration. And the endemic lack of respect often facing Latino stars would perhaps also once again play a not insignificant role. Immortality Cooperstown-style will almost certainly be Tiant's fate somewhere down the line, although it may well take the baseball writers (or members of the much-maligned Veteran's Committee, who can also confer glory at the ballot box), a few additional years to sanction what most fans already know with their collective wisdom. Statistically as well as artistically, only Marichal (who alone, along with Dennis Martínez, leads Tiant in victories, yet trails the Cuban for honors as all-time Latin American strikeout king) was a more accomplished Latino big-league pitcher.

If Latins were a big part of the major league baseball story during the fifties, sixties and seventies, they were nonetheless painfully tardy in integrating the hallowed halls of the sport's best-known shrine at Cooperstown. Clemente got there quickly enough, but only by way of an aberration brought about in the tragic wake of his untimely death. Marichal was next to relish enshrinement, but it was enshrinement that was much longer delayed (due largely to the aftertaste of an untoward bat-wielding attack on Dodgers catcher John Roseboro) than it likely should have been. Aparicio and Carew were the only two Latin American headliners who seemed to make it into Cooperstown's hall of heroes in a timely and routine fashion. Dihigo snuck into Cooperstown in 1977 largely unnoticed, just as he had always been unnoticed by American fans throughout his long and glorious career on backwater black league diamonds. Finally there was Puerto Rico's Cepeda

(1999) and then Cuba's Tony Pérez (2000) to expand the inventory of Latino idols ever so slightly. But in both cases the long-overdue recognition of these two seventies-era sluggers did not come without its own considerable infusions of heated controversy. Before Pérez belatedly broke through, Cuba remained deep in the shadows without a single organized baseball hall-of-famer. For Martín Dihigo was regrettably, through no fault of his own, not even a legitimate big leaguer.

An interesting contrast in playing style and career reputation is provided by Orlando Cepeda, Puerto Rico's "Baby Bull" who held a bigger spot in the hearts of San Francisco fans than even the incomparable Willie Mays, and Cuban slugger Tony Pérez, heavy-hitting infielder with the Big Red Machine Cincinnati Reds of the early and mid–1970s. Pérez slugged baseballs throughout the 1970s in Cincinnati just as Cepeda had done on the west coast during the 1960s, and in the end Pérez and Cepeda briefly stood apart as all-time Latin American home run leaders with 379 career round-trippers apiece. Yet while Cepeda was continually plagued by his destined lot with unappreciative and racist manager Al Dark in San Francisco, Pérez was blessed by his association with one of the most glamorous teams of the modern era. For half a dozen glorious summers at career's height Tony Pérez showcased his heavy-hitting wares in the constant media glare created by hall-of-fame teammates Johnny Bench and Joe Morgan, as well as the once-beloved (if now banished) Pete Rose. A personal-best 1970 season with high-water marks in four major hitting categories (40 HRs, 129 RBI, 107 runs, .317 BA) was sufficient to ignite a National League championship year with the powerhouse Reds contingent. Pérez in the end would appear five times in World Series play with Cincinnati (1970, 1972, 1975, 1976) and Philadelphia (1983). By career's close Pérez outstripped Cepeda in all major hitting departments save homers and batting average.

In the end it was the indelible image of a true winner, plus an always cordial relationship with working media and irreproachable personal lifestyle that stamped the Cooperstown credentials of Tony Pérez, even if those credentials were partially obscured by the glitter of several equally illustrious Big Red Machine teammates. Pérez's first Cooperstown votes (1992) totaled 215 of the needed 323, then a second time around (1993) 233 of the required 318; the numbers increased slight each subsequent January, even if they fell tantalizingly short with each passing year of the decade. By contrast, Cepeda remained a tarnished candidate in the general public perception, despite the fact that he actually outpolled Pérez in each of the three Cooperstown ballot counts where they squared off head-to-head (246–215 in 1992, 252–233 in 1993, 335–263 in 1994). With a spiffier public image like Tony Pérez, Cepeda would doubtless have much earlier been a hall-of-fame shoe-in. Once Cepeda's candidacy finally expired with the BBWAA elections of 1994, thus eliminating the obvious vote-splitting factor plaguing both Latino first sackers, Pérez eventually won enshrinement without having to wait for special backdoor sanction from the less universally respected Cooperstown Veterans Committee.

Whereas Cepeda had the clear misfortune of playing several seasons with bigoted skipper Al Dark and the racially insensitive SF Giants, Pérez was truly blessed with a slot on the Big Red Machine, positioned alongside hall-of-famers Joe Morgan and Johnny Bench. One recalls, however, that Tony Pérez did equally as much as Morgan, Bench, Rose, Foster, Concepción and Griffey to add true muscle to a bold Big Red Machine lineup that terrorized senior circuit rivals at the close of the 1960s and onset of the 1970s. When he finally hung up his spikes after 23 seasons in 1986, he was the number 14 RBI man in baseball history; for a full decade (1967–1976) he cemented an unparalleled Cincinnati batting order, six times topping 100 RBI (Bench also registered six 100-RBI seasons during the same stretch); during his decade anchoring the Cincinnati infield the Reds managed four pennants; his greatest single season (1970) matched Bench's (also 1970, with 45 HR, 145 RBI, .293 BA) and thus provided Sparky Anderson's champion Reds with one of the greatest single-season slugging tandems ever.

It is a difficult and perhaps pointless task to ferret out who was greatest between these two premier Latin sluggers of the 1960s and 1970s. Appropriately they finished lengthy careers tied with exactly 379 homers each, a Latino high water mark soon challenged and overhauled by Cuban-Americans Canseco and Palmeiro and then obliterated by Sammy Sosa. Pérez perhaps boasts superior hall-of-fame credentials in the eyes of an untutored fandom that mainly recalls pennants won and World Series appearances, alongside home run and RBI totals. Pérez also maintains a slight edge in rosy public image (an edge established as much by absence of off-field scandals or rumors of clubhouse agitations as by post-season heroism or any miniscule advantage in general slugging totals). Cepeda does, nonetheless appear to maintain a faint superiority in yearly batting totals, especially if one considers efficiency (batting and slugging averages, HR and RBI per game ratios, .300 seasons, and years with league-leading totals) and not mere raw power numbers.

Tony Pérez finally found his way into Cooperstown in 2000, several years later than may have been appropriate. Cepeda and Pérez will assuredly be joined among the immortals by Sosa (especially if he crosses the 600-homer plateau) and by Palmeiro (despite some delays inspired by a 2005 steroid-use suspension). Canseco is less likely ever to see the inside of Cooperstown, and this has less to do with his own late career image as flagrant substance-abuser and more to do with his on-field performance, which was admirable but hardly ever Ruthian or even Sosa-like. Sosa is without question the top Latin American slugger by raw numbers, though familiar questions of steroid use may also taint the Dominican idol's legacy of three 60-homer seasons. Debate between the others (Palmeiro versus Cepeda versus Pérez versus eventually Albert Pujols) is the classic stuff of winter hot stove league fare.

Comparison of career numbers between Pérez and Cepeda demonstrates considerable equality when it comes to judging relative hall-of-fame credentials. Once a trio of more recent batsmen — Sosa, Palmeiro and Canseco — are brought

Bert Campaneris with the author before a midsummer Cuban old-timers' game at Miami's Pro Player Stadium, September 1997.

into consideration the picture may indeed alter slightly relative to selecting a mythical all-time leader from within the ranks of Latino lumbermen. Sammy Sosa has charged to the head of the pack when it comes to home run numbers and the Cubs superstar will likely lengthen his lead substantially before his now rapidly fading career winds down completely. Canseco enjoyed only a brief period on top of the heap in several power categories. But the biggest surprise at the close of the millennium had to be Canseco's fellow Miami-Cuban compatriot, Rafael Palmeiro. Not even deemed worthy of comparison to the big guns a few years back, Palmeiro has ridden a late-career surge to astronomical numbers that almost assure his Cooperstown election by already positioning him as more than the equal of either Cepeda or Pérez. The jury may still be out on both Palmeiro and Canseco, but most of the evidence is already firmly in hand.

It is indicative of a still somewhat marginal acceptance for modern-era Latino ballplayers that so much controversy swirled around the Cooperstown candidacy of both Cepeda and Pérez. The former long remained tarnished by a single

Comparison of Top Latin American Major-League Sluggers

Category	Pérez (Cuba)	Palmeiro (Cuba)	Canseco (Cuba)	Cepeda (PuertoR)	Sosa (DomR)
Career	**23 years**	19 years	16 years	17 years	16 years
Games	2777	2721	1811	2124	2138
At-Bats	9778	**10,103**	6801	7927	8021
Runs Scored	1272	**1616**	1140	1131	1383
Base Hits	2732	**2922**	1811	2351	2220
Doubles	505	**572**	332	417	340
Triples	**79**	38	14	27	43
Home Runs	379	551	446	379	**574**
HR Pct*	3.87	5.45	6.56	4.78	**7.15**
RBI	1652	**1775**	1358	1365	1530
RBI/Game	0.594	0.652	**0.750**	0.643	0.716
RBI/100 ABs	16.9	17.6	**19.9**	17.2	19.1
Total Bases	4532	**5223**	3473	3959	4668
Batting Ave	.279	.289	.266	**.297**	.277
.300-Plus Yrs	3	6	2	**9**	4
Slugging Ave	.463	.517	.516	.499	**.545**
On-Base Pct.	.344	**.372**	.356	.353	.348
Bases on Balls	925	**1310**	861	588	856
Strikeouts	1867	1305	1867	1169	**2110**
Ks/100 ABs	19.1	**12.9**	27.5	14.7	26.3
Stolen Bases	49	95	198	142	**233**
World Series	**5**	0	3	3	0

Leader among Latin American sluggers in Bold Face

*Home Run Percentage = Home Runs per each 100 ABs (cf. *Total Baseball*, Thorn and Palmer, 1993)

Statistics for Rafael Palmeiro and Sammy Sosa are complete through the end of the 2004 MLB season.

post-career escapade (his 1975 conviction for marijuana possession) while the latter fell victim to playing on a celebrated team where he was but one of a half-dozen candidates for designated immortality. Pérez would suffer through a full decade of unsuccessful Cooperstown ballots precisely as Gil Hodges has long suffered in the eyes of skeptical Cooperstown voters; with Brooklyn teammates Robinson, Reese, Snider and Campanella already tabbed as immortals, how much of a giant could Gil Hodges actually have been? At least that was what logic seemed to dictate to balloters, first on the sportswriters panel and later the Veterans Committee, who year after year have bypassed Hodges in the annual voting. So goes the reasoning for many who throughout the nineties would debate the legacy of Tony Pérez, a workman-like hero who was similarly buried by an avalanche of Big Red Machine sympathy for flashier stars like Pete Rose, Joe Morgan, and Johnny Bench. For eight consecutive winter ballots the proud Cuban slugger finished consistently in the top four vote-getters before finally hearing a belated summons to overdue enshrinement in January 2000.

*   *   *

The Cuban presence in the big leagues faded rapidly by the late seventies and the early eighties. Those who had escaped Castro in the early years of the revolution were now retiring (Pascual in 1971, Oliva in 1976, Cuéllar in 1977, Tiant in 1982, Campaneris in 1983). Only four Cubans — Minnie Mendoza, Oscar Zamora, Orlando González, Bobby Ramos — entered the majors in the entire decade of the 1970s and none

were memorable. But there was still a slight trickle as the eighties witnessed a modest upswing to eight newcomers claiming at least Cuban heritage if not a birth site on the island. The number included a handful of Cubans who had left the island with their parents as infants — most notably José Canseco and Rafael Palmeiro.

Born in the Havana neighborhood of Regla and raised in Miami, José Canseco hardly matches the prototype of a classic Cuban ballplayer. González Echevarría cites veteran Havana sportscaster Eddy Martin reporting that his island countrymen normally refer to Conseco as *el pesado* (the boor) in light of his widely reported off-field peccadilloes. Most old-time Cuban fans look askance at Canseco as an immature player who generated little national pride for all his substantial on-field achievements. There is also the telling fact that Canseco did not grow up on the island and therefore did not hone his baseball talents there. For most Cubans back home Canseco is hardly ever mentioned among the U.S.–based pro ballplayers they proudly claim as their own.

Yet of modern-day players actually born on the island — especially among those who have played at the major league level, where indelible yardstick statistics are always available to underscore any batter's or pitcher's on-field achievement, Canseco is hard to ignore in any listing of the most substantial Cuban ballplayers. Three big league seasons with better than forty homers, two campaigns topping 120 RBI, and bragging rights as baseball's first 40–40 man (homers and steals in the same season) seem sufficient to stake any claim to lasting greatness.

González Echevarría even suggests that Canseco's rare combination of home run power, batting average and base path speed probably make him "the best Cuban baseball player ever" (*The Pride of Havana*, 360), yet for González Echevarría no player (for example, as Dihigo or Silvio García or Omar Linares or any of the numerous Olympic heroes) is to be considered for such deification without a major league stamp of approval. Certainly it can be said that Canseco has piled up numbers that serve to elevate him among the best of Latino-born sluggers.

José Canseco in the end is perhaps best compared to Tany Pérez. They both fit a similar prototype of the durable, muscular fence-buster who could produce needed runs in the clutch, often surprised with his adept fielding and sound base-running, and posted more than one MVP–quality season with pennant-bound ball clubs. After his first half-dozen seasons in Oakland as a "Bash Brothers" partner of Mark McGwire, Canseco did seem poised on the doorstep of true legendary status; when he overhauled Pérez and Cepeda's joint record for homers by a Latin American he still appeared fit for a bronze plaque in Cooperstown. But Sosa and Palmeiro have already usurped Canseco's temporary slot in the pantheon of Latino sluggers. And when several attempts at hanging on in Chicago, Tampa Bay and New York long enough to reach the magic number of 500 round-trippers met with failure, it was already beginning to appear likely that Canseco's future status in the history books would be more reminiscent of Dave Kingman or Dave Parker than it would of Gehrig, DiMaggio, or Cepeda.

Texas Rangers (ten seasons) and Baltimore Orioles (seven seasons) first baseman Rafael Palmeiro presents a case largely parallel to that of José Canseco. Of course Palmeiro has never sported the troublesome "bad boy" reputation that has remained Canseco's calling card and by contrast has quietly accumulated persuasive Cooperstown numbers with only a bare minimum of notoriety (at least before his 10-game suspension in mid–2005 after a positive drug test revealing use of banned supplements). But their resumes are otherwise nearly parallel.

Born in Havana but raised in Miami (where his parents fled when he was a toddler), Palmeiro found his way to the majors through the U.S. collegiate ranks as a slugging teammate of Will Clark at Mississippi State. Once in the big time the handsome southpaw swinger has never stopped hitting with machine-like proficiency. Consistency as been the recognized trademark of Palmeiro's game: he paced all big leaguers in games played in the 1990s, while smacking 20 or more homers every year between 1991 and 1999, and also posting six .300-plus averages during the same decade. Palmeiro has not only now superseded all of Canseco's top offensive numbers (100-plus more homers, 1000-plus more hits, 500-plus more runs scored), but he has outperformed both Pérez and Oliva to boot. He will never own three batting crowns like Tony Oliva, and it doesn't seem likely now that he will ever make it to a World Series. Cooperstown enshrinement, on the other hand, now looms as a sure thing for the all-time Latin American

leader in runs, hits, double, RBI and total bases (only Sosa may still catch him in the latter category). Yet Palmeiro is again (just like Canseco) a player who can only be legitimately deposited among the true Cuban stars on a mere technically of birthplace alone.

There have been other first and second generation Cubans who have poked their way into the majors throughout the nineties. Many of these are Cubans by bloodlines (American-born children of Cuban refugees and even of Cuban ballplayers) yet have little first-hand connection with the island and its baseball traditions. Most were raised in the Miami Cuban community or sometimes in more scattered parts of the United States.

Alex González, veteran shortstop with Toronto and later the Chicago Cubs, was born in Miami to Cuban parents. Fernando Viña with the Cardinals (earlier with the Brewers) is also the product of Cuban parents but was born and raised in Northern California. Right-hander Alex Fernández, who pitched with the White Sox and Marlins, and Alex Ochoa, who flashed brief promise with the Mets, boast similar family backgrounds. Orestes Destrade, a four-year performer with the Yankees, Pirates and Marlins and also a headliner in the Japanese Pacific League, was actually born in Santiago de Cuba but was again raised in South Florida. Outfielders Danny Tartabull (son of big leaguer José Tartabull and himself a native Puerto Rican) and Rubén Amaro (whose Mexican-born father of the same name also performed in the majors, while his grandfather Santos Amaro was a Mexican League standout of the forties) also can be added to this list of U.S. pros who boast a solid Cuban baseball heritage. Bobby Estalella (part-time catcher with the Phils and Giants in recent seasons) is a grandnephew of pioneering Washington Senators and Philadelphia Athletics slugger Roberto "Tarzán" Estalella; Eli Marrero, Cardinals backup receiver of the past few summers, claims precisely the same blood relationship to Conrado Marrero. Veteran first baseman David Seguí is a son of 1960s-1970s Cuban big league hurler Diego Seguí; journeyman outfielder Eduardo Pérez (lately in St. Louis) is the son of Cooperstown immortal Atanasio Pérez. Taken as a whole these contemporary players are perhaps only a weak link — but a true link nonetheless — to the ongoing Cuban big league legacy.

The biggest Cuban baseball story of the nineteen-nineties (big league story, that is) has to be the celebrated post-season pitching heroics of Liván and "El Duque" Hernández, along with the additional tiny trickle of recent dollar-seeking Cuban League defectors who have now made their way into the major leagues. These most recent island imports (especially pitchers Danys Báez and José Contreras) have substantially diverted media and fan interest from more Americanized Cubans like Canseco, Palmeiro or Eli Marrero, both in the Miami Cuban-American community and most certainly back in Cuba itself. The subject of Cuba's late–20th century and early–21st century baseball defectors is, however, fodder for a separate chapter and must therefore be postponed for later telling.

References and Suggested Readings

Bealle, Morris A. *The Washington Senators: The Story of an Incurable Fandom*. Washington, D.C.: Columbia Publishing Company, 1947.

González Echevarría, Roberto. *The Pride of Havana: A History of Cuban Baseball*. New York: Oxford University Press, 1999.

Lieb, Frederick G. *Baseball As I Have Known It*. New York: Coward, McCann and Geoghegan, 1977.

Oliva, Tony, with Bob Fowler. *Tony O! The Trials and Triumphs of Tony Oliva*. New York: Hawthorn Books, 1973.

Rogosin Donn. *Invisible Men: Life in Baseball's Negro Leagues*. New York: Atheneum, 1983.

Rucker, Mark, and Peter C. Bjarkman. *Smoke: The Romance and Lore of Cuban Baseball*. New York: Total Sports Illustrated, 1999.

Thorn, John, with Jules Tygiel. "Jackie Robinson's Signing: The Real, Untold Story" in: *The National Pastime 10* (1990), 7–12. Cleveland: SABR Publications.

Tiant, Luis, and Joe Fitzgerald. *El Tiante: The Luis Tiant Story*. Garden City, NY: Doubleday and Company Publishers, 1976.

Tygiel, Jules. *Baseball's Great Experiment: Jackie Robinson and His Legacy*. New York: Oxford University Press, 1983.

11

The World's Best Unknown Ballplayers

Perhaps the seminal English-language history of Cuba's national pastime contains what amounts to an extensive polemic disputing the legitimacy of Castro-era Cuban League baseball. In his widely reviewed *The Pride of Havana* (1999), Yale literature professor Roberto González Echevarría advances his belabored thesis that the "greatest failure of Cuba's post-revolutionary baseball comes from what only can be termed an 'epic deficiency' ... epic deeds need to be absolute in their greatness, unsurpassed in the strength, skill, and valor of the heroes who perform them" (p.366). At the outset of his final chapter — one that gives short shrift to contemporary Cuban baseball — González Echevarría unfolds his assertions that today's modern-era Cuban "amateur" league — a thinly disguised professional circuit by all reasonable measures — has little merit as top-level competitive baseball when held up to comparisons with major league teams, or even top-flight minor league circuits. Nor, furthermore, does today's island sport withstand a healthy comparison with the professional Cuban League of the professor's own forties- and fifties-era Havana youth.

Modern-era Cuban baseball, as González Echevarría sees it, represents a distorted and even distasteful employment of athletic contests for international political gain and thus closely parallels a Soviet-style model for organizing national sports machinery developed by Moscow at the mid-century height of the Cold War. Celebrated Cuban victories in world championship tournaments are not only seen as tainted in their propagandistic thrust, but also as holding little raw value given that they represent hollow victories over low-quality and thus thoroughly unworthy opponents. In making his argument the ex-patriot critic adopts a worn mantra that USA entries in world baseball tourneys for much of the past century have usually been lackluster clubs of untested college stars — that is, little more than rank amateurs.

Since Cuban ballplayers fall far short of major league quality (at least by González Echevarría's strict yardstick) the entire enterprise of league and Olympic play must have relatively little value for Cuban fans and even less status in the grander baseball universe at large. For Professor González Echevarría, as for most stateside ballpark devotees, the North American major leagues are the only true standard for measuring first-rate or legitimate baseball talent. And only top talent can provide top spectacle.

In simplest terms, for González Echevarría it apparently all comes down in the end to the issue of an objectively measured level — or at least a universally perceived level — of physical ball-playing skills. Cuban star slugger Omar Linares may be hyped as a near-equal to Brooks Robinson or Mike Schmidt by sympathizers and mouthpieces of the Cuban League; he may be adored by multitudes of Cuban fans; but just who has Linares faced, and on what playing fields has he achieved his reported feats of clutch hitting or rung up his legendary statistics? The baseball universe has, after all, its absolute yardsticks. Cuban national team victories so often touted by Fidel and legions of Cuban fans have been earned exclusively against little-prepared and inferior competition that often has consisted of raw and inexperienced American scholastic squads or Dominican, Japanese and Korean teams already picked clean of any budding pro prospects. Everyone knows, after all, that all the best young players from other sectors of the world (especially in baseball-crazy countries like the Dominican Republic, USA, Venezuela or Japan) turn professional at the earliest opportunity. Any Class AA team from U.S. organized baseball could naturally be expected to drub most editions of America's Olympic nine and thus could likely also handle the best Cuban national squads on a regular basis. At least thus runs the argument as presented in *The Pride of Havana* and all similar tomes (most North American press accounts, for example) celebrating baseball's professional enterprises.

But in strict fairness, González Echevarría's argument does seem also to boast a more sophisticated theoretical dimension to underpin it and carry it home. Or at least it offers the surface appearance of just such a philosophical position. This position appeals to the mythic trappings that cloak all sporting events, both amateur and professional. Epic heroes — whether drawn from the battlefield, the sports stadium, or the arena of political enterprise — are all sustained in the end by their relative stature within a culture; and it can be argued that this is especially true of our athletic heroes. We speak here of the dimension of "epic deficiency" attached to today's Cuban baseball as Professor González Echevarría assesses it. Epic heroes in classical literature (and by extension those in primitive if not also in modern cultures) hold their status because they have in the collective mind's eye demonstrated strength, skill and valor superior to anything else existing in the known universe. To qualify for such status, then, top-flight athletes must compete against and dominate only the very best that the known world has to offer. By this measure the Cuban League is, for González Echevarría at least, an unqualified failure. (Linares and company face the Australians and South Koreans, not the Yankees, Cubs and Tigers.) He cites as examples the cases of countless amateurs and minor leaguers in North American baseball lore (Clint "The Hondo Hurricane" Hartung of the early-fifties New York Giants serves as a prototype) who have earned in lesser leagues the highest praise (and often outrageous "bonus baby" contracts) and then failed to measure up to the standards of strenuous big-league competition.

The rhetoric is indeed engaging, but the thread of González Echevarría's argument is as hard to fathom as it is in the end to swallow. Is he simply claiming that the raw talent level (and thus by extension the proven performance level) is considerably higher in the major leagues than it is in international amateur championships? Or perhaps with NCAA baseball, or indeed anywhere outside of the major leagues themselves? Who after all would want to argue with this position? And what does it ultimately mean in the end? Millions who take pleasure in watching and even fanatically following NCAA college basketball instead of the NBA professional game, or who enjoy the intimate ballpark experience of lower-level minor league baseball, or who in other lands and other eras were devoted to the professional leagues of modern-day Japan or the long-lost Negro leagues of pre-integration days, all seem to provide viable exceptions to undercut any hypothesis that only top-level professional games can hope to satisfy sophisticated sports fans. College basketball junkies or fanatic minor league rooters could hardly feel cheated by the spectacle they watch simply because their heroes are not major leaguers. If the major leagues (or NBA, or NHL, or soccer's European Champions League) are the only leagues capable of creating and fostering true athletic heroes of legitimate or noble stature, then how indeed do we account for fanatic fan enthusiasm for minor league action across small-town rural America long before the age of television? Or the teeming devotion to Negro league players in thriving black neighborhoods from Kansas City to Baltimore during baseball's pre-integration days?

As one who relishes and defends the spectacle of Cuban baseball, I run head-on into this argument each time I try to explain to doubting listeners why the Cuban League ballgame is for me a far more enjoyable product than the version being sold to today's North American audiences by the corporate interests masquerading as organized baseball. I readily grant that the big leagues own far more talented athletes (not that some Cuban Leaguers might not indeed be big leaguers once given the opportunity, even if the majority are not). I grant also that the present-day structure of organized baseball offers wildly superior economic opportunities for its privileged athletes (though it arguably does so with many negative payoffs for the spectators who pay to watch them). But these are not my foremost measures of choice when assessing my ballpark pleasures. Baseball played in smaller and more intimate venues, with the absence of all-intrusive trappings of commercialism,

less electrified noise or blaring video distraction, and with a more leisurely pace and a far more competitive amateur spirit is to me more than a fair trade-off for slightly diminished levels of on-field skill. For me Cuban baseball is hands-down the most exciting brand of the sport anywhere available in today's baseball universe — and it all comes with an eye-catching level of talent to boot. I venture that few Cuban fans daily enjoying their own national pastime are in any sense crushed by the fact that it is not the big leagues. It is their baseball paradise, with its own extensive history, lore and epic heroes, and they embrace it with passion that is unsurpassed in any American city, where the local big league club now competes for attention with resident NFL, NBA or NHL franchises. One only needs to attend a single Cuban League game or immerse oneself in a heated street-corner debate among veteran fans in Havana's Central Park to grasp the raw baseball passion involved in Cuba's alternative baseball universe.

The element putting the final lie to González Echevarría's position about today's Cuban baseball is found in one of his own adjacent chapters. Earlier in *The Pride of Havana* (Chapter 6) González Echevarría convincingly establishes an indisputable fact that during the thirties and forties it was indeed amateur and not professional baseball that flourished as king of the island's sporting scene. In that earlier epoch the celebrity status of Cuba's pro stars — even if professional skill was a true measure of baseball legitimacy — had preciously little currency outside of Havana itself. In outlying towns the playing fields for sugar mill leagues were often of the most primitive construction, the grandstands were splintered plank, the uniforms were cheesy and tattered, the players were mostly local and hardly mythic in the epic sense González Echevarría prescribes as the standard for true heroism. But the local game was nonetheless unrivaled king for those legions of fans who had nothing else or little else to watch.

González Echevarría's "epic deficiency" thesis of course equally fails to account for the widespread popularity and viability of minor league baseball everywhere in the United States throughout the several eras before television hijacked and revamped the American sport. Or for the cherished blackball leagues that were a thriving centerpiece of black communities from coast to coast for more than three decades before integration at the past century's midpoint. Also for raw fanaticism among countless Japanese for their own sport of *besuboru* that long thrived in isolation (at least before the big league importations of Hideo Nomo and Ichiro Suzuki) after tours in the Orient by Babe Ruth, Lou Gehrig and Lefty O'Doul between the Two Great Wars. It also does little to explain why the professional Cuban League was nearly moribund by the middle and late fifties (a fact which González Echevarría partially excuses merely as the falloff in the Habana-Almendares rivalry after those two classic teams suffered dips in talent levels) while the newfound amateur circuit during the first decade after the 1959 socialist revolution brought teeming crowds and renewed passion to island stadiums which Cuban professional baseball had not witnessed for nearly two decades.

Yet there remains, nonetheless, at least one aspect in

which González Echevarría aims true in assessing baseball within contemporary Cuba. This is the observation that Cuban stars remain virtually unknown almost everywhere outside the closed world of Cuban League action, and thus that names triggering adulation in Havana or Camagüey or Cienfuegos have little or no currency whatsoever in other ballplaying nations. Outside of the widely celebrated Omar Linares — or a handful of big league defectors headed by Rey Ordóñez, José Contreras and the Brothers Hernández — American fans today know nothing of the current crop of Cuban ballplayers, leave aside the legendary stars of earlier decades, almost all of whom were relegated to the outlaw black leagues. There is a parallel here again, of course, with Cuba's popular amateur league stars of the 1930s and forties. Names that sparked endless discussion and impassioned debate in Havana during that bygone era would draw blank stares from American rooters — even in Cuban-infiltrated *barrios* throughout Miami Beach, Palm Beach, Key West or still further north in Tampa. Such anonymity elsewhere would hardly seem to make today's Cuban stars any less heroic or even less mythic for those who spend their lives watching them. Nor does it at all diminish the truly entertaining and competitive game that these ballplayers bring to the field of play. It is, nonetheless, a severe baseball loss for North American fans who have survived for decades thinking the true baseball universe is inevitably bounded by Yankee Stadium to the east, the Minneapolis Metrodome up north, Dodger Stadium out west, and Pro-Player Stadium down south.

* * *

A most lamentable circumstance surrounding Cuban baseball since the 1959 revolution is the fact that the island's numerous all-stars have rarely been seen or appreciated beyond Havana itself; it is a circumstance especially lamentable for fans throughout the world's other top baseball-loving nation — the United States of America. For four-plus decades a teeming fountainhead of rare baseball talent has remained effectively buried behind a Sugar Cane Curtain which still isolates Fidel Castro's Communist Cuba. Island stars the equal of journeyman big leaguers — and sometimes perhaps even near rivals of legitimate Cooperstown candidates — have come and gone across several decades without any more mention in the Yankee press than that received decades earlier by ghostly sluggers and shadowy hurlers performing in equal obscurity on America's hidden blackball circuits.

This is a regrettable circumstance that has begun to alter — however slightly — in recent summers. A handful of Cuban League defectors now performing in the major leagues, along with the two impressive performances by the Cuban national team versus the Baltimore Orioles, have together lately provided North Americans at least a passing glimpse of this untapped Cuban talent. Orlando Hernández with the Yankees and White Sox and Liván Hernández with the Marlins, Giants and Expos (lately the transplanted Washington Nationals) have inspired persistent rumors of perhaps dozens of such gifted pitchers idly waiting to be rescued by big league talent scouts from the apparent imprisonment of low-paid Cuban League careers.

Strapping young righty Danys Báez was reported to be incapable of making the starting rotation of his Cuban club back home in Pinar del Río (which featured José Contreras, Pedro Luis Lazo and venerable southpaw Faustino Corrales) before he jumped ship in Winnipeg (during the 1999 Pan American Games) yet only two years later was mowing down American League hitters for the Cleveland Indians. And stories have occasionally circulated in the stateside media that slick New York Mets (and later Tampa Bay Devil Rays) shortstop Rey Ordóñez originally defected as a teenager in 1994 largely because he perceived how slim his prospects were on the talent-rich island for garnering a spot on the elite national team. With the flashy Germán Mesa and the promising Eduardo Paret (first a star at the 1996 Atlanta Olympics and national team captain as late as the 2005 World Cup) already in line ahead of him, Ordóñez apparently saw the big leagues as a less difficult path to stardom.

Doubts of the kind voiced by González Echevarría may well be raised about the relative talents of, say, Omar Linares — Cuba's biggest diamond star of the post-revolution-era. But any such controversies are in the end little more than one of the irresistible charms of any baseball fan's off-season "hot stove league" sessions. The same tantalizing questions (Was Satchel Paige the equal of Lefty Grove? Or could Josh Gibson really be compared to Bill Dickey?) also dog Negro league stars of the 30s and 40s, now that they have been granted a belated second life in our baseball culture by modern-day revisionist historians; parallel debates also surround the Cuban leaguers of earlier generations who were also denied spots in the big leagues, either by racial restrictions (Oms, Dihigo and Torriente) or by personal choices to play on more familiar turf at home, or to gamble on more immediate financial rewards in Jorge Pasquel's cash-rich Mexican League of the mid-forties (Andrés Fleitas, Agapito Mayor, Juan Ealo or Quilla Valdés).

The plight of today's Cuban ballplayers does indeed parallel in rather eerie fashion the circumstances plaguing Negro leaguers during the sad days before organized baseball's belated progress toward racial integration. But during that era of exclusion at least there was a testing grounds for proving the parallel skills of excluded African-American and Afro-Cuban stars. Games matching barnstorming big leaguers in search of post-season paychecks against top black all-stars (Cuban and American) were October drawing cards in venues all across backwater America. Cuba itself was home to an integrated winter-season pro circuit that welcomed white major leaguers and talented Negro leaguers as teammates and rivals on big-league-level Cuban League rosters. Cristóbal Torriente did indeed face Babe Ruth in a sluggers' showdown in Havana in 1920, and also wreaked havoc with the best blackball pitchers up north for nearly two decades. Legendary Cuban hurler José Méndez did indeed face and at times thoroughly dominate touring contingents of Reds, Tigers, Athletics, Phillies and McGraw's Giants in a series of early-century "American season" Havana showdowns, even if these spirited games were only "staged" off-season exhibitions in which the motivations of the touring big leaguers might have been open to serious question.

But late–twentieth-century Cuban stars of the sixties, seventies, eighties and 1990s have been seemingly lost altogether to baseball fans residing anywhere outside of Cuba. Their fame has spread only as far as the island's compact shores. When the Cubans have taken their act on the road for top international tournaments, they have more often than not performed in European venues or in Australia or Taiwan — locales that would hardly be considered as center stage in the baseball universe. Even back home fame (to say nothing of financial fortune) for the top Cuban Leaguers has been muted somewhat by a reigning economic and social system that features little or no commercial advertising, few regular baseball publications, limited press coverage of the national sport, and nothing much in the way of media-fed celebrity glorification on a level expected in other sport-crazy nations. Cuba's eradication of professionalism in all sports has also meant the elimination of any commercial marketing of ballplayer-heroes as national treasures and thus envy-invoking popular culture idols.

Some recent stars of Cuban baseball have nonetheless enjoyed at least minor visibility on the North American scene. There has lately been exploding interest surrounding almost everything culturally Cuban. Ry Cooder's popular *Buena Vista Social Club* documentary film (followed by floods of spin-off CDs featuring earlier-generation Havana-bred salsa stars) first jump-started a minor North American craze surrounding long-dormant Afro-Cuban music. The ballyhooed Orioles-Cuba showdown series staged in March and May 1999 exploited an existing Cuban baseball mystique initially launched by inflated press accounts attached to Orlando Hernández — detailing El Duque's supposed dramatic flight by flimsy raft from communist tyranny and his subsequent miraculous rookie-season successes with New York's World Champion Yankees. The full-blown media circus chronicling absurd tug-of-war struggles between Miami-based relatives and Cuban authorities over repatriation of young Elian González spawned the most extensive U.S. interest in Cuba in more than three decades. At the same time, books like my own *Smoke: The Romance and Lore of Cuban Baseball* (with Mark Rucker), González Echevarría's *The Pride of Havana*, and S.I. Price's *Pitching Around Fidel* have raised consciousness about both the history and pageantry of the island's vibrant national pastime.

Continued big league success for both El Duque Hernández and half-brother Liván Hernández, along with the much-awaited Cuba-Orioles series — which for the first time matched the perennial amateur world champions against legitimate professional competition — cast an even brighter spotlight on the handful of top Cuban players who earlier reached U.S. soil either as political defectors or touring national team members. Nonetheless, North American fandom (in Canada as much as in the States) by and large remains woefully uninformed about the current state of Cuban baseball. And players who are true icons in today's Cuba still remain altogether unknown anywhere north of Miami.

Future big league ace Orlando "El Duque" Hernández in uniform with the 1992 Cuban Olympic champions.

Both the highest form of delight and the most egregious display of idleness in "hot stove league" discussions is to make comparisons between players from different eras (Lefty Grove versus Sandy Koufax) or from distinct baseball worlds (Josh Gibson up against Babe Ruth). Such speculations prove absolutely nothing in the long run, since the playing fields are never level and existing yardsticks are rarely relevant. But they are always a great deal of good pure fun, however inconclusive. And they always raise blood pressures of the participants at least a notch or two. This is just as true in the public squares and on the park benches throughout Cuba as it is anywhere else. I have been a frequent witness in Havana's *Parque Central* to many heated shouting matches among the local denizens over Ozzie Smith versus homegrown Germán Mesa, or Omar Linares as a certifiable big leaguer, or the merits of Havana-born Rafael Palmeiro for Cooperstown enshrinement, any of which would surely alarm a non–Cuban passer-by. Such debates — akin to small riots — often give the impression that blood will be spilt at almost any moment. Yet they are harmless daily occurrences that are the truest and most visible measure of fanaticisms inextricably attached to Cuba's favorite pastime.

What follows is a report on top Cuban League stars from the past decade, as well as from earlier periods, all of whom would likely have turned heads in the major leagues had a different political landscape allowed them to play there. This informal scouting report is offered in the spirit of the Hot Stove League debates that have long been baseball's greatest armchair pleasure. These are the players Cuban fans have worshipped and stateside fans have missed out on entirely. I emphasize before beginning that, unlike González Echevarría or Milton Jamail or the bulk of other observers of Cuban baseball here in the States, I do not for a moment bemoan the fact that these players have not been permitted by life's circumstance to earn untold millions of dollars in commercial baseball, or to gain a measure of fame and fortune beyond their homeland. I take no position on that issue, only observing that by staying at home these stars have likely provided far more ballpark pleasure and pride to Cuban fans than they would have as mere flickering television images beamed back from big league stadiums far from Cuban shores.

My regret — if there is one — is only that more true fans outside the rustic ballparks of Havana, Matanzas or Cienfuegos have not been able to witness and appreciate such exemplars of stellar ballpark play. And I regret also that I was myself unable to witness first-hand many of these island legends whose careers where already over (or largely diminished) before my own first regular island visits during the mid and late nineties.*

*   *   *

Omar Linares is always the first name raised when discussion turns to the grandest stars of contemporary Cuban baseball. Linares has easily been the most celebrated player both on and off the island, at least since the inaugural Olympic baseball tournament staged in Barcelona more than a dozen years ago. And many times over his considerable talent has been further colored by exaggeration or the aura of myth. But when all is said and done, Omar Linares almost assuredly was a far greater player than the amateur venues of world Olympic tournaments ever allowed him to demonstrate. I personally saw him for the first time at the Atlanta Olympics and became an instant believer. And nothing I have seen in Cuba (or at the 1999 Pan Am Games in Winnipeg and the 2000 Olympic Games in Sydney) over the final half-dozen years of his now faded career could convince me any differently.

Born on October 23, 1967, in rustic San Juan de Martínez, on the outskirts of Pinar del Río (Cuba's westernmost city), Linares inherited a valuable lineage from his athletic father Fidel, himself a noted star in the earliest years of the post–1960 Cuban League. Fidel Linares built his own Cuban

League legend by manning the outfield for two teams (Pinar del Río and Occidentales) across ten National Series seasons; the diminutive lefty-swinging outfielder also twice represented his nation on teams performing at the 1962 Central American Games (in Jamaica, where he batted .385 for a squad that limped home far out of medal contention) and 1963 Pan American Games (in Brazil, where his stellar defense contributed to a gold medal victory). But with only a .267 lifetime batting ledger and but eight career round-trippers, the elder Linares provided his greatest contributions to the Cuban national pastime in the persons of a pair of slugging offspring who would make their own indelible mark more than two decades after their father's 1971 retirement as an active player.

The baseball-playing genes that Fidel Linares passed down to a young Omar also visited his second son, Juan Carlos, a hard-hitting first baseman with Pinar del Río who has maintained an impressive 16-season .323 career batting mark while swinging from the left side like his lighter-hitting father. (Juan Carlos was retired as a player after the 2005 season and shipped to Nicaragua for coaching duties.) But neither pioneering father nor all-star brother were ever in quite the same league with the remarkable first-born Omar. Standing a shade over six feet and weighing around 200 during the most productive years of his career (1986–1996), Omar Linares fought through weight problems after several bouts with knee injuries in the final few seasons of the nineties. During late career years he thus took on the physical appearance of a right-handed dead ringer, in both stature and facial features (as well as batting prowess), for Cooperstown-bound big league icon Tony Gwynn. Always professionally courteous, even if exceeding soft-spoken and occasionally almost sardonic in dealings with international journalists, Linares remains even after retirement a fiercely loyal champion of the Cuban Revolution, which he unfailing praises for providing him with literally every opportunity and triumph that has come his way.

"El Niño" first broke onto the Cuban baseball scene in most dramatic fashion, appearing on the 1982 national junior team roster at a remarkable age of 14 and (despite his youth) batting a respectable if not eye-popping .250 during the Juvenile World Championships staged in Barquisimeto, Venezuela. That same fall the super-talented novice infielder surfaced as a raw Cuban League rookie with seemingly unlimited promise, appearing in 27 games for Vegueros (the team representing Pinar del Río) before his sixteenth birthday. Two seasons later, during a second Junior World Cup tournament — this time in Kindersley, Canada — the almost-18-year-

---

Some details of my time spent in Cuba might be necessary here to place my personal evaluations of recent Cuban ballplayers in more helpful perspective. My assessment of Cuban Leaguers is drawn from over forty trips to the island between February 1997 and November 2006, during which time period I witnessed in excess of 200 Cuban League ballgames either in person (visiting most of the island's regular league ballparks) or on Cuban television. I have also watched the Cuban national team extensively over the same span of nearly ten years, having viewed firsthand almost all tournament games either from the press box or grandstand, or on Cuban TV broadcasts, during each of the following events: 1996 Olympics (Atlanta); 1999 Cuba-Orioles series (Havana and Baltimore); 1999 Pan American Games (Winnipeg, Canada); 2000 Olympics (Sydney, Australia); 2001 World Cup (Taipei); 2002 Intercontinental Cup (Havana); 2003 World Cup (Havana); 2004 Olympics (Athens); and 2005 World Cup (The Netherlands).

I have also enjoyed personal contacts and numerous discussions with current Cuban League commissioner Carlitos Rodríguez (a personal and trusted friend); national team manager Higino Vélez; Cuban League managers Victor Mesa (Villa Clara), Jorge Fuentes (Pinar del Río) and Rey Anglada (Industriales); plus top Cuban League players Germán Mesa, Lázaro Vargas, Omar Linares, Javier Méndez, Juan Padilla, Yasser Gómez, Michel Enríquez, Pedro Luis Lazo, Eduardo Paret and Frederich Cepeda, among others. I also covered the 2005 World Cup tournament for the Havana-based Prensa Latina website and assisted with Cuban play-by-play radio broadcasts (serving as both statistician and spotter) beamed back to Havana from that most recent event.

old phenom first stunned international observers by crushing eight homers, blasting seven additional extra base hits, and posting a remarkable .511 BA to launch his burgeoning legend as perhaps the greatest world amateur tournament player of all-time.

Elevated to senior national team status by the mid-eighties, Linares appeared first in the Intercontinental Cup games at Edmonton in 1985, where he once more slugged away at a remarkable .467 clip for the nine-game tournament span. He next also lit up the Central American Games competitions held in the Dominican Republic the following year when he pounded the ball once more at a .497 clip; that same season he posted yet another glowing .457 mark in his first Amateur World Series (11 games) staged at Haarlem in The Netherlands. A year later at the late-summer Pan American Games in Indianapolis (while still but a teenager, though now a fully seasoned international circuit veteran) he maintained the remarkable momentum with an eye-popping .520 average (including a pair of triples) to outstrip the entire field of tourna-

ment sluggers, including potent future U.S. big leaguers such as Frank Thomas, Ty Griffin, Ed Sprague, and Tino Martinez. For an encore in October the prodigal teenager smashed 11 homers during Intercontinental Cup matches back in Havana as the loaded Cuban contingent again ran roughshod over yet another talented Team USA lineup, this one boasting future major leaguers Mickey Morandini, Chuck Knoblauch and Scott Servais, and mentored by University of Miami coaching legend Ron Fraser.

The exploding Linares legacy grew largely from an amazing collection of unparalleled batting achievements which began in the eighties and soon stretched across the decade of the nineties. Twice, in 1990 and 1993, he batted over .400 for a full season that included both the near-equivalent National Series (48 and 65 games) and Selective Series (63 and 45 games) campaigns; he completed four National Series schedules batting above the touchstone .400 plateau (admittedly all in the era of aluminum bats) and eventually reached 400-plus homers in only 1,700 games and 5,962 at-bats; his ratio of one round-tripper every 14.8 official at-bats thus rates favorably against the most legendary big-league bashers. Using *Total Baseball*'s telling Home Run Average calculation (homers per every 100 at-bats) as a yardstick and comparing Linares with veteran big league stars — admittedly a futile even if entertaining exercise — his 6.77 career mark would surpass all sluggers through the ages but McGwire, Ruth, Kiner and Killebrew.

But the oversized Linares reputation also grows from an uncanny ability to deliver in almost all truly clutch situations. In the slugfest gold medal shootout in Atlanta (1996) versus Japan, Linares saved the night with three booming homers, ironically after nearly proving the unfortunate "goat" with his crucial early-game throwing error that had let Japan back in the contest. In the opening Cuba-Orioles match in Havana (March 1999), despite coming off a season-long leg (calf-strain) injury that had limited his National Series play to only 30 games, and despite the dual handicaps of hitting for the first time with wooden lumber and debuting against major league pitchers, it was Linares unsurprisingly who delivered the crucial game-tying eighth-inning base hit.

A month later in Baltimore during Cuba's 12–6 pasting of the big leaguers, the veteran slugger reached base in every plate appearance, recording three singles, a double, and a pair of walks. After slumping badly throughout the Pan Am Games in Winnipeg during August of that same year, Linares unload at just the right moment (again against experienced professional hurling) with a vital homer in the do-or-die semifinal match with Canada that clinched Cuba's hard-earned qualification for the 2000 Olympic Games in Sydney. That Winnipeg homer, hit off of Canada's Mike Meyers, was indeed one of the most important long-balls in recent Cuban national team history. Veteran radio broadcaster Roberto Pacheco recalls the Linares late-inning blast as the ultimate highlight of his four-decade on-air broadcast tenure. Linares himself (in the pages of a recently published biography released during 2002 in Havana) recalls the Winnipeg circuit blast as his single brightest career moment, a landmark achievement among

Future Cuban League legend Omar Linares debuting in the National Series in 1982 with the Vegueros ball club at the remarkable age of less than fifteen. Linares would log 20 Cuban League seasons with 2,195 career hits in only 1,700 games.

Omar Linares's Career Cuban League Batting Records

*Seasons' totals include the National Series, Selective Series (1983–95) and Revolutionary Cups (1996–97)

Year	G	B.A.	H	R	2B	3B	HR	RBI	SLG	TB	SO/BB
1982–83	27	.247	19	12	3	1	0	4	.312	24	17/5
1983–84	112	.306	140	86	24	3	11	35	.444	203	55/37
1984–85	111	.364	160	96	24	11	18	59	.591	260	57/68
1985–86	96	.387	129	84	16	3	20	70	.634	211	39/67
1986–87	94	.341	116	88	14	2	24	59	.606	206	48/65
1987–88	94	.389	135	101	15	4	31	91	.723	251	33/63
1988–89	108	.377	160	106	21	2	36	87	.691	293	35/58
1989–90	110	.425	166	109	18	3	35	90	.754	295	46/87
1990–91	108	.374	136	109	23	3	26	75	.668	243	44/102
1991–92	107	.393	140	109	28	1	34	94	.764	272	36/107
1992–93	91	.423	129	91	18	5	26	73	.770	235	31/85
1993–94	99	.365	120	93	15	7	27	96	.699	230	29/93
1994–95	84	.357	100	93	19	0	25	71	.693	194	33/87
1995–96	95	.364	118	98	14	3	31	96	.713	231	44/88
1996–97	68	.387	91	69	16	2	23	63	.766	180	21/61
1997–98	61	.342	67	46	9	1	10	31	.551	108	18/48
1998–99	30	.272	28	21	4	0	2	12	.369	38	12/28
1999–00	92	.325	99	50	21	1	8	31	.479	146	31/75
2000–01	58	.390	71	47	14	1	9	40	.626	114	23/69
2001–02	46	.386	56	35	11	1	8	41	.641	93	21/29
Totals	**1700**	**.368**	**2195**	**1547**	**327**	**54**	**404**	**1221**	**.644**	**3842**	**675/1327**

his dozens and dozens of truly memorable clutch offensive performances.

The numbers posted by Linares in the Cuban League over 20 seasons (through the 2001–2002 campaign) are altogether staggering no matter what one thinks of aluminum bats or how quickly one dismisses the level of league competition. These numbers include a CL best-ever .367 batting average throughout nearly 7,500 plate appearances, 404 homers, 3,842 total bases, and 1,221 RBI. When early in the 2002 season the veteran Pinar del Río third sacker finally reached the 400-plateau (to stand alongside Kindelán and Lázaro Junco) he moved into third place all-time; he is also the league's top career run scorer and hitter for average, ranks second behind Kindelán in total bases, stands third in career hits, tops in slugging average (outstripping Kindelán by .644 to .600), second in intentional walks, and fifth in RBI.

But even the raw offensive numbers — impressive or even incomparable as they are — do not by themselves tell the complete story. Before finally being slowed by knee problems, excessive weight, and even a possible (if unacknowledged) dip in enthusiasm over the past few seasons, Linares was once clocked running 100 meters with 10.6 speed while dressed in full baseball flannels. His rifle-like right arm measured throws of over 90 mph to first base. His homers (especially in the days of aluminum bats) have been the stuff of legend in both Cuba and on the road during numerous international tournaments. But his spectacular fielding around third base has also been of a kind that would arrest the heartbeat of most veteran major league scouts.

There have been few if any players representing a more complete package among the thousands I have personally witnessed playing professionally, even at the big league level; and

I make this claim even though my brief experience watching Linares perform dates only from the final few seasons of his lofty career peak. I am most certain that he could have more than held his own on the same field with any shaky Cooperstown pretenders like Ron Santo, Scott Rolen or Jim Thome, or even with a fully legitimate hall-of-famer like Mike Schmidt. Many far more experienced bird dogs hold the same opinion and indeed it was a hot topic for debate when I shared a vantage point with a host of big league scouting acquaintances (including ex–big-league manager Preston Gómez and future Expos and Mets GM Omar Minaya) in Atlanta in 1996, and in both Baltimore and Winnipeg three summers later.

Many, even in Cuba, wrote Linares off his final few seasons, claiming his years of major productivity were far behind him. But despite limited play (46 games) during a final 2002 Cuban campaign, the wily veteran again turned it on during the post-season fray when he hit a spectacular .476 and helped carry Pinar del Río to the final game of a tense semifinal series versus upset-minded Sancti Spíritus. That final game of Linares' National Series career ended most fittingly (with two out in the bottom of the ninth) with his thunderous bases-loaded blast to deepest center field, a smash struck against phenom pitcher Maels Rodríguez that was only corralled by a spectacular game-saving, wall-crashing circus catch. Only a few days after the dramatic wrap-up of National Series #41 it was formally announced in the fine print of *Granma*'s limited sports report that the 35-year old Linares would be playing the upcoming 2003 campaign for the Chunichi Dragons of the Japanese Central League, thus becoming the first Cuban ballplayer sold to a foreign professional league in the full 40-year history of post-revolution baseball.

Linares was already performing remarkable feats in the

Cuban League and on the road in international play when he was still a mere teenager. These feats would quickly earn the nickname "El Niño" ("The Kid") that has subsequently stuck throughout a glorious two-decade career. It was in Canada in 1983 that he garnered his lasting moniker as "El Niño" — which drew largely upon his boyish appearance and young age, but which also prompted not entirely unreasonable comparisons with Cooperstown legend Ted Williams — the game's sanctioned greatest pure hitter and most perfectly disciplined slugger. Even an outspoken critic of contemporary Cuban baseball such as González Echevarría is at times almost effusive in his praise when the subject is the talent of Omar Linares. González Echevarría, in fact, seems to suffer considerable ambivalence about Linares, an ambivalence reflecting both his own anti–Castro political leanings and his simultaneous avowed pro–big-league stance. Downplaying the slugger's evident pro-ball potential, he nonetheless also exaggerates some of his loftiest international achievements (e.g., stretching the debut performance in Venezuela in 1982 from an actual .250 BA to an erroneous .307 mark). And commenting on the supposed decline of Cuban pitching and a resulting upswing in slugging in the eighties, the author of *The Pride of Havana* observes that "Linares, all by himself, could make pitching decline" (p.375–376).

Many outside Cuba have persisted over the years in labeling Linares as the greatest third baseman on the planet and also the best late–20th-century ballplayer not performing in the major leagues. The first contention can only stimulate much violent debate among major league purists, but the second will likely draw few serious counter-arguments. Linares, in the eyes of many, would almost assuredly have starred for a big league team if given the smallest opportunity. Major league third baseman Robin Ventura saw "El Niño" first hand back in 1988 as a member of Team USA at the Amateur World Series played in Italy. Ventura is quoted by *Baseball America* columnist Jim Callis in a 1992 Olympic preview article as saying that he had little doubt that the young Linares he saw back in 1988 could play successfully as an everyday big leaguer. Future Baltimore Orioles right-hander Ben McDonald, who pitched for the same 1988 Team USA, is also cited by Callis as claiming Linares had unquestionably the best arm at third base he had ever observed; McDonald later told this writer that assessment still stood, even including all the big leaguers he had subsequently faced.

Linares himself always adamantly denies that he would ever have desired or attempted to create (by abandoning Cuba) the opportunity for professional stardom. For him the thrill was always in playing for the greater glory of his beloved Cuban homeland. Cynics label him a "programmed pawn" of the Castro government and a victim of its dehumanizing sports machinery, and some even claim that he received special privileges such as fat pitches to hit simply because of his Communist Party loyalties. (The argument along these lines is muted, of course, by the fact that such favors were certainly not thrown his way by any USA, Japanese or Korean hurlers during international matches.) Yet those that have seen him in ac-

tion over the years and have solid basis for comparisons are quick to sing his ultimate praises. Ventura and McDonald certainly weigh in with a heavy opinion on the matter. And I myself have seen few better pure hitters (certainly Williams, Aaron, Mays and Bonds, but few others) or more naturally gifted infielders.

The slugging third sacker has posted singularly impressive statistics over the years and he has also performed legendary feats under immense pressures. (The entire Cuban nation lives and dies with almost every pitch in major international tournaments and stars like Linares therefore carry the weight of the nation on their shoulders with almost every Olympic or world championship at-bat.) One of the best among his vaunted performances on the international stage came in Baltimore on the heels of a season largely ruined by injury and nagging failures to return to past form. The numbers Linares has posted over the past two decades may mean relatively little as a true yardstick, given the career-long use of aluminum bats and the undeniable shortcomings of Cuban League and Olympic tournament play (at least before recent introduction of professional ballplayers). But it is nonetheless difficult to deny that Linares was a polished clutch player with remarkable natural abilities. His early career boasts consistent stellar hitting and dependable fielding in pressure-packed world tournaments. He rebounded brilliantly from a career-threatening slump at Winnipeg in 1999 and adjusted literally overnight to wooden bats and pro-level pitchers. In late-career campaigns Linares played injured, sometimes overweight, and increasingly shackled by the difficulty of sustaining his motivation and enthusiasm in a league that offers almost no financial rewards. But his talents in earlier campaigns were apparent beyond the realm of mere statistics; and his swan song outings in Atlanta, Winnipeg and Baltimore revealed time and again the oversized heart of a true champion.

It is hard for me to imagine a better all-around ballplayer performing anywhere without the immeasurable benefits of minor league and big league experience and coaching, or without the luxuries of perfectly groomed major league diamonds and pampered modern-era big league travel conditions. Cuban ballplayers, remember, travel on cramped yellow school buses and over pock-marked rural highways, under conditions rivaling those experienced by 1930s-era Negro leaguers, then bunk in sparse dormitories tucked under ballpark grandstands, and play on fields sometimes resembling untended sandlots. The non–big-league fields on which Omar Linares played only seemed to underscore his unparalleled talent. González Echevarría acknowledges that Linares did slug those three dramatic homers in the championship game of the Atlanta Olympics, but still derisively asks "against whom?" Such response seemingly misses the point entirely. When championships were on the line Linares seemed always to elevate his game to whatever level was necessary. His Atlanta blasts came against top Japanese professional pitching and not untried college scrubs. Future big leaguers like outfielder Jacque Jones, infielder Warren Morris and first sacker Travis Lee, who were anchoring Team USA in the same tournament, repeatedly failed to deliver against those same Japanese hurlers during Atlanta's semifinal match a day earlier. That fact alone should effectively close debate. To a smaller or larger degree Linares' achievements may be in some part a delusion caused by the level of competition performing on the same field with him down through the years. But in the end such natural abilities and spectacular performances are hard indeed not to apprehend or appreciate, no matter what type of venues may house them.

One can always cite the cases of New York Giants 1951 washout Clint Hartung and other spectacular major league busts, as does Roberto González Echevarría. These are the rare paragons of potential in lesser leagues who collapse spectacularly when they reach the recognized big-time. Yet the professor's easy downplaying of Linares by citing only big league standards in the end rings hollow. Others boasting more substantial credentials to judge baseball talent have been quick to tout Linares' skills. Fifties-era big league hurler and venerable Cuban pitching icon Conrado Marrero was one of those in his 1999 interviews with this author (Chapter 4). For Marrero, who once saw Martín Dihigo play and who faced the likes of Ted Williams and Mickey Mantle while toiling for the Washington American League ball club, is quick to label Linares the best post-revolution talent bar none and likely on a par with any big leaguer he faced in his own prime. Former major league manager and long-time scouting supervisor Preston Gómez has been still another among the Linares boosters. When told by the author of Marrero's assessments delivered in our lengthy Havana interview, Gómez was quick to add his own resounding second to Marrero's impassioned scouting report. The sage words of Gómez and Marrero are proof enough for me, even if my own eyes might prove unreliable touchstones.

When it comes to prognosticating potential big league stardom, rival Santiago de Cuba muscleman **Orestes Kindelán**— the all-time Cuban League home run leader — is a more difficult case to analyze. The thick-torsoed basher's impressive string of homers in Atlanta in 1996 (he led the Olympic tournament with nine impressive blasts) might well be discounted due to less-than-big-league pitching and the presence of rocket-launcher aluminum bats. As one clever *Sports Illustrated* scribe summed it up, Atlanta competition featured 133 often-mammoth home runs, non-stop pitching changes, and no broken-bat singles. Kindelán was assuredly a big leaguer, nonetheless, even once one recognizes that the bulk of his batting feats were achieved with aluminum wands. Nineties White Sox stalwart Robin Ventura was certainly not any less of a pro prospect when he was drafted from the Oklahoma State campus, simply because his collegiate 66-game batting streak was also a product of medal-assisted slugging. Kindelán's raw batting talent alone would seem sufficient to have guaranteed at least a major league trial during the years of his peak prowess. A case in point is the fact that organized baseball scouts climbed all over Habana Province third sacker Andy Morales (a nine-season .319 batter with 54 homers) when he defected from the island late in 1999, even if Morales was only a run-of-the-mill everyday player in Cuban League circles and

Santiago's Orestes Kindelán retired in 2002 with nearly 500 career homers and more than 1,500 life-time RBI.

was never a hitter remotely approaching Kindelán's level in either potential or actual achievement.

By career's end Orestes Kindelán had reached the elevated plateau of nearly 500 homers, all slugged in spacious stadiums and across a 21-year span that averaged between 75 and 90 annual games. Nobody in Cuba produced as much scoring: Kindelán himself tallied 1,379 times and is the league's all-time supreme RBI producer with 1,511. Defensively he was solid if not spectacular at first (earlier as a catcher) and it is tribute to his defensive skills that the Santiago slugger was used in most international tournaments as well as the Orioles contest in Baltimore as a position player and not a designated hitter. Few have ever hit balls as hard on a major league field as Kindelán did in Atlanta's Fulton County Stadium; one of his third-deck Olympic Games smashes was noted in the local press as easily the longest fly ball ever witnessed in the park's 30-year-plus history. It is difficult to doubt that any big league scout would have been thrilled with Kindelán's signature, even in later years when he was used mainly as a designated batsman.

Kindelán departed for Japan in "official retirement" after the 2001–02 National Series, playing briefly with teammate Antonio Pacheco on a Japanese semi-pro (industrial league) squad before returning home to Santiago as batting coach in time for the 2004–05 winter season. At the same time Linares was being loaned by INDER to the Central League Chunichi Dragons, Kindelán and Pacheco were farmed out as coaches — along with veteran national team stalwarts Germán Mesa and Luis Ulacia — a move clearly designed not only to reward loyal soldiers with coveted pro baseball salaries (unavailable to National Series players) but also to clear out slots on the potent national team roster for one of the best bumper crops of new prospects to arrive in years. As literal "payoff" for their string of international triumphs during the 1990s, this latest generation of superstars would be treated to a rare perk of overseas cash (80% of which returned to the Cuban government as was customary) for both training Japanese prospects (an INDER gesture of international goodwill) and also filling in as industrial league reserves. For Kindelán, however, the unexpected sports ministry handout of two cherished seasons abroad was balanced by the loss of a final few National Series seasons during which he potentially might further pad his already superior slugging records.

An impressive two-decade Cuban League career was now finally relegated to the pages of history, blighted only by the fact that INDER officials would not allow the league's all-time homerun king to suit up again even briefly in 2004 for a possible run at the still unattained 500 career plateau. It was a career — despite its disappointing end — that is matched for overall productivity throughout the eighties and nineties by none save Linares. Kindelán, like Linares, also always came up big in international tournaments season after season. He was the team slugging star in Atlanta for the 1996 Olympics, where he paced the field in both homers (7 in preliminary round games and a pair more in medal play) and RBI production. More than one of his stratospheric fly balls was widely believed among the longest ever witnessed in Fulton Country Stadium, the very park in which Aaron had overhauled Babe Ruth. And he authored numerous other moments of near-equal glory on the international scene, especially the vital home run (stroked against Team USA during the deciding contest) which ended an extended slump at the Pan American Games Olympic qualifying tournament in Winnipeg. Several times Kindelán has been batting champion of showcase tournaments (the 1998 World Cup matches in Italy and the 1990 World Cup in Edmonton top the list). A ratio of 98 international homers in 735 official ABs (one long ball every 7.5 times in the batter's box) also puts him squarely into Ruthian, Bonds-like or Aaronesque company. And his overall offensive numbers for career international tournament play would in the end fall only a fraction short of the ones Linares had posted.

Kindelán's Santiago teammate **Antonio Pacheco** never enjoyed the enthusiastic press notice accorded to Linares or Kindelán. For one thing he was never a flashy performer like the former, and he never boasted big power numbers or slugged eye-popping, towering fly balls like the latter. But

Pacheco was already a seasoned 10-year veteran of international tournaments by age 28, on the eve of the sport's debut in the Barcelona Olympics. He had already authored his own heroics on numerous occasions during international play. In the 1992 Olympic preview piece carried by *Baseball America*, Jim Callis refers to a then-unknown Pacheco as "another lethal hitter who would cause a bidding war among U.S. teams if he were available." A perennial league all-star second baseman, Pacheco was also a most durable (seemingly even indestructible) player. By the time his career was winding down at the end of the 1990s he had already become Cuba's all-time base hits leader (2,356) by a comfortable margin. He played for years with a top-flight team (Santiago de Cuba owned five league titles during his long service) and he himself largely made the difference between defeat and victory in a handful of those championships seasons. And Pacheco's remarkably consistent offensive production also left him at the top of a number of the Cuban career top-ten lists: fifth in runs scored, second in doubles, third in total bases, fifth in career average, third in RBI, as well as first in total base hits. And there were also the notable intangibles associated with a born on-field and off-the-field team leader.

Antonio Pacheco, Cuban League career base hits leader (2,356) and now manager of the Santiago de Cuba ball club, 2005 National Series champions.

Pacheco rose rapidly in stature in the Cuban League record books during his final several campaigns and ultimately would emerge as a kind of Cuban Pete Rose (in admirable on-field achievements, not in sordid off-field debauchery). Rarely among the league's two or three top hitters in any given single year, nonetheless he was never very far down the list. By shear longevity Pacheco, like Rose, would eventually overhaul all the top batsmen of past eras (Armando Capiró, Wilfredo Sánchez, Fernando Sánchez) to emerge as Cuba's all-time base hits pacesetter. At the time he moved on to better-paying industrial league games in Japan, Pacheco had left behind a legacy as one of the league's most solid all-around performers from any recent or distant era, even the current epoch in which Linares and teammate Kindelán were always grabbing most of the National Series headlines. Pacheco returned triumphantly to his home city in 2004 and directed his former team to an upset 2005 National Series title during his debut outing as rookie manager. Given his boundless popularity among the island's legions of fans, plus an unchallenged reputation as a loyal team soldier congenial to teammates and the Cuban press alike, it is not unreasonable to imagine Antonio Pacheco as Cuba's national team manager some day not too far down the line.

José Ariel Contreras— the most recent Cuban star to defect for major league riches — is a statuesque, jet-black and muscular "fireballer" who turned numerous big league heads back in May 1999 while stifling the lackadaisical Baltimore Orioles in Havana, and then did so again for an encore during crucial quarterfinal and final games at Winnipeg's Pan American Games tournament. On the latter occasion the stakes were raised measurably since a Cuban Olympic bid was now hanging tenuously in the balance. On tap first was the masterful 8-inning, 2-hit relief performance in Havana's Estadio Latinoamericano, played out before a huge, curious ESPN television audience back in the States, as well as fanatical radio and television throngs throughout the island. Three months later Contreras encored with an impressive domination (during a single 48-hour stretch) of big league and AAA hitters in Winnipeg's jam-packed Can West Global Park, clinching much-needed victories over the pesky Dominicans and formidable Americans. The latter two contests featured added pressures represented by team qualification for the Sydney Olympics and Pan American gold, which both rested squarely on the line. Legions of pro scouts were duly impressed at Winnipeg, even if most fans in the States saw or heard nothing of these clutch big-time performances. To appreciate Contreras's achievements during four brief seasons as pitching ace for the Cuban national team one only has to apprehend the pressures surrounding Cuban players back in their homeland whenever coveted trips to the Olympics or gold medals in the Amateur World Series, Pan American Games, or Intercontinental Cup are ultimately the prizes at stake.

When El Duque Hernández was first grilled by the New York press corps about the awe-inspiring experience of debuting in legendary Yankee Stadium, the refugee from the world's best amateur baseball had a ready-made answer. The American League playoffs or World Series were nothing, explained El Duque, compared with suiting up for his hometown Industriales club and facing arch-rival Santiago, before 55,000 screaming partisans at Havana's Latin American Stadium. For José Contreras the experience was altogether comparable: none among his several headlined outings against the Boston Red Sox during an American League pennant chase could represent any more of a heart-stopping, gut-wrenching moment than taking the mound for life-and-death games at Sydney or in Taiwan, with the shared dreams of an entire baseball-addicted nation of 11-million *fanáticos* attached to each and every toss.

Physically speaking, Contreras is a Lee Smith look-alike who — again reminiscent of the sure-bet Cooperstown reliever — was throughout ten National Series campaigns and eight Olympic-style venues an almost-always dominant force when any big game was on the line. No other Cuban pitcher has been used in so many crucial tournament situations during the recent history of international play. It was Contreras who was called upon for long relief in Havana versus the Orioles; it was also Contreras who was handed the ball for starting assignments twice in less than two days with Cuba's 2000 Olympic dreams about the crumble in Winnipeg (where the suddenly vulnerable Cubans had limped into the playoffs via a shaky 5–2 pool play showing); and it was inevitably the same Pinar del Río ace who was asked to deliver crucial semi-final wins (and thus lock-up an expected gold medal appearance) in Sydney during the 2000 Olympics and also at the 2001 World Cup in Taipei. The indomitable Cuban workhorse never failed on even a single occasion during these pressure-packed outings; Contreras's ability to deliver consistently in such trying settings was truly uncanny. His international tournament mark would by the time of his defection remain unblemished (13–0) and it was a record that had been earned with a true test by fire. For awhile at millennium's end it seemed that Team Cuba could only be toppled in vital matches (for example, the gold medal round at Sydney) when José Contreras was used up too early and thus no longer available for an ultimate sudden-death contest that represented the final championship clincher.

Equally hard-throwing **José Ibar** with Club Habana (the Havana Province team) was yet another paragon of pitching craftsmanship recently spawned by the fertile contemporary Cuban baseball landscape. For some knowledgeable scouts who roam the international circuit, José Ibar was — a year or two back — likely the most promising big league prospect in the entire Cuban arsenal.

Ibar suddenly emerged on the scene as a full-blown star several seasons back, after struggling to find himself during the early portions of his 16-year career. Entering the 1997–98 National Series (his true breakout campaign), at age 28 and with 11 seasons already under his belt, the portly right-hander boasted a 109–83 overall mark and a career 4.04 ERA; by year's end his career won-lost percentage had skyrocketed from a respectable .568 to an astronomical .603 (while his career ERA also plummeted to 3.77). Explanation for such a sudden turnabout — at least the one circulating in the streets of Havana — was simply that the Havana Province ace had finally shed excess pounds by overhauling his physical conditioning routine; yet it seems only logical that there had been something of a major attitude tuning in addition to any physical adjustments. Ibar did suffer a most disappointing setback in the Orioles series lid-lifter (honored with a starting assignment against the pros, he yielded a two-run homer to Charles Johnson in the second frame and was quickly lifted for Contreras) yet nonetheless made a huge splash later the same year at Winnipeg. There he earned redemption and then some by hurling a masterful near-complete game in the 3–1 semifinal triumph over Team Canada, with its loaded lineup of seasoned AAA and AA professionals. That Winnipeg outing came in one of the most memorable games in modern Cuban baseball history. Ibar's gutsy effort under trying circumstances (the game was briefly interrupted in the final frame but an on-field anti–Castro protestor who shamelessly charged the mound draped in a Cuban flag) assured Cuba of an all-important trip back to the Olympics in Sydney, where Castro's forces could once more defend the gold medal won handily in Atlanta.

Ibar was equally impressive in his initial outing against the MLB–flavored USA squad during Sydney's Olympics. His mastery of Team USA in the preliminary round (seven shutout innings with 10 Ks during a 6–1 victory) was perhaps the best performance by a Cuban against a talented American line-up since the legendary masterpiece unleashed by José Antonio Huelga against Burt Hooton in Colombia three full decades in the past. Ibar has been almost as rock-solid as Contreras when it comes to big-time tournament games with Cuba's national pride squarely tested. He boasts a 7–1 overall mark, with the lone defeat coming in his final major international outing at the 2001 Taipei World Cup (a 5–3 preliminary-round setback delivered by Japan). But he has done it with slightly different tools, relying mostly on tantalizing finesse and a devastating slider, while also featuring a fastball which is lively enough, but not quite in the same company as those scorched at helpless batters by Contreras or phenom Maels Rodríguez. There is no question that Ibar could have been the equal of Liván or El Duque in the big-time major leagues had he only gone that direction while still in the prime of such an impressive career.

No Cuban League pitcher as enjoyed more impressive consecutive seasons than José Ibar posted in 1998 and 1999, the first marking him as the only 20-game winner in Cuban League history, and the second falling only a pair of victories short of repeating that same unprecedented feat. Ibar's 20 victories in 1998 (with two more tacked on during league playoffs) was the top merit badge performance in Cuba until Maels Rodríguez bumped Ibar from the headlines with his glamorous strikeout performances of 2001 and 2002. Twenty wins is tough indeed to achieve in a Cuban League season, given the reduced number of games and the competitive balance among top teams. And Cuban pitchers are used differently and often even abused by major league standards. Starters often relieve on off-days and staff aces take the hill every three or four days, and always with the expectation that they will finish what they have started. Yet Ibar nearly won 20 two seasons running by ringing up 37% of his club's 1998 victory total and 35% for an adequate encore a season later. This was truly one of the most impressive individual feats post-revolution Cuban baseball has ever witnessed.

Pedro Luis Lazo joins the trio of contemporary hurlers who have most impressed MLB scouts catching at least brief glimpses of Cuban phenoms. An argument might easily be made that the easy-going and somewhat oversized Lazo (6–2 and 255 by official INDER measure) has been by consistency alone the most relentlessly effective Cuban League pitcher of the past five or six seasons. A huge bear of a man sporting a nevertheless gentle appearance and personality, Lazo has been all business on the mound the bulk of the time both in league games and foreign assignments. It has to be admitted that at times "King Kong" (his Havana handle) appears to lose concentration and is occasionally not the pitcher he otherwise might be (though this has rarely happened overseas). Part of the problem may be that Lazo's managers in Pinar del Río (Alfonso Urquiola, Jorge Fuentes, and now Juan Díaz) and on the national team (of late Higinio Vélez)) have never quite figured out how to best utilize his talents. He has thus shuffled back and forth between roles as a number one or number two starter (behind Contreras) in the National Series and a devastating closer or durable long reliever on the national team. That he has so easily made the transition between these distinct roles, with their vastly different demands, is perhaps as much a measure of his versatile talents as it is an excuse for any occasional inconsistencies.

Lazo, like Ibar or Contreras, has had his indisputably impressive moments, especially one pressure-packed outing in Winnipeg when he charged to the mound in the ninth to relieve Ibar and snuff out a final desperate ninth-inning Canadian rally (with sixth consecutive laser-beam strikes). But he has also stumbled badly at times, as in the memorable Sydney Olympic finals, where he was no match for revved-up big leaguer Ben Sheets when the latter tossed the game of his life to hand the Cubans a rare and bitter gold medal defeat. Lazo and his teammates would most likely have tasted defeat anyway with Sheets on that day pitching in another zone, but it didn't help for Lazo to get smacked around for three hits and a vital run in the first frame that put the crucial showdown game immediately out of reach.

Lazo first turned heads on the international scene in August 1995 at the World University Games at Fukuoka in Japan. It was there as an unseasoned youngster that he threw a no-hitter at a helpless USA squad in the semifinals, mowing down 17 strikeout victims in the process. The opposition on that occasion was an altogether outclassed American college nine that perhaps didn't measure up to seasoned world class competition. Yet it was after all the Florida State University squad, a perennial powerhouse of North American college baseball. It was Lazo's first no-hitter, but only barely. He had also tossed a brilliant one-hitter versus Chinese Taipei earlier in the same competition, that time around striking out 11 equally hapless

Taiwanese victims. A decade later he is still going strong. While Dany Betancourt was the anointed hero (with a mesmerizing seven-inning start) of the recent 2005 World Cup gold medal clash with South Korea, it was again Lazo who slammed the door with an array of unhittable offerings as the successful closer in all three medal-round games.

If Pedro Lazo is not Cuba's top contemporary pitcher, he is nonetheless an unforgettable centerpiece in my own favorite personal Cuban baseball experience. On the way back to Havana from a night game in Pinar del Río's Capitán San Luis Stadium, in February 1997, our contingent (including a pair of Cubadeportes officials) became disoriented among the side streets of the rustic city that is easily Cuba's quaintest baseball outpost. Forced to request help at a street-corner hole-in-the-wall market, we were more than a little surprised to encounter Lazo, still in uniform and on his own way home from the evening's just-ended contest. The Pinar ace promptly hopped on his rickety imported Chinese bicycle and enthusiastically led our cramped Russian-built Lata through the maze of narrow alleyways and onto a nearby highway entrance ramp. There is no more revealing anecdote available from my own experience to capture the innocent flavor of the big-time Cuban baseball scene. One can only imagine an still-uniformed Andy Pettitte, or perhaps Roger Clemens, peddling gleefully homeward on the dark side streets of some neighborhood surrounding Yankee Stadium.

Norge Luis Vera may be the most overlooked mound star on the current Cuban League scene. Vera's January 2001 no-hit masterpiece on the road versus Habana Province ranks among the standout moments of recent National Series seasons. More noteworthy still was the 0.97 ERA he rang up a year earlier during the first Cuban campaign in a quarter century played with wooden bats. But Norge Vera (his first name derives from the popular U.S. appliance brand of the forties and fifties, yet rhymes with *Porgy* and not with *forge*) has also been the most dominant hurler on the circuit throughout most of the past half-dozen seasons — at least until slowed by an injury sustained during the 2002 mid-season All-Star Game (he was smacked with a line-drive through the box).

Vera was the mound mainstay for Santiago de Cuba's three-peat league champions of 1999–2001 and his sub-par campaign three seasons back (1–2, 7.45 ERA, only 19 innings pitched) in the wake of his All-Star Game leg injury may contribute at least in small part to explaining Santiago's sudden free-fall out of the list of National Series title contenders. An unforgettable highlight moment nonetheless came against the MLB Orioles in Camden Yards and took the form of a brilliant relief stint stretching for 7 successful innings after a lengthy second-inning rain delay had kayoed starter José Contreras. But the World Cup matches have always provided Vera's most prominent stage. The slender right-hander was a linchpin in the 2001 Taiwan-based Cup matches when he one-hit the hapless Philippines during a one-sided 17–0 laugher and later also whitewashed a much tougher outfit representing Panama. Two autumns later in Havana he made World Cup history as the first hurler to gain victories in both the semifinals

(seven effective innings as a starter versus Taipei) and finals (seven whitewash relief innings against runner-up Panama) — games played two nights apart. The thirty-two year old silky-smooth hurler was, a year or two back, an ultra-cool fastballer with what once seemed to be almost limitless big league potential.

But of all the recent pitching talent on the island none rang up more imagined dollar signs in the eyes of lustful scouts and salivating agents than **Maels Rodríguez** — towheaded Sancti Spíritus flamethrower and all-time island strikeout king. Maels (pronounced Miles) first turned the heads of pro scouts with his brief appearance at Winnipeg's Pan Am Games, where he uncorked blistering fastballs yet also demonstrated an obvious tendency toward wildness. He soon captured further headlines back on the home front with phenomenal 2001 and 2002 campaigns that saw him obliterating most existing individual strikeout marks while performing truly legendary feats of mowing down enemy hitters and tossing pitch after blazing pitch at almost unfathomable speeds.

A 2001 National Series season was Maels' anointed personal stage from one end straight through to the other. He rang up the new National Series strikeout mark with 263, only the third pitcher to cross the lofty 200 plateau. He was also the league ERA pacesetter and tied for top slot in starts. And then for an encore in 2002 he again struck down more than 200 enemy hitters and also lifted his unheralded Sancti Spíritus team straight into the league championship series for the first time in better than two decades. If he lost the big games at the end of the playoffs (tasting defeat in half of his team's four championship-round losses) this was easily understandable. Having hurled unscheduled nine-frame exhibition matches on two occasions in the middle of interrupted post-season action — once against visiting pro Mexican Leaguers, then again in a game hastily arranged to entertain former president Jimmy Carter — the exhausted Maels won two decisions and dropped a third in the playoff quarterfinals, then won two more in the semis before two final starts during the championship face-off with Holguín. Maels started a playoff total of only four contests but nonetheless ultimately appeared in 11 and logged a workhorse 46.2 total innings in little more than two weeks.

Maels was easily the biggest story of the first two years of 2000-era Cuban League play. In December 1999 the youngster launched his relentless assault on the record books by performing the much-heralded feat of breaking a radar gun milestone with his 100 mph clocking in official game action; no Cuban Leaguer had been measured above the century mark before Rodríguez. This was followed with a perfect game versus Las Tunas barely two weeks later, also the first ever in league play. And finally there was the 2001 National Series countdown to a new single-season strikeout standard that gripped the island as it unfolded near season's end. The only notable strikeout feat that somehow escaped Maels during the incredible run was a new single-game high of 22 posted the same winter by veteran Pinar del Río southpaw Faustino Corrales. The 2001 campaign naturally proved a very hard act to follow. But Maels posted impressive numbers again in 2002 and this time around he also anchored a remarkably improved team that proved the biggest surprise of the entire season. Sancti Spíritus would ride the arms of Maels Rodríguez and two fellow aces (veteran Yovani Aragón and novice Ifreidi Coss) all the way to the league finals. Yet as just noted, the iron-willed and rubber-armed Maels would ironically drop both his decisions in that luckless championship showdown. He was obviously a double victim of both an acknowledged overuse by his desperate manager (Lourdes Gourriel) and an inevitable law of averages now manifesting itself in a sudden run of bad luck on the field. Sancti Spíritus lost three one-run decisions to Holguín, with Maels, Aragón and Coss each victimized once by a lack of timely run support.

But in the end it all came crashing down in the spring and summer of 2003 for Cuba's brightest prospect in decades. Overuse on the hill had wrought the inevitable, a string of nagging injuries to the strapping youngster's lower back and now-limp golden arm. With his fastball barely reaching 85 mph, Maels logged only 113 innings in 2002–2003 (compared with a record 255 the previous year), still capturing eight of 11 decisions but striking out only 117 (less than half his peak totals) and walking nearly as many (87). That summer and autumn he was left off both the Pan American and World Cup squads and the die had already been cast. On the very evening of Cuba's 2003 Havana World Cup victory word spread quietly through the Estadio Latinoamericano press box that Maels had fled the country with former national squad teammate Yobal Dueñas. What followed was a string of rather pathetic attempts by the fallen ace to impress MLB scouts in open tryout camps in Costa Rica during January 2004, all of which resulted in no offers and left Rodríguez griping about how badly Cuban officials had abused him ("These are things they invent to cut a little off the careers of some athletes."). Only 24 at the time of his October 2003 defection, the legend of Maels Rodríguez had crashed in flames, and the communist sports system's brightest phenom had seemingly become at one and the same time its most tragic human victim.

There were other top pitchers in Cuba in the early nineties, all arguably in the same class with early MLB defector Rolando Arrojo, or even the much ballyhooed El Duque. Industriales right-hander **Lázaro Valle** was for most truly knowledgeable Cuban fans the best talent on the island during the self-same years that El Duque was also ringing up his own impressive numbers with the same Industriales club. If El Duque had the better won-lost ledger, Valle (whose own 138–73 lifetime mark is only a shade off El Duque's record performance in that category) was the bigger star on Team Cuba during showcase international tournaments. Several of his performances are well worth highlighting: among them is the 8-inning perfect game tossed against South Korea at the 1989 Intercontinental Cup in Puerto Rico, where he struck out 13 of the 24 straight he retired; there was also a solid exhibition outing in 1993 (also in Puerto Rico) against the pro winter league San Juan Senators, a team featuring Javier López, Carlos Delgado and Carlos Baerga among others in their crack line-up. Valle was also subject of a brief portrait in a recent

book by S.L. Price entitled *Pitching Around Fidel* and purporting to capture highs and lows of being a star athlete under Fidel's ever-present watch. Valle is quoted throughout that account as an outspoken critic of a ballplayer's plight in present-day Cuba, but there is plenty of reason to question the accuracy of those quotes; Price's descriptions and accounts of locations across Havana (ones I myself visited within days of his own tour) suggest that the noted *Sports Illustrated* author often plays quite loose with facts whenever a good story seems to be looming on the horizon. However he is portrayed by Price, however, Lázaro Valle was one of Cuba's best pitchers of the recent generation. And he was again one who opted to turn his back on oft-rumored big league offers and thus to earn fame (if never much fortune) at home among his own countrymen.

Smooth southpaw **Jorge Luis Valdés** crossed a milestone plateau when he finally overhauled the career wins mark earlier established by 1970s-1980s legend Braudilio Vinent. Valdés was a over-skinny kid who demonstrated his worth with some clutch performances in international matches and also won games year-in and year-out for the Henequeneros team in the late eighties and early nineties. The stylish portsider was never close to overpowering, but in four straight World Cup tournaments between 1984 and 1990 he managed to capture seven victories without suffering a single losing decision. He also tossed the first-ever no-hitter in Pan American Games history back in 1991 on home turf in Havana. And for years he was a

Southpaw Jorge Luis Valdés tops the Cuban League career list with 234 lifetime pitching victories and also with 414 career starts.

league standout in domestic play also, racking up at least one (sometimes more) National Series individual crown for ERA (1986), won-lost ratio (1992), complete games (1986, 1989, 1992), wins (1983, 1989, 1991, 1992), and total innings pitched (1986). Valdés is perhaps more notable for his accumulated career numbers than he is for his raw pitching talent. But he is nonetheless a Cuban pitcher of recent vintage not to be quickly forgotten or blithely overlooked.

Omar Ajete, another graceful southpaw, might have been an even bigger star than he was for Pinar del Río and Vegueros (alternative names for teams representing the same province), but his volatile career always remained somehow strangely uneven. The lifetime 179-game winner was plagued by numerous nagging arm injuries, the same fate that befell his contemporaries Osvaldo Fernández (powerful righty from Holguín, who pitched with the MLB Giants and Reds) and also Rolando Arrojo, before their own separate departures to the big leagues. Ajete enjoyed few notable single seasons though he did own the year's only unblemished mark during the 1986 National Series. And he often faltered on the national team, though he was the number one Cuban starter during the 1991 Pan American

Southpaw Omar Ajete starred on several versions of the national team and won 179 Cuban League games. Nagging injuries nonetheless kept the Pinar del Río native from potential immortality as one of Cuba's greatest hurlers of the modern era.

Games in Havana, ranked ahead of big-league-bound Osvaldo Fernández. In the end Ajete never reached the promise inevitably generated by hard-throwing southpaws with intimidating mound presence. But if he had left Cuba early — say on the heels of his 1991 Pan Am Games showing, or during his lofty status as a top starter for the Barcelona and Atlanta Olympics, he would likely have attracted easily as much interest as that eventually surrounding Arocha or Arrojo, or even El Duque and the youngster Liván.

Injury problems also limited a once-bright career for yet another promising if meteoric hurler named **Omar Luis**, who first garnered plenty of attention with a 19-strikeout no-hitter against South Korea and a perfect 3–0 resume (0.86 ERA), all accumulated during 1995 Havana-based Intercontinental Cup action. Luis also enjoyed a singular moment of stardom in the Atlanta Olympics against Team USA, hanging on for seven tough innings as victorious starter in a celebrated 10–8 Sunday afternoon preliminary round matchup played before a huge NBC national television audience. He had his rare moments as well in several National Series campaigns, though he was never a dominant hurler like Lazo or Maels or José Contreras. Perhaps his biggest single triumph came after a freak 1997 accident (he crushed his non-pitching elbow in an automobile collision) put him on the shelf for more than six months. The following winter Omar Luis rebounded in remarkable fashion by striking out 147 batters in 137 innings while hurling for Camagüey, winning 13 of 18 decisions, and hanging up an impressive 1.77 ERA to finish high among the National Series leaders.

Not all top Cuban stars of the past decade have been ace pitchers or muscular home run sluggers. Some have been flashy and daring base runners and aggressive outfielders cut in the mold of Villa Clara stalwart Victor Mesa. And still others were stellar middle-infield glove wizards like **Germán Mesa** (unrelated by blood yet infused with the same bent for ballpark showmanship). The long-time shortstop for Industriales fell into brief disfavor with INDER officials in the mid-nineties but nonetheless strung together a remarkable 16-year career, both before and after the brief suspension from league and national team play that cost him a coveted appearance in the Atlanta Olympics. Germán Mesa has often been compared to Ozzie Smith (by the handful of scouts and journalists who have seen both defensive magicians play) and the comparisons may not have been totally unreasonable.

Germán Mesa's temporary suspension and subsequent return were two of the top sports stories emanating from Cuba in recent seasons. The suspension — which started out as a full banishment but was later rescinded as the result of a rare change of heart among top INDER officials — came under the murkiest of cloak and dagger circumstances. Both Mesa, the league's top infield performer, and Orlando Hernández, one of the best hurlers, had been dropped from the national team for reported lackluster performance on the eve of the 1996 Atlanta Olympics. In October, less than two months *after* the Cuban squad returned victorious from Atlanta, Mesa and El Duque, together with former national team catcher Alberto

Hernández (no relation to either Orlando or the already departed Liván) were together banished from further Cuban League play on never-substantiated charges of having accepted undercover payments from a pro scout representing Miami-based player agent Joe Cubas. (The agent, Cubas's cousin, Juan Ignacio Hernández Nodar, was earlier retained and is currently serving a fifteen-year Havana jail sentence for entering Cuba with false documents.) Further details were never forthcoming and Mesa quietly disappeared from the Cuban baseball scene for nearly two full years. El Duque, for his part, would soon make sensational headlines with his much heralded flight from the island little more than a year later.

The subsequent saga of Mesa's surprising full reinstatement was nearly as shrouded in mystery and intrigue as his original harsh banishment. The dramatic return was also a most emotional moment for Havana fans, since the talented Industriales defender was as universally beloved as any baseball figure on the island. The first Cuban ballplayer ever reinstated after suffering such serious charges of disloyalty to avowed INDER principles of amateur purity in sport, Mesa may well have benefited as much from sagging fan enthusiasm around the league as he did from his apparent exemplary be-

The greatest of many legendary Cuban shortstops, Germán Mesa drew frequent comparisons throughout the 1990s to Cooperstown Hall-of-Famer Ozzie Smith.

havior while quietly suffering his career-threatening punishment. But whatever the actual motives for the reinstatement, it stirred as much excitement among fans in the capital city and across the island as any baseball event of the past several decades. Mesa's celebrated reappearance transpired in Estadio Latinoamericano on opening day of National Series 38 (October 18, 1998) and was occasion for an emotional pre-game infield scene when players from both Industriales and rival Pinar del Río rushed on the field to shake his hand moments before the season's opening pitch. While ballplayers enacted their mutual love-fest, 40,000 patrons (the largest Havana opening game crowd in many a season) stood in unison to roar their own thunderous welcome to the long-absent hero in an equally spontaneous outpouring of love for Cuba's greatest modern-era shortstop.

I never had the special good fortunate to witness Germán Mesa play during his true apex of acrobatic performance in the late eighties and early nineties. But what I have observed since his return to action in late 1998 has been impressive enough to add my vote to those of his legions of boosters. Mesa is a phenomenal sure-handed defender, despite a reported lack of genuine motivation in recent years that seems endemic to many ballplayers in Havana. There is increasing speculation among the most knowledgeable Havana fans that top players seem to have little left to play for, with large collections of championship medals already in their possession but few prospects for easing their own financial hardships or those of their families, given their meager salaries paid only in under-valued Cuban pesos. Conditions seem especially difficult for Havana-based players who are daily exposed to fellow Cubans working in the tourist trade as waiters or hotel staff and raking in substantial pay in highly valued dollar-equivalent convertible pesos. Mesa, even if he may not have been playing all out at career's end, was nonetheless a rare talent who made the infield "circus stop" almost routinely game-in and game-out, and who amazed continuously with both his range and whip-like throwing arm. He no doubt slipped a notch after his lengthy forced retirement, but he still completed plays that would turn heads in any major league park, and he did so while playing on infields laced with pebbles ands ruts unacceptable even on most sandlots diamonds up north.

Earlier-mentioned Victor Mesa was just as bright a supernova in the earlier part of the nineties, and if never idolized like Germán, he was every bit as large a part of the Cuban baseball consciousness. **Victor Mesa** was best known throughout his playing days for daring base running skills, plus a desire to always play the game with the utmost joy and the most outrageous flair for the dramatic — even for the downright reckless. The Villa Clara native was a powerful and consistent hitter as well as a flashy outfielder with wide range and a rifle-like arm. But he was also what the Cubans call a *postalita* — a "hot dog" in English parlance. His appropriate nickname was "El Loco" ("The Crazy One") and throughout the decade of the 1980s and early nineties he lived up to his somewhat derogatory moniker at each and every opportunity. Mesa reigned as base-stealing champion half a dozen times in the

National Series and several times more in the Selective Series played during early summer months. But he ran the bases with a notably reckless style that had historically not been much appreciated in Cuba. The handsome and charismatic mulatto was an ever-present force who could be counted on to thrill home crowds in Santa Clara, but was almost always the target of opposition fan wrath in Havana or Santiago or elsewhere around the sixteen-city Cuban circuit.

Victor "El Loco" Mesa was the most flamboyant and colorful Cuban Leaguer of the eighties and early nineties and today manages perennial league powerhouse Villa Clara.

Victor Mesa was unquestionably one of Cuba's most colorful ballplayers of the recent epoch. He was also a dangerous opponent in world tournament play, which on several occasions turned him (despite his reported unpopularity in league cities outside Havana during National Series seasons) into something of a hero throughout all of Cuba. Such was the case in Brussels in late summer 1983 when Cuba reclaimed an Intercontinental Cup crown lost two years earlier, doing so largely on the strength of impressive slugging by Mesa which featured a leading .576 BA, plus the top tournament totals for runs scored, base hits, and home runs. Most recently "El Loco" has returned to the scene as an inconsistently successful manager with the team for which he played nearly twenty seasons. His pesky Villa Clara team was one of the big stories of the 2001 Cuban League season, though they did eventually collapse in the playoffs after posting the year's best regular-season mark. Many thought it was Mesa's brusque and highly emotional managerial style that more than anything explained the year-end swoon when his exhausted club immediately dropped three of four in quarterfinal action with weak-hitting Camagüey (a division rival Villa Clara outdistanced by six full games during the regular campaign).

A season later (2002) Villa Clara again charged into the playoffs looking like a serious championship contender. And again they wilted under the heat of a semifinal series versus a surprising destiny-driven team from Holguín. What made Mesa a star performer as a player now seems to be working against him on the manager's end of the bench. His moves are often the very epitome of over-managing: he yanks relief pitchers sometimes after only three or four tosses; at other times he punishes relievers or starters by leaving them on the mound to suffer an ERA-destroying barrage of hits and runs; he shows up his players in full view of opponents and spectators by flamboyant sideline displays of his displeasure at their failures or errors; in brief, he repeatedly calls attention to himself as the club's leading star figure. There may be considerable truth to an oft-repeated speculation that Mesa's Villa Clara players have little motive to sacrifice for the team or to go that extra proverbial mile for their unsupportive manager, especially by the time post-season rolls around.

Victor Mesa's career was marked from first to last by self-aggrandizing on-field displays, by a larger-than-life reputation for flamboyance, and by a ball-playing style that seemed largely out of synch with the normal smooth and controlled Cuban playing style. He was also a man unafraid of controversial words. Mesa even voiced his opinions freely to the North American press, something rare among Cuban athletes who have little to gain and much to fear from extroverted comments to foreign reporters. The typical Cuban baseball player employs such interviews like Omar Linares has so often done — to repeat what some would call a "party line" about the advantages and beauties of the Cuban amateur sports system. Mesa, however, was never afraid to step out of that mold. One such occasion was on the eve of the 1992 Barcelona Olympics when his words appeared in an article penned by Jim Callis for the pages of *Baseball America*. When asked about his own prospects, and those of his teammates, as potential major leaguers, Mesa boldly declared that the Cuban national team could win regularly on the big league diamond. Not at first perhaps, Mesa continued tongue in cheek, but "after a few years and with a little more pitching ... perhaps with Nolan Ryan, with Roger Clemens, with Dwight Gooden, and the rest of who we have here, we would definitely win." It was the kind of playful understatement altogether rare among cautious Cuban athletes faced with what might seem to be a hostile North American sporting press.

When Germán Mesa was unceremoniously left back home in disgrace during the Atlanta Olympics, another top-flight if lesser-known defensive wizard took his place and — as is so often the case with Cuba's second-line replacement players, once given a desperately awaited brief moment in the

Twenty-One Greatest Cuban League Hitters

Below is a listing of the likely best twenty-one hitters in forty-plus seasons of Cuban League baseball. Lifetime statistics here include play in the National Series and Selective Series, as well as the short-lived Ten Million Series, Super League and Revolutionary Cup. No attempt has been made to artificially adjust player stats to reflect the length and scope of big league seasons, as is done in many books and articles on Negro leagues baseball or various international leagues and tournaments. Cuban League statistics are taken strictly on their own terms, as they rightfully should be. Statistics are complete through 2003–04 season and active players (Osmani Urrutia, Alexander Ramos, Eduardo Paret) are here starred for easy identification.

Player	Seasons	At-Bats	B.A.	H	R	2B	3B	HR	RBI	TBases
Omar Linares	20	5962	**.368**	2195	**1547**	327	54	**404**	1221	3842
*Osmani Urrutia	11	2361	.360	849	316	115	12	70	410	1198
*Alexander Ramos	17	5665	.340	1926	914	250	31	104	685	2550
Antonio Pacheco	**22**	**7045**	.334	**2356**	1258	**366**	63	284	1304	3700
Pedro Luis Rodríguez	14	4793	.334	1599	871	281	53	193	802	2565
Wilfredo Sánchez	19	6565	.331	2174	891	228	69	16	523	2588
Lourdes Gourriel	20	6263	.323	2026	1122	326	39	247	1077	3171
Luis G. Casanova	17	5288	.322	1705	1144	288	41	312	1069	3011
Victor Mesa	19	6834	.318	2171	1282	351	46	273	1174	3433
Pedro Jova	17	5073	.315	1598	824	206	50	32	482	2000
Luis Ulacia	21	6961	.314	2183	1147	281	58	145	682	3015
Orestes Kindelán	21	6488	.313	2030	1379	330	36	**487**	**1511**	**3893**
Fernando Sánchez	**23**	**7204**	.307	2215	1115	338	65	280	1223	3523
Antonio Muñoz	**24**	6676	.302	2014	1281	355	45	370	1407	3569
Armando Capiró	14	3948	.298	1177	609	186	47	162	677	1943
Pedro Medina	17	4913	.295	1448	886	216	23	221	869	2373
*Eduardo Paret	14	4990	.293	1463	1059	235	55	114	541	2149
Félix Isasi	18	3902	.293	1142	571	181	17	45	445	1492
Agustín Marquetti	**22**	6725	.288	1935	853	279	31	207	1106	2897
Pedro José Rodríguez	15	4171	.287	1196	699	188	16	286	969	2274
Lazaro Junco	18	5780	.284	1641	1018	277	27	**405**	1180	3187

National Series and Selective Series Teams—**Linares** (Vegueros, Pinar del Río, Occidentales); **Urrutia** (Las Tunas, Orientales); **Ramos** (Isla de la Juventud, Occidentales); **Pacheco** (Santiago de Cuba, Serranos, Orientales); **P.L. Rodríguez** (Habana, Agropecuarios); **W. Sánchez** (Henequeneros, Citricultores, Matanzas); **Gourriel** (Sancti Spíritus, Las Villas, Centrales); **Casanova** (Vegueros, Pinar del Río); **Mesa** (Villa Clara, Las Villas, Centrales); **Jova** (Villa Clara, Las Villas); **Ulacia** (Camagüey, Camagüeyanos); **Kindelán** (Santiago de Cuba, Serranos, Orientales); **F. Sánchez** (Henequeneros, Matanzas); **Muñoz** (Azucareros, Sancti Spíritus, Cienfuegos, Las Villas); **Capiró** (Habana, Metropolitanos, Industriales); **Medina** (Metropolitanos, Industriales, Habana); **Paret** (Villa Clara, Centrales); **Isasi** (Occidentales, Henequeneros, Centrales, Matanzas); **Marquetti** (Habana, Industriales, Metropolitanos); **P.J. Rodríguez** (Azucareros, Cienfuegos, Las Villas); **Junco** (Citricultores, Henequeneros, Matanzas). *Note: Various teams listed for each ballplayer do not indicate player trades but rather year-to-year differences in team names as well as National Series versus Selective Series and Super League ball clubs. Players are listed here in descending order by batting average.

spotlight—filled in at the plate and in the field with more than adequate talent. **Eduardo Paret**, veteran of only a half-dozen seasons with Villa Clara but already considered an heir-apparent to the incomparable Mesa back home, provided the Cubans with a surprise fill-in at a key position. Paret hardly missed a beat defensively and was even more potent than the banished Industriales star once he had an aluminum bat in his hands. A steady .375 batting mark, a pair of key homers, and a collection of eye-popping defensive stops were enough to launch a new star on the always crowded Cuban baseball stage. Paret's own career thus seemed ready to explode on the Cuban League scene after Atlanta, until he also ran into his own problems with INDER authorities involving charges of reported contacts with undesirables ("baseball traitors" as INDER brands them) representing U.S. organized baseball. In this case the charge was that Paret and two teammates from Villa Clara had spoken secretly by telephone with earlier big league defector Rolando Arrojo, already under contract to the expansion Tampa Bay Devil Rays. Highly sensitive to continuous

efforts of clandestine scouts to raid their most promising prospects, INDER officials reacted in July 1997 with a suspension that put Paret safely on the shelf for the next couple of seasons. But like Germán Mesa, a contrite Paret apparently placated Cuban authorities with his subsequent humble displays of loyalty to Cuban baseball. The result was that the rehabilitated infielder was back in his Villa Clara uniform in time for a 2000 league campaign. Given the rare opportunity to rejoin the circuit, Paret was soon posting performances that made him one of the most productive and popular players on the Cuban League scene. It wasn't long before he had posted some record-breaking numbers and had quickly re-established himself as one of the top offensive threats on one of the league's most surprising teams.

Not surprisingly, in light of his feats in Atlanta, Eduardo Paret has emerged as a fearsome batsman as well as stellar shortstop since his return from suspension. He posted a bang-up year for Victor Mesa's Villa Clara team his second year back (in 2001) when he set a new record for runs scored (99 in a 90-game season) and stood near the top of the heap in numerous offensive categories. He passed the 100-hit mark, batted a solid .319, socked 16 homers, slugged 8 triples, and displayed sufficient speed to pilfer a league-third-best 31 bases. The 2002 National Series offered more of the same versatile production with 74 runs scored (runner-up to Matanzas outfielder Michel Abreu) and a league-wide base-stealing crown with 34. Three years later, approaching the advanced age of 33, national team captain Paret was the unchallenged star of the 2005 Holland-based World Cup, batting a tournament best .632 in pool-round play before being felled by a calf strain that kept him on the sidelines for the gold medal game with South Korea.

Paret had now inherited a mantle left by the recently retired Germán Mesa and at one point seemingly destined to be worn by another young prospect named Rey Ordóñez. Comparisons between the former New York Mets star infielder and the 5'8" 152-pound Villa Clara shortstop seem to fall favorably on the side of the Cuban who remained on the island to take his chances with less profitable amateur baseball in his isolated homeland. If Ordóñez sports a larger legend for brilliant defensive moves, it must be held in mind that he has enjoyed an advantage of scooping grounders on immaculately manicured major league diamonds; and while no mechanism exists for just comparisons of the difficulty of hitting consistently in the majors, versus weaker mound opposition faced by Paret, it would be difficult to mount any serious argument that the hard-swinging and swift-running Cuban Leaguer — with his triple-threat abilities as a long-ball basher, consistent contact hitter, and adroit base runner — is not a far superior offensive talent.

Another Villa Clara stalwart of top-flight ability is crack catcher **Ariel Pestano**, a svelte 180-pound 6-footer who has handled the talented national team pitching staff in most big international tournament games since his 1999 debut at Winnipeg. A slender but solid and powerful righty, Pestano is the best and one of the youngest (he turns 32 in January 2006) of several talented Cuban catchers. Others are perhaps equally as skilled, especially the three notable receivers laboring in Ciego de Avila (Roger Machado, Pestano's backup on the 2003 World Cup roster), Sancti Spíritus (Eriel Sánchez) and Santiago (Rolando Meriño). Eriel Sánchez was not only the second leading hitter on a surprising Sancti Spíritus club that reached the 2002 National Series championship finals, but he also adroitly handles an outstanding mound corps consisting of Maels Rodríguez, Yovani Aragón and Ifreidi Coss. On recent national teams (Athens Olympics and Holland World Cup) he has also doubled as DH and fill-in first sacker. Together the trio of Pestano, Machado and Sánchez have inherited the mantle as potential national team catcher from rugged Matanzas veteran Juan Manrique, the rock solid backstop at the Atlanta Olympics who was still potent enough at age 35 to have batted .345 in 2002 while slugging 14 homers and posting a .562 slugging mark.

What seems to elevate Ariel Pestano a notch above the others is his clutch hitting in big games and his skills handling stellar young hurlers on pitching-rich Team Cuba. Of the recent group of national team catchers, it is Pestano that major league scouts have had the most opportunities to see first-hand during recent seasons. Pestano caught every frame of the two Baltimore Orioles contests and stroked three singles during the surprise rout at Camden Yards. The fair-skinned six-footer could also not help but further impress the legions of pro scouts with his flawless work behind the plate in both Sydney (2000) and Athens (2004). At the most recent Olympics he was the tournament MVP on the strength of .512 opening-round batting; and during 2005 World Cup play in Haarlem he launched a titanic homer to open the literal floodgates of a rain-soaked 15–2 semifinal rout over outclassed Panama.

One of the most impressive ballpark performances I have witnessed first hand in Cuba was a recent three-homer night in Matanzas staged by the stalwart Villa Clara receiver. The three line-drive round-trippers were smacked to three different fields and two came on the first pitch delivered to Pestano in the second and fourth frames. Ironically the night of this memorable slugging event was also the same night that Pestano's manager, Victor Mesa, elected to act out one of his most infamous displays of explosive behavior that have unfortunately become the trademark of a brief tempestuous career as bench leader.

With Villa Clara up 7–0 after six and a half innings on the strength of Pestano's three long-range blasts, things suddenly began to come apart rapidly for visiting Villa Clara. Mesa subsequently yanked three pitchers during an eight-run Matanzas rally in the seventh frame, two relievers being sent to the showers after delivering but a single wide pitch. A third hurler was next allowed to remain on the hill even though he failed to retire any of nine consecutive batters. When the home team rally resumed again in the eighth frame (the game was eventually lost 13–7) the exasperated Mesa marched to the lawn in front of the Villa Clara dugout and gestured wildly for his entire remaining bullpen corps to depart for the team bus. To the delight of partisan Matanzas fans but quite obviously to the abject horror of his own ballplayers, the showboating manager remained for several minutes in front of the dugout steps performing an array of disgusted gestures aimed directly at his contingent of remaining relievers and bullpen catchers (those who had not yet been called into the game and therefore had not failed the club in any apparent sense) as they sheepishly passed him en route to their early showers.

The full list of contemporary Cuban league stars is too lengthy to review exhaustively. **Yobal Dueñas**, a converted second baseman who later patrolled center field in Pinar del Río throughout the late–1990s and early–2000s, was for a half-dozen seasons another touted prospect who occasionally came through with top-flight performances in national team nylons. Dueñas broke onto the main stage several seasons back as a surprising batting championship during the final year of aluminum bats (1999). He banged the ball from opening day that year straight through to his team's playoff elimination at well over .400 (finishing at .418, then the sixth highest mark in National Series annals) and at the same time showcased all the defensive and base running tools of a legitimate major leaguer. Dueñas eventually developed into a mainstay of the national team outfield, where he started the bulk of international tournaments between the Winnipeg Pan Am Games of 1999 and the Havana Intercontinental Cup in 2002. His one career highlight moment unquestionably came during the latter event, when he launched a towering line drive to the top reaches of the distant Estadio Latinoamericano leftfield grandstand. The dramatic homer in front of a packed stadium of Cuban fanatics provided all the scoring needed during a tense 2–1 gold medal victory over South Korea. But a year later (with 14 seasons and a .321 career average under his belt) Dueñas had fled Cuba in the company of Maels Rodríquez, after being left off the 2003 World Cup roster, reportedly for minor disciplinary infractions. By the summer of 2005, at the advanced age of 35, Dueñas was struggling to make the big time as a New York Yankees farm had, batting .271 and smacking only 3 homers in 76 outings with the Eastern League (AA) Trenton Thunder.

Another recent National Series batting champion, outfielder José Estrada, has been surprisingly far less inconsistent since the year he starred both in Matanzas and at the Atlanta Olympics. If Estrada faded quickly from the island scene after Atlanta, so did another yet Olympic outfielder, though under far different circumstances. Cuban baseball was shocked by a tragic automobile accident in early December of 2000 (after only a week of league play) which instantaneously killed Miguel Caldés — a notable Camagüey slugger who had once walked off with a national home run title during the season preceding Atlanta Olympic action — and also injured several of Caldés's teammates. It was an especially painful reminder of similar wrecks that took the lives of two star Cuban pitchers (José Huelga and Changa Mederos) several decades back. The Caldés accident was an indelible black mark hanging over much of the Cuban season which followed. Caldés had played exceptionally well for several years in the late nineties and sported a .289 average and 176 homers at the end of his truncated 14-season tenure. But he is best remembered as a tower of defensive strength in the Cuban lineup during the cherished Olympic victory at Atlanta.

If Linares, Kindelán, Pacheco and other sluggers of the 1990s seemed to leave a void in their absence at the outset of the new millennium this would be a short-lived perception indeed. Linares and company has been quickly replaced by a new set of seemingly equally potent bashers who were already writing their names in the record books and earning their spots on the international stage only four seasons after the shocking 2000 Olympic gold medal defeat in Sydney. Fidel Castro would boast in a televised speech in late 2005 that "traitors" to the Cuban sports system who had abandoned their homeland for the lure of professional dollars were being replaced at a rate of ten new stars for every single deserter. An inflated boast to be sure, but in the light of the team the Cubans had fielded for the 2005 World Cup in Holland only two months earlier it hardly seemed like an idle claim.

Pudgy right-handed hitting machine **Osmani Urrutia,** a 29-year-old veteran of a dozen National Series campaigns with Las Tunas, seems a prime example of the ability to generate almost endless supplies of big-level-talent on an island boasting a population barely equivalent to New York City. Across the first five seasons of the new century Urrutia has generated the biggest headlines in National Series play with a multi-season batting streak that has no parallel in organized baseball history. Grabbing four straight batting titles between 2001 and 2004, the chunky righty with a picture-perfect compact swing strung together four seasons of plus-.400 hitting, a feat never accomplished in the majors and to my knowledge also never duplicated at any level of legitimate organized baseball. "The streak" began with a .431 mark in 2001 that was the third highest in National Series history. Urrutia's .469 average three years later would easily outdistance Pedro Luis Rodríguez's .446 ledger (1988) as the all-time league mark. In 2003 Urrutia became the first National Series slugger to take home the league batting title three years running; his sensational 2004 season would next extend the record to four uninterrupted batting crowns.

Urrutia's improbable effort to run the string of .400-plus seasons to five fell painfully short during the recent 2005 campaign when a late-year slump left him with .385 at season's end. In mid–February, with but five weeks remaining, Urru-

Las Tunas outfielder Osmani Urrutia has boasted a remarkable string of .400-plus batting average across the past half-dozen National Series seasons and has inched ever closer to Omar Linares as Cuba's all-time career batting average leader.

tia had surged to .414 but couldn't maintain the momentum, though he did walk away once more as league batting champion. Batting .400-plus for Cuban League seasons of only 90 games is not the same thing, of course, as pulling off the feat over a much longer big league campaign; yet Urrutia's recent five-series string *does* nonetheless represent the 450-game equivalent of two and two-thirds major league years. While no claim comparing Cuban League and big league competition would rest on very solid ground, there is only one near-equivalent feat (in mere raw numbers at least) that can be culled from big league history. Hall-of-famer Rogers Hornsby (for many, the best right-handed swinger in big league history) surpassed the .400 barrier in three of five campaigns (1921–1925) during his own phenomenal run of six consecutive National League batting championships. The St. Louis Cardinals slugging wonder averaged .402 over his five stellar campaigns (compared with Urrutia's .422 in five shorter seasons) yet strung together only two back-to-back .400 outings (1921= .397, 1922=.401, 1923=.384, 1924=.424, 1925=.403). Urrutia thus remains the only four-time-consecutive .400-plus slugger at any level of organized baseball or anything approaching the stature of organized baseball.

One remarkable footnote to Osmani Urrutia's ongoing string of batting titles is the fact that he has remained an unknown on the international scene, overshadowed on the current national team by younger sluggers like Yulieski Gourriel and Michel Enríquez. Urrutia has not been the same dominate basher in his Olympic and World Cup outings, though he did post a respectable .333 hitting mark in Athens as the starting right fielder and delivered a number of clutch hits in the recent Holland World Cup (where his .417 BA trailed only Paret's .632 and Enríquez's .455). Part of the reason may be his positioning deep in the power-laden Cuban batting order. The line-up featured by manager Higinio Vélez's team in Holland in September 2005 likely represented the only occasion in baseball's long history (at any level, in any epoch) which witnessed a batter with a five-year string of .400-plus occupying the seventh slot in his own team's batting order.

There also have been numerous top performers of only slightly less notoriety. Michel Enríquez has recently put up impressive numbers as a heavy-hitting third sacker for a surprisingly strong Isla de la Juventud club which draws its players from all across the island. Juan Padilla teamed for a number of years with Germán Mesa as a crack keystone combination for Industriales, but an unfortunate non-baseball eye injury

shortly after the close of the 2000 season prematurely ended a still-productive career. Padilla, a Havana fan favorite who anchored second base for the 1996 Olympic squad, has now launched what promises to be an equally successful managerial tenure with the Havana-based Metros (Metropolitanos). Gabriel Pierre, for a dozen-plus years, proved a robust home run basher and climbed over the career 300 plateau for longballs in 2002; but the Santiago third sacker was always overshadowed in the heavy artillery department by teammates Kindelán and Pacheco, to say nothing of Pinar rival Omar Linares. Years of frustration playing behind Linares at third base on national team rosters seemed to boil over in recent seasons when Pierre suffered through a pair of prolonged suspensions after unseemly clashes on the field with umpires (he twice slugged a man in blue) and off the field with local INDER officials.

Among the new generation of young prospects, Havana outfielder **Yasser Gómez** has flashed as a gifted multi-tooled player in the capital city, first with Metros and then the more popular Industriales club. As 1999 rookie of the year with Metros, the all-lefty Gómez rang up solid batting numbers while displaying a remarkably strong throwing arm in right field. The diminutive spray hitter set a new rookie mark for base hits during National Series 37 with 112 safeties, and his robust .359 average was fifth highest in the entire league. A year later, now playing for Havana fan-favorite Industriales, Gómez put on one of the greatest individual hitting and fielding displays I have ever witnessed at Estadio Latinoamericano, blasting three long triples in three consecutive at-bats, all coming off deliveries from Granma ace right-hander Ciro Silvino Licea, and then for an encore also gunning down an opposing runner at home plate with a truly Clemente-like toss launched from deep in the right-field corner.

The transfer of Havana teams by Yasser Gómez is worth comment, as it demonstrates an unusual feature of Cuban League baseball structure. Players hardly ever switch teams since "trading" is not a recognized part of Cuba's socialist baseball system. But the occasional player move does take place, sometimes to accommodate the personal needs of a favored star performer, or at times for more pragmatic emergency reasons. José Estrada was transferred by the commissioner's office from his spot on the Matanzas roster into the shorthanded Pinar del Río lineup, in order to restore competitive balance (by replacing an injured and thus unavailable Omar Linares) at the time of the 2000 season's year-end playoffs. But Yasser Gómez was

Osmani Urrutia's Unparalleled Five-Year Batting Performance

Year	NS#	B.A.	AB	H	R	2B	3B	HR	RBI	TB	SLG Avg
2000–01	40	.431	290	125	62	14	0	16	64	187	.645
2001–02	41	.408	240	98	35	4	1	6	41	122	.508
2002–03	42	.421	292	123	43	18	0	13	72	180	.616
2003–04	43	.469	258	121	51	18	7	8	67	196	.760
2004–05	44	.385	291	112	47	23	1	16	60	185	.636
5-Year Totals		**.422**	**1371**	**579**	**238**	**77**	**9**	**59**	**304**	**870**	**.635**
12-Year Career		.362	2652	961	363	138	13	93	470	1383	.522

moved over to the Industriales line-up for yet another reason. League officials have made several such moves over the years to bolster the roster for the wildly popular Industriales club at the expense of the far less favored Metropolitanos team. Such official tampering happens only rarely but may nonetheless seem altogether inexplicable to fans oriented toward the free-agent system now practiced by major league baseball. A casual look at Cuban record books shows many players performing for several different teams. Charts of top Cuban hitters and pitchers presented in this present chapter serve as examples. But this misleading appearance of player movement results in almost all cases merely from shifting team names or evolving league structures down through the years, and only rarely from players actually having their province affiliations shifted.

Gómez was easily the best young player produced out of Havana in years, but only until **Kendry Morales** came along a mere three winters later. The switching-hitting 19-year-old Morales — featuring a strong physical resemblance to a young Mickey Mantle, or perhaps to current Texas Rangers phenom Hank Blaylock — put up truly startling numbers as a raw rookie. His 21 round-trippers (two short of the circuit leader) were a new league record for *novatos* (Cuban for "rookie"); his 203 total bases were also a new first-year mark and ranked third in the league; a .324 BA anchored the offensive thrust of a resurgent Industriales ball club; and his 27 game-winning hits were the season's top total. But the young slugger's campaign might have been better still under differing circumstances. Manager Rey Anglada moved Morales from his normal outfield slot to third (where his glove proved to be equally as iron-clad) for a lengthy stretch of mid-season games and the transition appeared to be a move that sapped much of the rookie's confidence and distracted heavily from his offensive concentration.

Morales was only one of a handful of young rookies or second and third year players who shown brilliantly during the 2002 season. Another was fleet-footed Sancti Spíritus second baseman **Yulieski Gourriel**, a first-year surprise with an extra special lineage. Playing for his manager-father, former national team star Lourdes Gourriel, Yulieski also ranked in the league's top ten for a handful of offensive categories (outpacing Kendry Morales in both doubles and plate appearances) while playing a significant role in carrying his unheralded and usually also-ran club to its first championship finals in a quarter-century. And just as promising is another Sancti Spíritus basher, **Frederich Cepeda**, a fifth-year player who slugged away with a .378 BA for the 2002 Western Division champions and by 2003 was entrenched as the front-line national team left fielder. Cepeda has proven in the last couple of years to be a special talent (shades of Luis Ulacia) whenever World Cup play rolls around. In the 2003 finals versus Panama in Havana, it was Cepeda's two solo shots that turned a sixth-inning 2–2 deadlock into a 4–2 gold medal victory. Two years later in Holland, despite a nagging wrist injury that forced him to swing from only the left side of the plate, it was again Cepeda who sprinted from first to home on a single to tally the deciding score of the gold medal finale versus South Korea.

With legitimate stars like this on the horizon, it appears that a strong future for Cuban baseball is hardly in doubt. This is certainly the case when it comes to a apparently inexhaustible supply of on-field talent still being rolled out year after year by the apparently always-resilient Cuban League.

One final contemporary player deserves a special mention. Honored for the past dozen years with an irrevocable place in the national team outfield and sporting Cuba uniform #1, switch-hitting veteran Camagüey outfielder **Luis Ulacia** has always saved his grandest performances for national team outings. Ulacia has rarely been a top echelon player in Cuban League seasons. The league record book carries his name only a single time, as 1988 Eastern Division batting champ during the first of several seasons in which the award was split between geographical regions. But during international tournament play Ulacia has always arisen Reggie Jackson–like to the head of the pack. He first made a mark in Atlanta, shining as a swift lead-off hitter with an astronomical .556 batting average (during what was admittedly an aluminum bat two-week slugfest) and also a stellar center field defender. He was also a

Luis Ulacia's two decades of steady offense left him fourth on the Cuban League career base hits list (2,183). The Camagüey fireplug was also a fixture as leadoff hitter in the national team lineup throughout the nineties.

crucial cog in Winnipeg, where his clutch hitting at the top of the order keyed a remarkable 1999 Olympic-qualifying Pan American Games come-from-behind victory. But the ultimate career moment for this gritty 38-year-old converted shortstop transpired during Taipei's World Cup championships in early November 2001. As Team Cuba racked up still another gold medal trophy, Ulacia was undisputed individual hero with his lofty .512 batting onslaught that locked up not only a string of team triumphs but also tournament MVP honors. It was a most remarkable swan song for a durable all-star who had so long played in the shadows of bigger guns like Linares, Pacheco, Kindelán and the entire host of big-league-quality Cuban pitchers.

* * *

Earlier post-revolution decades (1960s–1970s–1980s) owned their own larger-than-life stars and these were in truth some of the most revered names in all of Cuban baseball. González Echevarría muses on the difficulty of achieving personal stardom in Castro-era Cuba. He protests that individual stars have little or no chance to loom before the public under a socialist system which glorifies only collective achievement. Nothing could be much farther from capturing the essence of the contemporary Cuban scene, and one only has to hang out briefly among fans in Havana's noisy Parque Central to grasp the all-pervasive player adulation that dominates almost incessant daily street corner debates of the island's national pastime. And this occurs with athletes who are nothing like our American or European-style media celebrities — manufactured entertainment icons whose wide fame rests as much on cleverly orchestrated television and magazine commercial endorsements as on any actual ballpark heroics.

In contemporary Cuba a ballplayer's grass-roots notoriety always results strictly from on-field achievement — witnessed first hand at the ballpark or perhaps celebrated on radio — and Cuban fans follow that achievement with passionate devotion. It is a remarkable feature of such hero-status earned by word of mouth alone that it is indelibly entrenched in fan consciousness and rarely fades with arrival of a new season's batch of designated heroes. The dimension of such continued adulation for past-era diamond stars like Wilfredo Sánchez or Modesto Verdura from the sixties, or Braudilio Vinent and Armando Capiró from the 1970s, is more impressive still when one realizes that it stems largely from efforts of ballpark denizens themselves and not through calculated labors of advertising executives or television pitchmen bent on merely exploiting the sports scene for their own commercial ends.

Fidel Linares, diminutive and pesky southpaw-batting outfielder from the once baseball-poor province of Pinar del Río, was one such star of Cuba's first decade of National Series baseball. Linares would build a legacy in a handful of seasons that was far larger than anything explained by the offensive numbers he etched in the league record books. The senior Linares made an early name as a skilled hitter with the Occidentales ball club of the first few National Series campaigns,

but he would eventually leave an even greater mark on Cuban baseball in the figures of two heavy hitting sons he also sired during his decade of ball-playing. As a talented player in his own right the first Linares still holds a special niche in early Cuban League history. He was a leader in base hits in National Series II (1963) and also tied for the top slot in doubles a season later. He helped form a memorable outfield that also featured Erwin Walter (batting champion of the inaugural 1962 season) and Raúl Gonzalez (champion batsman of 1963). It was easily the best outfield trio of the first several seasons of National Series play and also the backbone of an Occidentales team that (under manager Fermín Guerra) earned the first league championship of novel post-revolution National Series baseball.

Linares celebrated his best individual campaign by hitting .310 in 1963, shadowing teammate Raúl González (.348) in the league batting race during only the second season of National Series competition. He roamed center field between a pair of early Cuban League legends, Miguel Cuevas (Orientales) and Pedro Chávez (Industriales), during that same year's Pan American Games triumph earned in Brazil. First starring in the middle and late fifties in the Pedro Betancourt amateur league (the first Cuban amateur circuit to admit black athletes on a large scale), the elder Linares was already thirty when he joined the Occidentales line-up for the inaugural National Series. On opening day of that 1962 season Linares captured a lasting measure of trivial immortality among fans and historians by smacking a crucial base hit in Estadio Latinoamericano (still known as Cerro Stadium at the time) to decide the first ball game ever played during a National Series campaign. Such was the stature of the father of Omar Linares that when Fidel Linares finally lost a lengthy and painful battle with cancer several years back (in 2000) his formal state funeral in Pinar del Río Province became a celebrated national event seemingly more fitting for a military hero than a mere one-time baseball star.

The two outfielders surrounding Linares at the Brazilian Pan American Games were also themselves luminous figures of a first half-dozen Cuban League seasons. **Pedro Chávez** had starred with Círculo de Artesanos in the popular pre-revolution amateur league and captured a batting triple crown in that circuit in 1957. He had also performed alongside Fidel Linares in the Pedro Betancourt League and thus as much as anyone provided a strong transition between the old and the new structures of Cuban amateur baseball. And he had starred with the surprising Cuban squad that had won such an emotional victory in the April 1961 Central American Games in Costa Rica (see Chapter 7). Chávez would walk off with two early National Series batting crowns (1964 with Occidentales and 1967 with Industriales) in his short post-revolution career. And he would later return to the spotlight as manager of several powerhouse versions of Team Cuba during the early eighties.

Miguel Cuevas, in turn, began his own National Series sojourn with Orientales, although he eventually also performed with the Granjeros team representing Matanzas Province. An talented infielder as well as part-time outfielder, the small but compact right-hander was the leading power hitter of the early and mid-sixties and rang up a then league record 86 RBI in National Series VII. He was also a base hits leader (in 1964), batting champion (1966) and home run king (1965) during his thirteen National Series seasons. Don Miguel (as he was always known to Cuban fans of the era) reached his international peak with a pacesetting three homers slugged during the Pan American Games outing in which he played alongside Linares and Chávez. Chávez — himself respected as a leading slugger and defender of the opening Cuban League epoch — would eventually be asked by Cuban media to pick an all-time league all-star team covering the sixties and seventies; when he did so, rival and teammate Miguel Cuevas was not surprisingly an automatic selection.

But as popular as players like Fidel Linares or Don Miguel Cuevas or Pedro Chávez may have been in those earliest National Series seasons, they would quickly enough be overshadowed by a second generation of stellar performers that were soon acknowledged as the best of any period save perhaps the present one. **Agustín Marquetti**, for one, was the first great Cuban slugger of the modern-day era. He was also the first Cuban Leaguer who left little doubt among the occasional professional bird dog who saw him perform about his unquestioned major league potential. A huge black slugger who served Havana Province as first baseman but also did occasional outfield duty, Marquetti truly dominated the Cuban League in individual offensive production throughout the late sixties and early seventies. He was best known for swatting towering home run blasts and his 19 round-trippers in the 99-game National Series of 1969 stood as a record for several seasons until surpassed by Armando Capiró. The number of homers Marquetti blasted that top season may not seem overly impressive by big league standards, until it is pointed out that his blasts came in spacious league ballparks and were stroked during a time noted for its abundance of overpowering pitching. Existing photos of Marquetti's roundhouse swing suggest the awesome power that accounted for 207 homers across 22 short seasons (approximately 50 National Series games followed by only a slightly longer Selective Series season) played in an epoch largely dominated by pitching skill, despite the presence of aluminum bats. By major league standards Marquetti's homers were not particularly frequent (he hit one about every 32 at-bats), but some of them were truly epic in proportion. Marquetti saved some of his top slugging feats for important international tournament play (he registered 31 homers and compiled a .346 BA in such events) where they always had the grandest impact. And he was a durable physical specimen who rarely suffered career-slowing injury, thus stretching out his talent-laden employment for 22 winters and summers in one of the longest tenures of Cuban League annals.

Agustín Marquetti also, at the top-end of his fabulous career, once fell victim to one of the strangest incidents ever witnessed in top-level baseball of any league or any country. This event came on a day when the young slugger knocked home a game-winning run with a blast to the outfield, but then

Agustín Marquetti, another hefty southpaw first sacker, rivaled Antonio Muñoz in the power department during the decade before Linares and Kindelán arrived on the scene.

saw his crucial single nullified with a rare play that can only recall famed New York Giants goat Bonehead Fred Merkle. After seemingly deciding a tense league game with his smack to right, the 20-year old rookie stood at home to embrace the teammate racing in with the winning tally. He was immediately gunned down at first by an alert opposition right fielder (nullifying the hit and the run and extending the game to extra innings) and thus suffered a painful moment truly as embarrassing as any etched in Cuban League history.

If the New York Yankees had their deadly M (Mantle) and M (Maris) Boys at the heart of the batting order in the early sixties, so did the Cuban national teams that came later in the same decade. **Antonio Muñoz** was the second great long-ball basher of the middle period of Cuban League history and in reality Muñoz was a much more impressive home-run slugger than Marquetti, especially if the raw numbers and frequency of homers is to be valued over the aesthetic impressions of mere distance brought on by raw power. Another black lefty of imposing stature, Muñoz labored for the Azucareros and Las Villas teams and also took up his defensive slot at first base. Marquetti drew as many headlines across the same era by having the advantage of playing in Havana, the nation's capital city in both politics and baseball. But it was Muñoz who always put up the bigger numbers.

The statistics posted by Muñoz are his ultimate legacy, of course, and most of those numbers were for raw power hitting. His career totals for 24 seasons (National Series and Selective Series) would feature 370 homers, a .302 BA, a .535 slugging mark, and 1,407 RBI. He garnered only two National Series home run titles and matched but never surpassed Marquetti's high of 19 in a single season. But he took individual honors six times in the spring-summer Selective Series, his 25 in 1979 fell three short of the record 28 stroked by teammate Cheíto Rodríguez, a mark which stood until Orestes Kindelán eventually surpassed it in the mid-eighties. Muñoz, affectionately branded by fans as "El Gigante del Escambray" (the Giant of the Escambray region), by career's end owned a career home run/at-bats ratio of one every 18 times to bat, almost twice as good as Marquetti though considerably short of Cheíto (and also of both Linares and Kindelán). But his career home run total nonetheless stood as the league high-water

Antonio Muñoz, slugging Havana first baseman, was the premier Cuban power hitter during the decades of the seventies and eighties. One noted *Sports Illustrated* scribe touted Muñoz during a 1977 visit as a near-clone left-handed version of Tony Pérez.

mark until it was surpassed eventually in the eighties by Lázaro Junco and then again in the nineties by Kindelán and Omar Linares. *Sports Illustrated* writer Ron Fimrite was especially impressed by Muñoz in his 1977 whirlwind tour of Cuban ballparks and described the towering southpaw quite fittingly as a near-clone left-handed version of fellow Cuban-born big leaguer and future Cooperstown hall-of-famer Antanasio "Tany" (Tony) Pérez.

Another potent Cuban batsman of note whose career overlapped Marquetti and Muñoz was a still more devastating pure hitting wizard, even if he rarely ever knocked balls completely over the fences. **Wilfredo Sánchez**, outfielder with several league teams representing the province of Matanzas, owned a colorful nickname — "El Hombre Hit" ("Mr. Hit" or "The Hit Man") — that seemed to capture so perfectly the essence of his illustrious career. A lefty all the way, Sánchez was a born hitter who sprayed the ball to all fields and lined his smashes like frozen ropes. He never hit the devastating long-ball, but he was nevertheless a most extraordinary singles and doubles hitter. His career batting average today still ranks fifth on the all-time list and his career total for base hits still leaves him in third place all-time. But in his own era he was the best natural hitter Cuba had ever produced with its post-revolution brand of baseball. Only the career of Omar Linares may today be enough to challenge the once indisputable claim that "El Hombre Hit" was and is the best all-around hitter ever to represent the island.

Armando Capiró (Habana and Industriales outfielder of the same late-sixties through early eighties era) was another of the acknowledged major league level Cuban hitters. Capiró was a rare combination of batting power and outfield grace and his tandem of pure scientific hitting and raw slugging power made him arguably the greatest Cuban all-around offensive threat on the scene before Linares. As a total package, he was one of the most prolific and colorful players of Cuban League history. Capiró was the first slugger to cross the 20 homer plateau in the National Series (in 1973) and he remained the only one to do so across the first 22 National Series seasons. He also produced remarkable slugging performances in international tournaments that further supplemented his stellar Cuban League play. And on top of his offense, Capiró owned a unique throwing arm that was frequently compared by those observers knowing major league action to the otherwise incomparable right arm of the immortal Roberto Clemente.

If the search for Cuba's sanctioned best at the plate over the past forty-plus seasons often leaves fans hopeless split over support for Capiró versus Wilfredo Sánchez, there are still others legitimately in the field and demanding consideration. Among Cuba's extensive roster of extraordinary hitters during the seventies and eighties, at least some witnesses would contend that perhaps the best of all was actually Pinar del Río outfielder **Luis Giraldo Casanova**. There are many Cuban fans around who will still argue quite vociferously in favor of Casanova against any support for rival immortals. One such rooter among Havana baseball connoisseurs is Antonio ("El Moro") Grenot, a personal friend of this author who himself pitched briefly with Havana's Metropolitanos and thus faced sluggers Capiró, Sánchez, Muñoz and Casanova in their heyday seasons. Grenot is enthusiastic to a fault when he speaks of the sweet swing and deadly line drives that Casanova would regularly unleash. Three hundred twelve homers, over 3000 total bases, and a .322 career average during 17 seasons are career stats that themselves speak volumes in support of the Pinar del Río outfielder.

And Luis Casanova had a special talent for remarkable national team performances. It was the international tournament stage, more so than the National Series, that made him such an enduring favorite throughout his homeland. In his first Amateur World Series in 1978 the trim yet muscular right-hander batted .444; two years later during the same event in Japan he tied teammate Muñoz as the top home run producer with seven; he shared the home run leadership again in 1984 with Cheíto Rodríguez and bested the field again in long-balls in 1988 when the same tournament returned to Italy. But the biggest display of slugging talent came with the 1981 Intercontinental Cup event held in Edmonton, when the top Cuban outfielder slugged his way to a tournament triple crown. Casanova was also a natural choice for one of the three outfield slots when Pedro Chávez picked his all-time Cuban League team for the editors of *Bohemia*, and at that point in time the Pinar del Río slugger was still only halfway through his impressive career.

When it came to extra special slugging feats performed on an international stage, another Cuban outfielder of the mid and late eighties and also the early nineties was every bit as spectacular as Pinar-native Luis Casanova. Lefty-swinging fly chaser **Lourdes Gourriel** of Sancti Spíritus was the most valuable performer in the 1994 World Cup staged in Nicaragua and swept by an undefeated Cuban contingent featuring a starting pitching rotation of four future big leaguers: Liván Hernández, Orlando Hernández, Osvaldo Fernández, and Rolando Arrojo. A full fourteen years earlier the same talented outfielder had registered a decisive base hit in the showdown match versus Team USA during the Tokyo-based Amateur World Series of 1980, and there were other memorable Team Cuba performances for Gourriel sandwiched in between. His finest hour was unarguably enjoyed during the 1989 Intercontinental Cup in Puerto Rico, where he batted a resounding .435, again homered and knocked in four runs in the title game against the Americans, and not surprisingly walked off with tournament MVP honors. Gourriel was also home run champion at the 1991 Pan American Games, and in a subsequent 1995 Pan American tournament he again slugged .464 to capture the individual batting crown.

Gourriel (like Robelquis Videaux, often also spelled Roberquis Videaux) has one of those names Cubans love to spell in a surprising variety of forms. Even the INDER-published league record book has featured chaotic alternative spellings from year to year (e.g. Gorriel, Gurriel, and Gourrial). But no matter how you spelled Gourriel, the ballplayer with the shifting moniker never failed to amount to a fearsome slugging force. That uncanny ability to find new paths toward

Pinar del Río's Luis Casanova had his numerous champions in the seventies and eighties for the mythical title of Cuba's greatest natural hitter.

victory has now translated to the manager's bench where four seasons ago Gourriel led a surprising hometown Sancti Spíritus team, long a league doormat, into its first National Series championship round (only its second ever) in 23 long years. He now manages a potent team that stars his sons Yunieski and Yulieski (one a top outfield prospect and the other a crack third baseman) and also boasts the strong pitching of veteran Yovani Aragón and youngster Ifredi Coss. It will not be much of a surprise if Lourdes Gourriel eventually arrives back in the international limelight as manager of some future edition of gold medal-bound Team Cuba.

Santiago "Changa" Mederos was a hard-throwing, bulky southpaw who mowed down opposing hitters for both Habana and Industriales during the early seventies and was also in retrospect something of an early coming of contemporary Cuban League ace Maels Rodríguez. Changa's calling card (like that of Maels) was the debilitating strikeout, and he first rang up record numbers in the successive National Series seasons of 1969 and 1970. In the earliest of those campaigns he had charged past Manuel Alarcón's record number of 200 Ks, a standard that stood for but a single campaign. The 208 strikeouts by Changa that winter would remain the league high water mark for the next thirty years, until Maels eventually came along at century's end. He also once posted 21 strikeouts in a single Central American Games outing versus hapless Mexico. Most observers of the era considered Mederos to have had no true peers in the Cuban League of the first three decades (1962–1992) other than legendary Braudilio Vinent and immortal José Huelga. He may arguably have been the best Cuban lefty of the entire 40-year revolutionary era. Hardly a one-dimensional flamethrower, Mederos's winning percentage was every bit as spectacular as his strikeout marks and he today still stands eighth all-time in the won-lost ratio department.

And all this came in a career that was somewhat shorter than it should have been — only fifteen seasons that might easily have been twenty or even more. Regrettably Changa also shared a tragic fate as well as a gifted talent with another of Cuba's pitching greats, the equally ill-starred José Antonio Huelga. On December 15th of 1979 — ten years after his sensational 1969 season — Santiago Mederos was tragically killed in a spectacular auto wreck along the desolate cross country highway a few miles outside Havana. He died within hours, of extensive burns suffered over most of his body — a horrible fate for one of Cuba's greatest athletes of the modern era.

Portly right-hander **Rogelio García** is Cuba's career strikeout king, having rung up one short of 2,500 in a stretch

Pinar del Río's durable Rogelio García was one of the island's four career 200-game winners.

that spanned 16 National Series and boasted 202 victories. The strikeout mantle is an honor he has shared down through the years with Braudilio Vinent, who fell some 300-plus short of García's mark but enjoyed four more seasons of work. Veteran Pinar del Río southpaw Faustino Corrales (who also boasts 20-plus campaigns) has recently also joined the 2000 career strikeout club, but it seemed more likely for awhile that it would be a strapping youngster named Maels Rodríguez who would eventually overhaul García's record, if he could only resist big league defection and the lure of promised millions on the professional circuit. But a dead arm would end Mael's meteoric career far short of any serious challenge, after a mere half-dozen seasons.

Together Changa Mederos (who was the equal of any Cuban strikeout ace but didn't live long enough to approach the top of the heap in career totals) and Rogelio García were the most fearsome hurlers in Cuban league annals before the appearance of the phenom Maels Rodríguez at the tail end of the millennium. A stocky black right-hander who hurled mostly for Vegueros, García captured six National Series strikeout crowns in seven years between 1977 and 1983; while he still stands in first place on the career strikeout list, he also had given up more walks than anyone in National Series history until Faustino Corrales overhauled that less fashionable mark late in the 2002 season. Unfortunately García's memory is somewhat tarnished for many longtime Cuban fans by his personal failure in one of Cuba's most painful losses ever suffered on the stage of international competitions. That regrettable moment came in a 1981 contest García started against future major leaguer Ed Vosberg and Team USA at the Intercontinental Cup finals in Edmonton. García did not last very far into the game and Cuba in turn suffered one of its most ignominious tournament defeats on record.

José Huelga might well have been Cuba's greatest pitching genius ever. And this includes any of the greatest big league hurlers (Pascual, Ramos, Cuéllar, even Luque) or blackball professionals (Méndez, Bragaña, Cocaina García) from lost decades before the society-altering 1959 revolution. Some contend that this slender righty was indeed the best ever seen on the island, especially given the brevity of his brilliant career. But the script that fate had in store for Huelga would only in the end make him Cuba's most tragic post-revolution baseball story. José Antonio Huelga will nonetheless live forever in Cuban baseball lore solely on the strength of his gutsy dual performances in two unforgettable playoff games with Team USA that decided the 1970 Amateur World Series showdown in Cartagena, Colombia. The first of these games was the celebrated duel with Burt Hooten (a 3–1, 11-inning victory) that most veteran Cuban baseball watchers to this day still judge the most artistic game ever played during top-level international competitions. A mere day later Huelga was again back on the field, this time in a relief role, to close the door in the deciding contest of the championship round. For those dramatic and pressure-packed performances José Huelga was immediately and officially proclaimed by Commander-in-Chief Fidel Castro as "the Hero of Cartagena" and thus etched for

Twenty-One Greatest Cuban League Pitchers

Below is a listing of the likely best twenty-one pitchers in forty-plus seasons of Cuban League baseball. Lifetime statistics include play in the National Series and Selective Series, as well as the short-lived Ten Million Series, Super League and Revolutionary Cup Tournament. No attempt has been made to artificially adjust player stats to reflect length and scope of big league seasons, as is done in many books and articles on Negro leagues baseball or various international leagues and tournaments. Cuban League stats are here taken strictly on their own terms, as they rightfully should be. Stats are complete through the 2004 season and still-active pitchers (Norge Vera and Pedro Luis Lazo) are here starred for easy identification.

Pitcher	Seasons	Games	W–L	Pct.	ERA	ShutO	SO	BB	INNS
José Huelga	7	160	73–32	.695	**1.50**	17	722	277	871.1
Manuel Hurtado	12	218	90–47	.657	**1.80**	21	860	380	1182.2
Walfrido Ruíz	12	234	102–50	.671	**1.88**	34	799	372	1314.0
Santiago Changa Mederos (LH)	15	253	123–67	.647	**1.97**	41	1420	633	1628.2
Aquino Abreu	14	232	63–65	.492	2.26	15	718	412	1116.0
Omar Carrero	17	338	149–105	.587	2.27	49	1225	460	2058.0
Maels Rodríguez	6	156	65–45	.591	2.29	14	1148	486	938.0
Rogelio García	16	398	**202**–100	.669	2.39	56	**2499**	1077	2609.0
Braudilio Vinent	**20**	477	**221**–167	.570	2.42	**63**	2134	989	3259.2
*Norge Vera	10	210	113–46	.711	2.47	29	851	322	1358.0
José Ariel Contreras	10	232	117–50	.701	2.82	26	1346	514	1473.0
Orlando "Duque" Hernández	10	246	126–47	.728	3.05	23	1211	455	1514.1
Jorge Luis Valdés (LH)	**20**	**519**	**234**–166	.585	3.13	46	1982	1024	**3134.0**
José Luis Alemán	17	406	174–125	.582	3.13	34	1447	692	2472.0
Lázaro de la Torre	19	495	**205**–132	.608	3.22	26	1679	888	2727.1
Faustino Corrales (LH)	**22**	437	169–131	.563	3.25	27	2327	**1183**	2505.0
Omar Ajete (LH)	16	449	179–96	.651	3.29	31	1777	681	2320.0
Lázaro Valle	15	334	138–73	.654	3.39	16	1351	613	1740.0
*Pedro Luis Lazo	14	391	181–102	.640	3.40	26	1826	750	2332.2
José Ibar	18	366	173–100	.634	3.45	31	1709	723	2371.0
Rolando Arrojo	13	359	154–98	.611	3.50	26	1138	442	2027.2

National Series and Selective Series Teams—**Huelga** (Azucareros); **Hurtado** (Industriales); **Ruíz** (Agricultores, Industriales, Habana); **Mederos** (Habana, Industriales, Agricultores); **Abreu** (Azucareros, Las Villas); **Carrero** (Ganaderos, Camagüey, Camagüeyanos); **Rodríguez** (Sancti Spíritus); **García** (Vegueros, Pinar del Río); **Vinent** (Mineros, Serranos, Santiago de Cuba, Oriente, Orientales); **Vera** (Santiago de Cuba); **Contreras** (Pinar del Río, Occidentales); **Hernández** (Industriales, Ciudad Habana); **Valdés** (Henequeneros, Matanzas); **Alemán** (Santiago de Cuba, Orientales, Serranos); **de la Torre** (Metropolitanos, Industriales, Habana, Ciudad Habana); **Corrales** (Pinar del Rio, Occidentales); **Ajete** (Vegueros, Pinar del Río, Occidentales); **Valle** (Industriales, Ciudad Habana, Habana); **Lazo** (Pinar del Río, Forestales, Occidentales); **Ibar** (Habana, Agropecuarios); **Arrojo** (Villa Clara, Las Villas, Centrales). *Note: Various teams for each player do not indicate trades but rather year-to-year differences in team names as well as National Series versus Selective Series and Super League clubs. Pitchers are listed here in order on the basis of career ERAs.

all time in the nation's collective memory as a true living monument of the barely decade-old socialist sporting system.

Back home on the island, during his mere seven National Series seasons, Huelga earned further plaudits with the lowest career ERA on record for a Cuban hurler. It remains an irony of his career, however, that he was never a single-season league leader in any major hurling category, ERA included. While he maintained remarkable consistency in the minimal earned runs department during an era of unmatchable league pitching, Huelga was edged out each winter in this department by the likes of Vinent (twice), Roberto Valdés, Rolando Castillo, Manuel Hurtado, Ihosvany Gallego and Juan Pérez Pérez. In the seven seasons covering his CL tenure there was never a league ERA pacesetter with a mark higher than the 1.13 posted by Pérez Pérez in 1974. But a far more tragic fate than mere on-field second-best awaited the young phenom from Sancti Spíritus. On July 4, 1974, Huelga's life was snuffed out in a fatal automobile accident on the highway near Mariel, a dozen miles west of the capital city. He had pitched only a fraction more than a half-dozen full seasons, and his memo-

rable victories in Cartagena were barely four years in the past. Today, three decades after his untimely demise, José Antonio Huelga is fittingly immortalized in his home province of Sancti Spíritus by the ballpark name which adorns the quaint Cuban League Stadium located in that provincial capital.

Manuel Alarcón was yet another giant figure in the renewal of Cuban baseball after the life-altering revolution. The workhorse hurler for a pair of Santiago Province teams christened Orientales and Mineros stands alongside Manuel Hurtado and Modesto Verdura as "the big three" among early pioneering Cuban League aces. A solidly built, square-jawed right-hander with a compact delivery and an impressive fastball, Alarcón became the first Cuban ace to reach 200 strikeouts in a single season when he rang up precisely that number for the Mineros squad in 1968 (National Series VII). Only Changa and Maels have reached the lofty milestone number of 200-plus in thirty-seven seasons since. Manuel Alarcón also posted several other impressive league milestones during National Series play: twice he paced the circuit in game starts (1963, 1965), he hurled the most complete games on three occasions (1963, 1964, 1967), and he tied Verdura for most wins in National Series #2, while he hurled the most innings in 1965.

Yet as a featured performer in international tournaments, Alarcón was somehow almost always inexplicably missing from the scene. He did appear briefly in the 1962 Central American Games in Jamaica where he split a pair of decision, then later won both starts at the 1963 Pan American tournament in Brazil, and also registered one victory in three starts when the same games renewed four years later in Winnipeg. Since Cuba did not send a team to the Amateur World Series of 1965 and Alarcón's own career had wound down by the time of AWS #17 in 1969, the Santiago ace was effectively shut out of any possible chance to perform in the most prestigious international venues. A versatile athlete owning a well-rounded personality, Alarcón also enjoyed a musical career after his short baseball sojourn had expired. But it was assuredly as a baseball pitcher and not as a salsa virtuoso that he will always be remembered by his appreciative countrymen. And many of his contemporaries (especially his arch rival Manual Hurtado) were quick to express a popular opinion that Alarcón was likely the best hurler among any produced during revolutionary baseball's initial pioneering era.

Modesto Verdura, a slender black-skinned righty with a whip-like throwing arm, is probably most famous in Cuban League legend and lore for the staged ceremonial base hit he casually (and cooperatively) yielded to *Commandante* Fidel Castro to open the second-ever National Series. But Verdura also enjoyed a most sensational league season during that same year. And he was always highly effective in international tournaments throughout the transitional era. Pitching for the Azucareros team, he posted the year's lowest ERA (1.58) for 1963; he simultaneously authored a 7–1 won-lost record on the hill; and he also was the league pacesetter in both games won and games started. For an encore, Verdura also logged the most total innings (79.2) that same winter. With a face almost suggestive of the young Michael Jordan, the almost overly trim Verdura owned a loose-jointed delivery yet always tossed a "heavy" baseball. No one of his era threw any harder than did Modesto Verdura. Unfortunately his career was not destined to be very lengthy as it stretched through only eight winter seasons. But it was indeed a spectacular and even meteoric career by almost any statistical or artistic measure.

Manuel Hurtado still owns one of the best winning percentages in Cuban League history (he now stands seventh) thirty years after his 1973 retirement and nearly a decade after his departure (as political defector) from his native island. He also stands nearly at the apex of the list for career ERA rankings (1.80), trailing only José Huelga (1.50) and another much less-heralded contemporary, Roberto Valdés (1.75). There were few better pitchers in the early years of the modern Cuban League and few who won more regularly. No less an authority than 221-game winner Braudilio Vinent himself has claimed that Hurtado may have been the best of them all when it came to rare native pitching talent. Manuel Hurtado was light in complexion and his facial appearance during playing

years was strongly suggestive of big leaguer Camilo Pascual, if one were to seek for comparisons. He threw with a distinctive over-the-head windup and an elevated leg motion that further suggested comparisons with accomplished big leaguer Pascual.

And Hurtado, again like Pascual, almost always threw most effectively, season-in and season-out, avoiding anything that resembled an all-too-common mid-tenure slump. He enjoyed the considerable good fortune of laboring for a strong Industriales club that was the powerhouse outfit of early league seasons. And his popularity was also certainly aided by pitching for the team based in the capital city and boasting, then as now, the country's most rabid fan base. He won twice as many games as he ever lost—a measure of excellence in any league—and he also put up some most impressive numbers in five international tournaments. A highlight of this final portion of his career came in 1970, when he first won a pair of starts at the Amateur World Series in Cartagena without allowing a single earned run, and then duplicated the feat in his single start at the Central American Games in Panama.

Diminutive and curly haired **Aquino Abreu**—league ace of the mid-sixties—holds a most special niche among Cuban pitchers. Like Cincinnati's Johnny Vander Meer in the majors, right-hander Abreu lives on in Cuban lore on the strength of two consecutive "masterpiece" whitewash games that etched in stone his lasting reputation. Beyond those games the career record is not a very spectacular one with more losses than wins and a hefty 2.26 14-season ERA that glows by present-day standards but is no more than run-of-the-mill for his own hit-stingy era. But Abreu did also have his stellar moments in international competitions, where he pitched almost flawlessly for a mediocre 1962 Central American Games squad, enjoyed two brilliant outings at the Pan American Games the very next summer, and also won his sole appearance at the 1966 Central American Games tourney to round out an unblemished 3–0 international ledger.

But it is the unmatched back-to-back no-hitters (also the first two of modern-era Cuban League history) that will always be associated with Abreu's league tenure. They came nine days apart in January of 1966 and Abreu himself has provided some interesting insights about those memorable games. He recalls today that the opening outing against Occidentales (10–0) was one in which his arm hurt throughout, and yet the constant pain didn't stop him from feeling he could seemingly place his mixture of fastballs and slow-breaking curves precisely where he wanted them on just about every pitch. The bizarre feature of that game was the fact that Abreu was unaware of his no-hit progress until his catcher pointed it out to him during an eighth inning mound visit. The succeeding match with Industriales (7–0) nine days later was one in which the tired arm still throbbed with a constant ache; he hadn't been able to hold it out straight from his side at the conclusion of the first masterpiece game, and it had showed very little improvement in the interim. The damaged wing seemed to improve, however, as it warmed throughout the action of the first five innings; but the pain returned with a vengeance during the final four frames and Abreu's historic feat was salvaged only by a supreme act of personal willpower to keep throwing, and also by several miraculous catches by a pair of his talented outfielders.

Abreu, Hurtado, Huelga, Alarcón or even Mederos aside, the greatest revolutionary-era pitcher of them all was — without debate — a durable right-hander from the Oriente who, before his 20-season tenure was complete, would break almost all existing records for individual pitching accomplishment. **Braudilio Vinent**, laboring over the years with four different National Series teams representing Santiago Province, was the first Cuban hurler to appear in 20 different National Series seasons, the first to log 200 career victories, and also the first to hurl 3,000-plus innings. While several of these marks for endurance and unparalleled achievement have now been outstripped by late-comers, his record total of 63 shutouts still seems safe from all future challenge. Rogelio García came the closest to Vinent with 56 whitewashes, and no active Cuban League hurler is much closer today than the half-way mark. Dubbed affectionately "The Meteor from La Maya," Vinent was not only the best league pitcher on the scene from the late sixties all the way down to the early eighties, but he also performed brilliantly in dozens of international contests (making a record 96 total appearances) and owned a special and much appreciated penchant for dominating rival American squads in several celebrated gold-medal showdowns. Vinent's international blue-ribbon outing came with Amateur World Series action in Managua in 1972 when he not only captured all four tournament appearances with a microscopic 0.62 ERA but also tossed a 8-hit complete-game whitewashing against a squad of tournament all-stars in the special exhibition contest that marked closing-day activities.

Among the offensive giants of earlier epochs, **Pedro Jova** holds a unique spot in Cuban baseball lore. His brightest achievements are arguably those garnered as a manager with Villa Clara in the early 1990s, when his team claimed three consecutive National Series titles. But he also earned his own brand of considerable and lasting fame on the field of play. Pedro Jova rarely appeared among the league leaders in major slugging departments for any individual seasons, nor did he ever hit with much long-ball power. His nearly two decades of action which totaled a combined 1,319 National Series and Selective Series games produced a mere 32 homers and a yawn-producing sub-.400 slugging percentage. But he did maintain a .315 career batting average and ultimately surpass the 1,500 career base hits plateau before the end of his 17 steady if not always spectacular Cuban League seasons. Tack together a .315 career batting mark with nearly 1,600 base hits and one of only three back-to-back-to-back league championships for a manager in the National Series and it is hard to find another Cuban baseballer who has achieved anything more while performing on both ends of the team bench.

Easily the most impressive home run blast I have so far witnessed on the island of Cuba (perhaps the longest I have seen struck anywhere) was a titanic smash clearing the cantilevered roof atop the left field bleachers of *Cinco de Septiembre* Stadium in the seaport city of Cienfuegos. This spectac-ular fly ball, measuring in the neighborhood of 600 feet, was struck in mid–February 2001 and flew from the bat of a muscular if somewhat chubby right-handed swinger named Pedro José Rodríguez, Jr. Adding to the drama of the moment was the fact that the young slugger who stroked the prodigious round-tripper was the well-endowed son of an older Cienfuegos ball-playing legend named Cheíto Rodríguez, one of Cuba's truly great long-ball sluggers of a not-too-distant aluminum-bat era.

The memorable fly ball struck by the younger Rodríguez was one of 15 he banged out during the second season after the return of wooden bats to Cuban League action. When I hastily inquired of local INDER officials sitting in a special box next to me if such an eye-popping blast had ever before been seen at this stadium, I was hastily informed that it had indeed happened on several previous occasions — all such earlier roof-clearing shots appropriately also delivered courtesy of none other than an elder Cheíto Rodríguez.

That elder Cheíto Rodríguez (formally listed as **Pedro José Rodríguez** in the Cuban record books) was a slugging righty-swinging third baseman boasting awesome aluminum-bat power while playing mostly for the Azucareros team (also Cienfuegos) between 1974 and 1988; Cheíto ("Little Che") logged 286 homers (ninth all-time), 2,274 total bases, and a .545 career slugging average (fifth best in Cuban League history). A solid 5–10 in stature and a muscular 190 pounds, Rodríguez was once the youngest player ever elevated onto the Cuban senior national team. (Omar Linares would later usurp that honor.) The dark-complexion athlete with a pencil-thin moustache first earned overnight fame with his hefty performance during February 1979 Intercontinental Cup competitions staged before hometown crowds in Havana's Latin American Stadium. In that one tourney outing alone Cheíto smacked seven long homers and paced the entire field in base hits (18), runs scored (15) and RBI (17) as well as in round-trippers. He also barely lost out for the batting crown to teammate Pedro Medina (.462), despite himself hitting .450 for the ten-game festival.

Merely 24 at the time, Rodríguez was touted by Cuban journalists at this early juncture in his career as owning a more proficient home-run frequency ratio than any among the celebrated big-league long-ball sluggers. (His one homer every 8.1 at-bats in international competition was one that Linares at 1/9.6 would fail to achieve, yet one which Kindelán's 1/7.5 would easily outstrip.) Cheíto's rare slugging feats continued in other international tournaments (he batted .378 in Brussels in 1983 and was also home run champ at the 1979 Pan Am Games in Puerto Rico) and across fourteen National Series seasons, during which he was league home run champion on four consecutive occasions. His shorter-than-usual career span left Rodríguez far behind Kindelán, Linares, Marquetti and others when it comes to his total career power numbers. He finished short of 300 homers and surprisingly only reached 969 career RBI. But his long-ball clouts were indeed legendary if not lasting, and until Omar Linares came along about the same time Cheíto was winding down, Pedro José Rodríguez was in his prime arguably the best offensive third baseman that modern-era Cuban baseball had ever produced.

Lázaro Junco, a right-side swinger and long-legged outfielder born in Matanzas Province on the eve of the revolution, never owned the national team stature of Cheíto Rodríguez or other great sluggers of the 1970s and '80s like Marquetti, Muñoz, or Capiró. Nonetheless Junco was a consistent power hitter with adequate defensive ability who would post impressive numbers throughout the eighties and most of the nineties, eventually winning or sharing the home run crown in a record ten different National Series outings. Junco would eventually break many of the league long ball records, notably becoming the first Cuban slugger to reach a career total of over four hundred homers. Since his retirement in the mid-nineties, only Kindelán and Linares have equaled or surpassed his career total of 405 circuit blows. (Linares actually fell one homer short of Junco, even though logging 892 more plate appearances and playing in 130 more games.) Junco still stands sixth in career RBI, his slugging average is also the fourth all-time best (trailing only Linares, Kindelán and Luis Casanova), and he sits in the top ten (currently still seventh) in career total bases. The lanky and graceful outfielder who performed with Matanzas-based Citricultores and Henequeneros teams was thus a mainstay performer throughout an era of diminished slugging talent, playing most of his career between more glamour-drenched epochs featuring first Marquetti and Muñoz and later Linares, Pacheco and Kindelán.

What unfortunately diminishes Junco's image somewhat for current fans is simply that he never enjoyed any single sensational campaign featuring eye-catching offensive numbers; instead he accumulated impressive totals rather quietly and mostly through longevity. In this sense he parallels another Cuban icon, one who was simultaneously garnering big-league fame. Junco is most suggestive of Rafael Palmeiro, the Cubs,

With 405 round-trippers, Matanzas fence basher Lázaro Junco stands between Kindelán and Linares on the Cuban League career home run list. A perennial league all-star with a record eight individual home run crowns, Junco remarkably never enjoyed success on the Cuban national team.

Rangers and Orioles standout who has finally in recent seasons garnered secure hall-of-fame stature with almost no real fanfare along the way. To make matters worse, Junco never boasted a shinning moment with the Cuban national team during any high-profile international events. Nonetheless, his highly productive 18 National Series seasons boast some of the loftiest overall numbers on record, and it was for this reason alone that he steadily if quite unspectacularly etched an indelible place for himself in league history.

Another Matanzas slugger, **Fernando Sánchez**, was for nearly a quarter-century almost as hefty a star (and equally as durable an icon) as was his more noted brother, "El Hombre Hit" Wilfredo Sánchez. Also an outfielder with demonstrable power from the right side of the plate, Fernando appeared in the National Series for 23 successive winters, a remarkable record for longevity matched or approached by only a tiny handful of other durable Cuban Leaguers. (Sánchez sits in second place behind Antonio Muñoz for total seasons served, yet outstrips all others with his 1,994 games played.) His total plate appearances (8,269) remain a league record and his total number of hits (2,215) not only surpasses his brother's ledger but also stood for years as the national standard until recently overhauled by Antonio Pacheco. Fernando also remains very near the top of the career list in doubles (fifth), triples (eighth) and total bases (again fifth). Like other stars of the National Series, he also boasted numerous highlight moments in international competitions. Fernando Sánchez paced the field in both base hits and doubles at the 1978 Amateur World Series #25 in Italy while batting a robust .432, and again slugged away at a .400-plus pace in the same tournament only two years later at Tokyo; yet he nonetheless could never quite overtake his hit-happy brother as a widely recognized and widely idolized international tournament all-star.

A final pair of memorable hitters has inexplicably never managed to receive the fan or media attention due them, even on the local Cuban home front. Havana's **Pedro Medina** in the seventies and **Alexander Ramos**, playing for the hinterland Isla de la Juventud club in the nineties, both were unjustly overshadowed year after year by bigger-name favorites who were their contemporaries. And Pedro Luis Rodríguez, also playing in Havana Province but not for one of the two popular capital city teams, similarly lived in the shadows of the like-named Cheíto (Pedro José Rodríguez) whose long-ball feats were always much more spectacular if only slightly more productive.

Medina, a multi-talented durable catcher serving eventually with both capital city teams and also with Havana Province, quietly rang up a .295 career batting average across 17 seasons and barely missed tallying 1,500 career base hits. He also later made his mark as a successful manager of Industriales, where he won a National Series championship in the mid-nineties. But Medina was rarely among the league leaders during an era that housed the two slugging Sánchez brothers alongside Luis Casanova, Armando Capiró and Lourdes Gourriel. Medina seemed to reach greater heights in his few chances to play with vaunted Team Cuba in overseas matches. Yet his most memorable hit — a late-inning clutch homer to knot the crucial deciding game with Team USA during the 1981 Intercontinental Cup affair at Edmonton — was buried by circumstance when the Americans prevailed in extra frames to hand the Cubans one of their most painful defeats ever in post-revolutionary baseball history.

Ramos, by contrast, only once enjoyed the opportunity of playing for Team Cuba, despite a lifetime batting average that now trails only Linares, Urrutia and Michel Enríquez, plus a career hits total that is today inching steadily beyond 2,000. Such is the disadvantage of playing for the make-shift team representing Isla de la Juventud, the quasi-province which sits isolated off the nation's southern coast and fills out its roster with leftovers drawn from other more populous regions. Ramos does own one distinction assuring at least a degree of diamond immortality: at the time of his retirement early in the 2005–06 campaign (timed to coincide with the opening of a new ballpark in the provincial capital, Nueva Gerona), he had extended his iron-man string of consecutive games to 1,112, a number which represented the sixth longest string found anywhere in the known baseball universe. Pedro Luis Rodríguez (a half-dozen seasons retired from the scene), much like Ramos, also stands in the top five all-time in batting average (tied for fifth with Antonio Pacheco) and did earn his numerous shots with the national team. Yet he never reached such milestones as 200 homers (finishing with 193) or 2,000 hits (posting only 1,599), and his popularity never approached that of some of the glamorous stars (Linares, Kindelán, Pacheco, Germán and Victor Mesa) he competed head-to-head against across the high-water mark seasons of the 1980s and early nineties.

There were indeed a handful of other early diamond notables that today occupy only a slightly lower echelon of Cuba's baseball Valhalla, and the list is certainly too lengthy to handle with full justice. Félix Isasi and Antonio Jiménez together graced the pioneering sixties with their substantial feats on offense and defense. Isasi, who grew up rooting for Almendares and especially for his boyhood idol Tony Taylor, was reportedly one of the first post-revolution Cuban Leaguers tempted with a contract offer from big league scouts; for 18 seasons he turned heads at shortstop as one of Cuba's most spectacular defenders, while also managing to hit consistently above .300 and twice also leading the circuit in runs scored. Jiménez, known popularly as Ñico and also weaned as a loyal Almendarista, was nearly as notable for his outfield "basket" catches in the style of Willie Mays as he was for his artful base stealing, a field in which he led the National Series circuit a record six times (a mark only recently broken by Metros and Industriales middle infielder Enrique Díaz). Matanzas native Rigoberto Rosique (remembered by Ñico Jiménez as easily the best center fielder of early Cuban League decades) flashed brightly across the subsequent seventies, both in the field (where he played shallow like Tris Speaker and relied on unparalleled speed to shag balls hit over his head) and at the plate (where he won a pair of league batting titles); Elpidio Mancebo, performing at the far eastern end of the island with Santiago-

based Mineros, was still another talented hitter of the same epoch who peaked in 1971 (base hits leader), 1972 (batting champion) and 1973 (leader in runs scored). By the late eighties Pedro Luis Rodríguez, as noted above, was briefly the island's top star until Omar Linares began approaching his own awesome potential. And there were some other brief comets like Héctor Olivera (a barrel-chested right-handed third sacker with both Las Villas and Cienfuegos), who in 1980 during a 60-game Selective Series campaign posted the first Cuban League .400-plus batting average. Omar Linares would not cross that threshold in the longer National Series season for another five full years.

These past-era diamond heroes today live on in collective island baseball memory, despite much less-extensive Cuban media coverage. Heroes born more of first-hand ballpark memories than from a flood of constant media chatter are more likely to survive onslaughts from each subsequent season's latest anointed paragons. Cuba has thus always been a land of grass-roots baseball which still finds fans creating their own myths and legends with endless street corner debates and nostalgic grandstand reminiscing.

Such was the untarnished stature of first-generation Cuban League idol Pedro Chávez, for example, that as 1984 Team Cuba manager he was asked to provide a mythical all-star team, drawn from the first two decades of revolutionary baseball and published by the popular Havana periodical *Bohemia*. The occasion was the celebration of Amateur World Series #28 to be held in Havana's Estadio Latinoamericano late that fall. Chávez's personal selections could hardly be controversial as far as they went. The catcher was Ricardo Lazo and Antonio Muñoz was the obvious-choice first sacker. The infield slots fell to Alfonso Urquiola at second, Cheíto Rodríguez at third and Rodolfo Puente at short. Cuevas, Victor Mesa and Luis Casanova provided the dream-team outfield. Alarcón was the right-handed pitching selection and Changa Mederos the designated southpaw. Not bad choices all of them. Yet so great was the constant influx into the league of new quickly proven talent that by the time Chávez's team appeared in print Marquetti, Capiró and Vinent were (for most fans) already replacing in stature some of the top stars on the list. It was one more demonstration that Cuban baseball possesses a remarkable capacity for seemingly endless and inevitable renewal.

How many of these Cuban standouts of recent decades could have earned their spurs it in the U.S. majors? Would Marquetti, Wilfredo Sánchez, Antonio Muñoz, Pedro José Rodríguez, flame-throwing Rogelio García, and finally Omar Linares, all have succeeded Miguel Cuéllar, Tony Oliva, Bert Campaneris and Tany Pérez in the uninterrupted string of Cuban greats donning professional uniforms? This is a moot question certainly impossible to answer in any conclusive manner. But the opinions of most big league scouts, managers and players who saw them in their primes seem to weigh quite heavily on only one side of the issue.

One thing is nonetheless certain beyond any reasonable doubt. One does not have to reach back to the early decades of the past century and into the lost era of separate (if perhaps not quite equal) Negro baseball leagues to find unheralded Cuban stars buried in obscurity by painful social and political circumstance. One can weigh in on either side of the heated argument regarding whether these ballplayers would have better served their destinies by laboring in the majors for untold dollars, or in the Cuban League for little beyond personal and national pride. But one can hardly fail to be saddened that such players were not better known everywhere off their native island. Lost legendary stars belong not only to baseball's embarrassing epoch of racial segregation in the early decades of the twentieth century. They are also to be found in considerable abundance only a stone's toss away in Communist Cuba, all throughout the past forty-plus years of mist-shrouded Cuban National Series baseball.

References and Suggested Readings

Bjarkman, Peter C. *Diamonds around the Globe: The Encyclopedia of International Baseball.* Westport, CT: Greenwood Publishing Group. 2005.

Casas, Edel, Jorge Alfonso, and Alberto Pestana. *Viva y en juego (Alive and In Play).* Havana: Editorial Científico-Techníca, 1986.

Callis, Jim (with Ken Rosenthal, George Rorrer, and Mark Ruda). "Could the Cubans Succeed in the Majors?" in: *Baseball America* (August 10, 1992), 5

Fimrite, Ronald. "In Cuba, It's Viva El Grand Old Game" in: *Sports Illustrated* (June 6, 1977), 69–80.

González Echevarría, Roberto. *The Pride of Havana: A History of Cuban Baseball.* New York: Oxford University Press, 1999.

Martínez de Osaba y Goenaga, Juan. *El Niño Linares (The Kid Linares).* Havana: Casa Editoria Abril, 2002.

Padura, Leonardo, and Raúl Arce. *Estrellas del Béisbol—El Alma en El Terreno (Baseball Stars—The Spirit on the Field).* Havana: Editorial Abril, 1989.

Rucker, Mark, and Peter C. Bjarkman. *Smoke: The Romance and Lore of Cuban Baseball.* New York: Total Sports Illustrated, 1999.

Statistics for Selected Cuban Post-Revolution International Tournament Stars (1962–2004)

Aquino Abreu (RH Pitcher; NS Teams: Azucareros, Las Villas)

1962–1975	GP	GS	W–L	IP	H	ER	SO	BB	ERA
National Series (14)	232	146	63–65	1116.0	849	280	718	412	2.26
International Series (3)	6	4	3–0	37	21	7	26	8	1.67

Cuban League Leader: W–L Pct. (1969); Games Started (1967); Innings Pitched (1964); Bases on Balls (1964); Hit Batsmen (1962, 1964)
International Series Appearances: Central American Games IX (1962 Jamaica); Pan American Games IV (1963 Brazil); Central American Games X (1966 Puerto Rico)

Manuel Alarcón (RH Pitcher; NS Teams: Orientales and Mineros)

1962–1968	GP	GS	W–L	IP	H	ER	SO	BB	ERA
National Series (7)	87	70	41–24	583.2	420	118	529	118	1.82
International Series (3)	7	7	4–3	53.1	40	12	64	13	2.00

Cuban League Leader: Games Won (1963); Games Started (1963, 1965); Complete Games (1963, 1964, 1967); Innings Pitched (1965); Strikeouts (1965, 1968)
International Series Appearances: Central American Games IX (1962 Jamaica); Pan American Games IV (1963 Brazil); Pan American Games V (1967 Canada)

Pedro Chávez (RH Outfielder; NS Teams: Occidentales, Industriales)

1962–1969	AB	H	2B	3B	HR	RBI	BB	SO	BA
National Series (8)	1389	399	53	19	22	192	228	63	.287
International Series (7)	197	75	165	1	9	45	21	7	.381

Cuban League Leader: Batting Champion (1964, 1967), Hits (1967); Triples (1964); RBI (1964); Sacrifice Flies (1964, 1966, 1967); Intentional Walks (1967)
International Series Appearances: Pan American Games III (1959 Chicago USA); World Cup XV (1961 Costa Rica); Pan American Games IV (1963 Brazil); Central American Games X (1966 Puerto Rico); Pan American Games V (1967 Canada)

José Ariel Contreras (RH Pitcher; NS Team: Pinar del Río; SS Team: Occidentales)

1993–2002	GP	GS	W–L	IP	H	ER	SO	BB	ERA
National Series/SS (10)	232	203	117–50	1473.0	1327	461	1346	514	2.82
World Cup Series (2)	—	—	4–0	29.2	—	1	—	—	0.30
Olympic Games (2)	—	—	3–0	34.0	—	11	—	—	2.91
Pan American Games (1)	—	—	2–0	18.1	—	2	—	—	0.98
Central American Games (1)	—	—	2–0	13.2	—	7	—	—	4.61
Intercontinental Cup (2)	—	—	2–0	25.2	—	7	—	—	2.46
International Totals	—	—	13–0	121.1	—	28	—	—	2.08

Cuban League Leader: (SS=Selective Series Season) Games Won (1997); Games Pitched (1995SS); Games Started (1997, 2001); Strikeouts (1997); Intentional Walks (1995SS)
International Series Appearances: Intercontinental Cup XII (1995 Havana); Olympic Games XXVI (1996 Atlanta USA); Intercontinental Cup XIII (1997 Spain); Central American Games XVIII (1998 Venezuela); World Cup XXXIII (1998 Italy); Pan American Games XIII (1999 Canada); Olympic Games XXVII (2000 Sydney); World Cup XXXIV (2001 Taipei)

Miguel Cuevas (RH Infielder; NS Teams: Orientales, Granjeros)

1962–1974	AB	H	2B	3B	HR	RBI	BB	SO	BA
National Series (13)	2821	786	118	15	75	522	348	331	.279
International Series (5)	76	24	7	2	5	8	7	13	.315

Cuban League Leader: Batting Champion (1966); Hits (1964); Home Runs (1963, 1965, 1971); RBI (1965, 1967, 1968); Sacrifice Flies (1968); Intentional Walks (1969)

Major International Series Appearances: Central American Games IX (1962 Jamaica); Pan American Games IV (1963 Brazil); Central American Games X (1966 Puerto Rico); Pan American Games V (1967 Canada)

Urbano González (LH Infielder; NS Teams: Occidentales, Industriales)

1962–1974	AB	H	2B	3B	HR	RBI	BB	SO	BA
National Series (13)	2864	792	97	18	18	320	244	67	.277
International Series (15)	296	92	9	3	2	47	9	7	.311

Cuban League Leader: Batting Champion (1965); Runs (1962); Hits (1962, 1964, 1965); Sacrifice Flies (1963)

International Series Appearances: Pan American Games III (1959 Chicago USA); World Cup XV (1961 Costa Rica); Central American Games IX (1962 Jamaica); Pan American Games IV (1963 Brazil); Central American Games X (1966 Puerto Rico); Pan American Games V (1967 Canada); Central American Games XI (1970 Panama); World Cup XVIII (1970 Colombia); World Cup XIX (1971 Havana); Pan American Games VI (1971 Colombia); World Cup XX (1972 Nicaragua)

José Ibar (RH Pitcher; NS Team: Habana; SS Team: Agropecuarios)

1987–2003	GP	GS	W–L	IP	H	ER	SO	BB	ERA
National Series/SS (18)	366	303	173–100	2371.0	2243	908	1709	723	3.45
World Cup Series (2)	—	—	2–1	16.0	—	8	—	—	4.50
Olympic Games (1)	—	—	2–0	16.0	—	3	—	—	1.69
Pan American Games (2)	—	—	1–0	12.1	—	2	—	—	1.46
Central American Games (1)	—	—	0–0	6.2	—	2	—	—	2.70
Intercontinental Cup (1)	—	—	2–0	17.0	—	5	—	—	3.75
International Totals	—	—	7–1	68.0	—	20	—	—	2.64

Cuban League Leader: (SS=Selective Series Season) ERA (1990SS, 1998); W–L Pct. (1998); Games Won (1995, 1998, 1999); Games Started (1997); Complete Games (1990SS); Shutouts (1990SS, 1995); Innings Pitched (1997, 1998, 1999); Hits (1997); Strikeouts (1998, 1999)

International Series Appearances: Pan American Games XII (1995 Argentina); Intercontinental Cup XII (1995 Havana); Central American Games XVIII (1998 Venezuela); World Cup XXXIII (1998 Italy); Pan American Games XIII (1999 Canada); Olympic Games XXVII (2000 Sydney); World Cup XXXIV (2001 Taipei)

Manuel Hurtado (RH Pitcher; NS Teams: Orientales, Industriales)

1962–73	GP	GS	W–L	IP	R	ER	SO	BB	ERA
National Series (12)	218	136	90–47	1182.2	315	237	860	380	1.80
International Series (5)	12	7	5–3	49.1	18	11	34	15	2.02

Cuban League Leader: ERA (1971); Games Won (1964)

Major International Series Appearances: World Cup (Amateur World Series) XVIII (1970 Colombia); Central American Games XI (1970 Panama)

Félix Isasi (RH Infielder; NS Teams: Occidentales, Centrales, Henequeneros; SS Team: Matanzas)

1964–1981	AB	H	2B	3B	HR	RBI	BB	SO	BA
National Series/SS (18)	3902	1142	181	17	45	445	472	294	.293
International Series (19)	584	185	37	4	20	41	—	—	.292

Cuban League Leader: (SS=Selective Series Season) Runs (1966, 1967); Stolen Bases (1964, 1966, 1967, 1975SS); Sacrifice Hits (1964); Hit by Pitch (1979SS)

Major International Series Appearances: Pan American Games V (1967 Canada); World Cup XVII (1969 Dominican Republic); World Cup XVIII (1970 Colombia); Central American Games XI (1970 Panama); World Cup XIX (1971 Cuba); Pan American Games VI (1971 Colombia); World Cup XX (1972 Nicaragua); World Cup XXI (1973 Havana); Central American Games XII (1974 Dominican Republic); Pan American Games VII (1975 Mexico); World Cup XXIV (1976 Colombia)

Orestes Kindelán (RH 1st Baseman/Catcher/DH; NS Team: Santiago de Cuba; SS Teams: Serranos, Orientales)

1982–2002	AB	H	2B	3B	HR	RBI	BB	SO	BA
National Series/SS (21)	6488	2030	330	36	487	1511	1232	1025	.313
World Cup Series (6)	222	94	—	—	23	78	—	—	.423
Olympic Games (3)	109	42	—	—	14	36	—	—	.385
Pan American Games (4)	119	41	—	—	13	48	—	—	.345
Central American Games (4)	103	50	—	—	20	50	—	—	.485
Intercontinental Cup (6)	182	72	—	—	28	68	—	—	.396
International Totals	735	299	—	—	98	280	—	—	**.406**

Cuban League Leader: (SS=Selective Series Season) Batting Champion (1989); Runs (1986SS, 1988SS, 1989); Doubles (1987SS); Home Runs (1984SS, 1986SS, 1987, 1987SS, 1988, 1988SS, 1989, 1993SS); RBI (1986SS, 1987SS, 1989, 1993SS); Walks (1989, 1989SS, 1990, 1990SS); Intentional Walks (1987SS, 1988, 1989, 1989SS); Strikeouts (1994SS); Sacrifice Flies (1984, 1992SS)

International Series Appearances: Intercontinental Cup VII (1985 Canada); Central American Games XV (1986 Dominican Republic); World Cup XXXIX (1986 Holland); Pan American Games X (1987 Indianapolis USA); Intercontinental Cup VIII (1987 Havana); World Cup

XXX (1988 Italy); Intercontinental Cup IX (1989 Puerto Rico); Central American Games XVI (1990 Mexico); World Cup XXXI (1990 Canada); Pan American Games XI (1991 Havana); Olympic Games XXV (1992 Barcelona); Central American Games XVII (1993 Puerto Rico); Intercontinental Cup XI (1993 Italy); World Cup XXXII (1994 Nicaragua); Pan American Games XII (1995 Argentina); Intercontinental Cup XII (1995 Havana); Olympic Games XXVI (1996 Atlanta USA); Intercontinental Cup XIV (1997 Spain); Central American Games XVIII (1998 Venezuela); World Cup XXX (1998 Italy); Pan American Games XIII (1999 Canada); Olympic Games XXVII (2000 Sydney); World Cup XXXIV (2001 Taipei)

Pedro Luis Lazo (RH Pitcher; NS Team: Pinar del Río)

1991–2004	*GP*	*GS*	*W–L*	*IP*	*H*	*ER*	*SO*	*BB*	*ERA*
National Series/SS (14)	**391**	**308**	**181–102**	**2332.2**	**2149**	**882**	**1826**	**750**	**3.40**
World Cup Series (3)	—	—	4–0	20.1	—	1	—	—	0.45
Olympic Games (3)		—	—	3–1	23.1	—	13	—	—	5.06
Pan American Games (2)	—	—	0–0	17.0	—	1	—	—	0.53
Central American Games (1)	—	—	1–0	6.2	—	1	—	—	1.35
Intercontinental Cup (2)	—	—	3–0	29.1	—	4	—	—	1.23
International Totals	—	—	**11–1**	**93.0**	—	**18**	—	—	**1.74**

Cuban League Leader: (SS=Selective Series Season) ERA (1997); W–L Pct. (1995SS); Complete Games (1995); Shutouts (1994)
International Series Appearances: Pan American Games XII (1995 Argentina); Intercontinental Cup XII (1995 Havana); Olympic Games XXVI (1996 Atlanta USA); Intercontinental Cup XIII (1997 Spain); Central American Games XVIII (1998 Venezuela); World Cup XXXIII (1998 Italy); Pan American Games XIII (1999 Canada); Olympic Games XXVII (2000 Sydney); World Cup XXXIV (2001 Taipei); Pan American Games XIV (2003 Santo Domingo); World Cup XXXV (2003 Havana); Olympic Games XXVIII (2004 Athens)

Fidel Linares (LH Outfielder; NS Teams: Occidentales, Pinar del Río)

1962–1971	*AB*	*H*	*2B*	*3B*	*HR*	*RBI*	*BB*	*SO*	*BA*
National Series (10)	1581	425	52	13	8	159	187	143	.267
International Series (2)	43	12	4	0	0	6	1	1	.279

Cuban League Leader: Hits (1963); Doubles (1964); Intentional Walks (1970); Hit by Pitch (1962)
International Series Appearances: Central American Games IX (1962 Jamaica); Pan American Games IV (1963 Brazil)

Omar Linares (RH 3rd Baseman/DH; NS Teams: Vegueros, Pinar del Río; SS Teams: Pinar del Río, Occidentales)

1983–2002	*AB*	*H*	*2B*	*3B*	*HR*	*RBI*	*BB*	*SO*	*BA*
National Series/SS (20)	**5962**	**2195**	**327**	**54**	**404**	**1221**	**1327**	**675**	**.368**
World Cup Series (6)	219	97	10	4	22	70	19	27	.443
Olympic Games (3)	108	48	3	0	13	27	13	20	.444
Pan American Games (4)	111	41	8	6	8	31	29	13	.369
Central American Games (4)	100	38	9	2	8	27	14	15	.380
Intercontinental Cup (6)	211	98	20	3	27	72	26	26	.464
International Totals	**749**	**322**	**50**	**15**	**78**	**227**	**101**	**101**	**.430**

Cuban League Leader: (SS=Selective Series Season) Batting Champion (1985, 1986, 1990, 1992, 1992SS, 1993); Runs (1985, 1987, 1989, 1990, 1991SS, 1992SS, 1993, 1995); Hits (1990SS); Triples (1985); Home Runs (1992SS); RBI (1988SS, 1992SS); Walks (1990, 1991SS, 1992, 1992SS, 1993, 1994, 1994SS, 1995, 1996); Intentional Walks (1986, 1990, 1991, 1991SS, 1992, 1992SS, 1993, 1994, 1994SS, 1996); Sacrifice Flies (1994SS)
International Series Appearances: Central American Games XV (1986 Dominican Republic); World Cup XXIX (1986 Holland); Pan American Games (1987, Indianapolis USA); Intercontinental Cup VIII (1987 Havana); World Cup XXX (1988 Italy); Intercontinental Cup IX (1989 Puerto Rico); Central American Games XVI (1990 Mexico); World Cup XXXI (1990 Canada); Pan American Games XI (1991 Havana); Olympic Games XXV (1992 Barcelona); Intercontinental Cup XI (1993 Italy); Central American Games XVII (1993 Puerto Rico); World Cup XXXII (1994 Nicaragua); Pan American Games XII (1995 Argentina); Intercontinental Cup XII (1995 Havana); Olympic Games XXVI (1996 Atlanta USA); Intercontinental Cup XIII (1997 Spain); Central American Games XVIII (1998 Venezuela); World Cup XXXIII (1998 Italy); Pan American Games XIII (1999 Canada); Intercontinental Cup XIV (1999 Sydney); Olympic Games XXVII (2000 Sydney); World Cup XXXIV (2001 Taipei)

Agustín Marquetti (LH 1st Baseman; NS Teams: Habana, Constructores, Metropolitanos, Industriales; SS Team: Habana)

1967–1986	*AB*	*H*	*2B*	*3B*	*HR*	*RBI*	*BB*	*SO*	*BA*
National Series (22)	6725	1935	279	31	207	1106	753	654	.288
International Series (27)	674	233	43	6	31	189	70	60	.346

Cuban League Leader: (SS=Selective Series Season) Doubles (1978, 1980SS); Triples (1966); Home Runs (1969, 1972); RBI (1969, 1972); Intentional Walks (1967); Hit by Pitch (1969, 1974); Sacrifice Flies (1974)
Major International Series Appearances: World Cup XVII (1969 Dominican Republic); World Cup XVIII (1970 Colombia); Pan American Games VI (1971 Colombia); World Cup XX (1972 Nicaragua); World Cup XXI (1973 Havana); Central American Games XII (1974 Dominican Republic); Pan American Games VII (1975 Mexico); World Cup XXIV (1976 Colombia); World Cup XXV (1978 Italy); Central American Games XIII (1978 Colombia); Intercontinental Cup IV (1979 Havana); Pan American Games VIII (1979 Puerto Rico)

Germán Mesa (RH Shortstop; NS Team: Industriales; SS Teams: Ciudad Habana, Habana)

1985–2002	*AB*	*H*	*2B*	*3B*	*HR*	*RBI*	*BB*	*SO*	*BA*
National Series/SS (16)	**4344**	**1239**	**195**	**33**	**112**	**527**	**688**	**550**	**.285**
World Cup Series (2)	48	14	—	—	1	11	—	—	.292

1985–2002	AB	H	2B	3B	HR	RBI	BB	SO	BA
Olympic Games (2)	48	18	—	—	0	7	—	—	.375
Pan American Games (3)	79	27	—	—	1	10	—	—	.342
Central American Games (2)	56	17	—	—	2	8	—	—	.304
Intercontinental Cup (3)	71	24	—	—	1	13	—	—	.338
International Totals	**302**	**100**	**—**	**—**	**5**	**49**	**—**	**—**	**.331**

Cuban League Leader: (SS=Selective Series Season) Hits (1988SS); Runs (1993SS); Triples (1988SS); Stolen Bases (1988, 1989, 1991); Sacrifice Hits (1993SS)

International Series Appearances: Intercontinental Cup IX (1989 Puerto Rico); Central American Games XVI (1990 Mexico); Pan American Games XI (1991 Havana); Olympic Games XXV (1992 Barcelona); Central American Games XVII (1993 Puerto Rico); Intercontinental Cup XI (1993 Italy); World Cup XXXII (1994 Nicaragua); Pan American Games XII (1995 Argentina); Intercontinental Cup XII (1995 Havana); Pan American Games XIII (1999 Canada); Olympic Games XXVII (2000 Sydney); World Cup XXXIV (2001 Taipei)

Victor Mesa (RH Outfielder; NS Team: Villa Clara; SS Teams: Las Villas, Centrales)

1978–1996	AB	H	2B	3B	HR	RBI	BB	SO	BA
National Series/SS (19)	**6834**	**2171**	**351**	**46**	**273**	**1174**	**662**	**843**	**.318**
World Cup Series (5)	218	83	15	4	9	55	11	27	.381
Olympic Games (1)	25	14	4	0	1	9	2	2	.560
Pan American Games (4)	101	36	7	2	5	42	16	12	.356
Central American Games (4)	117	35	2	2	2	18	5	10	.299
Intercontinental Cup (6)	183	67	11	4	13	45	9	22	.366
International Totals	**644**	**235**	**39**	**12**	**30**	**169**	**43**	**73**	**.365**

Cuban League Leader: (SS=Selective Series Season) Hits (1991SS); Runs (1981, 1983, 1983SS, 1984SS); Doubles (1980, 1990); Stolen Bases (1979, 1980, 1983, 1983SS, 1984, 1984SS, 1985SS, 1987SS, 1988SS, 1989, 1990SS, 1991 SS, 1992, 1992SS, 1993SS); Hits (1988SS); Runs (1993SS); Triples (1988SS); Stolen Bases (1988, 1989, 1991); Sacrifice Hits (1993SS)

International Series Appearances: Intercontinental Cup V (1981 Canada); Central American Games XIV (1982 Havana); Intercontinental Cup VI (1983 Belgium); Pan American Games IX (1983 Venezuela); World Cup XXVIII (1984 Havana); Central American Games XV (1986 Dominican Republic); World Cup XXIX (1986 Holland); Intercontinental Cup VIII (1987 Havana); Pan American Games X (1987 Indianapolis USA); World Cup XXX (1988 Italy); Intercontinental Cup IX (1989 Puerto Rico); Central American Games XVI (1990 Mexico); World Cup XXXI (1990 Canada); Pan American Games XI (1991 Havana); Olympic Games XXV (1992 Barcelona); Central American Games XVII (1993 Puerto Rico); Intercontinental Cup XI (1993 Italy); World Cup XXXII (1994 Nicaragua); Intercontinental Cup XII (1995 Havana); Pan American Games XII (1995 Argentina).

Antonio Pacheco (RH Second Baseman; NS Team: Santiago; SS Teams: Orientales, Serranos)

1981–2002	AB	H	2B	3B	HR	RBI	BB	SO	BA
National Series/SS (22)	**7045**	**2356**	**366**	**63**	**284**	**1304**	**741**	**834**	**.334**
World Cup Series (7)	266	112	—	—	21	32	—	—	.421
Olympic Games (3)	105	38	—	—	8	80	—	—	.362
Pan American Games (4)	112	52	—	—	9	50	—	—	.464
Central American Games (4)	102	43	—	—	8	29	—	—	.422
Intercontinental Cup (7)	242	88	—	—	12	46	—	—	.364
International Totals	**827**	**333**	**—**	**—**	**58**	**237**	**—**	**—**	**.402**

Cuban League Leader: (SS=Selective Series Season) Hits (1985SS, 1987SS); Runs (1987); Doubles (1987SS); Triples (1983, 1985SS); Sacrifice Flies (1985SS, 1988SS, 1997)

International Series Appearances: Pan American Games IX (1983 Venezuela); Intercontinental Cup VI (1983 Belgium); World Cup XVIII (1984 Havana); Intercontinental Cup VII (1985 Canada); Central American Games XV (1986 Dominican Republic); World Cup XIX (1986 Holland); Pan American Games X (1987 Indianapolis USA); Intercontinental Cup VIII (1987 Havana); World Cup XXX (1988 Italy); Intercontinental Cup IX (1989 Puerto Rico); Central American Games XVI (1990 Mexico); World Cup XXXI (1990 Canada); Pan American Games XI (1991 Havana); Olympic Games XXV (1992 Barcelona); Central American Games XVII (1993 Puerto Rico); Intercontinental Cup XI (1993 Italy); World Cup XXXII (1994 Nicaragua); Pan American Games XII (1995 Argentina); Intercontinental Cup XII (1995 Havana); Olympic Games XXVI (1996 Atlanta USA); Intercontinental Cup XIV (1997 Spain); Central American Games XVIII (1998 Venezuela); World Cup XXXIII (1998 Italy); Olympic Games XXVII (2000 Sydney); World Cup XXXIV (2001 Taipei)

Gaspar "Curro" Pérez (RH Pitcher; NS Teams: Henequeneros, Occidentales, Matanzas)

1964–1973	GP	GS	W–L	IP	H	ER	SO	BB	ERA
National Series (10)	222	106	76–63	1072.2	860	312	576	562	2.62
International Series (4)	17	7	9–1	96.0	NA	12	70	20	1.12

Cuban League Leader: Complete Games (1968); Wins (1965, 1966); Shutouts (1965); Innings Pitched (1968); Hits (1968); Bases on Balls (1965, 1966, 1967, 1969); Intentional Walks (1967, 1969); Hit Batsmen (1965, 1966, 1967, 1968, 1970)

International Series Appearances: World Cup XVII (1969 Dominican Republic); Central American Games X (1966 Puerto Rico); Pan American Games V (1967 Canada); Central American Games XI (1970 Panama)

Wilfredo Sánchez (LH Outfielder; NS Teams: Henequeneros; Citricultores; Matanzas; SS Team: Matanzas)

1967–1985	AB	H	2B	3B	HR	RBI	BB	SO	BA
National Series/SS (19)	6565	2174	228	69	16	523	503	310	.331
International Series (13)	776	264	38	9	NA	99	46	40	.340

Cuban League Leader: (SS=Selective Series Seasons) Batting Champion (1969, 1970, 1976, 1977SS, 1979, 1984); Runs (1970); Hits (1969, 1970, 1972, 1973, 1976, 1976SS, 1977SS, 1979, 1979SS, 1980SS); Triples (1969, 1976SS); Stolen Bases (1970, 1975, 1976, 1976SS, 1982)

International Series Appearances: World Cup XVIII (1970 Colombia); Central American Games XI (1970 Panama); World Cup XIX (1971 Havana); Pan American Games VI (1971 Colombia); World Cup XX (1972 Nicaragua); World Cup XXI (1973 Havana); Central American Games XII (1974 Dominican Republic); Pan American Games VII (1975 Mexico); World Cup XXIV (1976 Colombia); World Cup XXV (1978 Italy); Central American Games XIII (1978 Colombia); Pan American Games VIII (1979 Puerto Rico); Intercontinental Cup IV (1979 Havana); World Cup XXVI (1980 Japan)

Luis Ulacia (LH Outfielder/Shortstop; NS Teams: Camagüey; SS Team: Camagüeyanos)

1982–2002	*AB*	*H*	*2B*	*3B*	*HR*	*RBI*	*BB*	*SO*	*BA*
National Series/SS (21)	6961	2183	281	58	145	682	676	653	.314
World Cup Series (4)	127	51	—	—	3	19	—	—	.402
Olympic Games (3)	68	26	—	—	3	10	—	—	.382
Pan American Games (4)	83	34	—	—	1	7	—	—	.410
Central American Games (2)	38	17	—	—	0	4	—	—	.447
Intercontinental Cup (3)	93	31	—	—	2	11	—	—	.333
International Totals	409	159	—	—	9	51	—	—	.388

Cuban League Leader: (SS=Selective Series Season) Batting Champion (1987SS, 1988, 1991, 1996); Stolen Bases (1988)

International Series Appearances: Central American Games XV (1986 Dominican Republic); World Cup XXIX (1986 Holland); Pan American Games X (1987 Indianapolis USA); Intercontinental Cup VIII (1987 Havana); World Cup XXX (1988 Italy); Intercontinental Cup IX (1989 Puerto Rico); Central American Games XVI (1990 Mexico); World Cup XXXI (1990 Canada); Pan American Games XI (1991 Havana); Olympic Games XXV (1992 Barcelona); Pan American Games XII (1995 Argentina); Olympic Games XXVI (1996 Atlanta USA); Intercontinental Cup XIV (1997 Spain); Pan American Games XIII (1999 Canada); Olympic Games XXVII (2000 Sydney); World Cup XXXIV (2001 Taipei)

Modesto Verdura (RH Pitcher; NS Teams: Azucareros, Las Villas)

1962–1969	*GP*	*GS*	*W–L*	*IP*	*H*	*ER*	*SO*	*BB*	*ERA*
National Series (8)	110	47	32–20	475.1	407	135	310	221	2.56
International Series (2)	6	3	2–1	28.0	NA	5	22	4	1.61

Cuban League Leader: ERA (1963); W–L Pct. (1963, 1968); Complete Games (1963); Wins (1963); Innings Pitched (1963); Strikeouts (1963); Intentional Walks (1963)

International Series Appearances: Central American Games IX (1962 Jamaica); Pan American Games IV (1963 Brazil)

Braudilio Vinent (RH Pitcher; NS Teams: Mineros, Orientales, Serranos, Santiago de Cuba; SS Teams: Oriente, Orientales)

1968–1987	*GP*	*GS*	*W–L*	*IP*	*H*	*ER*	*SO*	*BB*	*ERA*
National Series/SS (20)	477	400	221–167	3259.2	2645	875	2134	989	2.42
International Series (36)	96	58	56–4	511.2	0	114	421	157	2.01

Cuban League Leader: (SS=Selective Series Seasons) ERA (1968, 1973); W–L Pct. (1976SS); Games Started (1971, 1975SS, 1976SS, 1979SS, 1981, 1981SS); Complete Games (1973, 1974, 1976SS, 1977SS, 1979SS, 1980, 1981SS, 1983SS); Wins (1973, 1974, 1976SS, 1980); Shutouts (1972, 1973); Innings Pitched (1974, 1976SS, 1977SS, 1979SS, 1980, 1981SS); Strikeouts (1971, 1972, 1979SS, 1981); Hit Batsmen (1971, 1981SS)

Major International Series Appearances: Central American Games XI (1970 Panama); Pan American Games VI (1971 Colombia); World Cup XX (1972 Nicaragua), World Cup XXI (1973 Havana); Central American Games XII (1974 Dominican Republic); Pan American Games VII (1975 Mexico); World Cup XXIV (1976 Colombia); World Cup XXV (1978 Italy); Central American Games XIII (1978 Colombia); Pan American Games VII (1979 Puerto Rico); Intercontinental Cup IV (1979, Havana); World Cup XXVI (1980 Japan); Intercontinental Cup V (1981 Canada); Central American Games XIV (1982 Havana); Intercontinental Cup VI (1983 Belgium); Pan American Games IX (1983 Venezuela); World Cup XXVIII (1984 Havana)

12

Playing with the Enemy: Player Defections, the Orioles, and Baseball Détente

I had heard that Cubans are a deeply religious people. In two days here I have learned that baseball is their religion.
— Sam Lacy, Baltimore Afro-American (circa 1920)

Cuban baseball and Cuban popular culture were both sizzling hot across the final decade of the recent millennium. Spurred by some notable player defections, the island nation's long-sequestered national pastime was again suddenly generating frequent notice in the North American sporting press. The Cubans made the baseball venue at the 1996 Atlanta Olympics their own personal showcase, doing so while Team USA stumbled in the semifinals versus Japan and had to settle for a consolation bronze metal. But the biggest headline-grabbers were a pair of Cuban half-brothers who defected to the majors and stamped their mark on MLB post-season play in two consecutive seasons of the late nineties.

Cuba's North American pop culture revival near millennium's end also reopened on several fronts beyond the small world of the baseball diamond. Fiery rhythms from Ry Cooder's *Buena Vista Social Club* music CD and movie soundtrack first spawned a new Latin music craze throughout the mid and late nineties. At the close of the same decade a heart-tugging family drama and frenzied media circus attached to Cuba's most notable political refugee, 9-year-old Elian González, fanned renewed debate over Washington's long-failed anti–Castro policies. And even Fidel himself was back on the front pages of U.S. dailies once the Elian *cause célèbre* handed the world's "last true communist" an unexpected gold-plated opportunity to rally literally millions of long-suffering Cubans unto Havana streets for unified mass demonstrations against policies of the demonized American government and actions by the feared Miami-Cuban "mafia." At the dawn of the 21st century, if it was at all Cuba-related it was seemingly now highly newsworthy.

But it was nonetheless Cuban baseball as much as anything else that again stoked the dying embers of a 40-year-old USA–Cuba political standoff. A much publicized and long-anticipated grudge series between Cuba's vaunted national all-stars and the big-league Baltimore Orioles during spring 1999 drew millions of curious fans to U.S. television sets and provoked more than mild surprise at the Cuban's shocking on-field successes. And each trumpeted addition to a small if note-worthy stream of Cuban national team defectors also grabbed sports-page headlines in the wake of surprisingly stellar and tantalizingly parallel 1997 and 1998 LCS and World Series performances by half-brothers Liván Hernández (Florida Marlins) and Orlando "El Duque" Hernández (New York Yankees)—the most celebrated escapees from Fidel Castro's communist-controlled baseball hotbed.

Considerable mystique surrounding the Cuban pastime also inevitably meant a spate of new stateside books and magazine features, and most of these unfortunately only served to muddy the waters. While Yale University distinguished literature professor Roberto González Echevarría likely reached the broadest audience with his bestselling volume *The Pride of Havana* (Oxford University Press, 1999), González Echevarría's painstaking scholarly effort was somewhat blunted by the renowned Cuban-born professor's choice to engage in "some unchecked mythmaking of his own" (to quote reviewer David Skinner). In a balanced and perceptive journal review (*Nine* 8:2, 153–157), Skinner — a veteran Cuba traveler and diehard Cuban League *aficionado* — tips his critical cap to González Echevarría for unprecedented comprehensive coverage of Cuba's rich baseball scene; yet Skinner also highlights the flaws diminishing this top-selling Cuban baseball book of recent literary seasons. Such flaws ("unsupported speculations about historical events, and ... irrational rejection of all things Castro") inevitably follow from the author's frequent decisions to treat his near-virgin subject matter more as nostalgia-inspired celebration and politically driven dialectic than as genuine historical canon.

González Echevarría's argument in a nutshell was that Cuban baseball had already reached its zenith in the winter of 1946–47, when his own beloved Habana Lions fell to the rival Almendares Scorpions during an exceptionally emotional Cuban winter league pennant chase, and then after that apparent unparalleled apex, the national sport rather abruptly simply died on the vine. In 400-plus pages the expert witness and dedicated chronicler offers no serious history of Cuban baseball's most recent and achievement-rich near-half-century

(1961–present), an era boasting Cuba's only true efforts at establishing anything approaching genuine island-wide league play.

González Echevarria unquestionably offers a most admirable history of Cuban baseball's earliest days — arguably the most thorough account found anywhere, in either English or Spanish; nonetheless, many thinly disguised political and personal preferences in the end discredit the thin portrait of Cuba's contemporary baseball scene. For González Echevarría the unrivaled heyday (and thus the true apogee) in Cuban baseball arrived in the forties, not surprisingly with the exact era of his own childhood fandom. His painstaking portrait of that particular epoch (focusing on a defining showdown series — "The Game, when Max Lanier beat Habana at the end of the 1946–47 season") is tinged with both political leanings (his fondness for the pre–Castro Batista era in which he himself was raised) and childhood nostalgia (fascination with forties-era clubs representing Almendares and his own favored Habana). He thus egregiously overrates one epoch (the penultimate decade for a strictly Havana-based professional league) and arguably also overrates comparative talents of both modern-day defectors (Liván and Orlando Hernández) as well as earlier-era Cuban-born big leaguers (José Canseco, and even Orestes Miñoso). More unfortunate still, he refuses to explore in any detail a full half of the vital Cuban baseball story — the engaging history comprising forty-plus seasons of a thriving country-wide and largely big-league-status circuit that since 1962 has provided a hidden parallel baseball universe, one existing alongside but totally independent from the "grand leagues" of North America's organized professional baseball. *The Pride of Havana* thus repeatedly belittles or largely ignores a large and vital segment — arguably even the main chapter — of Cuba's 15-decade-long baseball history.

Fortunately, Gonzalez Echevarría is not the only recent American chronicler of Cuba's baseball scene. In *Full Count: Inside Cuban Baseball* (Southern Illinois University Press, 2000), University of Texas researcher Milton Jamail—who has long doubled as astute correspondent covering current Latin American baseball for both *Baseball America* and *USA Today Baseball Weekly*— is far more lucid and informative on the topic of the contemporary Cuban pastime. For the record, I do not entirely adopt Jamail's opinions on the current status of Cuban League baseball any more than I share González Echevarría's views. But I do side with Jamail when it comes to his central conclusion that it is post-revolutionary (post–1962) Cuban baseball that holds prime interest and prime importance from both historical and contemporary perspectives.

Cuba's diehard baseball *aficionados*, especially those born on the island but now long-isolated by their expatriate experience in Miami or New York, seem to misapprehend repeatedly an altogether stark reality. If the pre–Castro-era Cuban professional circuit may well have provided an indispensable chapter in North America's Negro league baseball saga, its simultaneous impact on major league events was regrettably largely negligible. With the few exceptions of Dolf Luque, Orestes Miñoso and Camilo Pascual, Cubans in the big leagues from Almeida and Marsans down to Tony Oliva and Zoilo

Versalles were collectively little more than a minor blip on the wide screen of major league history. Oliva's pair of debut batting titles in the sixties and Louie Tiant's World Series heroics of the mid–1970s generated considerably less press at the time than that devoted to a pair of refugee Hernández half-brothers after their own October MVP performances in the late nineties. A small handful of Cuban "defectors" during the past dozen summers — Liván Hernández, Orlando Hernández, Rey Ordóñez, Danys Báez and José Ariel Contreras — are almost assuredly the best contingent of Cubans ever to perform in the stateside major leagues. Most certainly they represent the best refugee ballplayers among native Cubans who actually spent their early years learning the game back home on native soil and not as baseball exiles reared in Miami or other ports farther to the north.

Jamail's intimate examination of the workings of the contemporary Cuban League system (and the national sports program that supports it) also provides valuable insights nowhere else available. Jamail is anything but an apologist for the current Cuban baseball system: his entire book represents a sharp attack on what he sees as the way Cuba's government (especially Fidel Castro himself) has repeatedly usurped and distorted the national sport for seemingly cheap political posturing. In the end, Jamail assesses Cuban baseball of the 1990s and 2000s, especially the Cuban League and the crack Cuban national team that represents its highest achievements, as an institution that is today floundering on the brink of dire crisis.

Thus Jamail sets the tone for what has become a familiar drill for North American writers. The bulk of recent American press accounts treating Cuba's national pastime have been given over to chest-thumping stories about Cuba's recent rash of baseball defectors. And here again we find more than a small dose of misinformation and even outright distortion. Foremost among the exaggerated and romanticized accounts are those surrounding the reported dramatic escape from Fidel Castro's clutches by former New York Yankee star hurler Orlando "El Duque" Hernández.

The most outrageous "defector" account was the one penned for the pages of *Cigar Aficionado* (March/April 1999) by free-lance journalist Ken Shouler. Readers are tantalized by Shouler's gripping saga of a dangerous 12-hour and 35-mile harrowing escape to the distant haven of the Bahamas, reputedly made in a leaky raft, with little food or fresh water, surrounded by shark-infested seas. This heavily tweaked account would be soon enough exposed as entirely false, and it was one that hardly made much sense even at the time. The truth was that El Duque's departure from Cuban shores was aided and abetted from the start by his USA-based future agent. Any reader could barely image Miami-based player agent Joe Cubas at the time so incautiously risking his high-priced meal ticket by exposing a treasured pitcher headed for big league millions to such life-threatening dangers. In the end, Shouler's vivid if fictionalized tale reads suspiciously like little more than a press release orchestrated by El Duque's Castro-loathing attorney and business agent, Joe Cubas himself.

If the reported " miracle" escapes to freedom by departing Cuban national team stars have usually been heavily oversold, so has the reported talent level of many if not most of the journeyman Cuban Leaguers making up a large percentage of fleeing island ballplayers. This misperception of baseball talent in contemporary Cuba has been but one byproduct of the continuous flood of overblown defector stories. The notion has repeatedly been advanced by agents handling Cuban defectors (Joe Cubas, Gus Domínguez and Henry Vilar are the most prominent), and also by inaccurate press accounts filled with inflated Cuban League stats or bogus accounts of national team stardom, that a handful of defectors have been the true cream of the crop from Cuba's huge talent supply. This has hardly been the case, of course. Orlando Hernández did boast back in 1998 the best won-lost record in the history of post-revolutionary Cuban baseball. Ex-big-leaguers Rolando Arrojo (Devil Rays and Red Sox) and Osvaldo Fernández (Giants and Reds) both pitched successfully for the Cuban national team before their departures; the eleventh-hour flight of Arrojo in July 1996 was without question a potential major blow to Cuban victory hopes on the eve of the Atlanta Olympics. But it is not to be overlooked that in the end the Cubans won easily in Atlanta even without Arrojo to anchor their pitching corps. And if El Duque's won-lost record still stands at the top of the Cuban record book — largely because his career in Havana ended abruptly in mid-stream — this in itself does not rubber stamp him as the best Cuban pitcher of the nineties.

The last designation probably falls either to Duque's Industriales teammate Lázaro Valle, or to Santiago right-hander Norge Vera (see Chapter 11), a close second to El Duque in career winning percentage (.711 to .728), a potent force on the world tournament scene, and lately a wily veteran who two seasons back led his club to its fourth National Series crown in the past seven years. Vera has won nearly three-quarters of his outings; he performed an unparalleled feat by winning back-to-back pressure-packed semifinal and final games at the 2003 World Cup in Havana; and given his one shot at big leaguers, he mesmerized a lethargic Baltimore Orioles team at Camden Yards. Maels Rodríguez — the best pure physical specimen of the modern Cuban League era — departed the island only after arm injuries left his career in a shambles. And Pedro Luis Lazo is every bit the equal of José Contreras and just as devastating a force during Olympic play. There is also a plethora of talented young Cuban arms (headed by Yunieski Maya, Dany Betancourt and southpaw Yulieski González) that may well top the aces of either the 1980s or nineties.

Most often obscured, then, is an unalterable fact that the best Cuban pitchers have almost all remained back home; even recent celebrated departures by national team mainstay José Contreras (September 2002) and strikeout phenom Maels Rodríguez (October 2003) have merely opened coveted national team starting slots for such equally sensational young replacements as Vicyohandri Odelín, Ifreidi Coss, Adiel Palma and Frank Montieth. And if Cuba's best pitchers have remained loyal to the island's non-pro system, so have the most notorious sluggers like past-decade stars Omar Linares and Orestes Kindelán and the current heavy bashers Yulieski Gourriel, Frederich Cepeda and Osmani Urrutia. In light of ex-Japanese Pacific League batting king Ichiro Suzuki's potent big-league hitting, one can only wonder about Osmani Urrutia, author of five .400-plus Cuban League performances in the last half-dozen seasons.

The single major position-player departure has been Kendry Morales, who in early 2006 remains an unproven if promising talent in the Los Angeles Angels farm system. More insightful than any apocryphal Hollywood-scripted rags-to-riches legend glorifying El Duque is the more matter-of-fact defection scenario surrounding former New York Mets shortstop Rey Ordóñez. Ordóñez (the only position player among defectors to enjoy long-term success at the big-league level) fled Cuba back in 1993 (while his national junior team was in Buffalo, New York, for that summer's World University Games) largely because of a sub-

Omar Linares, top Cuban League star of the post-revolutionary era, was never tempted by the millions of dollars he might have earned as a big league headliner.

stantial roadblock of talented middle infielders (including legendary Germán Mesa and promising Eduardo Paret) lined up ahead of him for a coveted spot on the prestigious national team. Any notion that defections like those of El Duque or José Contreras foreshadowed imminent collapse of the wounded Cuban sports system remains pretty much a North American media pipe dream.

* * *

Cuba's national team juggernaut had reached full steam at the outset of a new century. Three straight IBAF World Cup victories without even a single individual game defeat — Tawain 2001, Havana 2003, Holland 2005 — would keep the momentum surging into the new millennium. And the recapturing of an Olympic crown at Athens in 2004 provided an indelible stamp of full recovery on the patient that had seemingly suffered from something of an undiagnosed malaise in the mid-nineties. With entry into Major League Baseball's first World Baseball Classic looming on the horizon for March 2006, Cuban baseball had never been more fun than it was by the close the first half-decade of the twenty-first century.

Despite the glories brought by uninterrupted international successes, all is not entirely well with the national game on Fidel Castro's hardscrabble home island. Home-front enthusiasm for the besieged Cuban League dipped noticeably in the late nineties and disillusioned fans seemed by 1997 (the first season after the impressive defensive of Olympic gold at Atlanta) to be abandoning ballparks everywhere around the island. A newly instituted 30-game short second season launched in June and July 2002 has been a total bust so far; the plan to collapse 16 National Series teams into four all-star clubs called Orientales, Oriente, Centrales and Habana has failed miserably to capture even a modest following among island baseball diehards and fans now shun these contests both at the park and on the television screen.

The continued trickle of big-league defections that has most recently erased two of the top league pitching stars — José Contreras and Maels Rodríguez — has unquestionably marred the image of Cuban baseball back home, even if it has failed to slow down perceptively the national team juggernaut on the field of play. Lifetime banishments (Germán Mesa in 1996 and Eduardo Paret in 1997, though both star players were soon reinstated) and brief suspensions (Yobal Dueñas and Bárbaro Cañizares, on the eve of 2003 World Cup play) along with forced retirements (Mesa, Kindelán, Linares and Ulacia all departed for Japan as player-coaches in 2002) have dealt a far deadlier blow to once indefatigable fan loyalties. And with ever-worsening economic conditions that today invade just about every element of daily existence, the central institution of Cuban sporting and cultural life appears now to be perilously poised at a crucial crossroads.

Much of the attendance drop-off, especially in Havana, can be attributed to bad economic times and lack of reliable public transportation. Back-to-back National Series crowns for local favorite Havana Industriales were nonetheless greeted with a revitalized rush to the ticket gates in the capital city the past couple of winters. While Cuban fans lately have seemed less willing to spend scarce pesos for seats at Havana's Estadio Latinoamericano, they nonetheless still gather in impassioned throngs on street corners of downtown Havana to heatedly debate both the triumphs and tragedies of their beloved national pastime. If the lengthy National Series campaign does not today pack seats in Havana's ancient stadium like it once did (especially when Industriales is not taking on a traditional rival like Santiago de Cuba or Pinar del Río), a raucous standing-room crowd of 55,000-plus did fill the grandstands for the semifinal and final games featuring Team Cuba at the October 2003 World Cup matches.

The bottom line is that while a continuous trickle of player defections may have drawn headlines here in the United States, such setbacks have indisputably failed to have the expected devastating impact on Cuban baseball that has been repeatedly predicted and even sometimes prematurely reported by American and Canadian journalists, or by legions of naysayers who continue to debunk modern Cuban League baseball as it is presently organized under a unique socialist-inspired and government-controlled amateur league system. It remains largely a myth that Cuban baseball can not survive in the glare of big-dollar contracts offered top stars if they can only escape communist clutches.

Nowhere was North American glee over what were usually heavily exaggerated reports of potential Cuban defections on more outrageous display than in Winnipeg, Canada, during two weeks devoted to July 1999 Pan American Games competitions. Local press outlets seemed far more interested in stoking the fires of political intrigue than in reporting daily results of the exciting competitions themselves. One Canadian daily ran a prominent box score of defections by Cubans as its front page banner. Bold-face oversized typeface trumpeted "Defectors 2, Fidel 0" after the departure from the Cuban camp of two champion Greco-Roman wrestlers during the first week of medal-round matches.

Department store windows directly across the street from Winnipeg's Convention Center housing the Pan Am Games press center also displayed a huge amateurish paper banner featuring a local phone number which disaffected Cubans were urged to ring up for immediate aid in planning defections. And the tense atmosphere turned more acrimonious still as the week progressed. A Cuban delegation including former Olympic track and field star and current INDER boss Alberto Juantorena was provoked into physical retaliation when accosted by flag-waving anti–Castro dissidents on a sidewalk outside the arena where they had just attended medal-round wrestling matches.

Baseball was an expected special focus of the anti–Castro and thus anti–Cuban Winnipeg media onslaught. I myself had agreed to an interview regarding the much inflated baseball career of President Castro (see Chapter 9), an interview I likely should have avoided. When the front page *Winnipeg Free Press* story (penned by staff reporter Grant Granger) appeared in print it predictably carried a tone most hostile to the Cuban camp, much to my own considerable embarrassment. The article headline boldly read: "Deconstructing the Castro myth" and a sub-heading carried a still more provocative claim: "Dictator never offered a contract."

But the most disagreeable incident by far was one that occurred in the crucial ninth inning of an all-important Canada-Cuba semifinal ballgame. With a 2000 Olympic berth on the line for both teams (only the two semifinal winners would qualify for the Sydney games) and Cuba trying to close out the contest in the top of the ninth, play was suddenly halted by a flag-draped anti–Castro protester who stormed the field and circled stunned Cuban pitcher José Ibar. Few security measures were in place at Can West Global Park and the Cuban players had to deal with the rude offender on their own for several tense minutes. Catcher Ariel Pestano took matters into his own hands by wrestling the intruder to the ground halfway between home plate and the pitcher's rubber. It was later confirmed that this was the identical rabble-rouser who had similarly disrupted the Cuba-Orioles contest in Baltimore only two months earlier before being body-slammed to the turf on that first occasion by Cuban second base umpire César Valdés.

The agitator — obviously a high-level security risk — had not only been allowed free entry into Canada during the week of the Pan Am festivities (a questionable decision, given his recent actions and his arrest at a nearly identical public sporting event in Baltimore) but had also encountered absolutely no impediments from Winnipeg security officers when he decided to jump the fence in an effort to ruin an exciting and important baseball game for the name of political ideology. Fortunately, order was finally restored once catcher Pestano and the Cuban bench had put the intruder's own health at considerable risk in full view of 10,000 stunned spectators. Although a visibly shaken José Ibar was now forced to the sidelines, ace reliever Pedro Lazo was able to close down the looming ninth-inning Canadian rally and thus preserve Cuba's immediate Pan Am gold medal hopes as well as all-important Olympic aspirations.

Defectors, or the implied threat of defectors, were thus the glamour story of the 1999 Pan American Games (baseball and all other sports included) as far as a Canadian press corps and likely also a good portion of the local hometown fans were concerned. In reporting the story in this monolithic fashion, the host Canadian journalists not only seemed to be more in the business of creating news than actually reporting it, but they also seemingly missed out on appreciating the actual headline feature of those games — one of the most outstanding amateur baseball tournaments ever witnessed.

Defections of Cuban athletes in any significant numbers simply did not materialize. One pair of frontline wrestlers had admittedly left for capitalist-style freedom almost before the games were underway. And smack in the middle of the action-packed baseball tournament a story broke that reserve Cuban pitcher Danys Báez had secretly departed from Winnipeg in the company of ubiquitous agent Joe Cubas. Cubas had openly staked out the Winnipeg athletes' village and had reputedly passed hand-written messages to all Cuban baseball players who would listen to his pitch. Despite the tireless efforts of

the Miami-based agent and his coterie, the single prize plucked from the tournament camp was Báez, only the number nine pitcher on a talented and obviously deep nine-man Cuban staff. Báez was hardly a worthless talent by any measure; but he was definitely an unknown commodity at the time. The strapping right-hander would eventually enjoy considerable success in the big leagues as a 98-mph smoke-throwing bull-pen closer with the American League Cleveland Indians and Tampa Bay Devil Rays. But the muscular Pinar del Río native (a few months short of 22 in July 1999) was not the hoped-for juicy plum that might guarantee front page headlines and hefty signing bonuses. In two National Series seasons with the league's strongest club in Pinar del Río, the untested righty had won only six of eleven decisions with an astronomical 4.70 ERA to round out his sparse credentials. His loss would not have the kind of impact back home that, say, the sudden departure of Rolando Arrojo had on the eve of the Atlanta Olympics.

When the Cuban national team visited Baltimore a few months earlier it had been more of the same sort of thing. During a pre-game press conference which also featured Orioles star Cal Ripken, Jr., two Cuban players selected to confront the media — Omar Linares and veteran outfielder Luis Ulacia — were peppered with questions about how they might like to play for the "real" major leagues for real dollars. Linares and Ulacia both politely expressed their desire to join the high-paying pros, as long as they could live in Cuba and travel regularly to their homeland. It was perhaps only a tongue-and-check answer. Ulacia remarked that he would play for free in the majors since baseball itself was far more vital than money. The obvious story here was that once more American sportswriters seemed more interested in player defections than in the intriguing on-field matchup ready to unfold. And outside Camden Yards Park on game day Joe Cubas again held forth with staged "interview" tirades to press representatives and passersby alike about his noble mission of bringing true freedom and unimagined dollars to abused Cuban ballplayers.

Cuban officials certainly did not keep their players under tight security lockdown in their Baltimore hotel. I myself freely entered the hotel lobby with ordinary press credentials and conversed openly with several Cuban ballplayers and other personal friends within the Cuban delegation, both before and immediately after the May 3rd game. But there was nonetheless some degree of caution exercised by Cuban officials. Only hours after the game ended, the entire Cuban delegation was suddenly spirited to the airport with little advanced notice. In the wee hours of the morning the entire delegation was back in the air winging toward Havana. Despite such precautions, one rather less-than-noteworthy member of Cuba's contingent had managed to stay behind. And in predictable fashion the story of this one "defector" was soon milked by the media for all it was worth.

The lone Cuban who jumped ship in Baltimore was former national team pitcher Rigoberto Betancourt, a southpaw of modest bygone stature who had played in the National Series for eight years throughout the sixties and achieved slightly more than modest successes. Betancourt labored for eight campaigns mostly with Havana-based clubs and had posted a 38–27 lifetime ledger with 12 career shutouts; he earned greatest plaudits with a league-best 10 wins in 1967, half of which were whitewashes. More recently he had been used as a youth-league pitching coach and was present on the Baltimore trip as part of a contingent of ex-players and other Cuban athletes brought along as reward for loyal service to the revolution. In the U.S. press Betancourt was immediately and almost predictably billed as a top national team pitching coach, which at the time he certainly was not. Interestingly enough, the Betancourt story would soon offer a strange twist and rather sad outcome. Within six months his name would reappear as subject of a magazine story published in Miami concerning at least one political defector's subsequent disillusionments once he could not find even menial employment in the United States. Betancourt (at least by his own account, told to *Miami New Times* correspondent Lissette Corsa) had apparently been promised some kind of work in organized baseball (perhaps as a coach) but was still wasting away unemployed in Miami, now very much regretting his decision to leave both his native land and his former life. Betancourt was one example of the risks inherent in any attempt by Cubans to trade in homeland, family and a past existence for a mere dream of riches and a better life somewhere in America's coveted Promised Land.

The term "defectors" is unpopular in most Cuban circles, especially among the nation's sports administration. INDER brass in Cuba would rather not have the issue discussed publicly; the official line always is that such athletes "have betrayed the Cuban people." It was also an altogether taboo subject for years in the island press and on Havana's popular radio call-in sports show *Deportivamente*. The ice was only somewhat broken in March of 2001 when I myself trod new ground during a detailed interview with Cubavision broadcaster Carlos Hernández Luján; on that fifteen-minute national telecast I was not only surprisingly allowed to mention players who had fled the country but was actually grilled by Luján concerning my opinions on the impact of top stars abandoning Cuban League teams for big league professionalism.

Even the leading baseball historian from within the anti–Castro exile community, Roberto González Echevarría, claims to be himself quite offended by the term "defectors" when it is applied to athletes rather than to soldiers or to government agents (cf., *The Pride of Havana*, 363). González Echevarría sees the term as implying "desertion" (in the military sense) by athletes who are simply electing where to live and work, and where to display their special talents; he thus faults Cuban officials for implying that their country is an "army led by the

Former Sugar Kings skipper and big league manager Preston Gómez (center) with the author (right) and a fellow journalist during the 1999 Winnipeg Pan American Games, one of the most dramatic international baseball tournaments ever staged.

Maximum Leader" and concludes that the concepts of "desertion" and "defections" are excellent examples of the totalitarian nature of the current Cuban regime. That INDER officials see players who skip the country as traitors to the Cuban people is unquestioned; but at the same time it should be emphasized that the term "defection" is not one Cuban officials themselves chose to use. The term is instead a favored creation of the U.S. and Canadian press corps, and it is the Americans equally as much as the Cubans (I would argue even more so) who have persisted in touting all ballplayer departures from Cuba as presumed political victories over Cuba's competing economic system.

"Defector" as a concept itself thus requires some further clarifications. Cubans in the streets (especially in Havana) talk quite freely about players who have left the country, especially those that have departed while still in their playing prime and those that have a crack at big league stardom. The typical Havana "fan in the street" is predictably fascinated by the accomplishments of his former heroes now playing in the big time. Cubans jam hotel bars (where tourists have access to Mexican Spanish-language ESPN broadcasts) and glue themselves to transistor radios to catch performances by Liván, El Duque and José Contreras during the big league playoffs. Ordinary Cuban fans seem to have none of the aversions to the topic of baseball "defectors" still being displayed by most representatives of Cuba's government-run baseball establishment.

Another mark of ambivalent attitudes toward baseball "traitors" is the fact that Cuban League annual guidebooks still carry full stats for defectors (along with an asterisk and note that the player "abandoned the country")—a sign that INDER has never "officially" deleted their past island achievements or obliterated their tainted memories. (By 2004 the * had been dropped, but El Duque and company are still listed in annual Cuban League guides.) It is thus fair to claim that Cuban authorities have adopted an official public stance branding such players are traitors to the socialist system, and (for good or bad) they obviously are. While some players are perhaps kept off national team traveling squads as perceived risks to escape overseas, there is certainly little visible effort to keep athletes under lock and key once they go on the road. It was easy enough for Arocha, Arrojo, Ordóñez, Báez and Contreras to walk away from delegations in Mexico and the USA and to join family members or agents ready and willing to offer shelter and provide sanctuary.

The American press nonetheless has been even more fascinated with rampant defection stories than their flag-waving Canadian counterparts. It may be only a small exaggeration to observe that seemingly every able-bodied Cuban male who leaves the island in search of wealth and freedom in Miami is bound to be portrayed as a potential Cooperstown hall of famer, or at the very least as a probable big-league all-star, or perhaps the most recent incomparable Cuban League sensation; at the same time, each new ball-playing refugee is claimed also to represent a direct blow struck for democracy and a smack in the face of Cuba's government, if not a vital moral victory against Fidel personally.

The elaborate effort to promote Cuba's baseball refugees has often reached near comical proportions. Some of the ballplayers agent Joe Cubas has showcased in hastily arranged tryout sessions were barely minor league prospects, let alone bona fide major leaguers. Some players ballyhooed as members of Cuba's national team have never played on any top-level Cuban squad and many never even performed on any traveling Cuban national team. One example was Cubas's attempt in August 1997 at marketing defector Osmani Santana. On the heals of Santana's arrival in Miami (with Cubas's assistance), the agent was quoted by *USA Today* as contending that the former Cienfuegos outfielder was a brilliant prospect at age 21 and "one of Cuba's top baseball players" as well as "winner of Cuba's 1996 equivalent of the Gold Glove." That there is no such award in the Cuban League was of little consequence compared to other distortions. Santana was a legitimate Cuban Leaguer to be sure: he had already completed seven full seasons and batted .302 overall during an era still marked by aluminum bats. But his previous seven seasons in the league likely made him no younger than 25 or 26 (not 21!), and he had yet to appear on any national team roster. When Santana abandoned the Cuban delegation in Mexico he was in training as part of the 40-man roster competing for spots (potentially the first for Santana) on the squad about to enter Intercontinental Cup games scheduled for Barcelona.

The ruse can be so easily pulled off because few in the general American public or in the major league scouting corps know much of anything about the Cuban national team — either what it is or how it is selected. So deep is the mystique surrounding Cuban players and so fixed is the mindset about finding the next Duque Hernández or Omar Linares that big league teams will apparently accept just about any line they are fed concerning the ages and potential abilities (and also the

Cuban League achievements) of these unscouted free-agent players.

A case in point came with the signing several years back of two minor prospects by the Texas Rangers. I was contacted at the time (March 2000) by Texas Rangers Media Vice President John Blake and asked about the players' existing Cuban League stats and also about their ages. I was able to supply both and also to point out to Blake that both men (shortstop Jorge Díaz and utility infielder Osmani García) were several years older than what was being billed. Two days later the players were signed and the Rangers released a hastily composed press notice touting the Cubans' incorrect younger ages. They were both billed as 25, but García had already logged 8 seasons with Villa Clara before defecting in August 1998; Díaz had played six years; both were at least three years older than advertised. At times it seems that some big league clubs are willing to throw money at overrated Cuban prospects if only for the immediate publicity value to be garnered. In this instance neither over-aged rookie ever made it out of the Rangers spring camp.

Recent books by Milton Jamail and S.L. Price suggest a Cuban baseball system that is wallowing in desperate crisis. The argument advanced by Jamail (*Full Count*) is cogent enough to require more detailed examination. There is little question that Cuban baseball is rapidly facing a crucial point of no return. The policy of maintaining an amateur system of baseball that might serve as a continuing model of the revolution — perhaps even the last successful vestige of the revolution — has been orchestrated and directed by Fidel himself. INDER's sports ministry is, just as Jamail claims, Cuba's most conservative government institution. The Cuban revolution will likely not last too many more years in its current form. There is certainly disillusionment among players (as there is today for all Cubans) about their continued existence entirely outside the tourist industry economic system based on a U.S. dollar exchange (since November 2004, dollar-equivalent Cuban convertible pesos). Tourist industry workers can help their families far more than ballplayers (or school teachers, lawyers and medical doctors, who are also paid only in Cuban pesos) and thus for all their status Cuba's baseball players are faced with daily economic frustrations. Until the 2002 shipping of five star players (including Linares, Kindelán and Germán Mesa) to Japan, Cuban baseball players did not enjoy the same freedoms to play in other countries and reap dollars that was already being offered to athletes in other sports and also to high profile musicians and graphic artists. And the Cuban fans were certainly dismayed in recent years by the forced retirements and the diminished quality of play all around the league. Jamail is nothing short of accurate when he portrays much of this current crisis facing the Cuban baseball structure. What blunts his critique for me is his offered proposed solutions, which taken together seem a good deal worse than the symptoms they would treat.

Jamail sees Cuban baseball as he sees all Latin baseball, as an important feeder system for the one legitimate baseball stage that exists only in the major leagues. A single salvation for Cuban baseball, from this point of view, would be an open door policy allowing all top Cuban players to move to the U.S. majors and minors to earn their full market value. And the relationship in Jamail's view would be entirely symbiotic: "For the baseball industry, Cuba represents the most important frontier in the increasingly important global search for players. Shortly after the turn of the century, Cuba will likely become the number one source of foreign-born players for the U.S. big-leagues." (*Full Count*, 2)

This is a devoutly wished circumstance that might have enriched Linares or Maels Rodríguez, or a dozen other top-flight Cubans (to say nothing of the investments to be reaped by moguls like George Steinbrenner or agents like Joe Cubas). But it would also likely be a certain death knell for baseball still played on the island. After all, it was nothing so much as the behind-the-scenes takeover of the pro Cuban League by organized baseball a half-century ago (Chapter 5) that spelled a quick demise for the once-thriving Cuban League of the pre-revolution era. It was also the rude intrusion of rampant major league signings of young prospects (mostly by Papa Joe Cambria) that scuttled the traditional hold of amateur play on the island in the early and mid-fifties. The majors (directly with its Arizona Fall League, and more indirectly with big-salary contracts making it unnecessary or prohibited for Latin imports to labor at home in the off-season) have already stripped the heart and soul out of winter league baseball as it today still tenuously exists in other Caribbean countries.

A Cuban League with most of the best players suddenly transferred to minor league clubs in the U.S. might be a welcomed windfall for dozens of elite Cuban ballplayers. It might even offer a short-term economic shot-in-the-arm for Cuba's cash-poor government (if Castro were able to reap profits by peddling stars to big league owners). But what would it do for several million diehard Cuban fans? Would there be any Cuban baseball left on the home front? (Forget talk of a major league or minor league team on the island; there is simply no economic infrastructure now in place that would allow it.) Would Cuban fans rather crowd bars to catch an occasional glimpse of Yulieski Gourriel or Frederich Cepeda and other young stars performing in occasional televised games beamed from Minnesota or Boston, or would they prefer to continue cheering their heroes in the flesh at stadiums in Havana, Holguín or Sancti Spíritus? What would happen to the unique rivalries between provinces that now sustain Cuba's traditional national game? I fear the solutions (the ones Jamail offers) far more than any current economic crisis, which for all its daily impact still allows for fan-pleasing baseball everywhere around the island.

There is little debate that Cuban League baseball is presently surviving in a full-fledged time warp. It can not last forever in its pristine form, isolated from and ignorant of the outside world's current baseball status quo of shopping mall stadiums, blaring electronic entertainment spectacles, games organized exclusively for television, soaring ticket prices, and a constant threat of salary-motivated player strikes. The Cuban League may well soon vanish in its present commercially naïve

Osvaldo Fernández, an early defector of the 1990s, never reached full pro potential after an arm injury suffered in Cuban League play.

format. But should we be further hastening its departure just to enrich even more the coffers of big league club owners? Cuban baseball, just as Jamail argues, has been in a state of turmoil in recent years — a crisis brought on largely by player suspensions and forced retirements and the resulting disillusionment of fans, then aggravated yet further by a larger crisis in the Helms-Burton-plagued Cuban economy. The crisis is real enough even if it may not be of the dire proportions Jamail has suggested. Fan interest has again surged in Cuba in the past three seasons, spiked by a series of redeeming international triumphs over perennial rival Team USA, and by thrilling Intercontinental Cup (2002) and World Cup (2003) victories staged at home in Havana. A new crop of young players headlined by sluggers Yulieski Gourriel and Frederich Cepeda and hurlers Ifredi Coss and Adiel Palma has seized the imagination of Cuban fans; interest has coalesced around four consecutive National Series seasons of .400-plus batting by Las Tunas stalwart Osmani Urrutia. The national team continues to rebound dramatically from its shocking losses in Barcelona and Sydney and would soon impress still further in its long-anticipated clash with big leaguers at the 2006 World Baseball Classic. And player defections remain little more than a distracting sidebar in Havana, for all the headlines they constantly generate in New York or Miami.

But the issue of capitalist sport versus socialist sport is

very much a two-headed monster. It is thus also worth noting that North American professional baseball (the big league version) is today facing its own state of worsening crisis — perhaps of even more severe proportions than that threatening the national game in Cuba. If Cuban fans are alienated by a dip in player performance and a staleness surrounding the National Series in recent winters, American fans are seemingly equally outraged by spoiled million-dollar athletes long out of touch with their anointed roles as public icons. Abuse of performance-enhancing drugs in pursuit of cherish hitting records clouds the game's genuine historic overtones. Major league baseball — despite, if not because of, its unlimited revenue sources, runaway ballplayer salaries and unchecked owner profits — again seems every bit as much on the verge of sudden collapse as does Cuban baseball, with its contrasting poverty of resources and restless under-compensated ballplayers. Neither institution will likely survive very much longer in exactly its present form.

Jamail is also widely off base with his treatment of Cuban defectors as a central story of contemporary CL baseball. I have few quibbles with Jamail's sensitive description of the economic difficulties Cuban players face and the personal issues they struggle with before deciding to abandon their homeland for promised big league riches. What is open to question, however, is his stated conviction that the existence of defectors has been most instrumental in throwing Cuban baseball into its current state of disrepair. Jamail seems to have overstated the case and read far too much into its implications. It is hard to image Cuban national teams winning top international competitions any more easily than they already have even with Arocha, Arroyo, El Duque and now Contreras. Outside of El Duque, Contreras and Maels Rodríguez, most defectors have been second-tier performers and not popular Havana idols; at that, Contreras, Maels, and recently Kendry Morales have been immediately replaced by the likes of Gourriel, Cepeda and Vicyohandri Odelín without so much as a skipped beat. Recent October and November 2003 results at both the World Cup and Olympic qualifier (where Cuba twice coasted to easy victory while Team USA suffered humiliating medal round knockouts) argues persuasively that defection-induced turnover in youthful stars has only strengthened (not hurt) an easily renewable Cuban juggernaut. Jamail's position on defectors is in large part due to his perception of Cuba as exploitable gold mine of free talent waiting for scavenging by big league clubs hoping to enrich their own coffers with exciting new talent.

One telling illustration of both pitfalls and exaggerations surrounding Cuban ballplayers escaping to the major leagues is found with the case of recent defector Rolando Viera, plucked by the Boston Red Sox organization from the July 2001 amateur player draft. An ESPN internet report of Viera's signing quotes Boston's international scout Ray Poitevint concerning supposed intrigue surrounding Viera's discovery in Mexico. Poitevint talks of a secret scouting mission to Mexico to watch the Cubans work out and get a line on top pitchers José Contrares and Pedro Luis Lazo. There Boston scouts apparently stumbled upon an impressive inter-squad game performance by the left-hander Viera, who pitched for Havana's Industriales in the Cuban League. Red Sox brass would subsequently use a late-round pick to gamble on the unknown Cuban.

Boston GM Dan Duquette would later admit that his club had in truth never seen Viera pitch before his drafting. Duquette was convinced nevertheless that the southpaw with an 18–10 CL record in his final two seasons before defecting was a solid enough gamble as so low a draft selection. Viera's six-year career record with Industriales was actually 22–19, with a 3.42 ERA. The reality was, of course, that Viera had never been on the Cuban national team, even for exhibition matches, nor had he ever left Cuban soil before his final permanent departure. Duquette sheepishly later revealed that his scouts may have confused the draftee with Norge Vera, a top Cuban ace with similar name who impressed the Baltimore Orioles during the May 1999 exhibition in Camden Yards and has been a mainstay of the Cuban national squad. Viera in the meantime was also several years older than his agent, Joe Kehoskie, had advertised (he was already 27 when drafted by Boston) and so far has not emerged from the lower echelons of the Boston farm system.

There is also the badly exaggerated case of one-time national team third baseman Andy Morales, who made an instantaneous splash here in the U.S. when he slugged a late-inning homer against the Orioles in Baltimore and then raced the base paths with arms raised in a joyous display of unrestrained enthusiasm. Morales later escaped from Cuba twice, the second time in early 2001 after being already returned once to his homeland by U.S. immigration officials. Finally reaching Miami on his second try, Morales eventually landed a welcomed contract with the Yankees and appeared with the New York club in more than a dozen spring training games before being shipped out to AA Norwich (48 games, .231 BA, one homer) and then unceremoniously released. What makes the Morales case noteworthy is that after signing on with agent Gus Domínguez, who arranged residency papers in Peru in a move which freed the player from organized baseball's free agent player draft, the nine-year Cuban League veteran inked an exorbitant Yankees contract reportedly worth at least $4.4 million. Morales had landed his big league tryout on the basis of credentials that included a brief appearance with the national team and Cuban League stats that suggested minor league potential (a .319 BA and 54 HR slugged mostly with aluminum bats) but hardly first-rank stardom back home in Cuba. When the Yankees finally released Morales as a washout they announced the voiding of his contact on the basis of the false age his agent had supplied the New York front office. Morales's legitimate age was hardly a dark secret, since it had appeared in the game-day program sold at the Orioles-Cuba exhibition in Baltimore. After his aborted trial with New York, Morales appeared in spring training with Boston in 2002 (now 28 years old) but was again sent packing after a few weeks and only a handful of Grapefruit League appearances. Morales was, in the end, another player clearly oversold by greedy agents and blindly overestimated by big league scouts, despite sufficient evidence at hand about his actual talents.

The biggest gloating about a Cuban defection came with the Christmas week escape of former national team ace Orlando "El Duque" Hernández in December 1997. The story of El Duque's departure was the pure stuff of Hollywood scriptwriting. First reports told of the star pitcher and several companions (including common-law wife Noris Bosch and second string national team catcher Alberto Hernández) being cast adrift on a flimsy raft that eventually reached the Bahamas after several harrowing days adrift. A convoluted saga then reportedly transpired, with Hernández winding up in Costa Rica under the watchful eye of eager agent Joe Cubas. Later accounts would reveal that Cubas had chartered a Lear jet to whisk El Duque into Costa Rica after retrieving the group from a detention camp in the Bahamas. In a celebrated staged spring tryout El Duque was subsequently impressive enough to land a contract with Steinbrenner's Yankees. But first, stories would circulate far and wide about an imminent pact with the Anaheim Angels that would have included a lucrative deal for a Hollywood film detailing the ballplayer's dramatic escape from the grip of communism, his improbable survival on the high seas, and his glorious arrival at the doorstep of the American Dream in Yankee Stadium.

El Duque's more-or-less fabricated tale of daring escape from Fidel's clutches was just what an American audience supposedly wanted to hear, and the facts could all be damned in the process of exploiting seemingly dramatic events for further lucrative gain. There were of course massive distortions in the entire harrowing escape saga and these quickly came to light. It might have seemed curious from the outset that any trip off the island arranged by Joe Cubas would have allowed a top prospect and likely meal ticket to risk his life and million-dollar limb against drowning, dehydration, or shark-infested waters. *Sports Illustrated* eventually published a story penned by investigative reporters Jon Wertheim and Don Yaeger which put the lie to much of the entire tale. As it turns out the escape vessel was not a leaky pile of rubbish but a solid 20-foot wooden fishing trawler equipped with a six-cylinder Russian-built engine. There was never any rough weather, dangerous leaking or shoreline shipwreck of any kind involved in the 10-hour, 35-mile voyage. If Cubas and his associates later romanticized the flight to freedom, at least in this instance the hyperbole-prone agent would not be guilty of exaggerating his new client's big league potential. But the story of the escape itself had been neatly dressed up for popular North American consumption.

It can never be denied that El Duque's sudden success with the Yankees was one of the top sports stories of the 1998 and 1999 major league seasons. Hernández demonstrated almost overnight that he had eye-popping big league talent and that he had kept himself in excellent pitching form during a brief forced retirement. He had sat on the sidelines in Havana under suspension after his half-brother Livián opted for exile and showed up in the majors briefly in 1996 (one game). He had worked at menial labor in a mental hospital (the one described in the opening pages of this book) and exercised his arm in private to maintain his pitching edge. The actions of Cuban authorities had forced the hand of the star pitcher and fears about Duque's own defection had quickly become a self-fulfilling prophecy. As Milton Jamail aptly put it, "A pitcher unable to pitch is like a sugar cane cutter without a machete."

Once given his chance, Hernández moved with lighting speed through a brief minor league trial and into the Yankees rotation. During his first autumn with AL champion New York he even matched almost pitch-for-pitch Livián's earlier MVP heroics in postseason play. For two full years the polished Cuban League veteran with a varied assortment of three-quarter-motion deliveries was a highly successful major league pitcher. But Duque was also quite predictably older than originally advertised. After a third season in the Yankee starting rotation (when he fell below .500 despite 12 wins and also saw his ERA balloon to 4.51) his career was already waning. At that, he remains to date (with a 70–49 career ledger after 2005) arguably the most successful Cuban League refugee so far to reach the majors.

José Ariel Contreras was arguably the best Cuban League hurler with Pinar del Río at the time of his 2003 defection to the American major leagues. Contreras also boasted a spotless ledger of 13–0 as national team ace in top international tournament competition.

There are some obvious explanations for the overnight successes of Orlando Hernández. While he may not have been the best Cuban League pitcher of his generation, he was nonetheless one of Cuba's top hurlers of recent memory. His stats for ten seasons — 126 wins and the top career victory percentage (.728) in 40 years of revolutionary baseball — back up any claims of all-star status. He was never the ace of the national team but he did pitch effectively in several international matches; he claimed one victory at Managua's 1994 World Cup and another in the 1992 Barcelona Olympics. And his best years may have still been ahead of him at the time of his permanent suspension.

Cuban League pitchers are trained and employed like our own workhorse major leaguers of a bygone generation. Hernández was a superb athlete and well-practiced craftsman and his success in the big time was thus hardly surprising. It was also not at all mysterious that El Duque's quick rise to stardom with the Yankees was subsequently followed by just as rapid a slide out of the limelight; the drop-off in performance also had its easy explanations. By the end of 2002 Hernández was 33 years of age and his arm had thrown literally tens of thousands of pitches. Injuries had also begun to slow his performance; he spent all of 2003 on the disabled list before a surprising rehabilitation in 2004 (8–2, 15 starts, 3.30 ERA). By 2005 he was still hanging on with the White Sox, where he won nine games for the World Champions and contributed mightily as "unofficial pitching coach" for fellow defector and staff ace José Contreras. The one real surprise may have been that he was quite as good as he actually was once he reached the majors at nearly thirty years of age.

A few years earlier, Duque's half-brother Liván Hernández stirred up an even bigger media blitz across MLB's version of the baseball world, though this time the drama played out in the minor media center of Miami and not the five-star media capital of New York. Twenty-year-old Liván had departed the Cuban junior team in Mexico in September 1995 after only three years in the Cuban League and a modest 27–16 record while pitching for one of the less notable clubs (Isla de la Juventud). There was not much question about Liván's potential, however, and his fast-track journey into the majors was almost as impressive as Duque's would soon be. Little more than a year after his quiet defection the younger Hernández bested Atlanta Braves ace Greg Maddux with a sterling three-hitter in Game 5 of the NLCS, thus trumpeting the potential of untold numbers of young Cuban pitchers likely lurking outside of organized baseball.

There were early detours in Liván's first-year trials with the National League Florida Marlins, largely brought by problems in adjusting to American fast food and a capitalist lifestyle; the youngster ballooned in weight after his initial season spent mostly with AAA Charlotte and AA Portland. But when Liván arrived in the big time to stay in mid-season 1997, he would make his first curtain call surrounded by considerable media hoopla. Winning his first nine decisions Hernández played a significant role in lifting the Marlins to a surprising wild card slot in post-season play; by the time Oc-

tober action had culminated with a world championship for the Cinderella Marlins, Liván Hernández — still a youthful 22 — had not only claimed a coveted Series ring but had walked off with both the NLCS and Series MVP honors. Liván Hernández was thus the first defector from Fidel Castro's camp to make a truly major impact on the big league scene. In the process he became an instant hero for Cuban fans in both Miami and Havana.

Liván like El Duque would also experience a dramatic dip in his pitching fortunes on the immediate heels of initial successes in Miami. The statuesque 240-pound right-hander would soon be pitching out in San Francisco (where he was traded in July 1999, after two losing seasons), one of the many victims of the rapid disbanding of the Florida Marlins team by cash-poor owner Wayne Huizenga. Liván has since bounced back from his brief dry spell, posting the Giants' top victory total (17 wins) in 2000 and enjoying a second resurrection as staff ace in Montreal (15–10, 3.20 ERA) during the 2003 campaign. By 2005 (still only 30) he was carrying the bulk of the work loan (15–10, 3.98, 35 starts) for the transplanted Washington Nationals. His career seems likely to continue on for some time (he may have five good years left to pad a 110–104 career ledger) and his overall impact in the majors may eventually be far greater than that of the more celebrated El Duque. Liván's decade-long career has also been followed intensely at home in Havana. But his reputation on the island is nonetheless quite mixed when compared with that of his half-brother and other earlier or later defectors like Arocha, Arrojo, Báez, Osvaldo Fernández and Contreras. For the most part, Cuban fans see Liván as at best undisciplined and at worst flaky and even self-absorbed like prototype "hot dog" José Canseco. Some of the baseball veteran debaters in Havana's *Parque Central* have told me repeatedly that, for them, Liván is a pitcher demonstrating little self-discipline both on-field and off, and is thus not a countryman to be entirely admired.

Liván and Orlando Hernández are both sons of Arnaldo "Duque" Hernández who pitched eight seasons in the Cuban League during its opening decade and won 26 of 50 decisions. The senior El Duque also logged time at shortstop, where he was adequate defensively but lacked substantial hitting prowess. It was his father's name, then, that New York's "El Duque" inherited and it is also his father's number "26" that the Yankees star (and recent Chisox mainstay) wears on his big league uniform. The baseball genes were also passed on to a third brother — also named Arnaldo like his father — who played only one season of Cuban League baseball before succumbing as a tragic victim of a cerebral hemorrhage. Orlando and Arnaldo share the same mother but the younger Liván was the product of his father's second marriage. Despite differences in physical appearance and personality, however, both surviving Hernández brothers are exceptional athletes who have more than adequately demonstrated the rare quality of Cuban League baseball with their sudden and largely unanticipated big league successes.

Media firestorms surrounding success stories like those of

Liván and El Duque have been repeatedly fanned by a handful of player agents who have shepherded Cuban defectors into the world of North American baseball — reputedly striking a blow for our free market system while enriching both themselves and their clients at the same time. Joe Cubas (the scion of a Cuban exile family in Miami) and Los Angeles-based Gus Domínguez (agent for the first significant defector, René Arocha) are the two most notable among these bird dogs turned into relentless talent sharks. Joe Cubas has claimed a competing pair of underlying motives for his work from its beginnings in the nineties, when he orchestrated and assisted the celebrated defections of El Duque, Liván and Rolando Arrojo. Foremost is his plan to embarrass Fidel Castro and the Cuban socialist political system by luring away its frontline ballplayers and thus sabotaging its showcase national team.

Cubas is also in the business of earning a substantial windfall for himself as well as his clients (who pay him a hefty percentage of each multi-million-dollar big league contract signed). Thus if he has enriched some of his ballplayers it has only been done in the process of also enriching himself in the name of true capitalist opportunism. We seem to have the American dream operating here at its most insidious level — the peddling of ballplayer flesh to the highest bidder, brazenly carried out in the guise of underpinning a cherished American value of free marketplace enterprise. Cubas's biggest *coup de grâce* has been not only to exploit the socialist Cuban baseball system that has trained his recruits but also to sabotage the regulations of organized baseball by obtaining third-country residence for his defectors (say in Peru, Costa Rica or Mexico) and thus securing top-dollar free agent contracts for athletes who would normally (if they remained in the United States) be subject to the major league amateur player draft.

Just as countless American politicians and Miami-based anti–Castro agitators have often handed Fidel unexpected favors (as with the celebrated case of boy-exile Elian González) and unwittingly made *El Jefe* look good from time-to-time even to American democratic eyes, so has Joe Cubas made the Cuban baseball system seem that much the purer by his own exploitative actions across the years. Several defectors would subsequently cut the their champion agent loose in apparent disputes over his excessive fees; Milton Jamail reports that Liván Hernández, Vladimir Núñez and pitching prospect Larry Rodríguez all abandoned Cubas and then signed up with new agents within a year of their arrivals in the United States. The biggest rap on Cubas's huckster-like techniques, however, has to do with truth in advertising: while he appears to promise freedom-of-opportunity for all the impoverished athletes he takes in tow, he does so in almost all cases through dishonest reports about the true baseball backgrounds of alleged "national team stars" (who in most cases are not that at all), shameless hyping of Cuban Leaguers' over-sold talents, and questionable tactics for luring players away from a Cuban League system that has trained and nurtured them.

Cubas and Domínguez also have repeatedly exploited to their own advantage the myths surrounding current Cuban baseball. One perception is that every ball-playing Cuban is

an outstanding talent destined for professional league stardom. As Jamail puts it, "[Cubas] often touts any Cuban male under the age of thirty who can walk and chew gum at the same time as a prospect" (*Full Count*, 83). Most Cuban defectors are passed off routinely as members of the vaunted national team, though few in the United States, including big league scouts, know quite what that means.

Cubas annually shadows Cuban teams in their frequent international tours and time and again has been most provocative in his behavior. At Winnipeg's Pan American Games in July 1999 he and his several aids held forth with impromptu news conferences at the local ballpark and in the process distracted attention whenever they could from an otherwise exciting tournament featuring equally matched Cuban, USA and Canadian national squads battling tooth and nail for two available 2000 Olympic slots. During 1996 Atlanta Olympics matches he announced he would charter a whole bus to carry the numerous ballplayers he predicted would flee the Cuban delegation (though none actually ever did). In Baltimore at the May 1999 Cuba-Orioles exhibition showdown Cubas again held court with a hastily manufactured press conference on the street corner fronting the Camden Yards ballpark. All this grandstanding has been staged in the name of bringing freedoms to abused athletes supposedly enslaved by the Cuban system. But it can also be seen as meddling in the internal politics and economic affairs of another sovereign nation; Cuban authorities empathetically judged it as such when they sentenced Cubas's cousin and partner Juan Hernández Nodar to fifteen years in a Havana prison in 1996 for attempting to lure players off the island. At the very least Joe Cubas's personal war against the Cuban baseball system is thoroughly tainted by the agent's own considerable cash interest in the entire sordid enterprise.

* * *

The bottom line seems to be that in the hands of agents like Cubas and Domínguez Cuban talent has been often overrated and repeatedly oversold. Danys Báez was handed $14.5 million by the Cleveland Indians despite never earning a starting slot in the rotation with hometown Pinar del Río; that investment was not without dividends, since Báez earned part (if not all) of his cash with ten wins in 2002, plus 25 saves after being converted to a closer by 2003. But Báez (signed as a free agent by Tampa Bay for the 2004 season) is no Contreras or Maels Rodríguez, and assuredly not a second coming of El Duque. Andy Morales is a better example of wide overestimation of defectors' talents — a career minor leaguer who was all-too-hastily swallowed by the Yankees as a can't-miss third base prospect. And there have been several other parallel cases, including Jorge Toca with the Mets and Roberto Colina who signed with Tampa's Devil Rays after scouts flocked to see him perform at Cubas-arranged tryout sessions during 1997 Florida spring training.

Two of the most notable cases of Cubans being hyped as owning far greater potential than they actually possessed were those of pitchers Vladimir Núñez and Larry Rodríguez, both penned to $1 million-plus deals with the Arizona D-Backs after abandoning their B-level national team during a 1995 tour of Venezuela. Núñez reached the majors in 1998 but has struggled to stay there since with Arizona, Florida and Colorado; his seven-season major league ledger now reads 20–32, with a hefty 4.83 ERA, and his only true highlight was 20 saves (all but one of his big-league total) for the Marlins in 2002. Rodríguez could never advance beyond the low minors and was eventually wiped out altogether by persistent arm problems. While Núñez (a three time performer on Cuba's junior national team but a sub-.500 starter with Havana Industriales) was a legitimate top prospect in Cuba, Larry Rodríguez was not, despite a 7–3 rookie-of-the-year performance with Habana Province.

Before last season's surprise Seattle debut by former Villa Clara shortstop Yunieski Betancourt, first baseman Jorge Toca was the only one among recent Cuban refugees to make the big leagues as a position player, after first establishing his potential with 100 homers and a .319 batting mark in eight Cuban League campaigns. But Toca has never been able to hang on for more than a cup of coffee in the National League (he played 12 games with 10 at-bats in 1999–2000); and explaining his team's total lack of interest in a January 2004 El Salvador workout session for recent ballyhooed defector Maels Rodríguez, a top Mets scout remarked that they were not much interested in getting roped in by another Jorge Toca.

The explanation here is simply that most ballplayers leaving Cuba are certifiable AA-caliber performers. Few have mirrored the cream of the island crop — El Duque and José Contreras aside — and their value has been constantly over-enhanced by the ubiquitous mystique shadowing Cuban ballplayers. Like Ordóñez or Toca, escapees have left home in some cases because their prospects for a top slot on the national team were slim at best. That is to say, most of the harvest so far has been ballplayers whose futures were not all that bright even back home in the Cuban League.

But this is not a claim that there hasn't been notable talent leaking out of Cuba and finding its way to the majors. El Duque and Liván were for a short spell legitimate big leaguers by any standards; Liván still fits that bill after his revival in Montreal and Washington. Rolando Arrojo may have been the most naturally gifted among Cuban pitchers seeking their fortune with the pros, and he performed admirably in both Tampa Bay and Boston despite his advanced age and a series of nagging injuries; owning a wicked slider, the thirty-four-year-old rookie broke in at Tampa Bay with 14 wins and a berth on the 1998 American League All-Star squad. A parallel case is Osvaldo Fernández, who labored gallantly for both the San Francisco Giants and Cincinnati Reds. If El Duque was the more brilliant performer back in Cuba, mainly on the strength of his record-book winning percentage with powerful Industriales, Arrojo (154–98, 3.50 ERA) and Fernández (82–62, 3.30 ERA) were barely a step behind. Arrojo (Villa Clara) and Fernández (Holguín) were disadvantaged on the island by being stuck on lesser teams; Fernández was the number one starter for the first Cuban Olympic winner at Barce-

lona, with Arrojo number two and El Duque in the fourth rotation slot. Fernández had also already experienced serious arm troubles back in Cuba — reportedly the result of throwing his breaking deliveries with inferior, almost seamless Batos-made balls — and was never able to throw one hundred percent after arriving in the United States. Nonetheless, the well-built right-hander would prove at times a most effective big league hurler and was sound enough to toss 172 innings during his 1996 debut with the Giants at age thirty.

One question needing answers is why most success stories among Cuban ballplayers transplanted to the majors have been veteran pitchers. The cases on display are Liván, El Duque, Osvaldo Fernández and Rolando Arrojo — and perhaps also Ariel Prieto and René Arocha. José Contreras with the 2003 AL champion Yankees and 2005 world champion Chisox only adds to a list of cases already long enough to clinch the point. Or, conversely, why have most of the failures or disappointments been non-pitchers? A trio of showcase ballplayers here are Toca, Colina, and Andy Morales. Roberto Colina has been the biggest bust, since he was easily the most hyped and by far the least productive. Sold by Cubas as a top national team star, the lefty-swinging 200-pound Colina was little more than a respected starter at first base for Industriales, averaging less that ten homers a season for a full decade and batting a shade under .300 in a league using aluminum bats. In the Devil Rays organization he was never able to advance beyond the low-rung minors and peaked with a .248 BA and five homers at A-level St. Petersburg in the Florida State League. Morales could not meet expectations at the plate after his moment of glory in Baltimore and soon bombed with a .248 batting mark during a 48-game trial with AA Eastern League Norwich (after being demoted from the Yankees 2001 spring training camp). Toca never materialized into an everyday big leaguer for the Mets and was still struggling in 2003 to hit above .275 in AAA with Norfolk. And despite brilliant fielding and considerable advantages earned from three seasons of solid U.S. minor league grooming, even flashy Rey Ordóñez was never the huge star a patient Mets organization hoped for and was finally shipped off to Tampa Bay for a song (two players to be named later) during December 2002 hot stove dealings.

Another mystery is why Cuban pitchers tasting big league successes have faded so fast once they reached AL or NL rosters and logged a passable season or two? One issue, of course, is nagging injuries. Arrojo and Fernández were already both damaged goods by the time they ever arrived on the scene in the majors. Age has also been a special issue, since every top-flight Cuban hurler except Liván (21 and 7 months, b. 2–20–1975) has broken into organized baseball (usually directly into the majors) beyond the downhill age of twenty-seven: René Arocha (27 and 2 months, b. 2–24–1966), Prieto (28 and 9 months, b. 10–22–1966), Fernández (29 and 5 months, b. 11–4–1966), El Duque (32 and 8 months, b. 10–11–1965), Arrojo (33 and 11 months, b. 5–29–1964), Contreras (31 and 4 month, b. 12–6–1971); three were beyond thirty. Cuban players have never turned out to have the ages advertised by their contract-hungry agents. (It is the contract-seeking agents and not INDER that distorts the true birthdates.) Arrojo was touted as only twenty-nine when he arrived with the Devil Rays, as was El Duque also when he debuted with the Yankees. Arocha and Fernández (still listed inaccurately in the most recent edition of *Total Baseball* as born in 1968, while Prieto is given a wrong birth year of 1969) had probably also left their better years behind them back in Cuba.

It is also interesting to note here that while René Arocha's assumed birth year of 1966 would have made him a raw 15 when he debuted in the Cuban League in 1981 (Jamail reports that he was one of only two Cuban League pitchers ever to start as young as age 15), defector Euclides Rojas (born 8–25–1964) has claimed that his childhood friend Arocha was a year older than he was; that would make Arocha's actual birth date fall in 1963 and thus his age a more likely 29 years and 2 months when he reached the majors.

There are no simple answers perhaps, but there are some obvious and quite reasonable guesses to be made regarding each of these issues. Pitchers have been the more successful simply because it is among pitchers that we find the few legitimate headliners leaving the island. Liván, Duque, Arrojo, Fernández, Arocha and Contreras were all national team regulars back in Cuba. Andy Morales was never a Team Cuba front-liner, nor were Colina or Toca. The three washout infielders had all made only brief appearances on national teams and never contributed as starters. Mets Gold Glover Rey Ordóñez was only a budding prospect when he left home at age 22-plus, with four seasons and 272 National Series games under his belt. It is also the case that since most of the defectors have been pushing thirty, the pitchers naturally have had a distinct advantage. Seasoned pitchers can be dropped straight into the majors with prospects of making some impact without first relearning their trade with years of apprenticeship in the minors (minor-league retooling being a requirement that would rule out position players, who would be simply too old if they entered the U.S. minors at, say, 27 and the majors at 32 or above). Pitchers with strong arms and lively deliveries have a measurable advantage over hitters who have not previously faced them and timed their motions. Position players— that is to say hitters—would face a stiffer transition, moving from aluminum bats (before 1999) to wood and learning how to hit major league pitching on an everyday basis. But the biggest factor here, then, is that no star infielder or outfielder or catcher has yet chosen to defect. Even aluminum-era batting champ and 2002 Intercontinental Cup hero Yobal Dueñas (who snuck out of Cuba in October 2003 with ace pitcher Maels Rodríguez) was already experiencing a severe career slide at age 31-plus and had lost his Team Cuba outfield slot to such emerging newcomers as Cepeda and Urrutia. This fact in itself underscores the miniscule impact such defections have actually had on the Cuban national team.

Among Cuban pitchers who have tasted at least moderate success after their flight to the big leagues, the groundbreaker was right-hander René Arocha, followed three years later by Ariel Prieto. Arocha was ace of the national team staff

One-time Industriales ace Orlando Hernández was the highest profile Cuban League defector of the nineties, and also one of the most successful after reaching the big leagues with the New York Yankees.

when he walked away from his teammates in Miami after a four-game series with Team USA in Millington, Tennessee. The July 1991 departure of Arocha must have been a shock to Cuban baseball officials since it represented the first disloyalty of this type in the three-plus decades of the revolution. After Arocha signed with the St. Louis Cardinals and subsequently debuted in the majors his career was followed avidly by fans everywhere in Cuba, even if it was never discussed openly on Havana sports radio talk shows or mentioned in the Cuban print media. Arocha's bold flight may have suggested to other Cuban players that such escapes to the big leagues, with a promise of riches and fame in top level professional leagues, was now a distinct (if previously unimagined) possibility. But if this was the case, the flood gates certainly did not open immediately or very widely. Ariel Prieto (a veteran of 10 Cuban

League seasons with a 67–66 career record) obtained a legal Cuban visa for USA travel and then stayed put in Miami in 1994, soon signing a $1.2 million deal with Oakland. Prieto's big league career never really got very far off the ground and after a few seasons elbow problems sunk his pro career prematurely. Though their stories were not followed closely at the time, top young prospects Rey Ordóñez and Edilberto Oropesa had already jumped from a lower-level Cuban national team at the World University games in Buffalo a year before Prieto's defection. Ordóñez would be a household name with the Mets by the late nineties but Oropesa would not make it into the majors for seven more years.

In actuality, the first Cuban ballplayer to escape the island after exiting the Cuban League and then also to appear in the big leagues was an unheralded journeyman outfielder named Bárbaro Garbey, who briefly played with the Detroit Tigers in the eighties and even appeared in the Fall Classic (without a hit) for the 1984 world champions. Garbey was a most special and somewhat controversial case and he is rarely mentioned today when talk turns to Cuban baseball, since he was technically neither a defector nor a noted loss to the Cuban national team. Right-handed swinging 5'7" Garbey had been a minor star in the Cuban League in the late seventies, with one national team appearance (1976 World Cup in Cartagena) to his credit and a .290 batting mark over five seasons. He also had been implicated in rumored game fixing scandals that swept the Cuban League on the eve of the 1980s and he was subsequently handed a lifetime ban from the sport by Cuban baseball authorities. Garbey next showed up in Miami in 1980 as part of the famed Mariel boatlift flight in which several thousand refugees were turned loose on America by the Cuban government. In the massive ex-patriot group were numerous reported criminals and undesirables that Fidel had apparently decided to dumb onto North American shores.

Garbey was tendered a major league contract and despite the trumpeted abhorrence of game fixing at the major league level, organized baseball simply looked the other way when his past history in Cuba eventually came to light. If anything, he was elevated as a hero for sabotaging Castro's socialist-inspired league. Given a new life in the majors Garbey took little advantage of the opportunity and suffered continued problems both on and off the field that made his big league stay in Detroit and Texas short-lived and unproductive. He does remain an answer to a trivia question; he was the first post-revolution Cuban League veteran to appear in a major league uniform, nine years before defector René Arocha.

After Arocha and Prieto the next Cuban "baseball traitor" to reach big-time professional baseball was Osvaldo Fernández (Rodríguez), a pitcher of considerable ability with the Holguín club in eastern Cuba who had won 82 career Cuban League games and headlined in several big international tournaments; the strapping righty known as *El Guajiro* (The Peasant) in his native eastern province posted 2–0 marks with microscopic ERAs in both the 1990 and 1994 World Cup matches, as well as in the Barcelona Olympics. A second Osvaldo Fernández (Guerra), pitcher with Havana-based Metropolitanos, would also soon defect yet never make it onto any big league roster. Fernández Rodríguez signed for $3.9 million with the San Francisco Giants and flashed temporary competence — with seven wins during his debut season — before recurrence of the nagging arm problems that had already troubled him in Cuba. He continued to hang around in the majors for five seasons and later also appeared as an occasional starter with Cincinnati, where he won five final games during his swan song campaign of 2001.

Still another island escapee did not enjoy the same successful outcome for his athletic dreams. Euclides Rojas never reached the majors, though he did get a shot at pro baseball. A top reliever in the Cuban League for several seasons, Rojas truthfully did take to the high seas as a *balsero* in order to make his way off the island on a crude fifteen-foot leaky raft — in precisely the manner that was later falsely attributed to El Duque. Risking his own life and that of a young wife and infant child, Rojas was genuinely desirous of leaving the Cuban socialist system behind and seeking a better life in Miami, a desire he would later speak about eloquently on film in a documentary entitled "Greener Grass" and aired on PBS shortly after the Baltimore Orioles exhibitions. Rojas was intercepted by American authorities during his desperate flight from his homeland and spent several months in forced detention at Guantánamo before being allowed entrance into the United States. He would eventually pitch in the minor league system of the Florida Marlins, the club that still employs him as a minor league pitching coach. Listed as only 30 in the Marlins 1998 media guide, Rojas was four years older than that, having reached the age of 32 by the time the Marlins released him in June of 1996. That age more than anything else might have been what prevented him from ever pitching a major league game.

Two earlier-mentioned defectors destined for the big leagues left the Cuban junior team at precisely the same time in July 1993, while performing at the World University Games in Buffalo. Their escape hardly made news at the time, though one of the pair would soon become the most visible Cuban in the major leagues outside of Liván and El Duque. Rey Ordóñez, who would need less than three years to reach the majors, was 22 years old when he walked away from the Cuban contingent to join his father-in-law, then a legal resident of Miami. The escape had been painstakingly planned out in advance and is described by S.L. Price in *Pitching Around Fidel.* (Price also relates mostly sorted details of Ordoñez's estrangement and divorce from the wife he left behind in Havana.) A day before Ordóñez fled, lefty pitcher Eddie Oropesa (age 23) jumped a chain-link fence outside Niagara Falls' Sal Maglie Stadium and joined relatives for the long car ride to Miami. It would be more than a half dozen years before Eddie (Edilberto) Oropesa would finally crack the big time with the Philadelphia Phillies (he also later joined the Arizona Diamondbacks) for a cup of major league coffee. In the interim the lanky southpaw (whose name is spelled *Oropeza* in Cuban League guides and who sported a mediocre Cuban League ledger: 20–26, 4.42 ERA) labored patiently in the minors hoping to earn his eventual shot at the big time.

The best pitcher abandoning Cuba has arguably been Rolando Arrojo. Arrojo skipped out before the Atlanta Olympics and angered most of his fellow national team members by doing so. Cuban ballplayers rarely criticize former teammates who have departed, but many in the Cuban camp thought Arrojo easily could have left after the games had ended and not handicapped his teammates on the eve of a possible gold medal. In the end the Cubans won easily enough even without Arrojo. Known as Luis Rolando Arrojo in Cuba, the hard-throwing right-hander won 154 games, which still places him fifteenth all-time (2005) in Cuban League history. Signed by the expansion Tampa Bay Devil Rays when he was nearly 33 (not 29 as Tampa Bay management claimed), the veteran had to wait an extra year to reach the majors; Tampa Bay was still a year away from its first expansion American League season. His debut was highly successful nonetheless and he not only won 14 games for a basement club and ranked fourth in *Total Baseball's* Total Pitcher Index (a measure of adjusted overall pitching efficiency) but also appeared in the big league All-Star Game (Denver). He was subsequently traded to Colorado and eventually to Boston where he was still pitching effectively as late as 2002. But age and injury were major villains in Arrojo's case as might have been expected. One can therefore only speculate about what he might have actually achieved in the big leagues if he had started there about ten years earlier.

More recently both Duquecito (Adrian) Hernández and Danys Báez have held high promise as big league pitching prospects. Adrian Hernández, who left Cuba in a cloud of mystery on January 1, 2000 and then quickly signed up with the Yankees for $4 million, is no blood relative of El Duque yet nonetheless appears physically to be a smaller-scale clone of the prototype original. Duquecito's delivery and colorful style of wearing his uniform socks at knee-high length earned him his complementary nickname in Havana. Duquecito ("Little Duque") pitched for Industriales, like his namesake predecessor, and rang up an 8–7 record during his final full Cuban season. He has made only three brief appearances with the Yankees (0–6, 6.55) and the jury is therefore still out on his possible major league future.

Báez is a more revealing case whose original defection speaks volumes about the whole issue of enticing Cuban players to leave their homeland. Báez was not by any stretch a star on the national team in Winnipeg during the 1999 Pan Am tournament; at best he was a promising future prospect who had been brought along simply for the international experience. That he was there in Winnipeg at all meant he was a prospect with distinct potential and thus also some calculated pro value. Agent Cubas was predictably also on hand in Winnipeg, dangling offers in front of whatever Cuban players he could fetch. Cubas had made so many boasts about corralling a handful of players during the Pan Am event that not getting any would have severely challenged his claims about the hunger of Cubans to leave socialist sports for blockbuster professional paychecks. Once Báez bit the hook he was sold to the press corps and to big league GMs as a hidden ace of the deep Cuban staff. Scrub the fact he was only the fifth starter on his

Solid but unspectacular infielder Andy Morales made brief headlines with his showy homer against the Orioles in Baltimore's Camden Yards, but later failed in two attempts to reach the big leagues after twice defecting in the early 2000s.

own Pinar del Río team back home, that he had posted a 6–5 record in the just-finished National Series, and that his two-year career ERA was 4.70 with 92 Ks in 122 innings. For all the false advertising there was no denying the raw potential of a 6–3, 225-pounder who threw in the high 90s, and Báez did eventually impress Cleveland scouts in a staged workout that snagged a mind-bending eight-figure contract. Half-a-dozen seasons later, it appears that the rawboned Cuban was indeed worth what the Indians spent, although a 2004 free agent signing with Tampa Bay meant the Devil Rays would reap the ripest harvest. But the successes of Danys Báez again raise a legitimate question about the stateside market values of his Pinar del Río teammates Faustino Corrales (recently retired as the most productive lefty in Cuban League annals), Contreras (who earned his spurs in the 2005 ALCS) and Lazo (still loyal to the Cuban national team, where he now functions as an intimidating closer)—all of whom back in 1999 were far superior talents.

Rey Ordóñez boasts the greatest success as a position player among the Cuban refugees (although Yunieski Betancourt's 2005 rookie season in Seattle now threatens to tip the scale). Like Báez when compared with Lazo or Corrales, Ordóñez and his achievement only seems to further raise the bar on island shortstops like Germán Mesa and Eduardo Paret who once barred his path to the national team roster. In the case of Rey Ordóñez the reasons for leaving Havana are at least somewhat more obvious. Milton Jamail (*Full Count*, Chapter 6) chimes in on the issue of Germán Mesa blocking Ordóñez's future in Havana, and I would also add Eduardo Paret to that equation. S.L. Price (*Pitching Around Fidel*, Chapter 5) offers details about deeper reasons for Ordóñez's defection, including the unhappy or inconvenient marriage he plotted to escape. After settling in with his father-in-law in Miami, Ordóñez became involved in a most unseemly string of soap-opera-like events which eventually had him marrying his father-in-law's stepdaughter. An ex-wife and son were left behind penniless in Havana and now remain there without communication or aid from the wealthy ex-big-leaguer. These personal matters seem like topics quite out of place in a strict baseball history, but they do shed light nonetheless on the fact that Cuban ballplayers do not always defect with political freedoms or economic prosperity as their sole or even top priority. There appear to have been numerous losers in the Rey Ordóñez defection saga and the Cuban baseball establishment was probably the least important among them.

What have been the lasting effects, if any, of the baseball defections back in Cuba itself? There has indeed been some rather noticeable fallout. Cuban ballplayers have never been under strict lock and key when on the road for international matches, but they have lately been watched more closely at home. Both Mesa and Paret were suspended in the wake of Liván's disparaged (by INDER) act of baseball treason. Germán Mesa was first left off the Olympic squad for fear he might defect in Atlanta, then sidelined permanently in October 1996 for allegedly receiving token cash gifts from an unnamed pro scout; Paret was temporarily shelved in July 1997 for reported telephone contacts with discredited ex-patriot Rolando Arrojo.

Other notable players have been similarly sanctioned and these include Paret's Villa Clara teammates Osmani García and Angel López (also in 1997, for similar communications with Arrojo) and more recently Yobal Dueñas, Kendry Morales and pitcher José Ibar, all supposedly for harboring defection plans. (Morales, it turns out, ran afoul of INDER officials for a number of indiscretions having little to do with big league contacts, and Ibar also had his own run-ins with authorities over illegal firearms possession.) There is also always palpable suspicion of Americans traveling on the island if they attempt to get too close to ballplayers. El Duque perhaps felt the greatest personal impact immediately after the illegal departure of his half-brother. But the subject of the defectors is itself not nearly so taboo as it once was. In 1997 and again in 1998 there were unconfirmed press reports outside Cuba of portable radios being confiscated in Central Havana from fans who were caught secretly listening to Miami transmissions of Liván and El Duque performing during the World Series. During my own nationwide television interview five full years ago (March 2001), conducted by Cubavisión sports analyst Carlos Hernández Luján, I was questioned quite openly before the gaze of all interested Habaneros about "those players that have left the country for capitalist baseball." My honest response (one I have repeatedly voiced elsewhere) was that, from my personal perspective, defectors' actions had only served to weaken a vital brand of baseball that was now struggling for survival on the island, no matter what personal rewards these players might have grabbed for themselves. I cite that interview here only to demonstrate that mentioning defectors in the Havana media is no longer taboo, and has not been so for half a decade or more.

For Cuban fans, on the other hand, the defection issue has been very much a mixed bag. There has undoubtedly been considerable pride generated among diehards in Havana and around the country by recent Cuban performances in the big leagues. Cuban fans hunger for scarce information bulletins on Liván and El Duque or Contreras and Ordóñez. These come mostly from contacts with American tourists, or from pirated ESPN Sports Center reports glimpsed in bars at tourist hotels like the *Habana Libre* or *El Telegrafo*. Cubans view any achievements of their former heroes now performing in distant New York or San Francisco as a positive measure of the league baseball they still watch nightly back on the island. But the recent government sanctions in the form of player suspensions and banishments on the home front have also weakened the league noticeably for fans and thus have caused wide frustration and sometimes mild outrage among loyal local rooters.

INDER, the Cuban sports ministry, has also been sensitive to the defector question. One amusing barometer of such sensitivities was the response encountered by this author and his collaborator Mark Rucker when copies of our earlier book *Smoke—The Romance and Lore of Cuban Baseball* began showing up on the island in late 1999 and early 2000. INDER had cooperated with us fully on that project from the start, back in 1997, by providing valuable ballpark access, interviews with league officials, and even much needed photos. Ministry and league officials with whom we had personal contact across the island between 1997 and 1999 all seemed genuinely enthusiastic that such an American book was in production. But when actual copies appeared, revealing mentions (however brief) of some of the defectors, plus a handful of photos of players who had left the country, the immediate response was generally a cold shoulder treatment from INDER personnel who had earlier been so supportive. Players like El Duque, Arrojo and Osvaldo Fernández are "officially" branded traitors to the Cuban system, and eyebrows were raised at a handful of images of these "unmentionables" (some of them on trading cards issued by INDER itself) in our final chapters on contemporary

Cuban League history. The reaction was for the most part only temporary, and in the end overall response to *Smoke* was almost universally positive. Most Cuban baseball officials felt that the book offered a fair and even quite stunning pictorial summary of their national pastime. It is hard not to be at least a little sympathetic toward official INDER outrage over pro baseball agents enticing their stars to abandon island play, even if one genuinely abhors any unwarranted governmental control of personal liberties. The painful reality is that continued inroads by the big leagues into Cuba's internal baseball structure will almost assuredly one day kill off the island's cherished pastime, just as it once killed off the thriving Negro leagues in urban Black America and has now also largely sabotaged once-booming winter leagues that for so long provided local entertainment to fans everywhere around the Caribbean.

Yet if there has been predictable negative reaction on the Cuban home front, some of it perhaps justified, the immediate impact of lost players on Cuban baseball has everywhere been much exaggerated. One small if telling example was Milton Jamail's mishandling of information on the Cuban team at the Sydney Olympics in his annual Cuban League summary published in the *Baseball America 2001 Almanac.* Jamail reported that young talents Yorelvis Charles and Michel Enríquez had been deleted from the Sydney roster due to fears of imminent defection to the majors. Perhaps worse yet was Jamail's suggestion that a second motive might be INDER officials' lack of confidence that the youngsters could perform under pressure. The truth was that both players were serving suspensions back home, the result of a minor shoplifting incident that occurred in Amsterdam while the two were traveling with the Cuban squad for pre–Olympic tune-ups. Jamail's inaccurate report angered a handful of my Cuban contacts who eventually saw it; furthermore it once again inaccurately emphasized a widespread view that Cuban baseball was driven by paralyzing fear that all top players were just itching to abandon their teams and their homeland.

Cuban teams have hardly been weakened by those who have jumped ship. In Atlanta it was victory as usual, with the only apparent chink in the armor being some reduction in Cuban pitching prowess. The gold medal game losses in Sydney in 1999 (Intercontinental Cup) and 2000 (Olympics) would most likely have occurred even if no Cuban players had ever left town. Both tournaments were lost through single momentary letdowns in the title games, events which are bound to occur from time to time. The loss to host Australia at the Intercontinental Cup came on an eleventh-inning dropped fly ball; in the Olympics the defeat in the final match with Team USA has to be attributed to a masterful three-hit pitching outing by future USA big leaguer Ben Sheets that stymied the best of the Cuban sluggers. Sometimes favorites lose baseball games and the Cubans had lost in showdown games before; what proved most remarkable was not that the Cubans had stumbled on these two occasions, but rather that anyone took the losses to be so uncharacteristic. No baseball team at any level has ever been expected to win absolutely every game: it is not in the nature of the sport — except perhaps when it comes to the Cuban national team. The law of baseball averages is to blame for the two Sydney collapses, not any smattering of defections from the world class roster.

There were reports circulated — anticipating Jamail's later charge in *Baseball America*— that the Cubans did not send their best team to the Sydney Intercontinental Cup matches, leaving the big guns like Kindelán and Linares on the sidelines in Havana in order to season youngsters like Michel Enríquez and Yasser Gómez. But its seems likely the reasons had nothing to do with reported fears of defections that were trumpeted by the U.S. media. There were so many good young players back home that it made sense to give some of them seasoning to prepare for imminent replacement of now fading stars like Linares, Germán Mesa or Antonio Pacheco. The Intercontinental Cup games were after all only an Olympic tune-up; and even with an inexperienced lineup the Cubans had every ex-

Santiago's Norge Vera — Cuban League runner-up to Orlando Hernández in career winning percentage — pitched brilliantly in relief against the lackluster Orioles in Baltimore. Vera would later toss a Cuban League no-hitter and win the final two games of the 2003 World Cup in Havana.

pectation of winning, and would have won, except for a single uncharacteristic misplayed outfield drive by talented fly-chaser Yasser Gómez late in the deciding game.

In some respects the defections have even helped Cuba's national baseball program. A case in point is the brilliant play of a youth-filled Cuban team that competed in both the World Cup in Havana and the Olympic Qualifier tournament in Panama City during October and November 2003. Novice super-sluggers like Yulieski Gourriel (sparkplug in a face-shaving come-from-behind win over Brazil), Michel Enríquez (World Cup MVP), Frederich Cepeda (two homers in the gold medal game) and a host of youthful pitchers — especially Yadel Martí, Vicyohandri Odelín and Adiel Palma — have already replaced retiring (Faustino Corrales, Juan Padilla) and defecting (Maels Rodríguez, Kendry Morales, José Contreras) older stars, plus 1990s luminaries like the Pachecos, Kindeláns and Mesas. Giving these promising next-generation aces a chance to emerge earlier than might have been expected has already proven a considerable boon to Cuba's continuing international prospects.

Cuban players have never been locked up in their hotel rooms or guarded like convicts-in-tow while out on the road. If professional player agents have been kept away from the Cuban camps in Winnipeg, Sydney or Millington, Tennessee, this is only understandable. (Recall the outrage of major league baseball officials during the mid-forties when the Mexican League mogul Jorge Pasquel dangled bundles of dollars in front of selected big leaguers in an effort to get them to jump to his teams south of the border; the ballplayer's democratic right to seek his fortunes with the highest bidder did not seem to be a rallying cry for organized baseball when players were fleeing in the other direction.) But there has been little attempt by Cuban officials to prevent players physically from leaving once they are traveling outside the homeland. If there were such heavy security measures in place, then Arrojo and Ordóñez and Liván and others (José Contreras and team manager Miguel Valdés in Mexico City in September 2002) would never have walked away from their delegations quite so easily. The fate of eventual outcast slugger Kendry Morales at the Olympic Qualifier tournament in Panama City during late 2003 is quite instructive in this regard. When INDER officials accompanying the team got nervous about Morales talking freely in a hotel bar with an American journalist (one wrongly suspected of being an agent) they ordered Morales to fly back to Havana; but the fact that Kendry Morales was wandering in hotel watering holes in the first place suggests a degree of freedom for touring Cuban athletes that is rarely reported in North American press treatments.

The most remarkable feature of the flight of Cuban ballplayers is that almost all the best players have willing stayed put at home. Only Orlando Hernández, Rolando Arrojo and José Contreras (at least before the most recent departures of Maels Rodríguez and Kendry Morales — both already under suspension) were Cuban League headliners at the time they jumped ship. The list of defecting athletes at chapter's end indicates just how small the baseball group actually has been

when compared to other sports. Defection is never easy since it involves leaving one's family and friends behind and abandoning a childhood home and culture (including food and language) that may never be revisited. But it also involves leaving a baseball culture and a social system that has provided a lifetime of training, camaraderie and elevated social standing on the home front.

In a thoroughly materialistic world it is easy enough to scoff at Omar Linares's repeated claim (echoed by other top Cuban stars in the seventies and eighties) that he would rather have the cheers of millions of his countrymen than the millions of dollars proffered by big league clubs; in fact it is too easy for those who have not stood in the shoes of the Cuban ballplayer. Whatever their personal reasons might be, numerous Cuban athletes see other alternatives to the material comforts of high-salaried professionals, and one is playing devotedly for national pride. Again, the outsider (especially the capitalist outsider) might claim this is all the result of communist brainwashing. But my own conversations with Cubans who are ballplayers, and Cubans who are not, reveals much more loyalty to country and to the prevailing socialist system than Joe Cubas or Gus Domínguez would ever have us believe. There are still corners of the world where not everything is for sale for the highest price tag offered.

Why then do ballplayers like Linares and Kindelán, or Paret and Mesa, opt for what the champions of the American capitalist system see as virtual slavery under Fidel, while El Duque or Liván or Contreras choose to take flight and pursue an American Dream with its untold financial rewards? The reasons are always highly personal to be sure and thus escape an easy analysis. In some cases, at least, athletes departing Cuba have done so for motives somewhat less pure than the always-touted specter of personal and political freedom. This is not to assert that notions of individual liberty have not been paramount for some; but any claim that most defecting ballplayers are motivated first and foremost by the American Dream is tainted by the very fact that many of these athletes have opted for residence in other Latin American nations like Costa Rica or El Salvador, simply in order to avoid the MLB free agent draft system and thus secure the heftiest possible free agent contracts (often with the New York Yankees). It is a lust for U.S. paychecks that often seems paramount, and not any lust for democracy-drabbed American citizenship.

Any belief that the Cuban League will soon collapse because of the drain of ballplayers enticed by big-dollar contracts is probably a false hope. Defections themselves will not kill off the Cuban League; witness only the replenished supplies of still unmatched talent that have recently filled the void and swept away all comers during the last several top international tournaments. The inevitability is nonetheless strong that Cuban baseball in its present form is quite likely already doomed. The 45-year-old Cuban administration under Fidel Castro seemingly can not hang on much longer in its present guise: it is doomed by the pressures of a continuing U.S. economic embargo, the ever-worsening economic crisis brought on by loss of most of the former international communist support system, and the increasing age and deteriorating health of Fidel himself. Some day soon there will more than likely be normalized business transactions in the form of player exchanges between U.S. organized baseball and the surviving Cuban League. It is these almost inevitable encroachments of the big leagues into Cuba that, when they come, will most likely ring the death knell on today's Cuban baseball. One of the last vestiges of high level baseball not yet controlled by profit-minded major league moguls is indeed very much living on borrowed time.

Major league baseball of course sees an untapped gold mine in Cuba. Jamail articulates the major league position frighteningly well throughout his book *Full Count*, especially with a chapter appropriately entitled "Bring on the Gold Rush"; Jamail quotes one-time Dodgers GM Fred Claire to clinch the point: "If the talent was available in Cuba, and all clubs could go in and scout, I can only envision a gold rush" (*Full Count*, 119–120). That teeming gold mine may well be exaggerated at times, especially in the press releases from Joe Cubas and his cronies. But there are indeed rich veins of ore to be exploited, even if they extend not much farther that the starting nine or four-man pitching rotation from the most recent Cuban World Cup team. Someday soon this mother lode will likely be fully exploited just as sugar, tobacco and other natural resources on the island were once pillaged wholesale by foreign-based capitalists. The sad truth about the history of Cuba is that except for the last forty-plus years under the socialist revolution — with all its negatives — Cuba has rarely had control of its own homegrown resources. Even on the baseball front, the big leagues had already taken over Cuba's professional league (under the protective umbrella of organized baseball in the wake of a firestorm surrounding Pasquel's Mexican League expansions) in the final decade before the revolution dawned. The dream for most American professional baseball people is now to get back to that one-time and one-sided status quo.

The argument that Cuban players deserve more money for their efforts on the field makes all the sense in the world. But, ironically, the real issue is not that these players are the privileged class that González Echevarría portrays in *The Pride of Havana*, pampered as state-sponsored athletes and exploited only because they can't operate as free agents and thus make the millions that big leaguers now make. The problem is better assessed by Jamail in *Full Count*, for all the latter author's orientations toward justifying big league recruitment programs as paramount in the baseball universe. Cuban ballplayers suffer today because they are forced to live outside the dollar-based half of the island's economy and thus are unquestionably underprivileged (and often frustrated) when measured against their compatriots who earn dollars by waiting tables in hotels or driving taxis catering to foreigners. This is the issue that INDER must resolve before more Cuban players become so disillusioned that they abandon the league more out of survivalist instincts than any greed for sharing the exalted life of a U.S. big leaguer.

There is also another side to the story, one that is unwelcome to most capitalist ears. Cuban fans in provinces from one end of the island to the other are today still enjoying entertaining baseball that has not been priced beyond their means as an entertainment spectacle designed mainly to the affluent consumer. The fans and the game itself have, to date, not been exploited by bottom-line ball club owners, me-first ballplayers, and greedy player agents, all of whom approach the national pastime strictly from the angle of profit motive. Cuban baseball has not yet been turned into an extravaganza made-for-television entertainment spectacle in which the game on the field is merely a sideshow to the main goal of luring fans into a shopping-center complex (disguised as a stadium) to sell them all the food, drinks and trinkets that support today's corporate sports teams. Nothing in contemporary Cuba is more delightful than a televised league game that finds play-by-play announcers staying on the screen between innings to analyze on-field action, since there are no commercial advertisements to be aired. The tradeoff has necessarily been a government-controlled socialist system of "amateur" sport that is short on personal freedoms and thus an anathema to most Americans and to all proponents of free-market capitalism. In short, Cuba is not paradise; but it is also not a consumer-crazed hell.

Several conclusions may in the end be drawn about the issue of Cuban baseball defectors. One is that this is not at all the front-page story that so many writers and a handful of greed-driven ballplayer agents have repeatedly attempted to make out of it. Nor should we assume that a handful of player defections have thrown Cuban League baseball into a hopeless and irreversible crisis. It would be far more accurate to state that the defections seem to have hardly jogged Cuban baseball at all, other than to thrust this previously ignored alternative baseball universe squarely into the limelight for many North American fans. A second deduction is that to date the exodus out of Cuba has for the most part consisted of the spare parts and marginal talents from national team rosters. If El Duque, Arrojo and Contreras were indeed top pitching stars from Cuba's number one roster, it is notable that they left home only *after* contributing heavily for several years to prestigious Cuban victories abroad. It is just as notable also that they were all quickly replaced by comparable talents. It is hard to make the case that defections have left any gapping holes in the Cuban juggernaut. The several dozen best prospects from the past two decades — outside Ordóñez and two or three pitchers — are all still on the island or have played out their career string at home before retirement. And finally, whatever happens to island baseball, a healthy outcome does not seem to be offered by the prospects of throwing open the doors to wholesale scavenging of Cuban League talent by scouts from big league baseball, who would quickly strip the island dry if given even half an opportunity.

The Cubans themselves do not seem to have any solution to the problem. Cuban baseball does indeed seem to be living on borrowed time. But the current crisis does not appear as deep-rooted as so often reported. The short-range crisis does not seem that severe at least: there was altogether little surprise in international baseball circles when Cuba's vaunted national team, behind the pitching of Adiel Palma and Dany Betancourt — overnight replacements for the likes of Contreras and Maels Rodríguez — swept the field at Athens in September 2004, easily garnering still another Olympic gold medal while an embarrassed USA contingent sat at home on the sidelines after elimination in the America's Olympic qualifier the previous November. And if anyone seriously believed that Cuban baseball was in genuine crisis mode, that confidence had to have been severely shaken when the Cuban juggernaut — behind the impressive slugging of new phenoms Yulieski Gourriel, Michel Enríquez and veteran Eduardo Paret — blasted a stronger-than-usual USA roster of AAA prospects in the quarterfinals of the September 2005 World Cup in Rotterdam, en route to a ninth straight World Cup championship.

No one should turn a blind eye to the ominous storm clouds now appearing on the near horizon. The threats nonetheless arise mostly from outside the system and not from inside the fortress of Cuban baseball. The fact that the Cuban League has held on in isolation for quite as long as it has is the biggest advertisement for today's Cuban baseball. Those of us who have been privileged enough to see it first hand have enjoyed a rare treat it may be difficult to appreciate fully. Baseball as a distinctive sport still operating aloof from the high-tech and homogenous corporate mass entertainment industry is almost entirely a thing of the past. This is true everywhere except on the mysterious island of Fidel Castro's revolutionary Cuba.

* * *

There is a considerable mystique surrounding seemingly all Cuban ballplayers. If a twenty-something (or even thirty-something) Cuban male makes it off the island and can stick a fielder's mitt on the correct hand without flinching he is likely to be taken as a serious big-league prospect. Part of it is pure tradition and a surviving notion that there is almost a genetic link between Cubans and baseball. Part is the American lottery mentality taken to the big-league level: hope springs eternal that another Babe Ruth or Omar Linares lurks around the next bend for every dedicated and tireless talent scout. Part is the carefully orchestrated propaganda campaigns carried out by self-serving player agents like Joe Cubas, Joe Kehoskie, Gus Domínguez, Don Nomura and company. One ploy of agents seeking their own cut of big-dollar contracts for any Cuban player they can corral is to claim that everyone who played on a Cuban League roster was a member of the prestigious national team. This confusion is often rampant even among otherwise well-informed big league scouts, who themselves usually have little concept of just what the Cuba national team actually is.

The first thing needing clarification, then, is the precise nature of contemporary talent now on the loose in Cuba. González Echevarría (*The Pride of Havana*, 401) dismisses today's Cuban League as approximating Class A baseball or lower. Another Stateside devotee, David Skinner, places the

bar (*Nine* 8:2, 156) somewhere above Class AAA. My own assessment, draw from considerably more island baseball viewing than either González Echevarría or Skinner, falls somewhere between these extremes. The Cuban League is easily better than A-ball; teams from organized baseball's rookie leagues (Class A) would certainly never beat up so regularly on all-star squads representing Japanese or Korean pro leagues, or humiliate respectable editions of Team USA in seemingly endless tournament after tournament.

There are two dozen or more legitimate big leaguers playing on the island at the time this book is going to press, and several — maybe as many as a dozen — would likely be almost immediate major league all-stars. Atop of any list of sure-fire big leaguers among current Cuban stars I would be forced to include at least the following: pitchers Norge Vera, Vicyohandri Odelín, Pedro Lazo and Adiel Palma; infielders Yulieski Gourriel, Michel Enríquez, Eduardo Paret, and Enríque Díaz; outfielders Frederich Cepeda, and Osmani Urrutia; and veteran catcher Ariel Pestano. A few others like Pacheco, Linares and surely Germán Mesa, and perhaps veteran southpaw Faustino Corrales, would have been easy bets, as well, if they had been snagged during their prime seasons a few years in the past. Yet the big league struggles of some recent defectors, plus outright failures by prospects like Andy Morales and Roberto Colina, have already proven beyond any shadow of a doubt that every frontline Cuban League starter (or even every national team standout) is not necessarily a no-brainer potential professional star of the highest caliber.

The strong point of contemporary Cuban baseball, especially in the most recent years, has been pitching. A handful of stellar mound aces of recent years are of unassailable major league caliber and (with the possible exception of "*Los Hermanos Hernández*" and the obvious exception of Contreras) a full step or two above those pitchers who have already defected to the big leagues. Among the defectors of the 1990s an overwhelming majority have been pitchers and some explanations for this trend have already been put forth (see Chapter 8). Among the legions that have stayed behind, at least several are (or recently were) dominant hurlers. Norge Vera and José Ibar were the cream of the crop during most of the past decade and demonstrated their skills both in Winnipeg and against the Orioles. Ibar mesmerized the eventual Team USA Olympic gold medal winners in a Sydney preliminary round showdown. Towering fastballer Pedro Luis Lazo is also formidable even if he may lack the consistency of a major leaguer, though he lacks little else. Several young starters with Industriales (Yadel Martí), Cienfuegos (Norberto González), Camagüey (Odelín), Pinar del Río (Yunieski Maya) and Granma (Ciro Silvino Licea) may now be even better.

More than one recent Cuban League season might be advertised as the landmark "year of the pitcher." Norge Vera unleashed a blockbuster performance for National Series #39 (1999–2000) with his 17–2 ledger and an almost unthinkable 0.97 ERA (157 innings); that same campaign, which welcomed the reintroduction of wooden bats, also counted sixteen other regular starters boasting sub–2.00 ERAs. Not to be outdone during the pitching-rich 2000 season, phenom Maels Rodríguez provided some super feats of his own while hurling for one of the league's weakest outfits. In late December Maels spun Cuba's first-ever post-revolution perfect game; and in early January the same Sancti Spíritus sensation also uncorked the first pitch in a Cuban League game ever officially clocked at better than 100 mph velocity. Pro scouts were soon drooling at the thought of such an unpolished gem hidden away just out of reach behind the Sugarcane Curtain; if Maels Rodríguez failed to impress during tryout camps in El Salvador after his 2003 defection it was only because by that time he had already battled several career-threatening arm injuries that had reduced his celebrated fastball by better than 15 notches on the radar gun. Similar potential was also displayed by slender righty Ciro Silvino Licea, although Licea's career-best 1999 outing (16–4 for a normally impotent Granma team, along with a league-leading 1.85 ERA and a 136–40 SO/BBB ratio) has not been matched by his more recent seasons. Vera, Maels (before his injury), and Licea are all the tested equals of defector Danys Báez who reaped millions from the Cleveland Indians and finally reached the majors with moderate successes after first toiling two summers in the low-level minors.

Another point sorely in need of sorting out involves the mechanisms by which the Cuban baseball system works. A detail account is fortunately now available in Milton Jamail's *Full Count*. A bare outline of Cuban League structure is more than enough for the casual fan, or for our immediate purposes here. The crucial element in the story is the manner in which all sports enterprises operate under Cuba's Soviet-inspired socialist system. There are without doubt some drawbacks for individual athletes who are repeatedly sacrificed to an organizational structure that is oriented toward mass-producing champions to carry the national banner. But there are also great advantages growing from the system as a whole, especially for Cuban baseball fans who get to watch thrilling competitive pennant races offering cheap accessible entertainment, even if the National Series is intended more as a five-month national team tryout camp than as leisure-time spectacles for the masses.

Baseball is unabashedly part of a national sports system which functions as part of the government's monolithic political agenda. The transparent goal is to produce athletes who will excel in international competitions and thus ultimately bring honor and glory to the system and to the nation's flag. The winter-long Cuban League action (usually played November until April) which thrills fans in all corners of the nation is not the end in itself but only a by-product of the system and thus a step toward a larger goal of selecting competitive national teams. The complex bottom-up organization of Cuban baseball features not only Cuban League squads at the apex of the pyramid, representing all 14 provinces, but also boasts leagues and tournaments at age-levels from nine through 18, again at the regional, municipal and neighborhood levels; there are even Cuban national teams for overseas events representing five distinct age groups. Thus while the senior national team was crushing the opposition at the 2005 World

Cup in Rotterdam, the national junior squad was also collecting a gold medal in Mexico in the IBAF World Cup 15–16 age division.

The current organizational structure with only small modifications has been in place since the early 1960s, and one of its proudest achievements is Cuba's near-total domination of international amateur baseball. On this point, at least, the record is unassailable and the system shines most luminously, no matter how much gnashing of teeth there may continuously be in the United States about the fact that American amateur teams do not represent the best of USA baseball and that Cuban victories in Olympic-style matches thus prove little if anything about either pure baseball or cloudy politics.

However sliced or presented, Cuba's record in the big world tournaments has been most impressive if not altogether miraculous, no matter who and what the annual international competition might be. In Pan American Games competitions held every four years since the early fifties, the Cubans have rarely lost even individual games let alone gold medals (see Chapter 7). It was therefore truly headline news when the Cubans were beaten a single time by the upset-minded Americans in a preliminary round of the 1987 tournament in Indianapolis (before ultimately embarrassing the same American squad in the more vital championship match-up). The Cuban juggernaut was soon on a tear that saw it win the next 154 straight "official" tournament games, without tasting a single international defeat. Such game-after-game success is unheard of in baseball; the sport by its nature almost doesn't allow such relentless winning. (One of the sport's most worn clichés holds that big league champions normally win at a 60% ratio.) It was thus bigger news still when the favored-as-usual Cuban squad was lodged in fourth place after preliminary round games at the 1999 Winnipeg Pan American event, before once again rebounding ferociously to sweep past Dominican, Canadian and USA challengers during the all-important championship showdown round.

Despite the gaudy won-lost records, it is indeed difficult to measure very precisely the achievements of Cuban national teams down through the years. There is some kernel of truth after all in González Echevarría's contention (*The Pride of Havana*) that Omar Linares and Cuban nonpareils will never be fully or adequately tested without daily measurements head-to-head against U.S. big league competition. But this is saying a quite different thing from panning Linares and the other Cuban stalwarts outright. Enough big-league scouts tracking international tournaments have been repeatedly impressed by Cuban sluggers and pitching aces to put a final rest to any lingering doubts about the depth of the country's top-level talent.

A less celebrated achievement of the Cuban system has been the thriving Cuban League winter scene (Chapter 8) that provides the island's alternative to professional big league baseball. The INDER-operated league (known formally as the National Series) was born in the early 1960s with only a handful of teams. Four Havana-based clubs battled for the first several championships and for a few winters the new "national baseball" remained an exclusive spectacle of the capital city. Genuine country-wide interest picked up only when the replacement amateur league was little-by-little expanded to provide a December through April competition that was truly national in more than name only. The league experienced its first burst of growth in the late sixties when the roster of teams ballooned from only six (National Series V, 1965–66) to a full dozen (National Series VII, 1967–68). Functional-if-rudimentary new concrete and steel ballparks were also constructed by the revolutionary government in most of the provincial capitals by the mid-seventies, and all remain in use today, though some now suffer from charming decay. From the outset there was a more-than-adequate supply of superb ballplayers and exciting pennant races, and as a result there inevitably was also spiraling fan interest. An anointed national sport that had been vir-

A star catcher on the national team for the past half-dozen years, Villa Clara's Ariel Pestano — 2004 Athens Olympics MVP — may be the top pro prospect to remain firmly rooted in his native Cuba.

tually dying on the vine in Cuba by the late 1950s — with sparse crowds in Cerro Stadium during pro games, dwindling support for the International League Sugar Kings, and waning interest everywhere outside Havana, once extensive big league scouting had plucked most local stars from regional amateur teams and dispatched them to the pro winter league circuit or faraway U.S. minor leagues — was suddenly revived everywhere across the island. The watershed years for Cuban baseball fell much more obviously in the 1960s and seventies, than it did in the 1930s or forties.

There once had been a thriving informal network of island-wide games under the old pre-revolution amateur baseball system. What had always been lacking was any single truly "national" league or even a confederation of such leagues spreading throughout Cuba. Top players on the island were traditionally split up between the pro leagues (strictly a Havana affair), hastily arranged semi-pro tournaments, and a pastiche of numerous sugar mill clubs and amateur industrial teams. Star players were also regularly found shifting their affiliations from season to season and even game-to-game, with loyalties being dictated only by the highest bidder (Chapter 7). Teams and all the leagues themselves, for that matter, were equally vagabond in nature. Almendares and Club Habana may have remained fixtures on the island. But other league teams came and went like overnight fads and the professional-league seasons themselves were frequently shortened, preempted, or even sometimes abandoned in midstream.

The present-day Cuban League is altogether unique in both structure and operations among the world's major baseball circuits, and thus there are organizational aspects that are totally foreign to the perceptions of North American fans. Teams represent strict geographical locales in actual fact and not just in token naming rights as in organized baseball. Players (with few noted exceptions mentioned in Chapter 8) are draw strictly from the local soil; players for Pinar del Río or from Camagüey were born and raised in those provinces and are thus true native sons. As we have seen, there is no such thing as ballplayer trades, and free-agency is a totally foreign concept for Cuba players and fans. As a result, I am constantly assaulted by acquaintances in Havana for details about high-dollar, multi-year big league contracts, which they have great difficulty in grasping.

The nature of the Cuban League as a development league for the national team must be held in mind in any overview of the rationale behind the National Series. But even if the annual pennant races have an ulterior motive on the island, there are nonetheless great payoffs for Cuban fans. The rosters of favored or rival clubs remain stable year after year, and a favorite local star is guaranteed to be there performing in the local ballpark for the duration of his playing days. It is for this latter reason that fans in Havana protested so vocally about recent INDER-orchestrated forced player retirements (like those in 2002 of Linares, Pacheco and Kindelán). The rooting interest is truly local and thus unfailingly passionate. It is always a case of my province against yours, and never a matter of our rented Dominicans (or Mexicans) beating your rented Venezuelans (or Puerto Ricans) as is customary in the big leagues. It is this factor—along with cramped old-style parks and complete absence of any commercial or electronic trappings—that so automatically appeals also to any visitor who comes to Cuba with a traditional baseball mindset.

If the current island economic crisis (undeniably severe) or the constant threat of player defections (often overblown by U.S. media) has thrown Cuban baseball into something of an upheaval in the past several seasons, the league nonetheless still boasts plenty of positives. The presumed crisis for one thing has repeatedly been exaggerated and sensationalized by an American press focused on eventual MLB harvests from available Cuban talent. A seemingly endless stream of replacement stars has continued to entertain island fans and some are likely among the best players Cuba has ever produced. Fifties-era big leaguer Conrado Marrero (alive and well in Havana at age 95) has told this author that his own choices for the nation's greatest ballplayers are blackball ace Martín Dihigo from a bygone generation and Omar Linares from the post-revolutionary era. And Marrero sees them as not that far apart. Politics may partially account for Marrero's view, but to dismiss his opinions as brainwashing is a clear oversimplification. Marrero unhesitatingly ranks Germán Mesa as the best short-stop he has ever seen. He is also quick to tout the advantages of today's Cuban pitchers over those of all earlier professional epochs. This is of course the reverse of assessments usually found north of Miami when it comes to comparing past-era pitching with modern-era hurling.

The post–1962 amateur Cuban League was a most-predictable byproduct of the revolution in its very conception as well as its carefully orchestrated structure. It provided Cuba's first truly "national" baseball in the process of its 45-year evolution. But it was also a circumstance forced upon Fidel Castro and his revolutionary government by both Washington economic policies (viz., the post–1962 embargo) and organized baseball's own reactionary political policies. And the tale of Cuba's transition forty-plus years ago from a free-enterprise professional baseball structure operating in the shadow of the big leagues to a state-controlled amateur affair that was part and parcel of the country's new socialist agenda also contains many of the seeds for the checkered history of failed attempts at baseball détente which have subsequently followed.

Havana lost its final organized baseball franchise when International League officers operating in tangent with the U.S. Department of State decided that Cuban playing fields were suddenly unsafe for visiting American ballplayers. Secretary of State Christian Herter (more so than International League Frank Shaughnessy) had called the shots and dictated the steps that removed minor league baseball from Havana (see Chapter 5). It can now be debated how accurate Washington's fateful assessments of dangers represented by a Castro regime were at the time. What did result from those strategies, of course, was something of a self-fulfilling prophecy. The loss of AAA baseball was likely a distinct blow to Fidel Castro's ego and severely challenged the new government's initial hopes for resuscitating baseball as a national institution on the island. But the robbing of he Sugar Kings (transplanted to Jersey City by the International League) and the erosion of the pro winter league turned out to be dual blessings in disguise. A cherished talent pipeline may well have been closed permanently for the big leagues. But this was not a worst-case scenario for the Cubans themselves. The best among Cuban ballplayers (actually all Cuban players) would now be kept home to entertain and inspire local fans. The empty stadium in Havana which had greeted most Sugar Kings games during the last years of the 1950s would soon again be teeming with fans to greet and celebrate a new kind of national baseball. In one of the great unintentional ironies of international baseball history, for the Cuban fans less suddenly became very much more.

There is little denying that a glorious baseball tradition was thriving on the Cuban island long before Castro's ascension to power. Baseball has always been embedded deep in Cuba's soul and has always provided its very lifeblood. But it is just as true — as every attentive commentator maintains — that Cuba's national pastime has from start to finish always been intimately tied to the island's politics. Baseball began in Cuba as a vital instrument of the Creole rebellion against Spanish rule. González Echevarría (*Pride of Havana*), especially, is at his strongest in recounting this part of the Cuban baseball saga. The origins of the island game are inseparable from the late nineteenth-century rebellion against a tyrannical Spanish colonial government. It is only consistent with the hoariest traditions of baseball on the island, therefore, that the national sport should maintain political overtones in the wake of the revolution and Fidel Castro's rapid rise to power. Fidel would, as a matter of course, uncover in Cuba's baseball heritage a well-laid precedent for relying on the national game both for political advantage at home and perhaps even greater propaganda advantages abroad.

Fidel admittedly utilized baseball as a political tool from the earliest years of the revolution. The first triumphs of the Cuban socialist system were not victories on the battle fields in Bolivia or Angola. Military and guerilla exploits aimed at exporting Cuban-style revolution to neighboring third world countries were met throughout the sixties and seventies with repeated and even shattering failures. It was rather on the baseball field that Fidel's new regime won its first muted victories. And the relentless triumphs have subsequently continued on to the present day.

Cuba's overall record in international competitions is indeed one of the most remarkable sports stories in the second half of the just-concluded century, and yet one that is only of late drawing much notice back here in the United States. Debunkers may belittle the lack of true competition encountered in events like the Caribbean-Central American Games, Pan American Games, or Intercontinental Cup. But what level of competition anywhere from T-ball to pony league to the industrial league sandlots or collegiate diamonds has ever witnessed a string of close to 150 uninterrupted victories? Such winning skeins are entirely unknown anywhere else on the baseball landscape, or in any other epoch since an inaugural 1869 cross-county tour by the legendary unbeaten Cincinnati Red Stockings launched the history of the professional sport. Harry Wright's crack Cincinnatians merely won 56 straight, not counting one tie with the Troy ball club (when the Haymakers quit the field to protect the interests of local gamblers) and several more games with inferior squads which manager Wright refused to count.

The Cubans would actually do those original "Reds" one better, and then some, by coming home a winner in all but one of the official senior-level international tournament games they played over an ten-year stretch, and they did so with constantly shifting rosters of new aluminum-wielding batters and brand new rubber-like pitching arms. The miraculous string stretched between a preliminary-round Pan American Games defeat by Team USA (Indianapolis in August 1987) and an Intercontinental Cup gold medal game loss to Japan (Barcelona in August 1997): the total ledger for that span was 143 games won and but one lost (a meaningless preliminary round game with Nicaragua during the 1991 Intercontinental Cup also held in Barcelona).

Across nearly four decades baseball in Cuba quite transparently remained an effective instrument of international politics. It has provided a singular opportunity to drub the Yankees (the ones in Washington, not New York) at their own

Preston Gómez spearheaded numerous futile efforts to reach a détente and schedule much-desired exhibitions between Cuban Leaguers and big leaguers during the seventies and eighties (courtesy Transcendental Graphics).

game and thus supposedly showcase the advertised superiority of a disciplined socialist national sports enterprise rooted in patriotism and idealism rather than capitalist profiteering. If one counts up the championship medals and head-to-head victories only, then this is one place where the revolution has wildly succeeded. What could be more satisfying in Havana than to witness the quintessential anti–American system— Fidel's communist-controlled sports machine—repeatedly dominating despised capitalists up north at the quintessentially American sport? And along the way there have been some truly epic struggles, especially a handful of politically charged matches against baseball "imperialists" representing Team USA. A first important showdown came in the 1970 Amateur World Series (IBA World Championships, now called the Baseball World Cup) in Cartagena, Colombia. The finals of that tournament brought a memorable square-off between USA and Cuban teams sporting identical 10–1 records. In the opener of a best-of-three title clash Cuban ace José Antonio Huelga topped future big leaguer Burt Hooton 3–1 during a truly unforgettable extra-inning duel that may well have been the most genuinely "classic" single contest of world amateur baseball history.

An equally dramatic if slightly less landmark victory was earned by the Cubans during the 1988 IBA World Championships at Parma, Italy — games staged in the aftermath of an "unofficial" Olympic tournament in Korea that the favored Cubans had regrettably boycotted (in sympathy with their allies, the Soviets). A dramatic Lourdes Gourriel homer stunned one-handed ace Jim Abbott and his American teammates after the future big-leaguer coaxed a 3–1 lead for eight innings. René Arocha and Antonio Pacheco—one Cuban ace who later defected and another who did not—played the starring roles as the Cubans defeated Team USA twice, both times rallying stubbornly in the ninth frame. And again in the summer of 1999 at Winnipeg, Manitoba, the gutsy Cuban nine scored one of its most heroic victories, overcoming a long layoff, the introduction of wooden bats, and Canadian, USA and Dominican squads stocked for the first time with seasoned pro players from high-powered AAA leagues. Clutch pitching from José Ibar, Pedro Lazo and José Contreras earned an uncanny comeback after early-round losses to the Canadians and Americans had threatened to sabotage a 2000 Olympic berth in Sydney and a renewed chance for the Cubans to again to defend their international domination.

But the many battles between Cuban and USA nines were for forty years fought only on amateur fields and thus always for American fans on less-than-notable stages. The dream, stateside at least, remained that of forcing a showdown between Cuba's best batters and pitchers and the only true measure of North American baseball talent—a major league team. As early as the late-sixties, efforts had already been launched to bring about just such an intriguing grudge match.

There have been many subsequent efforts across the years to force a showdown between the Cuban national team juggernaut and U.S. professionals, often proposed under the guise of some form of politically ripe baseball détente. Peter Angelos and the Baltimore Orioles brass did not invent this idea in 1998 or 1999 by any stretch of reasoning. Jamail reviews the cloak-and-dagger history of these efforts in fine detail with *Full Count* (Chapter 9). The purposes of the casual observer will be served with a brief summary that circumvents some of the convoluted details of specific ill-fated efforts. It is clear in each case that while there may have been a few enthusiastic supporters in Washington or in organized baseball for some of these ventures, few have had any weighty backing in either Washington circles or from the baseball commissioner's office.

Preliminary efforts at USA-Cuba baseball détente can be traced to the aftermath of the last big league game on Cuban soil, a spur-of-the-moment spring training visit in March 1959 by the Cincinnati Reds, featuring a sprinkling of former Cuban Sugar Kings, and the newly transplanted Los Angeles Dodgers with Koufax and Drysdale. The first spring of the new decade, a year later, witnessed some behind-the-scenes efforts to duplicate that series and bring the Cincinnati club back to Havana along with the American League Baltimore Orioles. But it never actually happened and the surrounding negotiations were never made very public. The remainder of the Viet Nam-ruined decade witnessed slim interest in baseball intercourse once Fidel's forces set out on a path of socialist reform causing nothing but consternation to North American politicians and citizenry alike.

It was not until summer 1971 that there were new rumblings of possible matchups between big leaguers and crack Cuban teams. Such rumblings surged to the foreground from time to time through the remainder of the decade and at least seven efforts at some form of détente can be documented during the 1970s. The Seditious Seventies, in fact, became the decade most filled with hopeful news and ultimate disappointment regarding possible USA–Cuba baseball reunions. Cuban-born big league manager Preston Gómez was, on several occasions, a leading figure in these ongoing backstage dramas. But in the end all efforts were always finally scuttled by Washington operatives or by the MLB commissioner himself. The reasons were not always quite the same, but the pervasive theme remained unchanged. And the dream of USA–Cuba competitions remained always well outside the shadowy intrigues of U. S. Cold War foreign policy.

In the end the two political systems were always too much at odds for realistic hopes that such potential "dream games" could ever succeed in materializing. If some proposals promised potential propaganda advantages for the Cubans they didn't usually offer sufficient economical or promotional windfalls for their organized baseball supporters. And those that would accomplish the latter could never seem to promise the former for Havana. Fidel Castro and organized baseball always had very different agendas when it came to the politics of international sports.

Why then was there, seemingly overnight, a breakthrough in early 1999; and why did the Orioles' historic visit to the island suddenly take place that spring after so many decades of posturing? The surprising events that would tran-

spire over several short months at century's end seemingly raised more questions than they answered. My own reading at the time was that the Cubans would never agree to such a showdown, especially one scheduled for the eve of a crucial Winnipeg Olympic qualifying tournament. Some of the top Cuban stars (notably Linares and several front-line pitchers) were just then coming off injury-riddled seasons. There were at least the trappings of a crisis in Cuban baseball and a resulting diminishing in the quality of play all around the league. The national team was itself in a state of transition, with veterans like Linares, Pacheco and Germán Mesa either slowed by injuries or slipping from the pinnacle of their game at the same time that replacements like Michel Enríquez or Yasser Gómez or promising pitcher Norge Vera were not yet tested in international waters. This was hardly a time to showcase Cuban talent in a big league park with high propaganda stakes squarely in the offering.

Major League Baseball's motives in pushing Washington for such a series were more clear-cut and obvious. There was an enticing prospect of getting a firsthand look at Cuban ballplayers (read here, potential defectors). ML persists in viewing international baseball as little more than another promising recruiting venue to be fully exploited in the face of diminishing resources back home. Cuba offered another pipeline supply of cheap talent to be pried open, as in the Joe Cambria era of the 1950s. MLB hangers-on like television executives and print media moguls of course also saw big dollar revenues to be pocketed.

Cooperation from the Clinton Administration also has its easy explanations. Democrats have historically leaned more lightly on the Cuba issue. President Carter had once before eased restrictions on American Cuba travel. Clinton's government team worked behind the scenes for a number of years to ease restrictions and temper the internationally (even domestically) unpopular economic embargo. But it never did so in all-out overt fashion that might risk crucial electoral votes in South Florida—a crucible of anti–Castro exile sentiment. Here perhaps was a chance to make further inroads against vocal conservative Castro haters in an arena that would garner large popular support. Wasn't this, after all, precisely what baseball détente was supposedly all about?

The agreement to such a series by Havana officials and thus first and foremost by Fidel — Cuba's lifelong baseball general manager — is perhaps less easily accounted for. There are several competing theories here. Perhaps a game versus big leaguers was finally needed to bolster waning fan interest on the island. More likely there was a jingoistic blindness to just how weak the Cuban team might be in the face of big-league opposition. Perhaps the prospects of financial gains for the sagging Cuban League itself were tempting, if these could be arranged in a way that did not compromise the communist system and a hard-line Castro stance concerning the sanctity of amateur baseball. My own theory at the time was that there was a large propaganda victory to be scored here, one that might even be worth the bundle of associated risks. It was certainly a bold move on the part of Fidel to bank on showing well in head-to-head matches with major leaguers. But Fidel has always survived on the shoulders of bold moves. Cuban ballplayers were also more prepared and motivated for the challenge that most at the time would have expected.

Whatever the complex reasons behind it, the baseball détente of spring 1999 was part and parcel of a sudden partial opening up of long-isolated Cuba to curious North American eyes. It would focus attention on Cuba that had not existed in years. And it supplemented momentum already building around almost all things Cuban by conspiring — alongside Ry Cooder's music and little Elian's soap opera saga — to spike the sudden vogue of Cuba watching. But it also only came to fruition after some very complicated negotiations regarding how the games would be handled, especially from a revenue standpoint. Several early U.S. and MLB proposals were quickly rejected outright in Havana. And the staging of the first game at Estadio Latinoamericano soon also led to some bizarre and unfortunate circumstances for Cuba's legions of diehard fans.

The games themselves—once they finally arrived—were a glowing and even shocking success, at least for the Cubans. A nip-and-tuck 11-inning Orioles victory in Latin American Stadium perhaps represented a disappointing defeat on the diamond, but nonetheless it was a major moral victory since it easily demonstrated that Cuban Leaguers could play head-to-toe with the big leaguers. It is true that few "real" fans found their way into the stadium that was jammed with government officials and party loyalists. But this would have been the case in the United States as well for any World Series or All-Star Game, where prime tickets would have gone to high rollers and not everyday fans. The Cuban patrons did all have access on television (without any commercial interruptions). And the home team played nobly and even heroically in defeat. A close loss was perhaps even better than a one-sided victory from the Cuban perspective, since it cancelled any claims that the big leaguers simply weren't trying. And such a loss built anticipation both at home in Havana and back in the States for an equally exciting rematch up in Baltimore.

The renewal at Baltimore's Camden Yards brought a more startling victory for Cuban baseball forces and also an unexpected windfall for Cuba's propaganda planners. American foreign policy has done much in recent years to revive Fidel Castro's slipping stature on the island. Elian González would soon provide even richer grist for Cuba's busy propaganda machinery. But perhaps the biggest blows in decades for Cuban national pride were those struck by Cuban bats on a rainy May night in Baltimore. The big leaguers were obviously unmotivated to play and were thus figuratively run off the field by a Cuban batting onslaught in the middle innings, following a lengthy tension-building early rain delay. But rather than diminish the Cuban team and its accomplishments, the sloppy performance by bored Baltimore players only seemed to enhance the image of Cuba's "play-for-pride" national baseball. The real victory came in simply showcasing a Cuban squad teeming with raw enthusiasm and almost childlike innocence. A key moment of the entire series unfolded after an otherwise meaningless ninth-inning homer by Andy Morales. Morales's

joyful arms-raised trot around the base paths (which the big leaguers later dismissed angrily as hot-dogging) provided a final and indelible contrast between two clashing baseball universes.

For big leaguers like Albert Belle or B.J. Surhoff the game was only an unwelcome burden ruining a scheduled "open-date" in the rat-race American League grind; for Morales and his teammates it was an much-savored and unmatched moment of proud victory over the giants of professional baseball.

What, then, were the measurable gains for the Cubans in this unique series? Clearly a major blow was struck in both Havana and Baltimore for recently sagging Cuban national morale. The whole affair was another unexpected propaganda windfall handed to Fidel when he least expected it. Washington politicos and big league baseball magnates have time and again done unexpected favors for Fidel Castro. The first, as it later turned out, was the pulling of the plug on professional baseball in Havana with the relocation of the Sugar Kings; without that sabotaging of USA-Cuban baseball relations forty years in the past most Cuban ballplayers would have been toiling in major and minor league parks outside the country and not winning trophy after trophy for the socialist sports system. But beyond another feather in Fidel's cap, it is unclear that there was much else done for Cuban baseball in Baltimore outside of the all-important propaganda arena. There was of course token financial payoff in the form of some cosmetic improvements at Estadio Latinoamericano, underwritten by MLB funds, and parallel improvements to league play brought by wooden bats and new Cuban League uniforms, also MLB gifts. But those paled beside the boasting right that had now temporarily been earned.

*   *   *

How serious is the baseball crisis in Cuba today? It is immediately obvious to any Cuba traveler that the surprising showing in Baltimore five-plus years ago has not completely gilded over Cuba's many baseball warts. The steady drain of bleacher fans and the slide of interest in league games, especially in Havana, seems now a far bigger blow to baseball health on the home front then the much-ballyhooed trickle of occasional defectors. It is highly likely that a deteriorating economy has had far more impact on empty ballpark seats at Latinoamericano than any loss of star attractions resulting from INDER policies of banishing or retiring disloyal and deadwood veteran stars. Fan enthusiasm around the country by all other measures seems as widespread as at any time in the recent or distant past. Havana's Parque Central still teems daily with its usual animated *aficionados* who ritualistically debate and celebrate the national pastime from dawn until dusk. And the league playoffs of recent seasons — especially those featuring Industriales the same week as the Orioles visit, and then again in 2003, 2004 and 2006 — have drawn some of the wildest Havana crowds witnessed in many a year.

What in the end, we should ask, is the future of baseball in Cuba and of the Cuba League as it currently functions? Jamail (*Full Count*, Epilogue) seems not far off the mark in his

Members of the Peña Deportiva (Cuba's version of the Society for American Baseball Research) in Havana's Central Park, January 1999. Fifties-era Cuban winter league star Asdrubal Baró is third from left. The author is at the far right and fellow American writer Milton Jamail is fourth from right.

suggestion that it was the Cuban government's own policies of selling and retiring players more than defections themselves that have recently threatened the game's health. From this perspective it is significant that in recent seasons there has been a reversal of INDER policy-making and also of league fortunes. Disgraced major stars like Germán Mesa and Eduardo Paret were rapidly returned to the Cuban League scene after brief banishments. And the sudden success of a newly restocked Industriales team — Cuba's most popular ball club — has rekindled fan interest in the nation's undisputed baseball capital. But it will take some time perhaps to see if this is a permanent or only a temporary reversal of sagging league fortunes, especially in a wake of another round of unpopular suspensions involving top Industriales stars (Kendry Morales and Bárbaro Cañizares) which came on the heals of that team's 2003 National Series championship. Another dip in fan support might have been anticipated once the Olympic gold medal hoopla of Athens 2004 had passed, or a giddy high following the Baltimore victory had begun to fade into the distant background. But Cuba's invitation to compete against the top big leaguers in a first-ever MLB World Baseball Classic has again already stoked the embers in March 2006.

Volatility on the current Cuban baseball scene has been appropriately reflected by up-and-down fortunes in recent years for the once invincible Cuban national squad. The slide in Cuban fortunes actually began on the heels of Atlanta's 1996 Olympics with a surprise drubbing by Japan at the Barcelona Intercontinental Cup finals of August 1997. The loss represented only a single ballgame; but Cubans have grown painfully unaccustomed to losing (it was their first international tournament game defeat since the opening round of the same event back in 1991) and an 11–2 lashing by the usually light-hitting Japanese was especially embarrassing. Fallout from this particular setback was truly earthshaking back on the home front and it even triggered the first public admission from INDER of full-blown crisis in Cuban baseball.

But the slide seemed temporary enough after a tremendous reversal in fortunes with the July 1999 Pan American championship at Winnipeg that locked up another Olympic title defense scheduled for Sydney. This was followed immediately — as the rollercoaster ride continued unabated — by further embarrassing losses in Nicaragua (Cuba dropped several exhibition games after sending a second-level national squad) and then in the Olympic tune-up in Sydney (where a second straight Intercontinental Cup was squandered with another disappointing letdown in the championship round versus host Australia). Finally there was the bitterest pill of all: the Olympic gold medal round whitewashing at the hands of the Americans. That ultimate loss to a more-solid-than-usual USA club with several major leaguers in the line-up — after so many years of beating the Americans as a matter of course — should perhaps not have been greeted as a national disaster of grandest proportions. But then the Cubans are not conditioned to losing gold medals, especially at the most highly showcased tournaments. The situation was not yet entirely stable at the close of 2003 — even after an impressive 2003 World Cup victory in Havana and also qualification for Athens 2004 and a chance at Olympic redemption — and baseball commissioner Carlitos Rodríguez and his staff (including a string of several national team managers that have followed since Sydney) continued to sit on a sizzling hot seat.

Are there likely to be more such Cuba-MLB match-ups? The answer was not at all obvious in late 2005, though Cuba was now penciled in to compete in MLB's World Baseball Classic, which is being billed by organized baseball as the eventually replacement for Cuba-dominated Olympic tournaments. But it is clear that true baseball détente was never really the goal of either side. And this likely will mean few if any renewed attempts at match-ups in coming years. The Cuban baseball machine won a considerable propaganda victory during March and May of 1999 and neither Fidel nor INDER brass would likely want to jeopardize this gain with further outings against more motivated big league teams. And the major league clubs, for their part, now realize there is slim chance of sudden windfall talent harvests likely connected with any more such games. Reportedly there was a plan afoot to bring the Cuban national team to Southern California for pre-season games during the spring of 2000. But it was a plan apparently aimed at circumventing MLB officials (the games were supposedly being arranged between the Anaheim Angels and Cubans directly, without involvement of the commissioner's office) and thus had little Stateside support. And such plans for renewed baseball friendship matches also predictably fell on very deaf ears in Havana as well as Washington during the height of the simmering Elian González crisis and its aftermath.

Cuba presumably will work out its own baseball fortunes in coming decades. Yet it will likely have to do so without the help of major league dollars, at least for a few years to come. And it will have to do so against the backdrop of the entrenched political machinery, with the handful of plusses and boatload of minuses which this might represent. Baseball people do not currently run baseball in Cuba and the result has been a huge drag on the entire enterprise. Those in charge of baseball administration are often INDER party soldiers whose task is always to protect the gains of the revolution and never to consider the health of baseball as an independent priority. Often these are men who have little or no actual baseball experience or even much of any sensitivity to the game's needs — a rare condition for Cuba, since this is a country with (in Milton Jamail's words) ten million expert managers hanging around everywhere on the nation's crowded street corners. But huge strides in the direction of repair have been made within the last two or three seasons. And they have come — unlike in the American big leagues — without ever throwing the proverbial baby out the window with the soiled bathwater. Cuban League baseball has remained foremost a game, free from the clutches of big business.

There will be much to be gained by certain Cuban ballplayers if there is any reconciliation with the organized baseball's professional leagues. Free-agency will immediately come to Cuban diamonds and fortunes will be made by top stars and journeymen alike. And huge fortunes will of course also be made by the slave traders known as agents. And there will even be some potential gains for Cuban fans. At last there will be Cubans — the very best Cubans — toiling again in the big leagues, for all the world to see. Cuban fans will again take pride in the accomplishments of their heroes playing against the best competition the sport has to offer. This will no doubt represent some compensation for fans on Havana streets, even if once-free ball games in Estadio Latinoamericano may quickly be priced well beyond their own modest reach.

But there will also be much that will be lost in the transition. The same way that much will be lost of Cuban innocence when rampant capitalism eventually embraces Havana's avenues, marketplaces and pristine waterfront. Once the old infrastructure is torn down and replaced willy-nilly with the new, much that was glorious on the Cuban scene will sadly disappear forever. And some of that loss will constitute the very best that Cuban baseball has long had to offer.

Sports Illustrated columnist S.L. Price has phrased it more or less correctly in his forthright examination of the government-controlled sports enterprise inside of Fidel Castro's Cuba. Cuba (with its absence of economic opportunity) is indeed the worst place imaginable to be an athlete. And as Price is also quick to admit, Cuba (where ballplayers remain national heroes rather than celebrity rock stars) is also the very best place of all to be an athlete.

References and Suggested Readings

Bjarkman, Peter C. *Diamonds around the Globe: The Encyclopedia of International Baseball*. Westport, Connecticut: Greenwood Publishing Group. 2005.

González Echevarría, Roberto. *The Pride of Havana: A History of Cuban Baseball*. New York: Oxford University Press, 1999.

Jamail, Milton. *Full Count: Inside Cuban Baseball*. Carbondale and Edwardsville: Southern Illinois University Press, 2000.

Price, S.L. *Pitching Around Fidel: A Journey in the Heart of Cuban Sports*. New York: HarperCollins (The Ecco Press), 2000.

Shouler, Ken. "El Duque's Excellent Adventures: How Cuba's Ace Pitcher Escaped Political Oppression to Become Part of the Great American Success Story" in: *Cigar Aficionado* (March/April 1999), 79–96.

Skinner, David. "Review of *The Pride of Havana: A History of Cuban Baseball* by Roberto González Echevarría" in: *Nine: A Journal of Baseball History and Social Policy Perspectives* 8:2 (Spring 2000), 153–157.

Wertheim, Jon, and Don Yaeger. "Fantastic Voyage — Three fellow refugees say the tale of Yankees ace Orlando (El Duque) Hernández's escape from Cuba doesn't hold water" in: *Sports Illustrated* 89:22 (November 30, 1998), 60–63.

Chronology of Failed Attempts at Cuba–MLB Baseball Détente

Cuba was a major supplier of big-league talent throughout the late-forties and the entire decade of the fifties, stocking the low-budget Washington Senators with nearly a third of its American League roster at one point. Cuba's big-league notables during the 1950s included Orestes Miñoso with the Indians and White Sox, pitchers Pedro Ramos and Camilo Pascual with the Senators, and relief ace Mike Fornieles with the Senators and Red Sox. When Fidel Castro outlawed pro baseball on the island after 1961 the Cuban pipeline quickly dried to a trickle, petering out with such last-minute escapees as Tony Oliva, Bert Campaneris, Zoilo Versalles, Cookie Rojas, Tito Fuentes, Tony González, Tony Taylor, Antanasio (Tany or Tony) Pérez and Luis Tiant, Jr. Havana's International League Sugar Kings enjoyed one final hurrah with their AAA championship captured during the Fall 1959 Junior World Series (when they defeated the American Association Minneapolis Millers in a series held mostly in Havana due to freezing weather up north).

March 20–21, 1959 — First two big league clubs to visit Cuba after Fidel Castro's January 1, 1959, rise to power are National League Cincinnati Reds and Los Angeles Dodgers. Clubs play rain-shortened two-game spring training series in Havana's Gran Stadium (later renamed Estadio Latinoamericano). Future hall-of-famers Don Drysdale and Sandy Koufax hurl for LA Dodgers in these two landmark exhibition games.

March 1960 — Talk circulates (in November 1959) of possible second spring training series between Baltimore Orioles and Cincinnati Reds in Havana, but proposed games are soon scrubbed due to disagreements between Washington officials and the Castro-led government about use of gate proceeds to underwrite Cuba's agrarian reform movement. Baltimore GM Lee MacPhail in the end officially cancelled this series, claiming his team refused to play under unsafe post-revolutionary conditions reportedly existing in Havana.

July 1960 — International League officials relocate Bobby Maduro's Cuban Sugar Kings AAA franchise in mid-season to Jersey City (while team is on road trip in Miami). U.S. Secretary of State Christian Herter petitions MLB Commissioner Ford Frick to initiate this move in order to protect U.S. ballplayers from possible "anti–American" aggressions during visits to Havana. Frick also orders all American players to avoid Havana's winter league, which holds its final season in 1960–61 with only native-born Cuban players.

Summer 1971 — Cuban-born Preston (Pedro) Gómez, former Sugar Kings skipper and the present San Diego Padres manager, announces plans to take big-league all-star team (with native Cubans Tony Pérez, Tony Taylor, Tony Oliva and Leo Cárdenas) to Havana during off-season tour. Frick initially approves proposed junket but MLB's tour is later denied formal approval by U.S. State Department officials and is thus abruptly cancelled.

February 1975 — Preston Gómez renews efforts to schedule a Cuba junket, meeting with Havana baseball officials and later Commissioner Bowie Kuhn about another possible island tour. This plan is touted by Gómez as akin to earlier "ping-pong diplomacy" with China but is nixed by Secretary of State Kissinger as being "politically inappropriate."

March 1976 — Kuhn's continued efforts to arrange a series between Cuban leaguers and big leaguers leads to talk of proposed match-up between Cuba's national team and major league "all-stars" supposedly to be televised in the United States by ABC. Kissinger again cancels proposed event, this time in anger over Cuba's military involvement with ongoing Angolan civil war.

March 1977 — Temporary semi-thaw in Cuba policy under new President Jimmy Carter and Secretary of State Cyrus Vance encourages renewed talk of possible visit to Havana by American League New York Yankees (reported to be Fidel's favorite team and Cuba's top choice for Havana exhibition visits). This time Kuhn cancels the plan as unacceptable since it might possibly "give the Yankees an unfair advantage in recruiting Cuban talent."

November 1977 — Houston Astros players and coaches quietly hold series of "secret" unsanctioned clinics for Cuban baseball players at Havana's Estadio Latinoamericano. Making this unauthorized trip (Commissioner Kuhn was not informed prior to the tour) were manager Bill Virdon; coaches Mel Wright, Deacon Jones and Bob Lillis; and then-active Astros players Bob Watson, Ken Forsch, and Enos Cabel.

March 1978 — Gabe Paul, a former International League official and now Cleveland Indians team president, again suggests visit of Cuban national team to Tucson, Arizona, for three early–April exhibitions with American League team, but once more MLB refuses to take any positive action on this latest plan.

July 1978 — Proposed August visit of Cuban national team to Quebec, Canada, to face the National League Montreal Expos quickly sabotaged by reported disputes between Castro government and MLB over shared TV rights to any such much-anticipated exhibition.

March 1982 — Decade of futile efforts at orchestrating baseball détente brought to climax when American League Seattle Mariners are forced to cancel hoped-for spring exhibition series versus Cuban all-stars due to virulent Miami-based Cuban-American protests.

Spring 1997 and Spring 1998 — Baltimore Orioles owner Peter Angelos twice denied an applied-for U.S. Treasury Department OFAC license that would legalize the MLB club's travel to Havana for possible exhibition games versus Cuba's national team. Speculations about Cuba's agreement to any such hoped-for series thus remain a moot point.

February 1999 — Orioles owner Angelos finally wins Washington and OFAC approval for exhibition series with Cuba to be played in both Havana and Baltimore. Nonetheless, American League Anaheim Angels denied in similar request to OFAC for U.S. Treasury Department sanction for additional exhibition series. Anaheim club had hoped to arrange MLB–Cuba matchup through team's special administrative assistant Preston Gómez.

Fall 2005 — Major League Baseball launches a formal attempt to corner the international baseball television market by announcing plans for its first World Baseball Classic, to be staged in March 2006. Preliminary games are scheduled for San Juan, Orlando, Scottsdale and Tokyo, with championship finals announced for San Diego's spiffy new $485 million Petco Park. Plans include teams featuring big league stars (from Puerto Rico, Panama, the Dominican Republic, Venezuela, Canada and the USA) suiting up for their native countries, with Cuba, Italy, The Netherlands, Korea, Taiwan, Australia and Japan (countries with too few big leaguers to staff an entire roster) also invited to participate. Penciled in for opening round action in San Juan, along with Panama, The Netherlands and host Puerto Rico, Cuba at first refuses to make clear-cut commitment to participating in the event, which IBAF officials go on record as labeling "an exhibition" and not a "world championship tournament with legitimate qualification rounds." OFAC first denies but later (after consider pressure from MLB) issues permission for Cuba's entry in the tournament and Fidel Castro announces his country's firm commitment to attend.

For the first time Cuba's all-stars will be matched head-to-head with all-star pros in a stellar round-robin event featuring baseball's highest-level players.

List of Cuba's Defecting Athletes (1960s–1990s)

The following alphabetical listing (compiled by this author from the various available published sources in May 2000) contains most of the known Cuban defectors through the 1990s, including athletes from all amateur sports. Baseball players are listed in boldface type, thus allowing the viewer a quick assessment of the percentage of defecting Cuban athletes representing the island's national pastime.

There are 47 baseball players included among a total 106 athletes on this list. Updates on the whereabouts and activities of defectors are complete only through May 2000.

Roberto Aldazabal, Gymnastics: Defected at 1993 Central American and Caribbean Games in Ponce, Puerto Rico. Assisted in leaving team by friend who had defected three years before. Won gold medal on uneven parallel bars at Ponce.

Ivan Alvarez, Baseball: Pitcher signed for $35,000 with San Francisco Giants in 1993; Retired from Burlington Bees in 1995.

Yamilet Amaro, Field Hockey: Defected at 1993 Central American and Caribbean Games at age 22. Uncle Tony Suárez earlier defected in 1988. Walked off field in Ponce with teammate. Current whereabouts unknown.

Jesús Amettler, Baseball: Second baseman defected in 1996 through Mexico. Batting .250 at Double A Arkansas (Cardinals) in May 2000.

Boris Anansibea, Judo: Defected from 1993 Central American Caribbean Games in Ponce, Puerto Rico hours before Cuban delegation was scheduled to fly home. Current whereabouts unknown.

René Arocha, Baseball: Signed for $15,000 bonus with St. Louis Cardinals in 1991; re-injured elbow (earlier damaged in Cuba) in 1996. Pitched in Mexican League in 1999 (1–7, 4.15 ERA).

Rolando Arrojo, Baseball: Top national team pitcher defected in 1996 (July 9 at Albany, Georgia) on eve of Atlanta Olympic Games. Signed for $7 million by Tampa Bay Devil Rays and made 1998 All-Star Game appearance; traded to NL Colorado Rockies after 1999 campaign but finished 2000 season with AL Boston Red Sox.

Danys Báez, Baseball: Pitcher defected at July 1999 Pan American Games in Winnipeg. Promoted to Double A Akron (Indians) in Spring 2000 after posting 2–2, 4.91 ERA in A-level minors. (Emerged in 2002 as one of top American League closers with Cleveland Indians.)

Jorge Enrico Blanco, Boxing: Walked away from Cuban team at 1967 Pan American Games staged in Winnipeg, Canada. Now lives in Texas (under the name Jesse Ravelo) and coaches professional and amateur fighters.

Norge Blay, Water Polo: Defected at 1993 Central American and Caribbean Games in Puerto Rico. Was 26-year-old forward on gold medal team before defecting. Left competition site in Ponce with teammate Antonio Pérez Sánchez. Resides in Puerto Rico, but often visits other exiled members of Cuban water polo team in Miami.

Lazaro Borrell, Basketball: Defected at Olympic qualifying tournament in July 1999 in San Juan, Puerto Rico. The 26-year-old center signed two-year contract with the Seattle Sonics in September 1999.

Felix Isasi Bustamante, Baseball: Outfielder defected in Spain (date uncertain) and to date remains unsigned by professional baseball. Current whereabouts are unknown.

Juan Carlos Bruzón, Baseball: Outfielder gained political asylum in Summer 1999 and later signed with Winnipeg Goldeyes of Independent Northern League in March 2000.

Alexis Cabreja, Baseball: Outfielder defected in 1992 (date uncertain); signed with Texas Rangers but never made it past A-level minor leagues. Current whereabouts unknown.

Ramon Campoallegre, Water Polo: Defected in 1998 from team training camp in Mexico. Currently serving as lifeguard in Miami area.

Joel Casamayor, Boxing: Defected in June 1996 at pre–Olympic training camp. Became ranked professional who recently won WBA super-featherweight title.

Elieser Castillo, Boxing: Came to U.S. in 1994 (exact date unknown, but harrowing escape reportedly made in small inner tube). Heavyweight professional fighter, who now trains in Atlantic City, New Jersey.

Elisio Castillo, Boxing: Came to U.S. in 1994 in inner tube with his brother Elieser Castillo. Cruiserweight professional, who now trains in Miami.

Angel Coballero, Basketball: National team 28-year-old

guard defected at Olympic qualifying tournament in July 1999 in San Juan, Puerto Rico. Currently still lives in Puerto Rico.

Roberto Colina, **Baseball:** First baseman (on second-level national team) defected in 1996; was released by Toronto Blue Jays in April 2000.

José Tejada Cortina, Gymnastics: Defected at 1993 Central American and Caribbean Games in Ponce, Puerto Rico. Claimed he was earning an equivalent of $1.75 a month while training in Cuba. Helped in Puerto Rico by exile group known as *Comite Cubano Por Derechos Humanos.*

Conrado Cabrera, Cycling: Defected after competing in 1993 Central American and Caribbean Games in Ponce, Puerto Rico. Current whereabouts unknown.

Juan Carlos Díaz, **Baseball:** Precise date of defection unknown. Declared free-agent by MLB in 1999 after his illegal signing (along with Josué Pérez) by Los Angeles Dodgers. First baseman (never played in Cuban League) was batting .275 with 4 homers for A-level Sarasota Red Sox in April 2000. Played four major league games for Boston in 2002.

Noel de la Cruz, Cycling: Defected immediately after competing in 1993 Central American and Caribbean Games in Ponce, Puerto Rico. Current whereabouts unknown.

Ana Santiago Díaz, Sharpshooter: Defected at 1993 Central American and Caribbean Games in Ponce, Puerto Rico. Reportedly plotted defection for months and didn't tell family of plans to depart Cuba. Current whereabouts unknown.

Jorge Díaz Olado, **Baseball:** Left under mysterious circumstances with four other players (including Maikel Jova and Osmani García) in August 1998. Second baseman played six seasons in Cuban League with Villa Clara; invited to extended spring training with Texas Rangers in 2000.

Ivan Domínguez, Cycling: Defected during 1998 Goodwill Games. Now trains with amateur cycling team based in Orlando, Florida.

Alfonso Donate, Archery: Coach who defected at 1993 Central American and Caribbean Games in Ponce, Puerto Rico. Current whereabouts unknown.

Alfonso Donate, Archery: Defected with father Alfonso Donate at 1993 Central American and Caribbean Games. Father reportedly trained son precisely so he could become member of national team and both could defect simultaneously. Left mother and sister behind in Cuba. Current whereabouts unknown.

Manuel Elizondo, Boxing: National team trainer defected in July 1994. Continues to train professional boxers in Miami area.

Osmany Estrada, **Baseball:** Precise date of defection uncertain. Infielder (with four years experience in Cuban League) drafted by Texas Rangers late in 1993; reached AAA-level minor leagues before his release from Texas organization. Played professionally in Taiwan in 2000.

Elsimo Felipe, Boxing: Came to U.S. in flimsy inner tube in 1995 (a year after brothers Elieser and Elisio Castillo, who used same escape method). Welterweight who no longer fights. Currently lives in Tampa.

Lázaro Fernández, Water Polo: Defected at 1994 Alamo Cup invitational event in Texas. No longer competes and now lives in Puerto Rico.

Osmany Fernández, **Baseball:** National junior team pitcher defected at Summer 1996 tournament in Illinois; currently lives in Dominican Republic.

Osvaldo Fernández Rodríguez, **Baseball:** Defected from national team in Millington, Tennessee in 1996. Pitcher who signed $3.2 million bonus contract with San Francisco Giants in 1997 but developed elbow problems (from earlier injury in Cuba). Enjoyed several quality major league seasons with San Francisco Giants as well as with Cincinnati Reds.

Osvaldo Fernández Guerra, **Baseball:** National team pitcher defected in Barbados in 1996; now out of the game. Current whereabouts unknown.

Ramón Garbey, Boxing: Defected in late June 1996 at pre–Olympic training camp. Currently trains in Denver, Colorado. Was scheduled to fight undefeated heavyweight Freston Oquendo on June 25, 2000.

Osmani García, **Baseball:** Left under mysterious circumstances with four other players (including Maikel Jova and Jorge Díaz) in August 1998. Third baseman played eight years in Cuban League with Villa Clara; invited to extended spring training with Texas Rangers in 2000.

Osvaldo Garcia, Sr., Water Polo: Defected with son at tournament in California in 1994. Former coach of Cuban national team and one-time Olympian; now works as physical education teacher.

Osvaldo Garcia, Jr., Water Polo: Defected with father at tournament in California in 1994. Former national team player; works with Miami Beach Patrol.

Andres Gilbert, Basketball: Defected at 1993 Central American and Caribbean Games in Ponce, Puerto. Was playing professionally in Europe in early 2000.

Juan Carlos Gómez, Boxing: Defected under largely unclear circumstances in late 1995. Professional cruiserweight world champion now based in Germany.

Jorge Luis González, Boxing: Defected in Helsinki, Finland on April 1, 1991, and was living in Las Vegas, Nevada in early 2000. *Boston Globe* reports that he was first major athlete to defect from Cuba; his defection launched major exodus of Cuban athletes during decade of nineties.

Alain Guillen, Water Polo: Precise date of defection unclear. Was national team player and now works with Miami Beach Patrol.

Arnaldo Guillen, Water Polo: Precise date of defection unclear. Was national team player and now also works with Miami Beach Patrol. Brother of Alain Guillen.

Adrian (Duquecito) Hernández, **Baseball:** Cuban League pitcher (top prospect with Industriales) defected under mysterious circumstances on New Year's Day 2000. Signed reported $4 million-plus bonus contract with New York Yankees and made it to major leagues for brief trials in 2001, 2002 and 2004.

Alain Hernández, **Baseball:** Pitcher smuggled out of Cuba in late 1998; never signed to professional contract in United States. Current whereabouts unknown.

Alberto Hernández, Baseball: Catcher (no Cuban League experience) played parts of two seasons in Taiwan and had tryout in Seattle Mariners minor league system; was living in Costa Rica in 2000.

Alexis Hernández, Baseball: Catcher (no Cuban League experience) gained political asylum in 1999; signed with Winnipeg Goldeyes of Independent Northern League in March 2000.

Liván Hernández, Baseball: Defected in Mexico while pitching for Cuban national junior team on September 27, 1995. World Series MVP for Florida Marlins in 1997; has enjoyed successful major league career with Florida Marlins, San Francisco Giants, and Montreal Expos. Half-brother of fellow defector Orlando Hernández. Enjoyed a major comeback season in 2003 while pitching for the Montreal Expos.

Michel Hernández, Baseball: Catcher defected in 1996. Batted .304 at Single A Tampa (New York Yankees) during 2000 minor league season.

Odalys Hernández, Softball: Pitcher defected at the 1993 Central American and Caribbean Games in Ponce, Puerto Rico. Current whereabouts unknown.

Orlando (El Duque) Hernández, Baseball: Defected in December 26, 1997 and has been subsequently the most famous of Cuba's baseball exiles. Posted 33–17 record in first two seasons with New York Yankees and won three World Series titles. Spent entire 2003 season on the disabled list but made comeback with Yankees during 2004 campaign. Pitched with 2005 world champion Chicago White Sox.

Rigoberto Betancourt Herrera, Baseball: Youth pitching coach and former Cuban League hurler, defected May 1999 in Baltimore while accompanying Cuban national team at exhibition game versus Baltimore Orioles. Reportedly promised coaching position with major league organization that never materialized. Still living with relatives in Miami, Florida.

Roberto Herrera, Basketball: National team 25-year-old guard defected at July 1999 Olympic qualifying tournament in San Juan, Puerto Rico. Son of Cuban Basketball Federation president, Ruperto Herrera. Brother Ruperto, Jr., had earlier defected in Argentina in May 1999. After playing one season at Hartnell College (California), briefly joined minor league Florida Sea Dragons in 2000; released after six games.

Usviel Himely, Kayaker: Defected sometime late in 1994. Entered several amateur competitions after arrival in United States. Current whereabouts unknown.

Diobelys Hurtado, Boxing: Defected in October 1994. Fought against Pernell Whitaker as pro welterweight in January 1997. Now trains with Joel Casamayor in Van Nuys, California.

Manuel Hurtado, Baseball: Pitcher in Cuban League for twelve seasons between 1962 and 1973 and member of the Cuban national team on several occasions. Current whereabouts unknown.

Mario Irribarren, Boxing: Defected in Denmark in 1994, where he requested political asylum. Currently based in Miami as professional boxer.

Maikel Jova, Baseball: Second baseman (son of Cuban League star Pedro Jova) defected in March 1997 on raft with several others including future major leaguer Jorge Toca; returned to Cuba in May by Bahamian government, but "redefected" with four other players in August of same year; signed for $150,000 with Toronto Blue Jays; played in Dominican rookie league for Toronto Blue Jays affiliate in Spring 2000.

Delia Lago, President of Cuban Diving Federation: Defected in 1999 at diving event in Ft. Lauderdale., Florida Mother of water polo player Armando Piedra. Now lives with son in Miami area.

Emilio Lara, Weightlifter: Defected at 1993 Central American and Caribbean Games in Ponce, Puerto Rico at age 23. Requested political asylum from Puerto Rican National Guard. Hid defection plans from older brother, Pablo Lara, who at time was also world-record-holding weightlifter and also part of 900-person Cuban delegation at Ponce Games. Reportedly currently living in Puerto Rico.

Iván Ledón, Boxing: Defected sometime in 1995. Junior welterweight in Cuba who departed the island with his uncle (Ramón) in a small inner tube. Current whereabouts unknown.

Ramón Ledón, Boxing: Defected sometime in 1995. Also a junior lightweight who accompanied his nephew (Iván) on flimsy inner tube. Current whereabouts unknown.

Mariano Leyva, Boxing: Cuban coach who sought political asylum during 1996 Atlanta Olympics. Now works as massage therapist in Miami area.

Angel López, Baseball: Twenty-nine-year-old catcher smuggled out of Cuba in March 1998, in group of ballplayers that included Jorge Toca. Earlier suspended in 1996 along with Germán Mesa and Eduardo Paret under suspicion of contacts with U.S. player agents. Boasted twelve years of Cuban League experience; returned to Cuba by Bahamian authorities but later "redefected" in August 1998. Due to advanced age, never signed to a professional contract in the United States.

Juan Carlos Martínez, Water Polo: Defected in 1993 after decade on Cuban national team. Currently lives in Miami area and works on Miami Beach Patrol.

Juan Median, Baseball: Pitcher (no Cuban League experience) defected sometime in late 1990s. Has never signed a professional contract in the United States.

Joel Monzón Mejia, Baseball: Pitcher (no Cuban League experience) defected in Spain. Never signed a professional contract in the United States.

José Menéndez, Cycling: Defected in Puerto Rico in late 1993. Reportedly now lives and works in Greater Miami area.

Neylan Molina, Baseball: Talented hitter on Cuban League Habana Province team before defecting to unspecified South America country sometime late in 1999; was awaiting U.S. residency papers in early 2000 baseball season. Played three Cuban League seasons with career .318 BA; hit .378 for Habana Province in 1999, fourth best average in league. Never subsequently signed professional baseball contract.

Daimara Muñoz, Swimming: Defected at Puerto Rican training camp in 1988. Left two-year-old daughter behind in Cuba. Current whereabouts unknown.

Liudmilla Montes de Oca, Swimming: Talented 18-year-old butterfly specialist defected at Puerto Rican training camp in 1988. Current whereabouts unknown.

Ihosvany Negret, Wrestling: Defected to United States (perhaps Florida) under unknown circumstances in May 1994. Current whereabouts unknown.

Vladimir Nuñez, Baseball: Pitcher (several promising seasons as Cuban Leaguer) signed for $1.8 million with Arizona Diamondbacks after defecting in Venezuela in 1995; continues to pitch in the major leagues with Florida Marlins.

Lino O'Cana, Weightlifter: Defected during 1993 Central American and Caribbean Games in Ponce, Puerto Rico. Later told stories to U.S. press about training on daily menu of sugar water, rice, beans and fish. Last known residence was in Puerto Rico in early 2000.

Edilberto Oropeza, Baseball: Defected at Buffalo World University Games in 1993. Signed with San Francisco Giants after defecting; first reached major leagues with Philadelphia Phillies in 2001 and also later pitched for Arizona Diamondbacks.

Rey Ordóñez, Baseball: Shortstop defected in 1993 at Buffalo World University Games. Won several Gold Gloves as defensive standout at shortstop with New York Mets. Also played with National League Tampa Bay Devil Rays.

William (Bill) Ortega, Baseball: Outfielder signed $200,000 bonus contract in 1997; was batting .354 with 11 HR and 43 RBI at AA Arkansas (St. Louis Cardinals) early in 2000 season. Reached major leagues with St. Louis Cardinals in 2001.

Michael Ortiz, Track and Field: Defected during Pan American Games in Winnipeg, Canada, in August 1999. Current whereabouts unknown.

Brayan Peña, Baseball: Talented catcher on national junior team before defecting in Venezuela in April 1999; signed $1.25 million bonus with Atlanta Braves in early 2000 at age 18. Reached major leagues in 2005.

Angel Pérez, Kayaker: Defected in 1993 by crossing Rio Grande River while traveling with national team in Mexico. Later trained for 2000 United States Olympic team.

José Pérez, Track and Field: Defected after winning bronze medal in 400-meter hurdles at 1997 San Juan (Puerto Rico) invitational meet. Whereabouts currently unknown.

Josué Pérez, Baseball: Outfielder signed $850,000 bonus with Philadelphia Phillies after being declared free agent by MLB (due to illegal signing, along with Juan Díaz by Los Angeles Dodgers); was batting .286 at A-level Clearwater (Phillies) in early 2000.

Miguel Pérez, Baseball: Exact circumstances and date of defection unclear. Pitcher who was still unsigned by U.S. pros in early 2000, but was reported to be having tryouts with big league scouts in Costa Rica.

Armando Piedra, Water Polo: Defected in September 1994 during competitions in Spain. Former national team member who now also works with Miami Beach Patrol.

Héctor Pino, Basketball: Talented 24-year-old center/forward defected during July 1999 Olympic qualifying tournament in San Juan, Puerto Rico. Played one season with Hartnell College in California and in early 2000 was still hoping to play professionally in Spanish League.

Ariel Prieto, Baseball: Came to U.S. in 1994 on legal visa and never returned to Cuba. Received $1.2 million signing bonus in 1995 with Oakland A's but suffered elbow problems; big-league career petered out in 2000 with fifteen career wins over five seasons.

Río Ramírez, Diver: Defected at 1993 Central American and Caribbean Games in Ponce, Puerto Rico. Was studying business administration at University of Miami in early 2000, where he also continued his diving career. Took semester leave in early 2000 to train for United States Olympic swimming and diving trials.

Lázaro Reinoso, Wrestling: Defected on route to 1994 amateur tournament in New Jersey. Competed for Division II Carson-Newman College during 1999–2000 season and won national title in his weight division.

Nataniel Reinoso, Baseball: Outfielder signed for $87,000 with Atlanta Braves in Spring 1999; Still playing in Atlanta minor league system during 2001 seasons.

Armando Rodríguez, Basketball: Team masseur defected at July 1999 Olympic qualifying tournament in San Juan, Puerto Rico. Current whereabouts unknown.

Larry Rodríguez, Baseball: Pitcher signed for $1.2 million with Arizona D-Backs after defecting in Venezuela in October 1995; pitched briefly with Habana Province team and was top Cuban League rookie for 1994–95 season. Released by Arizona after three seasons of struggling with arm troubles in lower minors.

Euclides Rojas, Baseball: Defected on raft in 1994; remains all-time saves leader in post-revolution Cuba League history, right-hander played in lower minors briefly. Now pitching coach in Florida Marlins minor-league system.

Nubis Rosales, Swimming: Defected under mysterious circumstances at Puerto Rican training camp early in 1988. Current whereabouts unknown.

Antonio Pérez Sánchez, Water Polo: Defected at 1993 Central America and Caribbean Games in Ponce, Puerto Rico. Reportedly works in auto parts warehouse in Miami area.

Osmani Santana, Baseball: Details of defection remain unclear, but left Cuban squad in Mexico during July 1997 while training for Intercontinental Cup. Signed contract in 1998; was batting .310 at Single A Kinston (Cleveland) in Spring 2000.

Francisco Santiesteban, Baseball: Catcher (played eight years in Havana with Industriales) defected in Colombia in 1997; signed minor-league contract with Seattle Mariners in 1998 and was released before opening of 2000 season.

Yalian Serrano, Baseball: Catcher defected at age 15 in 1996; signed to professional contract in U.S. by Tampa Bay Devil Rays but quickly released in 1999 after unsuccessful minor league trial.

Juan Carlos Suárez, Boxing: Reportedly came to U.S. in inner tube in 1994 but few details of his defection are verified. Reportedly currently living in Miami area.

Jorge Luis Toca, **Baseball:** Power-hitting first baseman who played on national team and logged eight seasons in Cuban League (.319 BA and 100 homers). Defected in March 1998 on raft with several other suspended Cuban League players. Signed $1.4 million contract in 1998 with New York Mets and had several unsuccessful stops in majors with New York before departing for Japanese pro leagues.

Tatiana Valdes, Kayaker: Defected in 1993 by crossing Rio Grande River with teammate Angel Pérez. She now lives and works in Miami area.

Jesús Ramón Valdivia, **Baseball:** Shortstop defected shortly after Atlanta Olympics in 1996 but never signed a pro U.S. contract. Briefly appeared in two Cuban League seasons but never played for Cuban national team at any level.

Juan Leopoldo Vázquez, Basketball: Defected at August 1999 Pan American Games in Winnipeg, Canada, receiving aid from Cuban American National Foundation. Current whereabouts unknown.

Alexis Vila, Wrestling: Defected at 1995 Pan American Championships in Argentina after taking gold medal at 54.0 kilograms. Lives in Miami and coaches youth wrestling.

Julio César Villalón, **Baseball:** Pitched six seasons in Cuban League with overall 26–33 won-lost record. Had brief stay in Tampa Bay Devil Rays minor-league camp in 1999 before being released.

Jesús Wilson, Wrestling: Defected (with Lázaro Reinoso) while en route to 1994 amateur tournament in New Jersey. Received U.S. citizenship before attending summer 2000 U.S. Olympic trials. Competed for Division III Upper Iowa University in 1998 and 1999 and was U.S. collegiate national champion at 133 pounds. Began new career at Upper Iowa University in 2000 as part-time wrestling coach.

PART IV

*Appendices and
Statistical Records*

Appendix A: Chronology (1866–2006)

June 1866 — Caribbean baseball reputedly born when U.S. sailors from American naval ship anchored at port in Matanzas Bay demonstrate diamond play for a crowd of Cuban dockhands employed loading sugar cane onto North American vessels. Cubans reportedly joke that American instructors seemed highly motivated by a desire to sell baseball equipment to their raw diamond recruits. One competing account of baseball's Cuban origins suggests that it was actually Nemesio Guilló (sometimes spelled Guillót) — an upper class youth educated in the United States — who first introduced equipment and demonstrations of this popular Yankee sport upon his return from Alabama's Spring Hill College to his native Havana in 1864.

April 1871 — Cuban-born Esteban "Steve" Bellán mans third base for Troy Haymakers during inaugural season of the National Association, pro baseball's first recognized big league circuit. Bellán, who honed his baseball skills while studying at Fordham University in New York City and later hit .236 in 59 games over a three-year professional career, thus becomes the first official Latin American big league ballplayer.

December 27, 1874 — Only eight years after the game's reported introduction in Matanzas, the same port city — known as the "Athens of Cuba" — hosts visiting Havana nine in first recorded organized ballgame between native Cuban teams. Playing for Club Havana are two early giants of Cuban baseball, ex-big-leaguer Steve Bellán and patriot-athlete Emilio Sabourín, himself later one of the organizing geniuses behind Cuba's own professional league. Bellán plays third base and socks two homers while Sabourín scores eight runs for Club Havana during its 51–9 rout of the talent-thin Matanzas nine.

December 29, 1878 — Cuban Professional Baseball League (Liga de Base Ball) launches play in Havana, thus making Cuban League the world's second oldest professional baseball organization, trailing only North American National League in seniority by a mere two seasons. Habana wins first game, 21–20 over Almendares, in contest featuring ten men to a side (extra position was "right short field"). Inaugural Cuban championship — ending on February 16, 1879 — consists of only three ball clubs (Habana, Matanzas, and Almendares) and Havana wins trophy with 4–0–1 record behind leadership of team manager and playing captain Esteban "Steve" Bellán.

November 23, 1879 — Imported American George McCullar, a catcher for Colón, smacks first reported Cuban League home run in 13–8 victory over Habana. The powerful smash was almost assuredly of the "inside-the-park" variety.

December 25, 1879 — Pitcher Carlos Maciá of Almendares credited (by fellow ballplayer-historian Wenceslao Gálvez) with first attempt to bunt, not for a sacrifice but for a base hit. Maciá's unique play comes a full dozen seasons before this same strategy is introduced in U.S. baseball by John McGraw and his Baltimore Orioles. Another account of this same event (by Roberto González Echevarría in *The Pride of Havana*) claims it occurred on this precise date, but in a game between Almendares and a visiting U.S. team called Hops Bitter (sponsored by the beverage company of that name) — the first touring American team to visit Cuba. González contends also that the Almendares batter performing a pioneering bunt was actually Carlos de Zaldo.

January 21, 1882 — Apparent single-game world record of sixty errors committed in Cuban semi-pro contest between Club Caridad (39 miscues) and Club Ultimatum (21 errors). It seems safe to assume ballplayers at this sloppy Havana spectacle wore no fielding gloves during their crude rag-tag match. The same winter witnesses the first switch-hitter recorded in Cuban baseball — José María Teuma of Club Fe, who also played all nine positions and posted 4–3 pitching record and .225 batting mark over seven (then brief) CL seasons. Original Almendares Park playing grounds also inaugurated on Carlos III Avenue in Havana during this action-packed season.

February 2, 1886 — Carlos Maciá, Almendares pitcher, blanks Club Fe 16–0 in first recorded Cuban League shutout. Maciá allows three base hits while Fe ballclub commits remarkable total 29 errors in this historic contest. At least one respected Cuban baseball handbook (Díez Muro) lists the Almendares pitcher for this game as actually being Miguel Granados and not Carlos Maciá.

May 1886 — Official statistics kept for first time in Cuban League and Wenceslao Gálvez is first formal batting champion (.345). Gálvez three years later publishes *El Base-Ball en Cuba,* Cuban baseball's first known printed history and perhaps the first-ever baseball historical chronicle published in any locale.

1886–1887 — Cuban Giants appear in U.S. as first salaried all–Negro team, but popular touring ball club ironically contains on its roster not a single native-born Cuban. Historic club is formed by Frank P. Thompson, headwaiter at the Hotel Argyle in Babylon, New York, who recruited pro players from the Philadelphia Keystones to work as waiters and entertain guests with ballplaying. More ballplayers were later added from the Philadelphia Orions and Washington Manhattens to form famed touring team at end of hotel tourist season.

February 13, 1887 — First professional league no-hitter pitched in Cuba by Carlos Maciá when Almendares defeats Carmelita by one-sided 38–0 margin. This is perhaps the first no-hit, no-run game anywhere in Latin America, though historical records remain cloudy on such matters. It is also easily the most one-sided no-hitter on record (with Almendares recording 32 base hits during its victory), and is further noteworthy for 28 errors committed by the losing ball club.

1889 — Sometime during this year José de la Caridad Méndez, Cuba's greatest blackball-era pitcher, is born in coastal town of Cárdenas within Matanzas Province. Several recent sources also report the birth year of Méndez as 1885, but the later year seems more likely correct.

July 14, 1889 — Second professional no-hit, no-run game in Cuba pitched by Eugenio de Rosas (Club Progreso) during 8–0 victory over Cárdenas. Game's highly unusual line score shows Cárdenas with no runs or hits yet astronomical total of 14 errors. This is final Cuban no-hitter for 47 years and only four more no-hit masterpieces will be tossed by Cuban hurlers during six decades preceding the 1961 suspension of professional baseball.

1890–1891—Cubans first introduce baseball playing in both Mexico and Puerto Rico, as well as in the Dominican Republic. For these efforts in spreading their national game the Cubans earn an appropriate designation as "the true apostles of baseball."

October 1891—First touring U.S. major leaguers visit Cuba for series of winter exhibitions (from October 25 to November 8) staged at Almendares Park. Young John McGraw is among group of barnstormers called "All-Americans" that posts 5–0 record, but only with help from some Cuban reinforcements provided by promoter Eduardo Laborde to fill out the Americans' shorthanded roster.

January 1892—Havana continues early domination of Cuban League play with ninth championship trophy in 14 years. Emilio Sabourín is now manager and captain of Habana ballclub. Sabourín's perhaps inflated role (by later Cuban historians, due to his stature as patriotic martyr) in organizing both the league itself and the champion Habana team fixes his reputation as true patriarch of Cuban baseball. Antonio Maria García ("El Inglés") captures second of three batting championships (1890, 1892, 1893), each with different club (Havana, Almendares, Aguila de Oro).

1893—Ricardo Cabaleiro (like Sabourín, later martyred in the War of Independence) posts first three-homer game in Cuba while playing for amateur team named Colombia versus Océano. Famed Negro leaguer James "Cool Papa" Bell would much later (1929) match Cabaleiro's feat during pro Cuban League game in Cienfuegos. Precise date for historic Cabaleiro slugging display is not known.

June 1894—Almendares, under manager Ramón Gutiérrez, wins its first league championship with 17–7–1 record. With arrival of Almendares as legitimate challenger to Club Habana, greatest rivalry in Cuban pro baseball is born. Over the succeeding three-quarters of a century Club Habana will gain an upper hand, but only barely with 30 championships (including 12 of first 14) to 25 for Almendares.

1895—Cuban Emilio Cramer, a wealthy tobacco grower, introduces baseball among his field workers in Venezuela. With most ballplayers now serving as soldiers in the Independence War against Spain, Cuban League baseball season is suspended for next several winters. Baseball pioneer and active patriot Emilio Sabourín is imprisoned by Spanish colonial authorities for his illegal revolutionary activities (and will die in North African prison on July 15, 1897).

February 1900—First team of touring U.S. black ballplayers visits Cuba for exhibition series. This team known as Cuban X-Giants is made up mostly of defectors from original Cuban Giants Negro touring club formed on Long Island in 1885 and now based in Trenton, New Jersey, and has no actual Cubans on its roster.

December 1900—Luis ("Mulo") Padrón leads Cuban League in both pitching victories (with 13) and also base hits (with 31). Lefty-throwing Padrón is first but not last to pull off this rare double, also accomplished by Martín Dihigo in 1936. Padrón later pitched two-plus decades in U.S. Negro leagues (1904–1926), appearing with Cuban Stars, All-Cubans and Cuban Stars of Havana.

May 1901—For first time a troupe of Cuban ballplayers tours in the United States (mostly Florida) under legitimate name of All-Cubans. Two years later Havana's popular *Score* magazine (May 22, 1903) would report that this same touring team led by promoter Abel Linares ran into considerable legal troubles in Florida because it was carrying three black ballplayers on its roster.

January 1902—Famed catcher and future Cuban hall-of-famer Gervasio ("Strike") González makes debut with stellar season for San Francisco. González achieves sterling two-decade (1902–1919) record as one of best Cuban defensive backstops of all time, earning special fame as the personal favorite catcher of José de la Caridad ("El Diamante Negro") Méndez. During this same season Habana finishes undefeated with unblemished 17–0 league record and with all 17 wins

(not so remarkably for that early era of iron-man pitchers) credited to ace hurler Carlos "Bebé" Royer.

1905—The Athletic Association League, Cuba's first senior-level championship amateur league, holds first season of play on Marino del Cerro playing grounds in Havana with three teams competing—Columbia, Vedado Tennis Club, and Havana University. The same summer (on an unknown date) in this same league, pitcher Armando Castellanos with Vedado Tennis Club reportedly throws first shutout in Cuban amateur baseball play.

May 25, 1906—Martín Dihigo born in Matanzas on this date. Dihigo will one day be universally dubbed the greatest Cuban ballplayer of all time and will also be the first Cuban elected to the United States Baseball Hall of Fame in Cooperstown, New York.

February 1908—José Méndez debuts with Almendares, pitching his first Cuban League game in relief on February 2 against Habana and making his first start on February 18 versus Matanzas—an 8–3 victory which includes eight shutout innings. Méndez wins all nine decisions of rookie season and leads Almendares to league championship.

November 1908—Matanzas-born black Cuban hurler José Méndez—later immortalized by New York Giants manager John McGraw as "Cuba's Black Diamond"—records string of impressive performances against touring Cincinnati Reds. Wiry 20-year-old phenom first posts 1–0 one-hit victory over stunned National Leaguers; two weeks later Méndez throws seven shutout innings in relief, plus second nine-inning scoreless performance as starter—a grand total of 25 scoreless innings against befuddled big-league visitors. Competing against Negro league stars during U.S. tour the following summer-fall, Méndez again distinguishes himself with an outstanding 44–2 single-season mound record.

November 18, 1909—Eustaquio "Bombín" Pedroso (Almendares) no-hits visiting American League champion Detroit Tigers who are playing without stars Ty Cobb and Sam Crawford. Detroit wins only four of twelve games versus Almendares and Club Havana during two-week Cuban barnstorming tour, yet twice Detroit defeats Cuban ace José Méndez.

November 1910—Philadelphia's World Champion Athletics (4 wins, 4 losses) and AL Detroit Tigers (7 wins, 4 defeats) again visit Cuba for winter exhibitions in Havana's Almendares Park. Big leaguers once again find Cubans to be challenging opponents, with José Méndez twice besting Philadelphia's future hall-of-famer Eddie Plank. One highlight is three straight "cutdowns" of Ty Cobb in steal attempts against crack Negro league catcher Bruce Petway and top Cuban receiver "Strike" González. Cobb, however, homers in very first at-bat in Cuba, an inside-the-park round-tripper in spacious Almendares Park.

July 4, 1911—Outfielders Armando Marsans and Rafael Almeida debut with Cincinnati Reds, becoming first 20th-century Cubans and first modern-era Latin Americans to appear in U.S. major leagues. Complaints about dark skin color of both ballplayers are met by official club press release (based on assurances of Cuban League officials) stating that these were "two of the purest bars of Castilian soap ever floated to these (Cuban) shores."

August 20, 1911—Mario Castañeda of Vedado Tennis Club pitches first no-hit, no-run game in Cuban amateur baseball, defeating Club Atlético de Cuba by tight 1–0 score.

November 1911—New York Giants featuring John McGraw are one of three professional North American teams renewing wintertime ballplaying visits to Cuba. New Britain of the Connecticut League (4 wins, 14 defeats) and National League Philadelphia Phillies (5 wins, 4 losses) join New Yorkers, who fare best with nine straight wins after three opening defeats. Cuban ace José Méndez beats Philadelphia twice but also loses once to Phillies and twice to Giants (including head-to-head battle with immortal Christy Mathewson).

March 1912—Julián Castillo of Club Fe accomplishes rare feat of slugging two homers in same contest against overpowering Almendares ace José Méndez on March 7, then less than three weeks later (March 24) repeats his unprecedented event with yet another pair of four-base-hits off the deliveries of often-untouchable Méndez.

1914—Cuban National League of Amateur Baseball (Liga National de Béisbol Amateur de Cuba) is first organized and Vedado Tennis Club team (with 13–3 record) captures initial championship of the new amateur circuit.

1915—Ramón Goizueta (laboring for powerhouse Vedado Tennis Club) pitches first no-hit, no-run game in new Cuban National League of Amateur Baseball while defeating Club Atlético de Cuba.

December 2, 1918—Baldomero "Merito" Acosta of Club Habana performs a most rare unassisted triple play, something done by an outfielder on only two other known occasions. Others to accomplish such an unusual feat are major leaguer Paul Hines (Providence, National League, 1878) and minor leaguer Harry O'Hagen (Rochester, 1902).

December 22, 1918—Bienvenido Jiménez (Cuban Stars) steals eight bases in one game against pitchers and catchers of Almendares ballclub. Jiménez records three steals each of second and third base and two more steals of home, yet his team nonetheless loses, 7–6.

October 3, 1919—Cuban Adolfo "Dolf" Luque becomes first Latin American to appear in World Series, pitching one inning as reliever for Cincinnati Reds in Game Three against Charlie Comiskey's infamous "Black Sox" in Chicago. Luque, who would later win 27 games for Reds during 1923 season, also pitches four more relief innings in Game Seven, at Cincinnati's Redland Field, on October 8.

October–November 1920—John McGraw's New York Giants arrive for much-heralded three-team tournament also featuring Habana and Almendares. The big leaguers are shorthanded in frontline pitching but include on their roster popular Yankees star Babe Ruth, who had just established new standards for home run slugging in the American League. Ruth joins big league squad somewhat late — two weeks into the tour on October 30 — yet nonetheless slugs base-clearing triple in very first at-bat in Almendares Park.

November 5, 1920—One of most legendary games ever played on Cuban soil highlights visit of Babe Ruth and John McGraw's Giants and establishes Cristóbal Torriente among the greatest of Cuban baseball heroes. Torriente outshines the hitless Ruth with three homers and a double during 11–4 Almendares rout of New Yorkers. Historians (like Cuban fans of the era) usually ignore in their accounts of this game the fact that New York team clowned throughout much of the contest and all Torriente's homers where hit off a non-pitcher, Giants first baseman Highpockets Kelly.

October 1923—At season's end, Cincinnati Reds ace hurler Dolf Luque owns major-league-leading won-loss record of 27–8 and ERA mark of 1.93, still the top single-season performance ever posted by a Latin American big league pitcher. Same fall (late November) Martín Dihigo makes debut as pitcher in Cuban League; Dihigo had played a handful of games one season earlier as an infielder with Habana.

1923–24—During season that begins in late October, is suspended in mid–January, and then witnesses make-shift second "championship" called the Gran Premio, Santa Clara Leopards field the best team of Cuban League history. Featuring an unparalleled outfield of Alejandro Oms, Pablo "Champion" Mesa, and top American star Oscar Charleston, Santa Clara outdistances the field so badly (at 36–11 with an 11½ game lead over runner-up Habana) that regular season action is suspended January 16 for lack of fan interest. Powerful Leopards also capture makeshift Gran Premio, but this time by only a single game over Almendares.

October 11, 1924—Oscar Levis of Club Habana no-hits rival Almendares, 1–0. This is first 20th-century no-hitter pitched in Cuban professional league play.

May 23, 1925—Cuban Miguel Angel "Mike" González traded from St. Louis Cardinals to Chicago Cubs, thus becoming first Latin player to appear with three different major league teams. Catcher González debuted with Boston Braves in 1912 and later joined St. Louis Cardinals in 1915.

1926—Cuba sends first team into international amateur competition by entering inaugural Central American and Caribbean Games staged in Mexico City. Cuban team takes three straight games from host Mexicans (the only other entrant for baseball competition) to capture first of what will eventually be numerous international baseball titles.

November 6, 1928—José de la Caridad Méndez dies in Havana at 39 years of age—a premature victim of tuberculosis—less than two years after completing final Cuban League season. Had the color-barrier not existed, Méndez—born in Cárdenas near Matanzas in 1889—might well have proven himself the greatest of all Cuban pitchers, once allowed to reach the major league stage. Méndez is buried in unmarked grave within Havana's Colón Cemetary.

November 15, 1928—Martín Dihigo (Habana) enters name in league record books with four doubles in single game against Cuba (Cuban League team playing under that name); Dihigo would remain only hitter ever to achieve such a feat in Cuba's eight-decade pro league.

December 24, 1928—Record consecutive-game hitting streak by Alejandro Oms (Habana) beginning on October 31 is finally stopped at 30 games. Six days later Oms—who hit .432 for the year—establishes another mark with six hits in six at-bats versus Cienfuegos.

January 2, 1929—Outfielder James ("Cool Papa") Bell, U.S. Negro leaguer playing for Cienfuegos, becomes first slugger to connect for three homers in single game during Cuban professional play. Bell's feat occurs at Aída Park (Cienfuegos) in 15–11 slugfest victory over Havana. Bell's three homers are struck against Oscar Levis, "Campanita" Bell, and hall-of-famer Martín Dihigo, although Bell himself later erroneously claimed all three came off blackball ace Johnny Allen.

October 10, 1930—Visiting all-star teams of U.S. big leaguers play first game at Havana's La Tropical Stadium (named for La Tropical Brewing Company), with Bill Terry, Al Lopez, Rabbit Maranville, Paul Waner, Sam Rice, Chuck Klein and Carl Hubbell (the losing pitcher) among the most notable big leaguers appearing. Tropical Stadium had originally opened for soccer games nearly a year earlier (December 1929) and would eventually host the second Central American and Caribbean Games (late in 1930) plus five additional Amateur World Series tournaments.

March 1931—Brooklyn Dodgers make brief spring training exhibition appearance in Havana, playing five games in La Tropical Stadium. Dolf Luque is on Brooklyn's roster and hurls in all three Dodgers victories.

October 7, 1933—Dolf Luque provides 4.1 innings of stellar relief to gain championship-clinching victory in Game Five of 1933 World Series. In notching Fall Classic title for New York Giants over Washington Senators, Luque becomes first Latin American pitcher to post a World Series pitching victory. Back in Luque's own island homeland worsening economic and political scene causes suspension of Cuban League play.

February 1935—Lázaro Salazar (splitting 56-game season between Marianao and Almendares) completes season with .407 batting average and is thus the last player ever to hit .400-plus in Cuban professional competition.

November 7, 1936—Legendary U.S. Negro leaguer Raymond "Jabao" Brown, toiling for powerhouse Santa Clara, hurls second 20th century no-hitter in Cuba, a one-sided 7–0 victory over Club Habana.

September 16, 1937—Black Cuban hall-of-famer Martín Dihigo (the only player enshrined in halls of fame in four different countries: United States, Mexico, Cuba and Venezuela) pitches first professional no-hit, no-run game on Mexican soil (in Veracruz) during 4–0 victory by Aguila over rival Nogales.

December 21, 1937 — First Cuban League night game played in La Tropical Stadium as Marianao defeats Almendares, 6–5. Martín Dihigo is fittingly the winning pitcher in this historic contest. Portable lights originally had been brought from Miami for use in scheduled all-star game between Cuban and U.S. pros on December 10, but when these lights proved somewhat unsatisfactory during test-run their use was postponed until December 21st league game. Later this same winter another pioneering night game is played in Havana suburb of Guanabacoa, this time between Regla Yacht Club and Casino Español of amateur Social League.

June 4, 1938 — Martín Dihigo strikes out 22 Mexican League batters in 13 innings while pitching for Aguila versus Comintra. Dihigo will be Mexican League's top batter (.387) and top pitcher (18–2, 0.90 ERA) during this same miraculous season.

September 18, 1938 — Versatile Cuban star Martín Dihigo, author of first Mexican League no-hitter, also becomes first Mexican League batter to register six hits in six at-bats while playing for Aguila against Agrario.

August 1939 — Havana hosts world amateur championships in Tropical Stadium and defeats Nicaraguan and USA teams for country's first world title. Cuba also hosts three of next four Amateur World Series (also known officially as World Championship of Amateur Baseball) and captures three of those championships, with future big leaguer Conrado Marrero pitching for Cuba in memorable 1941 (playoff loss to Venezuela) and 1942 (early round victory over Venezuela) tournament games. Cuba's Baseball Hall of Fame is also established during this year with ten initial inductees: Luis Bustamante, José Méndez, Antonio Maria García, Gervasio "Strike" González, Armando Marsans, Rafael Almeida, Valentín "Sirique" González, Cristobal Torriente, Adolfo Luján and Carlos "Bebé" Royer.

September 14, 1940 — United States, Hawaii Territory (not yet a State), Cuba, Mexico, Puerto Rico, Nicaragua, and Venezuela meet in Third World Amateur Baseball Championship, the first championship series to feature more than three participants and second held on Latin American soil. Host Cuba is easy victor for second consecutive year. An inaugural tournament (with only two teams and mostly American players) was staged in England in 1939 and was also won by the host nation, Great Britain.

October 23, 1941 — Conrado Marrero matched against Venezuelan ace Daniel "Chino" Canónico in deciding playoff game to determine champion in Fourth Amateur World Series at La Tropical Stadium. Venezuela scores three times in opening inning and then holds on for victory despite brilliant relief pitching by Cuba's Natilla Jiménez. This single dramatic game long remains true high-point of Cuban baseball lore among veteran Cuban aficionados.

January 3, 1942 — Ramón Bragaña (with Almendares) completes record string of 39.2 scoreless innings stretching over seven games, all against rival Habana.

October 4, 1942 — Connie Marrero and Chino Canónico are rematched in early round of much-diminished Amateur World Series V, played with only five teams and against overshadowing backdrop of World War II. The Cubans — en route to easy championship win — crush Canónico 8–0 this time around and game is highlighted by 500-foot homer off Canónico, smashed clear over distant center field scoreboard by outfielder Francisco Quicitus.

December 11, 1943 — Manuel "Cocaína" García of Club Habana pitches fifth no-hit, no-run game in Cuban League history, besting Marianao 5–0.

September 6, 1944 — Tommy de la Cruz, Cuban righthander, tosses first one-hitter by Latin American pitcher in the big leagues. Ironically, Tommy de la Cruz pitches but one wartime season for Cincinnati, recording 9–9 won-lost record and 3.25 ERA. De la Cruz exhibited exceedingly dark skin complexion, a fact (along with his age at 33) that may have speeded his hasty departure from Cincinnati immediately after 1944's concluding wartime campaign.

November 1944 — Cuba withdraws from finals of Amateur World Series VII in Caracas in protest over erratic and seemingly often partial umpiring. Controversies come during three-way tie-breaking playoff for championship between Cuba, Mexico, and host Venezuela, and also lead to withdrawal by Mexico's equally maltreated team. After this fiasco in Caracas, Cuba does not attend another world championship tournament until the 1950 event, held in Managua.

January 3, 1945 — Cuban professional baseball witnesses its sixth no-hit, no-run game, pitched by former big-leaguer Tommy de la Cruz of Almendares against rival Club Habana, losers by a 7–0 score.

January 7, 1945 — In the most violent incident of Cuban baseball history, Almendares outfielder Roberto Ortiz attacks umpire Bernardino Rodríguez during heated dispute at home plate and knocks the stunned and defenseless arbiter unconscious.

April 1946 — The Havana Cubans begin play in Class C Florida International League, marking Cuba's first entrance into U.S. organized baseball. Earlier this same spring Cienfuegos claims a championship in the last full Cuban League season played at Tropical Stadium. Later in the year Cuba loses for first time in Central American and Caribbean Games staged in Barranquilla, finishing third after suffering two shutouts at hands of Colombia's ace hurler Carlos "Petaca" Rodríguez.

October 9, 1946 — Team of National League All-Stars begins seven-game exhibition schedule against Cuban National All-Star team in Havana. NL team, featuring Buddy Kerr and Sid Gordon of the New York Giants, plus Brooklyn Dodgers Eddie Stanky and Ralph Branca, wins opening game of tour, 3–2.

October 26, 1946 — Estimated record-setting 31,000-plus fans attend inaugural game at impressive new Gran Estadio del Cerro in central Havana, witnessing Almendares defeat Cienfuegos 9–1. At the time, this was easily the largest crowd ever to turn out for a professional baseball game played in Cuba.

March 1947 — Jackie Robinson appears in spring training in Havana with Brooklyn Dodgers on eve of his historic appearance in National League, thus boldly breaking long-standing color line in major league baseball.

October 1947 — As a result of bitter ongoing dispute between organized baseball and Jorge Pasquel's ambitious Mexican League, inevitably leading to big-league suspensions of players who appeared in the latter circuit, Cuban winter league hosts two separate championship seasons staged at Gran Stadium (approved players) and La Tropical Stadium (banned players). Same winter brings retirement for two immortal figures of Cuban baseball — Adolfo Luque (after 34 seasons of Cuban League, U.S. minor league and major league action) and Martin Dihigo (after career of 23 Cuban League seasons).

August 21, 1948 — Representatives of Cuba, Panama, Puerto Rico and Venezuela meet in Havana and agree to stage novel four-country round-robin twelve-game tournament to be known as "Serie del Caribe" (Caribbean Series) and to be launched in Cuba during February 1949. This series, a future highlight of winter league play, continues uninterrupted through 1960 (Series XII), is resumed in 1970 (after 10-year hiatus), and survives to the present. In addition to the four founding countries, the Dominican Republic (replacing Cuba) and Mexico (replacing Panama) also later participate on regular basis.

February 25, 1949 — Agapito Mayor wins his third game during inaugural Caribbean Series while pitching for Almendares (Cuba) against Spur Cola (Panama), thus becoming first and only pitcher to capture three games in single year during 42 seasons of Caribbean Series play. Al Gionfriddo, 1947 Brooklyn Dodgers World Series hero (remembered for a miraculous catch of Joe DiMaggio's near home run in Game Six), completes three-game eight-for-fifteen batting rampage (.533) which makes him first Caribbean Series batting champion. Gionfriddo performs his heroics for Almendares (Cuba) in this first Caribbean Series, staged in Havana's Gran Stadium.

February 15, 1950—Seventh no-hitter of Cuban pro baseball history pitched by Rogelio "Limonar" Martínez in 6–0 Marianao victory over Almendares. Marianao hurler awarded league-sponsored prize of 1000 pesos for his rare effort.

December 1950—After finishing in three-way tie (equal 9–2 records) with the Dominican Republic and Venezuela, Cuba withdraws in protest from Amateur World Series XI held in Managua, claiming Puerto Rican team was using professional players. Nearly a year later FIBA officials meeting in Mexico uphold Cuba's protest, annul results of tie-breaking playoffs, and declare Cuba tournament champion.

December 6, 1950—Cuban catcher Carlos Colás (one of the fastest running receivers ever) provides one of greatest single-game batting displays ever witnessed in professional winter league play. Colás (a black-skinned star) collects five hits in five at-bats for Team Venezuela during 10–9 loss to Venezuelan League rival Vargas. Colás also registers the rare feat of three triples in a single contest.

October 1951—Minnie Miñoso of Chicago White Sox wins *The Sporting News* American League rookie-of-the-year honors. Miñoso trails New York Yankees' Gil McDougald by two votes for baseball writers' (BBWAA) rookie award, despite 50 more hits, 13 more RBI, and 20-point higher batting average. This same month in Mexico City FIBA (International Amateur Baseball Federation) meets to uphold Cuba's protest lodged at XI World Championships staged during previous November–December in Nicaragua.

February 21, 1952—Tommy Fine, diminutive U.S. right-hander who posted only four major league decisions with Boston Red Sox and St. Louis Browns, achieves immortality by pitching only no-hit, no-run game in five-decade history of Caribbean Series. Fine hurls for Cuba's Club Habana against Venezuela's Cervecería Caracas, striking out three and walking three in 1–0 victory during Caribbean Series IV held in Panama.

September 2, 1952—Mike Fornieles, Cuban righthander with Washington Senators, makes sensational major league entrance with rare one-hitter, thus becoming first Latin American pitcher and second American Leaguer to toss one-hitter in debut big-league outing. Only AL pitcher preceding Fornieles with this feat was Addie Joss (with Cleveland in 1902) and the achievement has been duplicated only once since, by William Rohr (with Boston in 1967). Only National League hurlers matching Fornieles' spectacular debut ironically were also Latin Americans—Juan Marichal of the San Francisco Giants in 1960 and Silvio Martínez with the St. Louis Cardinals in 1978.

September 6–26, 1952—Amateur World Series returns to Havana for its thirteenth tournament (first staged in Cuba since 1943) which Cubans capture with 9–2 overall record. Dispute between Cuban manager Clemente Carreras and local sportswriters triggers blackout of event by Havana newspapers.

May 24, 1953—New Cuban single-game strikeout record of 22 established during National Amateur championship tournament game by Evelio Hernández, pitching for Club Casino Español de Guines against Ferroviario (railroad workers) team from Havana. Earlier island record was 21 set by Julio "Jiqui" Moreno, future big leaguer with American League Washington Senators.

October 1953—Cuba (with sterling 11–1 record) captures Amateur World Series XIV championship when Antonio "Lindo" Suárez shuts out host Venezuela in front of 45,000-plus wildly enthusiastic Caracas fans during dramatic deciding contest. Cuba's only defeat comes in thrilling opening game in which Suárez is bested 3–2 by Venezuelan ace and tourney MVP Andrés Quintero.

September 1954—Cuban Sandy Consuegra (Chicago White Sox) becomes second Latin American pitcher to lead his league in winning percentage, completing year with sparkling 16–3 mark (.842). Cuban Dolf Luque, 27–8 with Cincinnati Reds in 1923, was first to gain such memorable distinction.

February 11, 1955—Perhaps most emotional and memorable game in history of Caribbean Series is played in University Stadium at Caracas. Emilio Cueche, legendary Venezuelan pitcher, throws brilliant two-hitter for Magallanes (Venezuela) yet loses 1–0 to Almendares (Cuba). A near riot in the grandstands, in dispute of close call on the base paths, delays game for over forty-five minutes as spectators throw objects onto the field of play. Major leaguers Vern Rapp, Rocky Nelson, Gus Triandos, and native Cubans Román Mejías and Willie Miranda are featured in Almendares starting lineup for this famous action-packed game.

October 4, 1955—Brooklyn defeats New York Yankees 2–0 in historic Game Seven to capture Dodgers' first-ever World Series championship. Cuban journeyman outfielder Edmundo "Sandy" Amoros is the ultimate Dodgers hero with his miraculous left field catch of Yogi Berra's sixth-inning line drive, a one-handed grab at the fence which launched a game-saving double play.

March 1956—Oscar Miranda, hurling for Santiago de las Vegas, authors first perfect game ever thrown in Cuba when he tosses 9–0 masterpiece against the ironically named Profesionales team in Union Atlética Amateur League action.

July 3, 1957—"The Pride of Havana"—the immortal Dolf Luque—dies in Havana, one month short of his sixty-seventh birthday.

November 23, 1957—Antonio Díaz of Cienfuegos tosses final no-hitter of Cuban League professional play, defeating Habana 2–0. It is eighth such masterpiece in Cuban League history and sixth of the 20th century.

July 25, 1959—Fidel Castro supporters, enjoying raucous "July 26th Celebration" in Havana's Cerro Stadium, halt International League contest between Rochester Red Wings and Cuban Sugar Kings with several random gunshots fired from grandstands. Rochester third base coach Frank Verdi and Havana shortstop Leo Cárdenas both suffer minor flesh wounds during infamous incident, causing Red Wings manager Cot Deal to pull his team from field and retreat to downtown hotel. International League officials promptly cancel remainder of Sugar Kings' home stand and will eventually relocate franchise to Jersey City during middle of 1960 season. But first, Havana-based Sugar Kings capture 1959 International League playoffs (Shaughnessy Cup) and also defeat Minneapolis Millers to claim AAA Little World Series.

September 1959—Cuba suffers one of its poorest showings ever in international competition with fourth-place finish at Pan American Games III in Chicago, Illinois. Cubans win two of three outings during pool play but drop all three contests during medal round, including painful losses to champion Venezuela (6–2) and third-place USA (3–2).

October 1959—Cuba's short stint in U.S. organized baseball reaches climax as Cuban Sugar Kings of International League defeat Minneapolis Millers of American Association (a team featuring future hall-of-famer Carl Yastrzemski) and thus lay claim to Little World Series and top prize of minor league baseball. Cuba, managed by Preston Gómez, had finished a mere third in 1959 International League standings yet surprisingly upset both Columbus and Richmond in post-season playoffs to reach AAA showdown series. After splitting two games in wintry conditions at Minneapolis, teams retire to tropical Havana for remainder of championship series. Against the backdrop of fuzzy reports about bearded revolutionary troops toting rifles while packing Cerro Stadium, Havana's Sugar Kings sweep to victory in three of final five games. Dramatic seventh game stretches to bottom of ninth, where Dan Morejón caps exciting Havana rally by producing game-winning single that plates pitcher Raúl Sánchez with the decisive tally.

July 13, 1960—Havana Sugar Kings franchise shifted by International League to new home as Jersey City (New Jersey) Reds, ending professional organized baseball in Cuba. Havana is playing in Miami at time of franchise shift and all 11 native Cuban players decide to remain with team in its new home (Raúl Sánchez, Orlando Peña, Andrés Ayón, Mike Cuéllar, Borrego Alvarez, Leo Cárdenas,

Joaquín Azcue, Daniel Morejón, Cookie Rojas, Orlando Tanner and Enrique Izquierdo). Manager Tony Castaños returns to Cuba and is replaced on the bench by former Cuban national team star Nap Reyes.

July 23, 1960—Kansas City outfielder Whitey Herzog hits into only all–Cuban triple play in major league history. Reverse round-the-horn putout action moves from Washington Senators pitcher Pete Ramos to first baseman Julio Bécquer to shortstop José Valdivielso.

April 1961—Cuba returns to Amateur World Series after eight-year absence and emerges with most surprising undefeated record (9–0) and still another championship at tournament played in Costa Rica. Cuba's top stars are Jorge Trigoura and Pedro Chávez during games played against backdrop of Bay of Pigs invasion back home on Cuban soil. This same spring and summer INDER (National Institute for Sports, Education and Recreation) is founded to manage renovation of Cuban sports and consequently professional baseball is formally banned on the island.

February–April 1962—First season of new Cuban League (amateur) held with Occidentales (18–9) emerging as champion under manager Fermín Guerra. Erwin Walter (.367) of the victors wins first batting title and Rolando Valdés of Orientales is home run leader with but three. Antonio Rubio (Occidentales) is first ERA champion with a stellar 1.39 mark.

July 10, 1962—Juan Marichal (Dominican Republic) becomes first Latin American pitcher to win major league All-Star Game with 3–1 National League victory during 1962's first Midsummer Classic (of two played) at Washington's DC Stadium. Ironically, Washington Senators ace Camilio Pascual (Cuba) is game loser, simultaneously becoming the first Latin-born pitcher to lose an All-Star Game in the majors.

August 13, 1962—Cuban native Bert Campaneris pitches two relief innings for Daytona Beach in Florida State League against Ft. Lauderdale, throwing both as right-hander and left-hander and allowing only one run during this rare stunt while striking out four. Normally an infielder, Campaneris later makes big-league history (on September 8, 1965) by appearing at all nine positions for Kansas City Athletics in a single nine-inning game.

April-May 1963—Cuba wins its first Pan American Games gold medal since inaugural tournament back in 1951, pounding the USA 13–0 in opening game and coasting to overall 7–1 record. This same spring witnesses another perfect game in low-level Cuban amateur baseball, this one pitched by Antonio "Chucho" Rubio for the Public Administration team versus Club Bauta during provincial-level tournament action in Havana.

May 2, 1964—Cuban rookie sensation Tony (nee Pedro) Oliva (Minnesota Twins) blasts first of big-league record-tying four consecutive Twins homers in 11th inning, pacing 7–4 victory at Kansas City. Following Oliva with round-trippers were Bob Allison, Jimmie Hall, and Harmon Killebrew, thus equaling earlier feat performed by Milwaukee Braves in 1961 and repeated by Cleveland Indians in 1963. Oliva, in his first big league campaign, leads junior circuit in hitting at .332, becoming first rookie to gain an American League batting crown.

May 20, 1964—Cuban pitcher José Ramón López (Monterrey) records 16 strikeouts, nine in succession, in 5–2 victory over Mexico City Red Devils, tying short-lived Mexican League record set in 1959 by Dominican Diomedes "Guayubín" Olivo (Poza Rica).

July 23, 1964—Cuban-born rookie Bert Campaneris of the Kansas City Athletics becomes only second man in big league history to hit two homers in his debut game, a first circuit blast coming on the initial pitch served up by Minnesota Twins hurler Jim Kaat. Bob Nieman of the St. Louis Browns earlier homered in his first two big-league at-bats (1951) while Campaneris accomplishes the same feat in his first and fourth trips to the plate.

October 1964—Minnesota Twins slugger Tony Oliva becomes first black ballplayer to win both batting title and Rookie-of-the-Year honors in same season. By pacing American League with .323 average, Cuban standout becomes only third Latin to win a big league batting championship.

February 21, 1965—Cuban Leaguer Inocente Miranda (Azucareros) plays entire game at first base without ever touching the ball, an event that has also occurred only five times in major league history (four times in 20th century and most recently involving Gene Tenace with the Oakland A's in 1974).

September 8, 1965—Infielder Bert Campaneris (Kansas City Athletics) becomes first player in big league history to play all nine positions in single contest. Versatile Cuban mans one position per inning versus Los Angeles Angels, recording single error (in right field), allowing one run and two hits while on the mound, and catching final inning during which he is injured in home plate collision with Ed Kirkpatrick and forced to leave the game. Campaneris would ironically later also be the first batter to face Venezuelan utility man César Tóvar during first inning of September 22, 1968 game in which Tóvar duplicates Campaneris's novel versatility feat.

October 1965—Cuban infielder Zoilo Versalles of American League champion Minnesota Twins blazes new trails as first Latin American ballplayer to earn MVP honors, being named junior circuit's most valued performer.

January 16 and January 25, 1966—One of the most overlooked performances in international baseball history occurs in Cuban League National Series when diminutive righthander Aquino Abreu (Centrales) hurls back-to-back no-hit games (beating Occidentales 11–0 and Industriales 7–0) thus matching Johnny Vander Meer's more recognized big-league feat. These are also the first two no-hit, no-run games ever pitched in post-revolution Cuban League, now in its fifth season.

August 13, 1966—Cuban-born Mexican League strikeout king José Ramón López establishes an all-time standard of 309 strikeouts for a single season, reaching 309 while hurling for Monterrey versus Reynosa. It is a small irony of the day's events that López, while striking out a dozen batters, loses the contest 2–0.

July 11, 1967—Cincinnati Reds third baseman Antanasio "Tany" (thus "Tony" in the USA) Pérez hits dramatic 15th inning home run off Jim "Catfish" Hunter to give Nationals 2–1 victory in Mid-Summer Classic at Anaheim. Hitting heroics by the Cuban slugger not only ended the longest contest in All-Star Game history, but also capped one of most bizarre games of the traditional series: third basemen accounted for all three runs with Dick Allen (Phillies) and Brooks Robinson (Orioles) also homering for the game's only other tallies.

August 1967—Team USA is Pan American Games baseball champion for the only time when George Greer singles off Cuban ace Manuel Alarcón in ninth inning of deciding playoff game. Cuba had won two earlier games (4–3 and 9–1) against Team USA in opening round play. This same fall all admission charges are dropped at Cuban sporting events, including Cuban League baseball games which will remain free to all citizens until the mid–1990s.

October 23, 1967—Omar Linares is born on this date in Pinar del Río Province. Son of stellar Cuban League outfielder Fidel Linares, Omar will emerge two decades later as arguably the greatest of all modern-era Cuban ballplayers.

January 28, 1968—Raúl Reyes (Industriales) produces 11 RBI and three homers during a one-sided 15–0 victory versus the Azucareros, making him the first hitter in amateur Cuban League with three homers in one contest.

January–April 1968—Seventh edition of the National Series provides Cuba's "year of the no-hit, no-run game" as five masterpieces are recorded, two on the same day (January 7, 1968). The quintet of successful pitchers included Leopoldo Valdés (January 7), Jesús Pérez (January 7), José Huelga (January 14), Orlando Figueredo (January 25), and Florentino González (April 4).

April 1969—Santiago "Changa" Mederos, lefthanded ace for Habana Province, completes National Series season with record 208 strikeouts—a mark that will remain the league record for more than three decades. In this same National Series season Agustín Marquetti is first to slug 19 homers and Wilfredo Sánchez sets new record for base hits with 140 safeties.

August 1969—Cuba claims Amateur World Series XVII championship contested in the Dominican Republic, winning in most sensational fashion when Gaspar Pérez and Rigoberto Rosique connect for consecutive singles in ninth inning of deciding game against American ace lefthander Larry Osborne.

November 1969—Cuba's Mike Cuéllar is first Latin American winner of coveted Cy Young Award, leading powerful Baltimore Orioles mound staff (2.83 team ERA, plus 20 staff shutouts) with his outstanding 23–11 won-lost record and sterling 2.38 ERA.

December 2 and December 4, 1970—José Huelga becomes instant legend of Cuban baseball when he earns victory in both playoffs games versus Team USA, leading Cubans to gold medal victory in 18th Amateur World Series at Cartagena, Colombia. Huelga tops future major league star Burt Hooton 3–1 in 11-inning classic and then returns two days later to garner another crucial victory in relief of Changa Mederos and Manuel Hurtado. Huelga will be killed in tragic automobile accident four years later, cutting short brilliant career that left him as all-time Cuban League ERA leader (1.50) and one of island baseball's undying legends.

May 20, 1971—"El Inmortal" Martín Dihigo dies in Cienfuegos at age 65 and is later buried in his wife's family plot in nearby Cruces.

November-December 1971—Havana's Estadio Latinoamericano given major facelift and expanded to seat 55,000 fans in preparation for December 1971 Amateur World Series (Number 19) hosted by Cuba and staged at sites all across the island. Cuba is easy tournament victor, winning all nine of its games and besting Colombia (7–2 record) for the gold medal.

November 1972—Agustín Marquetti slugs dramatic mammoth home run against the United States team in Nicaragua to decide championship round of Amateur World Series XX. This is Cuba's twelfth title in fifteen appearances at showcase world amateur event.

February 1973—Armando Capiró (Habana) surpasses Agustín Marquetti's existing record of 19 by blasting 22 round trippers in National Series XII. Braudilio Vinent (Serranos) also establishes milestone for pitchers during same season with 19 victories, a record that will last until José Ibar finally reaches 20-victory plateau in 1998.

July 4, 1974—Star pitcher José Antonio Huelga—hero of 1970 Amateur World Series XVIII held in Colombia—tragically killed in automobile crash on Mariel highway west of Havana. Twenty-six-year-old Huelga had pitched in seven National Series, compiled .695 career winning percentage, and still owns lowest career ERA in Cuban League annals.

April-May 1975—Structure of Cuban League baseball altered with addition of a 54-game Selective Series (super-provincial) season following shortened 39-game National Series (provincial) championship season. Oriente captures first Selective Series team title and future national team manager Alfonso Urquiola (Pinar del Río) is first Selective Series batting champion. Oscar Romero also hurls first Selective Series no-hitter (May 4) while pitching for Camagüey versus Havana-based Industriales.

January 4, 1976—Executives of International Amateur Baseball Association (IABA) meet in Mexico City to end lengthy feud between rival national delegations, creating new organization named Asociación Internacional de Béisbol Amateur (AINBA). With the USA returning to IABA fold after several-year absence, first AINBA world championship tournament is scheduled for Cartagena, Colombia and Cuban Manuel González Guerra is also named first AINBA president.

September 12, 1976—Minnie Miñoso becomes oldest player to record major league base hit, singling off Sid Monge in first game of doubleheader with California Angels. Seeing limited duty as DH in 1976, Cuban star has only one hit during eight plate appearances. Miñoso is nine months past 53rd birthday and thus eclipses mark set in 1929 by Nick Altrock, who collected his own final hit for the Washington Senators only days after turning 53.

December 1976—Aluminum bats are used for first time in Cuba during National Series XVI and Selective Series III. Aluminum "lumber" now also being used for world amateur play and will remain a fixture for Cuban baseball until 1999 post-season playoffs.

August 8, 1977—Black Cuban star Martín Dihigo, considered by most as greatest all-around Negro league performer, voted into Cooperstown shrine by BWAA Veterans Committee. Dihigo thus becomes second Latin hall-of-famer and first player ever enshrined in three different national halls (Cuba, Mexico, USA). Dihigo was top pitcher and also standout at every other position except catcher, was both batting and home run champion several times in Negro league play, and is credited with pitching first Mexican League no-hitter.

December 1977—Important rule change introduces designated hitter in Cuban League play, an innovation that had come to major league baseball only four seasons earlier. First Cuban DH is Lázaro Mádam, who serves in new lineup slot during pre-season exhibition game played between CDR and MININT Havana amateur clubs.

January 1979—Wilfredo Sánchez claims his fourth National Series batting title in tightest individual race in Cuban League history—the title being decided by four decimal places with Sánchez (Citricultores) barely edging Agustín Arias (Santiago de Cuba) by narrowest conceivable margin.

February 1979—Cuba's first appearance in Intercontinental Cup tournament (staged in Havana) becomes personal showcase for 24-year-old righty slugger Pedro José (Cheíto) Rodríguez. Cuban hero puts on one-man show by slugging seven homers, socking 18 hits and scoring 15 runs, plating 18 RBI, and posting slugging percentage of more than 1.000 (all top figures for the tournament). Cuba stands undefeated in its 10 games while a USA entry is the first American amateur ball club to visit the Communist-run island in 37 years.

December 15, 1979—Santiago "Changa" Mederos dies from burns suffered in highway auto crash—marking the second time this decade that a top Cuban pitcher is tragically killed in such a manner. Thirty-four-year-old Mederos, veteran of 15 National Series and five Selective Series, is rated best post-revolution southpaw hurler, and his single-season record of 208 strikeouts in 1969 will remain the National Series record until century's end.

April 12, 1980—For only time in amateur Cuban League history, two players from same team smack grand slam homers in same inning. Rey Vicente Anglada and Jorge Beltrán (Habana) ironically accomplish this rare feat on exact same day that Don Money and Cecil Cooper (Milwaukee Brewers) also pull it off in major league action. Anglada actually blasts two homers during big one-inning uprising against Matanzas.

June 1980—Outfielder Héctor Olivera of Las Villas posts highest average in Cuban League history while winning Selective Series individual crown with .459 mark posted during 59-game season. Olivera's feat also represents first .400-plus batting average registered in either the National Series or Selective Series.

October 4, 1980—After nearly four seasons as coach and ball club public relations executive, Minnie Miñoso makes token pinch-hitting appearance for Chicago White Sox. Miñoso thus becomes second player in big league history to appear in official league play during five different decades. Always-popular Miñoso had enjoyed four earlier stints in Chicago (1951–57, 1960–61, 1964, 1976) and is 57 at time of final pinch-hitting appearance, part of a promotional stunt orchestrated by Sox owner and ultimate showman Bill Veeck.

November 1980—At 26th Amateur World Championships—staged for first time in the Far East (Tokyo, Japan)—Cuba posts yet another perfect mark (11–0) under manager Servio Borges. Outfielder Lourdes Gourriel—several-times Cuban League batting champion and one of top league stars of late '70s and early '80s — records key hit in victory over third-place United States team.

August 1983 — During International Cup VI tournament in Belgium, Cuban star Victor Mesa blasts towering home run against USA pitcher Vincent Barger but is promptly ejected by home plate umpire for performing unsportsmanlike gesture while rounding base paths.

January 31, 1984 — Cuban League experiences game with fewest hits ever when southpaw Jorge Luis Valdés (Henequeneros) throws no-hitter against Villa Clara while opposing ace Reynaldo Santana allows only two safeties during 1–0 nail-biter.

August 1984 — Cuba hosts 28th IBA World Championships in Havana, defeating Chinese Taipei for gold medal and also beginning still-current string (as of 2006) of nine straight world titles. Subsequent victories will follow in 1986 (Holland), 1988 (Italy), 1990 (Canada), 1994 (Nicaragua), 1998 (again Italy) and 2001 (Taiwan).

January 1986 — Lázaro Vargas (Industriales) sets Cuban League consecutive-game hitting streak standard by collecting base hits in 31 straight games. Old mark of 29 by Felipe Sarduy had stood since 1969 season; Rey Isaac (Santiago de Cuba) will eventually extend record to 37 games in 1995.

November 27, 1986 — Braudilio Vinent becomes first Cuban League hurler to reach career milestone total of 2,000 strikeouts. Vinent will complete his career with lifetime total of 2,134, second all-time behind Rogelio García.

December 9, 1986 — Batters for Las Villas in Cuban League National Series bash ten straight singles against pitchers from Agropecuarios, thus matching feat not performed in major leagues since June 2, 1901.

February 11, 1987 — Outfielder Luis Ulacia (Camagüeyanos) becomes first and only Cuban League player to smack home runs from both side of plate in same game.

August 22, 1987 — Cuba rebounds from early-round loss to USA to defeat Americans 13–9 in dramatic come-from-behind championship match at Pan American Games in Indianapolis. Cuba rallies against future big-league pitcher Cris Carpenter for two runs in eighth and three more in ninth. Victory extends Cuba's Pan American Games gold medal streak to five straight (with three more to follow in 1991 and 1995 and 1999). Opening round defeat will be Cuba's final loss of any single game in international senior-level tournament competitions for next ten years (viz., until Intercontinental Cup finals in August 1997).

March 3, 1988 — Truly rare event occurs in Cuban League when Camagüey defeats Las Villas three times in same day. First loss for Las Villas results from previous night's contest that extends past midnight, while other two come in afternoon doubleheader. The same occurrence in major league play was recorded on June 2, 1903, when Brooklyn surrendered unusual triple-header to Pittsburgh.

September 23, 1988 — José Canseco, Cuba-born star with Oakland Athletics, becomes first major leaguer to record season with 40-plus home runs and 40-plus stolen bases. American League leader in both homers and RBI, Canseco is second Cuban to win MVP honors (Zoilo Versalles was first in 1965). Two seasons earlier Canseco was also second Cuban to win rookie-of-the-year honors (Tony Oliva being first in 1964).

August 22, 1989 — Right-hander Lázaro Valle hurls eight-inning perfect game (11–0) against South Korea while striking out 13 of 24 batters faced. Valle's masterpiece comes in Intercontinental Cup tournament at Puerto Rico, where Cuba grabs its fourth straight gold medal victory by beating Japan 8–2 in finals. Tourney MVP is Cuban leftfielder Lourdes Gourriel who bats .435 in eight games. Gourriel had opened the decade with key hit versus Team USA in 1980 Amateur World Series staged in Tokyo.

January 1990 — Omar Linares bats over .400 (.442) for third time in Cuban League play to win his third batting title. Linares already widely considered in amateur baseball circles and among professional scouts (major league scouts) as "the best non–big-league third baseman on the planet."

April 7, 1990 — Orlando Hernández — later the most celebrated among Cuban League defectors after departure from Cuba in 1997 — pitches his only no-hitter in Cuba. The 11–0 (7-inning mercy rule) blanking occurs in Habana Province victory at Victoria de Girón Stadium in Matanzas and is seventh and final no-hit, no-run game pitched during Selective Series action.

July 1991 — Catcher José Delgado smacks dramatic tenth-inning single to salvage 5–4 win over Japan in finals of 10th Intercontinental Cup in Barcelona, clinching Cuba's fifth straight ICC championship. Lefty Omar Ajete also tournament hero with his 0.00 ERA in preliminary round, a ninth-inning save in 2–1 semifinals victory over Chinese Taipei, and a successful starting role in gold medal game.

September 1992 — Cuba captures historic first-ever Olympic baseball gold medal competition (Barcelona) with undefeated record (8–0) and 11–1 triumph over Chinese Taipei in finals. Pitchers Omar Ajete and Giorge Díaz and slugger Omar Linares are Cuba's top gold medal heroes. Closest games for Cubans are 9–6 (opening round) and 4–1 (semifinals) victories over improved Team USA.

August 31, 1992 — Texas Rangers and Oakland Athletics swap Latin American sluggers José Canseco (Cuba) and Rubén Sierra (Puerto Rico) in most sensational trade to date featuring Hispanic superstars. Canseco joins Texas in exchange for switch-hitting Sierra, plus relief ace Jeff Russell and starting hurler Bobby Witt. With Canseco on same roster as AL home run leader Juan González (from Puerto Rico), slugger Rafael Palmeiro (Cuba), and former batting champ Julio Franco (Dominican Republic), Rangers boast most potent Latin American slugging lineup ever.

April 1993 — Tany Pérez debuts as Cincinnati Reds manager, yet his opening act is hardly successful and he is quickly fired only 44 games into first season. Hopes are high in Cincinnati for pennant challenge, and when Reds flounder early (20–24 on May 24th date of Pérez firing), even earlier stature as revered star of 1970s Big Red Machine teams is insufficient to save an ill-fated managerial career. Pérez will later return to managing with Florida Marlins during 2001 National League season.

April 9, 1993 — José Canseco, now with Texas Rangers, becomes first player since Ted Williams (1947) and 17th in baseball history to reach 750 career RBI plateau in 1000 games or less. Canseco's milestone RBI (in his 999th career game) comes against Royals at Kansas City.

June 7, 1993 — MVP Omar Linares smacks homer, double and sacrifice fly in three at-bats as Cuba defeats IBA World All-Star squad 8–2 in Tokyo Dome. IBA World All-Star Game III is first matchup of Olympic champion and all-stars from all other competing nations.

March 1994 — Lázaro Junco, Cuba's all-time longball slugger, wins eighth Cuban League home run crown. Junco (who played for Citricultores, Henequeneros and Matanzas) retires with Cuba's career home run record (later passed by Orestes Kindelán) of 405 round trippers.

August 31, 1995 — Pedro Luis Lazo tosses no-hitter and strikes out 17 as Cuba defeats USA 5–0 in semifinals of World University Games at Fukuoka, Japan. Lazo pitched six-inning 12–1 one-hit win earlier in same tournament versus Taiwan, striking out 11.

October 1994 — Cuban-born José Canseco tabbed American League Comeback-Player-of-the-Year after stellar season (his last with Texas Rangers ball club) in which he slugs 31 homers, drives in 90 runs, and bats a most respectable .282.

October 1995 — José Canseco now with Boston Red Sox finishes season with 300 career round trippers, becoming only third Latin player to reach 300-homer plateau. Canseco thus stands only 79 circuit blasts behind Tany Pérez and Orlando Cepeda for all-time top spot among Latin American sluggers.

July 1996 — Cuba (9–0 for tournament) again dominates international amateur scene by breezing to victory in Summer Olympics at Atlanta's Fulton County Stadium. Cuba defeats Japan 13–9 in gold medal game and Omar Linares (8) and Orestes Kindelán (9) perform awesome two-week display of aluminum-bat home run slugging. Kindelán blasts longest third-deck four-bagger ever witnessed in Fulton County Stadium.

April 8, 1997—Omar Linares of Pinar del Río slugs four homers in one game at hometown Captain San Luis Stadium, becoming only third player to accomplish the rare feat at any level in more than a century of Cuban amateur league or professional baseball. Linares matches Leonel Moa (for Camagüey on December 10, 1989) and Alberto Díaz (Matanzas on December 17, 1995) with his four round trippers. Veteran umpire Nelson Díaz ironically works all three of these games—at second base in first two and behind the plate for final historic contest.

August 10, 1997—Japan surprises Cuba 11–2 in finals of Intercontinental Cup play at Barcelona, Spain, thus ending ten-year Cuban domination of senior-level international tourneys, as well as string of seven straight titles for Cuba in Intercontinental Cup competitions. This loss on heals of 1996 Olympic victory shocks both Cuban fans and INDER officials and leads to dramatic changes in both the Cuban League format and leadership of Cuba's national team. Next Cuban League season will feature single National Series of 90 games and Jorge Fuentes is replaced as manager of both Pinar del Río and Team Cuba.

October 1997—Defector Liván Hernández stars in World Series for National League Florida Marlins and thus refocuses attention of U.S. fans on long and proud legacy of Cuban baseball. Most memorable World Series MVP performance by 22-year-old Hernández also creates considerable stir among diehard fans back in Cuba.

April 1998—Veteran José Ibar wins 20 games on mound for Habana Provine and becomes first pitcher in modern-era Cuban League to post 20 victories in single National Series season. Pinar del Río, featuring superstar slugger Omar Linares and mound aces José Contreras and Pedro Luis Lazo, captures Cuban League title for second straight year.

June 3, 1998—Orlando "El Duque" Hernández makes major league debut with world champion New York Yankees. Half-brother of 1997 World Series hero Liván Hernández, "El Duque" defected from Cuba in December 1997 and signed with New York club in February 1998 after much-publicized open tryout session held during winter league Caribbean Series in Caracas, Venezuela.

July 1998—José Canseco surpasses Cuban Tany Pérez and Puerto Rican Orlando Cepeda (379 each) to become Latin America's all-time career leader in big-league home runs. Regla-born and Miami-raised Canseco approaches 400 career homers before season's end.

August 1998—Cuba recaptures its long-standing reputation for international domination by winning IBA world championships in Italy, posting perfect 9–0 record for tournament and defeating South Korea 7–1 in one-sided finals. Cuba's stars are ageless Omar Linares (.500 BA), veteran slugger Orestes Kindelán (also above .500 and tournament's leading hitter), and power pitcher José Contreras, who hurls title game five-hitter. Cuba also beats Nicaragua (14–2) in semifinals and The Netherlands (12–1) in quarterfinals to capture its 25th senior-level world title in 27 outings since 1952 (including IBA world championships and Intercontinental Cup tournaments).

October 18, 1998—New National Series season (number XXXVIII) opens on dramatic note when popular star shortstop Germán Mesa makes emotional return to action in Estadio Latinoamericano after serving two-year suspension. High drama thus surrounds opening inning of game between Industriales and defending champion Pinar del Río when players from both teams jog onto field to shake Mesa's hand when he takes his position for first time since his controversial banning.

January 23, 1999—Up-and-coming young outfield star Yasser Gómez slugs three triples during same game in Estadio Latinoamericano versus Holguín. Teammate Germán Mesa joins Gómez in mad dashes around the base paths when the two Industriales stars hit back-to-back three-baggers during this same game.

March 28, 1999—Major leaguers appear on Cuban soil for the first time in 40 years for historic meeting between American League Baltimore Orioles and Cuban national team played before 55,000 frenzied fans in Estadio Latinoamericano. Omar Linares singles home tying run in eighth but major leaguers finally prevail 3–2 after 11 thrill-packed innings. Catcher Charles Johnson homers in second frame for Baltimore and José Contreras pitches eight dominant innings of relief for Cuba.

April 1999—During week following Orioles' historic visit baseball interest further revived in Havana by return trip of local favorite Industriales to National Series finals. Industriales takes commanding early 3–0 series lead before cross-island rival Santiago de Cuba sweeps final four games to earn National Series XXXVIII championship.

May 3, 1999—Two triples by shortstop Danel Castro, dramatic ninth-inning round tripper and joyous dance around basepaths by DH (and future defector) Andy Morales, and 6.2 innings of hitless relief hurling by Norge Vera all highlight stunning 12–6 romp by Cuban national team in their rematch with Baltimore Orioles at Camden Yards. The game—the first-ever meeting on U.S. soil between a Castro-era Cuban team and a major-league ball club—establishes Cuban League credibility and sets off wild celebrations within Havana and everywhere across Cuba.

July 1999—Cuba wins Pan American Games tournament in Winnipeg and thus qualifies for 2000 Olympic play upcoming in Sydney. Pan American tournament makes history as first international competition matching teams using professional players (mostly AAA minor leaguers). Dramatic final round of games provides perhaps the most exciting competition in long history of international baseball, as Cuba rebounds from two preliminary-round losses to take three straight from the Dominican Republic, Canada and the United States. José Contrares pitches brilliantly in quarterfinals and finals with but a single day's rest between games.

Summer 1999—Cuban baseball history first comes to widespread attention of North American fans with U.S. publication of two important scholarly books. Roberto González Echevarria's *The Pride of Havana* offers dense academic tome focused largely on pre-revolution Cuban baseball; Mark Rucker and Peter Bjarkman's *Smoke* offers colorful coffee table pictorial covering full 125-year span of Cuban national pastime.

November 1999—Cuba upset in gold medal game of Intercontinental Cup tournament played in Sydney, thus losing championship game of ICC tournament for second straight time after seven consecutive victories dating back to 1983. Surprise loss to host Australia, 4–3 in 11 innings, again shakes Cuban baseball establishment back home, even though Cuba did not send most of its veteran national team players to this tune-up event for 2000 Sydney Olympics.

December 1999—Rare unassisted triple play by third baseman occurs in Cuban League action when Villa Clara's Rafael Acebey tags two Industriales base runners along with the batter on slow roller off bat of Juan Padilla. Padilla himself facilitates the unusual play when he remains at home plate to argue with umpire that his weak roller had first hit him in the batter's box and was thus obviously a foul ball.

December 8, 1999—Maels Rodríguez cracks 100 mph barrier on speed gun in game at Sancti Spíritus. It is the first time that any Cuban League hurler has reached this ultimate three-figure standard for measuring pitching speed.

December 22, 1999—Maels Rodríguez throws first perfect game in Cuban League history when he blanks Las Tunas 1–0 on his home field in Sancti Spíritus. This game, along with remarkable 100 mph clocking only two weeks earlier, establishes 19-year-old phenom Rodríguez as Cuba's brightest new pitching star.

April 2000—Norge Vera, Santiago ace right-hander, completes year with sterling 0.97 ERA and leads host of pitchers who dominate first Cuban League season in 23 winters played with wooden bats. Other sterling performances are turned in by José Contreras (1.24 ERA) and Maels Rodríguez (177 strikeouts in 139 innings), and ten different starting pitchers all record ERAs of 1.75 or less.

July 2000—Antanasio "Tany" Pérez becomes first Cuban major leaguer inducted into major league baseball Hall of Fame in Cooperstown, New York. Pérez joins Martín Dihigo as only other Cuban hall-of-famer (Cooperstown) and also joins Puerto Rico's Roberto Clemente and Orlando Cepeda, the Dominican Republic's Juan Marichal, and Venezuela's Luis Aparicio among half-dozen legendary Latin Americans now enshrined in baseball's top hall of honors.

September 27, 2000—Cuba is upset by Team USA in Olympic gold medal match at Sydney. USA starter Ben Sheets hurls brilliant three-hit shutout in 4–0 American victory that ends Cuba's Olympic baseball domination. Cubans had earlier defeated the Americans by 6–1 score in preliminary round behind José Ibar's hurling and timely hitting of Oscar Macías and Miguel Caldés. Veteran Cuban manager Servio Borges likely committed crucial tactical error by deciding to start ace José Ariel Contreras in semifinal showdown versus Japan (a 3–0 Cuban victory) in order to save Pedro Luis Lazo for gold medal matchup vs. USA.

December 2000—Olympic team star and longtime national team outfielder Miguel Caldés—star player for Camagüey and former league home run champion—killed in tragic automobile accident outside hometown of Camagüey.

January 21, 2001—Santiago ace Norge Vera hurls no-hit, no-run game against Havana Province during Sunday doubleheader at Nelson Fernández Stadium in San José de las Lajas. This first-ever no-hitter by a Santiago de Cuba pitcher is also the 43rd such masterpiece of post-revolution Cuban League history and number 36 during National Series competitions.

March 3, 2001—U.S. author and historian Peter Bjarkman himself makes history with first-ever in-depth television interview of American baseball commentator during 40-plus years of Cuban Revolution. Interviewed by Carlos Hernández Luján on primetime Cubavision, Bjarkman discusses previously sensitive topics such as Cuban players leaving for professional big league baseball contracts and also controversial (at least in Cuba) competitions between Cuban national teams and squads stocked with minor league pro players staged during recent international tournaments.

May 2001—Twenty-year-old Maels Rodríguez shatters Cuban League strikeout record that had stood since 1969 (208 by Santiago "Changa" Mederos) and also posts circuit's top ERA. Maels' performance highlights the most exciting Cuban League season in years, with Santiago de Cuba capturing third straight pennant, and several other individual records and performances of note being recorded. Record breakers include: Alex Ramos (whose unmatched consecutive games streak extends to 712), Lázaro de la Torre (fourth CL pitcher to post 200 career wins), Eduardo Paret (with new league high of 99 runs scored), Orlis Díaz (who ties Oscar Machado's RBI mark at 87), and Antonio Pacheco and Orestes Kindelán (who extend their respective career marks for base hits and home runs).

November 2001—Cuba reclaims top spot in world amateur baseball with gold medal victory in 34th Amateur World Series staged in Taiwan. Sweet championship game victory comes against Team USA (by 5–3 score) and also avenges Olympic loss in Sydney one year earlier. Veteran outfielder Luis Ulacia—38 years old—enjoys a career swan song as tournament MVP. Tournament also marks likely final international appearances of long-time national team stars Omar Linares (all-time Cuban League batting leader), Orestes Kindelán (career home run leader), and Antonio Pacheco (career base hits pacesetter).

January 2002—Opening of 41st National Series season postponed until January, due both to world championship tournament action staged in Taiwan during November and to damage inflicted by a severe hurricane which sweeps the island in late October. New Cuban season also marks renewal of the suspended short-season Se-

lective Series (renamed the Super League and featuring thirty games and four teams named Occidentales, Habaneros, Centrales and Orientales) at the conclusion of National Series playoffs in late June.

June 2002—Surprising National Series XLI concludes with western provincial winner Holguín defeating eastern provincial champ Sancti Spíritus in a hotly contested seven-game finale. Unexpected match-up marked first-ever championship-series appearance for Holguín and only the second for Sancti Spíritus. Ace Maels Rodríguez performs yeoman service in the final playoff round as both a starter and reliever but suffers defeats three separate times.

July 2002—New ground is broken for Cuban baseball with the surprise announcement that five top stars will officially "retire" from league play and immediately join Japanese amateur and professional leagues as "rented" players and coaches. Long-time national team star Omar Linares is loaned to pro Chunichi Dragons; Orestes Kindelán and Antonio Pacheco sign on with amateur Sidas club; outfielder Luis Ulacia (MVP of 2001 World Championships in Taipei) and shortstop Germán Mesa are also designated as Japanese coaches.

September 2002—National team ace hurler José Ariel Contreras (sporting a perfect 13–0 record for major international tournaments) departs from Cuban squad in Mexico and later turns up in the United States, having defected from Cuban baseball alongside longtime team technical director (general manager) Miguel Valdés. Contreras will eventually sign a lucrative $30 million long-term contract with the New York Yankees and appear in the major leagues as well as at the AAA level (Columbus) during the upcoming 2003 season.

November 2002—Cuba breezes (with perfect 10–0 record) to another Interncontinental Cup championship on home turf in Havana and Matanzas. Pinar del Río's Yobal Dueñas is tourney batting hero with his dramatic game-deciding home run in 2–1 gold medal win over South Korea.

May 2003—Led by slugging third baseman-outfielder Kendry Morales and hard-hitting catcher Bárbaro Cañizares, Industriales captures National Series for first time in seven seasons with four-game rout of Villa Clara during playoff finals. Fan interest again peaks with the achievements of island's most popular ball club representing the capital city of Havana. On big league front Cuban-born Rafael Palmeiro slugs career homer number 500 for Texas Rangers, becoming second Latin ballplayer (after Sammy Sosa) to reach that Hall-of-Fame landmark milestone.

October-November 2003—Oblivious to recent defections by headliners Maels Rodríguez and Yobal Dueñas, young Cuban squad fronted by new leaders Yulieski Gourriel and Frederich Cepeda re-emerges at forefront of international competition by sweeping all opposition during Gold Medal wins at both the World Cup (Havana) and Pre-Olympic (Panama) tournaments.

August 2004—Cuba recaptures its seat atop the international baseball world with a third Olympic gold medal victory in four tries. Rebounding from a disappointing silver medal finish in Sydney four years earlier, Cuba brings its youngest and most inexperienced squad yet to the Olympic battleground and still manages to march through the nine-game event with only a single preliminary-round loss to third-place Japan. Cuba's surprise win is highlighted by a gutsy eighth-inning six-run comeback against Team Canada in the semifinal and a hard-fought 6–2 victory over upstart Australia in the finale. Top Cuban stars are catcher Ariel Pestano (the tournament batting champion) and southpaw Adiel Palma (the event's top pitcher). The tournament's biggest story, however, is the collapse of the favored Japanese team, which unaccountably suffers an upset 1–0 semifinal loss to Australia that dashes gold medal hopes for a Japanese Dream Team composed of top all-stars from the professional Japanese Pacific League and Japanese Central League.

May 2005—Las Tunas and national team outfielder Osmani Urrutia fades in the final weeks of the National Series 44 and misses a fifth successive Cuban League season of batting above .400—something never accomplished in the U.S. major leagues. Urrutia still manages to walk off with the league batting title, his fifth in a row, which cements his claim as the most dominant hitter in the history of (pre-revolution or post-revolution) Cuban baseball.

June 2005 — Major League Baseball announces plans for a World Baseball Classic under its auspices to be inaugurated in March 2006 and featuring all-star squads (mainly major leaguers) from sixteen competing nations. Opening rounds are scheduled for Japan, Puerto Rico, Holland and Miami, with the championship round planned for San Diego near the end of major league spring training. Cuba objects to the commercial nature of such a made-for-television tournament and announces that it will not participate. Cubans will later reverse their position and enter the showcase exhibition matches.

July 2005 — IOC officials vote to drop baseball from the roster of sports to be contested at the 2012 London Olympics. It is a shocking move that is felt most severely in Cuba, where Olympic tournaments have become a showpiece of the nation's baseball agenda.

September 2005 — Cuba once again successfully defends its world championship at the IBAF World Cup 36 tournament staged in The Netherlands (Rotterdam, Haarlem, Amsterdam). The victory runs Cuba's impressive total to 25 gold medals in 28 appearances at the prestigious World Cup event.

October 2005 — Former Cuban Leaguers Orlando Hernández and José Contreras team in the starting rotation for the American League Chicago White Sox and lead that team to an AL Central Division title and a first franchise World Series victory in eighty-nine years.

March 2006 — Cuban baseball history reaches its true apex moment with the stunning performance of the national team at the inaugural Major League Baseball-sponsored professional World Baseball Classic tournament. Cuba's entry in the event comes only after U.S. Treasury Department officials (under pressure from MLB and IBAF representatives) reverse an original decision to ban the communist country's participation. Competing for the first time against a full array of big league stars, the Cuban leaguers shock the collective baseball world by reaching the championship finals in San Diego's Petco Park, before falling to Japan in a 10–6 slugfest. Cuba's silver medal finish is highlighted by consecutive upset victories in Round 2 (San Juan) over Caribbean rivals Venezuela and Puerto Rico, teams boasting household big league names, and a third win against the star-studded pre-tourney favorite Dominican Republic club at the San Diego semifinals. Individual stars are Yoandry Garlobo (second leading tournament hitter), Yulieski Gourriel (tournament all-star second baseman), and Pedro Luis Lazo (whose brilliant relief hurling closes out wins over Venezuela and the Dominicans). These victories put to permanent rest a long-standing myth that Cuba's four decade domination of international baseball came only because the pseudo-professional Cubans had been competing against inferior squads of unseasoned amateurs and lesser professionals.

April 2006 — Osmani Urrutia of Las Tunas bats above .400 for the fifth time in six years of National Series play. Urrutia's half-dozen-year streak also vaults him into second place behind Omar Linares among career leaders in National Series batting average.

Appendix B: Blackball Register

Cuban Teams and Players in U.S. Negro Leagues (1904–1947)

The following list provides a partial roster of Cuban teams (i.e., teams with Cuban names that may or may not have included actual island-born Cuban players) and also most native Cuban players who performed in the various U.S. Negro leagues. The period covered stretches from 1904 (when the first Cuban-named ball club appeared in North American play) until 1947 (the summer when big league integration, in the form of Jackie Robinson with the Brooklyn Dodgers, ended the long-standing exclusion of blacks from organized baseball). While complete for most seasons (as complete, at least, as existing records allow), this listing of Cuban Negro leaguers is not exhaustive and thus remains in need of still further fleshing out.

Note: Some players with missing first names may also carry misspelled family names, such being the state of contemporary sports reporting in both Cuba and the U.S. (at least in the press that covered black baseball on a hit or miss basis). **Key:** UNKNOWN = first name unknown.

1904—*All Cubans* (Rafael Almeida, José Borges, Luis "Anguilla" Bustamante, Julián Castillo, José Figarola, Antonio María García ("El Inglesito"), Mamelo García, Gonzálo Sánchez, Joseito Muñoz, Emilio Palmero). *Cuban X Giants* (no native Cuban players on team roster).

1905—*All Cubans* (Rafael Almeida, José Borges, Luis "Anguilla" Bustamante, Alfredo "Pájaro" Cabrera, Bernardo Carrillo, Julián Castillo, Angel D'Meza, Antonio María García, Regino García, Eliodoro "Jabuco" Hidalgo, Armando Marsans, Joseito Muñoz, Emilio Palmero, Gonzálo Sánchez, Rogelio Valdés*). *Cuban X Giants* (Rogelio Valdés*). *Cuban Giants* (no native Cuban players on team roster). *Valdés played first with All Cubans and later with Cuban X Giants.

1906—*Cuban X Giants* (Antonio María "El Inglés" García, Joseito Muñoz, Julián "Fallenca" Pérez, Emilo Palomino, Rogelio Valdés). *Cuban Giants* (no native Cuban players on team roster).

1907—*Havana Cuban Stars* (Rafael Almeida, Luis "Anguilla" Bustamante, José Figarola, Héctor "Kiko" Magriñat, Pedro Medina, Joseito Muñoz, Esteban Prats, Ezequiel Ramos).

1908—*Genuine Cuban Giants* (no native Cuban players on team roster). *Additional Individual Cuban Player:* José de la Caridad Méndez (Brooklyn Royal Giants).

1909—*Cuban Stars* (Luis "Anguilla" Bustamante, Antonio María García, Manuel "Miguel" Govantes, Ricardo "Chico" Hernández, Héctor "Kiko" Magriñat, José de la Caridad Méndez, Joseito Muñoz, Juan Luis "Mulo" Padrón, Agustín Parpetti, Eugenio Santa Cruz).

1910—*Cuban Stars* (Luis "Anguilla" Bustamante, Antonio María "El Inglés" García, Luis "Chico" González, Gervasio "Strike" González, Valentín "Sirique" González, Ricardo "Chico" Hernández, Héctor "Kiko" Magriñat, Jesús Menderos, Agustín "Tinti" Molina, Eugenio Morín, Juan Luis "Mulo" Padrón, Agustín Parpetti, Eustaquio "Bombín" Pedroso, Eugenio Santa Cruz). *Stars of Cuba*

(Armando Cabañas, Pelayo Chacón, José Figarola, Manuel "Miguel" Govantes, Juan Guerra, Heliodoro "Jabuco" Hidalgo, José de la Caridad Méndez, Joseito Muñoz, Héctor "Monk" Pareda, Pablo "Tony" Valdéz, Roberto "Bobby" Villa).

1911—*All Cubans* (Luis "Anguilla" Bustamante, Julián Castillo, Antonio María García, Héctor "Kiko" Magriñat, UNKNOWN Marlotica, Jesús Menderos, Francisco Morán, Eustaquio "Bombín" Pedroso, Jaime Rovira, Rogelio Valdés). *Cuban Stars* (Luis Bustamante*, Pelayo Chacón, José Figarola, Gervasio "Strike" González, Miguel Angel González, Ricardo "Chico" Hernández, Heliodoro "Jabuco" Hidalgo, Jesús Menderos*, José de la Caridad Méndez, Eugenio Morín, Juan Luis "Mulo" Padrón, Eustaquio "Bombín" Pedroso*, Roberto "Bobby" Villa). *Bombín Pedroso, Luis Bustamante and Jesús Menderos began season with All Cubans and later jumped to Cuban X Giants.

1912—*Cuban Stars* (Julián Castillo, Miguel Angel González, Adolfo Luque, José de la Caridad Méndez, Inocente Mendieta, Eustaquio "Bombín" Pedroso, UNKNOWN Ramos). *Additional Individual Cuban Player:* José de la Caridad Méndez (All Nations).

1913—*Cuban Stars* (Bernardo Baró, Luis "Anguilla" Bustamante, Pelayo Chacón, José Figarola, Heliodoro "Jabuco" Hidalgo, José Junco, Héctor "Kiko" Magriñat, Francisco Morán, Monk Pareda, Agustín Parpetti, Eustaquio "Bombín" Pedroso, Joseito Rodríguez, Cristóbal Torriente, Roberto "Bobby" Villa). *Long Branch Cubans* (Angel Aragón, Jacinto "Jack" Calvo, Gervasio "Strike" González, Miguel Angel González, Eustaquio Gutiérrez, UNKNOWN Henríquez, Adolfo Luque, Inocente Mendieta, Juan Luis "Mulo" Padrón, UNKOWN Ramos, UNKNOWN Villazón). *Additional Individual Cuban Player:* José de la Caridad Méndez (All Nations),

1914—*Cuban Stars* (Pelayo Chacón, José Figarola, Miguel Angel González, Ricardo "Chico" Hernández, José Junco, Héctor "Kiko" Magriñat, Francisco Morán, Monk Pareda, Eustaquio "Bombín" Pedroso, Joseito Rodríguez, Cristóbal Torriente, Roberto "Bobby" Villa). *Additional Individual Cuban Player:* José de la Caridad Méndez (All Nations).

1915—*Cuban Stars* (Tatica Campos, Pelayo Chacón, José Figarola, Bienvenido "Pata Jorobá" Jiménez, José Junco, Héctor "Kiko" Magriñat, Agustín "Tinti" Molina, Juan Luis "Mulo" Padrón, Monk Pareda, Agustín Parpetti, Eustaquio "Bombín" Pedroso, Hermán Ríos, Carlos Rodríguez, Joseito Rodríguez, Cristóbal Torriente, Roberto "Bobby" Villa). *Long Branch Cubans* (José Acosta, Jacinto "Jack" Calvo). *Additional Individual Cuban Players:* José de la Caridad Méndez (All Nations), Juan Luis "Mulo" Padrón (New York Lincoln Stars).

1916—*New York Cuban Stars* (Juan Armenteros, Julián Fabelo, José María Fernández, Rodolfo Fernández, Juan "Marcelino" Guerra, Agipito Lazaga, Bartolo Portuondo, Ramiro Ramírez, Julio Rojo, José Sánchez, UNKNOWN Suárez, UNKNOWN Tampos, Recurvón Terán). *Additional Individual Cuban Players:* UNKNOWN Ballesteros (Long Branch Cubans), UNKNOWN Baranda (Long

Branch Cubans), Miguel Angel González (New York Lincoln Stars), Ricardo "Chico" Hernández (All Nations), Ramón "Mike" Herrera (Jersey City Cubans, Long Branch Cubans), Fidelio Hungo (Long Branch Cubans), José de la Caridad Méndez (All Nations), Joseito Muñoz (New Jersey Cubans, Long Branch Cubans), Juan Luis "Mulo" Padrón (Cuban Stars of Havana), Tomás Romanach (Long Branch Cubans), UNKNOWN Torres (Long Branch Cubans), Cristobál Torriente (All Nations).

1917—*Cuban Stars East* (Pelayo Chacón, Benito Calderón, Julián Fabelo, José María Fernández, UNKNOWN León, Alejandro Oms, Agustín Parpetti, Ramiro Ramírez, Julio Rojo, Pancho Canilla Rivas, UNKNOWN Suárez). *Cuban Stars West* (Bernardo Baró, Tatica Campos, Gervasio "Strike" González, Juan "Marcelino" Guerra, Bienvenido "Pata Jorobá" Jiménez, José Junco, Juan Luis "Mulo" Padrón, Eustaquio "Bombín" Pedroso, Bartolo Portuondo, Hernán Ríos, Joseito Rodríguez). *Additional Individual Cuban Players:* UN-KNOWN Baranda (Jersey City Cubans), Julián Fabelo (Havana Cuban Stars), José de la Caridad Méndez (All Nations), Juan Luis "Mulo" Padrón (Chicago American Giants), Ramiro Ramírez (Havana Cuban Stars), Cristóbal Torriente (All Nations) UNKNOWN Valos (Cuban Giants).

1918—*Cuban Stars East* (UNKNOWN Alderette, UNKNOWN Baranda, UNKNOWN Barbette, Benito Calderón, Pelayo Chacón, Rogelio Crespo, Isidro Fabré, José María Fernández, Bienvenido "Pata Jorobá" Jiménez, Agipito Lazaga, UNKNOWN León, Eustaquio "Bombín" Pedroso, Cristóbal Torriente, Ramiro Ramírez, Pancho Canilla Rivas, Julio Rojo, Recurvón Terán). *Cuban Stars West* (Bernardo Baró, Tatica Campos, UNKNOWN Gaideria, Juan Guerra, José Junco, Bartolo Portuondo, Joseito Rodríguez, Roberto "Bobby" Villa). *Additional Individual Cuban Players:* José Figarola (Brooklyn Royal Giants), Juanelo Mirabal (Atlanta Black Crackers), José de la Caridad Méndez (Chicago American Giants), Cristóbal Torriente (Chicago American Giants).

1919—*Cuban Stars* (Eugenio Abreu, Bernardo Baró, Tatica Campos, Bienvenido "Pata Jorobá" Jiménez, José Junco, UN-KNOWN Lavera, Julio José LeBlanc, Eustaquio "Bombín" Pedroso, Bartolo Portuondo, Hernán Ríos, Roberto "Bobby" Villa). *Cuban Stars of Havana* (Pelayo Chacón, Rogelio Crespo, Benito Calderón, Valentín Dreke, José María Fernández, Gervasio "Strike" González, Miles Lucas, Juan Luis "Mulo" Padrón, Ramiro Ramírez, Julio Rojo, Recurvón Terán). *Additional Individual Cuban Players:* Juanelo Mirabal (Atlanta Black Crackers, Birmingham Black Barons), José de la Caridad Méndez (Detroit Stars), Bartolo Portuondo (All Nations), Joseito Rodríguez (Detroit Stars), Cristóbal Torriente (Chicago American Giants).

1920—*Cuban Stars East* (Tatica Campos, Pelayo Chacón, Julián Fabelo, Isidro Fabré, José María Fernández, Eugenio Jiménez, José Junco, Miles Lucas, Armando Massip, Juan Luis "Mulo" Padrón, Ramiro Ramírez, Tomás Romanach, Recurvón Terán). *Cuban Stars West* (Eufemio Abreu, Bernardo Baró, Valentín Dreke, Juan Guerra, José Hernández, Ramón "Mike" Herrera, Bienvenido "Pata Jorobá" Jiménez, Julio José LeBlanc, Cando López, Pasquel Martínez, Eustaquio "Bombín" Pedroso, Hernán Ríos, Pablo "Tony" Valdéz). *Additional Individual Cuban Players:* Eugenio Jiménez (Philadelphia Giants), Jesús Mederos (Atlantic City Bacharach Giants), José de la Caridad Méndez (Kansas City Monarchs), Juanelo Mirabal (Birmingham Black Barons), José Pérez (Madison Stars), Bartolo Portuondo (Kansas City Monarchs), Ramiro Ramírez (Brooklyn Royal Giants), Joseito Rodríguez (Kansas City Monarchs), Julio Rojo (Atlantic City Bacharach Giants), Cristóbal Torriente (Chicago American Giants).

1921—*All Cubans* (Tatica Campos, Isidro Fabré, José María Fernández, Oscar Levis, Pasquel Martínez, Pablo "Champion" Mesa, Alejandro Oms, Juan Luis "Mulo" Padrón, Eustaquio "Bombín" Pedroso, Ramiro Ramírez, José Ramos, Joseito Rodríguez, Felipe Sierra, Pedro Silva, Antonio Susini, Roberto "Bobby" Villa). *Cincinnati Cubans* (Eufemio Abreu, UNKNOWN Barcello, Bernardo Baró,

Lucas Boada, Valentín Dreke, Rodolfo Fernández, Juan Guerra, UN-KNOWN Guilleu, Ramón Herrera, Bienvenido "Pata Jorobá" Jiménez, Eugenio Jiménez, Julio José LeBlanc, Monk Pareda, Hernán Ríos). *Additional Individual Cuban Players:* Juanelo Mirabal (Birmingham Black Barons), José de la Caridad Méndez (Kansas City Monarchs), Agustín Parpetti (Kansas City Monarchs), Bartolo Portuondo (Kansas City Monarchs), Julio Rojo (Atlantic City Bacharach Giants), Cristóbal Torriente (Chicago American Giants).

1922—*Cuban Stars East* (Bernardo Baró, Tatica Campos, Pelayo Chacón, Julián Fabelo, Isidro Fabré*, José María Fernández, Pedro Ferrer, Bienvenido "Pata Jorobá" Jiménez, José Junco, Oscar Levis, Pablo "Champion" Mesa, Juanelo Mirabal, Alejandro Oms, Juan Luis "Mulo" Padrón, José Pérez, Recurvón Terán). *Cuban Stars West* (Lucas Boada, Valentín Dreke, Isidro Fabré*, José Hernández, Agipito Lazaga, Juan Guerra, Eugenio Morín, Eustaquio "Bombín" Pedroso, Hernán Ríos, Gonzalo Rodríguez, Joseíto Rodríguez, Felipe Sierra, Pedro Silva, Roberto "Bobby" Villa). *Additional Individual Cuban Players:* José de la Caridad Méndez (Kansas City Monarchs), Juan Luis "Mulo" Padrón (Chicago American Giants), Bartolo Portuondo (Kansas City Monarchs), Ramiro Ramírez (Atlantic City Bacharach Giants), Julio Rojo (Atlantic City Bacharach Giants), Cristóbal Torriente (Chicago American Giants). *Isidro Fabré began season with Cuban Stars East and finished up with Cuban Stars West.

1923—*Cuban Stars East* (Bernardo Baró, Pelayo Chacón, Martín Dihigo, Julián Fabelo, Isidro Fabré, José María Fernández, Oscar Levis, Vidal López, Armando Marsans, Pablo "Champion" Mesa, Juanelo Mirabal, Esteban "Mayarí" Montalvo, Alejandro Oms, Juan Luis "Mulo" Padrón, José Pérez, Bartolo Portuondo, Recurvón Terán). *Cuban Stars West* (Eufemio Abreu, Lucas Boada, Tatica Campos, Pedro Dibut, Valentín Dreke, Rodolfo Fernández, Juan Guerra, Eugenio Morín, Eustaquio "Bombín" Pedroso, UNKNOWN Rigal, Hernán Ríos, Joseíto Rodríguez, José Sierra). *Additional Individual Cuban Players:* José de la Caridad Méndez (Kansas City Monarchs), Juan Luis "Mulo" Padrón (Birmingham Black Barons), Agustín Parpetti (Atlantic City Bacharach Giants), Ramiro Ramírez (Baltimore Black Sox, Richmond Giants), Julio Rojo (Baltimore Black Sox), Cristóbal Torriente (Chicago American Giants).

1924—*Cuban Stars East* (Bernardo Baró, Lucas Boada, Benito Calderón, Pedro Cárdenas, Pelayo Chacón, Martín Dihigo, Oscar Estrada, José María Fernández, Isidro Fabré, Bienvenido "Pata Jorobá" Jiménez, Oscar Levis, Juanelo Mirabal, Pablo "Champion" Mesa, Alejandro Oms, Bartolo Portuondo, UNKNOWN Salvat). *Cuban Stars West* (Eufemio Abreu, Angel Alfonso, Raúl Alvarez, Valentín Dreke, Juan Guerra, Pasquel Martínez, Esteban "Mayarí" Montalvo, Eustaquio "Bombín" Pedroso, José Pérez, UNKNOWN Petricola, Hernán Ríos, Lázaro Sálazar, Felipe Sierra, Recurvón Terán, UNKNOWN Tevera). *Additional Individual Cuban Players:* José de la Caridad Méndez (Kansas City Monarchs), Juan Luis "Mulo" Padrón (Chicago American Giants), Julio Rojo (Baltimore Black Sox), Cristóbal Torriente (Chicago American Giants).

1925—*Cuban Stars East* (Bernardo Baró, Pedro Cárdenas, Pelayo Chacón, Martín Dihigo, Oscar Estrada, Isidro Fabré, José María Fernández, Pedro Ferrer, Sijo Gómez, Oscar Levis, Armando Massip, Pablo "Champion" Mesa, Juanelo Mirabal, Alejandro Oms, Bartolo Portuondo, UNKNOWN Salvat). *Cuban Stars West* (Eufemio Abreu, Angel Alfonso, Raúl Alvarez, Luis, Lucas Boada, UNKNOWN Domínguez, Valentín Dreke, Juan Eckelson, David Gómez, Pasquel Martínez, Esteban "Mayarí" Montalvo, Eustaquio "Bombín" Pedroso, José Pérez, Felipe Sierra). *Additional Individual Cuban Players:* José de la Caridad Méndez (Kansas City Monarchs), Juan Luis "Mulo" Padrón (Arango Chicago American Giants, Brooklyn Royal Giants), Julio Rojo (Baltimore Black Sox), Cristóbal Torriente (Chicago American Giants).

1926—*Cuban Stars East* (Bernardo Baró, Pedro Cárdenas, Pelayo Chacón, Rogelio Crespo, Martín Dihigo, Isidro Fabré, José María Fernández, Oscar Levis, Pablo "Champion" Mesa, Juanelo Mirabal,

Alejandro Oms, Eustaquio "Bombín" Pedroso, Bartolo Portuondo, Alejandro San Pedro). *Cuban Stars West* (Angel Alfonso, Luis Arango, Benito Calderón, Marcelino "Cuco" Correa, Eliodoro "Yoyo" Díaz, Valentín Dreke, Manuel "Cocaína" García, David Gómez, Luis Gutiérrez, Cando López, Juan Luis "Mulo" Padrón*, UNKNOWN Pedamonte, Basilio "Brujo" Rosell, Felipe Sierra). *Additional Individual Cuban Players:* José de la Caridad Méndez (Kansas City Monarchs), Juan Luis "Mulo" Padrón* (Indianapolis ABCs), Cristóbal Torriente (Kansas City Monarchs), José Pérez (Harrisburg Giants), Julio Rojo (Baltimore Black Sox). *Mulo Padrón appeared with both Cuban Stars West and Indianapolis ABCs.

1927 — *Cuban Stars East* (Angel Alfonso, Raúl Alvarez, Bernardo Baró, Pelayo Chacón, Rogelio Crespo, Martín Dihigo, Isidro Fabré, José María Fernández, Oscar Levis, Pablo "Champion" Mesa, Juanelo Mirabal, Alejandro Oms, Bartolo Portuondo, Conrado Rodríguez, UNKNOWN Saabin, Alejandro San Pedro). *Cuban Stars West* (Rogelio Alonso, Benito Calderón, Pedro Cárdenas, Marcelino "Cuco" Correa, Eliodoro "Yoyo" Díaz, Valentín Dreke, Manuel "Cocaína" García, David Gómez, Cando López, Eustaquio "Bombín" Pedroso, UNKNOWN Rigal, Basilio "Brujo" Rosell, Felipe Sierra). *Additional Individual Cuban Players:* Esteban Montalvo (New York Lincoln Giants), José Pérez (Harrisburg Giants), Julio Rojo (New York Lincoln Giants), Cristóbal Torriente (Detroit Stars).

1928 — *Cuban Stars East* (Angel Alfonso, Bernardo Baró, Agustín Bejerano, Ramón Bragaña, Isidro Fabré, José María Fernández, Ramón "Paito" Herrera, Oscar Levis, Juanelo Mirabal, Emilio Navarro, Alejandro Oms, José Pérez, Silvino Ruíz, Alejandro San Pedro, Miguel Solís). *Cuban Stars West* (Rogelio Alonso, UNKNOWN Borges, UNKNOWN Celada, Marcelino "Cuco" Correa, Aurelio Cortez, Eliodoro "Yoyo" Díaz, Valentín Dreke, UNKNOWN Estenza, Cundo Gálvez, Manuel "Cocaína" García, David Gómez, Bienvenido "Pata Jorobá" Jiménez, Cando López, Vidal López, Jesús Lorenzo, Pasqual Martínez, Carlos Martínez, José Martini, Esteban "Mayarí" Montalvo, Busta Quintana, Conrado Rodríguez, Jacinto "Battling Siki" Roque, Basilio "Brujo" Rosell, Felipe Sierra). *Additional Individual Cuban Players:* Benito Calderón (Homestead Grays), Martín Dihigo (Homestead Grays), Julio Rojo (New York Lincoln Giants), Cristóbal Torriente (Detroit Stars).

1929 — *Cuban Stars East* (Angel "Cuco" Alfonso, Bernardo Baró, Agustín Bejerano, Antonio Castro, Marcelino "Cuco" Correa, Isidro Fabré, José María Fernández, Willie Gisentaner, José "Sijo" Gómez, UNKNOWN Lamberto, Oscar Levis, Juanelo Mirabal, Emilio Navarro, José Pérez, José Ramos, Basilio "Brujo" Rosell, Silvino Ruíz, Miguel Solís). *Cuban Stars West* (Rogelio Alonso, UNKNOWN Bema, UNKNOWN Celada, Aurelio Cortez, Eliodoro "Yoyo" Díaz, Cundo Gálvez, Ramón Hernández, Bienvenido "Pata Jorobá" Jiménez, Cando López, Vidal López, Jesús Lorenzo, UNKNOWN Molina, Conrado Rodríguez, Jacinto "Battling Siki" Roque, Felipe Sierra, UNKNOWN Ventura). *Additional Individual Cuban Players:* Martín Dihigo (Hilldale Daisies), Julio Rojo (New York Lincoln Giants).

1930 — *Cuban Stars East* (Eufemio Abreu, Raúl Alvarez, Bernardo Baró, Ramón Bragaña, Tatica Campos, Pelayo Chacón, UNKNOWN Cruz, Martín Dihigo, Carlos Etchegoyen, Armando Massip, Alejandro Oms, Eustaquio "Bombín" Pedroso, Miguel Solís). *Cuban Stars West* (Angel Alonso, Rogelio Alonso, Marcelino Bauza, Aurelio Cortez, Pablo Díaz, Eliodoro "Yoyo" Díaz, Ramón Hernández, Cando López, Jesús Lorenzo, UNKNOWN Molina, Alcibiades Palma, Lázaro Salazar, Felipe Sierra, Luis Tiant, Sr.). *Additional Individual Cuban Players:* Bernardo Baró (Kansas City Monarchs), Martín Dihigo (Hilldale Daisies), José María Fernández (Chicago American Giants), Oscar Levis (Baltimore Black Sox), Julio Rojo (New York Lincoln Giants), Cristóbal Torriente (Gilkerson's Union Giants).

1931 — *Cuban Stars East* (Raúl Alvarez, Luis Arango, Pelayo Chacón, Aurelio Cortez, Pablo Díaz, Isidro Fabré, José María Fer-

nández, Manuel "Cocaína" García, Oscar Levis, Cando López, Armando Massip, Alejandro Oms, José Pérez, Jacinto "Battling Siki" Roque, Miguel Solís, Fermín Valdés). *Cuban Stars West* (Oscar Estrada, Carlos Etchegoyen, Pedro Lanuza, Ramiro Ramírez, Luis Tiant, Sr., Fermín "Strico" Valdés). *Additional Individual Cuban Players:* Martín Dihigo (Hilldale Daisies, Baltimore Black Sox), Oscar Estrada (Cuban House of David), Carlos Etchegoyen (Cuban House of David), Oscar Levis (Hilldale Daisies).

1932 — *Cuban Stars East* (Eufemio Abreu, Raúl Alvarez, Luis Arango, Pablo Díaz, Isidro Fabré, José María Fernández, Rodolfo Fernández, David Gómez, Oscar Levis, Cando López, Armando Massip, Juanelo Mirabal, Ismael "Mulo" Morales, Alejandro Oms, José Pérez, Felipe Sierra, Miguel Solís). *Cuban Stars West* (Marcelino "Cuco" Correa, Pablo Díaz, Carlos Etchegoyen, Cuneo "Cundo" Gálvez, Pedro Lanuza, Ramiro Ramírez, Jacinto "Battling Siki" Roque, Lázaro Salazar, UNKNOWN Soldero, Luis Tiant, Sr., Fermín "Strico" Valdés). *Additional Individual Cuban Players:* Rogelio Crespo (Union Giants), Carlos Etchegoyen (Cuban House of David), Pedro Lanuza (Cuban House of David), Armando Massip (Washington Pilots), Cristóbal Torriente (Atlanta Black Crackers, Cleveland Cubs), Fermín "Strico" Valdés (Atlanta Black Crackers).

1933 — *Cuban Stars East* (Raúl Alvarez, Juanelo Mirabal, Busta Quintana, Aniceto "Nene" Rivera, Carlos "Snooker" Rivero). *Cuban Stars* (Luis Arango, Marcelino "Cuco" Correa, Eliodoro "Yoyo" Díaz, Isidro Fabré, José María Fernández, Rodolfo Fernández, Manuel "Cocaina" García, Cando López, Alejandro Oms, José Pérez, Lázaro Salazar, Miguel Solís). *Additional Individual Cuban Players:* Rogelio Crespo (Union Giants), Javier "Blue" Pérez (Atlantic City Bacharach Giants).

1934 — *Cuban Stars East* (Eufemio Abreu, Isidro Fabré, José María Fernández, Rodolfo Fernández, Oscar Levis, Cando López, Armando Massip, Juanelo Mirabal, José Pérez, Ramiro Ramírez, Conrado Rodríguez, Lázaro Salazar, Miguel Solís). *Padrón's Cuban Giants* (no native Cuban players on team roster). *Additional Individual Cuban Players:* Javier "Blue" Pérez (Atlantic City Bacharach Giants), Busta Quintana (Newark Dodgers), Luis Tiant, Sr. (Cuban House of David).

1935 — *New York Cubans* (Luis Arango, Ramón Bragaña, Marcelino "Cuco" Correa, Eliodoro "Yoyo" Díaz, Martín Dihigo, José Mará Fernández, Rodolfo Fernández, Manuel "Cocaina" García, Enrique Lantigua, Cando López, José Martini, Alejandro Oms, José Pérez, Basilio "Brujo" Rosell, Lázaro Salazar, Anastacio "Tacho" Santaella, Luis Tiant, Sr., Fermín "Strike" Valdés). *Additional Individual Cuban Player:* Javier "Blue" Pérez (Brooklyn Eagles).

1936 — *New York Cubans* (Raúl Alvarez, Marcelino "Cuco" Correa, Félix "Fellé" Delgado, Eliodoro "Yoyo" Díaz, Martín Dihigo, José María Fernández, Manuel "Cocaina" García, Cando López, Armando Massip, Julio Rojo, Lázaro Salazar, Anastacio "Tacho" Santaella, Miguel Solís, Luis Tiant, Sr.). *Additional Individual Cuban Players:* Javier "Blue" Pérez (Newark Eagles), Ramiro Ramírez (New York Black Yankees).

1937 — No Cuban-named teams and only a single individual Cuban player appeared in U.S. Negro leagues for this season. *Cuban Individual Player:* Javier "Blue" Pérez (Homestead Grays).

1938 — No Cuban-named teams and only a single individual Cuban player appeared in U.S. Negro leagues for this season. *Cuban Individual Player:* Bernard Fernández (Atlanta Black Crackers).

1939 — *New York Cubans* (Luis Arango, Esteban Carabello, Isidro Fabré, José María Fernández, Rodolfo Fernández, Ramón Heredia, Justo López, Pedro López, Vidal López, Francisco Martínez, Antonio Mirabal, Pedro Pagés, Antonio Rodríguez, Héctor Rodríguez, Silvino Ruíz, Luis Tiant, Sr., Armando Torres, Fermín "Strico" Valdés). *Additional Individual Cuban Players:* Bernard Fernández (Jacksonville Red Caps), Carlos "Snooker" Rivero (Baltimore Elite Giants).

1940 — *New York Cubans* (Clemente "Sungo" Carrera, Alejandro Crespo, José María Fernández, José "Tito" Figueroa, Silvio García,

Ramón Heredia, Rogelio "Mantecado" Linares, Antonio Mirabal, Silvino Ruíz, UNKNOWN Sigenero, Luis Tiant, Sr.).

1941—*New York Cubans* (Blacedo Bernal, Carlos Blanco, Heberto Blanco, Clemente "Sungo" Carrcra, Carlos Colás, Félix "Fellé" Delgado, José María Fernández, Ramón Heredia, Alberto Hernández, Silvino Ruíz). *Additional Individual Cuban Player:* Carlos "Snooker" Rivero (Ethiopian Clowns).

1942—*New York Cubans* (Heberto Blanco, Martín Crue, José María Fernández, Javier Pérez, Silvino Ruíz).

1943—*New York Cubans* (Martín Crue*, Pedro "Manny" Díaz, José María Fernández, Rodolfo Fernández, Rogelio "Mantecado" Linares, Javier Pérez, Carlos "Snooker" Rivero, Luis Tiant, Sr.). *Additional Individual Cuban Player:* Martín Crue (Homestead Grays). *Martín Crue appeared with both New York Cubans and Homestead Grays.

1944—*New York Cubans* (Luis Rafael Cabrera, Claro Duany, José María Fernández, Rodolfo Fernández, Rogelio "Mantecado" Linares, Javier Pérez, Carlos "Snooker" Rivero, Héctor Rodríguez, Luis Tiant, Sr.). *Additional Individual Cuban Players:* Luis Rafael Cabrera (Cincinnati-Indianapolis Clowns), Lazarus Medina (Cincinnati-Indianapolis Clowns), Carlos "Snooker" Rivero (New York Black Yankees), Fermín "Strico" Valdés (Cincinnati-Indianapolis Clowns), Armando Vasquez (Cincinnati-Indianapolis Clowns).

1945—*New York Cubans* (Luis Rafael Cabrera, Martín Dihigo, José María Fernández, Ramón Heredia, Rogelio "Mantecado" Linares, Orestes "Minnie" Miñoso, Rafael Noble, Fernando Díaz "Bicho" Pedroso, Javier Pérez, Santos Salazar, Luis Tiant, Sr.). *Additional Individual Cuban Players*: Avelino Cañizares (Cleveland Buckeyes), Sal "Chico" Hernández (Indianapolis Clowns), Lazarus Medina (Cincinnati-Indianapolis Clowns), Raúl Navarro (Cincinnati-Indianapolis Clowns), Armando Vasquez (Cincinnati Clowns).

1946—*New York Cubans* (Luis Rafael Cabrera, Francisco Campos, Alejandro Crespo, Martín Crue, José María Fernández, Silvio García, Rogelio "Mantecado" Linares, Orestes "Minnie" Miñoso, Rafael Noble, Oliverio Ortiz, Fernando Díaz "Bicho" Pedroso, Santos Salazar, Luis Tiant, Sr.), Armando Vasquez (Indianapolis Clowns). *Additional Individual Cuban Players:* Bernardo Fernández (Pittsburgh Crawfords), Lazarus Medina (Indianapolis Clowns), Raúl Navarro (Indianapolis Clowns).

1947—*New York Cubans* (Homero Ariosa, Lorenzo "Chiquitín" Cabrera, Luis Rafael Cabrera, Martín Crue, Lino Donoso, Claro Duany, José María Fernández, Silvio García, Orestes "Minnie" Miñoso, Rafael Noble, Pedro Pagés, Fernando Díaz "Bicho" Pedroso, Santos Salazar, Francisco Sostre, Luis Tiant, Sr.). *Additional Individual Cuban Players:* Ramón Bragaña (Cleveland Buckeyes), José Colás (Memphis Red Sox), Pedro Formental (Memphis Red Sox), Francisco Sostre (New York Black Yankees), Armando Vasquez (Indianapolis Clowns).

U.S. Negro leagues ceased to function as true major-league-level operation after organized baseball's limited racial integration began in 1946 (with Jackie Robinson in Montreal) and 1947 (Robinson with Brooklyn Dodgers).

Cuban-Born U.S. Negro League Players List

The following alphabetical listing of all Cubans (as accurately as can be determined) who played in the Negro leagues (1904–1947) includes positions (where they are known), years of service, and teams for which each player performed. Those Cubans who were light-skinned enough to pass as white ballplayers are indicated with an asterisk (*). Cuban Blacks who eventually played in the majors after 1947 are noted also (as #). Since Negro league statistics (especially for barnstorming games) are sketchy where they exist at all, no accurate reconstruction of career statistics is possible here. Brief sketches of many of the players are included in James A. Riley's *The Biographical Encyclopedia of the Negro Leagues* (1994) but — especially when it comes to the Cuban ballplayers — Riley often misspells names, bungles years of service, confuses one player under several different names, lists service with teams that did not exist in the indicated years, and repeats inaccurate hearsay anecdotes *ad nauseam*. In brief, Riley's player portraits, except for the most notable and familiar figures, are not a particularly useful or reliable source.

Eufemio Abreu (1919–1934) Positions: **catcher**, third base, outfield, first base, shortstop, pitcher. Teams: Cuban Stars West, Cuban Stars East.

José Acosta (*) (1915) Position: **pitcher**. Team: Long Branch Cubans.

Alderette (first name unknown) (1918) Position: **pitcher**. Team: Cuban Stars East.

Angel Alfonso (1924–1930) Positions: **shortstop**, second base, third base. Teams: Cuban Stars West, Cuban Stars East.

Rafael Almeida (*) (1904–1905) Position: **third base**. Team: All Cubans.

Rogelio Alonso (1925–1930) Positions: **pitcher**, outfielder. Team: Cuban Stars West.

Raúl Alvarez (1924–1933) Position: **pitcher**. Teams: Cuban Stars West, Cuban Stars East, Cuban Stars.

Angel Aragón (*) (1913) Positions: **second base**, shortstop. Team: Long Branch Cubans.

Luis (Pedro) Arango (1925–1939) Positions: **third base**, first base, shortstop. Teams: Cuban Stars West, Cuban Stars, New York Cubans

Mario (Homero) Ariosa (1947) Positions: **outfield**, second base, third base. Team: New York Cubans.

Juan Armenteros (1916). Position: **pitcher**. Team: New York Cuban Stars.

Ballesteros (*) (first name unknown) (1916) Position: **pitcher**. Team: Long Branch Cubans.

Baranda (first name unknown) (1916–1918) Positions: **third base**, outfield, first base. Teams: Long Branch Cubans, Jersey City Cubans, Cuban Stars East.

Barbette (first name unknown) (1918) Position: **first base**. Team: Cuban Stars East.

Barcello (first name unknown) (1921) Position: **pitcher**, catcher. Team: Cincinnati Cubans.

Bernardo Baró (1913–1930) Positions: **outfield**, first base, pitcher, catcher. Teams: Cuban Stars West, Cuban Stars East, Kansas City Monarchs.

Marcelino Bauza (1930) Position: **shortstop**. Team: Cuban Stars West.

Agustín Bejerano (1928–1929) Position: **outfield**. Team: Cuban Stars East.

Bema (first name unknown) (1929) Position: **pinch hitter**. Team: Cuban Stars West.

Blacedo (Sleepy) Bernal (1941) Position: **pitcher**. Team: New York Cubans.

Carlos Blanco (1938–1941) Positions: **first base**, third base. Teams: Cuban Stars, New York Cubans.

Heberto Blanco (1941–1942) Positions: **second base**, shortstop, outfield. Team: New York Cubans.

Lucas Boada (1921–1925) Positions: **pitcher**, outfield, first base, third base. Teams: Cuban Stars West, Cuban Stars East.

José Borges (1904–1905) Position: **second base**. Team: All Cubans.

Borges (first name unknown) (1928) Positions: **shortstop**, second base, third base. Team: Cuban Stars West.

Ramón Bragaña (1928–1947) Positions: **pitcher**, outfield. Teams: Cuban Stars East, Stars of Cuba, New York Cubans, Cleveland Buckeyes.

Luis (Anguilla) Bustamante (1904–1913) Positions: **shortstop**, second base, third base, outfield. Teams: All Cubans, Cuban Stars.

Armando Cabañas (1910) Positions: **second base**, first base, outfield. Team: Stars of Cuba.

Alfredo (Pájaro) Cabrera (1905). Positions: **first base**, shortstop. Team: All-Cubans.

Lorenzo (Chiquitín) Cabrera (1947). Position: **first base**. Team: New York Cubans.

Luis Rafael Cabrera (1944–1947) Position: **pitcher**. Teams: Cincinnati-Indianapolis Clowns, New York Cubans.

Calderin (first name unknown) (1917–1919, 1924) Positions: **pitcher**, right field. Teams: Cuban Stars East, Cuban Stars of Havana. **Note:** The player listed under this name by Riley (and others) was most likely actually **Benito Calderón** (below), whose name was misspelled in the North American press. An assumption is made in the above year-by-year listing of players that **Calderin** and **Calderón** are indeed one and the same player.

Benito Calderón (1926–1928) Positions: **catcher**, third base, pitcher. Teams: Cuban Stars West, Homestead Grays.

Jacinto (Jack) Calvo (*) (1913, 1915) Position: **outfielder**. Team: Long Branch Cubans.

Tatica Campos (1915–1930) Positions: **pitcher**, outfield, infield, catcher. Teams: Cuban Stars West, Cuban Stars East, Cuban Stars.

Francisco Campos (*) (1946) Position: **outfielder**. Team: New York Cubans.

Avelino Canizares (1945) Position: **shortstop**. Team: Cleveland Buckeyes.

Esteban (Esterio) Carabello (1939) Position: **right field**. Team: New York Cubans.

Pedro Cárdenas (1924–1927) Positions: **catcher**, outfield, first base. Teams: Cuban Stars East, Cuban Stars West.

Clemente (Sungo) Carrera (1940–1941) Positions: **second base**, outfield, third base. Team: New York Cubans.

Julián Castillo (1904–1905, 1911–1912) Positions: **first base**, pitcher. Teams: All Cubans, Cuban Stars.

Antonio Castro (1929) Position: **catcher**. Team: Cuban Stars East.

Celada (first name unknown) (1928–1929) Positions: **shortstop**, third base. Team: Cuban Stars West.

Pelayo Chacón (1909–1931) Positions: **shortstop**, second base, outfield. Teams: Stars of Cuba, Cuban Stars West, Cuban Stars East, Cuban Stars,

Carlos Colás (1941) Positions: **catcher**, outfield. Team: New York Cubans. (Brother of José Colás)

José Colás (1947) Position: **center field**. Team: Memphis Red Sox. (Brother of Carlos Colás)

Marcelino (Cuco) Correa (1926–1929, 1932–1933, 1935–1936) Positions: **shortstop**, left field, second base. Teams: Cuban Stars West, Cuban Stars East, New York Cubans.

Aurelio Cortez (1928–1931) Positions: **catcher**, first base. Teams: Cuban Stars West, Cuban Stars East.

Alejandro Crespo (1940, 1946) Position: **left field**. Team: New York Cubans.

Rogelio Crespo (1918–1933) Positions: **second base**, third base. Teams: Cuban Stars East, Cuban Stars of Havana, Union Giants.

Martín (Matty) Crue (1942–1943, 1946–1947) Positions: **pitcher**. Teams: New York Cubans, Homestead Grays.

Cruz (first name unknown) (1930) Position: **pitcher**. Team: Cuban Stars East.

Félix (Fellé) Delgado (1936, 1941) Positions: **outfield**, first base. Team: New York Cubans.

Angel D'Meza (1905) Position: **pitcher**. Team: All Cubans.

Eliodoro (Yoyo) Díaz (1926–1930, 1935–1936) Positions: **pitcher**, outfield, first base, catcher. Teams: Cuban Stars West, Cuban Stars, New York Cubans.

Pablo Díaz (1930–1932) Positions: **catcher**, first base. Teams: Cuban Stars West, Cubans Stars East.

Pedro (Manny) Díaz (1943) Position: **pitcher**. Team: New York Cubans.

Pedro Dibut (*) (1923) Position: **pitcher**. Team: Cuban Stars West.

Martín Dihigo (1923–1945) Positions: **pitcher, second base**, outfield, first base, third base, shortstop. Teams: Cuban Stars East, Homestead Grays, Hilldale Daisies, Baltimore Black Sox, New York Cubans.

Domínguez (first name unknown) (1925) Positions: **pitcher**, right field, third base. Team: Cuban Stars West.

Lino Donoso (*) (1947) Position: **pitcher**. Team: New York Cubans.

Valentín Dreke (1918–1928) Positions: **center field**, left field. Teams: Cuban Stars West, Cuban Stars of Havana.

Claro Duany (1944, 1947) Positions: **right field**, left field. Team: New York Cubans.

Juan Eckelson (1925) Position: **pitcher**. Team: Cuban Stars West.

Oscar Estrada (*) (1924–1925, 1931) Positions: **pitcher**, outfield, first base. Teams: Cuban Stars East, Cuban House of David.

Carlos Etchegoyen (1930–1932) Positions: **catcher**, third base, outfield. Teams: Cuban Stars East, Cuban House of David.

Julián Fabelo (1916–1923) Positions: **shortstop**, infield, outfield. Teams: Cuban Stars East, New York Cuban Stars, Havana Cuban Stars, Cuban Stars West.

Isidro Fabré (1918–1939) Positions: **pitcher**, outfield, first base. Teams: Cuban Stars East, All-Cubans, Cuban Stars, New York Cubans.

Bernard Fernández (1938–1939, 1946) Position: pitcher. Teams: Atlanta Black Crackers, Jacksonville Red Caps, Pittsburgh Crawfords.

José María Fernández (1916–1936, 1939–1947) Positions: **catcher**, first base, outfield. Teams: New York Cuban Stars, Cuban Stars East, Chicago American Giants, New York Cubans.

Rodolfo Fernández (1916, 1923) Position: **pitcher**. Teams: New York Cuban Stars, Cuban Stars West.

Rodolfo (Rudy) Fernández (1932–36, 1939, 1943) Position: **pitcher**. Teams: Cuban Stars East, Cuban Stars, New York Cubans.

Pedro Ferrer (1922–1925) Position: **second base**. Team: Cuban Stars East.

José Figarola (1904–1918) Positions: **catcher**, first base. Teams: All Cubans, Stars of Cuba, Cuban Stars, Brooklyn Royal Giants.

Pedro Formental (1947) Position: **outfield**. Team: Memphis Red Sox.

Gaideria (first name unknown) (1918) Position: **pitcher**. Team: Cuban Stars West.

Cuneo (Cundo) Gálvez (1928–1930, 1932) Position: **pitcher**. Teams: Cuban Stars West.

Antonio María (El Inglés) García (1905–1906, 1909–1912) Positions: **catcher**, first base, outfield. Teams: All Cubans, Cuban X Giants, Cuban Stars.

Mamelo García (1904) Position: **catcher**, outfield. Team: All Cubans.

Manuel (Cocaína) García (1926–1931, 1933, 1935–1936) Positions: **pitcher**, outfield, infield, catcher. Teams: Cuban Stars West, Cuban Stars, New York Cubans.

Regino García (1905) Position: **catcher**. Team: All Cubans.

Silvio García (1940, 1946–1947) Positions: **shortstop**, third base, outfield, pitcher, second base. Team: New York Cubans.

David Gómez (1925–1928) Position: **pitcher**, outfield, third base, first base. Team: Cuban Stars West.

José (Sijo) Gómez (1929) Positions: **pitcher**, catcher. Team: Cuban Stars East.

Gervasio (Strike) González (1910–1911, 1913, 1917) Positions: **catcher**, first base. Teams: Cuban Stars, Long Branch Cubans.

Luis (Chico) González (1910) Position: **pitcher**. Team: Cuban Stars.

Miguel Angel (Mike) González (*) (1911–1914, 1916) Positions: catcher, first base, outfield. Teams: Cuban Stars, Long Branch Cubans, New York Lincoln Stars.

Valentín (Sirique) González (1910) Position: **infield**. Team: Cuban Stars.

Manuel Govantes (1909–1910) Positions: **second base**, third base, outfield. Teams: Cuban Stars, Stars of Cuba.

Juan (Marcelino) Guerra (1910, 1916–1924) Positions: **first base**, outfield, catcher. Teams: Stars of Cuba, New York Cuban Stars, Cuban Stars West.

Luis Gutiérrez (1926–1927) Position: **right field**. Cuban Stars West.

Eustaquio Gutiérrez (1913) Position: **utility**. Team: Long Branch Cubans.

Henríquez (first name unknown) (1913) Position: **first base**. Team: Long Branch Cubans.

Ramón Heredia (1939–1941, 1945) Position: **third base**, shortstop, second base, first base, outfield. Team: New York Cubans.

Alberto Hernández (1941) Position: **outfield**. Team: New York Cubans.

Sal (Chico) Hernández (*) (1945) Position: **catcher**. Team: Indianapolis Clowns.

José Hernández (1920, 1922) Positions: **pitcher**, outfield. Teams: Cuban Stars West.

Ramón Hernández (1929–1930) Position: **third base**. Team: Cuban Stars West.

Ricardo (Chico) Hernández (1909–1911, 1914, 1916) Positions: **third base**, second base, outfield. Teams: Cuban Stars, All Nations.

Ramón (Mike) Herrera (*) (1916, 1920–1921, 1925–1926) Positions: **second base**, third base, shortstop. Teams: Jersey City Cubans, Long Branch Cubans, Cuban Stars West.

Heliodoro (Jabuco) Hidalgo (1905, 1910–1913) Positions: **outfield**, third base. Teams: All Cubans, Stars of Cuba, Cuban Stars.

Fidelio Hungo (1916) Position: **first base**. Team: Long Branch Cubans.

Bienvenido (Pata Jorobá) Jiménez (1915, 1917–1924, 1928–1929) Positions: **second base**, third base. Teams: Cuban Stars, Cuban Stars West, Cuban Stars East.

Eugenio Jiménez (1920–1921) Position: **left field**, right field. Teams: Cuban Stars East, Philadelphia Giants, Cincinnati Cubans.

José Junco (1913–1915, 1919–1922) Positions: **pitcher**, outfield. Teams: Cuban Stars, Cuban Stars East.

Lamberto (first name unknown) (1929) Position: **outfield**. Team: Cuban Stars East.

Enrique Lantiqua (1935) Position: **catcher**. Team: New York Cubans.

Pedro Lanuza (1931–1932) Position: **catcher**. Teams: Cuban Stars West, Cuban House of David.

Lavera (first name unknown) (1919) Position: **catcher**. Team: Cuban Stars.

Agipito Lazaga (1916, 1918, 1922) Positions: **right field**, left field, first base, pitcher. Teams: New York Cuban Stars, Cuban Stars East.

Julio (José) LeBlanc (1919–1921) Positions: **pitcher**, outfield. Team: Cuban Stars West.

León (first name unknown) (1917–1918) Positions: **outfield**, pitcher, catcher. Team: Cuban Stars East.

Oscar Levis (1921–1932) Positions: **pitcher**, outfield. Teams: Cuban Stars East, Baltimore Black Sox, Hilldale Daisies, All Cubans.

Rogelio (Mantecado) Linares (1940, 1943–1946) Positions: **first base**, center field, left field, right field. Teams: New York Cubans.

Candor (Cando) López (1920, 1926–1935) Positions: **center field**, left field, second base, third base, shortstop. Teams: Cuban Stars West, New York Cubans.

Justo López (1939) Position: **first base**. Team: New York Cubans.

Pedro López (1939) Position: **center field**, left field. Team: New York Cubans.

Vidal López (1923–1924, 1928–1929) Position: **pitcher**. Teams: Cuban Stars East, Cuban Stars West.

Jesús Lorenzo (1928–1930) Positions: **pitcher**, first base, right field. Team: Cuban Stars West.

Adolfo (Dolf) Luque (*) (1912–1913) Positions: **pitcher**, outfield, third base. Teams: Cuban Stars, Long Branch Cubans.

Héctor (Kiko) Magriñat (1909–1911, 1913–1915) Position: **left field**. Teams: Cuban Stars, All Cubans.

Marlotica (first name unknown) (1911) Position: **right field**. Team: All Cubans.

Armando Marsans (*) (1905, 1923) Positions: **outfield**, first base. Teams: All Cubans, Cuban Stars East.

Carlos Martínez (1928) Position: **catcher**. Team: Cuban Stars West.

Francisco Martínez (1939) Position: **pitcher**. Team: New York Cubans.

Pasquel Martínez (1920–1925, 1928) Position: **pitcher**. Teams: Cuban Stars West, All Cubans.

José Martini (1928) Position: **pitcher**. Team: Cuban Stars West.

Armando Massip (1920, 1925, 1930–1932, 1934) Positions: **first base**, outfield. Teams: Cuban Stars East, Washington Pilots.

Jesús Mederos (1910–1911, 1920) Positions: **pitcher**, outfield. Teams: Cuban Stars, All Cubans, Atlantic City Bacharach Giants.

Lazarus Medina (1944–1946) Position: **pitcher**. Teams: Cincinnati-Indianapolis Clowns, Indianapolis Clowns.

José de la Caridad Méndez (1908–1926) Positions: **pitcher**, shortstop, second base, third base, outfield. Teams: Brooklyn Royal Giants, Cuban Stars, Stars of Cuba, All Nations, Chicago American Giants, Detroit Stars, Kansas City Monarchs.

Inocente Mendieta (1912–1913) Positions: **second base**, outfield. Teams: Cuban Stars, Long Branch Cubans.

Pablo (Champion) Mesa (1921–1927) Position: **outfield**. Team: Cuban Stars East.

Orestes (Minnie) Saturnino Miñoso (#) (1945–1948) Position: **third base**. Team: New York Cubans.

Antonio Mirabal (1939–1940) Positions: **second base**, catcher, right field. Team: New York Cubans.

Juanelo Mirabal (1918–1934) Position: **pitcher**. Teams: Atlanta Black Crackers, Birmingham Black Barons, Cuban Stars East, New York Cubans.

Agustín (Tinti) Molina (1910) Positions: **first base**, outfield, catcher, pitcher. Teams: Cuban Stars.

Esteban (Mayarí) Montalvo (1923–1928) Positions: **right field**, first base, left field, pitcher. Teams: Cuban Stars East, Cuban Stars West, New York Lincoln Giants.

Ismael "Mulo" Morales (1932) Position: **outfield**. Team: Cuban Stars East.

Francisco Morán (1911, 1913–1914) Positions: **outfield**, third base. Teams: All Cubans, Cuban Stars.

Eugenio Morín (1910–1911, 1922–1923) Positions: **third base**, infield, catcher. Teams: Cuban Stars, Cuban Stars West.

Joseito (José) Muñoz (1904–1905, 1907–1910, 1916) Positions: **pitcher**, left field, center field. Teams: All Cubans, Cuban Stars, Stars of Cuba, New Jersey Cubans, Long Branch Cubans.

Emilio Navarro (1928–1929) Positions: **outfield**, infield. Team: Cuban Stars East.

Raúl Navarro (1945–1946) Positions: **outfield**, infield, catcher. Teams: Cincinnati-Indianapolis Clowns, Indianapolis Clowns.

Rafael (Ray) Noble (#) (1945–1947) Position: **catcher**. Team: New York Cubans.

Alejandro Oms (1917, 1922–1932, 1935) Positions: **outfield**, pitcher. Teams: Cuban Stars East, All Cubans, New York Cubans.

Juan Luis (Mulo) Padrón (1909–1926) Positions: **pitcher**, second base, outfield, third base. Teams: Cuban Stars, Long Branch

Cubans, New York Lincoln Stars, Chicago American Giants, New York Lincoln Giants, All Cubans, Birmingham Black Barons, Cuban Stars East, Brooklyn Royal Giants, Indianapolis ABCs, Cuban Stars West, Cuban Stars of Havana.

Pedro (El Gamo) Pagés (1939, 1947) Positions: **outfield**, first base. Team: New York Cubans.

Alcibiades Palma (1930) Position: **pitcher**. Team: Cuban Stars West.

Emilio Palmero (*) (1904–1905) Position: **outfield**. Team: All Cubans.

Héctor (Monk) Pareda (1910, 1914–1915, 1921) Positions: **pitcher**, first base. Teams: Stars of Cuba, Cuban Stars, Cuban Stars West.

Agustín Parpetti (1909–1910, 1913–1917, 1921–1923) Positions: **first base**, outfield. Teams: Cuban Stars, Cubans Stars East, Kansas City Monarchs, Atlantic City Bacharach Giants.

Pedamonte (first name unknown) (1926) Positions: **pitcher**, third base, outfield. Team: Cuban Stars West.

Eustaquio (Bombín) Pedroso (1910–1930) Positions: **pitcher**, right field, first base, catcher, shortstop. Teams: Cuban Stars West, All Cubans, Cuban Stars East.

Fernando Díaz (Bicho) Pedroso (1945–1947) Positions: **second base**, shortstop, outfield, third base. Team: New York Cubans.

Julián "Fallenca" Pérez (1906) Position: **pitcher**. Team: Cuban X Giants.

Javier (Blue) Pérez (1933–1945) Positions: **third base**, second base, outfield, first base. Teams: Atlantic City Bacharach Giants, New York Cubans, Brooklyn Eagles, Newark Eagles, Homestead Grays.

José (Pepin) Pérez (1920, 1922–1934) Positions: **first base**, infield, catcher, pitcher. Teams: Madison Stars, Cuban Stars West, Cuban Stars East, Harrisburg Giants.

Petricola (first name unknown) (1924) Position: **pitcher**. Team: Cuban Stars West.

Bartolo Portuondo (1916–1927) Positions: **first base**, second base, third base, catcher, left field. Teams: New York Cuban Stars, Cuban Stars, Cuban Stars East, Cuban Stars West, All Nations, Kansas City Monarchs.

Busta Quintana (1928–1934) Positions: **second base**, third base, shortstop. Teams: Cuban Stars West, Cuban Stars East, Newark Dodgers.

Ramiro Ramírez (1916–1936) Positions: **outfield**, second base. Teams: New York Cuban Stars, Cuban Stars East, Havana Cuban Stars, Brooklyn Royal Giants, All Cubans, Atlantic City Bacharach Giants, Baltimore Black Sox, Richmond Giants, Cuban Stars West, New York Black Yankees.

Ramos (first name unknown) (1912–1913) Positions: **pitcher**, first base, outfield. Teams: Cuban Stars, Long Branch Cubans.

José (Cheo) Ramos (1921–1929) Positions: **outfield**, third base. Teams: All Cubans, Cuban Stars East.

Rigal (first name unknown) (1923, 1927) Positions: **shortstop**, third base. Team: Cuban Stars West.

Hernán Ríos (1915–1924) Positions: **third base**, shortstop. Teams: Cuban Stars West, Havana Stars.

Pancho Canilla Rivas (1917–1918) Positions: **third base**, second base. Team: Cuban Stars East.

Aniceto (Nené) Rivera (1933) Position: **pitcher**, infield. Team: Cuban Stars East.

Carlos (Snooker) Rivero (1933, 1939–1944) Position: **shortstop**, second base, third base. Teams: Cuban Stars, Baltimore Elite Giants, Ethiopian Clowns, New York Cubans, New York Black Yankees.

Antonio Rodríguez (1939) Position: **pitcher**. Team: New York Cubans.

Héctor Rodríguez (1939, 1944) Positions: **third base**, shortstop. Team: New York Cubans.

Carlos Rodríguez (1915) Position: **pitcher**. Team: Cuban Stars.

Conrado Rodríguez (1922, 1927–1929) Positions: **pitcher**,

outfield, second base, third base. Teams: Cuban Stars West, Cuban Stars East.

José (Joseito) Rodríguez (1913–1923) Positions: **catcher**, first base, second base, shortstop. Teams: Cuban Stars, Cuban Stars West, Detroit Stars, Kansas City Monarchs, All Cubans.

Julio Rojo (1916–1930) Positions: **catcher, pitcher**, first base, third base, outfield. Teams: New York Cuban Stars, Havana Stars, Cuban Stars East, Atlantic City Bacharach Giants, Baltimore Black Sox, New York Lincoln Giants)

Tomás Romanach (1916, 1920) Position: **shortstop**. Teams: Long Branch Cubans, Cuban Stars East.

Jacinto (Battling Siki) Roque (1928–1929, 1931–1932) Positions: **outfield**, pitcher, catcher. Team: Cuban Stars West, Cuban Stars East.

Basilo (Brujo) Rosell (1926–1929) Positions: **pitcher**, first base. Teams: Cuban Stars West, Cuban Stars East.

Jaime Rovira (1911) Position: **third base**. Team: All Cubans.

Silvino (Poppa) Ruíz (1928–1929, 1938–1942) Position: **pitcher**. Teams: Cuban Stars East. New York Cubans.

Saabin (first name unknown) (1927) Position: **pitcher**. Team: Cuban Stars East.

Lázaro Salazar (1924–1936) Positions: **outfield**, pitcher, first base. Teams: Cuban Stars West, New York Cubans.

Santos Salazar (1946–1947) Positions: **second base**, shortstop. Team: New York Cubans.

Salvat (first name unknown) (1924–1925) Position: **pitcher**. Team: Cuban Stars East.

Alejandro (Eli) San Pedro (1926–1928) Position: **pitcher**. Team: Cuban Stars East.

Gonzálo Sánchez (1904–1905) Position: **catcher**. Team: All Cubans.

José Sánchez (1916) Position: **utility**. Team: New York Cuban Stars.

Eugenio Santa Cruz (1909–1910) Position: **center field**. Team: Cuban Stars.

Anastacio (Tacho) Santaella (1935–1936) Positions: **second base**, shortstop, third base, outfield. Team: New York Cubans.

Felipe Sierra (1921–1932) Positions: **second base**, infield, first base, outfield. Teams: All Cubans, Cuban Stars West.

Sigenero (first name unknown) (1940) Position: **pitcher**. Team: New York Cubans.

Pedro Silva (1921–1922) Positions: **pitcher**, outfield, first base. Teams: All Cubans, Cuban Stars West.

Soldero (first name unknown) (1932) Position: **pitcher**. Team: Cuban Stars West.

Miguel Solís (1928–1934) Positions: **third base**, second base. Team: Cuban Stars East.

Francisco Sostre (1947) Position: **pitcher**. Teams: New York Black Yankees, New York Cubans.

Suárez (first name unknown) (1916–1917) Positions: **pitcher**, right field. Teams: New York Cuban Stars, Cuban Stars East.

Antonio Susini (1921) Positions: **second base**, shortstop. Team: All Cubans.

Tampos (first name unknown) (1916) Position: **first base**. Team: New York Cuban Stars.

Recurvón (Julián) Terán (1916–1924) Positions: **second base**, third base. Teams: Cuban Stars East, Cuban Stars West.

Tevera (first name unknown) (1924) Position: **second base**. Team: Cuban Stars West.

Luis Tiant, Sr. (1930–1947) Position: **pitcher**. Teams: Cuban Stars West, Cuban House of David, New York Cubans. (Father of Luis Tiant, Jr.)

Torres (first name unknown) (1916) Position: **catcher**. Team: Long Branch Cubans.

Armando Torres (1939) Position: **pitcher**. Team: New York Cubans.

Cristóbal Torriente (1913–1928) Positions: **outfield**, pitcher, third base, first base. Teams: Cuban Stars, All Nations, Chicago American Giants, Kansas City Monarchs, Detroit Stars, Gilkerson's Union Giants, Atlanta Black Crackers, Cleveland Cubs.

Fermín (Strico) Valdés (1931–1944) Positions: **second base**, shortstop, pitcher. Teams: Cuban Stars West, Atlanta Black Crackers, New York Cubans, Cincinnati-Indianapolis Clowns.

Rogelio Valdés (1905–1906, 1911) Positions: **out field**, second base. Teams: All Cubans, Cuban X Giants.

Pablo (Tony) Valdéz (1910, 1920) Positions: **outfield**, first base, pitcher. Teams: Stars of Cuba, Cuban Stars West.

Valos (first name unknown) (1917) Position: **third base**. Team: Cuban Giants.

Armando Vasquez (1944–1948) Positions: **first base**, outfield, infield. Teams: Cincinnati-Indianapolis Clowns, Cincinnati Clowns, Indianapolis Clowns.

Ventura (first name unknown) (1929) Position: **pitcher**. Team: Cuban Stars West.

Roberto (Bobby) Villa (1910–1922) Positions: **pitcher**, right field, left field, second base, shortstop. Teams: Stars of Cuba, Cuban Stars West, All Cubans.

Villazón (first name unknown) (1913) Positions: **pitcher**, utility. Team: Long Branch Cubans.

* * *

All-Time Career Batting Statistics for African-Americans in the Cuban League

These statistics for U.S. Blacks compiled during Cuban League seasons are drawn largely from the ongoing research by Severo Nieto (veteran Havana sportswriter and baseball historian) and Jorge Figueredo (who left Cuba in the 1960s and now resides in Tampa, Florida); data has been amended where possible by my own investigation and cross-checking of available Cuban sources. **Symbols Key:** NA = No statistics now available for this category; ** = player also served as major leaguer; * = player also U.S. Negro league star performer; **Boldface** indicates incomplete (only partial) statistics for this category.

Player (Cuban Seasons)	AB	R	H	2B	3B	HR	RBI	B.A.
Newton Allen (1924–1938)	223	20	62	5	3	1	**25**	.278
Toussaint Allen (1920–1921)	9	1	2	0	0	0	NA	.222
George Altman (1959–1960)**	219	41	55	5	1	14	32	.251
Jabo Andrews (1936–1937)	234	37	66	11	5	5	37	.282
Walter Ball (1908–1911)	**111**	**9**	**29**	**1**	**2**	**0**	NA	**.262**
Sam Bankhead (1937–1941)**	802	139	238	24	10	10	123	.297
Jess Barbour (1910–1916)	179	15	40	5	1	0	NA	.223
Marvin Barker (1935–1936)	141	12	39	3	4	0	10	.277
Pepper Bassett (1946–1947)	61	4	11	3	0	0	0	.180
Harry Bauchman (1915–1916)	56	5	12	0	0	0	NA	.214
"Cool Papa" Bell (1928–1941)*	569	131	166	30	16	10	NA	.292
Jerry Benjamin (1940–1941)	46	6	7	0	0	0	1	.152
Gene Benson (1947–1948)*	239	22	57	9	2	1	20	.238
Chas Blackwell (1920–1923)	95	11	30	2	4	1	NA	.316
Bob Boyd (1949–1957)**	647	85	194	21	6	9	79	.300
Phil Bradley (1908–1909)	70	8	18	0	1	0	NA	.257
John Brazelton (1915–1916)	11	1	0	0	0	0	NA	.000
Barney Brown (1935–1940)	**329**	**50**	**94**	**10**	**1**	**1**	33	**.286**
Larry Brown (1924–1931)	500	62	126	10	10	0	NA	.252
Ray (Jabao) Brown (1936–1948)*	**353**	**51**	**94**	**9**	**5**	**6**	64	**.266**
Willard Brown (1937–1938)**	55	5	8	1	0	0	3	.145
Harry Buckner (1907–1909)	98	9	25	3	4	0	NA	.255
Pee Wee Butts (1947–1948)	285	26	71	8	3	0	28	.246
Joe Caffie (1957–1958)**	104	7	23	4	1	0	3	.221
Roy Campanella (1943–1944)**	128	15	34	9	3	0	27	.266
Walter Canady (1926–1940)	142	17	32	6	1	0	NA	.225
Tank Carr (1926–1927)	125	21	52	NA	NA	NA	NA	.416
Billy Cash (1947–1948)	224	23	48	10	2	1	24	.214
John Cason (1924–1925)	28	1	8	0	0	0	NA	.286
Oscar Charleston (1920–1931)*	996	219	360	44	25	19	NA	.361
Thad Christopher (1936–1937)	51	5	10	3	0	0	7	.196
Dell Clark (1920–1921)	32	3	13	1	0	0	NA	.406
Robert Clarke (1929–1930)	19	3	6	1	0	0	NA	.316
James Clarkson (1947–1948)	106	12	21	5	0	1	14	.198
George Crowe (1953–1954)**	75	3	12	2	0	1	10	.160
Ray Dandridge (1937–1953)*	2129	269	601	**69**	**14**	**10**	187	.282
Lloyd Davenport (1943–1948)	907	113	249	34	12	1	74	.275
Johnny Davis (1946–1948)	297	29	83	**5**	4	**0**	19	.279
Walter Davis (1927–1928)	82	10	22	2	1	2	NA	.268
Rap Dixon (1929–1930)*	175	36	46	10	6	5	NA	.263

Player (Cuban Seasons)	AB	R	H	2B	3B	HR	RBI	B.A.
Eddie Douglass (1923–1925)	172	19	42	**3**	3	**1**	NA	.244
Solly Drake (1956–1957)**	770	125	200	24	12	11	59	.260
Ashby Dunbar (1908–1909)	133	21	41	4	2	1	NA	.308
Pete Duncan (1915–1916)	58	5	20	2	0	0	NA	.345
Frank Duncan (1923–1938)	604	83	164	**21**	14	1	NA	.272
Donald Eaddy (1959–1960)	266	37	68	7	1	6	24	.256
Frank Earle (1908–1909)	36	8	12	3	1	1	NA	.333
Mack Eggleston (1923–1924)	99	6	21	3	0	0	NA	.212
Buck Ewing (1929–1930)*	112	23	34	2	3	0	NA	.304
Hooks Foreman (1928–1929)	5	0	1	0	0	0	NA	.200
Billy Francis (1908–1913)	123	13	17	1	1	0	NA	.138
Jude Gans (1908–1916)	**188**	**40**	**64**	7	4	**0**	NA	**.340**
Jelly Gardner (1924–1925)	118	22	34	0	1	0	NA	.288
Josh Gibson (1937–1939)*	224	61	79	10	5	14	52	.353
George Giles (1930–1931)	50	6	13	0	0	0	NA	.260
Junior Gilliam (1948–1949)**	1	0	0	0	0	0	0	.000
Charles Grant (1907)	70	4	13	0	0	0	NA	.186
Leroy Grant (1912)	10	1	1	1	0	0	NA	.100
Bill Handy (1914–1915)	97	11	25	4	1	0	NA	.261
Nate Harris (1909–1910)	134	4	26	3	0	0	NA	.194
Vic Harris (1939–1940)	116	18	30	1	0	1	7	.259
John Hayes (1938–1939)	32	2	4	1	0	0	2	.125
Joe Hewitt (1920–1921)	16	1	4	0	0	0	0	.250
Pete Hill (1907–1916)*	661	158	203	9	16	2	NA	.307
Crush Holloway (1924–1929)	252	44	73	10	6	1	NA	.290
Sammy Hughes (1939–1940)	175	19	43	9	2	0	15	.246
Monte Irvin (1947–49)**	358	66	95	16	7	11	61	.266
Louis Jackson (1958–1959)	48	4	11	3	0	0	6	.229
Sam Jethroe (1947–1955)**	663	126	192	22	17	10	62	.290
Chappie Johnson (1907)	99	10	17	0	0	1	NA	.172
Grant Johnson (1907–1912)	549	116	175	11	8	4	NA	.319
Oscar Johnson (1923–1924)	55	10	19	4	1	1	NA	.345
Judy Johnson (1926–1931)*	386	55	129	16	5	2	NA	.334
Newt Joseph (1928–1930)*	**110**	**16**	**30**	2	3	1	NA	**.273**
Henry Kimbro (1939–1949)	942	181	277	24	13	1	77	.294
Clarence Lamar (1940–1941)	73	6	14	2	0	0	10	.192
Buck Leonard (1936–1949)*	236	35	67	7	1	3	33	.284
John "Pop" Lloyd (1908–1930)*	**1327**	**210**	**436**	45	33	5	NA	**.321**
Dick Lundy (1920–1931)*	876	146	299	**31**	10	6	NA	.341
Jimmie Lyons (1912)	118	19	34	5	4	0	NA	.288
Biz Mackey (1924–1925)*	152	29	47	11	5	0	NA	.309
Oliver Marcelle (1922–1930)*	**957**	**148**	**292**	24	12	6	NA	**.305**
Tully McAdoo (1915–1916)	50	5	10	1	0	0	NA	.200
Dan McClellan (1907)	42	5	6	0	1	0	NA	.143
Sam Mongin (1908–1909)	134	4	26	3	0	0	NA	.194
Bill Monroe (1907–1908)	123	30	41	2	2	1	NA	.333
Dobie Moore (1923–1924)	281	38	100	**9**	6	1	NA	.356
Dink Mothell (1930–1931)	47	8	9	0	2	0	NA	.191
Buck O'Neil (1946–1947)*	116	12	25	3	1	0	14	.216
Leonard Pearson (1946–1951)	1299	160	340	54	5	28	218	.261
Charles Peete (1956–1957)	39	5	5	1	0	0	3	.128
Jim Pendelton (1952–1953)**	227	33	66	9	3	6	30	.291
Art Pennington (1947–1948)	77	6	18	3	1	0	10	.234
Bill Perkins (1935–1941)	902	146	260	25	10	9	135	.288
Bruce Petway (1908–1916)*	385	43	81	7	0	0	NA	.210
Zack Pettus (1912)	92	17	25	1	2	0	NA	.272
Bill Pierce (1910–1912)	82	8	19	2	0	2	NA	.232
Spotwood Poles (1910–1915)*	383	79	122	9	12	1	NA	.319
Alex Radcliffe (1938–1939)	169	14	45	5	1	1	24	.266
Larry Raines (1957–1958)**	165	16	42	2	4	4	21	.255
Orville Riggins (1924–1930)	266	40	80	7	10	1	NA	.301
Curt Roberts (1955–1957)**	560	74	143	17	6	7	53	.255

Player (Cuban Seasons)	AB	R	H	2B	3B	HR	RBI	B.A.
Neil Robinson (1946–1947)	12	1	0	0	0	0	0	.000
Branch Russell (1928–1929)	114	24	35	2	3	1	NA	.307
Louis Santop (1912–1921)*	33	4	8	3	2	0	NA	.242
George Scales (1927–1930)	375	63	112	12	8	3	NA	.299
William Serrell (1945–1947)	342	44	92	**14**	**3**	**2**	**29**	.269
Harry Simpson (1954–1955)**	132	13	28	10	0	1	8	.212
Chino Smith (1926–1931)*	565	83	189	**35**	**14**	3	NA	.335
Milton Smith (1955–1959)	705	104	189	27	11	11	75	.268
Felton Snow (1939–1940)	166	14	37	1	2	0	22	.223
Clyde Spearman (1936–1940)	774	121	211	20	4	4	105	.273
Henry Spearman (1939–1940)	127	15	35	3	0	0	24	.276
Turkey Stearns (1924–1925)*	58	13	13	0	2	3	NA	.224
Edward Stone (1937–1948)	352	52	93	19	4	4	42	.264
Mule Suttles (1928–1940)*	460	65	128	14	5	12	NA	.278
Willie Tasby (1958–1960)**	397	45	99	14	0	11	38	.249
Clint Thomas (1923–1931)	697	135	216	**12**	**10**	**5**	NA	.310
Dave Thomas (1936–1937)	253	32	79	8	4	0	36	.312
Hank Thompson (1946–1947)**	789	148	252	31	24	12	126	.319
Quincy Trouppe (1944–1951)*	307	46	78	13	6	5	37	.254
Felix Wallace (1908–1912)	13	0	2	0	0	0	NA	.154
Frank Warfield (1922–1930)*	**583**	**123**	177	17	**8**	4	NA	**.304**
Jap Washington (1928–1929)	106	7	28	3	2	0	NA	.264
John Washington (1939–1941)	374	44	95	13	5	0	34	.254
Speck Webster (1914–1915)	106	12	35	5	2	0	NA	.330
Willie Wells (1928–1940)*	1099	189	352	47	20	16	**113**	.320
Edgar Wesley (1923–1924)	101	14	24	1	1	0	NA	.238
Chaney White (1927–1930)	337	59	117	6	6	2	NA	.347
Charles Williams (1924–1925)	112	21	26	5	0	0	NA	.232
Chester Williams (1939–1941)	362	35	108	7	3	0	47	.298
Clare Williams (1910–1911)	15	0	2	0	0	0	NA	.133
Harry Williams (1936–1939)	597	79	186	27	4	6	84	.312
Jesse Williams (1946–1947)	121	11	32	4	1	1	11	.264
John Williams (1935–1936)	180	16	51	11	2	3	25	.283
Marvin Williams (1947–48)	42	5	12	1	0	0	4	.286
Jud Wilson (1925–1936)	769	165	286	38	27	18	NA	.372
Bob Wilson (1952–1953)	225	28	61	7	2	5	22	.271
Ray Wilson (1907)	36	3	7	0	1	0	NA	.194
Bobby Winston (1908)	177	41	47	0	2	0	NA	.266
Parnell Woods (1947–1948)	62	5	16	1	1	0	5	.258
Tom Young (1930–1931)	7	2	4	1	0	0	NA	.571

All-Time Career Pitching Statistics for African-American Players in the Cuban League

These statistics are again based on research by Severo Nieto and Jorge Figueredo; with data amended where possible by my own investigation and cross-checking of available Cuban sources. **Symbols Key:** NA = No statistics now available for this category; ** = player also served as major leaguer; * = player also U.S. Negro league star performer; **Boldface** indicates incomplete (only partial) statistics for this category.

Player	Cuban Seasons	Years	G	GG	W-L	Pct.
Emery (Ace) Adams	1940–1941	1	14	3	2–6	.333
Cliff (Crooks) Allen	1929–1931	2	21	12	10–6	.625
Walter Ball	1908–1911	3	26	20	9–16	.360
Bud Barbee	1940–1941	1	9	5	3–6	.333
Dave (Impo) Barnhill*	1947–1950	3	54	30	23–19	.548
Cliff Bell	1927–1931	4	58	27	25–17	.595
Joe Black**	1950–1952	2	43	17	20–13	.606
John Branahan	1922–1923	1	3	0	0–1	.000
Chet Brewer*	1930–1931	1	6	3	2–2	.500
Barney Brown	1935–1940	4	59	21	16–23	.410
Dave (Lefty) Brown	1922–1925	3	**31**	**15**	17–12	.586
Ray (Jabao) Brown*	1936–1948	5	89	57	46–20	.696
Harry Buckner	1907–1909	2	12	7	1–7	.125

Player	Cuban Seasons	Years	G	GG	W–L	Pct.
Walter (Lefty) Calhoun	1940–1941	1	14	2	2–5	.286
Ernest (Spoon) Carter	1937–1938	1	4	0	1–2	.333
Phil Cockrell	1920–1921	1	2	0	0–0	.000
Andy (Lefty) Cooper	1923–1929	3	37	13	15–17	.469
Willie (Sug) Cornelius	1939–1940	1	10	2	3–2	.600
Harry Cozart	1939–1940	1	4	0	0–1	.000
Reuben (Rube) Currie	1923–1924	1	11	6	10–5	.667
John Davis	1908	1	1	0	0–1	.000
Leon Day#	1937–1948	2	19	7	8–4	.667
William (Dizzy) Dismukes*	1914–1916	2	7	2	0–4	.000
Charles (Pat) Dougherty	1912	1	2	1	0–2	.000
Ed Dudley	1925–1926	1	13	6	2–6	.250
Louis Dula	1936–1937	1	21	4	5–8	.385
Frank Earle	1908–1909	1	3	2	1–1	.500
Jack Emery	1910–1911	1	1	1	0–1	.000
Felix (Chin) Evans	1937–1938	1	6	1	0–5	.000
Pud Flournoy	1920–1927	3	19	5	1–8	.111
Andrew (Rube) Foster*	1907–1916	4	34	24	17–12	.586
Willie (Bill) Foster	1927–1928	1	16	8	6–8	.429
Jonas Gaines	1946–1953	2	12	0	2–2	.500
Robert (Jude) Gans	1908–1909	1	5	3	1–4	.200
Willie (Lefty) Gisentaner	1926–1927	1	9	1	0–2	.000
Jim (Mudcat) Grant**	1957–1960	2	23	4	3–8	.273
Bill (Willie) Greason	1950–1951	1	7	2	2–2	.500
Claude (Red) Grier	1926–1927	1	14	6	5–3	.625
Bob Griffith	1937–1939	2	35	18	16–11	.593
Arthur (Rat) Henderson	1924–1925	1	14	7	8–5	.615
Bill Holland	1922–1939	4	50	23	27–22	.551
Len Hooker	1946–1947	1	3	0	0–1	.000
Willie Jefferson	1947–1948	1	8	0	1–0	1.000
Gentry Jessup	1946–1947	1	16	4	5–3	.625
Cliff (Connie) Johnson**	1954–1955	1	32	11	12–11	.522
Tommy Johnson	1939–1940	1	2	0	0–1	.000
Cecil Kaiser	1945–1946	1	15	2	3–3	.500
Jim LaMarque	1946–1948	2	53	7	18–13	.581
Rufus Lewis	1947–1949	2	55	16	19–11	.633
Max Manning*	1946–1950	4	88	27	27–33	.450
Jack Marshall	1922–1923	1	4	0	1–0	1.000
Leroy Matlock	1938–1939	1	18	7	6–8	.429
Dan McClellan	1907	1	3	2	0–2	.000
Bob McClure	1926–1927	1	14	6	3–8	.273
Booker McDaniels	1945–1948	3	49	10	15–14	.517
Terris McDuffie*	1937–1953	8	135	38	37–43	.463
Henry McHenry	1930–1945	3	30	3	8–7	.533
Henry Miller	1948–1949	1	3	0	0–1	.000
Percy Miller	1924–1925	1	4	0	0–3	.000
Squire (Square) Moore	1924–1925	1	8	2	2–3	.400
Barney Morris	1939–1940	1	25	15	13–8	.619
Don Newcombe**	1946–1949	2	9	1	1–4	.200
Leroy (Satchel) Paige*(**)	1929–1930	1	15	8	6–5	.545
Roy Partlow#	1939–1940	1	13	10	7–4	.637
Andy (Pullman) Porter	1939–1941	2	23	11	9–9	.500
William Powell	1949–1953	2	21	4	4–6	.400
Willie (Wee Willie) Powell	1927–1928	1	18	4	3–7	.300
Ted (Double Duty) Radcliffe*	1938–1940	2	35	12	12–11	.522
Connie Rector	1927–1930	2	13	5	3–3	.500
Dick (Cannonball) Redding*	1912–1923	5	62	32	18–23	.439
Wlbur (Bullet) Rogan*	1924–1925	1	18	5	9–4	.692
Merven (Red) Ryan	1920–1927	5	39	12	12–10	.545
Harry Salmon	1929–1931	2	16	5	4–5	.444
Ford Smith	1949–1950	1	19	6	8–6	.571
Hilton Smith	1937–1940	2	23	9	10–5	.667

Player	Cuban Seasons	Years	G	GG	W-L	Pct.
Robert Smith	1913	1	1	1	1–0	1.000
Theolic (Fireball) Smith*	1938–1948	2	19	8	5–9	.357
Sam Streeter*	1924–1930	5	39	11	10–10	.500
John (Steel Arm) Taylor	1912	1	1	0	0–0	.000
John Taylor	1936–1939	2	25	6	4–14	.222
Art Terrell	1924–1925	1	3	0	0–1	.000
Al Thomas	1908–1909	1	2	0	1–1	.500
Harold Treadwell	1922–1923	1	3	0	0–0	.000
Ted Trent	1928–1931	2	23	9	6–10	.375
Bill (Steel Arm) Tyler	1925–1926	1	6	2	1–2	.333
Frank Wickware	1912–1916	2	24	14	12–8	.600
Smoky Joe Williams*	1912–1916	3	48	26	22–15	.595
Johnny Williams	1946–1947	1	9	0	2–3	.400
Charles (Lefty) Williams	1928–1930	2	35	14	10–12	.455
Al (Apple) Wilmore	1950–1951	1	9	0	1–1	.500
Ray Wilson	1907	1	9	4	3–6	.333
Jessup (Nip) Winter	1923–1926	2	27	8	4–12	.250
Lamon Yokeley	1929–1930	1	11	4	2–4	.333

In a standard reference on Cuban League statistics (*Béisbol Cubano: Récords y Estadísticas*, 1955), Gabino Delgado and Severo Nieto provide data on the following U.S. Negro leaguers only: Bob Boyd, Sam Jethroe, Harry Simpson, Hank Thompson, and pitchers Joe Black, Connie Johnson, and Terris McDuffie. All were still active in 1955 and thus their listed numbers do not represent complete career statistics.

Appendix C: Major League Register

Cuban Major Leaguers by Debut Year (Chronological Listing)

151 Cuban Major Leaguers (players active during 2005 season appear here in **boldface** print)

Name	Debut	Position	Debut Team	Seasons (Games)	Career Statistics
Enrique Esteban Bellán	1871	Infield	Troy Haymakers (NA)	3 (60)	.252 BA
Armando Marsans	1911	Outfield	Cincinnati Reds (NL)	8 (655)	.269 BA
Rafael Almeida	1911	Outfield	Cincinnati Reds (NL)	3 (102)	.270 BA
Mike (Miguel) González	1912	Catcher	Boston Braves (NL)	19 (1042)	.253 BA
Merito (Baldomero) Acosta	1913	Outfield	Washington Senators (AL)	5 (180)	.255 BA
Jack (Jacinto) Calvo	1913	Outfield	Washington Senators (AL)	2 (34)	.161 BA
Angel Aragón	1914	Infielder	New York Yankees (AL)	3 (32)	.118 BA
Adolfo Luque	1914	RHP	Boston Braves (NL)	20 (550)	194–179, 3.24 ERA
Emilio Palmero	1915	RHP	New York Giants (NL)	4 (41)	6–15, 5.17 ERA
Joseito Rodríguez	1916	Infield	New York Giants (NL)	5 (58)	.166 BA
Manolo (Manuel) Cueto	1917	Outfield	Cincinnati Reds (NL)	3 (151)	.227 BA
Eusebio González	1918	SS	Boston Red Sox (AL)	1 (3)	.400 BA
Oscar Tuero	1918	RHP	St. Louis Cardinals (NL)	3 (58)	6–9, 2.88 ERA
José Acosta	1920	RHP	Washington Senators (AL)	3 (55)	10–10, 4.51 ERA
Ricardo Torres	1920	Catcher	Washington Senators (AL)	3 (22)	.297 BA
Pedro Dibut	1924	RHP	Cincinnati Reds (NL)	2 (8)	3–0, 2.70 ERA
Ramón (Mike) Herrera	1925	Infield	Boston Red Sox (AL)	2 (84)	.275 BA
Oscar Estrada	1929	LHP	St. Louis Browns (AL)	1 (1)	0–0, 0.00 ERA
Roberto Estalella	1935	Outfield	Washington Senators (AL)	8 (680)	.282 BA
Mike (Fermín) Guerra	1937	Catcher	Washington Senators (AL)	9 (565)	.242 BA
René Monteagudo	1938	LHP	Washington Senators (AL)	3 (46)	3–7, 6.42 ERA
Gilberto Torres	1940	Infield	Washington Senators (AL)	4 (44)	.262 BA
Jack (Angel) Aragón	1941	PR	New York Giants (NL)	1 (1)	.000 BA
Roberto Ortíz	1941	Outfield	Washington Senators (AL)	6 (213)	.255 BA
Chico (Salvador) Hernández	1942	Catcher	Chicago Cubs (NL)	2 (90)	.250 BA
Mosquito (Tony) Ordeñana	1943	SS	Pittsburgh Pirates (NL)	1 (1)	.500 BA
Nap (Napoleón) Reyes	1943	Infield	New York Giants (NL)	4 (279)	.284 BA
Tommy (Tomás) de la Cruz	1944	RHP	Cincinnati Reds (NL)	1 (34)	9–9, 3.25 ERA
Preston (Pedro) Gómez	1944	Infield	Washington Senators (AL)	1 (8)	.286 BA
Baby (Oliverio) Ortíz	1944	RHP	Washington Senators (AL)	1 (2)	0–2, 6.23 ERA
Luis Suarez	1944	3B	Washington Senators (AL)	1 (1)	.000 BA
Santiago (Carlos) Ullrich	1944	RHP	Washington Senators (AL)	2 (31)	3–3, 5.04 ERA
Roy (Rogelio) Valdés	1944	PH	Washington Senators (AL)	1 (1)	.000 BA
Jorge Comellas	1945	RHP	Chicago Cubs (NL)	1 (7)	0–2, 4.50 ERA
Sid (Isidoro) León	1945	RHP	Philadelphia Phillies (NL)	1 (14)	0–4, 5.35 ERA
Armando Roche	1945	RHP	Washington Senators (AL)	1 (2)	0–0, 6.00 ERA
Adrián Zabala	1945	LHP	New York Giants (NL)	2 (26)	4–7, 5.02 ERA
José Zardón	1945	Outfield	Washington Senators (AL)	1 (54)	.290 BA
Reggie (Regino) Otero	1945	1B	Chicago Cubs (NL)	1 (14)	.391 BA
Angel Fleitas	1948	SS	Washington Senators (AL)	1 (15)	.077 BA
Moín (Ramon) García	1948	RHP	Washington Senators (AL)	1 (4)	0–0, 17.18 ERA
Enrique (Julio) González	1949	RHP	Washington Senators (AL)	1 (13)	0–0, 4.72 ERA
Minnie (Orestes) Miñoso	1949	Outfield	Cleveland Indians (AL)	17 (1835)	.298 BA, 186 HR

Name	*Debut*	*Position*	*Debut Team*	*Seasons (Games)*	*Career Statistics*
Witto (Luis) Aloma	1950	RHP	Chicago White Sox (AL)	4 (116)	18–3, 3.44 ERA
Sandy (Sandalio) Consuegra	1950	RHP	Washington Senators (AL)	8 (248)	51–32, 3.37 ERA
Connie (Conrado) Marrero	1950	RHP	Washington Senators (AL)	5 (118)	39–40, 3.67 ERA
Limonar (Rogelio) Martínez	1950	RHP	Washington Senators (AL)	1 (2)	0–1, 27.00 ERA
Julio (Jiquí) Moreno	1950	RHP	Washington Senators (AL)	4 (73)	18–22, 4.25 ERA
Carlos Pascual	1950	RHP	Washington Senators (AL)	1 (2)	1–1, 2.12 ERA
Cisco (Francisco) Campos	1951	Outfield	Washington Senators (AL)	3 (71)	.279 BA
Willie (Guillermo) Miranda	1951	SS	Washington Senators (AL)	9 (824)	.221 BA
Ray (Rafael) Noble	1951	Catcher	New York Giants (NL)	3 (107)	.218 BA
Sandy (Edmundo) Amorós	1952	Outfield	Brooklyn Dodgers (NL)	7 (517)	.255 BA
Mike (Miguel) Fornieles	1952	RHP	Washington Senators (AL)	12 (432)	63–64, 3.96 ERA
Héctor Rodríguez	1952	3B	Chicago White Sox (AL)	1 (124)	.265 BA
Raúl Sánchez	1952	RHP	Washington Senators (AL)	3 (49)	5–3, 4.62 ERA
Carlos Paula	1954	Outfield	Washington Senators (AL)	3 (157)	.271 BA
Camilio Pascual	1954	RHP	Washington Senators (AL)	18 (529)	174–170, 3.63 ERA
Vicente Amor	1955	RHP	Chicago Cubs (NL)	2 (13)	1–3, 5.67 ERA
Julio Bécquer	1955	1B	Washington Senators (AL)	7 (488)	.244 BA
Juan Delís	1955	3B	Washington Senators (AL)	1 (54)	.189 BA
Lino Donoso	1955	LHP	Pittsburgh Pirates (NL)	2 (28)	4–6, 5.21 ERA
Vince (Wenceslao) González	1955	LHP	Washington Senators (AL)	1 (2)	0–0, 27.00 ERA
Román Mejías	1955	Outfield	Pittsburgh Pirates (NL)	9 (627)	.254 BA
Pedro (Pete) Ramos	1955	RHP	Washington Senators (AL)	16 (582)	117–160, 4.08 ERA
José (Joe) Valdivielso	1955	SS	Washington Senators (AL)	5 (401)	.219 BA
Chico/Humberto Fernández	1956	SS	Brooklyn Dodgers (NL)	8 (856)	.240 BA
Evelio Hernández	1956	RHP	Washington Senators (AL)	2 (18)	1–1, 4.45 ERA
Cholly (Lazaro) Naranjo	1956	RHP	Pittsburgh Pirates (NL)	1 (17)	1–2, 4.46 ERA
René Valdez	1957	RHP	Brooklyn Dodgers (NL)	1 (5)	1–1, 5.54 ERA
Ossie (Oswaldo) Alvarez	1958	Infield	Washington Senators (AL)	2 (95)	.212 BA
Pancho (Juan) Herrera	1958	1B	Philadelphia Phillies (NL)	3 (300)	.271 BA
Dan (Daniel) Morejón	1958	Outfield	Cincinnati Reds (NL)	1 (12)	.192 BA
Orlando Peña	1958	RHP	Cincinnati Reds (NL)	18 (427)	56–77, 3.71 ERA
Fernando (Fred) Rodríguez	1958	RHP	Chicago Cubs (NL)	2 (8)	0–0, 8.68 ERA
Tony (Antonio) Taylor	1958	Infield	Chicago Cubs (NL)	19 (2195)	.261 BA
Rudy (Rodolfo) Arias	1958	LHP	Chicago White Sox (AL)	1 (34)	2–0, 4.09 ERA
Mike (Miguel) Cuéllar	1959	LHP	Cincinnati Reds (NL)	15 (453)	185–130, 3.14 ERA
Zoilo Versalles	1959	SS	Washington Senators (AL)	13 (1400)	.242 BA, 95 HR
Borrego (Rogelio) Alvarez	1960	1B	Cincinnati Reds (NL)	2 (17)	.189 BA
Joe (Joaquin) Azcue	1960	Infield	Cincinnati Reds (NL)	11 (909)	.252 BA
Ed (Eduardo) Bauta	1960	RHP	St. Louis Cardinals (NL)	5 (97)	6–6, 4.35 ERA
Leo (Leonardo) Cárdenas	1960	Infield	Cincinnati Reds (NL)	16 (1941)	.257 BA
Mike (Miguel) de la Hoz	1960	Infield	Cleveland Indians (AL)	9 (494)	.251 BA
Tony (Antonio) González	1960	Infield	Cincinnati Reds (NL)	12 (1559)	.286 BA, 103 HR
Héctor Maestri	1960	RHP	Washington Senators (AL)	2 (2)	0–1, 1.13 ERA
Leo (Leopoldo) Posada	1960	Outfield	Kansas City Athletics (AL)	3 (155)	.256 BA
(Suspension of Professional Baseball in Cuba)					
Berto (Dagoberto) Cueto	1961	RHP	Minnesota Twins (AL)	1 (7)	1–3, 7.17 ERA
Manny (Manuel) Montejo	1961	RHP	Detroit Tigers (AL)	1 (12)	0–0, 3.86 ERA
Héctor (Rodolfo) Martínez	1962	Outfield	Kansas City Athletics (AL)	2 (7)	.267 BA
Marty (Orlando) Martínez	1962	Infield	Minnesota Twins (AL)	7 (436)	.243 BA
Orlando McFarlane	1962	Catcher	Pittsburgh Pirates (NL)	5 (124)	.240 BA
Tony (Pedro) Oliva	1962	Outfield	Minnesota Twins (AL)	15 (1676)	.304 BA, 220 HR
Cookie (Octavio) Rojas	1962	Infield	Cincinnati Reds (NL)	16 (1822)	.263 BA
Diego Seguí	1962	RHP	Kansas City Athletics (AL)	16 (639)	92–111, 3.81 ERA
José Tartabull	1962	Outfield	Kansas City Athletics (AL)	9 (749)	.261 BA
José Cardenal	1963	Infield	San Francisco Giants (NL)	18 (2017)	.275 BA, 138 HR
Marcelino López	1963	LHP	Philadelphia Phillies (NL)	8 (171)	31–40, 3.62 ERA
Tony (Gabriel) Martínez	1963	Infield	Cleveland Indians (AL)	4 (73)	.171 BA
Aurelio Monteagudo	1963	RHP	Kansas City Athletics (AL)	7 (72)	3–7, 5.05 ERA
Dagoberto Campaneris	1964	SS	Kansas City Athletics (AL)	20 (2328)	.259 BA
Tany (Atanasio) Pérez	1964	Infield	Cincinnati Reds (NL)	23 (2777)	.279 BA, 379 HR
Chico Ruiz	1964	Infield	Cincinnati Reds (NL)	8 (565)	.240 BA
Luis Tiant, Jr.	1964	RHP	Cleveland Indians (AL)	19 (573)	229–172, 3.30 ERA

Name	Debut	Position	Debut Team	Seasons (Games)	Career Statistics
Paul (Paulino) Casanova	1965	Catcher	Washington Senators (AL)	10 (859)	.225 BA
Tito (Rigoberto) Fuentes	1965	Outfield	San Francisco Giants (NL)	13 (1499)	.268 BA
Jackie (Jacinto) Hernández	1965	SS	California Angels (AL)	9 (618)	.208 BA
Sandy (Hilario) Valdespino	1965	Outfield	Minnesota Twins (AL)	7 (382)	.230 BA
José Ramón López	1966	RHP	California Angels (AL)	1 (4)	0–1, 5.14 ERA
Minnie (Minervino) Rojas	1966	RHP	California Angels (AL)	3 (157)	23–16, 3.00 ERA
Hank (Enrique) Izquierdo	1967	Catcher	Minnesota Twins (AL)	1 (16)	.269 BA
George (Jorge) Lauzerique	1967	RHP	Kansas City Athletics (AL)	4 (34)	4–8, 5.00 ERA
José Arcia	1968	Infield	Chicago Cubs (NL)	3 (293)	.215 BA
Chico (Lorenzo) Fernández	1968	Infield	Baltimore Orioles (AL)	1 (24)	.111 BA
José Martínez	1969	Infield	Pittsburgh Pirates (NL)	2 (96)	.245 BA
Minnie (Rigoberto) Mendoza	1970	Infield	Minnesota Twins (AL)	1 (16)	.188 BA
Oscar Zamora	1974	RHP	Chicago Cubs (NL)	4 (158)	13–14, 4.53 ERA
Orlando González	1976	1B	Cleveland Indians (AL)	3 (79)	.238 BA
Bobby (Roberto) Ramos	1978	Catcher	Montreal Expos (NL)	6 (103)	.190 BA
Leo (Leonard) Sutherland	1980	Outfield	Chicago White Sox (AL)	2 (45)	.248 BA
*Bárbaro Garbey	1984	Outfield	Detroit Tigers (AL)	3 (226)	.267 BA
José Canseco	1985	Outfield	Oakland Athletics (AL)	17 (1887)	.266 BA, 462 HR
Rafael Palmeiro	**1986**	**1B**	**Chicago Cubs (NL)**	**20 (2831)**	**.288 BA, 569 HR**
Orestes Destrade	1987	1B	New York Yankees (AL)	4 (237)	.241 BA
Nelson Santovenia	1988	Catcher	Montreal Expos (NL)	7 (297)	.233 BA
Israel Sánchez	1988	LHP	Kansas City Royals (AL)	2 (30)	3–2, 5.36 ERA
Tony (Emilio) Fossas	1988	LHP	Texas Rangers (AL)	12 (567)	17–24, 3.90 ERA
Ozzie Canseco	1990	Outfield	Oakland Athletics (AL)	3 (24)	.200 BA
Tony Menéndez	1992	RHP	Cincinnati Reds (NL)	3 (23)	3–1, 4.97 ERA
*René Arocha	1993	RHP	St. Louis Cardinals (NL)	5 (124)	18–17, 4.11 ERA
*Ariel Prieto	1995	RHP	Oakland Athletics (AL)	5 (67)	15–24, 4.88 ERA
*Osvaldo Fernández	1996	RHP	San Francisco Giants (NL)	4 (76)	19–26, 4.93 ERA
*Rey Ordóñez	1996	SS	New York Mets (NL)	9 (973)	.246 BA
***Liván Hernández**	**1996**	**RHP**	**Florida Marlins (NL)**	**10 (284)**	**110–104, 4.11 ERA**
Elieser (Eli) Marrero	**1997**	**Catcher**	**St. Louis Cardinals (NL)**	**9 (669)**	**.245 BA**
*Rolando Arrojo	1998	RHP	Tampa Bay Devil Rays (AL)	5 (158)	40–42, 4.55 ERA
***Orlando Hernández**	**1998**	**RHP**	**New York Yankees (AL)**	**7 (163)**	**70–49, 4.11 ERA**
*Vladimir Nuñez	1998	RHP	Arizona D-Backs (NL)	7 (230)	20–32, 4.83 ERA
*Jorge Toca	1999	Infield	New York Mets (NL)	3 (25)	.259 BA
***Michael Tejera**	**1999**	**LHP**	**Florida Marlins (NL)**	**5 (111)**	**11–13, 5.14 ERA**
*Adrian Hernández	2001	RHP	New York Yankees (AL)	2 (8)	0–4, 5.46 ERA
***Danys Báez**	**2001**	**RHP**	**Cleveland Indians (AL)**	**5 (284)**	**26–31, 102 S**
*Edilberto Oropesa	2001	LHP	Philadelphia Phillies (NL)	4 (125)	8–4, 7.34 ERA
Alex Sánchez	**2001**	**Outfield**	**Milwaukee Brewers (NL)**	**5 (427)**	**.296 BA**
Bill Ortega	2001	Outfield	St. Louis Cardinals (AL)	1 (5)	.200 BA
Hanzel Izquierdo	2002	RHP	Florida Marlins (NL)	1 (20)	2–0, 4.55 ERA
Juan Díaz	2002	1B	Boston Red Sox (AL)	1 (4)	.286 BA
***José Ariel Contreras**	**2003**	**RHP**	**New York Yankees (AL)**	**3 (81)**	**35–18, 4.28 ERA**
*Michel Hernández	2003	Catcher	New York Yankees (AL)	1 (5)	.250 BA
Brayan Peña	**2005**	**Catcher**	**Atlanta Braves (NL)**	**1 (18)**	**.179 BA**
***Yunieski Betancourt**	**2005**	**SS**	**Seattle Mariners (AL)**	**1 (60)**	**.256 BA**

*Played in post–1961 Cuban League before leaving Cuba (i.e., Cuban League Defector, except for Bárbaro Garbey)

Career Statistics of Cuban Major Leaguers (Alphabetical List)

One hundred fifty-one Cuban players (players born in Cuba) have now appeared in the major leagues, through 2005 season (below career statistics are all complete through October 2005).

Mérito Acosta (Baldomero Pedro Acosta Fernández) (b. 5-19-1896, Bauta; d. 11-17-1963, Miami, Florida USA) Debut: 6-15-1913 (1913–1916, 1918) Teams: Washington (A), Philadelphia (A) Position: Outfield (BL TL) Stats: 180 G, 436 AB, 111 H, 56 R, 0 HR, 37 RBI, .255 BA (Brother of Jose Acosta)

José "Acostica" Acosta (José Acosta Fernández) (b. 3-4-1891, Havana; d. 11-16-1977, Havana) Debut: 7-28-1920 (1920–1922)

Teams: Washington (A), Chicago (A) Position: Pitcher (BR TR) Stats: 10 W, 10 L, 213.1 IP, 4.51 ERA, 45 SO, 68 BB, 4 SV, 55 G (Brother of Merito Acosta)

Rafael "Mike" Almeida (Rafael D. Almeida) (b. 7-30-1887, Havana; d. 3-14-1968, Havana) Debut: 7-4-1911 (1911–1913) Team: Cincinnati (N) Position: Outfield, Infield (BR TR) Stats: 102 G, 285 AB, 77 H, 32 R, 3 HR, 46 RBI, .270 BA

Luis "Witto" Aloma (Luis Aloma Barba) (b. 6-19-1923, Havana; d. 4-7-1997, Park Ridge, Illinois USA) Debut: 4-19-1950 (1950–1953) Team: Chicago (A) Position: Pitcher (BR TR) Stats: 18 W, 3 L, 235.1 IP, 3.44 ERA, 115 SO, 111 BB, 15 SV, 116 G

Ossie Alvarez (Oswaldo Alvarez González) (b. 10-19-1933, Matanzas) Debut: 4-19-1958 (1958–1959) Teams: Washington (A),

Detroit (A) Position: Infield (BR TR) Stats: 95 G, 198 AB, 42 H, 20 R, 0 HR, 5 RBI, .212 BA

Rogelio "Borrego" Alvarez (Rogelio Alvarez Hernández) (b. 4-18-1938, Pinar del Río) Debut: 9-18-1960 (1960, 1962) Team: Cincinnati (N) Position: First Base (BR TR) Stats: 17 G, 37 AB, 7 H, 2 R, 0 HR, 2 RBI, .189 BA

Vicente Amor (Vicente Amor Alvarez) (b. 8-8-1932, Havana) Debut: 4-16-1955 (1955, 1957) Teams: Chicago (N), Cincinnati (N) Position: Pitcher (BR TR) Stats: 1 W, 3 L, 33.1 IP, 5.67 ERA, 12 SO, 13 BB, 0 SV, 13 G

Sandy Amorós (Edmundo Amorós Isasi) (b. 1-30-1930, Havana; d. 6-27-1992, Tampa, Florida USA) Debut: 8-22-1952 (1952, 1954–1957, 1959–1960) Teams: Brooklyn (N), Los Angeles (N), Detroit (A) Position: Outfield (BL TL) Stats: 517 G, 1311 AB, 334 H, 215 R, 43 HR, 180 RBI, .255 BA

Jack Aragón (Angel Aragón Valdés y Reyes) (b. 11-20-1915, Havana; d. 4-4-1988, Clearwater, Florida USA) Debut: 8-13-1941 (1941) Team: New York (N) Position: Pinch Runner (BR TR) Stats: 1 G, 0 AB, 0 H, 0 R, 0 HR, 0 RBI, .000 BA (Son of Angel Aragón)

Angel "Pete" Aragón (Angel Aragón Valdés) (b. 8-2-1890, Havana; d. 1-24-1952, New York USA) Debut: 8-20-1914 (1914, 1916–1917) Team: New York (A) Position: Third Base, Shortstop, Outfield (BR TR) Stats: 32 G, 76 AB, 9 H, 4 R, 0 HR, 5 RBI, .118 BA (Father of Jack Aragón)

José Arcia (José Raimundo Arcia Orta) (b. 8-22-1943, Havana) Debut: 4-10-1968 (1968–1970) Teams: Chicago (N), San Diego (N) Position: Infield, Outfield (BR TR) Stats: 293 G, 615 AB, 132 H, 78 R, 1 HR, 35 RBI, .215 BA

Rudy Arias (Rodolfo Arias Martínez) (b. 6-6-1931, Las Villas) Debut: 4-10-1959 (1959) Team: Chicago (A) Position: Pitcher (BL TL) Stats: 2 W, 0 L, 44.0 IP, 4.09 ERA, 28 SO, 20 BB, 2 SV, 34 G

René Arocha (Rene Arocha Magaly) (b. 2-24-1966, Havana) Debut: 4-9-1993 (1993–1997) Teams: St. Louis (N), San Francisco (N) Position: Pitcher (BR TR) Stats: 18 W, 17 L, 331.0 IP, 4.11 ERA, 190 SO, 75 BB, 11 SV, 124 G

Rolando Arrojo (Luis Rolando Arrojo) (b. 5-29-1964, Santa Clara) Debut: 4-1-1998 (1998–2002) Teams: Tampa Bay (A), Colorado (N), Boston (A), Pittsburgh (N) Position: Pitcher (BR TR) Stats: 40 W, 42 L, 700.0 IP, 4.55 ERA, 512 SO, 255 BB, 6 SV, 158 G

Joe Azcue (José Joaquín Azcue López) (b. 8-18-1939, Cienfuegos) Debut: 8-3-1960 (1960, 1962–1970, 1972) Teams: Cincinnati (N), Kansas City (A), Cleveland (A), Boston (A), California (A), Milwaukee (A) Position: Catcher, Infield (BR TR) Stats: 909 G, 2828 AB, 712 H, 201 R, 50 HR, 304 RBI, .252 BA

Danys Báez (Danys Báez González) (b. 9-10-1977, Pinar del Río) Debut: 5-13-2001 (2001–2005) Teams: Cleveland (A), Tampa Bay (A) Position: Pitcher (BR TR) Stats: 26 W, 31 L, 431.2 IP, 3.69 ERA, 351 SO, 184 BB, 102 SV, 284 G

Ed Bauta (Eduardo Bauta Gálvez) (b. 1-6-1935, Florida, Camagüey Province) Debut: 7-6-1960 (1960–1964) Teams: St. Louis (N), New York (N) Position: Pitcher (BR TR) Stats: 6 W, 6 L, 149 IP, 4.35 ERA, 89 SO, 70 BB, 11 SV, 97 G

Julio Bécquer (Julio Becquer Villagas) (b. 12-20-1931, Havana) Debut: 9-13-1955 (1955, 1957–1961, 1963) Teams: Washington (A), Los Angeles (A), Minnesota (A) Position: First Base, Outfield, Pitcher (BL TL) Hitting Stats: 488 G, 974 AB, 238 H, 100 R, 12 HR, 114 RBI, .244 BA; Pitching Stats: 0 W, 0 L, 2.1 IP, 15.43 ERA, 0 SO, 1 BB, 0 SV, 2 G

Esteban "Steve" Bellán (Esteban Enrique Bellán) (b. 1850, Havana; d. 8-8-1932, Havana) Debut: 5-9-1871 (1871–1873) Teams: Troy (NA), New York (NA) Position: Infield, Outfield (BR TR) Stats: 60 G, 278 AB, 69 H, 52 R, 0 HR, 42 RBI, .248 BA

Yunieski Betancourt (Yunieski Betancourt Pérez) (b. 1-31-1982, Santa Clara) Debut: 7-28-2005 (2005) Team: Seattle (A) Position: Shortstop (BR TR) Stats: 60 G, 211 AB, 54 H, 24 R, 1 HR, 15 RBI, .256 BA

Jack Calvo (Jacinto Calvo González) (b. 6-11-1894, Havana; d. 6-15-1965, Miami USA) Debut: 9-5-1913 (1913, 1920) Team: Washington (A) Position: Outfield (BL TL) Stats: 34 G, 56 AB, 9 H, 10 R, 1 HR, 4 RBI, .161 BA

Bert "Campy" Campaneris (Dagoberto Campaneris (Campaneria) Blanco) (b. 3-9-1942, Pueblo Nuevo) Debut: 7-23-1964 (1964–1983) Teams: Kansas City (A), Oakland (A), Texas (A), California (A), New York (A) Position: Shortstop, Infield (BR TR) Stats: 2328 G, 8684 AB, 2249 H, 1181 R, 79 HR, 646 RBI, .259 BA

Frank "Cisco" Campos (Francisco José Campos López) (b. 5-11-1924, Havana) Debut: 9-11-1951 (1951–1953) Team: Washington (A) Position: Outfield (BL TL) Stats: 71 G, 147 AB, 41 H, 13 R, 0 HR, 13 RBI, .279 BA

José Canseco (José Canseco Capas) (b. 7-2-1964, Regla) Debut: 9-2-1985 (1985–2001) Teams: Oakland (A), Texas (A), Boston (A), Toronto (A), Tampa Bay (A), New York (A), Chicago (A) Position: Outfield, DH (BR TR) Stats: 1887 G, 7057 AB, 1877 H, 1186 R, 462 HR, 1407 RBI, .266 BA (Brother of Ozzie Canseco)

Ozzie Canseco (Osvaldo Canseco Capas) (b. 7-2-1964, Havana) Debut: 7-18-1990 (1990, 1992–1993) Teams: Oakland (A), St. Louis (N) Position: Outfield (BR TR) Stats: 24 G, 65 AB, 13 H, 8 R, 0 HR, 4 RBI, .200 BA (Brother of José Canseco)

José Cardenal (José Rosario Cardenal Domec) (b. 10-7-1943, Matanzas) Debut: 4-14-1963 (1963–1980) Teams: San Francisco (N), California (A), Cleveland (A), St. Louis (N), Milwaukee (A), Chicago (N), Philadelphia (N), New York (N), Kansas City (A) Position: Outfield (BR TR) Stats: 2017 G, 6964 AB, 1913 H, 936 R, 138 HR, 775 RBI, .275 BA

Leo "Chico" Cárdenas (Leonardo Lázaro Cárdenas Alfonso) (b. 12-17-1938, Matanzas) Debut: 7-25-1960 (1960–1975) Teams: Cincinnati (N), Minnesota (A), California (A), Cleveland (A), Texas (A) Position: Shortstop (BR TR) Stats: 1941 G, 6707 AB, 1725 H, 662 R, 118 HR, 689 RBI, .257 BA

Paul Casanova (Paulino Casanova Ortiz) (b. 12-21-1941, Matanzas Province) Debut: 9-18-1965 (1965–1974) Teams: Washington (A), Atlanta (N) Position: Catcher (BR TR) Stats: 859 G, 2786 AB, 627 H, 214 R, 50 HR, 252 RBI, .225 BA

Jorge "Poncho" Comellas (Jorge Comellas Pous) (b. 12-7-1916, Havana; d. date unknown, Cuba) Debut: 4-19-1945 (1945) Team: Chicago (N) Position: Pitcher (BR TR) Stats: 0 W, 2 L, 12.0 IP, 4.50 ERA, 6 SO, 6 BB, 0 SV, 7 G

Sandy Consuegra (Sandalio Simeon Consuegra Castello) (b. 9-3-1920, Potrerillos) Debut: 6-10-1950 (1950–1957) Teams: Washington (A), Chicago (A), Baltimore (A), New York (N) Position: Pitcher (BR TR) Stats: 51 W, 32 L, 809.1 IP, 3.37 ERA, 193 SO, 246 BB, 26 SV, 248 G

José Contreras (José Ariel Contreras) (b. 12-6-1971, Sandino, Pinar del Río Province) Debut: 3-31-2003 (2003–2005) Teams: New York (A), Chicago (A) Position: Pitcher (BR TR) Stats: 35 W, 18 L, 446.0 IP, 4.28 ERA, 376 SO, 189 BB, 0 SV, 81 G

Mike Cuéllar (Miguel Angel Cuéllar Santana) (b. 5-8-1937, Las Villas) Debut: 4-18-1959 (1959, 1964–1977) Teams: Cincinnati (N), St. Louis (N), Houston (N), Baltimore (A), California (A) Position: Pitcher (BL TL) Stats: 185 W, 130 L, 2808.0 IP, 3.14 ERA, 1632 SO, 822 BB, 11 SV, 453 G

Bert Cueto (Dagoberto Cueto Concepción) (b. 8-14-1937, San Luís Pinar) Debut: 6-18-1961 (1961) Team: Minnesota (A) Position: Pitcher (BR TR) Stats: 1 W, 3 L, 21.1 IP, 7.17 ERA, 5 SO, 10 BB, 0 SV, 7 G

Manolo Cueto (Manuel Cueto Melo) (b. 2-8-1892, Guanajay; d. 6-29-1942, Regla, Havana Province) Debut: 6-25-1914 (1914, 1917–1919) Teams: St. Louis (F), Cincinnati (N) Position: Outfield, Infield (BR TR) Stats: 151 G, 379 AB, 86 H, 36 R, 1 HR, 31 RBI, .227 BA

Tommy de la Cruz (Tomás de la Cruz Rivero) (b. 9-18-1911, Marianao; d. 9-6-1958, Havana) Debut: 4-20-1944 (1944) Team:

Cincinnati (N) Position: Pitcher (BR TR) Stats: 9 W, 9 L, 191.1 IP, 3.25 ERA, 65 SO, 45 BB, 1 SV, 34 G

Mike de la Hoz (Miguel Angel de la Hoz y Piloto) (b. 10-2-1938, Havana) Debut: 7-22-1960 (1960–1967, 1969) Teams: Cleveland (A), Milwaukee (N), Atlanta (N), Cincinnati (N) Position: Infield (BR TR) Stats: 494 G, 1114 AB, 280 H, 116 R, 25 HR, 115 RBI, .251 BA

Juan Delís (Juan Francisco Delís) (b. 2-27-1928, Santiago de Cuba) Debut: 4-16-1955 (1955) Team: Washington (A) Position: Outfield, Infield, Shortstop (BR TR) Stats: 54 G, 132 AB, 25 H, 12 R, 0 HR, 11 RBI, .189 BA

Orestes Destrade (Orestes Destrade Cucuas) (b. 5-8-1962, Santiago de Cuba) Debut: 9-11-1987 (1987–1988, 1993–94) Teams: New York (A), Pittsburgh (N), Florida (N) Position: First Base (BB TR) Stats: 237 G, 765 AB, 184 H, 80 R, 26 HR, 106 RBI, .241 BA

Juan Díaz (Juan Carlos Díaz) (b. 2-19-1974, San José de las Lajas) Debut: 6-12-2002 (2002) Team: Boston (A) Position: First Base (BR TR) Stats: 4 G, 7 AB, 2 H, 2 R, 0 HR, 1 RBI, .286 BA

Pedro Dibut (Pedro Dibut Villafana) (b. 11-18-1892, Cienfuegos; d. 12-4-1979, Hialeah, Florida USA) Debut: 5-1-1924 (1924–1925) Team: Cincinnati (N) Position: Pitcher (BR TR) Stats: 3 W, 0 L, 36.2 IP, 2.70 ERA, 15 SO, 12 BB, 0 SV, 8 G

Lino Donoso (Lino Donoso Galeta) (b. 9-23-1922, Havana; d. 10-13-1990, Veracruz, Mexico) Debut: 6-18-1955 (1955–1956) Team: Pittsburgh (N) Position: Pitcher (BL TL) Stats: 4 W, 6 L, 96.2 IP, 5.21 ERA, 39 SO, 36 BB, 1 SV, 28 G

Roberto "Tarzan" Estalella (Roberto Estalella Ventoza) (b. 4-25-1911, Cárdenas; d. 1-6-1991, Hialeah, Florida USA) Debut: 9-7-1935 (1935–1936, 1939, 1941–1945, 1949) Teams: Washington (A), St. Louis (A), Washington (A), Philadelphia (A) Position: Outfield (BR TR) Stats: 680 G, 2196 AB, 620 H, 279 R, 44 HR, 308 RBI, .282 BA

Oscar Estrada (Oscar Estrada) (b. 2-15-1904, Havana; d. 1-2-1978, Havana) Debut: 4-21-1929 (1929) Team: St. Louis (A) Position: Pitcher (BL TL) Stats: 0 W, 0 L, 1.0 IP, 0.00 ERA, 0 SO, 1 BB, 0 SV, 1 G

Humberto "Chico" Fernández (Humberto Fernández Pérez) (b. 3-2-1932, Havana) Debut: 7-14-1956 (1956–1963) Teams: Brooklyn (N), Philadelphia (N), Detroit (A), New York (N) Position: Shortstop (BR TR) Stats: 856 G, 2778 AB, 666 H, 270 R, 40 HR, 259 RBI, .240 BA

Chico Fernández (Lorenzo Marto Fernández y Mosquera) (b. 4-23-1939, Havana) Debut: 4-20-1968 (1968) Team: Baltimore (A) Position: Infield, Shortstop (BR TR) Stats: 24 G, 18 AB, 2 H, 0 R, 0 HR, 0 RBI, .111 BA

Osvaldo Fernández (Osvaldo Fernández Rodríguez) (b. 11-4-1966, Holguín) Debut: 4-5-1996 (1996–1997, 2000–2001) Teams: San Francisco (N), Cincinnati (N) Position: Pitcher (BR TR) Stats: 19 W, 26 L, 387.0 IP, 4.93 ERA, 208 SO, 136 BB, 0 SV, 76 G

Angel Fleitas (Angel Félix Fleitas y Husta) (b. 11-10-1914, Los Abreus) Debut: 7-5-1948 (1948) Team: Washington (A) Position: Shortstop (BR TR) Stats: 15 G, 13 AB, 1 H, 1 R, 0 HR, 1 RBI, .077 BA

Mike Fornieles (José Miguel Fornieles y Torres) (b. 1-18-1932, Havana; d. 2-11-1998, St. Petersburg, Florida USA) Debut: 9-2-1952 (1952–1963) Teams: Washington (A), Chicago (A), Baltimore (A), Boston (A), Minnesota (A) Position: Pitcher (BR TR) Stats: 63 W, 64 L, 1156.2 IP, 3.96 ERA, 576 SO, 421 BB, 55 SV, 432 G

Tony Fossas (Emilio Antonio Fossas Morejón) (b. 9-23-1957, Havana) Debut: 5-15-1988 (1988–1999) Teams: Texas (A), Milwaukee (A), Boston (A), St. Louis (N), Seattle (A), Chicago (N), New York (A) Position: Pitcher (BL TL) Stats: 17 W, 24 L, 415.2 IP, 3.90 ERA, 324 SO, 180 BB, 7 SV, 567 G

Tito Fuentes (Rigoberto Fuentes Peat) (b. 1-4-1944, Havana) Debut: 8-18-1965 (1965–1967, 1969–1978) Teams: San Francisco (N), San Diego (N), Detroit (A), Oakland (A) Position: Second Base,

Infield (BB TR) Stats: 1499 G, 5566 AB, 1491 H, 610 R, 45 HR, 438 RBI, .268 BA

Bárbaro Garbey (Bárbaro Garbey Garbey) (b. 12-4-1956, Santiago de Cuba) Debut: 4-3-1984 (1984–1985, 1988) Teams: Detroit (A), Texas (A) Position: Outfield, Third Base, DH (BR TR) Stats: 226 G, 626 AB, 167 H, 76 R, 11 HR, 86 RBI, .267 BA

Moín García (Ramón García García) (b. 3-5-1924, La Esperanza) Debut: 4-19-1948 (1948) Team: Washington (A) Position: Pitcher (BR TR) Stats: 0 W, 0 L, 3.2 IP, 17.18 ERA, 2 SO, 4 BB, 0 SV, 4 G

Preston "Pedro" Gómez (Pedro Gómez Martínez) (b. 4-20-1923, Central Preston) Debut: 5-5-1944 (1944) Team: Washington (A) Position: Second Base, Shortstop (BR TR) Stats: 8 G, 7 AB, 2 H, 2 R, 0 HR, 2 RBI, .286 BA

Julio González (Julio Enrique González Herrera) (b. 12-20-1920, Banes; d. 2-15-1991, Havana Province) Debut: 8-9-1949 (1949) Team: Washington (A) Position: Pitcher (BR TR) Stats: 0 W, 0 L, 34.1 IP, 4.72 ERA, 5 SO, 27 BB, 0 SV, 13 G

Vince (Vincent) González (Wenceslao González O'Reilly) (b. 9-28-1925, Quivican; d. 3-11-1981, Ciudad del Carmen, Campache, Mexico) Debut: 4-13-1955 (1955) Team: Washington (A) Position: Pitcher (BL TL) Stats: 0 W, 0 L, 2 IP, 27.00 ERA, 1 SO, 3 BB, 0 SV, 2 G

Orlando González (Orlando Eugene González) (b. 11-15-1951, Havana) Debut: 6-7-1976 (1976, 1978, 1980) Teams: Cleveland (A), Philadelphia (N), Oakland (A) Position: Outfield, DH, First Base (BL TL) Stats: 79 G, 164 AB, 39 H, 16 R, 0 HR, 5 RBI, .238 BA

Mike González (Miguel Angel González Cordero) (b. 9-24-1890, Havana; d. 2-19-1977, Havana) Debut: 9-28-1912 (1912, 1914–1929, 1931–1932) Teams: Boston (N), Cincinnati (N), St. Louis (N), New York (N), St. Louis (N), Chicago (N), St. Louis (N) Position: Catcher, First Base (BR TR) Stats: 1042 G, 2829 AB, 717 H, 283 R, 13 HR, 263 RBI, .253 BA

Tony González (Andres Antonio González González) (b. 8-28-1936, Central Cunagua) Debut: 4-12-1960 (1960–1971) Teams: Cincinnati (N), Philadelphia (N), San Diego (N), Atlanta (N), California (A) Position: Outfield (BL TR) Stats: 1559 G, 5195 AB, 1485 H, 690 R, 103 HR, 615 RBI, .286 BA

Eusebio González (Eusebio Miguel González) (b. 7-13-1892, Havana; d. 2-4-1976, Havana) Debut: 7-26-1918 (1918) Team: Boston (A) Position: SS, Third Base, Infield (BR TR) Stats: 3 G, 5 AB, 2 H, 2 R, 0 HR, 0 RBI, .400 BA

Fermín "Mike" Guerra (Fermín Guerra Romero) (b. 10-11-1912, Havana; d. 10-9-1992, Miami, Florida USA) Debut: 9-19-1937 (1937, 1944–1951) Teams: Washington (A), Philadelphia (A), Boston (A), Washington (A) Position: Catcher (BR TR) Stats: 565 G, 1581 AB, 382 H, 168 R, 9 HR, 168 RBI, .242 BA

Adrian "Duquecito" Hernández (Adrian Hernández Ramírez) Debut: 4-21-2001 (2001–2002) Team: New York (A) Position: Pitcher (BR TR) Stats: 0 W, 4 L, 280 IP, 5.46 ERA, 19 SO, 16 BB, 0 SV, 8 G

Chico Hernández (Salvador José Hernández) (b. 1-3-1916, Havana; d. 1-3-1986, Havana) Debut: 4-16-1942 (1942–1943) Team: Chicago (N) Position: Catcher (BR TR) Stats: 90 G, 244 AB, 61 H, 16 R, 0 HR, 16 RBI, .250 BA

Evelio Hernández (Gregorio Evelio Hernández López) (b. 12-24-1930, Guanabacoa) Debut: 9-12-1956 (1956–1957) Team: Washington (A) Position: Pitcher (BR TR) Stats: 1 W, 1 L, 58.2 IP, 4.45 ERA, 24 SO, 28 BB, 0 SV, 18 G

Jackie Hernández (Jacinto Hernández Zulueta) (b. 9-11-1940, Central Tinguaro) Debut: 9-14-1965 (1965–1973) Teams: California (A), Minnesota (A), Kansas City (A), Pittsburgh (N) Position: Shortstop, Third Base (BR TR) Stats: 618 G, 1480 AB, 308 H, 153 R, 12 HR, 121 RBI, .208 BA

Liván Hernández (Eisler Liván Hernández Carrera) (b. 2-20-1975, Santa Clara, Villa Clara) Debut: 9-4-1996 (1996–2005) Teams:

Florida (N), San Francisco (N), Montreal (N), Washington (N) Position: Pitcher (BR TR) Stats: 110 W, 104 L, 1950.2 IP, 4.11 ERA, 1328 SO, 673 BB, 0 SV, 284 G (Half-Brother of Orlando "El Duque" Hernández)

Michel Hernández (Michel Hernández Nuñez) (b. 8-12-1978, Havana) Debut: 9-18-2003 (2003) Team: New York (A) Position: Catcher (BR TR) Stats: 5 G, 4 AB, 1 H, 0 R, 0 HR, 0 RBI, .250 BA

Orlando "El Duque" Hernández (Orlando Hernández Pedroso) (b. 10-11-1965, Boyeros, Havana) Debut: 6-3-1998 (1998–2005) Teams: New York (A), Chicago (A) Position: Pitcher (BR TR) Stats: 70 W, 49 L, 1004.2 IP, 4.11 ERA, 794 SO, 354 BB, 2 SV, 163 G (Half-Brother of Liván Hernández)

Mike Herrera (Ramón Herrera) (b. 12-19-1897, Havana; d. 2-3-1978, Havana) Debut: 9-22-1925 (1925–1926) Team: Boston (A) Position: Third Base, Infield (BR TR) Stats: 84 G, 276 AB, 76 H, 22 R, 0 HR, 27 RBI, .275 BA

Pancho Herrera (Juan Francisco Herrera Willavicencio) (b. 6-16-1934, Santiago) Debut: 4-15-1958 (1958, 1960–1961) Team: Philadelphia (N) Position: First Base, Infield (BR TR) Stats: 300 G, 975 AB, 264 H, 122 R, 31 HR, 128 RBI, .271 BA

Hank Izquierdo (Enrique Roberto Izquierdo Valdés) (b. 3-20-1931, Matanzas Province) Debut: 8-9-1967 (1967) Team: Minnesota (A) Position: Catcher, Pinch Hitter (BR TR) Stats: 16 G, 26 AB, 7 H, 4 R, 0 HR, 2 RBI, .269 BA

Hanzel Izquierdo (Hanzel Izquierdo) (b. 1-2-1977, Havana) Debut: 4-21-2002 (2002) Team: Florida (N) Position: Pitcher (BR TR) Stats: 2 W, 0 L, 29.2 IP, 4.55 ERA, 20 SO, 21 BB, 0 SV, 20 G

Jorge Lauzerique (George Albert Lauzerique) (b. 7-22-1947, Havana) Debut: 9-17-1967 (1967–1970) Teams: Kansas City (A), Oakland (A), Milwaukee (A) Position: Pitcher (BR TR) Stats: 4 W, 8 L, 113.1 IP, 5.00 ERA, 73 SO, 48 BB, 0 SV, 34 G

Sid "Izzy" León (Isidoro León Becerra) (b. 1-4-1911, Cruces, Las Villas Province; d. 7-25-2002, Miami, Florida USA) Debut: 6-21-1945 (1945) Team: Philadelphia (N) Position: Pitcher (BR TR) Stats: 0 W, 4 L, 38.2 IP, 5.35 ERA, 11 SO, 19 BB, 0 SV, 14 G

Ramón López (José Ramón López y Hevia) (b. 5-26-1933, Las Villas Province; d. 9-4-1982, Miami, Florida USA) Debut: 8-21-1966 (1966) Teams: California (A) Position: Pitcher (BR TR) Stats: 0 W, 1 L, 7.0 IP, 5.14 ERA, 2 SO, 4 BB, 0 SV, 4 G

Marcelino López (Marcelino Pons López) (b. 9-23-1943, Havana) Debut: 4-14-1963 (1963, 1965–1967, 1969–1972) Teams: Philadelphia (N), California (A), Baltimore (A), Milwaukee (A), Cleveland (A) Position: Pitcher (BR TL) Stats: 31 W, 40 L, 653 IP, 3.62 ERA, 426 SO, 317 BB, 2 SV, 171 G

Dolf Luque (Adolfo Domingo Luque Guzmán) (b. 8-4-1890, Havana; d. 7-3-1957, Havana) Debut: 5-20-1914 (1914–1915, 1918–1935) Teams: Boston (N), Cincinnati (N), Brooklyn (N), New York (N) Position: Pitcher (BR TR) Stats: 194 W, 179 L, 3220.1 IP, 3.24 ERA, 1130 SO, 918 BB, 28 SV, 550 G

Héctor Maestri (Héctor Maestri García) (b. 4-19-1935, Havana) Debut: 9-24-1960 (1960–1961) Team: Washington (A) Position: Pitcher (BR TR) Stats: 0 W, 1 L, 8.0 IP, 1.13 ERA, 3 SO, 3 BB, 0 SV, 2 G

Connie Marrero (Conrado Eugenio Marrero Ramos) (b. 4-25-1911, Las Villas) Debut: 4-21-1950 (1950–1954) Team: Washington (A) Position: Pitcher (BR TR) Stats: 39 W, 40 L, 735.1 IP, 3.67 ERA, 297 SO, 249 BB, 3 SV, 118 G

Eli Marrero (Elieser Marrero) (b. 11-17-1973, Havana) Debut: 9-3-1997 (1997–2003) Team: St. Louis (N) Position: Catcher, First Base, Outfield (BR TR) Stats: 525 G, 1425 AB, 339 H, 195 R, 43 HR, 187 RBI, .238 BA (Grandnephew of Conrado Marrero)

Armando Marsans (Armando Marsans) (b. 10-3-1887, Matanzas; d. 9-3-1960, Havana) Debut: 7-4-1911 (1911–1918) Teams: Cincinnati (N), St. Louis (F), St. Louis (A), New York (A) Position: Outfield, Infield (BR TR) Stats: 655 G, 2273 AB, 612 H, 267 R, 2 HR, 221 RBI, .269 BA

Héctor Martínez (Rodolfo Héctor Martínez Santos) (b. 5-11-1939, Las Villas) Debut: 9-30-1962 (1962–1963) Team: Kansas City (A) Position: Outfield (BR TR) Stats: 7 G, 15 AB, 4 H, 2 R, 1 HR, 3 RBI, .267 BA

José Martínez (José Martínez y Azcuiz) (b. 7-26-1941, Cárdenas) Debut: 6-18-1969 (1969–1970) Team: Pittsburgh (N) Position: Infield, Outfield (BR TR) Stats: 96 G, 188 AB, 46 H, 21 R, 1 HR, 16 RBI, .245 BA

Tony Martínez (Gabriel Antonio Martínez Díaz) (b. 3-18-1940, Perico; d. 8-24-1991, Miami, Florida USA) Debut: 4-9-1963 (1963–1966) Team: Cleveland (A) Position: Shortstop, Second Base (BR TR) Stats: 73 G, 175 AB, 30 H, 13 R, 0 HR, 10 RBI, .171 BA

Marty Martínez (Orlando Martínez Oliva) (b. 8-23-1941, Havana) Debut: 5-2-1962 (1962, 1967–1972) Teams: Minnesota (A), Atlanta (N), Houston (N), St. Louis (N), Oakland (A), Texas (A) Position: Infield, Catcher, Outfield (BB TR) Stats: 436 G, 945 AB, 230 H, 97 R, 0 HR, 57 RBI, .243 BA

Limonar Martínez (Rogelio Martínez Ulloa) (b. 11-5-1918, Cidra) Debut: 7-13-1950 (1950) Team: Washington (A) Position: Pitcher (BR TR) Stats: 0 W, 1 L, 1.1 IP, 27.00 ERA, 0 SO, 2 BB, 0 SV, 2 G

Orlando McFarlane (Orlando DeJesús McFarlane Quesada) (b. 6-28-1938, Oriente) Debut: 4-23-1962 (1962, 1964, 1966–1968) Teams: Pittsburgh (N), Detroit (A), California (A) Position: Catcher, Outfield (BR TR) Stats: 124 G, 292 AB, 70 H, 22 R, 5 HR, 20 RBI, .240 BA

Román Mejías (Román Mejias Gómez) (b. 8-9-1930, Abreus, Las Villas) Debut: 4-13-1955 (1955, 1957–1964) Teams: Pittsburgh (N), Houston (N), Boston (A) Position: Outfield (BR TR) Stats: 627 G, 1768 AB, 449 H, 212 R, 54 HR, 202 RBI, .254 BA

Minnie Mendoza (Cristóbal Rigoberto Mendoza Carreras) (b. 11-16-1933, Ceiba del Agua) Debut: 4-9-1970 (1970) Team: Minnesota (A) Position: Infield (BR TR) Stats: 16 G, 16 AB, 3 H, 2 R, 0 HR, 2 RBI, .188 BA

Tony Menéndez (Antonio Menéndez) (b. 2-20-1965, Havana Province) Debut: 6-22-1992 (1992–1994) Teams: Cincinnati, Pittsburgh, San Francisco (N) Position: Pitcher (BR TR) Stats: 3 W, 1 L, 29.0 IP, 4.97 ERA, 20 SO, 6 BB, 0 SV, 23 G

Minnie Miñoso (Saturnino Orestes Armas Miñoso Arrieta) (b. 11-29-1922, Havana) Debut: 4-19-1949 (1949, 1951–1964, 1976, 1980) Teams: Cleveland (A), Chicago (A), Cleveland (A), Chicago (A), St. Louis (N), Washington (A), Chicago (A) Position: Outfield, Third Base (BR TR) Stats: 1835 G, 6579 AB, 1963 H, 1136 R, 186 HR, 1023 RBI, .298 BA

Willie Miranda (Guillermo Miranda Pérez) (b. 5-24-1926, Velasco; d. 9-7-1996, Baltimore, Maryland USA) Debut: 5-6-1951 (1951–1959) Teams: Washington (A), Chicago (A), St. Louis (A), Chicago (A), St. Louis (A), New York (A), Baltimore (A) Position: Shortstop (BB TR) Stats: 824 G, 1914 AB, 423 H, 176 R, 6 HR, 132 RBI, .221 BA

Aurelio Monteagudo (Aurelio Faustino Monteagudo Cintra) (b. 11-19-1943, Caibarien; d. 11-10-1990, Saltillo, Mexico) Debut: 9-1-1963 (1963–1967, 1970, 1973) Teams: Kansas City (A), Houston (N), Chicago (A), Kansas City (A), California (A) Position: Pitcher (BR TR) Stats: 3 W, 7 L, 132.0 IP, 5.05 ERA, 58 SO, 62 BB, 4 SV, 72 G (Son of René Monteagudo)

René Monteagudo (René Monteagudo Miranda) (b. 3-12-1916, Havana; d. 9-14-1973, Hialeah, Florida USA) Debut: 9-6-1939 (1938, 1940, 1945) Teams: Washington (A), Philadelphia (N) Position: Pitcher (BL TL) Stats: 3 W, 7 L, 168.1 IP, 6.42 ERA, 93 SO, 95 BB, 2 SV, 46 G (Father of Aurelio Monteagudo)

Manny Montejo (Manuel Montejo Bofill) (b. 10-16-1935, Caibarien) Debut: 7-25-1961 (1961) Team: Detroit (A) Position: Pitcher (BR TR) Stats: 0 W, 0 L, 16.1 IP, 3.86 ERA, 15 SO, 6 BB, 0 SV, 12 G

Dan Morejón (Daniel Morejón Torres) (b. 7-21-1930, Havana)

Debut: 7-11-1958 (1958) Team: Cincinnati (N) Position: Outfield (BR TR) Stats: 12 G, 26 AB, 5 H, 4 R, 0 HR, 1 RBI, .192 BA

Julio "Jiqui" Moreno (Julio Moreno González) (b. 1-28-1921, Guines; d. 1-2-1987, Miami, Florida USA) Debut: 9-8-1950 (1950–1953) Teams: Washington (A) Position: Pitcher (BR TR) Stats: 18 W, 22 L, 336.2 IP, 4.25 ERA, 119 SO, 157 BB, 2 SV, 73 G

Gonzalo "Cholly" Naranjo (Lázaro Ramón Gonzalo Naranjo) (b. 11-25-1934, Havana) Debut: 7-8-1956 (1956) Team: Pittsburgh (N) Position: Pitcher (BL TR) Stats: 1 W, 2 L, 34.1 IP, 4.46 ERA, 26 SO, 17 BB, 0 SV, 17 G

Ray Noble (Rafael Miguel Noble y Magee) (b. 3-15-1919, Central Hatillo; d. 5-9-1998, Brooklyn, New York USA) Debut: 4-18-1951 (1951–1953) Team: New York (N) Position: Catcher (BR TR) Stats: 107 G, 243 AB, 53 H, 31 R, 9 HR, 40 RBI, .218 BA

Vladimir Nuñez (Vladimir Nuñez Zarabaza) (b. 3-15-1975, Havana Province) Debut: 9-11-1998 (1998–2003) Teams: Arizona (N), Florida (N) Position: Pitcher (BR TR) Stats: 17 W, 29 L, 382.2 IP, 4.68 ERA, 280 SO, 164 BB, 27 SV, 208 G

Tony Oliva (Pedro Oliva López) (b. 7-20-1940, Pinar del Río) Debut: 9-9-1962 (1962–1976) Team: Minnesota (A) Position: Outfield, DH (BL TR) Stats: 1676 G, 6301 AB, 1917 H, 870 R, 220 HR, 947 RBI, .304 BA

Mosquito Ordeñana (Antonio Ordeñana Rodríguez) (b. 10-30-1918, Guanabacoa; d. 9-29-1988, Miami, Florida USA) Debut: 10-3-1943 (1943) Team: Pittsburgh (N) Position: Shortstop (BR TR) Stats: 1 G, 4 AB, 2 H, 0 R, 0 HR, 3 RBI, .500 BA

Rey Ordóñez (Reynaldo Ordóñez) (b. 1-11-1971, Havana Province) Debut: 4-1-1996 (1996–2004) Teams: New York Mets (N), Tampa Bay (A), Chicago (N) Position: Shortstop (BR TR) Stats: 973 G, 3115 AB, 767 H, 291 R, 12 HR, 287 RBI, .246 BA

Eddie Oropesa (Edilberto Oropesa) (b. 11-23-1971, Colón, Matanzas Province) Debut: 4-2-2001 (2001–2004) Teams: Philadelphia (N), Arizona (N), San Diego (N) Position: Pitcher (TL BL) Stats: 8 W, 4 L, 92.0 IP, 7.34 ERA, 78 SO, 72 BB, 0 SV, 125 G

Bill Ortega (Guillermo "Bobadilla" Ortega) (b. 7-24-1975, Havana) Debut: 9-7-2001 (2001) Team: St. Louis (N) Position: Outfielder (BR TR) Stats: 5 G, 5 AB, 1 H, 0 R, 0 HR, 0 RBI, .200 BA

Baby Ortiz (Oliverio Ortiz Núñez) (b. 12-5-1919, Camagüey; d. 3-27-1984, Central Senado) Debut: 9-23-1944 (1944) Team: Washington (A) Position: Pitcher (BR TR) Stats: 0 W, 2 L, 13.0 IP, 6.23 ERA, 4 SO, 6 BB, 0 SV, 2 G (Brother of Roberto Ortiz)

Roberto Ortiz (Roberto Gonzalo Ortiz Núñez) (b. 6-30-1915, Camagüey; d. 9-15-1971, Miami, Florida USA) Debut: 9-6-1941 (1941–1944, 1949–1950) Teams: Washington (A), Philadelphia (A) Position: Outfield (BR TR) Stats: 213 G, 659 AB, 168 H, 67 R, 8 HR, 78 RBI, .255 BA (Brother of Baby Ortiz)

Reggie Otero (Regino José Otero Gómez) (b. 9-7-1915, Havana; d. 10-21-1988, Hialeah, Florida USA) Debut: 9-2-1945 (1945) Team: Chicago (N) Position: First Base (BL TR) Stats: 14 G, 23 AB, 9 H, 1 R, 0 HR, 5 RBI, .391 BA

Rafael Palmeiro (Rafael Palmeiro Corrales) (b. 9-24-1964, Havana) Debut: 9-8-1986 (1986–2005) Teams: Chicago (N), Texas (A), Baltimore (A) Position: First Base, Outfield, DH (BL TL) Stats: 2831 G, 10472 AB, 3020 H, 1663 R, 569 HR, 1835 RBI, .288 BA

Emilio "Pal" Palmero (Emilio Antonio Palmero) (b. 6-13-1895, Guanabacoa; d. 7-15-1970, Toledo, Ohio USA) Debut: 9-21-1915 (1915–1916, 1921, 1926, 1928) Teams: New York (N), St. Louis (A), Washington (A), Boston (A) Position: Pitcher (BR TR) Stats: 6 W, 15 L, 141 IP, 5.17 ERA, 48 SO, 83 BB, 0 SV, 41 G

Camilo Pascual (Camilo Pascual Lus) (b. 1-20-1934, Havana) Debut: 4-15-1954 (1954–1971) Teams: Washington (A); Minnesota (A); Los Angeles (N); Cleveland (A) Position: Pitcher (BR TR) Stats: 174 W, 170 L, 2930.2 IP, 3.63 ERA, 2167 SO, 1069 BB, 10 SV, 529 G (Brother of Carlos Pascual)

Carlos Pascual (Carlos Alberto Pascual Lus) (b. 3-13-1931, Ha-

vana) Debut: 9-24-1950 (1950) Team: Washington (A) Position: Pitcher (BR TR) Stats: 1 W, 1 L, 17 IP, 2.12 ERA, 3 SO, 8 BB, 0 SV, 2 G (Brother of Camilo Pascual)

Carlos Paula (Carlos Paula Conill) (b. 11-28-1927, Havana; d. 4-25-1983, Miami USA) Debut: 9-6-1954 (1954–1956) Team: Washington (A) Position: Outfield (BR TR) Stats: 157 G, 457 AB, 124 H, 44 R, 9 HR, 60 RBI, .271 BA

Brayan Peña (Brayan Eduardo Peña) (b. 1-7-1982, Havana) Debut: 5-23-2005 (2005) Team: Atlanta (N) Position: Catcher (BB TR) Stats: 18 G, 39 AB, 7 H, 2 R, 0 HR, 4 RBI, .200 BA

Orlando Peña (Orlando Gregorio Peña Quevara) (b. 11-17-1933, Victoria de Las Tunas) Debut: 8-24-1958 (1958–1960, 1962–1975) Teams: Cincinnati (N), Kansas City (A), Detroit (A), Cleveland (A), Pittsburgh (N), Baltimore (A), St. Louis (N), California (A) Position: Pitcher (BR TR) Stats: 56 W, 77 L, 1202 IP, 3.71 ERA, 818 SO, 352 BB, 40 SV, 427 G

Tony (Tany) Pérez (Atanasio Pérez Rigal) (b. 5-14-1942, Camagüey) Debut: 76-26-1964 (1964–1986) Teams: Cincinnati (N), Montreal (N), Boston (A), Philadelphia (N), Cincinnati (N) Position: First Base, Third Base, DH (BR TR) Stats: 2777 G, 9778 AB, 2732 H, 1272 R, 379 HR, 1652 RBI, .279 BA

Leo Posada (Leopoldo Jesús Posada Hernández) (b. 4-15-1936, Havana) Debut: 9-21-1960 (1960–1962) Team: Kansas City (A) Position: Outfield (BR TR) Stats: 155 G, 426 AB, 109 H, 51 R, 8 HR, 58 RBI, .256 BA

Ariel Prieto (Ariel Prieto Fernández) (b. 10-22-1966, Havana) Debut: 7-2-1995 (1995–1998, 2000) Team: Oakland (A) Position: Pitcher (BR TR) Stats: 15 W, 24 L, 348.2 IP, 4.88 ERA, 229 SO, 174 BB, 0 SV, 67 G

Bobby Ramos (Roberto Ramos) (b. 11-5-1955, Havana) Debut: 9-26-1978 (1978, 1980–1984) Teams: Montreal (N), New York (A), Montreal (N) Position: Catcher (BR TR) Stats: 103 G, 232 AB, 44 H, 20 R, 4 HR, 17 RBI, .190 BA

Pedro "Pete" Ramos (Pedro Ramos Guerra) (b. 4-28-1935, Pinar del Rio) Debut: 4-11-1955 (1955–1970) Teams: Washington (A), Minnesota (A), Cleveland (A), New York (A), Philadelphia (N), Pittsburgh (N), Cincinnati (N), Washington (A) Position: Pitcher (BB TR) Stats: 117 W, 160 L, 2355.2 IP, 4.08 ERA, 1305 SO, 724 BB, 55 SV, 582 G

Napoleón "Nap" Reyes (Napoleón Reyes Aguilera) (b. 11-24-1919, Santiago; d. 9-15-1995, Miami, Florida USA) Debut: 5-19-1943 (1943–1945, 1950) Team: New York (N) Position: First Base, Third Base, Outfield (BR TR) Stats: 279 G, 931 AB, 264 H, 90 R, 13 HR, 110 RBI, .284 BA

Armando Roche (Armando Roche Báez) (b. 12-7-1926, Havana Province; d. 6-26-1997, Chicago, Illinois USA) Debut: 5-10-1945 (1945) Team: Washington (A) Position: Pitcher (BR TR) Stats: 0 W, 0 L, 6 IP, 6.00 ERA, 0 SO, 2 BB, 0 SV, 2 G

Joseíto Rodríguez (José Rodríguez) (b. 2-23-1894, Havana; d. 1-21-1953, Havana) Debut: 10-5-1916 (1916–1918) Team: New York (N) Position: Infield (BR TR) Stats: 58 G, 145 AB, 24 H, 17 R, 0 HR, 17 RBI, .166 BA

Freddie Rodríguez (Fernando Pedro Rodríguez Borrego) (b. 4-29-1924, Havana) Debut: 4-18-1958 (1958–1959) Teams: Chicago (N), Philadelphia (N) Position: Pitcher (BR TR) Stats: 0 W, 0 L, 9.1 IP, 8.68 ERA, 6 SO, 5 BB, 2 SV, 8 G

Héctor Rodríguez (Héctor Antonio Rodríguez Ordenana) (b. 6-13-1920, Alquizar) Debut: 4-15-1952 (1952) Team: Chicago (A) Position: Third Base (BR TR) Stats: 124 G, 407 AB, 108 H, 55 R, 1 HR, 40 RBI, .265 BA

Minnie Rojas (Minervino Alejandro Rojas Landin) (b. 11-26-19, Remidios; d. 3-24-2002, Los Angeles, California USA) Debut: 5-30-1966 (1966–1968) Team: California (A) Position: Pitcher (BR TR) Stats: 23 W, 16 L, 261 IP, 3.00 ERA, 153 SO, 68 BB, 43 SV, 157 G

Cookie Rojas (Octavio Victor Rojas Rivas) (b. 3-6-1939, Havana) Debut: 4-10-1962 (1962–1977) Teams: Cincinnati (N), Philadelphia (N), St. Louis (N), Kansas City (A) Position: Infield (BR TR) Stats: 1822 G, 6309 AB, 1660 H, 714 R, 54 HR, 593 RBI, .263 BA

Chico Ruiz (Hiraldo Ruiz Sablón) (b. 12-5-1938, Santo Domingo; d. 2-9-1972, San Diego USA) Debut: 4-13-1964 (1964–1971) Teams: Cincinnati (N), California (A) Position: Infield (BB TR) Stats: 565 G, 1150 AB, 276 H, 133 R, 2 HR, 69 RBI, .240 BA

Alex Sánchez (Alexis Sánchez) (b. 8-26-1976, Havana) Debut: 6-15-2001 (2001–2005) Team: Milwaukee Brewers (N), Detroit (A), Tampa Bay (A), San Francisco (N) Position: Outfielder (BL TL) Stats: 427 G, 1527 AB, 452 H, 193 R, 6 HR, 111 RBI, .296 BA

Israel Sánchez (Israel Sánchez Matos) (b. 8-20-1963, Falcón Lasvias) Debut: 7-7-1988 (1988, 1990) Team: Kansas City (A) Position: Pitcher (BL TL) Stats: 3 W, 2 L, 45.1 IP, 5.36 ERA, 19 SO, 21 BB, 1 SV, 30 G

Raúl Sánchez (Raúl Guadalupe Sánchez Rodríguez) (b. 12-12-1930, Marianao) Debut: 4-17-1952 (1952, 1957, 1960) Teams: Washington (A), Cincinnati (N) Position: Pitcher (BR TR) Stats: 5 W, 3 L, 89.2 IP, 4.62 ERA, 48 SO, 43 BB, 5 SV, 49 G

Nelson Santovenia (Nelson Gil Santovenia Mayol) (b. 7-27-1961, Pinar del Río) Debut: 9-16-1987 (1987–1993) Teams: Montreal (N), Chicago (A), Kansas City (A) Position: Catcher (BR TR) Stats: 297 G, 884 AB, 206 H, 77 R, 22 HR, 116 RBI, .233 BA

Diego Seguí (Diego Pablo Seguí González) (b. 8-17-1937, Holguín) Debut: 4-12-1962 (1962–1977) Teams: Kansas City (A), Washington (A), Kansas City (A), Oakland (A), Seattle (A), Oakland (A), St. Louis (N), Boston (A), Seattle (A) Position: Pitcher (BR TR) Stats: 92 W, 111 L, 1807.2 IP, 3.81 ERA, 1298 SO, 786 BB, 71 SV, 639 G (Father of David Seguí, born in the USA)

Luis Suárez (Luis Adelardo Suarez) (b. 8-24-1916, Alto Songo; d. 6-5-1991, Havana) Debut: 5-28-1944 (1944) Team: Washington (A) Position: Third Base (BR TR) Stats: 1 G, 2 AB, 0 H, 0 R, 0 HR, 0 RBI, .000 BA

Leo Sutherland (Leonardo Sutherland Cantin) (b. 4-6-1958, Santiago) Debut: 8-11-1980 (1980–1981) Team: Chicago (A) Position: Outfield, Third Base (BL TL) Stats: 45 G, 101 AB, 25 H, 15 R, 0 HR, 5 RBI, .248 BA

José Tartabull (José Milages Tartabull Guzmán) (b. 11-27-1938, Cienfuegos) Debut: 4-10-1962 (1962–1970) Teams: Kansas City (A), Boston (A), Oakland (A) Position: Outfield (BL TL) Stats: 749 G, 1857 AB, 484 H, 247 R, 2 HR, 107 RBI, .261 BA (Father of Danny Tartabull, born in Puerto Rico)

Tony Taylor (Antonio Nemesio Taylor Sánchez) (b. 12-19-1935, Central Alara) Debut: 4-15-1958 (1958–1976) Teams: Chicago (N), Philadelphia (N), Detroit (A), Philadelphia (N) Position: Infield (BR TR) Stats: 2195 G, 7680 AB, 2007 H, 1005 R, 75 HR, 598 RBI, .261 BA

Michael Tejera (Michael Tejera) (b. 10-18-1976, Havana) Debut: 9-8-1999 (1999–2005) Teams: Florida (N), Texas (A) Position: Pitcher (TL BL) Stats: 11 W, 13 L, 238.1 IP, 5.14 ERA, 172 SO, 111 BB, 3 SV, 111 G

Luis "Looie" Tiant (Luis Clemente Tiant Vega) (b. 11-23-1940, Marianao) Debut: 7-19-1964 (1964–1982) Teams: Cleveland (A), Minnesota (A), Boston (A), New York (A), Pittsburgh (N), California (A) Position: Pitcher (BR TR) Stats: 229 W, 172 L, 3486.1 IP, 3.30 ERA, 2416 SO, 1104 BB, 15 SV, 573 G (Son of Luis Tiant, Negro leagues)

Jorge Toca (Jorge Luis Toca Gómez) (b. 1-7-1971, Remedios, Villa Clara Province) Debut: 9-12-1999 (1999–2002) Team: New York Mets (N) Position: First Base (BR TR) Stats: 25 G, 27 AB, 7 H, 4 R, 0 HR, 5 RBI, .259 BA

Gil Torres (Don Gilberto Torres Núñez) (b. 8-23-1915, Regla; d. 1-10-1983, Regla) Debut: 4-25-1940 (1940, 1944–1946) Team: Washington (A) Position: Infield, Shortstop, Pitcher (BR TR) Hitting Stats: 44 G, 61 AB, 16 H, 5 R, 0 HR, 2 RBI, .262 BA; Pitching Stats: 0 W, 0 L, 9.2 IP, 5.59 ERA, 3 SO, 3 BB, 1 SV, 5 G

Ricardo Torres (Ricardo Jiménez Torres Martínez) (b. 4-16-1891, Regla; d. 4-17-1960, Regla) Debut: 5-18-1920 (1920–1922) Team: Washington (A) Position: Catcher, First Base (BR TR) Stats: 22 G, 37 AB, 11 H, 9 R, 0 HR, 3 RBI, .297 BA

Oscar Tuero (Oscar Tuero Monzón) (b. 12-17-1898, Havana; d. 10-21-1960, Houston, Texas USA) Debut: 5-30-1918 (1918–1920) Team: St. Louis (N) Position: Pitcher (BR TR) Stats: 6 W, 9 L, 199.2 IP, 2.88 ERA, 58 SO, 53 BB, 4 SV, 58 G

Santiago "Sandy" Ullrich (Carlos Santiago Ullrich Castello) (b. 7-25-1921, Havana; d. 4-21-2001, Miami, Florida, USA) Debut: 5-3-1944 (1944–1945) Team: Washington (A) Position: Pitcher (BR TR) Stats: 3 W, 3 L, 91.0 IP, 5.04 ERA, 28 SO, 38 BB, 1 SV, 31 G

Roy Valdés (Rogelio Lázaro Valdés y Rojas) (b. 2-20-1920, Havana) Debut: 5-3-1944 (1944) Team: Washington (A) Position: Pinch Hitter (BR TR) Stats: 1 G, 1 AB, 0 H, 0 R, 0 HR, 0 RBI, .000 BA

René Valdez (Rene Gutiérrez Valdez) (b. 6-2-1929, Guanabacoa, Havana Province) Debut: 4-21-1957 (1957) Team: Brooklyn (N) Position: Pitcher (BR TR) Stats: 1 W, 1 L, 13.0 IP, 5.54 ERA, 10 SO, 7 BB, 0 SV, 5 G

Sandy Valdespino (Hilario Valdespino Borroto) (b. 1-14-1939, San José de Las Lajas) Debut: 4-12-1965 (1965–1971) Teams: Minnesota (A), Atlanta (N), Houston (N), Seattle (A), Milwaukee (A), Kansas City (A) Position: Outfield (BL TL) Stats: 382 G, 765 AB, 176 H, 96 R, 7 HR, 67 RBI, .230 BA

José Valdivielso (José Martínez Valdivielso y López) (b. 5-22-1934, Matanzas) Debut: 6-21-1955 (1955–1956, 1959–1961) Teams: Washington (A), Minnesota (A) Position: Shortstop (BR TR) Stats: 401 G, 971 AB, 213 H, 89 R, 9 HR, 85 RBI, .219 BA

Zolio "Zorro" Versalles (Zolio Casanova Versalles y Rodríguez) (b. 12-18-1939, Marianao, Havana; d. 6-9-1995, Bloomington, Minnesota USA) Debut: 8-1-1959 (1959–1971) Teams: Washington (A), Minnesota (A), Los Angeles (N), Cleveland (A), Washington (A), Atlanta (N) Position: Shortstop (BR TR) Stats: 1400 G, 5141 AB, 1246 H, 650 R, 95 HR, 471 RBI, .242 BA

Adrián Zabala (Adrián Zabala Rodríguez) (b. 8-26-1916, San Antonio de los Baños; deceased) Debut: 8-11-1945 (1945, 1949) Team: New York (N) Position: Pitcher (BL TL) Stats: 4 W, 7 L, 84.1 IP, 5.02 ERA, 27 SO, 30 BB, 1 SV, 26 G

Oscar Zamora (Oscar José Zamora Sosa) (b. 9-23-1944, Camagüey) Debut: 6-18-1974 (1974–1976, 1978) Teams: Chicago (N), Houston (N) Position: Pitcher (BR TR) Stats: 13 W, 14 L, 224.2 IP, 4.53 ERA, 99 SO, 58 BB, 23 SV, 158 G

José Zardón (José Antonio Zardón Sánchez) (b. 5-20-1923, Havana) Debut: 4-18-1945 (1945) Team: Washington (A) Position: Outfield, Infield (BR TR) Stats: 54 G, 131 AB, 38 H, 13 R, 0 HR, 13 RBI, .290 BA

Cuban Baseball Hall of Fame, Havana

(Players, Founders, Officials Selected Before 1961)

1939—Luis Bustamante, José de la Caridad Méndez, Antonio María García, Gervasio "Strike" González, Armando Marsans, Rafael Almeida, Valentín González, Cristóbal Torriente, Adolfo Luján, Carlos "Bebe" Royer (first class of inductees)

1940—Alfredo Arcaño, José Muñoz

1941—Emilio Sabourín, Regino García

1942—Agustín Molina, Alfredo "El Pájaro" Cabrera

1943—Luis Padrón, Heliodoro Hidalgo, Julián Castillo

1944—Carlos Maciá, Alejandro Oms

1945—Ramón Calzadilla, Carlos Morán, José "Juan" Pastoriza, Valentín Dreke, Bernardo Baró

1946 — Wenceslao Gálvez, Ricardo Caballero, Rogelio Valdés, Arturo Valdés, Francisco Poto

1947 — None

1948 — Juan Antiga, Antonio Mesa, Tomás Romañach, Jacinto Calvo, Rafael Hernández, Nemesio Guilló

1949 — Eduardo Machado, Julio López, Pelayo Chacón, Gonzalo Sánchez, Manuel Villa

1950 — Eugenio Jiménez, Eustaquio Gutiérrez, Rafael Figarola, Manuel Cueto, Ricardo Martínez

1951 — Martín Dihigo, José Maria Teuma, Alfredo Arango, Bienvenido Jiménez, José Rodríguez

1952 — None

1953 — Moisés Quintero, Juan Violá, Carlso Zaldo

1954 — Emilio Palmero, Pablo Ronquillo

1955 — Baldomero "Mérito" Acosta

1956 — Miguel Angel González

1957 — Emilio Palomino, Isidro Fabré

1958 — Adolfo Luque

1959 — Lázaro Sálazar, José Acosta

1960 — Ramón Bragaña, Armando Cabañas

1961 — Oscar Rodríguez, Tomás de la Cruz

Cuban Baseball Hall of Fame in Exile, Miami

(Players and Officials Selected After 1961)

First selection in 1962 (year of suspension of professional baseball in Cuba)

1962 — Eustaquio "Bombín" Pedroso, Rogelio Crespo, Agustín Parpetti

1963 — Pedro Dibut, Ramón "Paito" Herrera

1964 — Montalvo Mayarí, Pablo "Champion" Mesa, Eliodoro "Yoyo" Díaz

1965 — José Maria Fernández, Luis Tiant (Senior)

1966 — Rodolfo Fernández

1967 — Tony Castaño, Santos "Canguro" Amaro

1968 — Roberto "Tarzán" Estalella

1969 — Manuel "Cocaína" García, Fermín Guerra

1970 — Agapito Mayor

1971 — Regino Otero, Andrés Fleitas

1972 — Pedro Formental

1973 — Alejandro Crespo, Napoleón Reyes

1974 — Héctor Rodríguez

1975 — Silvio García, Roberto Ortíz

1976 — Julio "Jiqui" Moreno

1977 — Sandalio "Sandy" Consuegra, Conrado Marrero

1978 — Edmundo "Sandy" Amorós

1979 — Willie Miranda, Leo Cárdenas

1980 — Zoilo "Zorro" Versalles

1981 — Pedro Ramos, Tony Taylor

1982 — Pedro "Tony" Oliva, Octavio "Cookie" Rojas

1983 — Camilo Pascual, Orestes "Minnie" Miñoso, Alfredo Suárez, Emilio de Armas

1984 — Esteban Bellán, Justo Cando López, Julio Rojo, Pedro "Preston" Gómez, Adrián Zabala, Amado Maestri, Victor Muñoz, Miguel "Mike" Cuéllar, Mario Mendoza, Joe Massager, Rafael Conte, Dr. José López de Valle, Dr. Leopoldo de Sola

1985 — Lorenzo "Chiquitín" Cabrera, Bartolo Portuondo, Basilio "Brujo" Rosell, José "Cheo" Olivares, Rafael Noble, Miguel Fornieles, Antonio González, Roberto Maduro, Miguel Suárez, Pedro Galiana, Dr. Julio Sanguily

1986 — Francisco Correa, José Ramos, Pedro Arango, Marcelino Guerra, Jorge Comellas, Orlando Peña, Abel Linares, René Monteagudo, Julio Blanco Herrera, Bernardo Jiménez, Antonio "Tony" Pacheco, Dr. Rafael Inclán

1987 — None

1988 — None

1989 — None

1990 — None

1997 — Luis "Witto" Aloma, Joaquín "Joe" Azcue, Julio Becquer, Agustín Bejerano, Carlos Blanco, Heberto Blanco, Dagoberto "Bert" Campaneris, José Cardenal, Avelino Cañizares, Ramón Couto, Claro Duany, Vicento López, Humberto "Chico" Fernández, Rigoberto "Tito" Fuentes, Ramon Heredia, Salvador "Sal" Hernández, Román Mejias, Francisco "Panchón" Herrera, Isora del Castillo, Manuel "Chino" Hidalgo, Pedro Pagés, Luis Tiant, Jr., Rocky Nelson, Atanasio "Tany" Pérez, Antonio Rodríguez, Octavio Rubert, Raúl Sánchez, Diego Segui, Ramón Roger, Angel Scull, José Tartabull, Santiago Ullrich, Bobby Bragan, Oscar Charleston, Monte Irvin, Max Lanier

No Inductions Since 1997

Appendix D: Statistical Records

Cuban Professional League Records (1878–1961)

YEAR-BY-YEAR CHAMPIONSHIP RESULTS

Managers in **boldface** were also U.S. Major Leaguers (Key: † = Non-Cuban Manager)

Year	Series	Championship Team	Manager/Director	Record (W–L–T, Pct.)
1878–79	1	Habana	**Esteban Bellán**	4–0–1, 1.000
1879–80	2	Habana	**Esteban Bellán**	5–2, .714
1880–81		No Official Season		
1982		Season Not Completed (Dispute between Habana and Club Fe)		
1882–83	3	Habana	**Esteban Bellán**	5–1, .833
1883–84		No Official Season		
1885	4	Habana	Ricardo Mora	4–3, .571
1885–86	5	Habana	Francisco Saavedra	6–0, 1.000
1887	6	Habana	Francisco Saavedra	10–2, .833
1888	7	Club Fe	Antonio Utrera	12–3, .800
1889	8	Habana	Emilio Sabourín	16–4–1, .800
1889–90	9	Habana	Emilio Sabourín	14–3, .824
1890–91	10	Club Fe	Luis Almoina y Meléndez	12–6, .667
1892	11	Habana	Emilio Sabourín	13–7, .650
1892–93	12	Matanzas	Luis Almoina y Meléndez	14–9, .609
1893–94		Almendares	Ramón Gutiérrez	17–7–1, .708
1894–95		Season Not Completed (War of Independence)		
1895–96		Season Cancelled (War of Independence)		
1896–97		Season Cancelled (War of Independence)		
1898–98		Season Not Completed (War of Independence)		
1898–99	14	Habanista	Alberto Azoy	9–3–1, .750
1900	15	San Francisco	Patrocinio Silverio	17–10–1, .630
1901	16	Habana	Alberto Azoy	16–3–1, .842
1902	17	Habana	Alberto Azoy	17–0–2, 1.000
1903	18	Habana	Alberto Azoy	21–13, .618
1904	19	Habana	Alberto Azoy	16–4, .800
1905	20	Almendares	Abel Linares	19–11, .633
1905–06	21	Club Fe	Alberto Azoy	15–9–1, .625
1907	22	Almendares	Eugenio Santa Cruz	17–13–1, .567
1908	23	Almendares	Juan Sánchez	37–8–1, .822
1908–09	24	Habana	Luis Someillán	33–13–1, .690
1910	25	Almendares	Juan Sánchez	13–3–1, .812
1910–11	26	Almendares	Juan Sánchez	21–6–3, .714
1912	27	Habana	Eduardo Laborde	22–12–1, .647
1913	28	Club Fe	Agustín Molina	21–11–2, .656
1913–14	29	Almendares	Eugenio Santa Cruz	22–11–1, .667
1914–15	30	Habana	**Mike González**	23–11, .676
1915–16	31	Almendares	Alfredo Cabrera	30–12–3, .714
1917	32	Orientals	**Armando Marsans**	8–6–1, .571
1918–19	33	Habana	**Mike González**	29–19, .604

Year	Series	Championship Team	Manager/Director	Record (W–L–T, Pct.)
1919–20	34	Almendares	**Adolfo Luque**	22–5–2, .815
1920–21	35	Habana	**Mike González**	21–9–5, .700
1921	36	Havana	**Mike González**	4–1, .800
1922–23	37	Marianao	**Baldomero Acosta**	35–19–1, .648
1923–24	38	Santa Clara	Augustín Molina	36–11–1, .766
1924–25	39	Almendares	Joseíto Rodríguez	33–16–1, .660
1925–26	40	Almendares	Joseíto Rodríguez	34–13–2, .723
1926–27	41	Habana	**Mike González**	20–11, .645
1927–28	42	Habana	**Mike González**	24–13, .649
1928–29	43	Habana	**Mike González**	43–12–1, .782
1929–30	44	Cienfuegos	Pelayo Chacón	33–19–2, .635
1930–31		Season Not Completed		
1931–32	45	Almendares	Joseíto Rodríguez	21–9–4, .700
1932–33	46	Almendares (Tie)	**Adolfo Luque**	13–9, .591
		Habana (Tie)	**Mike González**	13–9, .591
1933–34		No Official Season		
1934–35	47	Almendares	**Adolfo Luque**	18–9–1, .667
1935–36	48	Santa Clara	Martín Dihigo	34–14–1, .708
1936–37	49	Marianao	Martín Dihigo	38–31–3, .551
1937–38	50	Santa Clara	Lazaro Sálazar	44–18–4, .710
1938–39	51	Santa Clara	Lazaro Sálazar	34–20–2, .630
1939–40	52	Almendares	**Adolfo Luque**	28–23–1, .549
1940–41	53	Habana	**Mike González**	31–18–5, .633
1941–42	54	Almendares	**Adolfo Luque**	25–19–4, .568
1942–43	55	Almendares	**Adolfo Luque**	28–20–1, .583
1943–44	56	Habana	**Mike González**	32–16, .667
1944–45	57	Almendares	Reinaldo Cordeiro	32–16–6, .667
1945–46	58	Cienfuegos	**Adolfo Luque**	37–23–4, .617
1946–47	59	Almendares	**Adolfo Luque**	42–24–2, .636
1947–48	60	Habana	**Mike González**	39–33–9, .542
1948–49	61	Almendares	**Fermín Guerra**	47–25, .553
1949–50	62	Almendares	**Fermín Guerra**	38–34–4, .528
1950–51	63	Habana	**Mike González**	41–32–1, .562
1951–52	64	Habana	**Mike González**	41–30–1, .577
1952–53	65	Habana	**Mike González**	43–29–1, .597
1953–54	66	Almendares	**Bobby Bragan**[†]	44–28–1, .611
1954–55	67	Almendares	**Bobby Bragan**[†]	44–25–2, .638
1955–56	68	Cienfuegos	Oscar Rodríguez	40–29–1, .580
1956–57	69	Marianao	Napoleón Reyes	40–28–1, .588
1957–58	70	Marianao	Napoleón Reyes	43–32–1, .597
1958–59	71	Almendares	Oscar Rodríguez	46–26–6, .639
1959–60	72	Cienfuegos	Antonio Castaño	48–24, .667
1960–61	73	Cienfuegos	Antonio Castaño	35–31–1, .530

INDIVIDUAL CUBAN LEAGUE BATTING LEADERS

Key: † 1921 and 1931 seasons were shortened and uncompleted

Year	Batting Average Leader	Home Runs Leader	Base Hits Leader	Runs Scored
1878–79	No Official Record	No Official Record	No Official Record	No Official Record
1879–80	No Official Record	No Official Record	No Official Record	No Official Record
1880–81	No Official Season			
1882	Season Not Completed (Dispute between Habana and Club Fe)			
1882–83	No Official Record	No Official Record	No Official Record	No Official Record
1883–84	No Official Season			
1885	Pablo Ronquilla (.350)	No Official Record	No Official Record	No Official Record
1885–86	Wenceslao Gálvez (.345)	No Official Record	Three Tied (10)	No Official Record
1887	Ricardo Martínez (.439)	None Hit	Ricardo Martínez (18)	No Official Record
1888	Antonio García (.448)	None Hit	Antonio García (26)	No Official Record
1889	Francisco Salabarría (.305)	None Hit	Francisco Hernández (24)	No Official Record
1889–90	Antonio M. García (.364)	Antonio M. García (1)	Antonio M.García (24)	No Official Record
1890–91	Alfredo Crespo (.375)	Two Tied (1)	Francisco Hernández (23)	No Official Record
1892	Antonio M. García (.362)	Alfredo Arcaño (3)	Francisco Hernández (34)	No Official Record

Year	Batting Average Leader	Home Runs Leader	Base Hits Leader	Runs Scored
1892–93	Antonio M. García (.385)	Two Tied (2)	Valentín González (36)	No Official Record
1893–94	Miguel Prats (.394)	Alfredo Arcaño (2)	Miguel Prats (41)	No Official Record
1894–95	Alfredo Arcaño (.430)	Valentín González (3)	Valentín González (32)	No Official Record
	No Official Record			
1895–96	Season Cancelled (War of Independence)			
1896–97	Season Cancelled (War of Independence)			
1897–98	Valentín González (.394)	No Official Record	Valentín González (13)	No Official Record
1898–99	Valentín González (.414)	No Official Record	Two Tied (12)	No Official Record
1900	Esteban Prats (.333)	No Official Record	Luís Padrón (31)	No Official Record
1901	Julián Castillo (.454)	No Official Record	Julián Castillo (30)	No Official Record
1902	Luis Padrón (.463)	Luis Padrón (2)	Valentín González (24)	No Official Record
1903	Julián Castillo (.330)	Julián Castillo (2)	Julián Castillo (37)	No Official Record
1904	Regino García (.397)	Valentín González (2)	Regino García (31)	No Official Record
1905	Regino García (.305)	No Official Record	Valentín González (32)	No Official Record
1905–06	Regino García (.304)	No Official Record	Regino García (28)	No Official Record
1907	Regino García (.324)	No Official Record	Regino García (36)	No Official Record
1908	Emilio Palomino (.350)	Luis Padrón (3)	Preston Hill (60)	Two Tied (53)
1908–09	Julián Castillo (.315)	No Official Record	Two Tied (46)	No Official Record
1910	Julián Castillo (.408)	Rogelio Valdés (1)	Two Tied (20)	Strike González (18)
1910–11	Preston Hill (.365)	No Official Record	Preston Hill (35)	Armando Marsans (22)
1912	Emilio Palomino (.440)	Julián Castillo (5)	Grant Johnson (43)	Carlos Morán (32)
1913	Armando Marsans (.400)	Julián Castillo (1)	Spotwood Poles (55)	Spotwood Poles (40)
1913–14	Manuel Villa (.351)	No Official Record	Manuel Villa (46)	Armando Marsans (28)
1914–15	Cristóbal Torriente (.387)	No Official Record	Cristóbal Torriente (48)	Cristóbal Torriente (33)
1915–16	Eustaquio Pedroso (.413)	No Official Record	Cristóbal Torriente (56)	Cristóbal Torriente (41)
1917	Adolfo Luque (.355)	None	José M. Fernández 16)	Mike González (9)
1918–19	Manuel Cueto (.344)	None	Two Tied (52)	Baldomero Acosta (30)
1919–20	Cristóbal Torriente (.360)	No Official Record	Bernardo Baró (37)	Bernardo Baró (21)
1920–21	Pelayo Chacón (.344)	No Official Record	Pelayo Chacón (32)	Two Tied (19)
1921[†]	Bienvenido Jiménez (.619)	Manuel Cueto (1)	Bienvenido Jiménez (13)	Bienvenido Jiménez (7)
1922–23	Bernardo Baró (.401)	Cristóbal Torriente (4)	Two Tied (61)	Cristóbal Torriente (37)
1923–24	Oliver Marcelle (.393)	Bienvenido Jiménez (4)	Dobie Moore (71)	Oscar Charleston (59)
1924–25	Alejandro Oms (.393)	Mayarí Montalvo (5)	Pop Lloyd (73)	Valentín Dreke (45)
1925–26	Johnny Wilson (.430)	Two Tied (3)	Johnny Wilson (64)	Two Tied (37)
1926–27	Manuel Cueto (.398)	José Hernández (4)	Manuel Cueto (41)	Paito Herrera (24)
1927–28	Johnny Wilson (.424)	Oscar Charleston (5)	Martín Dihigo (54)	Johnny Wilson (36)
1928–29	Alejandro Oms (.432)	James "Papa" Bell (5)	Alejandro Oms (76)	James "Papa" Bell (44)
1929–30	Alejandro Oms (.389)	Mule Suttles (7)	Chino Smith (67)	James "Papa" Bell (52)
1930–31[†]	Oscar Charleston (.373)	Three Tied (1)	Two Tied (19)	Pedro Arango (6)
1931–32	Ramón Couto (.400)	Alejandro Oms (3)	Alejandro Oms (44)	Alejandro Oms (28)
1932–33	Mike González (.432)	Bobby Estalella (3)	Two Tied (30)	José Abreu (17)
1933–34	No Official Season			
1934–35	Lázaro Sálazar (.407)	Eleven Tied (1)	Cando López (36)	Cando López (18)
1935–36	Martín Dihigo (.358)	Two Tied (5)	Two Tied (63)	Martín Dihigo (42)
1936–37	Harry Williams (.339)	Bobby Estalella (5)	Clyde Spearman (84)	Lázaro Salazar (47)
1937–38	Sammy Bankhead (.366)	Three Tied (4)	Sammy Bankhead (89)	Sammy Bankhead (47)
1938–39	Antonio Castaño (.371)	Josh Gibson (11)	Santos Amaro (78)	Josh Gibson (50)
1939–40	Antonio Castaño (.340)	Mule Suttles (4)	Sammy Bankhead (67)	Sammy Bankhead (41)
1940–41	Lázaro Salazar (.316)	Alejandro Crespo (3)	Helio Mirabal (59)	Pedro Pagés (37)
1941–42	Silvio García (.351)	Silvio García (4)	Silvio García (60)	Silvio García (24)
1942–43	Alejandro Crespo (.337)	Two Tied (2)	Alejandro Crespo (63)	Antonio Rodríguez (31)
1943–44	Roberto Ortíz (.337)	Saguita (Sal) Hernández (3)	Roberto Ortiz (64)	Roberto Ortiz (41)
1944–45	Claro Duany (.340)	Claro Duany (3)	Two Tied (59)	Four Tied (29)
1945–46	Lloyd Davenport (.332)	Dick Sisler (9)	Alejandro Crespo (72)	Roland Gladu (41)
1946–47	Lou Klein (.330)	Roberto Ortíz (11)	Andrés Fleitas (83)	Avelino Cañizares (47)
1947–48	Harry Kimbro (.346)	Jesús (Changuilón) Díaz (7)	Harry Kimbro (104)	Sam Jethroe (53)
1948–49	Alejandro Crespo (.326)	Monte Irvin (10)	Hank Thompson (85)	Hank Thompson (60)
1949–50	Pedro Formental (.336)	Two Tied (15)	Pedro Formental (99)	Pedro Formental (51)
1950–51	Silvio García (.347)	Four Tied (8)	Lorenzo Cabrera (88)	Orestes Miñoso (54)
1951–52	Bert Haas (.323)	Two Tied (9)	Johnny Jorgensen (85)	Pedro Formental (47)
1952–53	Sandy Amorós (.373)	Lou Klein (16)	Paul Smith (93)	Orestes Miñoso (67)
1953–54	Rocky Nelson (.352)	Two Tied (10)	Forrest Jacobs (94)	Forrest Jacobs (58)

Year	Batting Average Leader	Home Runs Leader	Base Hits Leader	Runs Scored
1954–55	Angel Scull (.370)	Rocky Nelson (13)	Bob Boyd (88)	Rocky Nelson (60)
1955–56	Forrest Jacobs (.321)	Ultus Alvarez (10)	Forrest Jacobs (91)	Orestes Miñoso (47)
1956–57	Orestes Miñoso (.312)	Archie Wilson (11)	Archie Wilson (76)	Solly Drake (52)
1957–58	Milton Smith (.320)	Four Tied (9)	Tony Taylor (83)	Milton Smith (46)
1958–59	Tony Taylor (.303)	Jim Baxes (9)	Tony Taylor (88)	Rocky Nelson (37)
1959–60	Tony González (.310)	Panchón Herrera (15)	Román Mejías (79)	Two Tied (41)
1960–61	Cookie Rojas (.322)	Julio Bécquer (15)	Cookie Rojas (85)	Tony González (42)

INDIVIDUAL CUBAN LEAGUE PITCHING LEADERS

Key: † 1921 and 1931 seasons were shortened and uncompleted

Year	Winning Percentage	Pitching Victories	Games Pitched	Complete Games
1878–79	No Official Record	No Official Record	No Official Record	No Official Record
1879–80	No Official Record	No Official Record	No Official Record	No Official Record
1880–81	No Official Season			
1882	Season Not Completed (Dispute between Havana and Club Fe)			
1882–83	No Official Record	No Official Record	No Official Record	No Official Record
1883–84	No Official Season			
1885	No Official Record	No Official Record	No Official Record	No Official Record
1885–86	Adolfo Luján (5–0 1.000)	Adolfo Luján (5)	Adolfo Luján (5)	Adolfo Luján (5)
1887	Adolfo Luján (5–0 1.000)	Carlos Maciá (7)	Carlos Maciá (9)	Carlos Maciá (9)
1888	Cisco Hernández (10–2 .833)	Adolfo Luján (11)	Adolfo Luján (15)	Adolfo Luján (15)
1889	Adolfo Luján (10–3 .769)	Adolfo Luján (10)	Enrique Rojas (20)	Enrique Rojas (18)
1889–90	Miguel Prats (11–2 .846)	Miguel Prats (11)	José M. Pastoriza (14)	José M. Pastoriza (14)
1890–91	Miguel Prats (9–4 .692)	José M. Pastoriza (10)	Two Tied (15)	Two Tied (12)
1892	Emilio Hernández (4–1 .800)	Miguel Prats (9)	José M. Pastoriza (17)	José M. Pastoriza (15)
1892–93	Cisco Hernández (4–1 .800)	Enrique García (6)	Three Tied (12)	Miguel Prats (8)
1893–94	José Pastoriza (16–7 .695)	José M. Pastoriza (16)	José M. Pastoriza (23)	José M. Pastoriza (18)
1894–95	Enrique García (12–4 .750)	Enrique García (12)	Enrique García (17)	Enrique García (15)
1895–96	**Season Cancelled (War of Independence)**			
1896–97	**Season Cancelled (War of Independence)**			
1897–98	Season Not Completed			
1898–99	José Romero (5–2 .714)	José Romero (5)	José Romero (9)	José Romero (7)
1900	Luís Padrón (13–4 .765)	Luís Padrón (13)	Salvador Rosado (20)	Two Tied (17)
1901	Carlos Royer (12–3 .800)	Carlos Royer (12)	Carlos Royer (15)	José Muñoz (14)
1902	Carlos Royer (17–0 1.000)	Carlos Royer (17)	Carlos Royer (19)	Carlos Royer (17)
1903	Cándido Fontanals (14–6 .700)	Carlos Royer (18)	Carlos Royer (28)	Carlos Royer (28)
1904	Carlos Royer (13–3 .813)	Carlos Royer (13)	Carlos Royer (16)	Carlos Royer (16)
1905	Angel D'Mesa (10–4 .714)	Two Tied (10)	José Muñoz (20)	Luís González (16)
1905–06	José Muñoz (8–1 .889)	Luís González (10)	Luís González (19)	Rube Foster (15)
1907	George Mack (4–2 .667)	Rube Foster (9)	José Muñoz (17)	Julián Pérez (13)
1908	José Méndez (9–0 1.000)	José Muñoz (13)	José Muñoz (19)	Julián Pérez (13)
1908–09	José Méndez (15–6 .714)	Two Tied (15)	José Méndez (28)	José Méndez (18)
1910	José Méndez (7–0 1.000)	José Méndez (7)	(Unknown) Marlotica (9)	Pastor Parera (8)
1910–11	José Méndez (11–2 .846)	José Méndez (11)	José Méndez (18)	José Méndez (12)
1912	José Junco (6–1 .857)	Fred Wickware (10)	Cyclone Williams (21)	Two Tied (13)
1913	Dick Redding (7–2 .778)	Eustaquio Pedroso (11)	Eustaquio Pedroso (22)	Eustaquio Pedroso (11)
1913–14	José Méndez (10–0 1.000)	Pastor Parera (11)	Pastor Parera (21)	Pastor Parera (12)
1914–15	José Acosta (5–1 .823)	Eustaquio Pedroso (10)	Eustaquio Pedroso (20)	Eustaquio Pedroso (12)
1915–16	José Acosta (8–3 .727)	Adolfo Luque (12)	Eustaquio Pedroso (21)	Eustaquio Pedroso (12)
1917	José Acosta (2–1 .667)	Two Tied (4)	Adolfo Luque (9)	Two Tied (6)
1918–19	José Acosta (16–10 .615)	José Acosta (16)	José Acosta (34)	José Acosta (17)
1919–20	Emilio Palmero (5–1 .833)	Adolfo Luque (10)	Two Tied (15)	José Acosta (11)
1920–21	José Hernández (4–1 .800)	José Acosta (6)	José Acosta, Oscar Tuero (13)	Oscar Tuero (8)
1921†	Julio LeBlanc (2–0 1.000)	Julio LeBlanc (2)	Emilo Palmero (3)	Oscar Tuero (2)
1922–23	Lucas Boada (10–4 .714)	Adolfo Luque (11)	Adolfo Luque (23)	Adolfo Luque (12)
1923–24	Bill Holland (10–2 .833)	Bill Holland (10)	Isidro Fabré (20)	Oscar Fuhr (9)
1924–25	José Acosta (4–1 .800)	Oscar Levis, Bullet Rogan (9)	O. Levis, Martín Dihigo (20)	Oscar Levis (12)
1925–26	César Alvarez (10–2 .833)	César Alvarez (10)	Oscar Levis (15)	César Alvarez (9)
1926–27	Juan Olmo (3–0 1.000)	Pedro Dibut, Claude Grier (5)	Raúl Alvarez (15)	Raúl Alvarez (7)
1927–28	Oscar Levis (7–2 .778)	Oscar Levis (7)	Willie Powell (18)	Willie Foster (8)
1928–29	Adolfo Luque (9–2 .818)	Adolfo Luque, Cliff Bell (9)	Charles Williams (19)	Campanita Bell (11)

Year	Winning Percentage	Pitching Victories	Games Pitched	Complete Games
1929–30	Yoyo Díaz (13–3 .813)	Yoyo Díaz (13)	Campanita Bell (23)	Yoyo Díaz (11)
1930–31†	Four Tied (1–0 1.000)	Several Tied (1)	Campanita Bell (3)	No Official Record
1931–32	Juan Eckelson (5–1 .833)	Rodolfo Fernández (8)	Luis Tiant (19)	Rodolfo Fernández (9)
1932–33	Jesús Lorenzo (3–0 1.000)	Jesús Miralles (6)	Jesús Miralles (14)	Jesús Miralles (6)
1933–34	No Official Season			
1934–35	Lázaro Salazar (6–1 .857)	Three Tied (6)	Gilberto Torres (13)	Tomás de la Cruz (7)
1935–36	Martín Dihigo (11–2 .846)	Martín Dihigo (11)	Tomás de la Cruz (23)	Martín Dihigo (13)
1936–37	Raymond Brown (21–4 .840)	Raymond Brown (21)	Martín Dihigo (30)	Raymond Brown (23)
1937–38	Raymond Brown (12–5 .706)	Two Tied (12)	Bob Griffith (24)	Raymond Brown (14)
1938–39	Martín Dihigo (14–2 .857)	Martín Dihigo (14)	Alejandro Carrasquel (26)	Raymond Brown (16)
1939–40	Rodofo Fernández (7–4 .636)	Barney Morris (13)	Tomás de la Cruz (31)	Barney Morris (15)
1940–41	Gilberto Torres (10–3 .769)	Vidal López (12)	Gilberto Torres (27)	Vidal López (16)
1941–42	Two Tied (6–2 .750)	Ramón Bragaña (9)	Ramón Bragaña (21)	Two Tied (11)
1942–43	Cocaína García (10–3 .769)	Cocaína García (10)	Two Tied (22)	Adrián Zabala (14)
1943–44	Martín Dihigo (8–1 .889)	Two Tied (12)	Coty Leal (26)	Tomás de la Cruz (10)
1944–45	Oliverio Ortíz (10–4 .714)	Oliverio Ortíz (10)	Luis Tiant (29)	Two Tied (9)
1945–46	Adrián Zabala (9–3 .750)	Natilla Jiménez (13)	Natilla Jiménez (32)	Three Tied (9)
1946–47	Cocaína García (10–3 .769)	Adrián Zabala (11)	Sandy Consuegra (31)	Adrián Zabala (14)
1947–48	Conrado Marrero (12–2 .857)	Two Tied (12)	Steve Gerkin (33)	Alex Patterson (18)
1948–49	Octavio Rubert (8–1 .889)	Dave Barnhill (13)	Max Surkont (31)	Dave Barnhill (13)
1949–50	Octavio Rubert (5–1 .833)	Thomas Fine (16)	Thomas Fine (35)	Al Gerheauser (11)
1950–51	Vicente López (7–3 .700)	Conrado Marrero (11)	Red Barrett (32)	Two Tied (10)
1951–52	Joe Black (15–6 .714)	Joe Black (15)	Thomas Fine (30)	Two Tied (12)
1952–53	Bob Alexander (10–3 .769)	Mario Picone, Al Gettel (13)	Hal Erickson (33)	Al Gettel (13)
1953–54	Cliff Fannin (13–4 .765)	Two Tied (13)	Joe Coleman (44)	Two Tied (12)
1954–55	Joe Hatten (13–5 .722)	Joe Hatten, Ed Roebuck (13)	Jim Melton (38)	Ed Roebuck (12)
1955–56	Pedro Ramos (13–5 .722)	Pedro Ramos (13)	Ben Wade (38)	Wilmer Mizell (13)
1956–57	Camilo Pascual (15–5 .750)	Camilo Pascual (15)	Two Tied (33)	Camilo Pascual (16)
1957–58	Billy O'Dell (7–2 .778)	Dick Brodowski, Bob Shaw (14)	Orlando Peña (37)	Bob Shaw (12)
1958–59	Orlando Peña (15–5 .750)	Orlando Peña (15)	René Guitiérrez (45)	Orlando Peña (15)
1959–60	Camilo Pascual (15–5 .750)	Camilo Pascual (15)	Manuel Montejo (40)	Camilo Pascual (13)
1960–61	Pedro Ramos (16–7 .696)	Pedro Ramos (16)	Manuel Montejo (36)	Pedro Ramos (17)

Pre-Revolution Cuban Professional Baseball Records and Milestones

CUBAN INDIVIDUAL BATTING RECORDS

Single Season Batting Average	Bienvenido Jiménez, .619 (1921, Short Season)
Single Season Batting Average	Julian Castillo, .454 (1901, 100 or more At-Bats)
Most Batting Titles Won	Antonio García, 4 (1887–88, 1889–90, 1891–92, 1892–93)
	Julián Castillo, 4 (1901, 1903, 1908–09, 1910)
	Regino García, 4 (1904, 1905, 1906, 1907)
Most Consecutive BA Titles	Regino García, 4 (1904, 1905, 1906, 1907)
Most Seasons Batting .300-Plus	Manuel Cueto (11) and Alejandro Oms (11)
Consecutive .300 Seasons	Alejandro Oms, 8 (1922–23 thru 1929–30)
Most RBI in Season	Pedro Formental, 57 (1952–53)
	Rocky Nelson, 57 (1954–55)
Most RBI in Single Game	Walt Moryn, 8 (October 14, 1952)
Most Career RBI	Alejandro Crespo (362) and Pedro Formental (362)
Most Seasons as RBI Leader	Leonard Pearson, 3 (1946–47, 1948–49, 1949–50)
Most Runs Scored in Season	Orestes Miñoso, 67 (1952–53)
Most Runs Scored in Game	Amado Ibáñez, 6 (January 10, 1954)
Most Career Runs Scored	Pedro Formental, 431 (1942–43 thru 1954–55)
Most Seasons as Runs Leader	Cristóbal Torriente, 4 (1915, 1916, 1921, 1923)
Most Base Hits in Season	Harry Kimbro, 104 (1947–48)
Most Base Hits in Game	Alejandro Oms, 6 (December 30, 1928)
	Antonio Castaño, 6 (December 25, 1938)
	Lloyd Davenport, 6 (January 17, 1946)
	Amado Ibáñez, 6 (January 10, 1954)
Most Career Base Hits	Silvio García, 891 (1931–32 thru 1953–54)
Most Seasons as Hits Leader	Valentín González, 5 (1893, 1895, 1899, 1902, 1905)
Longest Hitting Streak	Alejandro Oms, 30 Games (October 31 to December 24, 1928)
Most Home Runs in Game	James "Papa" Bell, 3 (January 1, 1929)

Most Home Runs in Game	Dick Sisler, 3 (January 24, 1946)
Most Career Home Runs	Pedro Formental, 54 (Lefthanded), 1942–43 thru 1954–55
	Roberto Ortíz, 51 (Righthanded), 1939–40 thru 1954–55
Most Home Runs in Season	Lou Klein, 16 (1952–53)

Cuban Individual Pitching Records

Seasons as Pitching Champion	José Méndez, 5 (1908, 1909, 1910, 1911, 1914)
	José Acosta, 5 (1915, 1916, 1917, 1919, 1925)
Most Games Won in Season	Carlos Royer, 21 (1903), Raymond Brown, 21 (1936–37)
Consecutive Wins in Season	Carlos Royer, 17 (1902)
Most Consecutive Wins	Carlos Royer, 20 (1902–1903)
Most Career Victories	Martín Dihigo, 105 (1922–23 thru 1946–47)
Most Consecutive Relief Wins	Thomas Fine, 9 (1949–50)
Most Career Complete Games	Martín Dihigo, 120 (1922–23 thru 1946–47)
Consecutive Complete Games	Carlos Royer, 69 (1901–1904) (Career Record)
	Carlos Royer, 33 (1903) (Season Record, with Playoffs)
Most Games Pitched (Career)	Adrián Zabala, 331 (1935–36 thru 1954–55)
Most Games Pitched (Season)	Joe Coleman, 44 (1953–54)
Most Shutouts (Career)	Adrián Zabala, 83 (1935–36 thru 1954–55)
Most Shutouts (Season)	Enrique Rosas, 14 (1888–89)
Most Seasons Shutout Leader	Luis Tiant, 5 (1932, 1936, 1937, 1940, 1941)
Most Strikeouts (Season)	Carlos Royer, 181 (1903, including playoffs)
Most Walks Allowed (Season)	Robert Darnell, 107 (1953–54)
Most Hits Allowed (Season)	Al Sima, 209 (1953–54)
Most Runs Allowed (Season)	Carlos Royer, 128 (1903)
Most Strikeouts (Game)	George McCullar, 21 (November 23, 1879)
Strikeouts (Modern Game)	Dave Barnhill, 15 (15 innings), January 10, 1948
Consecutive Strikeouts	Adolfo Luque, 7 (February 17, 1923)

Cuban Unassisted Triple Play

Player	Date	Teams
Baldomero Acosta	December 2, 1918	Havana versus Almendares

Cuban No-Hit Games Pitched

Pitcher	Series	Date	Score
Carlos Maciá	6	February 13, 1887	Almendares 38, Carmelita 0
Eugenio de Rosas	8	July 14, 1889	Progreso 8, Cárdenas 0
Oscar Levis	39	October 11, 1924	Habana 1, Almendares 0
Raymond "Jabao" Brown	49	November 7, 1936	Santa Clara 7, Habana 0
Manuel "Cocaína" García	56	December 11, 1943	Habana 5, Marianao 0
Tomás de la Cruz	57	January 3, 1945	Almendares 7, Habana 0
Rogelio "Limonar" Martínez	62	February 15, 1950	Marianao 6, Almendares 0
Antonio "Tony" Díaz	70	November 23, 1957	Cienfuegos 2, Habana 0

Post-Revolution (Amateur) Cuban League Statistics: Cuban Baseball Federation Records and Statistics (1962–2005)

National Series Champions and Batting Leaders in Post-Revolution Cuban League National Series Championships (Provincial)

Series	Year	Teams (Records) (Playoffs)	Manager	Individual Batting Champion
I	1962	Occidentales (18–9, .667)	Fermín Guerra	Erwin Walter(s) (Occidentales) .367
II	1962–63	Industriales (16–14, .533)	Ramón Carneado	Raúl González (Occidentales) .348
III	1963–64	Industriales (22–13, .629)	Ramón Carneado	Pedro Chávez (Occidentales) .333
IV	1964–65	Industriales (25–14, .641)	Ramón Carneado	Urbano González (Industriales) .359
V	1965–66	Industriales (40–25, .615)	Ramón Carneado	Miguel Cuevas (Granjeros) .325
VI	1966–67	Orientales (36–29, .554)	Roberto Ledo	Pedro Cháves (Industriales) .318
VII	1967–68	Habana (74–25, .748)	Juan Gómez	José Pérez (Azucareros) .328
VIII	1968–69	Azucareros (69–30, .697)	Servio Borges	Wilfredo Sánchez (Henequeneros) .354
IX	1969–70	Henequeneros (50–16, .758)	Miguel Domínguez	Wilfredo Sánchez (Henequeneros) .351
X	1970–71	Azucareros (49–16, .754)	Pedro Delgado	Rigoberto Rosique (Henequeneros) .352
XI	1971–72	Azucareros (52–14, .788)	Servio Borges	Elpidio Mancebo (Mineros) .327

Series	Year	Teams (Records) (Playoffs)	Manager	Individual Batting Champion
XII	1972–73	Industriales (53–25, .679)	Pedro Chávez	Eusebio Cruz (Camagüey) .341
XIII	1973–74	Habana (52–26, .667)	Jorge Trigoura	Rigoberto Rosique (Henequeneros) .347
XIV	1974–75	Agricultores (24–15, .615)	Orlando Leroux	Fermín Laffita (Cafetaleros) .396
XV	1975–76	Ganaderos (29–9, .763)	Carlos Gómez	Wilfredo Sánchez (Citricultores) .365
XVI	1976–77	Citricultores (26–12, .684)	Juan Bregio	Eulogio Osorio (Agricultores) .359
XVII	1977–78	Vegueros (36–14, .720)	José Pineda	Fernando Sánchez (Henequeneros) .394
XVIII	1978–79	Sancti Spíritus (39–12, .765)	Cándido Andrade	Wilfredo Sánchez (Citricultores) .377
XIX	1979–80	Santiago de Cuba (35–16, .686)	Manuel Miyar	Rodolfo Puente (Metropolitanos) .394
XX	1980–81	Vegueros (36–15, .706)	José Pineda	Amando Zamora (Villa Clara) .394
XXI	1981–82	Vegueros (36–15, .706)	Jorge Fuentes	Fernando Hernández (Vegueros) .376
XXII	1982–83	Villa Clara (41–8, .837)	Eduardo Martín	Juan Hernández (Forestales) .367
XXIII	1983–84	Citricultores (52–23, .693)	Tomás Soto	Wilfredo Sánchez (Citricultores) .385
XXIV	1984–85	Vegueros (57–18, .760)	Jorge Fuentes	Omar Linares (Vegueros) .409
XXV	1985–86	Industriales (37–11, .771) (6–0)*	Pedro Chávez	Omar Linares (Vegueros) .426
XXVI	1986–87	Vegueros (34–13, .723) (5–1)	Jorge Fuentes	Javier Méndez (Industriales) .408
XXVII	1987–88	Vegueros (39–9, .813) (5–1)	Jorge Fuentes	Pedro Luis Rodriguez (Habana) .446
XXVIII	1988–89	Santiago de Cuba (29–19, .604) (5–1)	Higinio Vélez	Juan Bravo (Industriales) .414
XXIX	1989–90	Henequeneros (37–11, .771) (4–2)	Gerardo Junco	Omar Linares (Vegueros) .442
XXX	1990–91	Henequeneros (33–15, .688) (6–1)	Gerardo Junco	Lázaro Madera (Vegueros) .400
XXXI	1991–92	Industriales (36–12 .750,) (7–1)	Jorge Trigoura	Omar Linares (Vegueros) .398
XXXII	1992–93	Villa Clara (42–23, .646) (8–3)	Pedro Jova	Omar Linares (Pinar del Río) .446
XXXIII	1993–94	Villa Clara (43–22, .662) (8–5)	Pedro Jova	Lourdes Gourriel (Sancti Spíritus) .395
XXXIV	1994–95	Villa Clara (44–18, .710) (8–2)	Pedro Jova	Amado Zamora (Villa Clara) .395
XXXV	1995–96	Industriales (41–22, .651) (8–2)	Pedro Medina	Luis Ulacia (Camagüey) .421
XXXVI	1996–97	Pinar del Río (50–15, .769) (8–0)	Jorge Fuentes	José Estrada (Matanzas) .391
XXXVII	1997–98	Pinar del Río (56–34, .622) (11–5)	Alfonso Urquiola	Robelquis Videaux (Guantánamo) .393
XXXVIII	1998–99	Santiago de Cuba (46–44, .511) (11–7)	Higinio Vélez	Yobal Dueñas (Pinar del Río) .418
XXXIX	1999–00	Santiago de Cuba (61–28, .689) (11–0)	Higinio Vélez	Yorelvis Charles (Ciego de Avila) .353
XL	2000–01	Santiago de Cuba (55–35, .611) (11–4)	Higinio Vélez	Osmani Urrutia (Las Tunas) .431
XLI	2001–02	Holguín (55–35, .611) (11–6)	Héctor Hernández	Osmani Urrutia (Las Tunas) .408
XLII	2002–03	Industriales (66–23, .742) (11–2)	Rey Anglada	Osmani Urrutia (Las Tunas) .421
XLIII	2003–04	Industriales (52–38, .578) (11–4)	Rey Anglada	Osmani Urrutia (Las Tunas) .469
XLIV	2004–05	Santiago de Cuba (55–35, .611) (11–2)	Antonio Pacheco	Osmani Urrutia (Las Tunas) .385

*Playoff between Western and Eastern Zone winners to determine championship after 1986 (National Series XXV)

NATIONAL SERIES HOME RUNS AND HITS LEADERS IN POST-REVOLUTIONARY CUBAN LEAGUE NATIONAL SERIES CHAMPIONSHIPS (PROVINCIAL)

Series	Years	Home Runs Leader	Base Hits Leader
I	1962	Rolando Valdés (Orientales) 3	Urbano González (Occidentales) 40
II	1962–63	Rolando Valdés (Orientales) 5	Fidel Linares (Occidentales) 36
		Miguel Cuevas (Orientales) 5	
III	1963–64	Jorge Trigoura (Industriales) 3	Miguel Cuevas (Orientales) 44
IV	1964–65	Miguel Cuevas (Granjeros) 5	Lino Betancourt (Industriales) 56
V	1965–66	Lino Betancourt (Henequeneros) 9	Urbano González (Industriales) 76
VI	1966–67	Erwin Walter(s) (Centrales) 7	Pedro Chávez (Industriales) 78
VII	1967–68	Felipe Sarduy (Granjeros) 13	Eulogio Osorio (Habana) 129
VIII	1968–69	Agustín Marquetti (Habana) 19	Wilfredo Sánchez (Henequeneros) 140
IX	1969–70	Raúl Reyes (Industriales) 10	Wilfredo Sánchez (Henequeneros) 98
X	1970–71	Miguel Cuevas (Granjeros) 10	Elpidio Mancebo (Mineros) 77
XI	1971–72	Agustín Marquetti (Industriales) 11	Wilfredo Sánchez (Henequeneros) 90
XII	1972–73	Armando Capiró (Habana) 22	Wilfredo Sánchez (Matanzas) 95
XIII	1973–74	Antonio Muñoz (Azucareros) 19	Lázaro Cabrera (Pinar del Río) 99
XIV	1974–75	Fernando Sánchez (Henequeneros) 6	Eulogio Osorio (Agricultores) 58
XV	1975–76	Antonio Muñoz (Azucareros) 13	Wilfredo Sánchez (Citricultores) 62
XVI	1976–77	Pedro José Rodríguez (Azucareros) 9	Armando Capiró (Metropolitanos) 52
XVII	1977–78	Pedro José Rodríguez (Cienfuegos) 13	Julián Villar (Industriales) 72
XVIII	1978–79	Pedro José Rodríguez (Cienfuegos) 19	Wilfredo Sánchez (Citricultores) 80
XIX	1979–80	Luís Casanova (Vegueros) 18	Lourdes Gourriel (Sancti Spíritus) 77
		Pedro José Rodríguez (Cienfuegos) 18	
XX	1980–81	Agustín Lescaille (Guantánamo) 15	Pablo Pérez (Isla de la Juventud) 76
XXI	1981–82	Lázaro Junco (Citricultores) 17	Fernando Hernández (Vegueros) 77

Series	Years	Home Runs Leader	Base Hits Leader
		Reynaldo Fernández (Camagüey) 17	
XXII	1982–83	Lázaro Junco (Citricultores) 15	Oscar Rodríguez (Guantánamo) 71
XXIII	1983–84	Lázaro Junco (Citricultores) 20	Lázaro Vargas (Industriales) 102
		Luis Casanova (Vegueros) 20	
XXIV	1984–85	Lázaro Junco (Citricultores) 24	Amado Zamora (Villa Clara) 115
XXV	1985–86	Reynaldo Fernández (Camagüey) 18	Lázaro Vargas (Industriales) 75
XXVI	1986–87	Orestes Kindelán (Santiago) 17	Luis Alvarez Estrada (Las Tunas) 66
XXVII	1987–88	Lázaro Junco (Henequeneros) 25	Pedro Luis Rodríguez (Habana) 87
XXVIII	1988–89	Orestes Kindelán (Santiago) 24	Luís Alberto Guerra (Vegueros) 78
XXIX	1989–90	Ermidelio Urrutia (Las Tunas) 20	José Estrada (Henequeneros) 77
XXX	1990–91	Lázaro Junco (Henequeneros) 17	Eddy Rojas (Villa Clara) 66
XXXI	1991–92	Romelio Martínez (Habana) 19	Luís González (Habana) 71
XXXII	1992–93	Lázaro Junco (Matanzas) 27	Remberto Rosell (Cienfuegos) 100
XXXIII	1993–94	Lázaro Junco (Matanzas) 21	Pedro Luis Rodríguez (Habana) 100
XXXIV	1994–95	Miguel Cáldes (Camagüey) 20	Alex Ramos (Isla de la Juventud) 100
XXXV	1995–96	Ariel Benavides (Guantánamo) 25	Jorge Safrán (Metropolitanos) 106
XXXVI	1996–97	Julio Fernández (Matanzas) 15	José Estrada (Matanzas) 104
XXXVII	1997–98	Oscar Machado (Villa Clara) 24	Reemberto Rosell (Cienfuegos) 132
XXXVIII	1998–99	Daniel Lazo (Pinar del Río) 18	Michel Enríquez (Isla Juventud) 152
XXXIX	1999–00	Ivan Correa (Industriales) 10	Orlis Díaz (Isla de la Juventud) 117
XL	2000–01	Oscar Macás (Habana) 23	Alex Ramos (Isla de la Juventud) 147
		Robelquis Videaux (Guantánamo) 23	
XLI	2001–02	Michel Abreu (Matanzas) 23	Luis Felipe Rivera (Isla Juventud) 136
XLII	2002–03	Joan Pedroso (Las Tunas) 28 (*new record)	Alexei Ramírez (Pinar del Río) 131
XLIII	2003–04	Reinier Yero (Sancti Spíritus) 19	Yordanis Scull (Las Tunas) 131
XLIV	2004–05	Joan Carlos Pedroso (Las Tunas) 27	Yulieski Gourriel (Sancti Spíritus) 126

NATIONAL SERIES STRIKEOUT AND ERA LEADERS IN POST-REVOLUTIONARY CUBAN LEAGUE NATIONAL SERIES CHAMPIONSHIPS (PROVINCIAL)

Series	Years	Strikeouts Leader	ERA Leader
I	1962	Manuel Hernández (Occidentals) 94	Antonio Rubio (Occidentales) 1.39
II	1962–63	Modesto Verdura (Azucareros) 55	Modesto Verdura (Azucareros) 1.58
III	1963–64	Rolando Pastor (Occidentales) 97	Orlando Rubio (Industriales) 0.63
IV	1964–65	Manuel Alarcón (Orientales) 101	Maximiliano Reyes (Industriales) 1.57
V	1965–66	Rigoberto Betancourt (Occidentales) 103	Alfredo Street (Industriales) 1.09
VI	1966–67	Rigoberto Betancourt (Occidentales) 126	Ihosvani Gallego (Occidentales) 0.80
VII	1967–68	Manuel Alarcón (Mineros) 200	Braudilio Vinent (Mineros) 1.03
VIII	1968–69	Santiago Mederos (Habana) 208 (*record)	Roberto Valdés (Mineros) 1.03
IX	1969–70	Santiago Mederos (Industriales) 143	Rolando Castillo (Mineros) 0.60
X	1970–71	Braudilio Vinent (Mineros) 112	Manuel Hurtado (Industriales) 0.67
XI	1971–72	Braudilio Vinent (Mineros) 127	Ihosvani Gallego (Industriales) 0.37
XII	1972–73	Alfredo García (Henequeneros) 160	Braudilio Vinent (Serranos) 0.85
XIII	1973–74	Julio Romero (Vegueros) 160	Juan Pérez (Camagüey) 1.13
XIV	1974–75	Santiago Mederos (Agricultores) 92	Walfrido Ruíz (Agricultores) 0.62
XV	1975–76	Omar Carrero (Ganaderos) 94	Omar Carrero (Ganaderos) 0.46
XVI	1976–77	Rogelio García (Vegueros) 97	Isidro Pérez (Azucareros) 0.90
XVII	1977–78	Rogelio García (Vegueros) 120	José Riveira (Villa Clara) 0.82
XVIII	1978–79	Rogelio García (Vegueros) 102	Nivaldo Pérez (Villa Clara) 0.86
XIX	1979–80	Rogelio García (Vegueros) 132	José Sánchez (Camagüey) 0.76
XX	1980–81	Braudilo Vinent (Santiago de Cuba) 90	Rogelio García (Vegueros) 1.31
XXI	1981–12	Rogelio García (Vegueros) 144	Julio Romero (Forestales) 1.45
XXII	1982–83	Rogelio García (Vegueros) 119	José Riveira (Villa Clara) 0.63
XXIII	1983–84	Faustino Corrales (Forestales) 143	Manuel Alvarez (Ciego de Avila) 1.17
XXIV	1984–85	Félix Nuñez (Las Tunas) 138	Andres Luis (Camagüey) 1.67
XXV	1985–86	Pablo Abreu (Industriales) 97	Jorge Luis Valdés (Henequeneros) 1.56
XXVI	1986–87	Juan Ramírez (Sancti Spíritus) 91	René Arocha (Metropolitanos) 1.31
XXVII	1987–88	Buenafe Nápoles (Camagüey) 96	Rogelio García (Vegueros) 2.21
XXVIII	1988–89	J.L. Alemán (Santiago de Cuba), Domingo Ordáz (Vegueros) 87	Lázaro Valle (Industriales) 1.93
XXIX	1989–90	Osvaldo Fernández G. (Metropolitanos) 118	Jorge Fumero (Metropolitanos) 1.44
XXX	1990–91	Juan Pérez (Las Tunas) 107	José Riscart (Villa Clara) 1.51

Series	Years	Strikeouts Leader	ERA Leader
XXXI	1991–92	Juan Pérez (Las Tunas) 134	Francisco Despaigne (Industriales) 0.92
XXXII	1992–93	Ernesto Guevara (Granma) 117	Jorge Pérez (Villa Clara) 1.74
XXXIII	1993–94	Liván Hernández (Isla de la Juventud) 132	Osvaldo Fernández R. (Holguín) 1.62
XXXIV	1994–95	Omar Luis (Camagüey) 108	Rolando Arrojo (Villa Clara) 1.88
XXXV	1995–96	Faustino Corrales (Pinar del Río) 128	Jorge Fumero (Industriales) 1.94
XXXVI	1996–97	José Contreras (Pinar del Río) 135	Pedro Luis Lazo (Pinar del Río) 1.15
XXXVII	1997–98	José Ibar (Habana) 189	José Ibar (Habana) 1.51
XXXVIII	1998–99	José Ibar (Habana) 158	Ciro Silvino Licea (Granma) 1.85
XXXIX	1999–00	Maels Rodríguez (S.Spíritus), Yovani Aragón (S.Spíritus) 177	Norge Vera (Santiago de Cuba) 0.97
XL	2000–01	Maels Rodríguez (Sancti Spíritus) 263 (*new record)	Maels Rodríguez (Sancti Spíritus) 1.77
XLI	2001–02	Maels Rodríguez (Sancti Spíritus) 219	José Contreras (Pinar del Río) 1.76
XLII	2002–03	Adiel Palma (Cienfuegos) 179	Alain Soler (Pinar del Río) 2.01
XLIII	2003–04	Luis Borroto (Villa Clara) 135	Luis Borroto (Villa Clara) 1.49
XLIV	2004–05	Adiel Palma (Cienfuegos) 143	Yunieski Maya (Pinar del Río) 1.61

SELECTIVE SERIES CHAMPIONS AND BATTING LEADERS IN POST-REVOLUTION CUBAN LEAGUE

Series	Year	Team (Records) (Playoffs)	Manager	Individual Batting Champion
I	1975	Oriente (33–21, .612)	José Carrillo	Alfonso Urquiola (Pinar del Río) .358
II	1976	Habana (34–20, .630)	Roberto Ledo	Bárbaro Garbey (Industriales) .328
III	1977	Camagüeyanos (36–18, .667)	Carlos Gómez	Wilfredo Sánchez (Matanzas) .381
IV	1978	Las Villas (35–25, .583) (3–2)*	Eduardo Martín	Pedro Jova (Las Villas) .372
V	1979	Pinar del Río (40–20, .667)	José Pineda	Sixto Hernández (Las Villas) .368
VI	1980	Pinar del Río (39–20, .661)	José Pineda	Héctor Olivera (Las Villas) .459
VII	1981	Orientales (38–22, .644)	Carlos Martí	Luis Casanova (Pinar del Río) .363
VIII	1982	Pinar del Río (35–22, .614)	Jorge Fuentes	Agustín Arias (Orientales) .404
IX	1983	Las Villas (42–18, .700)	Eduardo Martín	Gerardo Simon (Orientales) .350
X	1984	Pinar del Río (28–15, .651)	Jorge Fuentes	Luis Casanova (Pinar del Río) .391
XI	1985	Las Villas (26–19, .578)	Eduardo Martín	Amado Zamora (Las Villas) .361
XII	1986	Serranos (41–22, .651)	Frangel Reynaldo	Amado Zamora (Las Villas) .392
XIII	1987	Serranos (42–21, .667)	Higinio Vélez	Luis Ulacia (Camagüeyanos) .384
XIV	1988	Pinar del Río (40–23, .635)	Jorge Fuentes	Lourdes Gourriel (Las Villas) .430
XV	1989	Las Villas (45–18, .714) (2–0)*	Abelardo Triana	Amado Zamora (Las Villas) .413
XVI	1990	Ciudad Habana (46–17, .730)	Servio Borges	Antonio González (Ciudad Habana) .416
XVII	1991	Pinar del Río (41–22, .651)	Jorge Fuentes	Pedro Luis Rodríguez (Agropecuarios) .380
XVIII	1992	Serranos (36–27, .571) (4–3)*	Higinio Vélez	Omar Linares (Pinar del Río) .398
XIX	1993	Orientales (25–20, .556)	Frangel Reynaldo	Gerardo Miranda (Occidentales) .390
XX	1994	Occidentales (27–18, .600)	Jorge Fuentes	Juan Carlos Linares (Occidentales) .429
XXI	1995	Orientales (29–16, .644)	Higinio Vélez	Rey Isaac (Orientales) .424
SuperL I	2002	Habaneros (17–12, 586) (2–1)*	Armando Johnson	Andy Zamora (Centrales) .391
SuperL II	2003	Centrales (13–7, .650) (2–1)*	Victor Mesa	Frederich Cepeda (Centrales) .435
SuperL III	2004	Orientales (7–8, .467) (2–0)*	Angel Sosa	Rudy Reyes (Industriales) .417
SuperL IV	2005	Occidentales (15–13, .536) (2–0)*	Rey Anglada	Roger Poll (Centrales) .437

*Playoffs to determine champion for 1978 (Series #4), 1989 (Series #15), 1992 (Series #18), plus Super League

SELECTIVE SERIES HOME RUNS AND HITS LEADERS IN POST-REVOLUTIONARY CUBAN LEAGUE SELECTIVE SERIES CHAMPIONSHIPS (SUPER-PROVINCIAL)

Series	Years	Home Runs Leader	Base Hits Leader
I	1975	Antonio Muñoz (Las Villas) 12	Eusebio Cruz (Camagüey), Fernando Sánchez (Matanzas) 66
II	1976	Antonio Muñoz (Las Villas) 12	Wilfredo Sánchez (Matanzas) 66
III	1977	Pedro José Rodríguez (Las Villas) 16	Wilfredo Sánchez (Matanzas) 85
IV	1978	Pedro José Rodríguez (Las Villas) 28	Pedro Jova (Las Villas) 92
V	1979	Antonio Muñoz (Las Villas) 25	Wilfredo Sánchez (Matanzas) 81
VI	1980	Antonio Muñoz (Las Villas) 18	Wilfredo Sánchez (Matanzas) 88
VII	1981	Antonio Muñoz (Las Villas) 18	Antonio Muñoz (Las Villas) 82
VIII	1982	Lázaro Junco (Matanzas) 19	Agustín Arias (Orientales) 82
IX	1983	Antonio Muñoz (Las Villas) 14	Antonio Muñoz (Las Villas) 77
X	1984	Orestes Kindelán (Orientales) 12	Lázaro Madera (Pinar del Río) 63
XI	1985	Pedro Medina (Habana) 13	Fernando Sánchez (Matanzas) 60
XII	1986	Orestes Kindelán (Serranos) 30	Jorge García (Serranos) 96

Series	Years	Home Runs Leader	Base Hits Leader
XIII	1987	Orestes Kindelán (Serranos) 16	Antonio Pacheco (Serranos) 88
XIV	1988	Orestes Kindelán (Serranos) 28	Germán Mesa (Ciudad Habana) 91
XV	1989	Eddy Rojas (Las Villas) 25	Eddy Rojas (Las Villas) 100
XVI	1990	Leonel Moa (Camagüeyanos) 23	Omar Linares (Pinar del Río) 90
XVII	1991	Romelio Martínez (Agropecuarios) 20	Victor Mesa (Las Villas) 86
XVIII	1992	Omar Linares (Pinar del Río) 23	Reemberto Rosell (Las Villas) 96
XIX	1993	Orestes Kindelán (Orientales) 14	Juan Carlos Linares (Occidentales) 64
XX	1994	Romelio Martínez (Habana) 10	Juan Carlos Linares (Occidentales) 70
XXI	1995	Romelio Martínez (Habana) 16	Alex Ramos (Occidentales) 72
SuperL I	2002	Frederich Cepeda (Centrales) 7	Frederich Cepeda (Centrales), J.C. Linares (Occidentales) 35
SuperL II	2003	Frederich Cepeda (Centrales) 7	Michel Enríquez (Centrales), Luis Rivera (Occidentales) 32
SuperL III	2004	Eduardo Paret (Centrales) 5	Alexei Ramírez (Occidentales) 25
SuperL IV	2005	Joan Carlos Pedroso (Santiago) 14	Alexei Ramírez (Occidentales) 46

SELECTIVE SERIES STRIKEOUT AND ERA LEADERS IN POST-REVOLUTIONARY CUBAN LEAGUE SELECTIVE SERIES CHAMPIONSHIPS (SUPER-PROVINCIAL)

Series	Years	Strikeouts Leader	ERA Leader
I	1975	Julio Romero (Pinar del Río) 85	Gregorio Pérez (Oriente) 1.04
II	1976	Rogelio García (Pinar del Río) 97	Omar Carrero (Camagüey) 0.62
III	1977	Rogelio García (Pinar del Río) 122	Félix Pino (Pinar del Ríos) 1.28
IV	1978	Rogelio García (Pinar del Río) 111	Rogelio García (Pinar del Río) 2.21
V	1979	Braudilio Vinent (Orientales) 105	Juan Oliva (Pinar del Río) 1.97
VI	1980	José Darcourt (Habana) 91	Omar Carrero (Camagüeyanos) 1.87
VII	1981	Rogelio García (Pinar del Río) 114	José Luis Alemán (Orientales) 2.41
VIII	1982	Rogelio García (Pinar del Río) 116	Rogelio García (Pinar del Río) 1.70
IX	1983	Julio Romero (Pinar del Río) 109	Julio Romero (Pinar del Río) 1.67
X	1984	Reinaldo Costa (Pinar del Río) 60	Reinaldo Costa (Pinar del Río) 1.67
XI	1985	José Riveira (Las Villas) 63	Manuel Alvarez (Camagüeyanos) 1.98
XII	1986	Enrique Cutiño (Serranos) 111	Buenafe Napoles (Camagüeyanos) 2.36
XIII	1987	Pablo Abreu (Habana) 114	Rogelio García (Pinar del Río) 1.25
XIV	1988	René Arocha (Habana) 106	Orlando Hernández (Habana) 3.18
XV	1989	Buenafe Napoles (Camagüeyanos) 98	Fidel Azcuy (Pinar del Río) 2.85
XVI	1990	Omar Ajete (Pinar del Río) 106	José Ibar (Agropecuarios) 2.20
XVII	1991	Omar Ajete (Pinar del Río) 104	Osvaldo Fernández G. (Habana) 2.09
XVIII	1992	Faustino Corrales (Pinar del Río) 89	Orlando Hernández (Habana) 2.23
XIX	1993	Osvaldo Fernández Guerra (Habana) 58	Omar Ajete (Occidentales) 2.33
XX	1994	Omar Ajete (Occidentales) 55	Eliecer Montes de Oca (Centrales) 2.40
XXI	1995	Lázaro Valle (Habana) 53	Ernesto Guevara (Orientales) 3.63
SuperL I	2002	Maels Rodríguez (Centrales) 41	Orestes González (Occidentales) 1.13
SuperL II	2003	Norberto González (Centrales) 21	Luis Rodríguez (Orientales) 1.21
SuperL III	2004	Yovani Aragón (Centrales) 15	Luis Borroto (Centrales) 1.25
Superl IV	2005	Kenny Rodríguez (Habana) 36	Adiel Palma (Centrales) 2.10

CUBAN LEAGUE CAREER LEADERS (NATIONAL SERIES AND SELECTIVE SERIES, 1962–2004)

Career Individual Batting Records

Games	Fernando Sánchez (1994)
Innings	Sergio Quesada (16702.1)
At Bats	Sergio Quesada (7528)
Runs	Omar Linares (1547)
Hits	Antonio Pacheco (2356)
	Fernando Sánchez (2215)
Batting Average	Omar Linares (.368)
Doubles	Javier Méndez (381)
Triples	Enrique Díaz (84)
Home Runs	Orestes Kindelán (487)
Total Bases	Orestes Kindelán (3893)
Slugging	Omar Linares (.644)
Steals	Enrique Díaz (625)
RBI	Orestes Kindelán (1511)
Sacrifice Bunts	Eduardo Cárdenas (128)

Career Individual Pitching Records

Games	Carlos Yanes (588)
Games Started	Jorge Luis Valdés (414)
Complete Games	Braudilio Vinent (265)
Relief Appearances	Euclides Rojas (342)
Wins	Jorge Luis Valdés (234)
	Braudilio Vinent (221)
Losses	Carlos Yanes (194)
Winning Percentage	Orlando Hernández (.728)
Shutouts	Braudilio Vinent (63)
Saves	Euclides Rojas (90)
Innings Pitched	Braudilio Vinent (3259.2)
Strikeouts	Rogelio García (2499)
Bases on Balls	Faustino Corrales (1183)
ERA	José Huelga (1.50)
Runs Allowed	Carlos Yanes (1792)

Career Individual Batting Records

Sacrifice Bunts	Giraldo González (125)
Sacrifice Flies	Orestes Kindelán (91)
Hit-By-Pitch	Gabriel Pierre (225)

Career Individual Pitching Records

Runs Allowed	Gervasio Miguel (1483)
Wild Pitches	Faustino Corrales (211)
Hits Allowed	Carlos Yanes (3442)

Cuban League No-Hit and No-Run Games (1962–2005)

Number	Series	Date	Location-City	No-Hit Pitcher	Results (Game Line Scores)
01	NAC#5	1-16-66	Villa Clara	Aquino Abreu	Centrales 10–11–1, Occidentales 0–0–6
02	NAC#5	1-25-66	Havana (EL)	Aquino Abreu	Centrales 7–8–0, Industriales 0–0–2
03	NAC#6	2-14-67	Santiago de Cuba	Roberto Valdés	Orientales 12–16–0, Granjeros 0–0–6
04	NAC#7	1-7-68	Havana (EL)	Leopoldo Valdés	Habana 5–12–0, Pinar del Río 0–0–0
05	NAC#7	1-7-68	Artemisa	Jesús Pérez	Industriales 5–9–2, Vegueros 0–0–4
06	NAC#7	1-14-68	Villa Clara	José Huelga	Azucareros 1–7–1, Granjeros 0–0–1
07	NAC#7	1-25-68	Santiago de Cuba	Orlando Figueredo	Oriente 1–2–1, Azucareros 0–0–1
08	NAC#7	4-4-68	Camagüey	Florentino González	Camagüey 1–8–0, Matanzas 0–0–2
09	NAC#8	12-10-68	Havana	Raúl Alvarez	Pinar del Río 9–10–1, Camagüey 0–0–8
10	NAC#8	2-4-69	Havana (EL)	Andrés Liaño	Industriales 8–8–1, Pinar del Río 0–0–6
11	NAC#8	4-6-69	Villa Clara	Alfredo García	Henequeneros 1–5–3, Azucareros 0–0–0
12	NAC#9	1-7-70	Havana (EL)	Rigoberto Betancourt	Industriales 1–3–2, Oriente 0–0–1
13	NAC#10	1-16-71	Camagüey	Walfrido Ruíz (winner)* *with Elpidio Paez	Habana 10–9–2, Camagüey 0–0–6
14	NAC#10	1-21-71	Pinar del Río	Aniceto Montes de Oca	Azucareros 5–10–1, Pinar del Río 0–0–3
15	NAC#12	2-22-73	Camagüey	Juan Pérez	Camagüey 7–10–0, Serranos 0–0–3
16	NAC#13	4-25-74	Santiago de Cuba	Juan Pérez	Camagüey 1–10–0, Oriente 0–0–1
17	NAC#14	1-19-75	Camagüey	Juan Pérez	Ganaderos 2–7–0, Citricultores 0–0–0
18	SELS#1	5-4-75	Havana (EL)	Oscar Romero	Camagüey 4–11–1, Industriales 0–0–4
19	NAC#17	12-27-77	Pinar del Río	Porfirio Pérez	Forestales 3–7–1, Habana 0–0–2
20	NAC#18	2-18-79	Granma	Juan Gómaz (winner)* *with Pablo Castro and José Brizuela	Granma 14–18–3, Ciego de Avila 0–0–2
21	SELS#5	3-28-79	Villa Clara	Nivaldo Pérez	Las Villas 4–9–0, Camagüeyanos 0–0–1
22	NAC#20	1-27-81	Ciego de Avila	Omar Carrero	Ciego Avila 13–16–1, Las Tunas 0–0–4
23	NAC#21	1-16-82	Havana (EL)	Angel Leocadio Díaz	Industriales 2–6–3, Holguín 0–0–1
24	NAC#21	2-11-82	Matanzas	Carlos Mesa	Citricultores 6–9–0, Habana 0–0–3
25	SELS#*	5-18-82	Havana (EL)	José Pedroso	Habana 1–5–0, Camagüeyanos 0–0–1
26	NAC#22	12-30-82	Villa Clara	Mario Veliz	Villa Clara 3–11–1, Citricultores 0–0–2
27	SELS#9	3-9-83	Pinar del Río	Julio Romero	Pinar del Río 2–9–0, Camagüey 0–0–1
28	NAC#23	1-31-84	Villa Clara	Jorge Luis Valdés	Henequeneros 1–2–1, Villa Clara 0–0–3
29	SELS#13	3-1-87	Camagüey	Rogelio García	Pinar 10–11–0, Camagüey 0–0–1 (KO)
30	SELS#13	3-22-87	Pinar del Río	Rogelio García	Pinar del Río 3–5–2, Serranos 0–0–1
31	NAC#28	12-10-88	Havana (EL)	Osvaldo Fernández G.	Metros 6–9–3, Citricultores 0–0–0
32	NAC#29	12-13-89	Matanzas	Héctor Domínguez	Citricultores 2–3–1, Isla Juventud 0–0–1
33	SELS#16	4-7-90	Matanzas	Orlando Hernández	Habana 11–15–0, Matanzas 0–0–4 (KO)
34	NAC#31	11-19-91	Nueva Gerona	Faustino Corrales	Vegueros 7–10–1, Juventud 0–0–1
35	NAC#32	11-29-92	Havana (EL)	Osvaldo Fernández R.	Holguín 10–11–0, Metros 0–0–2 (KO)
36	NAC#32	12-8-92	Granma	Ernesto Guevara	Granma 2–7–1, Industriales 0–0–0
37	NAC#37	11-18-97	Las Tunas	Modesto Luis	Las Tunas 7–9–1, Granma 0–0–0
38	NAC#37	11-22-97	Guantánamo	Geovanis Castañeda	Guantánamo 8–9–2, Las Tunas 0–0–2
39	NAC#38	11-17-98	Havana (EL)	José Baez	Las Tunas 6–8–1, Metropolitanos 0–0–2
40	NAC#39	12-22-99	Sancti Spíritus	Maels Rodríguez	Sancti Spíritus 1–9–0, Las Tunas 0–0–2

(Maels Rodríguez pitched the only Perfect Game — allowing no base runners — in Cuban League history vs. Las Tunas)

Number	Series	Date	Location-City	No-Hit Pitcher	Results (Game Line Scores)
41	NAC#39	12-25-99	Cienfuegos	Adiel Palma	Cienfuegos 4–8–1, Las Tunas 0–0–2
42	NAC#39	5-3-2000	Nueva Gerona	Carlos Yanes	Isla Juventud 6–11–0, Villa Clara 0–0–1
43	NAC#40	1-21-01	Havana	Norge Vera	Santiago de Cuba 3–5–1, Habana 0–0–1
44	NAC#40	2-7-01	Villa Clara	Michel Pérez	Villa Clara 10–11–0, Las Tunas 0–0–0
45	SuperLg	8-21-02	Havana (EL)	Maels Rodríguez	Centrales 1–4–0, Habaneros 0–0–0

Symbols Key: NAC#Number = National Series, SELS#Number = Selective Series, FINALS = Playoff Finals of National Series, KO = game terminated by the ten-run mercy rule after seven innings, EL = Estadio Latinoamericano, Havana

Lifetime Top Ten Cuban Offensive Leaders (1962–2004)

Statistical career leaders through 2003–04 National Series XLIII season. Asterisk (*) indicates player is still active after 2003–2004 National Series XLIII. Team given in parentheses is a player's primary National Series/Selective Series team.

Total Series Played	(Series Nacionales/ Series Selectivas)
Antonio Muñoz (Azucareros)	24
Fernando Sánchez (Matanzas)	23
Agustín Lescaille (Guantánamo)	22
Augustín Marquetti (Habana)	22
Antonio Pacheco (Santiago de Cuba)	22
Lázaro Vargas (Industriales)	22
Javier Méndez (Industriales)	22
Felipe Sarduy (Granjeros)	21
Luis Ulacia (Camagüey)	21
José Luis Valdés (Henequeneros)	20 (most for a pitcher)
Braudilio Vinent (Serranos)	20 (most for a pitcher)

Plate Appearances	(Comparecencias al Bate)
Antonio Muñoz (Azucareros)	8377
Sergio Quesada (Camagüeyanos)	8310
Fernando Sánchez (Matanzas)	8269
Agustín Lescaille (Guantánamo)	8124
Orestes Kindelán (Santiago de Cuba)	7997
Lázaro Vargas (Industriales)	7968
Antonio Pacheco (Santiago de Cuba)	7955
Victor Vicente Bejerano (Granma)*	7923
Javier Méndez (Industriales)	7890
Luis Ulacia (Camagüey)	7808
Victor Mesa (Villa Clara)	7692

At-Bats	(Veces al Bate)
Sergio Quesada (Camagüeyanos)	7528
Agustín Lescaille (Guantánamo)	7326
Fernando Sánchez (Matanzas)	7204
Antonio Pacheco (Santiago de Cuba)	7045
Luis Ulacia (Camagüey)	6961
Victor Mesa (Villa Clara)	6834
Victor Vicente Bejerano (Granma)*	6816
Lázaro Vargas (Industriales)	6731
Agustín Marquetti (Habana)	6725
Antonio Muñoz (Azucareros)	6676
Wilfredo Sánchez (Henequeneros)	6565

Runs Scored	(Carreras Anotadas)
Omar Linares (Pinar del Río)	1547
Orestes Kindelán (Santiago de Cuba)	1379
Victor Mesa (Villa Clara)	1282
Antonio Muñoz (Azucareros)	1281
Antonio Pacheco (Santiago de Cuba)	1258
Enrique Díaz (Industriales)	1183
Luis Ulacia (Camagüey)	1147
Luis Casanova (Vegueros)	1144
José Estrada (Matanzas)*	1140
Javier Méndez (Industriales)	1139
Oscar Macias (Habana)*	1124
Lourdes Gourriel (Sancti Spíritus)	1122

Hits	(Hits)
Antonio Pacheco (Santiago de Cuba)	2356
Fernando Sánchez (Matanzas)	2215
Omar Linares (Pinar del Río)	2195
Luis Ulacia (Camagüey)	2183
Wilfredo Sánchez (Henequeneros)	2174
Victor Mesa (Villa Clara)	2171
Lázaro Vargas (Industriales)*	2132
Javier Méndez (Industriales)	2101
Eduardo Cárdenas (Matanzas)*	2077
Orestes Kindelán (Santiago de Cuba)	2030
Lourdes Gourriel (Sancti Spíritus)	2026

Batting Average (2000-plus At-Bats)	(Promedio de Bateo)
Omar Linares (Pinar del Río)	.368
Osmani Urrutia (Las Tunas)*	.360
Michel Enríquez (Isla de la Juventud)*	.358
Alexander Ramos (Isla de la Juventud)*	.340
Antonio Pacheco (Santiago de Cuba)	.334
Pedro Luis Rodríguez (Habana)	.334
Amado Zamora (Villa Clara)	.331
Wilfredo Sánchez (Henequeneros)	.331
Yasser Gómez (Industriales)	.330
Javier Méndez (Industriales)	.327
Lázaro Madera (Vegueros)	.324

Doubles	(Dobles)
Javier Méndez (Industriales)	381
Antonio Pacheco (Santiago de Cuba)	366
Antonio Muñoz (Azucareros)	355
Victor Vicente Bejerano (Granma)*	351
Victor Mesa (Villa Clara)	351
Fernando Sánchez (Matanzas)	338
Orestes Kindelán (Santiago de Cuba)	330
Omar Linares (Pinar del Río)	327
Fausto Alvarez (Santiago de Cuba)*	327
Lourdes Gourriel (Sancti Spíritus)	326

Triples	(Triples)
Enrique Díaz (Industriales)*	84
Evenecer Godinez (Santiago de Cuba)	81
Reemberto Rosell (Cienfuegos)*	75
José Estrada (Matanzas)*	74
Amado Zamora (Villa Clara)	70
Wilfredo Sánchez (Henequeneros)	69
Juan Padilla (Industriales)	68
Fernando Sánchez (Matanzas)	65
Antonio Pacheco (Santiago de Cuba)	63
Manuel Benavides (Santiago de Cuba)*	61
Sergio Quesada (Camagüeyanos)	60
Jorge García (Serranos)	60

Home Runs	(Cuadrangulares)
Orestes Kindelán (Santiago de Cuba)	487
Lázaro Junco (Citricultores)	405
Omar Linares (Pinar del Río)	404
Antonio Muñoz (Azucareros)	370
Romelio Martínez (Holguín)	370
Luis Casanova (Vegueros)	312
Gabriel Pierre (Santiago de Cuba)*	306
Julio Fernández (Matanzas)	302
Pedro José Rodríguez (Cienfuegos)	286

Home Runs (continued) (Cuadrangulares)

Oscar Macías (Habana)*	286
Antonio Pacheco (Santiago de Cuba)	284

Total Bases (Total de Bases)

Orestes Kindelán (Santiago de Cuba)	3893
Omar Linares (Pinar del Río)	3842
Antonio Pacheco (Santiago de Cuba)	3700
Antonio Muñoz (Azucareros)	3569
Fernando Sánchez (Matanzas)	3523
Victor Mesa (Villa Clara)	3433
Oscar Macías (Habana)*	3237
Lázaro Junco (Citricultores)	3187
Lourdes Gourriel (Sancti Spíritus)	3171
Javier Méndez (Industriales)	3137

Slugging Percentage (Promedio
(2000-plus At-Bats) de Slugging)

Omar Linares (Pinar del Río)	.644
Orestes Kindelán (Santiago de Cuba)	.600
Luis Casanova (Vegueros)	.569
Lázaro Junco (Citricultores)	.551
Pedro José Rodríguez (Cienfuegos)	.545
Romelio Martínez (Holguín)	.544
Pedro Luis Rodríguez (Habana)	.535
Antonio Muñoz (Azucareros)	.535
Frederich Cepeda (Sancti Spíritus)*	.534
Gabriel Pierre (Santiago de Cuba)*	.530

RBI (Carreras Impulsadas)

Orestes Kindelán (Santiago de Cuba)	1511
Antonio Muñoz (Azucareros)	1407
Antonio Pacheco (Santiago de Cuba)	1304
Fernando Sánchez (Matanzas)	1223
Omar Linares (Pinar del Río)	1221
Lázaro Junco (Citricultores)	1180
Victor Mesa (Villa Clara)	1174
Javier Méndez (Industriales)	1174
Julio Fernández (Matanzas)	1151
Agustín Marquetti (Habana)	1106

Stolen Bases (Bases Robadas)

Enrique Díaz (Industriales)*	625
Victor Mesa (Villa Clara)	588
Eduardo Paret (Villa Clara)*	410
Luis Ulacia (Camagüey)	355
Wilfredo Sánchez (Henequeneros)	339
José Estrada (Matanzas)*	337
Germán Mesa (Industriales)	335
Antonio Jiménez (Habana)	324
Sergio Quesada (Camagüeyanos)	284
Omar Linares (Pinar del Río)	246

Sacrifice Hits (Sacrificios
de Toque)

Eduardo Cárdenas (Matanzas)*	128
Giraldo González (Vegueros)	125
Armando Dueñas (Henequeneros)	117
Carlos Tabares (Industriales)*	107
Omar Arrozarena (Sancti Spíritus)*	94
Eduardo Paret (Villa Clara)*	92
Eusebio Rojas (Habana)	92
Reemberto Rosell (Cienfuegos)*	88

Juan Gordo (Las Tunas)	88
Evenecer Godinez (Santiago de Cuba)	84
Wilfredo Hernández (Serranos)	83

Sacrifice Flies (Sacrificios
de Fly)

Orestes Kindelán (Santiago de Cuba)	91
Antonio Pacheco (Santiago de Cuba)	88
Lázaro Vargas (Industriales)*	84
Antonio Scull (Industriales)*	80
Fausto Alvarez (Santiago de Cuba)*	77
Julio Fernández (Matanzas)	76
Victor Mesa (Villa Clara)	76
Lourdes Gourriel (Sancti Spíritus)	74
Javier Méndez (Industriales)*	74
Rafael Acebey (Villa Clara)*	72

Hit-By-Pitch (Golpeado por
Lanzamientos)

Gabriel Pierre (Santiago de Cuba)*	225
Romelio Martínez (Holguín)	186
Orestes Kindelán (Santiago de Cuba)	185
Rafael Acebey (Villa Clara)*	182
Oscar Macías (Habana)*	173
Victor Vicente Bejerano (Granma)*	150
Reutilio Hurtado (Santiago de Cuba)*	149
Luis Casanova (Vegueros)	147
Lázaro Vargas (Industriales)	136
Modesto Larduet (Santiago de Cuba)	135
Fernando Sánchez (Matanzas)	135

Walks (Bases on Balls) (Bases por Bolas)

Antonio Muñoz (Azucareros)	1551
Omar Linares (Pinar del Río)	1327
Javier Méndez (Industriales)	1244
Orestes Kindelán (Santiago de Cuba)	1232
Juan Manrique (Matanzas)*	1139
Romelio Martínez (Holguín)	1073
Luis Casanova (Vegueros)	1049
Lázaro Vargas (Industriales)	983
Gabriel Pierre (Santiago de Cuba)*	972
Pedro Medina (Industriales)	948

Intentional Walks (Bases
Intencionales)

Antonio Muñoz (Azucareros)	273
Omar Linares (Pinar del Río)	235
Agustín Marquetti (Habana)	191
Luis Casanova (Vegueros)	173
Orestes Kindelán (Santiago de Cuba)	168
Lourdes Gourriel (Sancti Spíritus)	155
Fernando Sánchez (Matanzas)	144
Alejo O'Reilly (Villa Clara)	141
Luis Ulacia (Camagüey)	140
Pedro José Rodríguez (Cienfuegos)	130

Strikeouts (Ponches)

Romelio Martínez (Holguín)	1078
Leonel Mario Moa (Camagüey)	1057
Orestes Kindelán (Santiago de Cuba)	1025
Lázaro Junco (Citricultores)	1007
Modesto Larduet (Santiago de Cuba)	917
Gabriel Pierre (Santiago de Cuba)*	914

Strikeouts (continued)   *(Ponches)*

Oscar Machado (Villa Clara)*   907
Victor Vicente Bejerano (Granma)*   906
Oscar Macías (Habana)*   895
Reinaldo Fernández (Camagüey)   890

Hit-Into-Double Plays   *(Bateo para Doble Jugada)*

Lázaro Vargas (Industriales)   234
Julio Fernández (Matanzas)   228
Gabriel Pierre (Santiago de Cuba)*   209
Yobal Dueñas (Pinar del Río)*   196
Victor Mesa (Villa Clara)   194
Lourdes Gourriel (Sancti Spíritus)   190
Antonio Pacheco (Santiago de Cuba)   187
Agustín Lescaille (Guantánamo)   186
Fernando Sánchez (Mantanzas)   180
Orestes Kindelán (Santiago de Cuba)   180

Lifetime Top Ten Cuban Pitching Leaders (1962–2004)

Statistical career leaders through 2003–04 National Series XLIII season. Asterisk (*) indicates player is still active after 2003–2004 National Series XLIII. Team given in parentheses is a player's primary National Series/Selective Series team.

Total Series Played   *(Series Nacionales/ Series Selectivas)*

Faustino Corrales (Pinar del Río)*   22
Carlos Yanes (Isla de la Juventud)*   21
José Riscart (Villa Clara)*   20
Oscar Gil (Holguín)*   20
Gervasio Miguel (Isla de la Juventud)*   20
José Miguel Baez (Las Tunas)*   20
Jorge Luis Valdés (Henequeneros)   20
Braudilio Vinent (Serranos)   20
Lázaro de la Torre (Industriales)   19
Roberto Almarales (Cienfuegos)   19
Julio Mantilla (Ciego de Avila)   19

Games Pitched   *(Juegos Lanzados)*

Carlos Yanes (Isla de la Juventud)*   588
José Miguel Baez (Las Tunas)*   541
Jorge Luis Valdés (Henequeneros)   519
Oscar Gil (Holguín)*   496
Lázaro de la Torre (Industriales)   495
Braudilio Vinent (Serranos)   477
Gervasio Miguel (Isla de la Juventud)*   465
Omar Ajete (Pinar del Río)   449
José Riscart (Villa Clara)*   447
Julio Mantilla (Ciego de Avila)   433

Games Started   *(Juegos Iniciados)*

Jorge Luis Valdés (Henequeneros)   414
Braudilio Vinent (Serranos)   400
Carlos Yanes (Isla de la Juventud)*   386
Faustino Corrales (Pinar del Río)*   373
Gervasio Miguel (Isla de la Juventud)*   341
José Luis Alemán (Santiago de Cuba)   333
Lázaro de la Torre (Industriales)   326

Rogelio García (Vegueros)   326
Oscar Gil (Holguín)*   322
Omar Ajete (Pinar del Río)   306

Complete Games   *(Juegos Completos)*

Braudilio Vinent (Serranos)   265
Jorge Luis Valdés (Henequeneros)   229
Rogelio García (Vegueros)   201
José Luis Alemán (Santiago de Cuba)   179
Félix Nuñez (Las Tunas)   163
Julio Romero (Vegueros)   162
Carlos Yanes (Isla de la Juventud)*   160
Lázaro de la Torre (Industriales)   159
Omar Carrero (Ganaderos)   146
Pedro Luis Lazo (Pinar del Río)   142

Relief Appearances   *(Juegos Relevados)*

Euclides Rojas (Ciudad Habana)   342
Jorge Tissert (Santiago de Cuba)*   314
Jesús Bosmenier (Vegueros)   293
Raúl Reyes (Camagüey)*   279
Julio Mantilla (Ciego de Avila)   274
Ruben Rodríguez (Santiago de Cuba)*   274
Francisco Despaigne (Industriales)   268
Felipe Fernández (Camagüey)   263
Orestes González (Pinar del Río)*   260
Jorge Martínez (Matanzas)*   260

Wins   *(Juegos Ganados)*

Jorge Luis Valdés (Henequeneros)   234
Braudilio Vinent (Serranos)   221
Lázaro de la Torre (Industriales)*   205
Rogelio García (Vegueros)   202
Carlos Yanes (Isla de la Juventud)*   187
Pedro Luis Lazo (Pinar del Río)*   181
Omar Ajete (Pinar del Río)   179
José Luis Alemán (Santiago de Cuba)   174
José Ibar (Habana)   173
Faustino Corrales (Pinar del Río)*   169

Losses   *(Juegos Perdidos)*

Carlos Yanes (Isla de la Juventud)*   194
Gervasio Miguel (Isla de la Juventud)*   185
José Miguel Baez (Las Tunas)*   172
Braudilio Vinent (Serranos)   167
Jorge Luis Valdés (Henequeneros)   166
Félix Nuñez (Las Tunas)   156
Oscar Gil (Holguín)*   149
Adiel Palma (Cienfuegos)*   135
Osvaldo Duvergel (Guantánamo)   134
Lázaro de la Torre (Industriales)   132

Winning Percentage   *(Promedio de Ganados)*
(120-plus decisions)

                                            (W–L)
Orlando Hernández (Industriales)   .728 (126–47)
Norge Vera (Santiago de Cuba)*   .711 (113–46)
José Ariel Contreras (Pinar del Río)   .701 (117–50)
Walfrido Ruíz (Habana)   .671 (102–50)
Rogelio García (Vegueros)   .669 (202–100)

Winning Percentage (continued) (120-plus decisions)	*(Promedio de Ganados)* (W–L)
José Luis Machado (Industriales)*	.664 (101–51)
Manuel Hurtado (Industriales)	.657 (90–47)
Lázaro Valle (Industriales)	.654 (138–73)
Omar Ajete (Pinar del Río)	.651 (179–96)
Santiago (Changa) Mederos (Habana)	.647 (123–67)

Shutouts	*(Lechadas)*
Braudilio Vinent (Serranos)	63
Rogelio García (Vegueros)	56
Omar Carrero (Ganaderos)	49
Jorge Luis Valdés (Henequeneros)	46
Santiago (Changa) Mederos (Habana)	41
José Riscart (Villa Clara)	36
Julio Romero (Vegueros)	36
José Luis Alemán (Santiago de Cuba)	34
Walfrido Ruíz (Habana)	34
Jesús Guerra (Vegueros)	33

Saves	*(Juegos Salvados)*
Euclides Rojas (Ciudad Habana)	90
Orestes González (Pinar del Río)*	69
Amaury Sanit (Industriales)*	58
José Miguel Baez (Las Tunas)*	55
Felipe Fernández (Camagüey)	53
Raúl Reyes (Camagüey)*	51
Jesús Bosmenier (Vegueros)	50
Jorge Tissert (Santiago de Cuba)*	49
Isidro Pérez (Villa Clara)	42
José García Sánchez (Habana)*	41

Innings Pitched	*(Entradas Lanzadas)*
Braudilio Vinent (Serranos)	3259.2
Jorge Luis Valdés (Vegueros)	3134.0
Carlos Yanes (Isla de la Juventud)*	3093.1
Lázaro de la Torre (Industriales)	2727.1
Rogelio García (Vegueros)	2609.0
Faustino Corrales (Pinar del Río)*	2505.0
Gervasio Miguel (Isla de la Juventud)*	2478.0
José Luis Alemán (Santiago de Cuba)	2472.0
José Miguel Baez (Las Tunas)*	2398.0
José Ibar (Habana)	2364.0

Hits Allowed	*(Hits)*
Carlos Yanes (Isla de la Juventud)*	3442
Jorge Luis Valdés (Henequeneros)	2980
Gervasio Miguel (Isla de la Juventud)*	2812
José Miguel Baez (Las Tunas)*	2696
Braudilio Vinent (Serranos)	2645
Lázaro de la Torre (Industriales)	2577
Oscar Gil (Holguín)*	2386
José Luis Alemán (Santiago de Cuba)	2322
Misael López (Granma)*	2282
Ormari Romero (Santiago de Cuba)*	2255
Omar Ajete (Pinar del Río)	2252

Runs Allowed	*(Carreras)*
Carlos Yanes (Isla de la Juventud)*	1792
Gervasio Miguel (Isla de la Juventud)*	1483
José Miguel Baez (Las Tunas)*	1443
Jorge Luis Valdés (Henequeneros)	1337

Oscar Gil (Holguín)*	1240
Misael López (Granma)*	1197
Lázaro de la Torre (Industriales)	1140
Osvaldo Duvergel (Guantánamo)	1133
Braudilio Vinent (Serranos)	1122
Félix Nuñez (Las Tunas)	1080

Earned Runs	*(Carreras Limpias)*
Carlos Yanes (Isla de la Juventud)*	1572
Gervasio Miguel (Isla de la Juventud)*	1282
José Miguel Baez (Las Tunas)*	1236
Jorge Luis Valdés (Henequeneros)	1090
Misael López (Granma)*	1031
Oscar Gil (Holguín)*	1021
Lázaro de la Torre (Industriales)*	975
Osvaldo Duvergel (Guantánamo)	966
Teofilo Pérez (Camagüey)*	931
José Ibar (Habana)	908

ERA (750 or more Innings Pitched)	*(Promedio de Carreras Limpias)*
José Huelga (Azucareros)	1.50
Roberto Valdés (Mineros)	1.75
Manuel Hurtado (Industriales)	1.80
Juan Pérez Pérez (Camagüey)	1.86
Walfrido Ruíz (Habana)	1.88
Santiago (Changa) Mederos (Habana)	1.97
Julio Rojo (Habana)	2.06
Rolando Macías (Las Villas)	2.17
Gregorio Pérez (Cafetaleros)	2.18
Florentino González (Pinar del Río)	2.20

Strikeouts	*(Ponches)*
Rogelio García (Vegueros)	2499
Faustino Corrales (Pinar del Río)*	2327
Braudilio Vinent (Serranos)	2134
Jorge Luis Valdés (Henequeneros)	1982
Pedro Luis Lazo (Pinar del Río)*	1826
Carlos Yanes (Isla de la Juventud)*	1808
Omar Ajete (Pinar del Río)	1777
José Ibar (Habana)	1709
Lázaro de la Torre (Industriales)	1679
Julio Romero (Vegueros)	1678

Walks (Bases on Balls)	*(Bases por Bolas)*
Faustino Corrales (Pinar del Río)*	1183
Rogelio García (Vegueros)	1077
Carlos Yanes (Isla de la Juventud)*	1061
Jorge Luis Valdés (Henequeneros)	1024
Braudilio Vinent (Serranos)	989
Rafael Rodríguez (Citricultores)	913
Gervasio Miguel (Isla de la Juventud)*	894
Lázaro de la Torre (Industriales)*	888
Oscar Gil (Holguín)*	878
José Miguel Baez (Las Tunas)*	854

Intentional Walks	*(Bases Intencionales)*
Lázaro Santana (Granjeros)	98
José Miguel Baez (Las Tunas)*	90
Jorge Luis Valdés (Henequeneros)	85
Oscar Romero (Granjeros)	82
Félix Nuñez (Las Tunas)	81

Intentional Walks (continued)   *(Bases Intencionales)*

Rogelio García (Vegueros)	77
Gervasio Miguel (Isla de la Juventud)*	77
Julio Romero (Vegueros)	76
Rafael Castillo (Holguín)	75
Gregorio Pérez (Las Tunas)	75
Osvaldo Duvergel (Guantánamo)	74

Home Runs Allowed   *(Cuadrangulares)*

Carlos Yanes (Isla de la Juventud)*	399
Gervasio Miguel (Isla de la Juventud)*	308
José Miguel Baez (Las Tunas)*	278
Osvaldo Duvergel (Guantánamo)	250
Ernesto Guevara (Granma)*	222
Jorge Luis Valdés (Henequeneros)	221
Misael López (Granma)*	207
José Luis Alemán (Santiago de Cuba)	207
Teofilo Pérez (Camagüey)*	202
Lázaro de la Torre (Industriales)	198
Félix Nuñez (Las Tunas)*	195

Hit Batters   *(Golpeados por Lanzamientos)*

José Miguel Baez (Las Tunas)*	237
Misael López (Granma)*	224
Eliecer Montes de Oca (Villa Clara)*	198
Pedro Luis Lazo (Pinar del Río)*	197
Carlos Yanes (Isla de la Juventud)*	185

Osvaldo Duvergel (Guantánamo)	181
Gervasio Miguel (Isla de la Juventud)*	172
Oscar Gil (Holguín)*	170
Rolando Arrojo (Villa Clara)	169
Teofilo Pérez (Camagüey)*	147

Balks   *(Balks)*

Gervasio Miguel (Isla de la Juventud)*	19
Wilson Hawthorne (Santiago de Cuba)	19
Luis Tissert (Santiago de Cuba)*	18
Eliecer Montes de Oca (Villa Clara)*	17
Remigio Leal (Pinar del Río)	17
José Luis Alemán (Santiago de Cuba)	16
Juan Ramírez (Sancti Spíritus)	16
Andrés Luis (Camagüey)	16
Wilson López (Santiago de Cuba	16

Wild Pitches   *(Wild Pitches)*

Faustino Corrales (Pinar del Río)*	211
Jorge Luis Valdés (Henequeneros)	189
Braudilio Vinent (Serranos)	178
Rogelio García (Vegueros)	175
Félix Nuñez (Las Tunas)	171
José Ibar (Habana)	168
Ariel Prieto (Isla de la Juventud)	164
Yovani Aragón (Sancti Spíritus)*	161
Julio Romero (Vegueros)	158
Alfredo Fonseca (Metropolitanos)*	154

Cuban National Team All-Time Roster and Lifetime Batting/Pitching Statistics

1962 (NATIONAL SERIES I) TO 2004 (NATIONAL SERIES XLIII)

Provided below are Cuban League (National Series and Selective Series combined) lifetime statistics of all players who have appeared on the Cuban National Team between 1962 and 2004 (43 years). This list includes all players (140 position players and 110 pitchers) on national teams that have competed in the Olympic Games, Pan American Games, Amateur World Series, Intercontinental Cup Games and Central American and Caribbean Games. For specific national team years and international tournaments participated in for each player, complete rosters are provided at the end of Chapter 7 above. Players not appearing in the below lists have not played on a national team representing Cuba in major international tournaments. Stats complete through National Series XLIII (2003–2004). **Boldface means active in 2003–04 and after.**

Statistics are drawn from records on file with INDER and published periodically in the recently revived annual *Cuban League Guidebook* (*Guía Oficial de Béisbol Cubana*). One flaw in the available Cuban League career statistics is that the specific years played are not available for individual players. Only total numbers of seasons played appear in these statistical summaries. **Note:** * = Player who has since left Cuba.

Cuban All-Time National Team Batting Statistics

(Statistics for games played in National Series and Selective Series seasons only)

Player (Primary NS/SS Team)	Series	AB	R	H	HR	RBI	SLG	B.A.
Abreu, Michel (Matanzas)	8	2194	386	691	115	432	.523	.315
Aguila, Germán (Industriales)	13	2634	277	592	21	237	.291	.225
Alvarez, Ubaldo (Industriales)	9	1773	189	433	4	150	.307	.244
Anglada, Rey (Industriales)	10	2773	422	806	40	303	.398	.291
Arias, Agustín (Oriente)	17	5165	691	1407	68	587	.370	.272
Baró, Juan Luis (Citricultores)	17	4425	700	1343	157	667	.486	.304
Bécquer, Julio (Azucareros)	3	257	32	56	1	22	.272	.218
Bejerano, Victor (Granma)	**21**	**6816**	**1092**	**1957**	**235**	**1017**	**.458**	**.287**
Benavides, Ariel (Guantánamo)	**13**	**3460**	**598**	**1098**	**165**	**601**	**.528**	**.317**
Betancourt, Lino (Henequeneros)	7	860	90	217	20	142	.380	.252
Blandino, Owen (Azucareros)	18	3473	406	883	52	367	.356	.254
Bruzón, Juan Carlos (Holguín)*	12	3633	533	1131	29	363	.405	.311
Caldés, Miguel (Camagüey)	14	4219	612	1220	176	683	.472	.289
Capiró, Armando (Industriales)	14	3948	609	1177	162	677	.492	.298
Carbonell, Francisco Javier (Villa Clara)	10	1155	82	291	6	94	.309	.252
Casanova, Luis Giraldo (Vegueros)	17	5288	1144	1705	312	1069	.569	.322

Player (Primary NS/SS Team)	Series	AB	R	H	HR	RBI	SLG	B.A.
Castro, Danel (Las Tunas)	**10**	**2426**	**408**	**729**	**67**	**437**	**.455**	**.300**
Castro, Juan (Pinar del Río)	16	3751	399	856	95	453	.347	.228
Cepeda, Frederich (Sancti Spíritus)	**7**	**2053**	**371**	**645**	**92**	**348**	**.534**	**.314**
Chapelli, Loidel (Camagüey)	**11**	**2874**	**444**	**925**	**80**	**497**	**.497**	**.322**
Charles, Yorelvis (Ciego de Avila)	**8**	**1755**	**262**	**571**	**44**	**253**	**.470**	**.325**
Chávez, Pedro (Industriales)	8	1389	215	399	22	192	.400	.287
Contreras, Lázaro (Henequeneros)	6	2057	344	616	54	259	.444	.299
Cuevas, Miguel (Orientales)	13	3144	396	876	83	573	.409	.279
Delgado, Jose Raúl (Sancti Spíritus)	20	4080	664	1112	183	698	.461	.273
Díaz, Raúl (Orientales)	2	96	14	19	2	5	.271	.198
Díaz, Vicente (Granjeros)	15	4808	602	1284	28	412	.331	.267
Dueñas, Yobal (Pinar del Río)*	14	5025	837	1615	136	763	.477	.321
Duvergel, Giorvis (Guantánamo)	**5**	**1561**	**252**	**489**	**30**	**164**	**.432**	**.313**
Enríquez, Michel (Isla de la Juventud)	**7**	**2398**	**469**	**859**	**72**	**374**	**.526**	**.358**
Estrada, José (Matanzas)	**18**	**6338**	**1140**	**2005**	**127**	**708**	**.450**	**.316**
Fernández, Julio Germán (Henequeneros)	19	6110	882	1820	302	1151	.496	.298
Fuentes, Angel (Industriales)	4	162	20	25	1	20	.198	.154
Garbey, Bárbaro (Metropolitanos)*	5	1128	148	327	19	140	.399	.290
García, Jorge (Serranos)	13	2442	387	715	43	346	.405	.293
Godinez, Evenecer (Santiago de Cuba)	17	5343	932	1556	107	704	.423	.291
Goire, Leonardo (Citricultores)	12	3850	488	1102	54	439	.380	.286
Gómez, Yasser (Industriales)	**7**	**2236**	**373**	**738**	**8**	**236**	**.406**	**.330**
González, Antonio (Occidentales)	11	2739	551	847	17	218	.369	.309
González, Giraldo (Vegueros)	15	4763	533	1219	61	482	.342	.256
González, Mario (Industriales)*	4	505	53	123	3	73	.315	.244
González, Urbano (Industriales)	13	2864	317	792	18	320	.342	.277
Gourriel, Lourdes (Sancti Spíritus)	20	6263	1122	2025	247	1077	.506	.323
Gourriel, Yulieski (Sancti Spíritus)	**3**	**1052**	**190**	**335**	**37**	**185**	**.530**	**.318**
Hechavarría, Ramón (Orientales)	17	2804	340	738	53	362	.373	.263
Hernández, Alberto (Orientales)	3	71	5	10	1	7	.197	.141
Hernández, Daniel (Orientales)	11	1563	206	358	22	188	.325	.229
Hernández, Evelio (Citricultores)	10	1747	223	431	33	220	.365	.247
Hernández, Fernando (Vegueros)	20	5627	866	1600	198	867	.449	.273
Hernández, Wilfredo (Guantánamo)	15	4018	438	1085	18	341	.326	.270
Herrera, Rafael (Henequeneros)	9	1690	166	417	1	151	.279	.247
Isaac, Rey (Santiago de Cuba)	**15**	**4228**	**742**	**1347**	**91**	**636**	**.443**	**.319**
Isasi, Félix (Occidentales)	18	3902	571	1142	45	445	.382	.293
Jiménez, Antonio (Industriales)	13	3185	522	802	5	225	.320	.252
Jova, Pedro (Villa Clara)	17	5073	824	1598	32	482	.394	.315
Junco, Lázaro (Citricultores)	18	5780	1018	1641	405	1180	.551	.284
Kindelán, Orestes (Santiago de Cuba)	21	6488	1379	2030	487	1511	.600	.313
Latiffa, Fermín (Orientales)	20	4712	625	1315	75	568	.378	.279
Lazo, Daniel (Pinar del Río)	**14**	**3894**	**626**	**1117**	**219**	**838**	**.503**	**.287**
Lazo, Ricardo (Industriales)	11	1367	140	347	11	174	.313	.254
Linares, Arturo (Occidentales)	14	3195	334	889	19	419	.365	.278
Linares, Fidel (Occidentales)	10	1581	172	425	8	159	.333	.269
Linares, Juan Carlos (Pinar del Río)	**16**	**4590**	**809**	**1481**	**101**	**689**	**.461**	**.323**
Linares, Omar (Pinar del Río)	20	5962	1547	2195	404	1221	.644	.368
López, Angel (Villa Clara)	12	2413	335	644	115	391	.462	.267
López, Lázaro (Cienfuegos)	17	3676	750	1080	184	616	.510	.294
Machado, Oscar (Villa Clara)	19	4050	726	1159	207	761	.504	.286
Machado, Roger (Ciego de Avila)	**11**	**2565**	**306**	**698**	**54**	**318**	**.404**	**.272**
Macías, Oscar (Habana)	18	6313	1124	1960	286	1080	.513	.310
Madera, Lázaro (Vegueros)	15	5774	909	1872	264	1093	.522	.324
Madera, Yosvani (Pinar del Río)	**14**	**2936**	**395**	**821**	**82**	**420**	**.419**	**.280**
Mancebo, Elpidio (Orientales)	17	4512	691	1271	54	523	.388	.282
Manríque, Juan (Matanzas)	**18**	**4583**	**909**	**1318**	**219**	**788**	**.489**	**.288**
Marquetti, Agustín (Habana)	22	6725	853	1935	207	1106	.431	.288
Martínez, Alberto (Las Villas)	16	3523	328	821	14	281	.282	.233
Martínez, Alfonso (Cienfuegos)	10	1208	118	279	13	87	.301	.231
Martínez, Isaac (Ciego de Avila)	**10**	**2338**	**354**	**718**	**50**	**333**	**.437**	**.307**
Martínez, Lázaro (Industriales)	17	3235	420	857	83	370	.394	.265

Player (Primary NS/SS Team)	Series	AB	R	H	HR	RBI	SLG	B.A.
Martínez, Romelio (Habana)	14	4710	924	1285	370	1055	.548	.273
Medina, Pedro (Industriales)	17	4913	886	1448	221	869	.483	.295
Méndez, Javier (Industriales)	22	6424	1139	2101	191	1174	.488	.327
Meriño, Rolando (Santiago de Cuba)	**14**	**3685**	**657**	**1082**	**102**	**529**	**.444**	**.294**
Mesa, Germán (Industriales)	16	4344	883	1239	112	527	.423	.285
Mesa, Victor (Villa Clara)	19	6834	1282	2171	273	1174	.502	.318
Millan, Juan Carlos (Habana)	11	3914	660	1146	221	778	.529	.293
Miranda, Danny (Ciego de Avila)	**8**	**2303**	**333**	**685**	**53**	**353**	**.437**	**.297**
Montejo, Silvio (Las Villas)	12	2343	328	619	33	245	.376	.264
Morales, Kendry (Industriales)*	3	871	147	287	37	170	.537	.330
Morales, Manuel (Habana)	12	2646	287	699	7	208	.317	.264
Moreno, Juan C. (Isla de la Juventud)	**11**	**3634**	**507**	**1059**	**88**	**485**	**.420**	**.291**
Muñoz, Antonio (Azucareros)	24	6676	1281	2014	370	1407	.535	.302
O'Reilly, Alejo (Ciego de Avila)	16	4683	664	1418	240	910	.509	.303
Oliva, Osvaldo (Azucareros)	16	4301	576	1156	67	467	.367	.269
Olivera, Héctor (Cienfuegos)	13	2703	337	854	78	488	.464	.316
Ortega, Raúl (Industriales)	3	171	13	39	0	13	.269	.228
Osorio, Eulogio (Industriales)	16	4329	555	1224	25	383	.359	.283
Otamendi, Ramón (Santiago de Cuba)	14	3525	456	869	132	451	.408	.247
Pacheco, Antonio (Santiago de Cuba)	22	7045	1258	2356	284	1304	.525	.334
Pacheco, Juan Emilio (Azucareros)	5	445	36	97	1	45	.285	.218
Padilla, Juan (Industriales)	16	5923	929	1828	148	880	.453	.309
Paret, Eduardo (Villa Clara)	**14**	**4990**	**1059**	**1463**	**114**	**541**	**.431**	**.293**
Pedroso, Carmelo (Forestales)	12	2745	336	765	44	345	.381	.279
Pedroso, Joan Carlos (Las Tunas)	**7**	**1993**	**331**	**605**	**87**	**347**	**.498**	**.304**
Perdomo, Michel (Villa Clara)	**13**	**3268**	**540**	**1011**	**120**	**549**	**.491**	**.309**
Pérez, Lázaro (Industriales)	18	2680	276	570	44	325	.311	.213
Pestano, Ariel (Villa Clara)	**13**	**2801**	**355**	**807**	**67**	**415**	**.435**	**.288**
Pierre, Gabriel (Santiago de Cuba)	18	5338	1031	1577	306	1043	.530	.295
Piloto, Luis (Isla de la Juventud)	10	1742	265	487	66	234	.452	.280
Puente, Rodolfo (Metropolitanos)	16	5109	690	1408	21	439	.330	.276
Ramírez, Alexei (Pinar del Río)	**4**	**1300**	**255**	**423**	**38**	**192**	**.498**	**.325**
Ramos, Alexander (Isla de la Juventud)	**17**	**5665**	**914**	**1926**	**104**	**685**	**.450**	**.340**
Reyes, Raúl (Industriales)	10	2351	335	590	62	310	.379	.251
Rodríguez, Pedro José (Cienfuegos)	15	4171	699	1196	286	969	.545	.287
Rodríguez, Pedro Luis (Habana)	14	4793	871	1599	193	802	.535	.334
Rojas, Ivan (Cienfuegos)	13	2677	377	736	98	461	.450	.275
Rosa, Félix (Industriales)	10	1984	243	533	18	197	.343	.269
Rosique, Rigoberto (Henequeneros)	13	2802	406	845	22	280	.379	.302
Sánchez, Eriel (Sancti Spíritus)	**11**	**2934**	**315**	**858**	**74**	**423**	**.418**	**.292**
Sánchez, Fernando (Matanzas)	23	7204	1115	2215	280	1223	.489	.307
Sánchez, Wilfredo (Henequeneros)	19	6565	891	2174	16	523	.394	.331
Sarduy, Felipe (Granjeros)	21	6109	825	1664	97	685	.371	.272
Sauquet, Eladio (Occidentales)	3	53	9	7	0	3	.208	.132
Scott, Santiago (Industriales)	4	356	51	92	2	45	.329	.258
Scull, Antonio (Industriales)	**18**	**4730**	**852**	**1485**	**189**	**975**	**.513**	**.314**
Tabares, Carlos (Industriales)	**12**	**3477**	**584**	**1074**	**47**	**426**	**.406**	**.309**
Telemaco, Andres (Orientales)	13	1791	268	465	25	143	.365	.260
Toca, Jorge Luis (Villa Clara)*	8	2497	411	796	100	465	.517	.319
Trigoura, Jorge (Industriales)	6	498	44	109	6	56	.295	.219
Ulacia, Luis (Camagüey)	20	6718	1107	2115	143	668	.436	.315
Urgelles, Yoandri (Metropolitanos)	**5**	**1137**	**167**	**370**	**12**	**149**	**.445**	**.325**
Urquiola, Alfonso (Pinar del Río)	19	4594	597	1314	89	566	.404	.286
Urrutia, Ermidelio (Las Tunas)	15	4904	845	1536	219	850	.515	.313
Urrutia, Osmani (Las Tunas)	**11**	**2361**	**316**	**849**	**70**	**410**	**.507**	**.360**
Vargas, Lázaro (Industriales)	22	6731	1109	2132	108	1064	.426	.317
Verde, Rolando (Industriales)	16	4970	725	1513	62	617	.405	.304
Videaux, Robelquis (Guantánamo)	**11**	**2620**	**459**	**835**	**107**	**440**	**.511**	**.319**
Villar, Julian (Occidentales)	12	2555	268	736	41	339	.396	.288
Walters, Erwin (Occidentales)	10	1505	179	407	27	206	.387	.270
Zamora, Amado (Villa Clara)	19	5143	851	1704	39	415	.415	.331
Zayas, Miguel (Camagüey)	16	3214	335	792	68	357	.356	.246

Cuban All-Time National Team Pitching Statistics

(Statistics for games played in National Series and Selective Series seasons only)

Pitcher (Primary NS/SS Team)	Series	GP	CG	INN	SO	BB	W–L	ERA
Abreu, Aquino (Azucareros)	14	232	46	1116.0	718	412	63–65	2.26
Abreu, Pablo (Ciudad Habana)	12	169	44	964.2	822	531	72–48	3.62
Ajete, Omar (Pinar del Río)	16	449	137	2320.0	1777	681	179–96	3.29
Alarcón, Manuel (Orientales)	7	87	43	583.2	529	188	41–24	1.82
Alemán, José Luis (Santiago de Cuba)	17	406	179	2472.0	1447	692	174–125	3.13
Alvarez, Ivan (Industriales)*	3	51	13	235.0	208	123	17–13	3.91
Aragón, Yovani (Sancti Spíritus)	**12**	**280**	**97**	**1791.0**	**1549**	**697**	**119–96**	**3.48**
Arocha, René (Metropolitanos)*	11	245	92	1412.2	1038	544	104–72	3.18
Arrojo, Luis Rolando (Villa Clara)*	13	359	129	2027.2	1138	442	154–98	3.50
Aspillaga, Franklyn (Occidentales)	7	78	12	270.2	131	73	23–13	2.86
Ávila, Orelvis (Holguín)	**9**	**224**	**33**	**972.2**	**445**	**345**	**55–66**	**3.92**
Báez, Danys (Pinar del Río)*	2	41	2	122.2	92	58	6–5	4.70
Barreiro, Luis (Habana)	6	79	8	313.1	240	111	23–11	1.84
Betancourt, Dany (Santiago de Cuba)	**4**	**96**	**16**	**504.1**	**364**	**221**	**37–24**	**3.37**
Betancourt, Rigoberto (Occidentales)*	8	108	25	569.0	573	209	38–27	2.51
Blanco, Jacinto (Azucareros)	1	1	0	0.0	0	3	0–1	——
Borroto, Luis (Villa Clara)	**3**	**80**	**16**	**380.2**	**383**	**148**	**33–19**	**2.93**
Carrero, Omar (Ganaderos)	17	338	146	1778.1	1029	610	110–110	2.94
Castillo, Rafael (Holguín)	14	280	119	3134.0	1982	1024	234–166	3.13
Castillo, Yoide (Villa Clara)	10	128	20	690.0	564	286	49–32	3.16
Contreras, José Ariel (Pinar del Río)*	10	232	76	1473.0	1346	514	117–50	2.82
Corrales, Faustino (Pinar del Río)	**22**	**437**	**124**	**2505.0**	**2327**	**1183**	**169–131**	**3.25**
Coss, Ifredi (Sancti Spíritus)	**3**	**79**	**12**	**402.1**	**334**	**105**	**29–15**	**2.51**
Costa, Reinaldo (Pinar del Río)	12	259	82	1364.2	814	466	110–67	3.14
Cutiño, Ariel (Serranos)	8	129	28	551.2	411	244	44–28	4.63
Darcourt, José M. (Metropolitanos)	14	296	132	1884.2	1344	753	129–107	2.83
De la Rosa, Lamey (Habana Province)	**10**	**192**	**9**	**616.0**	**468**	**317**	**47–34**	**4.08**
De la Torre, Lázaro (Industriales)	19	495	159	2727.1	1679	888	205–132	3.22
Díaz, Angel Leocadio (Industriales)	12	284	100	1627.0	816	455	112–74	3.20
Díaz, Giorge (Guantánamo)	10	237	73	1228.2	658	324	70–83	3.81
Díaz, Ricardo (Orientales)*	2	10	2	48.1	24	25	2–3	2.42
Duvergel, Osvaldo (Guantánamo)	15	394	135	2026.1	899	717	129–134	4.29
Fernández, Felipe (Centrales)	10	293	10	774.2	368	256	47–38	3.79
Fernández, Mario (Oriente)	11	157	47	784.2	482	234	44–51	2.72
Fernández Guerra, Osvaldo (Metros)*	11	206	43	943.2	778	358	70–42	3.12
Fernández Rodríguez, Osvaldo (Holguín)*	8	223	78	1160.2	844	356	82–62	3.30
Figueredo, Orlando (Mineros)	15	345	125	1937.1	1114	671	125–107	2.74
Fumero, Jorge (Industriales)	9	208	13	682.2	316	246	51–35	3.94
Galvez, Octavio (Cienfuegos)	7	134	57	778.0	335	170	47–40	2.98
García, Alfredo (Henequeneros)	10	204	68	1192.0	822	453	70–72	2.41
García, Rogelio (Vegueros)	16	398	201	2609.0	2499	1077	202–100	2.39
Garro, Lázaro (Matanzas)	**15**	**363**	**58**	**1547.1**	**686**	**674**	**86–99**	**4.58**
González, Bernardo (Habana)	7	89	15	401.0	364	170	30–21	2.04
González, Norberto (Cienfuegos)	**7**	**153**	**26**	**780.1**	**599**	**338**	**52–55**	**4.61**
Guerra, Jesús (Vegueros)	13	259	117	1668.1	819	451	114–84	2.36
Guevara, Ernesto (Granma)	16	345	104	2059.2	1238	541	133–108	3.75
Hernández, Livan (Isla de la Juventud)*	3	49	30	335.0	311	127	27–16	4.57
Hernández, Orlando (Industriales)*	10	246	75	1514.1	1211	455	126–47	3.05
Huelga, José Antonio (Azucareros)	7	160	56	871.1	722	277	73–32	1.50
Hurtado, Manuel (Industriales)*	12	218	60	1182.2	860	380	90–47	1.80
Ibar, José (Habana Province)	**18**	**366**	**129**	**2371.0**	**1709**	**723**	**173–100**	**3.45**
Ilivanes, Alfonso (Guantánamo)	11	268	99	1493.1	790	481	87–101	3.68
Jiménez, Antonio (Industriales)	11	210	37	846.2	530	392	63–37	2.37
Lazo, Pedro Luis (Pinar del Río)	**14**	**391**	**142**	**2332.2**	**1826**	**750**	**181–102**	**3.40**
Legon, Gaspar (Ganaderos)	15	377	105	2051.1	1247	645	141–101	2.29
Licea. Ciro Silvino (Granma)	**11**	**278**	**100**	**1738.2**	**1182**	**434**	**120–86**	**3.52**
López, Raúl (Industriales)	8	175	1	416.0	233	133	32–20	1.88
López, Wilson (Santiago de Cuba)	12	261	53	1239.1	719	475	74–56	4.47
Luis, Omar (Camagüey)	10	136	38	772.1	806	381	51–43	3.51

Pitcher (Primary NS/SS Team)	Series	GP	CG	INN	SO	BB	W–L	ERA
Macías, Rolando (Las Villas)	15	288	89	1551.0	801	387	110–65	2.17
Machado, Jorge Luis (Industriales)	**13**	**218**	**56**	**1301.1**	**829**	**310**	**101–51**	**3.40**
Madera, Abel (Pinar del Río)	8	124	5	444.0	263	158	33–17	3.43
Martí, Yadel (Industriales)	**6**	**161**	**15**	**572.2**	**368**	**186**	**42–24**	**3.50**
Martínez, Anselmo (Citricultores)	11	247	83	1392.2	869	580	87–80	2.94
Martínez, Jonder (Habana Province)	**8**	**189**	**28**	**1019.2**	**583**	**298**	**48–67**	**4.27**
Martínez, Jorge (Occidentales)	10	279	46	1149.2	469	314	72–54	4.22
Mederos, Santiago "Changa" (Habana)	15	253	106	1628.2	1420	633	123–67	1.97
Mesa, Carlos (Citricultores)	18	314	94	1642.2	1246	782	95–96	3.86
Montes de Oca, Eliecer (Villa Clara)	**15**	**316**	**96**	**1854.1**	**1038**	**624**	**126–83**	**3.54**
Montieth, Frank Andy (Industriales)	**1**	**32**	**0**	**75.1**	**64**	**21**	**4–4**	**2.51**
Nuñez, Félix (Las Tunas)	15	379	163	2248.2	1383	806	130–156	3.51
Odelín, Vicyohandri (Camagüey)	**7**	**153**	**42**	**857.2**	**618**	**210**	**66–40**	**2.76**
Oliva, Juan Carlos (Pinar del Río)	11	289	65	1330.0	749	393	101–57	2.46
Palma, Adiel (Cienfuegos)	**17**	**336**	**100**	**1900.2**	**1375**	**821**	**111–135**	**4.09**
Pastor, Rolando (Occidentales)*	3	42	10	199.0	197	131	9–16	2.89
Pérez, Gaspar (Matanzas)	10	222	58	1072.2	576	562	76–63	2.62
Pérez, Gregorio (Granjeros)	15	301	112	1791.2	976	363	110–107	2.18
Pérez, Juan Carlos (Las Tunas)	10	155	41	808.2	656	476	46–46	4.47
Pérez Pérez, Juan (Camagüey)	11	228	81	1301.1	974	523	89–58	1.86
Pérez, Santiago (Occidentales)	3	42	2	83.0	45	36	5–6	3.90
Pérez, Yosvani (Cienfuegos)	**11**	**217**	**61**	**1227.1**	**768**	**449**	**59–81**	**4.04**
Pino, Félix (Forestales)	9	184	49	925.1	575	453	55–46	2.82
Quesada, Walberto (Ciego de Avila)	10	155	20	614.2	402	236	31–40	3.97
Riscart, José Ramón (Villa Clara)	20	447	111	2172.2	1202	455	155–93	3.35
Rodríguez, Maels (Sancti Spíritus)*	6	156	42	938.0	1148	486	65–45	2.29
Rojas, Euclides (Industriales)*	13	365	6	847.2	625	285	59–42	2.93
Romero, Julio (Vegueros)	15	326	162	2174.2	1678	727	148–100	2.31
Romero, Ormari (Santiago de Cuba)	**15**	**388**	**107**	**2144.1**	**1065**	**524**	**158–99**	**3.51**
Romero, Oscar (Granjeros)	17	400	91	1948.1	1008	746	125–114	2.38
Rubio, Antonio (Occidentales)	6	43	10	216.2	143	102	14–8	2.37
Ruíz, Walfrido (Industriales)	12	234	76	1314.0	799	372	102–50	1.88
Salcedo, Francisco (Orientales)	4	22	2	79.2	44	43	4–5	3.28
Salgado, Emilio (Vegueros)	9	165	59	912.1	682	414	50–53	2.55
Sánchez, José (Camagüey)	13	270	43	1097.2	681	231	66–65	2.58
Santana, Lázaro (Granjeros)	17	418	101	2062.2	1054	695	140–116	2.35
Santana, Reinaldo (Las Villas)	10	296	24	1051.2	618	296	66–55	3.62
Street, Alfredo (Industriales)	8	120	26	549.2	396	252	33–26	2.01
Tamayo, Leonardo (Metropolitanos)	8	140	36	736.1	418	236	52–32	3.90
Tissert, Luis (Santiago de Cuba)	11	280	75	1345.0	665	340	94–55	3.14
Torriente, Jesús (Henequeneros)	8	116	38	651.2	427	240	43–39	2.22
Turcás, Leonides (Guantánamo)	8	159	39	861.0	539	367	49–62	4.28
Valdés, Jorge Luis (Henequeneros)	20	519	229	3134.0	1982	1024	234–166	3.13
Valdés, Roberto (Mineros)	10	159	66	977.1	633	268	77–40	1.75
Valle, Lázaro (Industriales)	15	334	84	1740.0	1351	613	138–73	3.39
Vega, Manuel Alberto (Granma)	**9**	**135**	**9**	**509.2**	**334**	**176**	**29–21**	**4.34**
Veliz, Mario (Habana)	11	265	95	1487.0	938	391	113–66	3.58
Verdura, Modesto (Azucareros)	8	110	15	475.1	310	221	32–20	2.56
Vera, Norge (Santiago de Cuba)	**10**	**210**	**84**	**1358.0**	**851**	**322**	**113–46**	**2.47**
Vinent, Braudilio (Serranos)	20	477	265	3259.2	2134	989	221–167	2.42
Yanes, Carlos (Isla de la Juventud)	**21**	**588**	**160**	**3093.1**	**1808**	**1061**	**187–194**	**4.57**

CUBAN NATIONAL TEAM VERSUS BALTIMORE ORIOLES
(GAME 1, HAVANA, MARCH 28, 1999)

Player	Position	Birth Date	Home Province (Cuban League Team)
Michel Abreu Martínez	Infielder	October 2, 1975	Matanzas (Matanzas)
Enrique Díaz Martínez	Infielder	September 2, 1968	Havana (Metropolitanos)
Yobal Dueñas Martínez	Infielder	April 4, 1972	Pinar del Río (Pinar del Río)
Eduardo Cárdenas Alcalá	Infielder	June 18, 1967	Matanzas (Matanzas)
Danel Castro Muñagorri	Infielder	July 2, 1976	Las Tunas (Las Tunas)
Omar Linares Izquierdo	Infielder	October 23, 1967	Pinar del Río (Pinar del Río)

Player	Position	Birth Date	Home Province (Cuban League Team)
Andy Morales Leon	Infielder	December 3, 1971	Havana (Habana)
Juan Carlos Moreno Pérez	Infielder	September 28, 1975	Isla de la Juventud (Isla de la Juventud)
Loidel Chapelli Jiménez	Infielder	November 14, 1971	Camagüey (Camagüey)
José Estrada González	Outfielder	January 22, 1967	Matanzas (Matanzas)
Oscar Machado Acosta	Outfielder	February 8, 1977	Villa Clara (Villa Clara)
Robelquis Videaux Martínez	Outfielder	February 15, 1976	Guantánamo (Guantánamo)
Luis Ulacia Álvarez	Outfielder	September 24, 196	Havana (Camagüey)
Daniel Lazo Monterrey	Outfielder	March 6, 1964	Pinar del Río (Pinar del Río)
José Ibar Medina	Pitcher (RH)	May 6, 1969	Santiago de Cuba (Habana)
José Ariel Contreras Camejo	Pitcher (RH)	December 6, 1971	Pinar del Río (Pinar del Río)
Pedro Luis Lazo Iglesias	Pitcher (RH)	April 15, 1973	Pinar del Río (Pinar del Río)
Ernesto Guevara Ramos	Pitcher (RH)	June 30, 1971	Matanzas (Granma)
Yovani Aragón Rodríguez	Pitcher (RH)	May 2, 1974	Sancti Spíritus (Sancti Spíritus)
Ciro Silvino Licea González	Pitcher (RH)	November 28, 1975	Granma (Granma)
Maels Rodríguez Carrales	Pitcher (RH)	October 15, 1979	Sancti Spíritus (Sancti Spíritus)
Lázaro Garro Menéndez	Pitcher (LH)	September 28, 1973	Matanzas (Matanzas)
Juan Manríque García	Catcher	August 26, 1967	Matanzas (Matanzas)
Ariel Pestano Valdés	Catcher	October 31, 1974	Villa Clara (Villa Clara)
Roger Machado Morales	Catcher	March 3, 1971	Ciego de Ávila (Ciego de Ávila)

CUBAN NATIONAL TEAM VERSUS BALTIMORE ORIOLES (GAME 2, BALTIMORE, MAY 3, 1999)

Player	Position (Shirt #)	Birth Date	Home Province (Cuban League Team)
Michel Abreu Martínez	Infielder (29)	October 2, 1975	Matanzas (Matanzas)
Enrique Díaz Martínez	Infielder (31)	September 2, 1968	Havana (Metropolitanos)
Germán Mesa Fresneda	Infielder (11)	May 12, 1967	Havana (Industriales)
Orestes Kindelán Olivares	Infielder (46)	November 1, 1964	Santiago de Cuba (Santiago de Cuba)
Danel Castro Muñagorri	Infielder (51)	July 2, 1976	Las Tunas (Las Tunas)
Omar Linares Izquierdo	Infielder (10)	October 23, 1967	Pinar del Río (Pinar del Río)
Andy Morales Leon	Infielder (53)	December 3, 1971	Havana (Habana)
Juan Carlos Moreno Pérez	Infielder (26)	September 28, 1975	Isla de la Juventud (Isla de la Juventud)
Loidel Chapelli Jiménez	Infielder (95)	November 14, 1971	Camagüey (Camagüey)
Gabriel Pierre Lazo	Infielder (33)	May 29, 1966	Santiago de Cuba (Santiago de Cuba)
Osar Macías Hernández	Infielder (38)	February 1, 1969	Havana (Habana)
Juan Padilla Alfonso	Infielder (7)	September 16, 1965	Havana (Industriales)
José Estrada González	Outfielder (23)	January 22, 1967	Matanzas (Matanzas)
Oscar Machado Acosta	Outfielder (15)	February 8, 1977	Villa Clara (Villa Clara)
Robelquis Videaux Martínez	Outfielder (21)	February 15, 1976	Guantánamo (Guantánamo)
Luis Ulacia Álvarez	Outfielder (1)	September 24, 196	Havana (Camagüey)
Daniel Lazo Monterrey	Outfielder (74)	March 6, 1964	Pinar del Río (Pinar del Río)
Javier Méndez González	Outfielder (17)	April 22, 1964	Havana (Industriales)
Norge Vera Peralta	Pitcher (RH) (20)	August 3, 1971	Santiago de Cuba (Santiago de Cuba)
José Ariel Contreras Camejo	Pitcher (RH) (52)	December 6, 1971	Pinar del Río (Pinar del Río)
Pedro Luis Lazo Iglesias	Pitcher (RH) (99)	April 15, 1973	Pinar del Río (Pinar del Río)
Omary Romero Turcas	Pitcher (RH) (19)	February 22, 1968	Santiago de Cuba (Santiago de Cuba)
Yovani Aragón Rodríguez	Pitcher (RH) (35)	May 2, 1974	Sancti Spíritus (Sancti Spíritus)
Carlos Yanes Artiles	Pitcher (RH) (32)	May 20, 1965	Isla de la Juventud (Isla de la Juventud)
Juan Manríque García	Catcher (45)	August 26, 1967	Matanzas (Matanzas)
Ariel Pestano Valdés	Catcher (13)	October 31, 1974	Villa Clara (Villa Clara)
Roger Machado Morales	Catcher (61)	March 3, 1971	Ciego de Ávila (Ciego de Ávila)

CUBAN LEAGUE HITTERS WITH MORE THAN 400 HOME RUNS (1962–2004)

Orestes Kindelán (Santiago de Cuba) 487
Lázaro Junco (Matanzas) 405
Omar Linares (Pinar del Río) 404

CUBAN LEAGUE HITTERS WITH MORE THAN 300 HOME RUNS (1962–2004)

Antonio Muñoz (Sancti Spíritus) 370
Romelio Martínez (Habana) 370
Luis Casanova (Pinar del Río) 312
Gabriel Pierre (Santiago de Cuba) 306
Julio Fernández (Matanzas) 302

CUBAN LEAGUE HITTERS WITH MORE THAN 200 HOME RUNS (1962–2004)

Pedro José Rodríguez (Cienfuegos) 286
Oscar Macias (Habana) 286
Antonio Pacheco (Santiago de Cuba) 284
Fernando Sánchez (Matanzas) 280
Victor Mesa (Villa Clara) 273
Leonel Moa (Camagüey) 272

CUBAN LEAGUE HITTERS WITH MORE THAN 200 HOME RUNS (1962–2004) (continued)

Lázaro Madera (Pinar del Río) 264
Lourdes Gourriel (Sancti Spíritus) 247
Alejo O'Reilly (Villa Clara) 240
Victor Bejerano (Granma) 235
Juan Millan (Habana) 222
Pedro Medina (Habana) 221
Ermidelio Urrutia (Las Tunas) 221
Juan Manrique (Matanzas) 219
Daniel Lazo (Pinar del Río) 219
Reinaldo Fernández (Camagüey) 212
Agustin Lescaille (Guantánamo) 212
Fausto Alvarez Santiago de Cuba) 210
Agustin Marquetti (Habana) 207
Oscar Machado (Villa Clara) 207

CUBAN LEAGUE HITTERS WITH MORE THAN 2000 BASE HITS (1962–2004)

Antonio Pacheco (Santiago de Cuba) 2356
Fernando Sánchez (Matanzas) 2215
Omar Linares (Pinar del Río) 2195
Luis Ulacia (Camagüey) 2183
Wilfredo Sánchez (Matanzas) 2174
Victor Mesa (Villa Clara) 2171

Lázaro Vargas (Habana) 2132
Javier Méndez (Habana) 2101
Eduardo Cárdenas (Matanzas) 2077
Orestes Kindelán (Santiago de Cuba) 2030
Lourdes Gourriel (Sancti Spíritus) 2026
Sergio Quesada (Camagüey) 2025
Antonio Muñoz (Cienfuegos) 2014
Agustin Lescaille (Guantánamo) 2009
José Estrada (Matanzas) 2005

CUBAN LEAGUE HITTERS WITH MORE THAN 1650 BASE HITS (1962–2004)

Oscar Macías (Habana) 1960
Victor Bejerano (Granma) 1957
Agustin Marguetti (Habana) 1935
Alexander Ramos (Isla de la Juventud) 1926
Reemberto Rosell (Cienfuegos) 1918
Juan Padilla (Industriales) 1914
Lázaro Madera (Pinar del Río) 1872
Eddy Rojas (Villa Clara) 1846
Julio Fernández (Matanzas) 1820
Luis Casanova (Pinar del Río) 1705
Amado Zamora (Villa Clara) 1704
Enrique Díaz (Industriales) 1682
Fausto Alvarez (Santiago de Cuba) 1676
Felipe Sarduy (Camagüey) 1664

Bibliography

The following incomplete but representative bibliography of books and articles in both English and Spanish provides essential references for any reader wishing to explore further into the history of Cuban baseball, and especially into the interconnectedness between Cuba's national pastime and the island nation's pre- and post-communist political history. The ambitious reader is also directed to the useful bibliographies found in Roberto González Echevarría's *The Pride of Havana* (1999) and this author's own *Diamonds Around the Globe* (2005).

Cuban Baseball (Books)

Bjarkman, Peter C. *Baseball with a Latin Beat: A History of the Latin American Game.* Jefferson, NC, and London: McFarland, 1994.

_____. *Diamonds Around the Globe: An Encyclopedia of International Baseball.* Westport, CT: Greenwood, 2005. See especially Chapter 1: Cuba — *Béisbol Paradiso,* pp. 1–67.

Brock, Darryl. *Havana Heat (A Novel).* New York: Total Sports Illustrated, 2000.

Casa, Edel; Jorge Alfonso, and Alberto Pestana. *Viva y en juego (Alive and playing).* Havana: Editorial Científico-Técnica, 1986.

Crespo, José R. *Memorias del Béisbol Espirituano.* Sancti Spitus, Cuba: Departamento Propaganda Sancti Spíritus, 1993. A brief history of baseball in Sancti Spíritus Province.

Delgado, Gabino, and Eduardo Navarro, et al. (editors). *Baseball Libro Azul, 1948–1949* (Baseball Blue Book). Havana: Editorial CENIT, 1948.

Delgado, Gabino, and Severo Nieto (editors). *Béisbol Cubano (Récords y Estadísticas).* Havana: Editorial Lex, 1955.

Díez Muro, Raúl. *Historia del base ball profesional de Cuba (Libro official de la Liga de Base Ball Profesional Cubana),* 3rd ed. Havana: no publisher indicated, 1949.

Fulgueiras, José Antonio. *Victor Mesa: El Béisbol en Vida.* Havana: Editorial Deportes, 2004.

Gálvez y Delmonte, Wenceslao. *El base-ball en Cuba. Historia del base-ball en la Isla de Cuba, sin retratos de los principales jugadores y personas más caracterizadas en el juego citado, ni de ninguna otra.* Havana: Imprenta Mercantil de los Herederos de Santiago, S. Spencer, 1889.

González Echevarría, Roberto. *La Gloria de Cuba: Historia del Béisbol en la Isla.* Madrid: Editorial Colibri, 2004.

_____. *The Pride of Havana: A History of Cuban Baseball.* New York: Oxford University Press, 1999.

Guía Oficial Cubana — Béisbol 63 (Official Cuban League Baseball Guide). Havana: Institutio Cubano del Libro (Ediciones Deportivas), 1963.

Guía Oficial Cubana — Béisbol 65 (Official Cuban League Baseball Guide). Havana: Institutio Cubano del Libro (Ediciones Deportivas), 1965.

Guía Oficial Cubana — Béisbol 69 (Official Cuban League Baseball Guide). Havana: Institutio Cubano del Libro (Ediciones Deportivas), 1969.

Guía Oficial Cubana — Béisbol 70 (Official Cuban League Baseball Guide). Havana: Institutio Cubano del Libro (Ediciones Deportivas), 1970.

Guía Oficial Cubana — Béisbol 71 (Official Cuban League Baseball Guide). Havana: Institutio Cubano del Libro (Ediciones Deportivas), 1971.

Guía Oficial Cubana — Béisbol 72 (Official Cuban League Baseball Guide). Havana: Institutio Cubano del Libro (Ediciones Deportivas), 1972.

Guía Oficial Cubana — Béisbol 92, Tomo I (Official Cuban League Baseball Guide). Havana: Institutio Cubano del Libro (Ediciones Deportivas), 1992.

Guía Oficial de: Béisbol 1998 (Official Cuban League Baseball Guide). Havana: Editorial Deportes (INDER), 1998.

Guía Oficial de: Béisbol 1999 (Official Cuban League Baseball Guide). Havana: Editorial Deportes (INDER), 1999.

Guía Oficial de: Béisbol 2000 (Official Cuban League Baseball Guide). Havana: Editorial Deportes (INDER), 2000.

Guía Oficial de: Béisbol 2001 (Official Cuban League Baseball Guide). Havana: Editorial Deportes (INDER), 2001.

Guía Oficial de: Béisbol 2002 (Official Cuban League Baseball Guide). Havana: Editorial Deportes (INDER), 2002.

Guía Oficial de: Béisbol 2002–2003 (Official Cuban League Baseball Guide). Havana: Editorial Deportes (INDER), 2003.

Guía Oficial de: Béisbol 2004 (Official Cuban League Baseball Guide). Havana: Editorial Deportes (INDER), 2004.

Holway, John. *Blackball Stars: Negro League Pioneers.* New York: Carroll & Graf, 1992 (Westport, CT: Meckler, 1988), 236–47. Includes useful if somewhat faulty chapters on José Méndez, Cristóbal Torriente and Martín Dihigo.

Jamail, Milton. *Full Count: The Inside Story of Cuban Baseball.* Carbondale: Southern Illinois University Press, 2000.

Letusé La O, Rogelio Augusto. *Béisbol Términos y Anécdotas.* Havana: Editorial Científico-Técnica, 2003.

Martínez de Osaba y Goenaga, Juan A. *El Niño Linares.* Havana: Casa Editorial Abril, 2002.

Miñoso, Orestes "Minnie" (as told to Fernando Fernández and Robert Kleinfelder). *Extra Innings: My Life in Baseball.* Chicago, IL: Regnery Gateway, 1983.

Nieto Fernández, Severo. *Conrado Marrero — El Premier.* Havana: Editorial Científico-Técnica, 2000.

_____. *José Méndez — El Diamante Negro.* Havana: Editorial Científico-Técnica (Colección Deportes), 2004.

Oliva, Tony (with Bob Fowler). *Tony O! The Trials and Triumphs of Tony Oliva.* New York: Hawthorn, 1973.

Padura, Leonardo, and Raúl Arce. *Estrellas de Béisbol — El Alma en el Terreno.* Havana: Editora Abril, 1989.

Pestana, Alberto. *Breve Historial de Las Series Mundiales de Béisbol Amateur.* Havana: Periodico Juventud Rebelde, 1965.

_____ (editor). *Memoria del Los Campeonatos Mundiales de Béisbol Aficionado.* Havana: Institutio Cubano del Libro (Ediciones Deportivas), 1971.

_____ et al. (editors). *Memoria del XX Campeonato Mundial de Béisbol Aficionado.* Havana: Institutio Cubano del Libro Ediciones Deportivas), 1973.

_____ (editor). *XIX Campeonato Mundial de Béisbol Aficionado.* Havana: Institutio Cubano del Libro (Ediciones Deportivas), 1973.

Pettavino, Paula J., and Geralyn Pye. *Sport in Cuba: A Diamond in the Rough.* Pittsburgh, PA: University of Pittsburgh Press, 1994.

Pietrusza, David; Matthew Silverman, and Michael Gershman (editors). *Baseball: The Biographical Encyclopedia.* Kingston, N.Y.: Total Sports Illustrated, 2000. Entries of value on Bert Campaneris, José Canseco, Leo Cárdenas, Martín Dihigo, Dolf Luque, José Méndez, Minnie Miñoso, Tony Oliva, Rafael Palmeiro, Camilo Pascual, Tony Pérez, Pedro Ramos, Zoilo Versalles and others.

Price, S.L. *Pitching Around Fidel: A Journey in the Heart of Cuban Sports.* New York: HarperCollins (The Ecco Press), 2000.

¿Quien es Quien en Series Nacionales? 1980–1981 (Who Is Who in the Cuban National Series, 1980–1981). Havana: INDER, 1980.

Riley, James A. *The Biographical Encyclopedia of the Negro Baseball Leagues.* New York: Carroll & Graf, 1994. This work contains numerous but sometimes jumbled and often inaccurate short entries on Cuban Negro league ballplayers of the pre-integration era.

Rucker, Mark, and Peter C. Bjarkman. *Smoke: The Romance and Lore of Cuban Baseball.* New York: Total Sports Illustrated, 1999.

Santana Alonso, Alfredo. *Martín Dihigo: El Inmortal del Béisbol.* Havana: Editorial Científico-Técnica, 1997.

Senzel, Howard. *Baseball and the Cold War — Being a Soliloquy on the Necessity of Baseball in the Life of a Serious Student of Marx and Hegel from Rochester, New York (A Novel).* New York and London: Harcourt Brace Jovanovich, 1977.

Terzian, James. *The Kid from Cuba: Zoilo Versalles.* Garden City, NY: Doubleday, 1967.

Tiant, Luis (with Joe Fitzgerald). *El Tiante: The Luis Tiant Story.* Garden City, NY: Doubleday, 1976.

Toot, Peter. *Armando Marsans: First Cuban Major League Baseball Player.* Jefferson, NC, and London: McFarland, 2003.

Torres, Angel. *La Historia del Béisbol Cubano.* Montebello, California (self-published), 1996.

_____. *La Leyenda del Béisbol Cubano, 1878–1997.* Miami: Review Printers (self-published), 1996.

Triana, Fausto. *Braudilio Venent: La Fama de la Consistencia.* Havana: Editorial Científico-Técnica, 1985. Biography of 1970s–1980s Cuban League pitching legend.

Wendel, Tim. Castro's *Curveball (A Novel).* New York: Ballantine Books, 1999 (also later paperback edition: Ballantine Books, 2000).

Cuban Baseball (Articles)

Alfonso, Jorge. "Conrado Marrero Ramos — ¿Guajiro o premier?" in: *Bohemia* 94:1 (2002), 42–44.

_____. "La Leyenda del Diamante Negro José Méndez" in: *Bohemia* 93:2 (2001), 17–18.

Bjarkman, Peter C. "Adolfo Luque: The Original 'Pride of Havana'" in: *Elysian Fields Quarterly* 20:1 (Winter 2003), 21–38.

_____. "Assessing the Cuban Pitchers" in: *International Baseball Rundown.* 7:10 (Winter 1998), 14–16.

_____. "Baseball and Fidel Castro" in: *The National Pastime* 18 (1998), 64–68.

_____. "Baseball Détente and the Current Cuban Scene" in: *International Baseball Rundown.* 8:2 (July-August 1999), 12–14.

_____. "The Baseball Half-Century of Conrado Marrero" in: *Elysian Fields Quarterly* 17:1 (Winter 2000), 27–44.

_____. "Behind in the Count — Cuban Baseball Hurt By Defections and Demotions" in: *Primera Fila (The New York Daily News* Spanish Supplement) 2:1 (April 1997), 12, 14.

_____. "Best and Worst of Times in Cuban League" in: *International Baseball Rundown.* 7:9 (October 1998), 17.

_____. "Campeones Eternos — Algunas Cosas Nunca Cambian ... Cuba Conquista Otra Copa Mundial" in: *Béisbol Mundial* 1:4 (November 2005), 22.

_____. "Covering the Latin Beat: Those Colorful Señores — Recalling the 1950s-Era Cuban Washington Senators," *Oldtyme Baseball News* 8:3 (March 1997), 22–24.

_____. "Cuban Blacks in the Majors Before Jackie Robinson" in: *The Inter-National Pastime* 12 (1992) (Special Issue: An Olympic-Year Appreciation of Baseball Around the Globe), 58–63.

_____. "The Cuban Comet" (Minnie Miñoso) in: *Elysian Fields Quarterly* 19:1 (Winter 2002), 22–36.

_____. "Cubans Complete Half-Century of Baseball Domination" in: *International Baseball Rundown.* 9:1 (January-February 2000), 5–9.

_____. "Dolf Luque, Baseball's First Hispanic Star" in: *The Perfect Game — A Classic Collection of Facts, Figures, Stories and Characters from the Society for American Baseball Research.* Mark Alvarez, editor. Dallas: Taylor Publishing, 1993, 113–122.

_____. "Fidel Castro's Pitching Career" in: *International Baseball Rundown.* 9:2 (March-April 2000), 8–9.

_____. "Fidel on the Mound: Baseball Myth and History in Castro's Cuba" in: *Elysian Fields Quarterly* 16:3 (Summer 1999), 31–41.

_____. "First Hispanic Star? Dolf Luque, Of Course" in: *Baseball Research Journal* 19 (1990), 28–32.

_____. "Four Decades of Cuban Amateur Baseball Tradition" in: *International Baseball Rundown.* 7:8 (September 1998), 14–15, 17.

_____. "History's Many Shades — Tracking Jackie's Latino Predecessors" in: *Primera Fila (The New York Daily News* Spanish-Language Supplement) 2:2 (October 1997), 12, 14.

_____. "Invasión Latina — Cubanos y Dominicanos Imponen Su Son en el Besuboro Japonés" in: *Béisbol Mundial* 1:2 (June 2005), 14.

_____. "Latin America's Game — History and the Latin Age: Exclusion, Prejudice Yield to a Latin Age" in: *Devil Rays Magazine* 3:3 (May-July 2000), 38–39, 40, 42, 44, 46, 48, 50.

_____. "Lifting the Iron Curtain of Cuban Baseball" in: *The National Pastime* 17 (1997), 31–35.

_____. "A Look at the Cuban Sluggers" in: *International Baseball Rundown.* 8:1 (Late Winter 1999), 12–14.

_____. "Martín Dihigo: Baseball's Least-Known Hall of Famer" in: *Elysian Fields Quarterly* 18:2 (Spring 2001), 22–39.

_____. "MLB Pros Fail to Test Cuba's Medal" (Pan American Games) in: *International Baseball Rundown.* 8:3 (October 1999), 1, 4–7.

_____. "Myth and Mystery Are Bywords of Cuban Baseball" in: *International Baseball Rundown.* 7:7 (August 1998), 1, 11.

_____. "New Cuban Talent Carries the World Cup Banner" (Cuban League 2006 Season Review) in: *Baseball America Almanac 2006,* in press.

_____. "¿Palmeiro Quien? En Cuba, aprecian más a los suyos que a los de aquí" in: *Béisbol Mundial* 1:3 (September 2005), 8–9.

_____. "The Real World Series — Cubans Again Dominate Olympic Action" in: *Baseball Research Journal* 26 (1997), 28–29.

_____. "Sangre Nueva: Renace El Béisbol Cubano" in: *Béisbol Mundial* 1:1 (April 2005), 16.

_____. "Santiago Captures Cuban Crown" (Cuban League 2005 Season Review) in *Baseball America Almanac 2006,* 355–356.

_____. "Waiting for Che — Chasing Illusions in the Modern-Era Cuban Ballpark" in: *Elysian Fields Quarterly* 21:2 (Spring 2004), 6–17.

Brock, Lisa, and Bijan Bayne. "Not Just Black: African Americans, Cubans and Baseball," in: *Between Race and Empire: African-Americans and Cubans before the Cuban Revolution.* Edited by Lisa Brock and Digna Castañeda Fuentes. Philadelphia: Temple University Press, 1998, 186–204.

Brown, Bruce. "Cuban Baseball" in: *Atlantic Monthly* 253:6 (June 1984), 109–114.

Burgos, Adrian, Jr. "Jugando en el norte: Caribbean Players in the Negro Leagues, 1910–1950," in: *Centro: Journal of the Center for Puerto Rican Studies 8,* nos. 1–2 (1996), 128–149.

Fagen, Herb. "Go Minnie, Go — Minnie Miñoso's Six-Decade Career Keeps Going and Going and Going..." in *The Diamond — The Official Chronicle of Major League Baseball.* March-April 1994, 54–58.

Fimrite, Ron. "In Cuba It's Viva el Grand Old Game" in: *Sports Illustrated* (June 6, 1977), 69–80.

González Echevarría, Roberto. "The Game in Matanzas: On the Origins of Cuban Baseball" in: *The Yale Review* 83:3 (1995), 62–91.

_____. "Peloteros cubanos: tres testimonios" in: *Nueva Sociedad* 154 (March-April 1998), 87–100.

Hoak, Don (with Myron Cope). "The Day I Batted Against Castro" in": *The Armchair Book of Baseball.* Edited by John Thorn. New York: Charles Scribner's Sons, 1985, 161–164 (reprinted from *Sport,* June 1964)

Holway, John B. "Cuba's Black Diamond (José Méndez)" in: *The Baseball Research Journal* 10 (1981), 139–145.

Jamail, Milton. "Holguin Wins First Championship" (Cuban League 2002 Season Review) in: *Baseball America Almanac 2003,* 374–375.

_____. "Santiago Wins Third Straight Title" (Cuban League 2001 Season Review) in: *Baseball America Almanac 2002,* 362–363.

_____, and Kevin Baxter. "Cuba Dominates Despite Defections" (Cuban League 2003 Season Review) in: *Baseball America Almanac 2004,* 357–358.

_____, and _____. "Cuban Season Comes Up Golden" (Cuban League 2004 Season Review) in: *Baseball America Almanac 2005,* 361–362.

Kritzer, Cy. "Memories of Baseball in Havana" in" *Buffalo Fan* (Summer 1977), 51–54.

Manuel, John. "New-look Cuba Wins Olympic Gold; Defending Champ U.S. on Sidelines" (Athens 2004 Olympics Review) in: *Baseball America Almanac 2005,* 423–424.

McCarthy, Eugene. "Diamond Diplomacy" in: *Elysian Fields Quarterly* 14:2 (Spring 1995), 12–15.

Miller, Tom (with photographs by Ernesto Bazan). "Cuba's All-Stars" in: *Natural History* (April 1999), 62–73.

_____. "Havana's Triple Play" in: *Hemispheres* (April 1993), 68–71.

Mortenson, Tom. "Tom Mortenson on Minnie Miñoso" in *Cult Baseball Players — The Greats, the Flakes, the Weird, and the Wonderful.* Danny Peary, editor. New York: Simon & Schuster (Fireside Books), 1990, 235–240.

Nowlin, Bill, and Kit Krieger. "La Tropical Park, Then and Now" in: *The National Pastime* 25 (2005), 3–8.

Peary, Gerald. "Gerald Peary on Conrado Marrero," *Cult Baseball Players — The Greats, the Flakes, the Weird, and the Wonderful.* New York: Simon & Schuster (Fireside Books), 1990, 231–34.

Pérez, Louis A., Jr. "Between Baseball and Bullfighting: The Quest for Nationality in Cuba, 1868–1898" in: *The Journal of American History* 81:2 (September 1994), 493–517.

Rathgeber, Bob. "A Latin Temper on the Mound — Adolfo Luque" in: *Cincinnati Reds Scrapbook.* Virginia Beach: JCP Corporation of Virginia, 1982, 54–55.

Santamaria, Everardo J. "The Hoak Hoax" in: *The National Pastime* 14 (1994), 29–30.

Shouler, Ken. "El Duque's Excellent Adventures: How Cuba's Ace Pitcher Escaped Political Oppression to Become Part of the Great American Success Story" in: *Cigar Aficionado* (March/April 1999), 79–96.

Silverman, Al. "Connie Marrero Throws a Cuban Curve," *Sport* XI (September 1951), 38–39.

Skinner, David. "Havana and Key West: José Méndez and the Great Scoreless Streak of 1908" in: *The National Pastime* 24 (2004), 17–23.

_____. "Twice Champions: The 1923–24 Santa Clara Leopardos" in: *From McGillicuddy to McGwire: Baseball in Florida and the Caribbean* (Yearbook of the SABR 30 National Convention), Summer 2000, 35–42.

Small, Collie. "Baseball's Improbable Imports," *The Saturday Evening Post* (August 2, 1952), 28–29, 88–90.

Smith, Marshall. "The Senators' Slow-Ball Señor," *Life* XXX (June 11, 1951), 81–82, 85–86, 89, 92.

Wagner, Eric A. "Baseball in Cuba" in: *Journal of Popular Culture* 18:1 (Summer 1984), 113–120.

Wertheim, Jon, and Don Yaeger. "Fantastic Voyage — Three Fellow Refugees Say the Tale of Yankees Ace Orlando (El Duque) Hernández's Escape from Cuba Doesn't Hold Water" in: *Sports Illustrated* 89:22 (November 30, 1998), 60–63.

Young, A.S. (Doc). "Comet from Cuba," in *Great Negro Baseball Stars (and How They Made the Major Leagues).* New York: A.S. Barnes, 1953, 165–179.

Cuban Political History and Culture (Books)

Brenner, Philip; William M. LeoGrande; Donna Rich and Daniel Siegel (editors). *The Cuba Reader: The Making of a Revolutionary Society.* New York: Grove, 1989.

Codrescu, Andrei. *Ay, Cuba! A Socio-Erotic Journey.* New York: St. Martin's, 1999.

Domínguez, Jorge I. *Cuba: Order and Revolution.* Cambridge: Belknap (Harvard University), 1978.

Gébler, Carlo. *Driving Through Cuba: Rare Encounters in the Land of Sugar Cane and Revolution.* New York: Simon & Schuster, 1988.

Gott, Richard. *Cuba: A New History.* New Haven, CT: Yale University Press, 2004.

Horowitz, Irving Louis. *Cuban Communism,* 7th ed. London: Transaction, 1989.

Kapcia, Antoni. *Cuba — Island of Dreams.* New York: Oxford University Press, 2000.

Miller, Tom. *Trading with the Enemy: A Yankee Travels Through Castro's Cuba.* New York: Atheneum, 1992.

Pérez, Louis A., Jr. *Cuba: Between Reform and Revolution*. New York: Oxford University Press, 1988.

_____. *On Becoming Cuban: Identity, Nationality and Culture*. Chapel Hill: University of North Carolina Press, 1999. See especially section entitled "Baseball and Becoming," 255–278.

Ryan, Alan (editor). *The Reader's Companion to Cuba*. San Diego: Harcourt Brace, 1997.

Simons, Geoff. *Cuba, from Conquistador to Castro*. New York: St. Martin's, 1996.

Suchlicki, Jaime. *Cuba: From Columbus to Castro*. Third Revised Edition. New York: Brassey's, 1990.

Thomas, Hugh. *Cuba, or The Pursuit of Freedom*. New York and London: Harper & Row, 1971 (also updated paperback edition: DeCapo Press, 1998).

Ward, Fred. *Inside Cuba Today*. New York: Crown Publishers, 1978.

Fidel Castro and Cuban Revolution (Books)

Anderson, Jon Lee. *Che Guevara: A Revolutionary Life*. New York: Grove, 1997.

Bourne, Peter G. *Fidel: A Biography of Fidel Castro*. New York: Dodd, Mead, 1988.

Castañeda, Jorge G. *Compañero: The Life and Death of Che Guevara*. New York: Alfred A. Knopf, 1997.

Castro, Fidel. *Nothing Can Stop the Course of History* (interview with Jeffrey M. Eliot and Mervyn M. Dymally). New York and Toronto: Pathfinder, 1986.

Conte, Agüero, Luis. *Fidel Castro: Vida y Obra*. Havana: Editorial Lex, 1959. First Fidel Castro biography, published in Havana.

Draper, Theodore. *Castro's Revolution: Myths and Realities*. New York: Frederick A. Praeger, 1962.

Dubois, Jules. *Fidel Castro: Rebel Liberator or Dictator?* Indianapolis: Bobbs Merrill, 1959.

Fidel Sobre el Deporte. Havana: INDER (Instituto Nacional de Deportes, Educación Fisica y Recreación), 1975.

Franqui, Carlos. *Diary of the Cuban Revolution*. New York: Viking, 1976.

Gerassi, John (editor). *Venceremos! The Speeches and Writings of Che Guevara*. New York: Macmillan, 1968.

Geyer, Georgie Anne. *Guerrilla Prince: The Untold Story of Fidel Castro*. Boston and London: Little, Brown, 1991.

Guevara, Che (Ernesto). *Reminiscences of the Cuban Revolution*. Translated by Victoria Ortíz. New York and London: Grove, 1968.

Halperin, Maurice. *The Rise and Decline of Fidel Castro*. Berkeley and Los Angeles: University of California Press, 1972.

James, Daniel. *Che Guevara: A Biography*. New York: Cooper Square, 2001.

Krich, John. *A Totally Free Man—An Unauthorized Autobiography of Fidel Castro (A Novel)*. Berkeley, CA: Creative Arts Books, 1981.

Lockwood, Lee. *Castro's Cuba, Cuba's Fidel*. New York: Vintage, 1969.

Mankiewicz, Frank, and Kirby Jones. *With Fidel: A Portrait of Castro and Cuba*. Chicago: Playboy Press Books, 1975 (also later paperback edition: Ballantine Books, 1976).

Matthews, Herbert L. *Fidel Castro*. New York: Simon & Schuster, 1969.

_____. *Revolution in Cuba: An Essay in Understanding*. New York: Charles Scribner's Sons, 1975.

Meneses, Enrique. *Fidel Castro*. Translated by J. Halcro Ferguson. New York: Taplinger, 1968.

Menton, Seymour (editor). *The Prose Fiction of the Cuban Revolution*. Austin: University of Texas Press, 1975.

Quirk, Robert E. *Fidel Castro*. New York and London: W.W. Norton, 1993.

Salas, Osvaldo, and Roberto Salas. *Fidel's Cuba: A Revolution in Pictures*. New York: Thunder's Mouth Press, 1998.

Sweig, Julia E. *Inside the Cuban Revolution: Fidel Castro and the Urban Underground*. Cambridge, MA: Harvard University Press, 2002.

Szulc, Tad. *Fidel: A Critical Portrait*. New York: William Morrow, 1986.

USA–Cuba Relations (Books)

Arboleya, Jesús. *The Cuban Counterrevolution*. (Translated by Damián Donéstevez). Havana: Editorial José Martí, 2002.

Elliston, John. *Psywar on Cuba: The Declassified History of U.S. Anti-Castro Propaganda*. Melbourne and New York: Ocean Press, 1999.

Franklin, Jane. *Cuba and the United States: A Chronological History*. Melbourne and New York: Ocean Press, 1997.

Leonard, Thomas M. *Encyclopedia of Cuban–United States Relations*. Jefferson, NC, and London: McFarland, 2004.

Oppenheimer, Andres. *Castro's Final Hour—The Secret Story Behind the Coming Downfall of Communist Cuba*. New York: Simon & Schuster, 1992.

Peterson, Thomas G. *Contesting Castro: The United States and the Triumph of the Cuban Revolution*. New York: Oxford University Press, 1994. This work contains a brief section on baseball in Cuban popular culture.

Rosendahl, Mona. *Inside the Revolution: Everyday Life in Socialist Cuba*. Ithaca, NY, and London: Cornell University Press, 1997.

Schwab, Peter. *Cuba: Confronting the U.S. Embargo*. New York: St. Martin's, 1999.

Smith, Earl E.T. *The Fourth Floor: An Account of the Castro Communist Revolution*. New York: Random House, 1962.

White, Mark J. *The Kennedys and Cuba—The Declassified Documentary History*. Chicago: Ivan R. Dee, 1999.

Wyden, Peter. *Bay of Pigs: The Untold Story*. New York: Simon & Schuster, 1979.

Index